FOURTH EDITION

Marketing Leadership in Hospitality and Tourism

Library of Congress Cataloging-in-Publication Data
Shoemaker, Stowe.
  Marketing leadership in hospitality and tourism : strategies and tactics for competitive
advantage / Stowe Shoemaker, Robert C. Lewis, Peter C. Yesawich. — 4th ed.
      p. cm.
  Lewis's name appears first on the earlier edition.
  Rev. ed. of: Marketing leadership in hospitality / Robert C. Lewis, Richard E. Chambers.
New York : John Wiley, © 2000.
  Includes bibliographical references and index.
  ISBN 0-13-118240-4
  1. Hospitality industry—Marketing. I. Lewis, Robert C. II. Yesawich, Peter C.
III. Title.
  TX911.3.M3L49 2007
  910.46068'8—dc22   2006049455

Editor-in-Chief: Vernon R. Anthony
Senior Editor: William Lawrensen
Managing Editor—Editorial: Judith Casillo
Editorial Assistant: Marion Gottlieb
Managing Editor—Production: Mary Carnis
Production Liaison: Jane Bonnell
Production Editor: Linda Zuk, WordCraft, LLC
Manufacturing Manager: Ilene Sanford
Manufacturing Buyer: Cathleen Petersen
Executive Marketing Manager: Ryan DeGrote
Senior Marketing Coordinator: Elizabeth Farrell

Marketing Assistant: Les Roberts
Senior Design Coordinator: Miguel Ortiz
Interior Design: Janice Bielawa
Cover Design: Robert Aleman
Cover Image: Jupiter Images/Picture Quest
Composition: Carlisle Publishing Services
Manager of Media Production: Amy Peltier
Media Production Project Manager: Lisa Rinaldi
Printer/Binder: R. R. Donnelley and Sons Company
Cover Printer: Phoenix Color

Previous editions published under the title *Marketing Leadership in Hospitality: Foundations and Practices,*
by Robert C. Lewis and Richard E. Chambers, copyright 2000.

Image credits appear on page 663.

Copyright © 2007 Pearson Education, Inc., Upper Saddle River, New Jersey 07458.
Pearson Prentice Hall. All rights reserved. Printed in the United States of America. This publication is protected by
Copyright and permission should be obtained from the publisher prior to any prohibited reproduction, storage in a
retrieval system, or transmission in any form or by any means, electronic, mechanical, photocopying, recording, or
likewise. For information regarding permission(s), write to: Rights and Permissions Department.

Pearson Prentice Hall™ is a trademark of Pearson Education, Inc.
Pearson® is a registered trademark of Pearson plc
Prentice Hall® is a registered trademark of Pearson Education, Inc.

Pearson Education LTD.
Pearson Education Singapore, Pte. Ltd.
Pearson Education Canada, Ltd.
Pearson Education–Japan

Pearson Education Australia PTY, Limited
Pearson Education North Asia Ltd.
Pearson Educación de Mexico, S.A. de C.V.
Pearson Education Malaysia, Pte. Ltd.

10 9 8 7 6 5 4 3 2 1
ISBN 0-13-118240-4

FOURTH EDITION

Marketing Leadership in Hospitality and Tourism

Strategies and Tactics for Competitive Advantage

Stowe Shoemaker
Donald Hubbs Distinguished Professor
Associate Dean of Research
Conrad Hilton College of Hotel and Restaurant Management
University of Houston

Robert C. Lewis
Professor Emeritus, University of Massachusetts, Amherst

Peter C. Yesawich
Chairman
Yesawich, Pepperdine, Brown & Russell

PEARSON

Prentice
Hall

Upper Saddle River, New Jersey 07458

This book is dedicated to my parents, Stowe and Ann Shoemaker; to my wife and best friend, Martha; and to Martha's mother, Peg McArdell: may she look down upon us and smile. All have sacrificed much so that I could pursue my dreams. I owe my success to them.

—Stowe Shoemaker

I dedicate this book to those students and professionals who will make a meaningful difference in the world of hospitality marketing.

—Robert Lewis

I dedicate this book to my parents, who always encouraged and supported my pursuit of education; to my wife, Paris, whose patience never waned during the many hours I spent preparing and reviewing manuscripts; to my sons Peter, Jr., Paul, and Logan, whom I hope will be equally inspired to pursue their intellectual and professional passions someday; and to our dog Rusty, who, although ostensibly an interested observer, slept through most of the entire process with great pleasure.

—Peter Yesawich

Brief Contents

Introduction / 2

PART I

Introduction to Hospitality Marketing / 13

Chapter 1   The Concept of Marketing / 14
Chapter 2   Marketing Services and the Hospitality Experience / 36
Chapter 3   The Marketing Mix and the Product/Service Mix / 58
Chapter 4   Relationship/Loyalty Marketing / 84

PART II

Marketing to Build a Competitive Advantage / 117

Chapter 5   Strategic Marketing / 118
Chapter 6   The Strategic Marketing System and Marketing Objectives / 148

PART III

The Marketplace / 167

Chapter 7   Understanding Individual Customers / 168
Chapter 8   Understanding Organizational Customers / 196
Chapter 9   The Tourist Customer and the Tourism Destination / 224

PART IV

Situational Analysis / 251

Chapter 10   Understanding Competition / 252
Chapter 11   Marketing Intelligence and Research / 280

PART V

Functional Strategies / 309

Chapter 12   Differentiation, Segmentation, and Target Marketing / 310
Chapter 13   Branding and Market Positioning / 346
Chapter 14   The Hospitality Pricing Mix / 372
Chapter 15   The Communications Mix: Advertising / 408
Chapter 16   The Communications Mix: Sales Promotions, Merchandising, Public Relations and Publicity / 432
Chapter 17   The Communications Mix: Personal Selling / 462
Chapter 18   Hospitality Distribution Systems: Bringing the Product to the Customer / 488
Chapter 19   Channels of Distribution: Bringing the Customer to the Product / 514
Chapter 20   Interactive Marketing: Internet and Database Marketing / 536

PART VI

Synthesis / 563

Chapter 21   The Marketing Plan / 564

Contents

Preface xvii
Acknowledgments xxiii
About the Authors xxv

Introduction 2
Marketing Executive Profile: Max and Greti Mennig / 3
Marketing in Action / 3
Quality / 6
Efficiency / 7
Customer Responsiveness / 7
Innovation / 8
Size / 8
■ REFERENCES / 10

PART 1

Introduction to Hospitality Marketing / 13

CHAPTER 1   The Concept of Marketing....................14
Marketing Executive Profile: Michael A. Leven / 15
Marketing in Action / 15
Foundations and Practices / 18
The Concept of Marketing / 19
The Purpose of a Business / 19
The Twofold Purpose of Marketing / 20
Solving Customers' Problems / 21
Management Orientations / 26
Operations Orientation / 26
Product/Service Orientation / 28
Selling Orientation / 28
Bottom-Line Orientation / 29
Marketing Orientation / 29
Marketing Leadership / 32
Opportunity / 33
Planning / 33
Control / 33
Marketing Is Everything / 33
■ SUMMARY / 34
■ KEY TERMS / 34

■ DISCUSSION QUESTIONS / 34
■ GROUP PROJECTS / 35
■ REFERENCES / 35

CHAPTER 2   Marketing Services and the Hospitality Experience..36
Marketing Executive Profile: Gary Leopold / 37
Marketing in Action / 37
Services versus Goods / 40
What Distinguishes the Marketing of Services? / 40
Intangibility / 40
Perishability / 43
Heterogeneity / 44
Simultaneity of Production and Consumption / 47
The Hospitality Product / 48
Other Aspects of the Service Component / 48
Components of the Hospitality Product / 49
Physical Product / 49
Service Environment / 50
The Service Product / 50
Service Delivery / 51
The Interrelationships of the Different Components / 51
Experience: The Result of Purchasing a Service / 52
Service Quality and Service Gaps / 52
Potential Gaps in Hospitality Service / 53
The Dimensions of Service Quality / 55
Zone of Tolerance / 55
International Gaps / 56
■ SUMMARY / 56
■ KEY TERMS / 57
■ DISCUSSION QUESTIONS / 57
■ GROUP PROJECTS / 57
■ REFERENCES / 57

CHAPTER 3   The Marketing Mix and the Product/Service Mix......................................58
Marketing Executive Profile: Peter Warren / 59
Marketing in Action / 59
The Four Ps / 62
The Seven Ps / 62
The 13 Cs / 63

The Hospitality Marketing Mix / 63
The Product/Service Mix / 63
The Presentation Mix / 64
The Pricing Mix / 64
The Communications Mix / 64
The Distribution Mix / 64
The Hospitality Product/Service Mix / 64
Designing the Hospitality Product / 65
The Formal Product / 65
The Core Product / 65
The Augmented Product / 66
The Complexity of the Product/Service Mix / 66
Standard Products / 67
Standard Products with Modifications / 68
Customized Products / 68
The International Product/Service / 69
Making the Product Decision / 71
The Product Life Cycle / 71
The Nature of Product Life Cycles / 72
Stages of the Product Life Cycle / 73
Locating Products in their Life Cycles / 79
Developing New Products and Services / 79
What Succeeds? / 80
■ SUMMARY / 81
■ KEY TERMS / 82
■ DISCUSSION QUESTIONS / 82
■ GROUP PROJECTS / 82
■ REFERENCES / 82

CHAPTER 4 Relationship/Loyalty
Marketing 84
Marketing Executive Profile: Adam Burke / 85
Marketing in Action / 85
What Relationship/Loyalty Marketing Is and
What It Is Not / 90
The Need for Relationship/Loyalty Marketing / 92
The Lifetime Value of a Customer / 93
Examining Customers Through the Stages of Their Life Cycles
with the Firm / 97
Building Loyalty / 98
The Evolution of Customer Loyalty / 98
The Loyalty Circle / 101
Frequent Guest Programs and Loyalty Programs / 103
What Frequency Programs Don't Do / 104
What Makes Frequency Programs Work? / 104
Customer Complaints and Service Recovery / 104
Employee Relationship Marketing or Internal Marketing / 108
Management Practices / 111
Noncontact Employees / 112
The Internal Marketing Concept / 113
The Past and Future of Relationship/Customer Loyalty
Marketing / 114
■ SUMMARY / 114
■ KEY TERMS / 115
■ DISCUSSION QUESTIONS / 115

■ GROUP PROJECTS / 115
■ REFERENCES / 115

PART II

Marketing to Build a Competitive Advantage / 117

CHAPTER 5 Strategic Marketing 118
Marketing Executive Profile: Christian Hempell / 119
Marketing in Action / 119
Strategic Marketing versus Marketing Management / 121
Strategy / 122
Strategic Leadership / 123
Strategic Marketing / 124
The Concept of Strategy / 124
Strategic Planning / 127
The Role of Strategic Planning / 128
The Levels of Strategic Planning / 129
Emergent Strategies / 134
Understanding the Environment / 136
Types of Environments / 137
Technological Environment / 137
Political Environment / 139
Economic Environment / 142
Sociocultural Environment / 142
Natural Environment / 143
■ SUMMARY / 146
■ KEY TERMS / 146
■ DISCUSSION QUESTIONS / 146
■ GROUP PROJECTS / 146
■ REFERENCES / 147

CHAPTER 6 The Strategic Marketing System and
Marketing Objectives 148
Marketing Executive Profile: Bruce Himelstein / 149
Marketing in Action / 149
The Mission Statement / 151
Master Marketing Strategy / 153
Situational Analysis / 154
Using the Strategic Marketing Systems Model / 156
Objectives and Master Strategies / 156
Business Strategies / 157
Target Market Strategy / 157
Product Strategy / 158
Competitive Strategy / 158
Market Strategy / 159
Positioning Strategy / 160
Functional Strategies / 160
Product/Service Strategy / 160
Presentation Strategy / 161
Pricing Strategy / 162
Communication Strategy / 162
Distribution Strategy / 162
Feedback Loops / 163

Strategy Selection / 164
Why Strategic Plans Fail / 164
■ SUMMARY / 165
■ KEY TERMS / 165
■ DISCUSSION QUESTIONS / 165
■ GROUP PROJECTS / 165
■ REFERENCES / 166

PART III

The Marketplace / 167

CHAPTER 7 Understanding Individual Customers 168
Marketing Executive Profile: Tom Storey / 169
Marketing in Action / 169
Characteristics of Customers / 172
 Needs and Wants / 172
 Application of the Theories / 173
The Buying Decision Process / 174
 Needs, Wants, and Problems / 174
 Search Process / 174
 Stimuli Selection / 175
 Perceptions / 175
 Reality Is Perception / 176
 Beliefs / 177
 Alternative Evaluation / 177
 Attitudes / 178
 Alternative Comparison / 178
 Expectations / 178
 Choice Intentions / 178
 Behavior / 178
 Perception versus Reality / 178
 Outcomes—Satisfaction or Dissatisfaction / 179
Types of Hospitality Customers / 180
 Business Travelers / 180
 Pleasure Travelers / 184
 Resort Market / 188
 The Package Market / 188
 Mature Travelers / 191
 International Travelers / 192
 Free Independent Travelers (FITs) / 193
■ SUMMARY / 193
■ KEY TERMS / 194
■ DISCUSSION QUESTIONS / 194
■ GROUP PROJECTS / 194
■ REFERENCES / 195

CHAPTER 8 Understanding Organizational Customers 196
Marketing Executive Profile: Charlotte St. Martin / 197
Marketing in Action / 197
The Generic Organizational Market / 200
Meeting Planners / 201

Planning the Event / 201
 Buy Time / 201
 Assess the Needs / 203
 Setting Measurable Goals / 204
 Developing a Plan / 204
 Resolving Conflicts / 204
 Executing the Meeting / 205
 Evaluating the Results / 205
The Corporate Travel Market / 205
 Knowing the Volume / 207
 Understanding Travel Patterns / 207
 Controlling Costs / 208
The Corporate Meetings Market / 208
Conference Centers / 210
The Incentive Market / 211
Association, Convention, and Trade Show Markets / 213
Convention Centers and Convention and Visitors Bureaus / 215
The Airline Crew Market / 216
The SMERF and Government Markets / 218
The Group Tour and Travel Market / 218
 Motorcoach Tour Travelers / 219
■ SUMMARY / 221
■ KEY TERMS / 221
■ DISCUSSION QUESTIONS / 221
■ GROUP PROJECTS / 222
■ REFERENCES / 222

CHAPTER 9 The Tourist Customer and the Tourism Destination 224
Marketing Executive Profile: Vincent Vanderpool-Wallace / 225
Marketing in Action / 225
Importance of Travel and Tourism / 227
Local Residents' Attitudes toward Tourism / 228
The Role of NTOs / 229
How Hotels and Tourist Destinations Work Together / 232
Destination Marketing Strategy / 232
 Macro Environment / 234
 Economic Environment / 234
 Technological Environment / 235
 Political/Legal Environment / 235
 Sociocultural Environment / 239
 Ecological Environment / 239
 Demographic Environment / 239
Competitors: Rivalry among Destinations / 242
Segmenting the Tourist Market / 242
Communicating with the Tourist Market / 244
 Importance of Image Promotion / 244
Travelers' Information Search Behavior / 246
 Familiarity / 246
 Expertise / 246
■ SUMMARY / 249
■ KEY TERMS / 249
■ DISCUSSION QUESTIONS / 250
■ GROUP PROJECTS / 250
■ REFERENCES / 250

PART IV

Situational Analysis / 251

CHAPTER 10 Understanding Competition............252
Marketing Executive Profile: Hirohide Abe / 253
Marketing in Action / 253
Macrocompetition / 256
  Marketing Threats / 257
Microcompetition / 257
Choosing the Right Competition / 259
Competitive Intensity / 260
Competitive Intelligence / 263
  Market Share / 264
  REVPAR / 265
  Yield Index / 265
  REVPOR / 266
  REVPAC / 266
  Internet REVPAR / 266
  Purchased Data / 267
  Restaurant Comparisons / 267
  Customer Satisfaction Index / 267
  Perceptual Mapping / 268
  Types and Objectives of Competitive Intelligence / 271
Competitive Analysis / 275
Competitive Marketing / 276
Finding Marketing Opportunities / 277
Feasibility Studies / 278
  ■ SUMMARY / 278
  ■ KEY TERMS / 279
  ■ DISCUSSION QUESTIONS / 279
  ■ GROUP PROJECTS / 279
  ■ REFERENCES / 279

CHAPTER 11 Marketing Intelligence and Research 280
Marketing Executive Profile: Dennis A. Marzella / 281
Marketing in Action / 281
Designing the Marketing Information System / 286
Collecting External Information and Public Domain Research / 286
Gathering Internal Information / 290
How Marketing Intelligence Can Be Used / 293
  Assessment of Area-Wide Demand / 293
  Product (Property) Research / 294
  Environmental Scanning / 296
Customer Research / 296
  Formal Marketing Research / 296
  Proprietary Research / 296
  Qualitative Research / 297
  Quantitative Research / 298
Research Design / 300
  Research Purpose / 300
  Research Problem / 300
  Research Objectives / 300
  What We Expect to Know / 301
  Research Method / 301

Reliability and Validity / 304
  Reliability / 304
  Validity / 305
Customer Satisfaction Research / 306
Program Measurement / 306
  ■ SUMMARY / 306
  ■ KEY TERMS / 307
  ■ DISCUSSION QUESTIONS / 307
  ■ GROUP PROJECTS / 308
  ■ REFERENCES / 308

PART V

Functional Strategies / 309

CHAPTER 12 Differentiation, Segmentation, and Target Marketing 310
Marketing Executive Profile: David W. Norton / 311
Marketing in Action / 311
Differentiation / 314
  Basis of Differentiation / 314
  Differentiation of Intangibles / 315
  Differentiation as a Marketing Tool / 316
  Differentiation—of Anything / 318
Market Segmentation / 318
  Which Comes First—Differentiation or Segmentation? / 319
  The Process of Market Segmentation / 320
Tailoring the Product to the Wants and Needs of the Target Market / 321
Segmentation Variables / 322
  Geographic Segmentation / 322
  Demographic Segmentation / 323
  Psychographic Segmentation / 324
  Usage Segmentation / 333
  Benefit Segmentation / 335
  Price Segmentation / 337
  International Segmentation / 338
  Fine-Tuning Segments / 340
Globalization of Markets / 341
Segmentation Strategies / 341
Target Marketing / 342
Mass Customization / 344
  ■ SUMMARY / 344
  ■ KEY TERMS / 345
  ■ DISCUSSION QUESTIONS / 345
  ■ GROUP PROJECTS / 345
  ■ REFERENCES / 345

CHAPTER 13 Branding and Market Positioning...346
Marketing Executive Profile: John Griffin / 347
Marketing in Action / 347
Salience, Determinance, and Importance / 350
  Salience / 350
  Determinance / 350
  Importance / 351
Objective Positioning / 351

Subjective Positioning / 351
Tangible Positioning / 352
Intangible Positioning / 354
Effective Positioning / 354
Positioning's Vital Role / 357
Repositioning / 358
The Art of Repositioning / 360
Developing Positioning Strategies / 361
Competitive Positioning / 362
Internal Positioning Analysis / 364
Branding and Positioning / 365
   Hotel Restaurant Branding / 366
   Multiple Brands and Product Positioning / 367
■ SUMMARY / *370*
■ KEY TERMS / *370*
■ DISCUSSION QUESTIONS / *370*
■ GROUP PROJECTS / *371*
■ REFERENCES / *371*

CHAPTER 14 The Hospitality Pricing Mix 372
Marketing Executive Profile: John Shields / 373
Marketing in Action / 373
The Basis of Pricing / 375
Pricing Practices / 376
   Hotel Room Pricing / 376
   Restaurant Pricing / 376
What Is Price? / 377
Pricing as One of the Seven Ps / 378
Types of Costs / 379
Cost-Based Pricing / 380
   Cost-Plus Pricing / 380
   Cost Percentage or Markup Pricing / 380
   Break-Even Pricing / 380
   Contribution Margin Pricing / 381
   $1 per Thousand Pricing / 382
Value-Based Pricing / 382
   The Components of Value / 383
   Prospect Theory / 385
   Reference Pricing / 386
Psychological Pricing / 387
   Veblen Effects / 390
   Value Added Service Pricing / 390
Pricing Objectives / 391
   Financial Objectives / 391
   Volume Objectives / 393
   Customer Objectives / 394
Determining Price / 396
Market Demand Pricing / 398
Price Customization and Revenue Management / 399
   What Revenue Management Is / 400
   Revenue Management Practices / 400
   Benefits of Revenue Management / 401
   Why Revenue Management Works / 401
International Pricing / 404
Pricing across Multiple Channels of Distribution / 405
The Last Word on Pricing / 405
■ SUMMARY / *406*

■ KEY TERMS / *406*
■ DISCUSSION QUESTIONS / *406*
■ GROUP PROJECTS / *406*
■ REFERENCES / *407*

CHAPTER 15 The Communications Mix:
Advertising 408
Marketing Executive Profile: Larry Tolpin / 409
Marketing in Action / 409
The Communications Mix / 412
Communications Strategy / 412
   To Whom to Say It / 413
   Why to Say It / 416
   What to Say / 416
   How to Say It / 418
   How Often to Say It / 419
   Where to Say It / 419
Research for the Communications Mix / 419
   Where Are We Now? / 419
   Why Are We There? / 419
   Where Could We Be? / 420
   How Can We Get There? / 420
   Are We Getting There? / 420
Push/Pull Strategies / 420
Word-of-Mouth Communication / 422
Budgeting the Communications Mix / 422
Advertising / 424
   Roles of Advertising / 424
   What Advertising Should Accomplish / 424
   Use of Advertising Today / 426
   Evaluating Advertising / 428
   Collateral / 429
■ SUMMARY / *430*
■ KEY TERMS / *431*
■ DISCUSSION QUESTIONS / *431*
■ GROUP PROJECTS / *431*

CHAPTER 16 The Communications Mix:
Sales Promotions, Merchandising, Public Relations
and Publicity...432
Marketing Executive Profile: Jennifer Ploszaj / 433
Marketing in Action / 433
Principles and Practices of Sales Promotions / 436
Sales Promotions and Marketing Needs / 437
Guidelines for Sales Promotions / 437
   Be Single-Minded / 438
   Define the Target Market / 438
   Decide Specifically What You Want to Promote / 438
   Decide the Best Way to Promote It / 438
   Make Sure You Can Fulfill the Demand / 438
   Make Sure Reality Meets Expectations / 439
   Communicate Your Promotion and All Related Aspects to the
      Market / 439
   Communicate the Promotion to Your Employees / 439
   Measure the Results / 439
Developing Sales Promotions / 440

Designing the Successful Sales Promotion / 442
  Identify the Gap / 442
  Design the Sales Promotion / 442
  Analyze the Competition / 442
  Allocate the Resources / 442
  Establish Goals / 443
  Research the Promotion / 443
  Understand the Break-Even Point / 443
  Execute the Sales Promotion / 443
  Evaluate the Sales Promotion / 444
Principles and Practices of Merchandising / 445
Basic Rules of Merchandising / 445
  Purpose / 446
  Compatibility and Consistency / 449
  Practicality / 449
  Visibility / 449
  Simplicity / 449
  Knowledgeable Employees / 450
Examples of Good Merchandising / 450
Public Relations and Publicity / 451
  Public Relations (PR) / 452
  Publicity / 458
■ SUMMARY / 460
■ KEY TERMS / 461
■ DISCUSSION QUESTIONS / 461
■ GROUP PROJECTS / 461
■ REFERENCES / 461

**CHAPTER 17 The Communications Mix:
Personal Selling** 462
Marketing Executive Profile: David Green / 463
Marketing in Action / 463
The Sales Process / 467
  Prospecting / 467
  Qualifying Prospects / 468
  Probing / 471
  Benefits and Features / 472
  Customer Attitudes / 472
  Closing / 475
  Follow-Up / 475
Sales Management / 476
  Account Management / 476
  Sales Action Plan / 477
  Organization of the Sales Team / 478
  Product Line Management / 481
Development of Personnel / 482
  Ethics / 482
  Motivation / 484
Sales and Operations / 484
■ SUMMARY / 486
■ KEY TERMS / 486
■ DISCUSSION QUESTIONS / 486
■ GROUP PROJECTS / 487
■ REFERENCES / 487

**CHAPTER 18 Hospitality Distribution Systems:
Bringing the Product to the Customer** 488
Marketing Executive Profile: Jens Thraenhart / 489
Marketing in Action / 489
How Distribution Channels Work / 493
Branded Hospitality Companies / 493
Franchises / 493
Reservation Services / 494
Representation Firms / 494
Channels for Manufactured Goods / 496
Channels for Hospitality Firms / 496
Structure of Distribution / 498
Distribution and the Building Blocks of Competitive
Advantage / 500
Ownership of Facilities / 501
Management and Ownership of One Facility or Multiple
  Facilities / 501
Management without Ownership / 503
Franchising / 504
  Franchise Support / 506
  The Future of Franchising / 507
Strategic Alliances / 508
Restaurant Distribution / 511
■ SUMMARY / *511*
■ KEY TERMS / *512*
■ DISCUSSION QUESTIONS / *512*
■ GROUP PROJECTS / *512*
■ REFERENCES / *512*

**CHAPTER 19 Channels of Distribution: Bringing
the Customer to the Product** 514
Marketing Executive Profile: Spencer Rascoff / 515
Marketing in Action / 515
Hospitality Channels of Distribution / 517
  Consortium / 517
  Incentive Travel Organizations / 518
  Traditional Offline Travel Agents / 518
  Central Reservation Systems / 521
  Global Distribution Systems (GDS) / 522
  Tour Operators/Discount Brokers/Consolidators/
    Wholesalers / 522
Corporate Travel Departments and Travel Management
  Companies / 523
Destination Management Organizations / 523
  Internet Channel Intermediaries / 525
Future Challenges of Online Distribution / 529
  Promotional Tie-Ins / 531
  Selecting the Channel of Distribution / 532
International Markets / 532
Channel Management / 532
  Relationships among Channels / 533
  Evaluation of the Channel / 533
  Motivation / 534

Recruitment / 534
■ SUMMARY / 534
■ KEY TERMS / 535
■ DISCUSSION QUESTIONS / 535
■ GROUP PROJECTS / 535
■ REFERENCES / 535

CHAPTER 20 Interactive Marketing: Internet and Database Marketing...**536**
Marketing Executive Profile: John Springer-Miller / 537
Marketing in Action / 537
The First Generation of Electronic Marketing (E-Marketing) / 540
The Role of the Internet in Transforming Marketing / 540
An Overview of Hospitality Website Design / 542
Managing Customer Information / 547
Database Marketing / 552
Database Marketing Components / 554
Using the Database / 557
Ways to Use the Database / 559
■ SUMMARY / 561
■ KEY TERMS / 561
■ DISCUSSION QUESTIONS / 561
■ GROUP PROJECTS / 562
■ REFERENCES / 562

PART VI

Synthesis / 563

CHAPTER 21 The Marketing Plan..........................**564**
Marketing Executive Profile: Terry Jicinsky / 565
Marketing in Action / 565
Requirements for a Marketing Plan / 568
Development of the Marketing Plan / 569
Data Collection / 570
External Environment / 570
Competitive Environment / 570
Internal Environment / 572

Data Analysis / 572
Environmental and Market Trend Analysis / 572
Competitive and Demand Analysis / 573
Property Needs Analysis / 573
Internal Analysis / 577
Market Analysis / 577
The Mission and Marketing Position Statement / 578
Opportunity Analysis / 579
Objectives and Methods / 579
Action Plans / 581
The Marketing Forecast / 582
The Marketing Budget / 582
Marketing Controls / 585
■ SUMMARY / 586
■ KEY TERMS / 586
■ DISCUSSION QUESTIONS / 586
■ GROUP PROJECTS / 586
■ REFERENCE / 587

Appendix to Chapter 9
Segmenting the U.S. Travel Market According to Benefits Realized...**588**

Appendix to Chapter 11
Understanding the Marketing Research Process: A Guide to Using an Outside Research Supplier.....**603**

Appendix to Chapter 13
Brand Positioning: An Example..................................**613**

Appendix to Chapter 14
Revenue Management **619**

Glossary / 627
Name Index / 637
Subject Index / 639
World Maps / 650
Image Credits / 663

Preface

Marketing begins and ends with the customer. Marketing is not just a series of tactical actions; rather, it is a way of thinking about how to incorporate the customers' views into all organizational decisions. The goal of marketing is also to gain a sustainable competitive advantage. This book illustrates these dual roles of marketing by:

- Providing a clear understanding of the customer decision process when making a purchase
- Examining ways to determine wants, needs, and problems through consumer research
- Exploring the impact of information on attitude and belief formation
- Detailing the various tactics that hospitality businesses can use to build a competitive advantage. We do this by not only examining the strategies and tactics of large multinational firms, but also examining the independent hotels, restaurants, and tourism entities that make up much of the hospitality industry.

Why a Separate Book on Hospitality and Tourism Marketing?

With all of the generic marketing texts available, the reader may wonder, why a separate book on hospitality and tourism marketing? Aren't the principles of marketing the same regardless of the industry? While we certainly believe that there are similarities across industries, we believe that the differences need to be highlighted and explored. One of the major differences pertains to the nature of services: the intangibility, the heterogeneity, and simultaneous production and consumption. These characteristics present unique challenges for our industry. How to meet these challenges is the subject of this book. Typically, generic marketing books do not cover such material.

Another major difference is the role that the guest "experience" plays in the hospitality purchase. Customers are buying not only rooms or meals, but memories. The role of marketing is to help define and create these memories. How marketing executives can do this is covered in this book. Again, generic marketing books do not cover such material.

We believe that textbooks should not merely educate students about the strategies and tactics used in marketing, but they should also educate students about the industry they plan to enter. This book is filled with examples that both educate students and excite them about the opportunities the hospitality industry presents. Our examples are international and include independent restaurants and hotels, as well as large multinational firms. The book also is filled with numerous examples that illustrate how tourism organizations use marketing to gain competitive advantage. These **Tourism Marketing Applications** are highlighted throughout the chapters.

Our Approach to Marketing

This fourth edition of *Marketing Leadership in Hospitality and Tourism* brings together what we, the industry, and academics have learned in the past few years—and a lot of what we are still learning. The foundation of marketing starts at the highest level by **deed** and **action**—not by words alone. These deeds and actions must permeate down to the lowest level of the organization. At the highest level, marketing shapes the corporate effort; at the lowest level, it means the porter doesn't mop where the customer is walking.

Taking a long-range perspective rather than an operational how-to approach, because marketing is long-range for any organization that seeks survival and growth, we explore the latest trends in marketing, distribution, and customer research and service.

The Latest Trends in Customer Loyalty

This edition examines the latest trends in marketing theory and practice, especially the emphasis on CRM—*customer relationship management*. Its focus on the 13 Cs (introduced in Chapter 3 of the text) of customer relationship marketing helps to reinforce how various marketing actions, such as interactive marketing, can be used to *customize* the service or product for the guest, and also demonstrate how firms can create value for and from customers by using *customer insight* and *channel management*.

Our thesis is that the sole purpose of creating value for and from the customer is to develop a competitive advantage. There is logic to marketing and this logic can be learned. There are ways to understand the vagaries of customer behavior. There are ways to get at the issues and reveal the essence of marketing problems and opportunities. There are underlying principles that appear time and time again.

The Latest in Pricing and Revenue Management

Pricing and revenue management are two critical areas to the hospitality industry. The greatly expanded pricing chapter (Chapter 14) explains why revenue management works and how to think strategically about pricing, including the latest thinking on behavioral pricing. An appendix on the theory and practice of revenue management is included.

The Latest Trends in Interactive Marketing

An entire chapter (Chapter 20) is devoted to interactive marketing, including how to use database marketing to create successful interactive and internet-based marketing programs, with the latest thinking from experts in this area, and offering the top ten secrets of e-mail campaigns, and how to develop web pages with the customer in mind.

Reaching an International Market

Throughout the text we include perspectives and examples from companies headquartered around the globe. Included in this text are:

- The marketing plan of the Czech Republic
- Interviews with the VP of Strategy and the Director of Worldwide Communications for InterContinental Hotels Group PLC
- An interview with the wife of the managing director of a large hotel casino resort in Uruguay to show how hotels can be a positive force in the local community
- A detailed description of how a resort in Fiji has developed a competitive advantage by focusing on sustainable tourism.

Distribution Channels

Chapter 18, Hospitality Distribution Channels, and Chapter 19, Channels of Distribution, have been completely rewritten to provide the student with a complete understanding of the various types of models used by travel intermediaries such as the online travel agent merchant model, the online travel commission model, and opaque models such as Hotwire.com and Priceline.com.

Consumer and Market Research

In response to the recent emphasis on the use of the scientific method, this edition reflects the latest trends in research (see Chapter 11), such as the use of web-based surveys. An appendix to the chapter on research presents an article on how to buy and use market research, providing students with a step-by-step guide to conducting research.

Features of the Fourth Edition

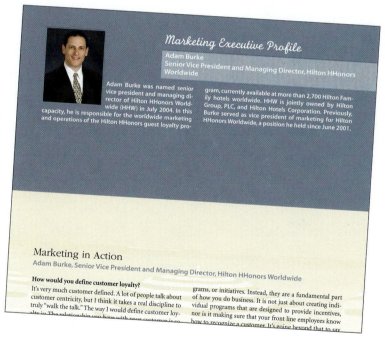

Tourism Marketing Application

A website called Destination Webrings, run by travelnotes.org (www.travelnotes.org/Webrings/destinations.htm), provides the consumer with a list of "some of the exceptional travel websites tucked away in a webring and not ranked highly on search engines." The website shows destination websites by country and things to do while there. For a destination that cannot afford a sponsored link on one of the major search engines, this may be a way to be noticed.

WebRing is a firm that businesses can use to create webrings (dir.webring.com/rw). A webring is defined this way: "similar sites are grouped together in rings and each site is linked to another by a simple navigation bar. Rings form a concentration of sites, allowing visitors to quickly find what they

Tourism Marketing Applications

These tourism sidebars provide numerous examples of how marketing is used to develop tourism. The tourism industry and the hospitality industry are interdependent. Both offer experiences to customers, both can be considered intangible, and simultaneous production and consumption occur in both fields. Our approach is to present the concepts of hospitality marketing and demonstrate the application of these concepts using hotels, restaurants, and tourism destinations.

Interviews with Executives in the Industry

Each chapter begins with an interview of a senior industry executive that provides insight into how the theory presented in that chapter is translated into real life. These executives work in restaurants, hotels, casinos, and tourism destinations. The distinguished executives and owners kind enough to be interviewed are:

Marketing Executive Profile

Adam Burke
Senior Vice President and Managing Director, Hilton HHonors Worldwide

Adam Burke was named senior vice president and managing director of Hilton HHonors Worldwide (HHW) in July 2004. In this capacity, he is responsible for the worldwide marketing and operations of the Hilton HHonors guest loyalty program, currently available at more than 2,700 Hilton Family hotels worldwide. HHW is jointly owned by Hilton Group, PLC, and Hilton Hotels Corporation. Previously, Burke served as vice president of marketing for Hilton HHonors Worldwide, a position he held since June 2001.

Marketing in Action
Adam Burke, Senior Vice President and Managing Director, Hilton HHonors Worldwide

How would you define customer loyalty?
It's very much customer defined. A lot of people talk about customer centricity, but I think it takes a real discipline to truly "walk the talk." The way I would define customer loyalty is: The relationship you have with your customer is so grams, or initiatives. Instead, they are a fundamental part of how you do business. It is not just about creating individual programs that are designed to provide incentives, nor is it making sure that your front line employees know how to recognize a customer. It's going beyond that to say

Max and Greti Mennig, Owners, Restaurant Zum See
Michael Leven, President, Vice Chairman, Marcus Foundation
Gary Leopold, President and CEO, ISM
Peter Warren, Chairman and CEO, Warren Kremer Paino Advertising, LLC
Adam Burke, SVP & Managing Director, Hilton HHonors Worldwide
Christian Hempell, VP Strategy, InterContinental Hotels Group
Bruce J. Himelstein, SVP Sales and Marketing, The Ritz-Carlton Hotel Company
Thomas Storey, EVP Development, Fairmont Hotels & Resorts
Charlotte St. Martin, President and CEO, St. Martin Enterprises
Vincent Vanderpool-Wallace, Secretary General, Caribbean Tourism Organization
Hirohide Abe, Director of Strategic Marketing, Global Hyatt Corporation

Dennis Marzella, Executive Vice President and Partner, Research & Brand Strategy, Yesawich, Pepperdine, Brown & Russell

David W. Norton, SVP Relationship Marketing, Harrah's Entertainment

John Griffin, VP Worldwide Marketing, Le Meridien

John Shields, Corporate Director of Revenue Management, Hyatt Hotels Corporation

Larry Tolpin, President & Chief Creative Officer, Yesawich, Pepperdine, Brown & Russell

Jennifer Ploszaj, Global Director of Brand Communications & Public Relations, InterContinental Hotels & Resorts

David Green, Chairman of the Board, David Green Organization

Jens Thraenhart, Executive Director, Marketing Strategy & Customer Relationship Management, Canadian Tourism Commission

Spencer Rascoff, CEO and Vice President of Marketing, Zillow.com

John Springer-Miller, President and CEO, PAR Springer-Miller Systems

Terry Jicinsky, SVP Marketing, Las Vegas Convention and Visitors Authority

Advertisements and Illustrations

The examples that appear in this book come from many sources. Concepts presented throughout the text are based on accepted principles and solid research. The examples and the advertisements used to illustrate the marketing concepts covered are primarily those of well-known international companies. Our worldwide readers will be familiar with their names and will be able to identify with these companies.

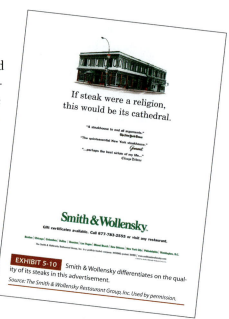

If steak were a religion, this would be its cathedral.

"A steakhouse to end all arguments."
The New York Times

"The quintessential New York steakhouse."
Gourmet.

"...perhaps the best sirloin of my life..."
Chicago Tribune

Smith & Wollensky.

Gift certificates available. Call 877-783-2555 or visit any restaurant.

Boston | Chicago | Columbus | Dallas | Houston | Las Vegas | Miami Beach | New Orleans | New York City | Philadelphia | Washington, D.C.

The Smith & Wollensky Restaurant Group, Inc. is a publicly traded company. NASDAQ symbol: SWRG | www.smithandwollensky.com

EXHIBIT 5-10 Smith & Wollensky differentiates on the quality of its steaks in this advertisement.
Source: The Smith & Wollensky Restaurant Group, Inc. Used by permission.

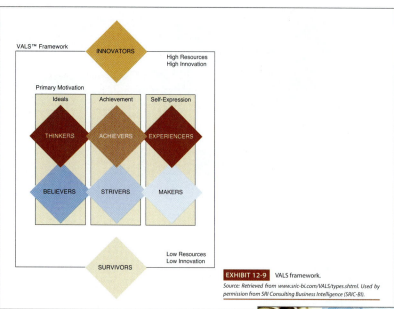

EXHIBIT 12-9 VALS framework.
Source: Retrieved from www.sric-bi.com/VALS/types.shtml. Used by permission from SRI Consulting Business Intelligence (SRIC-BI).

Case Studies

Case studies are available on CD-ROM and can be purchased with this book. These case studies are illustrative of the book's content and bring the concepts to life in real-world situations. All the cases are based on actual events, although in some instances names, places, and figures may be disguised. The Instructor's Manual provides recommendations for matching cases with chapters for optimal learning.

CASE 7

Holiday Inn Enters Salzburg

Walter Foeger looked at the stack of information before him. His new Holiday Inn, now under renovation, would open in about a year in Salzburg, Austria. Who would be the market and what would be the positioning of the hotel were at the top of his mind. He had to make a decision soon before the renovation went much further.

Walter had negotiated an "open" management contract with Holiday Inn management. "Open" meant that he had the option to position mid-market as a Holiday Inn, or up-market as a Crowne Plaza. He was fully aware that the company preferred a Crowne Plaza, the upscale hotel in its product line, other than InterContinental. But Walter had no illusions. He had observed the positioning problems of some of the other Crowne Plazas in Europe, such as the one in Amsterdam, and wasn't sure that an upscale position was the right one for the property in Salzburg. He was investing a lot of his

coach traffic, but very few stopped overnight. There was an excellent variety of tourist packages and a large choice of cultural highlights, such as all-day excursions in "Salzburger Land" and Mozart events.

The Salzburg economy was generally strong with unemployment less than 3 percent. Approximately 120 companies in Salzburg had annual gross revenues of over $100 million.

The soon-to-be Holiday Inn's location in the city center opposite the Congresshall and the Mirabellgarden was considered to be a unique selling point. It was one kilometer from the train station and seven kilometers from the airport. The downtown area was in easy walking distance. The property had originally been the long-standing 208-room Hotel Pitter, a well-known three- to four-star hotel that had fallen on hard times. Walter had maintained the existing frame of the building but had gutted the interior for renovation.

Web-Based Exercises

Web Browsing Exercise

Use your favorite search engine to look up information on WORLDHOTELS, Supranational, David Green Organization, Preferred Hotel Group, and Leading Hotels of the World. Compare and contrast the companies. What are the strengths and weaknesses of each firm? If you were the director of marketing for a hotel, would you use any of these services? Why or why not?

This edition includes many web-based exercises that encourage readers to seek current information on the topic under discussion. Information in this market is always changing and what is critical now may not be critical tomorrow. The web exercises will also keep the reader abreast of the latest information, while providing web addresses that the reader can refer to in the future. We have been very careful to use websites for firms that are long-term players in the industry.

Discussion Questions

Each chapter ends with a series of discussion questions that help students synthesize the material covered in the chapter.

■ Discussion Questions

1. What pricing lessons can the hospitality industry learn from the boom times of the early 1980s, the tough times of the early 1990s, the boom times of the mid-to late 1990s, and the tough times of the early 2000s?
2. Discuss the three types of pricing objectives (financial, volume, and customer), how they are different, and how they overlap.
3. Why is using only cost percentage pricing methods not recommended as a marketing-driven option, especially in the hospitality industry?
4. Discuss why it is possible for the hotel industry to have room rates that can change on a daily basis. How would you deal with a guest who complains about her room rate because she has found that her friend is paying $20 less per night for the same type of room?
5. Is the maintenance of a stable price a viable objective? Why or why not?
6. Discuss your personal pricing elasticity in terms of restaurants; that is, at what point in the price value mode will you trade down?
7. Discuss how psychological pricing can make a product seem to have a higher price–value relationship.
8. Choose two common mistakes in pricing and apply them to a real-life hospitality establishment.

Supplements for the Instructor

This textbook offers the instructor a multitude of options for covering the various subjects of marketing. Online instructor materials are available to qualified instructors for downloading. To access supplementary materials online, instructors need to request an instructor access code. Go to *http://www.prenhall.com,* click the **Instructor Resource Center** link, and then click **Register Today** for an instructor access code. Within 48 hours after registering, you will receive a confirming e-mail including an instructor access code. Once you have received your code, go to the site and log on for full instructions on downloading the materials you wish to use.

Instructor's Manual with Test Item File

The Instructor's Manual, available in print and downloadable formats, includes examples of various syllabi that can be used to teach different aspects of marketing. For example, we provide a plan—for both the quarter and the semester system—for instructors wishing to concentrate on marketing strategy. We also include discussion outlines for each class period, learning objectives, teaching tips, answers to end-of-chapter questions, recommendations for matching case studies (available on the Cases CD) with textbook chapters for optimal learning, and answers to case studies. The Test Item File includes multiple-choice, true/false, and short-answer questions.

TestGen Test Bank

The full Test Item File is available in this test generation software program.

PowerPoint Slides

A complete set of PowerPoint slides is provided for each chapter. The slides are comprehensive and include many of the exhibits. They have been designed so instructors can either use the slides as is or can incorporate their own material into the provided slides.

Instructor's Resource CD

This supplement contains all instructor materials on CD-ROM: Instructor's Manual with Test Item File, TestGen, and PowerPoint presentation.

For the Student

Companion Website

Discussions with our students led us to develop a study guide that students can access via a dedicated website (www.prenhall.com/shoemaker). This site contains review questions (multiple choice and true/false) with immediate feedback to test the students' understanding of the concepts in the text. Essay questions provide the opportunity to apply knowledge. PowerPoint slides, key-term searches, and chapter objectives provide the main points in each chapter.

Case Studies CD

Case studies on this CD-ROM are illustrative of the book's content and bring the material to life in real-world situations. All cases are based on actual events.

Acknowledgments

Many people—friends, former students, colleagues, industry people and customers, both advertently and inadvertently—have contributed to this book. Many will never realize how helpful they have been. We can mention only a few. We are grateful to these individuals, and to many others unmentioned, especially some great graduate and undergraduate students from around the world and executives with whom we have been privileged to work.

Those who have contributed directly to a case (on the CD-ROM) are noted on the first page of that case. Many of these contributors are graduate and undergraduate students at the University of Massachusetts/Amherst; the University of Guelph, Ontario, in Canada; and ESSEC Institute de Management Hotelier International (IMHI) in France. Still others are faculty and/or graduate students at other universities, as noted on the case. Others were participants in executive seminars.

We are especially thankful to Camille Robinson and Ashley Trevitz, both of the University of Houston; Julie Long, a longtime collaborator; and Jennifer Aiyer of the University of Houston. Camille served as an overall project director and provided many ideas, including the web exercises, for the book during its development. Ashley, among other things, obtained all the copyright permissions, a noble effort in itself. Camille, Jennifer, and Ashley provided the student perspective for this book: Camille and Jennifer at the graduate level and Ashley at the undergraduate level, as did a number of other students when the manuscript was pre-tested in the classroom. Julie provided research assistance for the text. Jennifer was responsible for the Instructor's Manual and all the supplementary material. The help of Camille, Ashley, Julie, and Jennifer cannot be overstated. This is a better book because of their efforts.

Richard Chambers, EVP of TravelClick Interactive, helped with this and earlier editions of the book. He conducted some of the interviews that appear at the beginning of each chapter and provided insight and material to various chapters throughout the text.

Peter O'Connor, professor at IMHI, and Bill Carroll, professor at Cornell University, helped greatly with Chapter 19, while Dogan Gursoy of Washington State University and Lydia Westbrook of the University of Houston contributed much to Chapter 9. We extend thanks to Tom Gorin, of Continental Airlines, for writing the appendix on Revenue Management. Mary Michele White, a student at the University of Houston, also helped supply research for the book and worked with Jennifer on the Instructor's Manual.

Still others contributed to this book in their own way through their support, experience, and knowledge in various discussions about the industry and its customers. These helpful individuals include Nan Moss, formerly of Hyatt Hotels and Resorts; Amy Weyman of Hyatt Hotels and Resorts; Judd Goldfeder of the Customer Connection; Jennifer Ploszaj of Intercontinental Hotels and Resorts; Valerie Cotter of University of Pennsylvania; Adam Burke of Hilton Hotels; Rick Mansur and Doug Leiber of JC Resorts; Dave Hanlon of Empire Resorts; Jim Eyster and Leo Renaghan, both of Cornell University; Emanuel Berger of the Victoria-Jungfrau; Bill Carroll of Cornell University; John Deighton of Harvard Business School and Meg Galliano of Las Vegas, Nevada.

Each of the executives profiled in the book deserves special thanks for taking the time to contribute their wisdom. Thanks also to the firms that graciously supplied advertisements and other information for the book.

Linda Zuk, of Wordcraft, was a wonderful editor and a pleasure to work with as we put together the final version. We are grateful to Ann Brunner, Judy Casillo, and Vern Anthony for their help and championing of this book at Prentice Hall.

And, of course, we thank our reviewers, whose helpful ideas and suggestions were well considered and often utilized: Ki-Joon Back, University of Houston; Jeff Beck, Michigan State University; Mark Bonn, Florida State University; Tim Dodd, Texas Tech University; Bradford Hudson, Boston University; Anna Mattila, Pennsylvania State

University; Ken McCleary, Virginia Tech; Hailin Qu, Oklahoma State University; Yvette Reisinger, Florida International University; Peter Ricci, University of Central Florida; Linda Shea, University of Massachusetts; and Karen Silva, Johnson & Wales University, Providence campus.

We would be remiss if each author did not personally acknowledge the following people for their wisdom over the years that, cumulatively, contributed to the final product: Frank and Jane Emanual of the Middlebury Inn, who are the ultimate hoteliers and who introduced me to this wonderful business (Stowe Shoemaker), Michael Leven of The Marcus Foundation (Robert Lewis), and Dr. Stanley Davis, former director of the SHA graduate program at Cornell (Peter Yesawich).

In spite of all this help and support, we stand responsible for the entire contents.

Stowe Shoemaker
Robert C. Lewis
Peter C. Yesawich

And to all our readers:

A truly good book teaches me better than to read it. I must soon lay it down, and commence living on its hint. What I began by reading, I must finish by acting.

Henry David Thoreau

About the Authors

Stowe Shoemaker is the Donald Hubbs Distinguished Professor and the Associate Dean of Research at the University of Houston's Conrad Hilton College of Hotel and Restaurant Management. He holds a Ph.D. from Cornell University in the School of Hotel Administration, an MS from the University of Massachusetts, and a BS from the University of Vermont. In addition to his role at the University of Houston, Dr. Shoemaker is on the executive education faculty at Cornell University.

Dr. Shoemaker's research has appeared in numerous hospitality journals, and his research has been honored as best yearly piece of research a total of four times. Dr. Shoemaker is co-author of a Harvard Business School Case Study on Hilton HHonors. Prior to moving to the University of Houston, Dr. Shoemaker taught at the University of Nevada, Las Vegas. Before earning his Ph.D., Dr. Shoemaker spent 15 years working in the hotel industry and in consulting.

Robert C. Lewis was a professor of marketing and strategy in hospitality, and graduate coordinator at the University of Guelph, Ontario, Canada, from which he is now retired. He previously served ten years in the same positions at the University of Massachusetts/Amherst, where he is Professor Emeritus. Dr. Lewis has also served as the Darden Eminent Scholar Chair in Hospitality Management at the University of Central Florida, and has been a visiting professor at Cornell/ESSEC *Institut de Management Hotelier International* in France. He spent a number of years in hotel management and airline food service management, and he owned and operated two French restaurants prior to completing his Ph.D. in 1980. He has consulted in the industry for 25 years.

Dr. Lewis is the author of *Cases in Hospitality Marketing Management,* second edition, and *Cases in Hospitality Strategy and Policy,* both published by John Wiley & Sons. He is the original and senior author of the first three editions of *Marketing Leadership in Hospitality.* He has published more than 80 articles in hospitality and other journals, including 25 in the *Cornell Quarterly,* and has written or supervised more than 100 case studies. He has taught, conducted executive seminars, and consulted on three continents.

Peter C. Yesawich is Chairman and Chief Executive Officer of Yesawich, Pepperdine, Brown & Russell (YPB&R), America's leading marketing, advertising, and public relations agency serving travel, leisure, and lifestyle clients. The agency represents clients in every category of the travel industry through seven offices across the United States and Europe.

Dr. Yesawich is a frequent commentator on travel trends in such publications as *The New York Times, The Los Angeles Times, The Wall Street Journal, USA Today, Time, Newsweek* and *Business Week,* on the CNN, CNBC, and MSNBC cable television networks, National Public Radio, and BBC World. He serves as a featured columnist in several industry trade publications and has authored numerous articles on marketing and advertising strategy in professional journals. Listed in *Who's Who in America,* Yesawich is the recipient of the World Travel Award from the American Association of Travel Editors, The Albert E. Koehl Award from the Hospitality Sales and Marketing Association International (HSMAI), and the Silver Medal from the American Advertising Federation. He was also named one of the 25 Most Extraordinary Marketing Minds by HSMAI, and is a former member of the board of directors of the Travel Industry Association of America.

Dr. Yesawich received three degrees from Cornell, including a doctorate in applied psychology, and is a graduate of the Advanced Management Program at Yale.

INTRODUCTION

Marketing Executive Profile

Max and Greti Mennig
Owners, Zum See Restaurant

Max Mennig began his career in 1969, spending several winter and summer seasons in hotels of top ski resorts such as Gstaad Palace, Alexander Palace, and Verbier, as well as eight months on the Holland America cruise line. It was on a cruise ship that he met Greti. Greti began her career helping her parents manage their hotel and restaurant in Ternberg, Austria.

The Mennigs lived and worked in Zermatt from 1976 until 1984. Max worked in the Zermatterhof for two years and then served as head chef at Hotel Pollux for six years. They opened Zum See Restaurant 22 years ago and have worked together there since: Greti in charge of the front of the house and Max in charge of the back of the house.

Marketing in Action
Max Mennig, Owner of Zum See Restaurant

What is the background and history of your restaurant and your involvement?

We started the restaurant 22 years ago and have been here for summer and winter seasons ever since. We started this restaurant after I was a chef in the Hotel Pollux in Zermatt and I had spent several seasons in seasonal places. Finally, we stopped in Zermatt and after eight years in Zermatt we started this restaurant in Zum See—a small village.

How many mountain restaurants are there in the Zermatt area?

In the Zermatt area, there are about 40 mountain restaurants, including self-service restaurants, but there are a lot of small restaurants like our place. Zermatt has a big tradition in mountain restaurants because they build a lot of restaurants out of stables, which are very cozy and charming.

What are the critical factors to your success?

I think one of the critical factors is that we are always there. My wife Greti and I know the customers. We also have a very high standard of quality. As I am always in the kitchen, I see everything and make sure it goes out the way I want it. I only use fresh meat—no frozen meat. In summer, I make the salads from our own garden. The important things are keeping the food fresh, fast, and hot—all of which are important to the overall quality.

What is your wife's role in the restaurant?

My wife is Austrian and she is very charming. She remembers the guests. She remains very cool—even when she is nervous. She stays very calm with the guests. She recognizes the clients, or sometimes they come to her and they have a small talk. Usually she doesn't have a lot of time for this, but she gives them each a little bit of time. In general, she is the boss of the restaurant outside. I am the boss in the kitchen, and she manages the restaurant.

What kind of guests do you have?

We have a few local people who come in quite regularly, but not a lot because there are so many restaurants and they have families and friends to visit. We are very happy with our local customers. In winter the most important guests are the skiers, who are very hungry. They enjoy what they are eating and relax after skiing until 1:00 or 2:00, finishing the day here before they go to the hotel. We also have hikers who stop by here for lunch.

How many people can you fit at one seating?

Inside we have a maximum of 75 seats, which are easily filled up, and we do it two and a half times if the weather is bad. You really have to organize your bookings and your reservations. If people reserve at 1:00, in the time from noon to 1:00 we can sometimes have another seating. Some people just stay for an hour, having a salad or a small plate, and they agree to leave their seat at 1:00. This way, the same table can be booked two or three times. Outside, we can seat about 100 people, and if the weather is nice, people want to sit outside in the sun and they sit everywhere. The arrangements are not complicated because it's a simple restaurant. We can put out extra tables even on the path and serve about 250 to 270 people in one day, which is probably the maximum.

Do you do that in all of your seasons?

Our winter season starts on the 15th of December, and this year, it goes until the 17th of April because Easter is very early, so the season is shorter. Sometimes we are open until the 28th of April, but it always depends on the snow and weather conditions—as long as people can get to us on skis, we remain open. In the summer we start about the 23rd of June, and it will go until the first weekend in October.

Have you ever thought of making the restaurant bigger?

I thought about it, not mainly for business reasons, but it is very difficult. I think about transformations to make it a little more organized for food supply. We have different cellars where we keep our food, and my cooks have to walk too far. For this reason, if I had a lot of money to invest, I would make the restaurant a little bit bigger inside to get some return on investment. Perhaps better toilets or something for the staff—like better changing rooms. If we transformed something, we would make a few more seats inside, if possible. Outside, I would not change anything because it's very original, very authentic, and to change it would disturb the tranquility. Some people tell me it wouldn't be good to make the restaurant bigger because it would lose some charm. In summer we hardly ever use the restaurant inside because everyone wants to be outside observing the beautiful nature around them. In winter you make more money than in summer because it's more crowded and so we may need to have more room.

Could you describe the kitchen and how you manage the cooks?

It is very difficult to work in a small kitchen, but you get used to it. It is so small that you can turn around and open a drawer, your meat is right behind you and the oven is just on the other side—you don't have to walk a lot. Every person has to work with it a little bit, and it takes new people a while to get used to the system. It is very organized because there isn't a lot of space. I try to create plates that we do not have to work on too much. The decoration is not fancy because the most important things are serving the food fast and warm. Sometimes you get into fancy restau-

rants and the plates are so fancily decorated that your food is no longer warm.

How do you get the food? It takes 25 minutes to walk up to the restaurant, and if you take the gondola, it's 20 minutes or you ski down. How do you get all of your materials and food up here to be able to serve the number of people you serve?

This is actually a little problematic for us, but we had to get used to it, and we make our own supplies. In summer we use a four-wheel ATV to bring materials up, which takes about 15 minutes. In winter I use my Ski-Doo, which takes only about 5 minutes, but I can only put so much food on it so I may have to go two or three times. I also have to bring down all the garbage and empty bottles; everything that I brought up that is not used, I have to bring down again.

How much planning do you do in terms of materials management?

In this place, there isn't a lot of storage room, so we have to be quite short with our orders. As a result, I only order fresh supplies. We can order every day in Zermatt because we have butchers and grocers for vegetables. You can actually buy everything here. We can order the fish two or three times a week from Zurich, and the meat can come every day. Some things, however, I have to order in advance. For example, calf's liver, I try to order that daily because it has to be fresh. It doesn't taste good if it's been vacuum sealed. There are other meats that come vacuum sealed that I can keep for easily up to two weeks or longer. Other things, like wines, you can store for the whole winter, and we start bringing them up in September. Usually, it's never enough and we have to get the rest of what we need quite frequently, about every week. The thing is, though, if you run out of something—calf's liver, sweet breads—people understand because they know we cannot go to the neighboring shop to buy supplies. You simply say, "Well, I'm sorry, but we are all out," because they know there is no time, especially if it is really busy.

What time do you get here and start preparing for the day?

Everyone comes in around 8:30, we open at 11:30, and we like to finish around 5:00 in the afternoon, but sometimes you have guests who come in a bit later. You're still cooking and you can do another four or five, depending on who is coming and how many. Sometimes you can get them to have one plate, or if there are four people, you can give them a choice of two plates, because they understand that we may have already started cleaning or closing up. My staff deserves their rest and I have to respect their working hours, so we try to do service from 11:30 to 5:00.

Do you keep a consistency in staff?

I try to keep a consistency as much as possible. Young people don't always want to stay for a long time. I have a waiter who has been with us for eight years and a man in the kitchen who has been with me for 11 years. It's very important to have some people who have worked for you for a lot of seasons because it's easier as well to keep the quality when you have someone who knows the place. We have to improvise a lot of the time, and new people are not always easily adaptable to new situations. Every day is different. Sometimes you think everything is fully booked, and then suddenly the weather changes and you have cancellations and empty tables. Luckily, we always have people who come by without reservations so it's not hard to keep the seats filled.

What makes your staff want to work here as opposed to working in another place?

For instance, the waiter who has been with us for eight years feels like he's at home, a bit like he's our son. We have a very good repetitive clientele and he knows the guests and they recognize him. He is happy to serve the guests from last year again and again. I think because it is a small team, it is a bit like family. When we sit, we sit at the same table and talk like family.

Any advice to people who wish to start careers in the restaurant business?

I think that if you ever want to work in this business, you have to love it. You cannot think about the money. If you do it with enthusiasm and you love what you do, the money will come on its own. The important issues are that you are serious and always run a restaurant with your own expectations in mind. I always tell my staff, if they want to serve something that I might not like, "Just imagine if you were to sit down at a table and get a plate like this or get a salad that was not nice anymore—you would say, 'What kind of cook do they have in that kitchen?' " I always think that I only want to serve what I would like to eat. Also, you always have to be nice to your clients, even if they are not so nice. Remember, they do not stay forever, and either they enjoy your food and your hospitality or they don't. If they don't, just keep in mind that in an hour or so, they will leave the place and then you will have other nice customers.

Used by permission from Max and Greti Mennig.

This textbook is about marketing. In addition to covering the usual topics one would find in a traditional text on marketing (e.g., the marketing concept, market segmentation, developing the marketing plan, and positioning), this book is designed to show how a firm uses the marketing function to create and sustain a competitive advantage. This is the main role of marketing, and all the strategies and corresponding tactics must lead to this end. The concept of competitive advantage is discussed in much detail in Chapters 5 and 6, where we discuss marketing strategy. However, we will briefly introduce the concept of competitive advantage in order to lay the foundation and "blueprint" for the text.

We define competitive advantage as the ability of a firm to develop and maintain distinctive competencies that enable it to capture a larger share of the market and earn higher-than-average profits. One example of a distinctive competency is management knowledge. By this we mean that the management of a particular firm has skills, knowledge, and know-how that enables the firm to do better than its competitors. Exceptional management skills also enable a firm to be successful when by all intuitive thinking the firm should fail. Knowledge is just one example of a competency that leads to competitive advantage. Other examples of competencies include, but are not limited to, features such as location, the firm's culture, creativity, access to scarce resources, exceptional employees, special patents, access to capital, and brand name. Of these competencies, management knowledge and skills are two of the most important.

To understand the importance of knowledge and skills, consider the Restaurant Zum See, which is located between Zermatt and Furi, Switzerland, literally in the middle of a mountain hamlet. The Restaurant Zum See is known as a mountain restaurant. There are 40 such restaurants in the Zermatt area. The market for these restaurants is hikers and skiers. The only way to get to the restaurant in the summer is to hike 30 minutes up the mountain from Zermatt or hike 20 minutes down from the nearest gondola. In the winter one reaches the restaurant on skis or snowshoes. All the supplies for the restaurant are brought in by tractor during the summer and on a motorized snow sled in the winter. The employees get to the restaurant by hiking and sliding down on a wooden sled. Despite being on the side of a mountain and not easily accessible, this little restaurant (between indoor and outdoor seating there is room for 165 customers) turns over its tables on average 1.5 times daily during its summer and winter seasons. (The restaurant is open from December through April in the winter and June through October in the summer.)

People come to Zermatt just to go to this restaurant. Max and Greti Mennig, the owners of the business, have created a competitive advantage because of their knowledge of the restaurant business, but more important, their knowledge of their customers—many of whom are repeat customers. It should be noted that, in order to get to the Restaurant Zum See, one must hike or ski by other mountain restaurants. Why do people walk by other restaurants to get to the Restaurant Zum See? The answer to this question is the heart of this book. This restaurant provides a prism through which we can illustrate the framework of the book.

All the actions Max and Greti Mennig take at their restaurant lead to a competitive advantage. One way to categorize the different actions the Mennigs and other firms take to gain a competitive advantage is to examine the functional areas of the firm. These functional areas are known as the value chain activities because they entail all the activities an organization undertakes to transform raw materials into the final product or service that the customer buys.[1] The functional areas are infrastructure, production, marketing, materials management, research and development, information sources, and human resources.

To illustrate the concept of the value chain, consider what happens at the Restaurant Zum See. One of the end products the customer buys is the meal that is served. For that meal to reach the customer, Max Mennig first needs to order the ingredients that comprise the product. These ingredients then need to be delivered, inventoried, and carried up the mountain. This is the *materials management* part of the value chain. For the ingredients to be properly put together, the *production* part of the value chain, Max Mennig needs to make sure that the right cooks are hired and trained. He also needs to ensure that there is a friendly and well-trained staff to deliver the food. Because of the restaurant's uniqueness (how many people want to work at a job where it takes 30 minutes to hike to and from work?), the Mennigs have had to create a culture that creates employee loyalty. This is the *human resources* part of the value chain. The *infrastructure* part of the value chain ensures that the restaurant has the correct equipment to prepare and serve the items desired by the patron. The *research and development* part of the value chain involves the activities Mr. Mennig undertakes to guarantee that the new items added to the menu are items customers like and items that the cooks can make. Of course, the *marketing* part ensures that there are customers to be served! This same process happens at a restaurant chain such as McDonald's, although many of the value chain activities are developed at the corporate level and implemented at the unit level.

These value chain activities are then focused on what Michael Porter, a professor of strategy at Harvard Business School, calls the generic building blocks of competitive advantage. These building blocks are quality, efficiency, customer responsiveness, and innovation. To this list we have added size, which for the hospitality industry can refer to either the number of properties or the size of the hotel. It can also refer to the number of seats available in a restaurant, the number of rooms on a cruise ship, and the number of seats on an airplane. We briefly discuss and provide examples of each building block.

Quality

To understand quality, consider what Mr. Mennig goes through before having one of the cooks make a specific item. First, he develops a recipe and records all the steps necessary to prepare the food item. Part of this planning involves measuring and recording all the food ingredients so that a specific taste will be delivered on a consistent basis. This is called "planning the work." When the cook makes the item, he or she essentially "works the plan." If the cook makes the item as specified in the recipe, then we can say we have a quality product. In this sense, quality refers to the fact that the products or services work as they were designed to and they work well.[2] The advertisement for Riedel glass shown in Exhibit 1 illustrates this point.

Most customers associate high quality with high price. However, the definition of quality does not necessarily mean this is the case. Consider, for instance, the Formule1 lodging chain that is located in Europe and owned and operated by Accor. The rate for a room in this chain in July 2006 was 29 Euros, or approximately $35, yet it offers high quality. It provides a comfortable, safe, and clean room at a very low price. The whole chain was designed to support this low price—the thread point count of the sheets, the size of the towels, the type of bedding, and the in-room amenities. The hotel works as it is designed to do for a price of $35. The George V in Paris also offers a comfortable, safe, and clean room, but at an average price of $1,000 per room. The thread point count of the sheets, the size of the towels, the type of bedding, and the in-room amenities are all designed to support this high price. This room also offers a quality product.

Quality of services is best understood in terms of the dimensions that define quality: reliability, assurance, tangibility, empathy, and responsiveness. These dimensions are referred to by the acronym RATER. These dimensions are discussed in more detail in Chapter 2.

As will be discussed throughout the book, one of the roles of marketing is to determine the price point at which customers are willing to buy and then design a quality product or service to match that price point.

EXHIBIT 1 This advertisement for Riedel Glassware illustrates how items such as glassware can be designed for a specific purpose. *Source: Riedel Crystal. Used by permission.*

of a restaurant firm that focuses on efficiency and, as such, offers lower prices. Its whole operation is designed to support an inexpensive taco without sacrificing taste. The company developed what was known as the K-Minus program, which changed the restaurant from 70 percent kitchen and 30 percent customer to 70 percent customer and 30 percent kitchen. They did this by making the kitchen for heating and assembly and transferring all cooking to central units.[3] In fact, in a video clip that accompanies a Harvard Business School case, although most fast-food companies give 27 cents on the dollar worth in food, Taco Bell attempts to provide 35 cents' worth. Southwest Airlines is an example of an airline that practices an efficiency strategy.

 Web Browsing Exercise

Visit the websites for Taco Bell (www.tacobell.com/) and Southwest Airlines (www.southwest.com/). How do these websites exhibit the companies' efficiency strategies? Compare and contrast.

One role of marketing is to determine whether there are enough customers to support this strategy and to ensure that efficiency does not negatively impact customers' willingness to buy the product or service. One of the authors of this text undertook countless studies on behalf of Taco Bell measuring the impact of the different types and quantity of ingredients on customers' attitudes about the product's taste. The goal was always to make sure that the drive for efficiency didn't compromise the focus on the customer.

Efficiency

Efficiency refers to the fact that the whole process of production is designed to minimize the cost of production. Referring to our earlier example of Formule1, the reason it can charge $35 per night relates to the design of the whole operation. Guests check themselves into the hotel and get their room key by inserting their credit card into a self-service kiosk. The top bed sheet and the bottom bed sheet are sewn together at the bottom so that the housekeeper can make the bed in one motion instead of two. The bed frame goes all the way to the floor so that housekeepers do not have to clean under the bed. As a result, they are able to clean more rooms per hour.

One of the characteristics of a firm that practices a strategy of efficiency is that it can offer lower prices than its competitors and still realize an acceptable return on invested capital. Taco Bell is perhaps one of the best examples

Customer Responsiveness

A third building block of competitive advantage is customer responsiveness. As the name implies, the focus of this strategy is to take care of the customer with the utmost detail. Although the other building blocks must also be concerned with taking care of the customer, this strategy is different because rather than focusing on market segments, firms practicing this strategy focus on the individual customer. For instance, Courtyard by Marriott focuses on the business traveler segment of the market. The product offered—from the size of the desk in the room to free access to high-speed Internet—is standardized to meet the need (or needs) of this segment. In contract, consider Ritz-Carlton, also a Marriott brand, which attempts to customize each hotel room. It does this by collecting the preferences of guests so that when guests check into the hotel, the room is customized to meet their needs. This includes having the minibar filled with their favorite drinks and snacks and having their favorite pillow type (e.g., goose down versus foam) on the bed. Firms that focus on this strategy develop elaborate database systems to keep track of their guests' preferences.

One of the roles of marketing in this strategy is to determine what individual customers want and then make sure they receive it.

Innovation

Innovation refers to a firm's ability to develop new products and services that either change the way an industry does business or the way a customer uses or interacts with the business. There has been considerable innovation in the hospitality business since Kemmon Wilson built the first Holiday Inn. Examples include the all-suite brands such as Embassy and the residence properties such as Residence Inns. Wingate Inns embraced technology early by offering high-speed Internet access in every room. They also added two-line speakerphones with data port, conference call, and voice mail capabilities. Other hotels have, of course, begun to offer the same. However, Wingate Inns was the first to innovate. Another example of innovation occurred when Club Med first offered all-inclusive resorts. Here, customers paid just one price for everything, including liquor and cigarettes. Now there is much competition in this space ("space" in this context refers to a type of business model in which firms compete).

Of course, innovation has also occurred in how customers make reservations. We provide two illustrations to make this point clear. First, consider for instance the importance of the Internet in terms of how customers search for information about hotels and how they make hotel reservations. Jupiter Research estimates that by 2007, 30 percent of total U.S. travel revenue will be booked online*. This represents $77 billion (an estimated 40 percent are "influenced" by the Internet according to the YPB&R/Yankelovich Partners 2004 *National Travel MONITOR*). This is up from 3 percent in the year 2000. This innovation has required hoteliers to develop strategies to manage this new channel of distribution. The department that this task usually falls to is the marketing department.

A second example of innovation pertains to the restaurant industry. Consider the impact of the rise of fish farming. Such methods of harvesting fish have provided restaurants with a steady supply of fish at a fairly stable price, which enables restaurateurs to focus on other facets of their business.

The role of those in marketing is to understand how innovations in other areas will impact their business and then adapt their strategies accordingly.

Size

The fifth building block of competitive advantage is size—that is, the ability of the firm to understand what size it should be in order to compete. As mentioned earlier, size in the hotel business refers to either the number of properties a firm has or the number of rooms an individual hotel has in a given market. For example, consider Hilton Corporation. In 2000 Hilton purchased Promus Hotels, which owned and operated Doubletree, Embassy Suites, Hampton Inns, Hampton Inn Suites, Homewood Suites, Harrison Conference Centers, and Red Lion. This purchase added 1,700 properties to Hilton's portfolio, raising the total number of rooms in the Hilton portfolio to 290,000 in 50 countries. The purchase of Promus was prompted in part by Hilton's desire to improve the viability of its frequent guest program—Hilton HHonors. In order to entice guests to join the program, it was important that Hilton have properties in a much larger number of locations. The purchase of Promus helped ensure that this would be the case.[4]

An example of an individual hotel is the MGM Grand in Las Vegas. This hotel, with 5,000 rooms, is the largest in Las Vegas. This size gives the property market power. Size is also a very important competitive advantage in the convention industry. According to *Tradeshow Week*, Las Vegas is the city where five of the ten largest trade shows are held each year.[5] In 2002 a total of 35 large conventions were held in the city. This number significantly outpaced the 21 large events held in the city of Chicago, the second preferred destination for such events during the same period. A study conducted by Merrill Lynch predicts that Las Vegas will continue to gain market share over its competitors and estimates that about 15 of the "*Tradeshow Week* 200 large conventions" are seriously considering relocating their events to Las Vegas during the next two years. On the other hand, only three trade show organizers are planning to relocate the events they currently held in Las Vegas somewhere else.[6] A major reason for this was the fact that Las Vegas has the largest convention space in the United States as well as the largest number of hotel rooms. The role of marketing is to determine whether size is a building block with which the firm can develop a compet-

---

*Website for Jupiter is www.clickz.com/stats/sectors/travelarticle.php/3433881

itive advantage, and, if so, how to exploit the size to create a competitive advantage.

The introduction of the Airbus A380 is an example of size in the aviation business. The A380 is the largest passenger aircraft in the world and holds 555 people. Two interesting facts about this aircraft are that it has 50 percent more floor space on the main cabin and 10 percent more in cabin baggage storage. The size does not increase cost. In fact, according to information provided by Airbus Industries, the A380 offers 15 to 20 percent lower per-mile cost than the traditional airplane.[7]

In 2006 Royal Caribbean Cruise Line will be launching Freedom of the Seas. This ship is large enough to have an ice-skating rink, rock-climbing wall, and Royal Promenade. In addition, it will offer some of the largest staterooms in the industry.

Size does not always have to mean big. Small boutique hotels, such as The Hotel in Luzern, Switzerland, are popular because they are exclusive. The Rittenhouse Hotel, a 98-unit luxury hotel in downtown Philadelphia, is another example. Editors of *Lodging Hospitality* ranked this hotel as one of the top performing hotels in 2002—a distinction it has earned for more than a decade.[8] The Rittenhouse Hotel has continued to earn awards, which it proudly displays on its website (www.rittenhousehotel.com/). We want to stress that size becomes a building block of competitive advantage only if the firm knows exactly what size it should be and why. We address this issue in the case of the Restaurant Zum See.

It is important to note that firms do not necessarily focus on one building block of competitive advantage and ignore all others. Very often a firm focuses on two or three at the same time. For instance, consider Harrah's Entertainment—the most profitable casino company in the world not because of its size, but because it focuses its marketing efforts on efficiency and customer responsiveness. Harrah's does this through its frequent player program, which is known as Harrah's Rewards. Harrah's has spent millions of dollars developing and defining their system so marketing dollars are spent very efficiently. Harrah's knows exactly when to mail a guest an offer and what that offer should look like in order to get the guest to purchase. The guest feels happy because Harrah's provides him with offers that matter to him (customer responsiveness), while Harrah's is happy because its marketing dollars are not wasted on customers who will never buy (efficiency).

Another example of an organization focusing on more than one of the building blocks of competitive advantage is the resort town of Arosa, Switzerland, which is a mountain town located in the eastern part of Switzerland. The closest town is approximately 28 kilometers (1 kilometer equals roughly 6/10 of a mile) and 360 sharp turns below (Arosa is at 3,000 kilometers and the next closest town is at 11 kilometers above sea level). The tourist bureau in this town has been able to get all those involved in the tourist industry to join forces in promoting Arosa as a destination (efficiency of marketing dollars). An example is the One Pass card, which enables visitors to Arosa to enjoy free transportation throughout the town. At the same time, the town is very customer responsive because it offers all levels of accommodations, a variety of ski trails with different levels of difficulty, and a variety of winter sports activities. Basically, it offers something for everyone.

The reader may have noticed that at the end of the discussion of each of the building blocks of competitive advantage, we briefly discussed marketing's role in developing and exploiting the specific building block to build a competitive advantage. Throughout the text we will expand on marketing's role in creating a competitive advantage by developing strategies and tactics to influence each of these building blocks. First, however, we provide the blueprint for the book, which can be seen in Exhibit 2.

Exhibit 2 shows that the book is divided into seven parts. The first three sections provide all the necessary background information to acquaint the reader with marketing strategy and the hospitality customer. Specifically, in Part I we discuss the essence of marketing and why hospitality and tourism marketing is different in many ways from traditional product marketing. We also discuss the marketing mix and product/service mix as well as relationship marketing, which is geared toward both the external and internal (i.e., employees) customers. Part II introduces the reader to the concept of strategy and the marketing environment and how hospitality firms should develop strategic plans and corresponding marketing objectives. Part III examines the hospitality customer. Reflecting the fact that there are multiple hospitality customers, the first chapter in Part III looks at individual customers, and the second chapter examines organizational customers.

Before those in marketing can develop strategies and tactics to focus on one of the building blocks of competitive advantage, they must understand their competition and how to effectively use marketing intelligence and research. This is the subject of Part IV. The first chapter in this section examines how to analyze the competitive environment in which one operates. The second chapter in this section is devoted to the use of marketing research and marketing intelligence.

Part V examines the functional strategies a firm undertakes with respect to the generic building blocks of competitive advantage discussed earlier. There are nine chapters, one chapter per functional strategy. Part VI reviews how the functional strategies developed are put into a coherent marketing plan. The figure also shows a feedback loop, which does need to be discussed in this book. The feedback loop is there only to remind the reader that

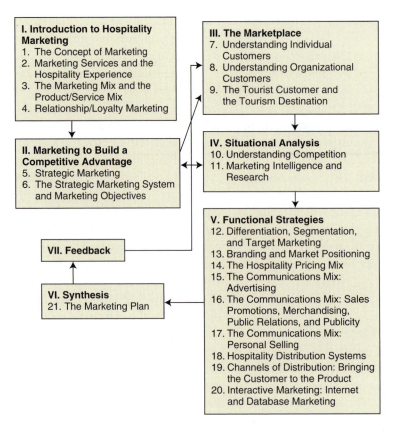

I. **Introduction to Hospitality Marketing**
1. The Concept of Marketing
2. Marketing Services and the Hospitality Experience
3. The Marketing Mix and the Product/Service Mix
4. Relationship/Loyalty Marketing

II. **Marketing to Build a Competitive Advantage**
5. Strategic Marketing
6. The Strategic Marketing System and Marketing Objectives

III. **The Marketplace**
7. Understanding Individual Customers
8. Understanding Organizational Customers
9. The Tourist Customer and the Tourism Destination

IV. **Situational Analysis**
10. Understanding Competition
11. Marketing Intelligence and Research

V. **Functional Strategies**
12. Differentiation, Segmentation, and Target Marketing
13. Branding and Market Positioning
14. The Hospitality Pricing Mix
15. The Communications Mix: Advertising
16. The Communications Mix: Sales Promotions, Merchandising, Public Relations, and Publicity
17. The Communications Mix: Personal Selling
18. Hospitality Distribution Systems
19. Channels of Distribution: Bringing the Customer to the Product
20. Interactive Marketing: Internet and Database Marketing

VII. **Feedback**

VI. **Synthesis**
21. The Marketing Plan

EXHIBIT 2   Model for the 4th edition of this text.

marketing is a continuous process, as the customer and the environment keep changing.

Exhibit 3 shows how the topics in the book relate to the responsibilities of those in marketing and how their actions help build a competitive advantage. For example, the responsibilities of the marketing department, listed under the value chain activities, include understanding the different types of customers (individual customers [Chapter 7] and organizational customers [Chapter 8]), the tourist customer and the tourism destination (Chapter 9), the internal and competitive analysis (Chapter 10), and marketing intelligence and research (Chapter 11). Concepts of positioning and branding are introduced in Chapter 13 and discussed with reference to efficiency, customer responsiveness, and size.

■ References

1. Porter, M. E. (1985). *Competitive advantage.* New York: Free Press.
2. Hill, C., & Jones, G. R. (2004). *Strategic management theory: An integrated approach.* Boston: Houghton Mifflin.
3. DeLong, D., Applegate, L., & Schlesinger, L. (2001). Taco Bell, Inc.—1983–1994 [Case study]. Harvard Business School Publishing. Case #9-398-129.
4. Hotel Online. (1999, September). Hilton acquires Promus for $4 billion [Press release]. Retrieved September 30, 2003, from www.hotel-online.com/News/Press Releases1999_3rd/Sept99_HiltonPromus.html.
5. Tufel, G. (2003, February 3). Five out of the ten largest tradeshows each year are held in Las Vegas. *Tradeshow Week.*
6. Jones, C. (2003, August 3). Las Vegas: Expo boom seen ahead. *Las Vegas Review-Journal.* Retrieved September 30, 2003, from www.reviewjournal.com/lvrj_home/2003/Aug03-Sun-2003/business/21842768.html.
7. www.airbus.com/A380/seeing/indexminisite.aspx. Retrieved September 25, 2005.
8. Watkins, E., & Wolff, C. (2003). The top performers. *Lodging Hospitality, 59*(11), 22.

EXHIBIT 3 The Responsibilities of Those in Marketing and How Marketing Leads to a Competitive Advantage

Value Chain Activities	Efficiency	Quality	Innovation	Customer Responsiveness	Size
Chapter 1: The Concept of Marketing Chapter 3: The Marketing Mix and the Product/Service Mix Chapter 5: Strategic Marketing Chapter 6: The Strategic Marketing System Chapter 7: Understanding Individual Customers Chapter 8: Understanding Organizational Customers Chapter 10: Understanding Competition Chapter 11: Marketing Intelligence and Research Chapter 21: The Marketing Plan	Chapter 12: Differentiation, Segmentation, and Target Marketing Chapter 13: Branding and Market Positioning Chapter 14: The Hospitality Pricing Mix	Chapter 2: Marketing Services and the Hospitality Experience Chapter 15: The Communications Mix: Advertising Chapter 16: The Communications Mix: Sales Promotions, Merchandising, Public Relations, and Publicity Chapter 17: The Communications Mix: Personal Selling	Chapter 18: Hospitality Distribution Systems Chapter 19: Channels of Distribution Chapter 20: Interactive Marketing: Internet and Database Marketing Chapter 9: The Tourist Customer and the Tourism Destination	Chapter 4: Relationship/Loyalty Marketing Chapter 12: Differentiation, Segmentation, and Target Marketing Chapter 13: Branding and Market Positioning Chapter 20: Interactive Marketing: Internet and Database Marketing	Chapter 13: Branding and Market Positioning

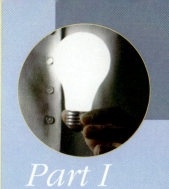

Part I

Introduction to Hospitality Marketing

Chapter 1
The Concept of Marketing

Chapter 2
Marketing Services and the Hospitality Experience

Chapter 3
The Marketing Mix and the Product/ Service Mix

Chapter 4
Relationship/Loyalty Marketing

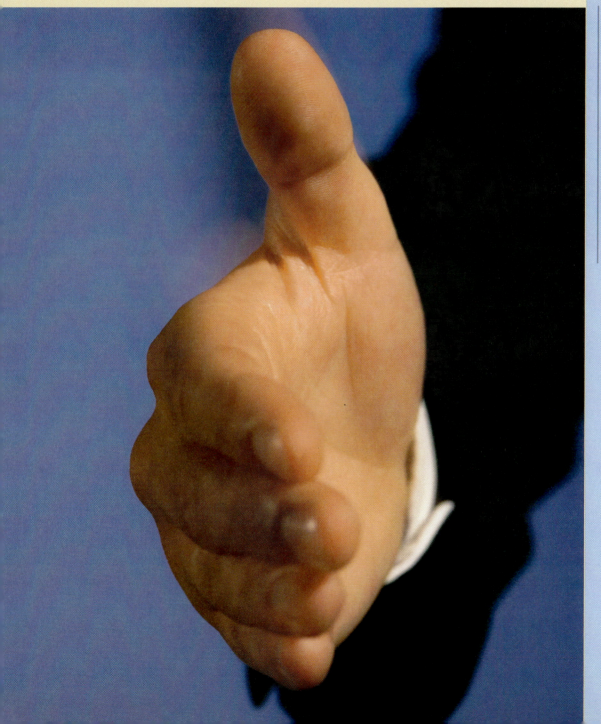

The Concept
of Marketing

Overview

Chapter 1 reviews the fundamentals of the **concept of marketing**. The chapter explains why every decision that a hospitality organization makes is an act of marketing and why every employee in an organization should be focused on either taking care of the customer or supporting someone who does take care of the customer. The marketing concept is explained early in the chapter and developed to be the text's foundation. Most important, this book is about the customers.

I. Introduction to Hospitality Marketing
1. *The Concept of Marketing*
2. Marketing Services and the Hospitality Experience
3. The Marketing Mix and the Product/Service Mix
4. Relationship/Loyalty Marketing

II. Marketing to Build a Competitive Advantage
5. Strategic Marketing
6. The Strategic Marketing System and Marketing Objectives

III. The Marketplace
7. Understanding Individual Customers
8. Understanding Organizational Customers
9. The Tourist Customer and the Tourism Destination

IV. Situational Analysis
10. Understanding Competition
11. Marketing Intelligence and Research

V. Functional Strategies
12. Differentiation, Segmentation, and Target Marketing
13. Branding and Market Positioning
14. The Hospitality Pricing Mix
15. The Communications Mix: Advertising
16. The Communications Mix: Sales Promotions, Merchandising, Public Relations, and Publicity
17. The Communications Mix: Personal Selling
18. Hospitality Distribution Systems
19. Channels of Distribution: Bringing the Customer to the Product
20. Interactive Marketing: Internet and Database Marketing

VII. Feedback

VI. Synthesis
21. The Marketing Plan

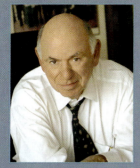

Michael A. Leven
Vice Chairman, Marcus Foundation

Mike Leven has spent more than 50 years in the hotel industry. Until recently, he was President and CEO of US Franchise Systems (USFS), a company he formed, that franchises the Microtel Inns & Suites, Hawthorn Suites, and Best Inns and Best Suites hotel brands. He was president and chief operating officer of Holiday Inn Worldwide, president of Days Inn of America, and president of Americana Hotels. Currently he sits on two hotel boards: Las Vegas Sands (Venetian Hotel) and Hersha Hospitality.

Leven cofounded the Asian American Hotel Owners Association (AAHOA). He is a former international president of the Hotel Sales & Marketing Association International (HSMAI) and a member of HSMAI's Hall of Fame.

Leven holds a bachelor of arts from Tufts University and a master of science from Boston University. He also holds honorary doctorate degrees from Johnson & Wales and Niagara University.

Marketing in Action
Mike Leven, Vice Chairman, Marcus Foundation

How do you define marketing?

For many years, the topic of conversation was, What is the difference between sales and marketing? because originally in the hotel business, there was no marketing—it really evolved through the selling function. I picked up a pamphlet once a number of years ago, and it very adequately defined the difference between sales and marketing, which is that sales is getting rid of something and marketing is knowing what to get rid of. From that, I developed my own definition of marketing as knowing what to get rid of. When you talk about establishing a product brand or line that you're going to deliver to customers, either from a service standpoint or a product standpoint, what marketing does is define what the customers' requirements are so that you can design the product or service to fill that requirement and then sales will sell it.

What does the marketing concept mean to you and your organization?

I think the marketing concept is essentially one that integrates the customer requirements with the requirements of the business to create more and more customers. Marketing to me is an all-encompassing function that each department in the corporation, all the way to the accounting department, participates in when the objectives that come from marketing are defined. The marketing concept is essentially a total business concept, without which you can't be successful in creating customers or repeating customers. The marketing culture is created by the leadership of the organization. It's not created by the chief marketing officer. It's created by the top senior person who puts the customer requirement on the front end of the burner and acts that way personally through every relationship that individual has with his staff in every department. Even the way they collect an account or the way an accounts receivable is passed through is part of a genuine marketing effort to develop the customer response mechanism. When you, as a leader, integrate your customer philosophy through each department as it works for you, that is how you generate the marketing culture.

Can you provide an example of a hospitality company that is truly marketing oriented?

There are some examples of specific marketing activities that go on in various corporations that one might identify as an appropriate activity, but there are no companies that represent true marketing philosophies. They all have some level of marketing conditions in them, but I do not feel that any of them really fit the profile as having the total marketing concept environment. The hotel business has been, for all practical purposes, an operation business and not a marketing business. You see examples of this from time to time, but it's generally not what would fall into the real definition of a marketing company. There are some companies that tend to move forward in this area, but since most hotel companies are run by finance people or development people, the marketing culture has had to be built from underneath them, and it is extremely difficult to do that. At Coca-Cola, they just eliminated their chief marketing officer position. That speaks as to what the leadership thinks is really important.

I think the students have come a long way over the course of my career. There were no sales or marketing courses when I started this business, at least not of any note. There's a lot more marketing philosophy and marketing technique and marketing understanding that comes out of the universities today. The difficulty is that for students, it takes a long time between when you graduate and when you lead a company, and many of the students may never get to the CEO position. They can *influence* the CEO, through marketing leadership positions, but the CEO is the one that sets the cultural framework. Over time, I think you'll have more of that, but I'm not sure if we'll see a significant difference in your lifetime or mine. There are gradual differences that I've seen taking place and there are elements of it, but nothing really significant.

One of the great marketers in the hotel business is a guy named Harris Rosen in Florida, and he's not even recognized by major companies. They look at him as a salesman of hotel rooms; I look at him as a great marketer. He builds a culture within his organization and his company, all the way down to the shoes that employees wear, their health care program, their uniform, and their benefits, which is part of the marketing effort—it's not a human resource decision. This is a decision as to how I am going to deliver services that I need to deliver through my distribution point or my people. It's a marketing decision and how he prices and what he does—I would say that he's the best I've seen, and he's not in a major corporation.

Starbucks is another company that is absolutely a prototypical marketing example. Most of the great marketing decisions are intuitive, and Howard Schultz's decision to build an environment—creating an environment where people wanted to be there and coffee became incidental—that's one of the most esoteric but most magnificent marketing decisions of this generation. Every time I go by, I am stunned by the number of people of all ages and demographics who would be there just to be there. He hit it right

on the button—he created an environment. With respect to hotels, W has done some of that for a particular market segment. You don't see that in your traditional companies—there is more of a "copycat" type of marketing.

How does your organization keep customers coming back?

If you don't have customers, you don't have a business. However, historically in the hotel business, repeat business has only been 60 to 65 percent for most. That essentially says you're only keeping two out of every three customers, which means you have to create a third customer every time. Some of the better companies have satisfaction rates of 80 percent now and they think that that is pretty good, but there's also now one out of every five customers that is not satisfied. That's not particularly good. You have an opportunity to satisfy a higher number of customers, but if the industry is willing to accept a 65 or an 80, that is not exactly what you call a satisfactory performance. If you were a manufacturing company and you had a defect rate of 20 percent, you'd be out of business. You could say, at best, we have a defect rate of 20 percent. How do you keep them? You focus on the defects.

In our company, what we decided was to go with noncorporate people who really would focus on the defect, and we found that over 90 percent of the defects took place in two places—the front desk and the reservations. Then we tracked it against different brands; even low price or midprice, the defects were exactly the same—they were on front desk and the reservations, check-in/checkout and the reservations. Now if I said to you, "If you have a 20 percent defect rate in which 18 points of the 20 come from essentially one of two areas, why do we not concentrate on fixing that?" Nevertheless, it continues.

We've made some dents in it, but not enough. There's in-room printing of your bill so that you don't have to receive it in an envelope or have it mailed. There's uniforming and grooming—ensuring the right profile of person is working at the desk. Are they getting paid properly? Are the hours right? If you were a manufacturer, you would be looking at it from the point of view that you wouldn't be able to stay in business with a defect rate like that. Hotels stay in business anyway. We've got all these people running around checking on life safety and checking on cleanliness and checking on this and that, and all this stuff comes back into the mystery shopping report and all of the problems stay in those two places. We've begun to try and concentrate in our small way, to focus on what we can do to change that particular thing, and we measure it. We historically had seven-hour shifts (excluding breaks) as long as I've been in the business—7 to 3, 3 to 11, 11 to 7. Maybe we need to decrease shifts to four hours.

Breaking the paradigm years ago was a free breakfast; breaking the paradigm now may be free local and long-distance calling and free high-speed wireless. But the paradigm really comes back to: What does the customer really want, can you afford to deliver to the customer, and can you charge the customer for those services by simply having the rate you charge move forward, as opposed to charging them on a nickel-and-dime basis? All-inclusive resorts from 30 years ago show a customer preference for getting one price and putting everything in it. Do you see a lot of all-inclusive resorts coming out? No, you see the same nickel-and-dime stuff you've seen since the 1960s.

How do you identify customers' problems?

First, it's experiential; second, it's intuitive; and only third would you back it up with some research. At the end of the day, when I was at Holiday Inn and we were coming out with Express, research indicated that people wanted a hot breakfast, but the research didn't indicate whether they would pay for it or not. I didn't really have the answer, but we went with a cold breakfast and it was very successful because I believed people wouldn't pay for it—that was intuitive. I assume that Howard Schultz designs something for Howard Schultz. His intuition says, "This is what is going to work." When we went to Microtel last year with free local, free long distance, and free high-speed wireless Internet, we didn't do research for that; we simply realized that the time had come for that and the economics as well as the customer want it—let's do it. It's only going to be a matter of time until the rest of the industry begins to do it, but it'll take a while. That is a decision based on customer needs—you don't have to research that, you just have to experience it. You have to experience going to a hotel in New York City, paying $400 for a room, and then being charged $1.00 for a local phone call; it's just ludicrous. Experience, intuition, and then, perhaps, the appropriate research.

What are traps organizations fall into that take them away from a customer orientation?

The answer to that is that nobody has enough drive to change it. The biggest trap is fear; the biggest trap is having to report to somebody. I was 24 years old starting as a sales representative at the Hotel Roosevelt in New York City, and I also had a secondary job there—my job was internal promotions. I was taking care of the signs in the elevators and the lobby—the various promotional cards and whatnot. I didn't really know what I was doing, but we had a bar there called the Club Car Bar that you had to walk by to go to the corridor to get to Grand Central Station. So there's a tremendous amount of traffic at 5.00 P.M. when everyone walks by the windows in the bar. I was there about a month or two and I was wandering around developing notes for all of these signs and things, and I saw that they had two rather large display cases at the front entrance of the bar (which was made to look like the club car of a train) and in the display cases were two vases of flowers. I looked at it and said to myself, "Why in the world would you have flowers in the window of a club car?"

The next day I looked in the yellow pages and I looked up the Lionel trains office and I stopped by and said that I would like to see their sales promotion manager. I asked if they could give me some trains so that I could replace the ridiculous flowers and put some Lionel trains in the window. It would be good promotion for Lionel and would be more applicable to the bar. The guy said, "sure," and the next day I got a couple of boxes of trains and the key to the window and I took out the flowers and put in the trains. About six hours later, I got a call from the controller. He got all aggravated because he was the one who put the flowers in, and he started yelling and screaming at me about putting the trains in the window. That was my first of many disputes with controllers over the years.

From a marketing perspective, people are going to run into individuals who do not quite understand what it's all about. I think this is a part of studying hospitality marketing. I think the focus has to be on how people have changed the parameters—how and why do these amenities and changes get in—so that they can have a better understanding of the process and the ability to get things through and to understand the results of the Howard Schultz kinds of decisions. You can't do without it, but you have to be prepared to fight for it.

Any other comments?

There used to be a poster with a woman on it around World War II when women were working in the factories and the title was "You've Come a Long Way, Baby." This industry continues to move, in an educational sense, dramatically, but in a practical delivery sense, it's a tortoise. It will get there one day, but not with a defect rate of 20 percent or more. The key is to identify the fight and create leaders like Sheldon Adelson, the owner of the Venetian Hotel in Las Vegas. The whole industry in Las Vegas laughed at him when he built the Venetian. He was the one to start the whole idea of a themed hotel in Las Vegas. Even in Vegas—which is very progressive, relatively speaking—he started the whole thing, and he was laughed at and not paid attention to. The only people who paid attention to him were the people who lent him the money. He did it with conventions as well, and this month's occupancy is 96 percent, which is down from last year's 98 percent. If you walk in there, it's the Venetian all the way through it.

Used by permission from Mike Leven.

Everyone knows McDonald's. Even in Zermatt, Switzerland, where the only way to get to the town is by train, *McDonald's* is a household word. Why is this? Some will say it is the products: the Big Mac or the Chicken McNuggets or the french fries or milk shakes. Others might repeat what McDonald's was initially known for: QSC—quality, service, and cleanliness. Both would be wrong. McDonald's had no monopoly on any of these features, yet for a long time its competition could not catch up with it. The reason *McDonald's* was a household word around the world was because for a long time its lifeblood was filled with the concept of marketing, and it practiced it in nearly everything it did.

Some fast-food chain manuals instruct management that the front windows must be cleaned every six hours, but the McDonald's manual states, "The front windows will never be dirty." In fact, some believe that the most innovative thing that Ray Kroc, founder of McDonald's, did was put large windows in front of every store. It was not enough that a McDonald's was clean inside; it was that people could look in and see that it was clean. Before McDonald's, you took your chances when you walked into a low-priced restaurant. Kroc went one step further. He also insisted that not only the outside of McDonald's be litter-free, but also the space next to it, even if McDonald's employees had to do the cleaning.

What do clean windows and clean sidewalks have to do with marketing? In hospitality, everything that management does affects the customer's image of the brand, and everything that affects the customer is marketing, good or bad. This cannot be repeated enough because it may be the most important thing that you will ever learn about marketing.

Practicing the concept of marketing means that organizations recognize that marketing and management in a service business, such as the hospitality industry, are one and the same. Practicing the concept of marketing means marketing leadership, which recognizes that it is marketing that shapes the total organization. This book is about marketing leadership in the hospitality industry. More specifically, it is about the causes and effects of marketing leadership. This book is about why people such as Ray Kroc and companies such as McDonald's succeed and why others do not succeed or succeed to a lesser degree. Or, why Bill Marriott and Marriott Hotels succeeded where Howard Johnson did not. It is about what it takes to succeed in the hospitality marketplace.

But this book is also about why the June 4, 2003, issue of the *Financial Times* discussed how, after years of double-digit growth, McDonald's announced its first quarterly loss since going public in 1965 and as a result closed 719 underperforming stores.[1] And why the American Customer Satisfaction Index in the fourth quarter 2002 rated McDonald's quality score a 61 (out of 100), while the average for all restaurants in the fast-food category was 71. As a point of perspective, the Internal Revenue Service in the United States earned a score of 62 for the same time period.[2] Where did McDonald's go wrong after such a good start? Essentially, it forgot the customer. While Jack M. Greenberg was CEO of McDonald's in the early 2000s, "his tenure was marked by the introduction of 40 new menu items, none of which caught on big, and the purchase of a handful of nonburger chains, like Boston Market, none of which were rolled out widely enough to make much of a difference."[3] None of these initiatives focused on the customer. Hence, this book is also about why companies fail. One can learn as much through failure as through success.

And this book is about why McDonald's may be turning things around. In January 2003, McDonald's brought the 59-year-old former vice president James R. Cantalupo out of retirement to replace the fired Mr. Greenberg. Mr. Cantalupo immediately claimed to the investment community that he would "bring the company back to the glory days by focusing on the basics: customer service, clean restaurants and reliable, appealing food."[4] Unfortunately, Mr. Cantalupo died suddenly, and it is now the responsibility of the team he put together to follow through with his strategy.

Foundations and Practices

Marketing-oriented companies and marketing-oriented people are the ones who are truly successful in the highly competitive hospitality marketplace. Does this mean that marketing has replaced operations and accounting? Of course not. The operations career individual will take fewer marketing courses, but must learn to apply marketing in his or her operations courses. When a menu is designed, the first question to be asked is, How will the customer react to it? When a hotel room is configured, the first question that needs to be asked is, How will the customer use it? When prices are established, the first question should be, How will the customer perceive the risk and the price–value relationship? When engineering is taught and electric consumption is measured, the first question is, Is the lighting appropriate for the customer? When food, liquor, or labor cost controls are taught, we must ask how all of these impact the customer. Specifically, we should ask, Are our costs so low that we are hurting customer satisfaction? We should also ask, What is the value of the product or service to customers, and might they pay more? The foundation of any business is the concept of marketing; the application is its practice.

No company can continue to operate without a profit. But, let's put first things first. No company can begin to operate without customers. Today we are in the "customer business." Without customers we cannot succeed. And the way to have customers is to offer them solutions to their problems. To keep them coming back, you must continue to solve these problems, satisfying their needs and wants and adding value to the core product or service. Although many often think of price when they hear the word *value*, Chapter 3 shows that value is much more than price. For instance, when organizations save the customer time by allowing a speedy check-in for loyal customers, this can be thought of as a temporal value. Resorts often provide activities where guests can interact with other guests. These gatherings provide social value for the guests. Other types of value are emotional, which is exhibited when guests are called by their first names and made to feel important.

The foundation of marketing starts at the highest level by deed and action, not just words, and it permeates down to the lowest level of the organization. Concern and responsibility for marketing are concerns and responsibilities of every person in a hospitality enterprise. At the highest level, marketing shapes the corporate effort; at the lowest level, it means the porter doesn't mop where the customer is walking.

The Concept of Marketing

For many, the term *marketing* conjures up images of selling and advertising with the hope of capturing as many new customers as possible, with little emphasis on getting customers to come back. Because of this long-standing and common belief, we emphasize that selling and advertising are only a part of marketing. Restaurant management advertises, so they think they are marketing. Hotel management has four salespeople selling, so they think they are marketing. Actually, however, selling and advertising are only two of the disciplines that make up the practice of marketing. Although they are important subsets, they are only subsets. Marketing is the integration of all of the professional disciplines required to determine the nature of customer demand, then develop, promote, and deliver the products and services that will satisfy that demand.

All phases of marketing, both foundations and practices, derive from a focus on the customer. Sales- and advertising-oriented management may think in terms of the virtues of their product and how they can persuade the customer to buy. Consciously or unconsciously, they may be selling the operations or physical end of the business. They often think in terms of what they have to offer the customer. In contrast, **nontraditional marketing**–oriented management thinks in terms of the entire buying process: from understanding the customer's needs when designing the service or product, to delivering the service and supporting the product after the sale is over. They think in terms of what the customer wants. Mr. Jim Cantalupo was an example of this new thinking when he stated, "McDonald's is changing its philosophy from building more stores to get more customers toward getting more customers in our existing stores."[5] McDonald's plans to do this by once again listening to the customers' wants and needs. Specifically, they are adding healthier items such as premium salads and fruit. In addition, in early 2003 McDonald's created a Global Advisory Council on Healthy Lifestyles, whose goal is to help guide the company on activities that address the need for balanced, healthy lifestyles, something that customers are striving for. McDonald's also plans to retrain employees and managers "in an effort to provide service that is more speedy, accurate and polite."[6] All of this is part of nontraditional marketing. Exhibit 1-1 presents lessons that hospitality firms can learn from McDonalds.

The Purpose of a Business

It is accepted without question that any for-profit business that fails to operate at a profit will eventually cease to exist. If the overall mix of goods and/or services cannot be offered at a price exceeding their total cost, then they should be removed from the market. The difference between the sale price and the cost of goods sold represents the "value" a customer assigns the service. The more a customer is willing to pay, the more profit will come to the business. A room at a Four Seasons hotel may cost $55 to service and is sold for $350. Another room in a Days Inn in the same city may cost $30 to service, yet the rate is only $80. The difference is clearly the premium a customer is willing to pay for the value of the room. Although essential to survival, however, profit is not the purpose of marketing but rather a way of measuring the success of marketing management decisions made by a company. As well-known management guru Peter Drucker stated:

> Profitability is not the purpose of but a limiting factor on business enterprise and business activity. Profit is not the explanation, cause or rationale of business behavior and business decisions but the *test of their validity* [emphasis added].[7] The only valid definition of business purpose is to create a customer. It is the customer who determines what a business is. For it is the customer and he alone, who through being willing to pay for a good or for a service, converts economic resources into wealth, things into goods. What the business thinks it produces is not of first importance—especially not to the future of the business and to its success. What the customer thinks he is buying, what he considers "value," is

---

EXHIBIT 1-1   **McDonald's Succeeds by Listening to the Customer**

An article in the April 14, 2003, issue of *Fortune* magazine described McDonald's as "really more of a landlord than a conventional fast-food chain." This description is given because McDonald's owns both the building and the land in many of its franchised operations (85 percent of McDonald's stores are run by franchisees). This means that McDonald's is able to earn revenue from rent as well as from the traditional franchise fees. The ability to drive revenue from real estate helps explain McDonald's strategy of growth and more growth.*

For years, revenue from real estate was able to hide many of the problems at McDonald's. These problems became readily apparent when the franchisee fees, which are calculated as a percentage of sales, were unable to compensate for the decline in real estate revenues caused by the lack of new locations.

McDonald's offers a good lesson for the hotel business, which often describes itself as a real estate business. As long as the real estate market is booming, revenues will be there. However, in an economic downturn, the **ROI (return on investment)** must come not from the appreciation on the asset, but from the EBIDTA (earnings before interest, depreciation, taxes, and amortization) and from the existing business. This EBIDTA comes from satisfied customers.

Hoteliers who like to think of themselves in the real estate business need to remember the lessons experienced by McDonald's.

* Grainger, D. (2003, April 14). Can McDonald's cook again? The great American icon ain't what it used to be. *Fortune,* pp. 120–127.

---

decisive—it determines what a business is, what it produces and whether it will prosper.[8]

Drucker wrote these words many years ago. No one since has said it better. Yet, amazingly, you can pick up a business publication or attend a conference to read or hear how someone has suddenly, in a stroke of genius, either "discovered" the customer or, like James Cantalupo of McDonald's, rediscovered the customer. The Restaurant Zum See is an example of the success a firm can have if it focuses on the customer. Unfortunately, some businesses, including hospitality firms, have still not discovered the customer or have lost a previous focus on the customer. You will read many current examples of this throughout this book.

The Twofold Purpose of Marketing

The **twofold purpose of marketing** is to create and keep a customer. **Creating a customer** is sometimes relatively easy. This usually occurs through the use of promotions and discounts, as exemplified by advertisements that get the customer to buy the product at an introductory price.

Promotions may get the customer to purchase the product once, but they won't, by themselves, induce the customer to buy additional products or services on this first visit or persuade the customer to return. That will depend on how well the organization handles customers after they get in the door. Thus, *creating* and *keeping* are two inherent and inseparable words that define marketing. Compare, for example, Exhibits 1-2 and 1-3. Exhibit 1-2 induces the customer to visit the South Seas Resort. Exhibit 1-3, on the other hand, shows a button worn by staff members at the Middlebury Inn, located in Middlebury, Vermont, which encourages guests to "stay another night."

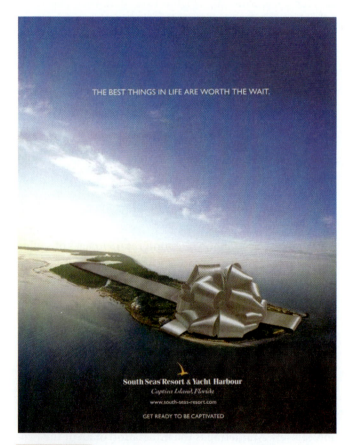

EXHIBIT 1-2   This advertisement induces the customer to visit the South Seas Resort.

Source: South Seas Resort. Used by permission.

The marketing challenge then is twofold: creating new customers and turning these new customers into repeat customers. Firms earn repeat customers not only by providing excellent service and satisfaction, but also by establishing relationships with them. These relationships can range from financial (e.g., the frequent guest programs that

EXHIBIT 1-3 Middlebury Inn employees encourage their guests to "stay another night" with these buttons.

Source: The Middlebury Inn. Used by permission.

reward guests with points that can then be used for free stays), to social (e.g., the vice president of marketing playing golf with a top travel manager), to structural (the organization keeps extensive records on the guest's preferences so that the guest's needs will be taken care of no matter who happens to be working that day). Chapter 4 examines these and other relationships in much more detail.

Solving Customers' Problems

There is a basic premise of marketing that we must understand. Simply put, customers do not buy something unless they have a problem to solve and believe that a purchase will provide the solution to the problem. An example, attributed to Charles Revlon, founder of Revlon cosmetics, is: "In the factory we make cosmetics; in the store we sell hope." Another example is that customers do not buy quarter-inch drills; they buy quarter-inch holes. That is, the drill just provides a mechanism for reaching the desired solution.

It should be noted, however, that customers also buy products or services because they are attracted to specific features. For instance, one of the authors owns an Apple iPod, even though he already owns another MP3 player. He did not need the iPod, but was attracted to both the amount of memory and its "coolness."

Exhibit 1-4 shows an advertisement that promotes a solution to a problem. Can you tell which problem is being solved? Customers also buy products or services that they hope will help them achieve certain images, aspirations, and dreams. Exhibit 1-5 shows an advertisement that is an example of this. If we can think of goods and services that we want to sell as solutions to problems, we are a long way on the road to successful marketing. Thinking this way forces us to stand in the customer's shoes, to think like the customer thinks, and to understand what problems the customer is trying to solve.

Customers may not be able to articulate what they really want or need, but they do know what their problems are. For instance, the meeting planner will not know exactly what a proper coffee service will look like, but she will know what one does not look like—cold coffee, hot water in a coffee pot so the tea tastes like coffee, and access to the coffee from only one side of the table. These are problems, which the hotelier will solve.

To illustrate this point further, one of the authors offers the following true story: I was working in a hotel when the first facsimile machines came on the market. When the salesperson approached me and asked if I would like to buy a facsimile machine so that I could send documents to other hotels in the chain, I replied, "I am a single hotel so I do not send documents to other hotels." The salesperson thanked me and left. I did not buy the facsimile machine despite the fact that I did have problems getting up-to-date rooming lists from tour operators who allowed customers to join the tour on the day of departure. Because facsimile machines were so new (yes, it is hard to believe there was a time when such items were new), I did not fully understand how they worked and how they could be useful. In other words, I did not know what I wanted; I just knew I had a problem. Unfortunately for the salesperson, he never asked if I had a problem, such as late rooming lists from tour operators; he just asked if I wanted a facsimile machine.

In the preceding story, the problem was not solved (and a sale not made) because the customer did not know the solution and it was not presented to him. At other times customers do not know they have a problem, but they buy anyway. An example is **impulse buying**. Advertising often induces impulse buying by heightening an interest or desire of customers. A good example is advertisements for hotels that remind customers that they should take a break now and then. This was illustrated in Exhibit 1-5.

At other times the customer knows the solution, as the following scenario illustrates. Perhaps you are driving down a highway and you become hungry. Or you become tired and need a place to sleep. These are needs, and basic ones at that. Needs create problems—namely, how to satisfy them—so what you do next is seek a solution. You

IT'S NOT WHAT YOU BRING.
IT'S WHAT YOU TAKE AWAY.

As we all know, it's not the destination, but the journey that matters. It's how our lives take shape. How our true selves are revealed. How we find joy. Canyon Ranch can guide you to a feeling so light, yet so powerful, it enhances your life forever. Your journey begins with us.

CANYONRANCH.
The Power of Possibility™
LIFE ENHANCEMENT RESORT™ • SPACLUB™
HEALTHY LIVING COMMUNITIES • SKIN CARE PRODUCTS

800.742.9000 • CANYONRANCH.COM

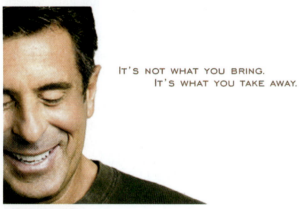

IT'S NOT WHAT YOU BRING.
IT'S WHAT YOU TAKE AWAY.

As we all know, it's not the destination, but the journey that matters. It's how our lives take shape. How our true selves are revealed. How we find joy. Canyon Ranch can guide you to a feeling so light, yet so powerful, it enhances your life forever. Your journey begins with us.

CANYONRANCH.
The Power of Possibility™
LIFE ENHANCEMENT RESORT™ • SPACLUB™
HEALTHY LIVING COMMUNITIES • SKIN CARE PRODUCTS

800.742.9000 • CANYONRANCH.COM

EXHIBIT 1-4   This advertisement for Canyon Ranch promotes a solution to a problem. Can you tell which problem is being solved?
Source: Canyon Ranch. Used by permission.

know the solution will have a cost. You have to give up something or make a sacrifice in order to get the solution. What emerges is a *trade-off* situation like that portrayed in Exhibit 1-6.

This is the trade-off thought process a customer faces when contemplating a purchase. In general, the decision-making process is more complicated as the cost of the item—both in terms of dollar amount and the associated risk of making a wrong decision—increases. A customer may spend months selecting a honeymoon destination and seconds selecting a can of soda. Nevertheless, the process takes place and the depth of deliberation depends on numerous factors, which will be discussed in Chapter 7.

For the moment, let's continue the illustration and assume that a solution presents itself: A sign on the highway announces a motor inn ahead with rooms at $59.50. Rooms provide a solution for the need to sleep, and $59.50 is an investment you are willing to make. You decide to head for the motor inn rather than continue driving.

Now the situation becomes complicated. You *expect* that the solution is at hand; that is, you *expect* that you can

get a good night's sleep at this motor inn. You *expect*, of course, that there will be a bed in the room, a bathroom, and other appointments. You also *expect* that the bed will be comfortable and that the room will be quiet so that you will sleep well. You may not verbalize these expectations, but subconsciously they exist. You also have, consciously or unconsciously, made another decision: You have decided that spending $59.50 is worth the *risk* that your expectations will be met, the solution will solve your problem, and the value you will receive will be worth the sacrifice. The **trade-off model** now looks like Exhibit 1-7. This figure is similar to Exhibit 1-6, except we have added these expectations to the triangle. It is the expectations part of the triangle that makes marketing in hospitality or other service industries unique.

Unlike buying an automobile, customers cannot take the hotel room for a "test drive" before they buy it. (Although some lodging brands now offer "satisfaction" or "service" guarantees, customers still have to buy and have a bad experience before receiving the service guarantee.) Instead, they purchase the solution at the same time they

EXHIBIT 1-5   In this advertisement, Doubletree capitalizes on customers' hopes that they will achieve certain images, aspirations, and dreams.

Source: Doubletree. Used by permission.

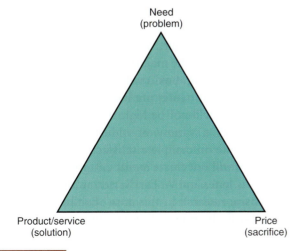

EXHIBIT 1-6   The trade-off of problem solutions.

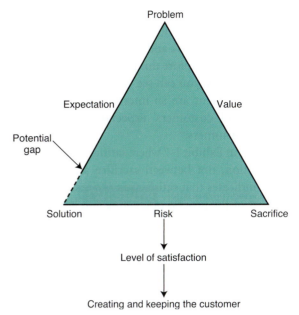

EXHIBIT 1-7   Expansion of the trade-off model.

consume it. Therefore, the customer has the expectation that the product or service will solve their problem. Once the decision is made to purchase, there is no backing out. It then follows that the greater the sacrifice, the greater the risk, the greater the expectation, and the more demanding the customer is of the solution. To put it another way, if the solution meets the expectation and the value justifies the sacrifice, the risk becomes more justifiable and a higher level of satisfaction becomes more likely. The result is a higher likelihood that we have created a customer. To put this in realistic terms, consider each element of Exhibit 1-6 in terms of going to eat at McDonald's versus Daniel, a famous restaurant in New York City where the three-course prix fixe menu without extras costs $96 and a five-course meal costs $132.

 Web Browsing Exercise

Visit the websites of both McDonald's (www.mcdonalds.com/) and Daniel (http://danielnyc.com/daniel/). Create your own consumer trade-off models for each restaurant. Compare and contrast. What did you learn from this exercise? How might this trade-off change depending on the person with whom you are eating?

Notice now what happens when the solution does not meet the expectation. This is the "potential gap" on the left-hand side of Exhibit 1-7 as indicated by the dotted line. We have made the dotted line, let's say, "Pizza Hut length." We might make it a hair shorter for "McDonald's length,"

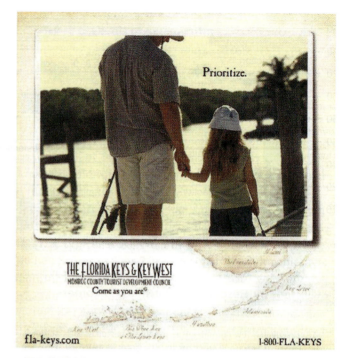

EXHIBIT 1-12 This advertisement from the Monroe County Tourist Development Council has created a solution for customers' problems that operations must fulfill.

Source: Monroe County Tourist Development Council. Used by permission.

EXHIBIT 1-11 Westin's marketing of their "heavenly bed" has created a need that only Westin can fulfill.

Source: Westin Hotels & Resorts. Used by permission.

the door; it is up to nontraditional marketing to *create* and *keep* the customer. For example, a well-known hotel in a major metropolitan area recently authorized the front desk staff to "make it right for the customer." What did this mean? That the front desk staff was authorized to refund up to $500 per guest without management's approval for any problem encountered during their stay. If a customer had a problem with the telephone, room service, wake-up call, or anything else, it was handled immediately. This is nontraditional marketing.

The trade-off model is critical to the understanding of marketing. The concept will be developed further in the chapters to follow, but first we need to see how marketing influences the total picture.

Management Orientations

All companies, firms, organizations, and other business entities operate under a basic philosophy or orientation. This philosophy may be spoken, written, or just simply implied. An organization's philosophy is a part of its corporate culture—it emphasizes that "this is the way we do business around here." It is what drives the firm, what makes it work.

The hospitality industry encompasses many philosophies and orientations at various times and places. These orientations may be operations, a product or a service, a selling orientation, or a bottom-line orientation.

Operations Orientation

An **operations orientation** is categorized by its emphasis on a "smooth operation," as symbolized by the anonymous person who once stated, "This is a great business to be in, if only the customers didn't get in the way." Operations manuals provide prescriptions for direction and behavior for almost every conceivable possible occurrence—until the customer decides to do something differently.

Operations-oriented hotels and restaurants sometimes forget the customer in the interest of a smooth operation. Although these facilities run well, customers are fickle and procedures cannot be written for every kind of demand or problem. This does not mean that manuals are not desirable for operations purposes. In fact, in today's large chains it would be impossible to obtain consistency in service delivery without these manuals.* Problems occur, however, when the manual becomes the "be all to end all" and there is no room for deviation on the customer's behalf. Or, what may be even worse, sometimes the manual is written only from an operations efficiency or cost perspective and without consideration for the customer. Consider a true story that occurred in a deluxe hotel in Paris: A former student of one of the authors was working in this hotel as a floor supervisor in housekeeping. She was told that at 14:00 every day (2:00 P.M.) the guests' rooms should be refreshed. When the student asked what to do if a "do not disturb" sign was on the door, she was told "Ignore the sign. Guests sometimes leave the sign on the door by mistake. Plus, this is the way we do things here and rooms need to be refreshed." Naturally, guests often complained to the former student, but her supervisors always said "policies are policies."

Operations philosophies, like all philosophies, come down from top management. When the company or the company's executives are very bottom line or profit driven, they tend to follow procedures based mainly on cost considerations, overlooking their impact on customers. Consider, for example, the restaurant that has a slow night. Typically, management will send wait personnel home (or in restaurant parlance, "cut the floor") and close part of the dining room. The section that is often closed may be the quieter section, away from the main dining room. This section may also be the most desirable from the customer's perspective. The part that remains open, of course, is closest to the kitchen because it is most convenient to serve. Similarly, you may have had the experience of saying to a dining room hostess, "Can we have that table over there?" (instead of the one you were led to) and receiving the response, "I'm sorry, but it's not that waiter's turn." These practices, of course, can lead to even emptier dining rooms.

One of the authors experienced a situation in an understaffed restaurant during the off season on Cape Cod, Massachusetts, with very different results. Upon entering the restaurant in midwinter, the author and his wife were approached by the owner, who said, "I had two people call in sick this evening. If you need to be seated right away and have dinner served quickly, let me call the restaurant down the road and they will take care of you. If you would like to be my guest for a glass of wine while we get your table ready and can be a bit patient with the service, I would be very grateful if you stayed." Nontraditional marketing at its best. The author and his wife had a very relaxed evening and recommended the restaurant many times over.

In another example, consider a large hotel of a major chain that claimed to be customer oriented but rewarded all of its people based on bottom-line results. This hotel was losing occupancy in the face of increasing competition and was responding by cutting costs and raising prices. Management spent $17 million on a new entryway that had little, if any, effect on business. The problems were inside, where staff had been cut to save payroll. Normal check-in time took 10 minutes, and that's when there wasn't a line. Checkout was about as bad. The widely advertised indoor pool didn't open until 9:00 A.M. (to save payroll), long after the business clientele had left for the day or were in meetings. The brightest light in the room was 67 watts (to save energy costs), difficult to use for paperwork or reading. The widest writing space in most rooms, including suites, was 16 inches.

These types of procedures are established in the name of operational or cost efficiency. Perhaps a better phrase might be "customer blindness efficiency." Hotels and restaurants that operate by these kinds of procedures pride themselves on their operational efficiencies, rather than on their solutions to customers' problems. Obviously, such efficiencies may well cause problems instead of solving them for guests seeking a hassle-free experience.

> ### Tourism Marketing Application
> Disneyland Paris is an example of a tourist destination that initially opened with a product orientation. The belief was, "If we build it, people will come." The destination was an exact copy of the destinations built in the United States. No consideration was given to the consumption habits of Europeans; for example, restaurants did not offer wine or beer. In addition, tour operators have a tremendous influence on the travel behavior of European travelers. Yet, because their needs were not met, sales suffered. Finally, no consumer research was undertaken to gain an understanding of Europeans' wants and needs. Cultures between the United States and Europe are different.

---

*Interestingly, when Bass Plc. of England, which is now part of InterContinental Hotels Group, took over Holiday Inns in 1990, it reduced the stack of operations manuals from about three feet to about three inches.

Product/Service Orientation

Hospitality properties that operate under the **product/service orientation** place their emphasis on the product or service. These properties market according to the concept of "build it and they will come." They trumpet that their property has the best food, the finest chefs, designer-decorated lobbies, or even the best location. In terms of service, they argue that they have the finest service available and that they know what service is best for the customer. The problem with this approach is that the firm may offer products and services that the customer does not want.

Consider the following situation that actually occurred when a group of hotel managers and meeting planners were asked to design a coffee break for a meeting.

> The executive committee diligently set out to design the "mother of all coffee breaks," including trilevel presentations, mirrors, ice carvings, lighting, flavored coffees, and so on. When costs were broken out, the break had to be priced at $32 per person to make a profit. The meeting's customers then turned in their "perfect" coffee break design: a simple coffee break with the table holding the break positioned about 10 feet from the back wall. The purpose, they explained, was to alleviate the congestion caused by a single line break. Their meetings could resume more quickly if the design of the table was simply moved a few feet!

This example shows how far management can be from the real needs and problems of customers. An example of how this emphasis on the **product or service** without regard to the customers' wants, needs, and problems, can creep into advertising can be seen in Exhibit 1-13.

The same can occur in both the restaurant industry and tourism destinations. An example of this orientation is the chef who says to the customer, "I only serve my tuna rare. If you want it cooked medium or well, you will need to order another item." In this case the chef believes that the only way to eat tuna is to eat it rare. The customer may desire something completely different. In tourism destinations, a product orientation may be the convention facility that prides itself on offering all the latest technology without regard to what the clients actually want to pay for. The addition of this technology requires that the facility raise its rates to cover the cost of this technology. If customers do not want to pay for this technology, they will go elsewhere.

Properties may have all the attributes they claim; sometimes they do not. Regardless, the claims, like the coffee break design, often fail to consider whether these factors are solutions to customers' problems. More than one group has been lost forever to a hotel because of inattentive personnel, inflexible policies, bad acoustics, or stale coffee, in spite of the beautiful and very expensive chandeliers and wallpaper. In the marketing sense, products and services should be defined only in terms of the *value and solutions they provide for the customer*. Whatever these products and service do, they should not create even more problems.

Selling Orientation

A **selling orientation** in hotel and restaurant companies is one in which the effort to obtain customers emphasizes finding someone who will come through the doors, as opposed to marketing a solution to a designated market's

---

EXHIBIT 1-13   Examples of Product/Service Orientation

A joint promotional brochure for some of Atlanta's hotels directed at meeting planners contained pictures of the hotels along with the following copy:

- At the Westin, after the hotel had spent $31 million, you could have a "more than successful" meeting because of "sumptuous new fabrics, elegant furnishings, Italian marble and breath-taking views" and, for "meeting inspiration" there were "twinkling arches and hidden courtyards."
- At the InterContinental, you could have "a chauffeur-driven Rolls Royce meet your private airplane," and you could dine in "surroundings of hand-polished wood, antique crystal and gleaming silver."
- At the Hyatt Regency, you would get to enjoy the hotel that, "20 years later continues to fulfill John Portman's vision."*
- At the Marriott Marquis, as a small group, you could "practically have the place to yourself . . . with its awesome atrium, ten restaurants, and lounges."

- At the Ritz-Carlton, on the other hand, they "concentrate on the fine points of innkeeping like luxurious rooms, afternoon tea served in English bone china and richly paneled walls graced by 18th and 19th century oils."

  In the same brochure, there was the Colony Square Hotel, a Preferred Hotel, which "assigns individuals who work behind the scenes to oversee every detail of your meeting—from planning to follow-up." The ad also contained a picture of and a quote from the manager of the Coca-Cola U.S.A. Training Center, who said, "The thing I appreciate most is the flexibility. They respond quickly to our last minute requests."

  Tens of thousands of dollars were spent on these ads. Which of all of the attributes listed by the various properties do you suppose meeting planners most preferred?

* In case you didn't know (and few today would), John Portman is the architect who created this hotel with the first-of-its-kind atrium lobby in the 1960s.

needs. Hotel companies with this kind of orientation often have large sales forces and/or large advertising budgets. They are very conscious of their open periods, and they push their salespeople to "go out and fill them" and to meet their sales quotas. Sale-oriented restaurants may run frequent promotions and special offers or flood their market with discounts and coupons. Whichever, everything is based on the "sell, sell, sell" edict rather than identifying customers' needs and wants.

Bottom-Line Orientation

Although the orientations mentioned previously all have their place in different companies, the **bottom-line orientation**—without regard to its impact on customers—does not. Certainly, it is important to yield a satisfactory return on invested capital; as such, one needs to be concerned with profitability and ROI. However, to do this without thinking of the impact on the customer is a dangerous orientation that has destroyed a number of companies in many industries. Twenty years ago this was very prevalent in hospitality companies, many of which did not survive. It is not as prevalent today. We'd like to think it is gone completely, but unfortunately, it still prevails in some places—from small owner-operated restaurants to some large companies.

The bottom line, of course, is profit. A bottom-line orientation means that most things, if not everything, are done in the name of profit. In these cases, profit or its reciprocal, cost, is the basis for decisions, not the test of their validity as noted earlier. This manifests itself most often in terms of cost—food cost, labor cost, beverage cost, marketing cost, refurbishment cost, and so forth. We discuss the fallacy of this more in the pricing chapter, but suffice it to say for now that when the emphasis is on cost, the customer is soon forgotten.

One of the authors confesses to being guilty at one time of this marketing crime when running his own restaurant. After all, he had gone to hotel school, where he learned that the only thing that really mattered was 40 percent food cost, 30 percent labor cost, and 20 percent beverage cost. By this time, however, these standards had been dropped to 36, 26, and 18 percent. That's how he operated until he woke up one day and thought, "Boy, do I run a good operation—just look at those costs. Just one problem—there aren't too many customers."

Liquor bars in airports run a very low liquor cost, but they have a captive audience. Some exclusive resorts get away with the same, but they have other attractions. For many businesses the mandate is cost-driven prices, not price-driven costs, which should be the case.

There is obviously nothing wrong with running a good operation, having a good product or service, and employing an effective sales force (these should be advanced as targeted goals!). Well-run and successful companies accomplish all of these and do them well. A truly marketing-oriented company, however, views these achievements as subsets of marketing. That is, they are accomplished with the customer as the focal point. The operations manager says, "I run a tight ship," but only after making sure that the customers' needs and wants have been considered. The service manager considers first what the service will do for the target market.[10] And the sales manager sells those benefits that will solve customers' problems and make their experiences hassle-free.

Examples of bottom-line restaurant companies that lost sight of the customer and no longer exist today or exist in a reincarnated form include Howard Johnson, Victoria Station and Boston Market, Planet Hollywood, China Coast restaurants, and many individual proprietor restaurants. Hotel firms include Prime Motor Inns, Sheraton Hotels, and many individual proprietor hotels. Can companies who are focused on the bottom line change? Of course they can, although they usually change with new management and a customer orientation.

Web Browsing Exercise

Search the websites of both Boston Market (www.bostonmarket.com/index.jsp) and Sheraton Hotels (www.starwoodhotels.com/sheraton/index.html). How have these companies incorporated their new customer orientation into their websites?

The Sheraton story is worth telling at some length because it demonstrates many of the principles that we have been discussing. When we were writing the earlier editions of this book, we sometimes wondered how Sheraton Hotels, a well-known bottom-line organization noted for inconsistent service and poor maintenance, managed to survive. Well, guess what—it didn't. Starwood Hotels and Resorts completed its purchase of ITT Sheraton in 1998. Since that time, they have become much more marketing oriented, with great success, as illustrated in the Sheraton story that is told in Exhibit 1-14. Starwood shows that companies can change.

Marketing Orientation

The **marketing orientation** is based on the premises that the customer is king; the customer has a choice; and the customer does not have to buy your product or service. Thus, the best way to ear a profit is to serve the customer better.

EXHIBIT 1-14 **The Sheraton Story**

Sheraton was long noted for its bottom-line mentality. Staff was often short, service was poor, maintenance was deferred, and the concept of value for price was a stigma. Sheraton general managers and their staffs were rewarded for their low-cost efforts, largely based on percentages. Sheraton was in trouble and top management knew it, but they weren't sure why. ITT bought the company in 1968 when Sheraton was as much a real estate company as a hotel company. The long time CEO was soon "retired" in the 1970s. The successful manager of Sheraton's European operations became president and CEO, but operating Sheraton for ITT wasn't like managing hotels in Europe. In 1979 Rand Araskog became CEO of ITT, and in 1980 he became CEO of the Sheraton division of ITT as well.

THE NEW SHERATON

In the early 1980s, Sheraton celebrated its 50th anniversary with a huge party in Hawaii that cost millions of dollars. All GMs, top staff, and sales and marketing people worldwide were flown at company expense to Hawaii. Festive meals, cocktail hours, and high-priced entertainment complete with plenty of ice carvings, decorations, music, golf, and other sports ensued for four days.

But there was a company message along with all this festivity, and it was pushed incessantly at many meetings throughout the conference. This message was called "the New Sheraton." Sheraton was going to change, and the attendees were expected to understand the message—better quality, better service, and better care for the customer. Costs were barely mentioned—this was the New Sheraton and it was understood that things needed to improve if the company wanted to survive.

At a gala banquet on the last night of the festivities, CEO Rand Araskog made a rousing closing speech that ended with words to this effect, "Sheraton will never forgo quality or the customer, but let everyone in this room understand their responsibility, obligation, and contribution to the profits of this company."

What happened? Everyone went back to their jobs, some grousing about the money spent that might have given them raises instead. When back home, many asked, "What's the New Sheraton?" The reply was, "Business as usual."

SHERATON PROBLEMS

Five years later, the newly appointed vice president—North America (a very successful, by bottom-line standards, previous Sheraton GM) invited one of the authors to the corporate office in Boston to discuss "strategy." His idea was to have strategy meetings with groups of GMs across the country. "What do you want to tell them?" the author asked. "Well, I just think we should get them to start thinking strategically," was the response.

"What are your problems?" was the next question. "Oh, we don't have any problems," he replied. "I just think we should talk to them." The author had spent the previous night at the Sheraton Boston, the company's flagship hotel (in a large luxurious suite, in fact, due to a foul-up in room assignments). He related to the vice president a multitude of things that had "gone wrong" in that short 16-hour stay. The response was, "No, no, that's impossible. Those things don't happen at a Sheraton."

When they got down to the nitty-gritty, the VP admitted that Sheraton had a very bottom-line mentality and somehow this had to be changed. Stacked on the credenza behind his desk were maybe 50 to 100 copies of a book that had just been published. It was *Service America* by Karl Albrecht and Ron Zemke (Dow Jones-Irwin, 1985), probably the first—or at least first best-seller—of all the "service and customer" books that spewed out in the 1980s and 1990s. The VP was going to give a copy to each of his GMs. (He also gave one to the author.) That's as far as the meeting went. The strategy meetings were never held, and about five years later the VP left Sheraton to become VP of a Canadian hotel chain.

THE SPLIT-UP

Rand Araskog, once referred to by the *Wall Street Journal* as the "poster boy for overpaid executives" after he made $11.4 million in 1990 when ITT stock was grossly underperforming (when queried, his response was, "I feel I earned it") marched forward. In 1995 he split ITT into three companies with himself as CEO of ITT Sheraton Hotels and Casinos company. He started the Sheraton Grand line of luxury hotels, putting millions into properties such as the St. Regis in New York City, buying CIGA Hotels (a small luxury Italian chain) and other trophy hotels around the world. Mr. Araskog reportedly loved the grand life and was especially enthralled with the casino division. Knowing little about running casino hotels, however, he brought in at least two experienced casino operators, one after the other, to run that division. They soon left, in a matter of months. After all, Mr. Araskog knew how to squeeze profits out of these properties.

One good thing did happen along the way. Frank Camacho, head of research at Marriott, was hired as the senior vice president of marketing and instituted a bonus system based one-third each on customer evaluations, employee evaluations, and return on investment. The old culture, however, by this time was too deeply embedded, and this was not enough to save Sheraton.

THE END OF SHERATON

Fast forward to the year 1996. Steve Bollenbach—a financial wizard who had proven himself a highly capable turnaround artist with stints at Holiday Inn, with Donald Trump, and at Marriott and Disney—was named CEO of Hilton Hotels in 1996. Hilton had long been a stagnant company—like Sheraton, never a leader—under Barron Hilton. Although Barron Hilton owned a sizable portion of Hilton stock, he was usually preoccupied with his polo ponies and hot air balloon adventures or other personal interests. The Hilton board finally made him hire a new CEO with full, 100 percent authority. Hilton's stock went up 16 percent in four days after Bollenbach's hiring; within a year it was up 80 percent versus ITT Sheraton's 6 percent in the same period.

Within months, Bollenbach had bought Bally Casinos. On January 27, 1997, he led a $6.5 billion (later raised to $8.3 billion), plus assumption of $3 billion of debt, hostile takeover bid for ITT Sheraton. Among other things, he cited poor, weak, inefficient, self-serving top Sheraton management. Hilton would clean this up and turn Sheraton around. Well, you might as well have hit Mr. Araskog (now 65) over the head with a baseball bat. He hired investment bankers Lazard Freres & Co. and Goldman, Sachs and Co., who had previously helped him fight off other predators such as the Pritzker family (owners of Hyatt Hotels) for $20 million in fees, plus the renowned top New York City law firm of Cravath, Swaine & Moore (about $500 an hour) and planned his defense strategy.

Among other things, Araskog sold off side businesses and some Sheraton hotels, postponed the annual shareholders' meeting (all directors were up for election at the same time—something Bollenbach was counting on to replace them with his own), and took many other defensive actions including refusing to meet with or respond to Bollenbach. You might say that Mr. Araskog was slightly infuriated.

Finally, he found a "white knight" that came along in the form of 36-year-old Barry Sternlicht, CEO of Starwood Hotels and Resorts. Sternlicht had just completed the acquisition of Westin Hotels, the latest of many acquisitions, and was on the prowl for more with his tax-advantaged paired share REIT.* Starwood won the bidding over Hilton and bought ITT Sheraton with a stock swap.

A NEW BEGINNING

Since his tenure at Starwood, Sternlicht has made the customer the top priority. One of the first strategies implemented by Sternlicht and his team was to initiate a loyalty program, which they called Starwood Preferred Guests

(SPG). This program was the first program in the hospitality industry to offer no blackout dates and no capacity controls. The success of the program is evidenced by the fact that from 1999 to 2002 it was named by customers as the Hotel Program of the Year. Of course, marketing is more than loyalty programs, as will be discussed in Chapter 4. Sternlicht also focused on providing consistent service at all Sheraton hotels to keep guests coming back.

In the fall of 2002, Starwood announced a program called the Sheraton Service Promise, which gives guests credit if something should go wrong during their stay. It should be noted that this was not a new idea, but one that was very appropriate for Sheraton given the perception of declining quality of guest service. At the time of the program's launch, slow check-ins, billing problems, or a shortage of towels earned guests $15 credit or 500 SPG points. Other problems earned credits from $25 to $75. The message to the guest was that Starwood was committed to making sure guests enjoy their stays. As Geoff Ballotti, vice president of North American hotel operations, stated: "Basically, this program is going to force our general managers to maintain the same top-quality service at all Sheraton properties. We're backing up our product with a promise and if something's wrong we'll make it up to them instantly, in a way where they can feel it."* Starwood also retrained many of its employees.

The emphasis on the customer is paying off for Starwood. In June 2005, the stock for Starwood was close to $58, which was an increase of 93 percent for the year. Clearly, taking care of the customer does pay.

* REIT stands for real estate investment trust. These trusts get special tax treatment because they are required by law to pass 95 percent of their profits on to shareholders. They are not, however, allowed to operate the real estate. When this last ruling was made, a special exemption was allowed for four existing publicly traded "paired share" trusts. These are REITs that own real estate and a management company that manages it, but trade as one stock. Starwood is one of the four. Steve Bollenbach, of course, cried foul, and he and others are trying to get Congress to revoke this special status. There was much speculation, however, that the consolidation of hotel brands by REITs may put the bottom line back before the needs of the customer. See, for example, Christina Binkley, "Young Mr. Sternlicht Built Hotel Empire; Now, He Must Run It," *Wall Street Journal*, March 5, 1998, pp. A1, A17.

Developed from trade publications, published news items, industry sources, and personal experiences and contacts.

Harris, B. (2002, September 7). Sheraton to offer credit for bad service. *Los Angeles Times*, p. C-2.

Tourism Marketing Application

Like all the orientations we have discussed, a marketing orientation is, essentially, the culture of the organization.

A "yes" answer to the following questions indicates a firm with a marketing orientation:

- Does the firm focus on the customer?
- Do the various departments within the firm work together to respond effectively to customers' wants and needs?
- Is the market intelligence on customers, competitors, and market conditions shared throughout the organization?
- Does the firm's reward system support the emphasis on the customer?

As defined by Kohli and Jaworski, marketing orientation is "simply the implementation of the marketing concept.[11] The marketing concept is based on the premises that the customer is king: he or she has choices and the best way to earn a profit is to serve the customer.

According to the marketing concept, an organization should try to provide products [and services] that satisfy customers' needs through a coordinated set of activities that also allows the organization to achieve its goals. . . . The organization must continue to alter, adapt, and develop products to keep pace with customers' changing desires and preferences. . . . The marketing concept stresses the importance of customers and emphasizes that marketing activities begin and end with them.

In attempting to satisfy customers, businesses must consider not only short-run, immediate needs but also broad, long-term desires. Trying to satisfy customers' current needs by sacrificing their long-term desires will only create future dissatisfaction. . . . To meet these short- and long-run needs and desires, a firm must coordinate all its activities. Production, finance, accounting, personnel and marketing departments must work together. . . . This is what a firm with a marketing orientation does.

The marketing concept is not a second definition of marketing. It is a way of thinking or a culture—a management philosophy guiding an organization's overall activities. This philosophy affects all efforts of the organization, not just marketing activities. . . . The marketing concept stresses that an organization can best achieve its goals by [fulfilling customer expectations and solving customer problems].[12]

The marketing concept does not just consist of advertising, selling, and promotion. It is a willingness to recognize and understand the customer's needs and wants and a willingness to adjust any of the marketing mix elements, including product, to satisfy those needs and wants. In other words, communicating effectively to customers is part of the concept.

Having a marketing orientation is necessary, but not sufficient. We can believe that we are in the business of solving customers' problems and serving their needs and wants, and we can have this philosophy permeate the entire firm, but until we do something about it—put it into practice—it will not suffice. Perhaps a better way of stating this is: You have to put your money where your mouth is. Practicing the marketing concept does exactly that.

There is a fine but important distinction here: *A company can have one without the other.* A company that has a marketing orientation without practicing the marketing concept is off to a good start, but it will not succeed in the long run. When the company dies, people will say, "They were such nice people. I wonder why they didn't make it." On the other hand, practicing the marketing concept without a marketing orientation is like giving lip service to marketing; it constructs marketing as a company policy without permeating the firm as a shaper of the corporate effort. How many times have we seen the poster "The customer is number one" in the hotel employee cafeteria, only to have it ignored by both management and staff? A marketing philosophy and marketing concept must both exist before we can define the firm as a true marketing company.

Practicing the marketing concept means putting oneself in the customer's shoes. It means identifying, profiling, and selecting market segments that can be served profitably. This translates into profitable products and services that the company can produce. Practicing the marketing concept means making the business do what suits the customer's interests. For management, it has implications of integrating and coordinating the research, planning, and systems approach of the firm. Practicing the marketing concept is a management approach to marketing that stresses problem solving and decision making to enhance the objectives of the entire firm. Marketing is not the clever selling of what you have to sell. It is, rather, the creation of genuine customer value. It is helping your customers to become better off.

> Probably the most important management fundamental that is ignored is staying close to the customer to satisfy his needs and anticipate his wants. In too many companies, the customer has become a bloody nuisance whose unpredictable behavior damages carefully made strategic plans, whose activities mess up computer operations and who stubbornly insists that purchased products should work.[13]

Tourism Marketing Application

Golf tourism is a growing industry worldwide. One company that designs golf courses around the world is Golfplan (www.golfplan.com). Rather than simply designing the course (product orientation), they practice a marketing orientation by helping developers with feasibility studies, land use planning, construction design, and construction management, among other activities. They also work to reduce the courses' annual maintenance expenditures.

Marketing Leadership

The guiding philosophy in any firm is established by the top management, which provides the leadership and direction for the organization. These leaders must believe in the marketing philosophy and the marketing concept and ensure that they pervade all levels of the organization. Marketing leadership accepts change as a constant. It not only recognizes the needs and wants of the customer, but it also recognizes that the customer changes. The customer is not in a static state, and any successful company must change with, if not before, the customer. Business obituaries are replete with companies that failed to recognize changes in the marketplace.

An excellent example is that of the "old" Howard Johnson. In 1965 Howard Johnson annual sales were greater than the combined sales of McDonald's, Burger King, and KFC. By 1970 its sales were about the same as McDonald's. In 1984, when the company was broken up, its sales were less than 750 million dollars; McDonald's had grown to almost 3.5 billion dollars.

When the customer changed, Howard Johnson did not; slowly but surely its customer base eroded. As things got worse, Howard Johnson concentrated on cutting costs rather than recognizing its customers' problems and finding out what the customer wanted. Howard B. Johnson, son of the founder, said they ran a very tight operation. They were on top of the numbers daily. Others said that if he'd eaten in his own restaurants more instead of lunching at Club 21 in New York City, he might have learned something. Among other things, Howard Johnson failed in its communications strategy.

Today, Howard Johnson has gained in stature. Under new ownership (Cendant, Inc.), it has divested many of its inferior properties, has built or converted a number of new ones, and has expanded internationally where it does not have to fight a previous image. The roofs, however, are still orange, and much of the negative image lingers on in the United States. Franchise ads still talk about "turning around."

On the other hand, take the example of Jan Carlzon. In 1981 he was picked by the Scandinavian Airlines System (SAS) board of directors to be its president, with the challenge of turning around an ailing company. In what were tough times for the airlines, most other companies were cutting back. Carlzon went the other way; he poured it on. In a little over a year, Carlzon took SAS from an $8 million loss to a gross profit of $71 million. He did it by going to the trenches, where the customer was. Carlzon initiated the marketing concept in SAS. He convinced employees that customer loyalty could be developed if employees fulfilled the needs and demands of travelers quickly and efficiently. SAS soon became one of the leading and most profitable international airlines. Carlzon understood the importance of the marketing concept, advocated it, and provided the leadership to permeate the marketing philosophy throughout the organization. In recent years, we have seen companies as large as General Motors, IBM, Compaq, American Express, Sears Roebuck and Company, Holiday Inns, and Hilton Hotels turned around by new, customer-oriented leaders with new strategic plans. We will discuss this further in Chapters 5 and 6.

Carlzon understood the three components of marketing leadership. Howard Johnson did not. One survived and prospered; the other did not. Next we will briefly discuss the three components of marketing leadership: opportunity, planning, and control.

Opportunity

Great success stories in business almost always include tales of visionary leaders who saw and grasped opportunity, people like Howard Johnson (the founder); Kemmon Wilson, founder of Holiday Inns; Bill Marriott of Marriott International; and Ray Kroc, founder of McDonald's. These men were visionaries. They didn't create the need, wants, or problems, but recognized them as opportunities.

Very few opportunities are as grand as these. To find the smaller ones, marketing concept managers don't look for opportunity first; they look for customer problems because they are easier to identify. What is perceived as a customer problem may well be the symptom of an operations problem. This, then, becomes an opportunity. For example, as previously mentioned, 67 watt lightbulbs are real customer problems to this day, caused by the management problem of wanting to cut costs.

Opportunity continues to be the lifeblood of successful marketing. It doesn't start with fancy draperies or upholstered walls; it starts with customers' problems. Look for a problem, the real problem, and you will find an opportunity. No industry, no business, and no product enjoys automatically ensured growth. Only seeking, finding, and successfully exploiting opportunities can ensure growth.

Planning

Another element of practicing the marketing concept is planning. Planning is defining what has to be done and allocating the resources to do it. It means proacting rather than reacting. It means shaping your own destiny.

Although one would expect planning to be a given in most companies, it is not difficult to find companies that do not plan, plan haphazardly, or plan only as an exercise. Good planning follows from good leadership. Growth must be carefully planned. Opportunities must be sought and planned for in a systematic manner. This means planning with the customer in mind.

Many hotels develop annual marketing plans (independent restaurants rarely do, whereas chain restaurants do), but they often have very little to do with planning. These marketing plans often turn into promotional objectives, advertising and sales allocations, budgets, and day-by-day occupancy forecasts. Rarely do they address the creation of customers or changes in current operating procedures to keep these customers coming back. Although financial planning is often routine, true marketing planning has yet to achieve that status. This is odd because without customers there are no finances to manage.

Control

Control is the third element of marketing leadership, but it is also the glue that holds the others together and makes them work. When control is lacking, leadership and planning founder. Control in the marketing sense means control of your destiny through leadership, planning, and opportunity by controling the customer, the market, and the product.

Control is the feedback loop of the system that tells whether the system is working and provides information to management on who the market is and what the customer's problems, expectations, perceptions, and experiences are. Control is knowing whether perceptions equal reality, why the customers come or don't come, how they use the product, how their complaints are handled, and whether they return. In short, control is knowing and serving the customer. Control is also knowing your employees because, as we will see later, every employee is an integral part of the marketing effort.

Control in marketing requires a good management information system, which we will also discuss later in greater detail.

Marketing Is Everything

Technology is transforming choice, and choice is transforming the marketplace. Almost unlimited customer choice accompanied by new competitors is seen as a threat by many marketers. But the threat of new competitors is balanced by the opportunity of new customers. We address the issue of identifying this opportunity in Chapter 10 when we discuss research.

These new customers don't know about the old rules, the old understandings or the old way of doing business—and they don't care. What they do care about is a company that is willing to adapt its products or services to fit their strategies. This represents the evolution of marketing to the market-driven company.[14]

The alternatives to old traditional marketing approaches are what McKenna called knowledge-based and experience-based marketing.

Knowledge-based marketing includes mastering the technology in which a company competes with knowledge of competitors and customers; the competitive environment; and its own organization, capabilities, and way of doing business. With this knowledge, companies can integrate the customer into the process to guarantee a product or service that solves customer problems; to identify segments of the market that the company can own; and to develop an infrastructure of suppliers, partners, and users to sustain a competitive edge.

Experience-based marketing means spending time with customers, constantly monitoring competitors, and developing a feedback system that turns this information into new product/service intelligence.

We have written (and will write more) about creating and keeping a customer and about customer loyalty. But today, with so much choice, it is extra hard to maintain loyalty. The only way to keep a customer is to integrate him or her into the company and create and sustain a relationship between the customer and the company. This is marketing's job. Marketing will do more than sell. It will define the way a company does business.

> The old notion of marketing was based on certain assumptions and attitudes, but marketing today is not a function. It is a way of doing business. . . . Marketing has to be all-pervasive, part of everyone's job description. . . . Its job . . . is to integrate the customer into the design of the product and to design a systematic process for interaction that will create substance in the relationship.[15]
>
> . . . Technology permits information to flow in both directions between the customer and the company. It creates the feedback loop that integrates the customer into the company, allows the company to own a market, permits customization, creates a dialogue and turns a product into a service and a service into a product.[16]
>
> . . . The critical dimensions of the company—including all the attributes that together define how the company does business—are ultimately the functions of marketing. That is why marketing is everyone's job, why marketing is everything and everything is marketing.[17]

Better yet, we might add, the customer is everything. The rest of this book is about customers.

■ Summary

This chapter has introduced marketing as a philosophy and a way of life of the hospitality firm. We have defined marketing in terms of the customer, and we have demonstrated how a marketing orientation or concept—or the lack of it—impacts the entire organization. We have examined the concepts of internal and relationship marketing (although without using those terms), which will be discussed in detail in Chapter 4.

We have shown that marketing is far more than selling and advertising, the traditional concepts of the field. In fact, it has been shown that advertising and selling are only subsets of marketing. A philosophy of marketing is needed before any communications vehicles are employed. In some cases, these activities may not even be necessary to marketing, as demonstrated by the many successful establishments that never advertise or practice direct selling.

The other side of this coin should also be apparent. You don't have to be a marketing professional to engage in marketing. Marketing is an integral part of management and the day-to-day business of running an operation.

Those readers for whom this chapter is their first real introduction to marketing may, in fact, be a little bewildered with this concept of marketing. Not to worry. In services industries (of which the hospitality industry is certainly a part) more than 80 percent of marketing may be nontraditional marketing. In Chapter 2 we will explain why.

■ Key Terms

concept of marketing	traditional marketing
marketing leadership	selling orientation
nontraditional marketing	operations orientation
return on investment (ROI)	product/service orientation
twofold purpose of	bottom-line orientation
marketing	marketing orientation
creating a customer	knowledge-based marketing
impulse buying	experience-based marketing

■ Discussion Questions

1. A very successful restaurateur says, "Who needs marketing? That's for big corporations and business students. I operate by hunch and common sense." Discuss this statement.

2. Give examples of hospitality operations with which you are familiar or that you have read about that seem to operate by the different philosophies discussed in the chapter. Relate their philosophy to their success or lack of it.

3. From some of your own experiences, apply the consumer trade-off model. How do you balance risk against problem solution? How does this affect your price/value perception and your expectations? Develop a scenario for how a hospitality customer might do the same thing.

4. The chapter states, "Having created expectation, marketing needs to reduce perceived risk." Discuss the ways marketing might do this in the hospitality industry.

5. Discuss the application of the marketing philosophy and why it is needed before using advertising and sales efforts.

■ Group Projects

1. Design the "perfect" hotel room based on customer needs and wants. Be prepared to discuss it in class.

2. Design the "perfect" restaurant experience based on customer needs and wants. Be prepared to discuss it in class.

3. Design the "perfect" tour package based on customer needs and wants. Be prepared to discuss it in class.

■ References

1. Healthier options are in demand. (2003, June 4). *The Financial Times Limited,* p. 3.

2. ACSI 4th Quarter 2002. Retrieved from www.theacsi.org August 23, 2003.

3. Gogi, P., & Arndt, M. (2003, March 3). Hamburger hell. *Business Week,* pp. 104–109.

4. Day, S., & Elliott, S. (2003, April 8). At McDonald's, an effort to restore lost luster. *New York Times,* p. C1.

5. Grainger, D. (2003, April 14). Can McDonald's cook again? The great American icon ain't what it used to be. *Fortune,* pp. 120–127.

6. Day & Elliott

7. Drucker, P. F. (1974). *Management: Tasks, responsibilities, practices.* New York: Harper & Row, 60

8. Drucker, P. F. (1954). *The practice of management.* New York: Harper & Row, 37.

9. Jones, T. O., & Sasser, W. E., Jr. (1995, November to December). Why satisfied customers defect. *Harvard Business Review,* 88–99. Copyright 1995 by the President and Fellows of Harvard College; all rights reserved.

10. See Lewis, R. C., & Nightingale, M. (1991). Targeting service to your customer. *Cornell Hotel and Restaurant Administration Quarterly, 32 (2),* 18–27.

11. Kohli, A. K. and B. J. Jaworski, (1990) "Market Orientation: The construct, research propositions, and managerial implications," *Journal of Marketing,* 54 (April), 1–18.

12. Pride, W. M. (1997). *Marketing: Concepts and strategies* (8th edition). Boston: Houghton Mifflin, 13–14.

13. Peters, T. J., & Waterman, R. H., Jr. (1982). *In search of excellence.* New York: Harper & Row, 156.

14. McKenna, R. (1991, January-February). Marketing is everything. *Harvard Business Review,* 65.

15. Ibid., 69.

16. Ibid., 78.

17. Ibid., 79.

Marketing Services and the Hospitality Experience

Overview

Chapter 2 focuses on services, the cornerstone of hospitality in both marketing and operations. Hospitality is first and always a service industry. The differentiation between goods and services and the impact these differences have on both customers and marketers are fully covered. The chapter also examines the four components of a service and explains the characteristics of services that make each of the components unique. A model of service "quality gaps" is introduced. Finally, we discuss how marketers can use this information to increase revenues.

I. Introduction to Hospitality Marketing
1. The Concept of Marketing
2. *Marketing Services and the Hospitality Experience*
3. The Marketing Mix and the Product/Service Mix
4. Relationship/Loyalty Marketing

II. Marketing to Build a Competitive Advantage
5. Strategic Marketing
6. The Strategic Marketing System and Marketing Objectives

VII. Feedback

VI. Synthesis
21. The Marketing Plan

III. The Marketplace
7. Understanding Individual Customers
8. Understanding Organizational Customers
9. The Tourist Customer and the Tourism Destination

IV. Situational Analysis
10. Understanding Competition
11. Marketing Intelligence and Research

V. Functional Strategies
12. Differentiation, Segmentation, and Target Marketing
13. Branding and Market Positioning
14. The Hospitality Pricing Mix
15. The Communications Mix: Advertising
16. The Communications Mix: Sales Promotions, Merchandising, Public Relations, and Publicity
17. The Communications Mix: Personal Selling
18. Hospitality Distribution Systems
19. Channels of Distribution: Bringing the Customer to the Product
20. Interactive Marketing: Internet and Database Marketing

Over the years, Gary Leopold has served as an adviser to many leading travel, hospitality, and leisure organizations, including Four Seasons Hotels and Resorts, Sheraton Hotels, Hong Kong Tourist Association, Barbados American Express, Emirates, and Harley-Davidson. Prior to joining ISM, Leopold was the corporate director of public relations for Sonesta International Hotels Corporation. Leopold is a past president of the Hospitality Sales and Marketing Association International (HSMAI) and currently serves on their board of directors as well as on the board of the HSMAI Foundation. He is the founder of the HSMAI Golden Bell Public Relations Awards and Golden Click Web Awards and a cofounder of the Annual Travel Awards Night dinner.

Most recently, he was named the 2004 recipient of the HSMAI Albert E. Koehl award for lifetime achievement in advertising and marketing, joining a prominent list of past winners, including Richard Branson and Michael Eisner.

Marketing in Action

Gary Leopold, President and CEO, ISM

Explain the difference between marketing services and products.

Service marketing is much more emotional than the product environment. There is a dynamic relationship between the consumer and the service offering that is missing from product marketing. Product marketing tends to be static with innate offerings and latent consistency—there is a reason people buy Kleenex and chocolate bars. Service marketing blends a myriad of personalities and includes interaction with people and the moods of the people. Service marketing allows the delivery to be molded to the needs of the customer.

One of the criticisms that some people have always had about Ritz-Carlton, for instance, is that the experience is a little stiff, pretentious, or forced. It's ladies and gentlemen serving other ladies and gentlemen, which already in that statement has a sense of formality about it. In contrast, at Four Seasons, the whole service marketing philosophy behind their business model is "do unto others as you would have others do unto you." It's the golden rule that they apply to everything, and there is a real commitment to taking care of the people that are guests there. The interactions between you and the service people are real human interactions—it doesn't feel contrived, forced, formal, or trained.

One can say they have a high staff count per guest so they're able to do such things, but I do think there is a certain service mentality there that's very real, very caring, and very engaging. They will tell you that they oftentimes will hire people based more on their personalities and interpersonal skills rather than on the amount of experience they have servicing other people. You have the beautiful facilities, but it's also held together by a team of people who really seem to be committed to the guest and not in a contrived way. I think that combination has propelled that brand to its tremendous success.

Others that do it don't do it very well and that's one of the challenges. Often what happens is that there are people within organizations who do it really well or there are parts of the experience that are done really well, but these things usually then sit side by side with something that isn't done as well. For example, you might check into a hotel after a long flight and be greeted warmly by a great front desk person. You haven't talked to anyone for the last 10 hours, and it's nice to have some human interaction. I'm a big believer that everybody isn't really hoping to check in at a kiosk. So you have a great front desk experience and then you'll go up to your room and it will take 15 rings of the telephone before room service answers.

The challenge of business today is how to create wonderful experiences throughout the customer touch points in an organization, and it's a challenge with automation. We have a client that's contemplating ripping out the voice prompts in their call center, because they are finding that it is more efficient to have human beings answer the phones because a great percentage of the people on the voice prompts get into the wrong bucket and they end up having to redirect them anyway. Wouldn't it be eminently more efficient to have a person answer the phone to start with? One, you would fall off your seat if a human being answered the phone and two, if the human being can then ask you, "How may we help you?" and you say, "I'm looking for *x, y,* and *z,*" then they can put you right into a specialist or the right department or better direct your call. It's infinitely more efficient than waiting on hold in the wrong queue.

I think we are at a place as consumers where little signs of human interactions, involvement, access, and empathy go a long way. For instance, I just joined Saks frequency program, SaksFirst, and they sent me my membership kit containing a little handwritten note from the general manager. I enrolled in New York, but when I got the kit, there was a handwritten note from the general manager of the Boston store near my home, along with his business card just saying welcome and telling me to feel free to call if I ever need any assistance. Will I ever call the person? Probably not, but I thought that was pretty impressive.

Years ago, Sheraton had an ad campaign that's become a bit of a cliché, which was "Little things mean a lot." The reality is that your experience is based on all these little things that customers remember, and many of them are not over-the-top things. People simply being friendly is so welcome today, because in many instances they are not or there's a real sense that it's been too scripted.

Describe how perishibility affects the marketing strategy.
We constantly need to decide when to get rid of the inventory and at what price. Cars in the parking lot can be sold today or not and at a discount or not. The hotel has to decide if 50 percent occupancy is acceptable at a high rate or 80 percent occupancy at a mix of rates. The perception of the product in the marketplace is also affected. Where is the value proposition in terms of the prices offered? This perishibility creates thinking on multiple levels. Marketing travel is challenging. All points of contact are interrelated. In today's environment there are no longer "image" campaigns and "tactical" campaigns; there's now a need to blend them together.

In the past, campaigns would have an image followed up by a price point type of ad. Why is there a need to merge tactical and imaging campaigns in today's environment?
One is that the cost of marketing today has skyrocketed and people's budgets generally have not increased proportionately. The ways in which we need to communicate to people keep multiplying because in the old days, you could buy mass markets. You would be in the newspaper and on television and you have covered 95 percent of the marketplace. Today, you've got a certain audience that wants everything online, a certain audience that still is loyal to newspapers, and a certain audience that still wants to watch television to get a lot of information. You are forced to do more with your money, because your budget hasn't increased as rapidly as the channel fragmentation has increased.

In the old days, a lot of companies had their brand ads where they would talk about their brand—very ethereal and very emotional—and they were used to establish the value of the brand in the marketplace. Because of the Internet and the immediacy of being able to make bookings and do research, what's happened now is there's been more of this conversion where we want to create advertising that still conveys the brand, the value of the brand, and portrays the image of the brand. But after we've described the emotional reasons you should come, now, here's how much it is or here's a value-added opportunity, or here is the tactical method that then completes that transaction. I think in the old days, we used to feel we'll engage them as a brand and then we'll sell to them in a different environment. Now, what we're saying is we're going to engage you in the brand and sell to you all in the same breath. I think it's worked.

Clearly, a lot of the tactical advertising we're doing with Four Seasons has a very strong brand message emphasizing the quality of the experience and what that experience will be like in that property, and then in a smaller, elegant way, we're saying, "Now you can take advantage of it with a 'Buy four nights, get a fifth night free'" or a special rate or a special golf package or whatever it may be. In the old days, what you would do would be to just have an ad that shouted, "Golf Package, $299" and show the hotel. We've tried to reverse that and continue to use the dollars that we're spending in a way that's not just tactical and not just brand. There's more of this need to help people understand your brand and help people understand what it costs to engage that brand and what opportunities there are to engage that brand.

Can you give an example of marketing a message that overcomes the intangibility of service marketing?
Our agency is currently managing the marketing for the country of Barbados. We came up with the tag line "Experience the authentic Caribbean." Our research showed that

the consumer had very little knowledge of any Caribbean island's actual location, that all the islands were perceived as somewhat the same—sun and sand. Or, that Barbados is a destination perceived as far away and expensive. There's a certain truth to that, and a lot of what we've done in our marketing is turn that into an advantage—that this is a destination that takes a little longer to get to and it's a little farther away, but that's also what has allowed it to stay so authentically Caribbean. It attracts a certain type of traveler, so it's not your typical Americanized destination like the Bahamas. Not all customers want McDonald's, Gold's gym, and other American icons at their Caribbean destination—not that this is a bad thing. Some customers want a different experience, so we began to think about the island of Barbados as hard to get to and hard to leave. We discovered that the oldest synagogue in the Western Hemisphere is on this island. 'God's Trail' gives visitors tours of ancient churches and houses of worship on the island.

We work with a triangle approach. Imagine three circles: customer needs, product offering, and guest experience. At some point, these circles intersect, and that's what we market. This is the branding "sweet spot." We develop a list of all of the rational reasons for choosing the destination and then make a list of all of the emotional reasons for visiting. The lists relate to each other, but the emotional reasons are what truly call to the customer, and understanding how your rational attributes can fuel emotional desires is key.

Can you tell us a little bit about how it's working, some metrics that you're measuring, or some sense of how it's come together?

We tend to measure across the variables that are available to us. We measure things like total visitation from the U.S., for instance, or Canada, if that's where our marketing is designed to drive people. So we look at the customs and immigration statistics that they have relative to overnight visitors coming to the island. We tend not to measure friends and families because they're a given and are generally staying with friends and family, not in hotels. So, we measure something like that, but in the case of Barbados, we do a lot of things in concert with partners because at the end of the day, we don't really take any bookings, which is true of most destinations. We don't run a reservation system. We don't really have anything to sell but the island itself, and our job is to drive demand, which we tend to drive through existing channels. So we're driving it through Expedia, Travelocity, Orbitz, etc., online, or we're driving it through American Express Vacations or Liberty Travel or something like that.

We've helped to market their "Best of Barbados" package that offers some extra value—at different times, it's been an added night or sometimes it's been a credit

towards the airfare—but a fairly attractive package. This year, we'd only budgeted for a certain amount of volume. We only have room allocations for a certain amount, and we've sold it out for the first time to the point that we've had to go back and get the partners to provide us with more availability and more inventory. So, the good news is that this year, the message seems to be working, as does the combination of creating a demand and a desire and an interest to go to an island that's a little bit farther away but delivers a more authentic experience. Combining this message with that of making the experience a little more affordable for this off-season and shoulder season is really driving some excellent sales and numbers.

If you had to look back at the campaign, what would you have done differently?

Anytime you're dealing with a public organization, things take longer because decisions are often made by committee. On the other hand, in a private enterprise where you own all your hotels, you can decide this is what we're going to do, it starts on Tuesday, let's go. In this public environment, you have to go out and solicit hotels' participation, you have to get people to buy in, and if there is copy written talking about different hotels, they need to approve certain things—it has to run through a marketing committee. We'd like to be able to move very fast, so if there's anything that we would do differently, it would be to have a little bit more lead time in the sense of getting things approved so we can find some additional promotional opportunities or some other ways to get messages into the market.

How do you see the changes in service marketing over the past 10 years?

It is becoming harder and harder to differentiate the service offerings. It is not about ads or taglines, but about all of the touch points of the consumer experience. In the past, there was a television campaign and that positioned the brand. Then, everyone tried to build a brand on the Internet, and this proved much harder than it was first thought. We know that the brand is built around a number of different touch points: when the telephone is answered, when the request for information is made, the materials used for fulfillment, confirmation pages for reservations, and a hundred other areas of touching the customer.

Today's marketing environment is more connected. Customers have much more information from the Internet and get information from many more points of contact. The customer is increasingly taking control and your brand needs to wrap around them in ways that they find relevant and meaningful.

Used by permission from Gary Leopold.

Today, people doing "knowledge work" and "service work" account for three-fourths, if not four-fifths, of the workforce in all developed countries—and their share is increasing. In 1955 these people represented less than one-third of the workforce.[1] Currently, the service sector generates over three-fourths of the gross domestic product for the United States.

The hospitality industry is a service industry. The professional disciplines required to manage the marketing function are slightly different from those used in marketing goods. The basic concept of marketing will not change, however; it remains the fulfillment of customers' needs and wants, regardless of the industry.

We argued in Chapter 1 that every act of management in the hospitality industry is also an act of marketing. When this notion is contrasted with the management of a manufacturing plant and the marketing of the goods produced by that plant, it can be seen that many differences exist between the two types of industries. These differences and the differences between services marketing and goods marketing are worth examining before we proceed to the special case of hospitality marketing.

Services versus Goods

The major differentiation between services and goods is the notion of intangibility. Yet, there is no such thing as a pure good without some elements of service attached to it. For example, an automobile is a manufactured good, but few of us are strangers to the service aspects of buying and owning a car. Thus, even the purchase of a manufactured good will have some element of intangibility. Similarly, most services contain some element of **tangibility**. Airlines are considered part of the service sector, but the seat in which you sit is very tangible. Our focus, however, is on the intangible aspects of the product, namely, the service that accompanies it.

As the state of the art of marketing services has developed over the past 20 years, it is clear that not only are services different from goods, but there are also different classifications of services. In fact, one marketing scholar argued that services can be classified by how one answers the following five questions:

1. How is the service currently delivered?
2. What is the nature of the demand for the service?
3. What are the attributes of the service experience?
4. What type of relationship does the service organization have with its customers?
5. How much room is there for customization and judgment on the part of the service provider?[2]

The services provided by a doctor, lawyer, or dentist would yield different answers to the previous questions than the services provided by an airline, hotel, or car rental agency. For example, with the first group of service providers, the customer normally visits the service provider and is predisposed to spend as much time with the provider as necessary to meet the customer's service expectations. There is little the customer can do to speed up this interaction. In the latter group, the customer wants to spend as little time as possible with the service provider, as the customer is the "expert" and usually in a hurry. Self-service technologies are much appreciated by the latter, but not the former.

The challenge for marketing executives is to understand what customers want from the service organization and then adapt accordingly. This is why airlines, hotels, and rental car companies have adapted self-service technologies that allow customers to do most of the work, thus avoiding long check-in lines.

All of these elements (the intangibility and the emphasis on the **experience**) make the marketing of hospitality products so special. We next provide more detail on the differences between goods and services.

What Distinguishes the Marketing of Services?

There are a number of important differences between services and manufactured goods. Four of these have been referenced previously: intangibility, perishability, heterogeneity, and simultaneous production and consumption. It is important to understand these differences because they have major implications for marketing practice. For each difference, we will discuss the implications from the perspective of both the customer and the marketer.

Intangibility

The word *intangible* is strictly defined as "incapable of being touched or perceived by touch; incapable of being defined or determined with certainty or precision."[3] The services marketing literature tends to use the term more loosely as being unable or difficult to be perceived by the five senses and by conceptualization. That is, one cannot taste, feel, see, smell, or hear a service, at least until one has consumed it, and one cannot easily grasp it conceptually. Although services will differ in some of these respects (and it is obvious that this description is not appropriate for hospitality products in all cases), we will continue to use the term.

Services are experienced, rather than possessed. There is no passing of title when a service is purchased. Buyers have nothing to be displayed, to be shown to friends or family, to put on the shelf, or ever to use again. In sum, buyers leave the transaction empty-handed. They do not, however, go away empty-headed. They have memories of the experience that they can recall and share with associates and friends. The wording in the advertisement shown in Exhibit 2-1 illustrates this point.

The Customer.   The intangibility of services has profound implications for customers and thus for marketers. In the extreme, buyers are not sure what they are buying or what they will get. Even if they have purchased the service before, they cannot go back and say, "I want one of the same" and show the seller what it is that they want or be sure they will get the same thing again. Even in the same restaurant, ordering the same meal on the same evening the following week can present a very different experience. Buyers cannot kick the tires, turn up the sound, measure the size, or taste the flavor before buying. Customers are

buying based on what they think they might receive; in other words, they are buying the service based on their expectations. The role of marketers is to set and manage these expectations.

Customers' expectations are formed in a variety of ways. When buyers have not purchased the service previously, they may rely on similar experiences to create their expectations. More often than not, they rely on expectations formed through exposure to advertising and promotion, as well as word-of-mouth endorsements. For a customer who always stays at a Ritz-Carlton, the expectations of a first visit to a Four Seasons will be based on what he has received at the Ritz-Carlton. Customers may also choose to rely on the experiences of others to set their expectations. This is why word-of-mouth advertising becomes so important. Finally, customer expectations may be set by traditional marketing communication methods—advertising, public relations, and promotional events.

The first service experience creates expectations for future experiences. This point demonstrates why each service experience should be thought of as a marketing effort. It is the only true way customers have of valuing the purchase and determining whether it is worth the price they are paying. Even then they are not sure if it will be repeated in an identical fashion. These factors increase the risk for customers.

Web Browsing Exercise

Browse "Hotel and Conference Center" on a search engine. What are some of the similarities offered by these properties? What are some of the differences? Are there differences between branded and unbranded properties? What are the different types of management structures you see? What features seem to be promoted? Are they tangible or intangible features? How do they convey the intangible side of the business?

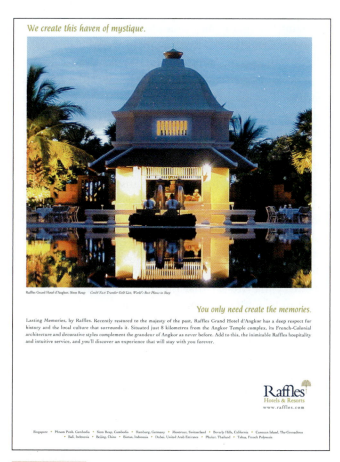

EXHIBIT 2-1   This advertisement for Raffles shows that services are experienced, not possessed.

Source: Raffles Hotels & Resorts. Used by permission.

In hospitality marketing, creating the right customer perception and expectation is critical. Practitioners need to be careful about promising what they cannot deliver. A Radisson hotel may advertise itself as a "hotel and conference center." Similarly, a dedicated conference center such as Doral Arrowwood in Westchester County, New York, also advertises itself as a conference center. Customers will have expectations of what it means for a building to be considered a "conference center" based on previous experience with properties that use the moniker "conference center," what friends have told them, and what advertising they have seen. Yet, a conference center that is part of a hotel and a conference center that is dedicated solely to conferences are vastly different structures. A customer who has just held a meeting at the Arrowwood Conference Center would be very disappointed at the Radisson version of a conference center. Conversely, the Radisson customer would presumably be overwhelmed by the cost of holding a similar meeting at the Arrowwood Conference Center. Buyers who have only the advertising or promise of the seller on which to rely may be buying something completely different from their expectations. The visit to the Radisson and the Arrowwood conference centers will be very different intangible experiences, just as guests will have very different experiences at any hotel or restaurant. Thus, hotels often advertise the intangibles as shown in Exhibit 2-2. This advertisement, while stating the specifics of the convention center, is selling the intangibles of the area.

Business centers represent another service offered to hotel customers with varying degrees of comparability. Hotel A may have a state-of-the-art business center, with secretarial help, fax machines, computers, copiers, and so on. Hotel B's business center may be the administrative assistant to the general manager. Both advertise "business centers," or tangible goods, as an amenity to their guests, but both offer very different levels of service and intangible experiences.

EXHIBIT 2-2 This advertisement for Beau Rivage, while stating the specifics of the convention center, is selling the intangibles of the area.

Source: MGM Mirage. Used by permission.

Terms such as *conference center*, *fitness center*, and *business center* create perceptions that may be far from the reality when encountered. Good marketing seeks to equate perception with reality because, as we will see later, perception *is* reality for the customer.

The Marketer. The intangibility of services creates several other challenges for marketers. It is not easy to display and communicate intangible services. Marketers must convince prospective buyers that they offer the right solution to buyers' needs or problems, while at the same time not promising what cannot be delivered. The first step in this process is to develop the expectation. Traditional methods of doing this include advertising, direct marketing, personal selling, and publicity. Contemporary methods include all of these plus online (Internet) marketing. Hospitality companies use these methods in many cases, but there are inherent problems—it is not easy to advertise or sell an intangible service. You can use words, but often these are as abstract as the service itself and may serve only to compound the intangibility (e.g., "the finest," "the ultimate") or you can use tangible cues, sometimes called "tangibilizing the intangible." One example of tangible cues is shown in Exhibit 2-3. Here, the picture of the airplane inside the Mirage tangibilizes the intangible because, without a frame of reference, it is hard to tell how large a meeting space is. The use of an airplane suggests to the meeting planner, "If it is big enough to hold an airplane, it must be very big, indeed."

Marketers, by definition, must make promises; and the greater the intangibility and corresponding promise, the greater the risk for buyers because they do not know what they are getting until they make the purchase. Customers have no choice but to believe the representations of one particular marketer or rely on those of another marketer, in which case they will likely get the same promise and be faced with the same dilemma. It is because of this quandary that we say that the marketing of services is so different from the marketing of goods.

Advertising of goods is a very common practice, but some have raised serious questions about the value of advertising hospitality services except for purposes of creating awareness and as reminder, or "maintenance" advertising. Research has shown that, barring firsthand experience, buyers of services assign greater credibility to word of mouth than any other source of information. To create positive word of mouth, a hospitality organization must create positive experiences for customers. Thus, it is clear that one of the most important elements of marketing a service is the consistent delivery against customers' expectations. The example is compounded even further. Customers who experience poor room service may not complain only about

EXHIBIT 2-3 This advertisement of an airplane in the Mirage tangibilizes the intangible.

Source: MGM Mirage. Used by permission.

room service; they are as likely to complain about the total service in that hotel. The same analogy can be made for restaurants. It is for this reason that we discussed in Chapter 1 that the marketing philosophy must permeate the whole business.

Intangibility also makes pricing decisions difficult. How much more will a customer pay for excellent service versus good service? In addition, buyers are more likely to equate higher prices with better quality. Consider this example: Prospective attendees of a large convention are sent a list of hotels and their rates for the city in which the convention is to be held. If one does not have any previous experience with hotels in that city, room rates may be the only indicator of quality. The brand name used to be a moniker of quality. The Internet has changed this for the most part. High-priced brands are offering rooms at $99 in major destinations. The differentiation between brand name and price has been blurred by increasingly opaque distribution models. Buyers may speculate that lower room rates indicate a poor location or poor upkeep or, very likely, poor quality and service, which is not necessarily the case. Branding, of course, attempts to assuage the fears of customers by giving them a sense of expectation at any price level. Nevertheless, the buyer cannot experience the service before making the choice. Without any other cue to use, they may rely on price. A similar dynamic governs the sale of wine, as the novice buyer will usually use price to determine the quality.

Marketers are also challenged by the fact that services, unlike tangible products, cannot be protected by patents. No single organization has the exclusive right to provide excellent service. In addition, most new services that a hotel may introduce may be easily copied by the competition, but the intangibility of customer satisfaction is not easily copied and is far more elusive.

Perishability

The second primary characteristic of services is their **perishability**. Consider an airline seat or a hotel room: If a seat is not sold on a particular flight or a room is not sold on a particular night, the opportunity to sell it is gone forever. The seat or hotel room cannot be stored and sold the next day. It is therefore the task of marketing management to create demand for these rooms or seats so that there is always 100 percent occupancy.

The issue of perishability is compounded by the fact that most **services** have fixed capacity. There are only a certain number of seats on a plane and only a certain number of rooms in a hotel. Similarly, someone selling professional services (e.g., an attorney or a doctor) has only a limited about of time in which to perform the services. The combination of perishability and fixed demand has implications for both the marketer and the customer, as we discuss next.

> **Tourism Marketing Application**
> An article in *USA Today* described how it is easy to manipulate pictures. For example, it explains how a wide-angle lens can be used to make rooms look larger and describes airbrushing in an ocean view where none exists. While these tactics may create great pictures, they create GAP 4.[4]

EXHIBIT 2-10	Four Components of a Service			
Industry	**Physical Product**	**Service Product**	**Service Environment**	**Service Delivery**
Full-service five-star restaurant	Food served	Plan for how order is to be taken by waitstaff	Use of pressed and starched tablecloths and fine china and silverware	How the waiter actually takes the order
Casino	Game of roulette	Procedures for dealing the game	Atmospherics of the casino	Friendliness and competency of the dealer
Hotel	Firmness of the mattress	Procedures for turn-down service	Colors and decor of the room	Attitude of service personnel

what "well" is), does the customer say, "Boy, this is a well-managed hotel"? Probably not. But if one thing is not executed well, she may well say the opposite. Why should this be? Because it is *expected* to be executed well. That is the solution to the customer's problem. That is how the customer measures the price–value relationship. This is why the "risk" was taken. *All* these lead to the level of guest satisfaction. There is no opportunity to return room service for another room service in the same way a good can be exchanged. You can see now that room service, like every other aspect of hospitality operations, is *marketing*—it solves or causes problems; it can keep or lose a customer.

Experience: The Result of Purchasing a Service

The result of consuming all four components of a service is an experience. Although customers of the hospitality product may not always seek an experience per se, that is inevitably what they come away with and remember most. Consider the value of experience from the viewpoint of the humble coffee bean. It begins life as a *commodity*. At about 3 dollars a pound, it translates to 3 or 4 cents a cup. Someone grinds and packages it, turning it into a *good*, costing 5 to 25 cents a cup. Brewed and served in a diner, it becomes a *service* at perhaps 1 dollar per cup. Then we add the *environment* of, say, an upscale restaurant or an espresso bar and customers gladly pay 2 to 5 dollars a cup. At a place like Fouquet's on the Champs-Élysées in Paris, a single cup of coffee may run 15 to 20 dollars a cup.

So coffee is a commodity and a good. It is purchased as a service in an environment. But how can one purveyor charge more than another, up to 15 or 20 dollars? Because each adds a distinctive *experience*. Experiences are a distinct economic offering, as different from services as services are from goods.[14]

How are experiences different from goods and services? Experiences are *memorable*, experiences *unfold over a period of time*, and experiences are *inherently personal*. Thus, experiences can create new and greater economic value. They are not merely entertainment, such as the experiences one finds at theme restaurants such as Planet Hollywood, where food is just a prop for what has become known as an "eatertainment" experience. Rather, they *engage* customers, connecting with them in a personal, memorable way. Effective service providers use experiences to increase the attractiveness of their offering—to bring customers back to the same hotel or restaurant. As services increasingly become copied and commoditized, successful hospitality operators will create memorable experiences to acquire and keep customers.

Service Quality and Service Gaps

In Chapter 1 we considered the potential gaps that may occur in expectations between the problem and the solution. Exhibit 2-11 is a model that illustrates potential gaps in service delivery and where they may occur. This model is based on the premise that customers' evaluation of a service purchase (e.g., their satisfaction) is determined by how well the actual purchase experience compares to what was expected. Exhibit 2-12 shows the determinants of customer expectations. The service experience often does not exactly meet expectations, but may exceed or fall below expectations. The range in which the service experience falls below expectations but customers are still satisfied is known as the **zone of tolerance**. We discuss what leads to the zone of tolerance after we examine each of the potential service gaps.

 Web Browsing Exercise

Look up SERVQUAL on a search engine. Develop a brief analysis of how it is used in different industries. How is it similar to how SERVQUAL is used in the hospitality industry? How is it different?

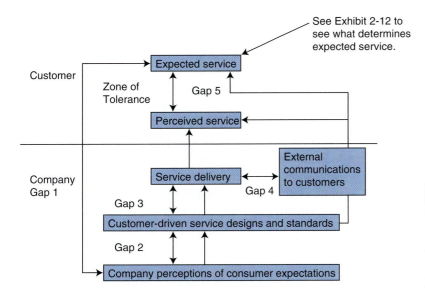

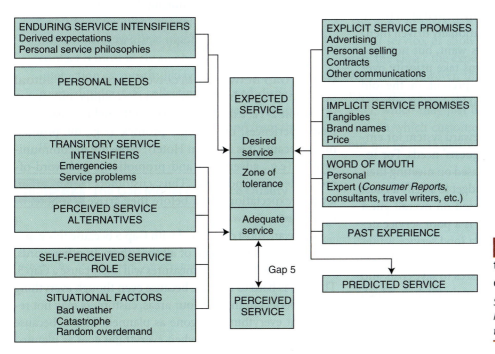

EXHIBIT 2-11 The SERVQUAL model illustrates potential gaps that may occur during service delivery.

Source: Adapted from Zeithaml, V. A., & Bitner, M. J. (2003). Services marketing (3rd ed., international). Boston: McGraw-Hill/ Irwin, 31.

EXHIBIT 2-12 The zone of tolerance and the nature and determinants of gaps.

Source: Adapted from Zeithaml, V. A., & Bitner, M. J. (2003). Services marketing (3rd ed., international). Boston: McGraw-Hill/Irwin, 31.

Potential Gaps in Hospitality Service[15]

There are five gaps identified in the gap model of service quality. The role of management is to understand how the five gaps are created and then develop strategies to close them.

Gap 1: Gap between services expected by the customer and managements perceptions of customers' expectations.
This gap refers to the discrepancy between what the company thinks customers' wants and needs are and the actual wants and needs of the customers. This gap occurs as a result of a lack of upward communication between management and customers and between contact employees and managers.

The first of these is generally the result of inadequate customer research. Many companies do not ask their customers what their problems, wants, needs, or expectations are. The second occurs because even though customers may communicate their wants and needs to employees in general conversation, there is no mechanism for these comments to get passed up "the chain of command"; as such, they will remain with the employee and be forgotten. The final way this gap may occur is if there is an inadequate process for handling complaints (a.k.a., service recovery).

CHAPTER 3

The Marketing Mix and the Product/Service Mix

Overview

This chapter explains the hospitality marketing mix and one of its elements, the product/service mix, by which the hospitality firm decides what **products** and **services** to offer. The hospitality marketing mix comprises five submixes:

1. The product/service mix
2. The presentation mix
3. The pricing mix
4. The communications mix
5. The distribution mix

We discuss each submix in detail in this chapter after first providing a brief description.

I. Introduction to Hospitality Marketing
1. The Concept of Marketing
2. Marketing Services and the Hospitality Experience
3. *The Marketing Mix and the Product/Service Mix*
4. Relationship/Loyalty Marketing

II. Marketing to Build a Competitive Advantage
5. Strategic Marketing
6. The Strategic Marketing System and Marketing Objectives

VII. Feedback

VI. Synthesis
21. The Marketing Plan

III. The Marketplace
7. Understanding Individual Customers
8. Understanding Organizational Customers
9. The Tourist Customer and the Tourism Destination

IV. Situational Analysis
10. Understanding Competition
11. Marketing Intelligence and Research

V. Functional Strategies
12. Differentiation, Segmentation, and Target Marketing
13. Branding and Market Positioning
14. The Hospitality Pricing Mix
15. The Communications Mix: Advertising
16. The Communications Mix: Sales Promotions, Merchandising, Public Relations, and Publicity
17. The Communications Mix: Personal Selling
18. Hospitality Distribution Systems
19. Channels of Distribution: Bringing the Customer to the Product
20. Interactive Marketing: Internet and Database Marketing

Peter Warren
Chairman, CEO, Warren Kremer Paino Advertising, LLC

Peter Warren has been in the advertising business for nearly 40 years.

His company has handled advertising, promotion, and direct response for a wide range of domestic and international accounts, including Marriott, Holiday Inns, Four Seasons Hotels, Intercontinental Hotels, Hershey Resorts, The New York Convention and Visitors Bureau, American Express, Stock Imported Vermouth, Bulova, Nestlé, as well as islands and resorts throughout the Caribbean.

He has written numerous articles and lectures frequently on the topics of hospitality and destination marketing, direct response, and business-to-business advertising and new technology. He is listed in *Who's Who is Advertising*.

Marketing in Action

Peter Warren, Chairman & CEO, Warren Kremer Paino Advertising, LLC

In your opinion, how has the hotel industry evolved?

I have been in the business for about 14 years and have seen its transitions. Hotels were all about location and amenities before—what the lobby looked like, what the restaurant looked like, the exterior. Marketing was a question of showing the building, what the pool looked like. While we are moving in another direction, some are still stuck in that mind-set.

We are now moving forward with the help of smarter, more sophisticated marketing and more information, better research and understanding of the traveler's mind-set. In the 1980s we started to get a little smarter about understanding who this traveler is and what their expectations are. What a thought! I mean, build a product around the customer's needs—what a concept! We started evolving into what now has become a cliché: "the experience economy." Selling the experience, training and hiring people to deliver the experience—this is what is important. What we were selling was no longer real estate, but that experience. And once you start to recognize that everybody has different experiences and different pocketbooks, you start to fragment more. The thing that comes immediately to mind is the effort that Barry Sternlicht, founder of Starwood Hotels and Resorts, took to improve in the area of the boutique hotel concept.

What are your thoughts on the boutique hotel concept?

Barry Sternlicht is a genius. He is only around 40 years old and is a financial guy who saw a space in the marketplace for this kind of individualized product or experience. It's like something that you wear. People have asked me about this, that when it comes to boutique hotels, more and more people "wear" their hotel like they wear a watch.

For example, take the leisure market. Invariably when you talk to people, they ask where you went on your last vacation. They want to know which "in" hotel you stayed at. "Oh, you were in Cancun, where did you stay?" Or, "When you are in New York, where do you stay?" "Oh, I stay at the Hudson," or the Pierre or at the Doubletree Metropolitan. Each one of those makes a different statement, like the watch you wear. Or like the car you drive—a BMW versus a Mercedes, versus an Oldsmobile. It has to do with style, it has to do with how hip you are, how young you are or how young you think you are, how big your pocketbook or wallet is, and so on. And there is the classic hotel and the boutique hotel.

Returning to Barry, Barry saw Ian Schrager, founder of Ian Schrager Hotels and former owner of Studio 54, with this idea and he wondered, "You know, is there a business here?" So Barry took it and made a chain out of it. Of all the Starwood Brands, I think W is the strongest brand. Now he realized there are a lot of people who can't afford a W, so now they are going to come out with a low end or budget W, so customers can be hip, but low budget. More and more, you are going to have a tougher time doing this. You are going to need more people with brains like Barry. Different brands are going to promise different experiences. You can certainly see that out in Las Vegas. You see that now with these themed hotels. And then you have the individual boutique hotels like Delano. The problem with the boutique hotels is everything that is hip doesn't last long. "Today" isn't necessarily "in" next year. So the marketing team is going to have to keep their concept if necessary, fresh and reinvent themselves all the time. And their advertising is a big challenge—how do you keep the message hip and relevant, because the market is always changing? Somebody interviewed me yesterday from the *New York Times* about generation X versus baby boomers. I love questions like that because it gets me to clear my head about whether there is a difference.

What were your thoughts on the difference?

The difference between generation X and baby boomers is age, but a lot of the difference in terms of defining travel, is not demographic—it is more psychographic. It is about people's personalities. If you work at the Palace Hotel, you may see gen Xers and baby boomers, but the reason they are both staying there is because there is a mind-set for that kind of classic elegance. As opposed to someone who comes to New York and will spend just as much but wants to stay at a hip hotel. It's not this simple, but clearly generation X or the younger generation doesn't want to stay at their father's hotel. The dilemma will be what we do when the baby boomers start getting into their 60s and 70s and generation Xers are going to be taking over. They are becoming the core of travel, whether it is family travel or corporate travel, but not necessarily the luxury market. But it's a trend we have to watch and go through to create the product or experience, if you will. We have to recognize what gen X wants. And, of course, some of the things you're seeing is their desire for technology, their desire for meet and greet, and time becomes the most precious commodity. Technology will enable us to have instant check-in, where you can go right to your room, you can have room amenities shaped or customized to your needs. Whether it's toiletries or a bar or newspapers or whatever, they want recognition, they want quality, and many are willing pay for it because time and convenience have become valuable commodities.

What do we do with the standard Sheraton, Marriott, and Hilton products that are not really customized? They were built more for the masses. What do we do with the Holiday Inns of the world? Where are those types of hotels going?

The promise that chains give you is consistency. If I am Marriott, I need to find out how I can support my product. I can succeed financially by delivering consistency. I am not going to be as individualistic as some of the boutique hotels or some of the independent hotels, but that is not my game. My game is consistency and so I have to deliver it. Roger Dow—before he was with TIA, he was with Marriott—said something that maybe has become a cliché: that Marriott's core belief was to do the basics with brilliance. I don't think that is ever going to change. You can't walk away from the fact that you are initially in the hospitality business, and you need to get down to the basics and make sure you do them brilliantly.

How do you find hotel companies matching the service to the products?

It's like the "sizzle in the steak" issue. Sometimes in this business you end up with a product that is less than what the owners and the managers believe, but we have to go out there and make it into a silk purse. I sometimes marvel at some of the things we are asked to claim, when we know that the product can't deliver. You still come back to a consumer who is getting smarter but, more important, they have greater access to information. Word of mouth is critical. It is the most powerful force, and buzz can work both for you and against you. So if you try to "pull the puppet strings," as the old cliché says, good advertising and good marketing only accelerates success or failure of a product.

Can you give a sense of how you see the product life cycle? If you are starting out with a brand new hotel, how does it mature as it goes along in its life?

We have a perfect example of a hotel in its beginning stages—the Alex Hotel on the East side of New York City. Here is a product that they came to us with. When I met the owners, the only other hotel experience they ever had was that they opened the Flatotel. They came to us and they had already named the hotel after both their children. One had a child named Alexi and one Alexa. So Alex became the hotel name. We sat down while it was under construction and started asking questions. What was their vision? What was going to be different about their hotel? We pushed them and pushed them, and we said, "Guys, you are in New York. This is the toughest town, like Frank Sinatra said. So, you've got to come up with things. Every hotel thinks they have a distinguishing quality, so what are you going to do that is different?"

They showed us the model and the subzero refrigerator and what they were going to do about martinis and so on. They talked about these customized services in a small luxury residential hotel. They had a well-known, respected interior designer and a well-known builder, so everything was first-rate and we played off of that. The ads never show the hotel. They never show anything about the real estate. They only talk about the service. One ad had green tea ice cream and said it would be waiting for you in the refrigerator, and their martinis are shaken, not stirred and are made in your room. It's a more subtle way of showing some of what the hotel offers. For example, we have a picture of bamboo and it says, "Soothing décor, flawless design, sublime amenities. What can we do for you? The Alex—overnight or overtime." Then we described the 203 impeccable guest rooms and deluxe suites, designed by David Rockwell. We also talked about the flat screen televisions in all guest rooms, bathrooms, and living rooms; 24-hour room service from Riingo, which is the award winning restaurant; a good location and friendly staff. Overall, the experience is extraordinary, very distinctive and very different. What happened in the past year is they have been terribly successful. I think their average daily rate is between $300 and $400.

Mary Lou [Pollack, general manager of the Alex Hotel] is extraordinary. This woman knows luxury service. Which other general manager goes out and gets a cab for her guest? She is just phenomenal. She is relentless, and I think she sets an example and a pace for the rest of the staff.

So this is a case study where they developed the product and then matched it with the service?

Exactly. They recognize relationship marketing and all of those basic things that you need to do to build that business. They are extraordinarily careful with building guest recognition. They customize the experience to each guest, and the more they know, the more they can profile a guest and the more they can customize the experience. And they are getting celebrities, dignitaries, very demanding clientele, and they're succeeding. For some reason, Mary Lou gives us a lot of credit for this, which I don't think we deserve, but I thank her for it. I mean, they are the delivery system. We can only make promises. The magic is in the property, just like any retail establishment—whether it be a store or a hotel—the magic is in the experience on the delivery side. And if you don't have your act together, I can promise the world, but it's just not going to happen.

How do you think the Internet has affected the whole product/service mix?

First of all, the most powerful thing it has done is it has armed the consumer. In all my 40 years in this business, I have never seen the consumer more powerful than now. I remember when I was in college and I told people I was going to go into advertising. My intellectual friends said, "Ah, you know you just color the consumer's mind . . . " and I said, "No, the consumer is king." Well, if the consumer was king back then, then they are immortal today. For example, the Internet has transformed car buying. You can go into a dealer and there is no negotiation unless you want it. Everything is transparent.

Are you aware of the trend of selling cars at an employee rate? I'm surprised some hotels haven't done the same thing. What are your thoughts?

That's not a bad idea, but I think all those car guys are in such desperate shape. They have got to do something just to get those cars off the lot. Thank God we are not in that position. We are having a great year. Next year is projected to be even better. So, we are going to ride this for a while. The hotel industry took a lot of knocks for three years, so why not win some project back. Fortunately what I am seeing is the growth of the luxury markets. You have people now who have more taste, are much more demanding, who expect more, and you have to deliver it. And if you deliver it, they will reward you. They will pay your price, but then you have to keep delivering. I think the Internet has enabled this market. First of all, as marketers, we have to make sure we harness this. Our website is our "storefront," and I don't think marketers have really embraced it yet as they should. It is going to take some time. The experience online is not as good as it should be or can be, but give it a couple of years. Then it will be the first place we go for everything.

I think we have an enormous market that is growing; demographically, by the way it's going—from old to young, from rich to poor—it's going to accelerate the buying process. I was with the Palace General Manager yesterday and we started talking about the renovations of the group and banquet facilities. I said we really need to go out and start announcing it now and he said they are filling the space they have as fast as they're creating it. He said they just booked a $100,000 party, two or three days before the event. And the whole thing is this Internet mind-set, that we can do things literally overnight, so our lead times are shrinking. Travel has become an impulse item, like the kind of thing you buy at the cash register like chewing gum.

For students who are thinking of going into the advertising side of the hotel business, what kind of skill sets do you think they should possess to be successful?

I am involved at New York University and talk to a lot of students taking internships—even on the high school level. Many of them want to go into marketing and advanced communications; to marry both travel and marketing, which is a double dream. The first quality you need is curiosity. You have to be inquisitive. You can't stop. You have to keep looking and exploring. Fortunately, with the wonderful tool of the web, you have access to this—research companies and their competitive profiles. It is amazing what people share with you on their sites. In terms of personality, you have to like people. You cannot be in the hospitality business of any dimension, whether it's marketing or sales, if you don't like people. It's amazing how many

people fell into this business that don't have that, even in the advertising business. I want the receptionist to smile when she answers the phone. Marketing is a business of optimism. It's a business of the positive—that the glass is half full. You must start positively. You have to walk into a room as a ray of sunshine. If you don't have that outlook, fine. Go into insurance.

Used by permission from Peter Warren.

The marketing mix involves developing and implementing an appropriate mix of marketing activities directed toward market segments and target markets. These activities include the creation and presentation of products and services; the methods used to get the customer to these products and services (or vice versa) for an appropriate price; and the various techniques employed to communicate with customers. In this chapter we will define the marketing mix, especially as it relates to the hospitality industry, and then discuss in detail its first element, namely the product/service mix. The other elements will be discussed in future chapters.

The marketing mix is the stage of marketing management and strategy that directly affects the customer, but it is also a stage at which the company has the most control. We can decide what kind of products and services to offer or the kinds of hotels and restaurants we want to build. We can also select the magazines or radio stations to carry our message, and, of course, we determine the price. Finally, we select the distribution channels. Naturally, all these activities will take place only after we have studied the external environment and learned the needs and wants of our target markets and determined our positioning. The marketing mix is the ultimate outcome of the company's philosophy and mission statement and the final delivery of the company's offering to the marketplace. The marketing mix is often known as the four Ps.

The Four Ps

The marketing mix was originally developed by Professor Neil Borden of Harvard in what have come to be known, through subsequent alteration, as the **"four Ps."**[1] Borden's six original elements—product planning, pricing, distribution, promotion, servicing, and marketing research—were later reduced to four elements by McCarthy—product, price, place (distribution), and promotion.[2] Although we

will change the names of these elements to better fit the hospitality industry, it is necessary to understand the concept.

The problem that we have with the four Ps in hospitality marketing is not their concept, but the elements of the mix that are essentially based on the marketing of goods. Consistent with our previous arguments in Chapter 2, we believe that the marketing of hospitality services is different from the marketing of goods and thus requires a different approach to the marketing mix. The point in redefining the mix elements for this purpose is not to change their meanings—essentially, they remain the same—but to make the concept of the marketing mix more useful and applicable for hospitality marketing decisions.

The Seven Ps

In order to account for the uniqueness of services, three Ps were added to McCarthy's four elements. These Ps are process, physical attributes, and people. The process is discussed first.

Recall from Chapter 2 that two of the four components of a service are the service product and the service delivery. As discussed in that chapter, both the service product and the service delivery reflect in part what the customer has to do to purchase the service. For instance, guests who do not use the self-service technology option when checking into a hotel must visit with the front desk clerk. This is why we discussed the need to "plan the work"—that is, make sure that the guest and staff interaction is designed to help the guest reach the desired objective (in this case, check into the hotel). Once the guest begins the check-in process, it becomes critical to "work the plan" designed. Both "planning the work" and "working the plan" are a process; hence the fifth P.

The sixth P is the physical product. Because services have various degrees of intangibility, the goal of management is to tangibilize the intangible so consumers will gain an understanding of what they will be purchasing. The use of linen tablecloths, fish forks, and multiple wine glasses indicates a very upscale restaurant, whereas a table set with placemats, paper napkins, and perhaps an old wine bottle stuffed with a candle suggests something completely different. This last P is related to the service environment, which was discussed in the last chapter.

The 13 Cs

The trouble with the four or seven Ps is that an organization that truly practices the marketing concept is involved in many activities beyond those presented in the seven Ps. To account for this, one author suggested looking at the 11 Cs.[3] Sean Darlington, of British Airways, added a 12th C to this list—capacity control. And the 13th C is competition. The 13 Cs of marketing are shown in Exhibit 3-1. Notice that the 13 Cs help define and articulate the marketing concept much better than the four Ps and seven Ps do. In fact, one of the Cs is customer. There is no direct mention of the customer in any of the Ps. This book is all about the customer. The typology of both the four Ps and seven Ps focuses on creating a product or service *for* the customer, whereas the 13 Cs suggest that the focus is on creating a product or service *with* the customer. Many of the 13 Cs are discussed in more detail in this text.

The Hospitality Marketing Mix

In addition to the seven Ps and 13 Cs of marketing discussed earlier, another way of examining the marketing mix for the hospitality industry was developed by Renaghan.[4] The hospitality marketing mix, according to Renaghan, contains three major submixes: the product/service mix, the presentation mix, and the communications mix. To this trio we add back two of the original elements defined by Borden—price and distribution.

The Product/Service Mix

The **product/service mix** is the combination of products and services, whether free or for sale, that are offered to satisfy the needs of the target market. The product service mix is what customers see, get, and perceive when they go to a hotel, restaurant, or other hospitality entity. It is the physical product. It is one of the Ps suggested by Borden.

This definition is consistent with our discussion of the hospitality product in Chapter 2. Specifically, it is one of the four components of a service. An important addition here, however, is the word *free*. This, again, is an important distinction between the marketing of manufactured goods and the marketing of hospitality services. We can infer "free" as including those supporting goods that the customer does pay for, but indirectly. Swimming pools, exercise

---

EXHIBIT 3-1 **The 13 Cs of Marketing**

- **Customer:** Everything the organization does should be designed for and with the customer.
- **Categories of Offerings:** Hotels offer many types of rooms; in addition, they can offer customers many ways to spend their money, whether it be at a spa, restaurants, or a lounge.
- **Capabilities of the Firm:** A company should focus on attracting those customers it is best able to serve.
- **Cost, Profitability, and Value:** It is important to examine the cost to serve every guest and focus on those that are the most profitable; for instance, if a hotel has one room available and two guests want the room, it should go to the guest who has spent and will continue to spend the most money with the hotel.
- **Control of Process:** The goal is to make the service process as homogeneous as possible and remove any variability that could interfere with guests' expectations.
- **Collaboration within the Firm:** Departments within an organization should work together to best take care of the customer. An example is housekeeping and front desk; another example is the chef and the wait staff. Traditionally, these different departments have had adversarial relationships because each has different goals (get people to their room as quickly as possible versus make sure all rooms are thoroughly cleaned and checked).
- **Customization:** Each product and service should be customized for the guest; in the simplest example, this involves en-

suring a specific bed type and filling the minibar with products that the guest requests.
- **Communications:** This is more than advertising and promotion. It involves creating a two-way dialogue with the customer, which means that the timing of the communication, the information presented, and the form of the communication (e.g., e-mail, telephone, or mail) is determined by the customer.
- **Customer Measurement:** All customers are not equal; some are more valuable than others. In order to determine the value of the customer, it is necessary to collect data on the customer.
- **Customer Care:** Once the organization is designed around the customer's wants, needs, and problems, it is necessary to ensure that all effort is focused on taking care of the customer.
- **Chain of Relationships:** Organizations need to take a holistic view of the customer and at times may need to partner with another organization to best care for the customer. An example is hotels that partner with cab companies to take guests to and from the airport.
- **Capacity Control:** If a room is not sold on a given day, the revenue is lost forever. This is unlike products that if not sold today can be sold tomorrow. The challenge becomes managing capacity to maximize revenue.
- **Competition:** Because firms do not operate in a vacuum.

The formal product, what customers think they are buying, is the meeting room and the seating capacity, and that's what the hotel is selling. The meeting space will be unacceptable unless it meets a minimum standard. The formal product is also known as the salient product. On the other hand, the core product, which is determinant and important, is what they are really buying. Therefore, the core product in this situation is a quiet, controlled, hassle-free, successful meeting. It is how the entire facility deals with the meeting planner's problems. That's what the hotel should be marketing.

The Augmented Product

The **augmented product** is the totality of all benefits received or experienced by the customer. It is the entire system with all accompanying services. It is the way the customer uses the product. The augmented product may include both tangible and intangible attributes. These attributes range from the manner in which things are done, the assurance that they will be done, the timeliness, the personal treatment, and the no-hassle experience, to the size of the bath towels, the linens used, the cleanliness of the restrooms, the décor, and the honored reservation.

The augmented product even includes the sun and the moon. As any resort manager can testify, there is nothing worse than three or four rainy days with all your guests locked inside on their vacation or a ski area with unsuitable ski conditions. The frequent effect is that customers go away angry over something management can do nothing about. Or can it? For a marketing-oriented management the answer is yes. This is a customer problem that management anticipates and for which it prepares by developing alternative activities.

The augmented product is the total product bundle that should solve all the customers' problems and even some they haven't thought of yet. In designing the product, it is critical to understand the augmented concept and its basis in customer problems. This is different from simply augmenting for the sake of augmenting. Mints on pillows don't make up for poor lighting. Elaborate bathroom amenities don't make up for a businessperson's having no place to write or for a couple not having two chairs to sit in.

The success of the all-suite hotel concept is based on the augmented product. This concept provides guests with a total living experience rather than simply meeting their basic needs. The success of McDonald's was based on the augmented product, which included, among other things, cleanliness and fast service. In fact, the success of any hospitality enterprise begins with an understanding of the core product and its augmentation to solve customers' problems.

Examine the ad in Exhibit 3-2. What do you consider to be the formal, the core, and the augmented products?

EXHIBIT 3-2 What do you consider to be the formal, the core, and the augmented products for this advertisement of The Canyons?

Source: The Canyons. Used by permission.

The Complexity of the Product/Service Mix

Now that we understand what a product is and what it does, it should be easy enough to go out and design a hotel or restaurant that will solve customers' problems. If only life were that simple! Obviously, we have a multitude of customers with a multitude of problems, and we can never hope to satisfy all the customers or solve all the problems. We narrow the problem down, of course, by segmentation and target marketing, which is why these strategies are so critical to effective marketing. Even within these submarkets, however, we can never hope to be all things to all people.

It is clear, however, that we need to go beyond the basic and formal product when designing the hospitality product/service. Certain characteristics of products and services come to be taken for granted by customers, especially those concerned with basic functional performance. If these are missing in a product, the user may well be up-

EXHIBIT 3-3   **User-Friendly Guest Rooms**

Staying recently in a five-star, five-diamond hotel, the guest rooms were oversized and expensively decorated by a well-known hotel designer who, apparently, never stayed in a hotel room:

- The blackout draperies did not protect against the morning sunrise and allowed a "halo of light" to penetrate around the periphery of the draperies.
- The lamp on the light table did not encourage reading in bed. Its 65 watt bulb was inadequate even when the lamp shade was tilted.
- The guest room doors had no electronic door locks, but the old fashioned metal key and lock cylinder.

- A low-quality clock radio-alarm perched on the night table, but the variety and quality of music was nil.
- The television did not provide recent release movies.
- The desk chair and upholstered chair were too low to allow comfortable dining from the room service table.
- There was no telephone on the desk. One had to sit, unsupported, on the edge of the bed to make calls.

Source: Adapted from Stanley Turkel, MHS, ISHC (stanturkel@aol.com), hotel consultant. Used by permission.

set. But if they are present, the seller gets no special credit because quite logically every other seller is assumed to be offering the equivalent.

This is why we discussed the use of the RATER system in Chapter 2. Firms can use the RATER system to get credit for what they do normally; specifically, the RATER system reminds the guest of the quality of service being given by the service provider. Without using the RATER system, the values that are salient in decision making are the values that are problematic, but also those that differentiate one offering from another. One thing is certain—the product or service shouldn't *cause* problems. Consider, for example, the experiences of Stanley Turkel, a hotel consultant, described in Exhibit 3-3. Too often, designers, architects, or whomever don't understand how people use a hotel room.

Today's hospitality customers are much more well traveled and sophisticated than those of previous generations. Thus, the basic functions served by a hotel are taken for granted. Customers expect a good location, clean room and bath, comfortable beds, and pleasant service from all hotels. However, customers look for other benefits that may be unique to a particular hotel, benefits that differentiate one hotel from others. For example, business travelers will look for a hotel that offers services that will increase their productivity. A family on vacation will look for services that allow them to be together as a family or perhaps separate, in order to enjoy their own activities, as advertised in Exhibit 3-4. This resort caters to families. Product offerings can be presented as standard products, standard products with modifications, or customized products.

EXHIBIT 3-4   Smugglers' Notch has been named America's number one family destination.

Source: www.smuggs.com. Used by permission.

Standard Products

Standard products have the advantage of providing a cost benefit derived from standardization. They are also more amenable to efficient national marketing. Holiday Inns' original motels are an example of a successful standardized product. No matter where in the country customers stayed at a Holiday Inn, they could just about find their way blindfolded to the front desk, their room, the lounge, or the dining room, Today, Microtel and the Accor properties

Web Browsing Exercise

Using your favorite web browser, type in "resorts with children's programs". What do you learn about the different resorts that offer kids' programs? What is the core product? The augmented product? Is their offering unique? Why or why not? Is it sustainable?

EXHIBIT 3-5 Companies such as McDonald's incorporate local tastes and customs into their restaurants.

Source: Jack Parsons, Omni-Photo Communications, Inc.

Formule1 and Etap would be prime examples. As seen in Exhibit 3-5, fast-food chains such as McDonald's and Burger King are also prime examples. In hospitality, this kind of standardization exists, justifiably, almost entirely at the lower end of the price scale. Upscale properties, however, do provide standardization as well, mostly to ensure proper service.

A problem with standardized products, however, and one that befell Holiday Inns for a while, is the emphasis placed on cost savings, which means that sometimes more expensive variations in the product in certain markets are ignored. Eventually, this results in a loss of customers who either want something different or want a more modified or customized product. Even McDonald's, which has been successful with a highly standardized product, allows its **franchisees** to make variations on the theme. The effect has been a major contribution to their success. In Canada, for example, McDonald's allows franchisees to incorporate a maple leaf (the national symbol) into the traditional golden arches. Canadian customers feel that the restaurant has addressed their nationalist needs, while serving the same fare as the next town over the U.S. border. In the same vein, McDonald's in Japan added promotional products such as its Gratin Croquette Burger that appeal to Japanese tastes. In France, McDonald's added a hot ham-and-cheese sandwich dubbed the Croque McD, similar to the common Croque Monsieur.

Standard Products with Modifications

The **standard product with modifications** is a compromise between the standard product and the customized product. An example is the concierge floor of a hotel. In such cases, the scale economies of building and furnishing a standard room remain unchanged; the modifications are easily added to only those rooms requiring them, and an additional charge is often extracted for them.

This strategy has one considerable advantage: The modifications or added amenities are sometimes easily added, removed, or changed as the market changes. Thus, the property maintains a flexibility that in itself may be perceived as a desirable attribute because the property can more easily meet customer requirements and encourage new uses of the product. Another advantage that accrues is differentiation within the product class, while maintaining the same strategic position. In restaurants, one example of a standard product with modifications is to offer different-size portions of menu items. Such a policy has a high level of flexibility as well as the ability to cater directly to changing market needs. (The popularity of doggie bags indicates that many people don't eat all they order.) Burger King's "We do it your way" campaign had considerable impact on McDonald's method of doing it only their way. Many fine-dining restaurants offer different options for their wines by the glass. Customers can choose to order a tasting size (usually two to three ounces), a glass (usually four to six ounces), a half bottle, or a whole bottle. Starbucks coffee shops are a very successful standard product with modifications. To see the different modifications, all one has to do is stand in line at a Starbucks and listen to how customers modify what they order. For example, a single-shot latte is usually made in a tall cup and comes with caffeinated coffee. However, many have been known to modify this to a Grande size cup with extra foam and decaffeinated coffee. Exhibit 3-6 describes how Starbucks has added additional products and mechanisms to increase sales of their product.

Customized Products

Customized products are based on the premise of designing the product to fit the specific needs of a particular target market or even one individual. Price may not be a large

---

EXHIBIT 3-6	Starbucks: New Products

As competition increased, so too did the demand for new twists to classic products. Starbucks responded by introducing the iced Frappuccino blended beverages. These new products, some of which did not contain coffee, were a way to attract and lure in the anticoffee customer—the person who otherwise would not have come to Starbucks. By mixing up their product presentation, they began attracting a whole new kind of customer.

In an effort to extend its long-term growth, Starbucks did such things as form alliances with Breyer's Ice Cream and Coca-Cola to promote their product in new, innovative ways. They now have the best selling coffee ice cream in the United States. Starbucks also worked with the Jim Beam company to create a high-quality brand of Starbucks coffee liqueur.

EXHIBIT 3-7	Examples of Customized Products Aimed at the Business Traveler

WESTIN'S GUEST OFFICE

Available at most hotels in North America and Asia, Westin's Guest Office® offers business travelers the option of staying in rooms that double as offices for just $20 above the standard room rate. Developed to meet the increasing needs of business travelers, Westin's Guest Office combines the efficiency and technology of an office with the unsurpassed comfort and luxury of a private guest room. Each Guest Office room includes a comfortable work area complete with an ergonomically designed chair, multi-function laser printer/fax/copier, speakerphone with data port, printer cables, voice messaging and free, unlimited local calls and long distance access. Westin's Guest Office also includes convenient late checkout privileges.

THE QUIET ZONE BY CROWNE PLAZA

The Quiet Zone offers drape clips, soft nightlights, sleep CDs, a sleep kit including ear plugs, an eye mask and lavender spray and the Guaranteed Wake Up Call (you'll get a refund for the night's stay if you do not receive the requested call).

Sources: Retrieved October 4, 2004, from *www.starwood.com/westin/service/;* and Thrasher, P. C. (2004, August 13). Beds: Hotels jump into luxury. Retrieved October 4, 2004, from *www.ajc.com/travel/content/travel/content/0804/13bedwars.html.*

---

consideration for buyers of customized products because they expect to pay a premium to have it exactly the way they want it. On the other hand, with their Courtyard line, Marriott has demonstrated a customized product for the price-conscious business traveler. Business traveler rooms with all of the business amenities are examples of customized products that are now branded with names such as Smart Room (Sheraton), The Room that Works (Marriott), The Guest Office (Westin), Wyndham by Request (Wyndham), The Business Plan (Hyatt), The Business Class Room (Loews), and the Quiet Zone (Crowne Plaza). Exhibit 3-7 describes The Guest Office from Westin and The Quiet Zone from Crowne Plaza.

The growth of all-suite hotel concepts has led to both modifications in the standard product and some degree of customization. Free breakfasts and free cocktail hours have been two of the modifications, while the perceived price–value relationship of the suite is still maintained. One all-suite in San Francisco, however, charges a much higher rate than any other all-suite hotel. This property stocks the suite with cooking and eating equipment, foods and snacks, liquors and wines, stereo, cassette recorders, and a VCR with a choice of movies and free exchange for other ones. The concept is customized to a very specific target market.

In 1998 Chicago's Ritz-Carlton, which is actually run by the Four Seasons Hotel Company, introduced "allergy sensitive" rooms. These rooms include special cleaning products, nonallergenic pillows, nonfeather duvets, and hypoallergenic bath products. Since this introduction, many other hotel companies have offered similar amenities.

Hotel bathrooms may be the latest version of customized products in the hotel industry. In the world's deluxe hotels, the bathroom frills once considered lavish (telephones, TV, marble) have now become commonplace. Designers are looking for new attractions. Drew Limsky, in *USA Today,* suggested that what brings customers back to hotels are the bathrooms. He provides an example of a three-foot-wide Jacuzzi bathtub in the Maison Orleans located in New Orleans' French Quarter. According to one guest, the tub "is so serene, so beautiful. You could party in there. There is nothing like it in the city." Limsky additionally quoted the editor of a business travel magazine who stated that hotel bathrooms have "become a sanctuary, because most people don't have full marble baths or Bulgari products at home. It's very pampering."[5]

The International Product/Service

The question of standardization versus customization is an even more complex one when dealing with international markets. "Think global, act local," say some. "Think local, act global," say others. Theodore Levitt, the noted retired Harvard Business School professor, says that high-touch products are as global as high-tech ones and the global organization should seek global standardization. The answer to the question of standardization versus customization, like all product decisions, should lie in the needs and wants of the marketplace and the degree of difference among the markets being served.

There are pitfalls in either case. Hilton International's standardization of products helped it to establish a common image worldwide so that first Americans and then other international travelers became accustomed to it and bought Hilton when available. This standardized product, however, did not match the conditions in every market. Holiday Inn, by contrast, has been more successful in foreign markets where it has adapted the product than in those where it has not. Fast-food firms have been quick to adapt internationally, as discussed earlier. In Australia, KFC has delivery service and a "smorgasbar" deli case; Pizza Hut has spicy sauces, barbecue, and all-you-can-eat dessert bars; and Sizzler includes pumpkin soup on its menu. In India, McDonald's has mutton burgers. All of these are adaptations to popular items in the countries, as shown already in Exhibit 3-5.

Jollibee, a burger chain in the Philippines, however, has taken advantage of McDonald's pattern of standardization. First, it borrowed every trick in McDonald's book—from child-friendly spokes-characters to prime locations. Instead of selling a generic burger, however, it caters to a local penchant for sweet and spicy flavors, which it also puts in its fried chicken and spaghetti. It is the dominant chain in the Philippines with over 900 outlets. In 2004 Mr. Tony Tan Caktiong, the chairman of the organization, was named the Ernst and Young's 2004 World Entrepreneur of the Year. As shown in Exhibit 3-8,

their marketing strategy seems quite similar to that of McDonald's.

Web Browsing Exercise

Compare and contrast the websites of Jollibee (www.jollibee.com.ph/default.htm) and McDonald's (www.mcdonalds.com/). How are they similar? How are they different? Does their commitment to standardization come through in their websites? Explain.

Each international expansion requires designing the product line for the location and the markets to be served. Products such as hotels and restaurants may need to be adapted to different countries and cultures. The product objectives for each country and market must be clearly delineated and related to the local situation as well as to the overall corporate objectives. On the other hand, sometimes it is not good to totally adapt. For example, TGI Friday's adapted to French customs when it opened in Paris with a dismal performance. Research finally revealed, "If we're going to go to an American concept, we want it to be American." This is in contrast to results discussed in Chapter 2 regarding Disneyland, Paris. While there appears to be a contradiction, the message is that one needs to understand the customer before doing anything—that is, practicing the marketing concept. Jain stated the case this way:

> [The international] product decision must be made on the basis of careful analysis and review. The nature, depth and breadth of the product line; the possibilities of new product development and product innovation . . . the adaptation and customization of products to suit local conditions vis-à-vis standardization, . . . and a planned screening and

---

EXHIBIT 3-8	Jollibee's Marketing Strategy

Jollibee's advertising is deeply rooted in the traditional Filipino values of family and love for children. Fueled by Filipino creativity, its expression "Atin ang Langhap Sarap!" is anchored on its products' unique taste and superiority.

It aims to be perpetually in the public consciousness through television, radio, print, cinema advertisements, and billboards. The company also sponsors selected community activities. Moreover, premium items and toys are offered to bring home and display on the toy shelf.

Likewise, as a way to ensure that the superior equity is sustained and a strong, cohesive and comprehensive visual identification in all Jollibee stores is created, a system-wide Jollibee retail identity was initiated. The international graphic design group, Addison, was commissioned to formulate the new retail identity that is more dynamic and fun-oriented. The new retail identity is an integrated system encompassing the total restaurant design from the menu-board and various signage, the dining equipment and area, to the Playland and other facilities.

The product menu is continually reviewed to sustain customer excitement. Existing products are improved and re-launched. New products are test-marketed in keeping with the strategy of having a continuing fresh lineup of products—all of these to respond to customers' changing needs and preferences, which has been a major factor in Jollibee's success.

At the forefront of innovative marketing and advertising programs are the Value Meal product upgrades and additions. This concept has indeed proven to be an effective response to the narrowing customer spending power brought about by the current economic crunch. Jollibee owns the children's market and will endeavor to keep its stronghold on this segment. Hence, Jollibee continues with its Jolly Kiddie Meal promotions, offering a choice of Regular Yum, Spaghetti Special, or Chickenjoy.

Source: Retrieved October 4, 2004, from www.jollibee.com.ph/corporate/marketing.htm.

elimination of unsuccessful products bear heavily on success in foreign markets.[6]

Making the Product Decision

Standardizing, modifying, and customizing are important marketing decisions in designing the hospitality product service. Although the examples used here have been on a fairly large scale, these decisions also apply to all facets of the product. To illustrate this point, let's examine a relatively minor product decision in light of the criteria that have been proposed.

If a restaurant has rack of lamb on its menu or Dover sole or Caesar salad, does it carve, fillet, or mix these in the kitchen or at tableside? To do it in the kitchen is to standardize it. This provides cost efficiencies and presumably the finished product offered to the customer is identical to the one offered when the work is done at tableside.

The decision, however, is a marketing one, not a cost one. To perform the work at tableside has elements of both the core and augmented product in it. First, we would have to identify the target market. Does this market expect, want, and appreciate the additional effort and cost to customize the product at tableside? Is it willing to pay an additional price for it? What does the modified or customized product do for customers? Does tableside service make customers feel better and more prestigious? Does it impress their guests, add perceived quality, or add romance or mysticism to the product? Or, does it simply delay the service delivery?

What business are we in? Are we in the business of serving quality food at a fair price or providing a dining experience? Are we providing elegance, flair, or entertainment? We discuss these decisions in the next chapter.

Finally, do we have the capabilities? Is the staff properly trained, or can they be trained? If trained to do the carving, filleting, or mixing properly, can they do it with flair and finesse? If not, we may defeat the entire purpose.

The hospitality product/service includes everything we have to offer the guest whether "free" or for sale. It contains the basic elements of what guests think they are buying, what they really hope to get, and the total augmentation of the product that constitutes the entire experience in purchasing it. From the budget motel in North Overshoe to the Bristol Hotel in Paris, from the hot dog vendor at Fenway Park to Max and Greti Mennig's restaurant in Switzerland, the hospitality product/service determination is a marketing decision based on the target market. The problem for the marketer is to determine the effective demand for the various product features and the total benefit bundle.

Exhibit 3-9 provides a checklist for analyzing the hospitality product. This is a marketer's checklist for an existing product, because the answers will give the marketer the necessary tools to market the product. When applying the list, keep in mind the two critical definitions of a product: How is it perceived, and what does it do for the customer? See if you can apply these criteria to the ad in Exhibit 3-2 or other ads in this book. Is the product standardized, modified, or customized?

There is one more thing to be said about designing the hospitality product, which has been said before but bears repeating: No matter how successful your product is now, never forget that the customer changes. The hospitality product requires constant evaluation and reevaluation. We will discuss this in more detail in the next section on the product life cycle.

The Product Life Cycle

The concept of the **product life cycle** is basic to the marketing literature. It rests on the premise that a product goes through various stages during its lifetime, much as individuals do. There is the introductory or embryonic stage followed by the growth stage, the mature stage, and the stage of decline. Each stage calls for different strategies and tactics, as shown in Exhibit 3-10. The product life cycle may be applied in four ways. It may refer to all products

---

EXHIBIT 3-9 **Analyzing the Hospitality Product/Service**

As seen by the target market:
- What is it in terms of *what it does for the customer*?
- How does it solve problems?
- What benefits does it offer?
- How does it satisfy demand?
- Who uses it? Why? How?

- How does it compete?
- What are the occasions for its use?
- What are its attributes?
- What is the perception of it?
- How is it positioned?
- Which attributes are salient? Determinant? Important?

EXHIBIT 3-10	Strategies and Characteristics of Product Life Cycle Stages			
Strategies	**Introduction**	**Growth**	**Maturity**	**Decline**
Customer	**Innovators**	**Early adopters**	**Middle majority**	**Laggards**
Categories of offerings	Focus on one or two products/services	Begin to augment the product/service	More augmentation	Begin to reduce number of offerings
Capabilities of the firm	Innovative, product/ service champions	Focus on managing the process of service delivery	Focus on reducing cost of service delivery	Focus on reducing cost of service delivery
Cost, profitability, value	Negative; high cost per customer	Rising profits; average cost per customer	High profits; low cost per customer	Declining profits; low cost per customer
Control of process	Try to understand the process	Focus on managing the process of service delivery	Focus on reducing cost of service delivery	Focus on reducing cost of service delivery
Collaboration within the firm	High	High	High	High
Customization	No customization	Some customization	More customization	More customization
Communications	Targeted to loyal customers; higher spending to build awareness	Begin broad-based advertising; increase in spending	Continue broad-based advertising; maintain level of spending; focus on points of differentiation	Targeted to loyal customers; decrease levels of spending
Customer measurement	Understand how product can be improved; satisfaction and word of mouth	Measure satisfaction and word of mouth	Measure satisfaction and word of mouth	Measure satisfaction and word of mouth
Customer care	High	High	High	High
Chain of relationships	Create selective chain	Expand chain of relationships	Continue to expand	Begin to decrease, keeping only profitable relationships
Capacity control	Not an issue as low sales	Begin to save for best customers	Save for best customers	Not as much an issue as sales declining
Characteristics				
Sales	Low sales	Rapidly growing	Peak sales	Declining sales
Competitors	Few	Growing number	Stable number beginning to decline	Declining number

Source: The idea and some of the information in this table comes from Kotler, P., & Armstrong, G. (2005). *Principles of marketing,* 11th ed. Upper Saddle River, NJ: Pearson, Prentice Hall.

within a product class, such as all fast-food restaurants or all-suite hotels, sometimes called an industry life cycle. On the other hand, the product life cycle may be used in reference to one particular brand, such as McDonald's or Burger King or one particular property such as the Waldorf-Astoria. Finally, it may apply to one specific product line such as Burger King's Whopper or McDonald's Arch Deluxe, which died in about a year. The traditional and widely used perspective of the product life cycle is shown in Exhibit 3-11.

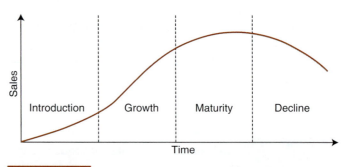

| EXHIBIT 3-11 | Classic stages of the product life cycle. |

The Nature of Product Life Cycles

Life cycles of products can vary widely in time span. Researchers have identified some as long as 100 years (Ivory soap) and some as short as six months (pet rocks). The life cycle of the fast-food industry, which is now considered to

be in the mature stage in the United States, had its major introduction in the 1950s. Products with very short life cycles are usually referred to as fads.

Product life cycles do not always follow the familiar S-shaped curve shown in Exhibit 3-11. An example of a variation of the curve is the growth of the highway motel. This product had a fast growth period following World War II and the end of gas rationing. It never really matured. It fell into disrepute (as well as disrepair), went into decline, and became moribund, to finally emerge on a new growth curve as the motor inn with full hotel facilities. Today, there is another new growth curve in what was the motel life cycle fueled by the boom in budget properties without full facilities such as Courtyard by Marriott, residence hotels such as Residence Inn by Marriott, and mid-priced suite hotels such as Hawthorn Suites by Hyatt.

Product life cycles may be in different stages in different parts of the world. The hotel industry is considered mature in the United States but is still in its introductory stage in China. Upscale hotels are in the mature stage in India while middle-tier properties are in the growth stage. The reason for this is that upscale hotels tend to be built in the major cities for international travelers. As the country gains more income, country residents begin to travel, hence the need for middle-tier properties. Similarly, the fast-food industry is in an introductory phase in Russia and in a growth phase in parts of Asia.

Regarding brands, Rodeway Inns had been in the decline stage for some time, which took it through six owners. Now franchised by Choice Hotels International, it is being revitalized as senior citizen hotels with special senior citizen pretested amenities. Planet Hollywood has reached maturity, although may be on a rebound in a different form. The restaurant emerged from bankruptcy in 2002 and reorganized as a private company. In 2004 it purchased the Aladdin Casino in Las Vegas. Rainforest Cafe was in the mature stage and then was purchased by Landry's Restaurants of Houston for $7 million dollars. At the time of writing there are 27 restaurants in the United States and 8 outside the country. Time will tell if Landry's continues to grow the chain. Boston Market was in decline and then was sold to McDonald's, which, as discussed shortly, is trying to revitalize the brand.

 Web Browsing Exercise

Visit the website for Rainforest Cafe (www.rainforestcafe.com/). Do you think Landry's has been successful in revitalizing this chain? Why or why not?

It is well to keep in mind that the introductory, growth, and decline stages of the product life cycle must, at some point in time, come to an end. The mature stage, at least theoretically, could go on forever. Our argument, then, is that the mature stage is the most critical to the marketer. This is not to say that introduction and growth are not marketing challenges as well. It is at the mature

stage or that of early decline that the introductory and/or growth stage must be reincarnated if the product is to survive in some form. To "restart" Boston Market, McDonald's is testing home delivery in different markets across the country and working to put the product in deli counters of major supermarkets.

The growth of a product is to some extent a function of the strategy being pursued. Thus, a product is not necessarily predestined to decline as propounded by the traditional concept of the product life cycle, but can be kept profitable and mature by proper adaptation to the evolving market environment. As an analogy, Crest toothpaste has been reintroduced several times with special plaque fighters, new flavors, baking soda, a new dispensing cap, a whitening gel, and other alterations. This is what we mean by *more augmentation* in Exhibit 3-10 in the row titled "categories of offerings." Fast-food hamburgers, started by White Castle in 1921, have had numerous incarnations and a strong cult following. White Castle has over 380 restaurants in 10 states, mostly in the Midwest. Clothing stores such as Lord and Taylor, Hot Topic, and Urban Outfitters sell quite a number of shirts with the White Castle logo. There was even a movie that featured White Castle: *Harold and Kumar go to White Castle.*[7] On the other hand, many products just decline and die.

Perhaps what is most important, then, is to recognize the stage in which the product presently resides—for instance, to see that one's product is in the mature stage. Too often, management may be unaware of the product's stage, believing that growth will go on forever. We discuss the different stages next and how to identify the specific stage the product is in.

Tourism Marketing Application

One destination that clearly illustrates the change in product life-cycle over the years is Las Vegas, Nevada. This city constantly reinvents itself. Las Vegas is now one of the top convention cities in the world. Over the past 15 years, Las Vegas has changed itself from a sleepy gambling town to a place for themed resorts, to a destination focused on children and families, to a destination focused on adults, to one of the top convention cities in the world.

Stages of the Product Life Cycle

The Introductory Stage. The **introductory stage** of a product is its entry into the marketplace; the new restaurant that opened down the street or the new hotel that was just built in Las Vegas are entering the introductory phase of their product life cycles. As well, some products in the later years of their product life cycles begin anew with new names. The Park Suites Hotel in Boca Raton, Florida, entered the decline stage with declining occupancies and revenues. By reflagging the hotel with the Embassy Suites name and investing capital for refurbishment, the existing real estate structure entered a new introductory stage of its life cycle. Oftentimes, a repositioning of a refurbished individual property does exactly that.

Exhibit 3-10 shows how the 13 Cs are used during the introductory stage. Notice that in this phase of the product life cycle those who first buy the product are referred to as innovators (customers). Firms tend to introduce the simplest rendition of the product or service (category of offering) in order to understand the process (control of the process). Promotions are geared to loyal users, and money is spent to build awareness (communication). For the introductory phase to succeed, product/service champions need to both ensure that it receives the necessary support from upper management (capabilities of the firm) and to think creatively to confront the many problems that occur with a new opening.

The very nature of the hospitality product often may make test marketing prohibitive before introduction, although not for a new brand or new restaurant item. Ideally, the product should be developed on the basis of as much customer research as possible. Frequently, however, this is not done, and a new hotel or restaurant is opened on the opinions of the owner, developer, and/or management. An exception was the Marriott Courtyard concept. Extensive customer research was conducted before three Courtyards were built in the Atlanta area to test the concept before further expansion ensued. Darden Restaurants tested two Bahama Breeze units in Orlando before deciding to take the concept elsewhere. In 2004 there were 32 units in 22 cities across the Untied States. If the property is truly innovative, the marketer holds a two-edged sword: The product will be easy to differentiate, but may create resistance to achieving trial and acceptance.

The introductory stage may also be one of high costs. Before McDonald's could open its first restaurant in Moscow, the company had to build a 100,000-square-foot distribution center that included a meat plant, a bakery, a potato plant, and a dairy. McDonald's even had to work with Russian farmers to raise the appropriate breed of cattle, from which the meat would be obtained, and the appropriate potato for its french fries.

Whereas goods manufacturers often shroud their new products in secrecy as long as possible before introduction (Gillette's new razor introduced in 1998 was a closely guarded secret in development for five years), hotels and restaurants do not have the same luxury. Construction time may be as long as three to four years and is often pre-ceded by publicity because of the zoning changes, financial arrangements, and other events that must occur long before the actual opening. This is considered an advantage to the property because it is all free publicity.

Whereas goods manufacturers may work with only two or three months of lead time to promote the introduction of their product, hotels seek two to three years of lead time, and restaurants may use up to a year. For hotels this is because groups, conventions, corporate accounts, and others must be solicited well in advance of actual purchase and usage. Thus, the property's marketing team arrives well in advance of the opening.

Introduction begins with a "soft" opening that may be a few days to a few weeks before the official opening. Word of mouth brings some customers, small groups (sometimes large ones) are booked, and various people, such as dignitaries, are invited to "test" the facility. This is the shakedown period, when management hopes to get a smooth operation going before the expected deluge.

Marketing's concern is very different with hospitality than with a manufactured good. In the case of goods, they have been built to specification and tested. Many units have been produced and distributed, and one hopes they will be sold. Hospitality marketers have a different problem. Instead of producing just so many units to be sold, they must produce on demand. They hope they can "handle the crowds," that the staff is trained and ready, that everything has been thought of, and that there are no major crises. Chances are that the product is not even totally complete since construction never seems to finish quite on time and the furniture and equipment never all arrive on time. Hospitality products depend on repeat purchases. Business may boom initially; the question is, Will they come back?

In the marketing sense, initial hospitality customers are less likely to be innovators than are initial goods buyers, although initial hospitality customers may be more innovative with restaurants. More likely, people who try new hotels or restaurants are variety seekers who want to try something different and may not be too willing to forgive when everything doesn't go right the first night. Also, competitors may be many, and customers can always go back to where they came from. Switching costs are low.

The same factors apply, only to a lesser degree, to the introductory stage of a new cocktail lounge or restaurant concept. The lead times will be shorter, more publicity and advertising will be needed to create awareness, but the same concerns pertain. This is also true for a new service, menu item, or other smaller part of the product mix. Obviously, advance time is less, if it exists at all, and the risk is far lower, but the elements are the same. The marketing objectives at this stage include creating product awareness, inducing trial, and establishing a position in the marketplace. When the property is part of a known chain, this is easier to do than if it is an independent entity. However, brand name alone is insufficient to establish a firm's position because of the often wide variations between properties, especially in the case of hotels. Research has shown that businesspeople, at least, judge far more by the individual property than by the chain name.

There is still a far more important marketing objective in the case of introducing the hospitality product. For a product to enter the growth stage, the customer must be persuaded in the introductory stage. If the demand forecast is accurate, awareness and trial will come relatively easily through advance publicity, advertising, and word of mouth. It is what happens to the customer during trial that determines the slope of the growth curve. Although selling and advertising to get new customers is important, it is secondary to the critical need for relationship marketing and creating loyalty. We discuss this in the next chapter.

Consider a case in point. A new large hotel opened in Atlanta with existing ample competition and wholesale rate-cutting being practiced. The corporate office of the hotel company was so convinced that they had a winner and that there would be a deluge to stay at the new hotel that it issued orders not to offer discounts to get business. The sales staff was literally laughed at, and advance bookings remained minimal. After six months, corporate rescinded the order. The sales staff was laughed at again—they had alienated a major part of the market. The hotel survived because it was one of a large national chain with an excellent reputation, but millions of dollars in revenue had been lost in the process.

New product introductions rarely go perfectly, especially when they are major products such as a hotel or restaurant. This is the high-cost, low-profit stage of the life cycle. It is the stage when the customer has to be wooed and won at any cost. Failure to recognize this can be suicidal. Most of all, the emphasis must be on internal and relationship marketing.

Growth Stage. Many newly developed manufactured goods—in fact, most—fail in the introductory stage and never reach the **growth stage**. This is not as true in the hospitality world, where there is large investment capital. If a new menu item does not sell, of course, it can be discontinued with minimal loss. McDonald's twice pretested pizza in selected restaurants and withdrew it from the market when it did not receive a favorable reception. If the new product is a $50 million hotel or a $5 million restaurant, however, it is more difficult simply to "discontinue" it. Generally, the property will find a new owner who buys it

at the right price and has pockets deep enough to ride out the slow growth period. It may also emerge in a new form such as condominiums. There is an old saying in the restaurant industry that it is the third owner who succeeds, having bought it at the right price after two failures. But even the high rate of restaurant failures occurs mostly in the growth stage.

Customers in the growth stage are referred to as early adopters. They are not the first people to try a new restaurant or hotel, but they are there before everyone starts going. During the growth phase firms begin to change the product or service to better meet customers' needs, and they focus on managing the process of service delivery to make sure customers are happy. At this point communication methods go to a more broadly defined audience as awareness continues to be built. Again, Exhibit 3-10 details how the 13 Cs are used in this phase.

The growth stage of a hospitality entity is one of excitement and pitfalls. Sales may be growing monthly, there may not be enough seats in the restaurant, or the hotel is filled on many nights. Customers who tried the facility in the introductory stage have told others who are now trying it. Business is booming, but there are many marketing issues at hand.

Survivors of the introductory stage will proceed into a period of slow or rapid growth or somewhere in between. During the growth stage the previous relationship marketing pays off. Customers come back and they tell others. This is what the growth stage of a hospitality product is all about. Although, like goods, new customers are needed for rapid growth, the hospitality product depends far more on repeat customers. Good relationship marketing must, of course, continue. The hospitality customer is very fickle, and management must be ever alert. Consider the following, which was written about a new trendy restaurant in New York City that treated its customers haughtily and closed a few months after opening.

> If the evening is ruined and the dinner a disaster, if all the complaining—oral and written—is to no avail, the offended customer still might get some consolation from the certain knowledge that at least some of this month's most popular and crowded restaurants will, soon enough, be empty has-beens.

As one restaurateur stated: "The trendy places take success for granted and that hurts many of them eventually.... You see places that were hot a year ago become lackadaisical, then sales drop precipitously and they fold."[8]

The growth stage is also the time of product refinement. Continuous customer research and feedback should result in both elimination of flaws and fine-tuning of the product to the target market. This is by no means a time to

EXHIBIT 3-12	Examples of Management Decisions that Potentially Alienate the Market Following a Successful Introduction

- Charge for coffee formerly included with the meal
- Raise prices of alcoholic beverages
- Raise prices of menu entrees that are selling well
- Create artificial levels of guest room product and restrict access to affordable accommodations during busy periods
- Stop taking reservations or fail to honor them on time
- Move tables closer together to get more people in
- Refuse to serve arrivals who come at closing time

- Do not provide the rooms requested
- Raise room rates
- Overbook and have to "walk" too many customers
- Dismiss complainants as a nuisance
- Overcharge for small extras or room service items
- Fail to honor special requests such as bed boards, which are used to make mattresses firmer

rest on one's laurels because the introductory stage has been a booming success. Products must be improved, and ways must be found to serve the target markets better than ever before. A frequent mistake made with hospitality products is for management to assume that initial fast growth gives them automatic license to raise prices. In the short term, this means higher profits; in the long term, it can mean disaster. This is the time for building loyalty, not for gouging the customer.

Exhibit 3-12 shows some of the tactical things that managements do to alienate the market after a successful introduction.

Operations makes the decisions listed in Exhibit 3-12 99 times out of 100, but you can see that they are really marketing decisions. Every one affects the customer. It is poor management that would make such decisions without a marketing perspective. Once again, we repeat: Hospitality management is inseparable from hospitality marketing. Typically, instead, while these decisions are being made, management is exhorting its salespeople to "get out there and get more customers." And, believe it or not, when the decline stage occurs, the only question management can ask is, "What happened?" Many will answer, "Overbuilding," "Too much competition," "Everyone's going to Europe these days," or, "They rerouted the highway." No one ever says, "We took our eyes off the customer." This is what they should be saying, of course.

The growth stage of a product is the time for fortification and consolidation. It is the time to plow back both money and goodwill, not take away; it is the time to sow, not reap. It is the time to reward your good staff and to keep them enthusiastic and motivated. It is the time to listen to your customers and your employees for constant improvement of the product. It is the time to steal customers from the competition.

The marketing objectives at this stage are to solidify, to price for penetrating the market, and to keep customers. Every customer you keep at this stage will create other cus-

tomers. This is the stage when you not only have to do things right, you also have to do the right things. This is the stage that will make or break the product. Finally, it is the time to start planning, if you haven't already, for extension of the mature stage.

Mature Stage. The **mature stage** of the product life cycle, as we have already said, can continue for a long period of time. It can also end very abruptly. Once more, complacency is a bitter foe. If the product has successfully and correctly traversed the introductory and growth stages, the market should now be pretty well in place. The product's positioning should be established, its niche carved out, and its target market steady and loyal. There is a temptation at this stage to say, We've got it made! Nothing could be further from the truth. Never forget that fickle customer out there, the one who says, What have you done for me lately?

Exhibit 3-11 shows how the 13 Cs are used during the mature stage. Notice that in this phase of the product life cycle those customers who now buy the product are referred to as the middle majority. The product or service has been augmented quite a bit and continues to be augmented as the firm tries to differentiate itself from other "me too" products (categories of offerings). At this point, the process is well understood and the goal is to focus on reducing the cost of the service delivery, while at the same time improving customer satisfaction. Promotion dollars are still spent and geared to both loyal and broad-based users (communication).

The characteristics of the mature stage are usually easy to diagnose—leveling off of sales levels, good repeat business, and general settling down of the operation. Things finally seem to be getting easier, but now is the time for marketing management to be at its best.

At the mature stage, the product sometimes begins to get a little frayed around the edges—not just the furniture, carpet, and drapes, but also the concept and the execution. All elements need refurbishing. Too frequently, manage-

EXHIBIT 3-13	The Mature Life Cycle Stage for a Hotel

Consider a 1,400-room hotel in a large city, for years the largest hotel and the major convention property in town. Other chains started to move into the city with brand-new state-of-the-art properties. Occupancy in this hotel began slipping. The corporate office's decision was to put $27 million into refurbishing the property. Instead of putting the money into meaningful renovations, two-thirds of the monies went into building a new exterior carriageway.

This hotel essentially had the market to itself for a number of years with relatively little effort. It had stayed in the mature stage largely because there was no serious competition to stop it. It did need refurbishing, but probably could have done what was necessary for less than half the amount spent—but that wasn't the real problem.

The real problem was that management didn't communicate with the customer. It virtually ignored complaints or dismissed them with trite responses. It was notorious for problems at the front desk—lost reservations, overbooking and walking, putting people in rooms not made up, making people wait until 5:00 P.M. to get into a room, long lines and waiting, incredibly slow room service, lost telephone messages, overpricing, and other related problems.

The hotel also had waited too long for refurbishment because management thought it had a captive market. Instead of building customer loyalty at the right time, according to many who stayed there, the hotel seemed to delight in alienating customers even to the point of refusing such simple requests as to split a bill on two credit cards. One large group that occupied a very sizable block of rooms four times a year had been complaining for years, to no avail, about both the services and the prices. This group, for one, moved en masse as soon as another hotel opened that could handle it.

ment thinks that a face-lift is all that is needed and then wonders why business continues to slip. Exhibit 3-13 gives an example.

The example in Exhibit 3-13 is a classic case of management not understanding the ramifications of having reached the mature stage of its life cycle, of not having prepared for that stage, and of not taking the appropriate actions when it reached that stage. Even a customer research study showing that this hotel was perceived as the poorest in the city in its product class failed to daunt management. The hotel survived because of its size, location, and membership in a large chain, but it took years and new management to recover its former position.

In the mature stage of the product life cycle, the product has to run harder just to stand still. Competition abounds, market segments have been tapped, and the product and product concept are both old hat. The best defense at this stage is to have built the loyalty and fortification in the growth stage, but this alone will not be enough to contend with the newcomers on the block. One must also go on the offensive.

The best offenses are being innovative, staying close to the customer, finding new markets, seeking and solving customers' problems, and doing this better than the competition. McDonald's, for example, reached this stage around the mid-1970s. It developed the breakfast concept and Egg McMuffin. It researched its market to see what it could do better. It went overseas, into malls, office buildings, museums, and other unsuspected places to find new markets. It developed new products such as Styrofoam take-out containers to solve customers' problems—and it did this all better than the competition. As we saw in Chapter 1, McDonald's took its eyes off the customer for a while with tragic results. The company now seems to be on the right track.

You don't have to be a McDonald's to survive in the mature stage. You can be Joe's Bar and Grill down on the corner. The concepts, principles, and practices are the same; the difference is only a matter of scale. Sales growth slows down in this stage; that is to be expected. This is a **maintenance stage**, not of creating interest, but of maintaining it. This is a stage of developing new users and new uses and new variations on the theme. It is a stage when product quality is paramount, and to slip now is to court disaster. This is a stage when customers have gotten to know us well and will not tolerate our blunders. This is the time to augment the product. This is the stage when **total quality management (TQM)** proves itself. TQM is a classic example of the principle that, in services, management and marketing are the same. This is also the time to evaluate the RATER system discussed in Chapter 2. Are we providing reliability, assurance, tangibility, empathy, and responsiveness to guests' complaints? More important, are we reminding the guests that they are receiving quality?

If the product is not maintained during the mature stage, it will enter into the decline stage. In some cases, this is a natural and appropriate thing to happen when the product was a short-lived fad and has run its course. Menu items lose their freshness, tastes change, the customer changes, and it is time to go on to bigger and better things. When the product is a hard piece of real estate, however, the situation is somewhat different. To avoid decline, sooner or later the product must be reanalyzed, refurbished, renovated, reformatted, redesigned, repositioned, and/or remarketed. This is the time to reverse the curve before it heads south with abandon.

McDonald's did it with innovativeness and new markets. Burger King did it with head-on competitive advertising. Days Inn did it with new leadership. The Greenbriar and Homestead Resorts in West Virginia and Virginia did it by targeting convention business instead of primarily the leisure market. Pinehurst Resort, in the golf capital of North Carolina, did it by repositioning from a golf resort to a family sport resort. Many properties are now turning themselves into spa resorts. Las Vegas went from gambling to families and now conventions.

Although all this may sound fairly easy, it is not. It takes real marketing leadership to know which way to go, to understand the market, and to take the risk involved. Often it demands a change in attitude, as with the case of the hotel discussed in Exhibit 3-13. The main point is that the mature stage is the critical stage: Sooner or later it will end in decline if something isn't done, and done right.

Decline Stage. Decline has a tendency to accelerate even faster than growth. Actually, some of the previous examples of reversing the life cycle curve have occurred in, or very close to, the **decline stage.** Alert leadership does not wait that long; it knows when it is in the mature stage and that something has to be done. Even more alert leadership starts planning before it reaches the mature stage. We use the term *decline stage* here, then, to mean that the end is near. Although there may be a rebirth in some other form, for all intents and purposes the product, as we know it, is finished.

Customers in the decline stage are referred to as laggards. They are the last group to try a new restaurant or hotel. During the decline phase firms continue to reduce the cost of service delivery. At this point, communication methods go to more narrowly defined audiences that can be reached very inexpensively. Again, Exhibit 3-10 details how the 13 Cs are used in this phase.

Howard Johnson failed because it waited too long, couldn't change its attitude, was too solidified in a negative position, and didn't understand the customer. Its third owner has revitalized it. Victoria Station and Valle's Steak House failed because they waited too long, didn't understand what was happening, and didn't know what to do. Sambo's Restaurants, once a chain of 1,200 coffee shop restaurants, failed in part because it took away management's incentive and didn't understand its employees. The company has now disappeared. Many restaurants fail simply because they allow product quality to slip. Some hotels fail because management thinks the way to survive when the product slips and business declines is to raise prices and cut costs. These responses only serve to grease the skids. Exhibit 3-14 shows a simple schematic of what can happen in the decline stage of the product life cycle, called the product **death spiral.**

> ### Tourism Marketing Application
> An example of a destination that could never reinvent itself is the Catskills, located in upstate New York in Sullivan and Ulster Counties. New Yorkers traveled to the Catskill Mountains to escape New York City in the summer. In the 1950s, there were more than 900 hotels that attracted over a million people a year. In addition to hotels, there were numerous summer camps that attracted thousands of children. The decline of the Catskills began in the early 1970s as airfare became more affordable. Suddenly destinations around the world became easily accessible. Today none of the Catskills hotels exists. However, entrepreneurs are trying to bring the Catskills back to their glory days by introducing gaming.

Management, faced with declining revenues, takes the easiest course of action: reducing expenses. This is done by reducing the number of desk clerks, housekeepers, servers in the restaurant, telephone operators, and others. Other reductions follow such as no new carpet for the ballroom, cheaper soap in the bathroom, and smaller shrimp on the menu. Customers begin to notice the decline in service and product. With so many options in the marketplace, they begin to go to competitors. The results are more revenue decline, resulting in more dissatisfied customers, resulting in further revenue declines. The product death spiral continues until someone finally wakes up and says, "Hey, let's do some marketing to bring in customers instead of cutting costs." Of course, by that time it may be too late.

Some products, of course, should die. They have lived their time and served their purpose. We may even push them into oblivion to make room for new products. Others, such as many fast-food franchises of the 1960s and 1970s, simply become extinct. When demise is not natural, not anticipated, and not desired, however, marketing probably has not done its job.

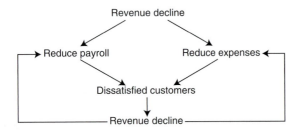

EXHIBIT 3-14 The product death spiral in the decline stage.

Locating Products in Their Life Cycles

How do you know what stage the product is in at any given point in time? Such an evaluation is highly subjective, prone to error because of irregularities in the S curve, and inconclusive. There are guidelines that, along with good management acumen, marketing leadership, and willingness to objectively accept reality, make determining the life cycle stage for hospitality products not as difficult as it might seem.

 Web Browsing Exercise

Visit In-N-Out Burgers at: www.in-n-out.com/. Which stage in the product life cycle are they in? Why?

The first step in locating a product in its life cycle is to study its performance, competitive history, and current position and match this information with the characteristics of a particular stage of the life cycle. Past performance can be analyzed by examining the following:

- Sales growth and market share progression in comparison with the best-fitting curve that one would expect for the particular product
- Alterations and enhancements that have to be made to the product
- Sales and profit history of similar, related, complementary, or comparable products
- Casualty history of similar products in the past
- Customer feedback
- Repeat and new business ratios (heavy repeat business with declining overall business is a sign of maturity or decline)
- Competitive growth and decline
- New competition and new concept introduction
- Number of competitors and their strengths and weaknesses
- Industry life cycle progressions
- Critical factors for the success of the product

Current situations should be reviewed to gauge whether sales are on the upswing, have leveled out, or are heading down; whether any competitive products are moving up to replace the product under consideration; whether customers are becoming more demanding vis-à-vis price, service, or special features; whether additional sales efforts are necessary to keep the sales going up; and whether it is becoming harder to work through the distribution network.

Such an analysis is not a task for amateurs; managerial intuition and judgment are critical. As our thinking tends to be strongly tainted or biased after the fact, a wise move could be to develop a model, based on the preceding list, prior to introducing the product. The model will then serve as a yardstick for future measurement.

Developing New Products and Services

It is clear by now that the development of a new product or service should start with an examination of customers' needs and wants and problems. This does not prohibit someone with a stroke of genius from shouting, "Eureka, I've got it!" and coming up with just the right new idea that customers will love. It also does not necessarily mean that finding new ideas comes from asking customers what they want. In fact, research has long shown that customers are really not very good sources for new product ideas if we ask them directly. Customers have difficulty articulating just what it is they would like to have in a new product. Nevertheless, it is around the customer that most new products should be developed.

Having said that, we hasten to add that this is often not the case in the hospitality industry. It is doubtful that anyone has ever asked customers whether they wanted mints on their pillows or their beds turned down. If they had, of course, the reply would no doubt have been a unanimous "Yes. Why not? It doesn't hurt and it's free."

When the bathroom amenities "war" started, no one asked customers what amenities they wanted; management made that decision. Since then, customers have been surveyed as to which ones they use. One company found, to no one's surprise, that soap is the most frequently used bathroom amenity. No one has yet scientifically determined, to our knowledge, which of the amenities people take and use at home.

When frequent traveler plans were developed, how often were customers asked what should be included? When a hotel is built, how many ask customers how they "use" it? (Actually, today, some chains do ask.) How often are the members of a target market for a new restaurant asked which items they would like to see on a menu? (Some restaurant chains do ask.) Or how they would prefer the seating and lighting in a restaurant? Or whether they really like that loud music or blaring TV in the lounge (often the preference of the employees who work there), especially when the lounge is empty most of the time?[9]

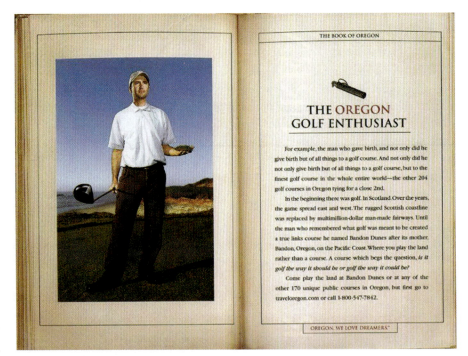

EXHIBIT 3-15 This advertisement for Oregon demonstrates the relationship between product and need.

Source: Travel Oregon (The Oregon Tourism Commission). Used by permission.

The point of all these questions is to emphasize that too many new hospitality products originate from the mind of someone other than the customer—yet their purpose is usually to enhance the product, increase satisfaction, create and keep a customer, and generally fulfill the customer's needs and wants. With these objectives, the customer should be consulted more often. There is, however, a definite emerging trend with more and more companies conducting customer research.

Those operators who do, in fact, introduce successful new products are usually those who have based the product on solving customers' problems. Adding a sports bar to some hotels was a trend of the early 1990s; it separated those who wanted to watch sports on TV from those who didn't and were annoyed by it. Champions was introduced at the Marriott Copley Place in Boston and then was copied by other Marriotts and convention hotels throughout the United States. No-smoking sections came from an obvious customer problem even though, in most cases, it had to be mandated by law before restaurants would offer a solution. All-suite hotels came from customers' problems of where to stay on extended stays. Directories in hotel rooms came from problems of wanting information, and keyless door locks came from customers' problems with security.

But mints on pillows, turn-down service, the extravagance of bathroom amenities, and TVs in bathrooms (but not telephones) were ideas that originated from management. As we have noted, the worst part of this kind of product development is that once the competition does the same thing, the differential advantage is lost and what remains is a higher cost structure.

What we are saying is not that a new or improved product should not be developed to try to gain a marketing edge and differentiate from the competition. What we are saying is that products and services should be developed for the purpose of creating and keeping a customer, and that if you are in the new product development game, the best place to start is with customer needs. Exhibit 3-15 demonstrates this point. Exhibit 3-16 provides a checklist for evaluating new products.

What Succeeds?

Many new products fail, as we have previously said. What about those that succeed? Researchers have found the following factors most likely to be associated with successful new products:

- Ability to identify customer needs
- Use of existing company know-how and resources
- Developing new products in the company's core markets

EXHIBIT 3-16	Checklist for New Product Appraisal	
Question	**Worth Doing**	**Non Worth Doing**
Is it compatible with current product line?	Complements and reinforces	No fit; will hurt present line
Do we have know-how and appropriate skills?	Can handle with minimal training	Will need new staff and training
Will it be stable?	Will always have high use	Fad—short lived
Will target market grow?	Increasing demand	Declining
Size of target market?	Large; need only small share	Not large enough to support
Can we reach target market?	Easily	Difficult, expensive
Communication efforts?	Easy, present channels	Difficult
Price–value relationship?	Excellent	Difficult to sell
Versus competition?	Clear advantage	No advantage
Loyalty impact?	High	One shot; no repeat
Differentiation	Original; fills need	No distinctive advantage
Copy possibilities?	Unique to us; difficult to copy	Would be copied immediately
Market life?	Long	Quick obsolescence
Customer acceptance?	Eager	Nil
Marketing ease?	Easily advertised, sold, promoted	No promotable advantages
Measure of success	Dollar and customer increases	Hard to tell
Capital available?	No problem	Will be costly
Continuing costs?	Minimal	High
ROI?	High	Minimal
Profit margin?	High	Minimal
Contribution margin?	High	Minimal

- Measurement of performance during the development stage
- Screening and testing ideas before spending money on development
- Coordination between research and development and marketing
- Organizational environment that encourages entrepreneurship and risk-taking
- Linking new product development to corporate goals

New product development is a total company effort. Successful new products very often come from the bottom up rather than the top down. This is especially true in the hospitality business because it is the bottom line of employees that is closest to the customer. These people can often best tell you what the customers' problems are. Of course, you can always ask customers as well. Do not ask what they would like to see, however; ask what their problems are. Marriott Suites Hotel in Downers Grove, Illinois, has a general manager's breakfast twice a week. Ten guests are treated to a complimentary buffet. Each is asked to bring questions and concerns of the hotel operation to discuss.

Summary

The marketing mix consists of various activities directed toward the customer. Most day-to-day marketing efforts take place in the implementation of this stage of the marketing effort. The importance of the marketing mix is evident in the marketing of any good or service. Because of this, Borden's original marketing mix and McCarthy's popularization of it have made the four Ps common terms in the language of marketers. The four Ps have survived for many years, and it has been difficult for marketers to break away from this constraint in terms of marketing services. One way the breakaway occurred was with the introduction of two new Ps—the process and the physical product. Renaghan, however, has shown that traditional marketing mix concepts have limited utility for hospitality marketers because they reflect strategies for marketing goods and ignore the unique complexities of marketing hospitality services.

The product/service mix represents what the hospitality firm has to offer to the customer, both tangible and intangible, both "free" and for sale. The product/service mix drives the other elements of the marketing mix; in some cases it may even drive the strategy of the firm. Accordingly, it is not just the marketer's job to "sell" the product/service. More important, it is the marketer's job to design in accordance with the needs and wants of the target markets.

A product/service has three elements: the formal element, the core element, and the augmented element. These elements are closely related to the concepts of salience, determinance, and importance. The astute marketer will develop products/services with these relationships in mind.

The product life cycle is concerned with the various stages of a product's growth in the marketplace. The best use of the product life cycle is not so much to predict the future, but to recognize its existence and preplan for it and to recognize the product's present stage and the appropriate actions necessary.

Product innovation is a characteristic of marketing leadership. The place to look for new product ideas is in customers' problems. Too many new products are designed without considering the customer's real needs.

■ Key Terms

products	standard product
seven Ps	with modifications
thirteen Cs	customized products
product/service mix	product life cycle
presentation mix	introductory stage
pricing mix	growth stage
communications mix	mature stage
distribution mix	maintenance stage
formal product	total quality management
core product	(TQM)
augmented product	decline stage
standard products	death spiral
franchisees	

■ Discussion Questions

1. Discuss the virtues of the hospitality marketing mix against those of the four Ps. Do you think, as some do, that the four Ps are adequate for the hospitality market? Argue why they are or are not.
2. List the formal, core, and augmented products of an all-inclusive resort hotel in the Caribbean.

3. Give examples of various hospitality products that are in various stages of the product life cycle. How do you define which stage they are in? What specific implications does this have for marketing them?
4. Discuss the following: Hospitality customers really have no choice in product determination. They can't articulate what they want until they have it. Therefore, there really is no alternative but to determine the product for them.
5. Consider some common customer complaints—for instance, waiting for the elevator, waiting at the front desk, hearing the telephone ring 15 times before somebody answers. Develop a new product or service that is economically feasible to solve these customer problems.
6. Which part of the hospitality product is most important to the customer—the tangible or the intangible? Discuss.

■ Group Projects

1. Analyze the product/service mix at a local establishment. Does it fulfill the criteria outlined in the chapter? Why or why not?
2. Develop a new product or service for a hotel, restaurant, or travel and tourism company and match it against the criteria in Exhibit 3-16.

■ References

1. Borden, N. (1964, June). The concept of the marketing mix. *Journal of Advertising Research, 4*, 2–7.
2. McCarthy, E. J. (1975). *Basic marketing: A managerial approach.* Homewood, IL: Richard D. Irwin, 75–80.
3. Gordon, I. (1998). *Relationship marketing: New strategies, techniques and technologies to win the customers you want and keep them forever.* Toronto: John Wiley & Sons Canada, Ltd., 61–63.
4. Renaghan, L. M. (1981, April). A new marketing mix for the hospitality industry. *Cornell Hotel and Restaurant Administration Quarterly*, 31–35.
5. Limsky, D. (2003, September 17). To-die-for bathrooms separate the best hotels from the rest. *USA Today.* Retrieved October 4, 2004, from www.usatoday.com/travel/bonus/2003-05-17-bathrooms.htm.
6. Jain, S. C. (1984). *International marketing management.* Boston: Kent, 345.

7. Retrieved October 4, 2004, from www.whitecastle.com and http://seattlepi.nwsource.com/business/180754_whitecastle05.html.

8. Hughes, K. A. & Landro, L. (1986, November 12). A lot of restaurants now serve rudeness with the rigatoni. *The Wall Street Journal*, p. 22.

9. An insight into new product development in restaurants, as well as an excerpt on the development of Courtyard by Marriott, can be found in Feltenstein, T. (1986, November). New-product development in food service: A structured approach. *Cornell Hotel and Restaurant Administration Quarterly*, 63–71.

CHAPTER 4

Relationship/Loyalty Marketing

Overview

The concept of relationship marketing (also known as loyalty marketing) is introduced in this chapter. In this concept, customers are considered valuable assets with whom firms should develop an ongoing relationship in order to promote repeat purchase, positive word of mouth, emotional bonding, and partnership activities (e.g., letting the firm know when a service failure has occurred). Relationship/loyalty marketing is also applied to employees to develop the same level of commitment to the organization as guests provide. The chapter deals with the "whys" and "hows" of relationship/loyalty marketing.

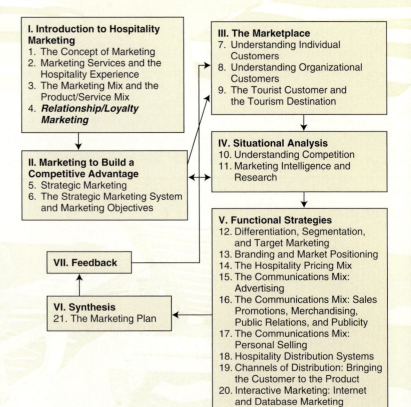

I. Introduction to Hospitality Marketing
1. The Concept of Marketing
2. Marketing Services and the Hospitality Experience
3. The Marketing Mix and the Product/Service Mix
4. ***Relationship/Loyalty Marketing***

II. Marketing to Build a Competitive Advantage
5. Strategic Marketing
6. The Strategic Marketing System and Marketing Objectives

III. The Marketplace
7. Understanding Individual Customers
8. Understanding Organizational Customers
9. The Tourist Customer and the Tourism Destination

IV. Situational Analysis
10. Understanding Competition
11. Marketing Intelligence and Research

V. Functional Strategies
12. Differentiation, Segmentation, and Target Marketing
13. Branding and Market Positioning
14. The Hospitality Pricing Mix
15. The Communications Mix: Advertising
16. The Communications Mix: Sales Promotions, Merchandising, Public Relations, and Publicity
17. The Communications Mix: Personal Selling
18. Hospitality Distribution Systems
19. Channels of Distribution: Bringing the Customer to the Product
20. Interactive Marketing: Internet and Database Marketing

VII. Feedback

VI. Synthesis
21. The Marketing Plan

Marketing Executive Profile

Adam Burke
Senior Vice President and Managing Director, Hilton HHonors Worldwide

Adam Burke was named senior vice president and managing director of Hilton HHonors Worldwide (HHW) in July 2004. In this capacity, he is responsible for the worldwide marketing and operations of the Hilton HHonors guest loyalty pro-gram, currently available at more than 2,700 Hilton Family hotels worldwide. HHW is jointly owned by Hilton Group, PLC, and Hilton Hotels Corporation. Previously, Burke served as vice president of marketing for Hilton HHonors Worldwide, a position he held since June 2001.

Marketing in Action

Adam Burke, Senior Vice President and Managing Director, Hilton HHonors Worldwide

How would you define customer loyalty?

It's very much customer defined. A lot of people talk about customer centricity, but I think it takes a real discipline to truly "walk the talk." The way I would define customer loyalty is: The relationship you have with your customer is so differentiated that the barriers to switching to a competitive product are extremely high. Unless you really drop the ball on that relationship, they remain invested in your products and services. The motivators that would give an individual reason to have that type of loyalty to an organization are going to be extremely varied, depending on each individual's needs. So when you talk about being customer centric, that has to stem from what each of your customers is looking for from your products and services.

Do you see hospitality firms moving in that direction or just some of them?

Everyone in the industry is talking about it in some form. I think the difference is the degree of operational discipline that you want to put behind it. To give an example, we talk about driving loyalty from the standpoint of truly being customer centric. It means that terms like *customer relationship management* can't simply be buzzwords, pro-grams, or initiatives. Instead, they are a fundamental part of how you do business. It is not just about creating individual programs that are designed to provide incentives, nor is it making sure that your front line employees know how to recognize a customer. It's going beyond that to say that, at every possible touch point where a customer interacts with your enterprise, you have indoctrinated everyone to look at things from a customer perspective. You can talk all you want about loyalty, and you can talk about the fact that you've thought about the obvious things—recognizing the customer when they arrive at the hotel, for example. That's all great, but what happens when that loyal customer calls an individual hotel because they have a billing inquiry and ends up with the night auditor? What's the likelihood that the night auditor is going to treat the customer the way we would hope to treat them at all of our touch points? The answer to that question illustrates how well we've educated our broader organization on the value of customer loyalty.

When we talk about what people are trying to do in the industry, the first point I would make is that there is a lot of lip service paid to putting the customer at the center of the organization, but the proof is in terms of how well

chain, it's likely because we simply haven't found the thing that is most relevant and most important to them. Now, that's not to say there aren't customers out there who will never consolidate their stays. For the vast majority of travelers, however—particularly the most frequent travelers—they would rather have a relationship with an organization that knows them as an individual and, as a result, is able to consistently deliver a superior experience at all of their properties. I think the key is that if you don't consolidate your stays and you don't get to the point where a company knows you well enough that they can deliver a customized experience, it means that you're not going to experience everything that a hotel company can offer. Above all else, though, no matter what we promise, flawless execution and consistent service delivery is going to be crucial for long-term success.

What advice can you give to students who wish to pursue a career in marketing?

The first thing I would say is, if you want to pursue a career in marketing, particularly as it relates to the hospitality industry, you've got to start with a broad understanding of the operation overall. I think the pitfall of a lot of marketers is that perhaps they look too much into the theoretical world of how to run a good marketing program and not enough into the nuts and bolts of their industry and what the implications are for how you can integrate that into the overall operation. So if I am talking about the hotel space, it's critical that you have an understanding of the front office operation. It's critical that you have an understanding of the franchise environment. It's critical that you have an understanding of the financial part of the operation and how to structure things in a way that makes sense within those parameters. It's also equally critical, as a marketer, that you are completely versed in the customer service and reservations operations of the company. My first piece of advice is, if you really want to pursue a marketing career in the hospitality industry, don't forget that, first and foremost, you are in the hospitality industry.

The second thing I would say is that you have to have a commitment to viewing business from the customer's perspective. There's a lot written out there about CRM [customer relations management]—about what it is and what it should be. But ultimately, if you really want to plan on long-term success, then I believe that you've really got to be willing to make the commitment to put the customer at the center of your decision-making process. That means that you stop looking at things from a short-term focus and start talking about how you cultivate true loyalty over a long-term relationship with your customers. This requires taking a very different look at things like financial invest-

ment, cost containment, and ROI, and it means that you have to be willing to take some risks to really cultivate that long-term relationship.

How important are the partners you work with, and what are some of the criteria in choosing partners to work with?

Partners are absolutely vital to the program. There are a few key points. One is something that I alluded to earlier, which is that we do not rent or sell our lists. To us, having a relationship with a customer means that both explicitly and implicitly, there is a responsibility to use that information properly. So, the only way that someone can contact our customers is if they are a strategic business partner of ours. And we are the ones who approve not just the offer, but the content and the communications as well. We have to recognize that anything a customer receives because of their affiliation with us will be viewed as an extension of that relationship. Partnerships are one of the key ways that we extend value to the customer, but in ways that respect the customer's preferences.

Within that context, partnerships broaden the appeal and relevance of a program. For example, when you talk about the currencies that people value—some people really value airline miles. Our relationships with airline programs are crucial in making sure that we can provide that incentive for our customers. Similarly, we look for partners that allow our members to earn HHonors points outside of the hotel space, so that the currency becomes more meaningful to them. This includes partnerships in the financial services arena, for example.

Another important consideration is that we look for partners who are also among the best in their respective industries, because an important aspect of being part of the Hilton organization is being brand stewards. We need to recognize that there's such tremendous equity in our brands that we shouldn't affiliate with companies that are not of that same stature because we have a responsibility to our brands and customers. It takes a fair amount of infrastructure and support to maintain these relationships, so it has to be about the quality of these partnerships and making sure that they deliver additional value to our customers and to our owners.

Other comments?

A huge opportunity in working with a loyalty program is recognizing your role as one of the strongest customer advocates within your organization. Let's face it—across a variety of industries, there are a lot of more conservative ways of looking at the business. Those perspectives aren't necessarily wrong, but they don't always take the customer perspective into account. So if you're sitting in a meeting where some of those more traditional approaches come up, I think you have to be willing to view yourself as the voice of the customer in those settings because that's who you're representing. That's not to say that you shouldn't be financially responsible—far from it. It's just your opportunity to ensure that the voice of the customer is an integral part of your organization's business decisions.

Used by permission from Hilton Hotels Corporation.

Customers are assets. They are the most important assets a company can have. Firms spend large amounts of money on such things as insurance and elaborate alarm systems to protect their assets such as buildings and warehouses. In the same way, firms need to spend money protecting their customers. One way to define relationship/loyalty marketing is to say that it is marketing that protects the customer base. (We will define it in other ways later on.) **Relationship marketing** sees the customer as an asset. Its function is to attract, maintain, and enhance customer relationships. To put this in perspective, consider the hypothetical abbreviated balance sheets in Exhibit 4-1.

Exhibit 4-1 shows two balance sheets: a traditional balance sheet and a second that includes customers. As discussed in finance, **total assets** always equal total **liabilities** plus shareholders' equity. To improve shareholders' equity, you must either increase assets, decrease liabilities, or do both. Looking at the second balance sheet, one can see that if management can increase both the number of customers that are likely to come and definitely come, while at the same time decreasing the number of customers who will either defect because of not being satisfied or not come at all because they have heard negative comments, then shareholder equity will increase in order to "balance" the balance sheet.

It is clear from the customer balance sheet that the goal of an organization should be threefold:

1. To get more customers
2. To keep more customers coming back (that is, to reduce the number of customers defecting)
3. To lose fewer potential customers because unhappy current customers say unflattering things about the property or organization

This is essentially what marketing is all about. But relationship/**loyalty marketing** adds a new dimension; specifically, the goal is to not only encourage guests to return, but to get them to tell their friends how wonderful the property or organization is. One metric used to determine the word-of-mouth influence is to ask the following question: How likely is it that you would recommend _____ to a friend or colleague? This is done on a

---

EXHIBIT 4-1	**Customers as Assets on the Balance Sheet**

Hypothetical Standard Balance Sheet for a Hotel

Current Assets:	
Cash and investments	$120,000
Receivables	30,000
Inventory	50,000
Total current assets	200,000
Fixed Assets:	
Properties and land	25,000,000
Investments	2,500,000
Total assets	27,700,000
Liabilities:	
Current debt	100,000
Accounts payable	50,000
Long-term debt	20,000,000
Shareholder's equity: capital stock	7,550,000
Total liabilities and equity	27,700,000

Hypothetical Customer Balance Sheet for the Same Hotel

Current Assets:	
Probable customers: 2,000 @ $2,000 a year	$4,000,000
Receivables: 1,000 customer prospects @ $2,000 a year	2,000,000
Inventory (guaranteed customer deposits for future year): 1,400 @ $500	700,000
Total current assets	6,700,000
Fixed Assets:	
Investments: 10,500 loyal customers @ $2,000	21,000,000
Total assets	27,700,000
(6,700,000 + 21,000,000)	
Liabilities:	
Current debt: loss of upset customers 500 @ $2,000	1,000,000
Accounts payable: pay back irate customers	100,000
Long-term debt: loss of customers by word of mouth	19,050,000
Shareholders' equity: capital stock	7,550,000
Total liabilities and equity	27,700,000

---

0 to 10 scale. The percentage of people who respond with a 9 or 10 are called promoters; those who score from 0 to 6 are called detractors. Those who score 7 or 8 are indifferent. The net promoter score is the difference between the percentage that are promoters and the percentage that are detractors.[1]

EXHIBIT 4-2	Undoing a Relationship

A couple had gone to a certain hotel within 25 miles of their home following their marriage. The time was early December, when the hotel traditionally ran 20 percent occupancy. They had been going there on their anniversary for the last four years, each time spending about $600. They also went there other times or ate there, sometimes with friends.

On the fifth year, they arrived about 7:00 P.M and were welcomed by the desk clerk, whom they had come to know. They went to their room and ordered champagne and dinner. They also had their remaining meals in the hotel and spent time in the hotel lounge. When they checked out three days later, they asked for the 10 percent room discount they were entitled to as members of an organization with which the well-known hotel chain had an agreement. The same clerk's response was that he could not grant the discount because they did not ask for it when they checked in, according to the standard operating procedure. When they got home,

they wrote to the general manager, asking for the discount. In a two-page letter, the discount was refused in no uncertain terms. They then wrote to the vice president of marketing of the company, including a copy of the manager's letter.

Shortly afterward, they received a polite letter from the general manager starting, "We are always glad to know of our customers' complaints because it helps us to improve our operations." It included an invitation to spend a weekend at the hotel as his guest. No mention was made of the 10 percent discount—the main purpose of the letter. Nor did management mention the changes that had been made to ensure that the problem did not happen again. The couple never went back and never will, nor will many of their friends.

Consider the cost of granting the discount, about $25, against the business lost.

The goals of loyalty marketing also include two more items:

1. To have customers spend more money while on the property
2. To have customers tell management when things go wrong, instead of just walking away and never coming back

Of course, when guests do tell management when things go wrong, management must not only solve the problem, but also put in place systems to ensure that the same mistake does not happen again. Consider the situation in Exhibit 4-2, which examines the poor response of management to a guest's complaint. It was a poor response because management did not address the guest's complaint nor did management mention anything about new systems to ensure the problem would not happen again. Rather, it appeared that management was just trying to buy loyalty by giving away a free room. We address the issue of complaint management in more detail later in this chapter.

What Relationship/Loyalty Marketing Is and What It Is Not

Relationship/loyalty marketing is not, contrary to some beliefs, database marketing, frequent traveler programs, partnerships, or relationship selling. Although some of these may be used to enhance relationships, they are not, in themselves, the bases of relationships. The true sense and purpose of relationship/loyalty marketing is to maintain customer relationships and build loyalty with the expectation that both parties in the relationship will continue long

after the formal production/consumption process has ended, seeking not only to keep customers but to bring them back as well. Levitt compared the relationship to something like a marriage.

> The sale merely consummates the courtship. Then the marriage begins. How good the marriage is depends on how well the relationship is managed by the seller. That determines whether there will be continued or expanded business or troubles and divorce and whether costs or profits increase. . . . It is not just that once you get a customer you want to keep him. It is more a matter of what the buyer wants. He wants a vendor who will keep his promises, who'll keep supplying and stand behind what he promised. The age of the blind date or the one-night stand is gone. Marriage is both more convenient and more necessary. . . . In these conditions, success in marketing, like success in marriage, is transformed into the inescapability of a relationship.[2]

Like a good marriage or a good relationship, both parties have to "get something." For the firm, it is repeat patronage, the expectation that the guest will spread positive word of mouth, and the belief that the guest will tell management when things go wrong. These are just a few of the firm's expectations. For the guest, the expectation is that the firm will do everything in its power to ensure an error-free and customized experience, and that the firm will look after the guest's best interest.

A good relationship involves commitment and trust, and, as in our personal lives, there are numerous antecedents that bring this about. There are also numerous consequences when they do not exist. Exhibit 4-3 shows a model of service relationships developed by Bowen and Shoemaker based on their research in the luxury hotel industry. This model illustrates the antecedents and consequences of commitment and trust in service relationships, as indicated by the plus and minus signs. The numbers rep-

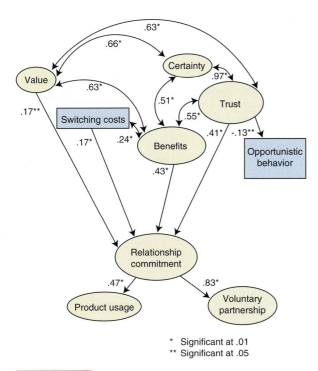

* Significant at .01
** Significant at .05

EXHIBIT 4-3 Model of service relationships.

Source: Adapted from Bowen, J. T., & Shoemaker, S. (1998, February). Loyalty: A strategic commitment. Cornell Hotel and Restaurant Administration Quarterly, 14-17. Adapted from SAGE Publications. Used by permission.

resent linear correlation coefficients. Theoretically, these can range from −1 to +1, with numbers closer to 1.0 (−1.0) indicating stronger relationships. We explain the model after first defining what we mean by trust and commitment.[3]

Trust is the belief that an individual or exchange partner can be relied on to keep his or her word and promise. Trust is an antecedent of loyalty because the customer trusts the organization to do the things that it is supposed to do, implicitly or explicitly. Any actions taken to increase feelings of trust will lead to commitment. Conversely, any action taken to decrease trust will lead to a lack of commitment.

Commitment is the belief that an ongoing relationship is so important that the partners are willing to work at maintaining it and are willing to make short-term sacrifices to realize long-term benefits.

Web Browsing Exercise

Go to the website of any hotel loyalty program. Examine the benefits they offer. Examine each of the benefits and prepare a list of those that can be considered "hard" benefits and those that can be considered "soft" benefits. In addition, which ones are rewards, and which are recognition? Put all this information in a 2 × 2 table with the type of benefit in the columns (hard, soft) and outcome in the rows (reward, recognition).

Antecedents and consequences of commitment include trust, value (e.g., saving time, experiential and emotional), certainty (firm does what it says it will do), benefits (all the things the customer receives), and switching costs. Notice that opportunistic behavior will cause a lack of trust. This means that we cannot arbitrarily take advantage of our best customers. If we do, we violate the trust. If we have trust, there is a greater likelihood that we will have commitment.

Consequences also include increased product usage (e.g., using the hotel's restaurant versus going elsewhere) and voluntary activities that one partner is likely to undertake on behalf of the other (e.g., strong word of mouth and business referrals). Note that the preceding are all positive outcomes of commitment. Negative outcomes result from lack of commitment.

Clearly this focus on loyalty is different from the old-fashioned view of marketing that focused on "getting customers into the door." Relationship/loyalty marketing means thinking in terms of the customers we have, rather than just in terms of the ones we hope to acquire. This is crucial in the hospitality industry. Competition is standing by all too ready and willing to take the customers you can't keep.

What specific things create trust and loyalty? There are many things to be sure, and not always the same things at different properties or for different types of customers. Bowen and Shoemaker found, for example, that the features in Exhibit 4-4 have the greatest impact on the creation of trust and loyalty for business travelers in luxury hotels.

Relationship/loyalty marketing, then, can be defined as *an ongoing process of identifying and creating new value for individual customers for mutual value benefits and then sharing the benefits from this over a lifetime of association.* In this sense, it differs from our usual definition of marketing, although it is certainly part of it in the following ways:

- ▪ It seeks to create *new* value for customers and *share* the value so created.
- ▪ It recognizes the key role of *individual* customers in defining the value they want—that is, value is created *with* customers, not *for* customers.
- ▪ It requires that a company define its organization to support the value that individual customers want.
- ▪ It is a continuously cooperative effort between buyer and seller.
- ▪ It recognizes the value of customers over their purchasing *lifetimes.*
- ▪ It seeks to build a chain of relationships between the organization and its main stakeholders to create the value that customers want.
- ▪ It focuses on the processes and whatever else is needed to advance the customer relationship.[4]

EXHIBIT 4-4   Features of a Hotel that Create Trust and Loyalty

Trust:
- I always feel safe at this hotel.
- The management of this hotel knows the luxury hotel business.
- When an employee at this hotel says they will do something, I am sure it will get done.
- If I ask management or an employee a question, I feel they will be truthful with me.
- If I make a request, no matter how trivial, it gets taken care of.
- Any communication including reservations will always be accurately received and recorded or filed.

Loyalty:
- The hotel provides upgrades.
- You can check in and check out at a time that suits you.
- The hotel uses information from previous stays to customize service for you.
- You can request a specific room.
- Employees communicate the attitude that your problems are important to them.
- When you return to a hotel, your registration process is expedited.

Adapted from Bowen, J. T., & Shoemaker, S. (1998, February). Loyalty: A strategic commitment. *Cornell Hotel and Restaurant Administration Quarterly,* 19. Adapted from SAGE Publications. Used by permission.

EXHIBIT 4-5   Comparison between Relational and Traditional Marketing

RELATIONAL MARKETING
- Orientation to customer retention
- Continuous customer contact
- Focus on customer value
- Long time scale
- High customer service emphasis
- High commitment to meeting customer expectations
- Quality is concern of all staff

TRADITIONAL MARKETING (A.K.A. TRANSACTIONAL MARKETING)
- Orientation to single sales
- Discontinuous customer contact
- Focus on product features
- Short time scale
- Little emphasis on customer service
- Limited commitment to meeting customer expectations
- Quality is the concern of the production staff

Tourism Marketing Application

Loyalty programs can also be used to determine where consumers would like to travel. For example, the *Royal Bank of Canada Avion Visa Summer Travel Poll* was conducted in June of 2005. Participants were given four choices: (1) selected sightseeing or visiting a seaside villa in Europe; (2) lying on a beach somewhere or taking a Caribbean cruise; (3) an adventure holiday in South America or Africa; or (4) a golf holiday in Hawaii. Option number one was the choice of 38%; option number two was chosen by 32%; number three was the choice of 14%; and number 4 was the choice of 7%. (The choices of the other 9% are uncertain.) (www.colloquy.com/cont_breaking_news.asp?ix=53343, retrieved March 18, 2006)

Exhibit 4-5 summarizes how loyalty marketing is different from traditional marketing. Later in this book we will talk about segmentation and target marketing. With loyalty marketing we take this one step further to develop customer-specific objectives and strategies that are unique to each customer or to each group of similar customers, which are part of a larger target market.

The Need for Relationship/ Loyalty Marketing

Before discussing the need for relationship/loyalty marketing, it is important to understand what we mean by loyalty. One definition suggested by Shoemaker and Lewis is illustrative of the emotional side of loyalty, as compared to the frequency side. They stated that loyalty occurs when

> The customer feels so strongly that you can best meet his or her relevant needs that your competition is virtually excluded from the consideration set and the customer buys almost exclusively from you—referring to you as their restaurant or their hotel. The customer focuses on your brand, offers, and messages to the exclusion of others. The price of the product or service is not a dominant consideration in the purchase decision, but only one component in the larger value proposition.[5]

Reichheld proposed a second definition of loyalty:

> A loyal customer is one who values the relationship with the company enough to make the company a preferred supplier. Loyal customers don't switch for small variations in price or service, they provide honest and constructive feedback, they consolidate the bulk of their category purchasers with the company, they never abuse company personnel and they provide enthusiastic referrals.[6]

Tourism Marketing Application

Frequency programs are not just for hotels, restaurants, or cruises; they're used to market baseball as well. In the spring of 2006, The Los Angeles Dodgers created Think Blue Rewards, which gives fans the opportunity to earn such experiential rewards as sitting in the dugout, meeting players, and access to tickets. Points are earned at concessions within the ballpark and at partner merchants in the Los Angeles area. Additionally, fans can earn points online at the Think Blue mall, which features more than 250 e-retailers such as Lands' End, Overstock.com, and Teleflora. (www.colloquy.com/cont_breaking_news.asp?industry=Entertainment&region=All, retrieved March 18, 2006)

Loyalty is important because it provides critical inoculation across multiple areas. For instance, loyal customers are less likely to ask about price when making a reservation. They are also less likely to shop around; hence, competitive offers face a higher hurdle. The customer becomes more forgiving when you make a mistake because there is goodwill equity. In fact, loyal customers are more likely to report service failures. *Loyalty begets loyalty.* Further, marketing and sales costs are lower, as are transactions costs. Research has shown that if companies increase their customer retention by 2 percent, it is the equivalent of cutting their operating costs by 10 percent.[7]

Relationship/loyalty marketing is most applicable under the following conditions:

- There is an ongoing and periodic desire for service by the customer.
- The service customer controls the selection of the service supplier.
- There are alternative supplier choices.
- Customer loyalty is weak and switching is common and easy.
- Word of mouth is an especially potent form of communication about a product.

These conditions are obviously quite prevalent in the hospitality industry. We don't sell one-time services, and the customer has many choices. In an era of heavy hotel building, numerous restaurant openings, and excess capacity, any hotel or restaurant is especially vulnerable to competition. Just about everyone likes to try a new place. The question is, Will they come back? Do we offer a competitive product on dimensions that are meaningful to customers, solve customer problems, and are difficult for competitors to duplicate? Do we have a meaningful relationship? This is what relationship/loyalty marketing is all about, and when the preceding conditions pertain, the opportunities to practice it are abundant.

The fundamental reason loyalty marketing is important is because of the lifetime value of the customer, which we discuss next.

The Lifetime Value of a Customer

The lifetime value of a customer, in short, is the net profit received from doing business with a given customer during the time that the customer continues to buy from you. As stated by members of the Harvard Business School faculty, "The lifetime value of a loyal customer can be astronomical—especially when referrals are considered." These researchers calculated that the lifetime revenue from a loyal pizza customer can be greater than $8,000.[8]

 Web Browsing Exercise

Go to Google and search the term "lifetime value." What do you find?

Others estimate that a 5 percent increase in customer loyalty can produce *profit* increases from 25 to 85 percent. These authors concluded that *quality* of market share, measured in terms of customer loyalty, deserves as much attention as *quantity* of market share. Taco Bell, in fact, measures "share of stomach" to compare the company's sales against all other food purchases a customer can potentially make. As a result, Taco Bell tries to reach customers through kiosks, carts, trucks, and the shelves of supermarkets.[9]

Worksheets can be developed for calculating the lifetime value of customers.[10] What one needs to know is the retention rate, the spending rate, the variable costs, and the discount rate to compute net present value (i.e., the value today of the customer over a period of time). For instance, consider Exhibit 4-6, which shows that in the first year, the customer is worth $75 to the firm. If, however, the customer stays five years with the firm, the actual profitability

EXHIBIT 4-6 Lifetime Value Calculation Worksheet

Revenue	Year 1	Year 2	Year 3	Year 4	Year 5
A Number of customers (same customers tracked one year to the next)	1,000	400	180	90	50 (at the end of five years, only 50 of the initial 1,000 are still customers)
B Retention rate (% of those who return from one year to the next)	40% (400/1000)	45% (180/400)	50% (90/180)	55%	60%
C Average yearly sale	(Total sales/total customers) $150	$150	$150	$150	$150
D Total revenue of customers from original group) $A \times C$	$150,000	$60,000	$27,000	$13,500	$7,500
Costs					
E Cost percent or calculate any way that makes sense for your company	50%	50%	50%	50%	50%
F Total costs $(D \times E)$	$75,000	$30,000	$13,500	$6,750	$3,750
Profits					
G Gross profit $(D - F)$	$75,000	$30,000	$13,500	$6,750	$3,750
H Discount rate $D = (1 + i)^n$	$1\ D = (1 + .20)^0$	$1.2\ D = (1 + .20)^1$	$1.44\ D = (1 + .20)^2$	$1.73\ D = (1 + .20)^3$	$2.07\ D = (1 + .20)^4$
I NVP profit = profits/discount rate	$75,000	$25,000 ($30,000/1.2)	$9,375 ($13,500/1.44)	$3,902 ($6,750/1.73)	($3,750/2.07) = $1,812
J Cumulative NPV (Y1 + Y2. . . + Y5)	$75,000	$100,000 ($75,000 + $25,000)	$109,375	$113,277	$115,088
K Lifetime value (NPV)	$75	$100	$109.38	$113.28	$115.09

Source: Reprinted from International Journal of Hospitality Management, Vol. 18, No. 4, Shoemaker et al, Customer loyalty in hotels, pp. 345–370, copyright 1999 with permission from Elsevier.

of the customer is $115.09. This $115.09 includes future profits the firm will earn from this customer discounted backwards to current dollars. What this means is that if the guest had a problem that would cost $80 to solve, the firm should solve it, because the profitability of the guest's lifetime will still be positive. Without the understanding of lifetime value, it might be tempting to let the guest leave unhappy.

Exhibit 4-7 gives one view on profits from loyal customers. This figure shows that customers' profitability increases over their lifetimes because they tend to spend while staying on the property, they bring other guests via positive word of mouth, and they cost less to serve.

Exhibits 4-6 and 4-7 illustrate that we have switched from product and service profitability to customer profitability. Exhibit 4-8 shows the questions that form the basis of understanding customer profitability.

With the answers to the questions in Exhibit 4-8 we can now begin to develop a **customer analysis,** in a sense, for each customer. Which customers are profitable, now and in

the future? Some customers add value, while others may have negative value; that is, they require too much time and effort to ever make them profitable. A customer matrix like that shown in Exhibit 4-9 helps to make the point.

Exhibit 4-9 is a little confusing at first glance. The way to interpret it is to first look at future customers. Looking up from future customers you see two columns: unprofitable and profitable. Now, look at current customers. Looking across, you see two rows: profitable and unprofitable. To interpret each cell, you must consider both the customers' current behavior and their potential future behavior. For instance, consider the cell labeled A. Here, the customer's current behavior is profitable, but his or her potential in the future is unprofitable. In the hotel industry, this situation could occur because the person is going to change jobs that will require less travel. In the casino industry, it could change because the person may be moving away and the casino is no longer convenient. We find out this information by listening to our customers and by asking them questions.

In the cell labeled B, the customer's current behavior is profitable, as is his or her future behavior. Perhaps the customer plans to travel more in the future, or perhaps he or she has recently come into more money so will be able to gamble more. The cell labeled C exhibits the current customer who is unprofitable and his or her potential in the future is also unprofitable. Finally, the customer who is currently unprofitable, but shows great potential in the future, is located in the cell labeled D.

Exhibit 4-9 suggests that different customers have different priorities on the part of management, depending on their income statement or worth to the firm both now

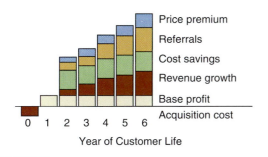

| EXHIBIT 4-7 | Profits throughout the hotel guest life. |

(chart labels: Price premium, Referrals, Cost savings, Revenue growth, Base profit, Acquisition cost; x-axis: 0 1 2 3 4 5 6, Year of Customer Life)

EXHIBIT 4-8 **What One Needs to Know to Understand a Customer's Profitability**

1. How much does it cost to get a new customer?
2. How much does it cost to keep that customer?
3. What is the revenue from that customer—each visit, annually, lifetime?
4. What is the cost of serving that customer—each visit, annually, lifetime?
5. What are the retention rates of customers?
6. If we are losing loyal customers for reasons beyond our control (e.g., death, moving away), are we replacing them, and with whom? (We will address this later, but keep in mind that grandiose statements such as, "We have 80 percent repeat customers" can be dangerous if you are not also acquiring new ones. See next question.)
7. What is a repeat customer? Is it someone who comes only on Saturday night when the restaurant is always full? One that stays every time he is in town but that's only once a year? One that wants us to stay as we are when we know we have to change? One that stays in this hotel but in other cities goes to a different

chain? One that is loyal as long as we give him an upgrade? You can imagine that this list could go on and on. You can also turn the questions around to make them positive.

8. What is the revenue and profitability from repeat customers versus those we might replace them with? (For example, in hotels, do they buy the cheapest rooms and always eat out—that is, what is the total revenue and profitability?
9. What other opportunities are there for revenue from our customers for things that we don't now provide?
10. Do our customers really want all the things in our package bundles?
11. If our customers weren't here, where would they be or where might they go?
12. What value do our customers get from us?
13. Do we have a relationship with our customers, or are they just customers?
14. How frequently do we communicate (Internet, telephone, mail, and mass media) with our customers? Is this favorable to them and to us?

		UNPROFITABLE	PROFITABLE
CURRENT CUSTOMERS	**PROFITABLE**	**A** Manage Issues need to be addressed. Create mutual value that will enhance business prospects.	**B** Reward and Invest Ideal customers. Assign priorities. Invest time. Reward with special benefits.
	UNPROFITABLE	**C** Fire Analyze and assess. If no benefits, now or future, have friendly parting of ways.	**D** Discipline Make profitable. May be able to reduce costs or to charge more while maintaining the relationship.
		UNPROFITABLE	PROFITABLE
		FUTURE — CUSTOMERS	

EXHIBIT 4-9 Customer analysis.

Source: Gordon, I. (1998, April). Relationship marketing. Toronto: Wiley Canada, 9.

and in the future. Perhaps the best example of this matrix being put into practice in the hospitality industry is in the casino business, where the individual income statement is based on the customer's theoretical win. This is the amount the casino can be expected to win from the customer. For instance, consider a customer who plays $5 slot machines; that is, every spin of the wheel costs $5. If the machine pays the customer 97 percent of the time, then for every spin of the wheel the casino "earns" 15 cents. If a customer makes 240 spins per hour (one spin every 15 seconds), then the theoretical win for this customer is $36. Depending on the theoretical worth of the customer, he or she is likely to get free rooms (possibly suites), maybe even free airfare and lots of management attention.

The strategy for members of Cell A (profitable current customers but unprofitable in the future) is to manage the relationship, but not invest in a long-term relationship. Because we do not expect them to stay with us for a long time, we want to keep them happy during their current stays, but we will not spend money to get them to stay with us in the future.

The strategy for members of Cell B (profitable customers currently with potential for them to be more profitable in the future) is to reward and invest in them. A casino, for instance, might provide these guests with free upgrades, show tickets, and the like, on their current visit even though their current theoretical worth does not jus-

tify these additional rewards. Harrah's Entertainment uses sophisticated mathematical modeling to identify the customers' potential worth (lifetime value) based on a variety of proprietary features and then rewards and invests in these customers.

The strategy for Cell C members is to fire them. Not all customers are worth having. They may be too costly to serve. They may buy only specials and low-margin items. They may not be personally desirable by dress or manner. They may be constant complainers who require undue attention. The customers we "fire" are just not profitable now and never will be. We don't want to alienate them, so we have to be careful. Perhaps if they do not receive enough attention, they will go elsewhere. We usually fire customers by removing them from our mailing list and no longer sending them special offers. When they ask for something on the casino floor, we say no.

The members in Cell D are not profitable now, but in the future they can be profitable. These are the customers that need to be disciplined. A major casino in Las Vegas invested in these types of customers. Very high rollers, or "whales" in Las Vegas parlance, were provided with free airfare and free rooms and food and beverage, as long as they gambled a certain amount of money for a certain period of time. Unfortunately, these gamblers did not live up to their part of the bargain and left the gaming tables early. Because they had the potential to be such high-revenue sources, the casino did not ask them to leave; instead, they applied "the carrot and the stick." That is, they told the customers that they were reducing their allowance for food and beverage and rooms unless they stayed longer at the gaming tables.

The previous discussion shows that different types of customers require different types of relationships. In a way, we seem to be contradicting our definition of marketing. Not really. We need to determine the *target market* and then apply the marketing concept. Remember too from Chapter 1 that the resulting profits are the *test of the validity* of our decisions. If we cultivate too many of the customers in the "fire" category, we may have many completely satisfied customers that we've created and can keep, but we will not have a profitable business that will survive.

Examining Customers Through the Stages of Their Life Cycles with the Firm

Exhibit 4-10 shows what can be called the **customer loyalty ladder**. The obvious effort is to move the customer from the state of awareness (suspect/prospect) to being a brand **advocate**. The strategies one would select for each rung of the ladder are discussed next.[11]

On the first two rungs of the ladder are suspects and prospects. A suspect is anyone who might buy our product or service. They are called suspects because we suspect they

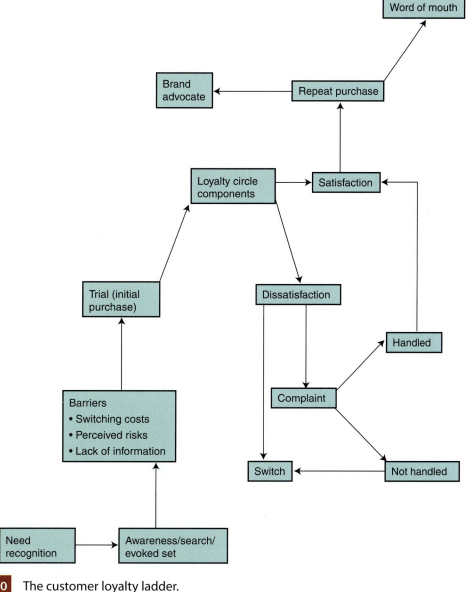

EXHIBIT 4-10 The customer loyalty ladder.

might buy our service, but we don't know enough about them to be sure. A prospect is someone who has a need for our product or service as well as the ability to buy. The prospect has heard of us, but has not yet purchased. The strategy for this group is to overcome apprehension with empathy and encouragement, **client** "success stories," site visits, or product/service guarantees. For instance, Hampton Inns gave an unconditional guarantee starting in 1990. In the first year, they sold about 157,000 rooms to first-time users because of the guarantee. This grossed an additional $7 million. Of those who invoked the guarantee, 3,300 returned the same year, and 61 percent of these said the reason was the guarantee. The payout on the guarantee was $350,000. The total additional revenue was $8 million.

In the search for prospects, it is possible to come across disqualified prospects. These are customers who we have learned enough to know that they do not need or do not have the ability to buy our product or service. This group may also represent customers who are unprofitable and likely to remain so. Our strategy with this group is to fire or not pursue them, as discussed in Exhibit 4-9.

On the next rung of the customer loyalty ladder are first-time customers. These may have come from the competition or may be new to the product or service category. The strategy for this group is to meet or exceed their expectations, as discussed in Chapter 3. The staff also needs to subtly remind guests what a great job they are doing in providing quality service. This is because it is far easier to determine when quality is not delivered than when it is. One way to remind customers that the experience they are receiving meets their expectations is to focus on the dimensions of service quality discussed in Chapter 3. Again, these were reliability, assurance, tangibility, empathy, and responsiveness. This is also known as RATER. The example from the earlier chapter involved the RATER and room service. The firm should also build a promise for return visits, thank them for their business, and invite them to return.

Repeat customers are on the next rung of the ladder. These are customers who have purchased two or more times. The strategy for this group is to provide value added benefits with each repeat purchase and to seek regular feedback.

Repeat customers eventually become clients. These are customers who buy regularly all or most of the firm's products/services. The firm's strong ongoing relationship with them makes them immune to the competition. The strategy for this group is to tailor the service to their needs. It is important for employees of the firm not to take business for granted. They need to remind customers that it's smart to do business with them. Like with members of other groups, it is important to continually seek input and feedback.

On the final rung of the ladder are the advocates. These customers are like clients, but they also encourage others to buy from us. They do our marketing for us and bring additional customers. The strategy for this group is to get them to sell for us. Encourage advocacy through letters of endorsement and referral acknowledgments. Communicate with them regularly.

Firms often have inactive customers or clients. These customers have not bought from the firm in a period longer than the normal purchase cycle. The strategy here is to develop a "win back" plan based on inactivity diagnosis. If defection is certain, ask, What can we do to win you back? and listen closely. Exhibit 4-11 provides an example of research one of the authors conducted for a casino company that undertook focus groups to determine why people defected or played at the casino less often. A similar set of questions was asked of the regular customers to look for differences. Focus groups and other research methods are discussed in more detail in Chapter 11 and the Appendixes.

Building Loyalty

The Evolution of Customer Loyalty

Exhibit 4-12 shows the evolution of building loyalty. Initially, the focus of marketing was purely on sales, not loyalty. The goal was to get as many new customers as possible. In this phase, there was little targeting, little measurement, and lots of discounts. As marketing developed, marketing managers began to focus on specific market segments, but the mentality was still on pushing traffic to the property.

 Web Browsing Exercise

Go to the TARP website (www.tarp.org). What types of studies does the firm undertake? What do they say about the latest trends in complaint management? What types of firms are represented in their research?

Frequency programs were the next element of the evolution of loyalty. We discuss frequency programs in more detail later in the chapter, but these programs initially were used to reward frequent purchasers. Exhibit 4-13 illustrates the process of setting up a frequency program. S&H Green Stamps started this movement in the 1950s by giving customers stamps every time they purchased certain brands. These stamps were then pasted into books that were exchanged for free merchandise. Today, companies award points or airline miles that are exchanged for free travel, as well as other items. The points are also used to keep track of customers' purchase behaviors across multiple retail outlets. Consider, for instance, the different names of locations

EXHIBIT 4-11 **Guidelines for Focus Group Questionnaire**

1. Introduction (welcome, introductions, opportunity to get people to relax, etc.)
2. Ask respondents to think about visiting casinos. Ask how frequently they visit and how long they stay.
3. Ask respondents which casinos they gamble in and why.
4. Ask respondents about promotions in general.
   a. Which casinos have good promotions?
   b. What makes a good promotion?
   c. What is the best way for a casino to tell you about a promotion?
5. Ask respondents about the client casino company Fe.
   a. What comes to mind when you think of this casino?
   b. What is this casino known for?
   c. The best thing at this casino is _____.
   d. The worst thing at this casino is _____.
   e. Are you playing here more or less frequently?
6. Ask respondents about promotions at the Santa Fe.
   a. What type and name of promotions were offered here?
   b. What specific promotions does this casino offer (40-coin bonus when you redeem a coupon, bonus for a specific four of a kind, double points, $1 comp for 575 bonus points.
   c. Which promotions, both current and past, did you particularly like? Dislike? Why?
7. Ask respondents what type of nongaming events could casinos offer (e.g., miniature golf tournaments).
8. Ask respondents about reel machines and video poker machine.
   a. How do you pick a particular machine?
   b. Are all the machines the same?
   c. What makes a good machine?
   d. On video poker machines, what do the numbers mean?
   e. How do the machines here compare to machines at other places?
9. Ask respondents about "tight machines" (e.g., machines that do not pay well).
10. Ask respondents about the current ad campaign. Show an advertisement and ask the following questions:
   a. Have you seen it?
   b. What does it mean to you?
   c. Is it believable?
   d. What would you tell your friends about this advertisement?
11. Ask respondents what customer service issues are important.
12. Ask respondents about service issues at client casino.
   a. What service issues do you particularly like?
   b. What service issues do you particularly dislike?
13. What are respondents opinions of the slot club program?
   a. What do you like and dislike about the slot club program?
   b. Do you understand True Value Rewards and how points are accrued?
   c. Can you understand how to read the brochure?
   d. Do you understand the reader box? Is the idea of full disclosure important?
   e. How do points work (i.e., what is the ratio)?
   f. How does client's program compare to other programs where you play?
   g. Where would you like to be able to spend your points?

14. Ask respondents about the buffet. Issues to address:
   a. Food quality
   b. Food variety
   c. Value for the money
   d. Cleanliness of food area
   e. Appearance of food items
   f. Cleanliness of dining area
   g. Improvements?
   h. Staffing issues: wait times to enter restaurant, friendliness of service personnel, promptness of service personnel for drink orders, etc.
15. Ask respondents about the coffee shop. Issues to address:
   a. Food quality
   b. Food variety
   c. Value for the money
   d. Cleanliness of food area
   e. Appearance of food items
   f. Cleanliness of dining area
   g. Improvements?
   h. Staffing issues: wait times to enter restaurant, friendliness of service personnel, promptness of service personnel for drink orders, etc.
16. Ask respondents about the steak house. Issues to address:
   a. Food quality
   b. Food variety
   c. Value for the money
   d. Cleanliness of food area
   e. Appearance of food items
   f. Cleanliness of dining area
   g. Improvements?
   h. Staffing issues: wait times to enter restaurant, friendliness of service personnel, promptness of service personnel for drink orders, etc.
17. Ask respondents about the Italian restaurant. Issues to address:
   a. Food quality
   b. Food variety
   c. Value for the money
   d. Cleanliness of food area
   e. Appearance of food items
   f. Cleanliness of dining area
   g. Improvements?
   h. Staffing issues: wait times to enter restaurant, friendliness of service personnel, promptness of service personnel for drink orders, etc.
18. Ask respondents about bars. Issues to address:
   a. Speed of service
   b. Availability of drinks
19. Ask respondents about drink service on the floor (if not covered earlier). Issues to address:
   a. Friendliness
   b. Speed of service (time of order to time of delivery)
20. Ask respondents what the Santa Fe could do to encourage more frequent visitation.
21. Wrap-up and thank you.

owned by Marriott. With so many locations, it would be almost impossible to keep track of individual purchase behavior by name alone. The membership number provides an easy way for firms to track behavior. The points then determine a person's status, which means more frequent purchasers get certain benefits not available to less frequent purchasers. For instance, airlines often hold the most desirable seats (e.g., those up front or in the bulkhead) for their

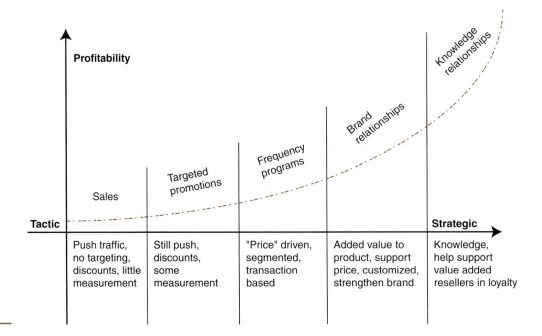

EXHIBIT 4-12 Evolution of building loyalty.

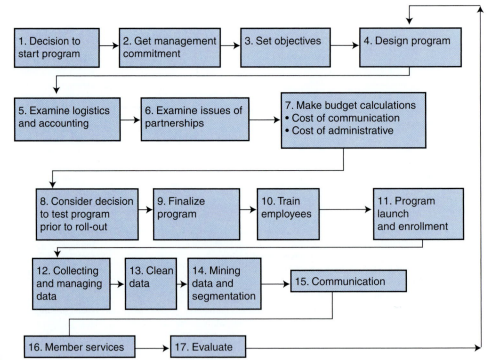

EXHIBIT 4-13 The process of setting up a frequency program.

Source: Adapted from Campbell, T. (1996, December 9-10). Presentation by Frequency Marketing Inc. for the Strategic Research Institute, Chicago, IL.

frequent travelers, while less frequent travelers get the less desirable seats.

The advent of a mechanism to track multiple stays enables marketing executives to provide customized services, such as preferred seating on airplanes. In addition, management can customize the service. There is tremendous opportunity to learn about particular customers and their specific problems and to tailor the service to solve those problems. For example, at Caneel Bay Resort on St. John in the Caribbean, guests are allowed to store anything that they do not want to carry back home, including such things as suntan lotion, swim suits, and snorkel gear. For their next visit, these belongings are placed in their rooms before arrival. Other methods of customization include asking hotel guests if they want help to get to their room or are happy to find their own way and carry their own bags. Video checkout and bed turn-down *on request* are still others.

In the final phase of the evolution of relationship marketing, the firm fully understands the customer.[12] Although customization also occurs in this phase, the focus is on knowing the customer and using that knowledge to augment the product to better serve the customer. Service augmentation means building extras into the service that help improve the customer's stay. We call this final phase *knowledge relationships*. This is the one-to-one marketing popularized by Peppers and Rogers.[13] An example of one hospitality firm that is beginning to move in this direction is Wyndham Hotels with their Wyndham ByRequest program. This program is not a point- or mileage-based program found with many hotel programs. Rather, guests customize their hotel stay by providing Wyndham with information on their room preferences (e.g., smoking versus nonsmoking, bed type, and the like) and the types of snacks they would like to see in the honor bar.[14] The information provided by the customer is then stored in a central database so that the room will be customized in any Wyndham location the customer chooses.

A second example of this move toward knowledge relationships is Hilton Hotel's Corporation's OnQ, which was launched in May 2003 across all Hilton brands (e.g., Double Tree, Hampton Inns, and Hilton Garden Inns). This system is billed as the first and only system that gives front desk personnel real-time information on every HHonors member that checks into any one of the Hilton brands worldwide. Exhibit 4-14 shows the benefits customers receive from this new system. Unlike the Wyndham system, information comes from two sources: information provided by the guest and information provided by the individual property that observes the guest's behavior. Clearly, the more one stays at a Hilton, the more information Hilton collects. And, the more information collected, the more the stay can be customized to meet the guest's needs. This customization makes it harder for the guest to switch to another brand.

The Loyalty Circle

A way to think about creating customer loyalty is **the loyalty circle**, as shown in Exhibit 4-15. The three main functions on the circle are process, value, and communication. Notice that at different points along the circle, there are places where the customer might exit the circle and hence the relationship. The goal of hoteliers is to keep the customer in the circle by executing equally well the three functions of the circle. Equality is the key to the loyalty circle. If hoteliers are great on creating value, for instance, but do not effectively communicate with the customer, then that customer may leave the relationship.

On one side of the loyalty circle is the process, which is "how the service works." It involves all activities from both the guest's perspective and the hotelier's perspective. Ideally, there should be no gaps in this process. For guests, the process includes everything that happens from the time they begin buying the service (e.g., calling to make a reservation) to the time they leave the property (e.g., picking up their car from a valet.) All interactions with employees are part of this process.

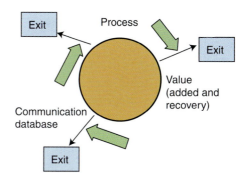

EXHIBIT 4-15   The loyalty circle.

EXHIBIT 4-14   **The Hilton Guest Profile Manager**

The Hilton Guest Profile Manager enables the front desk team members to recognize guests at check-in and provide more personalized service, including:

- Welcoming a guest who typically stays at another of our hotels in the Hilton Family back to our Family when that guest is staying for the first time at one of the sister brands;
- Delivering top four guest preferences such as: smoking or non-smoking room; type of bed (king or double/double); floor level; and, room location relative to the elevator, among other preferences;
- Accessing real-time information about an HHonors member's reward status;

- Making requested adjustments to a guest's personal profile; and changing a future reservation from the hotel in which a guest currently is staying; and
- Addressing service issues that may have arisen during a past guest stay, resulting in increased service recovery and follow-through dedication to guest satisfaction.

Source: Shoemaker, S., & Bowen, J., (2003). Antecedents and consequences of customer loyalty: An update. *Cornell Hotel and Restaurant Administration Quarterly, 6* (4), 31–52. Used by permission.

For the hotel, the process includes all interactions between the employees and the guests; the design of the service operations; the hiring and training of service personnel; and the collection of information to understand customers' needs, wants, and expectations. Much of the specifics of the process were discussed in Chapter 2 when we introduced the gap model of service quality. One way to monitor the process is through the use of consumer research and intelligence techniques. One such technique is mystery shopping. With this technique people hired by the service organization or by a third party act as customers and report everything that occurred during the purchase of the service. Another way is to conduct focus groups with customers. Focus groups consist of 10 to 12 customers (or noncustomers) who are asked to focus on one or two topics of interest to the service organization. A moderator leads the discussion and keeps participants focused on the topics of interest to management. Exhibit 4-11, shown earlier, is an example of the types of questions participants might focus on. A third way is to undertake large-scale survey research with current customers as well as past customers.

Web Browsing Exercise

Go to Google and type in "focus group facilities." Choose one of the firms and write one page about the company. Include the types of focus groups they run and what they believe to be the strengths of their firm.

A second component of the loyalty circle is value creation. Value creation is subdivided into two parts: value added and value recovery. Value added strategies increase loyalty by providing guests with more than just the core product; that is, for hotels, offering more than just a place to sleep. Value added strategies increase the long-term value of the relationship with the service firm by offering greater benefits to customers than can be found at competing firms who charge a comparable price. Features that pertain to value added are of six types: *financial* (e.g., saving money); *temporal* (e.g., saving time); *functional* (e.g., the product does what it was designed to do); *experiential* (e.g., enhancing the experience such as by offering an upgrade); *emotional* (e.g., more recognition and/or more pleasurable service experience); and/or *social* (e.g., interpersonal link with a service provider). Temporal value is important because business travelers have stated that they value their time at $100 per hour and anything that saves them time saves them money.

Consider, for instance, the check-in process of a hotel. Research reveals that many frequent business travelers want to go immediately to their rooms and do not want to wait in line to check in. If they have to wait in line for 15 minutes, they mentally figure that they have spent $25 to check in. Waiting in line is especially annoying if the guest is a member of the hotel's frequent guest program and all of her information is already stored on file. Certain technologies (e.g., blue-tooth software that works with PDAs) allow guests to check in, receive their room numbers, unlock their rooms, and have charges automatically billed to their credit cards without having to check in at the front desk. Moving these guests to this form of check-in would have the benefit of shortening the line for those guests who want to speak with a front desk clerk. This new check-in procedure speeds up and improves the process (*functional value*) and adds value because it saves guests time (*temporal value*).

The importance of value added strategies in creating customer loyalty is illustrated in a study (conducted by one of the authors) of business travelers who both spend more than $120 per night for a hotel room and take six or more business trips per year. The study revealed that 28 percent of the 344 who spend more than 75 nights per year in hotels (38 percent of the total sample) claimed that the feature "is a good value for the price paid" is important in the decision to stay in the same hotel chain when traveling on business. A similar percentage rated the features "collects your preferences and uses that information to customize your current and future stays" and "accommodates early morning check-in and late afternoon checkout" important in the decision to stay with the same chain. Both these tactics are examples of features that add value to the core product offering.

Value recovery strategies are designed to rectify a lapse in service delivery. The goal is to ensure that the guest's needs are taken care of without further inconveniences. Empowering employees to solve problems and offering a 100 percent guarantee are examples of value recovery strategies. The key to value recovery strategies is that the complaints be taken seriously by the hotel and that processes be put in place so that the same mistakes do not happen over and over again. We discuss complaints later in this chapter.

The final component of the loyalty circle is communication. This side of the circle incorporates database marketing, newsletters, and general advertising. It involves all areas of how the hotel communicates with its customers. When communicating with guests, firms must be sure that external communications do not overpromise what the service can deliver; this would create Gap 4, as discussed in Chapter 3. It is also critical that communications reflect the needs of the customer and that customers do not receive offers in which they have no interest.

If marketers can focus the organization on these components, they will create loyal customers who will return over and over again. If they do not focus on the components of the circle, they will be forced to focus on getting more and more customers to replace those who have left the circle.

Frequent Guest Programs and Loyalty Programs

Two questions are often asked: Are frequency programs the same as loyalty programs? and, Do frequent guest programs build loyalty? The answer to the first question is no, frequency programs are not the same as loyalty programs. We state this even though many firms call their frequent guest program a loyalty program. We define a loyalty program as *a strategy undertaken by a firm to manage the three components of the loyalty circle to create an emotional bond with customers so that they give the firm a majority of their business, provide positive word of mouth, act in partnership with the firm, and spend more with the firm than a nonloyal guest would.*

Tourism Marketing Application

Frequency programs are also used to market resort destinations. Consider, for example, Vail, Colorado. The Vail Resort Company operates the lifts and many of the resorts and restaurants in Vail, Beaver Creek, Breckenridge, Keystone (all in Colorado), and Heavenly (Lake Tahoe, California). The Peaks program enables members to earn rewards on their purchases at multiple restaurants, hotels, mountain activities, and other related activities. The "soft" rewards enable members to purchase ski tickets in advance, charge all their purchases on a credit card so members do not have to carry cash, and receive exclusive offers and e-mail letters. They can redeem points for activities such as lift tickets and ski lessons. (www.snow.com/info/peaks.asp, retrieved March 18, 2006)

In contrast, we define a frequency program as *any program that rewards guests with points, miles, stamps, or "punches" that enable them to redeem such rewards for free or discounted merchandise.* The potential trap is to confuse purchase frequency with customer loyalty—that is, to confuse the ends with the means. Frequency in itself does not build loyalty as we define it; it is loyalty that builds frequency. Frequency can create loyalty if the firm uses the information gathered on frequent visits to focus on the components of the loyalty circle; however, if the firm ignores this opportunity, then it ignores the emotional and psychological factors that build real **commitment**. Without that commitment, customers focus on the "deal," not the brand or product relevance. Consider the coffee shops that provide a free coffee after so many purchases, as shown in Exhibit 4-16. Notice that after 12 purchased coffees, guests of It's a Grind receive a free cup of coffee. If no mechanism is in place to track specific customers' requests or identify

EXHIBIT 4-16 It's a Grind gives customers free coffee after they have made a certain number of purchases.

Source: It's a Grind Coffee House. Used by permission.

---

the customer, the customer focuses only on the deal. At It's a Grind, however, store managers and staff are taught to recognize guests and learn their names. The names of those guests that redeem for a free coffee are especially important names to remember. Colleen Brown, owner and manager of It's A Grind in The Woodlands, Texas (north of Houston), stresses the importance of this to all her employees. It is not unusual to hear her employees call most of the guests by their first names. In fact, Ms. Brown runs a contest called Beat the Manager. The goal of the contest is to be able to list the names of as many guests as possible and provide an interesting fact about each guest named. The two winners, Caleb Narvaez and Heather Shrum, each could name over 100 customers. Interestingly, they each work the same shift but had very few overlapping names. (One name was one of the authors of this text, who spent too much time drinking coffee while writing this book.)

Tourism Marketing Application

The Jurni Network, (www.jurni.com) owned by Sabre Holdings (www.sabre-holdings.com) is a network of independent leisure travel agents based in the United States. The network offers travel agents the opportunity to earn points by attending training sessions, booking specific travel products, and using specific tools promoted by Jurni. Points earned can then be redeemed for familiarization trips (i.e., trips travel agents take to learn about an area, usually free), scholarships for travel certifications, and gift cards at such stores as Target, Crate&Barrel, and amazon.com. (www.colloquy.com/cont_breaking_news.asp?industry=Miscellaneous&region=All, retrieved March 18, 2006)

An interesting twist is that customers often keep the coffee sleeves in their cars, which constantly reminds them of the brand. Colleen states that it is not unusual for a person to pick up hot coffee in the morning and then a cool drink on the way home in the afternoon. The sleeves are also ecology friendly, as customers save them rather than throw them away.

With frequency programs, sales may increase, as they would with price discounts. Repeat purchases may also increase, but the focus is on the rewards, not on product superiority or brand relevance. Thus, awards programs are tactical solutions to a strategic problem—an awards program for unprofitable customers, parity instead of differentiation. This behavior focus makes bribing the customer the line of reasoning. Over time, the economics of bribery begin to collapse with greater and greater bribes, eventually eroding the brand image and diminishing product/service differentiation. The differences between frequency and loyalty are shown in Exhibit 4-17.

What Frequency Programs Don't Do

Sometimes the wrong things are expected from loyalty programs. These programs are not "quick fixes." They will not fix an essential problem in the operation that may be costing customers. They won't show a profit in the short run—these are dedicated long-term efforts. They are not a promotion that is temporary or, worse, becomes part of the product and adds to the cost. And they won't bring in new customers. The brand has to overcome the barriers to first trial before the loyalty program can kick in.

What Makes Frequency Programs Work?

According to Richard Dunn at Loyaltyworks, the following elements are essential to a successful frequency program:

- A vital database—the relationship foundation
- Targeted communications—the relationship dialogue
- Meaningful rewards—relationship recognition
- Simplicity—easy to participate and understand
- Attainability—motivational rewards must be attainable (e.g., upgrades)
- Sustainability—don't let it lapse; keep it active
- Measurability—make sure it is working in the right ways
- Management—full commitment and behind it all the way
- Manageabiity—don't let it get out of hand
- Profitability—is it really working in the long term?

Further caveats from Dunn are these:

- Don't treat the program like a promotion.
- Don't focus excessively on rewards, but on the relationship.
- Don't short-change the communications component.
- Don't underestimate the importance of internal support.
- Don't pretend to care more than you really do.
- Tailor the value of benefits to specific customers based on their achieved or expected value.

Customer Complaints and Service Recovery

When we discussed the loyalty circle earlier in the chapter, we mentioned that a component of value is value recovery; that is, how the firm manages and addresses service failures.

EXHIBIT 4-17	Frequency versus Loyalty	
	Frequency	**Loyalty**
Objectives	Build traffic, sales, profit	Build sales, profit, brand desirability
Strategy	Incentivize repeat transactions	Build personal brand relationship
Focus	Segment behavior and profitability	An individual's emotional and rational needs and their value
Tactics	Free/discounts/rewards, profitability	Individual value, tenure, preferred status, "insider," value added upgrades, add-ons, tailored offers/messages, emotional rewards
Measurement	Transactions, sales growth	Individual lifetime value, attitudinal change, emotional

Source: Shoemaker, S., & Bowen, J. (2003). Antecedents and consequences of customer loyalty: An update. *Cornell Hotel and Restaurant Administration Quarterly 6*, (4), 31–52. Used by permission.

Firms that are committed to relationship/loyalty marketing are proactive in terms of service recovery strategies. By this we mean that they encourage guests to speak out when things go wrong; after all, there can be no service recovery if the firm does not know when something goes wrong. Proactive firms believe in the adage, A complaint is a gift.[15]

Customer complaints deserve special treatment in this chapter because they are one of the most misunderstood and mishandled areas of customer relations in the hospitality industry. Let us look first at what customer complaints are.

- ■ **Inevitable**   Nothing is perfect. The diversity of the hospitality customer and the heterogeneity of the hospitality product absolutely ensure that there will be complaints. This will be true even when everything goes according to plan. Of course, when everything doesn't go according to plan (and it almost never does), there will be additional problems and there will be complaints.

- ■ **Healthy**   The old army expression is, If the troops aren't griping, look out for trouble. An absence of complaints may be the best indication management has (along with declining occupancies or covers) that something is wrong. Hospitality customers are never totally satisfied, especially over a period of time. Probably, instead, they are simply not talking to you or you are not talking to them. The communication process is not working; the relationship is deteriorating. By the time it explodes, it will be too late. Some say, If it isn't broken, don't fix it. First, you have to know if it's broken, and the ones who know first are your customers. And, incidentally, the ones they tell first are your employees, which means that you should listen to your employees as well.

- ■ **Opportunities**   Customer complaints are opportunities to learn of customers' problems, whether they are idiosyncratic or caused by the operation itself. If it's broken, you have an opportunity to fix it. If it's not broken, you have an opportunity to make it better, to be creative, to develop a new product, to learn new needs, and to keep old customers. A study by TARP, a research firm located outside Washington, D.C., found that customers who complain and are satisfied are up to 8 percent more loyal than those who had no problem at all.[16]

- ■ **Marketing tools**   If marketing is to give customers what they want, then marketing must know what they want. All the customer surveys in the world won't tell you as much as customer complaints will tell you.

- ■ **Advertising**   Yes, advertising. The advertising is negative if you don't resolve the problems, and there is nothing more devastating in the hospitality business than negative word of mouth. It is positive if you fix the problem. Research has shown that one of the best and most loyal customers is the one who had a complaint that was satisfactorily resolved. And this customer loves to tell others about it.

TARP undertook the initial research on complaint handling. Tom Peters, author of *On Achieving Excellence*, stated, "TARP is perhaps [America's] premier customer service research firm."[17] TARP's initial research occurred in the late 1970s and has been replicated in multiple industries and 20 countries. The replicated studies revealed that the initial findings still hold today. Following are some of the major findings:[18]

- ■ On average, across all industries, 50 percent of customers will complain about a problem to a front line person.
- ■ Only 1 to 5 percent of customers will escalate their complaints to a local manager or corporate headquarters. For packaged goods and other small ticket items, TARP found that 96 percent of customers either do not complain or complain to a retailer where they bought it.
- ■ Complaint rates vary by type of problem. Problems that result in out-of-pocket monetary loss have high complaint rates (e.g., 50 to 75 percent), whereas mistreatment, quality, and incompetence problems evoke only 5 to 30 percent complaint rates to the front line.
- ■ On average, twice as many people are told about a bad experience than they are about a good experience.

TARP also developed what they called the tip of the iceberg phenomenon. This is shown in Exhibit 4-18.[19] The basic idea is that top management, which is ultimately responsible for the organization, rarely hears what the customer is asking for. Unless there is a mechanism to get these comments throughout the organization, management will never hear them.

Research shows that once the cause of the complaint has occurred, the level of stress becomes a function of the handling of the situation. The disturbance level can be reduced if the complainant actively believes in management. This means that it is important for management to direct its efforts toward creating an attitude that will minimize the negative effect of the complaint.

Complainants want to feel that management is sincere and will make a sincere effort to correct the situation. If this belief is supported, they will probably choose the same hotel, restaurant, or travel and tourism company again. The tendency of complainants, however, is not to believe. One of the authors found that 29 percent of the still unsatisfied complainants indicated they would have been

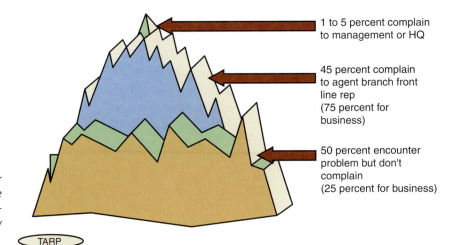

EXHIBIT 4-18 The tip of the iceberg phenomenon.

Source: Goodman, J. (1999). Basic facts on customer complaint behavior and the impact of service on the bottom line (p. 5). White paper published by TARP. Retrieved from www.e-satisfy.com/research2.asp. Used by permission.

satisfied simply with a proper response from management rather than what they felt were token gestures.

TARP found that if complaints were resolved quickly, complainants were more likely to make repeat purchases. The opposite is also true, as can be seen in Exhibit 4-19.

Exhibit 4-20 shows the results of two studies that examined complaints and a person's country of origin. Specifically, one study revealed that American consumers, who are from an individualistic culture, are more likely to voice dissatisfaction to the company, whereas South Korean consumers, who are from a collectivist culture, are more likely to avoid confrontation and instead just leave. South Korean customers are more likely to engage in negative word of mouth to prevent friends and family members from having the same bad experience.

The second study presented in Exhibit 4-20 comes from hotel guests in Hong Kong. Results from this study suggest that with services, unsatisfied customers tell 11 people, whereas satisfied customers tell 6 people.

These studies demonstrate the opportunities inherent in the proper handling of customer complaints. Appropriate complaint handling just may be relationship marketing at its finest; certainly it is a tremendous marketing opportunity, which is why a marketing-oriented management should actually seek out complaints.

Practicing relationship marketing through customer complaint handling is not the easiest task in the world. Many discontented customers will not take the trouble to complain. Actually encouraging complaints becomes the necessary objective. Research has shown that people do not complain for three primary reasons:

1. It is not worth the time and effort.
2. They don't know where or how to complain.
3. They believe that nothing will be done even if they do complain.

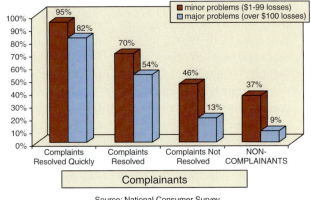

Source: National Consumer Survey

EXHIBIT 4-19 How many of your customers with problems will buy from you again?

Source: Goodman, J. (1999). Basic facts on customer complaint behavior and the impact of service on the bottom line (p. 3). White paper published by TARP. Retrieved from www.e-satisfy.com/research2.asp. Used by permission.

Marketing's task is to overcome these obstacles by making it easy to complain, making it known where and how to complain, and truly doing something about the complaint if it is reasonable, which over three-fourths of all complaints appear to be. This means setting up specific procedures.[20] Such an action will also constitute internal marketing; when employees see management taking complaints seriously, they will feel more inclined to do likewise.

Categorically, there are four ways firms usually handle complaints, as shown in Exhibit 4-21. It should be clear that the cell in the lower right corner is the cell where the service organization should be. Firms in this cell will follow the eight steps to complaint handling, which follow.

There are many reasons for encouraging customers to complain. The one we would like to point out here is the opportunity that this unhappy customer is giving to the

EXHIBIT 4-20	**Customer Complaint Research**

Research has shown that there are several differences across countries and industries with regards to customer complaint behavior. In a comparative study between an individualistic culture (the USA) and a collectivist culture (South Korea), the following was observed:[a]

Actions	USA	South Korea
Voice dissatisfaction to the company	American customers were more likely to inform the company about the problem and to try to solve it with them.	To avoid such confrontation, South Koreans would rather not say anything and leave.
Private actions such as switching companies, engaging in negative word of mouth	More inclined to directly complain to the company; Americans engaged in private actions much less than South Koreans did.	South Koreans were more likely to switch to another company and then engage in negative word of mouth to prevent family members and friends from having the same bad experience.
Third party responses such as writing a letter to a local newspaper or consumer agency, taking legal action	No significant differences between the two countries. In both countries, dissatisfied customers are more likely to take one of the preceding actions than take a third party action.	

Research conducted for hotel restaurants in Hong Kong suggested that young, well-educated, and female customers tend to be the heaviest complainers.[b] In general, twice the negative word of mouth is generated by dissatisfied customers as positive is generated by satisfied customers.[c] Below you can find the amount of word of mouth generated for some industries:

	Cars[d]	Packaged Goods[e]	Soft Drinks[f]	Services[g]
Unsatisfied	22 people	10 people	10–16 people	11 people
Satisfied	8 people	5 people	5–8 people	6 people

THE MONETARY VALUE OF CUSTOMERS—WHY YOU SHOULD NOT LOSE ONE

Looking at the other side of the coin, a survey on the UK market dated December 2002 of over 2,500 holidaymakers found that serious failings in the management of complaints is costing the holiday industry over £280 million per year.[h]

a. Liu, R. R., & McClure, P. (2001). Recognizing cross-cultural differences in consumer complaint behavior and intentions: An empirical examination. *Journal of Consumer Marketing*, 18 (1), 54–75. Available online from www.emeraldinsight.com.
b. Heung, V. C. S., & Lam, T. (2003). Customer complaint behavior towards hotel restaurant services. *International Journal of Contemporary Hospitality Management*, 15 (5), 283–289. Available online from www.emeraldinsight.com.
c. Retrieved December 18, 2004 from www.tarp.com.
d. Barlow & Møller.
e. Retrieved December 18, 2004 from www.tarp.com.
f. Goodman, J., Maszal, J., & Segal, E. (2000, March-April). Creating a customer relationship feedback system that has maximum bottom line impact. *Journal of Customer Relationship Management*. Available online from www.emeraldinsight.com.
g. Hart, C. W. L., Heskett, J. L., & Sasser, W. E., Jr. (1990, July-August). The profitable art of service recovery. *Harvard Business Review*, 148–156. Extracted from Hallowell, R. (2002, March). Service recovery. *Harvard Business Review*.
h. Retrieved December 21, 2004 from www.e-satisfy.co.uk.

company to solve the problem and transform him into a satisfied customer with repurchase intentions. According to a study conducted on the hotel industry, the way complaints are handled is the major factor determining whether someone will return for another night's stay.[21]

The following steps for effective complaint handling were extracted from the book *A Complaint Is a Gift*:[22]

1. **Say 'thank you'.** Before you apologize about the incident, thank the customer for sharing this valuable information with you.
2. **Explain why you appreciate the complaint.** Tell the customer how you are grateful to learn about this problem and to be given another chance to resolve it.
3. **Apologize for the mistake.** Apologize to the customer about the incident and any inconvenience it may have caused. Tell him or her that you sincerely hope you will be given a chance to serve them again in the future.
4. **Promise to do something about the problem immediately.** Once you have apologized, tell the customer that you two should try to work things out immediately.
5. **Ask for necessary information.** Ask the customer all the essential information about the incident so you can more effectively try to resolve it.
6. **Correct the mistake, promptly.** This would be the ideal situation, so that the customer could walk out

EXHIBIT 4-21	Complaint Matrix: How Companies Respond to Complaints

Company's Response

	Defensive	Corrective
Passive	Management apologizes to unhappy customer and does nothing.	Management solves complaint but does nothing to prevent it from happening again.
Active	Management encourages customers to complain but does nothing about the complaints.	Management solves complaint, finds out why it happened, and fixes cause. It then follows up with the customer and encourages him or her to return.

Source: Barlow, J. (1996). *A complaint is a gift: Using customer feedback as a strategic tool.* Williston, VT: Berrett-Koehler.

satisfied and remember what an effective recovery system your company has.

7. **Check customer satisfaction.** Before the customer leaves, check once more if they are entirely satisfied with the outcome and see if and/or how you can be of help. Thank them again for the opportunity they gave you.

8. **Prevent future mistakes.** Make sure you take the appropriate actions so this incident does not happen again.

Once complaint-handling procedures have been put in place, it is important to measure how well the procedures are working. Specifically, firms should know the following:

■ What percentage of guests have a problem during their stay?

■ Of those who have a problem, what percentage is reporting the problem to management?

■ Of those who report a problem, what percentage is claiming their problem was solved to their satisfaction?

■ Of those who report a problem, what percentage is claiming their problem was not solved to their satisfaction?

■ What is the impact of complaint procedures on customers' willingness to return, overall satisfaction, and net promoter score?

Luckily, one question can provide all the preceding information. This question is shown in Exhibit 4-22. Exhibits 4-23 a and b show with one question that it is easy to determine how many people had no problem and how many of those who had a problem said something. It also shows how well the form responded to those complaints.

The data in Exhibits 4-23a and b come from an in-flight survey one of the authors conducted for an airline company. As noted, 84 percent of the respondents experienced no problems. A total of 16 percent experienced a problem, but less than two-thirds (61.6 percent) reported the problem to management. Clearly, more needs to be done to get the 38.4 percent who did not speak up to talk about the problems they experienced. Notice that of those who reported a problem, 70.1 percent claimed it was resolved in a friendly and effective manner. The airline should be concerned that 30.9 percent of those who complained felt their problem was not solved in a friendly manner. Exhibits 4-23a and b show what happens when controlling for repurchase intent. Repurchase was measured on a 1 (*definitely will not fly again*) to 5 (*definitely will fly again*) scale. As noted in Exhibit 4-23, 40.3 percent of those who claimed their problem was solved in a friendly manner rated their likelihood of flying again a 5. If the problem was reported but not handled in a friendly manner, just 12.1 percent claimed they would definitely fly again. This is less than the percentage of customers who had a complaint but did not report it. The message? If you cannot solve the problem, it is best not to ask if there was a problem.

The benefits are clear: long-term profit from loyal customers and more positive and less negative word-of-mouth advertising. Ancillary benefits include new product ideas, new product information, improved image, better-educated customers, and higher productivity and service. For line employees, there are also the benefits of less customer conflict, better image and word of mouth about the company, and better respect for the company and the product.

Each company must devise its own system for soliciting and handling complaints. Handling satisfied customers is easy; handling dissatisfied customers is the acid test of marketing and management.

Employee Relationship Marketing or Internal Marketing

Employee relationship marketing, often referred to as **internal marketing**, means applying marketing principles and the components of the loyalty circle to the people who serve the customers. The emphasis of internal marketing is on the employee as the internal customer who also has needs, wants, and problems. What this customer is buying is his or her job. Thus, the job is the product that satisfies the needs and wants of these internal customers so that they, in turn, will better satisfy the needs and wants of the external customers.

The service profit chain model developed by James L. Heskett, W. Earl Sasser, and Leonard A. Schlesinger in 1997 illustrates the importance of the employee. This is shown in Exhibit 4-24. It evolves around the idea that there are di-

| EXHIBIT 4-22 | A Tool to Measure the Effectiveness of Complaint-Handling Procedures |

1. Please indicate if you reported any problems during your visit and how they were resolved.
   a. No problems experienced   Skip Question #2
   b. Problems reported and were resolved in a friendly, effective manner   2
   c. Experienced problems, but did not report to staff   3
   d. Problems reported and were not resolved in a friendly, effective manner   4
2. What problem did you experience? _____

Source: Reprinted with permission from *Marketing Management,* published by the American Marketing Association, Rust, R., & Subramanian, B. (1992). Making complaints a management tool, Vol. 1, No. 3, pages 40–45.

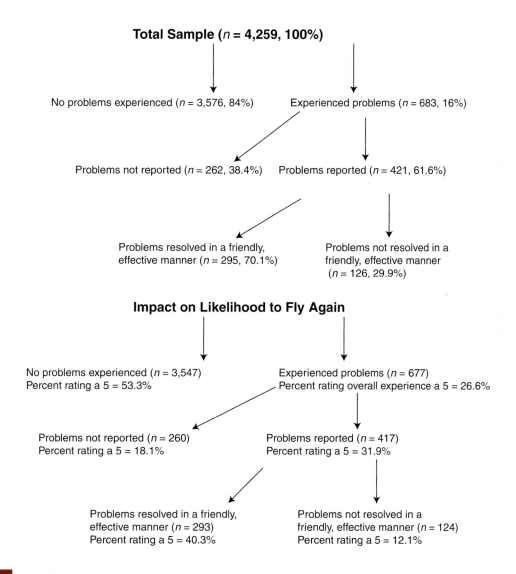

Total Sample (*n* = 4,259, 100%)

No problems experienced (*n* = 3,576, 84%)   Experienced problems (*n* = 683, 16%)

Problems not reported (*n* = 262, 38.4%)   Problems reported (*n* = 421, 61.6%)

Problems resolved in a friendly, effective manner (*n* = 295, 70.1%)   Problems not resolved in a friendly, effective manner (*n* = 126, 29.9%)

Impact on Likelihood to Fly Again

No problems experienced (*n* = 3,547) Percent rating a 5 = 53.3%   Experienced problems (*n* = 677) Percent rating overall experience a 5 = 26.6%

Problems not reported (*n* = 260) Percent rating a 5 = 18.1%   Problems reported (*n* = 417) Percent rating a 5 = 31.9%

Problems resolved in a friendly, effective manner (*n* = 293) Percent rating a 5 = 40.3%   Problems not resolved in a friendly, effective manner (*n* = 124) Percent rating a 5 = 12.1%

| EXHIBIT 4-23 | What happens when controlling for repurchase intent and satisfaction with the overall experience. |

rect and strong relationships between profit and growth; customer loyalty and customer satisfaction; the value and quality of goods and services delivered to customers, and employee satisfaction, loyalty, capability, and productiv-ity.[23] What Heskett, Sasser, and Schlesinger refer to as the "satisfaction mirror" suggests that the success of a company results from "employee satisfaction being 'reflected' in terms of customer satisfaction."[24]

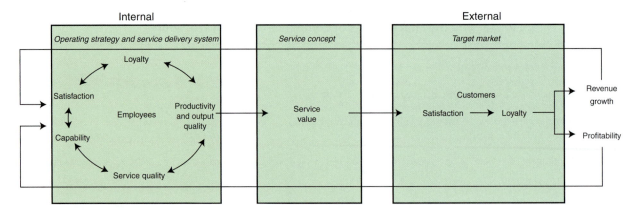

- *Step 1:* Through internal marketing, managers are primarily worried about their employees' necessities, capability, and productivity. The goal is to increase employee confidence and provide them with the right tools, so they can do their jobs more easily. Training programs are developed to achieve that, with employees being the central focus of the company. These, in turn, gain confidence about their jobs and their level of satisfaction toward the company increases.
- *Step 2:* With the proper tools in place and the employees gaining more self-confidence, a higher consistency in the product/service being offered is achieved. Consequently, there is an improvement in service quality and value.
- *Step 3:* As the service quality and value improves in the eye of the customer, a higher level of satisfaction is achieved. Happy customers are likely to return and are less prone to overtures from the competition, as suggested by Fornell.*
- *Step 4:* As customers become more loyal and return to the establishment more and more often, a **trust** relationship is built and the company experiences an increase in profit. This might be attributed to various reasons, such as lower sales and marketing costs and lower transaction costs, among others.

*Fornell, C. (1992). A national customer satisfaction barometer: The Swedish experience. *Journal of Marketing, 56,* 6–21. Available online from www.emeraldinsight.com.

EXHIBIT 4-24 The service profit chain, step by step.

*Source: Rust, R. T., & Subramanian, B. (1992). Making complaints a management tool. *Marketing Management 1(3),* 40–45. Adapted from Emerald Group Publishing Limited. Used by permission.*

Taco Bell, by examining employee turnover records for individual stores, found that 20 percent of the stores with the lowest turnover rates had double the sales and 55 percent higher profits than did 20 percent of the stores with the highest turnover rates.[25] Sheraton found likewise. It determined that its employee satisfaction index accounted for 50 percent of the variance in its customer satisfaction index, which, in turn, accounted for 50 percent of the variance in its revenue per available room (REVPAR).

To create customer value, the company must create employee value. Employees, after all, manage the process, provide the imagination, implement the policies, and derive the insight to help deepen customer bonding. This is especially true when we are dealing with so many intangibles that make for customer value and can never be explicit in the policies ordained. Without the commitment of employees, relationship marketing is doomed to fail. This may mean looking at employees in a new light, like customers. To do this, it is useful to apply the matrix in Exhibit 4-9 to employees with some minor adaptations. We can replace the words *profitable* and *unprofitable* with *creates customer value* and *doesn't create customer value.* This, of course, is the view of the employer, who must also create value for the employee.

At first glance, this may appear to be a strange way to look at marketing; it is certainly not the way we look at the marketing of goods. However, a closer look makes the case obvious: One of the first tasks of marketing and management is to have the employees believe in their job, which is the product that they represent to the customer. The successful hospitality firm must first sell its jobs to employees before it can sell its services to its customers. If this is not done, we end up with dissatisfied customers (employees) who will, one way or another, express their dissatisfaction to the paying customers. Paying customers, in turn, find that their problems are not adequately solved, so they go elsewhere. Clearly, this is not the way to keep customers. Thus, what firms practice in the creation and keeping of customers they must also practice in the creation and keeping of employees. Relationships with customers often depend on employees to go beyond standard policies and procedures to make a big difference in problem resolution and the feeling a customer has for the company.

Again, Bowen and Shoemaker shed some light on what this means. When asked, What does it mean to have trust in a luxury hotel? respondents said the following:

■ The hotel does things as promised.
■ The feeling that my personal property is safe in my room.
■ If I receive a fax, I know it will be delivered to my room.
■ Employees provide quick and correct answers.
■ *I trust a hotel that trusts its employees* [emphasis added]. One respondent commented that if management could not trust an employee with a $30 decision (of another guest), he could not feel comfortable leaving a $4,000 computer and other valuables in his room.[26]

Management Practices

Keeping good employees leads to keeping good customers. The quality of services depends in large measure on the skills and attitudes of the people producing the services. An acceptable product is necessary to appeal to the external market. The same is true of the internal market. Employees, an integral part of the product in hospitality, must also be marketing oriented. Unless a firm has something to offer to its employees, it should not expect marketing-oriented behavior. Just as we select customers whose needs we can best meet, we must select employees whose needs can be met through a job in our organization.

Understanding the simultaneous production and consumption nature of services is helpful in understanding what has just been stated. Many companies conduct employee courses in customer handling, including what trainees have dubbed "smile training." Smile training, as we have previously said, is not enough. Consider the previous example of a room service waiter who arrived an hour late with breakfast, a big smile, and a "How are you folks today?" instead of a somber, "I'm sorry." Or, consider the following anecdote told by a front desk clerk of a large convention hotel:

A large convention was checking into the hotel all day, and we never had a chance to get away from the desk and take a break for coffee or even for lunch. We were smiling our hardest dealing with all the problems, and things were going fairly smoothly considering the circumstances. After a while, however, all the problems began to get to us so we devised a little sing-song communication and banter among us that helped to keep our sense of humor and keep us going. While all this was going on, our supervisors were sitting in a room behind the front desk, talking and drinking coffee. Occasionally, one would step out and, seeing that all was going well, would go back to the room leaving us to carry on. When they heard our banter, however, things changed. One of us was called into the backroom and told to tell the others to cut it out. Our attitudes changed immediately. We kept on working, but we couldn't have cared less about the customers and it showed.

The impact of this anecdote is that marketing principles have not been applied to these employees' jobs. Customer satisfaction has been given token attention rather than being treated as a philosophy. Employees will not "buy" the product, customer service, when it appears that management is not willing to deliver on its promise of what it is "selling." The old expression "practice what you preach" is also the essence of internal marketing.

There is a natural conflict between company policies and the ability of the employee to satisfy customers. The very nature of the service business implies that it is impossible to anticipate all the needs and wants of customers. Obviously, there must be policies to guide employee actions, and no one is suggesting that there are easy solutions to these conflicts. But it is just as obvious that there must be flexibility. Progressive companies, such as Marriott, are embracing the concept of employee empowerment. Line employees are allowed to make decisions that will solve guests' immediate problems, without seeking prior approval of their supervisors. Exhibit 4-25 is from the website of the government of Canada and profiles Delta Hotels (www.deltahotels.com). As shown, Delta Hotels is a firm believer in employee empowerment, and it translates this into everything it does.

The Peabody Hotel in Orlando, Florida, and the Opryland Hotel in Nashville, Tennessee, are two properties that haves managed to "break the mold" for customer service. Visiting these hotels, both over 1,000 rooms, one is completely impressed with the level of service offered by *everyone*. Each of these hotels has 800-plus employees continuously interacting with the guests. Every employee verbally and visually engages the customer and is empowered to satisfy that customer's needs and ask questions later. Ritz-Carlton employees are empowered to spend up to $2,000 to satisfy a customer. According to Patrick Mene, head of quality control at Ritz-Carlton, "To us, empowerment means giving the employees responsibility for solving guests' problems."[27]

Consider the following anecdote from Eddystone C. Nebel, who followed and observed 10 hotel general managers as part of a qualitative research study:

This general manager . . . tries very hard to communicate what is important to his employees. He's developed a series of sayings to help guide the thinking and actions of the entire hotel staff. His first saying which he preaches with missionary zeal to his staff of 850 employees and executives is, "Talk to the guests." Talking to the guest is meant to convey a number of things. It means that a pleasant hello from all

EXHIBIT 4-25 Delta Hotels is a firm believer in employee empowerment, and it translates this into everything it does.

Source: Organizational Profiles: Delta, www.sdc.gc.ca/en/lp/spila/wlb/ell/06delta_hotels.shtml. Social Development Canada, 2001. Reproduced with permission of the Minister of Public Works and Government Services Canada, 2006. Retrieved October 11, 2005.

Employee Empowerment

Delta believes that key to a healthy bottom line is a healthy culture, one in which employees feel empowered enough to be able to freely walk into their manager's office and say "I think this really needs to be changed", or "This is what I need in order to get my job done". Therefore, it is consistently communicated to employees, from their first days, that they are key to the hotel's success and that their opinions matter. Delta has set up numerous mechanisms in order to ensure that feedback is encouraged and operationalized. Numerous training and empowerment programs also contribute to Delta's commitment to employee development.

Program Initiatives

Measurement

A commitment to continuous quality improvement makes identifying areas of strength and weakness key. Therefore, Delta measures all aspects of its performance throughout the organization, including its performance with employees, and develops action plans based on the findings. For example:

- **Employee Satisfaction Surveys:** Employees are surveyed annually, and results are worked into plans that respond directly to identified areas of dissatisfaction. Each hotel conducts its own employee survey, and is then given three months to create an action plan based on the outcomes.
- **Quality Assessment:** Following the NQI model, business assessments are conducted every two years in each Delta hotel by internally trained assessors.
- **Balanced Scorecard:** Delta has been using a Balanced Scorecard approach, including human resources measures, for seven years.

Accountability

Understanding that managers are one of the two key drivers of employee morale and satisfaction (along with culture), Delta has created management development reviews — including 360° feedback — that examine specific managerial competencies such as flexibility, ability to handle stress, ability to work with a team, and interpersonal sensitivity.

- Results of the performance reviews, including the people management scores, are tied to manager's bonuses.
- At a senior level, employee satisfaction scores, broken out at a departmental or unit level, are tied directly to bonuses.

"Let's make it easy for everybody," says Pallett. "Let's just link it to compensation. That'll drive it."

the staff is a sign of hospitality, even in a 1,000-room hotel. But talking to the guests means much more; it means finding out from the guests if things are going well or if they need anything. In short, "talk to the guests" means constant and total communication, one-on-one, between as many employees and as many guests as possible. How is your stay? What do you need? Are there any problems? How can I help? These are the kinds of questions his staff is continuously asking the guests. . . . [His] goal is to not only talk to the guest but also to get the *guest talking* [emphasis added].[28]

Customers have a wide variety of expectations. Although the customer is *not* always right, there is not much to be gained in proving the customer wrong. Employees, instead, must be empowered to make the customer "feel right." This constitutes marketing to both the customer and the employee—what influences customers must be marketed to all employees.

Noncontact Employees

We have discussed internal marketing from the point of view of the customer-contact employee. This is certainly the most obvious way to look at it. But it doesn't stop there. The engineers, the housekeepers, the night porters, the cooks, the dishwashers, the storeroom people, and even the accountants are part of the internal marketing effort in hospitality. Management's task is to get employees to realize and feel that they are part of the effort.

A dishwasher, for example, can stop a chipped glass or stained plate from going back into the dining room. The storeroom person can make certain that the right degree of freshness is received. The housekeeper can make sure that all the lightbulbs in a room are working. ALL employees in hospitality are part of the marketing effort. If you said this to back-of-the-house employees, most of them would probably say, "Huh?" What influences customers must be *marketed* to all employees. Consider, for example, housekeepers talking (or even shouting) in a hallway at 8:00 A.M. One could tell them not to do this; better, one could tell them the effect it has on customers in their rooms.

Employees will need not only to understand how what they do impacts the customer, but also to broaden their scope of knowledge of more processes, technologies, and people with whom they must interact. They need to understand how everything the company does comes together for the customer as each customer expects. Gordon suggested the following:

1. Identify the relationship marketing skills required from employees who are to participate in all the processes that impact customer value.
2. Assess the performance of employees with respect to these skills and determine any knowledge gaps by working this through with employees and communicating effectively in real time, not just in an impersonal manner.
3. Develop training programs and technology support to re-skill and/or de-skill processes where employees require additional knowledge or context.[29]

As Gordon pointed out, "many companies establish major training initiatives, putting vast amounts of information into three-ring binders and then attempting to drill this into the skulls of their staff."[30] More often than not, this approach is likely to fail.

The Internal Marketing Concept

Motivating employees is not a new management task, but neither is it only a function of the organization's personnel department. The effort that supports the concept of internal marketing starts with top management and involves management at every level of the organization. Lower-level employees, whether they are customer contact or not, cannot be expected to be customer conscious if management above them is not similarly involved. Management style and decisions must support this orientation, not counteract it. Personnel policies, likewise, must reflect this orientation and practice it in the form of job selection, recruitment, and promotion. We can take this one step further: If internal marketing is not incorporated into the management culture, the direction of the firm may make implementation of internal marketing difficult or even impossible at lower levels. Successful internal marketing considerably eases the task of implementing relationship marketing or the primary task of keeping customers.

In fact, Bowen and Shoemaker discovered that a final barrier to loyalty can be employees. Their findings indicate that if employees do not communicate the attitude that a guest's problems are important to them, guests will not become loyal to a hotel.[31]

Traditional marketing activities can also play a role in influencing personnel as much as they are designed to influence customers. Employees should know about new products, new developments, and new customer promises even before the customer does. If a customer wishes to claim an advertised benefit, it is self-evident that the employee to whom the claim is made should know exactly what the customer is talking about and be enthused about promoting it. Too many times have we called the 800 reservation number of a national chain to request a rate advertised in a full-page newspaper ad to find that the reservation agent knows nothing about it. "It's not on my screen," is a frequent response. Here's a great story that makes the point:

> Mike Leven, now CEO of US Franchise Systems, was once honored by Washington State University as Hotel Marketer of the Year. Two students from the hotel school picked him up at the Seattle airport. "Tell us about marketing," they said. "Just watch," said Mike. When they got to the Holiday Inn in Pullman (the other end of the state), there on the hotel sign in large neon lights were the words, "Welcome Mike Leven, Hotel Marketer of the Year." "Neat," thought Mike. When he went to check in, however, the clerk proclaimed that he had no reservation. More than a little tired and now a little irate, Mike asked how that could be when his name was in neon lights at the front of the ho-

tel. "How would I know that?" responded the clerk, "I came in the back door."

Clearly, figuratively speaking, employees need to come in the front door to understand the customer. Okay, but was this the clerk's fault or management's?

Keeping employees aware of what is going on is not just so they can respond to customers. Unawareness leads to embarrassment, disappointment, reduced motivation, and lack of support for marketing efforts. Employees are, in fact, as much vital recipients of marketing campaigns as are customers. Robert Kelley put this all together quite well in a "Manager's Journal" column in the *Wall Street Journal*:

> Service providers treat customers similar to the way they, as employees, are treated by management . . . . The employees in turn convey the identical message to the customer. If management treats employees' concerns with indifference, then employees will not care about the customers' complaints.
>
> It is a rare employee who can rise above the effects of such poor management . . . . If managers want to improve service quality they must treat employees the same way they want employees to treat customers. Managers are the servants of employees, not just the bosses. They must provide services to the employees in a friendly, helpful and efficient manner that will enable those employees to better serve the customers. Customers thus become the beneficiaries of high-quality service that mirrors the organization's inner working.[32]

Kathy Ray was the new GM of the Sheraton Grand in Washington, D.C., when it was in bad shape. Occupancy was down, employee morale was low, and, it was said, "it was beyond hope"—and this was the Sheraton flagship hotel in the city. Ray gathered all employees together for a meeting. She put an organizational chart of the hotel on the wall. Front line employees were at the top of the organizational chart. She ate in the employees' dining room. Former GMs had never done that. She went into the kitchen to talk to the employees, not to have coffee with the chef or to have a special omelet prepared. She made her employees "believe." The customers noticed, and she turned the hotel around.

The success of the internal marketing concept ultimately lies with management. Lower-level employees cannot be expected to be customer conscious if the management above them does not display the same focus. Operations-oriented managers who concern themselves primarily with policies and procedures, often instituted without regard to the customer, undermine the firm's internal marketing effort, reducing employees' jobs to mechanical functions that offer little in the way of challenge, self-esteem, or personal gratification. Moreover, by requiring employees to adhere rigidly to specific procedures, the

EXHIBIT 4-26	Traditional versus Relationship Marketing Organization

Traditional	Relationship
Functional departments	Process teams with customer focus
Simple tasks, checking, monitoring	Little checking on, trust
Lots of controls	Empowerment
Hire for skills	Hire for team spirit, broad education, self-discipline
Teaching *how* of job	Teaching *why* of job
Boss appraisal	Customer appraisal, impact on satisfaction
Small merit increases	Bonuses
Advancement based on performance	Advancement based on ability and leadership potential, customer handling
"Boss pays my salary"	"Customer pays my salary"
"I'm just a cog in the wheel"	"Every job is important; I make a difference"
"The higher my title, the more important I am"	"My importance is based on my contribution to customer loyalty"
"Tomorrow will be just like today"	"We live with constant change—I must constantly learn"

operations-oriented manager ties their hands and restricts their ability to satisfy the customer. All of this means that the organization that practices relationship marketing has to change from the old traditional style. Exhibit 4-26 delineates these differences.

The Past and Future of Relationship/Loyalty Marketing

Although, as we have said, everyone talks about the customer and relationship marketing, that isn't the way it necessarily works in the organization. In fact, too many organizations work as follows:

1. Some organizations only talk about treating customers better. Management doesn't always understand what outstanding service looks like and isn't ready to turn its organization upside down to provide it. Managers paint happy faces on front line people. Or they conduct a service program for employees, but don't make it a part of their core strategy. Rhetoric does not become reality.
2. The organization tries to be everything to everybody. Customers are lumped together as one big mass. Their separate expectations are not known or aren't weighted and prioritized.

3. Customer surveys are acknowledged when they are positive, but negative data is often denied. Budget priorities are set and resources allocated with little, if any, connection to customer expectations. Priority is on what management or the company thinks is important.
4. Customers are not part of research and development of new services and products.
5. Employees are seen as the cause of service breakdowns when research shows that a large majority of service breakdowns are caused by the system, the process, or the structure and only a few from the people in the trenches.
6. The focus is on customer acquisition rather than customer retention. Sales and marketing efforts are aimed more at bringing in new customers than at keeping or expanding the business of old customers.

The future promises something different for those companies that deal with these negatives and focus on the positives. In today's technological world, there is little reason for not understanding customers and what they expect. But technology only provides the means; it doesn't by itself change attitudes or behavior, and if it's not paid attention to it becomes no more than a costly, fruitless expense.

Innovative leaders in the hospitality marketplace are not only translating guest experience and expectation data into operational changes, but also forging links among data acquisition, analysis, and delivery. They are rethinking customer and service strategy and improving customer services and value by providing front line employees with the information they need to provide higher-quality customer service and retention. These will be the companies with the sustainable competitive advantage of the future.

 Web Browsing Exercise

Go to the website for ICLP (international customer loyalty programs). What kind of firm is this? Who are their clients? What do they believe are their strengths and weaknesses?

■ Summary

A technique of nontraditional marketing is relationship marketing. Relationship marketing creates the customer bonding and understanding that is an integral part of any company's sustenance and growth. Relationships must be developed and sustained so they build loyalty and increase the **lifetime value of a customer**. In a service business, this is hardly possible without similar employee relations. The principle of internal marketing is to market hospitality jobs to employees just as we market hotels or restaurants to customers.

Establishing good customer relations also involves creating an atmosphere in which customers' complaints are sincerely addressed. We call this value recovery. One way to do this is to talk to the customer and to make it easy for the customer to talk back. Complaints are healthy, customer problems are opportunities, and marketers must be opportunists. Innovative relationship marketing will give a sustainable competitive advantage to tomorrow's leaders and their companies.

■ Key Terms

relationship marketing	client
total assets	loyalty circle
liabilities	commitment
loyalty marketing	internal marketing
customer analysis	trust
customer loyalty ladder	lifetime value of a customer
advocate	service augmentation

■ Discussion Questions

1. Which is the end and which is the means—frequent patronage or loyal patronage? Why? Discuss.
2. Discuss what relationship marketing is not. Why is this so?
3. What are the important elements in computing the lifetime value of a customer? How can you establish the value?
4. What is the importance of doing a customer analysis when establishing a relationship marketing program?
5. What is the difference between a customized service and **service augmentation?**
6. What are the problems with frequent guest/dining programs? What are the virtues?
7. What are some reasons that relationship marketing doesn't work?
8. Consider a complaint you have made in a hotel or restaurant. How was it handled? How would you have handled it?

■ Group Projects

1. Develop a model for determining the lifetime value of customers for a hotel, restaurant, or a travel and tourism company. Put some numbers to it.

2. Develop a loyalty program for a specific hotel or restaurant with which you are familiar.

■ References

1. Adapted from Reichheld, K. (2002). [Letter to the editor]. *Harvard Business Review, 80* (11), 126.
2. Levitt, T. (1981, May-June). Marketing intangible products and product intangibles. *Harvard Business Review*, 94–102. Copyright 1981 by the President and Fellows of Harvard College; all rights reserved.
3. Adapted from Bowen, J. T., & Shoemaker, S. (1998, February). Loyalty: A strategic commitment *Cornell Hotel and Restaurant Administration Quarterly*, 14–17. Adapted from SAGE Publications. Used by permission.
4. Adapted from Gordon, I. (1998). *Relationship marketing*. Toronto, Canada: John Wiley & Sons, 9. Readers interested in learning more on this subject than we can cover in one chapter are urged to read this book.
5. Shoemaker, S., & Lewis, R. (1999). Customer loyalty: The future of hospitality marketing. *Journal of Hospitality Management, 18*, 349.
6. Reichheld.
7. Shoemaker & Lewis.
8. Heskett, J. L., Jones, T. O., Loveman, G. W., Sasser, W. E., Jr., & Schlesinger, L. A. (1994, March-April). Putting the service-profit chain to work. *Harvard Business Review*, 164.
9. Reichheld, F. F., & Sasser, W. E., Jr. (1990, September-October). Zero defections: Quality comes to services. *Harvard Business Review*.
10. The objective is to get as close as possible to an evaluation of the net present value of all future profits from a particular customer. The profit from a customer is the profit margin on sales to that customer, less the cost of maintaining the relationship, plus any incremental benefits the customer brings, such as recommendations to other customers. For formulas see, for example, Cannie, J. K. (1994). *Turning lost customers into gold*. New York: AMACOM Books.
11. Shoemaker & Lewis.
12. Much of the information found in this phase of the evolution of loyalty comes from Shoemaker, S., & Bowen J. (2003). Antecedents and consequences of customer loyalty: An update. *Cornell Hotel and Restaurant Administration Quarterly, 6* (4), 31–52. Used by permission.
13. Peppers, D., & Rogers, M. (1996). *The one to one future*. New York: Doubleday.
14. Piccoli, G., & Applegate, L. M. (2003). Wyndham International: Fostering high-touch with high tech [Case

study]. Case no. 9-803-092, pp. 1–42. Cambridge: Harvard Business School.

15. Barlow, J., & Møller, C. (1996). *A complaint is a gift.* San Francisco: Berrett-Koehler.

16. Goodman, J. (1999). Basic facts on customer complaint behavior and the impact of service on the bottom line. White paper published by TARP. Retrieved from www.e-satisfy.com/research2.asp.

17. TARP. (2002). [Electronic brochure]. Retrieved July 22, 2004, from www.tarp.com/clients.html.

18. Goodman.

19. Goodman, 5.

20. For more discussion of this subject, see Lewis, R. C., & Morris, S. V. (1987, February). The positive side of guest complaints. *Cornell Hotel and Restaurant Administration Quarterly,* 13–15.

21. Gilly, M. C. (1987). Post-complaint processes: From organizational response to repurchase behavior. *Journal of Consumer Affairs, 21* (2). Extracted from Barlow & Møller.

22. Barlow & Møller.

23. Morris, B. (1998). Book reviews. *International Journal of Service Industry Management, 9* (3), 312–313. Available online from www.emeraldinsight.com.

24. Silvestro, R., & Cross, S. (2000). Applying the service profit chain in a retail environment. *International Journal of Service Industry Management, 11* (3), 244–268. Available online from www.emeraldinsight.com.

25. Heskett, Jones, Loveman, Sasser, & Schlesinger, 169–170.

26. Bowen & Shoemaker, *Restaurant Administration Quarterly,* 24. Used by permission.

27. Quoted in Partlow, C. G. (1993, August). How Ritz-Carlton applies TQM. *Cornell Hotel and Restaurant Administration Quarterly,* 20.

28. Nebel, E. C., III. (1991). *Managing hotels effectively: Lessons from outstanding general managers.* New York: Van Nostrand Reinhold, 37.

29. Gordon, I. (1998). *Relationship marketing.* Toronto: John Wiley & Sons, 275. Used by permission.

30. Ibid. Used by permission.

31. Bowen & Shoemaker, 25. Used by permission.

32. Kelley, R. E. (1987, October 12). Poorly served employees serve customers just as poorly. *Wall Street Journal,* p. 20.

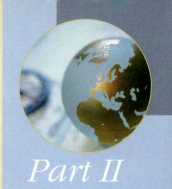

Part II

Marketing to Build a Competitive Advantage

Chapter 5
Strategic Marketing

Chapter 6
The Strategic Marketing System and Marketing Objectives

Strategic Marketing

Overview

This chapter discusses the concept of strategic planning and how it should impact and guide whatever a firm does. We examine the differences among strategy, operational effectiveness, and marketing management. The importance of strategic leadership and strategic vision is also emphasized. Strategy takes a long-range view. It is about creating "fit" between the firm and the environment to develop a competitive advantage. Once business objectives have been established, the strategies for obtaining those objectives must be developed to fit the rest of the organization's activities. Strategy must not be confused with tactics, which are the specific steps implemented to execute the strategy. The strategy is what guides the day-to-day tactical decisions.

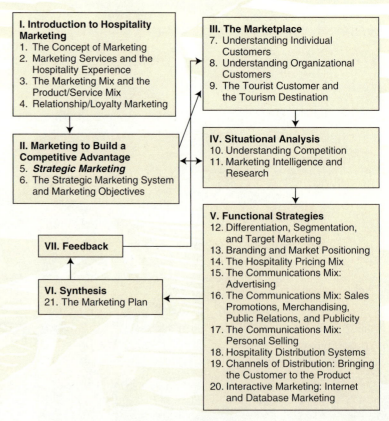

I. Introduction to Hospitality Marketing
1. The Concept of Marketing
2. Marketing Services and the Hospitality Experience
3. The Marketing Mix and the Product/Service Mix
4. Relationship/Loyalty Marketing

II. Marketing to Build a Competitive Advantage
5. *Strategic Marketing*
6. The Strategic Marketing System and Marketing Objectives

VII. Feedback

VI. Synthesis
21. The Marketing Plan

III. The Marketplace
7. Understanding Individual Customers
8. Understanding Organizational Customers
9. The Tourist Customer and the Tourism Destination

IV. Situational Analysis
10. Understanding Competition
11. Marketing Intelligence and Research

V. Functional Strategies
12. Differentiation, Segmentation, and Target Marketing
13. Branding and Market Positioning
14. The Hospitality Pricing Mix
15. The Communications Mix: Advertising
16. The Communications Mix: Sales Promotions, Merchandising, Public Relations, and Publicity
17. The Communications Mix: Personal Selling
18. Hospitality Distribution Systems
19. Channels of Distribution: Bringing the Customer to the Product
20. Interactive Marketing: Internet and Database Marketing

Christian Hempell
Vice President, Strategy, InterContinental Hotels Group

Christian Hempell is vice president, strategy, for InterContinental Hotels Group, PLC, the world's most global hotel company with over 3,500 properties under 7 brands in nearly 100 countries. He joined in the strategy function in 2003 and is based in London, UK. Hempell is responsible for supporting the development of the company's global strategy and managing the internal strategic planning process. Prior to joining IHG, Hempell served as practice manager for Andersen's Hospitality Consulting Group in the United States. He holds a BS degree from the School of Hospitality Management at Cornell University and an MBA degree from Harvard Business School.

Marketing in Action
Christian Hempell, VP Strategy, InterContinental Hotels Group

How does IHG practice strategy, and who is involved in the strategic planning in this organization?

Speaking generally about the hotel industry, I do not think there is one single way to practice strategy. It is based on the capabilities and the culture of the company and the way in which it chooses to compete. Therefore, although the strategy function operates differently by company, all hotel players invariably practice strategy very deliberately. The way it works at InterContinental Hotels Group is we do have a central strategy function and we work with our regional business units (the Americas, EMEA, and Asia Pacific) through a "top down" and "bottom up" approach. The "top down" looks at the overall position of the company and understands what we need to focus on at a global level to drive up value for our shareholders, as well as meet the needs of our stakeholders—be it owners, employees, or consumers. The central function supports the overall development of strategy and strategic objectives that drive the company's decision making. On the global scale, we know which areas we need to focus on, and that's based on a series of analyses into market opportunities, consumer trends, our existing position in various markets versus competitors, our scale in supply share, the strength of our brands, and management capabilities on the ground needed for execution. We know which are the biggest markets—we call them the "pools of growth"—and how we should go after them. The business units—the regions—will develop specific plans to capture share in those pools of growth from the bottom up. So, they will develop specifics on how many hotels we could add into our system and which consumer brands would be most successful in each market.

The real trick, in my opinion, is the iteration that happens among the different trade-offs that you have to make across business units. For example, a business unit may find an attractive opportunity to invest and grow, but they don't know if that's a better return relative to something in another part of the world. So, they submit these opportunities, and then it's the job of the center and the business units collectively to pick and choose which ones are the most meaningful for the company. Strategy is about trade-offs. It's about saying no more often than it is saying yes, so it has to be done in a culturally vibrant way. There are many good growth opportunities, but some are better than others. Picking up these opportunities on a relative basis to one another allows you to make your best choices.

Every company, regardless of how big it is, has limited resources, and one of the scariest resources is management focus. Capital is important, and the number of staff, employees, etc., is important, but really, it's about having the top managers of the company focusing on a handful of things that are really going to drive the biggest profit for the company. There are a lot of things that are worth doing, but they won't have the same return or impact on achieving your strategic objectives. Time is limited and focus is finite, so companies needs to pick the big drivers that really matter.

We talk about the value chain and the five forces model to help look at strategy and the strategic process. How involved is that in terms of companies using those to help guide their strategic thinking?

I think the principles behind the five forces model and value chain are absolutely fundamental to really understanding your position versus competitors and why each player derives different levels of profit out of the industry. It is important to understand how much negotiating power your customers (owners) have, the level of competitive rivalry, and how high the threat of substitution or new entrants is. Being able to define what we call the industry "rules of the game" comes from using the five forces model. You have to realize that each company is unique and different in their industry position, and the attractiveness of an industry is based on who you are. Some companies have better capabilities in hotel management and in standardized processes. Others might be better at branding and innovation, while still others might be better in different segments of the market, be it midscale or upscale. Depending on where your standing point is, you have a different set of strategic options that look attractive to you.

Coming back to the five forces model, understanding which things you can influence and which things you cannot is really important. For example, in the franchise business model, almost every franchise owner in the United States charges similar fees for their franchise, which is generally about 5 percent of room revenues for the franchise. However, you don't see strong franchisor pricing power in the industry, and the reason for that is there are so many different brands out there, you couldn't raise your royalty rate to 8 or 10 percent because of the competitive pressure from rivals. This presses down the pricing (and profit) power of the franchisor.

Another example would be on the consumer side, and that is the brand premium that we get as a branded hotel. In other industries, their premiums are often 50 or 75 percent—for example, the price between a generic cola and a Coca-Cola. In the hotel business, the brand premiums are more limited. If you had two midscale hotels of the exact same quality in the exact same location and one was branded

and the other independent, you would rarely see brand premiums of 50 percent or more. Understanding how and how much brands drive premiums helps define the nature of the industry. Understanding the different pressures, their implications, and how they interact with each other with respect to the five forces model is really quite fundamental.

The value chain is very important as well—especially when you see the revolution in electronic distribution with third party intermediaries (Expedia, Travelocity, etc.), which have seen phenomenal growth in the last 5 to 10 years. In some ways, they are attempting to commoditize hotels by stepping in between consumer and brander and having guests make hotel decisions primarily on price and location. Understanding how to compete in the value chain and how we can claim a large share of value as a franchisor is therefore very important. Altogether, the principles behind the five forces model and the value chain help a strategist understand who creates and captures value—how many pieces of the profit pie each player is getting—more effectively.

What do you think some of the biggest strategic challenges are today and in the future for the hotel industry?

One of the challenges is going to be the way the industry can innovate in an economically viable way. Some of the hotels in the last five years have innovated with respect to the product, whether it's the bed and bath experience or some of the service elements. If you think about how far different industries have come in the last 50 years, be it television or automobiles or retail experience, and then compare that to the typical hotel experiences, I would submit that perhaps the hotel business hasn't evolved or innovated as quickly as other industries. One reason for this lack of innovation is the inability to keep anything proprietary. Once a hotel or brand starts using a certain bed product, it can easily be copied by all of the competitors. This limits the ways in which companies can create a viable long-term competitive advantage.

I think another strategic challenge is how the industry's value chain changes with the continued growth of Internet distribution companies. These players will have different impacts on brand franchisors, management companies, and owners. It's interesting to see a new technology changing the economics of an industry. How this plays out will depend on how consumer loyalty shifts over time, whether it increasingly moves toward hotel brands or the online agency itself.

Somebody once said, "The hotel that your parents stayed in isn't necessarily the hotel you want to stay in." Do you acknowledge this idea?

I think that statement is directionally true. As the industry matures, particularly in the USA, consumers are looking for more specialized experiences that require niche positions and more tailored product offerings. The hotel industry must be careful not to commoditize itself, and I think moving forward with innovations and better understanding consumer insights will help people to see value in the differences created by branders and owners. We have enough consumer understanding to know that the basic hotel need is similar to previous generations, but how it is delivered can be improved upon.

How do you measure or track the success of your strategy?

One of the most important functions of our strategy team is to track the progress and success of the corporate strategy. We have two methods of measuring how our strategy is performing. One is the level of total shareholder return, which is essentially how the shareholders benefit from the actions we take. A share price is simply the earnings per share times the price/earnings multiple. We have direct control of our earnings per share through our operations, and we can influence (but not control) the multiple based on management credibility, a good track record on delivery, and a lot of future growth opportunities. This, however, is only the financial measure of our strategy.

We also track our strategic progress by taking our relationships with stakeholders into account—owners, consumers, and employees. We monitor how many new contracts we have signed with owners and how many renew their agreements. We measure our brand premiums and loyalty program to ensure long-term relevance and preference with consumers. And we assess the talent base of the company to develop a deep pipeline of management capability and high employee engagement. These measures describe more of our future earnings growth and long-term viability as a company.

How many people tend to work in the strategy department in your field?

There is a difference between the strategy department and the strategy function. The actual department is a rather small group of individuals who are available to do analysis on corporate-level initiatives and on big strategic decisions that arise. The actual strategy function involves putting together ideas for growth opportunities, looking at your competitors, assessing your capabilities and what you can execute upon, and being very clear on how they work together—that requires a much wider group of people. Whether it is our head of franchising, head of finance, head of management operations, or the president of a region, the entire senior management team is involved in the strategy function. The strategy process is balanced and integrated with our budget and operations plans for the next year. However, each company will do this differently based on how they're structured, the role of the corporate office, and where decisions are made.

Strategy is both an art and a science. The science part is more what people think about in regards to the branding, the financial modeling, and competitors—the analytical side. Then there is the art side, which is where people get together and come up with different ideas that seem equally plausible and at the end of the day the chief executive and executive committee decide how best to grow the company. There is not necessarily one clear answer, and this is where the art comes in. Being able to pick and integrate the best strategy overall not only involves numbers or a column in a spreadsheet, but it also involves creativity to come up with the management team's best assessment about choosing and achieving your strategic objectives.

Used by premission from Christian Hempell.

Today's complex hospitality industry environment requires organizations to be better prepared and proactive to address both internal and external changes. Successful achievement of a firm's objectives depends on the ability of management to understand the environment and to respond to opportunities in an ever-changing environment. Strategic marketing encompasses all the decisions and actions used to formulate and implement strategies designed to achieve the firm's objectives.

First, we will clarify the use of the word *strategy* in the marketing or management context. We will then briefly elaborate on the process of strategic marketing and demonstrate its importance in any marketing context. Finally we will discuss how to understand the environment and the different types of environments that help determine a firm's strategy.

Strategic Marketing versus Marketing Management

First, it is important to differentiate between strategic marketing and marketing management. Some authors place strategy largely at the corporate or strategic business unit (SBU) level and marketing management at the local level; we believe that true marketing leadership derives from the practice of strategy and marketing management at both levels.

It is essential, then, that one understands the difference between strategy and **management effectiveness**. Management effectiveness refers to activities that allow a company to operate more smoothly and produce better results. It includes such things as employee motivation, technological advances, total quality management (TQM), better salesmanship, revenue management, global distribution, and employee empowerment, among others. For example, consider Southwest Airlines. While other airlines are facing bankruptcy, Southwest's profits continue to grow. Management effectiveness keeps employees happy and loyal to the airline. Management effectiveness also enables Southwest to realize the need to lock in fuel prices (called hedging), thus enabling them to lower their fuel costs. This is in contrast to many other carriers where there is an adversarial relationship between employees and management. This adversarial relationship means management is focused on other issues and not on issues that can help it gain a competitive advantage, such as the hedging of fuel costs.

Web Browsing Exercise

Visit Southwest Airlines' website (www.southwest.com/about_swa/). Which areas on this website show management effectiveness? How? Which areas show strategic effectiveness? How? Compare and contrast Southwest's management effectiveness and its strategic effectiveness.

Management effectiveness is necessary for a company to produce better results, but it is not sufficient. In other words, management effectiveness alone will not lead to better results. A solid, well-thought-out, and well-executed strategy is equally important. Too often, management effectiveness is emphasized in lieu of strategic thinking—the long-range view.

Management effectiveness means performing activities that are different from competitors' or performing similar activities in more effective or meaningful ways. A company can outperform others only if it can preserve an established difference. In addition, members of the target market must be able to see this difference and find it of value. Southwest Airlines' strategy of flying point to point to "secondary airports" instead of the traditional hub-and-spoke system favored by many "legacy" airlines and its emphasis on keeping operating costs to a minimum enabled the airline to survive higher fuel prices and the economic impact of 9-11 when other airlines could not. Southwest's strategy is to perform things differently; for example, no assigned seating, no meals, and flights to secondary air-

ports that still provide convenient access to major destination cities. Southwest is successful because it sticks to what it does best and it delivers on its promises to customers.

Many casino companies have player reward programs, which are similar to hotel frequency programs. The more a customer spends gambling, the more rewards he earns. Many firms have these programs, yet no casino company is as successful as Harrah's in using the reward program to drive business. The success of their program comes from the knowledge and skills of the employees who run the program. Basically, they have hired mathematicians—or, as they call them, "propeller heads"—to analyze data and to determine the specific type of rewards to offer to specific customers and the timing of these rewards. The success of their program provided Harrah's with the resources necessary to buy Caesars Entertainment, a company much larger than Harrah's Entertainment. This is an example of a firm performing activities similar to those of their competitors, but in different ways.

Strategy

Competitive strategy is about being different. Strategic competition is the process of perceiving new market positions that bring new customers from competitors or bring new customers into the market. Often these positions open up or close because of environmental change or because they have been ceded by competitors. Consider, for example, the development of the Internet. The Internet has changed the way people book airlines and hotels. This change of booking method has made many travel agents obsolete. It has also forced those travel agents who have survived to change their business model. Specifically, rather than relying solely on commissions, they now charge fees per transaction.

What, then, is strategy?[1]

1. Strategy is the creation of a unique and valuable market position. If there were only one ideal position, there would be no need for strategy. In reality, there are many ways a firm can conduct its business. The idea is to choose the products, services, and methods of promotion that are different from those of competitors and valued by members of the target market.
2. Strategy is making trade-offs. Companies cannot be all things to all customers. Trade-offs purposefully limit what a company offers. An essential part of strategy is also choosing what not to do.
3. Strategy is creating "fit" or directing all activities that occur in an organization toward the same goal. Consider the case of Starbucks Coffee. Its competitive advantage comes from the way its activities fit and complement one another. Fit locks out com-

petitors by creating a chain that is as strong as its strongest link. The best fits are strategy specific because they enhance the company's uniqueness. The whole matters more than any individual part, and sustainable competitive advantage grows out of the entire system of activities. Prior to Starbucks, getting a cup of coffee was routine. Starbucks offered not only many different varieties of coffee, but also a great place to sit and enjoy the coffee. Starbucks has higher per store revenues than the local coffee shop because of these two differences.

Unfortunately, many companies lack marketing strategies or fail to make strategic choices or let their strategies disintegrate and disappear. Although this may be due partially to external causes (e.g., changes in technology or competition), more often it comes from within—from a misguided view of competition, organizational failure, or the undisciplined desire to grow "bigger and better."

Managers are under increasing pressure to deliver measurable performance growth. Managerial effectiveness becomes the goal, and strategic thinking gets bypassed. Companies imitate one another in a kind of herd behavior. This has been especially true in the hotel industry. Consider the hotels in Las Vegas. After Steve Wynn built the Mirage with its volcano and Siegfried and Roy magic show, other companies copied this idea of a themed resort. Although each hotel has a different theme, the strategies of the hotels are essentially the same.

Then there is the desire to grow with steps that blur a company's strategic position. Attempts to compete on many fronts can create confusion and cause organizational chaos. The goal is for more revenue even if profits fall. Meanwhile, uniqueness is fuzzy, compromises are made, fit is reduced, and competitive advantage is lost. Rather than deepen a strategic position, it is broadened and compromised. Consider Darden Restaurants, operators of Red Lobster and Olive Garden. They tried to grow through the introduction of a Chinese food concept called China Coast. After 55 units were opened across the United States, they were all closed and the concept abandoned because China Coast lacked strategic fit and competitive advantage. Another chain, P.F. Chang's, has been very successful with Chinese cuisine in multiple locations. P.F. Chang's had a better strategic fit and a strong competitive advantage. The Chinese food at P.F. Chang's is excellent, and they offer signature dishes served in a hip environment with a great local bar scene.

On the hotel side, consider the successful growth strategies of Marriott International, which has acquired Residence Inn, Renaissance, and Ritz-Carlton and developed a number of successful new product lines, such as Courtyard and Fairfield Inn. How does Marriott do it? According to Arne Sorenson, formerly executive vice president of strategy for Marriott Corporation and now chief financial officer, they apply four major criteria to growth and acquisitions:

1. The strategic fit
2. The net present value 10 years out
3. Earnings per share
4. The reputability of the company

Success, ironically, can be one of the greatest threats to survival and future success because it may invoke the attitude, We can do no wrong. Following are some examples of the past:

- IBM
- General Motors
- Apple
- Mirage Resorts (now part of MGM Mirage)
- Caesars Entertainment (now part of Harrah's Entertainment)
- Digital Equipment (initially part of Compaq and now part of Hewlett-Packard)
- Sears Roebuck
- International Harvester
- K-Mart
- Coca-Cola
- Sheraton (now part of Starwood)
- Planet Hollywood

Some of these companies were able to turn things around; others were purchased by other companies. Bill Gates of Microsoft, an astute observer of business strategy, has vowed never to be afflicted by the same mentality. He is constantly challenging the company to seek new business opportunities and new ways to use computers.

Strategic Leadership

Strategic leadership is the fundamental element necessary to establish or reestablish a clear strategy. This requires strong leaders willing to make choices. Michael Porter of Harvard Business School describes his view of strategic leadership in Exhibit 5-1.

The views laid out in Exhibit 5-1 make more sense and are easier to grasp when applied to a real situation. It is important to grasp it before we move on to more detailed explanations and applications of strategic thinking, strategic planning, and strategic choice; therefore, we provide real situations in Exhibits 5-2 (Marriott International) and 5-3 (McDonald's).

Exhibit 5-2 presents a timeline of the history of Marriott starting with the founding of Hot Shoppes, Inc., in 1929 to 2004, when Marriott reported sales in 2003 of $19

EXHIBIT 5-1	Michael Porter's View of Strategic Leadership

General management is more than the stewardship of individual functions. Its core is strategy: defining and communicating the company's unique position, making trade-offs, and forging fit among activities. The leader must provide the discipline to decide which industry changes and the customer needs to which the company will respond, while avoiding organizational distractions and maintaining the company's distinctiveness. . . . One of the leader's jobs is to teach others in the organization about strategy—and to say no when appropriate.

Strategy renders choices about what not to do as important as choices about what to do. . . . Deciding which target group of customers, varieties, and needs the company should serve is fundamental to developing a strategy. But so is deciding not to serve other customers or needs and not to offer certain features or services. Thus strategy requires constant discipline and clear communication. Indeed, one of the most important func-

tions of an explicit, communicated strategy is to guide employees in making choices that arise because of trade-offs in their individual activities and day-to-day decisions.

. . . A company may have to change its strategy if there are major structural changes in its industry. In fact, new strategic positions often arise because of industry changes and new entrants unencumbered by history often can exploit them more easily. However, a company's choice of a new position must be driven by the ability to find new trade-offs and leverage a new system of complementary activities into a sustainable advantage.

Source: Reprinted by permission of *Harvard Business Review.* From "What is strategy?" by Michael Porter, Nov-Dec 1996, 77–78. Copyright © 1996 by the Harvard Business School Publishing Corporation; all rights reserved.

billion and reported gross profit of $476 million. The interesting point of Exhibit 5-2 is how over time Marriott has focused on what it does best—running hotels—and sold those businesses that require different skill sets. Such businesses include Senior Living Service Communities (sold in 2003), Marriott Distribution Services (also sold in 2003), the food service business (e.g., Bob's Big Boy), facilities management businesses (each sold in 1998), and theme parks.

Exhibit 5-3 examines McDonald's again. You will recall that we began Chapter 1 with the example of McDonald's—because McDonald's is a **marketing concept** company that demonstrates all the principles of marketing. Later in that chapter we took a different and more current view of McDonald's and some of its problems. In 2010 will McDonald's still be the leader in the quick service category? Let us say now that the answer to that question may well depend on the strategic leadership of Jim Skinner, the new CEO. Exhibit 5-3 shows how McDonald's lost its strategic leadership, but found it under the late Jim Cantalupo. Time will tell whether Jim Skinner can continue the success of the late Cantalupo. At the time of this writing, it appears Skinner can: Stock price is up, as are same-store sales.

Strategic leadership is the ability of the leader to articulate a strategic vision for the company or division of the company (e.g., one hotel in a chain) and to motivate others to buy into that vision. Characteristics of this type of leadership also include commitment, being well informed, a willingness to delegate and empower, and an astute use of power.

Strategic Marketing

We now examine the differences between strategic marketing and marketing management. Strategic marketing takes an overall view, allocating resources and setting objectives after defining the market; marketing management develops

the product or service, prices it, tells the customer about it, and gets it to the customer. Thus, strategy must precede management. A hotel's restaurant, for example, cannot be appropriately designed without first correctly designating the market it is to serve. Exhibit 5-4 delineates the differences between strategic marketing and marketing management.

Strategic marketing addresses the long-term view of the market and the business to be in; marketing management stresses running that business and the implementation of the strategies on a daily basis. We emphasize this distinction for a specific reason. Far too many annual marketing plans fail because they are based on the wrong strategy or fail to flow from the right strategy. An excellent example of this is the strategy of a hotel to target an upscale market when that market does not exist or is already overcrowded or the product is not adequate to serve it. A marketing plan is then developed to implement the strategy and fails.

If the strategy cannot be implemented, it may be the wrong strategy. Too often a marketing plan is developed with the final conclusion drawn before the work begins and the data collected are summarily "fitted" to the conclusion. The result is a marketing plan that is both unrealistic and unworkable.

The Concept of Strategy

We begin with the standard textbook definitions of strategy and tactics, which derive directly from the military: Tactics are the way to win the battle; strategy is the way to win the war. In a simplistic example, we could demonstrate this as follows:

- *Objective:* Surround the enemy.
- *Strategy:* Take one area at a time.
- *Tactic:* Use armored tank divisions.

EXHIBIT 5-2   **The Marriott Timeline**

2004

Marriott ExecuStay hits the 30-market franchise mark; broadens reach through new agreements in Southern California, St. Louis, and Wisconsin.
MARSHA celebrates 20 years of successful service.
Ramada International opens 200th hotel in Amsterdam.
Marriott revenues total $19 billion in 2003 and $476 million in gross profits. Marriott adds more than 31,000 rooms and time share units in 2003, bringing the global system to 2,718 hotels and time share units (490,564 rooms).
500,000th room opens in London, located at the West India Quay Marriott Hotel in the Canary Wharf district of London.
Marriott Rewards welcomes its 20 millionth member.
Marriott Vacation Club International celebrates its 20th anniversary.

2003

Marriott completes the sale of its Senior Living Service Communities and Marriott Distribution Services.
Courtyard opens its 500th hotel in downtown Minneapolis.
SpringHill Suites opens its 100th hotel in Dallas-Addison, Texas.

2002

Marriott celebrates its 75th anniversary. The company now has over 2,300 hotels, 156 Senior Living Services Communities, 200,000 associates, and operations in 63 countries and territories with annual sales of $20 billion.
Marriott announces the sale/spinoff of its Senior Living Services Communities and Marriott Distribution Services.
Marriott opens its 500th extended stay hotel, representing a total of 400 Residence Inns and 100 TownePlace Suites.
Fairfield Inn opens its 500th hotel in Rogers, Arkansas.
Marriott opens its 2,500th hotel worldwide, with the completion of the 950-room JW Marriott Desert Ridge Resort & Spa in Phoenix, Arizona.
Marriott increase its North American market share to 8 percent.

2000

The 2,000th Marriott property opens in Tampa, Florida.

1990s

1990: Pathways to Independence, Marriott's Welfare to Work Program, established.
1993: The company splits into Marriott International and Host Marriott Corporation.
1995: Marriott acquires the Ritz-Carlton Hotel Company.
1997: Marriott acquires the Renaissance Hotel Group and introduces TownePlace Suites, Fairfield Suites, and Marriott Executive Residences brands.
1998: 1,500th hotel opens; sales reach $8 billion; Sodexho Alliance acquires Marriott's food service and facilities management businesses.
1999: Marriott acquires the ExecuStay corporate housing company.

1980s

1981: 100th hotel opens in Hawaii.
1982: The company acquires Host International, Inc.
1982: Marriott acquires Gino's and converts to Roy Rogers.
1983: First Courtyard hotel opens.
1984: Marriott enters the vacation time share and senior living markets.
1985: J. Willard Marriott, Sr., passes away; Marriott Distribution Center opens in Savage, Maryland.

1987: Marriott acquires Residence Inn Company and enters the lower-moderate lodging segment with Fairfield Inn.
1989: 500th hotel opens in Warsaw, Poland. Bridges: Marriott Foundation for People with Disabilities established.

1970s

1972: J. W. Marriott, Jr., is named CEO.
1973: The company obtains its first hotel management contracts.
1975: Marriott opens its first European hotel in Amsterdam, Holland.
1976: The company opens two theme parks, both called Great America, located in Santa Clara, California, and Gurnee, Illinois.
1977: The company celebrates its 50th anniversary; sales top $1 billion.
1979: A new corporate headquarters is built in Bethesda, Maryland.

1960s

1964: J. W. Marriott, Jr., is named president.
1965: Marriott Foundation established.
1967: Corporate name is changed from Hot Shoppes, Inc., to Marriott Corporation; the company opens Fairfield Farm Kitchens, a food production and purchasing facility in Beaver Heights, Maryland; In-Flite opens a facility in Venezuela; Marriott acquires Camelback Inn, its first resort property; and buys Bob's Big Boy Restaurants.
1969: Marriott's first international hotel opens in Acapulco, Mexico.

1950s

1953: Marriott stock becomes public at $10.25/share and sells out in two hours.
1955: Marriott Food Service lands its first institutional and school feeding contracts at Children's Hospital and American University; Marriott's Highway Division opens several Hot Shoppes on the New Jersey Turnpike.
1957: Marriott opens its first hotel, the 365-room Twin Bridges Motor Hotel in Arlington, Virginia.

1940s

WW II: Hot Shoppes feeds thousands of workers who move to the nation's capital to work in the defense industry.
1945: The first Hot Shoppes cafeteria is established at McLean Gardens, Washington, D.C.; Hot Shoppes lands its first government feeding contract; In-Flite lands its first airport terminal food service contract at Miami International Airport.

1930s

1934: Hot Shoppes expands to Baltimore, Maryland.
1937: Airline catering business begins at Hoover Field (currently site of the Pentagon). The division is named In-Flite Catering and serves Capital, Eastern, and American Airlines.
1939: Marriott lands its first food service management contract with the U.S. Treasury.

1920s

1927: J. Willard Marriott marries Alice Sheets in Salt Lake City, Utah, and moves to Washington, D.C. with his new bride. That spring, J. Willard and Alice open a nine-stool A&W Root Beer stand, which they later call "The Hot Shoppe."
Winter 1927/1928: Hot Mexican food items are added to the menu.
1929: Hot Shoppes, Inc., officially incorporated. Invents curb service.

Source: www.marriott.com/corporateinfo/culture/heritageTimeline.mi.

EXHIBIT 5-3	McDonald's: An Initial Loss of Strategic Leadership, Now Found

Ray Kroc is reported to have said something like, "I don't know what we'll be serving in the year 2000, but we'll be serving more of it than anybody." As America's tastes changed, McDonald's changed with them. The changes were vital, but never radical. The Golden Arches became one of the world's most recognized symbols. For 40 years, the future of McDonald's seemed assured, but as McDonald's approached its 50th birthday in 2005, there was some doubt that this was true. In fact, McDonald's may have lost some of its relevance to American culture—a culture that it helped to shape. And overseas the same thing is happening. Some facts:

- The last new successful product was Chicken McNuggets in 1983.
- Tests with pizza, veggie burgers, fajitas, pasta, McLean Deluxe, Arch Deluxe, and discount promotions have confused the public, and most were discontinued shortly after they were initiated.
- Since 1987 McDonald's share of fast-food sales in the United States has declined two percentage points to 16.2 percent even as it has increased its number of restaurants by 50 percent.
- Operating profits haven't kept up with inflation—they have risen just 2 percent in 10 years. Per store profits have declined over 20 percent in the same period, from $125,000 to $97,000.
- In two years, McDonald's stock price increased just 3 percent compared to Coca-Cola's 71 percent and Walt Disney's 78 percent, companies that changed their position, made trade-offs, and created better fits. The S&P 500 had a 63 percent increase in the same period.
- A price promotion in 1997 offering 99 cent Big Macs caused a furor among franchisees and was quickly and embarrassingly abandoned.

In short, McDonald's has been unable to use its brand strength to grow beyond its basic formula of hamburgers and french fries.

In 1997 CEO Michael Quinlan reorganized and decentralized the management team in an attempt to recreate some entrepreneurial spirit. Fundamentally, however, McDonald's didn't change. "Do we have to change?" asked Quinlan. "No, we don't have to change. We have the most successful brand in the world. We will extend our line, rather than go in more radical, different directions."

One industry observer put it this way: "McDonald's seems to have fallen into the hell that traps many of the best companies at some point in their lives. Having established a dominant position under a previous generation, it is bedeviled by a reverence for the old formulas, while its leadership takes weak steps and then denies all problems."

In 1997 top management outlined plans to improve its domestic business, calling for "value" pricing and improvements to the current menu, but no new products. They said they would restore momentum by concentrating on improving the taste of current products and reemphasizing clean restaurants and fast, accurate service.

In 1998 McDonald's announced that it would kill the year-old Arch Deluxe sandwich (designed to attract adults), which Quinlan said had exceeded all expectations when everyone knew it hadn't, and pushed franchisees to upgrade their kitchens. Made-to-order sandwiches would be the new feature based on a new computerized production system called Made for You. This system would send orders directly from the cash register to the griller or sandwich maker even before the customer had finished ordering. Heat lamps would be phased out.

In essence, McDonald's had asked, How can we sell more hamburgers? rather than What does our brand allow us to consider selling to our customers? McDonald's tried to make the same formula appeal to everyone. It could have used its credibility to develop new approaches, but it was stuck in a 50-year-old rut lacking innovation.

This all changed when Jim Cantalupo took over the company and was continued by Charles Bell and currently by Jim Skinner. The goal was to move McDonald's from being an old company selling fattening products to one that is hip and selling healthier meals. The new slogan in 2004 was "I'm Lovin' It." To attract more diet-conscious customers, it offers Adult Happy Meals that consists of bottled water and salads. The children's happy meals consist of apple slices and yogurt. Cantalupo, Bell, and Skinner also changed the focus from new store sales to increases in same-store sales by investing in upgrades and cleaning up the stores. The strategy seems to be working. The stock price moved from a low of $12 in March 2003 to $33.12 in August 2005.

This section is taken from various industry sources and trade and business publications. Direct quotes, however, are from Leonhardt, D. (1998, March 9). McDonald's. Can it regain its golden touch? *BusinessWeek*, 70–77; Jenkins, H. W., Jr. (1998, March 18). How to save McDonald's. *The Wall Street Journal*, p. A23; Stires, D. (2004, May 4). McDonald's keeps right on cookin'. *Fortune*. Retrieved from www.fortune.com/fortune/subs/print/0,15935,632557,00.html; and Buckley, N. (2004, April 20). McDonald's has big shoes to fill after Cantalupo. *The Financial Times*.

EXHIBIT 5-4	Major Differences between Strategic Marketing and Marketing Management

Point of Difference	Strategic Marketing	Marketing Management
Timeframe	Long-range; i.e., decisions have long-term implications	Day-to-day; i.e., decisions have relevance in a given financial year
Orientation	Inductive and intuitive	Deductive and analytical
Decision process	Primarily bottom-up	Mainly top-down
Relationship with environment	Environment considered ever-changing and dynamic	Environment considered constant with occasional disturbances
Opportunity sensitivity	Ongoing to seek new opportunities	Ad hoc search for a new opportunity
Organizational behavior	Achieve synergy between different components of the organization, both horizontally and vertically	Pursue interests of the decentralized unit
Nature of job	Requires high degree of creativity and originality	Requires maturity, experience, and control orientation
Leadership style	Requires proactive perspective	Requires reactive perspective
Mission	Deals with what business to emphasize	Deals with running a delineated business

Jain, S. C. (1997). *Marketing Planning and Strategy*, 5th ed., p. 141. Cincinnati: South-Western. Reprinted with permission of South-Western, a division of Thomson Learning: www.thomsonrights.com. Fax 800 730-2215.

Actually, marketing is not much different. The objective is to increase revenues. Strategy is the way to gain and keep customers; tactics are the step-by-step procedure of how to do it. For example:

- *Objective:* Increase revenues 6 percent during the next fiscal year by being perceived as the hotel of choice.
- *Strategy:* Always give customers better value.
- *Tactics:* Always have their reservation and room (tables) ready; call them by name; make sure they receive their wake-up call; have full-length mirrors and good bathroom lighting in their rooms; offer fresh-brewed coffee as soon as they sit down for breakfast; have room service delivered on time; provide complimentary Internet access from guest rooms; have the print on the menu large enough to read; offer a selection for those who are light eaters; and so forth.

From this example it can be seen that tactics flow from strategy. That means that the first thing we have to do is develop an appropriate strategy. It is the strategy that drives the firm and specifies the direction in which it is going. You might ask, If no strategy has been developed, what drives the firm? The answer is that there is always a strategy, in one way or another. If there is no explicit strategy, then there is an implicit one. In fact, too often strategies exist by default. Here's a simple example:

One of the basic tenets of marketing strategy is market segmentation, which involves dividing the total market into smaller groups of customers who have similar needs. We then select those markets that we can serve best. Suppose no one has even given this a thought, much less developed a strategy. The result is that "we'll take any customers we can get." The strategy, by default, is to take anyone as customers. Along comes a bus tour group; we take it and it fills the lobby. The result may be our corporate customers saying, "What's going on here? We thought this was a business person's hotel. Let's go somewhere else next time."

The default strategy in this case is counterproductive. That is why strategy should never be left to chance. It should be both planned and executed very carefully, although it may also emerge, as we discuss later.

Strategic Planning

The essence of **strategic planning** is "how to get from here to there." This proces follows, in short, strategic visioning and is demonstrated by the model in Exhibit 5-5. (We will explain this model more thoroughly in the rest of this chapter.)

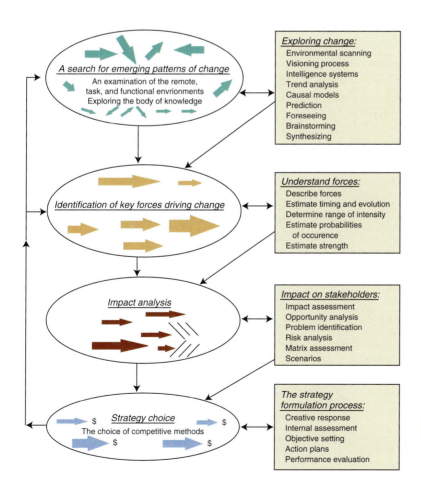

EXHIBIT 5-5   Strategic visioning model.

Source: Michael D. Olsen, Michael D. Olsen Associates, Blacksburg, VA. Used by permission.

It naturally follows that there are two things inherent in such a statement: If you want to get from "here," you have to know where "here" is; if you want to get to "there," you have to know where "there" is. In strategic planning, the first is called a situational analysis or "where we are now"; the second is called objectives or "where we want to go." Strategic planning fills the gap: How do we get from where we are now to where we want to go?

In a more formal sense, strategic planning is concerned with **environmental scanning**, estimating the impact of the environment, setting business objectives, matching products and markets, choosing competition, allocating resources, proactively planning, and choosing the competitive methods needed to reach the objectives. Although some people believe that strategic planning is complicated and difficult to understand, it is really an everyday, basic concept. We'll explain this with another simple example:

> Consider a high school graduate. Where are they now? Seventeen years old, no real skills, no profession, and certainly little chance for professional growth in a solid career path. Where do they want to be? A solid candidate for a good job in a firm that will offer opportunities for growth and advancement. Strategy? Get a good education and enhance their capabilities and potential in the business world. Tactic? Go to college.

Although most strategic planning is done at the higher levels of a business organization, this should not necessarily be the case. Strategic marketing planning is appropriate at any level. We repeat this because of the common perception to the contrary. In fact, this has been one of the major failings of strategic planning: It often takes place only at higher levels and doesn't filter down to strategic management that focuses on implementation of the strategic plan.

For example, giving the customer better value can be a strategy at any level. If this is the actual corporate strategy of a 300-property hotel chain, let's see how it translates down to the strategic management of a coffee shop in only one of those 300 units.

> The manager, a recent college graduate, thinks, "If that's the corporate strategy, then how does it affect me—how do I give better value?" She looks around and says, "Right now (situational analysis) we're just another coffee shop. What we'd like to be (objective) is the best coffee shop in town. The answer is (strategy) giving the customer better value (competitive advantage). How that is done (tactics) is always to have fresh orange juice and freshly brewed coffee, offer coffee as soon as a customer is seated for breakfast, never close off the most desirable part of the dining room no matter how slow it is, don't 'push' customers so we can turn the tables over, don't put singles next to the kitchen door, and be sure that prices are competitive."

In contrast to the coffee shop example, a fast-food operation works on volume. The objective is to maximize patronage and turnover. The strategy is to give the customer every reason to move on quickly. The tactics are to have food all ready, accept pay for food when it is picked up, and minimize table setting so the table can be ready for another party almost immediately.

This, then, is the concept of strategic planning: Decide where you are now, decide where you want to go, and develop and manage the strategy that will get you there. From that strategy flows everything else that you do, including all tactics.

The strategic marketing planning and management process has many interrelationships among the various elements and requires a systems perspective. The strategic framework model for this perspective is illustrated later in this chapter; we will first discuss the levels of strategic planning and then discuss the systems model step by step and cover each step in more detail in this and later chapters.

The Role of Strategic Planning

As stated earlier in the chapter, the essence of strategic planning is "how to get from here to there." The reason for the need to get from here to there is to ensure the long-term viability of the organization. As mentioned in the Introduction of this text, a way to ensure the viability of an organization is to achieve a competitive advantage over the firms with which the organization competes. To review, we define competitive advantage as the ability of a firm to develop and maintain distinctive competencies that enable it to capture a larger share of the market and earn higher-than-average profits. These higher-than-average profits can then be used to grow the business.

Strategic planning is used to help the organization focus on one or more of the building blocks that lead to competitive advantage. These building blocks, again discussed in the Introduction of the text, are quality, efficiency, customer responsiveness, innovation, and size. For the hospitality industry, size can refer to either the number of properties or the size of the hotel. The same can be said for restaurants. For instance, the restaurant can be very small with a small number of tables to create a feeling of intimacy, or it can be big enough to hold three or four wedding receptions at a time. An example of a large restaurant is the Wayne Manor in Wayne, New Jersey.

 Web Browsing Exercise

Look up the Wayne Manor, which is located in Wayne, New Jersey (www.thewaynemanor.com/aboutus.html). What did this website tell you? How do they balance size with intimacy? What is the Wayne Manor's strategy? Will it work? Why? Why not?

The Levels of Strategic Planning

Although we have clearly stated that **strategic thinking** and planning are necessary at every level of management, there are usually certain strategic functions at certain levels within the organization. These levels are commonly called corporate, business, and functional. To illustrate these levels, consider MGM Mirage Resorts, which owns multiple casinos around the world, including the Bellagio in Las Vegas. The corporate level refers to those whose responsibilities include determining the direction the whole organization takes. For instance, the decision for MGM Mirage Resorts to buy Mandalay Resorts occurred at the corporate level. In contrast, the business level refers to those who are involved in running the Bellagio or any one of the other casino resorts. Finally, the functional level refers to strategies directed at improving the effectiveness of functional operations within a company, such as manufacturing, marketing, materials management, research and development, and human resources. This is not to say that, depending on the business, all three levels (corporate, business, and functional) may not all come together in the same place. For example, all these strategies fall on the shoulders of Max and Greti Mennig, the owners and operators of the Restaurant Zum See in Zermatt, Switzerland. They make the corporate, business, and functional strategic decisions. Keep this in mind as you continue reading this chapter.

Corporate-Level Strategy. Strategy at the corporate level must address the issue of what business you should be in to maximize the long-run viability of the firm. This involves not only issues of position, trade-offs, and **fit**, but also how to maximize these capabilities to take advantage of one or more of the building blocks of competitive advantage. There are a variety of strategies a firm can use to ensure long-term viability. Many of these strategies will be discussed in your strategy class. However, we discuss a couple here to provide an example.

One type of strategy is **vertical integration**. This means moving backward into the production process (upstream) or forward into the distribution process (downstream) to better manage the business. The building blocks of competitive advantage most influenced by vertical integration include quality and efficiency. Suppose Max and Greti decide to make their own ice cream because they can make it better themselves (the building block is quality). This is upstream integration. Or, instead of waiting for customers to hike up the mountain to visit their restaurant, they can hire staff to deliver food to a place of their choosing (downstream). Nouvelles Frontières, a French travel agency, bought an airline and hotels (upstream) for its customers and had exclusive arrangements with tour operators and agencies (downstream) to sell its packages.

Web Browsing Exercise

Go to www.nouvelles-frontieres.fr/nf. What can you learn about the company from this website? What destinations are popular?

Exhibit 5-2 shows that Marriott opened a distribution center in 1985 to supply its businesses with the materials needed to take care of guests. According to company information, Marriott Distribution Services, based in Washington, D.C., was one of the largest limited-line distributors in the United States in 2000. It provided food and related supplies to both external customers and Marriott facilities and carried an average of 3,000 product items at each of its 13 distribution centers. This is upstream integration. However, in 2003 Marriott sold this division to Services Group of America, Inc.,[2] because it decided to focus on its core competencies—running hotels.

A second type of strategy is **diversification**. This means entering into a new business activity that complements (related) the present business or uses extra resources to enter into a different business (unrelated). Max and Greti may decide to set up a catering business (related), or they can decide to set up a ski rental business (unrelated). Entering the catering business allows them to take advantage of their core competencies (i.e., knowledge of the restaurant business) while at the same time grow their business. The additional size may provide economies of scale that will provide a competitive advantage—for example, the ability to better handle swings in demand in its core business. Entering the ski rental business may bring in extra money, but it does not take advantage of Max and Greti's knowledge of the restaurant business.

Exhibit 5-6 shows how InterContinental Hotels Group was formed from a diversification strategy of Bass Breweries. As can be seen, a change of the laws in the United Kingdom led Bass Breweries to focus on the hotel business and not the pub business.

Web Browsing Exercise

Visit IHG's website (www.ichotelsgroup.com/). What promotions are they currently running? How do you think this fits in with their strategic plan? Why? Why not?

Other strategies available at the corporate level include acquisitions, new ventures, and restructuring. All companies, especially publicly traded ones, have a mandate

EXHIBIT 5-6	History of InterContinental Hotels Group

1777 TO 1988

The origins of InterContinental Hotels Group can be traced back to 1777 when William Bass established a brewery in Burton-on-Trent, trading under his own name. The business thrived under William and his son, Michael Thomas, developing into a leading domestic brewer and exporter. In 1876 their red triangle trademark became the first trademark to be registered in the United Kingdom.

As the business grew, it actively participated in the consolidation of the industry, acquiring several well-known regional companies. Bass merged in 1967 with Charringtons in London. Each regional brewery had large pub estates, and as a result Bass became one of the largest brewers and pub owners in the country.

1989 TO 1995

In 1989 the government sought to reduce vertical integration in the brewing industry through the Beer Orders legislation, which limited the number of tied pubs that each of the major brewers could own. This signaled a major restructuring of the industry, the effects of which are still being felt and have had a profound impact on the companies involved.

The group's response was to reduce dramatically the number of pubs that it owned and focus on larger outlets, more specifically targeted toward the new growth areas of the markets, which were being created by changing social and demographic trends. At the same time, it chose to direct the cash flow generated by its more mature businesses into developing an international hotel business.

Bass already owned a small chain of hotels. But the first significant international move into the hotel industry came in 1988, with the purchase of Holiday Inns International, followed by the acquisition of the remaining North American business of Holiday Inn in 1990, already the leading midscale hotel brand in the world. In 1991 Holiday Inn Express was launched, adding a complementary brand in the limited service segment, and Crowne Plaza was launched in 1994 to move the group into the upscale market. As the business became more purely brand focused, it sold its U.S.-owned midscale hotel assets in 1997, while retaining the branding through franchise agreements.

1996 TO 1999

In 1996 Bass acquired half of the Carlsberg-Tetley brewing business in the UK, in order to form a joint venture with Carlsberg, consolidate its position in the UK, and form the platform for further overseas expansion. However, this move was blocked by the UK government and led to a renewed focus on developing the hotels and pubs divisions.

Over the next few years a number of smaller, noncore businesses were sold along with more pubs, including the group's leased pub business. Nonetheless, the pubs business grew and was becoming increasingly branded. The acquisition of Harvester in September 1995 was a turning point for the business, marking a significant commitment to the growing eating-out market.

During 1997 Bass entered the profitable U.S. upscale extended stay segment with the introduction and development of Staybridge Suites by Holiday Inn. The brand's rapid growth in the Americas demonstrates the company's ability to create and launch brands in the hotel market.

A further significant advance for the hotels division came in March 1998, with the acquisition of InterContinental. Not only did it serve as a quality hotel brand, meeting international travelers' needs, but it also took care of the 40,000 airline crew and staff as they flew the airlines' routes. InterContinental added an upper upscale brand to the hotel portfolio with an important global position and complemented the wide range of brands, encompassing the midscale and upscale markets. This brought considerable synergies and cost savings.

The acquisition of Southern Pacific Hotels Corporation (SPHC) in Australia in January 2000 confirmed Bass Hotels & Resort's position as the leading hotel company in Asia Pacific. Shortly afterward, Bass acquired Bristol Hotels & Resorts, a U.S.-based hotel management company comprising 112 hotels operating mainly under leases, giving the group a stronger management contract presence in the world's largest hotel market.

2000 TO 2004

With the pace of consolidation in the global brewing business starting to accelerate, the group saw the opportunity to realize significant value from its brewing business and entered into an agreement to sell Bass Brewers to a major Belgian brewer in June 2000, for £2.3 billion. The sale was subsequently cleared by the European Commission and completed unconditionally in August. This marked the final step in the refocusing of the group from being a vertically integrated domestic brewer to being a leading international hospitality retailer—a process that had taken over 10 years to complete. It also involved the sale of the Bass name and the subsequent name change to Six Continents to reflect better the global spread of the group's businesses.

The Britvic soft drinks business is also part of the group. Britvic is a leading UK producer of soft drinks, combining an excellent range of successful brands in the carbonated and stills sector, excellent product development, strong management, and effective marketing to address this dynamic market. Britvic's brands include Robinsons, Tango, Purdey's, J$_2$O, and Red Devil.

On October 1, 2002, Six Continents PLC announced the proposed separation of the group's hotels and soft drinks businesses (to be called InterContinental Hotels Group PLC) from the retail business (to be called Mitchells & Butlers PLC) and the return of £700 million of capital to shareholders.

This separation process was completed in April 2003, and InterContinental Hotels Group PLC (IHG) is now a distinct, discrete company, listed in the UK and the United States.

IHG is the world's most global hotel company and the largest by number of rooms. The group has more than 3,500 owned, leased, managed, and franchised hotels and approximately 538,000 guest rooms across nearly 100 countries and territories.

IHG owns a portfolio of well-recognized and respected brands, including InterContinental Hotels & Resorts, Crowne Plaza Hotels & Resorts, Hotel Indigo, Holiday Inn, Express by Holiday Inn, Holiday Inn Express, Staybridge Suites, Candlewood Suites, and Priority Club Rewards.

Source: www.ihgplc.com/aboutus/history.asp

---

to grow in order to increase shareholder value. As shown in Exhibit 5-2, Marriott used acquisitions to grow. In the luxury category, the JW Marriott brand was growing too slowly, so Marriott acquired Ritz-Carlton Hotels to take a strong position in the luxury market. This is an example of an acquisition strategy. In 1998 Marriott wanted to grow faster internationally (having already acquired Renaissance Hotels, based in Hong Kong, for the same reason) and made a bid for InterContinental Hotels. Bass Breweries of England, however, which had already acquired Holiday Inns, had the same strategy and outbid Marriott. Again, the history of Bass Breweries is shown in Exhibit 5-6.

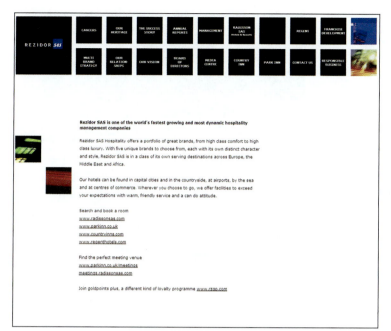

| REZIDOR SAS | CAREERS | OUR HERITAGE | THE SUCCESS STORY | ANNUAL REPORTS | MANAGEMENT | RADISSON SAS Hotels & Resorts | | REGENT | FRANCHISE DEVELOPMENT | |
| | MULTI BRAND STRATEGY | OUR RELATION- SHIPS | OUR VISION | BOARD OF DIRECTORS | MEDIA CENTRE | COUNTRY INN | PARK INN | CONTACT US | RESPONSIBLE BUSINESS | |

Rezidor SAS is one of the world's fastest growing and most dynamic hospitality management companies

Rezidor SAS Hospitality offers a portfolio of great brands, from high class comfort to high class luxury. With five unique brands to choose from, each with its own distinct character and style, Rezidor SAS is in a class of its own serving destinations across Europe, the Middle East and Africa.

Our hotels can be found in capital cities and in the countryside, at airports, by the sea and at centres of commerce. Wherever you choose to go, we offer facilities to exceed your expectations with warm, friendly service and a can do attitude.

Search and book a room
www.radissonsas.com
www.parkinn.co.uk
www.countryinns.com
www.regenthotels.com

Find the perfect meeting venue
www.parkinn.co.uk/meetings
meetings.radissonsas.com

Join goldpoints plus, a different kind of loyalty programme www.rzgp.com

EXHIBIT 5-7   Website for Rezidor SAS.

Source: Retrieved October 11, 2005, from www.rezidorsas.com. Used by permission of Rezidor SAS.

An example of a new venture strategy is Courtyard by Marriott. Marriott developed this new limited service venture called Courtyard and, eventually, franchised it for faster growth. In 2003 the 500th hotel opened in downtown Minneapolis. Marriott also started a new restaurant venture called Allie's. However, when Marriott decided to exit the restaurant business, they sold off Allie's. The sell-off of the restaurant business is an example of restructuring.

Marriott's growth provided certain economies of scale, which lead to efficiency—one of the building blocks of competitive advantage. An example of this is the MARSHA system. MARSHA stands for Marriott's Automated Reservation System for Hotel Accommodations; according to one article in *Network Computing*, "MARSHA allows guests to call in at any property and have a reservation agent allocate and book reservations." The Marriott Rewards System is also kept on this system so that guests can tabulate their points. All major airlines and travel agencies link into MARSHA by T1 and 56-Kbps connections as well.[3] As shown in Exhibit 5-2, MARSHA celebrated it 20th birthday in 2004.

General Mills restructured by divesting its restaurant unit, which became Darden Restaurants. PepsiCo did the same with Pizza Hut, Taco Bell, and KFC, now all part of a company called Yum! Brands with the stock symbol YUM. Both Darden and Yum! Brands retained their management. Thus, these are also referred to as management buyouts or spin-offs.

More strategic alliances and joint ventures occur when two or more parties get together to enhance the overall value of each. Rezidor SAS Hospitality (SIH) of Brussels wanted exposure outside of Europe and formed a strategic alliance with Radisson Hotels, which wanted exposure in Europe. Radisson SAS now has rights to the brand in Europe, the Middle East, and North Africa. Radisson has the rest of the world. Both share the same worldwide reservation system (Pierre), and together they have tripled their marketing clout through economies of scope. The website of Rezidor Hotels, shown in Exhibit 5-7, promotes the brands of both companies.

Four Seasons found it could not handle the growth of the Regent brand after buying it and formed a strategic alliance with Carlson Hospitality (owners of Radisson), which now has all rights to the expansion and growth of Regent. US Franchise Systems (USFS) was started in 1995 by acquiring Microtel. In 1996 it formed a joint venture with Hawthorne Suites (then controlled by the Pritzker family) to expand that brand and, in 1998, acquired all the rights to the brand. It later did the same thing with Best Inns. In 2000 USFS was purchased by business interests of the Pritzker family, who are the owners of Hyatt Hotels and Resorts.

These kinds of corporate-level strategies, although financially oriented, are definitely corporate marketing strategies. Although they may reduce costs, provide better management, and have other benefits, their primary objective is to reach different markets or the same markets differently and gain competitive advantage. The building block on which these strategies focus is size. This is **strategic visioning** and leadership. These companies saw their industries consolidating, understood the forces of branding, analyzed the opportunities and risks, and chose expanded branding and international growth as prime competitive methods.

Business-Level Strategy.   Business-level strategy is reflected in the overall competitive theme of a company and

EXHIBIT 5-8 Formule 1 has proven that cost leadership strategies work.

Source: Retrieved October 11, 2005, from www.accor.com/gb/groupe/activities/ hotellerie/marques/formule1.asp. Used by permission.

EXHIBIT 5-9 Four Seasons differentiates on their level of service, as exhibited in this advertisement.

Source: www.fourseasons.com. Photograph by Robb Aaron Gordon. Used by permission.

the way it positions itself in the marketplace.* We will cover this in more detail in a moment in connection with the strategic marketing systems model. For now, we take a broader view based on Porter's three generic competitive strategies at the business level.[4] These three approaches are cost leadership, differentiation, and focus.

Cost leadership strategy The cost leadership strategy means outperforming competitors by producing goods and services at a lower cost. This enables a business to charge a lower price but realize the same profits or charge a similar price but make higher profits. The low-cost leader chooses a low level of product differentiation or uniqueness. It usually targets a mass market, and its distinctive competency is the management of the materials and production process. Southwest Airlines has proven that this strategy works. McDonald's and Burger King also come to mind. So do Microtel of the United States and Formule 1 of France (an Accor brand) (see Exhibit 5-8), both low-budget properties with tremendous cost savings built into their design as well as their operations.

For instance, Formule 1 is designed so that the bathroom, which is shared by other guest rooms, is self-cleaning and self-sanitizing. In the bedroom, top and bottom sheets are sown together at the bottom of the sheet to make it simple and quick to make the bed. Guests get their room keys by entering their credit cards in outdoor kiosks. Cus-

tomers may not be totally happy with these products, but they are attracted by the lower prices. Any customer loyalty is likely based on that factor.

Differentiation strategy The differentiation strategy is designed to achieve a competitive advantage by creating a product or service that is perceived to be unique in some meaningful way—with "meaningful way" defined as the preferences of customers, not of the firm. This strategy may target a number of different market segments and may often charge a premium price. Firms that practice this strategy often have distinctive competencies in research, development, sales, and marketing because all are needed to see in the market what other firms cannot.

Planet Hollywood falls into this category. So, too, do all-suite hotels and all-inclusive resorts. Four Seasons differentiates on its level of service (Exhibit 5-9). Smith & Wollensky differentiates on the quality of its steaks (Exhibit 5-10). Rosewood Hotels differentiates on the fact that all of its hotels are

---

*This also applies to the strategic business units (SBUs) of a company, which, is a sense, are companies by themselves, but are subject to the corporate-level strategies discussed earlier.

If steak were a religion,
this would be its cathedral.

"A steakhouse to end all arguments."
The New York Times

"The quintessential New York steakhouse."
Gourmet

"...perhaps the best sirloin of my life..."
Chicago Tribune

Smith & Wollensky.

Gift certificates available. Call 877-783-2555 or visit any restaurant.

Boston | Chicago | Columbus | Dallas | Houston | Las Vegas | Miami Beach | New Orleans | New York City | Philadelphia | Washington, D.C.

The Smith & Wollensky Restaurant Group, Inc. is a publicly traded company. NASDAQ symbol: SWRG | www.smithandwollensky.com

EXHIBIT 5-10 Smith & Wollensky differentiates on the quality of its steaks in this advertisement.

Source: The Smith & Wollensky Restaurant Group, Inc. Used by permission.

There are no formulas here.
It's a different culture, a different world.
It's an individual experience,
every time. Is it possible to have
more than one trip of a lifetime?

LAS VENTANAS · AL PARAISO · A ROSEWOOD RESORT   CANEEL BAY · A ROSEWOOD RESORT   LITTLE DIX BAY · A ROSEWOOD RESORT   JUMBY BAY · A ROSEWOOD RESORT   ACQUALINA · A ROSEWOOD RESORT

A SENSE OF PLACE®

THE CARLYLE New York · HOTEL SEIYO GINZA Tokyo · THE MANSION ON TURTLE CREEK Dallas · LAS VENTANAS AL PARAISO Los Cabos, Mexico
HOTEL CRESCENT COURT Dallas · CANEEL BAY St. John, USVI · LITTLE DIX BAY Virgin Gorda, BVI · JUMBY BAY Antigua, West Indies
AL FAISALIAH HOTEL Riyadh · HOTEL AL KHOZAMA Riyadh · KING PACIFIC LODGE Princess Royal Island, BC, Canada
CORNICHE Jeddah (Opening Early 2006) · ACQUALINA Sunny Isles, Miami Beach (Opening February 2006)

CONTACT YOUR TRAVEL PROFESSIONAL. CALL 888-ROSEWOOD OR VISIT WWW.ROSEWOODHOTELS.COM.

ROSEWOOD
HOTELS & RESORTS
CELEBRATING
25 YEARS

EXHIBIT 5-11 This advertisement shows how Rosewood Hotels differentiates on the uniqueness of its hotels.

Source: Rosewood Hotels & Resorts. Used by permission.

unique (Exhibit 5-11). Customer loyalty in these cases is based, in part, on these unique characteristics. The difficulty with this strategy may be the long-term ability to maintain the perceived uniqueness of the product or service.

Tourism Marketing Application

The Orient Pacific Century Company, a marketing research firm in Asia (www.orientpacific.com), conducted a study on behalf of the Malaysian Tourism Promotion Board to understand consumers' perceptions of different destinations in Asia. The study was conducted in 1998, but was not allowed to be made public until 2003. The study found the following perceptions of travelers and tourist agents from the United States, Japan, India, Germany, Australia, the United Kingdom, and Sweden for various destinations in Asia:

- Singapore was perceived by many of those polled as "clean, modern, and safe."
- "Culture" was perceived as China's dominant image and attraction.
- Malaysia was perceived as "multicultural with many beaches."
- Thailand had a brand image of "exotic, fun, and friendly people."

(www.asiamarketresearch.com/columns/tourism-branding.htm, retrieved January 24, 2005)

It is one thing to say "differentiate"; it is another thing to do it. There are many who say that hotel rooms and airline seats have become commodities, like a pound of salt, in that there is very little left to differentiate between them within the same product class. It is at this point, however, that marketing imagination comes to the forefront. Sometimes the way a company manages its marketing may be the most powerful form of differentiation. For example, the Palms in Las Vegas is like many casinos in Las Vegas. However, its marketing efforts have created the impression that it is the "hip" place to be. The MTV show *The Real World* was filmed there, and many celebrity sightings are always reported, which reinforces the "hip" image.

Focus strategy The focus strategy is aimed at serving the needs of a limited customer group or segment, one or a few, based on any kind of distinctive competency. Using a focus strategy, a company specializes in some way. This may be by differentiation or as a cost leader, but in a more specialized sense than when those two are used as a core generic strategy. Normally a large hotel could not compete with the 360-room Four Seasons in New York, which targets a smaller and more select market of individuals. By creating the Towers, which are 173 of the total 890 rooms, the New York Palace was able to create a specialized product offering to compete directly with the smaller luxury hotels of New York City. Other unique hotels fit this category of a focus strategy such as the Pierre in New York; the Ritz or Bristol in Paris; the Claridge, Savoy, and Connaught in London; and so forth.

Other examples of firms that pursue a focus strategy are Hotwire.com and Priceline.com. These are Internet companies that focus on booking travel for those who are brand agnostic. That is, consumers who use these services are focusing their decision criteria on price alone. Chapter 19 provides more information on these firms.

Some companies use both a cost leadership and a differentiation strategy. Southwest Airlines is an example of such a company. Its low cost comes about because of the tactics the company uses to lower the variable and overhead cost of flying airplanes. One such tactic, in addition to those discussed earlier, is flying the same kind of aircraft. Southwest's differentiation strategy focuses on the use of point-to-point fares instead of the hub-and-spoke system.

Those pursing a focus strategy may also use either a cost leadership or a differentiation strategy, so that in many cases there is not a clear-cut distinction. This does not, however, void the need to determine which strategy to use. Without doing so, a company may easily be "caught in the middle," to its detriment.

Firms that are caught in the middle have no defined strategy; as such, they never know which opportunities to respond to and which to neglect. In addition, the consumer is often confused.

Functional-Level Strategy. Functional-level strategies are aimed at improving the effectiveness of functional operations. Here we will discuss, again in a generic sense, what is commonly referred to as the **value chain**. Each activity in the value chain adds value to the final offering of the product/service, presentation, communication, and distribution.[5]

As discussed in the introduction to this text, value chain activities are divided into two parts: primary and support activities. The primary activities pertain to the physical creation of the product or service. These are manufacturing and marketing. Marketing is a primary activity because marketing connects the customer to the product or service. The support activities allow the primary activities to take place. These are infrastructure, human resources, research and development, and materials management.

Similar to strategies developed at the corporate and business levels, the strategies that pertain to the value chain activities also focus on the generic building blocks of competitive advantage. Exhibit 5-12 provides an example of how the different functional areas can impact the competitive advantage of a firm. For instance, the human resources area can focus on total quality management and "six sigma" initiatives to build quality as a competitive advantage. Ritz-Carlton did this and won the Malcolm Baldrige National Quality Award twice; once in 1992 and then again in 1999.

The materials management function can improve both quality and efficiency by reducing the number of suppliers and purchasing for multiple organizations rather than one, which provides economy of scale. For instance, the hotel companies Hyatt Hotels, InterContinental, ClubCorp USA, Marriott, and Fairmont Hotels & Resorts joined together to form Avendra—a firm that provides products to the hospitality industry. Avendra also supplies consulting services to those who wish to buy such products and services. As they say on their website (www.avendra.com):

> Avendra's purchasing programs give you access to a $2 billion supply chain of goods and services. Avendra has over 50 contracting experts who work deep into the supply chain, going beyond the distributor to negotiate attractive pricing with manufacturers and sometimes raw material suppliers. Avendra's purchasing programs span every aspect of: Food & Beverage, Rooms Operations, Engineering, Golf Pro Shop, Golf Grounds Maintenance, Spa Equipment and Products, Administrative, Professional & Financial Services, Gift Shop & Retail and Replenishment (replacement kitchen equipment and decorative furnishings).[6]

The focus of this book is how the marketing function can be guided by strategies and tactics to develop a competitive advantage. Review Exhibit 3 in the Introduction of the book to see how the chapters in this book address each specific building block of competitive advantage.

Emergent Strategies

All strategies are not carefully and rationally planned and followed. In fact, many seem to emerge in response to unforeseen circumstances. These are called **emergent strategies**. Henry Mintzberg, a strategy expert at McGill University, said that strategy is more than what a company intends or plans to do; it is also what it actually does, which may be more appropriate than what was intended.[7]

Mintzberg also talked about crafting strategy and likened this to working at a potter's wheel. As the wheel turns, the potter crafts the vase with his hands, slowly de-

EXHIBIT 5-12 **Building Blocks of Competitive Advantage**

Size	Value Chain	Efficiency	Quality	Innovation	Customer Responsivenes
A	Infrastructure	1. Provide company-wide commitment 2. Facilitate cooperation between functions	1. Provide leadership and commitment to quality 2. Find ways to measure quality 3. Set goals and create incentives 4. Get input from employees 5. Encourage cooperation between functions	1. Overall project management 2. Facilitate cross-functional cooperation	1. Through leadership by example; build a company-wide commitment to customer responsiveness
B	Manufacturing	1. Pursue cost economics 2. Implement flexible manufacturing systems	1. Shorten production runs 2. Trace defects to source	1. Cooperate with R&D in designing products that are easy to manufacture 2. Work with R&D on developing process innovations	1. Achieve customization by implementing flexible manufacturing 2. Achieve rapid response through flexible manufacturing
C	Marketing	1. Adapt aggressive marketing to ride down experience curve 2. Limit defections by building brand loyalty	1. Focus on the customer 2. Provide customer feedback on quality	1. Provide market information to R&D 2. Work with R&D on developing new products	1. Know the customer 2. Communicate customer feedback to appropriate functions
D	R&D	1. Design products for ease of manufacture 2. Seek process innovations	1. Design products/services for ease of manufacture/use	1. Develop new products/ processes	1. Bring customers to the product development process
E	Materials Management	1. Implement JIT systems	1. Reduce number of suppliers 2. Help suppliers implement TQM 3. Trace defects to area responsible		1. Develop logistics systems capable of responding quickly to unanticipated customer demand
F	Human Resources	1. Training to build skills 2. Self-managing teams 3. Pay for performance	1. Institute TQM training programs 2. Organize employees into quality teams		1. Develop training programs that make employees think of themselves as customers

A: Control processes to manage financial side of business; e.g., SAP, PeopleSoft
B: Reduce costs because of purchasing cloud
C: Test on one or two restaurants/hotels before introducing to the system; learn from creativity at one property and introduce to all
D: Create loyalty program to track purchases across different locations
E: Proces innovations
F: Provide opportunities for promotion from within

Intended Strategy

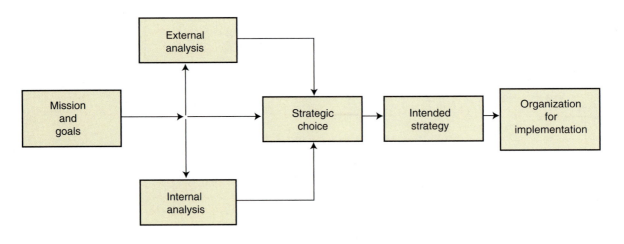

Emergent Strategy

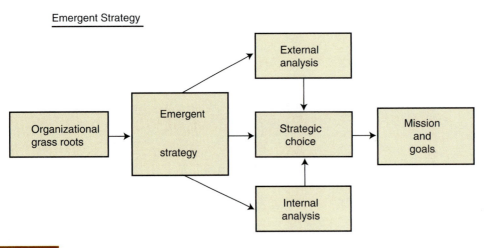

EXHIBIT 5-13 Intended and emergent strategies.

veloping the final product in a form that he likes.[8] In the final analysis, strategies are probably a combination of planned, crafted, and emergent forces. All incorporate strategic thinking, but the formulation of intended strategies is essentially a top-down process, crafted strategies are ongoing adjustments to strategies, and emergent strategies derive from a bottom-up process. Exhibit 5-13 shows the intended and emergent strategies; **crafted strategies** would apply to either.

Undertanding the Environment

As discussed earlier in this chapter, a careful assessment of the environment is necessary before any strategic plans can be implemented. As the world's economies become more intertwined and as the world becomes flat—a phrase coined by Thomas Friedman, an op-ed writer for the *New York Times*—the environment of companies has become larger and more complex than ever before. Events in faraway places have an impact close to home. Customer needs and wants are also ever changing, creating an environment that is dynamic and demanding.

Marketing leadership means planning for the future. Trying to determine what the future holds in store has come to be known as environmental scanning. This simply means asking, What is going on out there in the environment that is likely to impact our business? What this also means is having an awareness of the need to be proactive, rather than reactive, and the need to constantly perceive what is happening and to anticipate what will occur. Environmental scanning as a systematic approach is an essential leadership tool. All of this, of course, is relative to the competition, which is also an environmental force.

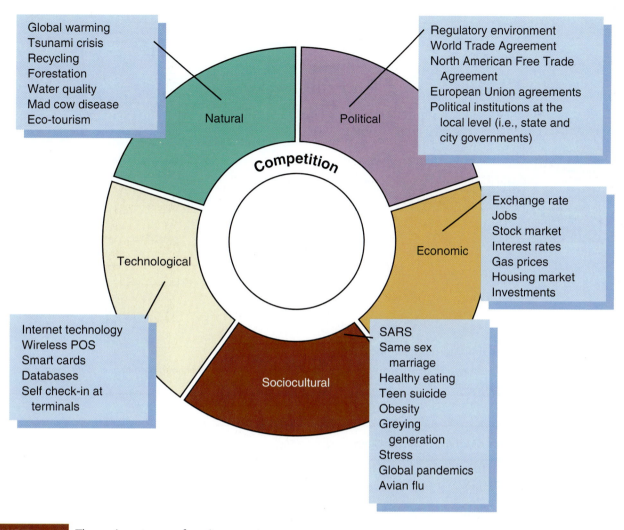

Global warming
Tsunami crisis
Recycling
Forestation
Water quality
Mad cow disease
Eco-tourism

Regulatory environment
World Trade Agreement
North American Free Trade
    Agreement
European Union agreements
Political institutions at the
    local level (i.e., state and
    city governments)

Exchange rate
Jobs
Stock market
Interest rates
Gas prices
Housing market
Investments

Internet technology
Wireless POS
Smart cards
Databases
Self check-in at
    terminals

SARS
Same sex
    marriage
Healthy eating
Teen suicide
Obesity
Greying
    generation
Stress
Global pandemics
Avian flu

Natural
Political
Economic
Competition
Technological
Sociocultural

EXHIBIT 5-14 The various types of environments.

Source: Ian W. McVitty, Jr. Used by permission.

Types of Environments

Macro environmental forces, other than competition, can be broadly classified into technological, political, economic, sociocultural, and natural (also known as the ecological) environments. Exhibit 5-14 details some examples of macro environmental forces, each of which will be discussed in detail.

It must be noted that these components are dynamic and often tied to each other. The major task of environmental scanning is not only to identify those elements that will affect the firm, but also to assess the nature of the effect. A favorable effect is an opportunity, whereas an unfavorable effect is often a threat. Exhibit 5-15 is a model demonstrating the flow of environmental scanning information to the development of strategy and marketing planning. Exhibit 5-16 details the steps of environmental planning.

Technological Environment

Technology impacts both how managers run their businesses and how consumers use these businesses. For instance, consider customer relationship management. Customer relationship management would not have occurred had there not been advances in computer hard disk storage. The advances increased both the amount of storage available and the price of this storage. To put this in perspective, consider that in the late 1980s a personal computer with a 20-megabyte hard drive was considered large. "In the latter half of the 1990s, hard drives with capacities of 1 gigabyte and greater became available. As of early 2005, the 'smallest' desktop hard disk in production has a capacity of 40 gigabytes, while the largest-capacity internal drives are a half terabyte (500 gigabytes), with external drives at or exceeding one terabyte."[9]

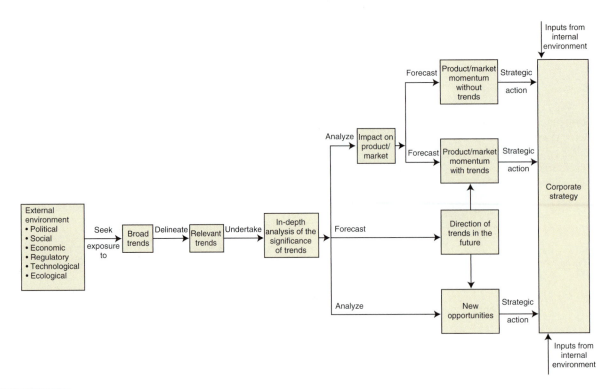

EXHIBIT 5-15 Linking environmental scanning to marketing.

Source: Jain, S. C. (1997). Marketing planning and strategy (5th ed.). Cincinnati: South-Western, 141. Reprinted with permission of South-Western, a division of Thomson Learning: www.thomsonrights.com. Fax 800 730-2215.

EXHIBIT 5-16 **The Steps of Environmental Scanning**

1. WATCH FOR BROAD TRENDS

Examples of broad trends are the American change in social mores regarding drinking, smoking, later marriages, two-income families, increased travel, diet consciousness, and "grazing" eating habits. Even locally, broad trends may occurring. For example, as more New Yorkers bought second homes in Vermont, the demand for better restaurants there increased dramatically. In Europe and Asia, more vacation time and discretionary income are examples of broad trends.

2. DETERMINE RELEVANT TRENDS

Not everything that happens in the environment is relevant, nor can an organization adapt to everything that is relevant. The problem is determining what is relevant and what is irrelevant. Certainly, there are no hard-and-fast rules. Creativity, imagination, and farsightedness play important roles in this process. Some people are better at this than others, and these people should be singled out. Another method is to circulate a short memo to key people (these could very well include line employees who are close to the action) and ask for reactions.

3. ANALYZE THE IMPACT

Assuming relevance, what is the possible impact of the change, both sooner and later? Analyze it in terms of product, price, target market, competition, cost, employee attitude, and other variables that could be affected. Does it present a threat or an opportunity? If it is a threat, can it be turned into an opportunity? Again, get reactions from key people and from line employees where appropriate. At the same time, beware of those who automatically resist change and will try to minimize any impact. Two examples of very noticeable trends that were virtually ignored for years by many hoteliers were the increase of single women travelers and the price sensitivity to increasing rack rates. Substantial competitive advantage was gained by those who acted early on these trends, such as those who moved into the middle-tier market.

4. FORECAST DIRECTION

This is a difficult stage. One method is to use people to develop scenarios. For example, when the forthcoming increase in women travelers became apparent, companies might have brought together groups of its women employees to do this. Although that does not constitute scientific research, it is a start. The general manager or marketing director of an individual hotel could do the same, as could the manager of a restaurant. Another method is to use an outside consultant who is unconstrained by past experiences and personal biases. Intuitive reasoning by one person alone should not be used. That person's view may be too narrow—for example, one might see the marketing impact but not the financial implications or vice versa. Alternatively, one's impact may be clouded by one's own set of values, beliefs, experiences, likes, and dislikes. Playing off opposites may not lead to consensus, but it can certainly help in getting all viewpoints. This helps particularly when management may perceive a trend but can't conceive of its relationship or impact. Serious research is another way to develop forecasting accuracy.

5. ASSESS OPPORTUNITY

Often it is too easy to look at the bad side of things, such as the 1986 tax act, the banning of happy hours, the raising of drinking ages, and the banning of smoking. Look too for the opportunities. Remember that necessity is the mother of invention.

6. RELATE THE OUTCOME

Relate the outcome of the preceding five steps to the marketing strategy or marketing plan, now, next year, and five years from now. Are changes needed? If so, what are the full implications? Environmental scanning is too important to any organization to be approached haphazardly. A systematic method is needed to fully use this critical marketing tool.

EXHIBIT 5-17 Wyndham ByRequest allows customers to specify what they want in their hotel room when they arrive.

Source: Retrieved October 11, 2005, from www.wyndham.co/wbr/join.wnt?. Used by permission of Wyndham Worldwide.

Tourism Marketing Application

In order for a foreign traveler to enter the United States if she or he is not a citizen of one of 27 countries that are members of the VWP (visa waiver program), a nonimmigrant visa will be needed. It is a hassle to obtain such a visa, and the cost is $100. Those who are citizens of one of the 27 VWP countries will be required to present passports that contain biometric identifiers in order to enter the United States. According to the Travel Industry Association of America (TIA) 13.8 million visitors currently come from VWP countries. It is not known how many countries have biometric identifiers in their passports. Countries that are not members of the VWP have until October 2006 to become members; otherwise their citizens will need visas. (This information comes from a report by the Travel Industry Association of America and appeared in *Travel Insights:* August 2005, Vol. 1, page 7.)

The advent of inexpensive mass computer storage has enabled management to collect large amounts of information about its guests, which can then be used to customize the stay for the guest. An example of such customization is the Wyndham ByRequest program. This program, shown in Exhibit 5-17, allows customers to specify what they want in their hotel room when they arrive. Although Wyndham requires the guest to input this information, firms such as Four Seasons and Ritz-Carlton collect it automatically.

Technology can also create and destroy businesses. The rise of the Internet as a distribution channel is perhaps the most obvious example of this. Firms such as Expedia.com, Hotwire.com, and Travelocity were not around when the first edition of this text was published. There were also many more travel agents back then than there are today. According to Yesawich, Pepperdine, Brown & Russell/Yankelovich Partners' 2005 *National Business Travel MONITOR*, almost 7 out of 10 business travelers now use the Internet to plan some aspect of business trips.[10] The comparable percentage for leisure travelers is just over 60 percent. The Internet has provided consumers with an infinite number of choices, as well as access to large amounts of information—information that used to be available only through travel agents.

While technological advances have brought other benefits to organizations, such as better and faster elevators, self-service kiosks, immediate credit card approval, electronic door locks, and many other amenities, it is the impact of technology on consumer behavior with which hospitality marketing executives need to be most concerned. Marketing executives must determine whether a technological solution can be used to improve the nontechnological amenity and thereby increase customer satisfaction. For instance, when the guest states that she would like a phone on the desk, she is really stating that she would like a phone that is more accessible. Perhaps putting a portable in the room would better suit her needs versus two traditional phones. Similarly, the additional data line accessible to the desk can best be met by a wireless solution. Finally, the desire for express check-in/checkout is currently being met by self-service kiosks, as evidenced in Exhibit 5-18.

 Web Browsing Exercise

Go to your favorite search engine and type in the words "technological impacts" or "impact of technology." Choose one of the sites listed, read the information, and be prepared to report to the class on what you discovered and the implications for the hospitality industry.

Political Environment

The political environment refers to the rules and regulations that can either encourage growth and trade or impede it. One group that helps monitor and set the rules and regulations of trade is the World Trade Organization. As described on its website, "the World Trade Organization

EXHIBIT 5-18	Hilton Hawaiian Offers Guests Self-Service Hotel Check-In at Honolulu International Airport

Hilton Hawaiian Village® Beach Resort & Spa and the Honolulu International Airport partnered in 2004 to become the first hotel and airport in the United States to offer self-service kiosks that allow Hilton guests to check into the hotel and get their room keys—before they even claim their baggage and leave the airport.

Hilton installed four kiosks at the airport, two each in Baggage Claim areas "G" and "H," which serve United, Continental, Northwest and American Airlines. The kiosks are readily identifiable with Hilton signage.

Hilton and IBM developed the kiosk hardware and software and began testing it in lobbies of selected hotels on the U.S. mainland in January 2004. Hilton installed 100 kiosks in 45 hotels in 2004. However, Honolulu International was the first airport in the nation with hotel self-service kiosks. Hilton Hawaiian Village also installed three kiosks in its main lobby to provide guests with an alternative to the high touch service associated with a traditional front desk check-in. The kiosks may also be used for check-out or as a private check-in solution for large groups.

"We are delighted to work with the team of the Honolulu International Airport and Hawaii Department of Transportation on this important leap forward in the travel and tourism industry," said Gerhart Seirbert, area vice president and managing director of Hilton Hotels Corporation—Hawaii. "Cooperative efforts such as this are yet another example of the commitment by the state and the tourism industry to keep Hawaii at the forefront of customer service and technology."

The kiosks function in much the same way as airline self-service kiosks for air travelers using e-tickets. After inserting a credit card for identification purposes, guests follow a set of simple on-screen instructions and utilize the touch screens to check into the hotel. The kiosk displays the traveler's reservation information, offers a room based on the customer's known preferences, which the customer can accept or change, issues a room key and provides printed room directions and information. The kiosks can also offer guests the opportunity to upgrade to more premium accommodations than originally reserved, should the guest desire.

Hilton guest service agents are on-hand at the airport to answer questions and assist guests in the check-in process. Hilton's long-term commitment to personal service and a warm welcome adds to the convenience, control, and efficiency the kiosk check-in provides. Guest service agents also have access to Hilton's entire technology platform OnQ via Xybernaut Atigo wireless, handheld computers.

At the end of the stay, the traveler can checkout at a kiosk in the same fashion by reviewing and confirming their bill and printing out a receipt for their records. At checkout customers can also change their payment credit card, enter Hilton HHonors® and airline frequent flier account numbers, and request an email copy of their receipt.

"This is the trend of the future," said Seibert. "Seasoned travelers, whether on business or vacation, value time and convenience. At Hilton, we continue to explore new technologies to meet their needs and we hope to roll out this technology in other locations around the country in the future."

"These kiosks are an exciting addition to an array of high-tech services we already provide our guests at Hilton Hawaiian Village," continued Seibert. "With high-speed internet access in place in all of our guest rooms, wireless internet access in many of our meeting and public areas, and an impressive array of technology-based services throughout the resort, even the most tech-savvy guest can stay connected at the Village."

Source: gohawaii.about.com/od/oahulodging/a/hiltonhv090804a.htm. Used by permission of Hilton Hotels.

(WTO) is the only international organization dealing with the global rules of trade between nations. Its main function is to ensure that trade flows as smoothly, predictably and freely as possible."[11] The political environment is particularly critical for large and multinational companies in many areas of the world because in addition to the WTO, each government also sets trade rules. In India, for example, foreign corporations can now hold more than 50 percent ownership in a business, but only with prior approval of the finance minister. To invest in a business in India, non-Indian firms can only do so in the following way:

1. Through financial collaborations
2. Through joint ventures and technical collaborations
3. Through capital markets via Euro issues
4. Through private placements or preferential allotments[12]

Foreign direct investment (FDI) is not permitted in the following industrial sectors:

1. Arms and ammunition
2. Atomic energy
3. Railway transport
4. Coal and lignite
5. Mining of iron, manganese, chrome, gypsum, sulfur, gold, diamonds, copper, and zinc

In another example, consider the People's Republic of China. The opening of China led to many opportunities for both hotels and fast-food companies. In 2004 there were more than 1,000 KFC restaurants in China, and the number is increasing at an annual rate of 200 per year.[13] Of course, it is not just U.S. companies creating businesses outside the United States. Companies based outside the United States have also expanded into the United States. The prime example is Accor, which is a French company. In March 2005, 17 percent of Accor sales came from North America. Accor operates 1,248 hotels in North America: 10 Sofitel, 1 Novotel, 850 Motel 6, 40 Studio 6, and 347 Red Roof Inns.[14]

Government regulations that occur within a nation's borders can either be taken advantage of or counteracted. That is, the firm can use the rules to their advantage as Barry Sternlicht did when he used regulations on real estate investment trusts (REITs) to form Starwood Hotels. The lobbying actions of many companies against potential regulation are an example of at-

---

| EXHIBIT 5-19 | Swedish Hotel and Restaurant Association's (SHR) Political Objectives |

The hotel and restaurant industry is a highly staff-intensive industry and as Sweden is a country with high taxes (in particular when it comes to employers' contributions), staff-related costs constitute an unreasonably large portion of a company's overall costs. *SHR therefore demands a reduction in employers' contribution.*

Restaurant VAT [value-added tax] is an unjust and excessive tax, which distorts the general view of competition between restaurants and food stores. When a store can sell a lunch meal at only 12 percent VAT while the restaurant around the corner must pay 25 percent, the result is far from competition on equal terms. Sweden has, together with Denmark, Europe's highest restaurant VAT. *SHR demands that the restaurant VAT be lowered.*

Companies in the traditional manufacturing industry are fully exempt from paying energy tax. Not so hotels and restaurants, however, who have to pay the same tax as private households. Factory-made meatballs are therefore exempt from taxation while restaurants pay tax for the same manufacturing process. *SHR demands equal terms for the manufacturing industry and hotels and restaurant companies with regard to energy tax.*

Where it comes to property tax, the situation is similar to energy tax. Properties with hotel or restaurant operations pay 1 percent of the assessment value in tax while the tax on industry premises is 0.5 percent of the assessment value. *SHR demands equal terms for the manufacturing industry and hotels and restaurant with regard to property tax.*

Sweden has Europe's highest tax on alcohol. This has led to an increase in both legal imports of alcoholic beverages from our neighboring countries as well as a strong increase in smuggled goods and home-distilled alcohol. For the Swedish government this means losses in tax income and less control over how and where people consume alcohol. For the restaurant industry, this means intolerable competition from the illegal market. *SHR therefore demands the tax on alcohol to be lowered.*

The limit for business-hospitality deductions was reduced in two stages in the latter half of the 1990s. Today it is down to SEK 90 [approximately US $11.90]. Business lunches or dinners cannot possibly be accommodated within this limit and if this creates a scenario where businesses refrain from entertaining clients at restaurants, the restaurant business will, of course, suffer in consequence. *SHR demands a more realistic level for the hospitality deductions.*

Sweden is a long way behind other EU countries when it comes to the development of its tourism industry. Our politicians have found it hard to view tourism as one of Sweden's key industries, despite the fact that it employs well over 100,000 people and, in terms of exports, exceeds Swedish exports of pharmaceuticals, for example. The Swedish government's allocation for marketing the country is much smaller than the other Scandinavian countries. *We also demand that the state allocation for marketing Sweden as a tourist country be raised to the same level as our Scandinavian neighbors.*

Source: Retrieved September 15, 2003 from www.shr.se/shr.html?c5171&ni5267&location51. Used by permission of Swedish Hotel & Restaurant Association.

---

tempts to counteract specific legislation. Within the United States, both the National Restaurant Association and the American Hotel & Lodging Association maintain lobbyists in Washington, D.C., to fight taxes and minimum wage laws and lobby for a greater emphasis on tourism. Consider the case of Sweden. The information presented in Exhibit 5-19 is from the website of the Swedish Hotel and Restaurant Association (SHR), which is trying to reduce the tax burden paid by restaurants and hotels, clearly a political decision.

State and provincial politics can be equally important. Florida (United States), Ontario (Canada), the Loire Valley (France), Algarve (Portugal), Costa del Sol (Spain), and the Bosporus (Turkey) are examples of locations where state and provincial politics have had major impacts on helping or impeding tourism.

Local politics are also equally critical. No operator can afford to ignore them. When the state of Louisiana licensed a casino in New Orleans, the local restaurant association lobbied to prevent the casino from having any substantial food and beverage services that would compete with existing local restaurants. The casino was also forced to restrict the number of hotel rooms it could build. At the even more local level, politics—town, village, or city—control such things as liquor licenses, zoning variances, building permits, and hours of operation.

Tourism Marketing Application

Tourism experts project that the requirement of a passport to enter the United States from Canada and Mexico starting January 1, 2008, will have a huge impact on tourism in the United States because the majority of residents of those countries do not have passports. The expectation is that, rather than going through the aggravation of obtaining a passport, they will simply stay in their own country. Cruise operators are also worried that U.S. passengers will stay home rather than go through the hassle of getting a passport—which they will be required to have in order to reenter the United States.

Web Browsing Exercise

Pick any country in the world. Using your favorite search engine, find the rules and regulations for starting a business in that country. Be prepared to answer the following questions:

1. Can a foreigner own more than 50 percent of a business?
2. Can the profits be sent out of the country?
3. Are the laws and regulations business friendly? Why? Why not?
4. What type of rights do employees have?
5. What are the tax rates?

Economic Environment

Many of the economic factors that affect any business include recessions, inflation, employment levels, interest rates, the price of oil, and personal discretionary income. One that has a particularly significant impact on international travel is the fluctuation in currency values. For example, if the U.S. dollar is strong relative to other international currencies, it means that items in the United States are more expensive than the same items in other countries; as such, the United States is a less attractive place to visit. In the late 1990s, when the U.S. dollar was worth about twice the Canadian dollar, Americans flocked to Canada for the bargains on everything from ski vacations to Canadian fashions, while many Canadians decided to "visit" their own country. In 2005, however, the situation changed. The U.S. dollar was at an all-time low against the euro and the Canadian dollar. For Canadians, America became less expensive. For Europeans, America became a very inexpensive place to visit while Europe became very expensive for Americans. To make Europe more affordable to American meeting planners, InterContinental Hotels & Resorts ran a promotion of $1 = €1. This is shown in Exhibit 5-20.

Price resistance is another economic factor impacting the hospitality industry. The expense account customers whom many hoteliers had classified as "non-price-sensitive" are now resisting higher prices. Corporate controllers have forced cutbacks in expense accounts, and organizational travel planners and buyers are seeking reduced-price contracts with both airlines and hotel companies. Corporate travel planners reduce airline costs by negotiating a flat per mile charge per ticket used. Under such arrangements, tickets cost the company the same per mile from New York to Paris as from New York to Boston. Hotel costs are reduced by the same travel managers who choose two or three hotels in a given travel destination. Once rates are negotiated with these properties, they are placed on a directory for use by company travelers, who can use only the selected properties if they wish to have their hotel expenses reimbursed.

Sociocultural Environment

The sociocultural environment refers to the personal beliefs, aspirations, values, attitudes, opinions, lifestyles, interpersonal relationships, religion, and social structure of the members of a society. Understanding sociocultural trends is critical to the hospitality industry because much of the hospitality experience is dependent on such trends. An example is the low-carbohydrate trend that occurred in the United States in the early 2000s. This trend impacted not only the frequency in which consumers dined out but also their menu choices. In response, many restaurants listed the number of carbohydrates in menu dishes or offered dishes that were specifically "low-carb."

BE AN EXPERT IN OVERSEAS MARKETS.

Do you live an InterContinental life?

INTERCONTINENTAL.
HOTELS & RESORTS

EXHIBIT 5-20 InterContinental Hotels & Resorts attempts to make Europe more affordable to American meeting planners.

Source: Intercontinental Hotels Group. Used by permission.

Tourism Marketing Application

The *Journal of Tourism and Cultural Change* is an academic journal that examines the impact of sociocultural changes on tourism destinations. The website is www.multilingual-matters.net/default.htm (retrieved February 27, 2005). In addition, the Travel Industry Association presents a Minority Traveler Report. Results publicized in this report indicate that minorities exhibit a greater likelihood than travelers in general of choosing group tours, engaging in gambling and nightlife activities, and visiting theme parks and amusement parks. Minorities generate about 17 percent of all U.S. travel expenditures. (This information comes from a report by the Travel Industry Association of America and appeared in *Travel Insights*, August 2005, Vol. 1, page 7.)

The growth of resort spas is another example that resulted from consumers' desires to relax and reduce the stress in their lives. As one academic stated, "The ultimate test of a business is its social relevance. This is particularly true in a society where survival needs are already met. It therefore behooves the strategic planner to be familiar with emerging social trends and concerns."[15]

The sociocultural environment also includes demographic trends (e.g., the aging of the population), socioeconomics (e.g., increasing dual-income households), cultural values (e.g., the changing role of women), and consumerism (e.g., certain "rights" such as full information, safety, and ecology). Contained in the sociocultural environment is the marketplace itself and the characteristics of society. Many of these trends started in the United States and have moved, or are moving, abroad. Others have come to the United States from abroad. Although the hospitality industry has not been oblivious to these trends, it is sometimes slow in catching up with them. This is hardly surprising given that so many have come so quickly. An organization that is constantly alert and adapts to cultural change will have a lead on the others.

Let us consider an example. The female traveler, now approaching 50 percent of the U.S. business travel market, looks at business travel differently than does her male counterpart. Exhibit 5-21 shows the results of a proprietary study undertaken for a major hotel brand in 2000. The goal of this study was to better understand the trends of women business travelers. Although the study was undertaken some years ago, it is useful to see how men and women are different in terms of their travel behaviors. The interested student may wish to update this information for an honors paper or master's thesis.

From this table it is worth noting that women are more likely than men to claim that they always do the following:

- Pack sleepwear (70.2 versus 32.7 percent)
- Eat the turn-down mints, if provided (46.5 versus 37.4 percent)
- Carry medical information with them (36.9 versus 28.4 percent)
- Read up on the destination prior to arrival (24.3 versus 14.7 percent)
- Bring a spouse, significant other, or friend (24.3 versus 8.4 percent)
- Take some of the hotel's bathroom toiletries home (22.0 versus 14.8 percent)
- Take a bath instead of a shower (14.6 versus 4.7 percent)

In restaurants, sociocultural changes are affecting menus and entire dining concepts. Trends toward healthier foods have increased the consumption of salads, fish, pasta, and chicken at the expense of red meat. Interesting food and presentation is replacing quantity. Decaffeinated coffee and tea, substitutes for sugar and salt, truth-in-menu, spa menus, and nonsmoking sections are "in." Increasingly, in fact, *all* smoking is "out." Exhibit 5-22 provides a commentary on food service trends.

Natural Environment

The ecological environment refers to the natural environment and includes everything relating to the care and preservation of the environment. It also includes natural disasters such as the SARS outbreak of 2003, the tsunami that occurred in 2004, the devastating 2005 hurricane season, and earthquakes.

As customers become more aware of the fragility of our natural environment, issues relating to ecology have risen to the forefront. In fact, one of the growing segments of the travel industry is ecotourism. Belize, a small country nestled between Mexico and Guatemala, has created an image of an ecotourism paradise. With many unspoiled natural resources ranging from tropical mountains to the second largest barrier reef in the world, Belize is approaching tourism with caution and has positioned itself to attract the growing number of environmentally conscious travelers.

Environmental concerns such as waste disposal, recycling, and pollution are attracting attention not only from customers but from regulators as well. Cruise ships are no longer allowed to dump their wastes into the sea, and some even have biodegradable golf balls so that their customers

■ Summary

The concepts discussed in this chapter, along with those discussed in the next chapter, if followed correctly, lay the foundation for the eventual success of the hospitality firm. This chapter explained the differences among strategy, operational effectiveness, and marketing management. Strategic leadership and strategic vision must come first, as strategy takes a long-range view. It is about creating "fit" to develop competitive advantage. Part of the fit is understanding the environmental factors that impact a business. Once objectives have been established, the strategies for obtaining those objectives must be developed to fit the rest of the organization's activities. This leads to operational effectiveness. Without a firm strategy, the organization may end up doing "the wrong things" very well. This will lead to failure. Strategy must not be confused with tactics, which are the specific steps implemented to execute the strategy. The strategy is what guides the day-to-day tactical decisions. The strategy ensures "the right things," while the tactics help guide and monitor the operational effectiveness.

This chapter also discussed how the corporate-level strategy leads to the business-level strategy, which in turn leads into the functional-level strategy. In the next chapter we develop the concepts introduced in this chapter in much more detail.

■ Key Terms

management effectiveness
competitive strategy
strategic leadership
marketing concept
strategic planning
environmental scanning
strategic thinking

fit
vertical integration
diversification
strategic visioning
value chain
emergent strategies
crafted strategies

■ Discussion Questions

1. Discuss the key differences between strategies and tactics. List three examples of each as they apply to the hospitality industry. Do the tactics flow from the strategies?
2. Why does marketing strategy have to come before the marketing plan?
3. Explain the differences and similarities among corporate-, business-, and functional-level strategies.
4. How does Mintzberg's emergent strategy view differ from traditional views of strategy? What are the implications of the differing viewpoints for hospitality firms?
5. What is meant by the statements "strategy is making trade-offs" and "strategy is creating fit"?

■ Group Projects

1. Take a hospitality firm, tourist destination, or any other public organization that reveals its strategy to the public. Review the overall strategy in terms of the material discussed in this chapter. Evaluate the effectiveness of the tactics in promoting or fulfilling the stated marketing strategy. If you cannot find all the information you need, develop a list of questions you would ask the CEO if you had the opportunity to do so.
2. Look at Exhibit 5-13, on the building blocks of competitive advantage that are combined with the value chain activities. Find a hospitality firm or a tourist destination and then recreate the table using specific examples in as many cells as possible.

■| References

1. We have borrowed some ideas here and in other parts of this section from Porter, M. (1985). *Competitive advantage.* New York: Free Press; and Porter, M. (1996, November-December). What is strategy? *Harvard Business Review,* 61–78.

2. Services Group buys Marriott distribution. (2002, December 23). *Nation's Restaurant News.* Website: www.nrn.com. Retrieved from www.findarticles.com/p/articles/mi_m3190/is_51_36/ai_96058052.

3. Litt, M. R. (n. d.). Marriott International's accommodating network. *Network Computing.* Retrieved September 5, 2004, from www.nwc.com/909/909centerfoldtext.html.

4. Porter, M. E. (1980). *Competitive strategy: Techniques for analyzing industries and competitors.* New York: Free Press.

5. For a more detailed discussion on the value chain, see Chapters 2 and 3 in Porter, M. (1985). *Competitive advantage.* New York: Free Press.

6. Retrieved September 12, 2004, from www.avendra.com/buyers_purch.asp.

7. Mintzberg, H., Ahlstrand, B., & Lampel, J. (1998). *Strategy safari: A guided tour through the wilds of strategic management.* New York: Free Press.

8. Mintzberg, H. (1987, July-August). Crafting strategy. *Harvard Business Review,* 66–75.

9. Retrieved from http://en.wikipedia.org/wiki/Hard_dish#History.

10. Yesawich, Pepperdine, Brown & Russell. (2005). *National Business Travel MONITOR,* 78.

11. Retrieved from www.wto.org/english/thewto_e/whatis_e/inbrief_e/inbr00_e.htm.

12. Retrieved from http://business.indiaserver.com/direct-foreign-india-investment.html.

13. Retrieved from www.chinatoday.com.cn/English/e2004/e200406/p26.htm.

14. Retrieved from www.accor.com/gb/groupe/accor_monde/carte.asp.

15. Jain, 134.

16. Retrieved from www.norcalwaste.com/press/prrestaurantrecycling.htm.

17. Ibid.

The Strategic Marketing System and Marketing Objectives

Overview

This chapter imparts a good grasp of strategy and the importance of developing a strategic plan before developing a marketing plan. Specifically, the chapter begins with the mission statement and leads into a full discourse of the strategic marketing system, including SWOT analysis and developing a strategic marketing plan.

The strategic system begins with a mission statement. The mission statement identifies what the business entity wants to be and where it wants to go in terms of owners, customers, employees, and other stakeholders. The master marketing strategy entails a review of the situational analysis and shapes the firm's long-range marketing objectives through its distinctive competence.

I. Introduction to Hospitality Marketing
1. The Concept of Marketing
2. Marketing Services and the Hospitality Experience
3. The Marketing Mix and the Product/Service Mix
4. Relationship/Loyalty Marketing

II. Marketing to Build a Competitive Advantage
5. Strategic Marketing
6. *The Strategic Marketing System and Marketing Objectives*

VII. Feedback

VI. Synthesis
21. The Marketing Plan

III. The Marketplace
7. Understanding Individual Customers
8. Understanding Organizational Customers
9. The Tourist Customer and the Tourism Destination

IV. Situational Analysis
10. Understanding Competition
11. Marketing Intelligence and Research

V. Functional Strategies
12. Differentiation, Segmentation, and Target Marketing
13. Branding and Market Positioning
14. The Hospitality Pricing Mix
15. The Communications Mix: Advertising
16. The Communications Mix: Sales Promotions, Merchandising, Public Relations, and Publicity
17. The Communications Mix: Personal Selling
18. Hospitality Distribution Systems
19. Channels of Distribution: Bringing the Customer to the Product
20. Interactive Marketing: Internet and Database Marketing

Prior to joining The Ritz-Carlton Hotel Company, Bruce J. Himelstein was senior vice president, sales and marketing, for Marriott International.

A 25-year veteran, Himelstein has held various positions in sales and marketing from national sales to pre-opening resorts. His career started as a bellman and has escalated to senior vice president. He was the recipient of Marriott's Director of Sales of the Year Award and has been responsible for developing division-wide sales and marketing initiatives.

Himelstein is currently global chairman of the Hospitality Sales and Marketing Association International (HSMAI), which has over 6,000 members worldwide. He received his BA in communications from the State University of New York at Geneseo.

Marketing in Action
Bruce Himelstein, Senior VP—Sales and Marketing, The Ritz-Carlton Company, LLC

Describe the process of developing a mission statement.

It is almost the last thing you do after the dialogue has been put on the table. A mission statement as a mission statement is fairly worthless unless all of the dialogue and all of the emotion about what you and this group of people are going to do is put on the table. The mission statement is a paraphrase or just an abbreviation of all that emotion and commitment that has been put on the table, so I have always strived for that first. The goal is never to come up with a mission statement. The goal is to come up with what we are going to do as a team. What are the priorities? What is the commitment? What are the ideas that we have? What is it that we can all hold each other accountable for? When all that is done, then you look back and say, "How do I check that in a sentence or two?"—versus the goal being to come up with a mission statement. I am not a big fan of that exercise, so that is really how I approach it.

Can you describe some SWOT analyses [strengths, weaknesses, opportunities, and threats] you have done in the past? How do you go about generating that exercise on a strategic level? If you had to develop a SWOT analysis for an individual hotel that is opening or one that is experiencing some competition, how would you set about getting that document produced? Who would participate on the team, and what type of resource would you be looking for in order to bundle this all together?

The approach would change and the players would change, depending on the situation. There is no one generic approach to something like that, but I will give you an example. We just came back from a six-day trip to Asia where we are developing about seven properties. When you look at development deals on paper, it's one thing, and when you actually go see the site, it is another. The director of international sales offices, the VP of marketing, the VP of sales strategy, the VP of revenue management, and I met at each point with customers. We met with demand generators, whether they were accounts or government officials. We also met with the movers and shakers, the buzz makers of the market, to get a feel from the ground level what the market potential would be. We then culled all the data and discussions into a format that anyone could read and understand. In this case, it is all preopening, but if I was working on an existing problem, there would have to be some pretty tight time frames put against it to see whether or not all that effort made a difference.

How did you find the awareness of the brand over there?

That is an interesting question. We are at a very exciting turning point for Ritz-Carlton. Because of the nature of the success and the respect that the Ritz-Carlton Shanghai has earned, it is a well-known brand to many people in Asia, to many of the developers, and the government. The consumer doesn't necessarily know the brand outside of Shanghai. Maybe they have been to Hong Kong, but as much equity as the brand possesses, we're confident of our success in Asia. These owners could have flown any flag they wanted to, but they selected Ritz-Carlton because of the experience, the reputation that our hotel currently enjoys. Essentially, it clarifies and validates how vital every hotel operation is because that becomes the brand experience for them.

I am sure that when the Shanghai property was built, the thinking was beyond just operating a profitable hotel—to creating a foothold into China.

That is exactly right. For the third year in a row, they achieved the special recognition of being voted the best employer in Asia. What the ladies and gentlemen have created over there is bench marketable at any level. They are an industry leader and are building a destination. They are not just building a hotel, they are developing cities—malls, high-end retail, hotels, residential—and the Ritz-Carlton acts as the anchor for the development.

Can you tell me a little bit about the type of feedback loops that Ritz-Carlton has in place? You mentioned that you talk to customers who are the demand generators (that is, firms that are in your area that provide business because people who come to see them stay in your rooms). Are there any other feedback loops in terms of employees? You mentioned governments or internal structures that you gather data from to make strategic decisions.

We keep our ears pretty close to the ground at the corporate level, and research the feasibility of the market we are contemplating. Each executive committee member spends approximately half of their time in the field. I am gone half of the time and visiting hotels, meeting with customers, with executive committees, reviewing competition, finding trends. There is very little value in spending the majority of your time in a corporate environment. So the internal feedback mechanisms are critical, especially when

you are trying to evolve a brand like we are doing with Ritz-Carlton. If you don't get the buy-in internally, don't bother. You need that support in order to move forward, and you get that by understanding the people who are on the front line and what it is they have to tell you. Therefore, we are out a lot.

You talked about the success of your Asian strategy. Can you relay a couple of other strategies that you have been instrumental in developing that have worked well for your company?

At the beginning of July, we introduced a new advertising campaign that it is a new look for the brand. We have put it in magazines but for the first time we have put this look outside the traditional media and have embellished it with lifestyle media. We are really shifting the image, the mindset of who this brand is. It has been met with incredible, favorable results. A lot of research went into that and a lot of my gut, and what we have done is to start to send the message out to the consumers of the world that this brand perhaps may be up to something. It was significant enough that the *Wall Street Journal* did a piece on it, and the reaction from our customers has been overwhelming. We are advertising in places that we typically haven't been, with an image that we haven't used. It is starting to send the message. So that has been pretty exciting because you don't get that opportunity every day.

Can you describe a little about what type of research you did that went into the campaign?

We interviewed and did significant focus groups in Chicago, Los Angeles, New York, Miami, and London with Ritz-Carlton loyalists and competitive loyalists. We focused on luxury, lodging, travel, trends, lifestyle. We rolled a lot of that up and looked at where we were as a brand. It was a solid 90-day exercise.

What was your gut reaction on this?

My gut was that the brand had to start changing its image a little bit, that the consumer had shifted, that this whole mass luxury trading dialogue was creating enough buzz that brands that stood still and didn't stay relevant were probably going to be left behind.

What type of measurable response have you had?

The press has been very kind and enthusiastic about the new campaign. *Vanity Fair's* results for ad recall placed us in the #1 spot for ad recall this past June. We also started running ads with price points and things that typically did well for us almost doubled this time because we were at places we hadn't been before, talking to people we hadn't talked to before. So we had more call volume, more room nights, more revenue.

Some strategic plans fail because they take too long to implement. There is not enough sense of urgency. There is lack of accountability, lack of fluidity, and lack of good internal salespeople. You know, you have two stakeholders in any given set of circumstances: external and internal. I think strategies fail sometimes because the proper sale wasn't made internally, and probably by the time it got to marketing, it was watered down and trying to meet a common denominator and then you lose the original punch of what should have been out there.

Would you say that some strategic plans fail because they didn't get the buy-in of some of the stakeholders, that it was kind of just sent down by e-mail that this is what we are doing and the troops just kind of said, "Fine," and got to marching.

Yes, you know it's the classic push–pull strategy. Until you get the buy-in at the market level, it doesn't' work. The Internet has added resources to our organization. It has added a whole other component from a distribution channel standpoint as to what our brand should be to the end user and to anyone looking at us on the Internet. It has created an explosion of white paper thinking, so it has been phenomenal for us.

If a student were contemplating going into strategic planning and using a strategic marketing system, what type of skill set do you think that person would need to have to be successful?

The first skill set is they would have to be a phenomenal listener. Their listening skills would have to be the best in the organization. After that, they would have to be a really good project manager at the same time. When you are an air traffic controller for an organization, one of your roles is that listening component, but then absolutely taking that and putting it into a format that everyone gets and everyone understands. Chances are, if you are in strategic planning, you are going to be working in a matrix organization because you are probably not going to have a staff of 20 people below you doing things. You are probably going to be a lone pony out there, or you will have two people you work with. But you are going to have to influence, so your influencing skills are going to have to be honed very sharply, which means you are going to have to be working under a matrix organization. So you are going to have to have influence over people that can help the process along without you actually controlling them.

Used by permission from Bruce Himelstein.

Exhibit 6-1 shows the **strategic marketing system** model, which starts with the firm's mission statement. This is true whether you are Hilton Hotels Corporation or the Restaurant Zum See's owners Max and Greti Mennig. Both Hilton and Max and Greti Mennig have specific objectives and missions. Hilton's may be put together by an executive committee of senior vice presidents. Max and Greti may carry theirs around in their heads and, if you asked them, they might be unable to articulate them. It doesn't matter; the objectives and mission are still there, and they will drive the operation of the Restaurant Zum See, for better or for worse, every bit as much as Hilton's will guide the operations of that multinational corporation. The mission statement usually includes the broad, long-term goals of an organization.

The Mission Statement

Any firm has certain financial objectives, and we will not dwell on those here, keeping in mind that profit is the ultimate test of the validity of decisions. In addition, the firm has competitive objectives, customer objectives, and company objectives, all of which are related. These objectives are brought together in what constitutes the **mission statement**.

The mission statement defines the purpose of a business. It states why the firm exists, who the firm competes against, who the target market is, and how to serve the constituents—those who have an interest in what the firm does. These include customers, employees, owners, financial backers, and the local community, all of whom are commonly called stakeholders. It is the corporate mission statement from which all other mission statements in the organization flow, as shown in Exhibit 6-1.

Tourism Marketing Application
Tourist destinations can also have mission statements. For example, consider Victoria, Canada. The Tourism Victoria Corporation, which promotes tourism in Victoria, espouses the following mission statement: "Maximize employment and the long-term economic benefits of tourism to Victoria by developing and marketing the State as a competitive tourist destination." (www.tourismvictoria.com.au/index. php?option=displaypage&Itemid=126&op=page retrieved March 5, 2006)

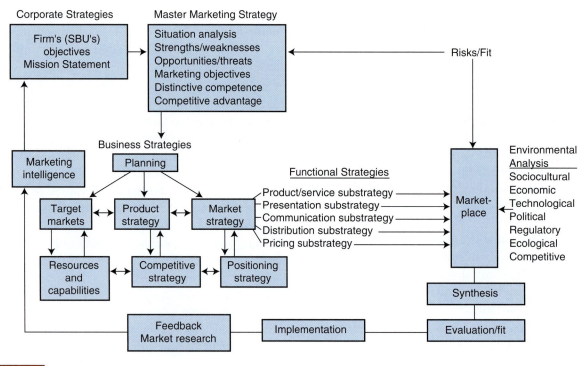

EXHIBIT 6-1 The strategic marketing system model.

Mission statements exist not only at the corporate level, but also at the level of every **strategic business unit (SBU)** within the firm. An SBU is a unit of a business that serves a clearly defined product–market segment with its own strategy, but in a manner consistent with the overall corporate strategy, its own mission, and its own identifiable competitors.

As Marriott Hotels and Resorts has a mission, so too does the Courtyard by Marriott division, the Fairfield Inns division, and the Residence Inn division. The same is true of the Marriott Long Wharf and the Marriott Copley Place, both in Boston. These hotels not only have their individual competitors but also compete against each other, not to mention three other Marriotts in the Boston area. By the same token, the restaurants and lounges at the Marriott Copley Place should each have their own objectives and mission and their own identifiable competitors.

Strategic planning occurs at every level where a strategic business unit exists. Bear this in mind as we discuss the remainder of the strategic marketing systems model.

A firm's (or SBU's) objectives may include growth, return on investment, profit, leadership, industry position, or other factors. These are included in the mission statement. Thus, developing the mission statement is a crucial assignment. Because the mission statement indicates the purpose of the business and is a statement of why the business exists, it drives all subsets of the business. Most im-

portant, mission statements must be realistic. For a mission statement to say, as some do, "We will be known as the leader in the hotel industry" when such a possibility is not realistic or meaningful only leads to confusion at lower levels of the organization.

The mission statement should be something in which all employees can believe. It sets goals and it urges everyone in the organization to meet those goals. Properly, it is communicated throughout the organization for all to follow. That, in fact, is one of its purposes—to unify the organization. When the response at lower levels is, "Who are they kidding?" the entire effort becomes a meaningless and self-defeating endeavor. Although some mission statements are quite brief, an effective mission statement, which is nothing less than an overall strategy statement, should fulfill the criteria shown in Exhibit 6-2, either implicitly or explicitly.

It is important to note that three entities should be equally represented in the mission statement: employees, customers, and shareholders. Too often, mission statements reflect the needs of the owners: more profits. Profits can only be achieved with satisfied customers and employees. Conversely, if customers enjoy prices that are too low and employees are paid too much, the owners will not be satisfied. All three entities must be represented in any successful mission statement.

Consider the mission statement of Ritz-Carlton, probably one of the most complete ones in hospitality, in Exhibit 6-3, and that of Numi Tea, in Exhibit 6-4. You

EXHIBIT 6-2	Criteria of an Effective Mission Statement

1. *It states what business the company (or SBU) is in or will be in.* This goes considerably beyond being in the hotel, restaurant, or food business. Instead, it is more specific and states how we serve our customers and specifies who they are. For example: Hotel XYZ is in the business of providing the traveling and price-sensitive public with modern, comfortable, and clean accommodations at a very reasonable price. Accordingly, Hotel XYZ recognizes the basic needs of travelers as well as the need for a pleasant and hassle-free experience, but without the amenities for which this market is unwilling to pay. Hotel XYZ wants to be known as the best buy at the moderate price level, satisfying all essential needs for the motoring public.

    You can see that this statement has numerous ramifications such as how, what, when, and where. These are enumerated later in the strategic plan, but the answers will be driven by the mission statement.

2. *It identifies the special competency of the firm and how it will be unique in the marketplace.* Hotel XYZ is and will continue to be a leader in its field because of its special identification with the budget-minded traveling public and its needs. By continuous communication with its market and regularly adapting to the changing needs of that market, Hotel XYZ will maintain its position as the hotel of choice of its customers.

    Again, the mission statement has committed the firm to a definite course of action. Its competency and uniqueness is special knowledge of the target market and a commitment to maintain and implement that knowledge.

3. *In a market position statement it defines who the competition will be—that is, it actually chooses whom it will compete against and does not leave this to chance.* Hotel XYZ's niche in the market will be between the full economy, highly price-sensitive market that

chooses accommodations almost solely by price, and the middle-tier market that will pay $20 more for additional amenities and services. Accordingly, XYZ competes only tangentially against ABC and DEF, on the one hand, and GHI and JKL, on the other hand. XYZ competes directly for the same market against MNO and PQR as well as other companies that choose to enter this market.

   As Burger King knows it has to beat McDonald's and Pepsi-Cola knows it has to beat Coca-Cola, XYZ knows it has to beat MNO and PQR and will watch these competitors very closely.

4. *It identifies the needs of its constituents.*
    a. *Customers:* XYZ will conduct ongoing research of its customers needs, both at the corporate and unit levels. It will continuously seek to satisfy those needs within the constraints of its mission.
    b. *Employees:* XYZ recognizes all employees as internal customers with their own varying needs and wants. Accordingly, it will attend to those needs and wants with the same attitude it holds toward its paying customers and will maintain an open line of communication for that purpose.
    c. *Community:* XYZ recognizes its position in the economic, political, and social communities. Thus, it will maintain a role of good citizenship in all endeavors and efforts.
    d. *Owners:* XYZ has committed itself to a 15 percent ROI for its investors as well as a positive image of which they can be proud. XYZ will function both in the marketplace and in its operations to maintain these commitments.

5. *It identifies the future.* Hotel XYZ will develop and expand through controlled growth in suitable locations. Its strategy will be to develop regional strength as a gradual development toward national strength, with the objective of reaching that goal by the year 2005.

---

should evaluate both of the mission statements in light of the criteria in Exhibit 6-2.

 Web Browsing Exercise

Search the World Wide Web for restaurants, travel and tourism companies, or hotels (other than Ritz-Carlton and Numi). Find two companies that have different positions in the marketplace and evaluate their mission statements. How effective are these mission statements as measured by Exhibit 6-2? Next, compare and contrast the mission statements. In what ways are they similar? Different?

Master Marketing Strategy

Developing the **master marketing strategy** is the next stage in the strategic marketing system, as shown in Exhibit 6-1. The master strategy is designed to be long term, not short. This does not mean it will never change; if market conditions change, then so too should the master strategy.

Consider again Marriott, which was initially founded as a food service organization. In the 1980s Marriott's

Restaurant Division pursued a master strategy of growth and acquisition. To implement this, one substrategy aimed at creating a midpriced restaurant chain (named Allie's) to complement Marriott's fast-food branch (Roy Rogers). The long-term objective of the division was to have 3,000 Allie's units after 10 years; 600 of these were to be completed in three years at a budgeted cost of $250 million.[1]

By the end of 1989, however, and after completing another **situational analysis**, Marriott decided to divest its entire restaurant division. A company that was founded on food service had to face the realities of the environment. It changed its corporate master strategy and placed its emphasis where its strengths and **opportunities** lay—in hotels and institutional feeding. Later, as shown in Chapter 5 (Exhibit 5-2), Marriott decided to divest itself of the institutional feeding segment.

The original intention, however, of master strategies is that they will endure for some time. This means that they take a long-range perspective of the environment as opposed to the short-range perspective of the marketing plan, even though many of the issues are the same.

THE RITZ-CARLTON®
HOTEL COMPANY, LLC

MISSION STATEMENT

The Ritz-Carlton Hotel Company will be regarded as the quality and market leader of the hotel industry worldwide.

We are responsible for creating exceptional, profitable results with the investments entrusted to us by efficiently satisfying customers.

The Ritz-Carlton Hotels will be the clear choice of discriminating business and leisure travelers, meeting planners, owners, partners and the travel agent community.

Founded on the principles of providing a high level of genuine, caring, personal service; cleanliness; beauty; and comfort, we will consistently provide all customers with their ultimate expectation, a memorable experience and exceptional value. Every employee will be empowered to provide immediate corrective action should customer problems occur.

Meeting planners will favor The Ritz-Carlton Hotels. Empowered sales staff will know their own product and will always be familiar with each customer's business. The transition of customer requirements from Sales to Conference Services will be seamless. Conference Services will be a partner to the meeting planner, with General Managers showing interest through their presence and participation. Any potential problem will be solved instantly and with ease for the planner. All billing will be clear, accurate and timely. All of this will create a memorable, positive experience for the meeting planner and the meeting participants.

Key account customers will receive individualized attention, products and services in support of their organization's objectives.

All guests and customers will know we fully appreciate their loyalty.

The Ritz-Carlton Hotels will be the first choice for important and social business events and will be the social centers in each community. Through creativity, detailed planning, and communication, banquets and conferences will be memorable.

Our restaurants and lounges will be the first choice of the local community and will be patronized on a regular basis.

The Ritz-Carlton Hotels will be known as positive, supportive members of their community and will be sensitive to the environment.

The relationships we have with our suppliers will be one of mutual confidence and teamwork.

We will always select employees who share our values. We will strive to meet individual needs because our success depends on the satisfaction, effort and commitment of each employee. Our leaders will constantly support and energize all employees to continuously improve productivity and customer satisfaction. This will be accomplished by creating an environment of genuine care, trust, respect, fairness and teamwork through training, education, empowerment, participation, recognition, rewards and career opportunities.

EXHIBIT 6-3 The Ritz-Carlton mission statement.
Source: Ritz-Carlton. Used by permission

Mission Statement

Numi's mission is to be the most innovative tea company in the world dedicated to quality, sustainable values and a commitment to community. Within the United States, Numi will be among the top five tea companies in the Natural Food industry and among the top ten in Food Service by 2008. Numi will also make an impact in the international market becoming a globally recognized brand by 2010.

EXHIBIT 6-4 Numi Tea mission statement.
Source: Numi. Used by permission.

The master strategy shapes objectives of the firm. This occurs after developing and weighing alternative strategies. It specifies where the firm is going and provides the framework for the entire marketing effort. The marketing strategy must be derived from the mission statement and firm's objectives. It is the marketing strategy that fulfills the firm's objectives and missions.

The mission statement of the hypothetical hotel company XYZ in Exhibit 6-2 noted that it wanted to be perceived as the best buy at the moderate price level. The master marketing strategy, then, should deal with that accomplishment to make it happen.

Situational Analysis

The master strategy begins with a situational analysis of strengths and weaknesses, again asking the questions, Where are we now? and Where do we want to go? It is the "where" of the strategic marketing system that shapes objectives and sets the stage for all decision aspects. A master strategy deals with the generic stages we have just discussed such as positions, trade-offs, and fit. It also deals with such issues as new markets, growth sectors, customer loyalty, re-

peat business, quantity versus quality, cheap versus expensive, best versus biggest, high or low markups, quick turnover, product/service range, building brand name, customer awareness and perception, and a host of other things that will guide the **business strategies**. Marketing objectives are identified in the master strategy in these contexts.

Tourism Marketing Application

The Bulgarian Association for Alternative Tourism has prepared a SWOT analysis for alternative tourism in Bulgaria. This organization defines alternative tourism as travel that is "personal and authentic and encourages interaction with the local environment, people, and communities"—in contrast to mass tourism. The organization believes that by 2007 Bulgaria will be a leader in alternative tourism. Their report details the SWOT analysis of this type of tourism. (www.alternative-tourism. org/english/index.php?page=15, retrieved March 18, 2006)

To address these issues, it is clear that one must first define their current state. We continue with an environmental analysis, looking especially at the long-range trends and effects. These trends could be economic (the state of the international, national, or local economy), sociocultural (the graying of America, generation X), lifestyle (interest in fitness and health), legal (laws pertaining to employees such as minimum wage requirements and smoking bans), ecological (a greater awareness of environmental concerns), political (room taxes to terrorism), technological (Internet reservations), or competitive (industry consolidation). The major purpose of environmental analysis is to identify external opportunities and **threats** to the organization.

An opportunity is a favorable trend in the environment such as an emerging market segment or a need or demand for certain specialized services. On the other hand, a threat is an unfavorable trend, such as reduced demand or new competition. When various questions are asked in a situational analysis about the organization, external opportunities and threats, along with strengths and weaknesses, will evolve. An analysis of strengths, weaknesses, opportunities, and threats is often called a SWOT analysis. Examples are shown in Exhibit 6-5.

The main objective of a SWOT analysis is to identify strategies that fit a company's resources and capabilities to the demands of the environment in which the company operates. The purpose of the strategic alternatives developed by a SWOT analysis is to build on a company's strengths by exploiting the opportunities, countering the threats, and overcoming the weaknesses, thus developing distinctive competencies and a competitive advantage.

The **distinctive competency** of an organization is more than what it can do; it is what it can do particularly well. It often takes a great deal of self-analysis to understand this and to abide by it. Objective situational analysis is the tool to lay bare the facts. Abiding by it is sometimes more difficult. Marriott learned this when it diversified into different businesses in which it lacked strength or distinctive competency. As shown in Exhibit 5-2, the company rectified these mistakes by selling many of the different businesses. In many cases, failure to recognize strengths and weaknesses results in targeting the wrong markets. Strategically speaking, a firm should do only what it has the competency and resources to do well. Ignoring this fact may result in a colossal strategic error.

Too often SWOT analysis primarily provides indications of past performance that are unlikely to produce assessments of future opportunities. Following are some methods to avoid this error:

- Involve the managers who will make the final strategic choices.
- Test alternative strategies against strengths and weaknesses.
- Evaluate strengths and weaknesses in terms of the future and their strategic significance and relative to the competition.
- Separate weaknesses from simple problems to be overcome.

EXHIBIT 6-5   **Some Elements of a Situational Analysis**

INTERNAL—STRENGTHS AND WEAKNESSES

- *Brand Demand:*   Who is our customer? Why? What is our position? Who are our market segments and target markets? To which do we appeal the most? What use do they make of our product/service? What benefits do we offer? What problems do we solve or not solve? What are the levels of brand awareness, preference?
- *Customer Profile:*   What do our customers look like—demographically, psychographically, behaviorally? Are they heavy users or light users? How do they make the decision? What influences them? How do they perceive us? What do they use us for? Where else do they go? What needs and wants do we fulfill? What are their expectations?
- *Organizational Values:*   What are the values that guide us? What is the corporate culture? What drives us in a real sense? Do these limit alternatives?
- *Resources:*   What are our distinctive capabilities and strengths? What do we do particularly well? How do these compare to the competition? What are our physical resources? Are there any conflicts among our resources, our values, and our objectives? Do we have a good fit?
- *Product/Service:*   What is our product/service? What benefits does it offer or problems does it solve? How is it perceived, positioned? What are the tangibles/intangibles? What are our complementary lines? What are our strengths and weaknesses?
- *Objectives:*   Where do we want to go? What do we want to accomplish? Are our objectives quantifiable and measurable? How do we want to be perceived? What are the long-range and short-range considerations? What trade-offs do we need to make?
- *Policies:*   What rules do we have now? How do we operate? What guides us? Are any rules conflicting?
- *Organization:*   How are resources, authority, and responsibility organized and implemented? Do we become proactive rather than reactive? Does the organization enhance the strategy, or does the organization need to be changed?

EXTERNAL—OPPORTUNITIES AND THREATS

- *Generic Demand:*   How are we positioned? Why do people come here, and why do they use this product? Where else do they go? What do they need, want, demand? Are there unmet needs? What do users and nonusers look like? What are the segments for this product category? What are the alternatives? What are the trend patterns—cyclical, seasonal, or fashion?
- *Competition:*   Who are our competitors? Where are they? What do they look like? How are they positioned against us? In what market segments are they stronger or weaker? Why do people go there? What do they do better or poorer than we do? What is their market share? What are their strengths and weaknesses? What are their expectations? What are their strategies? What are they doing, and where are they going? Are there new ones coming?
- *Environment:*   What are the impacts of technology and sociocultural, economic, political, and regulatory trends?

EXHIBIT 6-6	Chronology of Howard Johnson's Failure as a Result of Lack of Diligent SWOT Analysis and Strategic Planning

1979

Daiquiris, discos, and candlelight dinners: that's what Howard Johnson is serving up these days. The bastion of the highway travel market is out to change its image. Said Johnson, "We know where our operations will be in the 1980s, but the question is 'will we be in the right spot?'" "I still don't think the food business is a marketing business." "I'm sure that we're making the right long-term moves."[a]

1983

The wraps are slowly coming off a new strategic business plan at the Howard Johnson company. Key to the sluggish giant's assault on its problems is a carefully planned major reorganization of the way the company manages and markets its restaurants and lodges. "It's just a case of reorienting the thinking under new leadership."[b]

1983

"Everybody has a theme restaurant, but I think Ground Round [a restaurant concept division of Howard Johnson] has a unique niche among them. Both families and singles are comfortable with us. We have done the one thing older chains have failed to do: marry the family trade with strong liquor sales."[c]

1984

Bettering the chain's infamously undependable service has suddenly become a priority.[d]

1985—AFTER THE FALL

"Howard Johnson's restaurants had become overpriced and understaffed purveyors of pallid food, hamstrung by outdated ideas. Howard Johnson's troubles [were blamed] on everything but incompetent management. Howard Johnson stood fast with a diversified menu while it was being 'segmented' to death for two decades, what an opportunity was blown!"[e]

TODAY

In 2005 Howard Johnson is a hotel company with nearly 500 hotels in 14 countries. The brand is owned and franchised by Cendant Corporation.

a. The Howard Johnson team: Razing the orange roof. (1979, February 1). *Restaurant Business*, 123–134.

b. Hojo unveils new strategy to overcome sluggish sales. (1983, January 17). *Nation's Restaurant News*. p. 1.

c. Welcome back, Howard Johnson's. (1983, December 28). *Restaurants and Institutions*, 88.

d. Howard Johnson: Is it too late to fix up its faded 1950s image? (1984, October 22). *BusinessWeek*, 90.

e. The sad case of the dwindling orange roofs. (1985, December 30). *Forbes*, 75–79.

The final output should be a list of the most significant strengths, on which the future should be planned, and the most important weaknesses, which should be targeted for solution and avoided as underpinnings of strategy.

Solid strength and weakness analysis may be the most neglected phase of strategic planning in the hospitality industry. Without a doubt, this lack was a major contributor to the failure of Howard Johnson, the stages of which are shown in Exhibit 6-6. In less than 10 years, Howard Johnson went from boom to bust. Eventually, it was broken up and sold off in pieces, all because management failed to understand its strengths and weaknesses or to see its opportunities and threats. Many opportunities and threats spring from the changing environment, as seen in this case, as well as from customers' problems, which you can conjecture from Exhibit 6-6.

Web Browsing Exercise

Go to the Howard Johnson website (www.hojo.com/HowardJohnson/control/home). What did you learn about the company's industry? The power of its brand name? How one division can fail while another division continues to grow?

Using the Strategic Marketing Systems Model

Rather than discourse further on the model in Exhibit 6-1, we will make it come alive by illustrating the stages with excerpts from the actual strategic marketing plan of an international hotel we will call the International. The mission of this hotel was to be the top upscale hotel of choice for international travelers to its destination. Without enclosing the full situational analysis (covered earlier) that serves as the foundation for the strategy, we have placed some key questions in brackets. Three years after this strategic plan was drawn, this hotel was devastated by new competition. Examine its analysis and plan to see if you can understand why.

Objectives and Master Strategies

Marketing Objective. To be perceived as a premier super deluxe hotel marketed to the connoisseur customer.

Master Marketing Strategy. To create an image of exclusivity and uniqueness with premium-quality facilities and services.

Strengths.

- Personalized and professional service
- Prime strategic location
- Part of chain that has already made its mark
- High standards of food and service
- Newly refurnished outlets
- Renowned shopping arcade on premise
- Wide variety of excellently appointed suites

[Do these strengths represent unique competitive differences perceived by the customer that build defenses against competitive forces or find niche positions in the market? What is the hotel's distinctive competency?]

Weaknesses.

- Higher room and food and beverage rates make it difficult to secure international conference business
- Market sensitivity that we are more pro-foreigner and have less identification with the local community
- Lower percentage of national clientele
- Marketing is more product oriented than customer oriented
- Lack of exclusive executive club
- Absence of well-located properties in chain that reduces chain utilization

[Are these weaknesses, or problems that need to be solved?]

Opportunities.

- The commercial market in the city is very active and our location is strategic.
- Development in this area is strong and has strong affiliation with our hotel.
- The entrepreneurial market is growing and most businesses are locating in this area.

[Is this a matching of strengths and competencies to opportunity?]

Threats.

- Foreign traffic will depend on the political stability of the country.
- Corporations are developing their own facilities to encourage privacy and reduce expenditures.
- Biggest competitor has renovated rooms.
- Some corporations are moving to suburbs.

[Are these threats caused by weaknesses? Can they be avoided? Can resources be better deployed?]

Business Strategies

The next stage in strategic marketing, and one flowing directly from the master strategy, is the planning stage (see Exhibit 6-1). It consists of both operational and business-level strategies. These strategies are the "how" of strategic marketing—that is, *how* we're going to get from *here* to *where* we want to go. Strategies at this point are easily measurable and may have time and performance requirements.

This is the stage at which the organization acts in advance, rather than reacts, by planning for change. It is here that the organization shapes its own destiny. At this stage the company attempts to minimize risk, maintain control, and allocate resources to keep in focus and reach its objectives.

The planning stage is also the stage of specific matching of the product to the market, of understanding where the business is going to come from, of developing new products and services, and of influencing demand. You should take special note of the interrelationship among the various elements of the business strategies.

Target Market Strategy

Target market strategy clearly depends on, among other things, resources and capabilities. To target a market with similar needs and wants is grossly insufficient, if not fatal, when the resources and competencies are not there to serve that market. The appropriate strategy is to target not just markets that appear to have the most opportunity, but also those that the firm can serve best and, one hopes, better than the competition.

A common failing in this respect may be observed among hotels that target the upscale market and price accordingly, but do not have the resources or capabilities to sustain an advantage against this market segment. The hotel then has to accept lower-rated business while management continues to vehemently maintain that it is serving the upscale market. The result is a confused image and failure to fulfill potential. Such strategies are often built on egos and wishful thinking rather than on unbiased analysis. Another potential peril derives from targeting too many different markets—a strategy of providing something for everyone, which lacks focus and results in confusion for all.

Target market strategy means defining the right target market within the broader market segment. The strategy of the International hotel we have been discussing is to target the following market.

- Age: 35 plus
- Income: High

- Lifestyle: Results-oriented professional businessperson, aristocratic with a modern outlook on life, respected in the community, voices an opinion, a leader, and an active socializer
- Desired customer response:
  - Rational: I like staying here because the rooms are spacious and beautiful. I like the computerized telephone exchange with its automatic wake-up call and direct international dialing. The executive club with computers and fax machines is time-saving, smooth, and trouble-free. Check-in/checkout is fast and efficient. Because the hotel is so exclusive, I don't encounter undesirable people. Service is smooth, courteous, and efficient.
  - Emotional: I like staying here because everyone knows me and takes care of me. I feel very much at home with the room service and restaurants. They know my likes and dislikes and make it a point to remember. It is so exclusive; I like to be seen here.

Product Strategy

Product strategy is concerned with the offering of different products and services to satisfy market needs. It deals with the benefits the product provides, the problems it solves, and how it differentiates from the competition. Product strategies should be based on opportunities in the environment and customer needs rather than just owners' or managements' concept of what the product should be. For example, it is quite common in southeast Asia for upscale hotels to have as many as five formal dining rooms. These will inevitably be Chinese, Japanese, and French, plus one native to the country. The other is likely to be Italian or American. The reasoning, of course, is that all these geographic markets are served by the hotel. Each room usually seats 100 or more, and in most cases is fortunate if it is 50 percent occupied.

The low patronage does not occur because there is no market need. Demand exists for all these ethnic foods, but at varying levels. Further, there are numerous freestanding restaurants in the city also filling these needs—at least the Chinese, Japanese, and natives. Regardless, the product strategy is to have something for everyone instead of defining the specific needs of the target market.

The essence of marketing is to design the product to fit the market. Sometimes, however, the product, like a hotel, already exists and the situation is reversed: The market must be found that fits the product. Such a case might exist when the market changes or new competition takes it away.

Competitive Strategy

In developing competitive strategy, the firm actually chooses its competition and when and where it will compete, as well as whether it will be a low-cost producer, a differentiator, a focuser, or some combination of these. This is realistic provided the choice is realistic and if it is based on an objective situational analysis.

Take the case of Wendy's restaurants, which used a **focus strategy** when it started its first restaurant in Columbus, Ohio, on November 15, 1969.

> In the late 1960s, when McDonald's and Burger King were already well established, industry experts did not think that there was room for another hamburger chain to enter the market and grow to any substantial size. However, in March 1978, Wendy's had grown to a chain of 1,000 units. A year later, it opened its 1,500th unit. Wendy's did not compete head to head with McDonald's or Burger King, but rather it focused on a special niche in the crowded hamburger market. For instance, it became the first fast-food chain to introduce the salad bar. It went after the baby-boomers, who were young adults in their 20s and 30s. Surveys showed that over 80 percent of Wendy's business came from those over 25. Compare this with McDonald's, which derived 35 percent of its business from those under 19.

The secret to a successful competitive marketing strategy is to find a market in which there is a clear advantage or a niche in the market that can be defended. The trick, then, is to match the firm's product strengths with the market or niche. It does not matter whether this niche occurs in the high or low end of the market, it is generally prudent to consider examples on both ends of the spectrum.

Ritz-Carlton uses a **differentiation strategy** and is positioned at the top of the market. Its product is "top drawer," and it is almost never compromised. Even after being bought by Marriott, Marriott clearly indicated it will never put the Marriott name on the Ritz-Carlton brand. On the other hand, Microtel has maintained its position in the budget segment as a low-cost leader. Both these companies chose their competition, stuck to it in the marketplace, and were realistic about the choice. This is the essence of clear and compelling competitive strategy. These are single-product companies that compete in a single niche.

Other companies, such as Choice International, choose their competition in different niches with different brand lines—Clarion, Quality, Comfort, and Sleep Inns—and market them together, giving the customer a choice. Taj Hotels in India uses one brand name on six different product lines (Exhibit 6-7), while Groupe Accor of France

EXHIBIT 6-7   Taj Group offers one brand with six product lines.

Source: Retrieved September 12, 2005 from www.tajhotels.com/AboutTaj/ CompanyInformation/default.htm. Adapted from Taj Hotels, www.tajhotels. com. Used by permission.

EXHIBIT 6-8   Groupe Accor of France has 13 brand lines.

Source: Retrieved October 11, 2005, from www.accor.com/gbgroupe/activities/ hotellerie/marques/formule1.asp. Courtesy of Groupe Accor. Used by permission of AccorHotels.com.

has 13 brand lines, as shown in Exhibit 6-8. Each of the brand lines is marketed separately.

On the other hand, poor strategic planning leads to choosing the wrong competitors to compete against with the wrong product. When Omni Hotels took over the New York Sheraton and refurbished it, management chose as its competition upscale hotels such as the Essex House and the Parker Meridien without offering a comparable product and thereby damaging its identity. Gross operating profit doubled when new management chose instead to compete against the lower-scale hotels in the marketplace. The New York Sheraton is now Parc Central Hotel, part of Interstate Hotels.

In some companies with widely varied product carrying the same name, each property has to choose its own competition. This is sometimes difficult when the brand name is carried on all products. For example, prior to being purchased by Starwood, Sheraton operated the five-star Sheraton St. Regis in New York City, the convention hotel Sheraton New York a few blocks away, tiny Sheraton Russell on Park Avenue, and franchises in Bordentown, New Jersey (50 miles away), and Westchester County, a half an hour from New York City. Each of these Sheratons had markedly different competition and customers, but all were marketed together under the Sheraton flag. To correct this situation, Starwood rebranded many of the properties by creating different classifications of hotels. For instance, they established the Four Points (by Sheraton) hotel brand for lower-tier properties. Other brand names now include St. Regis, the Luxury Collection, Sheraton, Westin, and W.

 Web Browsing Exercise

Visit Starwood's website (www.starwoodhotels.com/), as well as the websites for their different brands (you can link to these from the preceding web address). How do the brands' individual websites highlight their different competitive strategies? Compare and contrast the brands' individual websites. How are they similar? How are they different?

Market Strategy

Market strategy is founded on the premise of reaching the right market with the product. In the final analysis, if you can't reach the market, the best product and the most well-defined strategy will fail. For the hospitality industry, reaching the market can be looked at in two ways. The first is taking the product to the market; the second is bringing the market to the product. By contrast, with manufactured goods, taking the product to the market is a major commitment and, in some cases, a major capital investment. For multi-unit hotel and restaurant companies, taking the product to the market is part of the distribution system. This is the area where location becomes a major factor. The strategy involved concerns the appropriate markets to enter.

For multi-unit companies that seek growth, the case is multiplied many times. When McDonald's saw its growth limited in freestanding, drive-up stores, it changed its market strategy. Soon McDonald's appeared in inner-city locations, office buildings, universities, and almost anywhere else one looked. It then headed overseas to both the European and Asian markets. In Singapore, on the main road of the city and right next to the Hilton International, sits what became the highest-grossing McDonald's in the world, later supplanted by the one in Red Square,

Moscow. Market strategy has been a major factor in McDonald's success.

Hilton International's market strategy was to be in major capital cities throughout the world. InterContinental was developed for cities where Pan American Airlines, its former owner, flew. Le Meridien Hotels chose to enter primary cities such as Boston, New York, and San Francisco when it expanded into the United States. Marriott likes to saturate an area with multiple units, as it has done in Boston; Washington, D.C.; Atlanta; Dallas; and other cities.

Getting the market to the product involves a new set of strategies. When resources are scarce, as they usually are, the market strategy must designate where to use those resources. A restaurant may choose the surrounding neighborhood and concentrate on word of mouth. McDonald's, on the other hand, uses national television to cover the entire United States, as well as other countries. Hyatt concentrates heavily on airline magazines, meeting planner journals, and travel agent media. Marriott concentrates on its frequent traveler program and business publications. Many hotels, especially in Asia and southern Europe, rely heavily on tour operators to get their customers to them.

> **Tourism Marketing Application**
> The city of Dublin, in Ireland, presents its marketing strategy and its plans to reach its goals on the website www.trade.visitdublin.com/trade/marketing/default. asp. This website is a nice example of concepts discussed in this chapter. (Retrieved March 18, 2006)

Positioning Strategy

The last, but by no means least, of the business strategies is the positioning strategy. This entails the creation and/or enhancement of a specific brand image in the customer's mind. Positioning strategy is no less than the presentation of the product strategy directed at the target markets, consistent with the resources and capabilities of the firm, aimed at specific markets, vis-à-vis the competition.

Functional Strategies

Functional strategies (refer again to Exhibit 6-1) are the "what" of the strategic system—that is, the *what* we are going to do to get *where* we want to go. The important thing to remember is that these are still strategies, not tactics, which come immediately afterward. It is this set of strategies that flows directly to the customer in the form of the value chain. For example, the communication strategy might be to portray luxury; the presentation strategy to price exclusively with luxurious rooms; the product/service

strategy to render personal attention (e.g., butler service); and the distribution strategy to use exclusive referral systems and select travel agents. The functional strategies represent the substrategy implementation of the business strategies. They are commonly referred to as the marketing mix. Strategies at this level of the hierarchy represent shorter-term and more flexible strategies. As mentioned in Chapter 5, all include value chain elements.

In Chapter 3 we identified the different components of the marketing mix. We now reexamine each of these in terms of marketing strategy.

Product/Service Strategy

The product/service mix is defined as follows: The combination of products and services, whether free or for sale, aimed at satisfying the needs of the target market.[2]

In the better-known four Ps (product, price, place, and promotion) developed for goods marketing, this is the product. Ritz-Carlton has a top-of-the-line product/service strategy at the master and business strategy levels. At the functional strategy level, strategic decisions must be made regarding the level of service to offer and when and how to offer it. The same criteria, of course, apply: What is important to the target market? What does the target market expect? What problems does the target market have?

Let's say that the product/service strategy is to provide luxury. This would be a natural derivation from the master strategy and the business strategies. The question is how to put it into practice. These are the tactics. Consider terry-cloth bathrobes in each room—is this important to the market? Does the market expect it? Does it solve a problem for the customer? For Ritz-Carlton the answer may be yes and the customer is willing to pay the additional cost. For most other hotels the answer is probably no.

For a destination area, the product/service strategy is to provide family entertainment. This is certainly the case for Orlando. The tactics to put this into practice include all the theme parks, family-friendly restaurants, and family activities.

The Oberoi Hotel chain in India once changed its master strategy and decided to aim at the super-luxury market. Into the rooms went antique desks, personalized stationery, beautiful brass ashtrays, and terry-cloth bathrobes, among other things. The rooms themselves weren't much different; it was the symbols of luxury that made the difference, and the product/service strategy had to change. Many other changes were also made in the hotel's marketing mix to carry out this strategy. Exhibit 6-9 gives some examples of tactics that failed to support the strategies of various hotel properties.

These examples demonstrate that product/service functional strategies concern the level of product and ser-

| **EXHIBIT 6-9** | **Tactics That Failed to Support Strategies** |

Hyatt Hotels once had a policy that every dish that went out of its restaurant must have fresh fruit on it. Strawberries showed up in the strangest places, but the tactic, at least, was consistent with the strategy of fresh quality. This was also the communications strategy at that time, and ads portrayed fresh fruit (tactic). In other situations, this was not the case. The Sheraton Boston Hotel (formerly the Sheraton Towers Hotel) had a product/service strategy of exclusivity and provided bathrobes, but didn't open the pool until 9:00 A.M., and all the lightbulbs in the rooms were only 67 watts. Marriott's Courtyards didn't open the pool until 10:00 A.M., in spite of people trying to get in at 8:00 A.M.. The Fairmont Hamilton Princess in Bermuda (formerly the Southampton Princess Hotel) emphasized service and convenience and told you that its coffee shop was open until 1:00 A.M., but closed it if no one happened to be there at 10:00 P.M. It also closed its lobby restrooms and waterfront pool and bar in the slow season to keep costs down, but maintained expensive bathroom amenities and high room rates in the largely empty rooms.

The Grosvenor Hotel in Orlando (formerly the Americana Dutch Inn) once offered nightly dancing, but only disco, and only locals went. The hotel was full of families, its target market. The Crowne Plaza in Kuala Lumpur offered fresh orange juice, but not before 10:00 A.M. (because "the juicer is in the bar") and targeted Americans. The Asia hotel in Bangkok, catering to an American and European market, had minibars in the rooms, but no wine in them. The Westin Harbour Castle in Toronto had Do Not Disturb signs to hang on your doorknob. The maid knocked at 8:00 A.M. anyway.

The Marriott Copley Place in Boston had drapes that didn't close all the way to shut out the morning light, no pull-out clotheslines in the bathroom because they're "too much trouble," and a restaurant with coffee shop decor, appointments, and service, but fine dining room prices. The Walaker Hotel in Sognefjord, Norway, billed itself as the finest hotel in Norway, charged $200 for a double room, but had tiny soap bars (albeit in fancy boxes) reminiscent of the early American motels.

All of these examples show how tactics executed at the hotel level may not support the mission statement at the corporate office.

vice offered consistent with higher-level strategies. Higher-level strategies must be built around the target markets and the product, as should the functional strategies that flow from them and the tactics that are implemented. As shown in Exhibit 6-9, this is sometimes not the case in practice.

Presentation Strategy

The presentation mix is defined as follows: All elements used by the firm to increase the tangibility of the product/service mix in the perception of the target market at the right time and place.[3]

The presentation strategy addresses the physical plant, atmospherics, employees, customers, location, and price. The same rules apply to this strategy as to the product/service strategy. Much of what we have said earlier could also be applied here—that is, this strategy is no less than a carryover of the product/service strategy. This mix has no true counterpart in the four Ps but includes price.

Physical plant and atmosphere must be consistent with the product/service strategy. This means that they shouldn't be overdone or underdone.

Employees must be hired and trained accordingly. Certainly we expect a bigger smile and quieter maids at a four-star than at a two-star hotel and better service at a three-star than at a one-star restaurant. In either case, we expect an emphasis on the customer rather than on the service. This difference, in fact, is why Ritz-Carlton does so well at what it does. The reverse is also true: At McDonald's we expect service to be consistent with the product strategy; for example, McDonald's expects you to clear your own tray when finished!

The *customer mix* strategy is very important. In some deluxe hotels in Paris and London, men don't get in the

door without a coat and tie. At other places, you may feel out of place if you have them on. Some restaurants also require a coat and tie, as well as regulate the footwear of their clientele. There is a basic strategy here that really applies in almost all cases: Don't mix incompatible markets if you can possibly help it; if you have to deal with incompatible markets, keep them separated in both time (e.g., seasonally) and space (e.g., separate dining rooms).

Location strategy means being where the customer can get to you or you can get to the customer. Again, McDonald's, in its infinite ubiquitousness, is a prime example of this strategy in practice with stores located in just about every conceivable facility or location.

Pricing strategy, again, should be consistent with the other functional strategies. In too many cases, in fact, there seems to be no strategy at all. Prices sometimes seem to be set totally independent of all other strategies and without regard to their interrelationship. Price creates many expectations, which is why we consider it both a part of the presentation mix, as well as a separate part of the marketing mix.

Consider the airline passenger who pays $6,000 to fly business class on an international flight versus the passenger who pays $600 in economy. They leave and arrive at the same time and travel at the same speed. What does the $1,400 difference in price tell you? That's an easy one: leg room, good food, personal service, movies, and so on. What does $200 for a hotel room tell you? Or $100? Or $75? Or $35? In Toronto we found a hotel that charged $150 for a room service imperial quart bottle (40 ounces) of liquor, plus tax and tip, which sold in the liquor store for under $30. The room cost $119. Although the customer is the same for both, there is clearly no relationship between the pricing strategies.

Pricing Strategy

The pricing mix is the combination of prices used by the firm to represent the value of the offering. The pricing mix is how the customer values what is being offered and what is received.

The following points have been considered in developing the pricing strategy:

■ Special features of the product
■ Spending power of the market
■ Traffic movement of the market
■ Possibility of losing regular users of high-rate rooms to lower-rate rooms
■ Pricing of the competition
■ Management policy to avoid discounted business, group business, and any upgrading to the new rooms
■ The fact that the rates will be raised in three months

While you consider the last point, also consider what Jain stated:

> Increase [in price] should be considered for its effect on long-term profitability, demand elasticity and competitive moves. Although a higher price may mean higher profits in the short run, the long-run effect of a price increase may be disastrous. The increase may encourage new entrants to flock to the industry and competition from substitutes. Thus, before a price increase strategy is implemented, its long-term effect should be thoroughly examined. Further, an increase in price may lead to shifts in demand that could be detrimental.[4]

All of the possibilities Jain mentioned have happened in the hotel and restaurant industries in recent years because of overpricing in the short run. We will discuss pricing in a later chapter, as a separate part of the marketing mix, so it will not be belabored further here. Suffice it to say that pricing is both a powerful and dangerous strategic tool.

Communication Strategy

The communications mix consists of all communications between the firm and the target market that increase the tangibility of the product/service mix, that establish or monitor customer expectations, or that persuade customers to purchase.[5] The communication mix replaces promotion in the four Ps.

The issue here is obviously the strategy to be used to communicate all of the preceding to the marketplace. The strategic issue is what to say, not how to say it. The "how to say it" requires exceptional creativity in many cases and is often best left to those with that kind of expertise. The "what to say," however, is a strategic management decision and should not be left for advertising agencies to decide without extensive consultation.

Management's failure to clarify its strategy will not stop the agency from being creative. But it could, and too often does, result in advertising that does not clearly communicate the desired or appropriate message. The finished ads, the "how to say it," should always be filtered through the strategy to be certain that is what they are really saying.

An example that happens quite frequently in practice is advertising copy that positions a hotel or restaurant at a higher level than its strategy calls for. The property may be at a three-star level and aimed at the corresponding target market. The "creative" agency, however, gets inflated with terms such as *luxurious* and *elegant*. The appropriate target market feels it cannot afford it, and the upscale market, which is attracted, is disappointed. The result is a net loss for everyone.

Advertising, of course, is not the only part of the communications mix strategy. The strategy will also dictate the methods of communication. This is likely to include some combination of advertising, personal selling, public relations, promotion (including frequent traveler programs), merchandising, direct mail, and, today, marketing on the World Wide Web. The strategy will dictate where the emphasis and proportion of the budget should be placed on each.

An excerpt from the strategic plan of the International hotel follows.

■ *Objective:* To creatively highlight the uniqueness of the product.
■ *Strategy:* To convince customers, especially the FIT (foreign independent traveler) and corporate segments, that we have a unique hotel in terms of its being traditional in decor, equipped with the most modern business aids, and having a greater accent on personalized service. To create awareness of the new F&B outlets.
■ *Mix:* [This is followed by an extensive list including advertising media, in-house materials, sales materials, direct mail, publicity materials, brochures, sales trips and blitzes, research, personal invitations, travel agencies, and other strategic and tactical plans.]

Distribution Strategy

The distribution mix is made up of all channels available between the firm and the target market that increase the probability of getting the customer to the product.

Strategies for distribution deal with channels and, in the case of most hospitality services, how to move the customer physically to the product. These include travel agents, tour brokers, wholesalers, referral services, reservation systems, websites, airlines, travel clubs, and so forth. Strategies involve the emphasis placed on each (or none) as well as the channels used. Distribution replaces place in the four Ps.

Destination hotels and resorts will place special emphasis on using these channels. Distribution systems have become increasingly complex in the hotel industry and for many companies require far more attention today than they did 10 years ago.

Club Med presents a somewhat unusual situation. The Club Med vacation is generally all-inclusive (meals, transfers, hotel room, and sometimes airfare are packaged on a per person basis). Accordingly, Club Med tended to act largely as its own travel agent. This strategy was less than optimally effective in penetrating the American market. The revised strategy was to cultivate specific markets and select travel agencies. Club Med personally trained the agents in the "Club Med concept" and made them "Club Med specialists." This strategy established a special distribution channel that turned out to be very effective.

Restaurants are also involved in distribution channels. Restaurants in Brussels where there is heavy convention and tourist traffic, work closely with tour operators and incentive travel planners to bring in customers. There are other special cases, too. Many restaurants use the services of concierges at hotels to make recommendations to out-of-town guests. This distribution channel in many cases is worked every day, with financial rewards to the concierges that send the most business to certain restaurants.

In fact, destination management companies (DMCs) are increasingly becoming strong channels of distribution. Originally designed to handle the land transportation needs of groups upon arrival, the DMCs quickly recognized the ability to steer potential customers to restaurants, catering facilities, attractions, and other related hospitality providers.

Feedback Loops

There are two **feedback loops** in the strategic marketing system model in Exhibit 6-1. One is the risk/fit loop. Feeding back to the master strategy, this loop questions the risks if the strategy is pursued and the strategic fit. Some of the critical risk questions that must be asked are, What can happen? Will it work? What if it doesn't? How will competitors react? What are the economics? Does it meet objectives? and Is there a fit between the marketplace and the master strategy? If answers are negative, reevaluation must

take place. This is far better than following hunches that often end in failure.

The second loop starts with **synthesis** of all the analysis that has been done. Through analysis, we learn to break a problem into its many parts such as the marketing, financial, organizational, and environmental components. Many students and managers are good at this, but what they often do not do is put the pieces back together again. Too often the ability to analyze is valued over the ability to synthesize. Miller stated it this way:

> Analytical skills are fine for delving into problems, but they are inadequate for generating the insight needed for a workable solution. Analysis requires systematic probing, thoroughness and logic. Synthesis, on the other hand, calls for artful pattern recognition, receptiveness and magical insight—traits much neglected in the western world.[6]

In other words, synthesis means putting the pieces back together in a meaningful way that separates the wheat from the chaff. This means restating the pertinent elements in a concise, clear summation that is configured in a way that considers the needs of the firm, the needs of its customers, and the challenges of its competitors. It means identifying a theme or a vision for a configuration that is durable, defensible, and feasible.

Synthesis is followed by evaluation/fit. Here we ask some of the same questions that we asked in the risk loop. We also make value judgments about whether the strategy matches capabilities and whether the organization can support it; that is, can it be successfully implemented, and, if so, what will it take? Evaluation is the summation of the upside and the downside.

Once the strategy is planned and approved, it has to, of course, be implemented. Unfortunately, this is sometimes where it all falls apart, especially if the previous planning stages haven't been analyzed thoroughly. Implementation may require a number of events.

First, there is the organization. Strategy is implemented through organizational design. This means creating an organizational structure that will spot its own weaknesses and make the strategy work. Too often, a strategy is put in place with the existing organizational structure, which doesn't allow it to work, or, worse, the strategy is designed around the existing structure. Structure follows strategy. This is critical. Employees' activities must be coordinated, and employees must be motivated to make the strategy work—to create value and to obtain competitive advantage. The organization must also be designed to have an effective control system that compares actual performance against established targets, evaluates the results, and takes action if necessary.

Because this is a marketing text, we won't elaborate further on organizational structure and implementing change. These issues, however, are not to be taken lightly and should be considered in any strategic plan.

The second feedback loop continues with the feedback on whether the strategy is working once it is in place. Marketing research is fed into the marketing intelligence system. This is the control that warns management to act before the possibility arises of the system's being out of control.

Strategy Selection

As we have progressed through the strategic marketing system model illustrated in Exhibit 6-1, we have provided a framework on which we can later expand. We have probably raised more questions than we have provided answers. That is because there is no single right marketing strategy for any situation; there are simply right alternatives. The situational analysis, if done objectively, should lay bare the facts. The environmental analysis provides the bases for assumptions. From these sources, the strategic planner develops alternative courses of action.

Which one should be chosen? That is a simple question that has no simple answer. When you consider that there are also alternatives at every step of the strategic planning process, you find that you have dozens, perhaps hundreds, of choices to make. That seems like a formidable task, and it may well be. Some are better at it than others. Good common sense, wisdom, judgment, and intuition still have their place. Interpreting information, while objective, is not mechanical. The functions of strategic planning are to define objectives in terms other than profit, to plan ahead, to influence and not just react to change, and to inspire organizational commitment. Once the strategy has been formulated, it should also be evaluated for content. Exhibit 6-10 is a checklist for that purpose. Strategy selection should also include understanding the customer's role in the process:

A business . . . is defined by the want the customer satisfies when he buys a product or service. . . . To the customer, no product or service and certainly no company, is of much importance. . . . The customer only wants to know what the product or service will do for him tomorrow. All he is interested in are his own values, his own wants and his own reality. For this reason alone, any serious attempt to state "what our business is" must start with the customer, his realities, his situation, his behavior, his expectations and his values.[7]

Why Strategic Plans Fail

The best formulated strategy in the world can fail if it is badly implemented. In some quarters, strategic planning has acquired a bad name because of these failures. It is better to understand the reasons for failure than to blame the process. Research has shown the following reasons for failure. We have added some comments to each.

- *Poor preparation of line managers* Too often managers are rewarded solely or largely on bottom-line profits. The emphasis remains on short-term objectives. Owners' demands become the compelling decision process.
- *Faulty definition of business units* Too often structure comes before strategy, and the organization does not support the development and execution of strategy. The role of top management is not to spot and solve problems as much as it is to create an organization that can spot and solve its own problems. Organizations need to determine whether they have the right structure to implement the preferred strategy.
- *Vaguely formulated goals* Too often goals are largely financially oriented or based too much on average rate, occupancy, and/or market share rather than on share of customer, customer loyalty, or long-range strategic advantage.
- *Inadequate information bases for action planning* Planning in detail should be used as a further test of a strategy's feasibility, requiring the participation of

---

EXHIBIT 6-10   **Strategy Checklist**

- Is it identifiable and clear in words and practice?
- Does it fully exploit opportunity?
- Is it consistent with competence and resources?
- Is it internally consistent, synergistic?
- Is it a feasible risk in economic and personal terms?

- Is it appropriate to personal values and aspirations?
- Does it provide stimulus to organizational effort and commitment?
- Are there indications of responsiveness of the market?
- Is it based on reality to the customer?
- Is it workable?

middle and lower management and the workforce. Lower-level participation is essential to working out practical steps. Pushing strategic planning out into the organization by exhortation or one-way communication is not effective.

■ *Inadequate linkage of strategic planning with other control systems* Other control systems can include such things as budgets, information systems, and reward systems. Strategic planning is a way of thinking about a business and how to run it.

■ Summary

Strategic planning is a difficult but essential process. At the highest level of the firm, it drives the firm. At the lowest operational level, it drives day-to-day activities. It is an essential phase of marketing and management leadership. In the short term, however, it is the annual marketing plan, which makes the strategic plan work.

Good strategic planning rests on knowing where you are now and where you want to go and finding the best way to get there. Its success rests on objective analysis, knowing what business you are in, understanding markets, integrating within the firm, and creating an organizational structure that will facilitate the implementation. In essence, there is no substitute for strategic planning and execution in today's competitive environment.

At the same time, all strategic thinking and planning need not take place only at the corporate or higher levels of management. Unit managers have to be involved in strategic planning. We have given numerous examples of what happens when strategic planning is not done, is done poorly, or is poorly executed. At the least, every manager should be thinking strategically at every level.

Strategic planning occurs at the functional level following the strategies set forth at the higher levels. It may occur for a 60-seat coffee shop or a 20-unit motel. Regardless, it is strategy that drives tactics and that, when done and executed properly, will optimize marketing performance. Even Max and Greti's Restaurant Zum See will sell more food when they plan strategically. The functions of strategic planning are to define objectives in terms other than profit, to plan ahead, to influence and not just react to change, and to inspire organizational commitment.

■ Key Terms

strategic marketing system
mission statement
strategic business unit (SBU)
master marketing strategy
situational analysis
opportunities
business strategies

threats
distinctive competency
focus strategy
differentiation strategy
functional strategies
feedback loops
synthesis

■ Discussion Questions

1. Discuss why a mission statement and objectives are needed at the highest and lowest levels of management.
2. How is the product/service strategy different from the target market strategy in strategic planning?
3. What are the most critical factors in strategy selection? Why?
4. Apply the information in Exhibit 6-5 to a hospitality company of your choice. Read information from a variety of sources, not just information on its website or a corporate report. Is the information consistent?
5. Go to a company you either currently work for or one you have worked for in the past. Ask to see the mission statement for this company. Does the organization live by its mission statement? What evidence do you have for your decision? If you are not working or have never worked, go to a company with which you are familiar.

■ Group Projects

1. Use the strategic marketing system model in Exhibit 6-1 to analyze a local operation with which you are all familiar such as a bar, restaurant, or even campus food service. Pinpoint each stage of the model.
2. From a recent publication, choose an article on the problems of a hospitality enterprise. Analyze the organization in terms of the model in Exhibit 6-1. Where did the company go wrong? Where could it or should it have corrected the situation? How?

CHAPTER 7

Understanding Individual Customers

Overview

This chapter reviews the process consumers go through when attempting to meet their needs and wants, solve problems, and make decisions and choices. Special emphasis is placed on hospitality purchases. The consumer begins by realizing that she has a problem (need) that may be solved or satisfied by the hospitality offering. Initially, she searches past experiences for a solution to this problem/need, but may graduate to searching outside information; for example, she may call a friend, go to a website, or seek information from a travel agent. The search process can be either high involvement (an important decision for the consumer) or low involvement (a relatively unimportant decision). Customer perceptions of the importance of the purchase decision are critical in the buy decision process. Beliefs are derived from these perceptions, and these perceptions in turn reflect the attitudes and opinions toward the hospitality offering.

I. Introduction to Hospitality Marketing
1. The Concept of Marketing
2. Marketing Services and the Hospitality Experience
3. The Marketing Mix and the Product/Service Mix
4. Relationship/Loyalty Marketing

II. Marketing to Build a Competitive Advantage
5. Strategic Marketing
6. The Strategic Marketing System and Marketing Objectives

VII. Feedback

VI. Synthesis
21. The Marketing Plan

III. The Marketplace
7. *Understanding Individual Customers*
8. Understanding Organizational Customers
9. The Tourist Customer and the Tourism Destination

IV. Situational Analysis
10. Understanding Competition
11. Marketing Intelligence and Research

V. Functional Strategies
12. Differentiation, Segmentation, and Target Marketing
13. Branding and Market Positioning
14. The Hospitality Pricing Mix
15. The Communications Mix: Advertising
16. The Communications Mix: Sales Promotions, Merchandising, Public Relations, and Publicity
17. The Communications Mix: Personal Selling
18. Hospitality Distribution Systems
19. Channels of Distribution: Bringing the Customer to the Product
20. Interactive Marketing: Internet and Database Marketing

Marketing Executive Profile

Thomas Storey
Executive Vice President, Development, Fairmont Hotels & Resorts

Tom Storey was appointed executive vice president, development, of Fairmont Hotels & Resorts in June 2004. Tom is responsible for defining and executing the growth plan for the firm and also oversees new business development and Fairmont Heritage Place.

Storey joined the company as executive vice president, business development and strategy, in February 2001. Prior to Fairmont Hotels & Resorts, he was with Promus Hotels, a hotel management and ownership company, as executive vice president, strategic planning and venture operations, from 1998 until 2000, and executive vice president, marketing, from 1997 to 1998. Prior to joining Promus Hotels, Storey was executive vice president, sales and marketing, at Doubletree Hotels.

Marketing in Action

Thomas Storey, Executive Vice President, Development, Fairmont Hotels & Resorts

How do you segment your different individual customers (e.g., business, leisure), and would this be typical of all hotels?

At a macro level, we do segments in business and leisure. We also segment them as direct or through a third party—typically a travel agent—and we also segment them by how they book us—whether they go to the hotel direct through the reservations center, through the GDS [global distribution system], or through an e-commerce site. Plus, we do segmentation from a clustering perspective relative to their spend levels, their stay patterns, their geographic source, etc. I think it is typical of most hotel companies.

Are business travelers one segment or many? How are they different?

The ideal segment is the segment of one, and that is where the business is moving, towards customerization* by individual. From a marketing perspective, it's still more difficult to attract one person than it is to cluster people together and look for commonalities that you can market to. In the business travel segment, people would segment from the perspective of whether they're booking themselves or booking through an intermediary. They would also probably segment by some sort of product purchase intent. For example, we have a Gold product, which is a higher service product bundle that is within our hotel, so people who purchase that product will be different from people who are just purchasing the standard Fairmont room. Hotel companies have multiple segments within business travel that either relate to the types of products they offer, to the price point that they offer them at, or again, in terms of how their decision is ultimately made.

We reach these travelers through general marketing communications that would get them through the traditional media vehicles that you would normally think of, such as print, TV, and cable. There's also an increasing use now of various online search tools as well as online aggregators that we would set parameters with and try to market to individuals in that respect. For example, keyword marketing has become a pretty aggressive form of marketing on

---

Customerization can be defined as a "buyer centric company strategy combining mass customization with customized marketing." For more information, visit www.smeal.psu.edu/ebrc/publications/res_papers/1999_06.pdf.

the Internet. We market through out own databases and also through various corporations that we would be working in partnership with. In large cases, we would create a corporate account with a company and then use their marketing vehicles to get to their customers and encourage them to stay at Fairmont.

What are the needs of business travelers today by segment? How have these needs changed over time?

They're always evolving. The key evolution in the past five years has been the increased use of technology—whether that's high speed Internet in the room, wireless networks, plasma televisions, the fact that many consumers now are carrying their own content, whether they are doing that through their own computers, memory sticks, or iPods, or some other format. For a while, the content was resonant in the TV, then the content was resonant in the traveler's laptop, then it became resonant on the network, and now it's really in all of the above. Being able to access multiple forms of content through multiple technologies is probably the latest need of the business segment. In a hotel, we need to make sure that, if a person is carrying their information on a JumpDrive, that there is a place in the hotel where they can access that JumpDrive. If a customer accidentally forgets the power cord for their iPod, we need to make sure that we have those available at the front desk or an in-room stereo system that they can plug that equipment into. There are multiple ways of looking at it. The comfort level with technology that business travelers have today is dramatically different than what it was in the past.

It used to be that business travel was considered "price inelastic." Is this still true today? If not, what brought about these changes?

Price plays a couple of different roles in the hotel industry. For business travelers, there's typically a price band determining what they can spend. So, if I am the CEO of a company, then I have a price band that probably has a very high top end on it—if any at all. If I'm a corporate officer, maybe I have a price band that says I can stay in a luxury hotel but I can't stay in a boutique hotel, and if you're a traveling salesperson, maybe you can't stay anywhere above $120. As a result, business travelers really need to look at the options they have within a band and look at the upper limit of that band to see what's in the band or not. So, in a certain band, I may be able to choose a high-end hotel, but I really can't have a luxury hotel on my expense report. Price plays a role in limiting their options, and then they can choose within that band as a function of what's most convenient for them, what offers the best services, best food and beverage, etc. I think price for the business traveler has always had an impact. Within a price band, I think people are looking at

other factors, like loyalty programs and such, which help them make a decision as to where to stay.

What role do travel managers or organizations play in arranging business travel? Is their power getting stronger or weaker?

They tend to work with most of the major companies, but for a corporate account, they are looking at where the bulk of their travelers would usually go. If that's one location, then they'll negotiate between multiple hotel companies in that location that have roughly comparable quality amenities. But if there are multiple locations, which many corporations have, they will then manage across those multiple destinations, leveraging one destination against another to try to get the best overall pricing for the company. So companies that have broad distribution typically can be more effective negotiators when they're negotiating with a company that has multiple destinations that they're trying to deal with.

However, hotel companies that have various owners, particularly when they are franchising hotels, are sometimes in a more difficult situation trying to negotiate those deals, because they're negotiating across multiple owners. If you have a more uniform ownership group, it becomes a little easier to leverage the high-demand destinations against the lower-demand destinations and improve the overall business for the company. In regards to the amount of power these managers have, I would say it has gotten weaker. On the one hand, they're getting better tools at their disposal in order to be able to negotiate transactions because the expense-tracking technology has gotten better. But on the other hand, the online booking channels have surpassed or supplanted the corporate travel managers in some cases, particularly as it relates to business travel as opposed to group travel, because people will just go online and book themselves.

Are leisure travelers one segment or many? How are they different?

They are the same as business travelers, but they have a wider array of segments because leisure travelers have multiple trip occasions. They could be traveling with family or friends, they could be attending an event, it could be personal leisure, or it could be vacation. I think that any one leisure traveler could have multiple reasons for booking a leisure trip, which could actually cause them to fall into different segments.

How do hotel firms attract the leisure segment?

Promotions and price are the two big ones, with price being more for short-term demand and promotion more typically being used for when a person is looking for some type of value added type of booking. In terms of how you reach leisure travelers, it is largely the same tools as you would use to reach business travelers. I think for long-haul destination leisure travels, travel agents play an even greater role. Travel agents come more into play the more expensive the trip gets, because if somebody just wants to book a weekend someplace, it's less likely that they're going to use a travel agent. If they're booking a week, 10-day, or perhaps two-week vacation—especially if it's overseas, because there's a lot of risk in that vacation—they might research it online, but still talk to a travel agent to give them a bit of a security blanket. Additionally, it's still relatively difficult to do a multisegment booking online—using air, car rental, and multiple hotels, for example. It's often easier to have a travel agent put something like that together, and obviously the suppliers are paying the agents, not the traveler.

How important are packages to the leisure segment?

We have multiple tiers of packages. Some are what we call positioning packages. For instance, we have a package where you can stay at a suite at the San Francisco Fairmont, rent a 911 Carrera 4S Porsche, and then stay at the suite at our Sonoma property, which is a four-day package for about $17,000. That's what we call a Prestige package. It's more about the positioning of the experience. We have packages that are more experience-based packages, where you would be interacting with the destination, amenities at the hotel, etc. We also have price-based packages, where you stay three days and get the fourth day free or receive X kind of discount or bonus miles—that type of thing.

What advice can you give to companies designing packages?

I think packages need to do a few things. Firstly, they have to be unique to the competition. They also have to be easy to understand, and they have to be attractively priced from a value perspective.

Do the needs of travelers change depending on their country of residence? If so, how?

One key difference is language. It may not seem like a big thing, but it is when you're taking people from Asia to the Rockies or from some parts of Europe to someplace like Bermuda—language is key.

Food is also key. You need to be able to offer people food that is consistent with their typical diet. Whenever you have people that are traveling in larger groups such as tour groups, you need to be able to help them coordinate all the ground handling activities, whether that is transport or sightseeing or any sort of destination type product that they might experience beyond the hotel. People like to be able to experience the food in the culture they are visiting, but at the same time, they like to see types of food that they are used to back home as a sort of fallback. When we bring Asians to Banff, we typically try to have Asian food like sushi, rice, etc., that would fit a traveler coming from Asia. It's not that it replaces the indigenous foods, but rather is a complement to them.

How much market research do you do as a company?

We do a lot of ongoing research through a number of different vehicles. We obviously have comment cards. We do our own forms of research with J.D. Power and Associates, plus we do both ad hoc and annual customer surveys. There are a lot of different research vehicles going on, and we are constantly trying to triangulate them on what is going to most differentiate us and what is going to be the most relevant to our customer.

Do you do a lot with lifetime value of a customer?

We do, although I won't say we use it as our single criterion. It's one of the criteria that we look at when we're trying to balance our short-term revenue needs against our long-term customer loyalty needs. We typically do calculate it, and we try to calculate it by segment. Our bias is probably more towards loyalty, as opposed to more towards the short term, in regards to where we place our marketing effort. It's somewhat difficult to calculate because it's a bit of a moving target in that customers book in many different ways, which have different cost structures, and customers consume at the hotels in many different ways, which also affects the lifetime value calculation.

What advice can you give to those studying marketing?

I think there is a continuing evolution towards customization, so I think that students need to focus more on the intricacies of market research, both qualitative and quantitative, to really understand how to develop hypotheses, how to test hypotheses, and how to monitor behavior. Those are all critical components in being an effective transient marketer.

I think that gaining a high level of comfort with technology and how to use technology is also important—again, to do the research, but also to deliver a customized product. I would carry that through to operations research from the standpoint of being able to create service bundles that truly are differentiated and customized.

The hotel industry still operates within a lot of paradigms around the way the service is delivered, and it tends to be from the hotel out, rather than from the customer in. I think the hotelier of tomorrow is going to be even better at identifying and recognizing somebody as an individual, providing them with a customized set of products and services, and then maintaining a dialogue with them over time so that it becomes a community of one, rather than trying to dump them into segments. Fairmont is continuing to go in that direction. It's more challenging in larger hotels when you're dealing across multiple customer segments. Some customer segments are better served by being able to handle large numbers of people, and some customer segments—transient in particular, especially high-end transient—are more oriented toward intimacy and personalization. Blending the two of these together is somewhat of a challenge, especially doing it in a portfolio where you probably have upwards of one and a half million a year going through the hotel. Luckily, technology has come a long way, so it's easier than it used to be, but it's still not an easy task in general.

Used by permission from Thomas Storey.

If the first step in marketing is to recognize customers' needs, wants, and problems, then it is obvious that we must understand how and why customers behave the way they do, as well as what leads them to behave in that manner. This is no small task.

There are no easy and definite answers to these questions. Instead, many theories, concepts, and models have been developed to explain the complex customer. These have been derived from many disciplines such as sociology, psychology, social psychology, anthropology, philosophy, and economics; all these approaches must be integrated before we can approach even a limited understanding of the customer. Our ultimate goal, of course, is to be able to influence buyer behavior.

It is important to begin with some basic and generally agreed upon **tenets of consumer behavior,** because effective marketing must be based on these premises. Managerial decisions that ignore these premises will tend to lead to marketing failures.

- ■ *Premise 1:* The behavior of the consumer is purposeful and goal oriented. What may appear to be completely irrational to the outside observer is, nevertheless, the action that an individual views as the most appropriate at the time. To assume otherwise is to underestimate the customer.
- ■ *Premise 2:* The consumer has free choice. Messages and choices are processed selectively. The frequency of these messages is increasing daily. Those that are not felt to be pertinent are either ignored, disregarded, or forgotten.
- ■ *Premise 3:* The behavior of the consumer is a process. The specific act of buying is only an intermediate stage in that process. There are many influences on consumer behavior both before and after purchase. The purchase may be a culmination of the marketing effort and its influence on the process.
- ■ *Premise 4:* Consumer behavior can be influenced, but only if we address perceived problems and potential needs and wants, a task of marketing.
- ■ *Premise 5:* There is a need for consumer education. In all their wisdom and purposeful behavior, customers may still behave unwisely, against their own interests Marketers have a responsibility in this effort.

Are hospitality customers any different from customers of other goods and services? Probably not. After all, they are the same people regardless of the type of purchase they are contemplating or making at any given time. It would seem, then, that basic buyer behavior theories would apply, and we could confine ourselves to that domain. There is a difference, however, which lies in the context of the purchase.

Buying a stereo is certainly not in the same context as buying a hotel room or a restaurant meal. The characteristics that distinguish services from products, such as intangibility, perishability, heterogeneity, and simultaneous production and consumption, create different contexts in which hospitality purchases take place. In the first part of this chapter, we will look at a few theories of consumer behavior that have been developed in other contexts and then apply them to the hospitality context. In the second part, we will look at specific types of hospitality customers.

Characteristics of Customers

Needs and Wants

Abraham Maslow was a psychologist who wanted to explain how people are motivated. What he learned was that motivations are based on different needs in different contexts. Maslow labeled his theory of motivation the "hierarchy of needs."[1] This hierarchy model has stood the test of time and is the basis of much of what we know about human behavior. The model is shown in Exhibit 7-1.

The thrust of Maslow's hierarchy is that lower-level needs have to be met before the higher-level needs become important. Thus, until the physiological needs of hunger

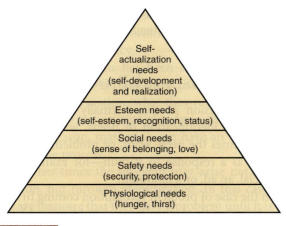

EXHIBIT 7-1   Maslow's hierarchy of needs model.

and thirst are satisfied, they remain primary in human motivation. Once these are satisfied, our safety needs of security and protection become primary, and so forth on up the pyramid. Of course, all of us will not act in exactly the same manner, but it has been shown, in a general sense, that the order prevails. (Recall from Chapter 1 that in marketing jargon we translate these into problems to be solved.)

Maslow *did not claim that the hierarchy was completely rigid or necessarily exclusive.* In fact, it should be noted that we may seek to satisfy two or more diverse needs at the same time; for instance, reserving a hotel suite instead of just a room might be an attempt to satisfy needs at opposite ends of the hierarchy. Or, in another marketing sense, we might *need* a room but *want* a suite.

Maslow also identified two categories of cognitive needs that he did not specifically place on the hierarchy, but that he felt belonged fairly high on the scale. These additional needs are *the need to know and understand* and *aesthetic needs,* which are designated as needs for things that are pleasing to the eye. These needs, of course, certainly apply to hospitality.

It should also be noted that we may satisfy the same need in different ways, depending on the occasion, the availability, and the appropriateness at the time. This leads us into a second-level theory called **behavior primacy theory.** This theory holds that behavior is a reaction to the environment—that is, behavior changes as the environment changes or, to use the same term used previously, as the context changes.

Application of the Theories

In marketing, theories are important because they help us understand why certain behaviors occur. The "why" may be more complicated than you think. For instance, consider eating. We eat because we are hungry, but the process of being hungry may also be related to being depressed, be-

ing with friends, or being with family. Theories also help explain why we have higher-level needs of belonging, esteem, and self-actualization. This will become clearer when we discuss segmentation and target marketing, both of which involve pinpointing particular customers. In the meantime, let us consider the need–context relationship.

Businesspeople who travel have the need to sleep, shower, eat, and change their clothes. These are basic needs, so almost any hotel will satisfy them. But they also may have the need for esteem and will select a hotel to fulfill that need.

At the same time, they will have other needs, such as a desk on which to write, good lighting to read by, good telephone service, a wake-up call that occurs on time, and wireless connectivity for their laptops. These are not needs in the sense of Maslow's hierarchy; they are better described as wants. We can also see that they are problems—customers need to wake up on time, they need to read material for the next day's meeting, and so on. They seek solutions to those problems and are willing to pay for them (or have their companies pay).

Beside these, they have other wants. According to Market Metrix, a firm specializing in customer satisfaction in the hotel industry, in the luxury hotel segment key loyalty-inducing emotions include feeling pampered, feeling relaxed, and appearing sophisticated. For economy hotels key loyalty-inducing emotions are feeling comfortable, feeling welcome, and being practical.[2]

Web Browsing Exercise

Go to www.marketmetrix.com/services.html to learn about Market Metrix. What type of research do they provide hospitality firms? What other needs do consumers have that can be derived from the research conducted by Market Metrix?

Customers definitely do not want to stand in line, to wait an hour for breakfast to be delivered, to have the telephone ring 15 times before the operator answers, and to hear the housekeepers yelling at each other in the hallway. In this sense, customers have **contrary needs,** or things they do not want, which really means that needs are not being satisfied.

For the sake of example, consider the businessperson who arrives home on Friday night after a very hectic week. She may say to her family, "Let's go to a hotel where I can relax and the children can have fun." Let's say she takes her family to a hotel where she stayed on business. Her basic needs haven't changed; she still needs to sleep, shower, and change her clothes, but the environment or context of her visit has changed. Now price may be a factor because she is paying for the trip with the family's money instead of the firm's. The phone is unnecessary because she definitely does not want to be disturbed, and there is no need for a work area. She wants to other choices, such as for a restaurant or hotel. It is self-explanatory, so further discussion here is unnecessary. However, you should trace through the steps to see how they fit the elements of consumer behavior we have discussed thus far. This analysis will make the theory more practical. You might even attempt fitting to the model your own particular mental process on a recent or proposed purchase to see how it fits. Better yet, think of how marketing could impact each stage of the process. You will find ads (only one phase of marketing) in this book that address each step.

Exhibit 7-4 is an oversimplification of a very complex process. In fact, this process is so complex that only one's own mind can process it for oneself because it is full of many different variables. The process in an overall consumer behavior sense, however, is important, and marketers should understand it. Here, we tie them together to understand how they are interrelated. So far we have discussed hospitality customers and their purchase behavior in a general sense. Now we will look at some specific types of customers, as commonly defined in the industry.

Types of Hospitality Customers

There are various ways of grouping different types of hospitality customers based on common needs and wants, which is called segmenting. Here we will try to understand these customers in broad category types so that we can make an effort to influence their purchase behavior.

Business Travelers

The business traveler market segment is one of the most desirable for the hospitality marketer. This market consists of over 50 million travelers a year in the United States alone. It is not only the largest major segment, but is also considered the least price-sensitive market available. The business traveler is defined as a customer who is using the product because of a need to conduct business in a particular destination area. Although the hotel facility or restaurant may be used during business, the facility is not the sole reason for the buy. Purposes of the business trip include company-related business, consulting, sales trips, personal business, and trips required to fulfill managerial functions. Most of these travelers spend between two and three nights away from home on each trip.

On the surface, the needs of this market are simple; in practice, they are far more complex and not so simple to deliver. One thing is certain: The business traveler group contains the greatest "demanders"—best explained by considering the nature or purpose of their travels. They would rather be home, they may have had a bad flight or business dealing, they are quickly in and out, and they want everything to go like clockwork.

Business Traveler Needs. Whereas business travelers (like others) once complained loudly about the small towels and the soap bar, they now have other things to complain about. The industry has changed radically, and so has the customer. In the past, a hotel served the purpose of providing a place to sleep while a customer was on a business trip. Today, a hotel has to provide the services for a successful business trip and may just happen to be a place to sleep as well. Research has shown that when business travelers are asked open-ended questions on their first consideration when selecting a hotel, convenience of location receives the highest response. This is followed by reputation and price. It is useful to go through the actual decision process.[4]

First, business travelers consider location, and many hotels emphasize it in their ads. If the location is inappropriate, it's out of the running. This rarely happens because they look at location first and only then at what hotels are situated within that location. Many hotel companies try to circumvent the location by emphasizing other amenities.

Second, business travelers look at rate ranges impacted by any company mandates or personal limitations. This is a determination by product class—that is, all hotels within the product class are assumed to be in the appropriate rate range, be it upscale, middle tier, or budget. This is why descriptive research with closed-ended questions often does not indicate price as an important factor—that decision has already been made by the company and is no longer a factor. Furthermore, price is a factor only relative to what is available. If the product class desired is middle tier (Courtyard), and the only other available choice is upscale (Four Seasons), then price may be the single most important factor in the decision, including location.

Most hotels have what are called corporate rates. To get them, all you have to do is ask. These are not necessarily the lowest rates, but often are better rooms, better furnished for the business traveler at a discount from the rack rate. Some are on concierge floors, where, at a higher price, special services, a lounge, and complimentary continental breakfast are available. The concept is that the business traveler will pay more for less hassle. In other cases, corporate rates apply to specific corporations that book so many room nights a year, either at a particular hotel or at any hotel of a chain.

Today, in many locations all over the world, there is an alternative to high prices that includes clean, comfortable rooms and good locations as well as security, prompt and courteous service, friendliness, and other factors. In understanding the business traveler, one has to understand the *role* of price—its role lies in designating a price range. Once that price range is determined, price is a minor factor unless, of course, the same or better value can be found at a lower price.

Business travelers do not really think much about cleanliness when making an initial choice; they assume it exists unless they have had a previous bad experience. Cleanliness is almost never given as a reason for choosing a particular hotel at a particular time, but it is always an important reason when they get there. What they want to know next is the reputation of the hotel or, barring that, the chain. This will come from their personal experiences or from conversations with others.

We are now past the "threshold" items and are at a level where the issues become myriad and idiosyncratic depending on the individual, but can be lumped together by target market. These are the service aspects. Each hotel should do its own research on these aspects because these will often be the determining factors in choosing among competitors in similar locations at similar rates. Again, most of these will be based on reputation and previous experience. If these are unknown, the first two items, general location and price, will prevail.

One most important aspect, according to one hotel company's research, is covered by the question, 'Will they have what I ordered and have it on time?' This may include things such as floor level, exposure, bedroom configuration, type of bed, working space, telephone location, lighting, and so on. This is consistent with the notion that hotels today have a greater role to play in the success of a business trip. This was echoed by Nan K. Moss, formerly assistant vice president of Hyatt Hotels. Although she made this comment many years ago, it is truer now in today's highly competitive market: "Customers tell us that they basically want what they need when they need it. They need a hotel to be flexible in meeting their needs because what they are looking for is enhanced productivity."[5]

Other concerns are check-in lines, employee attitudes, deferential treatment, lighting, skirt hangers, mirrors, security, type of clientele, coffee makers, business services, noise (some business travelers avoid convention, atrium-lobby hotels and prefer more boutique, smaller properties), operational efficiency, hotel "rules," limousine service to the airport, and a host of other things.

On the whole, business travelers who are choosing a hotel do not consider bathroom amenities, shoe polishers, bathrobes, turn-down service, chocolates on the pillow, and other such factors, except perhaps in luxury hotels where they are expected. These may be nice "extras," but are not critical. Customers have come to expect certain amenities, such as a decent size bar of soap. Goat's milk shampoo,

herbal soap, and bubble bath are mostly "take home" items. Even when some are used, their absence wouldn't be considered serious. These travelers are more concerned with how the shower works.

An even better example is that of a new president of a major hotel company in India. Seeing competition increasing, he decreed that business travelers would get a box of chocolates, a bathrobe, a copy of *Time* magazine (expensive in India), and other amenities adding about $10 to the variable room cost. "Whoa!" said the director of marketing in the London office that booked many of these guests. "What our customers want is to get through the airport hassle-free," a real issue in India but easily accomplished with a little know-how. The president prevailed, but he added only costs by adding amenities. He did not add revenue, and he left the company soon afterward.

For many hotels, superfluous amenities have become a cost they can no longer afford at the prices travelers are willing to pay. A better way, perhaps, is the approach now taken by some hotels to provide amenities only when really needed, as one hotel chain did. In each bathroom, they had a sign that said something to the effect of, "If you find you are missing anything from your overnight kit, please call the front desk and we will be happy to supply it." Many hotels, for example, now promote the amenities that customers really care about, as exhibited in Exhibit 7-5. Further, simply having a swift, friendly check-in with all of the information being correct the first time solves many problems and greatly improves customer satisfaction.

Most business travelers visiting cities do not consider hotels' restaurants as a determinant factor, simply because there are usually numerous alternatives available. A good breakfast room is assumed, and a quick and easy "grazing" restaurant open all hours is desired; having other restaurants in a hotel is considered convenient, sometimes, but not totally necessary. A majority of city hotel customers in most developed countries eat out for lunch and dinner. This somewhat contradicts the notion of convenient location, which tends to reappear when staying at a roadside hotel. (This does not mean that an upscale hotel should not have good restaurants, but that they are seldom determinant in the choice of hotel.) These are generalizations. As we have said, each hospitality establishment has to know its own target market.

The YP&B/Yankelovich *National Business Travel MONITOR* for 2004 provided some interesting statistics, which are shown in Exhibit 7-6. Exhibit 7-7 shows what business travelers are looking for in a hotel/motel experience and some differences between men and women.

Dealing with the Business Segment.   While the corporate office is saying, Raise the rates, the local marketing

Many destinations have recognized the value and significance of tourism, and there is intense competition among countries and states to attract the pleasure traveler. For example, residents of New Orleans are exposed to advertising campaigns from the states of Texas, Arkansas, Mississippi, and Tennessee, all of which compete heavily for visitors from that area. Malaysia seeks Singaporeans and vice versa. Advertising campaigns have raised the awareness of customers of their many vacation choices, such as that shown in Exhibit 7-8. Thus, demand for hospitality services is being created and spurred on by foreign, state, and local governments, which reap their share from taxes levied on visitors. The international tourism market has grown huge and is still growing with many different needs and wants.

The pleasure market is a high-growth-potential market. Whereas business travelers remain relatively stable and travel and eat out when they have to, a large portion of the pleasure market stays home and has yet to be developed. This is even truer in countries other than the United States. Many countries have only recently seen a large growth in the so-called middle class with more discretionary income. Because they are not "big spenders," however, they are often closed out of a market that caters and prices to the expense account customer. Lower-cost options of hotels and restaurants in some countries have expanded this market.

A major part of the pleasure market is made up of family travelers. Even in tough economic times a family vacation has become an essential part of many lifestyles. This market is more price sensitive than the business segment and is more fickle about choices of destinations and hotels. Just as hotels must learn the needs of business travelers, however, they must also determine the underlying reasons and needs of pleasure travel. Rebecca Gardyn, editor of *American Demographics* magazine, revealed the results of research on the family vacation market: "There are many overlooked and underserved niches within the family travel market, the biggest being grandparent/grandchild travel, multigenerational travel and single-parent travel. Gay/lesbian family travel, extended family member travel (such as aunts and uncles taking trips with nieces and nephews) and even pet travel are also emerging trends."[6]

Exhibit 7-9 shows some research results on what people are looking for in a pleasure travel hotel experience. You can contrast this with Exhibit 7-7 to see some of the differences between business and pleasure travel needs among the different generational groups.

Another important pleasure market is made up of people traveling to visit friends and relatives. Although many of these travelers stay with friends and relatives at their final destinations, they often seek out lodging accommodations along the way. This is generally a value-conscious market that is attracted to budget hotels and eating places such as McDonald's and family restaurants. In these lower-tier markets, pleasure travelers are actually less demanding than customers in almost any other market. One reason for this is the lack of experience. Travelers may not realize just what is available, or they may simply not know how to demand. (The exceptions, of course, are the business travelers now turned pleasure travelers.) They do, however, have long memories. These customers are prone to simply walk out of a bad experience without complaining, never to return. They also are very prone to spread negative word of mouth. They are and will become, however, more demanding as their travel experience increases.

EXHIBIT 7-8 Advertising campaigns have raised the awareness of customers of their many vacation destination options.

Source: Los Cabos. Used by permission.

Web Browsing Exercise

Use your favorite search engine and type in phrases such as "gay travel," "lesbian travel," "multigenerational travel," and "pet travel." What do you find? What might you recommend to those in the hospitality industry?

EXHIBIT 7-9 **What People Are Looking for in a Leisure Travel Experience**

Age Differences[h] 2004

	Echo-Boomers %[e]	Xers %[e]	Boomers %[e]	Matures %[e]
Attributes Considered Extremely/Very Desirable:[f]				
Experimentation/Fantasy/Ambiance:				
Beautiful scenery	82	91	87	88
A place I have never visited before	83	87[c,d]	78	76
A beach experience	71	74	69	49[a,b,c]
An opportunity to eat different and unusual cuisines	58	66	57	53
A hotel with casually elegant atmosphere and décor	52	55	54	40[c]
Nightlife and live entertainment	73[b,c,d]	56	45	47
The option of scheduling vacation activities in advance of arrival	54	56	49	51
A hotel with a historical atmosphere and décor	43	50	42	43
Going to theme parks	63	58	40[a,b]	18[a,b,c]
A destination that is remote and untouched	38	65[a,c,d]	44d	23
A hotel or resort with a distinctive theme or atmosphere	47	45	42	34[a,b,c]
A hotel with a formal and elegant atmosphere and décor	43[c,d]	38	33	31
Going to a spa	47	39	32[a,b]	24[a,b,c]
A small "boutique" hotel with unusual atmosphere and décor	34	29	33	32
Learning a new skill or activity	41	29	31	24[a]
Being able to gamble	29	25	25	23
Physical Activities:				
Getting exercise	61[b,c,d]	42	45	39
Hiking and outdoor adventure	52	52	42[a,b]	25[a,b,c]
Snorkeling or scuba diving	58	48	37[a]	20[a,b,c]
Participation in water sports	50	42	35[a]	9[a,b,c]
Whitewater rafting	38	37	28	4[a,b,c]
Bicycling trips through the countryside	24	29	28	19
Snow skiing	32	23[a]	13[a,b]	6[a,b,c]
Playing golf	15	14	16	17
Mountain biking	29	27	8[a,b,]	8[a,b]
Snowboarding	27	15[a]	7[a,b]	1[a,b,c]
Playing tennis	11	5	8	4
Other Activities:				
Participating in activities with children while on vacation[g]	62	77[a,c]	63	39[a,b,c]
Visiting arts/architecture/historical sites	47	51	54	54
A hotel having a kids' club or organized family activities[g]	43	44	36	35
Shopping	42	44	36	35
Familiarity/Control:				
Safety of hotel or motel	75	85	86	83
Safety of destination	69	81	83[a,d]	72
A place I have visited before	54	55	54	60
Having a separate children's/teen program	37	36	28	26
Having access to the Internet or an online service to stay in touch with the home or office	40	27	30	17[a,c]
Pricing:				
An all-inclusive vacation price (one that includes air transportation, accommodations, food, transfer to the hotel or resort, and some recreation)	70	69	64	56[a,b,c]
An all-inclusive resort price (one that includes my accommodations, food, beverage, and recreation)	76[b,c]	67	62	49[a,b,c]

a = statistically significant difference from Echo-Boomers, b = significant difference from Xers, c = significant difference from Boomers, d = significant difference from Matures.

e Asked in versions of the questionnaire. Interview base varies.

f Top two box score on a scale of one to five where one equals not at all desirable and five equals extremely desirable.

g Asked among respondents who have taken or plan to take one or more leisure trips with children.

h Echo-Boomers = those adult consumers born since 1979, Xers = those adult consumers born 1965 through 1978, Boomers = those adult consumers born from 1946 through 1964, and Matures = those adult consumers born before 1946.

Source: Yesawich, Pepperdine, Brown & Russell. (2004). *National Business Travel MONITOR*, 97–98.

187

Resort Market

The resort leisure market is also unique from the customer viewpoint. Business travelers stay at a hotel or resort because they have business to do or a conference to attend. The resort leisure market, however, travels to resorts because it wants to be there and to get away from it all. This has led to a proliferation of both upscale and downscale resorts and quiet country inns where you can spend a week in a rocking chair on the front porch. Again, the wants and needs of these customers are different from those of the nonresort traveler. We showed the decision process of these customers in Exhibit 7-4, but the possibilities are almost endless.

Resort leisure guests need to fulfill their idea of a vacation. Whether it be total quiet relaxation or a sports/recreation schedule busier than their job back home, they must feel satisfied that their idea of relaxation was met.

The complexion of resort guests is different from that of guests at commercial hotels. Almost two-thirds may be pleasure travelers, while the rest are attending a conference, participating in an incentive junket, or on business (or vice versa), depending of course on the hotel and the location. This varied market poses inherent problems—especially when it comes together at the same time, which should be avoided when possible. The hotel staff must be trained to deal with the diverse needs of the leisure traveler on vacation, at the same time that it executes complicated conferences with infinite details. The needs of the meeting planner and the leisure resort market can conflict. A hotel has to be prepared to serve them both.

For example, a major conference at a hotel may want to use the pool area for a cocktail reception, worth $20,000 to the resort. Should the manager shut down the pool area to leisure guests to accommodate the needs of the conference? (It too often does!) This integration of diverse customers is more amplified in the resort setting. Many times, the exclusive nature of the facility lends itself to these conflicts. For example, when there are so many conferees on the golf course, it is impossible for an individual to get a tee time. The marketing-driven manager will understand the needs of both customers, develop operating standards for both, and sell the facility so that revenues will be maximized without losing guests.

Weekend escape travel is another part of the pleasure market. Dual-income households provide better incomes for people, but make the scheduling of vacations much harder. There is a trend toward shorter, more frequent vacations taken by travelers who will be more demanding during the use of their precious vacation time. Much of this is part of the package market.

Tourism Marketing Application

It is also important to understand the motivations for vacations and trips. While the outcomes of these motivations are reflected in what people are looking for, the understanding may lead to other offerings that are not currently available. Motivations for travel include: (1) to observe the lifestyle of exotic peoples, such as a trip to India to study yoga and meditation; (2) to experience or participate in festivals or living museums, such as those found in Williamsburg, VA; (3) to visit historic sites, such as the Coliseum in Rome; (4) to visit natural and environmental attractions, such as national parks; (5) to participate in sports, such as skiing or swimming; and (6) to attend business meetings, conventions, or other functions. (From Valene Smith. 1977. *Hosts and Guests*. Philadelphia: University of Pennsylvania Press, pp. 2–3.)

The Package Market

This increasingly popular method of attracting customers during low-demand periods is becoming more crowded with offerings every day. In the *New York Times* Sunday Travel Section, hotels from the upscale Ritz-Carlton on Central Park and the Carlyle on the Upper East Side, to the Waldorf-Astoria on Park Avenue, to the convention-type Hotel Pennsylvania in the garment district and the downscale Milford Plaza on Broadway are all offering weekend packages. The same is true in major cities throughout the United States; at resorts, and in London, Paris, Rome, Athens, Singapore, Bangkok, and just about any other place you look. Some include airfare (see Exhibit 7-10). Another popular version of packages is the "escape" or "getaway" theme. One of each of these is shown in Exhibit 7-11 and 7-12.

The hotel package market is defined as the offering of a combination of room and amenities to customers for an inclusive price. Although normally these packages are designed to boost occupancy during low-demand time periods, such as weekends and off-seasons, sometimes packages are used to maximize revenues at all times.

An example of this might be a resort whose package includes three nights' accommodations and breakfast and dinner daily. The purpose of this combined package is to ensure that while the hotel is full, the guests are required to make use of the food and beverage facilities. Also, the three nights are sold at once, ensuring their occupancy over the period. If sold individually, one night might sell out before the others, eliminating longer, more desirable bookings. Naturally, the hotel would have to forecast some significant

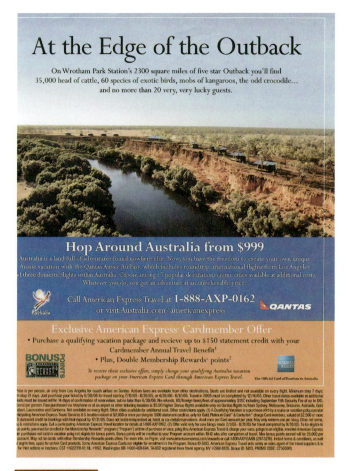

EXHIBIT 7-10 This package for Australia includes airfare.

Source: American Express Travel. Used by permission.

EXHIBIT 7-11 This advertisement for Starwood exhibits an "escape" package.

Source: Starwood Hotels Hawaii. Used by permission.

demand to be able to force the customer to purchase that type of package.

We define a package as bundling of goods and services, be it food and beverage, coupons to a nearby retailer, or a welcome gift upon arrival. Often the term is misused to describe blatant discounting. Offering a guest room at a significant discount is nothing more than that; it certainly does not package anything for the customer.

In developing packages, the needs and problems of the customer must be first understood in order to succeed in developing the target package market. What works in one section of the country or the world may be completely foreign in another market.

Once the needs of the target package customer have been identified, the competition needs to be analyzed. As was mentioned earlier, there are very few places left that do not have a myriad of packages for the customer to buy. Again, the key is the differentiation of the product to the target market. With so many different packages available and plenty of availability on weekends, during the off-

season, or, for some resorts, midweek, the creation must clearly be better from an offering or price standpoint in order to capture the market.

From the customer's point of view there are four different advantages to packages, assuming the initial motivation is there from the needs and wants perspective. In other words, why buy a package when you can do the same thing on your own?

1. *Package prices imply that the sum is cheaper than the individual parts.* This is usually, but not always, true and depends heavily on the quality of the parts. A low-rated, obscure room and an inexpensive split of champagne might have been bought cheaper on your own, but many people don't know this and either don't want or don't know how to take the trouble to find out, so they buy on price. Even when the price is not less, there is a *perception* of value in packages.

2. *Packages offer something that people want but probably would not request by itself—for example, breakfast in*

ST. KITTS
RESORT
& THE ROYAL BEACH CASINO
Marriott.

**SOMETIMES OUR
WATER SPORT
ACTIVITIES REQUIRE
NO ACTIVITY AT ALL.**

Captivating St. Kitts offers
every type of recreation you
can imagine on sea and shore
including a first-class spa and
spectacular golf. And it's all
surrounded by pristine beauty
and unspoiled Caribbean
splendor. With Marriott's
exemplary service, you'll have
everything you need, no matter
what you choose to do — even
if you choose nothing at all.
St. Kitts Marriott Resort & The
Royal Beach Casino. Where
you've always wanted to go
and never want to leave.℠
IT'S THE MARRIOTT WAY.℠

Special Caribbean
Resident Rates
From **$89***/night

For reservations, please call
800-228-9290 and ask for
code LCCU. Or, visit us at
www.stkittsmarriott.com

*Rates are per room, per night, based on double
occupancy and vary by season. Promotion is
subject to availability and the $89 rate is valid
through December 23, 2004. Must show proof of
Caribbean residency. This promotion is not valid
for existing reservations, nor for groups of 10
rooms or more, and cannot be combined with
other offers, coupons, etc. Other restrictions may
apply. Rates exclude tax and service.
©2004 Marriott International, Inc.

EXHIBIT 7-12 This advertisement for St. Kitts Resort & Royal Beach Casino exhibits a "getaway" package.

Source: Marriott International, Inc. Used by permission.

bed. "It's too expensive, but look, it's included." Or perhaps it's something like horseback riding: "I always wanted to do that but never would have thought of it." Packages remove the worry of "how to," and make it easier for the customer to do whatever it is.

3. *Packages should be hassle-free.* The customer doesn't have to make decisions about where to eat, where to dance, where to go to the theater, how to get there, and so on. This is particularly true for the inexperienced traveler. It is also why carefully thought-out packages can be priced at more than the sum of their parts. The package removes much of the hassle for customers, and they will pay for that, even though they probably think they are getting it cheaper. Packages make the multiple-purchase decision much simpler.

Club Med has become a master at this art by offering a total week's experience at their resorts, including airfare, ground transportation, all food, wine, and sports activities. All you pay for are drinks, and you do that with beads, for which you are charged on departure. In fact, Club Med is an excellent example of a marketing-oriented packaging company.

When Club Med was first conceived, packages appealed to the younger single set that wanted to get away and meet members of the opposite sex. There was a definite hedonistic overtone to the advertising messages. The market has since changed. Customers are more conservative, and many of today's Club Med customers are older and married with children. Club Med's product has changed with them, offering a much more wholesome package including a staff pediatrician in some locations.

Other companies have taken this one step further to what is called the all-inclusive resort—for instance, Sandals in Jamaica, PlanHotel Resorts, which has all inclusive properties in the Maldives, Kenya, Egypt, and Zanzibar. Some of the packages don't include airfare, but they include everything else—all you can drink, for instance and golf in their Jamaica and St. Lucia resorts. The price is high, but is paid only once. The customer feels that a problem is solved: "I can do whatever I want and don't have to worry about what it costs." The following Web exercise has you search for other examples of all inclusive resorts.

 Web Browsing Exercise

Use your favorite web search engine to look for all inclusive resorts. Be prepared to compare and contrast the different offerings of the different resorts you investigate.

The fourth appeal of some packages is that buyers get something they would not get without the package. That something appeals to a particular interest. One example is the "murder weekend" packages that started in England and had mixed success in the United States. With these packages, a couple went to a hotel for the weekend and spent the weekend, with other couples, trying to solve a murder that was literally enacted before their eyes, with all the appropriate clues. With the package, of course, came room, food, and beverages. Murder mystery nights are now sometimes available at restaurants. Other packages of this type are designed for "buffs." For example, there are rock buffs, sea shell buffs, bird-watcher buffs and others. Special activities are planned for these buffs, who know they will be sharing the experience with others of like interest.

An important warning about packages too often is violated: Provide what you promise in the package! This advice is obvious but is not always followed, resulting in very negative feedback for the property. For example, we know of one small city hotel that offered the usual weekend package. The main appeal of this package in the winter in New England was the indoor pool and lounge area. People from only a few miles away bought the package for that reason. More often than not, the hotel had a wedding party every Saturday afternoon that was held by the pool. Including setup and break-down time, package customers could not use the pool for much of their stay.

Too often hotels do not deliver on the promises made with their packages. The main reasons for this seem to be that they do not plan for packages and consider them secondary, low-rated business. This is self-defeating and results in extremely negative word of mouth. Research on customer complaints has revealed a disproportionate number of complaints about package "promises."

Another kind of package—the tour group package that includes airfare and accommodations—will be described in the chapter on distribution.

Mature Travelers

The mature traveler market, actually a subsegment of the pleasure market, is another important growth segment for both the hotel and restaurant marketer. Usually defined as ages 55 and over, this market's size is on the increase because people tend to live longer and better. This segment is important to the hospitality industry not just for its size but for other reasons. They travel extensively, spending over 50 percent more of their time away from home than the younger pleasure segments. Members of this market today live longer, healthier, and more vigorous lives; are better educated; and have wider interests and activities than previous generations at their age. Their children are grown; their mortgages are paid; and they have the time, energy, and inclination to travel.

The needs and wants of the mature market are different from those of other segments discussed in this chapter. Studies have reported that "to visit new places" was the number one reason for trips taken by mature travelers, followed by "to visit friends and family." Many mature travelers are price sensitive, and getting a discount is an important attraction. Because they have the flexibility to plan trips any time, they can take advantage of the lowest prices. These travelers use hotels of all price ranges, from luxury to budget, but hotels must be able to provide those attributes that are important to this segment. Some of these attributes include increased security, well-lit public areas, legible signage, no-smoking rooms, easily maneuverable door handles, grab-bars and supports in bathrooms, and wide doorways to accommodate wheelchairs and walkers.

The mature market is not homogeneous. This market can be segmented in a variety of ways: Travel habits of mature travelers differ depending on retirement status; travel habits are likely to be affected by travelers' life stage as they grow older and encounter physical restrictions; and mature travelers may prefer to travel as part of a group, whereas others travel in pairs.

Many hotel chains are aggressively pursuing this market, especially those over 65, sometimes called seniors. Choice Hotels has long featured famous but active seniors in its television advertising. Hilton has a Seniors HHonors program where members can receive up to a 50 percent discount on room rates. Radisson SAS once gave discounts by age starting at age 65.

Restaurants also tap into this market. Active senior citizens spend a large proportion of their food budgets on food away from home, and most prefer midscale restaurants. Many are bargain hunters who are conservative in their eating habits. Restaurants should have good lighting to avoid safety hazards, and menus should be easily readable with enough variety to satisfy senior citizens' nutritional needs. Service staffs should be trained to recognize changes in vision and hearing so that people with special needs can be provided better service without calling attention to their impairments.

The restaurateur can fill some seats early in the evening because seniors tend to eat dinner earlier. In fact, "sunset dinners" or "early-bird specials" have become quite popular in attracting diners from 5:30 to 7:30 P.M., before regular patrons arrive. These menu offerings normally include beverage and dessert at an attractive price.

The needs of the senior citizen (again, those 65+) are basically simple. They are not, as a group, demanding. They want rooms close to the lobby, they want help with luggage, and they want information. Like most customers they want clean rooms, convenient location, and value. They do not want to be publicly singled out for service, but at the same time hospitality employees must recognize their special needs and provide them in a subtle way. Seniors tend not to rush through their stays the way conferees or businesspeople do.

Senior citizens tend to travel outside traditional patterns, such as the businessperson's Monday through Thursday, the weekend package guest's Friday and Saturday, or the busier times of the year. They are also more flexible in rearranging their schedules. Senior travelers can often check in on a Thursday and stay through Monday, making their stay attractive to the hotelier.

As the baby-boom generation in the United States matures, it is quite possible that the needs of this market will further evolve and change, as it has in only the past 10 years. It is up to hospitality corporations to research these needs as they evolve so that this market can be better served.

International Travelers

Tourism is already the world's largest retail industry, and travel between nations is expected to continue to grow. Although international tourism was on the rise before September 11, 2001, international traveler spending in 2003 consisted of only 11.6 percent of total U.S. tourism spending. However, international tourism is expected to increase in the upcoming years.

Canada and Mexico provide the most tourists to United States, and vice versa, because of their contiguous borders. Overseas visitors are led by the Japanese, followed by Europeans from the United Kingdom, Germany, France, and Italy. Growth markets in the future are visitors from Argentina and South Korea, which have shown huge increases. Singapore targets Australians and Japanese. Thailand targets Germans. Portugal, Spain, and Turkey target the British. And so it goes.

The international market is staggering in its size and complexities. Over 400 million people travel outside their own countries every year. This market is obviously not homogeneous, and hospitality marketers must be sensitive to the cultural differences of visitors from different nations. Because it is expensive and risky to try to directly market to individual international visitors, hospitality operators often seek out an intermediary, such as a consortium, reservation system, referral network, or tour operator with which to establish marketing relationships.

International trade shows such as the Travel Industry Association's International Pow Wow are also essential for reaching this market. This show brings together tour operators from all over the world who meet with hospitality industry representatives to conduct business. The tour operators account for over 70 percent of all international tourist arrivals to the United States. As the number of international travelers has increased, hospitality corporations and tourist destinations have become more user-friendly. However, much can be done.

Web Browsing Exercise

Type www.tia.org/PowWow into your favorite web browser. Read about the Pow Wow and the list of attendees and find answers to the following questions:

1. What is TIA's International Pow Wow?
2. How is this meeting different from traditional trade shows?
3. Where are the future meetings being held?

Not long ago, most U.S. hospitality companies, both small and large, could disregard the international market unless they deliberately chose to enter it. This situation is changing quickly. To this day, foreign visitors to the United States can go to only a very few select hotels in major cities such as New York and expect to find someone who speaks their language and exchanges their money, not to mention understanding their needs. The situation is even worse in restaurants; the singular hope for a foreign speaker in this case is to go to a purely ethnic restaurant or hope to have an immigrant waiter or waitress who speaks the same language.

On the other hand, an American can travel almost anywhere overseas and find hotels and restaurants in which at least someone will speak English or make an honest attempt at it. The overseas hospitality enterprise has long recognized the value of the American market. Even in some remote European or Asian villages it is possible for Americans to communicate basic needs and wants. Contrarily, foreign visitors to the United States are too often greeted with a "Huh?" when trying to communicate in an American hospitality enterprise. This problem goes far beyond the problem of language difficulties; it extends into the area of basic customer needs and wants. Because many foreign visitors to the United States are able to speak some English, Americans are relieved of the burden of understanding another language, but this does not relieve them of the burden of understanding the customer.

The basic principles of marketing to the international traveler are no different wherever you go—they always involve the needs and wants and solutions of problems of customers. Likewise, the concepts of positioning, segmentation, and marketing planning or strategy are no different. What changes, of course, are the customers. International marketing does not involve changes in marketing concepts; instead, it involves understanding the changes in customers.

Worldwide, customers are looking for the same things: to establish relationships and to be sure that they will be taken care of on arrival. Communicating the message that a property will do this may vary by country of origin, but the meaning will be the same. Vagaries such as a Japanese breakfast or directional arrows to Mecca for Arabs are like mints on the pillow—nice to have, but without trust and relationship, they become nonissues.

When McDonald's first opened in Moscow, they served 35,000 customers a day. Russians, however, ate with utensils and were not accustomed to picking up food with their hands. So McDonald's created brochures and tray liners explaining *how* to eat a hamburger, not *why* to buy one. Burger King had similar experiences in Venezuela—hamburger buns no longer have sesame seeds (the Venezuelans kept brushing them off), the ketchup is sweeter, as are milkshakes, the menu includes ice cream (everyone's favorite dessert there), and the outlets stay open as late as 1:30 A.M. because Venezuelans eat late.

Burger King also realized that mere adaptation to cultural differences does not mean that one gets to know the market. Burger King originally served wine in its restaurants in France, but customers tended to linger longer over glasses of wine. This slowed table turnover, so wine was removed from the menu. Conversely, Disney did not allow alcoholic beverages to be served at EuroDisney. The French were outraged, and Disney now sells wine.

But what do you do when your customer mix originates in 20 or more countries, as is the case for many hotels worldwide in major destination areas and some not so major? This is the challenge that faces hospitality firms that have an international focus.

Free Independent Travelers (FITs)

A final category of individual travelers is somewhat of a catchall for everyone that is left over. In fact, in many hotels' segment breakdowns of their customer base, this may be quite a substantial proportion. That is because everyone that is not known to fit some other category will fall into this one.

The **free independent traveler (FIT)** is a "nonorganized" visitor who does not belong to a group. Although these travelers may well participate in tours during their visit, they essentially come on their own and do as they please. Unidentified business travelers will also be lumped into this category. Hotels catering to the FIT market will usually set aside a block of rooms a year in advance and fill them in as reservations are made. The lead time may be three to six months in advance. The hotel releases the unused blocked space according to its buy-time schedule.

Both wholesalers and retail agents (who will be discussed in the chapter on distribution) handle the FIT. This segment is normally willing to pay higher rates than group customers. However, a conflict arises with this situation. Whereas the FIT is willing to pay a higher rate because of a lack of volume, the wholesaler and retailer are able to negotiate large discounts as a result of aggregate FIT bookings.

The resulting savings are not always passed on to the traveler. Therefore, the guest may pay a high price while the hotel receives a relatively low room rate. Often the FIT booked by an intermediary may get the poorest room in the house based on the rate being paid to the hotel. The traveler is at a disadvantage in these situations and is surprised at the accommodations. This can hurt the hotel that is caught in the middle.

Incidentally, the term *FIT* is also used by some to designate "free individual traveler" or "free international traveler."

■ Summary

There is a tremendous amount of research on the topic of consumer behavior, and it is impossible to review all of it in any one chapter. However, we have tried to show how some of these theories can be applied to understand the behavior of hospitality customers. This chapter has also shown that this can be very difficult because we cannot be sure what goes on in a person's mind. **Maslow's hierarchy** of needs forms a foundation, but perceptions and expectations play important roles. Differences between perceptions and expectations create many challenges for hospitality marketers as seen in the gap model.

Perceptions lead to beliefs, which in turn affect attitudes, and much of marketing deals with attitudes and the changing of attitudes. Positive attitudes toward a product or service are required before customers will include it among their choices. Consumer behavior is a complex process, and the different stages are need or problem recognition, search, stimuli selection, **alternative evaluation,** alternative comparison, and choice.

The key to marketing today is to understand the customer. Good theory provides the basis for that understanding. Applying it will put you light years ahead of those who are still selling when they should be marketing.

In the latter part of this chapter we reviewed the most common broad individual market segments, both business and pleasure, that are encountered in the marketing of hospitality. There are numerous other segments, as well as more specifically defined target markets. The most important point to remember is that market segments represent groupings of customers with similar needs and problems. Ideally, the scenario would be to operate a hotel or restaurant that catered to one market segment year-round. Unfortunately, this is seldom realistically possible.

In fact, different segments will often be on premise at the same time, making service and execution of the product difficult. The marketing-oriented team responds to this challenge by truly understanding the needs of the customer and communicating these needs to the staff that will deliver the promised product. When all is said and done, relationship marketing provides the tie that binds.

■ Key Terms

tenets of consumer behavior	attitudes
behavior primacy theory	cognitive dissonance
contrary needs	FIT (free independent
buying decision process	traveler)
selectivity	Maslow's hierarchy
reference groups	alternative evaluation
beliefs	

■ Discussion Questions

1. Consider Maslow's hierarchy of needs in terms of a hotel, restaurant, or tourism company. In each case, name as many attributes as you can that fit each level of the hierarchy. Be prepared to discuss.
2. Collect a half-dozen hotel, restaurant, or tourism ads from a recent paper or magazine. Discuss them in terms of perception, expectation, beliefs, attitudes, and intentions.
3. List the reference groups that you belong to and explain how they can shape your choices of hospitality facilities.
4. Explain the relationships among beliefs, attitudes, and intentions. Discuss how all these interrelate in hospitality consumer behavior.
5. Consider Exhibit 7-2. Take an example of something you have done or might want to do in terms of a hospitality purchase. Apply the model.
6. What are the major factors that business travelers consider when selecting a hotel or restaurant? Pleasure travelers?
7. Discuss this statement: We do not sell hotel rooms to business travelers; we improve their productivity.
8. Discuss this statement: Mature travelers' needs will change as the baby-boom generation ages into this market.

■ Group Projects

1. Consider a particular market segment, such as students on a spring break. Develop and price realistically the "perfect" package for this segment.
2. Apply Project 1 to mature travelers. This will be a lot harder because you are not one of them, so you may have to do some research. This is more realistic than Project 1 because hotel marketers usually do not belong to the groups for whom they design packages.
3. Consider either the business or pleasure market. Develop a mini marketing plan that considers the needs and wants of both men and women.

■ References

1. Maslow, A. H. (1954). *Motivation and personality.* New York: Harper & Row.
2. Barsky, J., & Nash, L. (2003, October-December). Customer satisfaction: Applying concepts to industry-wide measures. *Cornell Hotel and Restaurant Administrative Quarterly,* 173–183.
3. This discussion of consumer information processing is quite limited. Those who would like to take it a step further are recommended to Ajzen, I., & Fishbein, M. (1980). *Understanding attitudes and predicting social behavior.* Upper Saddle River, NJ: Prentice Hall.
4. This discussion is based on extensive research by the authors and others.
5. Reported in 1993 Outlook for Travel and Tourism. *Proceedings of the U.S. Travel Data Center's 18th Annual Travel Outlook Forum,* 94.
6. Gardyn, R. (2001, August). The new family vacation. *American Demographics,* 43–44.

CHAPTER 8

Understanding Organizational Customers

Overview

The organizational customer is described as the purchaser of hospitality products for a group or an organization that has a common purpose. Following are several subsegments of the organizational customer that are described in detail in this chapter:

- Generic organizational market
- Corporate travel market
- Corporate meetings market
- Incentive market
- Association, convention, and trade show market
- Airline crew market
- Social, military, education, religious, and fraternal (SMERF) and government markets
- Group tour and travel market

I. Introduction to Hospitality Marketing
1. The Concept of Marketing
2. Marketing Services and the Hospitality Experience
3. The Marketing Mix and the Product/Service Mix
4. Relationship/Loyalty Marketing

II. Marketing to Build a Competitive Advantage
5. Strategic Marketing
6. The Strategic Marketing System and Marketing Objectives

VII. Feedback

VI. Synthesis
21. The Marketing Plan

III. The Marketplace
7. Understanding Individual Customers
8. *Understanding Organizational Customers*
9. The Tourist Customer and the Tourism Destination

IV. Situational Analysis
10. Understanding Competition
11. Marketing Intelligence and Research

V. Functional Strategies
12. Differentiation, Segmentation, and Target Marketing
13. Branding and Market Positioning
14. The Hospitality Pricing Mix
15. The Communications Mix: Advertising
16. The Communications Mix: Sales Promotions, Merchandising, Public Relations, and Publicity
17. The Communications Mix: Personal Selling
18. Hospitality Distribution Systems
19. Channels of Distribution: Bringing the Customer to the Product
20. Interactive Marketing: Internet and Database Marketing

After 28 years with Loews Hotels, Charlotte St. Martin left Loews to start her own company, St. Martin Enterprises. The company specializes in marketing, branding, and operations for the hospitality industry.

St. Martin served as executive vice president of marketing and sales for Loews Hotels, where she was responsible for all of sales and marketing for the chain's 20 hotels and resorts. Since joining the company in 1977 as director of sales and marketing for the former Loews Anatole Hotel, where she also served as president and CEO from 1989 to 1995, St. Martin rose through the ranks to become one of the highest-ranking female executives in the lodging industry. From 1990 to 1996, she simultaneously held the position of executive vice president of operations, but turned her full attention back to marketing in 1996 as a result of the chain's unprecedented $1 billion expansion.

Currently, St. Martin serves as chair for the Meeting Professionals International Foundation. In addition, she is a recent past chair of the New York Society of Association Executives, the first associate member ever to serve as a chair not only of NYSAE, but of any major Society of Association Executives in the country. She has also served as both vice chair and treasurer of the New York Convention and Visitors Bureau and served on the executive committee from 1990 to 2003. She currently serves on its board of directors.

Marketing in Action

Charlotte St. Martin, President and CEO, St. Martin Enterprises

What is the customer actually purchasing when "buying" a meeting? How do hoteliers provide this? Are they providing it now?

The customer is buying the services of a group of professionals who provide a site that, ideally, is problem free so that the meeting is all about achieving the desired results for the organization. Hotels are providing it now, although we can continue to improve our understanding of the purpose of the meeting so that we can deliver that problem-free meeting. For example, if we know that one of the goals of the meeting is to get an interactive dialog going, we would not recommend a theater or schoolroom setup. If we simply "follow orders," we aren't helping to ensure the success of a meeting.

What do you think meeting planners are looking for these days in hotel services?

I think they are looking for more bells and whistles online and they are looking for no reduction in services at the hotel level. They want 360-degree views of ballrooms, meetings layouts that they can access online, online menus, RSVPs online—essentially they want everything made easier for them. They want you to have the very best technological capabilities to make their lives easier. And when they arrive at the hotel, they want to have everything be exactly the same as it was online. They want the 24-hour room service. They want all the bells and whistles. It has certainly created an interesting relationship for hotels and has increased the capital budget because it is difficult to do it all.

Do you think hotels are doing a good job of responding to the needs of these group planners?

I think we are, for the most part. I think that, for awhile, we were not. I think there was definitely a time when we put too much money into the bells and whistles and not enough into the service. I think that, fortunately, the business is getting better right now because room rates are returning, so the hotels are once again making enough money to put the service back in. But there was some time when it was one or the other, but not both.

Do you think that convention and visitors bureaus today are more or less influential in terms of where business is placed? How do they fit in the overall selling mix?

I don't think they have changed for the really big conferences. You know that, if you need 5,000 rooms for 10,000

197

people, you are still going to use your bureau. Although many people don't think they are as necessary for the smaller meetings and the midsize meetings, I think that is a mistake. I think bureaus can do so much more for the planners than they realize, but the bureaus haven't done a good job of communicating their capabilities.

Can you share with us some strategies you aimed towards a particular segment at Loews that seemed to work pretty well?

Certainly. The "one stop stopping" strategy has been very successful for Loews. To my knowledge, Loews is still the only company that has a conference management department, which is the same thing as a meeting planning department, only for big meetings. If you have a 1,000-room meeting or a 500-room meeting, you have one contact for that meeting and that person does all the food and beverage arrangements, the meeting arrangements, the rooming list—they really do everything. Instead of having to work with the rooms division, the food and beverage division, the convention services division, the customer has only one contact person. It is something that we are known for, and I think it has really made a difference.

What do you feel the impact of the Internet has been on corporate meeting planners?

There have been some very positive impacts and some not so positive impacts. One positive impact is that, with meeting departments being downsized, a meeting planner can reach out and get a lot of information quickly. They used to have to make phone calls and write letters, but now they can reach out to a lot of different people quickly through the Internet and, of course, email. They also get more information more quickly online. They are able to compare rates quoted in a proposal format to prices available to customers booking directly online. In other words, if I am doing a proposal for the American Medical Association for December and I am quoted a rate of $180, I can go online and try to get the same hotels for those dates. If, on the other hand, I get a rate of $129, then there is a possibility for the customers that the negotiations will sour. The Internet allows planners to get a better sense of what the hotel is charging.

That issue of rate parity is interesting. How can companies deal with the fact that planners can go to the Internet just as quickly as any businessperson or vacationer and see what the rate is?

The reality is that there is no way hotels can give the planner the same rates they are giving individuals because they are making so many more concessions such as the meeting space, comps, and things like that. And the more sophisticated meeting planner is aware of that, but they don't want to see a huge barrier. As you know, a lot of the rates quoted on various websites are for the smallest rooms, so it is a way of using the Internet to create dialog to make sure that the hotels are giving a really good negotiated rate. The other side of that is that a meeting attendee simply doesn't understand why they see a room for $99 on the Internet, but the corporate rate is $155. They don't understand that the group is getting all kinds of other compensations that are, in effect, being paid for by the room rate—or that these are last minute rooms and the hotel is not obligated to hold a lot of rooms for a long time. These misunderstandings have had a very negative impact on the relationship between the customer and the meeting planner or the meeting planner and their own attendees. It is a never-ending battle.

You have been involved in the meeting business for many years. How have you seen it change over time and where do you see it moving in the future?

Although relationships have always been important—and still are—the technology that has been added has provided a degree of pace and efficiency that was not a factor years ago. We as an industry went through a period several years ago during which relationships were put on a back burner. Online RFPs were replacing the personal nature of the business, but the meeting planners and their suppliers soon learned that, although technology is terrific and helps us a great deal, we need to have personal interaction to do the best job for our organizations. I don't see this changing in the future. While procurement will be involved in the meetings industry increasingly in the future, personal relationships are still important to providing the best meetings possible.

I think that the biggest trend will be the continuation of outsourcing. But I honestly believe that the last trait that I just mentioned—developing the ability to bring an ROI component to the meeting—will be the factor that enables meeting planners to keep their job and be very valuable. Otherwise, companies would simply outsource.

Do you see advances in technology replacing the need for smaller meetings? For example, rather than meeting in a hotel, the meeting could occur via videoconferencing?

Technology replaces a lot of rhetoric and saves meeting planners and hoteliers a great deal of time. But there is NO substitute for face-to-face interaction. Technology will help prepare the participants for meetings, and will insure that the meeting can be more targeted. This should provide for better meetings.

How does a firm compete successfully in the meeting business?

One of the key mistakes hoteliers/vendors make is not understanding what they do best—what their "hook" is . . . what makes them unique or especially qualified to handle a meeting. To successfully compete (unless you happen to be lucky with a perfect location during a high-demand market), you need to demonstrate that you know who you are and what you provide best and be very clear about delivering that message to your customers. Additionally, a vendor that fills the need of a planner will be the most successful in creating a relationship and developing long-term relationships.

How has the repositioning of Las Vegas as a major meeting and convention town impacted the rest of the industry?

Las Vegas has done an amazing job of reminding the meetings industry that people attending a meeting are still people and they want to be entertained, enchanted, and surprised—and they want it "packaged." Although Las Vegas initially didn't understand how to serve meetings, it has learned quickly. They were smart to recognize the trend of more but shorter vacations, enabling them to go after those meetings whose attendees could come early or stay after and make a vacation of it . . . saving time and money. Orlando has done the same thing.

You are very involved in MPI and other organizations. Can you indicate how these organizations have impacted your career? The industry?

MPI, ASAE, PCMA and CIC are all organizations in which I have held leadership positions. I believe that volunteering and getting involved in them is probably the single biggest factor in my success in the early stages of my career. I held leadership roles in organizations prior to these, and they helped me learn things that I hadn't yet learned in my paid positions, enabling me to gain respect by my bosses for being more accomplished than the average person at that point in my career. Also, being in sales and marketing, being visible, certainly helped our brand. As President and CEO of the then-Loews Anatole Hotel, I once analyzed our local business and found that over 75 percent of our local customers came about as a result of a relationship I had developed in one of my leadership roles. Additionally, as I noted above, these roles helped me understand my customer, which is so crucial in being successful in the sales/marketing arena. The industry has raised the visibility of meetings and has made work in the meetings industry a "real career." Although there is still much to be done, we wouldn't be where we are without them.

You have spent your entire career with one firm. Would you say this is quite unique? What advantages/disadvantages has it brought you?

Actually it's two: Fairmont Hotels for 7 years and Loews for 28 years. It is absolutely unique. Probably I could have moved up faster if I had wanted titles, but as a woman who started in the industry during a time when there were very few women, I was fortunate to be with a company that rewarded performance regardless of gender. They not only appreciated my talents, but encouraged me to ensure that we delivered that message to all of our hotels. In the end, I think financially I had no disadvantages, although certainly early in my career I sacrificed salary and incentives for the ability to work for a company that really cared about me.

You have been very successful in this industry. What lessons have you learned that can be passed on to those reading this text?

The most important thing I've learned is that listening to your customer is critical for long-term success. Truly understanding their business, their needs, and what you can do to make them more successful is such an important thing that I did during my career. There is no substitute for caring about the customer. I attend industry organization meetings, learn about their concerns, challenges, needs, and wants; and then I do my best to meet those needs and challenges. Volunteering for leadership roles in their organizations has been the cornerstone of my success, both in the meetings industry and within my own company. Integrity follows you throughout your career. Not having it will kill you in the long term.

What types of skill sets would be needed by a student interested into going into the meeting planner side of the business?

Actually, I would recommend they have two opposite skills: the first is to be extraordinarily detail-oriented because a meeting is all about the details. But the meeting planners who are getting the bigger jobs with higher pay and bigger incentives are the ones who understand that their jobs are much more than just details. They are much more strategic. They are able to actually develop a strategy for the meeting with their client and are able to measure the results of that meeting. They build that into their processing, so at the end of the meeting they can go to the CEO or the VP of marketing or whomever and discuss the outcome of the meeting: how the meeting ranked, how much money was made, or how much they saved. They make themselves much more valuable in that process.

Used by permission from Charlotte St. Martin.

The **organizational customer** is defined as the purchaser of hospitality products and services for a group or organization that has a common purpose. These customers are particularly important to hotels and resorts that offer extensive meeting facilities and, in many cases, represent the majority of such properties' annual occupancy. These customers' needs are somewhat different from those of the individual customers described in Chapter 7. Although all of the basic principles of purchase behavior are the same as described in Chapter 7—stimuli, search, perceptions, beliefs, attitudes, and so on—organizational customers are typically the "purchasers" for the end "users." Although both the meeting planner or travel manager and the actual user are organizational customers, we will use the term *user* (or *end user*) for the actual user who is not the purchaser. We will use the term *planner* for the buyer who is not the end user.

Planners and managers act as intermediaries to satisfy the needs and wants of the users as a group, which is why this is referred to generically as the group market. They may "sell" to the organizational customer, just as travel agents, tour operators, and incentive travel planners do; or, as is the case with meetings and **convention planners**, they may organize and plan meetings for the organizational customer. As in the case with travel managers, they may also "manage" the travel arrangements for organizational customers.

Although there are a number of target market categories in the organizational market, we can define them in seven major segments:

- Corporate travel market
- Corporate meetings market
- Incentive market
- Association, convention, and trade show/exhibition market
- Airline crew market
- Social, military, education, religious, and fraternal (SMERF) and government markets
- Group tour and travel market

An acronym for the first four segments listed above (meeting, incentive, conference, and exhibition markets) is **MICE**.

The Generic Organizational Market

When a couple books a hotel room on a weekend package, they know what their expectations will be because the expectations are their own. Similarly, business travelers may choose to be close to their place of business for the next day, sometimes at the expense of comfort. The needs and purpose of these customers are individualized. The meeting planner or manager, however, intends to satisfy the needs of multiple travelers at the same time. Although the group may have a common purpose, such as a business meeting of a corporation, a computer industry convention, or an incentive trip for insurance salespeople, each member of the group may have somewhat different needs. This makes the overall task somewhat more complex for the planner or manager. The similarity, of course, is that if expectations are not met in either case, the customer may go somewhere else the next time.

The challenge of planners has amplified in recent years because of the corporate trend toward downsizing. Large corporations have trimmed their workforces by tens of thousands of employees. Many meeting planners and travel managers have been victims of the downsizing, leaving these tasks to administrative assistants, who lack experience in this field, or to travel agents or travel planners, who don't know the organization as intimately. This gives the hotel marketer an even more critical need to understand the buyer. This has also led to the growth of more independent professional meeting planners, who do not work for just one company but plan meetings for numerous corporate clients.[1]

Specifically, the planner or manager must try to anticipate the needs of the group, as well as select the proper facilities to accomplish the group's common purpose. For example, the meeting planner of a corporation may be given the task of planning a sales conference for the international division. The planner must understand the needs of that particular department within the company, with which she normally has very little contact, as well as the needs of the individual members.

At times, planners or managers may not even visit the hotels or restaurants to which they send their organizational groups. Thus, to make the right decision, they need to rely on a different set of stimuli from those used by other customers. Yesawich, Pepperdine, Brown & Russell revealed in their 2004 *Portrait of North American Meeting Planners* that if planners do not make a site visit (by far the most important source of information when selecting a site), then they rely heavily on property sales staff. Word-of-mouth referrals from fellow planners or managers are also very influential factors when choosing one facility over another. About 4 out of 10 professional meeting planners rely on information in brochures or other collateral, regional hotel/resort sales staff, and hotel/resort representation company sales staff. Advertising in meeting trade directories, business press, meeting trade press, and direct mail all rank far down the list on the reliance hierarchy,[2] thereby underscoring the importance of a property or destination's sales staff in soliciting this type of business. However, advertising is used to gen-

Anticipation can be quite grueling.

Meetings. Come to order April 28, 2005.
To book your next meeting please call us at (866) 770 7031.
Or visit us at wynnlasvegas.com.

Wynn LAS VEGAS

Circle #374 on Free Information Card

EXHIBIT 8-1 This advertisement from Wynn hotels targets meeting planners' need for success.

Source: Korey Kay & Partners. Used by permission.

erate leads and "get meeting planners talking," as shown in Exhibit 8-1 for Wynn Resorts and in Exhibit 8-2 for Tarrytown House.

Meeting Planners

Planners rely heavily on hotel salespeople. Also, conference service managers of the hotel, who handle the details during an event, become extremely important in the decision to book and to rebook after the event is over. Even the chef, who is going to be serving perhaps 300 attendees three meals a day, becomes critical. The **organizational planner** is at far more risk from a bad meal than is the weekend package customer who is not pleased with room service.

As planners gain more experience on the job, however, they are less influenced by salespeople. Corporate meeting planners are far more likely to rely on site inspections than on sales staff when selecting meeting destinations.[3] These

people and many other planners want to see for themselves and will often visit the property before booking it. There is an increased professionalism among experienced planners, which is evident in the way they go about inspecting properties and setting up meetings. All planners, no matter what their depth of competence, are most concerned that the hotel and its staff perform so that their meetings are successful. Quite often a planner's promotion—or even his or her job—is on the line, and hotels often reflect this in their advertising (see Exhibit 8-3). Even if the hotel is entirely at fault, the responsibility ultimately falls on the planner, who chose the wrong site for the meeting.

The leading concerns of meeting planners, both corporate and association, are shown in Exhibit 8-3.

One planner explained what customers need:

> You can have the most gorgeous facility in the world. . . . I still need professional staff to augment what I do. . . . I often follow the same people as they move from hotel to hotel. The people I do meetings for like to be pampered a little bit. A property may be less than desirable, but if they can provide service and if the food is good we can overlook the other things. What's important to me is . . . that everything I've ordered is there. Problems occur when hotels don't deliver what they say they can deliver.[4]

Exhibit 8-4 shows the highest 18 site-selection criteria generally agreed on by association and corporate meeting planners.

Planning the Event

To begin to understand the needs of the organizational planner, it is important to see how the planning process should go for a meeting or function. Understanding this, the sales and operations departments of a hotel can anticipate problems before they happen, perhaps preserving the success of an entire meeting. We next discuss critical issues related to working with the organizational planner.

Buy Time

Different segments of customers have different buy times (also called purchase cycles or **lead times**) for purchasing the hotel product. A corporate traveler may make reservations one week in advance of an upcoming trip. According to a study undertaken by PKF Consulting on behalf of *Convention South* magazine, the average booking lead times for large events has moved from 21.6 months in 2002 to 23.4 months in 2004.[5] The tour operator will have routes calculated a year or more in advance. For smaller meetings, the lead time is less. For example, Yesawich, Pepperdine, Brown & Russell found in their 2004 *Portrait of North American Meeting Planners* that for meetings of less than

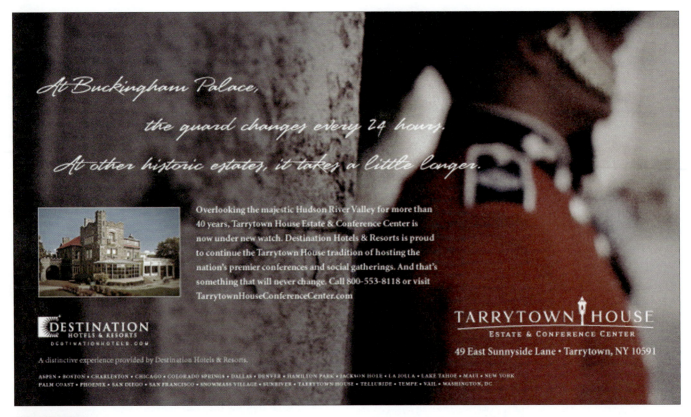

At Buckingham Palace, the guard changes every 24 hours. At other historic estates, it takes a little longer.

Overlooking the majestic Hudson River Valley for more than 40 years, Tarrytown House Estate & Conference Center is now under new watch. Destination Hotels & Resorts is proud to continue the Tarrytown House tradition of hosting the nation's premier conferences and social gatherings. And that's something that will never change. Call 800-553-8118 or visit TarrytownHouseConferenceCenter.com

DESTINATION HOTELS & RESORTS
DESTINATIONHOTELS.COM

A distinctive experience provided by Destination Hotels & Resorts.

ASPEN • BOSTON • CHARLESTON • CHICAGO • COLORADO SPRINGS • DALLAS • DENVER • HAMILTON PARK • JACKSON HOLE • LA JOLLA • LAKE TAHOE • MAUI • NEW YORK
PALM COAST • PHOENIX • SAN DIEGO • SAN FRANCISCO • SNOWMASS VILLAGE • SUNRIVER • TARRYTOWN HOUSE • TELLURIDE • TEMPE • VAIL • WASHINGTON, DC

TARRYTOWN HOUSE
ESTATE & CONFERENCE CENTER
49 East Sunnyside Lane • Tarrytown, NY 10591

EXHIBIT 8-2 The Tarrytown House focuses on tradition to entice meeting planners to consider them for their next meeting.

Source: Destination Hotels and Resorts. Used by permission.

EXHIBIT 8-3 Top 12 Factors with Which Meeting Planners Are Extremely or Very Concerned

Factors of Concern	Corporate Planners	Association Planners
Making the meeting agenda relevant	1	1
Convention services staff	2	3
Room rates	3	2
Accessibility of the destination by air	4	6
Cost of food, beverage, and entertainment at the destination	5	5
Cost of flying to the destination	6	7
Availability of low-cost air carrier service to the destination	7	9
Hotel or resort security services	8	N/A
Internet access from all meeting rooms	9	N/A
Meeting attendance projections	10	4
AV company services	11	N/A
Adequacy of the high-speed Internet	12	N/A
Popularity of the destination	N/A	8
Availability of new/interesting speakers	N/A	10
Popularity of the hotel or resort	N/A	11
Accessibility of the destination by car	N/A	12

Source: Yesawich, Pepperdine, Brown & Russell. (2004). Portrait of North American meeting planners, 42.

100 people, the average lead time is 6.3 months; for 100 to 200 attendees it is 9.5 months; for 201 to 400 it is 13.2 months; for 401 to 600 it is 15.2 months; for 601 to 800 it is 16.6 months; and for 801 to 1,000 attendees the average lead time is 18.2 months.[6]

Knowing the timing of the purchase is important in selecting potential market segments because it will determine the scheduling of sales, advertising, and related marketing activities. To maximize revenues, the ideal business mix of segments may include a variety of group customers.

EXHIBIT 8-4	Hotel or Resort Selection Criteria of Association Meeting Planners and Corporate Meeting Planners (% stating extremely important or very important)		
		Corporate Planners	**Association Planners**
Small meeting rooms		82%	75%
Internet access from guest rooms		82%	57%
Free Internet access from guest rooms		79%	57%
Ability of "headquartered hotel" to accommodate all delegates together		76%	81%
Ballroom		61%	68%
Bar or lounge on premises		63%	62%
Internet access my attendees can trust is secure		56%	76%
On-site convention service manager		74%	76%
Working desks in guest rooms		74%	46%
Business Center		72%	63%
Hotel/resort brand's reputation in the meetings industry		70%	59%
Casual, three-meal restaurant on premise		68%	68%
Complimentary transportation to/from airport		67%	69%
Ability of on-site technical support for high speed Internet in the meeting rooms		67%	58%
Internet access from the meeting rooms		67%	54%
Professional on-premise support for Internet/AV		66%	67%
Secure high-speed Internet to protect data		64%	45%
Fine dining restaurant on premises		64%	44%

Source: Yesawich, Pepperdine, Brown & Russell. (2004). *Portrait of North American meeting planners*, 33.

With the different room rate potential of each customer grouping, managing the inventory becomes critical.

For example, a 400-room hotel may have an opportunity to sell out to a midweek convention three years in advance at a rate of $100 per night. At first glance, this might appear to be a good sale; the sales department can spend its time trying to fill other, less busy time periods. More careful analysis, however, might show that this hotel has an average of 300 rooms per night occupied by business travelers during the week. The rate this year is $125 per night, and in three years it is expected to be $150.

Few, if any, business travelers plan business trips three years in advance. These travelers will be calling the hotel a few days in advance for their room reservations, unaware of the convention that is being held there at that time. If all patterns hold, the hotel will "lose" $50 per room on the 300 rooms that it could have held for the segment that pays a higher rate, but books the shortest lead time. Mistakes like this are very subtle, because the hotel is sold out, yet the room revenues are decreased by $5,000 a night. The hotel may also alienate some regular customers who cannot get rooms when they need them. It does not take many miscalculations like this to understand the importance of the lead time on profitability.* We discuss pricing more in a later chapter. Managing this forecast revenue has led to a practice called yield management, which will also be discussed in detail in the chapter on pricing.

Another buy time variable is the use of a property at different periods of time. City hotels generally target business travelers and conventions during the week and pleasure travelers on weekends. The same variation may occur between summer and winter. Thus, many hotels offer "package" meetings at special rates during slow periods just as they do for individual travelers. Resort hotels have similar situations depending on the season of the year. At one time, many resorts simply closed during the off-season. Now most stay open year-round, but seek a different mix of occupied rooms that includes more meetings and conventions.

Assessing Needs

Each collection of people with a common purpose has different needs. For example, the convention of the Elks Club, a fraternal organization, certainly has different reasons for a meeting than does the new product development team for Eastman Kodak, yet both of these organizations may meet in the same hotel at the same time of the year. Both the planner and the hotel employees must understand the purpose of each meeting. If, in fact, the meeting is purely a social one, theme parties, golf outings, fashion shows, and so on, are expected and welcomed. If, on the other hand,

*With convention: 400 rooms at $100 = $40,000. Without convention: 300 rooms at $150 = $45,000. This calculation, of course, ignores F&B revenues from the convention, which could change the picture. Still, the question of alienation remains.

the purpose of the meeting is to devise strategies that will bring a corporation out of bankruptcy, the entire agenda and tone of the meeting will be altered accordingly. These are obvious differences; many are far more subtle.

The most common complaint planners have about hotel salespeople does not relate either to high-pressure selling or "cold calls"—though they don't particularly like either one. Rather, it is that the salesperson has not taken enough time to find out about their business. They may be pitched by a property unsuited to their needs and resent the fact that their time is being wasted by someone who didn't make enough effort to find out what they were like. In part, this refers to Gap 1 discussed in earlier chapters.

Setting Measurable Goals

For the planner, it is critical that the needs of the meeting be translated into measurable results. Corporate planners can measure results from their agenda. If the meeting purpose is to brainstorm for a new product, the success of the meeting may be partially judged on how the hotel helped to facilitate the process. For the incentive planner, post-trip evaluations are helpful. The goal may be that 90 percent of the winners of the incentive would return to the hotel or resort next year if given the opportunity. From the hotel side, if the planner does not have measurable goals set, success for the meeting becomes subjective rather than objective, and minor discrepancies are subject to magnified scrutiny.

Developing a Plan

The plan needs to be concise and to lead directly from the goals and needs of the organization. The planner should include hotel- and nonhotel-related activities. Airline tickets, ground transportation to and from the airport, excursions, and transportation of materials are all items that must be incorporated into the plan. An organizational planner without a plan is one who must be helped through the process by the hotel staff.

It is the responsibility of the hotel that wants satisfied customers to assist inexperienced planners with all phases of the meeting. Many hotels have been accustomed to working with meeting professionals. Now, these duties in some cases have been assigned to corporate staff with little experience in this area. For example, the bylaws of the organization may stipulate that the secretary of the group is responsible for the annual convention. If the newly elected secretary has no prior planning experience, the hotel staff needs to give assurance that all phases of the meeting will be accommodated. It will do the hotel no good to have a disorganized function, no matter whose fault it is. Once the salesperson senses an absence of knowledge, a different selling scenario should be employed.

During the planning process, for example, it may be found that the planner did not allow the proper timing between sessions for the group to move from the meeting rooms to the ballroom for lunch. The conference coordinator must be knowledgeable enough to steer the planner toward the correct time frame. An example occurred in the city of Boston, where three hotels formed a strategic alliance to market themselves. The Copley Connection is a joint venture among the Westin Hotel Copley Place, the Boston Marriott Copley, the Sheraton Boston Hotel, and the Copley Place Shopping Galleries. The hotels were marketed together as one destination for a meeting. Although the hotels are connected by a skywalk, planners soon found out that it took 30 minutes to move a group from the ballroom of the Marriott to a function room at the Westin. Experienced planners adjusted their agendas accordingly; others found the spaces and distances to be problematic.

On the other hand, professional planners are also becoming more educated as to what is best for their meetings. For example, a hotel salesperson might book another group into the meeting room next to the general session of the conference. The planner might, in this instance, insist that the space be used for a luncheon, thereby preventing any unanticipated interruptions from the group next door. This occurred in a hotel in Hong Kong where a major record label held a meeting to introduce new artists to retail stores and radio stations. A very serious meeting of a manufacturing concern was in the room next door. This latter group had a hard time holding their meeting while all of the artists were singing in the room next door.

Resolving Conflicts

Planners have to work in tandem with both the hotel and their own organizations to anticipate and resolve potential problems. Although planning may alleviate possible conflicts, the hotel may be only half of the problem. The organization itself presents problems that must be addressed before the function occurs. There may be a hierarchy of attendees within the organization that needs suites, first-class travel, and seats at the head table. Failing to accommodate these needs can cause conflicts that ruin the meeting through no fault of the hotel. A hotel staff can anticipate these needs by asking to review the VIP list and discussing its needs.

There are numerous other potential issues. Non-smoking guest rooms and meeting rooms are entering into the spectrum of worries. Individual special meals during a banquet are no longer limited to just kosher or vegetarian meals. Today guests have many different dietary needs and restrictions, and hotels must work hard to cater to these to satisfy the needs of attendees.

The best way to resolve possible conflicts for both sides is to have a **preconference meeting**. The term *preconference* is generic and can be applied to incentive trips as well as to corporate meetings. At this meeting, the planner reviews the details of the meeting with each department to ensure that communications have not been distorted through the conference service manager. The front office, housekeeping, banquet managers, and general manager, if the situation warrants, should be in attendance with the salesperson and conference service manager to ensure that all potential conflicts are discussed and remedied before the function ensues.

Executing the Meeting

Executing the meeting may be the simplest phase of the planner's job if all the previous steps were followed and done well. If they were not, this is certainly the hardest portion of the process. The execution of the meeting could occur without the planner being in attendance. The needs of the planner are now being transposed onto the group.

Sometimes, even if the organizational planner is on site, the end users' needs are not met. For example, the association planner may want the general session set up theater style, with the room having chairs that face the podium for a guest speaker. The guest speaker might demand that the room be set up classroom style, with each chair having a desk in front of it so that participants can take notes during the presentation. One of the authors attended a function in Chicago where the meeting specifications called for a podium on the platform. At the last minute it was decided that a sit-down panel format would be more appropriate. The flustered setup man was clearly annoyed at the last-minute change.

These are classic examples of how the planner is not the end user and how the needs of the group can change right up to the last minute. The hotel that adjusts accordingly will be the one that receives the future business. There are no right and wrong sides to this scenario. The task must be completed to satisfy the needs of both the end user and the organizational planner. It really does not matter how many times a group changes the setup of a room. The hotel is responsible for making the changes. This is what marketing is all about—giving customers what they want at a time and place of their choosing.

Evaluating the Results

Based on the goals of the organization, was the meeting a success? The hotel should be as interested in the results as the planner is. The evaluation process can take place in a **postconference meeting** held shortly after the conclusion of the function. Department heads and the planner can review face-to-face all the things that went right, as well as those that went wrong. The marketing-oriented organization will take immediate steps to correct the malfunctions and to reinforce the positive aspects.[7]

The evaluation process is also critical for the planner. When these customers are the buyers, but may not be present at the actual event, it may be difficult for them to understand exactly what took place. Even when the hotel delivered as promised, the organization may not have accomplished its goals. The planner will need to assess the results before starting to plan the next similar function and should be made aware of the problem areas by the hotel that wants to recapture the business.

The Corporate Travel Market

The corporate travel manager or coordinator plans travel and entertainment for a company's employees. Corporate travel managers are different from corporate meeting planners in that they plan individual travel schedules. A common purpose still may exist, since the corporate entity is relatively homogeneous, but people at different levels of the organization will be traveling on different missions. In some organizations, the travel manager and the **meeting planner** are the same person. Corporate meeting planning will be discussed in the next section.

The size of the corporate travel market is very large, running into tens of millions of business travelers worldwide. Behind salaries and technology, travel and entertainment costs are the third largest controllable expense of private sector companies in the United States.[8] About half of these end users are directed or influenced by the corporate travel manager who plans, controls, mediates, negotiates, evaluates, and/or approves travel expenditures of those companies having corporate travel managers.[9] In 2003 the typical travel manager managed $4.2 million in U.S. booked air volume and $5.1 million in travel and entertainment. This travel manager was responsible for an average of 5,190 U.S. and foreign travelers.[10] This market is very desirable for hotels because it tends to pay good rates, is large in size, and delivers business consistently throughout most of the year. Exhibit 8-5 shows what travel managers are managing.

EXHIBIT 8-5	What Travel Managers Are Managing	
Hotel	89%	
Car rental	87%	
Air travel	86%	
Policy creation, enforcement	75%	
Online booking	68%	
Car services, including limo	67%	
Travel agency	64%	
Meeting planning	61%	
Airport parking	53%	
Rail	52%	
Intranet travel site	50%	
T&E charge card program	49%	
Global distribution system selection	42%	
Leisure travel for employees	39%	
Incentive planning	36%	
Traveler security	36%	
Emergency plans/evacuations	35%	
Traveler tracking software	32%	
Corporate housing and relocation	31%	
Telephone calling cards	31%	
Travel data warehouse	31%	
Business charter and aircraft	30%	
Online expense reporting	29%	
Travel insurance	27%	
Corporate car fleet/leasing	24%	
Mobile phone contracts	24%	
Procurement cards	21%	
Other	67%	

Source: Warcholak, E. S. (2004, August 2). Travel manager salary and attitude survey. Business Travel News. Retrieved November 14, 2005, from www.btnmag.com/businesstravelnews/headlines/breaking_news.jsp, © *copyright VNU Business Media. All rights reserved. Distributed by Valco IP.*

The corporate travel manager needs to find the correct products and services for the entire group of corporate travelers. Once the product is identified, the best rates are negotiated. The supplier needs to understand the culture of the organization to fulfill its needs. For example, some companies go to the top of the line for their hospitality and service needs. From first-class airplane seats, to limousines for ground transport, to the best hotel in the area, some companies spare no expense when entertaining themselves or their customers.

Some corporate cultures are just the opposite. They use hotel rooms sparingly, have meetings in their own offices, and use cabs or airport shuttles to reach hotels. Negotiations with a large corporate planner at the Embassy Suites Hotel in Boca Raton revealed this culture. After renovation, the hotel approached its major customer for a rate increase. During the sales call, the customer did not disagree that the hotel was new and worth more money. The customer simply said that the company at this time would not pay more than $125 per night for a hotel room, even if it was the Ritz-Carlton. The Embassy Suites lost this business. Most companies are somewhere in between.

Typically, corporate executives get the best treatment and company trainees the least. It mostly comes down to examining the purpose of travel, who is traveling, and their position in the corporate hierarchy.

Many companies have come to realize the extent of their travel and entertainment budgets. In some cases, this can be as much as 25 percent of an organization's costs. Thus, many corporations are tightening the screws on travel costs. As one corporate travel manager told us, "You can't believe what $5 a night means to this company over a year's time." Exhibit 8-6 shows an advertisement for Hershey Resorts. Notice the last line of the advertisement: "An easy drive from anywhere in the mid-Atlantic." The implication is that you do not need to fly to reach this destination.

The way corporations manage their travel and entertainment dollars significantly affects the revenues of the hospitality industry. The emergence of corporate travel buyers is a result of this cost control effort. Essentially, their task is to control these costs without losing the quality of the product. Corporate travel buyers first ascertain the level and service of product that the organization is willing to accept; then they negotiate the prices.

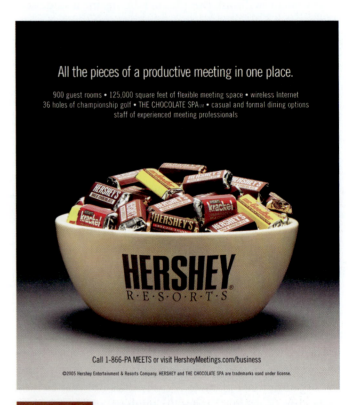

EXHIBIT 8-6 Hershey Resorts addresses the budget needs of the corporate travel manager.

Source: Hershey Entertainment and Resorts Company. Used by permission.

In order to work with the corporate travel market, certain things should be known: volume, travel patterns, and cost control.

Knowing the Volume

It is difficult to negotiate anything without knowing the parameters with which both parties are dealing. A hotel might give a discount based on expected volume, only to find that the volume never materializes. A corporation, on the other hand, might underestimate its true rooms requirements at a destination and be paying more than it could negotiate at the actual volume. The same is true with airline travel, where companies can often negotiate volume discounts. Most major airlines even have a special website for corporate travel managers.

 Web Browsing Exercise

Visit the website of Northwest Airlines for corporate travel managers (www. corporate.nwa.com). Compare and contrast this with their regular website (www.nwa.com/). What differences, if any, are there? What makes this website unique for the target audience? If you were a corporate planner, would it make you want to join the program?

If hotel rack rates are high, the travel manager has come to expect a discount no matter what the volume. One of the authors once received a call from a corporate travel department asking for a discounted rate. The company, which happened to make shoes, claimed its volume would be about 100 room nights annually. The hotel happened to enjoy high occupancies and rarely discounted rooms, even for 1,500 room nights a year. The shoe company planner was not convinced that his perception of volume did not apply in this case. Finally, the author asked whether he could get a discount on shoes if he bought three pairs a year. The response was, "Of course not! You have to be a big retailer to command a discount!" The point was finally made.

Hotel room rates are negotiated initially from the published or rack rates. Rarely today do customers pay the rack rate unless they are uneducated enough not to ask for one of the myriad other rates available or are traveling during peak demand periods. From rack rates come corporate or commercial rates, which are usually at least 10 to 15 percent lower than the rack rate.

Hotels now negotiate individual corporate rates with individual corporate customers. Volume corporate customers recognize the wide-scale availability of corporate rates for anyone and demand their own corporate rate relative to their volume. These rates can run 15 to 35 percent below the rack rate. This, of course, makes the rack rate a ridiculous pretension, so hotels may raise their rack rate (say, 10 percent) to raise the corporate and volume rates.

Large travel agencies or consortia provide volume purchasing power for their customers. Woodside Travel in Boston, American Express in New Jersey, or Rosenbluth Travel in Philadelphia are examples of consortia or a consolidated purchaser under which smaller agencies can access the technology and buying power of larger entities by combining the volume of a number of corporations to get the best fares and rates for all.

These specific corporate fares and rates are called "volume negotiated rates," which are framed in "**rate buckets**," based on volume. An example is shown in Exhibit 8-7.

Corporate travel managers also like hotel chain representatives to negotiate rates that will apply chain-wide. A chain that provides the convenience of "one-stop shopping," or one place where corporate travel managers can negotiate room rate agreements for all hotels in the chain, would have a competitive advantage in this market.[11]

Understanding Travel Patterns

The corporate travel manager uses knowledge of corporate travel patterns to negotiate with hotel suppliers; the supplier responds in kind. For example, if the corporation has people traveling to a given city mainly when occupancy is already high, the manager will have far greater difficulty negotiating preferred rates. On the other hand, if travel can

EXHIBIT 8-7	Volume Negotiated Corporate Rate Buckets

Hotel Rate Structure

Rack[a]	$200
Corporate[b]	$180
Consortia[c]	$170

Rate Buckets

Volume Promised per Year	Negotiated Rate
250 plus rooms	$165
400 plus rooms	$160
500 plus rooms	$155
1,000 plus rooms	$145

a. Rack rate is the published room rate.
b. Corporate rate is the rate quoted to anyone asking for a corporate rate.
c. Consortia rates are given to large groupings of travel agencies that pool their buying power for the purpose of getting lower rates. To be accepted into their distribution channel, consortia demand rates at least 15 percent below rack and below the available corporate rates. Salespeople use these sales to negotiate with large rooms producers in a destination.

be planned during low-occupancy periods, the manager may obtain not only discounted rates but also preferred availability during periods of high occupancy. The corporate customer tries to anticipate travel patterns and reserve in advance, not just react to travel trends.

Controlling Costs

When low room rates are negotiated, the corporate customer tries to ensure that they are used. If rates are negotiated on the basis of volume, then lack of volume may result in forfeiture of the rate. This stipulation is often inserted in the contract by the hotel. Of course, if lower rates are negotiated and company personnel don't use the rooms, the cost savings are not realized.

Some companies develop policies to enforce their negotiated rates. The corporate travel manager might go into a marketplace and negotiate (or ask for bids) with hotels at various levels of product class and cost. For example, in Denver a company might have three preferred hotels: Holiday Inn, Sheraton, and Hyatt; who stays at which brand may depend on the management level of the employee. To enforce compliance, the company may not reimburse hotel bills at alternative hotels unless the others are sold out.

There is a trend by companies to hire outside professionals or organizations to handle this phase of the business, such as American Express. As rates for hotels and airlines become more complicated, along with the benefits of frequent traveler programs, the task of managing individual travel for corporations has become increasingly complex.

Another solution has been the hiring of "in-plants" by companies with large travel budgets. An **in-plant** is a division of a travel agency that is located inside the offices of the organizational customer. The equipment and employees belong to the travel agency, but their use is dedicated to the host company's needs. These employees become the corporate travel manager, although they technically work for the travel agency. The in-plant receives either straight fees, commissions on bookings, or a combination of both for services rendered.

In-plants offer unique resources to the corporation that might not be otherwise accessible. Specifically, the in-plant can leverage its business with the host company, plus other companies also served by the agency, to negotiate even lower rates. For example, XYZ Company may have 500 rooms being used annually in Denver. This volume might justify a 10 percent discount off rack rates. The in-plant agency, however, might also represent four other companies with equal room usage in Denver. Thus, the in-plant can negotiate on the basis of 2,500 room nights to re-

EXHIBIT 8-8	Meeting Destination Selection Decision Factors (unaided mentions by 8 or more percent of sample)
Cost/price/rates of hotel rooms	55%
Convenience of location for attendees	34%
Travel/transportation/access to airport	23%
Amenities at hotel/conference center included in hotel	18%
Entertainment options/shopping	18%
Accessibility	16%
Size/capacity of meeting rooms	16%
Available hotels and dates	9%
Service staff at hotel/venue attends to our needs	9%
Quality of hotel/reputation	8%
Climate/weather/time of year	8%

Source: Yesawich, Pepperdine, Brown & Russell. (2004). *Portrait of North American meeting planners,* 28.

ceive a 25 percent discount for all, the same as the travel agent consortia mentioned earlier. For example, according to the Accenture Global Travel Management Study, firms that used American Express Business Travel services achieved 19 percent savings on air travel, 13 percent savings on hotel accommodations, and 15 percent savings on car rental charges.[12]

Of course, cost is not the only consideration of travel managers. The most important factors and their relative priority by travel managers are shown in Exhibit 8-8.

The Corporate Meetings Market

The corporate meetings market covers a wide range of organizational customers. In 2003 this market spent $44.7 billion dollars over 1,058,800 meetings attended by 84.6 million people.[13] The average corporate meeting expenditure was $262,000 in 2003, with hotel and F&B costs representing up to 56 percent of this figure.[14] Some hotel companies aim to specifically attract this business, as shown in Exhibits 8-1 and 8-9.

The most common type of corporate meeting is a management meeting, wherein executives gather to discuss company business. These tend to be smaller with only senior mangers attending. An additional type of corporate meeting is the sales meeting, which is usually organized once or more a year to discuss and review company sales goals and strategies and "pump up" the sales team. Another common type of corporate meeting is the training meeting or seminar. These provide corporations avenues to exchange information and improve personnel performance.

Productive meetings arise from a harmonious setting.

222 MASON STREET · SAN FRANCISCO, CA 94102 · 415.394.1111· FAX 415.421.0455
HOTELNIKKOSF.COM · In Partnership with Le Meridien Hotels & Resorts

hotel nikko san francisco
Meetings

EXHIBIT 8-9 Some companies, such as Hotel Nikko, specifically pursue the corporate meetings market.

Source: © 2005 Hotel Nikko San Francisco. Used by permission.

EXHIBIT 8-10 Hotel Sofitel is appealing to meeting planners.

Source: Sofitel. Used by permission.

They are often for new recruits to ensure their indoctrination into the corporate culture. The corporate planner is responsible for all three types of meetings and any others. Some incentive meetings are also in this bailiwick, but this unique type of meeting is usually handled by specialized incentive companies.

To understand the needs of the corporate meeting planner, one must review all the components of the organizational customer. In a nutshell, meeting planners need to "look good." They need to look good to their boss, to the person whose meeting they organize, and also to the hotel if they want to continue to look good to the first two people. At least one hotel company was advertising to appeal to this need of meeting planners, as shown in Exhibit 8-10.

What meeting planners do not need is for hotels to mislead them with regard to the capabilities of the physical plant and the personnel. The sometimes short-term thinking of the hotel business may lend itself to misrepresentation and eventual loss of the customer. With as much as a 70 percent annual turnover in many hotel sales offices and bonuses based on room nights sold, the reward system essentially mandates how fast you can make your quota to increase your income or get promoted. Sales offices are told to "book

it, not cook it," meaning get the signed contract and go find more business. Many experienced planners, however, have little need for the salesperson, requiring instead the attention of a professional conference service manager, who works for the hotel, to service the meeting. Conference service managers are the on-site need fulfillers. All the detail work will be done through this person who, like the salesperson, may also be on a similar "fast track," often leaving the meeting planner in the hands of inexperienced new people.

Meeting planners need meeting rooms that will suit the purpose of their event. They also want quiet rooms. Often, hotel ballrooms are divided by thin movable walls that allow noise from the meeting next door to filter through. One of the authors recently gave an all-day seminar on research methods directly across a narrow hallway from a national convention of gospel singers. You can imagine the problem.

Hotel employees may also be a source of disruptive noise. Although it is operationally convenient to have the kitchen right next to the ballroom, meeting attendees are justifiably annoyed when the kitchen crew bangs pots and pans throughout a meeting. Doors that bang when people

LAS VEGAS

Wynn

Meetings. Period.

READY & RUNNING SPRING 2005
Call our Sales Office at 877 770 7077 to check remaining availability.

www.wynnlasvegas.com

EXHIBIT 8-11 The Wynn Resort uses this advertisement to attract the meeting business.

Source: Wynn Las Vegas. Used by permission.

go in and out of meeting rooms are another source of high irritation.

The meeting planner also needs an efficient front desk that will assign rooms to the right people: the VIPs in the suites and the attendees in the regular rooms. The billing needs to be right: Some rooms may be billed to the organization, while some attendees may have to pay for their own. The meeting planner needs meeting rooms to be set up on time and coffee breaks to arrive when ordered. The audiovisuals need to be in the meeting room at the right time and in working order. The spare bulb for the projector should be on the cart, not locked in a closet at the other end of the building.

Meeting planners, like all customers, do not need excuses. It is not their problem that the banquet manager did not show up for work or that the linen was supposed to be delivered at 10:00 A.M. or that they should not have scheduled the break so close to lunch time. The hotel staff assumes all responsibility for the "well-being" of the meeting.

In short, meeting planners expect all of the details to be handled absolutely professionally. If a hotel is able to provide planners not only with what they think they need,

but also with what they don't realize they need, the planners will return. All of these concerns, and many more, fall on the shoulders of the conference service manager assigned to service a group.

From the hotel's perspective, there may be problems with the corporate meetings market. Although attendance at these meetings is usually compulsory, thus assuring the planned rooms and meal counts, cancellation of the entire meeting is often a threat. At the last minute, a corporation may cancel a meeting for hundreds of people that has been in the planning stage for months. Economic conditions, failure to develop a new product on schedule, or simply whim may provoke such a decision. This has led to the imposition of more large up-front and nonrefundable deposits.

Corporate meeting planners need as much help as they can get and may require a great deal of guidance in accomplishing their company's meeting objectives. On average, corporate planners in 2004 arranged 16.7 meetings in the United States and 9.9 international meetings.[15] A total of 87 percent of these meetings were in hotels, 39 percent at resorts, and 20 percent at **conference centers**. The hotel staff provides the right guidance in order to ensure a successful meeting. Exhibit 8-11 shows an advertisement for a hotel that hopes to capture a share of the meeting planning business.

Conference Centers

Meeting planners may choose from a multitude of hotels. With this additional supply in most marketplaces, the need to attract meeting planners' business has grown. Some hotels attempt this by claiming to be conference centers and adding the words to their name, believing they can establish a new identity (i.e., XYZ Motor Inn becomes XYZ Motor Inn and Conference Center). Howard Johnson properties have, for example, in many areas, adopted the practice of adding the term *conference center* to their signs. These properties are not, however, conference centers in the true sense. In fact, many are far from it and may, in the long run, be hurting themselves with this pretension. On the other hand, many large hotels have excellent conference centers connected to them or on the same grounds, as shown previously in Exhibit 8-2.

One way the industry has responded to the unique needs of meeting planners is by developing "dedicated" conference centers that offer carefully designed facilities and services that are reserved mainly for meetings and do an excellent job specializing in this market. Pure conference centers cater almost exclusively to meetings. The National Conference Center in Leesburg, Virginia, or Babson Executive Center outside of Boston are true conference centers as defined by the sole trade association that repre-

According to the IACC, the big difference between a combined hotel and conference center and a true conference center is not just technical services but human services. The IACC claims that the business of the typical hotel is transient, limiting the attention and service it can give to every meeting, and that a conference center has a greater commitment to managing conferences as essentially the only market it serves.

In some cases, the combination of hotel and conference center works well when the markets are separated by day of the week or season. In other cases, conflicts are created that can be detrimental. The ballroom that is ideal for weddings or for **trade shows** may be entirely inappropriate for meetings. For example, in the first case, wedding guests would probably not hear noise from the kitchen. During a sales presentation meeting, however, those noises can break the concentration of the speaker and ruin the meeting. The dividing walls of the same ballroom may be ideal for the separation of a cocktail reception and a dinner, but too porous for the hosting of two meetings simultaneously. Very few facilities are ideal for all markets.

True conference centers attempt to serve one market only, the conference meetings market, and they do so in a controlled environment. With soundproof meeting rooms, dedicated audiovisual rooms with state-of-the-art equipment, and conference service managers whose sole job is to facilitate the needs of the meetings, these properties offer a serious environment for conducting meetings. Most are located outside and away from major cities so that recreational distractions are also held to a minimum.

Many conference centers offer an "inclusive pricing" option called a complete meeting package (CMP). This rate typically includes accommodations, meals, snacks, basic recreational amenities, meeting room rental, and even audiovisual services, all priced per person per night. These centers are dedicated to the needs of meeting planners and serve them well. At the same time, some are having a difficult time making ends meet financially. High occupancy occurs during selected time periods, and low periods incur very high costs without compensating revenues. For this reason, most dedicated conference centers attempt to fill in open dates with the social transient market.

The Incentive Market

The incentive meeting planner has a unique problem (need) when compared with other customers of the hospitality product. The incentive planner has to plan not only for the meeting and sleeping room requirements of a group, but also for the group's idea of "fun," such as entertainment, golf, sightseeing, and a multitude of other activities. This is

EXHIBIT 8-12 The website for ARAMARK Harrison Lodging, which is a division of Aramark Services Inc.

Source: Retrieved September 15, 2005, from www.aramarkharrisonlodging.com/home/flash.php. ARAMARK Harrison Lodging is a division of Aramark Services, Inc. Information submitted 1/5/06. Used by permission.

sents the category: IACC (International Association of Conference Centers). This organization has established a number of exacting criteria that must be met by a facility to use the "conference center" designation, including a requirement that at least 60 percent of available meeting space be dedicated, single-purpose conference space. These rooms must be separated from living and leisure areas and made available to clients on a 24-hour basis for material storage. In addition, a minimum of 60 percent of total revenue from guest rooms, meeting space, food and beverage, conference technology, and conference services must be conference related. The average group size must be 75 people or fewer.[16] The needs of the conference attendee are very different from those of leisure guests or business travelers. Exhibit 8-12 shows the website for Aramark Harrison Lodging, which is a division of Aramark Services, Inc.

Web Browsing Exercise

Visit the website for the International Association of Conference Centers (www.iacc-online.org/). How does this organization help move the planner through the buying process model discussed in the previous chapter? Why would an organization want to belong to this association? Why would a planner want to use this organization? Why would a planner not want to use this organization? If you work for a conference center that is not part of this organization, how do you compete?

a difficult task. When you think of your own idea of a good time, it is probably quite different from that of some other people you know. This problem of disparity challenges the incentive meeting planner.

The incentive meeting planner organizes travel as a reward for superior performance within a group. As stated by the Sales Marketing Network, "What distinguishes incentive or motivational travel from traditional travel is the focus on creating an extraordinary experience for the winner or one that builds morale, communicates the corporate message or fosters improved communications between employees and/or the company and its customers."[17] For example, the sales team of a computer manufacturer may have exceeded its sales quota by 30 percent. The reward is a trip to the Caribbean for a week, with spouses. Managers of a retail store chain may be eligible for travel incentives if their profit margins are above a certain quota.

The Society of Incentive Travel Executives, SITE, defines incentive travel as follows: "Incentive travel is a modern management tool that motivates salespeople, dealers, distributors, customers and internal employees by offering rewards in the form of travel for participation in the achievement of goals and objectives."[18]

Exhibit 8-13 reveals the results of a study undertaken by *Incentive* magazine (www.incentivemag.com). This table shows how many incentive programs are run annually, the objectives of incentive travel programs, the annual expenditure for incentive travel programs, and the amount spent on trip delivery per participant.

The U.S. incentive travel market generates over $27 billion a year, including revenues from airfare and ground services. Over 50 percent of expenditures are hotel related. Group sizes range from 2 to 2,000 people, with an average of over 100 people per trip. Most incentive trips include spouses. About 50 percent of the selected venues are resorts.[19]

Travel certainly is not the only form of incentive reward, but it is one that projects an image of excitement and relaxation away from the job. When this is done in the group format, teamwork and morale increase with the sense of accomplishment. Merchandise rewards, such as televisions, stereos, and cash bonuses, are the competition to travel rewards. Travel rewards are preferred by many companies, however, and managing that travel becomes an important task.

This has led to the growth of "**incentive houses**," companies that provide professional incentive planning services and hope to ensure no-hassle, successful, and satisfying trips. As the value of the incentive travel market has become recognized by the hotel industry, companies are trying to better meet this market's needs. According to J. J. Gubbins, former vice president of Sheraton,

---

EXHIBIT 8-13	2003 Incentive Travel Facts

Number of Programs Run Annually

1	22%
2	24%
3	2%
4	8%
5	7%
6 or more	37%

Objectives of Incentive Travel Programs (35% or more mentions)

Increase sales	86%
Recognize performance	74%
Build morale	63%
Increase market share	54%
Improve employee loyalty	49%
Sell new accounts	48%
Build customer loyalty	40%
Create new markets	36%
Foster teamwork	35%

Annual Expenditure for Incentive Travel Programs

Under $25,000	20%
$25,000–$49,999	9%
$50,000–$99,999	7%
$100,000–$149,999	7%
$150,000–$199,999	6%
$200,000–$249,999	7%
$250,000–$499,999	10%
$500,000–$999,999	15%
$1 million or more	19%

Amount Spent on Trip Delivery per Participant

Under $1,000	19%
$1,000–$1,999	28%
$2,000–$2,999	21%
$3,000–$3,999	20%
$4,000 or more	12%

Source: Retrieved November 13, 2005, from *www.incentivemag.com/incentive/ reports_analysis/index.jsp.*

Incentives really taught the hotel industry to be creative. It got us to focus on the idea of travel as entertainment. Through servicing incentives we learned how to develop the creative aspects of our own industry, which has affected nearly every aspect of our operation—even in the way hotels and resorts are designed.[20]

The incentive planner often becomes involved in the development of criteria for incentive success. In order to have winners to send on trips, the framework of the incentive must be established. In order to have a successful incentive, the reward must be different and worth the extra effort required to achieve it.

Once the framework of the incentive has been developed, the incentive planner must formulate the appropriate travel prizes. Even if **incentive planners** do not specifically design the promotion, it is critical for them to have a full understanding of the composition of the group and its achievements. Incentive planners need to establish the perceived level of incentive and plan accordingly.

The actual incentive trip can take three forms: pure incentive, incentive plus, and incentive weekends. The pure incentive trip is dedicated to having a good time without any business-related activities. The incentive plus is a more popular form of incentive trip and represents over 70 percent of the trips taken. Incentive plus trips combine pleasure with some form of meeting or new product introduction. In this way, companies maximize the use of their incentive travel dollars. The company can disseminate valuable information without having another sales meeting elsewhere. Incentive weekends are increasingly being used as rewards for good, but less than superior, performance. Companies recognize that although incentive trips are productive, they also take time away from the workplace. Three-day weekend incentives are more cost effective from a time management viewpoint.

The incentive planner has a multifaceted job when planning the actual trip. Specifically, all phases of the excursion must be minutely planned to enhance the end user experience. This is different from planning corporate or association meetings or conventions. In those cases, the planner plans the functions but leaves it to the individuals to get there and participate. The incentive planner, on the other hand, arranges for literally everything: air and land travel, hotel, food, excursions, sightseeing, entertainment, sports, and anything else that might take place during the trip. Each of these categories can be critical to the success of the trip.

This is why incentive planners almost always visit the host site and the hotels, restaurants, and ground operators at the site before developing the package. They want to make sure not only that everything is up to par, but also that every detail will be taken care of. As a final security measure, they or their representatives go on the trip. This means that a hotel has a special challenge in booking and handling incentive travel. We know of one case, for example, in which the planner ruled out an upscale hotel on an inspection trip because the sand urns had cigarette butts in them and facial tissue was missing in some of the rooms. "If they can't take care of the little things, they'll never take care of the big ones," was this planner's comment.

Incentive trip planning also differs from that of other organizational customers in that the popularity of the destination is of primary importance. The corporate customer or meeting planner may choose a facility because of the hotel itself or because of its proximity to business-related activities; for the incentive planner, the choice of hotel comes after the choice of destination.

Many companies are not large enough or skilled enough to develop incentive trips through their internal organization. A company may have a full-time corporate **travel manager** and a meeting planner, but the complexities of the incentive purchase are entirely different. For example, staying familiar with different destination areas and necessary ground arrangements is incredibly time-consuming. Incentive houses are a popular intermediary for the companies that need the dedicated attention of a professional. The incentive house is more than a travel agent; professional incentive planners help in all phases of incentive management.

Overall, the incentive organizational customer has a unique job among hotel customers. The "fun" aspect of the planning can be anything but that. Hotels that want a greater share of the incentive market must be extremely flexible in their approach to this market. Standardized approaches to capturing this market are likely not to be fruitful. An ad aimed at this market can be seen in Chapter 9, Exhibit 19-8.

Association, Convention, and Trade Show Markets

The association, convention, and trade show markets overlap. Association and convention customers have similar needs, although they are somewhat different types of groups. Both tend to have large guest room and meeting/function space requirements. An **association meeting** can comprise a group of people convening on a social basis to elect officers, have social functions, and organize activities on a regional or national basis. This category of organizational customer also tends to meet throughout the year in smaller groups, and social contacts are a major reason for attendance. Of course, innumerable professional (e.g., American Medical Association) and business associations (e.g., National Association of Manufacturers) meet both regionally and nationally to present papers, have board meetings, and set policy.

Convention planners are more focused on annual activities, such as annual meetings of delegates for a political caucus. Other examples are union gatherings to decide policies for the coming year or a commercial fishermen's convention to plan lobbying efforts. The participants may or may not meet throughout the year, and dissemination of information, more than social contacts, is the primary objective.

Finally, the main purpose of **trade shows** is to showcase and sell products. This requires wide open space, as

EXHIBIT 8-14 Atria solicits trade show business on its website.

Source: Retrieved September 16, 2005, from www.accor.com/bg/groupe/ activities/hotellerie/marques/atria.asp. Used by permission of AccorHotels.com.

advertised in Exhibit 8-14, which promotes Atria. The hotel's task in booking trade shows is to provide the space; ease of access for products to be brought in; and the facilities, such as electric power and lighting, to display the products. This requires a great deal of work, which can be disruptive to other guests. In addition, the hotel sells rooms and meals to exhibitors and those who attend. Exhibitors also make wide use of "hospitality suites," where they entertain customers. This puts heavy pressure on the hotel's room service division. However, the hotel does make money on these hospitality suites.

While the planners for each of these events (association, convention, and trade show) have different reasons for purchasing the hospitality product, their needs are similar and sometimes interchangeable. For example, an association may meet as a convention in connection with a trade show. At times, an entire facility will be booked for a two- or three-day period. Usually, the planner arranges for guest rooms to be held, but reservations are made individually by the participants. The organizer will have a list of VIPs, but the majority of guest rooms are booked by direct calls or through the use of reservation forms.

Reservation forms are essentially order forms that are provided by the hotel and are designed specifically for the use of attendees. Attendees, of course, are always free to stay somewhere else if they prefer. Thus, the hotel sales department tries to make it desirable for them to stay there. Handling reservations in this manner can make coordination difficult. The hotel must be flexible to accommodate the needs of the attendees, many of whom are buying the hotel sight unseen. Strict inventory control is necessary. If, for example, the hotel accepts more king-size bedroom requests than it can accommodate, it may have many unhappy customers. In addition, the sales department needs

to coordinate with reservations and revenue management to ensure that attendees cannot book a room at the same hotel less expensively by going through a different distribution channel such as the Internet.

Food and beverage is also a unique proposition for hotels in these markets. The organizational buyer tries to be as precise as possible when forecasting the number of people who will attend meal functions, but the actual attendance can vary widely. If there are alternatives, as in a large city, many attendees will go out for meals. Attendance at different meal functions can vary widely even within the same meeting. The first night's awards banquet might have close to 100 percent attendance. The following night might have a boring speaker, and half the attendees will go elsewhere.

Association, convention, and trade show planners need extremely good convention service managers within the hotel to execute all phases of the event. These managers are far more important than the salespeople in delivery of the final product. Rutherford and Umbreit found that convention service managers of hotels had the greatest number of encounters with meeting planners during the process of planning and executing an event than any other personnel.[21] This may be true for any meeting of size, but it is especially true for these large and complex ones. Technical details such as the voltage in the main ballroom, the delivery space for exhibits, and the audiovisual support for the speakers are all critical to the success of the meeting.

The hotel staff also needs to have good relations with the unions that are involved in handling large affairs. Not only are union members within the hotel used, but often members of other unions set up booths, deliver products to the display area, and so forth. A convention planner may be unaware of the vagaries of local unions, and a mistake in procedures can ruin the setup or breakdown of a function very easily.

Delegates to these kinds of functions often will not stay for the duration of the meeting. They may book for three nights and stay two and not give any notice of doing it (although hotels are beginning to penalize this behavior). Many are small businesspeople who cannot make definite plans for the future; others will simply feel they've had all they want and decide to leave.

Delegates to these functions also tend to be quite price sensitive. To keep the delegates happy, the organizer looks for low rates and for low-cost or free meeting space. All three of these markets are tough to sell and tough to service, but they can represent lucrative business, especially if booked during slow business periods.

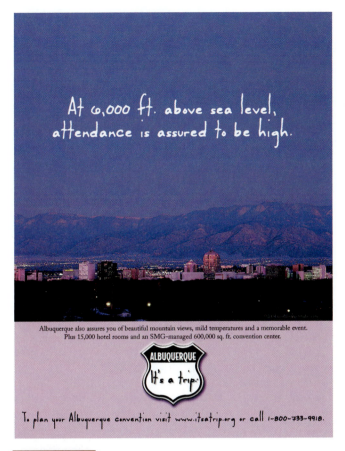

EXHIBIT 8-15   Albuquerque has a freestanding convention/ conference center.

Source: Albuquerque Convention and Visitors Bureau. Used by permission.

Convention Centers and Convention and Visitors Bureaus

Two external bodies often closely involved in the handling of association, convention, and trade show marketing need brief mention. The first is the freestanding convention center, sometimes called a conference center, but generally meaning a freestanding, independent property such as that shown in Exhibit 8-15. Most major cities in the world and many secondary and tertiary cities, especially in the United States, have such convention centers. In these cases, the "main event" takes place in the convention center, which is usually publicly owned but privately operated. The trade show or convention itself, on the other hand, may be handled by a private organizing firm.

The annual National Restaurant Association (NRA) trade show in Chicago or the annual Consumer Electronics

EXHIBIT 8-16   This is the website for the convention and visitors authority of Las Vegas.

Source: Las Vegas Convention and Visitors Authority. Used by permission.

Show in Las Vegas are examples of trade shows held in convention centers. Either booths or space are sold to purveyors, and attendees peruse the offerings under one roof. Although informational seminars may be given during the show, the main purpose of the event is to display products and take orders. The trade show organizer makes money from the booth or space sales. In turn, the purveyors hope to write enough business to make their expenses worthwhile.

The convention center works closely with the city's hotels and restaurants for lodging and feeding delegates. In New York City, for example, the annual AH&LA (American Hotel & Lodging Association) trade show is held in the Jacob Javits Convention Center. The collateral sent out by the show operator includes hotels' locations and rates, free bus schedules, and restaurant and theater ads to make it easier for attendees to plan their stays. Hotels may book individual groups and functions from this event, but they are not the main focus.

Many such events are arranged, at least initially, through **convention and visitors bureaus (CVBs)** such as the one for the San Diego Convention and Visitors Bureau, shown in Exhibit 8-16. These organizations are publicly and privately supported by those they serve—convention centers, hotels, restaurants, merchants, theaters, airline, and so forth.

CVB organizations are nonprofit, serving their constituents, who pay annual fees. They exist in both large and small cities. Their mission includes promoting the city as a destination area, assisting groups with meeting preparations,

---

EXHIBIT 8-17 What Every Meeting Planner Needs to Know about CVBs

Misconception #1: CVBs solely book hotel rooms and convention space.
Fact: CVBs represent the gamut of visitor-related businesses, from restaurants and retail to rental cars and racetracks. Therefore, they are responsible for introducing planners to a full range of meeting-related products and services the city has to offer. Basically, they match needs to a city's resources.

Misconception #2. CVBs only work with large groups.
Fact: More than half of all meetings involve less than 200 people. These meetings are just as important to a CVB as larger ones. In fact, larger bureaus often have staff members specifically dedicated to small meetings.

Misconception #3: Bureaus own and/or run the convention center.
Fact: Only 5 percent of CVBs run the convention center in their location. Nevertheless, CVBs work closely with local convention centers and can assist planners in getting what they need from convention center staff.

Misconception #4: Planners have to pay CVBs for their services.
Fact: In truth, the services of a CVB are free. Michael Gehrisch, president of the International Association of Convention & Visitor Bureaus (IACVB), points out, "Convention bureaus are both a hotel's and a meeting planner's best friend. They don't charge either one, but book business for the hotel without a fee and provide the same service, for free, to planners." Most bureaus are primarily funded through hotel occupancy taxes. Some bureaus also charge membership fees.

Some may question the need to work through a CVB when planning a meeting, particularly in cases where the bulk of an event takes place at one hotel or at the convention center. The bureau can help you work with those entities and can help fill out the convention schedule with off-site activities (including spouse tours and pre- and post-conference tours). An objective resource, the bureau can direct planners to products and services that will work best to accommodate their needs and budgets. In summary, a CVB acts as a mediator, matching meeting needs to the products, services and speakers available in a community.

Why use a CVB? CVBs make planning and implementing a meeting less time-consuming and more streamlined. They give meeting planners access to a range of services and packages.

Before a meeting begins, CVB sales professionals can help locate meeting space, check hotel availability and arrange for site inspections. CVBs can also link planners with the suppliers, from motorcoach companies and caterers to off-site entertainment venues, helping meet the prerequisites of any event.

What are some of the specific services CVBs offer planners?

- CVBs can offer unbiased information about services and facilities in the destination.
- CVBs serve as a vast information database and a one-stop shop, thus saving planners time, energy and money in the development of a meeting.
- CVBs act as a liaison between the planner and the community. For example, CVBs are aware of community events that may beneficially coincide with your meeting (like festivals or sporting events). They can also work with city government to get special permits and to cut through red tape.
- CVBs can help meeting attendees maximize their free time through the creation of pre- and post-conference activities, spouse tours and hosting of special evening events.
- CVBs can provide hotel room counts and meeting space statistics and will keep a convention/meetings/events calendar in order to help planners avoid conflicts and/or space shortages.
- CVBs can match properties to specific meeting requirements and budgets.

Other services provided to planners include:

- Collateral material
- Help with on-site logistics, including registration
- Housing bureaus
- Auxiliary services, such as production companies, catering and transportation
- Site inspections/familiarization tours and site selection
- Speakers and local educational opportunities
- Security
- Access to special venues

The overall job of a CVB is to market and sell a destination. A CVB wants every single client to be happy. It will do everything it can to match every client with the perfect setting and services for their meetings. The bottom line—the CVB is working for you.

Source: Retrieved November 13, 2005, from www.pema.org/resources/convene/archives/displayArticle.asp?ARTICLE_ID=4622. Used by permission. Reprinted with permission of *Convene*, the magazine of the Professional Convention Management Association. © 2006. www.pcma.org.

---

providing promotional material to encourage attendance, and working with hotels to coordinate room blocks. Hotels and restaurants usually work very closely with CVBs. If the CVB can sell the city to a group, it then provides information on hotel accommodations, restaurants, and other attractions that are part and parcel of the overall enticement.

Exhibit 8-17 details what every meeting planner should know about CVBs. Clearly, CVBs offer many services.

Web Browsing Exercise

Visit the San Jose CVB website (www.sanjose.org/). Look at the misconceptions of CVBs listed in Exhibit 8-17. How does this website prove that the misconceptions are wrong? What information, if any, is missing from Exhibit 8-17?

The Airline Crew Market

The airline crew market is defined as the housing of airline employees and crew members on a contract basis. When an airline's employees fly a designated number of hours, as established by government aviation authorities, the airline has to provide a place for the crew to rest for a designated number of hours. In the past, hotels chosen for this purpose were low priced and located near the airport for reasons of reduced transportation costs. Two factors have changed the traditional scenario, however:

1. The supply/demand ratio in the hotel marketplace
2. The unions that participate in the bargaining process on behalf of their members

In the first case, as more hotels have been built in relatively stable demand centers, the competition for customers has increased. This has put pressure on hotels to find new customers to fill their hotel rooms, especially in soft economic periods. In the second case, although airline unions may not get the wage increases they would like, they have been successful in keeping and improving other benefits for their members, such as housing. Crew unions have hotel committees, members of which go on hotel inspection trips with their airlines' hotel buyers. They keep databases of crew complaints and a list of the hotels they dislike.

The net result has been that the airline buyer, who negotiates for crew accommodations, finds a number of better products from which to choose, with pressure from the unions to make the best possible facilities available to their members. On the hotel's part, however, facilities alone will not hold the contract. Unless the hotel understands these customers and their unique needs, it will not be able to deliver the product and will eventually lose the business to the hotel that understands airline crew members' problems. Some airlines have a "chief of flight crew accommodations" who regularly evaluates contracted rooms and facilities for their suitability. One hotel in South America even washes the crews' uniforms as a way to keep the crews happy and their stays as convenient as possible.

Airline crew members have many needs and problems that are different from those of other travelers. Because of tight flight schedules, there are relatively few hours available to rest between flights. Airline crews must have all of their rooms available and assigned before they arrive (which may be at odd hours) for instantaneous check-in. The aircraft captain is always in charge of the crew, even off the plane. All unusual situations need to be discussed with him or her before any decisions can be made.

Once in their rooms, airline crews do not necessarily like street views with street noises! Here is a market segment that would gladly take the rooms facing an inner courtyard or another building in the interest of getting a good night's rest. Some airline crews have very unusual hours of sleep—for instance, some international flight crews check in at 8:00 A.M. and need to sleep immediately. Heavy blackout drapes are also necessary to enable crew members to sleep during the day, a feature that would not affect most other customers of the hotel. Flight crews abhor any kind of noise and want 24-hour room service, inexpensive meals, and free coffee.

Coordination is needed in all phases of the operation. For the corporate client who is at a meeting, 11:00 A.M. may be the best time to have a houseman vacuum the hallways, but this is not true for the airline crew that checked in at 8:00 A.M. Wake-up calls are critical. Delayed flights can cost an airline thousands of dollars because someone forgot to make wake-up calls at 3 P.M. Numerous other seemingly small details are critical for crew members, such as locating them away from elevators and ice machines and assigning crew members to adjacent rooms.

Finally, integration of the food and beverage offerings needs to occur. Recognizing that crews are not on expense accounts (like many government employees, they are on **per diem**—a fixed daily allowance), they will probably not eat at a restaurant where lunches average $18. However, there is potential in these customers, and special menu discounts can provide additional revenues and profits. Many hotels provide a 20 percent discount on meals, including room service. As one pilot told one of the authors, "After flying all night, I want to go to my room, order room service, and be away from people. I don't want to pay full room service prices, so the 20 percent discount is very important to me."

How much is too much? Airline crews were once largely contracted on a yearly basis for a set number of rooms, but this has changed as the airlines insist on short-term contracts to give them more flexibility. Rates can sometimes be very low (as low as 40 percent off the prevailing rate) compared to the printed rack rates or even the corporate rates. At one time, many hotels displaced their crew rooms because demand was so strong from more lucrative market segments. However, the pendulum always seems to swing back; many hotels are once again pursuing the airline crew market.

Airline contracts are obtained by a low-rated bid practice. Some managers shy away from airline business because of the low rates, because they think it gives a negative image to a hotel, or because of the hassles they cause. Airline crews may not be considered "appropriate" in the lobby of a luxury hotel in the United States; in some countries, however, they are accepted as adding prestige to the hotel.

In fact, many hoteliers admit that the clients who annoy them most are flight crews, with whom they have a love–hate relationship. Hotels cater to crews because their business is sizable and steady, providing a comfortable cushion when the economy is soft.

Besides the image and trouble factors, the real test of accepting airline business depends on the net revenue generated by the business and the compatibility with the segment mix. To determine the profit margins of an airline contract, a displacement study needs to be done. First, management must estimate how many nights during the contract period the hotel will run a high enough occupancy that it could not accommodate under the crew contract. For example, if an airline wants 100 rooms in a 500-room hotel, how many nights would the hotel likely have between 80 and 100 percent occupancy? The number of possible lost nights becomes the basis for calculating revenue displacement. In other words, how many nights could the guest rooms be sold to a guest at a higher rate, and what would be the net gain or loss?

Revenue can be calculated for both scenarios—with and without the crew contract. From this should be deducted variable cost. For example, if the variable cost to service a room is $20 and the airline contract is for $60 a room and the otherwise obtainable rate is $120, the hotel has to sell two and a half airline rooms to make the same gross margin as one regular room. It may also be wise to calculate additional margins, such as from food and beverage sales, where crews tend to spend very little money. If the gross margin earned from an airline crew contract is greater than the gross margin from the displaced rooms, then the airline business should be considered.

The SMERF and Government Markets

The **SMERF market** (social, military, education, religious, and fraternal) is not solicited by many major hotels because their inventory is used by more upscale corporate customers and associations. In poor supply/demand positions, however, many hotels are soliciting SMERF customers. The SMERF market is considered a "segment" by the Professional Conference Managers Association (PCMA). SMERF customers include all organizational customers that do not fit into the other categories; hence, they are considered to be part of a "catchall" market.

So what is the SMERF market? It is a price-sensitive, nonprofit organization market. All social-related group business is considered SMERF. Wedding parties needing overnight accommodations, rehearsal dinner parties, society events, fund raisers, and so forth, are all considered to be part of this market. So are gospel singers and military customers. The education subsegment consists of groups such as faculty and school sports groups. Religious groups include large Baptist conventions filling cities or the Order of the Rising Star meeting in hotels. Finally, fraternal orders such as the Masons fall into the SMERF segment.

Although the SMERF segment has the reputation of being low rated, the customers nevertheless fill guest rooms, ballrooms, and local restaurants, especially during slow periods. The head of an Elks group can be no less important a customer to some hotels than a corporate meeting planner.

The **government market** is also low rated, but in the United States it is a $12 billion market and is large in other countries as well. Again, economic slumps in bookings may lead hoteliers to see government as an attractive mar-

ket. This market is a reliable source of incremental revenue for many budget and midlevel properties. Upscale properties also cannot ignore the upper end of this business.

Government at all levels is engaged in many activities that tend to be travel intensive: research, regulation, investigation, enforcement, oversight, litigation, education, and coordination. Government employees travel anywhere and everywhere people are to be found.

Although government employees may be end users, they may not be the customers to whom to make the sale. Government travel planning is a bureaucratized affair. A program manager or travel coordinator is probably responsible for their reservations, and per diem rates are set by state or national edict. Hotels can target this market for rooms that might otherwise be left empty, similar to their approach to airline crews. Careful planning and marketing is needed, and, again, segment mix must be considered.

Web Browsing Exercise

Go to your favorite search engine and search the word *SMERF*. What entries do you find? In addition, look up different fraternal organizations such as Free Masons, Elks Club, and Rotary International. What is the purpose of these organizations? How can hospitality firms help these organizations reach their objectives? Do you believe such organizations will be around in 10 or 15 years? Why or why not?

The Group Tour and Travel Market

The group tour and travel market is defined as leisure travelers who travel in groups, with or without an escort. This is a wide-ranging market that has changed dramatically in recent times and is no longer characterized by hordes of ignorant travelers visiting five countries in four days. Tours may range from trekking in the Himalayas to whale watching in the Pacific; from a ladies garden club tour of Japan to a high school senior trip to Spain. Group tour travelers have different motivations for selecting this form of travel, the most important of which is generally the convenience of having all arrangements made for them. Other motivations include companionship (especially among mature travelers), lower travel costs, and planned itineraries that will ensure that travelers do not miss the "must-see" places.

Regardless of motivation or type of tour, hotel accommodations are the most important part of a group tour package. Exhibit 8-18 discusses how Middlebury Inn caters to group travelers, which it has been doing for over 25 years. As Plog stated:

> An adequate hotel room is important in travelers' itineraries because it becomes a stable base for almost everything that vacationers want to do, whether they are the venture-

EXHIBIT 8-18 Motorcoach Tours at the Middlebury Inn in Middlebury, Vermont

The Middlebury Inn has been catering to the motorcoach tour market for the past 25 years. Two types of group tours visit the Middlebury Inn—those who come as predefined groups (for example, a senior citizen group belonging to a specific senior citizen center) and those who come as individual travelers on tours sponsored by bus tour companies, such as Perkiomen Tours.

Tour groups at the Middlebury Inn typically stay for three nights and four days. On the first day of arrival, the motorcoach is met approximately 30 minutes prior to arriving at the hotel. This allows the staff to welcome the guests, pass out room keys, and go over other pertinent information prior to arriving at the inn. Tour members typically want to exit the bus as quickly as possible when it arrives at the front door. The prearrival greeting allows members to do just that. While guests are enjoying an arrival greeting, bell persons take the luggage immediately to the rooms.

The Middlebury Inn has designed a variety of programs for its motorcoach tour guests. These include guided tours to area attractions, themed dinners, and after-dinner entertainment activities. An example of a typical tour is shown in Exhibit 8-19. Tour offerings vary by season. For instance, in the fall there are Fall Foliage Tours; in the winter, Christmas Tours and Winter House Parties; in the spring, Maple Sugar Tours; and in the summer, tours to Vermont's many attractions.

some types or the more timid souls. They do not want to worry about making wrong choices, in terms of quality or price, because so much of an always short vacation can be ruined by the discomforts and indignities that accompany the wrong choice of hotel. The assumption exists that the travel organizer, whether an airline or a tour wholesaler, can obviate the need for the vacationer to go through the learning curve on how to select hotels of adequate quality and that they will do this for a relatively reasonable price because of the buying power of large organizations.[22]

There are over 2,000 tour operators in the United States and many more around the world. Tour operators usually belong to trade associations such as the Cross-Sphere (formerly known as the National Tour Association), the American Bus Association, or the United Bus Owners of America. Member directories provide useful information and are a good starting point for hospitality marketers interested in pursuing this type of business. Although there are many kinds of tours, a common type is the escorted **motorcoach tour** or the group inclusive tour (GIT) arranged by wholesale tour brokers.

Motorcoach Tour Travelers[23]

In the United States, the motorcoach tour market segment has traditionally consisted of older travelers. In other parts of the world, however, where owning cars is not as prevalent, motorcoach tours have long been a popular mode of sightseeing and vacationing. Things are changing in the United States as well. Many younger travelers are using motorcoach tours to see domestic sights inexpensively. Exhibit 8-20 discusses Tauck Tours, a global leader in motorcoach tours.

Web Browsing Exercise

Compare and contrast Tauck Tours (www.tauck.com/index.html) and Perkiomen Tours (www.perkiomentours.com/). What differences, if any, exist between these two firms? How would you market to each tour company? To which market segments does each company appeal?

The Middlebury Inn
4 Days and 3 Nights
History and Agriculture

Arrival Day
Arrival (between 3:00 & 5:00). Welcome refreshments. Walking tour of town [if time allows]. Wine & cheese party. Dinner. Entertainment. Nighttime snack.

Touring Day
After eating a bountiful breakfast, we will board the motorcoach for a day of touring. Our first stop is at the **UVM Morgan Horse Farm** where we enjoy a guided tour of the buildings and enjoy a video show about the history of the property. Next we'll visit the **Shelburne Museum** where we can explore selected buildings of Americana. So that we may enjoy the museum at our leisure, we will eat lunch on our own in the Museum's cafeteria. Dinner and Entertainment at the Inn.

Touring Day
Breakfast. **Maritime Museum**, Luncheon cruise aboard the **Spirit of Ethan Allen III**, and some "free-time" to explore the downtown **Middlebury** area. Dinner. Entertainment. Nighttime snack.

Departure Day
Breakfast. 9:00 Departure from the Inn. Our last stop in the Middlebury area will be at the **New England Maple Museum**. You will learn of the history of maple sugaring and also enjoy samples. A wide variety of maple products are available in their gift shop for you to take home with you.

	Per Person Net Rates		
May/June 2006	Single $435	Double $299	Triple/Quad $265
July/August	Single $449	Double $320	Triple/Quad $280
September/October	Single $465	Double $335	Triple/Quad $295

email: chantal@middleburyinn.com
14 Courthouse Square Middlebury, VT 05753
802-388-4961 800-842-4666 FAX 802-388-4563

EXHIBIT 8-19 The Middlebury Inn pursues overnight business from motorcoach tour travelers.

Source: The Middlebury Inn. Used by permission.

The motorcoach tour market for hotels and restaurants may be defined as five or more travelers arriving at a hospitality establishment by motorcoach, as part of a total leisure tour package. This market really has to be separated from other travelers arriving at the hotel by bus, simply because of their original reason for the purchase. A group of corporate businesspeople could arrive at a hotel

EXHIBIT 8-20	The Tauck Tours Difference

TAUCK TOURS MISSION STATEMENT

Our mission is to offer enriching travel experiences that enhance people's lives by broadening their knowledge and fulfilling their dreams. To that end, we strive to create unique and imaginative travel itineraries.

By conducting each Tauck vacation with pride and enthusiasm, we bring to our guests the best possible experience in every destination. It's a difference that's uniquely Tauck.

CAREFREE TRAVEL, BOTH RELAXED AND REFINED

An important benefit of "Tauck Style" is the freedom to relax and travel as an individual because your needs and expectations are anticipated. Our carefully designed and choreographed itineraries are a refreshing mix of sightseeing, leisure, adventure and culture. You'll experience spectacular scenery and exciting events other travelers only dream about. Every detail is handled seamlessly. Imagine . . . luggage usually in your hotel room before you arrive and preferred seating at shows! Your time is truly your own to enjoy.

UNIQUE AND DISTINGUISHED HOTELS IN THE BEST LOCATIONS

When you travel with Tauck, you enjoy some of the best rooms at the world's finest hotels. With Tauck, you may stay in oceanfront rooms at the Royal Hawaii Hotel, lake view rooms at Chateau Lake Louise and you'll be on the Grand Canyon rim at Kachina Lodge. Many of our hotels, such as the Raffles Hotel in Singapore, the Grand Hotel in Paris and the Westin Excelsior Hotel in Rome, are rated among the world's finest.

EXCEPTIONAL DINING AND FREEDOM OF CHOICE

The enjoyment of dining is a delightful and integral part of travel. That's why Tauck selects restaurants that offer a true "taste" of each region you visit. You have the freedom to dine from regular restaurant menus—whether you're in the mood for a sophisticated Chateaubriand in a hotel's "signature" restaurant or a specialty salad in the café. You even have the freedom to dine anytime and with anyone you wish. You simply sign the check "Tauck World Discovery."

INSIGHTFUL TOUR DIRECTIONS

During your travels, you have the advantage of being with a Tauck Tour Director who is fully knowledgeable about the destination, its history and its culture. You can relax knowing that you are accompanied by a professional who manages the flow of events . . . a problem-solver should one arise . . . an insider who saves you precious time . . . and a friend who will help transform your trip into a truly memorable journey.

EVERY TRAVEL EXPENSE IS INCLUDED

When you travel with Tauck, you will save up to 40 percent from the cost of traveling the same itinerary on your own. Virtually every travel expense is included . . . hotels, meals, cruises, sightseeing, entertainment—even taxes and gratuities. Guests are delightfully surprised how much is included—you can practically leave your wallet at home! A Tauck vacation offers you both superb quality and extraordinary value.

FREQUENTLY ASKED QUESTIONS

How do you describe Tauck World Discovery and how is your brand different?
For three generations we have focused on providing travel experiences that truly enhance people's lives. We create journeys that go beyond the ordinary; they are innovative, authentic and unique experiences that our guests couldn't get "on their own." Our company is different in many ways; predominately in our highly knowledgeable and passionate staff that helps others to broaden their horizons and see a destination in a new way. We are very different from mass market "tours" in that we offer "in-depth experiences" in a variety of different ways, such as luxury small-ship cruising, Heli-hiking and rail journeys. We include the finest accommodations available, our tours are all-inclusive and we take care of all the details. This is what makes our brand different!

What new travel patterns have emerged for 2004/2005?
The upscale travel market is on a fast rebound and Tauck is experiencing some significant new trends in travel. Most notably, travel to Europe is up 75 percent, with incredible growth in interest to Eastern Europe, Scandinavia, Russia, Italy, Great Britain and Ireland. Family travel remains strong, including family reunions and three-generation family travel, as evidenced by a 150 percent growth in Tauck's family-focused sister company, Tauck Bridges. Tauck's small ship cruises are seeing significant growth as the market seeks a higher quality, intimate cruise experience to fantastic, remote destinations. For the long term there continues to be growing interest in exotic destinations, including the Galapagos Islands, Costa Rica, Australia, New Zealand and South Africa. More than ever guests are seeking the finest "all-inclusive," guest protection and "done for you" services as they venture abroad once again.

For many people, vacations are becoming shorter (such as one-week tours to Europe) and multi-generational family travel is very popular. Europe is a treasure trove of experiences and there is growing interest in year-round travel to Europe—by train, riverboat and lightly traveled roads—all unique ways to explore cultural "hidden gems" of the Old World.

Source: Tauck World Discovery website. Retrieved January 3, 2006, from www.tauck.com/.

by bus, yet their sole purpose for the visit would be to attend a corporate meeting, making them a corporate group. A convention could have an entire delegation from a similar geographic area arrive by bus, but again the reason would be to attend the convention, not to visit local attractions.

The size of the motorcoach tour market is ever expanding. Although the majority of these trips are within one day, almost 40 percent stay overnight in a lodging establishment. Motorcoach tours from the United States to Canada generate over $1 billion a year in Canada according to the National Tour Association. Every "bus night"

(average of 40 passengers) generates many thousands of dollars. More than one-third of this goes to hotels.

Motorcoach tours are arranged in two formats, series and ad hoc groups. A tour series is a prearranged link of stopovers, usually carrying a theme. An example is a motorcoach tour to see the New England autumn foliage. Stopovers include country inns and landmark restaurants, with occasional visits to local museums.

An ad hoc group has a specific destination in mind—for example, Walt Disney World in Orlando, Florida, or EuroDisney. A group arranges to travel there by motorcoach and stay several nights to take advantage of the attraction.

Although ad hoc groups might also have stopovers, they are not the initial reason for the trip.

When soliciting the motorcoach market, hoteliers should respond to its specific needs to make the approach more successful. Tours employ tour leaders responsible for the well-being of the group as well as the satisfaction of its individual members. Tour leaders are also, in essence, sales representatives for the tour company. The hotel salesperson sells the hotel to the tour company, but the tour leader is the one who has to travel with the group and ensure their satisfaction. As with most other products, many similar tours are available to the customer, and often the tour leader develops a following of repeat customers.

The group requires special room key assignments, all being preassigned before the bus arrives. The keys are distributed by the tour leader, and the baggage is unloaded and tagged. The luggage is a critical need for this customer. It is unacceptable to have to wait over half an hour for luggage to arrive in the guest rooms after a long day on the road and before an inflexible dinner time. Whether luggage is carried to the rooms by bell persons or by the customer directly, this relatively simple yet unusual situation can, if not handled correctly, create many unsatisfied customers. The Middlebury Inn had a very unique way of getting keys to its customers. A representative would meet the bus approximately 20 miles from the inn. They would then board the bus and pass out the room keys during the final journey to the inn. Thus, when passengers exited the coach onto the red carpet, they were able to go immediately to their rooms.

Although the median age of motorcoach tour travelers is dropping into the 50s, older travelers typically prefer rooms that do not require the use of stairs. They prefer rooms with views, they like being close to each other, and they want the correct bedding configuration—all requirements around which some misunderstanding may arise. A weekend package user might ask for a double room and be completely satisfied with a queen bed assignment. The same double room for the motorcoach guest may indicate a need for two beds in the same room—and a roll-away is not an acceptable substitute.

Motorcoach tour groups are a viable market for many hotels; in fact, some hotels survive on them. The warning here is the one we have mentioned before: These customers may mix well with some other market segments, and special care is needed to see that this mix is not a problem. Unlike with other travelers, the needs of these travelers arise all at once. An average busload of 40 means 40 bags all at once (maybe 80), 40 luncheons all at once, and 40 breakfasts all at once. Staffing to handle this is critical, especially when these customers don't tip well and employees are not especially eager to serve them. Disgruntled tour groups make a great deal of noise!

■ Summary

Organizational meeting planners and travel managers are unique to the hospitality industry in that they often represent the "purchasers" but not the "users." These planners/managers are responsible to the organizations they represent and have to anticipate the wide variety of needs of the members of these organizations.

Overall, organizational planners and travel managers are better educated about, and have more experience in, the hospitality industry than the individual purchasers of hotel and restaurant products. The single most important factor in their destination and hotel decision-making process remains the word-of-mouth endorsement of their fellow professionals. References from someone within their organization also help steer this customer toward a specific hotel or resort. And the conference service manager at the host hotel probably plays a more significant role than the salesperson in creating and keeping customers.

■ Key Terms

organizational customer
convention planner
MICE
organizational planner
lead time
preconference meeting
postconference meeting
meeting planner
rate buckets
in-plant
conference center

incentive houses
incentive planner
travel manager
association meetings
trade show
convention and visitors bureaus (CVBs)
per diem
SMERF market
government market
motorcoach tour

■ Discussion Questions

1. What is the essential difference between the organizational customer and other customers discussed earlier in this book?
2. Why do hotel convention and conference planners play a more important role in the decision-making process of the organizational customer than the individual business traveler?
3. How do corporate travel manager customers and corporate meeting planner customers differ?

4. Describe the three types of incentive trips. How would each of these affect the choice of destination and hotel?

5. Why is the preconference meeting and the postconference evaluation process critical for organizational customers?

6. Describe the similarities and differences among the association, the convention, and the trade show segments in terms of the end users.

■ Group Projects

1. Act as a meeting planner for a designated group and develop a list of their needs and a list of their requirements that you would expect a hotel to deliver.

2. Act as a corporate travel manager for a designated well-known corporation where employees at all levels travel frequently. Develop a request for proposal (RFP) that you would send to hotel chains to get them to bid on your business.

■ References

1. In the 2003 "State of the Industry" report prepared by Successful Meetings, the average number of full-time meeting planners in an organization had dropped from seven in 2000 to four in 2002. In the 2003 "State of the Industry" report, 33.7 percent of participants identified themselves as corporate planners. Another 27.4 percent claimed they were association planners, and 13.1 percent claimed to be independent planners. Retrieved December 4, 2004, from www.successmtgs.com/successmtgs/ images/pdf/2003-01-coverstory.pdf. See also www. successmtgs.com/successmtgs/search/search_display.jsp?vnu_content_id=1957337.

2. Yesawich, Pepperdine, Brown, & Russell. (2004). *Portrait of North American meeting planners*, 5.

3. Ibid., 59.

4. Seal, K. (1987, July 20). Staff, service, top priorities for planners. *Hotel & Motel Management*, 40–43.

5. Mandelbaum, R. (2004, December). Understanding the recovery occurring in the meeting's market—Special report. Hotel Online. Retrieved from www.hotel-online.com/News/PR2004_4th/Dec04_PKFConventions.html.

6. Yesawich, Pepperdine, Brown, & Russell, 23.

7. Some details of meeting rights and wrongs are revealed in a critical incident study that is recommended for additional insight into this critical process. See Rutherford, D. G., & Umbriet, W. T. (1993, February). Improving interactions between meeting planners and hotel employees. *Cornell Hotel and Restaurant Administration Quarterly*, 68–80.

8. *American Express 1994 Survey of Business Travel Management*. New York: American Express Travel Related Services Company.

9. Ibid.

10. Warcholak, E. S. (2004, August 2). Travel manager salary and attitude survey. *Business Travel News*. Retrieved from www.btnmag.com/businesstravelnews/headlines/breaking_news.jsp.

11. Bell, R. A. (1993, April). Corporate travel-management trends and hotel-marketing strategies. *Cornell Hotel and Restaurant Administration Quarterly*, 31–39.

12. American Express website. (2004, July/August). *Business Travel Connexions*. Retrieved from http://corp.americanexpress.com/gcs/travel/us/resources/default.aspx.

13. Meetings and Conventions. (2004). Meetings market report. Retrieved from www.mcmag.com/mmr2004/index.html.

14. Ibid.

15. Yesawich, Pepperdine, Brown, & Russell, 18.

16. IACC North America website. (2004). Retrieved from www.iaccnorthamerica.org/about/index. cfm?fuseaction=memcrit.

17. Sales Marketing Network website. (2004). Incentive travel overview: Resources & statistics [no. 4010]. Retrieved from www.info-now.com/moshow/article55#stat.

18. Shaw, M. (1985). The group market: What it is and how to sell it. Washington DC: The Hotel Sales and Marketing Association International Foundation, 45.

19. Successful Meetings. (1993, July). State of the industry report, 7, 30.

20. Alonzo, V. (1991, August). A wider world for winners. *Meetings and Conventions,* 101.

21. Rutherford, D. G., & Umbriet, W. T. (1993, February). Improving interactions between meeting planners and hotel employees. *Cornell Hotel and Restaurant Administration Quarterly,* 68–80.

22. Plog, S. C. (1991). Leisure travel—Making it a growth market again. New York: John Wiley & Sons, 98.

23. To see how one independent hotel captured the senior citizen bus tour market, see Shoemaker, S. (1984). Marketing to older travelers. *Cornell Hotel and Restaurant Administration Quarterly,* 25(2), 84–91.

The Tourist Customer and the Tourism Destination

Overview

In this chapter, the focus of the book shifts to the importance of travel and tourism and the current trends in tourism (and factors that contribute to these trends) are discussed briefly. Then we discuss the importance of local residents' support for the success of a destination and the types of marketing activities that national tourism organizations (NTOs) perform in the marketing of countries and subsets of countries, as tourist destinations. To explain how public and private sectors collaborate to market a destination, we provide an interview with the VP of marketing of the Hilton Waikoloa to show how a specific hotel works with a destination to promote itself and the destination. In this section, current macro environmental trends and the factors that are likely to influence them are examined. This is followed by an explanation of competition and how competing destinations may influence a destination's marketing strategies. Finally, tourist market segmentation and communicating with target markets are discussed.

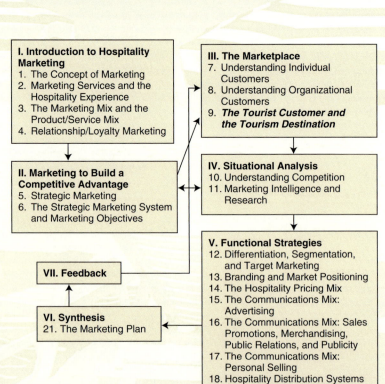

I. Introduction to Hospitality Marketing
1. The Concept of Marketing
2. Marketing Services and the Hospitality Experience
3. The Marketing Mix and the Product/Service Mix
4. Relationship/Loyalty Marketing

II. Marketing to Build a Competitive Advantage
5. Strategic Marketing
6. The Strategic Marketing System and Marketing Objectives

VII. Feedback

VI. Synthesis
21. The Marketing Plan

III. The Marketplace
7. Understanding Individual Customers
8. Understanding Organizational Customers
9. *The Tourist Customer and the Tourism Destination*

IV. Situational Analysis
10. Understanding Competition
11. Marketing Intelligence and Research

V. Functional Strategies
12. Differentiation, Segmentation, and Target Marketing
13. Branding and Market Positioning
14. The Hospitality Pricing Mix
15. The Communications Mix: Advertising
16. The Communications Mix: Sales Promotions, Merchandising, Public Relations, and Publicity
17. The Communications Mix: Personal Selling
18. Hospitality Distribution Systems
19. Channels of Distribution: Bringing the Customer to the Product
20. Interactive Marketing: Internet and Database Marketing

Before being selected as secretary general of the Caribbean Tourism Organization, Vincent Vanderpool-Wallace was director-general of the Bahamas Ministry of Tourism. Prior to that he had been involved in the tourism industry for more than 15 years, holding senior management positions in both the private and public sectors.

Born in Nassau, Bahamas, Vanderpool-Wallace graduated from Harvard University and then worked for the Ministry of Education and Culture from 1975 to 1977. Joining the Ministry of Tourism's marketing department, he rose to the position of deputy general manager of marketing which he held from 1979 to 1982. In 1982, Vanderpool-Wallace joined the staff of Resorts International (Bahamas) Ltd., where he held various managerial positions including senior vice president in the Office of the President.

Marketing in Action
Vincent Vanderpool-Wallace, Secretary General, Caribbean Tourism Organization

Please briefly explain the role of the Caribbean Tourism Association.

Right now we have 32 member states within the Caribbean, from Barbados to Bermuda. We all get together—recognizing that tourism in this area is the dominant industry—and try to find ways to collaborate for the greater good of tourism development for the entire region. Each member country pays dues that are proportionate to the total number of visitors that they receive. It has been in existence for over 50 years.

What are the key challenges in marketing a destination such as the Caribbean?

Each member country is an individual sovereign nation that has a right to develop tourism in any way, shape, or form they wish. So, although we have established certain policies that we think would make their development of tourism travel more efficient, they don't have any obligation to follow our lead in anything that we're doing. We are always trying to allow enough leeway for our members to do what is necessary in their individual interests while at the same time advancing the cause for the Caribbean as a whole.

The other issue that we have been trying to grapple with is that you have different markets that the individual members are going after and also individual products within each of those segments. It is a peculiar situation in that we are trying to market diversity, which is very important, we think, to the long-term success of the Caribbean, and many people see this variety of products and variety of markets as a problem.

How does your organization identify key market segments and key competitors?

We've got some emerging trends that we can clue our numbers onto, so that we can prepare a long time in advance for them. These trends are in terms of the types of products and services that need to be delivered in any kind of product you have or any market you're going after. We are always on the lookout for the best piece for a particular market so

---

Note: The authors acknowledge the help of Dogan Gursoy, Ph.D., Washington State University, who contributed greatly to this chapter. Lydia Westbrook of University of Houston also was instrumental in writing the majority of this chapter.

we can learn the lesson of being more efficient—not inventing anything and certainly avoiding any mistakes that any other member states make within our league towards a particular market or any mistakes somebody not in our league has made in a particular market.

Our key competitors are really anyone taking a vacation anywhere. In the United States, for instance, we compete with Orlando, Las Vegas or other vacations people may pick within the United States. Our job is always to get people to leave the country of the United States and come to our part of the world. In New York, for example, the United Kingdom and the Caribbean are equidistant, so our competition, a lot of times, really depends on where the customer is coming from. We recognize that any other place a customer can chose as a destination is our competitor.

How much consumer research is undertaken on behalf of your organization?

The integral members of the association conduct a fair amount of consumer research themselves, so we try to fill in the gaps. Before we undertake anything, we consult with our individual members to see if somebody has already reviewed that issue. But beyond that, we are constantly collecting as much data as we can and only rarely do our own consumer research because many members undertake their own research for their own behalf. We pay for this with dues and a marketing promotion that also comes with being a member. Beyond that, an extensive part of our budget comes from grants from the European Union and the American States. We normally get a substantial part of what we need for research from these international organizations, as opposed to member contributions. This is a great benefit with membership, since they don't have to pay for it directly.

What factors influence consumers' decisions to visit the Caribbean? Have these factors changed over time? How do you monitor these changes?

It certainly has changed over time. One of the things that you will notice is that there used to be a very sharply defined season—of people escaping the cold. The market would really die after that. Then, as people began looking for and selling the "experience," we got more than the people who were merely escaping the cold. The focus has now changed more towards what the experience is that we can give our customers, and the customers are looking for great value. This has probably been the most significant change over the years and means a lot more business on a more year-round sort of basis.

Some of our members have the most sophisticated data-gathering techniques and technologies in the world, such as the reservation card, which collects data from every single piece of data about people coming into the country—where they come from, why they are coming, e-mail addresses, the flight they came on, and which hotel they're staying in. There's a piece of the card that you hand back in on your way out of the country that has a questionnaire on the back of it asking what they did enjoy and what they didn't enjoy. That is used for guidance in terms of seeing trends, seeing what is happening, and looking at who is coming through travel agents versus who is booking online.

We also have some fairly sophisticated data-gathering techniques that give information about what people thought about their vacation and what you need to fix in order to increase their level of satisfaction. One of the things that we want to do is aggregate the information that is being taken for each country so we can look at trends on a global basis—especially where people are coming from.

How do destinations sell "off season"?

Unfortunately, a significant part of selling during the off-season is price. We reduce the price compared to other destinations. We have looked at research of the people who do vacation during the off-season to try and get an idea of what it is they are looking for and try and promote that idea instead of lowering prices so that our destination can continue to be sold more effectively. At the same time, one of the other options is that even though we are kind of in the Northern Hemisphere, we are considered cooler than the southern parts of South America and you will see a shift in terms of us focusing on a much more global market, particularly with the use of the Internet and other technologies. We believe in discounting those markets that are harder to reach during a certain time, but try to sell a whole experience to a certain type of customer so that we can eliminate reducing costs.

What impact has the growth of the cruise ships had on your members' businesses?

One of the things that our preliminary research shows is that for at least three and maybe four groups of people on a cruise ship, one group really chose to cruise. The other group is the multidestination traveler that wants to go to all of these places, but simply could not afford flying individually from place to place. Then there's a third group, who, by reason of price, chose because they get total value for their money as they see it. We have a fourth group, which we call convertible. Until we know the size of these individual groups, we won't know what kind of impact it has in terms of reducing business. However, on the other side, people from these groups spend an incremental amount in our destinations that we clearly would not have had without the cruise ships.

What advice can you give to students who want to be involved in destination marketing?

There is no doubt in my mind that it is the most exciting area of any career I could ever think of. The one thing about the tourism business is that it is broader in depth and scope than any other business on earth because it affects and is affected by so many areas. If you think you are somebody who can think in very broad terms and also see the large numbers and information and choose a course of action from that, then this is a great field for you. In our constituency, it is the people who live and work in the destination that you rely on to treat the customers very well and very fairly. You have to satisfy the tourists and locals equally, which is one of the peculiarities of destination marketing that many people forget and often run into trouble with because they focus on the local constituencies and you need more than that for long-term success.

How critical is it to create "events" to drive tourists to the Caribbean?

We think it's very important because what happens in a number of cases is that you're introducing people to the Caribbean that would not come without the event. If we have a meeting association and there is a group of people, there has to be something relevant to the Caribbean that makes it work well. You can't have an arms trading show in the Caribbean because it doesn't fit, it doesn't work—you need something that can involve music, food, and cultural exchanges. In addition to bringing large amounts of people, these events can also bring a large amount of publicity to the destination, so that's the great dual power of events and something that we support considerably.

How do you manage the news reports that come from different islands in the Caribbean?

We provide a great deal of assistance in that area. We have a coalition of public relations companies that represent the entire Caribbean, so we are getting things that go beyond the individual destination. In many respects, we are not controlling the news, obviously, but one of the things we do is tell people how best to react to any particular situation, which entails making sure we are fully prepared before something happens. I think you would be surprised at how expensive some of our plans have been in the past years that have had to do with addressing certain issues. We don't execute very well yet, but we are getting better and better. We are prepared for a whole variety of things, one of which is giving people advice. In the particular case of Aruba right now, we are trying to constantly monitor what the volume of news coverage is in terms of negative reports of our Aruba Island in order to monitor the levels of people coming in. In the middle of all of the things happening in Aruba right now, business is up higher than most other destinations. We think that, contrary to popular opinion, they have managed that far better than people think, despite the stories that are pouring out on the news. We function by giving advice on how to get prepared before something happens.

Used by permission from Vincent Vanderpool-Wallace.

Importance of Travel and Tourism

According to the UN World Tourism Organization (UNWTO), tourism comprises the activities of persons traveling to and staying in places outside their usual environment for not more than one consecutive year for leisure, business, and other purposes (official UNWTO definition). Tourism can also be defined as the processes, activities, and outcomes arising from the relationships and interactions among tourists, tourism suppliers, host governments, host communities, and surrounding environments that are involved in the attracting and hosting of visitors. Both of these definitions suggest that tourism is made up of a number of tangible and intangible components, often taken to include the tourist, the tourist-generating region, the transportation system, the tourist destination, hospitality services, and the tourism industry. All of these components are highly interrelated, and they are very sensitive to changes in macro and micro environmental trends. Any small change in any of the environments that may influence one of the components of tourism is likely to have some effect on all or most of the other components because of their close interrelatedness. This makes the whole industry very volatile and susceptible to external influences.

Even though the tourism industry is very volatile and susceptible to external influences, many countries and destinations heavily depend on travel expenditures by domestic and international travelers as a source of taxation and as a source of income for the companies that provide hospitality services to these travelers. Tourism has been described as a global phenomenon and a global industry.

It affects the economy of every country and of every city and local community in the world. According to the UNWTO, tourism is the number one industry in many countries and the fastest-growing economic sector in terms of foreign exchange earnings and job creation. International tourism became the world's largest export earner and an important factor in the balance of payments of most nations. For tourist-receiving destinations, it has become one of the most important sources of employment and an enormous stimulant for investment in infrastructure and superstructure. It is "one of the most remarkable economic and social phenomena of the past century."[1] Its enormous growth and influence has spread widely since World War II, particularly since 1960. International recessions in 1982–1983 and 1991 caused slight declines, but recovery was swift and strong. In 2001–2003, the worldwide tourism industry contracted as the result of a series of events. The attacks in the United States on September 11, 2001 and subsequent tightening of travel restrictions, the SARS outbreak in Asia, expanded military operations in the Middle East, and an increase in terrorist attacks worldwide further weakened the global economy and contributed to an overall decrease in international travel. There are indicators, however, that global travel is overcoming these challenges; 2004 experienced a dramatic turnaround in international arrivals, with an increase of 10.7 percent.

According to the UNWTO, international tourist arrivals (the term used to indicate that travelers leave their home country and visit another) increased at a phenomenal average annual growth rate of 6.5 percent from 1950 to 2004.

The fastest-growing destinations in recent years have been outside the traditionally economically stronger continents of North America and Europe. While Europe and the Americas have lost tourism market share in the last 50 years (10 percent and 13 percent, respectively), Asia and the Pacific have grown by an average of 13 percent a year, and destinations in the Middle East have grown by 10 percent a year. Explanations for the rapid growth of tourism in regions outside of North America and Europe include the following:

- Robust economic growth
- Relatively stable political environments
- Relaxed visitation regulations
- Ability to finance infrastructure development
- Aggressive marketing efforts by national tourism organizations (NTOs) of host countries
- Increase of tourism demand worldwide

Even though tourism is the world's fastest-growing industry and the number of travelers is likely to reach a record in the next decade, communities that are planning on developing tourist destinations and existing tourist destinations need to understand that competition among the destinations is fierce, travelers needs and wants constantly change, and tourism is susceptible to changes in the macro environment. To be successful in today's environment and sustain success, tourist destinations need to thoroughly know their situation, local residents' attitudes toward tourism, the type and level of tourism products and services offered, their competitors, and the changing needs and wants of the current and prospective markets and their characteristics.

Local Residents' Attitudes toward Tourism

Understanding local residents' attitudes toward tourism development is crucial for local governments, policy makers, and businesses because the success and sustainability of any sort of tourism development depends on the goodwill of the local residents and their active support. Once a community becomes a tourist destination, the quality of life of the local residents is affected by the consequences of tourism development. These include an increased number of people, increased use of roads, and various economic and employment-based effects. The success of any tourism development project is threatened to the extent that the development is planned and constructed without the knowledge and support of the local residents. While successful tourism depends on attractions and services, it requires the hospitality of local residents. Anger, apathy, or mistrust on the part of the local population will ultimately be conveyed to the tourists and is likely to result in reluctance on the part of the tourists to visit places where they feel unwelcome. In addition, active opposition can lead to delays, legal action, and abandonment of projects if they become financially unfeasible. The importance of local residents' support has been widely recognized by both planners and businesses.

Several factors affect the level of local residents' support for tourism development. Residents are likely to support tourism development as long as they believe that the expected benefits of development exceed the cost of the development. Because the most visible benefits of tourism are its contribution to the local economy and the employment opportunities created, some local residents are likely to see tourism as an economic development tool, and therefore, they are likely to support tourism in their community. However, not all residents place such an importance on the economic benefits of tourism. Some are apt to view tourism as having both positive and negative impacts;

some are likely to perceive tourism as having negative social and cultural impacts; and some are inclined to view tourism as having positive economic, social, and cultural impacts. If residents believe that tourism creates more benefits than costs for the community, they tend to have a favorable view of tourism and as a result support tourism development. On the other hand, if they believe that tourism brings more costs than benefits, they are not likely to endorse tourism development (Gursoy & Rutherford 2004).[2]

Several factors are likely to influence how locals view tourism and their support for tourism. One of those factors is the state of the local economy. Many communities have been going through substantial changes over the past decade. Many primary industries on which community residents have depended have departed, leaving behind economic difficulties and a search for alternative development strategies. Many of these communities, faced with a narrow resource base, embraced tourism as a panacea for their economic malaise. Evidence suggests that in economically depressed communities, residents underestimate the cost of tourism development and overestimate the economic gains. They are willing to put up with some inconvenience in exchange for tourist money. The perception of the state of local economy has a significant impact on both the perceived costs and benefits of tourism and on the support for tourism. If the economy of the community is depressed, residents are likely to place more importance on the perceived benefits of tourism and consequently support tourism development even though they are aware of the potential for tourism to result in negative impacts (Gursoy, Jurowski, & Uysal 2002).[3]

To be successful over time, destination managers need to make sure they have local residents' support and endorsement for tourism development. However, having that support alone is not enough. Destination managers also need to know their situation and must be in tune with their external environment and changing customer needs and wants. There must be a strategic fit between what the market wants and what the destination has to offer, as well as between what the destination needs and what the market can provide. This requires a marketing strategy that is endorsed and supported by all stakeholders to guide the product development and all marketing activities. However, it should be remembered that in most destinations, public agencies such as national tourism organizations (NTOs) and convention and visitors bureaus (CVBs) are likely to promote the tourist business for the whole destination or country while the private businesses such as hotels and restaurants are likely to promote their own businesses.

The Role of NTOs

At the national level, governments promote their countries in the international tourism market through national tourism organizations (NTOs). In some countries, such as Mexico and Canada, government leaders have recognized the importance of tourism to a nation's economy and have elevated the status of the NTO to cabinet level, instituting a Ministry of Tourism. Regardless of their position in governments, NTOs have similar objectives. They promote their countries through the following:

- Publicity campaigns
- Research
- Plans for destinations

As a result of increased competition in world tourism, NTOs today spend much more on their tourism marketing budget than at any other time. A significant part is spent to publicize a country as a destination, through outlets in major source countries, to create public awareness and to promote positive images.

After the Indian Ocean tsunami at the end of 2004, several Southeast and South Asian countries increased their tourism budgets to educate travelers about the geography of the region, promoting locations that were not directly affected by the tragedy and publicizing the recovery of impacted areas.

The United States Travel and Tourism Administration (USTTA), under the Department of Commerce, functioned as the NTO for the United States until 1996. At that time its funding was cut, leaving the United States as the only major country without a federally funded NTO. The Travel Industry Association of America (TIA), established in 1941 as a consortium of industry trade organizations and private companies, has attempted to fill this gap by promoting and facilitating increased travel to and within the United States. In 2005, TIA teamed up with the Travel Business Roundtable to further strengthen its influence with government lawmakers and to promote travel-friendly regulation in the United States.

Historically, the principal marketing roles of NTOs have been fairly narrow in scope—creating and communicating overall appealing destination images and messages to the target market. However, NTO functions are changing as today's international tourism industry becomes more competitive and tourists become increasingly more sophisticated in their destination choice behavior. Because tourism industry leaders in many countries recognize the importance of collaboration between the public and private sectors, they launch and implement various collaborative marketing programs. The Greater Mekong (river) Subregion (GMS) is being marketed as a single destination; it includes the

Southeast Asian countries of Myanmar, Laos, Thailand, Cambodia, Vietnam, and southeastern China.

In 2003 tourism to East Asian countries was severely affected by incidences of the SARS virus. Even countries with no record of SARS cases were negatively affected. In one month Thailand experienced a 46 percent drop in arrivals compared to the prior year.[4] Tourism marketing budgets in the region were boosted by the millions in a post-SARS strategy to attract tourists. By October 2004 UNWTO reported that Northeast and Southeast Asian countries had "bounced back stunningly from the losses suffered in 2003 due to SARS."[5] However, 2005 and news of a looming threat of an avian flu epidemic originating in Asia had the World Tourism Organization warning that an overreaction could once again damage international tourism.[6]

The marketing activities of an NTO are mainly centered on the promotion of the country as a whole. Subsets, however, are common. States, provinces, regions, areas, cities, and other small parts of a country participate in similar activities to promote their unique destinations. Advertisements for some of these locations are shown in Exhibits 9-1 to 9-5.

EXHIBIT 9-1 This image illustrates the promotion of states.

Source: Vermont Department of Tourism & Marketing and Stowe/Smugglers' Notch Region. Used by permission.

EXHIBIT 9-2 This image illustrates the promotion of regions.

Source: St. Petersburg/Clearwater Convention & Visitors Bureau. Used by permission.

NTOs also play a facilitation role that typically includes the following:

- Collecting, analyzing, and decimating market research data
- Establishing a representation in the markets of origin
- Participating in trade shows
- Organizing and coordinating familiarization trips
- Supporting the private sector in the production and distribution of literature

An analysis of the pleasure travel market potential for various countries may involve looking at the following important characteristics that relate to the volume of travel and associated spending:

- Total number of potential travelers
- Incidence rate of long-haul adult pleasure travelers
- Actual number of visitors
- Potential for more visitors
- Potential for additional market penetration
- Current receipts from pleasure travelers
- Per capita pleasure traveler receipts
- Total potential receipts
- Potential for additional pleasure travel receipts

When comparing countries, each item can be assigned a mathematical weight relative to its importance, and the target countries can then be ranked according to these numbers.

Noting that "a growing economy is one of the strongest indicators of tourism growth,"[7] TIA has put additional resources into studying the potential of outbound travel to the United States by four emerging markets: China (PRC), India, Russia, and Poland. All have been identified as having more affluent populations with growing middle-class segments that have the resources for international travel. These countries are targeted in addition to the traditional U.S. markets—the UK and Japan.

Because the United States has no national tourism offices, the Nevada Commission on Tourism was able to obtain certification by the China National Tourism Administration (CNTA) to operate an office in China. Nevada is now the only state tourism office in China, putting it in a unique position to capture Chinese travelers to the United States.

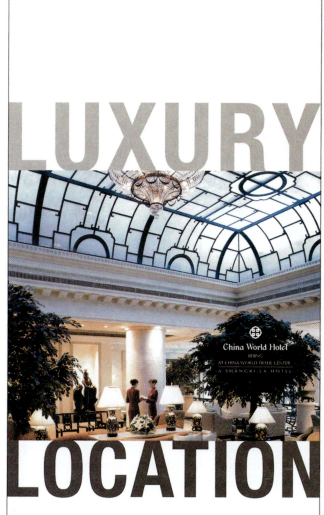

China World Hotel, Beijing.
What will your reason be?

For some, it's the inspired setting
in the city's commercial and diplomatic heart.
For others, it's the legendary Shangri-La hospitality.
But perhaps most of all, it's the luxurious accommodations
unmatched anywhere else in the city, if not the world.
www.shangri-la.com

EXHIBIT 9-3 This image illustrates the promotion of countries.

Source: Developed for Shangri-la Hotels and Resorts. Used by permission.

 Web Browsing Exercise

Go to the Peru Tourism Bureau website (www.visitperu.com). What major aspects of Peruvian culture are highlighted to attract tourists to the country? Is it possible to make a hotel booking from the Visit Peru website?

 Web Browsing Exercise

Go to the Nevada Commission on Tourism website (www.travelnevada.com). Besides China, in which other countries will you find a Nevada tourism promotion office?

watch Mother
Nature light
up the night.

This fall...

The Outer Banks

**Click now for your
free Getaway Card.**

EXHIBIT 9-4 This image illustrates the promotion of areas.

Source: Outer Banks Visitors Bureau. Used by permission.

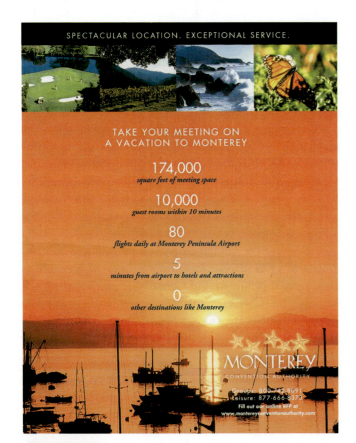

SPECTACULAR LOCATION. EXCEPTIONAL SERVICE.

TAKE YOUR MEETING ON
A VACATION TO MONTEREY

174,000
square feet of meeting space

10,000
guest rooms within 10 minutes

80
flights daily at Monterey Peninsula Airport

5
minutes from airport to hotels and attractions

0
other destinations like Monterey

MONTEREY
CONVENTION AUTHORITY
Groups: 800-717-8091
Leisure: 877-666-8373
Fill out our online RFP at
www.montereyconventionauthority.com

EXHIBIT 9-5 This image illustrates the promotion of cities.

Source: Monterey Convention Authority. Used by permission.

How Hotels and Tourist Destinations Work Together

To provide an example of how the marketing executive of a specific hotel might work with a tourism office to promote both the hotel and the destination, we conducted an interview with Leanne Pletcher, who is the VP of marketing for the Hilton Waikoloa on Hawai'i—the Big Island. Tourism is the number one source of revenue for the state of Hawaii; as such, much money is used to promote Hawaii as a destination. A critical issue for a hotel in such a destination as Hawai'i is to maintain its identity and not get lost in the promotion of the destination. That is, Leanne Pletcher wants the traveler to say, "I am going to the Hilton Waikoloa in Hawai'i" rather then, "I am going to Hawai'i."

Pletcher explains how this is done in Exhibit 9-6. The advertisement in Exhibit 9-7 promotes the destination, whereas the advertisement in Exhibit 9-8 promotes the individual property. Both of these advertisements would appear together in a magazine or newspaper, just as they do in this book.

Destination Marketing Strategy

Before a destination can begin to formulate a marketing strategy, management must understand the external environment to identify possible opportunities and threats.

EXHIBIT 9-6   Interview with Leanne Pletcher of the Hilton Waikoloa on Hawai'i

DO THE HILTONS IN HAWAII PROMOTE THE DESTINATION FIRST AND THE HILTONS SECOND, OR IS IT THE OTHER WAY AROUND?

Whether the promotion carries destination versus property-specific information depends on the nature of the message and the size and scope of the target market. For a broader appeal—if the guest is coming from a further distance and more apt to spend a longer amount of time on their trip—the message will incorporate more of a destination message for the Hilton Hawaii property: Hilton Waikoloa Village, Hilton Hawaiian Village, or Doubletree as the main attraction. Because the three properties have their own unique characteristics, each has its own separate marketing plan, as well as joint advertising messages for Hilton Hawaii.

Hilton Waikoloa Village recognizes the importance of promoting not only the resort, but also the destination. When a visitor is making the commitment to travel to Hawaii, they should be informed of all there is to offer at our resort and the Big Island.

Hilton Waikoloa Village promotions typically incorporate a message about the property along with the destination, as the two go hand in hand. Especially on the Big Island, we recognize the importance of conveying to the visitor that Hawaii's Big Island is part of the Hilton Waikoloa Village experience. It is also important to sell the destination to groups because they are inclined to do activities both on and off the property.

With our local or "kama'aina" markets, which can encompass on-island residents or visitors from the outer islands, Hilton Waikoloa Village focuses promotional efforts on special events, dining, spa, and room packages. Kama'aina business complements our group and FIT business, especially during the "shoulder" periods. Kama'aina promotions include radio and newspaper advertising, pitching local media writers, and e-mail communications.

WHAT SORT OF ACTIVITIES DOES A PROPERTY IN A DESTINATION LIKE HAWAII DO TO GET NOTICED OR TO STAND OUT?

A resort like no other, Hilton Waikoloa Village is really a destination in itself. Hilton Waikoloa Village stands out amongst other resorts and properties in Hawaii due to the following:

- Set on 62 ocean-front acres on the sunny Kohala Coast of the Big Island with tropical gardens, abundant wildlife, nine international restaurants, world-class shopping, art and culture, golf and tennis.
- Dolphin Quest Learning Lagoon—offering guests the unique experience of a dolphin encounter.
- Largest amount of indoor/outdoor meeting space combined with room availability on the outer islands.
- Special events like Dolphin Days Summer Fest, Return to Paradise, and Big Island Festival, which showcase the unique culture, agriculture, art and foods of Hawaii.
- Guests can explore the resort by air-conditioned trams; take a leisurely stroll on flagstone walkways with $7 million in Polynesian, European, and Asian artwork; or cruise on mahogany canal boats along waterways throughout the property.

Being owned and managed by Hilton, Hilton Waikoloa Village has the advantage of Hilton Hotels Corporation's brand marketing campaign, collateral pieces, and electronic media vehicles. Hilton Hawaii also partners with strong marketing companies, like American Express, on strategic mailings.

HOW DOES A PROPERTY OVERCOME THE LENGTH OF TRAVEL TIME NEEDED TO REACH THE DESTINATION?

While the length of time certainly varies with the origination of the traveler, the number of direct flights continues to increase, making it easier

to travel to Hawaii, and especially to Hawaii's Big Island. Marketing and public relations efforts are targeted to the cities and regions that provide the direct lift.

One marketing strategy is to work with the airline partners of the Hilton HHonors program to cross-promote the resort and the airline to the target markets. Hilton Waikoloa Village also works with Big Island Visitors Bureau (BIVB) on special promotions and events that are in conjunction with new flights/airlines coming to Keahole-Kona International Airport.

Given the amount of activities available and the time commitment for travel, we also try to recommend at least a week stay at the resort.

WHAT SORT OF ACTIVITIES ARE UNDERTAKEN TO PROMOTE THE HILTON AND HAWAII IN YOUR FEEDER MARKETS?

- Direct sales efforts to groups, companies, organizations through Hilton Waikoloa Village–based national sales managers, and Hilton Corporation–based national sales team on the mainland.
- Media/marketing plan incorporates targeted advertising in publications that have distribution and frequency in the feeder markets. Direct mail pieces are targeted to the same areas. Efforts are also made to capture repeat visitors in these markets.
- Strong website presence and e-communication programs in place.
- Providing information, packages, and specials to travel agents and wholesalers.
- Targeted press releases to major metro markets.
- Invitations to media based in feeder markets to take individual or group press trips to the resort.
- Media blitzes several times annually to feeder markets.

HOW DOES AN INDIVIDUAL HOTEL WORK WITH THE TOURIST AND VISITORS CONVENTION BUREAU TO PROMOTE ITS PROPERTY?

Hilton Waikoloa Village works with Big Island Visitors Bureau on a number of levels:

- Co-op advertising opportunities.
- Representation on media trips to top market destinations in order to pitch stories (articles published in top magazines).
- Offering accommodations to Big Island Visitors Bureau–sponsored media/writers visiting the Big Island. The Hawaii Visitors and Convention Bureau is also a major partner, as well as the Kohala Coast Resort Association. Both groups also sponsor media/writers.
- Participation in Big Island Visitors Bureau–sponsored trade shows and special events on the mainland or other target markets.
- Participation on the board level to give input on marketing plans and sales efforts.
- Being a part of "aloha" greeting committee to new flights/passengers coming into the Keahole-Kona International Airport.
- Promotions, sweepstakes, and other partnership opportunities with the bureaus.

HOW DO INTERACTIONS WITH TRAVEL WRITERS FIT INTO YOUR OVERALL PROMOTIONAL STRATEGIES?

Interactions with travel writers are key to the success of a public relations program. Relationships with trust must be developed with writers so that they can call on a public relations professional at any given time for information. Speedy, accurate response to writers' requests will guarantee optimum coverage.

Travel writers provide the unique opportunity to convey our messages through magazines, newspapers, website, and broadcast media. Articles can capture more detail and give the reader the essence of a true

(continued)

TAKE ME TO

HAWAII

TO A PARADISE I'VE DREAMED ABOUT.

TAKE ME TO THE HILTON.™

HILTON HAWAIIAN VILLAGE

Located on the world-famous Waikiki Beach on the island of Oahu, Hilton Hawaiian Village® Beach Resort & Spa offers the most extraordinary ways to experience this island paradise. Along with stunning oceanfront settings, a sunny tropical climate and world-class service, you will also find the perfect mix of exceptional hotel accommodations and classic Hawaiian hospitality— Waikiki's only complete resort.

For reservations visit
Hilton.com
or call **1-800-HILTONS**.

Ⓗ
Hilton
Hawaiian Village®
Beach Resort & Spa
Travel should take you places™

2005 Kalia Road
Honolulu, Hawaii 96815
Phone 808-949-4321
HiltonHawaiianVillage.com

Fall is a Perfect time to escape to Hawaii,

HILTON HAWAIIAN VILLAGE

Lose yourself on famous WAIKIKI Beach, in a picture perfect setting.

BEACH FRONT SUPER POOL

Hilton Hawaiian Village® Beach Resort & Spa occupies 22 lushly landscaped oceanfront acres on the widest stretch of famous Waikiki Beach.

- Set amidst tropical gardens, waterfalls, and exotic wildlife
- Relax by the stunning Super Pool framed by towering palms just steps from the beach
- Village setting with an international selection of 22 restaurants and lounges, over 90 shops and specialty boutiques and the world-renowned Mandara Spa‡
- Fireworks spectacular and a Polynesian show every Friday evening

To learn more, tour online at
HiltonHawaiianVillage.com

‡*Independently owned and operated.*

VARIETY OF DINING EXPERIENCES

EXHIBIT 9-7 An advertisement that promotes a destination.

Source: Hilton Hotels. Used by permission.

and the Spectacular Resorts of Hilton Hawaii.

HILTON WAIKOLOA VILLAGE

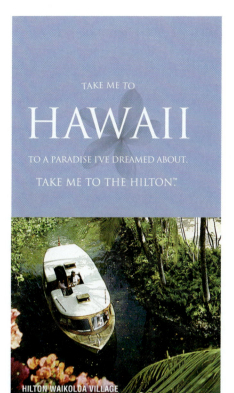

TAKE ME TO

HAWAII

TO A PARADISE I'VE DREAMED ABOUT.

TAKE ME TO THE HILTON.™

HILTON WAIKOLOA VILLAGE

A lush oceanfront oasis, cradled by miles of untamed coastline. You have found paradise on Hawaii's BIG ISLAND.

Hilton Waikoloa Village® is a spectacular destination resort set on over 62 acres on the sunny and exclusive Kohala Coast of Hawaii's Big Island. Recently ranked as a Departures Magazine readers favorite hotel in Hawaii.

- Explore aboard mahogany boats that cruise tranquil waterways or in Swiss-made trams
- Enjoy award-winning dining, shopping, Hawaiian arts and culture
- Snorkel or kayak in a private ocean-fed lagoon
- Experience an interactive experience with dolphins*
- Play 36 holes of championship golf or renew body and spirit at the Kohala Sports Club & Spa

For a complete resort tour, visit
HiltonWaikoloaVillage.com

Independently owned and operated.

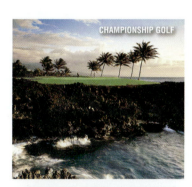

CHAMPIONSHIP GOLF

DOLPHIN QUEST LEARNING LAGOON*

At this stunning destination resort on the sunny Kohala Coast of Hawaii's Big Island, Hilton Waikoloa® Village is set on over 62 oceanfront acres of breathtaking scenery surrounded by 36 holes of championship golf. Enjoy endless activities and experience Hawaii art and cultural treasures at this spectacular destination resort. Truly a world-class resort with service to match—a resort like no other.

For reservations visit
Hilton.com
or call **1-800-HILTONS**.

Hilton
Waikoloa Village®
Travel should take you places®

425 Waikoloa Beach Drive
Waikoloa, Hawaii 96738
Phone 808-886-1234
HiltonWaikoloaVillage.com

EXHIBIT 9-8   An advertisement that promotes an individual property.

Source: Hilton Hotels. Used by permission.

EXHIBIT 9-9 The Multiplier Effect

Tourism not only creates jobs in the tertiary sector, it also encourages growth in the primary and secondary sectors of industry. This is known as the multiplier effect, which in its simplest form is how many times money spent by a tourist circulates through a country's economy.

Money spent in a hotel helps to create jobs directly in the hotel, but it also creates jobs indirectly elsewhere in the economy. The hotel, for example, has to buy food from local farmers, who may spend some of this money on fertilizer or clothes. The demand for local products increases as tourists often buy souvenirs, which increases secondary employment.

The multiplier effect continues until the money eventually "leaks" from the economy through imports—the purchase of goods from other countries. A study of tourism "leakage" in Thailand estimated that 70% of all money spent by tourists ended up leaving Thailand (via foreign-owned tour operators, airlines, hotels, imported drinks and food, etc.). Estimates for other Third World countries range from 80% in the Caribbean to 40% in India. Exhibit 1 presents a chart of the tourist multiplier effect.

Source: Courtesy of Barcelona Field Studies Centre S. L. Used by permission. Retrieved January 3, 2006, from www.geographyfieldwork.com/Tourist Multiplier.htm.

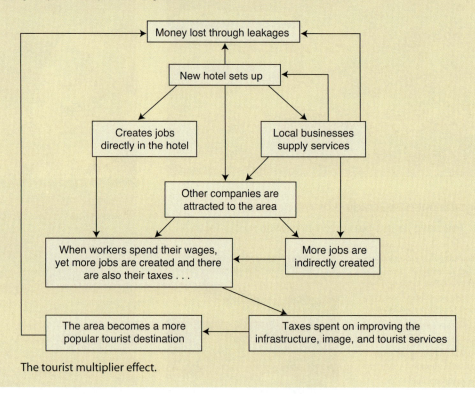

The tourist multiplier effect.

World Tourism Organization [UNWTO] and the International Air Transport Association [IATA]). International politics also play a significant role in the volume of travel and tourism business. After the terrorist attacks in the United States on September 11, 2001, international travel to the United States experienced a 16 percent drop—the worst decline in the history of international arrivals. Part of this decrease was a result of the travel restrictions put in place by the U.S. government. For example, the Western Hemisphere Travel Initiative will require all travelers to and from the Americas, the Caribbean, and Bermuda to have a passport or other accepted document to enter or reenter the United States. The implementation schedule is as follows:

■ **December 31, 2005:** All travel to or from the Caribbean, Bermuda, Central and South America
■ **December 31, 2006:** All air and sea travel to or from Mexico and Canada

■ **December 31, 2007:** All air, sea, and land border crossings.[12]

Conversely, nearly a quarter million Americans have visited Vietnam since the two countries normalized relations in 1995.

The air transport industry was liberalized in most tourist-generating countries in the 1980s. The deregulation of the airline industry in North America generated a significant increase in intercontinental flights, which, in turn, positively contributed to the growth of world tourism. The adoption of an "open sky" policy in Asian countries resulted in a substantial increase in air traffic within Asia and fostered the introduction of new carriers such as Eva Airways (Taiwan) and Asiana Airlines (South Korea). The advent of low-cost carriers in Europe—for example, Air Berlin, Easy Jet, and Ryan Air—have also contributed to the increase in tourism among countries.

Relaxed travel restrictions and increasing leisure time and income of residents in newly industrialized countries contributed significantly to a growth of tourism within and from Asia. In the past, both the Taiwanese and South Korean governments restricted or limited overseas travel by their citizens. With rapid economic growth and an increase in consumer disposable income, the concept of leisure travel became widespread in these countries, and their governments gradually lifted overseas travel bans. In the past, for example, the Korean government prevented its citizens from obtaining passports for "sightseeing" purposes. Previously, to obtain a passport for pleasure travel, an applicant had to be at least 50 years old in 1983, 40 in 1987, and 30 in 1988. In 1989 the government eliminated all age restrictions on the issuance of passports to its citizens. The Taiwanese government followed the same course. The number of outbound tourists from Taiwan increased more than threefold in four years. The number of South Korean outbound travelers increased fivefold during the same period.

In 2004 the Chinese government increased the number of "approved" countries its citizens are able to visit to 90. This in turn has spawned considerable activity in tourism-related organizations in the approved countries to attract and accommodate Chinese visitors. Buoyed by the sheer number of potential visitors, *BusinessWeek* magazine dubbed 2005 the "Year of the Chinese Tourist" for Europe because more than 25 European countries were added to the approved destination list.[13]

Web Browsing Exercise

Use your favorite search engine to find the most up-to-date travel requirements for inbound passengers to the United States. What requirements exist? Do these requirements vary by the passport carried? That is, are travel restrictions different for those who carry Chinese passports then they are for those who carry UK passports? For comparison, choose another country and examine its travel restrictions. How do these restrictions compare to those of the United States?

Sociocultural Environment

Social and cultural considerations involve the beliefs, values, attitudes, opinions, and lifestyles of those in the market environment, as developed from their cultural, ecological, demographic, religious, educational, and ethnic conditioning.

A key element in the tourism marketing process is the significant demographic shifts affecting the population, particularly in selecting target markets. In 1970, 24 percent of the U.S. population was between 25 and 45 years of age. By 1990 this age group accounted for 33 percent of the population, a 38 percent increase. A major turning point in the United States will be in 2010, when the majority of the population will be 45 years and older. Another continuing phenomenon is the growth rate of the over-60 segment, a group that likes to travel. Other countries have had similar demographic shifts. Moreover, as social attitudes change, so too do the leisure patterns of consumers. The popularity of "ecotourism" in recent years is one good example.

Web Browsing Exercise

Go to the World Travel & Tourism Council website (www.wttc.org). Click on "Blueprint for New Tourism." What are the three fundamental conditions for the Blueprint for New Tourism? After looking at the "Case Studies of the Blueprint for New Tourism in Practice," which initiative is of most interest to you and why?

Ecological Environment

A growing awareness of planet Earth's finite resources and the impact of travel on a destination's ecology have spurred new consciousness on the part of some international travelers and host communities alike. In a landmark survey of American travelers by TIA and the National Geographic Society, nearly three quarters claimed that it is "important to them that their visit not damage the environment."[14]

Host governments of popular tourism destinations—for example, the Great Barrier Reef in Australia and the Galapagos Islands of Ecuador—have taken steps to manage the carrying capacities of these destinations. It is hoped that measures such as limiting the number of tour operators and increasing visitor fees will minimize the ecological impact of tourism.

In late 2005 the government of Mexico received a $200.5 million loan from the World Bank "to promote sustainable development by balancing socioeconomic development with sound environmental management." The money is to be used in part to promote sustainable action plans in selected tourist destinations and to make improvements in areas such as wastewater and solid waste disposal.[15]

Exhibit 9-10 provides an example of a resort at a destination area that has successfully used sustainable tourism to create a strong market.

Web Browsing Exercise

Go to www.unep.net and search the topic "tourism." Be prepared to discuss the type of information on this site. Review one of the pieces of information in detail and be prepared to discussion it in class.

Demographic Environment

Although demographic change is a constant process, it has received a lot of public attention in recent years because it is

EXHIBIT 9-10 Turtle Island Resort: To Be a Vital Resource to its Community

In the early 1970s, having sold a successful cable TV network in the Pacific Northwest, Harvard-educated Richard Evanston was 36 years old and burned out from his fast-paced life in the United States. Evanston sought refuge in the South Pacific and in 1972 bought the uninhabited island of Anaya Levu, renaming it "Turtle Island."

The island, however, was in not much better shape than its new owner. Uninhabited and largely barren, decades of overgrazing, neglect and abuse had resulted in only 15 percent of the valleys on the 500-acre island still supporting forest growth. Significant soil erosion was also evident and as a result the island's many eco-systems (mangroves, coral reefs and beaches) were under threat. Native fauna were few and far between.

Even though the idea of a resort was still many years away, Evanston, who remains the owner and the Managing Director, made a commitment to restoring the island to its original state—not because he anticipated living there indefinitely, but because he perceived it as the natural, necessary and "right" thing to do. As a result of this ethos and commitment, Turtle Island is now internationally recognized as a prime example of how environmental and cultural sustainability can be integrated into a quality tourist operation. Turtle Island has demonstrated that a resort can achieve financial success by being a socially and environmentally responsible operator; and that Turtle Island's ethos of responsible tourism is in fact fundamental to the success of the operation.

THE VISION

The Turtle Island Vision is that Turtle Island will provide a genuine and loving Fijian experience for caring people and will be a vital resource to its community. During over 20 years of operation (the resort opened in 1980), a number of unique and innovative programs have been undertaken, setting Turtle Island apart from other tourism developments. Reflecting Turtle Island's vision and commitment to its community, these programs and activities represent aspects of a sustainable future for tourism and provide a model for other tourism operators—not only in the Pacific, but in other developing nations as well.

The Turtle Island vision also includes several broad statements of commitment:

- to be staffed by a team of people who are committed
- to high standards and who exhibit a caring and
- loving attitude towards the guests and each other;
- to provide an environment which facilitates a positive and unique guest experience;
- to be regarded as one of the leading ecotourism resorts in the world;
- to be recognized by their communities as a vital resource.

THE TURTLE COMMUNITY

Turtle Island seeks to establish itself as an indispensable and valuable resource to its communities. All strategies and action plans for Turtle Island are measured against this ideal. "Communities," in the sense of Turtle Island, span a range of stakeholders including:

- the guests of Turtle Island;
- the 160 staff at Turtle Island;
- all of the close to 3,000 residents of the seven villages in their Ticino (region);
- all of the residents of the Yamahas (the island group in which Turtle Island is located); and
- the population of the Fiji Islands.

Turtle Island guests play a vital role in the success of community development programs through financial and in kind contributions to various programs. The "Turtle experience" as it is known, is predicated on a unique sense of "family" created on the island that is shared between the guests and the staff. Turtle Island staff and management take the formation of this sense of family very seriously. The intentional facilitation of a collective and shared experience engenders an intercultural sense of community between employees and guests, as well as among the guests themselves. Staff are encouraged to take an active interest in the lives of the guests and vice-versa. Through shared events, activities and experiences, guests develop a sense of closeness and community not often seen in the tourism arena. Clearly, the guests who choose to stay at the resort appreciate these efforts—36 percent of its guests are returnees.

YAMAHAS COMMUNITY FOUNDATION (YK)

Turtle Island Resort encourages guests to take an active role in protecting and enhancing the lives of local people. They are often so touched by their experience on Turtle Island and the warmth and hospitality of staff and local villagers that they want to give something back by making a contribution. The Yamahas Community Foundation (YK, formerly known as the Turtle Island Community Foundation) was created in 1992 to generate guest donations and ensure that they are applied to projects which provide solutions to real problems facing local residents. The foundation supports a number of innovative community projects in healthcare, education and employment.

EDUCATION

The area faces a number of educational barriers. There are no secondary schools in the local area of Macula Ticino (the area in which Turtle Island is located), and many families cannot afford to send their children to boarding school on the mainland. As a result, the attrition rate between primary school and secondary school is close to 50 percent.

To help families send their children to high school, Turtle Island identified two strategies:

- to create employment opportunities so families could afford to send their children to school; and
- to build a school on Turtle Island so that the children from the seven local villages can live in their home village and commute to school by boat each day. (This goal was realized in 2002, with the first class of seven students commencing study. It is anticipated that the high school will be finished in 2005. Ultimately, it will cater to 100 local students.)

HEALTHCARE

In addition to other health concerns, Fiji also has a particular problem with blindness-causing cataracts and diabetic retinopathy. The healthcare facilities in the Yukawa Islands, the group in which Turtle Island is situated, are rudimentary at best. There has been no resident doctor for many years, and nursing stations lack electricity, running water, significant expertise and medical equipment.

Turtle Island recognized that this was a serious problem within its extended community. So for the last 12 years, they have closed the resort for one week each January to conduct eye clinics, during which they host medical teams of up to 20 people. Since they began this program, more than 11,000 Fijians have had their eyes tested, more than 9,000 pairs of glasses have been issued without charge, over 800 operations have been conducted (mainly cataract or pterygium operations) and more than 20 corneal transplants have been done. In addition to the eye clinics, Turtle Island also sponsors other medical clinics during the year, including dermatology, general practice, women's health, pharmacology and dentistry.

EMPLOYMENT

In the Yamahas, fishing and subsistence agriculture provide enough food, and adequate housing is available. However, employment opportunities outside tourism are nonexistent. As a result, villages have high rates of unemployment, which leads to urban drift. This affects the youth of the Yamahas in particular. Those young people fortunate enough to go to the

EXHIBIT 9-10	Turtle Island Resort: To Be a Vital Resource to its Community, *(Continued)*

mainland for their education are unlikely to return, since there are no employment options.

In order to expand employment opportunities, Turtle Island has worked with three villages as a "social entrepreneur" to build budget and backpacker accommodations. These properties are owned by the local villages, subject to an obligation to repay Turtle Island the cost of the building (on an interest-free basis), from the profits generated.

Turtle Island has also been instrumental in creating an association of local budget and backpacker operators (inclusive of the three properties discussed above) called the Macula Ticino Tourism Association (NTTA). Members of the NTTA have adopted their own Code of Conduct for Responsible Tourism and have agreed to implement and be bound by its principles in their resort operations.

BENCHMARKING AND EVALUATION: MEASURING AND IMPROVING FOR A SUSTAINABLE FUTURE

Turtle Island believes that regular "check-ups" are vital to the health of its operations. In the words of Richard Evanston: "The difficulty in measuring what you are achieving is knowing where you are on the sustainability continuum at a particular time." It is a fundamental part of Turtle Island's philosophy to test and measure the impact of operations on its environment, community, marine resources and overall health and to seek to improve its operations on this basis. This is done through the commissioning of both environmental and cultural audits. Such is Turtle Island's commitment to this process, the results of the audits "warts and all" are available to all guests to peruse.

TURTLE ISLAND: A LEADER IN THE NEW TOURISM PARADIGM

Both the resort and foundation successfully address the three legs of sustainability: community, environment and economy. The benefits of their community initiatives are clear. Their environmental practices are equally strong and both programs have helped the resort's brand identity. For more

information on environmental audits, reforestation and environmental self-sufficiency go to the Turtle Island Resort Web site (www.turtlefiji.com).

Turtle Island's vision expresses a strong commitment to its communities. Turtle Island lives that vision because it is good for guests, its communities and Turtle Island itself. It sees community commitment as fundamental to achieving environmental and social responsibility, which it believes is the new paradigm through which the future of tourism must be seen. By adhering to sound principles of sustainable tourism, tourism operations can be of great benefit to the stakeholders involved, in both a commercial and ideological sense. To that end, Turtle Island has shown that an owner and operator can remain profitable while also behaving ethically and professionally, creating benefits for all stakeholders.

BEST HISTORY

BEST was started in 1999 with a grant from the Ford Foundation. It served as an incubator for a variety of activities aimed at encouraging the adoption of sustainable practices, stimulating the demand for such practices by travelers, and helping communities start pilot programs.

BEST was under the direction of Michael Seltzer until late 2003, and many conferences and programs were attended and launched.

In late 2003, BEST became a part of the Prince of Wales International Business Leaders Forum (IBLF) as a program of the International Tourism Partnership. It continues to be a resource for anyone interested in the vital task of encouraging sustainable travel practices by the travel and tourism industry, communities, educators, and individual travelers.

BEST's mission is to serve as a leading source of knowledge on innovative travel industry practices that advance community, business and travelers' interest and support the economic and cultural sustainability of destinations.

Source: www.sustainabletravel.org. Information on Turtle Island used by permission.

---

seen as one of the important drivers for new trends in consumer behavior. Global demographic trends are likely to have far-reaching consequences for the future of destinations. One of the major demographic trends that is likely to have a significant impact on tourism and the future of destinations is the rapidly aging population of the developed world. For example, many baby boomers in the United States are at the peaks of their careers and possess the highest earning power of their lives, resulting in the highest level of discretionary income. They are reaching their retirement age rapidly, but even after retirement they are likely to stay active and retain their independence for a long time. Research has shown that people do not change their travel behavior just because they turn 60 or 65, or because they retire. In most cases they stick to the travel patterns acquired until the middle of their lives. This fact allows for predictions of the tourist behavior of future senior generations.

The new senior citizens in 5 or 15 years' time will be different from the present senior citizens when it comes to travel behavior. While senior travelers today are already relatively active, the senior generations to come are more than

likely to surpass them. The effects of demographic change (more and bigger share of older people) and consumer behavior patterns (sticking to learned travel patterns) will show up as more senior trips with different preferences. For example, it is estimated that in Germany within 15 years the number of tourists in the age group 70 to 80 years will rise by more than 50 percent (from 4.2 million in 2003 to 6.6 million in 2018) with more than two thirds choosing destinations abroad. Studies also suggest that participation in cultural and heritage activities increases through middle age, peaks between 45 and 65, and subsequently falls off, which makes this group a prime target for these kinds of activities. This group also has more available time than they had previously, and those with older children choose to expose them to enriching educational experiences. In addition, this group is likely to be one of the best target markets for tourism focusing or health, spas, and keeping fit.

Another demographic trend that is likely to influence the future of tourism destinations is the shrinking population of the developed world as a result of lower fertility rates in many industrial countries. This combined with the dissolution of traditional family patterns may require destinations to develop products and marketing strategies that will attract visitors from developing countries.

Another important demographic trend is rising education levels. This is likely to result in consumers with unprecedented sophistication and depth. Destinations may need to develop products that can satisfy their sophisticated needs and wants.

The increasing economic role of women worldwide is another demographic trend that may influence the future of tourism and destinations. More women are working, and they are earning more money and controlling more discretionary income. Women typically make the decisions regarding the educational experiences of their children and set vacation plans. They also account for a large majority of bus tour passengers, trip planners, and elementary schoolteachers who make decisions on field trip destinations for their students. Women account for 60 to 65 percent of museum attendance and are more likely to support and participate in heritage and cultural activities. As more women move into positions of power and influence, funding for these interests will tend to increase.

These demographic trends suggest that tourism will have the largest, wealthiest, and best-educated market for the next 20 years.

Competitors: Rivalry among Destinations

In today's global marketplace, hundreds of destinations are competing for the market share. To maintain a competitive position in the market, a destination must be able to accurately evaluate its competition. To do this, destination management must have a sound understanding of the market in which they operate: their customers, market boundaries, market conditions, and their competitors.

In the tourism industry, destinations are mutually dependent. A competitive move by one destination can be expected to have a noticeable effect on its competitors, such as retaliation or counter efforts. For example, if one destination starts offering deeply discounted packages or rates to all leisure customers, chances are good that other destinations will develop discounted packages to maintain their market share.

Identifying competitors is especially crucial because it influences all marketing decisions such as pricing, promotion, distribution, products development, attraction design, and positioning. It also provides the basis for competitive analysis, which assesses the industry structure, market scope, and focus of competitive advantage. Destinations must also understand on what dimensions they compete when assessing and selecting a competitive strategy.

A destination can identify its competitors using one of two approaches: an industry or supply-based approach or a market or demand-based approach. The industry approach defines competitors as those brands that operate in the same industry offering similar products and services to similar customers. This is also called the supply-based approach because it requires identifying competitive destinations through the similarity of their offerings, resources, and strategies. The market approach classifies competitive destinations as those satisfying the same customer need. This method is also called a demand-based approach because it requires identifying competitors by the similarity of their customers (i.e., their attitudes, behaviors, and motivations). Research indicates that managers tend to use an industry (or supply-based) approach more often than a market (or demand-based) approach because of its ease. Basically, managers identify destinations that appear outwardly similar—for example, Malta and Cyprus. This approach ignores the fact that customers choose between competitive brands. Competition takes place in the mind of customers, which makes it very important for destinations to create and clearly communicate a strong image of the destination. In addition to creating and communicating a strong image, a destination must be able to distinguish itself from the competition and promote its superiority and relevance to target customers. By providing a point of distinction to its target customers, the destination may be able to entice the target customer to choose that destination over others.

The context and situation in which destinations are considered as travel options can be influenced by a variety of factors such as the customer's cultural orientation, knowledge level, available time, discretionary income, and perception of safety, as well as major catastrophic events, terrorism, and so on. For example, tourists from an English-speaking country may seek holiday destinations where people also speak English. Similarly, people from Muslim countries may purposely limit their destination choice to other Muslim destinations. Available time and discretionary income are likely to play a significant role in determining which destinations are likely to be included in a tourist's consideration set. If a person has limited time or limited money to travel, that person's choice is likely to be restricted to cheaper, closer-to-home destinations rather than expensive and or long-distance destinations.

Segmenting the Tourist Market

Like any product, destinations cannot be everything to everyone. It is almost impossible for a destination to offer travel and tourism products that will satisfy the needs of everyone. Travel markets consists of travelers who may differ in their wants, needs, resources, locations, buying attitudes, and buying processes. Because travelers have unique needs and wants, each traveler can potentially be classified as an individual market. However, modifying the marketing strategy and developing customized product for each traveler may not be feasible for destinations because of their limited resources. Therefore, destinations may need to identify groups of travelers who have common interests and share common values. For example, students who travel for spring break purposes are likely to have similar interests and share similar values. The same may be true for those who travel for the purpose of visiting ancient Roman ruins. Destinations can identify their target markets in two ways. One is to gather information about current visitors to develop profiles of the current market segments. What are they? Where do they come from? Why do they visit the destination? What push and pull factors affect their destination selection? What are their demographic characteristics? How do they make their vacation decisions? Basically, the destination uses the market segmentation approach to develop profiles of its current visitors using some or all of the bases for market segmentation.

Another way to identify target markets is to inventory the kind of attractions, services, and facilities the destination offers and then identify market segments that may be interested in what the destination has to offer. This approach enables a destination to identify underused attractions, services, and facilities and provides an opportunity to increase the visitation levels by going after the segments that may be interested in those underused attractions, services, and facilities. While developing an inventory of what the destination has to offer, managers should also identify the variables, or internal strategic factors, within their destination that may be important to the operation. These internal strategic factors are likely to determine whether a destination can take advantage of external opportunities such as the changing needs and wants of its target markets or opportunities offered by emerging market segments, while also avoiding threats. Experts in the area suggest that differences in performance among destinations in the same market may be explained best through the differences in destinations' capabilities and resources and their application. To gain and sustain a competitive advantage, destination managers need to understand the destination's capabilities and resources and know how to use those capabilities and resources to maintain current visitation levels and attract new segments. If competitors also have similar capabilities and resources, the manager needs to make sure that the operation uses those capabilities and resources better than competitors do. Otherwise, competitors are likely to start stealing customers.

To identify capabilities and resources, destination managers list and describe the service(s) the destination offers. For each offering, managers identify the main points, in-

cluding what the attraction, service, and facilities are; how much they cost; what sorts of customers make purchases; and why. What customer need does each service fill? It is always a good idea to think in terms of customer needs and customer benefits, rather than thinking of the destination side of the equation, such as how a destination generates the service. After identifying the attractions, services, and facilities it offers, the destination needs to determine what it does better than its competitors. These are the destination's distinctive, or core, competencies, the products and services the destination provides better than any other destination in the marketplace. As a destination lists and describes its attractions, facilities, and services, it may run into one of the serendipitous benefits of good planning, which is generating new ideas. Describing the offerings in terms of customer types and customer needs may enable managers to discover new needs to fill and new kinds of market segments to target.

After identifying the current and prospective market segment, destination managers need to conduct marketing research to find out who those people are, where they are located, and so on. For example, a destination may identify several market segments from Germany and France. However, different segments or groups of travelers from Germany and France may visit the destination for different purposes. To identify segments that visit or that may be interested in a destination, destination marketers need to know who comes to the destination and why. In other words, destination marketers may need to develop a profile for each segment, making sure they include the location of the segment and the reasons they travel.

Most destinations have limited marketing budgets and are under constant pressure to maximize the rate of return on every marketing dollar they spend. It is always financially more feasible to go after market segments that are heavily concentrated in fewer locations. If most of the members of a market segment are located in a few major cities, the destination can develop very cost-effective localized promotion strategies to attract those customers. If the market segment members are located all over the country, it may be cost prohibitive to go after that segment.

Markets can be described in terms of geographic, demographic, psychographic, and behavioral attributes. Analyzing the market from this perspective can be a useful way to categorize the people one wants as customers and may lead to identifying and confirming opportunities that the market presents. **Market geographies** address where the members of each segment are physically located. Destination managers are likely to attempt to identify regions and cities where most customers are located (for each product) in order to develop cost-effective promotion strategies and communication materials. **Market demographics** refers to travelers' wants and preferences and the frequency of their purchases because they are often associated with travelers' demographic characteristics. Travelers' demographics include information about their age, gender, nationality, education level, household composition, occupation, and income. Travelers with common demographic factors are likely to be in the same market segment. However, destination marketers need to make sure that segments of travelers with common characteristics also describe the visitors whom they expect to be potential visitors. That is, in the search for new customers, it is important to make sure that it is the demographics to lead to behavior and not some other factor, as we discuss next and in previous and future chapters. **Market psychographics** describes the market segments in terms of psychographic information. It is more challenging than the previous categories because it is less quantifiable and more subjective. Psychographics categorize people on the basis of their lifestyle or personality attributes. For example, the lifestyles and personality attributes of people in a large metropolitan city are likely to be very different from those of people living in a small agriculture-based community. Destination marketers may use this segmentation base to identify the general lifestyles or personalities of their market segments. **Market behaviors** categorizes travelers based on their knowledge, attitude, use, motivation, or response to an attraction, facility, or service. These behavioral variables may include the occasions that stimulate a visit, the benefits they realize, the status of users, their usage rate, their loyalty, their buyer-readiness stage, and their attitude toward the attractions, facilities, and services a destination offers.

For example, a market segment may be described in these terms:

Geographic: They are located in the suburbs of Seattle, Chicago, and Los Angeles that have populations of 65,000.

Demographic: The average incomes of this predominately couple group is $70,000 or more, most have attended college, they are between the ages of 35 and 50, and they have children at or out of the home.

Psychographic: They consider time their most limited resource, and security—both physical and financial—is important.

Behaviors: After checking with people they know and trust, they choose destinations that offer unique and authentic cultural heritage attractions. They are likely to keep visiting such destinations. However, while they may be loyal to a destination, they may eventually stop visiting the destination because of their desire to visit someplace new.

After developing profiles of each market segments and identifying where they are located, destination mar-

keters identify the segments that are likely to yield the highest return on each marketing dollar spent to attract those travelers. Once the most profitable segments are identified, destination marketing managers develop promotional campaigns and communications materials to communicate with each of those segments.

Communicating with the Tourist Market

In today's dynamic global environment, understanding how travelers acquire information is important for making marketing decisions, designing effective marketing communications campaigns, and delivering services. It is during information search that marketers can provide information and influence travelers' vacation decisions. However, before designing communication materials for specific target market segments, destination marketers need to understand what kind of image the destination travelers have in their minds. This is because a destination image is one of the factors most likely to influence travelers' destination selection.

Importance of Image Promotion

Every communication related to a destination helps consumers form an image of that place; websites, books, movies, television, postcards, songs, photographs, news stories, and advertising all contribute. Favorable images, of course, greatly improve the chance of increasing tourist traffic. *The Lord of the Rings* movie trilogy spawned a number of operators in New Zealand to offer tours to the movie locations. Similarly, two of America's popular television series, *Survivor* and *The Amazing Race*, increased Americans' interest in adventure travel destinations around the world.

On the other hand, negative images can also have a profound impact by increasing the challenge for NTO marketers to promote a country's tourism overseas. The book and movie *Midnight Express*, which depict the story of the convicted drug smuggler Billy Hayes' treatment in a Turkish prison before he escaped after 5 years (he was sentenced to 30 years as an example to others), hurt tourism to Turkey. Turkey was portrayed as having a corrupt and inhuman government, and as a result, people were afraid to visit. In another example, India had difficulty promoting itself as a tourist destination because of the image of poverty that people associated with the country. The scenic beauty and many cultural attractions of India were overshadowed by the negative scenes of starving people and squalid living conditions. In recent years, however, India has been able to overcome these challenges and has seen double-digit increases in foreign tourist arrivals since 2003.[16] In the United States, tourism in the entire state of Florida suffered following the

YOU'LL BE TEMPTED TO CALL THE GAME DUE TO WEATHER.

Sure, we've got incredible sports facilities here. And yes, we do host every type of tournament from baseball to soccer to volleyball, and every sort of sport from triathlons to gymnastics to cheerleading. But, when all is said and done, what really makes holding a sports event here a hit is the beach. Our beach. And that's just the beginning. Call 1-800-PCBEACH or visit thesportsloversbeach.com. And discover all the other ways to play at Panama City Beach.

PANAMA CITY BEACH
The Sports Lover's Beach
thesportsloversbeach.com

EXHIBIT 9-11   Tourism officials have had to make efforts to overcome the negative images of Florida as a hurricane target.

Source: Panama City Beach Convention & Visitors Bureau, Inc. Used by permission.

massive hurricanes in 2004 and 2005. Tourism officials had to make efforts to overcome the negative images of Florida as a hurricane target. Exhibit 9-11 is an advertisement for St. Petersburg/Clearwater Beach showing that the hurricanes that struck Florida did not affect these beach areas.

Images of a destination are so important that states and countries spend millions of dollars to build positive images of their destinations (see Exhibit 9-12). Some researchers postulate that a tourist's experience is nothing but a constant modification of the destination image. As shown in Exhibit 9-13, a tourist makes a destination choice based on a previously held image of the destination. The tourist's *actual* experience in the destination provides comparison with the previous image—a "reality check"—and determines the tourist's level of satisfaction or dissatisfaction with the overall experience.

The following example illustrates the process of choosing a destination: Ken is a 21-year-old college student from Pittsburgh who decides to take a vacation over spring break and reads brochures for spring travel packages to Cancún, Mexico. He has never been to Mexico and is excited about the idea of going to Cancún. At this point, Ken's image of Cancún is mainly based on three things: the written information from the tour package brochure, "Visit Cancún" websites, and his previous knowledge about Mexico acquired through books, mass media, and friends. Ken's image of the destination is most important here because his expectations of Cancún (and also Mexico in general) are based on his images of the area.

moments.

occasions.

CAYMAN ISLANDS
Grand Cayman • Cayman Brac • Little Cayman

Close to home. Far from expected.

EXHIBIT 9-12   Images of a destination are so important that states and countries spend millions of dollars to build positive images of their destinations.

Source: Department of Tourism, Cayman Islands. Used by permission.

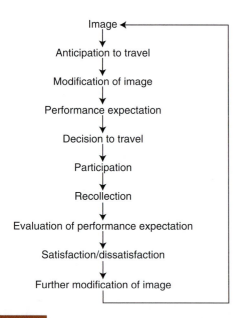

Image

↓

Anticipation to travel

↓

Modification of image

↓

Performance expectation

↓

Decision to travel

↓

Participation

↓

Recollection

↓

Evaluation of performance expectation

↓

Satisfaction/dissatisfaction

↓

Further modification of image

EXHIBIT 9-13 Destination image modification and travel decision making.

Source: Adapted from Chon, K. (1990). The role of destination image in tourism: A review and discussion. The Tourist Review, 33 (2), 2–9.

Spring Break comes and Ken travels to Cancún. He participates in water sports and also meets new friends. When he returns home, he will go through a "recollection" stage in which he evaluates his overall experience, including a comparison of his expectations and actual experiences. If the actual experiences lived up to his expectations (based on his images of the destination), he will be satisfied; if the actual experiences did not live up to his expectations, he will be dissatisfied. Depending on his level of satisfaction or dissatisfaction, Ken will decide whether to return to Cancún, as well as other places in Mexico, in the future. More important, he'll talk about his experiences with his friends, which will, in turn, help his friends form images of Cancún and Mexico.

Travelers' Information Search Behavior

As with the purchase of any product, when it comes to making a vacation decision, travelers are likely to go through a decision-making process, which includes a prepurchase information search. Information acquisition is a necessary step for tourists in selecting a destination and for on-site decisions such as selecting accommodations, transportation, activities, and tours. Understanding the information search behavior of key current and prospective markets can help destination managers and marketers develop effective communications. Using travelers' information source utilization patterns as either a segmentation base or descriptor can enable focused positioning and media selection.

Even though most of the hospitality and tourism researchers who examined the prior product knowledge construct as part of an information search model have utilized prior knowledge as a unidimensional construct, recent hospitality and tourism studies and marketing and consumer behavior literature suggest that a consumer's prior product knowledge comprises two components: familiarity and expertise. Familiarity represents the early stages of learning and expertise represents the later stages of learning. As consumers' familiarity with the product increases, their expertise with the product increases as well.

Familiarity

Familiarity with a product category has been recognized as an important factor in consumer decision making. Consumers' familiarity with a product category is measured as a continuous variable that reflects their direct and indirect knowledge of a product category. Familiarity has been defined as the consumer's perception of how much he or she knows about the attributes of various choice alternatives being considered. However, several researchers suggest that what people think they know and what they actually know often do not correspond because familiarity represents a traveler's subjective knowledge of the destination, whereas the traveler's expertise represents his or her objective knowledge.

Because familiarity represents early stages of learning, consumers are likely to gain knowledge and, therefore, familiarity through an ongoing information search such as reading guidebooks or other related books, seeing advertising and write-ups in newspapers and magazines, watching advertisements on TV, listening to advertising on radio, and talking to friends and relatives. Studies show that product familiarity has direct impact on consumers' information search behavior. In both familiar and unfamiliar product categories, consumers first search their memory for some information to help guide them to make decisions. Consumers' familiarity with a product category is likely to lead to direct acquisition of available information from memory. If the consumer has sufficient information in his or her memory, there may be no need to search for additional information and the consumer can make a decision based on internal information.

Expertise

Expertise can be defined as product-related experiences such as advertising exposures, information search, interactions with salespersons, choice and decision making, purchasing, and product usage in various situations. The term *consumer expertise* is also used in a very broad sense to include both the cognitive structures (e.g., beliefs about product attributes) and cognitive processes (decision rules for acting on those beliefs) required to perform product-related tasks successfully. However, the type of expertise required to perform a product-related task varies because different tasks require different types of expertise. Moreover, more than one type of knowledge is generally required for the successful performance of a particular task.

At the most basic level, mere exposure to a brand name may result in perceptual enhancement of it during visual search. Repeated exposure to a single brand or attribute may lead to easy retrieval of information about that single brand or attribute. Wider experience results in the accumulation of more information, which enables consumers to include more brands in their memory-based evoked sets and to recall and use more attributes during internal information-based decision making. When decisions are based on internal information, knowledge may offer an expert consumer an opportunity to use processing decision strategies that are very different from the ones used by the consumer who is low in expertise. When a consumer who is high in expertise and a consumer who is low in expertise learn the same information and later must make a decision, the expert consumer may be able to rely on memory, whereas the consumer who is low in expertise may again need to engage in external search in order to avoid making an ill-informed decision.[17]

Certainly, understanding external information source utilization can help marketers effectively tailor the promotional mix. In addition, understanding the similarities and differences in familiar travelers' and expert travelers' external information search behavior and identifying which information sources are most likely to be used by familiar travelers and expert travelers can help marketing managers design effective marketing programs and communication strategies.

Past research in the area of information search has focused on developing typologies of consumer information search strategies using nearly 60 variables that are likely to influence external information searches. These typologies included several aspects of the environment (e.g., the difficulty of the choice task, the number of alternatives, and the complexity of the alternatives), situational variables (e.g., previous satisfaction, time constraints, perceived risk, and the composition of the traveling party), consumer characteristics (e.g., education, prior product knowledge, involvement, family life cycle, and socioeconomic status), and product characteristics (e.g., the purpose of the trip and mode of travel). Based on these research studies, Gursoy and McCleary (2004) developed an integrative model that conceptualizes travelers' information search behavior as a series of interrelated behaviors, as seen in Exhibit 9-14.

Prepurchase information search is defined as information search activities that are related to a recognized and immediate purchase intension. For immediate prepurchase information needs, a consumer is likely to use either internal or external information sources, or both. Studies suggest that the type of prepurchase information search (internal or external) is influenced directly by the perceived cost of internal and external information searches and the level of travelers' involvement. Travelers' familiarity and expertise (prior product knowledge), learning, and previous visits influence their information search indirectly. The influence of travelers' familiarity and expertise (prior product knowledge) is likely to be mediated by the cost of internal and external information searches (Gursoy and McCleary 2004). An increase in familiarity is likely to decrease the cost of an internal search and increase the cost of an external search, whereas an increase in expertise is likely to decrease the cost of both an external and internal information search.

The cost of an external information search includes both financial and time costs, whereas the cost of an internal search includes the cognitive effort required and the expected outcome of the search. An increase in the cost of either type of search is likely to decrease the level of search activity.

Travelers' involvement is also likely to have a positive effect on familiarity and expertise. Highly involved travelers are likely to be more familiar with the product and to remember the product information, develop better category structures, analyze the information in more detail, elaborate on it, and make automatic decisions. A traveler's involvement may also positively influence intentional learning. A traveler who is highly involved is likely to pay more attention to incoming information such as commercials about the destination.

A traveler who has been to the destination before is likely to have more familiarity and expertise on the destination than a traveler who has never been to the destination. The previous visits may also have a positive influence on a traveler's involvement. Previous studies suggest that as the number of previous visits to a specific destination increases, a traveler's involvement is likely to increase as well.

Learning is also likely to influence a traveler's information search behavior. Studies suggest that travelers' learning has two dimensions: intentional learning and incidental learning. Intentional learning is likely to increase a traveler' expertise and familiarity, whereas incidental learning is likely to increase a traveler's familiarity. Travelers who gather information through intentional learning are likely to pay more attention to incoming information and process the information thoroughly and therefore increase their objective knowledge and expertise. On the other hand, travelers who learn through incidental learning are not likely to process information thoroughly. However, because incidental learners

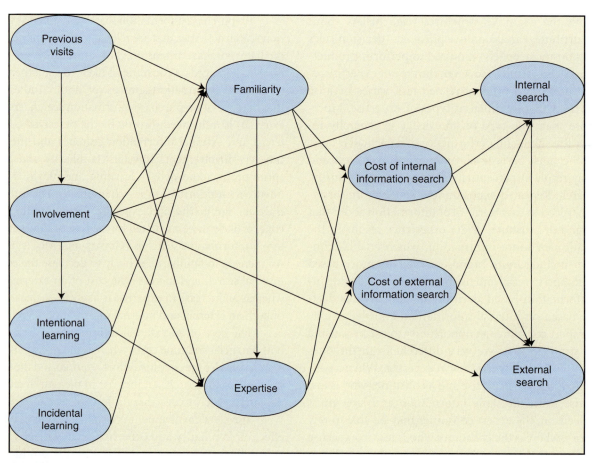

EXHIBIT 9-14 Integrative model of tourists' information search behavior.

Source: Adapted from Gursoy, D., & McCleary, K. W. (2004). An integrative model of tourist's information search behavior. Annals of Tourism Research, 31 (2), 353–373.

have some information about the destination and its attractions, their learning is likely to increase their subjective knowledge and therefore their familiarity with the destination and its attractions.

It is crucial for destination managers to understand the importance of the perceived cost of an information search. The negative relationship between the perceived costs of external information and the amount of information received should cause marketers to take steps to make external searches as inexpensive and time efficient as possible. This is often not the case in travel marketing. For example, a perusal of destination websites quickly reveals sites that are difficult to navigate, take a long time to load, and are linked to empty sites and incomplete information. This increase in time cost to acquire information can cause travelers to look elsewhere for information. Destination marketers should also be aware of the fact that the more information there is available about a destination, the more likely travelers are to increase both incidental and intentional learning. These two factors are likely to lead to increased familiarity and expertise, which, in turn, decrease information search costs, reduce the necessity for an ex-

tensive external search, and help focus the search on specific attributes rather than on general information.

Marketers recognize the value of actual visitation to a site for improving marketing outcomes. Indeed, previous visits may positively affect involvement with a destination while increasing familiarity and expertise, which lead to the outcomes discussed earlier. Both familiar and expert travelers are likely to use external information sources to varying degrees. However, travelers' use of external information is likely to be influenced by their perception of the cost of the information search. Therefore, marketers and advertisers need to develop different communication strategies for familiar and expert travelers. Because unfamiliar travelers are likely to have a hard time examining the information gathered from external sources because of their limited processing ability, they may require a different communication strategy than expert travelers. Communication strategies developed for unfamiliar travelers should provide simple information about the overall destination. They may also need to include a comparison of the destination with other destinations that target the same market to make it easier for the traveler to digest the information.

In other words, communication materials should clearly identify the unique selling propositions of the destination to differentiate the destination from competitors and to make positioning of the destination easier for unfamiliar travelers. Establishing a good and understandable communication with unfamiliar travelers is critical in convincing them to choose a destination over other destinations because low familiarity is associated with higher perceived importance of, and receptivity to, new information.

Another method of communicating with unfamiliar travelers is through word of mouth. Unfamiliar travelers may have a hard time comprehending and evaluating product-related information because of their inferior ability to comprehend and evaluate product-related facts. Because of their limited ability to process the product-related information, unfamiliar travelers are more likely to sample the opinions of others such as their friends and family. Because positive word of mouth is the result of satisfaction, special attention needs to be given to customer satisfaction and complaint handling. Customer satisfaction should be constantly monitored in order to identify the problem areas and to make necessary modifications to enhance customer satisfaction. In addition, customers' complaints should be handled delicately and quickly to ensure satisfaction and positive word of mouth.

Communication materials developed for expert travelers should include detailed information about the attributes that are important to the target market. These attributes can easily be identified by conducting formal or informal research. In addition, destinations also need to monitor changing consumer needs and wants that may shift the importance placed on attributes. Destinations can design surveys or conduct focus groups to find out and monitor what attributes are most important to expert travelers. Managers may also identify the important attributes by just talking to their existing customers. Destinations need to pay special attention to identifying expert travelers. If destination managers and marketers fail to ask the right questions to the right audience, they may end up making the wrong conclusions and developing ineffective communication strategies.

After the important attributes are identified, destinations will need to communicate them to expert travelers. Expert travelers are more likely to search for detailed information. Therefore, destinations need to develop communication materials (i.e., brochures, direct mailing materials, etc.) that provide detailed information about the destination and its important attributes. These materials need to be modified as expert travelers' needs and wants change.

Destination managers and marketers should understand that different travelers have different information needs. While unfamiliar travelers need simple, understandable, and general information, expert travelers need detailed information about the destination and attributes to make their vacation decisions. Destination managers and marketers can use travelers' level of prior product knowledge (familiarity and expertise) as a segmentation tool to develop communication strategies that are most appropriate for each segment.

It is important for travel marketers to have an overall picture of how travelers acquire information. It is also important to know the major components of the search process and how they fit together. With this understanding, marketers can design communication strategies aimed specifically at different stages in the information search process, which will lead to the efficient use of resources and more success in attracting tourists to their specific destinations.

■ Summary

Marketing destinations is no different than marketing hospitality products. External macro and micro environmental factors that are likely to influence the marketing efforts of any hospitality organization are likely to influence any destination marketing efforts. The only difference between hospitality marketing and destination marketing is that most destination marketing activities are likely to be undertaken by public agencies such as NTOs with the support and help of private hospitality organizations.

A factor that is likely to influence the success of any tourist destination is local residents' attitudes toward tourists and tourism. Any tourism development in a destination and any marketing activity that is not supported by local residents is likely to fail. To make sound marketing decisions, an NTO or its subset needs to constantly monitor any changes occurring in the environment and travelers' behaviors and take a proactive posture in its marketing programs.

Because of the importance of building positive destination images, in the future, NTOs and their subsets will continue to play an important image building and image communication role in the marketplace. However, to communicate the desired image, an NTO needs to understand the factors that are likely to influence travelers' information search behavior and develop communication strategies that are aligned with their search behavior. At the same time, NTOs will play a greater role as facilitators for market research and as collaborators of market efforts by the private sector of the tourism industry.

■ Key Terms

market geographies   market psychographics
market demographics   market behaviors

■| Discussion Questions

1. Choose a little-known or remote destination of the world. Research and discuss the environmental influences that affect tourism in that destination.
2. Choose a destination in the world that has a negative image for you. What created this image? Research and show what this destination could do to overcome it. If it does, can it meet expectations?
3. Describe how you would promote your own hometown. What research would you do?

■| Group Projects

1. Visit the following official sites by ministries of tourism of nations in the Eastern Mediterranean and then answer the questions that follow:
   - www.tourismturkey.org/
   - www.syriatourism.org/
   - www.lebanon-tourism.gov.lb/
   - www.tourism.gov.il/tourism/default/homepage.aspx
   - www.tourism.jo/Home/index.htm
     a. Which nation's site gives you the best idea about the geographic location of the nation?
     b. How many clicks are required from the first web page to find visa requirements for you to visit this nation (whatever nationality you are)? If U.S. passport holders are not required to have a visa, is the nation using that fact in a positive way to lure U.S. passport holders?
     c. How convenient is it to access a hotel reservation site from the first page?
     d. Which nation appeals to you most as a potential place for a relaxation holiday or a holiday of exotic exploration?

■| References

1. World Tourism Organization. Historical perspective of world tourism. Retrieved from www.world-tourism.org/facts/menu.html. November 1, 2005.
2. Gursoy, D. and Rutherford, D. (2004). Host attitudes toward tourism: An improved structural model. *Annals of Tourism Research*, 31(3): 495–516.
3. Gursoy, D., Jurowski, C., and Uysal, M. (2002). Resident's Attitudes: A Structural Modeling Approach. *Annals of Tourism Research*, 29 (1), 79–105.
4. East Asian countries launch campaigns to revive tourism lost to SARS. (2003, June 9). *Travel Agent*, 83–84.
5. UNWTO World Tourism Barometer. (2004 October), 2 (3), 6.
6. World Tourism Organization. (2005, October 18). Avian flu: Overreaction could damage tourism industry, says WTO [press release]. Retrieved November 29, 2005, from www.world-tourism.org/newsroom/menu.htm.
7. Travel Industry Association of America. (2004). *Emerging international tourism markets: Trends and insights*, 2004 Edition.
8. World Tourism Organization. (2005, May 19). Asian destinations on the rise in world tourism ranking [press release]. Retrieved November 7, 2005, from www.world-tourism.org/newsroom/menu.htm.
9. Japanese Ministry of Land Infrastructure and Transport. White Paper on Transport. (1987). Realization of more comfortable life and transport in a society open to the world. Retrieved November 7, 2005, from www.mlit.go.jp/english/white-paper/unyu-whitepaper/1987/1987010101-123.html.
10. Pacific Asia Travel Association PATA. (2005, September 27). Russia's middle classes trip out [press release]. Retrieved October 9, 2005, from www.pata.org/patasite/index.php?id=1133&backPID=1133&tt_news=211.
11. Salma, Umme. (2002, Spring). Indirect economic contribution of tourism to Australia, 1997-98 to 2000-01. *Australian Bureau of Tourism Research Report*, 4 (2).
12. Retrieved January 3, 2006, from www.allstays.com/Services/2005/04/new-us-travel-restrictions.htm.
13. Tiplady, R. (2004, December 13). The Year of the Chinese Tourist. *BusinessWeek Online*. Retrieved November 8, 2005, from www.businessweek.com/magazine/content/04_50/b3912081_mz054.htm.
14. Travel Industry Association of America. (2003). Geotourism: The new trend in travel. Executive Summary.
15. The World Bank. (2005, September 6). Mexico: World Bank approves $200.5 million for sustainable development [press release]. No. 2006/06/LAC.
16. Tourism statistics for India. (2005, October 4). *Federation of Hotel & Restaurant Associations of India (FHRAI) Magazine*. Retrieved November 8, 2005, from www.fhrai.com/mag-news/magTourismStatisticsIndia.asp.
17. Gursoy, D. and McCleary, K. W. (2004). An integrative model of tourist's information search behavior. *Annals of Tourism Research*, 31(2): 353–373.

Part IV

Situational Analysis

Chapter 10
Understanding
Competition

Chapter 11
Marketing Intelligence
and Research

Understanding Competition

Overview

This chapter provides a thorough examination of the subject of competition: the different types; how to defend against it; and how to determine it, compare it, and measure it. Businesses need to know and choose with whom they compete and not leave this critical consideration to chance or pick the wrong competition. This chapter also refers to competitive intelligence or the collective insights and knowledge about competitors to which you need access in order to gain a sustainable competitive advantage. Finally, we discuss market feasibility studies, which involve analyzing projects to see whether they are feasible in terms of customers and finances.

I. Introduction to Hospitality Marketing
1. The Concept of Marketing
2. Marketing Services and the Hospitality Experience
3. The Marketing Mix and the Product/Service Mix
4. Relationship/Loyalty Marketing

II. Marketing to Build a Competitive Advantage
5. Strategic Marketing
6. The Strategic Marketing System and Marketing Objectives

VII. Feedback

VI. Synthesis
21. The Marketing Plan

III. The Marketplace
7. Understanding Individual Customers
8. Understanding Organizational Customers
9. The Tourist Customer and the Tourism Destination

IV. Situational Analysis
10. *Understanding Competition*
11. Marketing Intelligence and Research

V. Functional Strategies
12. Differentiation, Segmentation, and Target Marketing
13. Branding and Market Positioning
14. The Hospitality Pricing Mix
15. The Communications Mix: Advertising
16. The Communications Mix: Sales Promotions, Merchandising, Public Relations, and Publicity
17. The Communications Mix: Personal Selling
18. Hospitality Distribution Systems
19. Channels of Distribution: Bringing the Customer to the Product
20. Interactive Marketing: Internet and Database Marketing

Hirohide Abe has been director of strategic marketing at Hyatt International Corporation, a subsidiary of Chicago-based Global Hyatt Corporation, since 2002. In this role, he oversees the company's strategic marketing including business intelligence, marketing communications, advertising, brand standards, and budgeting. He supports more than 90 hotels located in over 40 countries worldwide. Previously, he served as director of marketing at Park Hyatt Tokyo.

Marketing in Action
Hirohide Abe, Director of Strategic Marketing, Global Hyatt Corporation

How should a hospitality firm define the competition?

We are surrounded by dynamic business environments. Traditionally, we have defined our competitive set by looking at those hotels with similar price range, product type, and location. However, we should define our competitive environment from our customers' point of view. Customers compare hotel dining with local independent restaurants. They look at our spa against their local spas. Hotel weddings compete with independent banquet facilities. Customers may choose videoconferencing rather than staying at a hotel for a meeting. They may prefer catering at home rather than entertaining at an outside venue. Customers also have access to diverse booking channels and packaging, which means we must compete to sell our brand rather than be shown as a commodity. We need to understand how our customers see us, product by product, channel by channel, and market by market.

How does a firm ensure that it identifies the "right" competition?

We use various competitive intelligence data to determine competitor performance, including booking trends, etc. However, this data is not enough to understand our markets. We tend to think we know customers, but their attitudes are always changing. We constantly talk with customers and ask them why they would or would not choose us, what percentage of their business they give to us, what alternatives they consider besides Hyatt, and what new products and services appeal to them.

How do you ask the customers this information?

Market and consumer research is critical to our understanding of customers. We have such diversified emerging markets around the world that we would be lost without it. Wherever we do research, we discuss the items I mentioned in the previous question.

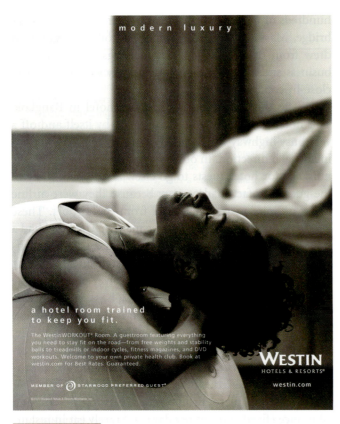

EXHIBIT 10-3 This advertisement for Westin Hotels & Resorts is trying to steal customers from the competition.
Source: Westin Hotels & Resorts. Used by permission.

Tourism Marketing Application
Use your favorite web browser and type in the words "competition tourism destination." You will find many articles on this topic. Read one of the articles and be prepared to discuss it in class.

First, deliberately choose with whom you want, and can, compete. Rarely do markets simply appear out of nowhere; most of the time you have to entice them away from a competitor. Exhibit 10-3 provides an example of advertisement for a firm trying to steal guests from the competition. Specifically, the WestinWORKOUT Room is competing against other hotels that claim to have gyms. They are going one step further. As Michael Porter pointed out in his extensive writings on competition, choosing with whom you want to compete is one of the first decisions that has to be made in developing a product or business.[3] Of course, as we discussed in the beginning of the book, the first decision that has to be made is which customer need we are trying to fill or which customer problem we are trying to solve.

The second way to determine how we compete is to ask customers where they would be if they were not at your property. This is easy to do as guests are checking into your property. After welcoming the guest, first ask, "If you had not come here, where would you have stayed?" Then ask, "Why?" Or, if you're developing a new product, research the market. Investigate what problems customers currently have. Attempt to determine their needs. Then investigate where they go now to solve their problems or fulfill their needs. Why? The answers to these questions will tell you, at least, who the market perceives to be your competition. The answers will also reveal what you have to compete against in terms of attributes and services. If the market identifies properties that are different from the ones against which you have chosen to compete, it is clear that your perception differs from the market's.* You may need to rethink your competitive strategy.

We can illustrate these two points with further reference to hotel F&B outlets. Astute marketers will first determine whom they desire as customers and what their needs, wants, and problems are. (This includes in-house customers and the local market.) Then they will ask where these customers go now or will go. Next, they will undertake a thorough analysis of the potential competition. Then they will go to the architect, the F&B director and other involved parties, and say, "This is what we need to do to keep, steal, or create these customers." Then, and only then, should concept development begin, because you have now chosen with whom you will compete. You have also determined the weapons you will need to compete.

Competitive Intensity

The **competitive intensity** in a marketplace is the fierceness with which competing companies do battle with each other. It is an important measurement in competitive analysis because the level of intensity will often dictate the way a firm does business. In general, competitive intensity is very high in the hospitality industry. This can lead to less-than-wise decisions to gain competitive advantage. Jain put it as follows:

The degree of competition in a market depends upon the moves and countermoves of the various firms active in the market. It usually starts with one firm trying to achieve a favorable position by pursuing appropriate strategies [or tactics]. Because what is good for one firm may be harmful to rival firms, however, rival firms respond with counter strategies [or tactics] to protect their own interests. Intense competitive activity may or may not be inju-

---

*In a study we did in Boston, the Parker House management viewed its major competitor as the Ritz-Carlton. Very few of its customers, however, gave the Ritz-Carlton as an alternative; no Ritz-Carlton guests gave the Parker House as an alternative.

rious to the industry as a whole. For example, while a price war may result in lower profits for all members of an industry, an advertising battle may increase demand and actually be mutually beneficial.[4]

Exhibit 10-4 shows some factors contributing to competitive intensity in the hospitality industry.

It is a marketing truism that all opportunities are not necessarily competitive advantages. Consider the so-called hotel amenities wars in the 1980s:

> The amenities wars started in the United States in the early 1980s with one hotel chain adopting the European custom of putting a mint on the pillow and turning the bed down. Other hotel chains followed suit and the mints got better and more expensive. Then someone started with special soaps, soon followed by shampoos, body lotions, shoe horns and so on and then a choice of soaps, body lotions, shampoos, bubble baths and so on. In some cases, all this added well over $10.00 per occupied night to the cost of the room for the hotel.

No hotel company bothered to do research to determine what effect all these amenities really did have on the customer or read the research others were doing.[5] At the same time, hotel guests were filling their suitcases with the amenities and stocking their home medicine cabinets. Finally, Michael Leven, then president of Holiday Inn, Americas Division, and now president of Microtel, called a halt: "Bubble bath is not [in]. We are off Vidal Sassoon and into reality."[6] Today, in the lower-tier segments, the amenities wars are over with no winners except the manufacturers who made them. However, they are starting again in the luxury segment.

The amenities wars story demonstrates some important things about competitive intensity. First, services that can be easily duplicated offer only short-term advantage, if that, when you have aggressive competitors. When those services are not perceived as a determinative advantage by customers and instead end up costing them more for the core product, such services may in fact become a negative factor for the entire product class. At one point, Marriott quietly cut down its bathroom amenities package from a cost of five dollars to less than one dollar and suffered no ill effects. However, the definition of an amenity has changed. It is no longer just soap, but other things, as shown in Exhibit 10-5.

 Web Browsing Exercise

Go to your favorite web browser and type in "hotel amenities." Prepare a list of the amenities that you see being promoted. Which are unique? How do the hotels promote their amenities?

Second, when introducing an additional service, you need to anticipate how your competitors will react. Third, competitive tactics should, as much as possible, be based on the needs of the customer and not on the competition, unless this is necessary for the firm's self-protection. It is also critical to realize that competitors may have different strategies, different ownership structures, and different cost structures that may allow them to do things that your firm cannot do. Blindly copying them may be a financial catastrophe. Just because one firm adds something, it does

---

EXHIBIT 10-4   Factors Contributing to Competitive Intensity

- *Opportunity Potential:*   A promising market increases the number of firms interested in sharing the pie, thus increasing the rivalry.
- *Ease of Entry:*   When entry into an industry is relatively easy, the existing firms try to discourage potential entrants by adopting strategies that increase competition.
- *Nature of Product:*   When the products offered are perceived by the market as more or less similar, properties are forced into price and service competition, which can be quite severe in some locations.
- *Exit Barriers:*   High investments in assets for which there may not be a readily alternative use and top management's emotional attachment force companies into competitive methods in order to improve or even survive.
- *Homogeneity of the Market:*   When segments of the market are more or less homogeneous, the competitive intensity is increased to gain market share.
- *Industry Structure:*   When the number of firms active in the market is large, one or more may aggressively seek an advantageous position, leading to intense competitive activity as other firms retaliate.
- *Commitment to the Industry:*   When a company has committed itself, it will do most anything to hang on without worrying about the impact on either the industry or its own resources.

- *Technological Innovations:*   In industries where these are frequent, each firm tries to cash in on the latest technology by quickly copying what other firms do, creating competitive activity.
- *Scale Economies:*   Attempts to gain scale economies may lead a firm to aggressively compete for market share, escalating pressure on other firms. Or, when fixed costs are high, a firm tries to spread them over larger volume.
- *Economic Climate:*   When the economy is down and growth is slow, competition is much more volatile as each firm tries to make the best of a bad situation.
- *Diversity of Firms:*   New entries into an industry do not necessarily play by the rules of a kind of industry standard of behavior. Instead, they may have different strategic perspectives and be willing to go to any lengths to achieve their goals.

Source: Adapted from Jain, S. C. (1997). *Marketing planning and strategy* (5th ed.). Cincinnati: South-Western, 77–78. Reprinted with permission of South-Western, a division of Thomson Learning: www.thomsonrights.com. Fax 800 730-2215.

EXHIBIT 10-5 Swissotel New York shows that a hotel room is much more than a bed.

Source: Swissotels & Resorts. Used by permission.

EXHIBIT 10-6 Renaissance Hotels & Resorts makes a play for its competition's customers.

Source: Marriott International, Inc. Used by permission.

not mean your customers want the same thing. Consider the case of Hilton's HHonors frequent guest program. This program bases it differentiation on the fact that it rewards guests with both hotel points and airline miles. In principle, it would be easy for other hotel firms to offer the same. However, the other hotel chains chose not to. Why? Because their research showed that their customers would rather these chains spend money on other things.

Does this mean that a hotel or restaurant should not try to gain competitive advantage by introducing services that are easily duplicated? No, it does not or else there would never be growth or improvement. There is also something to be said for being there first. After all, it took the major hotel firms many years to copy Westin's Heavenly Bed. It does mean, however, that the intensity of the competition is a critical factor and should be carefully weighed before making the decision.

It also means going back to the customer first. Does the amenity create or keep customers? If yes, at what cost to them and at what cost to the property? Does the amenity increase the price–value relationship or just price? If it is to be done, in what meaningful way can it be done—that is, do we know what the customer really wants? If the competition follows suit, do we retain an advantage or just an additional cost? The best competitive advantages are those that are sustainable.

When the needs of the market are similar, the intensity of competition is much greater as many entries in the market are competing for the same customer (see the example in Exhibit 10-6). Small competitive advantages can become large ones if they can be sustained. On the other hand, it may be mandatory for one firm to copy another that is aggressively seeking an advantageous position, if it can do so, in order to eliminate the advantage. The hotel "business room," for example, has been copied by so many that the advantage has not been sustainable by the first provider. It has, however, filled a need, solved problems, added value for the customer, and today is an essential part of the product offering for many commercial hotels.

EXHIBIT 10-7	**Competitive Innovations in Hotels over the Past 20 Years**

- *Frequent Guest Programs:* Programs designed to build customer loyalty by providing special privileges and free travel opportunities to frequent guests.
- *Strategic Alliance:* Efforts made by firms to formally cooperate in such programs as advertising and marketing, sharing products and customers and financing activities designed to maximize hotel occupancy.
- *Computer Reservation Systems:* First pioneered by Holiday Inn, these programs work similarly to airline reservation systems. Designed to fill rooms at rates that maximize the revenue yield per room, these programs also make it easier for the customer and travel agent to secure desired accommodations at appropriate prices.
- *Amenities:* Added products and services available to the guest once they have registered. Often include toiletries and in-room services.
- *Branding:* Attempts by hotel companies to create and deliver new products to the customer. Often thought of as levels of service such as budget, economy, luxury and business class hotels. Each product is associated with specific products and services to differentiate it from the competition. Brands are available in several of these segments as well.
- *Technological Innovation:* This method includes a wide array of advancements designed to improve the products and services offered by hotels. They include all elements of communication systems, decision support systems for management, accounting services, safety and security programs, energy and conservation programs, automated check-in and check-out services, etc.
- *Niche Marketing and Advertising:* These programs were designed to zero in on specific target markets emphasizing special products and services to those markets.
- *Pricing Tactics:* This method is generally viewed as discounting and yield management (maximizing the revenue per room based upon demand projections).
- *Cost Containment:* The attempt to operate as efficiently as possible by reducing all costs associated with running a hotel.
- *Service Quality Management:* The attempt by hotels to improve service quality by such techniques as Total Quality Management, continuous process improvement, etc.
- *International Expansion:* As current markets become saturated, hotel firms seek expansion into new overseas markets.
- *Travel Agent Valuation:* This method seeks to improve relations with the travel agent industry in order to secure greater volumes of business. This includes agent reward and incentive schemes.

- *Franchising and the Management Fee:* This method of growth is viewed as a competitive method for those firms that possess unique capacity to deliver the necessary capabilities in each case.
- *Employees as Important Assets:* This method places new value on the role of the employee in delivering and executing high quality products and services.
- *In-Room Sales and Entertainment:* This method offers an array of possibilities to improve the revenue yield of each rented room by providing such items as pay-per-view on-demand movies, beverages, snacks and concierge services.
- *Special Services for Frequent Guests:* This program goes beyond the early frequent guest programs and offers such attributes as automated check-in and out, special seating, lounges, merchandise discounts in the hotel and overall improved choices and upgrades for all products and services. (As discussed in Chapter 4, the frequent guest programs for the large chains enable this to happen.)
- *Conservation/Ecology Programs:* Methods in this category are designed to address the guest's growing awareness for conservation and desire for clean air in the hotel and its rooms. It is seen as a way of attracting guests who value these efforts.
- *Business Services:* Designed to meet the needs of the increasingly pressured business traveler, these methods include a full range of business services in the hotel and/or room as well as a full range of communication services.
- *Database Management:* This method takes advantage of growing technological capabilities to fully track the guest and his or her habits. This information is now being fully integrated into all other information systems utilized by the hotel.
- *Core Business Management:* The recognition of doing one or few things well underpins this method. Firms have divested themselves of peripheral business units in order to concentrate on the core business of hotel management.
- *Direct Customer Marketing:* The information highway and advancing technology now make it possible for firms to sell directly to the customer using information provided by database marketing programs. This method will grow in popularity as more travelers seek to make their own travel plans through such channels as the Internet.

Source: Olsen, M. D., Zhao, J. L., Cho, W., & Tse, E. (1997). Hotel industry performance and competitive methods: A decade in review: 1985–1994. In *Into the new millennium, a white paper on the global hospitality industry*, 33. Paris: International Hotel and Restaurant Association. Used by permission.

Michael Olsen and his colleagues' extensive international research uncovered major hotel industry competitive innovations over the past 20 years. Their findings are shown in Exhibit 10-7. All were quickly copied by competitors. Some have added value; some have not. In other words, some were successful and some were not in both gaining and keeping customers.

Web Browsing Exercise

Go to your favorite web browser and type in the words "hotel innovations." What do you find that has been innovative lately in hotels? Are these innovations easily copied by others? What consumer needs are being fulfilled by the innovation(s)?

Competitive Intelligence

As in war, one always wants to know what the enemy is doing, their position and intentions, strengths and weaknesses, where they are most vulnerable and least vulnerable, and where the best place is to attack. There are a number of ways to get this information, and it is well worth getting. It goes beyond physical property descriptions. The movie *Godfather II* taught us one thing about this: Be close to your friends, but closer to your enemies.

First, there is public information. The media (especially the World Wide Web today), articles in the trade press, information available through trade associations, annual reports for publicly traded firms, company brochures, flyers and ads, publicity releases, and so forth, are examples of some sources. Mission statements, discussed in earlier chapters, essentially lay out the strategy of the firm. Then there is trade gossip—information from vendors and others who deal with the competition; for example, consulting and accounting firms, universities, local convention and visitors bureaus, and local hotel and restaurant associations.

Another technique for getting information is simply to talk to your competitors. You might do this one on one or at industry conferences and trade shows. You can also talk to your customers, who might have been your competitors' customers. You can talk to your employees, who might have been your competitors' employees or at least might know some of their employees. Finally, there is always merit to visiting or using the competitor's product. Do not forget, of course, that while you are doing this, so is the competition! Finally, there are measurable differences that can be determined, which are outlined in the following sections.

Market Share

In some areas, hotels exchange room occupancy percentages and average rate figures nightly by mutual arrangement. In addition, firms such as Smith Travel Research, TravelCLICK, and the Daily Bench provide competitive information on a daily basis. Many restaurant operators do likewise. (An old restaurant trick is to drive around and count cars in parking lots, but beware of employee cars!) These arrangements are beneficial because they tell you how you are doing relative to the others. Refusing to share this information or lying to each other is generally self-defeating. It still remains to discover why you are doing better or worse.

Comparison figures of occupancy and restaurant covers are called **market share** figures and are used to compare **actual market share** with **fair market share**, or that amount of business you could expect if you received your proportional share of the total business conducted by the properties that comprise the competitive set. In computing fair market share, you must be sure you are comparing apples with apples—in other words, with other properties in the same competitive set (those that are directly competitive in the same product class who are competing for the same customers). Management needs to be realistic about identifying the proper competitive set. This means that you will often make this calculation multiple times. For instance, you would make calculations for the leisure travel segment, for the group segment, and the like. To calculate your fair market share, you divide your capacity by total capacity in the product class. This is the share you should get if every competitor is performing equally well. To compute actual market share, divide your actual occupancy (or covers) by total competitive set occupancy. Then compare actual to fair market share as a measure of how well you are doing relative to the competition. The goal is for your market share to exceed your fair share. We illustrate this with an example.

Consider the hypothetical example shown in Exhibit 10-8 for one city area for one night. All of the participants in the analysis are not in the same product class. This does not mean that you are not interested in their occupancy—for instance, it would be worthwhile to know why middle-tier properties are running at higher occupancy than upper-tier properties. It might indicate that the upper-tier properties are pricing themselves out of the market, or it could mean something entirely different, for instance, concerning the type of business that was in town last night.

Now consider the market shares of the properties in your competitive set. Hotel C's actual share is considerably lower than its fair share (46.2 percent versus 35.2 percent). But look at the size of this hotel; it is still filling more rooms than any of the others in the analysis. Perhaps this is prima-

EXHIBIT 10-8	Hypothetical Example of Market Share				
Hotel	Actual Rooms	Rooms Sold	Occupancy %	Fair Share %	Actual Share %
Upper-Tier Hotels					
A	300	220	73.3	11.5	15.5
B	500	350	70.0	19.2	24.7
C	1,200	500	41.7	46.2	35.2
Yours	600	350	58.3	23.1	24.7
Total	2,600	1,420	54.6	100.0	100.0
Middle-Tier Hotels					
E	275	220	80.0	31.3	39.6
F	425	360	84.7	48.3	50.0
G	180	140	77.8	20.4	19.4
Total	880	720	81.8	100.0	100.0

rily a convention hotel with widely fluctuating occupancies; perhaps it should not be included in the same competitive set. What this means is that one has to interpret these figures with discretion before making judgments.

As you can see, your hotel is getting slightly more than its fair market share (actual share is 24.7 and fair share is 23.1) and would not be doing so even if Hotel C's occupancy were up. Hotels A and B, however, are substantially exceeding their fair share (15.5 versus 11.5 for Hotel A and 24.7 versus 19.2 for Hotel B for actual share and fair share). What, you might ask, are they doing right? Or, what are you doing wrong? This calls for an examination of their segments and marketing strategies.

REVPAR

While market share is one method of measuring relative performance in the marketplace, the calculation of **revenue per available room (REVPAR)** is another method commonly employed in the hotel industry. REVPAR is calculated by dividing the room revenue by the number of rooms available for sale. It can also be calculated by multiplying the average daily rate (ADR) by the occupancy percentage. The fallacy of market share is that a competitor can gain actual share in the market at the expense of room rates. By dropping its rates $10, more people may book at that hotel. REVPAR measures the revenue generated per available room and essentially controls for pricing decisions. REVPAR is the method most widely used in the industry today.

The REVPAR calculation more accurately measures the balance of marketing efforts as shown in Exhibit 10-9. The middle-tier hotels indicate better asset management. Their REVPARs are comparable to the upper-tier hotels or better, and they undoubtedly are lower-cost producers. One possible conclusion is that they are stealing business from the upper-tier hotels with lower rates. Another is that, on this particular day, the upper-tier hotels had booked lower-rate conference groups. In any case, the reason needs to be examined on a regular basis. Trends are more enlightening than calculations performed to evaluate single days, and other conclusions might be drawn.

Yield Index

Given that a firm knows the REVPAR and revenue in the market, it is possible to calculate the yield index. The **yield index** is calculated two ways. One way is to divide the property REVPAR by the market REVPAR. The second way is to examine the yield in terms of revenue. Here, the calculation is share of revenue divided by the share of supply in the market. An index of greater than 1.0 indicates that the hotel is outperforming the market, whereas an index of less than 1.0 indicates that the hotel is underperforming the market. The yield index is shown in the last column of Exhibit 10-10. What conclusions can be drawn?

> **Tourism Marketing Application**
>
> The demand for tourist destinations is based on three measures: visitor arrivals, visitor-days or visitor nights, and amount spent. Visitor arrivals is easy to determine if travelers arrive by airplane or other form of public transportation. However, statistics from the U.S. government are more difficult to collect; those provided by state governments are much easier to collect. The visitor days/visitor nights is simply the number of visitors times the average number of days or nights at the destination. The amount spent is usually based on a percentage of sales tax collected. (From The Howard Johnson Team, February 1, 1979, Razing the orange roof, *Restaurant Business*, 123-134.)

EXHIBIT 10-9	**Hypothetical Example of REVPAR**

Hotel	Actual Rooms	Rooms Sold	Occupancy %	Average Daily Rate (ADR)	Revenue	REVPAR	Yield Index
Upper-Tier Hotels							
A	300	220	73.3	$120	$26,400	$88.00	1.17
B	500	350	70.0	130	45,500	91.00	1.21
C	1,200	500	41.7	150	75,000	62.50	0.83
Yours	600	350	58.3	140	49,000	81.67	1.08
Total	2,600	1,420	54.6	137.96	195,900	75.35	1.00
Middle-Tier Hotels							
E	275	220	80.0	$110	$24,200	$88.00	1.06
F	425	360	84.7	100	36,000	84.70	1.02
G	180	140	77.8	90	12,600	70.00	0.85
Total	880	720	81.8	101.11	72,800	82.70	1.00

REVPOR

Another, less widely used measurement tool is **revenue per occupied room (REVPOR)**. It is gaining in popularity, however. This method includes all revenue attributed to each occupied room such as food and beverage expenses, telephone and minibar charges, room service, and so forth. Assume, in the example in Exhibit 10-9, that in your hotel you had additional room charges that night of $10,000. Your REVPOR would be $10,000 plus $49,000 divided by 350 rooms or $168.57. This tool can also look at the type of guest (market segment) to reveal who your most valuable customers are in terms of how much they spend in total. In the previous example your average is $168.57. Any customer exceeding this amount would be more valuable in terms of his or her average total expenditures than any customer spending less than this amount.

Of course, you could apply the same logic to REVPAR only we would have to find a new acronym (maybe TOTREVPAR, total revenue per available room?). We have not seen this done yet but it may still come and has merit. The caveat in either case, however, is whether people charge these additional expenses to their room or pay in some other manner. For example, one might use a credit card or pay cash in the restaurant. Or, to confuse it more, how do you handle the restaurant room charge when someone takes others to dinner and charges it all to his room or even a conference food bill? All of this would have to be sorted out to develop a protocol. However, for some hotels, this would be revealing information.

REVPAC

What some consider a major measurement tool of the future is **revenue per available customer (REVPAC)**. The method requires advanced technology in a fully integrated system tying reservations to the property management system (PMS) across all units of the company including all strategic business units (SBUs). What is being measured is total yield per available customer.* From a marketing point of view this makes a great deal of sense.

Consider this: Marriott has a business traveler who stays regularly at its hotels and charges everything in the hotel to his room. At conferences, he often stays at a Marriott Marquis. For getaway weekends, he stays at a Marriott Courtyard, except when he goes on a golfing vacation, when he plays on a Marriott golf course. When he goes to see his grandchildren, he likes a Marriott Fairfield Inn nearby. For vacations he buys a Marriott time share. When his company relocates him, he stays at a Marriott all-suite Residence Inn until he finds a place to live. When he travels to the Far East, he prefers a Marriott-owned Renaissance Hotel. For his 25th wedding anniversary, he stays at a Marriott-owned Ritz-Carlton. An integrated system to keep track of all this is putting it mildly, but the marketing information derived could be a very powerful tool for use in developing profiles for others.

In a lesser form, REVPAC is used today primarily by resorts to measure total spending of the customer including golf, skiing, spa, tennis, and so forth. REVPAC is used in the casino industry. Part of the calculation of REVPAC is what is known as the "theoretical win" of the customer. This calculation multiplies the following pieces of information together: the average bet per hand or spin of the wheel, the house advantage of the game, the length of playing time, and the number of bets made during the playing time. For instance, consider a person who plays roulette for one hour and bets $10 per spin. The house advantage in roulette is 5.25 percent, which means that for every $1 bet, the house earns 5.25 cents. If there are 60 bets per hour, the theoretical win of our player would be $10 \times 60 \times 1 \times .0525$. This equals $31.50. To this value the casino would add money spent in the hotel, at shows, in the lounges, and so on.

> **Tourism Marketing Application**
>
> To determine the demand for a destination, look at the following factors: (1) economic distance: the cost and time required to go from origin to destination; (2) cultural distance: the difference between the culture of the origin and the culture of the destination; (3) cost of services at the destination: hotels, restaurants, etc.; (4) quality of services offered at the destination; (5) seasonality of the destination: time of year vacation is planned; (6) psychographics of the traveler: attitudes, interests, and opinions; (7) demographics of the traveler; and (8) effectiveness of the marketing of the destination. (From Charles R. Goeldner, J. R. Brent Ritchie, and Robert W. McIntosh (2000). *Tourism: Principles, Practices, Philosophies*, Eighth Edition. New York: John Wiley & Sons, pages 396–398.)

Internet REVPAR

As the Internet is becoming a more significant channel of distribution and source of business, many hotels are beginning to track this as well. Internet REVPAR is calculated by dividing the revenue generated by Internet sources (lo-

---

*REVPAC is somewhat akin to, but still different from, the lifetime value of a customer, which we discussed in Chapter 4.

cal website, brand website, and third party sites) by the number of available rooms in the hotel. This calculation can then be measured against competitive hotels to determine the percentage of business generated by the Internet.

Purchased Data

More sophisticated operators use third party services to gain market share data (and avoid possible antitrust violations). Smith Travel Research (STR) of Hendersonville, Tennessee, is the primary provider of this information to the hotel industry in the United States. Each month and now each day, STR generates STAR reports for the majority of lodging establishments in the United States. Exhibit 10-10 is an example of this information.

Other types of competitive data include information from TravelCLICK, which offers competitive data from the GDS channels. The Daily Bench, a firm based in the United Kingdom, is similar to Smith Travel Research (for their websites, see the Web Browsing Exercise on page xxx).

Exhibit 10-10 is for a fictitious property located near the Nashville airport for the month of November. The data for the ABC Inn is real (derived by adding the performance of several properties in the area and dividing through by a constant), and the results shown on the report are valid. A brief review indicates a property with below-average performance. We explain this in Exhibit 10-11.

Web Browsing Exercise

Go to the websites for TravelCLICK (www.travelclick.net), the Daily Bench (www.thedailybench.com), and Smith Travel Research (www.smithtravelresearch.com). Compare and contrast the different offerings. What other information do they provide that can be helpful to the marketing executive? Be sure to read their sample reports.

Restaurant Comparisons

Revenue per square foot (RSQFT) and **revenue per available seat (REVPAS)** are two very new market share methods developed for restaurants. Both calculate competitive restaurant share by measuring one restaurant's position against that of the competition. Exhibit 10-12 shows how this is done.

Customer Satisfaction Index

Another way to understand how a firm is perceived relative to the competition is to calculate a customer satisfaction index (CSI). The CSI is a weighted average of the importance and performance scores that are generated when conducting customer research. The CSI is only relevant if the correct features are measured. The higher the CSI, the more the property meets customers' needs on an overall basis. Because it is a weighted average, the influence of individual variables is minimized. The calculation

---

EXHIBIT 10-10	Example of a STAR Report from Smith Travel Research

	Performance Report			Market Share Report		
	Occupancy %	Average Room Rate	Room Sales per Available Room	Room Sales	Room Supply	Room Demand
Market Segment						
ABC Inn	56.8	$41.93	$23.81			
Market Segment						
Nashville, Tenn.	66.1	$58.07	$38.38	100.0	100.0	100.0
ABC Inn				0.4	0.6	0.5
Price Level						
Mid-Price	62.5	$42.90	$26.81	21.4	30.7	29.0
ABC Inn				1.7	2.0	1.8
Selected Competitors						
Competitors	75.0	$46.74	$35.06	4.4	4.8	5.5
ABC Inn				8.5	12.5	9.5
Market Tract						
Nashville E.						
Airport	68.1	$68.44	$46.61	51.8	42.6	43.9
ABC Inn				0.7	1.4	1.2
Tract by Price Tier						
Middle Tier	57.1	$41.87	$23.91	9.5	18.6	15.5
ABC Inn				7.6	7.6	7.4
Tract by Segment						
Small Chains/Independent	62.6	$41.60	$26.04	16.0	28.7	26.4
ABC Inn				4.5	4.9	4.5

Source: Smith, R. A. (1996, February). How to succeed by the numbers. *Lodging*, 19. Used by permission.

EXHIBIT 10-11	Explanation of the STAR Report in Exhibit 10-10

With occupancy of 56.8 percent, the ABC occupancy is nearly 10 percentage points below the Nashville market and 12 points less than the Nashville East airport tract. The difference narrows somewhat when you compare the ABC Inn's occupancy performance with its specific price tier and chain segment. Relative to other properties in the middle price tier in this tract, the ABC Inn is comparable in terms of both occupancy and room rates.

The most important comparison is with its competitive set. These properties have a substantial occupancy premium and nearly a five dollar rate premium above the ABC Inn. As a result, REVPAR for the competitive set is nearly $12, or 50 percent more than the ABC Inn. This difference is highlighted in the market share section of the report where the ABC Inn has 12.5 percent of the supply, but only 9.5 percent of the demand and 8.5 percent of the room sales.

Based on this data, the ABC Inn has a penetration index of 76.0 (computed by dividing 56.8 percent property occupancy by 75 percent competitive set occupancy or by dividing 9.5 percent demand share by 12.5 percent supply share) and a yield index of 68 percent (computed by dividing $23.81 property room rate by $35.06 competitive set room rate or by dividing 8.5 percent revenue share by 12.5 percent supply share). Since both indices are less than 100, the property is not achieving its fair market share of rooms sold or rooms revenue. Further, REVPAR has declined by 1.6 percent for ABC, but rose 4.9 percent for the competitive set.

All this does not bode well for ABC. One next step might be to review the competitors' facilities. This might indicate a need for renovation to restore ABC's competitive position. Another review might be that of the marketing program and sales effort. In any case, a competitive analysis is called for. A competitive market analysis is an essential first step in evaluating whether a problem is property specific or a function of the competitive market.

Source: Olsen, M. D., Zhao, J. L., Cho, W., & Tse, E. (1997). Hotel industry performance and competitive methods: A decade in review: 1985–1994. In *Into the new millennium, a white paper on the global hospitality industry*, 19–21. Paris: International Hotel Association.

of the CSI is visually shown in Exhibit 10-13. The steps are as follows:

1. For each attribute, multiply the importance score by the performance. Although this could be done for each individual customer, it is often calculated using averages. This necessitates that the CSI be calculated by customer segment. As shown in the tables, the numbers in Column A are multiplied by the numbers in Column B for Brand A and the numbers in Column A are multiplied by the numbers in Column D for Brand B. The results of the multiplication appear in Column C for Brand A and Column E for Brand B.
2. Sum the importance ratings for all features. These numbers are in Column A in Exhibit 10-13. Multiply this sum by the number of scale points. In the example presented, the scale was 1 to 10.
3. Sum all numbers in Column C and Column E. Multiply this sum by the number of scale points (in this case 10, as a 10-point scale was used).
4. Calculate the CSI for each brand. For Brand A, this is calculated by dividing the company total score in Column C by the total score in Column A. For Brand B, this is calculated by dividing the company total score in Column D by the total score in Column A. Then, multiply each response by 100.
5. Interpretation: The higher the number, the greater the overall satisfaction. The CSI is best used to compare one property against a multiple of other properties.

Please note that the numbers in Exhibit 10-13 do not reflect real figures. Rather, they are provided only to demonstrate the calculation. The results in Exhibit 10-13 reveal that Company A performs better than Company B on the features measured. Exhibit 10-14 provides an example of the questionnaire wording used to generate the responses.

Perceptual Mapping

Another way to analyze competitive intelligence is through the construction of **perceptual maps** that plot customers' perceptions of your property versus those of your competitors. This technique may involve simple plotting or sophisticated statistical methods known as multidimensional scaling or discriminant analysis. The technique may be used to evaluate a single property or multiple properties. Consider Exhibit 10-16, which shows how a single firm performs on features that are important to the customer.

The numbers on the axis in Exhibit 10-15 represent the scale used in the questionnaire (see Exhibit 10-12 for an example of how the features were measured). In this example, a scale of 1 to 10 is used, where 1 means *not at all important* or *does not describe the casino at all* and 10 means *very important* or *describes the casino perfectly*. Exhibit 10-15 shows that the feature *good entertainment* is of very low importance to the customer. However, customers believe that the casino offers *good entertainment*. This is in contrast to the feature *value of promotions*. This feature is very important to the customer, but customers do not believe the casino delivers on this feature. The feature *slot club* is important to the customer, and customers believe the casino has a *great slot club*. The same interpretation can be made for the feature *feel safe*.

The main advantage of the type of analysis presented in Exhibit 10-15 is that it visually displays to management

EXHIBIT 10-12   RSQFT and REVPAS Calculations

1	2	3	4	5	Revenue per Square Foot (RSQFT)				10	Revenue per Available Seat (REVPAS)			
					6	7	8	9		11	12	13	14
Comp Set	Avg. Check	Covers	Revenue	AMS % of TR	Available f²	Revenue per f²	FMS % of f² Available	Penetration Index on f²	Available Seats	FMS %	Rev. per Available Seat	AMS %	Penetration Index on Avail. Seats
Istana	$45	7,500	$337,500	10.0	60,000	$5.63	11.8	-1.8%	3,300	12.2	$102.27	9.7	-2.5
Tokyo Rose	$70	5,250	$367,500	10.9	60,000	$6.13	11.8	-0.9%	2,800	10.4	$131.25	12.5	2.1
Marty's	$63	9,000	$567,000	16.9	80,000	$7.09	15.7	1.2%	2,100	7.8	$270.00	25.7	17.9
Dice	$73	6,000	$438,000	13.0	75,000	$5.84	14.7	-1.7%	4,000	14.8	$109.50	10.4	-4.4
Balche	$77	6,300	$485,100	14.4	70,000	$6.93	13.7	0.7%	3,600	13.3	$134.75	12.8	-0.5
Fellini	$78	5,700	$444,600	13.2	70,000	$6.35	13.7	-0.5%	3,800	14.1	$117.00	11.1	-3.0
Sushi House	$76	7,000	$532,000	15.8	60,000	$8.87	11.8	4.0%	4,100	15.2	$129.75	12.3	-2.9
Cellantro	$48	4,000	$192,000	5.7	35,000	$5.49	6.9	-1.2%	3,315	12.3	$57.92	5.5	-6.8
Average	66.25	6,344	$420,462			$6.54			3,377		$131.56		
Totals		50,750	$3,363,700	100	510,000		100		27,015	100	$1,052.44	100	

Column:

1 is the competitive set of restaurants

4 is average check × covers = revenue

5 AMS = % of total revenue is a restaurant's revenue / total revenue

7 revenue per square foot is revenue / square footage

8 FMS is square footage / total square footage

9 penetration index (PI) on square footage is FMS subtracted from AMS

Cellantro's PI is a negative 1.2 so it is not getting its FMS; Sushi House is getting the largest market share with a penetration index of 4.0.

10 available seats = number of seats × days in the month

11 is FMS percentage of all available seats

12 is revenue / available seats

13 is AMS percentage of revenue per available seat

14 penetration index on available seats is FMS subtracted from AMS

Cellantro's PI is a negative 6.8 so it is not getting its FMS, but, in this case, based on available seats, Marty's is doing the best with a 17.9 PI. Average checks, number of covers, or some combination can be reviewed to ascertain where the differences lie.

EXHIBIT 10-13 Calculation of Customer Satisfaction Index, AKA Competitive Index

	Importance	Brand A		Brand B	
		Rating	Score	Rating	Score
Column	A	B	C	D	E
Feature	Scale: 1–10	Scale: 1–10	A × B	Scale: 1–10	A × D
It is a place friends like to go	7.30	7.60	55.48	6.40	46.72
Atmosphere is very pleasant	8.80	7.70	67.76	7.60	66.88
One place seems to have better odds	7.40	6.80	50.32	6.00	44.40
Slot machines filled in a timely manner	7.50	6.80	51.00	6.80	51.00
Types of promotions offered	7.40	7.70	56.98	6.80	50.32
Total	384.00		281.54		259.32
Index			73.32		67.53

EXHIBIT 10-14 Questions Used to Determine Importance and Performance

IMPORTANCE QUESTION

Next, please think for a moment about the reason for visiting a specific legalized gambling establishment in Las Vegas. Please tell me how important each reason is for you in your decision to choose one specific property over another. Please use a 1 to 10 scale where a 1 means the reason is not at all important and a 10 means the reason is very important in your decision to choose one legalized gambling establishment over another. You may use any number on this 1 to 10 scale. Do you understand how this 1 to 10 scale works? How important is _____ in your decision to choose one place to visit over another?

PERFORMANCE QUESTION

Now I am going to read you a list of features that may or may not describe some of the casinos in the Las Vegas area. We'll use a 1 to 10 scale where 1 means it *does not describe the casino at all* and 10 means it *describes the casino perfectly*. If you have not been to the casino personally, please base your answers on what you have heard or what you believe to be true. The first feature is _____. How well does this feature describe casino _____?

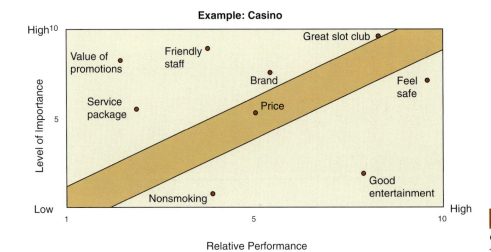

Example: Casino

EXHIBIT 10-15 Matrix of competitive advantages.

---

where they should be spending their money to better take care of the customer. In this example, management would do well to spend less on entertainment and more on increasing the perceived value of their promotions. The perceived price is equal to what is important. Ideally, as discussed in Chapter 2, importance should equal performance.

A second way to visually display how your firm does relative to the competition is to plot both CSI scores and prices charged. In this map, the prices charged are plotted on the vertical axis and the CSI scores are plotted on the horizontal axis. Your hotel's CSI score and price is plotted in the center of the map, so that it is easy to tell which com-

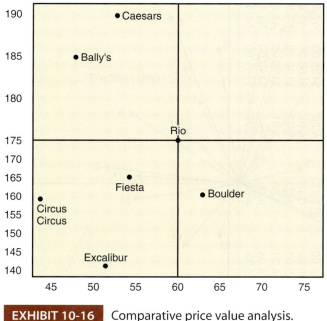

EXHIBIT 10-16   Comparative price value analysis.

petitors are below or above your firm both in terms of CSI scores and price. This is illustrated in Exhibit 10-16 with data from Exhibit 10-17.

Exhibit 10-16 shows the Rio (your hotel) positioned in the center with a rate of $175 and a CSI of 60.0. The positioning map reveals that Bally's and Caesars have higher rates than the Rio ($185 and $190, respectively). More important, both of these brands have a CSI lower than that of the Rio. This indicates that the Rio could probably raise its prices because its customers are generally more satisfied than are those of Bally's and Caesars, which are both earning a higher rate than the Rio. Boulder Station could also probably charge a higher rate because its CSI score is the highest. This analysis should be done for each market segment. It should be noted that although these hotels exist, the numbers are fictitious.

In Exhibit 10-18 we show a more sophisticated mapping, based on discriminant analysis. Discriminant analysis enables the researcher to categorize the different perceptions of the restaurants. The net effect of this is the ability of the restaurant that commissioned the research to see not only how it is perceived, but also who represents true competition in that category. The data used to create the map are shown in Exhibit 10-19. These data represent average scores for each of the restaurants.

The interpretation of a positioning map is detailed in Exhibit 10-20. This table reveals that proper interpretation includes both a review of the positioning map and the table of average scores used to create the positioning map. The perceptual map in Exhibit 10-18, combined with the data in Exhibit 10-19 shows the following information:

- The Den is perceived more than Belle's or the Short Stop to be *a place where I can study or work*—#23 (5.48 versus 3.15 and 3. 46. for Belle's and the Short Stop).
- The Den is perceived as a place that *I can relax with my friends/colleagues*—#11 (6.00 versus 5.16 and 5.12, for Belle's and the Short Stop).
- The Den is perceived as *a place that accepts my debit/credit card*—#12 (6.59 versus 4.47 and 5.75).
- The Short Stop is perceived as a place that *I can purchase food to go if I desire*—#8 (7.08 versus 6.37 for The Den and 6.46 for Belle's)
- The Short Stop, more so than the Den, is perceived as a place where *I am able to order, receive, and pay for food quickly*—#5 (7.88 versus 7.22 for the Den).
- The Short Stop, more so than Belle's, is perceived as a place where *The pricing is fair and provides good value for the money*—#13 (8.66 versus 8.17 for Belle's)
- Belle's, more so than the Den, is perceived as a place where *I do not have to wait in long lines*—#3 (8.09 versus 7.40 for the Den).
- The average score of Belle's is directionally higher than both the Den and the Short Stop for the feature *serves freshly prepared, quality food that I like to eat*—#18 (8.69 versus 8.48 for the Den and 8.51 for the Short Stop). This means customers are slightly more likely to perceive Belle's as having this feature relative to the other brands.
- The average score of Belle's is also directionally higher than both the Den and the Short Stop for the feature *hours of operation are convenient*—#17 (8.11 versus 7.65 for the Den and 7.79 or the Short Stop).

Types and Objectives of Competitive Intelligence

Competitive intelligence involves close observation of competitors to learn what they do best and why, and where they are weak and why. There are three major types and objectives of this information. *Defensive intelligence* refers to that type of intelligence that keeps track of competitors' moves to avoid being caught off guard. For example, the restaurant across the street is planning to feature early bird specials. *Passive intelligence* is obtained in order to make specific decisions. For example, what markets do a competing hotel's sales forces cover? What discounts do they offer to groups? *Offensive intelligence* is sought for the purpose of identifying new opportunities. For example, some hotels have their salespeople spend nights in competitor hotels to learn where there may be opportunities to do something better.

Either kind of competitive intelligence has three major objectives:

| EXHIBIT 10-20 | Interpretation of Positioning Maps Developed Using Discriminant Analysis |

The positioning map in Exhibit 10-18 reveals how respondents perceive each of the different restaurants based on how well the attributes describe each restaurant. These features are the independent variables measured using the wording in Exhibit 10-19. Because there are three brands, the perceptual map is two-dimensional (the number of dimensions equals the number of brands minus one). If there were more brands, multiple maps would need to be drawn. For instance, for four brands it would be necessary to draw three perceptual maps: dimension I versus II, dimension I versus III, and dimension II versus III. In many cases, it is possible to get most of the information in the plot of dimension I versus dimension II.

The lines on the positioning map are called vectors. A vector represents each independent variable, and its length represents its importance in differentiating one group from another. The independent variables with short lines are not necessarily unimportant; they just do not differentiate the groups as well as other variables.

For instance, note that the vector labeled #18 (*It serves freshly prepared, quality food that I like to eat*) is relatively short, indicating that it does not differentiate the restaurants. A review of the means in Exhibit 10-19 reveals that the means for the vector labeled #18 for the three restaurants are 8.48 (the Den), 8.69 (Belle's) and 8.51 (the Short Stop). It is clear that respondents rated the three restaurants approximately the same. Had the scores been more different, the vector would have been longer.

By drawing a perpendicular line from the restaurant centroids, representing the mean of each restaurant, to each vector, one can see which independent variables are important in separating the groups; that is, which variables differentiate the restaurants. The farther away from the

coordinate intersection this crossing is, the more important the variable is in differentiating the restaurants. When reading a perceptual map, it is important to consider that each restaurant's individuality is dependent not only on which factors are most important to respondents, but also on which are less important. Therefore, it is also necessary to consider the continuation of the vectors in the "negative" direction. (Note that the negative direction of the vectors was not shown for the majority of variables in order to keep the perceptual map easier to read.)

For instance, on the positioning map it is clear that the vector labeled #12 (*It is a place that accepts my debit/credit card*) is one of the longest. This feature separates the Den and the Short Stop from Belle's. Notice that for these two restaurants the perpendicular line crosses the vector in the positive direction, whereas it would cross Belle's in the negative direction. This would indicate that the Den and the Short Stop are thought to have this feature, whereas customers believe Belle's does not have this feature. A check of the means shows that the Den has a mean of 6.59 on this feature and the Short Stop has a mean of 5.75. In contrast, Belle's has a mean of 4.47. Clearly, this feature separates the restaurant brands.

The perceptual map of dimension I versus dimension II shows that some of the vectors are pointing up toward the Short Stop and away from the Den and Belle's. Another set of vectors is pointing toward the Den and away from the Short Stop. This is not surprising when one examines the means for each restaurant. For instance, vector #23 (*It is a place where I can study or work*) points toward the Den and away from the Short Stop and Belle's. The mean for the Den is 5.48, whereas the means for the Short Stop and Belle's are 3.46 and 3.15, respectively.

Similar interpretations can be made for the other vectors.

| EXHIBIT 10-21 | Obtaining and Using Competitive Intelligence |

A. Setting up the process
   - Identify competitors in all relevant market segments.
   - Identify your target (i.e., define your competitive set).
   - Identify the unique characteristics of the customers in each market segment.
   - Determine what specific information you need. The most commonly sought data are on pricing, sales statistics, strategic plans, market share changes, key customers, new product developments, and growth plans, but there are obviously many others as shown below.
   - Decide who will get and use the intelligence and what will be done with it.
   - Identify the most likely sources of the data.
   - Develop research strategies and techniques, not hit-or-miss methods.
B. Collecting the raw data
   - Determine the performance record of each competitor. This includes such things as market share, REVPAR, pricing, sales growth, and profitability.
   - Determine the offerings of each competitor such as discounts, packages, guest amenities, loyalty programs, room sizes, physical condition, F&B outlets, and so forth.
   - Construct a profile of each competitor's marketing strategy. This includes goals and objectives, strengths and weaknesses, distinctive competence, target markets, resources, positioning, sales efforts, and the full marketing mix.
C. Evaluating and analyzing the data
   - Ask, Where are competitors most vulnerable?
   - Predict any future strategies and tactics. This is a qualitative exercise for managers. It is based on the information gathered in the previous stages and managers' own experience in the industry.
   - Evaluate the impact of competitors' strategies and tactics on the property or firm.
D. Drawing conclusions and using the data
   - Are the data reliable? Do we have all we need?
   - Develop, on an ongoing basis, defensive, passive, or offensive strategies and tactics that will counter or lead to a competitive advantage.

1. To understand your position of comparative advantage and disadvantage
2. To understand competitors' strategies and tactics
3. To help you develop your own strategies and tactics that may create a competitive advantage.

Exhibit 10-21 pulls all this together in a step-by-step procedure for gathering and using competitive intelligence.

In the final analysis, the management that obtains the most information will be the one that moves around, keeps its eyes and ears open, and uses good intuitive judgment.

Close observation can tell you a lot about what the competition does best and why, where they are off the mark and why, what their strengths and weaknesses are, and what they plan next. All this is good marketing intelligence, and it can go a long way in helping you to develop your own marketing strategy.

Competitive Analysis

The purpose of competitive intelligence, of course, is to use it to your best advantage. Exhibit 10-22 provides a model of broad dimensions for competitor analysis. If you are behind, you need to seek and increase competitive advantage. If you are ahead, you need to sustain and increase competitive advantage. In the first case, you need to overcome barriers to move ahead. In the second case, you need to erect barriers to stay ahead.

A barrier may be raised based on the size of the targeted market, better access to resources or customers, and limitations on what competitors can do. Scale economies, for ex-

ample, may provide an unbeatable cost advantage. In the hotel industry, this is especially true today in the use and cost of the latest technology. This technology also gives a firm preferred access to customers. This helps to explain at least one reason the industry has been in such a consolidation stage.

Barriers may also be raised based on cost differentials or on price and service differentials. A successful barrier returns higher margins if it is sustainable and unreachable by the competition; that is, it must cost the competition more to overcome it than it costs the firm to defend it. Exhibit 10-23 shows the Bellagio's approach to this. It would be very expensive for other hotels in Las Vegas to obtain the AAA Five Diamond Award.* New Zealand, on the other hand, has found a very simple approach to competitive advantage (see Exhibit 10-24).

Another example of a cost barrier is in advertising. Marriott, for example, can get twice the impact from national advertising as that of a firm with half the market share. In other words, the same advertising spreads over a

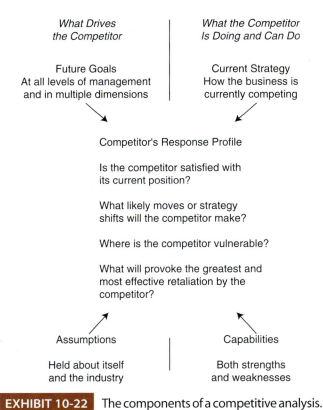

EXHIBIT 10-22 The components of a competitive analysis.

Source: Porter, M. E. (1980). Competitive strategy: Techniques for analyzing industries and competitors. Adapted with permission of the Fress Press, a Division of Simon & Schuster Adult Publishing Group. Copyright © 1980, 1998, by the Free Press. All rights reserved.

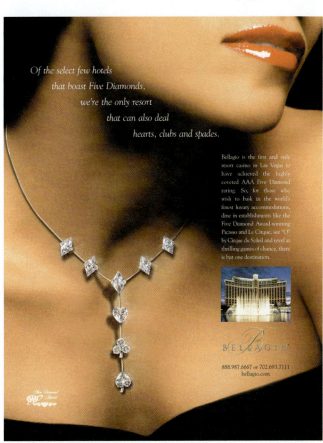

EXHIBIT 10-23 Bellagio has raised barriers based on cost differentials or on price and service differentials.

Source: MGM Mirage. Used by permission.

---

*Five Diamonds is the highest and most exclusive rating given by the American Automobile Association (AAA), a respected authority that personally inspects all rated properties.

EXHIBIT 10-24 New Zealand features a sustainable competitive advantage with simplicity.

Source: Tourism New Zealand. Used by permission.

much larger customer base and quantity of hotel rooms. A wide product line, large sales and service forces, and systems capabilities (again Marriott) are other examples of major barriers. Each is effective against smaller competitors who are attempting to overcome the leader but have less volume over which to spread the costs.

These, and many more, are all reasons hotel and restaurant companies grow larger and develop some sustainable advantages as they do so. On the other hand, there is an anomaly in this situation that is peculiar to the industry. In many cases, each unit (hotel or restaurant) largely succeeds or fails on its own. Although all chains have loyal customers, many hospitality customers make their choices based on the individual properties. Thus, the Mansion on Turtle Creek in Dallas, for example, can and does compete against the Four Seasons with some premium service advantages that are unique and sustainable in spite of being one of a kind and not having economies of scale or scope.

A **sustainable competitive advantage** in marketing strategy happens only when (1) customers perceive a consistent difference in important attributes between one firm or property and its competition, (2) the difference is the result of a capability gap between the firm and its competi-

tors, and (3) both the difference in important attributes and the capability gap can endure over time.[7]

The essence of opportunity is beating the competition. Intense competition in an industry is neither coincidence nor bad luck. It is a fact of business life. The competitive objective is to find the most vulnerable position that, if broken, would eliminate a competitive barrier or one that would enable you to erect the best defense barriers. This means finding what makes the competition vulnerable. Attacking vulnerability, as in the military sense, means attacking the weaknesses and avoiding the strengths in the line. The latter is as important as the former. Wendy's is one fast-food operator that has proven this point. Wendy's attacked where McDonald's was weak in two areas. One was the area of "adult" hamburgers. Wendy's saw that McDonald's was not really serving this market so it set out to carve its own niche. The second area was in the product. Wendy's saw a dislike in the market for the frozen, precooked hamburger, especially among a portion of the adult market, and offered fresh hamburgers. Wendy's has survived where many others that copied McDonald's failed. The budget portion of the hotel industry has done likewise.

Avoid the competition's strength, at least until you are strong enough and have the resources to challenge them with meaningful differentiation. Look for the weaknesses. These may be in the product line, in positioning, in value, in segmentation and target markets, in capacity, in resources, in cost disadvantages, in product differentiation, in customer loyalty, or in distribution channels.

Competitive Marketing

Porter suggested three strategies for beating the competition:

1. Positioning to provide the best defense
2. Influencing the balance by taking the offense
3. Exploiting industry change[8]

Defensive positioning means matching strengths and weaknesses against the competition by finding positions where it is the weakest (as Wendy's did with McDonald's) and developing strengths where the company is least vulnerable. Four Seasons Hotels have accomplished this by maintaining their level of service at all costs.

Influencing the balance by taking the offensive or being proactive means attempting to alter the industry structure and its causes. It calls for marketing innovation, establishing brand identity, or otherwise differentiating the product. Darden is a restaurant example with Olive Garden, Red Lobster, Bahama Breeze, and Smokey Bones. This has also happened with all-suite hotels, conference center hotels, and, especially, "luxury budget" hotels.

Web Browsing Exercise

Visit the websites of Darden Restaurant company (www.darden.com/) and Brinker International (www.brinker.com/). Have they distinguished their brands? If so, how?

Exploiting industry change means anticipating shifts in the environment, forecasting the effect, constructing a composite of the future, and positioning accordingly. Taco Bell and Domino's pizza delivery are two examples. Robert Hazard accomplished this in his successful metamorphosis of Quality Inns (now Choice International) in the early 1980s, when he offered three different product levels to the marketplace. All-suites have done the same thing, as has SAS Hotels in its strategic alliance with Radisson.

A successful company must look beyond today's competitors to those that may become competitors tomorrow (such as convenience stores and take-out versus the fast-food industry). It must also watch out for new entries in the race (e.g., condominium and private home rentals and conference center hotels) and the threat of substitute products (e.g., supermarket "make your own meal" bars). As gambling has become popular, many have gone to destinations that offer gambling.

The key to growth, even survival, is to obtain a position that is less vulnerable to direct attack, old or new, and less vulnerable to customer manipulation and substitute products. This may be done through relationship marketing, actual or psychological product differentiation, and constant and foresighted competitive awareness and analysis.

Finding Marketing Opportunities

To be sure, all marketing opportunities begin with the identification and quantification of customers' problems. Well-known management author Peter Drucker called these opportunities "incongruities."[9] Incongruities here are discrepancies between what is and what ought to be. As far as the customer is concerned, this may be the difference between expectation and reality; it may also be the difference between what the customer would like it to be and what is available. These are both true opportunities. Drucker stated:

> Of all incongruities, that between perceived and actual reality may be the most common. Producers and suppliers almost always misconceive what it is that the customer actually buys. They must assume that what represents "value" to the producer and supplier is equally "value" to the customer. . . . And yet, no customer ever perceives himself as buying what the producer or supplier delivers. Their expectations and values are always different.[10]

Even if Drucker is only half right, it is clear that within customer incongruities there are tremendous opportunities. Everyone is familiar with the expression: There ought to be a better way. It is in that better way that opportunities reside. Consider the case of the atrium hotel lobby, now common all over the world:

> John Portman was an architect who decided there ought to be a better way to design a hotel. At the time, hotel architecture had reached a degree of sameness that was so "commodity-laden" that no one thought hotels could ever be other than what they were, architecturally speaking. The first Portman-designed atrium hotel was opened by Hyatt in Atlanta in 1967, and the industry was shocked, primarily because of the perceived energy costs. Everyone criticized, but the customers kept coming and Hyatt became a major chain as a result.

Was the atrium hotel lobby a customer problem solved? Was this a case of customer expectations being unfulfilled? Of course it was. Hotels were dull, dreary places with long, dark corridors and dull lobbies with couches built around the antiquated concept of "a home away from home." Customers did not want a home away from home; they wanted a new and exciting experience. They wanted something different, and Hyatt gave it to them. The decision by Hyatt to build an atrium lobby hotel did more than start Hyatt on its way; it started hotel architecture on its way, and today's many examples are a result of that initial Portman design and Hyatt decision.

Consider the now popular restaurant salad bar. Who knows where or when it started. Someone saw an opportunity arising from a customer problem. Fine wine by the glass (and increasingly, various sizes of pours), thanks to improvements in the storage of open wine bottles, and coffee, juice, and roll carts on hotel elevators solved other customer problems. Environmental changes present other, more macro problems and opportunities. If you want to find an opportunity, look for a customer problem.

Opportunity solutions, to be effective, have to be simple. They have to be easily understandable by the customer. They have to avoid increased customer risk. Opportunities call for innovation, leadership, and a constant awareness that there ought to be a better way. Opportunities are out there crying for solutions, but innovation to fulfill them does not fall in your lap. Sometimes it takes hard work, sometimes just a little common sense, and sometimes great timing and a streak of good luck!

The search for opportunity begins with knowing your market, knowing your customers, and understanding your customer's problems. But never forget the first rule of marketing when you get a great opportunity idea: Will it create or keep a customer? When you can answer yes, then and only then ask what it will cost to develop and implement and whether you can afford it.

All opportunities to create and keep a customer are not "great" ideas. Some are just common sense. We previously mentioned an American chain hotel in Kuala Lumpur, Malaysia, that offered freshly squeezed orange juice, but you could not get it until after 10:00 A.M. Why not? The juicer was in the bar, and the bar did not open until 10:00 A.M. The service personnel did not tell you this; they simply served canned orange juice until 10:00 A.M.! Opportunity lost and common sense.

Marketing intelligence and marketing research are critical activities in marketing and getting to know the customer. It is a particularly vital part of environmental scanning and opportunity and competitive analysis. It is also, of course, a subject of its own. We offer a detailed treatment of marketing research in a separate chapter. We urge you also to take a marketing research course.

Feasibility Studies

Another form of marketing opportunity differs somewhat from that in the previous discussion. Instead of looking for opportunities, market feasibility studies are conducted to verify whether an opportunity exists. When feasibility studies are conducted, someone already believes that there is an opportunity, such as to build a hotel or open a restaurant in a certain location. The purpose of the **feasibility study** is to evaluate that belief in a quantitative manner (and prove to the lender or investor that it is a viable one). Measurement of market potential or feasibility offers knowledge of market size, market growth, market segments, profitability, demand and types of buying decisions, and competition. In essence, the feasibility study should ask these questions:

- Is there a market for this property (business, concept, operation) in this location? If so, where is it? How large is it or will it be? What are its needs?
- How is the market currently served by the competition?
- What market share can be captured? At what rate? At what REVPAR? At what cost?
- Will customers use our property?

Other related questions will follow naturally.

How does the answer to the first question project into financial realities—for example, room rates or check averages, revenue, profit, return on investment, and other quantitative financial considerations? Our interest here is only in the first question. The answers to the second question obviously depend on the answers to the first question.

Feasibility studies focus on the proposed financial performance of a proposed business and rely on an evaluation of marketing opportunities and competitive analysis. They deserve an entire chapter to themselves, but that is not within the scope of this text. Instead, we place the emphasis on the analysis of the marketing opportunity. Studying markets, as we know by now, involves studying customers or consumer groups and how they will respond (in this case) to a given offering. In other words, having decided that we would like to do something (e.g., build a new hotel or restaurant), we seek to determine whether the opportunity is there and, if so, to what extent. The opportunity, of course, lies in customers who are ready, willing, and able to buy.

The marketing opportunity depends on the customer. If the customer is not responsive to the offering, there is no marketing opportunity. By the same token, the competitive analysis of any marketing opportunity should be restricted to focus on those who are competing for the same customer under the same conditions. Six motels within a five-mile area have little to do with the competition of a proposed 300-room conference center.

A market feasibility study should have only one purpose: to evaluate the opportunity to attract customers who are willing to pay a specific price over a sustained period of time. That's the hard part. Once done, the easier part is to estimate revenue, subtract cost, predict net and cash flow, and determine whether the project is "feasible"—that is, evaluate the financial opportunity.

A true market feasibility study depends, totally, on the predispositions and behaviors of customers, whether they will come and what they will pay. This is the competitive opportunity or lack thereof. Unfortunately, most feasibility studies crunch numbers with only a remote idea of where the customers are, whether they will come, or who the real competition is. In marketing, real opportunities depend on the ability to create paying customers—nothing else.

Web Browsing Exercise

Go to your favorite web browser and type in "hospitality feasibility studies." What do you find? What types of firms provide feasibility studies? Does the information provided explain what makes a good feasibility study? What does this information tell you?

■ Summary

Although we tend to think of marketing as a managerial activity that reaches the customer, we have shown in this chapter that other elements are involved. Marketing, in fact, is akin to enemy warfare and includes outwitting, outflanking, and outdoing the competition in the battle for customer trial and, ultimately, loyalty. Marketing does not live in a vacuum in solving customers' problems and satisfying their needs and wants. A firm's marketing must perform these tasks better than the competitors do. This is the only way to achieve a sustained advantage and growth in the hospitality industry.

Without doubt, many firms in the hospitality industry maintain the status quo and still survive, but maintenance and survival are not the preferred outcomes of effective marketing. Neither objective will fulfill the potential of the firm.

This chapter has shown that identifying and understanding the competition does not mean just understanding bricks and mortar. Rather, understanding all facets of competitors' businesses and the actors who make them work requires constant analysis. Without this understanding and often good research to explain it, marketing is doomed to ignore opportunity, and the property is doomed to the status of "also ran" when the final count is in.

Sustainable competitive advantage is hard to come by in the hospitality industry. Regardless, it is an essential competitive element. As we said in Chapter 3, we think that, at least in the immediate future and for some time to come, sustainable competitive advantage will lie in understanding the competition and the ever-evolving lifestyles, habits, and preferences of customers.

■ Key Terms

competitive intelligence
conceptitis
competitive intensity
market share
actual market share
fair market share
revenue per available room (REVPAR)
yield index
revenue per occupied room (REVPOR)

revenue per available customer (REVPAC)
revenue per square foot (RSQFT)
revenue per available seat (REVPAS)
perceptual maps
sustainable competitive advantage
feasibility study

■ Discussion Questions

1. What are the basic elements of strategic competition? Discuss.
2. Identify, with examples, different sources of competition.
3. How does industry structure affect the intensity of competition?
4. What are the major sources of competitive intelligence?
5. How can a company or property maintain sustainable competitive advantage?

6. Consider a local restaurant or hotel. What is its competition in a macro sense? In a micro sense? Explain.
7. Explain competitive intensity. How does it affect marketing? Give examples and discuss.
8. Develop a new acronym and formula for applying REVPAR analysis to a restaurant.
9. Make a list of new competitive advantages that a hotel or restaurant might achieve. Could they be sustainable?

■ Group Projects

1. Consider a hotel or restaurant chain with which you are familiar, such as Sheraton. Delineate how it should develop marketing strategy in order to build and sustain competitive advantage for the next 10 years.
2. Marriott needs a hand in establishing protocol to measure REVPAC. Develop a model that would provide a framework to address this.
3. Blindly, have each member of your group categorize along specified dimensions that might be competitive advantages a restaurant or hotel with which you are all familiar. Draw a positioning map for this property.

■ References

1. Jain, S. C. (1997). *Marketing planning and strategy* (5th ed.). Cincinnati: South-Western, 70.
2. Porter, M. E. (March-April 1979). How Competitive Forces Shape Strategy, *Harvard Business Review*. Copyrighted 1979 by the President and Fellows of Harvard College; all rights reserved.
3. Porter, M. E. (1980). *Competitive strategy: Techniques for analyzing industries and competitors.* New York: Free Press.
4. Jain, 76–77.
5. In one study, for example, of 1,314 hotel guests of six hotels, amenities were found to be nonsignificant in determining the choice of hotel and nonsignificant in importance when staying at a hotel, for both business and pleasure travelers. See Lewis, R. C. (1985, February). Predicting hotel choice: The factors underlying perception. *Cornell Hotel and Restaurant Administration Quarterly*, 82–96.
6. Industry rethinks amenities and value (1993, September 27). *Business Travel News*, 20.
7. Jain, 96–98.
8. Porter, M. E. (1975). Note on the structural analysis of industries. Harvard Business School Case Services, 22.
9. Drucker, P. F. (1985). *Innovation and entrepreneurship.* New York: Harper & Row, 57.
10. Ibid, 66.

How is research different for the hospitality field versus the packaged good fields?

The gap has narrowed considerably over the years that I've been in the business, as companies are much more research oriented today and marketing has gotten a lot more sophisticated. There is still that intuitive development, and a lot of times our marketing budgets or advertising budgets are nowhere close. In hospitality, you might spend $8 million on advertising, whereas with packaged goods, they spend many more millions on something because they're looking at things in a lot more detail.

Any other comments about using research as a decision tool in marketing?

I think the big thing is for people to try to get comfortable with research, particularly in operations. They're very used to financial data going into infinite detail with income statements, balance sheets, or cost control programs, and they need to think at that same level of detail about knowing your consumers and what they want. It's applying that same very detailed kind of analytical thinking from a consumer needs standpoint.

Used by permission from Dennis A. Marzella.

Effective marketing programs are founded in comprehensive marketing research. This is not to say that prudent decisions cannot be made on intuition alone. Max and Greti Mennig have never undertaken a formal marketing research project. However, for every Max and Greti who has used intuition to create and run a successful business, there are tens of thousands of others who also "knew it would work"—only to find that it did not. The world today is not what it was when Max and Greti started their restaurant. Today's world is far more competitive, and accordingly, the depth of insight required to make the best decisions requires access to the "intelligence" that can help guide these decisions.

There is another reason marketers need better intelligence today—the consumer. The consumer is changing and has a seemingly endless array of choices. Choices mean decisions, and making more decisions means acquiring more information, even if only to verify intuitive thought. Understanding these consumer decisions is critical for successful marketing. Today, virtually no business makes a decision without acquiring some sort of market intelligence about the consumer. To make decisions without such information on the consumer is to create Gap 1, which we discussed at length in Chapter 3.

As with many other subject areas in this text, marketing intelligence is not restricted to one chapter. In fact, much of the discussion throughout the text has been about the information that is needed to make marketing decisions or to handle marketing problems. In particular, one of the best sources of marketing intelligence comes from the customer, as discussed in Chapter 4, Chapter 7, and Chapter 8. Environmental scanning, discussed in Chapter 5, is another area from which intelligence flows and is obviously very critical to marketing decisions. Chapter 9 dealt with the use of intelligence for competitive analysis. In this chapter we review some of the information discussed in earlier chapters, as well as deal more specifically with intelligence needs and their acquisition.

Insights acquired through market intelligence are used to guide decision making at every level of the hospitality organization, thereby enhancing the overall quality of customer service while simultaneously ensuring the ongoing creation and evaluation of products and services that meet emerging customer needs. "Market intelligence" is gleaned in myriad ways and typically includes the following:

- Analysis of the general economic environment in which the hospitality enterprise operates
- Creation of customer profiles (both existing and prospective)
- Assessment of new market opportunities
- Pretesting of new product(s)
- Pricing and communication strategies
- Overall measurement of the impact of the marketing plan

Restaurant firms, as well as food service firms (such as university dining services), require the same type of information, but also use research to determine the following:

- Changes in menu offerings
- Sales opportunities
- Hours of operation
- Changes in design, decor, and atmosphere
- Market position strategies

Although the responsibility for the development and implementation of a comprehensive marketing research program clearly resides with management of the hospitality enterprise, outside expertise is frequently commissioned to assist with the capture and analysis of research information. In the appendix of this chapter, we provide insight into working with a marketing research supplier or outside consultant. Outside data may also be purchased to provide the hospitality organization with a broader view of the economic, social, and political variables most likely to affect the business in the years ahead. For example, many chain hotel companies (and individual hotels and resorts) in the United States subscribe to occupancy tracking reports—such as the STAR report published by Smith Travel Research. These reveal the subject property's performance against a defined set of competitors. Outside the United States, the firm the Daily Bench provides similar information. Exhibit 11-1 shows an advertisement for Decision Analyst, Inc.

Large restaurant chains are more prone to subscribe to data services that track consumer trends. The best known of these is probably **CREST (Consumer Reports in Eating Share Trends)**, conducted by a division of NPD, Inc., a marketing and research firm. Companies that subscribe to this service and others receive regular reports on expenditures and behavior in the commercial food service industry by type and classification of restaurant and by meal period. Essentially, these reports track broad trends (useful for environmental scanning), but for individual companies, it can provide specific information on their product as well as market share percentages.

A publication popular to many firms in Europe, the Middle East, and Africa is *Foodservice Europe and Middle East*. This magazine, published by Gretel Weiss, tracks food service trends and holds a yearly conference for food service executives. Exhibit 11-2 shows the cover of one of the issues of this magazine. Notice the trends listed in this issue.

Another resource for market intelligence that is used by many travel service marketers is the Yesawich, Pepperdine, Brown & Russell/Yankelovich Partners *National Travel MONITOR*, an annual survey of the travel habits, preferences, and intentions of Americans. The same firm authors a variety of "vertical" market studies on affluent travelers, family travelers, meeting planners, and American gamblers.[1]

We look at other ways to collect market intelligence from external and internal information after we provide an overview of collecting market intelligence by designing a proper marketing information system.

Why Consider INTERNET RESEARCH?

The primary reason to consider the Internet for marketing research is the quality of the data. Respondents take the survey at a time of their own choosing, when they can give it their full attention (in contrast to the "interruption" of the telephone or mall-intercept). Respondents see the questions and the answer choices (instead of only hearing them) and can reread them if needed. Respondents can take as much time as they need to think about the answer to a question. Pictures, sounds, and video can be integrated into the questionnaire.

Since Decision Analyst panelists are paid for their time, Internet surveys can be longer and more detailed than phone surveys. Concerns over the representativeness of Internet samples are diminishing as Internet penetration grows. Currently, over 70% of adults in the U.S. and Canada have access to the Internet at home or work, and Internet penetration is increasing rapidly around the globe.

Decision Analyst, Inc.
The global leader in Internet research systems
www.decisionanalyst.com

EXHIBIT 11-1 An advertisement for Decision Analyst, Inc. Internet research systems.

Source: By permission; Decision Analyst, Inc.

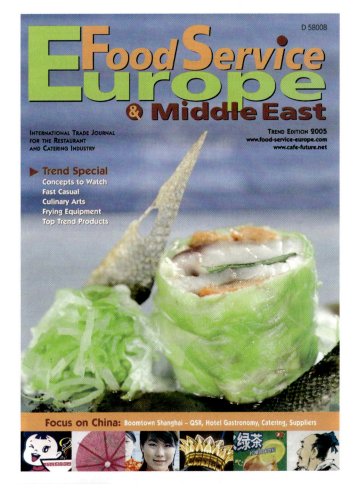

EXHIBIT 11-2 *Foodservice Europe and Middle East* is an example of one source of market intelligence.

Source: Food Service Europe. Used by permission.

research. Such research may, however, be very useful in environmental scanning when one wishes to observe broad trends.

Web Browsing Exercise

Visit www.pkfcanada.com. What information is available to download? How can this information help those in the hospitality industry? Download one of the reports and prepare a one-page summary of the reported information.

Of particular concern to the marketing manager is the representativeness of the data collected for analysis. Specifically, appropriate controls need to be in place to ensure that the observations are taken from individuals who have been properly prequalified and are drawn to reflect the presumed random distribution of attitudes and behaviors across the population under study. When examining any type of external data, marketing managers need to see whether these controls were in place.

To illustrate this point, consider the case of the *Literary Digest* issue that predicted that Alfred Landon would defeat Franklin Roosevelt in the 1936 U.S. presidential election. This decision was based on a research study of 6 million registered voters. Obviously, Roosevelt was the actual winner. What happened? The sample consisted of registered automobile owners and those with telephones. In 1936 people with automobiles and telephones were a minority. The sample was biased and the results, incorrect.

Gathering Internal Information

The hospitality industry as a whole has access to more information about its customers than perhaps any other industry in the world. The reason is probably obvious—guests of hotels and resorts are required to disclose a great deal of information about themselves, such as their name, contact address, travel preferences, and so on, both before and while they consume the "product." The decrease in the cost of memory now enables hospitality firms to keep track of this information to better cater to customers' needs. We discussed some of this in Chapter 4 and will discuss more of it in Chapter 19, when we discuss interactive marketing, which includes database marketing.

The discussion that follows refers mainly to hotels. This does not mean, however, that restaurants and tourist destinations cannot gather similar types of information. As discussed in Chapter 4, one of the main reasons for frequent guest programs is to gather this type of information.

The creation of a comprehensive customer profile is a fundamental step in the development of an effective marketing strategy. A profile of *existing customers* is relatively easy to construct from historical registration and/or consumption information. However, the profile of *prospective customers* is more difficult to construct and typically requires some form of primary marketing research (direct interaction with individuals who meet the targeted market profile). Suggested techniques of primary research are discussed later in this chapter.

Two sources of data that should be tracked to profile existing customers are as follows:

1. The information they provide at the time of reservation (for hotels and resorts)
2. The information they yield throughout the course of their stay

It is possible to develop a remarkably clear picture of existing customers simply by compiling "transaction" data from the time a hotel or resort reservation is taken. For example, the following information is typically requested and provided at the point of reservation:

■ Correct spelling of the customer's name
■ Source of the reservation (e.g., website, central reservation office, travel agency, etc.)
■ Date of the reservation
■ Type of guest (e.g., market segment defined by purpose of trip and method of travel)
■ Any special rate or package plan information
■ Primary "snail mail" address, including the zip code of the origin market
■ Primary e-mail address
■ Intended date of arrival
■ Intended length of stay
■ Expected number of people in the party (including adults and children)
■ Preferred accommodations
■ Any special requests

The following information may also be "sampled" unobtrusively during the course of the customer's stay and contribute significantly to the richness of the resulting database:

■ First time or repeat guest (typically discerned at the point of registration)
■ Food and beverage charges
■ Recreational amenity charges
■ Total of all room, food, beverage, and miscellaneous charges
■ Method of payment

The data should be verified for accuracy after checkout and then stored in a master database for use in the identification of customer travel patterns (and subsequent direct marketing programs).

The analysis of the information contained in your existing customer database should be governed by three considerations:

1. The criterion unit under study (e.g., registrants or room nights)
2. Mutually exclusive market segment classifications
3. The media markets from which the customers originate

Most marketing managers elect to use room nights as the criterion unit of analysis because the distribution of room nights bears a specific relationship to the number of registrants over time. The classification of registrants by mutually exclusive market segments is also critical to the conduct of a meaningful customer analysis. Although marketing managers display considerable creativity in labeling "segments" of existing guests, the classifications presented in Exhibit 11-5 provide a useful segmentation model. Specifically, all segments are defined with reference to two criteria:

1. The customer's primary reason for the trip (business or pleasure)
2. Whether the customer is traveling individually or part of a formal group for which the accommodations have been reserved by a third party (meeting planner)

Hence, there are four mutually exclusive lodging market segments as follows:

■ Individual business travelers
■ Individual pleasure travelers
■ Group business travelers
■ Group pleasure travelers

These are illustrated in Exhibit 11-5.

The "local market" should be not excluded from this analysis because it may be a significant contributor of room nights.

The four mutually exclusively market segments revealed in this taxonomy may be subdivided further if appropriate. For example, the individual pleasure market may be subdivided to include several subsegments, such as the following:

■ Weekend package guests
■ Honeymooners
■ Golf enthusiasts, etc.

Similar subsegment classifications may be developed for the group business market:

■ Corporate meeting planners
■ Association meeting planners, etc.

It is essential to establish appropriate criteria for the identification of individual market segments because the "purchaser" of the accommodations may not necessarily be the "consumer." By way of illustration, individuals who are traveling to participate in a corporate sales meeting probably had very little, if anything, to do with the selection of the host hotel or resort. The latter was probably the sole responsibility of a corporate meeting planner. In this example, the corporate meeting planner is the "purchaser," whereas the individual delegates attending the meeting are the "consumers." This is an important distinction to make because the advertising and sales promotional techniques used to influence each market segment's purchase patterns differ as well.

Exhibit 11-6 reveals the pitfalls of making advertising decisions based solely on the aggregate distribution of room nights by origin market (without delving further into the individual market segment analysis). In the absence of appropriate segmentation information, one might obtain a distribution similar to that shown in the "all registrants" column, whereas the use of appropriate segmentation criteria would yield the more useful distributions shown in the middle and right-hand columns (group and individual registrants, respectively). Advertising and sales promotional programs targeted toward individual registrants would clearly be misdirected if based on the aggregate room night distribution rather than the distribution shown for individual guests. Regrettably, this type of strategic oversight occurs every day in hospitality marketing.

EXHIBIT 11-5 Lodging Market Segments

Purpose of Trip		Individual	Group
	Business	Individual Business	Group Business
	Pleasure	Individual Pleasure	Group Pleasure

EXHIBIT 11-6 Mix of Business by Designated Market Area (DMA)

Designated Market Area (DMA)	% All Registrants	% Group Registrants	% Individual Registrants
New York	19	11	8
Boston	16	10	6
Philadelphia	12	3	9
Chicago	10	7	3
Detroit	9	7	2
All Others	34	14	20
Total	100	52	48

The task of defining the origin markets of customers must also be approached carefully because there is frequently a difference in the markets from which the "registrants" and "reservations" originate. This is true for commercial hotels that enjoy a significant volume of business from "local" referrals, typically the case for city center commercial hotels. Moreover, the geographic boundaries of origin markets should be defined with respect to media coverage, not political boundaries. We discuss media coverage shortly.

Suppose the top five markets for a given hotel's registrants and reservations are as shown in Exhibit 11-7. Clearly the distributions are different. Which should be used to guide marketing and media strategy? This situation would arise when, for example, an individual who resides in New York plans a business trip to Chicago. He calls the office he intends to visit in Chicago and requests assistance with hotel arrangements. The room reservation then originates from the office he is visiting in Chicago, even though the guest actually travels from and resides in New York. The "smart money" in marketing typically focuses on the markets from which the *reservations* originate.

Regrettably, many marketing managers overlook this critical distinction in their analysis of existing customers, and the data used to develop advertising and sales promotional programs are distorted as a result. Additionally, it is generally more effective for properties to focus their promotional efforts in origin markets that account for the highest percentage of reservations (not registrations), particularly if the "consumers" of the accommodations are not the "purchasers" as illustrated in the preceding example. Another common example may be found in hotels and resorts that cater to a high percentage of group business because the "consumers" (delegates) are generally not the "purchasers" (typically meeting planners). It is therefore essential to identify and track both distributions.

The classification of origin markets should also be an issue of concern to hospitality marketing managers. In this regard, many hotel and resort property management systems trace registrants by origin markets that are defined by some political boundary (e.g., city or state), although these generally do not provide any "actionable" insights when it comes time to formulate marketing or media strategy. For example, knowing that 13 percent of your individual commercial room nights originate from New York State is of little value because the state comprises several disparate metropolitan markets, each of which is served by different radio, television, and print media. Accordingly, a more precise definition of origin markets is required.

The preferred solution is to define origin markets by media coverage. The preferred unit of analysis is the **designated market area (DMA)** tracked by Nielson Media Research. Simply defined, a DMA is the geographic area within which the majority of households consume media that emanate from a central source. Each DMA has specific zip code correlates, which change over time to reflect population migration patterns and changes in media coverage. There are currently 210 DMAs in the United States and 15 DMAs in Canada. Comparable measures are in use in developed markets worldwide. A sample DMA map is shown in Exhibit 11-8.

With the unit of analysis properly specified, the market segments classified in the mutually exclusive manner, and the origin markets properly delineated, one is now prepared to commence the market analysis. Unless there are unique requirements, frequency distributions and cross tabulations should provide most of the required information. It may also be appropriate to evaluate the relationship between one or more variables, in which case multivariate analysis would be required.

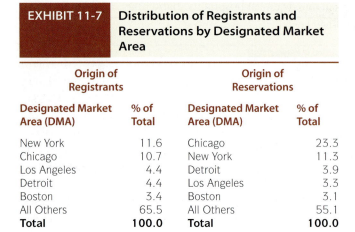

EXHIBIT 11-7	Distribution of Registrants and Reservations by Designated Market Area

Origin of Registrants		Origin of Reservations	
Designated Market Area (DMA)	**% of Total**	**Designated Market Area (DMA)**	**% of Total**
New York	11.6	Chicago	23.3
Chicago	10.7	New York	11.3
Los Angeles	4.4	Detroit	3.9
Detroit	4.4	Los Angeles	3.3
Boston	3.4	Boston	3.1
All Others	65.5	All Others	55.1
Total	**100.0**	**Total**	**100.0**

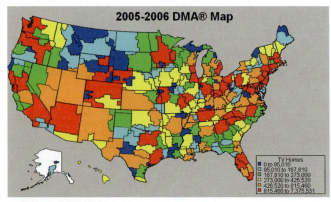

2005-2006 DMA® Map

EXHIBIT 11-8	2005–2006 DMA map.

Source: Retrieved November 11, 2005, from www.softill.com/dma.html. Used by permission of Software Illustrated.

Once the database of information has been assembled on current customers, the analysis should be conducted to reveal trends

- over time (both monthly and quarterly),
- by market segment (individual versus group registrants),
- by media market, and
- by any relevant combination of attributes that would help sharpen the focus of future product development and marketing communication strategy

Unfortunately, comprehensive information on the demography, travel habits, and media habits of existing customers is generally not readily available through the guest reservation/registration process. The acquisition of this information entails direct customer contact and the use of properly developed survey forms to obtain representative data. Many hospitality operators will accept information from in-room or tabletop comment cards as a surrogate for this data, yet caution should be exercised because of the manner in which the data are sampled. Specifically, apart from deficiencies that may be inherent in the composition of the survey instrument, the data from comment cards are potentially deceptive because each guest does not have an equal probability of being drawn into the sample. As a result, the data from in-room comment cards is typically skewed to reflect an extreme—positively or negatively—than one would otherwise expect simply because most customers complete these cards only when they have had a particularly positive or negative experience.

To avoid this potential deception, the survey instrument should be composed to capture relevant information on the following:

- Demography (age, income, household size, marital status, educational achievement, and so on)
- Behavioral information
- Product evaluations where appropriate
- Travel habits
- Media habits

Distribution of the survey instrument should be random or otherwise systematic (to every nth customer) to yield a representative sample both by time of year and type of guest. A modest incentive (financial or otherwise) may be required to promote participation, but should have little effect on the survey results. Should you question whether the results are truly representative, however, it may be appropriate to conduct a parallel survey of nonrespondents (those who were initially contacted but declined to participate). These data may then be compared statistically to those from the initial group to determine whether the differences reveal that you have sampled information from two different populations. It might seem odd to measure nonrespondents because, if they responded, why are they considered nonrespondents? The difference is that when a person refuses to complete the survey, they are asked, "May I just ask you five to six very short questions?" The responses to these questions are then compared to the responses to similar questions of those who completed the full survey.

How Marketing Intelligence Can Be Used

The following sections show how marketing intelligence can be used. For marketing intelligence to be accepted by others in the organization, it must be useful to management. Collection of data for the sake of having data on hand is not only expensive, but it creates a culture in which people believe that money spent on research is wasteful. Then, when money is really needed for research, it will not be granted. In the following section, we discuss various ways to collect actionable research.

Assessment of Area-Wide Demand

One research task is typically that of determining the market area's sources of demand for lodging accommodations or related hospitality services. This entails the following:

1. Quantifying total demand for accommodations by both type and source
2. Calculating the subject property's share of total demand (market share) in aggregate and by individual market segment
3. Identifying any anticipated changes in demand generators that may affect both short- and long-term demand for accommodations and services

Area-wide demand is typically expressed in aggregate by the number of occupied rooms in lodging accommodations. Of particular interest is the number of occupied rooms in a defined "competitive set" of properties—those that are determined to be directly competitive with the subject property. Accordingly, the first task in the development of an effective marketing strategy is to quantify the demand for accommodations by market segment within the defined competitive set of properties under study, followed by an examination of the demand generators responsible for this business.

We discussed area-wide demand in the previous chapter on competition. However, we present a second example to reinforce this important concept. A simple way to estimate area-wide demand is to multiply the total inventory of rooms within the defined competitive set (your property plus those with which you compete directly) by the aggregate occupancy of all properties for the most recent 12-month period. The resulting information represents a summary of the total occupied rooms within the competitive set, providing a baseline from which you can then estimate demand by individual market segment. A sample area-wide demand calculation is provided in Exhibit 11-9.

Demand generators include the following:

■ Local manufacturing, retail, and service establishments
■ Tourist attractions
■ Convention centers
■ Special entertainment or cultural events

Specific demand estimates may be established by determining how many room nights are produced by each demand generator in a typical 12-month period. Estimates on transient visitation may also be constructed through historical trends in air, auto, bus, and rail arrivals. Once the aggregate demand has been determined for the competitive set, the subject property's "share" of the total demand may then be calculated and expressed as a percentage of occupied room nights and indexed with reference to the average achieved by all properties that are part of the analysis. An example of this calculation follows.

In this example, the subject property has 25 percent of the available rooms in the competitive set, yet enjoys an indexed share of occupied rooms of 104 percent (4 percent above the number it would expect to receive if it received its "fair share") because of its superior performance against the listed competitors, as shown in Exhibit 11-10.

Product (Property) Research

The product, or property, aspect of the marketing research program entails the identification and quantification of the subject property's most marketable features. These may be classified as either "tangible" (physical) or "intangible" (qualitative) in nature and, once inventoried, will enable a comparative analysis revealing the subject property's competitive strengths and weaknesses. When profiling a hospitality operation, one must assess the two different but equally important sets of attributes:

1. Tangible features—those for which you can prepare a physical inventory
2. Intangible features—those subjective assessments that are ascribed to various aspects of your operation by guests

Tourism Marketing Application
Conversion research studies are conducted to address the questions of how many inquirers from travel ads convert to visitors and to determine the converters' demographic and travel-behavior characteristics, including length of stay, travel-party size, destination activities, and expenditures. The formula is the number of inquiries divided by the number of people who actually visit. Conversion studies are usually accomplished by surveying consumers. Problems can occur with conversion studies under certain conditions: nonresponse bias (people do not respond to the survey and they are different than those who do answer); sample is not random (not everyone has an equal chance of being

EXHIBIT 11-9	Area-Wide Demand Analysis				
	Subject Property	**Competitor A**	**Competitor B**	**Competitor C**	**Competitive Set Total**
Available rooms	350	400	300	325	1,375
Occupancy	68.5%	67.5%	72.3%	63.4%	67.8%
Occupied rooms	87,509	98.550	79,169	75,208	340,436

EXHIBIT 11-10	Actual versus Fair Share Analysis				
	Subject Property	**Competitor A**	**Competitor B**	**Competitor C**	**Competitive Set**
Available rooms	350	400	300	325	1,375
Occupied rooms	87,509	98,550	79,169	75,208	340,436
Share of available rooms	25.45%	29.09%	21.82%	23.64%	100.00%
Share of occupied rooms	25.70%	28.95%	23.26%	22.09%	100.00%
Indexed share of occupied rooms	1.01	1.00	1.07	0.93	1.00

included in the survey); overreliance on memory recall; and failure to understand why someone is requesting information. (www.wisc.edu/urpl/people/marcouiller/projects/clearinghouse/Conversion.htm, accessed March 19, 2006)

Tangible features include the physical assets of the property, such as the following:

- Number and configuration of guest rooms
- Number and configuration of seats in a restaurant
- Number and size of meeting rooms
- Size and configuration of public space
- Number and type of food and beverage outlets
- Number and quality of recreational facilities, etc.

Intangible features include such elusive things as the following:

- Perceived quality of guest service
- Cleanliness
- Friendliness of the staff
- Reputation of the facility
- Popularity of the destination in which the subject property is located

It is important to note that although intangible features are difficult to quantify, they are often more important than the tangible features to both existing and prospective customers.

 Web Browsing Exercise

Use your favorite web browser to search for articles on tourism conversion studies. One you may wish to access is the following: www.tourism.umn.edu/research/nonbias.html, accessed March 19, 2006. Be prepared to discuss methods to improve tourism conversion studies.

The simplest way in which to profile the most marketable attributes of the hospitality enterprise is through the use of standardized checklists that are completed by appropriate department heads or employees who are expected to make a contribution to the development and execution of the annual marketing program. Their observations should then be compiled to create an overall "property profile" that may be used to compare the subject property with the other properties that are determined to be part of the competitive set.

The determination of whether a particular property attribute constitutes a competitive advantage depends on its importance to your customers and the features offered by the properties that comprise your competitive set. Accordingly, you must first identify the properties with which you compete directly and subsequently inventory their strengths and weaknesses along the same attributes for comparative purposes.

Which properties should be considered part of the competitive set? This question must be answered clearly (and consistently) in order to provide an appropriate framework for the comparative analysis. Specifically, three criteria should be used to determine whether a specific property is directly competitive with the subject property: geographic proximity, substitutability, and price.

Geographic Proximity. All other things being equal, hotels and restaurants that are located in the same geographic proximity are generally competitive. But do those adjacent to an airport compete directly with those located downtown? It depends on the destination in which the two are located. They may be competitive in a smaller market, but are clearly not competitive in larger markets such as New York, Mexico City, or London. The issue of geographic proximity, therefore, is one of whether a guest would be significantly *inconvenienced* by having to stay in one of the other properties if the subject property were not available.

Substitutability. Substitutability is a subjective assessment of whether prospective guests view the other properties as *acceptable alternatives* when the subject property is not available. Stated another way, would a Sheraton property be an acceptable alternative to a Marriott if the latter were not available to a traveler who prefers to stay with Marriott? If yes, the two brands may be deemed "substitutable." If not, the two brands are probably not directly competitive because one is not perceived to be an acceptable alternative for the other.

Price. In general, properties that are priced within plus or minus 15 percent of the subject property will be directly competitive *if they meet the other two criteria referenced previously*. A property's competitive set usually comprises other properties that

- are in close geographic proximity,
- offer a quality of accommodation,
- have service that is perceived to be "substitutable" by prospective guests, and
- achieve an actual rate within plus or minus 15 percent of that achieved by the subject property.

Not all properties that meet these three criteria will be 100 percent competitive within each individual market segment; therefore, your competitive analysis should be conducted on a segment-by-segment basis to account for any such differences.

Once you have determined the properties that comprise your competitive set, you can apply the same checklist to profile the subject property's individual strengths and weaknesses compared to the others. After these have been compiled, you can develop a comparative matrix to assess strengths and weaknesses. This analysis will help you to discern distinctive characteristics that may become the foundation for an effective marketing strategy. It is particularly insightful to prepare this analysis by individual market segment, then rank each property's attributes in terms of their perceived importance to the targeted segments. This will highlight differences that may be emphasized in marketing communications.

Environmental Scanning

Another important application of marketing research is to "forecast the future" in order to anticipate changes in such things as the following:

- Consumer behavior
- Distribution systems
- Product and brand preferences
- Evolving preferences for specific product and service features

This type of research is typically conducted over multiple points in time and the results are reviewed to assess emerging shifts in customer preferences or buyer behavior. An example from the Yesawich, Pepperdine, Brown & Russell/Yankelovich Partners 2005 *National Business Travel MONITOR* is shown in Exhibit 7-6.

There appear to be two preference shifts underway among business travelers in the United States:

1. Growing interest in "independent" accommodations (not chain affiliated)
2. Growing preference for hotels with fewer than 300 guest rooms

The survey goes on to speculate why these changes are taking place and, importantly, their implications for future hotel development and operations. Developers and franchisors of hotels would presumably be very interested in tracking these trends over time because they could have significant implications for the types of hotels and motels they build, operate, and/or franchise.

This type of environmental scanning information is published by a number of national trade organizations in the United States, including the Travel Industry Association, the National Restaurant Association, and the American Resort Development Association. Private sector firms such as Ernst & Young; PricewaterhouseCoopers; and Yesawich, Pepperdine, Brown & Russell are also excellent resources for this type of information.

Customer Research

This aspect of the marketing research program typically entails the development of comprehensive profiles on two customer groups:

1. Existing customers—specifically those who have patronized the subject property within the past 12 months
2. Prospective customers—individuals who meet some predetermined demographic or travel habit profile and currently patronize one or more competitive brands

This aspect of the research program should also include a comprehensive review of the intermediaries, if any, who direct business from these individuals to your establishment. The latter would include travel agents, tour operators, meeting planners, and convention or congress organizers.

Formal Marketing Research

Formal marketing research—and we use the word *formal* to distinguish it from the ad hoc collection of data, such as that provided by comment cards—is the objective and empirical collection of information about consumers. In this same sense, it means primary data as opposed to secondary data. Secondary data are those collected from some other source (typically in the public domain) that may be useful to our purpose. What was discussed earlier under the heading of external data are largely secondary data. Primary data, on the other hand, are collected for a specific purpose and constitute what is called formal, or primary, marketing research.

Proprietary Research

Proprietary research is research conducted on behalf of a particular organization for the particular use of that organization—as opposed to a general use. It may be conducted by the organization itself or by an outside "supplier"—a firm commissioned to do the actual data collection for another firm. Regardless of who conducts it, the research requirements are the same. Absolute rigor and control are necessary for the findings to have validity and reliability. There are two broad categories of research—qualitative and quantitative. Both have their place; the important thing is to know what that place is. Exhibit 11-11 is an example of Sweet Tomatoes inviting guests to participate in an online survey.

EXHIBIT 11-11 One method used by firms to find out how well they are doing is e-mail surveys.

Source: Sweet Tomatoes. Used by permission.

Qualitative Research

Qualitative research consists of "directional" information on consumer attitudes and behavior that is typically gathered from small samples of respondents. It is largely exploratory in nature, and the findings cannot be generalized to a larger population with any degree of confidence. Its purpose is usually to learn more about a subject, to understand how consumers use a product to test a new product concept, or to provide information for developing further quantitative research.

The most common form of qualitative research is the **focus group**. A focus group consists of 8 to 10 people who represent the type of people expected to use the product (a judgment obtained by screening in their selection). Exhibit 11-12 shows an example of a screener used to recruit gamblers. These people are brought together in a room where a skilled moderator leads the discussion. Characteristics of moderators are discussed in the appendix.

As an illustration, suppose a restaurateur was considering a radically new menu. She has a mock-up of the menu made, but before she goes ahead with the change, she wants to see how her customers might react. She invites eight of her customers on each of four different days of the week to have a free dinner if they will agree to participate in a two-hour focus group about their reactions to the new menu. She hires a skilled moderator (she would not do this herself because of her lack of skill and potential bias), who leads the group in discussion. The moderator not only asks questions but also attempts to build a rapport with the group and spends a great deal of time probing. The relationship between the moderator and the group is important because a reluctant group will not provide thorough information.

It is common to audiotape or videotape focus groups. Thus, more complete "content" analysis is possible after the session is over. Also, while the session is being conducted, the restaurateur and some of her staff may sit behind a one-way mirror and observe the proceedings, watching for special nuances and signs that the moderator might miss. Exhibit 11-13 shows an example of a moderator's guide to understand players' desire to play slot machines.

The other common form of qualitative research is the personal interview. This constitutes a structured exchange in which the interviewer probes for specific comments and reactions.

Following are some pragmatic reasons for using qualitative research:

- It can be executed quickly in a short period of time.
- It is relatively economical.
- The environment can be tightly controlled.
- It permits direct contact with consumers.
- It permits greater depth by probing for responses.
- It permits customers to open up.
- It develops new creative ideas.
- It establishes consumer vocabulary.
- It uncovers basic consumer needs and attitudes.
- It establishes new product concepts.
- It interprets previously obtained quantitative data.
- It is used to help develop survey items for a quantitative data

The major deficiency with qualitative research, however, is that you cannot generalize from it. The best you can say is that this is what these particular people say. It does, however, help in providing some directional insights on consumers' attitudes and intentions. It helps to define problems and oftentimes forms the basis for quantitative research to follow. Sometimes we think we understand the problem but really do not; we are unable to put ourselves into the consumer's perspective. Other times we simply don't know what the problem is. Comment cards may be positive, customer comments are good, and everything

---

EXHIBIT 11-12   **Example of a Screen Used to Recruit Those Who Play Slot Machines**

CHECK QUOTA FOR GENDER. APPROACH BASED ON QUOTA. LOOK FOR PEOPLE AROUND SLOT MACHINES.

GENDER   Male or Female   NO MORE THAN 60% OF ONE GENDER

1. Today we are asking about legalized gambling. About how often do you participate in legalized gambling, where you gamble at least 15 minutes? GIVE RESPONDENT CARD AND RECORD. CHECK QUOTAS.

More than 5 times a week	1
About twice a week	2
About once a week	3
About twice a month	4
About once a month	5
About once every two months	6
About 4 times a year	7 T&T*
About 2 times a year	8 T&T
Once a year or less	9 T&T
Do not gamble	10 T&T

   (T&T means Thank you and terminate)

2. Which category describes your age? GIVE RESPONDENT CARD AND RECORD. CHECK QUOTAS.

Less than 21	1 T&T
21–34	2
35–44	3
45–54	4
55–64	5
65–74	6
75+	7 T&T

3. Are you a:

Local _____ resident?	1
Out-of-town visitor?	2

4. When visiting a legalized gambling establishment, what percentage of your time is spent playing traditional slot machines, new multiline video slot machines, or video poker games? IF TOTAL LESS THAN 50%, THANKS AND TERMINATE.

Traditional reel slots	_____
Multiline video slots	_____
Video poker	_____
Total	100%

5. How many hours do you normally gamble per session? _____ IF LESS THAN 1 HOUR, THANKS AND TERMINATE.

6. What denomination do you play most often? _____

7. How many coins do you play per spin? _____

8. Which machine do you play most often? _____

Today we are asking customers about slot machines. It will take about 75 minutes, and we will pay you $35 for your time. Plus, you will help us decide which new games to introduce. All interviewing will take place in a meeting room in this hotel-casino. GAIN COOPERATION. TRY TO GET THEM TO COME TO NEXT SESSION. IF NOT, SIGN UP FOR LATER SESSION. The interviewing times are: _____.

INTERVIEWS TAKE PLACE.

GET NAME: _____

GIVE INSTRUCTION SHEET ON WHERE AND WHEN TO MEET.

EXHIBIT 11-13   **Moderator's Guide**

- Introduction
- Complete first page of questionnaire that asks basic demographic and usage characteristics
- Type of slot machines respondents' play most often and why
- Name of the game respondents play most often
- How slot machine player behavior has changed over time
- Possible reasons people choose to play a specific slot machine
- Features people would like to see in slot machines that are currently unavailable
- Awareness, trial, and usage of different brands of slot machines
- Attitudes and beliefs toward the different manufacturers' machines

- Impact of the specific machine or game on the machine in the decision to play one machine over another; for example, players often request to have machines locked down. How will this impact server-based gaming?
- Frequency of playing progressive machines and why
- Which jackpot option is more enticing (small, frequent payouts; big, less frequent payouts; or it does not matter) and why
- When playing slot machines, which behavior describes respondents (play alone not talking to anyone else, play with little discussion with others, play with frequent discussion with others) and why
- What other activities compete for the gambler's entertainment dollars?

---

looks rosy, except business is declining. Through qualitative probing it may be possible to uncover some problems that otherwise would never reveal themselves. Exhibit 11-14 shows a focus group facility.

Quantitative Research

Quantitative research consists of information that is collected in such a manner that the corresponding conclu-sions may be "projected" to the entire population under study with a certain degree of confidence. **Descriptive quantitative research** tells us how many, how often, whether they like or dislike something, and the demography of the respondents. For instance, it might show that there were 362 females interviewed (48 percent of the total interviewed), these females ate in a restaurant 2.3 times last week, and 36 percent of them have at least a college education. Using statistics, descriptive quantitative research also helps to deter-

EXHIBIT 11-14 A focus group facility is used to collect qualitative data.

Source: Personal Marketing Research, Inc. Used by permission.

mine whether any differences by gender or age grouping are likely to have occurred by chance. Descriptive quantitative research does not tell us why these differences occur, nor does it identify the real reasons consumers behave as they do and make the decisions they make. The frequency of consumers' citing an attribute—for example, location—does not necessarily indicate its relative importance in the selection process, especially when subjects are allowed multiple responses.

Allowing multiple responses on limited choice questions introduces a bias problem that is particularly common in both public and proprietary descriptive research and often diminishes the validity of the findings. For example, the makers of Dial soap commissioned a study on frequent travelers.[4] The questionnaire provided limited lists of items to be rated by the respondents on their degree of importance or expectation of each of the items when staying at a hotel. This list had 29 items on it, one of which was a "bar of soap." Respondents evaluated each item. Thus, it is conceivable that all 29 items could be rated as "expected." It is difficult, at least in the United States, to conceive of anyone who, given 29 items from which to choose, would not expect to find a bar of soap in her hotel room. Apparently, however, that is not the case, because only 96.2 percent of the respondents who patronize luxury hotels indicated that they expected to find a bar of soap! Because this was the highest percentage of all items chosen from the list, the conclusion of the study was that the most important amenity expected in a hotel is a bar of soap and that hoteliers should put more personal care items in their rooms. From a research perspective, such an interpretation is invalid for two reasons.

The first reason is because of multiple responses. When allowed to name as many items as desired with no rank ordering or choices to be made, very salient items such as soap will almost always be mentioned. The second reason is the bias of the list. Under the category of services, besides the bar of soap (which is not a service) were items such as wake-up call, direct dial phone, cable TV, check cashing, free newspaper, tennis courts, swimming pool, and fresh flowers in the room, all of which are either services or augmented products. None of the 29 items, with the singular exception of soap, is offered by all hotels. Because soap is always present and expected in a hotel and the other items are not, the results of this research were preordained. In other words, it was a no-lose situation for Dial.

To further emphasize this point, let us carry it one step further. Suppose that now we know that only 96 percent of guests expect soap and had wanted to prove that soap was not the most expected item. We could very easily do so. In our limited choice list, besides soap, we would include the following: bed, sheets, pillows, blanket, chair, lamp, toilet, hot and cold running water, and carpet. With this list we would likely "prove" that, in fact, soap was 10th on the list of expected items. You may think this somewhat absurd (and this case is a particularly blatant one), but this type of research is prevalent in much published research today.

Inferential quantitative research, unlike descriptive quantitative research, allows us to generalize to a larger population based on the findings from a probability sample, in which each person in the population being studied (e.g., business travelers) has an equal chance of being selected. Since it is rarely feasible to survey everyone in whom we might be interested (called a population), we have to select a few people from the larger group (called a sample). With inferential statistics, it is possible to draw conclusions about the population on the basis of just a sample—so long as the sample is representative of the population.

Inferential methods also enable the multivariate analysis of interaction effects among the data collected, and this, in turn, assumes probability sampling. An example would be measuring various effects of different factors on a specific market segment's choice of a particular restaurant. A sample from the segment could be surveyed and asked to rate the importance of food quality, service, ambience, location, and price in their decision. In **multivariate analysis**, each of these attributes would interact with the others. The analysis would then reveal relative weights—that is, the respective influence of each attribute in choosing the restaurant. This would reveal both the relative relationship of the various attributes and their predictive capability in restaurant choice.

With the findings from the preceding, assuming we had surveyed a representative sample of all people who choose that restaurant, we could then generalize the results to all those people (the population) as to why they make that choice. This would tell us what is important in influencing people to choose the restaurant, or, perhaps, why they would not choose it. Thus, inferential data are far more powerful and useful than descriptive data. They are also more complex, take more skill to obtain, require more computer analysis, and are more expensive both in collection and analysis. Further, although they are more powerful, inferential and multivariate data are also more susceptible to misinterpretation.

Research Design

Developing the research design may be the most important part of all research. This is because perfectly executed and analyzed research is virtually worthless if it is not based on the appropriate design. The design is what guides the research from beginning to end, as shown in Exhibit 11-15. Whether you are conducting research, commissioning it, or reading it, you should understand the requirements of the research design. The first four steps are the most critical ones for building the research foundation, which we will discuss in detail. They include specifying the research purpose, defining the research problem, establishing the research objectives, and determining what we expect to find out.

Research Purpose

The first step in designing research that will provide useful managerial information is to make sure that you correctly identify the research purpose. The research purpose is what you intend to do with the findings—that is, what kinds of business decisions you plan to make after you have the results. You might want to develop an advertising campaign, change your menu, refurbish your decor, run a special promotion, or any number of other things.

The research purpose flows from the management problem, which may seem very obvious. In truth, that is not necessarily the case. For example, you might say that the purpose of a research is to find out why business is declining. You might learn that it is declining because three new competitors have come to town and your former customers are going to them. Simply knowing that you had new competition, which you probably knew anyway, would not help much in making these decisions. What you want the research to tell you is how to stop business from declining. Knowing your purpose will lead to obtaining the information you need to fulfill that purpose.

Research Problem

The research problem is how to provide the information that addresses the management problem. We can use the

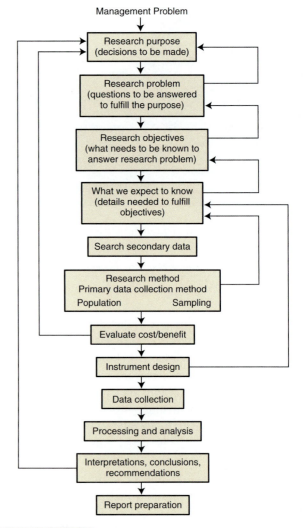

EXHIBIT 11-15 A flowchart of the research process.

same example as before. The management problem is that business is declining. The research purpose is to learn how to stop the business from declining, or we could say that the research purpose is to gather the information needed to develop a marketing strategy to stop the decline in business. The research problem, then, is to answer the question, What is causing business to decline? or, to put another way, Why are our customers going to the competition?

Learning that our customers are going to new competition is not enough. We need to know why they are going there, or, perhaps, why they are not coming here anymore. It is often useful to state the research problem even more specifically in the form of a question: What needs to be done to stop the decline in business?

Research Objectives

The specific objectives are what we want to find out. This follows from the research problem. Following the previous example, the research problem is, What needs to be done to stop the decline in business? The research objectives, then, might be to find out what people do and why. For instance:

- What are people's present eating-out habits?
- What are people's perceptions of our restaurant?
- What would people like to see in a restaurant?

From the objectives flow the answers to the question, What do we expect to know after the research is completed?

What We Expect to Know

What we expect to know is all the pieces of information that are necessary to fulfill the objectives, for instance:

- Where do they go now?
- How often do they go there?
- Why do they go there?
- How much do they spend there?
- What do they order there?
- Why do they dine out at all?
- What do they think of us?
- What do they seek that they can't find at a restaurant?
- What would persuade them to go to a different restaurant?

It should be clear now that if we simply deal with the issue of why business is declining, we might not come up with answers that would be very useful in changing the pattern. That is why the preceding four steps are so critical to good research and why each must flow from the previous one. What each step does, in turn, is simply to narrow the parameters of the research so that it focuses directly on what is needed to make management decisions. This process continues. The first four parameters will establish who the population is; the sample that is needed; the questions that need to be asked; and whether the research should be qualitative, descriptive, inferential, or some combination of these.

Research Method

The remainder of the research design is called the research method. This includes defining the population and corresponding sample, the sample size, the method of data collection, the questions asked, and the type of analysis that will be applied.

Tourism Marketing Application

On the CD-ROM that accompanies this text there is an article by one of the book's co-authors on the use of marketing research to study destinations. The paper examines a variety of destinations and divides tourists into various segments based on reasons for travel and type of destination they would like to visit. The research shows that there are differences between what consumers say they want and what they actually buy. This finding stresses the importance of asking, not what they prefer, but what they actually buy or have bought. For example, I prefer to go golfing for my vacation, but my wife would rather visit museums; we do what my wife says.

Population. The **population** consists of all those individuals who display the characteristics or behavior of interest. This might mean all present customers, all potential customers, or both. It might mean all people who eat at restaurants in this area or all those who come from another area. It might mean all businesspeople or leisure travelers or those who eat beef or those who do not. It might be all those who use a certain restaurant category (fast food) or a certain restaurant brand (McDonald's).

In the broadest sense, the population consists of all those people who display some criterion measure of behavior (e.g., took an overnight vacation, flew on a commercial airline during the past six months, etc.). The population should be as homogeneous as possible—that is, its members should display similar characteristics along the dimensions we wish to measure.

Consider the following example: The operators of a restaurant want to determine the opinions of a particular group of people concerning their restaurant operation. The populations involved could be classified in the following ways:

- All people who eat out
- People who like to dine out in the type of restaurant operated by this restaurateur
- People who have an opportunity to dine at this type of restaurant
- People who know about this particular restaurant and:
  - have never dined there
  - have dined there in the past but do not dine there now
  - dine there now on an irregular basis
  - dine there now on a regular basis

Sample. The **sample** is derived from the population. Because it is generally too expensive and time consuming to survey everyone, we will have to survey only a sample of the entire population. Exhibit 11-16 shows an advertisement for a firm that sells telephone samples. From these few we hope to learn the characteristics of the many. The techniques that should govern the selection of an appropriate sample and corresponding sample size are beyond the scope of this book. Prescribed methods for doing this may be found in any survey research text. Our main concern here will be with the type of sample.

A probability sample is one in which every member of the population (or the sample frame, which is a subset of the population when the population is very large) has an equal chance of being drawn into the sample. This means that the sample is collected randomly without any bias as to who is selected. A simple method of randomly selecting a sample group of 50 would be to put all the names of the population in a bowl and then reach in and pick out the 50 names one at a time.

Statistically, it can be shown that results calculated from a random sample will closely approximate the true characteristics of the population. This is why we can make inferences from a sample to the broader population. It can also be shown that we can state with a certain degree of confidence that what we have learned could not have occurred by chance. Demonstrating these points mathematically is also beyond the scope of this book. Suffice it to say that the larger the sample, the smaller the possible margin of error.* It is only with probability samples that one can legitimately use inferential analysis. This is true because of the statistical controls that are possible with this kind of sample.

A nonprobability sample obviously means just the opposite—that is, everyone in the population does not have an equal chance of being drawn into the sample. This is called a convenience sample, in which people are selected simply because they are convenient. We might choose to sample the first 50 people who check out of the hotel one morning. This does not allow us to generalize our findings to everyone who stayed there the night before. People who check out later or on another day might have very different characteristics from the first 50.

Another kind of nonprobability sample is called a judgmental or quota sample. In this case, it might be decided that some specified variation is needed, such as a mixture of sexes, members of certain age groups, individuals by travel purpose, and method of arrival at a hotel. We might choose the first 10 of each category who check out. Judgmental samples are often used for focus group selection because focus group respondents are usually selected to represent certain characteristics. In these cases, subjects are first screened to be certain that

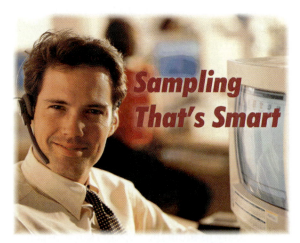

Scientific Telephone Samples (STS) offers a comprehensive array of random digit (RDD), listed, and business samples for marketing research. Since 1988, our commitment to quality, innovation, outstanding customer service, and the lowest prices has made STS the smart choice for accurate, timely, and productive sampling. Smart - because you'll always have the most current data, on time, every time. Smart - because each sample is 100% guaranteed for quality. Smart - because you're saving money. Smart - because you can rest assured that our added dimension of broad-based research knowledge will help guarantee every sample developed by STS will be the finest available anywhere.

 RDD samples from 2¢ to 5¢ per number. Listed samples from 6¢ to 12¢ per number.

(800) 944-4-STS · (949) 461-5400 · www.stssamples.com · info@stssamples.com

EXHIBIT 11-16 Scientific Telephone Samples sells samples to research companies around the United States.

Source: Scientific Telephone Samples (STS). Used by permission.

they meet certain criteria such as demography or product/service usage.

A common method of creating judgmental samples is what is called a mall intercept. This means, essentially, that we go to a shopping mall and intercept people (Exhibit 11-17). If they consent to respond, we screen them by asking, for example, "Do you eat dinner in a restaurant two or more times a week?" If the answer is no, we move on; if it is yes, we proceed with further questions. Of course, all so-called mall intercepts don't take place in malls; they may also take place in airline terminals, restaurant entryways, or hotel lobbies.

Another type of nonprobability sample is composed of the people who fill out guest comment cards in hotel rooms. This is a biased "default" sample. Although you

---

*Large sample sizes do not, however, overcome sample biases or aberrations in the sample that will distort the data and the findings. In fact, in nonprobability samples, larger sample sizes will only magnify the bias and distort the data even further. Further, very large samples are almost always likely to produce statistical significance. How large, then, should a sample be? Many variables affect that answer. An extensive discussion is beyond the scope of this book, but can be found in any good research book. We will add only that bigger is not necessarily better, and statistical confidence levels should be employed to arrive at the correct answer.

EXHIBIT 11-17 One way to collect data is through a mall intercept.

Source: Bob Daemmrich, The Image Works

could argue that everyone who stays in a hotel room has the same opportunity to fill out the comment card, this does not constitute a probability sample because the researcher has no means of controlling the probability of any one guest completing and returning the comment card. This results in a default selection. The bias comes from the fact that the sample would represent only those people who are prone to fill out comment cards (presumably because they had an either delightful or dreadful experience). These people may differ drastically from people who have never filled out a comment card.

Data Collection. The data collection design comes next. However, data collection should clearly be in mind when the sample was selected because the two are closely related and must be coordinated. It should also have been already decided whether the research will be qualitative, quantitative, or a combination of the two.

Regardless of the form of data collection, some written preparation is required beforehand. If focus groups are to be used, a moderator's guide must be prepared. This will be needed to direct the dialogue of the group and to ensure that all intended topics are covered satisfactorily. It will also enable the group moderator to allocate adequate time to probe the topics of greatest interest to the researcher. In other forms of qualitative research, such as personal interviewing, the interviewer will use a guide for the same reason. Additionally, it may be desirable to ask specific questions and write down specific responses for later analysis.

In quantitative research, a questionnaire (survey instrument) is prepared, whether the data is collected by telephone, personal interview, regular (snail) mail, or through an online survey. A mailed questionnaire will require more care in its preparation in terms of format, design, appearance, and other factors that will both induce respondents to complete it and make it easier for them to do so. It is also important that the data collected be easy to tabulate or feed into the computer for analysis. Exhibit 11-18 shows an advertisement for IHR Research Group.

Questionnaire design is not a simple task. Questions must be clear and unambiguous. Each question should, as nearly as possible, have the same meaning for all respondents. This means that if an abstract term such as *quality* is used, it should be defined so that everyone interprets it in the same way.

The subject of questionnaire design is covered in research textbooks and will therefore not be discussed here. We only caution that if you are not measuring what you think you are measuring, you will obtain invalid data and findings. For this reason, too, it is always necessary to pretest questionnaires. This means trying them out on people who will not be included in the final sample to get feedback on the wording, the time it takes, clarity, the understanding of terms, possible omissions, and other factors that might confuse respondents or invalidate the findings.

The decision of whether to use personal interviews, focus groups, or probability samples, as well as the actual method of implementation (e.g., mail, web-based surveys, telephone, or some other distribution method), is an important one in the research design. Each has its trade-offs in terms of time and money. Although the budget is always a limiting factor, the most important criterion is the method that will provide the most valid and reliable data for the problem at hand. There is no one answer to this because each case is individual and must be weighed on its own merits.

An issue of increasing concern to marketers is the extent to which consumers are willing to participate in primary research. Specifically, random digit dialing telephone surveys are increasingly difficult to execute because of consumers' growing reluctance to take the time to participate and the logistic barrier created by the "do not call" legislation enacted in 2003, which enabled consumers to block unsolicited telephone calls from designated residential numbers. One of the outcomes has been the increased need to provide respondents with more attractive incentives to secure their participation. This, in turn, has contributed to an increase in the cost of conducting primary marketing research. Locating prospects who qualify for inclusion in a qualified sample has also become increasingly difficult because of the "fragmentation" of society. As a result, researchers oftentimes purchase access to regional and

Creating Satisfied Customers For Over 25 Years.

At I/H/R Research Group, customer satisfaction isn't just a goal - it's a reality. That's why our customers return again and again. Our intensive interviewer hiring and training process yields superior interviewers. Superior interviewers means superior results, with a higher level of productivity. Plus, our state-of-the-art systems combined with innovative phone center management software, such as CATIHelp and Collective InfoSystems, make the I/H/R experience second to none.

Let I/H/R Research Group make customer satisfaction a reality for you on your next project, with top quality data collection at the lowest prices, on-time results, and the attention to detail you deserve.

I/H/R Research Group
(800) 254-0076 · (702) 734-0757
www.ihr-research.com · info@ihr-research.com

EXHIBIT 11-18 An advertisement for IHR Research Group.

Source: Scientific Telephone Samples (STS). Used by permission.

national "panels" of consumers who have been assembled to reflect the general population and consent to participate in primary research in exchange for compensation.

The arrival of the Internet has also altered the techniques used to conduct primary marketing research, with more surveys now being conducted online. Web-based survey instruments provide a much faster and more economical way to capture and analyze data. Exhibit 11-19 shows one company that provides software for web-based surveys. (Interested students should note that colleges and universities that actually use the software as part of the teaching process can get the software free through Web-Surveyor's Academic Grant process. Check with your professor to see if your college or university uses this software.)

Analysis. The data obtained must, of course, be analyzed very carefully. The method of analysis will have been decided beforehand, since it will affect the way questions are asked, the type of response solicited, and the scale that is used to measure the results. Inferential data used in multivariate analysis, for example, require responses to be collected on an interval or ratio scale (e.g., 1 to 7) instead of simple nominal scale (yes/no) or ordinal scale (rank-ordered data). Such data also require a dependent variable—that is, a measurement such as *likelihood to return*—that can be used as an overall scale to measure the impact of the other (independent) variables. Data analysis is beyond the scope of this book; instead, we refer readers to any good marketing research text.

Exhibit 11-20 includes a minicase and a very brief research design to illustrate the points that have been covered.

EXHIBIT 11-19 WebSurveyor is a leader in software designed to collect data over the Internet.

Source: Retrieved November 11, 2005, from www.websurveyor.com/gateway. asp. Used by permission of Web Surveyor.

Reliability and Validity

The research design, the sampling, the data collection, and the data analysis must be all rigorously controlled when doing research. Each step is critically important, none more or less so than the others. Two supreme tests are applied to research findings—reliability and validity. Because these tests are so critical, we will discuss them further.

Reliability

Reliability in research refers to the consistency of the measurement over different points in time. Stated another way, a reliable measure is one that will produce consistent re-

EXHIBIT 11-20	Taco Gourmet Minicase

A successful restaurateur decided to start a Mexican fast-food chain offering "gourmet" tacos and other Mexican foods in order to cash in on the latest fast-food trend but at a higher level of quality. His pilot effort was called Taco Gourmet. The food quality was superior because he used only the best ingredients. He priced his items about 30 percent higher than the competition for the same items.

Business was excellent the first month, then started falling off. After three months, it was only half of what it had been the first month. The owner noticed that few of his customers were repeat customers. He inquired among his friends to see whether they had heard complaints. The only complaint that seemed to appear was about the prices. The owner decided to conduct some formal research. After analyzing the situation, a consultant developed the following research design:

- Purpose of the research: To determine product and pricing strategies.
- Research problem: What is the market looking for in a Mexican fast-food restaurant?
- Objectives:

  To determine quality perceptions of Mexican fast food
  To determine the price–value relationships of Mexican fast food
  To determine market demand for Mexican fast food at different price and quality levels
- What we expect to find out:

  Do people know and appreciate the difference between quality and ordinary Mexican fast food? If yes, on what basis?

How much are they willing to pay?
How frequently do they eat it?
Where do they go now? How often? How much do they spend?
What is the present awareness and trial of Taco Gourmet?
What is the present perception of Taco Gourmet?
How much more, if anything, will people pay for "different" Mexican fast food?

- Population: All people over the age of 16 within a five-mile radius who eat Mexican fast food at least once a month
- Sample: Assuming 50 percent of the population appreciates the difference in quality, with a 5 percent margin of error and a desired confidence level of 95 percent, a sample of 384 is required.* With an expected response rate of 25 percent, a probability sample of 1,600 names will be drawn from street listings.
- Data collection: Four focus groups divided by sex and age will be convened. Data collected from these groups will be used to develop a written questionnaire to be mailed to the sample.
- Data analysis: Frequency statistics will be derived and data will be cross-tabulated by demography. Regression analysis will be used to predict intention to purchase Mexican fast food at various price and quality levels.

*The computation of sample size is done here using the proportional method, which is described in research texts.

sults over different samples taken from the same population over time. It is important to note, however, that data may be reliable (consistent), but not necessarily valid.

Validity

Validity in research refers to whether the data represent true and accurate measures of the variables under study. Stated another way, do the data really measure what they purport to measure? Valid data will always be reliable.

Here is a humorous example to illustrate the difference between the two concepts. Let us say a particular psychologist believes that the true measure of human intelligence may be defined by the circumference of an individual's skull. He then measures the circumference of the skulls of his various students and declares those with the largest skulls to be the most intelligent. He takes another set of measurements one year later only to find similar results and makes the proclamation once again. Is this a valid measure? Clearly, the answer is no. Although the circumference measurements were consistent (reliable), they did not represent a valid measure of human intelligence. So, valid measurements will always be reliable, but reliable measurements may not necessarily be valid. Both characteristics are required to make the data useful.

Some of the critical forms of validity are as follows:

- *Face Validity:* Is the instrument (questionnaire) measuring everything it is supposed to measure? Is the sample representative of the behavior or trait being measured?
- *Construct Validity:* Is the construct being measured the one we think we are measuring? For instance, if we want to find out why people choose a restaurant and they tell us that the most important factor is the quality of food, are they really telling us that this is the reason they choose a given restaurant?
- *Internal Validity:* Are the findings free from bias? Are they true, or are they an artifact of the research design? For instance, are there intervening, interactive, additive, or spurious effects that affect the responses and are extraneous to the causal relationship? An example of this is research on "best" hotels. If 100 people are asked their opinions of a hotel and 50 have been there and 50 have not, then having been to the hotel is an intervening variable—that is, it "intervenes" in their opinion. Such variables must be controlled. In this case, we would control by asking whether they had been there. We could then compare the responses from each group to see whether they differed.

Without validity, research findings projected to a larger population are meaningless. Anyone who wants to use research for decision-making purposes should always verify its validity first. Lack of validity is the most common cause of faulty research. Other common faults of research projects, presented more or less in order of the frequency of occurrence and importance, are contained in the following list:

1. Lack of construct validity
2. Failure to control for intervening variables
3. Unwarranted conceptual leaps, unsupported conclusions, and presumptive judgments
4. Failure to apply tests of statistical significance
5. Errors in sample size and selection
6. Failure to identify the issue, problem, or purpose of the research
7. Failure to capture the richness of the data (whether because of poor research instruments or poor statistical analysis)
8. Failure to define or limit variables
9. Poor writing
10. Failure to notice spurious relationships[5]

Customer Satisfaction Research

Some form of customer satisfaction research is conducted by most hospitality enterprises in order to maintain a contemporary perspective on precisely how customers feel about the business and its delivery of the services it provides. In its simplest form, this type of information is gathered through in-room or at-table comment cards. However, caution should be exercised about the interpretation of information gleaned in this manner because of the lack of control exercised over the way respondents have been sampled (i.e., not on some random or systematic basis). More sophisticated customer satisfaction measurement programs entail the discipline of sampling respondents on some regular frequency (both while they are "consuming" the product and postdeparture), the analysis of the results against some predetermined standard of success (e.g., a minimum of 90 percent of customers should provide a "satisfied" or better rating), or against the normative ratings of other properties that may belong to the same chain or franchise system. These ratings may also be conducted and evaluated by third party organizations such as J.D. Power & Associates.

> **Tourism Marketing Application**
> The Mexico Ministry of Tourism conducted a study of foreign visitors' satisfaction with their visit to Mexico. A total of 62,452 questionnaires were answered between November 2001 and April 2002, the result of which was an overall level of satisfaction of 82.1 points, on a scale of 1 to 100. The complete methodology and other levels of satisfaction can be found on the website www. sectur.gob.mx/wb2/securing/sect_8978_study_of_ tourist_pr accessed March 19, 2006.

Program Measurement

Marketing research may also be used to yield one or more metrics by which entire marketing programs are measured. If the assumption is that the marketing program is intended solely to increase revenues (it may not be), then management should evaluate the standard metrics of occupied rooms, business mix, room rate, REVPAR, and total revenue to declare success or failure. But the marketing plan may also be designed to create or change a property's image, communicate the news of a renovation, or simply enhance the reputation of the enterprise as a caring corporate citizen. If so, then the standard financial metrics alone won't reveal the entire story. Rather, in this instance, management may elect to supplement the traditional performance measures with "surrogate" measures of market awareness, image, and intention to act. Each of these will require some form of qualitative research, but may prove invaluable in the overall evaluation of campaign performance. For example, the research may reveal that unaided awareness (e.g., not prompted by any mention of the brand name) increased from X to Y percent as a result of a well-orchestrated advertising and public relations campaign, or that the image of the destination has changed to appeal to younger adults 25 to 34 years old. When combined with traditional performance metrics, the results provided by this type of marketing research can prove invaluable.

■| Summary

The most effective marketing programs are those guided by the continuous collection, evaluation, and interpretation of marketing research. In its most basic form, this research entails an assessment of the market forces responsible for area-wide demand. It also includes a comprehensive understanding of how the hospitality enterprise compares to its direct competitors and a thorough assessment of the origins, habits, preferences, and intentions of customers. Marketing research may also be used to illuminate answers to specific questions about operations and to assist with an evaluation of the impact of the overall performance of the marketing plan.

Marketing research provides the insights that help frame managerial decisions, but it does not make them for you. It should be designed to provide specific information to answer the questions to which an operator needs answers. This is not a simple matter. Too much research is conducted without a complete understanding of what management hopes to learn. On the other hand, too much research is conducted to confirm decisions already made or to feed an ego. When the decision fails, the research is blamed.

The results of valid research should be accepted and used, even if they refute existing beliefs. Too much research ends up buried in a file drawer because it did not corroborate someone's prior assumptions. Regardless of what management believes, it is customers' perceptions that count.

It is difficult to overemphasize the importance of marketing information systems in the hospitality industry today. Whether it is environmental scanning, internal data, competitive analysis, or insights on consumer perceptions and behavior, the time has come when management will no longer survive, except in rare cases, by intuitive decisions only. Management at every level of a hospitality organization needs information not only to manage effectively but also to both anticipate and manage the future. It is not as easy as it seems to set up the systems that will provide the information, nor will the systems come until management fully understands what its needs are and demands the systems to fulfill them.

On the other hand, the problem may be one of having too much information. Computer technology and information services provide an abundance of information too unwieldy for ready digestion. The additional problem, then, is one of selection. Effective marketing information systems will come only after defined and selective informational needs are established.

Marketing research is an area of the marketing information system just coming into its own in hospitality. Remarkably, hospitality, an industry that is physically closer to its customer than most, is one that knows the least about its customers. The result has been both the loss of customers and the winning of customers by default. Essentially, this has resulted in the "trading" of customers. The firm that wants to keep customers is simply going to have to know its customers better.

There is a myth that marketing research is used only to make big decisions and has little to do with daily operations. Although this argument might have some merit in, say, manufacturing tires, it bears little weight in an industry where brand loyalty is fleeting and every product unit has a personal relationship with the individual who purchases it. The value of research is tied more to the level of uncertainty than to the level of risk in making the decision.

■ Key Terms

CREST (Consumer Reports in Eating Share Trends)
secondary research
designated market area (DMA)
proprietary research
focus group
descriptive quantitative research

inferential quantitative research
multivariate analysis
population
sample
reliability
validity

■ Discussion Questions

1. Why are management information systems and marketing research more important today than they were 10 or 15 years ago?
2. Describe how inferential quantitative research is different from descriptive research. What implications does this have for understanding the hospitality customer? Give examples of situations in which you would use each or both.
3. Describe the difference between a probability and a nonprobability sample. Be prepared to discuss when you would use each and why.
4. Discuss the different versions of validity and reliability.
5. What questions need to be asked when considering selecting a sample?
6. Explain the pros and cons of comment cards.

■ Group Projects

1. You, as a manager of a hotel, have run a unique weekend package promotion for six weeks. It was an unqualified success. You wonder why and decide to commission some research to find out. Define the research purpose, the research problem, the objectives, what you would expect to know when done, the population, the sample, data collection, and analysis (in general terms).

2. How is the hospitality industry unique in its ability to gather internal information? Give some examples of how this can be done. Make a list of things you would want to know about your customers if you managed a hotel or restaurant. Discuss how this information would help you make management decisions.

■ References

1. Visit www.ypbr.com.
2. Geller, A. (1984). *Executive information needs in hotel companies.* Peat, Marwick, Mitchell & Co.
3. Jain, S. C. (1985). *Marketing planning and strategy.* Cincinnati: South Western, 159.
4. Knutson, B. (1987). *Frequent traveler study perceptions of economy, mid-price, and luxury market segments.* E. Lansing: Michigan State University. Prepared for the Dial Corporation.
5. Lewis, R. C., & Pizam, A. (1986, August). Designing research for publication. *Cornell Hotel and Restaurant Administration Quarterly,* 57.

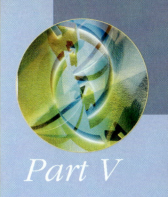

Part V

Functional Strategies

Chapter 12
Differentiation, Segmentation, and Target Marketing

Chapter 13
Branding and Market Positioning

Chapter 14
The Hospitality Pricing Mix

Chapter 15
The Communications Mix: Advertising

Chapter 16
The Communications Mix: Sales Promotions, Merchandising, Public Relations, and Publicity

Chapter 17
The Communications Mix: Personal Selling

Chapter 18
Hospitality Distribution Systems: Bringing the Product to the Customer

Chapter 19
Channels of Distribution: Bringing the Customer to the Product

Chapter 20
Interactive Marketing: Internet and Database Marketing

Differentiation, Segmentation, and Target Marketing

Overview

The concepts of differentiation, segmentation, and target marketing are discussed in this chapter. These concepts, while related, are really separate tools used in marketing. Differentiation refers to the task of making your products and services different, or appear different, from those of the competition. Firms differentiate the offering on some combination of features and/or benefits in an attempt to satisfy the specific needs of a well-defined group of prospective customers. For differentiation to work, customers have to perceive the difference as adding value, which encourages them to want your product over another. Product marketing differentiates by the size and appearance of the package, the components used in the making of the product, and/or the actual performance of the product. Services are more difficult to differentiate within the same product class, but there are both tangible and intangible ways to differentiate services, as we will discuss in this chapter.

(continued on page 312)

310

I. Introduction to Hospitality Marketing
1. The Concept of Marketing
2. Marketing Services and the Hospitality Experience
3. The Marketing Mix and the Product/Service Mix
4. Relationship/Loyalty Marketing

II. Marketing to Build a Competitive Advantage
5. Strategic Marketing
6. The Strategic Marketing System and Marketing Objectives

VII. Feedback

VI. Synthesis
21. The Marketing Plan

III. The Marketplace
7. Understanding Individual Customers
8. Understanding Organizational Customers
9. The Tourist Customer and the Tourism Destination

IV. Situational Analysis
10. Understanding Competition
11. Marketing Intelligence and Research

V. Functional Strategies
12. *Differentiation, Segmentation, and Target Marketing*
13. Branding and Market Positioning
14. The Hospitality Pricing Mix
15. The Communications Mix: Advertising
16. The Communications Mix: Sales Promotions, Merchandising, Public Relations, and Publicity
17. The Communications Mix: Personal Selling
18. Hospitality Distribution Systems
19. Channels of Distribution: Bringing the Customer to the Product
20. Interactive Marketing: Internet and Database Marketing

David W. Norton
Senior Vice President, Relationship Marketing,
Harrah's Entertainment

David Norton is the senior vice president of relationship marketing at Harrah's Entertainment, which operates more than 40 casinos nationwide and has been recognized for its outstanding marketing practices by the *Wall Street Journal, Info Week*, and *CIO* magazine.

Norton is responsible for the company's direct marketing strategy, VIP marketing, revenue management, teleservices, the Total Rewards customer loyalty program, Internet marketing, marketing reinvestment, operational CRM, and Travel Services.

Prior to joining Harrah's in October of 1998, Norton worked in the credit card industry with American Express, Household International, and MBNA. He has a BS in finance from Boston College, an MBA from Loyola College, and a master's in management of technology from the University of Pennsylvania and the Wharton School.

Marketing in Action

David Norton, Senior Vice President, Relationship Marketing, Harrah's Entertainment

Do casino companies segment their customers? If so, how do they do that?

Certainly we do. I'm sure other casino companies think about slots versus tables and VIP versus non-VIP. We do, in terms of slots versus tables, daily value, customer frequency, are they a lodger or not, and then we try to ascertain how loyal they are to us using models to try to predict value and compare that to our observed behavior.

How do you develop and identify different market segments?

We can't know who a non-Total Rewards member is and that's why it's so important for us to encourage people to sign up, because it gives us a lot of insight into the business. When we started a number of years ago, we were only tracking about half of our gaming revenue, and now it's close to 80 percent. As we've bought Horseshoe and Caesars, we see that their tracked play was a lot less than ours, so we've focused a lot of energy on the value proposition of Total Rewards and why it's in your best interest to have your play tracked. At the same time we're going to be very respectful of your privacy, and we hold that promise as a very important standard for us. Because of that, we have a lot of information about the customers in terms of how we identify market segments. It's

really looking at the data initially to say what trends are there and what makes sense. With any degree of segmentation, you have to figure out what you are going to do differently—whether it's different service or a different marketing message or different marketing offers—so we don't do segmentation for segmentation's sake. As long as you have something different to do, then the segmentation is worthwhile.

In terms of updating it, frankly, the segmentation we launched back in mid-1999 for our original direct mail program is still in place. We've added to them and we've added other capabilities to get more refined in different applications, but the basic premise of the segmentation has stayed stable for a number of years, which gives us a lot of learning within a property and across properties as well.

What are some key things that one should know to effectively segment and target a given market?

I think you need to have the data to figure out who these people are and their behavior, and you have to have the ability to execute against it. For us, we can have all this segmentation, but if it required people to spend days and days writing a query to get at that segmentation, then they're just going to say that's too burdensome. So, the data has got to inform a segmentation and then you have to be able to

Continued on page 312

Overview *(continued)*

Market segmentation is a complementary strategy to differentiation. True market segmentation refers to the task of identifying and classifying groups of "like" customers according to some shared characteristics or behaviors. Target markets are really subsegments. Many of the same principles of segmentation apply, but are refined. Undifferentiated target marketing assumes that all customers within a segment represent equally good prospects and have similar needs and wants, so only one type of product or service is offered. Concentrated target marketing identifies one target market among a number and allocates all of its resources to attracting those customers.

Marketing in Action *(continued)*
David Norton, Senior Vice President, Relationship Marketing, Harrah's Entertainment

make it easy for people to execute so they can think through what the segment is all about, what to do differently, or what test to do. The automation of execution is critical, especially when you have a lot of segments.

There are programs like SRI Consulting Business Intelligence's VALS, Cohorts, and Claritas' PRIZM that help give a psychographic segmentation. Do you do any of that?

We've dabbled in it and there might be a little bit of opportunity there, but that certainly has not been a core part of our success to this point. It's really been more about the transactional data and the little bit of demographic information we get when people sign up, but it's hard to predict who's likely to be passionate about gaming. Two people could be 55 years old and have the same income and live on the same street and yet one loves to game and one does it once a year. This is why psychographics are better than demographics. It's hard to predict with external data, and it isn't until you see the transactional data that you get more accuracy and are able to develop some models.

How do you attract new customers? Do you look at the characteristics of your current customers and try to identify others like them?

No, we've tried acquisition through direct mail, and the returns are poor. We've just about given up on direct mail acquisition, which is obviously different than other industries. For us, it's all about advertising and doing promotions that draw people in and sign them up for Total Rewards with the immediate gratification of the promotions. We do about four big national promotions a year, which reward our existing customers, but also provide a hook for new people to sign up. We do some predictions based on that first observation and figure out who we think has the potential to become a loyal Harrah's customer and do everything we can to get them in the fold.

Is that similar to what was done in the credit card industry?

It's quite different. In credit cards, acquisition is a huge part of what they do, so that's why you get all those solicitations in the mail. Again, in a different industry, direct marketing acquisition works, but we've just found it doesn't for us. It is different in the credit card industry. You also have a better predictor of their value with credit bureaus, so you can see what kind of share you're getting because you can see what someone is doing with all their various cards. For us, we don't know that as explicitly. We just try to predict it.

So, it's more about getting the customer in the door using the traditional methods, such as advertising, and once a customer selects Harrah's versus some other property, you do what you can to get them to keep coming back to you.

It could be that someone is staying at the Mirage and playing there primarily, and then they come across the street to Harrah's just to change their luck or see what it's all about. Or, they're drawn in by Carnival Court at Harrah's or the Show in the Sky at the Rio. So, they may give us a little bit of play. Then, how do we convince them that their casino choice should be a Harrah's Entertainment property? You convince them to come in with that immediate gratification, but it doesn't mean that they're inherently going to be loyal. How do you have them overcome those loyalty effects they have to somebody else, to get them in the fold? That's where we spend a lot of our energy.

In its simplest form, differentiation means distinguishing your products or service from the competition in ways that are both identifiable and meaningful for the customer. How does this occur in the casino business, because you have multiple properties?

I think that in terms of the differentiation, the product is pretty consistent. Obviously, the mix of table games or the mix of denomination might differ from property to property, but we try to match the product to what the core customers want, and I think we've done a pretty good job with that. We know which customers play which games, and we lay out the floor particularly because of that. If Diamonds gravitate to an area, we'll have more employees in that area to make sure we can give differentiated service. So, there's something there with the product, even though at the highest level, it's fairly consistent across not only our own properties, but across the competition as well. However, our offers, incentives, and messages are going to be customized based on where somebody is in our segmentation strategy. Clearly, a big part of what we've done is differentiated service that's delivered through the tier program, and we make sure our Diamond customers get fantastic service. We want all customers to receive good service, but we realize that some customers are worth more because of their loyalty and ensure that they get the differentiated service experience that they want.

Is this differentiation method that you're following sustainable over the long run, and do you think it could be easily copied?

I think it's sustainable for a couple of reasons. Internally, we have the measurement tools in place to figure out how we're doing in terms of the differentiated service or offers. This allows us to ensure that the differentiation is being used well from both a marketing and operations perspective, so people don't drop their eye off the ball. If you look at what we've done over the years, we continue to evolve and refine. We're not resting on our laurels; in fact, we're doing more and more each year to try to get closer and closer to the customer.

Externally, I think a lot of companies are still focused on the facility. I don't see many that have taken the loyalty program or marketing efforts to quite the same level. I think, in general, people in our industry try to distinguish themselves by spending their energy building beautiful facilities—especially in Las Vegas and, to some extent, in other markets as well.

But the reality is, people are coming in partly for the facilities, but they're also coming in for the gaming experience. That's really where you're going to make your money.

Right, though nongaming revenue is a very significant part of the business, especially in Las Vegas.

You have properties around the country. Do the segments change for Las Vegas versus Tunica versus Atlantic City, or are they fairly consistent because a gaming customer is a gaming customer?

The spirit of the segmentation is consistent across all properties, but the specifics might vary. Obviously, the frequency in Las Vegas is not the same as it is in Atlantic City or St. Louis, but we still think that the segmentation makes a lot of sense. What defines a high-frequency customer in Las Vegas is quite different than what defines a high-frequency customer in St. Louis—in terms of the number of trips they can make to the market.

How much decision making occurs at the property level for different offers, or are decisions made at the corporate level?

Specifics are generally done at the property level, but they do it within the framework and tools that we've developed centrally that should make them more effective. We have several roles in my group that are responsible for partnering with the properties, evaluating how they're doing. The execution really happens decentrally, but within a fairly structured framework.

How do you test the effectiveness of different promotions you do for different segments?

With any segment, we can split it up into the standard offer, the test offer, and, if we want to hold out a control group, we can do that as well. So we'll take a like group of customers at a fairly refined level and split them into those three groups and figure out what the incremental value of the marketing intervention is. You can look at that versus the control group, or if we want to test food versus cash, we can see how the two groups perform from a response perspective or a revenue perspective. The key measure that we look at is net profitability, and if we see Offer B worked, then we can roll that out, not only across that segment, but maybe other segments as well. It's very easy to set up tests on the front end, and then we've got a pretty strong mechanism to evaluate what worked and what didn't. Because the segmentation stays stable, we can translate that within a property and across properties as well.

And do you do these tests and control groups for most of your offers or just for a sampling?

Generally any program should have a few tests out there so we can constantly learn and refine and try to get to optimal profitability at a segment level, so we've created a pretty good culture of testing and learning that should be happening every month with the key programs.

Are recency, frequency, and monetary value still metrics that are used fairly often, or have we gone beyond that?

I think we go beyond that. We certainly look at frequency, the recency of their visit, and really how that varies to their pattern is a big part of it. But basically what we act upon is somebody's annual value. It's very clear in the tier program, but also a lot of our marketing is based on frequency, daily value, and stage of the life cycle, as well as changes in behavior—all of which drive what segment a person is going to be in.

For students wanting to get into the casino business in marketing and segmentation, what kinds of courses would you recommend or advice would you give them?

To be successful at our company or just to be a successful marketer, you have to be comfortable with analytics and be analytically inquisitive. What we've done is built a lot of tools where it's pretty easy to evaluate what's going on in the business from a marketing program perspective. It's not about creating the reports, but rather being comfortable with the data, finding insights, and being innovative and creative enough to come up with recommendations based on those insights. Depending on where you are in a corporate role, interpersonal skills are important because you're trying to influence people that you don't necessarily have responsibility for directly. But in summary, what's critical is the comfort in analytics and the ability to take insights and turn them into action.

Used by permission of David W. Norton.

Differentiation

In previous chapters we touched on differentiation, market segmentation, and target marketing. In this chapter we will elaborate on how these tools are used by the marketer to outflank the competition, seize marketing opportunity, maximize marketing efforts, and satisfy customer needs and wants. They are separate concepts and tools, but, at the same time, are highly interrelated—that is, all three are almost always used to market the same product or service. We will define how they are different and how they work together.

Differentiation

Differentiation in its simplest form means distinguishing your product or service from that of the competition in ways that are both identifiable and meaningful for the customer, so that customers will chose your product or service over that of the competition. The assumption is that the customer will *perceive* greater utility, better price value, and/or better problem solution in your product or service. Notice the use of the word *perceive*; it is not necessary that there be an actual difference, only that the potential customer perceives there to be one. It is just as important to note the converse situation. If the market does not perceive a difference, then for all intents and purposes a difference does not exist. It is the role of the marketer to convince the customer that a difference exists. It is the role of operations to deliver the difference.

There are numerous examples of differentiation in the hospitality industry. One is that of Peabody Hotel Group, which differentiates its properties in a unique way: A family of ducks is housed in each hotel and is brought down an elevator each morning to spend the day at a fountain in the hotel lobby. In the evening, the ducks troop back into the elevator to return to their quarters. This daily ritual attracts many camera-toting spectators to the Peabody lobbies. The lobby bar does a roaring business every evening as people wait to see the ducks march into the elevator. In fact, the logo of the Peabody Hotels is a duck (Exhibit 12-1). Does this make the Peabody a better hotel? Probably not, but it certainly differentiates it in an interesting and entertaining way. Another, more functional basis of differentiation may be observed among most all-suite hotel brands such as Embassy Suites, Comfort Suites, and the like, who typically invite guests to "stay in a suite for the price of a room."

Web Browsing Exercise

Visit the Peabody Hotel Group's website (www.peabodyhotelgroup.com/). How does this company market its differentiation strategy on its website? Does this strategy come across on the website?

Basis of Differentiation

Minor product features can serve as the basis for differentiation. In themselves, they may be unimportant, but they can be very effective when

- they cannot be easily duplicated,
- they appeal to a particular need and/or want, and
- they create an image or impression that goes beyond the specific difference itself.

Consider the Plaza Hotel or the Waldorf-Astoria, both in New York City. Both are premier hotels with a great deal of history behind them, and both have been frequented by people of international fame. Their histories cannot be duplicated by other hotels in New York. This basis of differentiation has considerable appeal for customers who like the Old World and the feeling of blending with the past. Further, there is an image or impression that these hotels, because of their past, will deliver great service and unmatched elegance. In sum, companies that differentiate their products must also instill

EXHIBIT 12-1 The Peabody Hotel Group has a unique way of differentiating itself.

Source: Retrieved from www.peabodymemphis.com/asp/ home.asp. Used by permission of Peabody Hotels.

EXHIBIT 12-2 This advertisement for Ritz-Carlton shows an example of tangiblizing the intangible.

Source: © 2005 The Ritz-Carlton Hotel Company, L.L.C. All rights reserved. Reprinted with the permission of The Ritz-Carlton Hotel Company, L.L.C.

an image of those products in the minds of customers that distinguishes them from others and causes the customer to react more favorably toward them.

Differentiation of Intangibles

Because much of the hospitality product is largely intangible, differentiation in traditional marketing often centers largely on "tangibilizing the intangible," which we discussed earlier in the book. Exhibit 12-2 is an example of this. Ritz-Carlton uses a couple hugging and kissing to tangibilize romance. The use of trick photography shows the couple on a silver tray, suggesting that the Ritz-Carlton serves up romance.

Making a tangible representation out of something abstract, such as using an atrium lobby (tangible) to represent an "exciting" (intangible) hotel experience, was an example of this in the first atrium hotels. Today atriums are so common that few differentiate any more. Many hotels try to differentiate on the basis of better service quality. However, this expectation is typically set as a function of

the rate paid (e.g., the higher the room rate, the higher the expected level of service) and is somewhat suspect until customers experience the actual service first, then later decide if it was indeed better. If tangible proof is offered, then differentiating on this basis can be successful. For example, as shown in Chapter 10, Bellagio is perceived to have the best service in town. Proof: The Bellagio is the only five-diamond hotel in Las Vegas. Hotels and restaurants also try to tangibilize their service by evoking issue of tradition, as shown in Exhibit 12-3 for the Langham Hotel, Boston and Exhibit 12-4 for the Waterlot Inn. Similarly, restaurants sometimes differentiate by their tradition.

The Roger Smith Hotel has differentiated itself in the New York City marketplace by creating a guest experience built around art. The exterior, lobby, and restaurant all feature original art designed by the owner and others. This "thinking man's" boutique hotel is unique in a city full of medium to large commercial hotels. Starwood's W concept promises to uniquely differentiate by offering "business chic" to attract the generation X businesspeople who are upwardly mobile and "looking for an experience" in their choice of lodging.

INSTEAD OF SIMPLY PAYING BOSTON'S
FASCINATING SITES A VISIT, STAY IN ONE.

The Langham London, built in 1865.

A world-renowned landmark in luxury that forms the cornerstone of Boston's city center.
A location just minutes from Newbury Street shopping, the museums and Quincy Market.
A grand hotel that not only brings you the best of Boston, but lets you live it firsthand.

THE LEGEND LIVES • SINCE 1865

EXHIBIT 12-3   Langham Hotel tangiblizes its service by evoking tradition.

Source: Adapted from Langham Hotels International (www.langhamhotels. com). Used by permission.

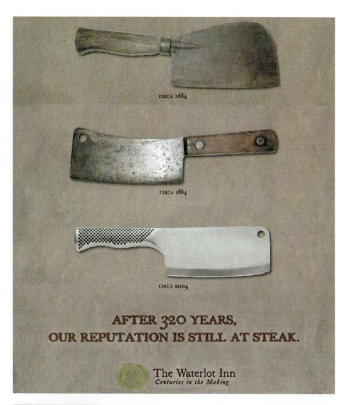

AFTER 320 YEARS,
OUR REPUTATION IS STILL AT STEAK.

The Waterlot Inn
Centuries in the Making

EXHIBIT 12-4   The Waterlot Inn also tangiblizes its service by evoking tradition.

Source: Fairmont Hotels Bermuda. Used by permission.

Differentiation as a Marketing Tool

Differentiation is an important marketing tool, whether the differences are real or only perceived. For one thing, differentiation helps to create awareness and trial by the customer. Atrium lobbies once did that, artifacts once belonging to famous people do it for Planet Hollywood, "infinite attention to detail" service does it for Mandarin Oriental hotels, ducks do it for Peabody Hotels, superior steaks do it for Ruth's Chris Steak House, all-suite accommodations do it for Embassy Suites, chocolate chip cookies do it for Doubletree, and consistency of service does it for Marriott. Note that these differentiating factors are both tangible and intangible, and all, more or less, fit our three previous criteria. Yes, some can be duplicated, but not really that easily.

As we will see later in this chapter, sometimes the only thing we can do when we compete with others in the *same* market segment or product class is attempt to differentiate the product. It is a world of limited opportunities, in this respect, when the product approaches commodity status, and differentiation may occur only in marketing.

When these attempts violate our three rules previously stated (they cannot be easily duplicated, they appeal to a particular need and/or want, and they create an image or impression that goes beyond the specific difference itself), however, such as extensive bathroom amenities and mints on the pillow, the differential advantage is soon lost. The cost of delivering these differentiating amenities can also be very high.

There is a way out of this endless spiral of adding amenities or things that cost money that can be easily duplicated (facetiously referred to by many practitioners as "amenity creep"), and it lies in marketing in its truest sense. This means, of course, refocusing on the customer. Days Inn research in 1985 revealed that guests prefer in-room coffee service over such basic amenities as shampoo, lotions, and shower caps: 87 percent of those customers asked indicated that they would even pay an increased room rate if rooms were supplied with such a service; 78 percent indicated that an in-room coffee service would influence their selection of a hotel the next time they traveled. In-room coffee service, of course, can be easily duplicated and has been many times over.

Days Inn, however, set itself apart by inaugurating this service in budget hotels. They appealed to a particular

Restaurant Latitude…
une invitation au voyage.

Toute latitude est laissée à notre Chef de Cuisine pour vous faire entrevoir et apprécier les saveurs du monde ou encore découvrir les spécialités culinaires de notre pays. Ouvert tous les jours midi et soir

Mövenpick Hotel & Casino Geneva
Route de Pré-Bois 20
1215 Genève, Suisse
Téléphone +41 (0)22 717 11 11
hotel.geneva.airport@moevenpick.com

www.moevenpick-hotels.com
True Excellence in Swiss Hospitality.

MÖVENPICK
Hotel & Casino Geneva

EXHIBIT 12-5 This image clearly creates a perceived differentiation of a restaurant.

Source: Copyright © Mövenpick Hotels & Resorts Management. Used by permission. All rights reserved.

Web Browsing Exercise

Go to the website www.leye.com. What brands does the company offer? How does it differentiate these brands from other restaurants?

Hotel management has also begun to realize the need to differentiate restaurants and have developed more creative concepts. The traditional hotel had a coffee shop, a fine dining room, and a lounge, often with little imagination or creativity and often not fulfilling customers' needs. Rather than being creative and seeking new opportunities, hotels simply accepted that food and beverage departments would hopefully operate at a small profit and there wasn't much that could be done about it. The frequent customer reaction was, "That's hotel food; let's go out to eat."

The situation is quite different outside the United States. Both in Europe and Asia it is not uncommon for hotel dining rooms to be among the best restaurants in the city. Both hotel guests and the local populace patronize them heavily. In France, for example, one can find a two-star hotel with minimal rooms that includes a dining room superior to most in New York City. In Japan, where eating out is such a common practice, F&B can contribute as much as 70 percent of a hotel's revenue. The same is true in Dubai, where such chains as the Rotana Hotel Group are known for their restaurants.

If a hotel restaurant is going to compete with a freestanding restaurant, management has to think, look, and act like its freestanding competition. Jim Nassikas did this when he opened the Stanford Court Hotel in San Francisco, which is now a Renaissance Hotel. Nassikas opened Fournou's Ovens, an upscale restaurant, within the hotel, but didn't tell the hotel guests. There was no mention of the restaurant in the guest rooms or within the hotel. To get there, guests were instructed to go out the front door and around the corner. In fact, one of Nassikas' favorite stories is of the hotel guests who hailed a cab to get to the restaurant. Nassikas' strategy not only added a mystique to the restaurant, but also differentiated it in the eyes of nonguests who fastidiously avoided "hotel food." The result was a very successful, differentiated hotel gourmet restaurant. The New York Palace leased its restaurant space to Le Cirque, creating tremendous differentiated in-house dining experiences for guests, as well as outside customers.

Today there are hotels with "fast-break" bars for juice, coffee, and rolls; lounges with deli bars as well as liquor bars; lobby lounges with entertainment; grazing restaurants; and so forth. When the basic hotel room doesn't change much, these are excellent opportunities to differentiate in ways that are not susceptible to copying and can offer unique and distinct advantages. Marriott spawned the

need and created an impression that went beyond the service itself. The St. Regis in New York set itself apart from its competitors in a different way. There are many "luxury" hotels in New York City. The St. Regis differentiated itself from the rest by offering "butler service." What better ways to travel than having a butler unpack and store your garments and bring hot tea on a moment's notice? Days Inn differentiated one way; St. Regis, another.

Food service establishments actually have greater opportunity to differentiate their product than do hotels. Although some food service product classes may be somewhat close to commodity status, there are many ways that restaurants can differentiate their product; in other words, it is much easier to be creative, economically, with a menu and decor in a restaurant than with a hotel room. Mövenpick Hotel & Casino Geneva has been very successful with its creativity. Exhibit 12-5 clearly creates a perceived differentiation of a restaurant.

sports bar concept with "Champions" in the Marriott Boston that has been replicated successfully in many other Marriotts around the world. As a result, there is an increasing frequency of leased restaurants in hotels by established operators such as Champions, TGI Friday's, Henry Bean, Todd English Restaurants, and others. This trend is explored further in the chapter on branding.

> **Tourism Marketing Application**
> The province of KwaZulu-Natal is located in South Africa. The goal of the Tourism Commission for this region is to be recognized as Africa's premier tourism destination. To reach this goal, the commission has created a website, www.zululand.kzn.org.za (accessed March 25, 2006) that provides information about the various destinations in the region. Each destination is positioned on different features, whether cultural attractions or natural wildlife reserves.

Differentiation—of Anything

Goods manufacturers seek competitive differences through features that may be seen and measured or sometimes just implied. This is also true, said Levitt in a classic article, with services.

> Commodity exchange dealers trade in totally undifferentiated generic goods such as pork bellies and metals; what they sell is the claimed distinction of their execution, their efficiency, their responsiveness to customers' buy and sell orders . . . In short, the "offered" product is differentiated, although the "generic" product is identical. When the generic product is undifferentiated, the offered product makes the difference in getting customers and the delivered product in keeping them.[1]

Product differentiation, then, may be defined as any *perceived difference* in a product when compared with competitive products. It is what makes Smirnoff premium vodka when it is fairly well established that all American vodkas are, by legal specification, very much the same. It is what makes Grey Goose or Belvedere vodka even more premium than Absolut, even when used in a mixed drink where the subtle difference is indistinguishable to most. It is what makes waiting in a single line at a Burger King different from waiting in multiple lines at a McDonald's. It is what makes a person respond, "I just like it there," when asked why he goes to a particular restaurant. It is what makes one hotel appear more friendly; another, more efficient.

In short, the marketer seeks differentiation whether perceived or real. The differentiation may be product specific, message specific, and even brand specific. The latter is more difficult to achieve in the hospitality industry because of the heterogeneity of services but, because of that,

even more desirable for chain operations. Levitt stated the case for differentiation as follows:

> To attract a customer, you are asking him to do something different from what he would have done in the absence of the programs you direct at him. He has to change his mind and his actions. The customer must shift his behavior in the direction advocated by the seller. . . . If marketing is seminally about anything, it is about achieving customer-getting distinction by differentiating what you do and how you operate. All else is derivative of that and only that. . . . To differentiate an offering effectively requires knowing what drives and attracts customers. It requires knowing how customers differ from one another and how those differences can be clustered into commercially meaningful segments. If you're not thinking segments, you're not thinking.[2]

Differentiation also separates product classes. The luxury hotel is different from the budget hotel. Choice International tries to differentiate Sleep Inn from Comfort Inn and Quality Inn from Clarion Hotels. Within the same product class, differentiation separates the competition. Days Inn strives to be different from La Quinta, and Wendy's differentiates from McDonald's and Burger King. In traditional marketing, differentiation is essentially a promotional or advertising strategy that attempts to control demand. In nontraditional marketing it is an internal strategy that attempts to create demand. For this reason, the best differentiation may be in the marketing itself, such as relationship marketing. Differentiation provides an opportunity to strengthen competitive strategy, and it forms the basis of positioning strategy. Exhibit 12-6 shows how one area plans to differentiate itself from other areas.

Market Segmentation

Differentiation and market segmentation are not competing, but complementary, strategies. Whereas the first refers to the unique characteristics of a product or service, the second applies to customers. Product or service differentiation starts with the product or service. These differences need to be identifiable and meaningful to the target audience. Segmentation, on the other hand, starts with the customer. It assumes that the market is made up of customers whose needs and wants are different. The total market is divided into smaller markets that are comprised of people who are in some way alike—that is, who have the same needs or wants on one or more dimensions. We will discuss these groups specifically later in the chapter.

The product or service is defined for specific market segments based on the differences within each segment. For example, Steve Wynn's new property in Las Vegas was designed for customers who want more than the five-star services traditionally found at such hotels as Ritz-Carlton

EXHIBIT 12-6   This advertisement for Seven Canyons of Sedona shows how an area plans to differentiate itself from other areas.

Source: © 2005 Young/Wells. Used by permission.

and Four Seasons. His property is more in line with six-star properties such as the Burj Al Arab in Dubai. Because he was going after this market, there had to be more precise adjustment of the product to address the requirements of specific market segments.

Tourism Marketing Application

Brian Kurth started his company, Vocation Vacations, in 2004. His company enables consumers to "test drive their dream job" without quitting their regular job. On the company's website (www.vocationvacations.com, accessed March 25, 2006), interested consumers can choose multiple-day "vocations" in a variety of industries. They can also choose to act as general manager of a hotel. Clearly this company is designed for those truly seeking a different type of experience.

Which Comes First—Differentiation or Segmentation?

Which comes first is not the proper question, because firms do not undertake either strategy separately. Rather, firms

undertake a combination of both at different times. For example, the firm may first segment the total market into smaller markets and then perform differentiation within each segment. Differentiation can lead to market segmentation, and market segmentation can lead to product differentiation. This first requires knowing how people differ, segmenting them accordingly, and then developing the specific products to meet their needs and wants.

This practice has hotel companies featuring a number of product lines such as budget, economy, suite, middle-tier, and upscale properties. As an analogy, this is no different from General Motors offering five different product lines of automobiles. An example of when differentiation may have first occurred in the hotel industry is when Robert Hazard became CEO of Quality Inns (now Choice International), a hotel franchisor. Hazard inherited a wide variety of franchisees with diverse properties, ranging from the barely adequate to the middle tier of quality—all called Quality Inn. The result had been a very confused customer image with mixed expectations and a high risk factor. To counteract this, Hazard differentiated the product into three categories: Comfort Inns, Quality Inns, and Quality Royale (now called Clarion) and advertised to create different perceptions of each category. What resulted was a market segmented by the product. Hazard's concept was highly successful, and other operators soon began to follow similar strategies.

Both market segmentation and differentiation strategies are part of the marketing concept. In fact, a major reason for studying consumer behavior is to aid in the development of segmentation and differentiation strategies. An example is the development of Marriott's Courtyard by Marriott product line. Marriott went to self-employed, independent, restricted, or non-expense-account customers, a subset of the business traveler market, and asked what they wanted in a relatively low-cost hotel room, what trade-offs they would make, and what they would give up to pay less. The product was then designed to fit the demand. The result, of course, was copied by others. In fact, some hotel chains blatantly stated that their new products would be copies of Marriott's Courtyard. Hilton, for example, followed years later with Garden Inns. Today many hotel companies are competing in the same market segment as Courtyard. The astute marketer now must turn back to differentiation within this new product class.

  Web Browsing Exercise

Visit the websites for Garden Inn (http://hiltongardeninn.hilton.com/) and Courtyard (http://marriott.com/courtyard/default.mi). Compare and contrast how these two companies compete for the same segment of business travelers. What appear to be the strength and weaknesses of each brand?

Another example is the all-suite hotel concept pioneered by Granada Royale Hometels. The all-suite hotel was designed for the extended-stay business traveler who wanted a little more room to spread out. At the time, the all-suite hotel was a differentiated product; today, it is a full-blown market segment with a number of individual target markets, with both upscale and down-market offerings. Hyatt Hotels recently acquired Amerisuites to gain share in this growing market.

The Process of Market Segmentation

With all of the preceding in mind, let us proceed through the market segmentation process. The basic assumption, once again, is that the marketplace is heterogeneous; customers have different needs and wants. If we are to establish a more precise definition of the needs and wants of the marketplace, it is clear that we will need to identify those segments of the market with similar needs and wants—in other words, we need to break the market down into smaller homogeneous segments. Our need is better served if we take this in stages, since there are a number of elements that we will need to consider along the way.

Step 1: Needs and Wants of the Marketplace. In an oversimplification of the problem, we could conduct a giant research survey in which we ask customers what they want in a hotel or restaurant. The complexity of this question is immediately apparent. As we discussed in Chapter 7 on buyer behavior, we first need to understand such constraints as the context of the purchase (e.g., for business or pleasure), the time element (e.g., do we have lots of time or little time), and the target (e.g., what type of hotel and at what price). Clearly, we will not get very far with this approach, so the first thing we will have to do is to set parameters. Let us proceed with a hypothetical example.

We are considering opening a restaurant in a city whose population is 1 million people. We have decided that this will not be a fast-food restaurant, but could be anything from an inexpensive family restaurant to a very expensive gourmet restaurant. We analyze what already exists and find that there is no high-quality French restaurant in the area. With this existing void, we could go this route and, without too much difficulty, clearly differentiate our restaurant from the competition, based on French cuisine.

But what if no one wants French cuisine? We would be in serious trouble. Already we see the hazards of differentiating before segmenting. Instead, at this stage, let's ignore the competition and what already exists because, even if it exists, we really don't know if it is satisfying the needs and wants of the marketplace. Maybe it is not as successful as it looks; maybe it is successful only because there is no alternative.

Therefore, let us reset the parameters. To simplify the example, let's say we have found a location and we have decided to open for lunch and dinner. Otherwise, there are no restrictions. Now we can conduct our survey.

Assume that we take a random sample of those with household incomes of $40,000 or more per year. The questions we could ask are almost unlimited but we will have to narrow them down:

- How often do you go out for lunch/dinner?
- Where do you go?
- What do you order?
- Are you satisfied with the offering?
- What would you like to have instead?
- How much do you spend?
- How far do you travel?
- Do you like the atmosphere?
- Would you like a different atmosphere?
- If so, what would this atmosphere be like?
- Where would you like to go?
- How often?
- How much would you be willing to spend?
- What would you order?

There could be many more similar questions.

Our survey shows that 20,000 people or 20 percent of the population (100,000 people) with incomes greater than $40,000 would go to a gourmet restaurant with some frequency. They will go there an average of twice a month for lunch with an average of three other persons and once a month for dinner with an average of two other persons. They would spend $18 per person for lunch and $45 per person for dinner.

Of course, the other 80 percent of the same population is saying something else that, having open minds, we could not ignore. For purposes of illustration, however, let us concentrate on this 20 percent. This is a market segment: a relatively homogeneous segment of the market that likes and will patronize a gourmet restaurant. Armed with this information, we proceed to the second step.

Step 2: Projecting Wants and Needs into Potential Markets. This step is called **demand analysis**. Demand analysis includes an evaluation of needs and wants plus willingness and ability to pay. Willingness and ability to pay are critical, and we cannot afford to overlook them. For example, we may truly need a car to get to work every day and we may truly want a Mercedes, but if we are unwilling or unable to pay the price of a Mercedes, we are clearly not in the demand segment for that car. Demand analysis means projecting needs, wants, willingness, and ability to pay into a potential market.

Our survey has shown that we have needs, wants, willingness, and ability to pay. What does this mean in terms of potential market? If we can believe the figures (again, this is an oversimplification to make the point), we have calculated that 20,000 people in the market segment (20 percent of 100,000) would be interested in the restaurant. If we accept the frequency of dining out (twice a month for lunch and once a month for dinner) and assume that those who would accompany them (three people for lunch and two people for dinner) are also in the population surveyed, we calculate 10,000 [(20,000/4) × 2] lunch covers a month for a gross of $180,000 (10,000 at $18 each). For dinner we calculate 6,667 covers [(20,000/3) × 1] a month for a gross of $300,000 (6,667 at $45 each). The total potential of this market is perceived to be approximately $480,000 gross per month or $5,760,000 a year. This appears to be sufficient, so we proceed to Step 3.

Step 3: Matching the Market and Capabilities. Recall that when we surveyed the market, we had open minds about the type of restaurant we would open. Now that we have found an effective level of demand, the question is, Do we have the capabilities to meet that demand? In this case, because we are starting from scratch, we have to consider dollar resources and all the financial implications of a major undertaking; designing and equipping a gourmet restaurant is not the same as designing and equipping a family restaurant. But we also have to consider the expertise in the firm:

- Who will manage it?
- What is their experience?
- Is this our mentality or philosophy?
- Does it fit with other things we are doing?
- Do we need outside help?

It is important, but often overlooked, that a firm's capabilities be matched to the market it is trying to serve. If we have successfully passed the first three steps, we can proceed to Step 4.

Step 4: Segmenting the Market. We have determined the needs and wants of the marketplace, projected them into potential markets, and matched them with our capabilities. But gourmet is a very broad category; in fact, it is quite heterogeneous in composition. Not only does gourmet mean different things to different people, there are also many forms of gourmet. So we turn to further segmentation. To simplify the case, let's assume that we found a strong preference for French food in our survey; we decide to segment the market on those who have a high preference for French food. Now we have to go back through Steps 2 and 3 and reevaluate the situation.

Step 5: Selecting Target Markets from Identified Segments. Just as gourmet food is not all the same, neither is all French food. This fact was learned the hard way by a restaurateur in a midsized New England city. This operator opened a French restaurant because "there weren't any around." He managed to build a small, loyal, steady clientele as well as an infrequent special-occasion following. When he closed, unsuccessful, two and a half years later, his comment was, "The people in this city think French cuisine is quiche Lorraine."

So we have to select specific target markets from the broader market segment. This will be discussed in more detail later, but we might target on occasion, on nouvelle French, on income bracket, on age, on business entertaining, or any number of other things.

Tailoring the Product to the Wants and Needs of the Target Market

Now we see the advantages of segmenting and target marketing in terms of the marketing concept. Let's look at these advantages more specifically.

- **We are better able to identify and evaluate opportunities in the marketplace.** By knowing our target market, we can track it, identify what is missing, find niches, and discover customers' problems.
- **We can better mesh our product with the needs of the market.** Consider the survey we did of the entire population, an expensive and time-consuming chore. Now we can be more specific as to which customers comprise the market. We can ask more specific questions and get higher response rates because we now have people interested in the subject. We can better identify who those people are. We can have a much better idea of the acceptance of any innovation.
- **We can optimally allocate and direct our resources.** As in the case described earlier, we wouldn't build a fancy French restaurant for a market that wanted quiche, nor would we need the same level of manpower and expertise. Perhaps we could determine that there is a take-out market for quiche and develop that end of the business. In short, the potential for wasting resources is greatly decreased.
- **We can use relevant market intelligence to sense change and to change strategies.** Because we now have a smaller market and are closer to it, we can keep in touch with it better. We have more opportunity to "talk" to the customer. We are better able to determine cultural and reference group influences, to understand beliefs and attitudes, to recognize and

influence perceptions, to use tangible evidence of intangible constructs, to understand the information processing of the customer, and to give more "control" to both customers and employees.

■ **We have greater ability to tailor our behavior, promotion, logistics, distribution channels, and marketing mix to the market.** Essentially, this means we are better able to reach customers by knowing where they are, what appeals to them, what they pay attention to, what they react to, and what media they use.

■ **We are better able to be unique and to differentiate from the competition.** We can determine more readily what the competition is doing for this segment or target market. We know better what to copy, what not to copy, and what we do that will be copied. We have more opportunity to find competitive advantage and to exploit the weaknesses of the competition.

■ **We are better able to determine strategies to develop and enlarge the core market.** Take again the example of take-out quiche. Initially, we might not think this was a viable opportunity at all; by knowing our market, we might learn that it was and start offering take-home quiche to our customers. Eventually, we could expand this market by selling it to noncustomers—those who would not come to eat but would come to pick up a quiche and take it home.

Segmentation Variables

There is no one best way to segment the market, but there is no shortage of different ways to do so. What's more, they are certainly not mutually exclusive. First, we will discuss some of the more commonly used segmentation variables, and then we will take a look at how they overlap.

Geographic Segmentation

Geographic location is probably the original segmentation variable and one of the most widely used in the lodging and restaurant industries. It has its strengths and its weaknesses. Geographically speaking, we can segment by country, city, media market, town, part of city, or even neighborhood. The essence and the substance of geographic segmentation is that certain geographic locations are the major sources of our business. A hotel in San Francisco might draw most of its business from Los Angeles and New York. A hotel in Singapore might draw most of its business from Australia and Japan. A restaurant in New York City might draw most of its business from a five-block radius. A restaurant in Hartford, Connecticut, might draw most of its business from suburban towns.

If geographic segments can be pinpointed, then the problem of reaching those segments is greatly facilitated, especially if they are in concentrated areas. Both direct mail and media forms of communication are more easily specified. It is also possible to use available resources to learn more about the denizens of these areas.

The U.S. federal government defines large metropolitan areas in terms of supposed economic boundaries called **metropolitan statistical areas (MSAs)**—for example, the New York City MSA. The government produces reams of data on these areas—population, ethnic mix, growth, income, discretionary spending, household size, occupations, and so forth. The use of MSAs in hospitality marketing is limited, but probably of greatest value when the market is being segmented on certain demographic variables. MSAs can be analyzed for the existence of these variables.

Another geographic division is the designated market area (DMA), developed by Arbitron and now used by the AC Nielsen media research company. These designations are defined by specific zip code correlates and reflect the geographic areas served by television stations located in a central geographic point. Their data also include demographic characteristics that can be used for reaching specific audiences by television. Most sophisticated advertisers use these designations.

The primary purpose of the DMA analysis is to aid firms in planning media coverage. For instance, if a firm wanted to advertise to customers living in Orange County, California, the firm could look at DMA maps to see which TV stations reach this area.

Geographic segmentation is the easiest segmentation to define, but it is also the most fallible for the hospitality industry because it doesn't necessarily reflect the locus of the "buy decision." That is, the markets from which the registrants come from may not necessarily be where the reservation came from. For instance, the reservation of a particular guest may be the result of a decision in the corporate office that all employees would stay at a specific brand when traveling. The local neighborhood eatery doesn't have to employ MSAs or DMAs to know where its business comes from. Broader-based operations draw from a wide variety of geographic locations and need to use more specific and economical means to reach their markets. In fact, one of the problems of individual restaurants is that they cater to numerous small segments that are difficult and prohibitively expensive to reach through traditional advertising media.

 Web Browsing Exercise

Type "designated market area" into your favorite web browser. What are the top 50 markets? What are the different DMA codes?

The primary problem with geographic segments is that they may not reflect where the actual buy decision is made. For example, a business traveler from New York may have one of his associates in Chicago book him a room on his next business trip to Chicago. His registration record will reflect an address in the New York DMA, but the reservation actually originated in the Chicago DMA. Failure to understand this distinction would ultimately lead to the erroneous allocation of marketing resources. Thus, a simple segmentation of guests by geographic origin is incomplete.

If analyzed properly, however, geographic segmentation can be very useful in concentrating resources. The tourism board of Bermuda knows that most of Bermuda's tourism comes from the northeastern United States, eastern Canada, and the United Kingdom, and their advertising dollars are concentrated in those three areas. The New York City restaurant that knows most of its business comes from within a five-block radius can use direct mail and flyers to reach that market. Singapore can spend a major share of its marketing resources in Australia and Japan.

Although all this is both true and helpful, it helps us only to reach the market; it is not of much assistance in determining the needs and wants of the market, because geographic segments, unless they are very small ones, are still very heterogeneous in terms of customer profiles, needs, and wants.

Demographic Segmentation

Demographic segmentation is widely used in almost all industries. One reason for this is that, like geographic segments, demographics are easily measured and classified. Demographic segments are based on income, race, age, nationality, religion, gender, education, culture, and so forth. For some goods, demographic segments are clearly product specific—for instance, children's clothes, lipstick, Rolls Royce automobiles, and denture cleaners.

Demographic segmentation, however, may be somewhat moot. Knowing that someone is 30 years old, earns $40,000 a year, is married, and has a child may not be too helpful in separating a truck driver, a college professor, and an accountant. Each of these people will have different needs and seek different benefits, but for a large majority of both products and services, the demographic profile of the users will not distinguish among them.

Demographic lines have, in many cases, become very blurred and fuzzy. Plumbers may have higher incomes than accountants with MBAs. Everyone wears jeans, regardless of social standing. Executives check into hotels on weekends looking as though they have just finished mowing the lawn. Some of the wealthy get wealthier by eating cheap, staying at budget motels, and fighting over the last nickel on their check. In fact, demographic lines have become so blurred that it is hard to tell what they mean anymore.

For the hospitality industry today, one of the most useful demographic parameters may be age—age in the sense of attracting children who bring with them parents, or age in the sense of senior citizens, a vast and rapidly growing market with distinctive needs and wants, not to mention discretionary income. Another demographic variable that may be useful in some operations, particularly restaurants and resorts, is the family life cycle stage. The **family life cycle** has been defined as follows:

> The emotional and intellectual stages you pass through from childhood to your retirement years as a member of a family are called the **family life cycle**. The stages include the following: childhood, independence, coupling or marriage, parenting: babies through adolescents, launching adult children and retirement or senior stage of life.[3]

Increasingly, today there are dual-income couples with no children, single parents and nonparents, and second and third marriages. Each of these stages contains, for most people, its own level of discretionary income, personal time, specific buying needs, and patterns of behavior. Marketers can tap into this information, as has been demonstrated by singles resorts, early-bird dinners, special tours, and packages. Econo Lodge, a segment of Choice Hotels, claimed to have generated of over $1 million of additional revenue in the first four months after introducing designated "senior rooms." This room type was introduced in 1993 and was the first chain to offer such amenities as "senior-friendly" rooms. Rodeway Inn began offering "senior" rooms with brighter lighting, grab bars in showers, lever handles on doors, and large buttons on phones and alarm clocks.[4]

Some of the acronyms for lifestyle segments are **DINK** (dual income, no kids), **DEWK** (dual employed, with kids), and **echo boomers** (the children of the baby boomers). Demographic market segments, like geographic ones, are also largely nonpredictive because they too are post hoc. We may know that older people with high incomes come to our property, but we still need to find out why; what needs and wants of these people are being satisfied or not? Age, income, education, nationality, and other demographic or sociodemographic characteristics are limited in informing us of the needs and wants of these segments.

Does this mean that demographics are an unimportant segmentation variable? No, it does not. It means that we have to understand the meaning of those demographics and how they relate to other segmentation variables. Demographics serve as gross market definition parameters within which are found more specific subsegments, as shown in Exhibit 12-7. For example, notice that this advertisement appeals to women.

EXHIBIT 12-7   This advertisement for Grand Cypress appeals to women.

Source: Grand Cypress Golf Resort. Used by permission.

Tourism Marketing Application

The Ontario Tourism Marketing Partnership Corporation (OTMPC) has segmented the primary North American markets (Ontario and the U.S. border states) into four market segments that they call Youth, Senior, Mature, and Family. These four groups are further segmented by lifestyle choices and demographics. (www.tourismpartners.com/TcisCtrl?language=EN&site=partners&key1=research&key2=setgReports, accessed March 25, 2006)

EXHIBIT 12-8   **Lifestyle Dimensions**

Activities	Interests	Opinions	Demographics
Work	Family	Themselves	Age
Hobbies	Home	Social issues	Education
Social events	Job	Politics	Income
Vacation	Community	Business	Occupation
Entertainment	Recreation	Economics	Family size
Club membership	Fashion	Education	Dwelling
Community	Food	Products	Geography
Shopping	Media	Future	City size
Sports	Achievements	Culture	Life cycle stage

Source: Reprinted with permission from Plummer, J. T. (1974, January). The concept and application of life style segmentation. *Journal of Marketing*, 34. Published by the American Marketing Association.

Psychographic Segmentation

Psychographic segments are segments based on **activities, interests, and opinions (AIO)**, self-concepts, and lifestyle behaviors. AIOs are personality traits; the word *psychographic* actually means "the measurement of personality traits." First, we need to understand what psychographics are.

According to Joseph Plummer, a former advertising executive and one of the leading proponents of lifestyle segmentation, the concept is defined as follows:

Life style as used in life style segmentation research measures people's activities in terms of (1) how they spend their time; (2) their interests, what they place importance on in their immediate surroundings; (3) their opinions in terms of their view of themselves and the world around them; and (4) some basic characteristics such as their stage in life cycle, income, education and where they live [i.e., demographics and geographic locations].[5]

Lifestyle dimensions, as defined by Plummer, are shown in Exhibit 12-8.

Those who are strong advocates of psychographic segmentation argue that lifestyle patterns combine the virtues of demographics with the way people live, think, and behave in their everyday lives. Those who study psychographics attempt to correlate these factors into relatively homogeneous categories using descriptive classification terms such as *homebodies, traditionalists, swingers, loners, jet-setters, conservatives, socialites, yuppies*, and so forth. The classifications are then correlated with product usage, desired product attributes, and media readership and viewing. **VALS** is a psychographic system.

The VALS system, originally developed by SRI International, is now run by SRI Consulting Business Intelligence (SRIC-BI). The U.S. VALS system, Japan-VALS, and U.K. VALS have proven to be effective tools for categorizing American, Japanese, and British consumers into various segments based on psychological characteristics and four key demographics. Merrill Lynch replaced its "Bullish on America" herd of bulls with one bull in their television

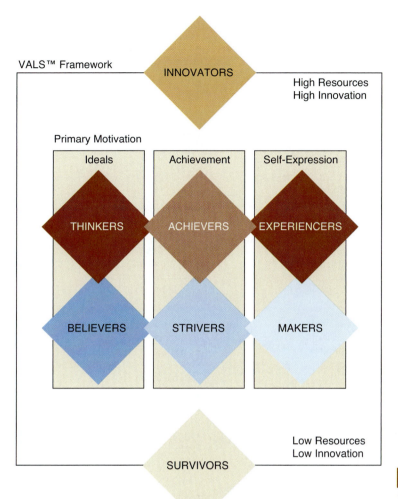

EXHIBIT 12-9 VALS framework.

Source: Retrieved from www.sric-bi.com/VALS/types.shtml. Used by permission from SRI Consulting Business Intelligence (SRIC-BI).

and print advertising campaign. The VALS analysis revealed that the target market that Merrill Lynch wanted to attract saw themselves as self-made visionaries rather than as part of a herd.

The U.S. VALS system categorizes U.S. adult customers into eight segments using dimensions of primary motivation and level of resources (high or low), as shown in Exhibits 12-9 and 12-10. Customers are thought to be driven to buy products and services by three main motivations—ideals, achievement, or self-expression. Customers who are primarily motivated by ideals are guided by knowledge and principles. Customers motivated by achievement look for products and services that demonstrate success to their peers. Finally, customers motivated by self-expression seek social and physical activity, variety, and risk.

Resources include education, income, health, eagerness to buy, energy level, and self-confidence.

VALS is linked to extensive databases of consumer behavior including Media Mark Research Inc. (MRI) and Consumer Financial Decision's Macro Monitor. GeoVALS estimates the proportion of the eight VALS types by U.S. zip code or block group, Japan VALS, and U.K. VALS products.

Cohorts is another company that provides psychographic segmentation. Cohorts' database is broken into 31 segments, as shown in Exhibit 12-11. Notice that Cohorts uses first names to describe each segment to make the segments more real. Cohorts also is linked to extensive behavioral information from Simmons Market Research Bureau and Scarborough Research. Behavioral data categories include the following:

- Retail shopping behavior
- Radio and television behavior
- Credit cards used
- Travel behavior
- Cable networks watched
- Sports watched on TV/cable
- Telephone services used
- Newspaper sections read
- Attitudes and opinions and more[6]

EXHIBIT 12-10	VALS Psychographic Segments

Segment	Lifestyle Characteristics	Psychological Characteristics	Customer Characteristics
Innovators	• Successful, sophisticated • Value personal growth • Wide intellectual interests • Varied leisure activities • Well informed, concerned with social issues • Highly social • Politically very active	• Optimistic • Self-confident • Involved • Outgoing • Growth oriented • Open to change • Established and emerging leaders in business and government	• Enjoy the "finer things" • Receptive to new products, technologies, distribution • Skeptical of advertising • Frequent readers of a wide variety of publications • Light TV viewers
Thinkers	• Moderately active in community and politics • Leisure centers on home • Value education and travel • Health conscious • Politically moderate and tolerant	• Mature • Satisfied • Reflective • Open-minded • Intrinsically motivated • Value order, knowledge and responsibility	• Little interest in image or prestige • Above average customers of products for the home • Like educational and public affairs programming on TV • Read widely and often • Look for value and durability
Achievers	• Lives center on career and family • Have formal social relations • Avoid excess change or stimulation • May emphasize work at the expense of recreation • Politically conservative	• Moderate • Goal oriented • Conventional • Deliberate • In control	• Attracted to premium products • Prime target for a variety of products • Average TV watchers • Read business, news and self-help publications
Experiencers	• Like the new, offbeat and risky • Like exercise, socializing, sports and outdoors • Concerned about image • Unconforming, but admire wealth, power and fame • Politically apathetic	• Extraverted • Unconventional • Active • Impetuous • Energetic • Enthusiastic and impulsive	• Follow fashion and fads • Spend much of disposable income on socializing • Buy on impulse • Attend to advertising • Listen to rock music
Believers	• Respect rules and trust authority figures • Enjoy settled, comfortable, predictable existence • Socialize within family and established groups • Politically conservative • Reasonably well informed	• Traditional • Conforming • Cautious • Moralistic • Settled	• Buy American • Slow to change habits • Look for bargains • Watch TV more than average • Read retirement, home and garden and general interest magazines
Strivers	• Narrow interests • Not well educated • Unconcerned about exercise and nutrition • Politically apathetic	• Reward-oriented • Unsure • Impulsive	• Trendy • Limited discretionary income but carry credit balances • Spend on clothing and personal care products • Prefer TV to reading
Makers	• Enjoy outdoors • Prefer "hands on" activities • Spend leisure with family and close friends • Avoid joining organizations except unions • Distrust politicians, foreigners and big business	• Practical • Self-sufficient • Constructive • Committed • Satisfied	• Shop for comfort, durability, value • Unimpressed by luxuries • Buy the basics • Listen to radio • Read auto, home mechanics, fishing, outdoors magazines
Survivors	• Limited interests and activities • Prime concerns are safety and security • Burdened with health problems • Conservative and traditional • Not innovative	• Narrowly focused • Risk averse • Conservative	• Brand loyal • Use coupons and watch for sales • Trust advertising • Watch TV often • Read tabloids and women's magazines

Source: ■ Retrieved September 16, 2005, from www.d.umn.edu/~rvaidyan/mgts4731/vals2tbl.htm. Used by permission from SRI Consulting Business Intelligence (SRIC-B1).

EXHIBIT 12-11	2004 Brief Description of All Cohorts Segments

The right message to the right household

Married Couples

	Cohort Segment Name	Description	U.S. Median Age	U.S. Median Income
	Alex & Judith	<u>Affluent Empty-Nesters</u> Dual-income, older couples who use their high discretionary incomes to enjoy all aspects of the good life.	61	$144,000
	Jeffrey & Ellen	<u>Affluent Couples with Kids</u> Urban families who, despite having children at home, have sufficient financial resources to own the latest high-tech products and to lead very active recreational and cultural lifestyles.	43	$141,000
	Barry & Kathleen	<u>Affluent Professional Couples</u> Educated, dual-income, childless couples who have connoisseur tastes and are focused on their careers, staying fit, and investing.	46	$133,000
	Stan & Carole	<u>Upscale Middle-Aged Couples</u> Unburdened by children, these credit-worthy, dual-income couples divide their time between the great outdoors and domestic hobbies.	49	$75,000
	Brett & Tracey	<u>Hyperactive Newlyweds</u> Young, dual-income, educated couples whose energies are channeled into active sports, outdoor activities, careers and their home lives.	31	$65,000
	Danny & Vickie	<u>Teen-Dominated Families</u> Middle-aged, middle-income families whose teen-dominated households keep busy with outdoor activities, computers, and video games.	42	$58,000

(continued)

EXHIBIT 12-11	2004 Brief Description of All Cohorts Segments, *(Continued)*

Married Couples *(continued)*

	Cohort Segment Name	Description	U.S. Median Age	U.S. Median Income
	Burt & Marilyn	<u>Mature Couples</u> Comfortable, close-to-retirement homeowners who are active investors and who engage in charitable activities, travel, politics and their grandchildren.	66	$57,000
	Todd & Wendy	<u>Back-to-School Families</u> Families with mid-range incomes, pre-adolescent kids, pets, and lots of video, computer and outdoor activities to keep them occupied.	38	$55,000
	Chad & Tammie	<u>Young Families</u> Up-and-coming young families who curtail their lifestyle expenses through less-costly outdoor activities and working around the house.	31	$52,000
	Frank & Shirley	<u>Older Couples Raising Kids</u> Conservative grandparents and older parents whose home-oriented lifestyles include pets, do-it-yourself workshops, gardening and sweepstakes.	60	$49,000
	Ronnie & Debbie	<u>Working-Class Couples</u> Moderate-income couples with active, traditional interests including fishing, hunting, automotive work and crafts.	48	$38,000
	Eric & Rachel	<u>Young Married Starters</u> Young, childless renters whose lifestyle patterns include outdoor activities like camping, fishing and running, as well as automotive work and video games.	28	$20,000

EXHIBIT 12-11	**2004 Brief Description of All Cohorts Segments, *(Continued)***

Married Couples (continued)

	Cohort Segment Name	Description	U.S. Median Age	U.S. Median Income
	Elwood & Willamae	<u>Modest-Income Grandparents</u> Retired couples with modest incomes who dote on their grandchildren and engage primarily in domestic pursuits.	72	$19,000

Single Females

	Cohort Segment Name	Description	U.S. Median Age	U.S. Median Income
	Elizabeth	<u>Savvy Career Women</u> Affluent, working women with sophisticated tastes, very active lifestyles, and good investing habits.	42	$174,000
	Virginia	<u>Upscale Mature Women</u> Older women approaching or enjoying retirement, who travel and have upscale interests, including charitable causes and investments.	60	$72,000
	Allison	<u>Educated Working Women</u> Childless, professional women building their careers, developing sophisticated tastes, and staying fit.	32	$52,000
	Andrea	<u>Single Moms with Careers</u> Successful, professional single mothers who balance their careers with the demands of raising their children.	39	$50,000

(continued)

EXHIBIT 12-11	2004 Brief Description of All Cohorts Segments, *(Continued)*

Single Females *(continued)*

	Cohort Segment Name	Description	U.S. Median Age	U.S. Median Income
	Bernice	<u>Active Grandmothers</u> Home-oriented women who enjoy handicrafts, indoor gardening, and their grandchildren.	62	$36,000
	Penny	<u>Working-Class Women</u> Childless female office workers who are concerned with their appearance; enjoy music, pets and handicrafts; and add intrigue to their lives with the prospect of winning the big sweepstakes.	43	$18,000
	Denise	<u>Single Moms on a Budget</u> Single mothers with modest incomes who indulge their kids with video games, movies, and music, and who try to find time for themselves.	36	$17,000
	Megan	<u>Fit & Stylish Students</u> Young, fashion-conscious, career-minded female students who enjoy music, aerobic sports, and the latest in high tech.	26	$16,000
	Minnie	<u>Fixed-Income Grandmothers</u> Older single women who spend lots of time on their grandchildren, handicrafts, and religious reading.	73	$11,000

A third psychographic segmentation is proposed by Claritas. They use what is called the **PRIZM NE** system, which stands for *Potential Rating Index Zip Code Markets*. The idea is that people choose to live near people who are similar to themselves. Therefore, if a firm knows the zip code of its customers, the best place to find new customers is in either the same zip code or a zip code with similar characteristics. There are 66 different zip code clusters in the United States. One such cluster is shown in Exhibit 12-12. More information on Claritas can be found at the website (see Web Browsing Exercise on page 332).

EXHIBIT 12-11	2004 Brief Description of All Cohorts Segments, *(Continued)*

Single Males

	Cohort Segment Name	Description	U.S. Median Age	U.S. Median Income
	Jonathan	Elite Single Men High-powered career-driven men with sophisticated tastes, extensive investments, and the means to travel the world.	43	$174,000
	Sean	Affluent Guys Affluent, health- and fitness-minded men with investments and upscale interests.	44	$96,000
	Harry	Well-to-Do Gentlemen Mature men who are savvy about their investments, travel, and politics.	58	$49,000
	Ryan	Energetic Young Guys Younger, physically active men with strong career drives and upscale interests, including electronics and technology.	33	$47,000
	Randy	Single Dads Single fathers who enjoy outdoor activities, their home workshops, and electronic entertainment with their kids.	37	$45,000
	Jerry	Working-Class Guys Blue-collar men who spend their free time in the garage or outdoors.	47	$19,000

(continued)

EXHIBIT 12-11	2004 Brief Description of All Cohorts Segments, *(Continued)*

Single Males (continued)

	Cohort Segment Name	Description	U.S. Median Age	U.S. Median Income
	Jason	<u>Male Students & Grads</u> Physically active, technologically inclined young men finishing school or embarking on their first job.	26	$17,000
	Elmer	<u>Sedentary Men</u> Aging, sedentary men with fixed incomes and few interests beyond their grandchildren and their gardens.	73	$17,000

Households That Defy Classification

Ω	**Omegas**	Omegas are people who are impossible to classify distinctly. They may be married or single, homeowners or renters, 18 to 65 years old, have incomes that range from very low to six figures, and enjoy numerous and diverse interests.

Source: Cohorts. Used by permission.

Web Browsing Exercise

Visit the website for Claritas (www.claritas.com). On the website find "You are where you live" and enter the zip code for your area as well as other areas. What does this information tell you? How accurate do you believe it is? Next, visit www.sric-bi.com. Navigate the website to find the VALS survey. Take the survey and be prepared to discuss your grouping.

The assumption of Cohorts, VALS 3, PRIZM, and other such psychographic segmentation techniques is that product attributes can be tailored to psychographic segments and that the product will thus have special appeal to those segments. The greatest proponents and users of psychographics are advertising agencies, which use the classi-fication elements to reach the segments via specific creative treatments and media strategies and to communicate the product attributes via the lifestyle factors. Lifestyle research provides advertisers with insight into the setting, the type and appearance of the characters, the music, the tone, self-perceived roles, and the rewards people seek. Thus, in the past, we saw on television the "typical" housewife, whose main concern was taking care of her family and standing by the washing machine extolling the virtues of a laundry detergent. Today, different kinds of women and men wash clothes.

Psychographics may be used in developing hospitality advertising messages such as those of McDonald's and

EXHIBIT 12-12 ZIP code cluster.

Source: Retrieved November 21, 2005, from www.claritas.com/MyBetSegments/ Content/tabs/filterMenuFrameWork.isp?page=/Segments/snapshot.jsp&m enuid=91&submenuid=911.

Burger King. As shown in Exhibit 12-13, The Venetian in Las Vegas used Cohorts to help gain a better understanding of its player database.

Critics of psychographics express concern about whether these variables can be defined, are valid, and are stable. Lifestyle variables not only are difficult to define but also overlap greatly. Because of this, there is considerable room for error variance in establishing the classifications. Furthermore, people change, and do so rapidly, in today's society—today's lifestyle may not be tomorrow's.

Regardless of the criticisms and failings of psychographic segmentation, it remains a rich area for marketing effectiveness in the hospitality industry. New hotels and restaurants are sometimes designed and built and old ones refurbished by architects, designers, and developers with little attention to customers and how they "use" a property. Architects and designers want their creations to be artistic, developers want them to be built at minimum cost, operators want them to be functional, and marketers want them to be marketable. It is possible that psychographic research can tell us a great deal about what the customer wants and how to build and market to those wants. Exhibit 12-14 shows an example of a lifestyle advertisement in hospitality.

Usage Segmentation

Usage segmentation is a broad umbrella that covers a wide range of categories that probably apply more specifically to hospitality businesses than any other type of segmentation. Although we often accept these categories as givens, some are not always well used in **market segmentation** strategies. The basic question of all is, How do customers use the product or service? We will discuss the segmentation categories one at a time.

Purpose. The purpose of the purchase is a common segment category. Often market breakdowns of occupancy are kept on a daily basis, categorized by the purpose of visit. Approximately 80 percent of urban hotel occupancy in the United States, on average, derives from business travelers. The business expense account customer is also a source of sizable patronage in many restaurants. Business purpose can be broken down into submarkets such as conventions, corporate meetings, expense account, non-expense-account, and so forth. These subcategories are important because each one will have somewhat different needs and wants and should be marketed to accordingly.

EXHIBIT 12-13 **The Venetian Adds Cohorts to All Customer Databases**

After a successful execution of Cohorts' Proof of Concept (POC) testing in fall 2003, The Venetian Resort-Hotel-Casino has agreed to add Cohorts segmentation to its entire Venetian Player's Club membership and hotel guest databases.

The Cohorts-segmented POC testing utilized e-mail and direct-mail marketing campaigns, targeting Player's Club members and hotel guests who normally would not have been selected for the mailing because of previous play levels. This group was targeted because of their propensity to play up to the level of the other players.

Under a new, annual agreement, Cohorts will be used as an ongoing element of campaign development and analysis for The Venetian. According to the agreement, The Venetian will continue to use Cohorts segmentation for direct-mail and e-mail marketing campaigns and will add the use of list suppression to avoid reinvesting in players who should not receive mailings. Originating at the household level, Cohorts segmentation enables The Venetian to enhance name and address customer databases with unique Cohort designations. By appending segment codes to its customer database, the company understands the differences—some subtle, some profound—between its key Cohort segments, such as Jonathan (Elite Single Men) and Jeffrey & Ellen (Affluent Couples with Kids). Armed with this knowledge, The Venetian can create versioned, relevant offers that resonate with each distinct audience.

For example, the Burt & Marilyn Cohort (Mature Couples) might respond better to a promotion offering a midweek stay that includes restaurant comps and Madame Tussaud's wax museum passes, while the elite single men in the Jonathan Cohort might be more responsive to a promotional message about a table game tournament with golf and Canyon Ranch SpaClub comps.

Source: Courtesy of The Venetian Resort Hotel Casino. Used by permission.

I NEVER KNEW

HAPPY HOUR

COULD LAST ALL DAY.

At first, we noticed the little things. The tip of a hat. A door held open. A "pardon instead of 'huh?' Somehow in the warm little mountain town of Steamboat, the Code of the West is alive and well. Maybe it's the mountain. Maybe it's waking up to the kiss of Champagne Powder® snow. But, as we checked out, I found myself holding the door open for another family checking in.

This is my Steamboat.

Steamboat

877.239.2628   STEAMBOAT.COM/SKI

EXHIBIT 12-14   An example of a lifestyle advertisement in hospitality.

Source: Steamboat. Used by permission.

The other major purpose category is called social, pleasure, or leisure. Because this market actually has a number of specific purposes, a better term would probably be simply either *nonbusiness* or *personal*. This segment will represent a larger proportion of business for restaurants than for hotels.

Frequency.   The frequency of purchase segments has to do with regularity of usage. Repeat business is well recognized as highly desirable, and programs such as frequent traveler plans are geared toward this behavior. Again, however, there are subsegments that should not be ignored. High frequency might mean once a week to a restaurant, once a month to a commercial hotel, and once a year to a resort. Low frequency can also be an important segment, especially if it occurs with regularity. A restaurant might have certain customers who come only once a year on an anniversary date. A few hundred of these, however, constitute an important segment that needs special attention.

Monetary Value.   Monetary value refers to how much the customer is worth to the organization. For instance, in the casino business, monetary value is often referred to as

the "theoretical value." The theoretical value takes into account the length of time a person plays a game and the amount being bet for each decision (i.e., spin of the wheel at roulette.) We might call the important members of this segment "big spenders," or in the case of Las Vegas, "whales." Purchase size is the high check average in a restaurant or the expensive wines; even the big tippers can be a vital segment. In hotels, this segment might use the better rooms or suites, eat in the hotel's restaurants, or order expensive room service. Obviously, this type of behavior should be encouraged by marketing. Purchase size also considers the low spenders who may not be desirable customers.

Recency.   Recency refers to how recently the customer consumed the product or service. This is used quite often in direct mail promotions. For instance, a firm may send a mailing piece to those who have not visited the establishment in the last 30 days.

RFM.   RFM stands for recency, frequency, and monetary value. Each of the terms has already been identified. RFM analysis is used to identify groups of customers in the database. Essentially, the database is sorted by each specific measure. For instance, with monetary value, the sort would be from the largest value to smallest value. For recency, the sort would be by most recent visit to least recent visit, and for frequency the sort would be from most frequent to least frequent. Once the sort has been accomplished, the database is divided into five equal parts labeled 5 to 1, with 5 representing the highest category and 1 the lowest. A customer with a score of 555 has visited the property most recently, visits frequently, and has a high monetary value. A customer with a score of 111 is just the opposite. Companies use the RFM score to direct targeted mailings. For instance, a person with a 555 score would get a very different offer than would a person with a 333 score.

Timing.   Timing deals with days, months, or seasonal periods of the calendar. The Monday night customer can be icing on the cake for a restaurant; the weekend customer, for a hotel; and the off-season customer, for a resort. These segments may include people who don't like crowds or simply those on different schedules. Of course, those who come at busy times also represent a timing subsegment.

Timing segments also can be based on when the customer buys. For an anniversary dinner, it might be two weeks ahead; for a wedding, six months; for a simple dinner out, two hours. A meeting planner may book accommodations one or more years in advance; the business traveler, two days in advance.

Nature of Purchase.   Consumer behaviorists often categorize buyers by the nature of purchase:

- ■ **Convenience:** buy a particular product because it's convenient to do so
- ■ **Impulse:** buy products on impulse without much forethought
- ■ **Rational:** buy only after careful consideration

Each of these subsegments is susceptible to a different approach.

Convenience buyers, for example, are probably more apt to use in-room refrigerator bars or room service if it is convenient to get the food items elsewhere. Impulse buyers are highly subject to suggestions, such as menu clip-ons, wine carts, the server's dessert suggestions, and a higher-priced room with a view. Rational buyers need more information; they are more apt to be influenced by descriptions on wine lists, in-room descriptive materials, and ads or brochures with more detailed information.

Where They Go. Some segments can be identified by where they go. Many might go to certain destinations on a regular basis. For vacation, they might always go to the Caribbean; for a hotel, they might always go near the theater district; for a restaurant, they might always go to the suburbs. Some, in fact, might always go someplace different. We can direct our marketing efforts according to these inclinations.

Purchase Occasion. Purchase occasion represents special occasion segments. They go to restaurants for birthdays and anniversaries or use hotels for the same occasions. Some may use hotels only for visiting relatives or when on vacation or when going to the theatre in a large city. Some people take a trip with the goal of seeing as much as possible, whereas others go on vacation with the goal of just sitting and relaxing.

Heavy, Medium, and Light Users. Heavy, medium, and light users often get special attention from marketers. A marketing truism states that 80 percent of purchases are made by 20 percent of those who consume the product or service (often referred to as the 80/20 rule). Any marketing research needs to pay special attention to separating these categories. As a total group, customers might have a mean of 2.5 on a scale of 5 when evaluating an attribute. Broken down, it might be that light users have a 1.7, medium users a 3.2, and heavy users a 4.4. Changes made to please heavy users might alienate light users, a consideration that management must evaluate before making changes.

There tends to be a heavy concentration in marketing circles on the heavy user. This is probably advisable, but at the same time should not distract from the light user or, to coin a new phrase perhaps, the "other user." Hypothetically, let's suppose that the heavy user represents 80 percent of an establishment's patronage, whereas the other 20 percent represents a mix of various segments. That 20 percent may also represent five more percentage points of occupancy or, in a volume-sensitive business, 90 percent of its spending may drop down to the bottom line. The RFM analysis is a method of classifying usage.

It would not be too difficult to suggest even more user segments than those mentioned. The point that has to be made is that each of these segments has some different needs and wants. They may also have many needs and wants in common, but catering to the different special needs and wants is what creates and keeps customers.

A given restaurant or hotel may well have every segment mentioned earlier as customers or potential customers. This is not as impossible a situation as it may at first seem; it is simply the nature of the hospitality business and demonstrates why paying attention to only broad segments such as business/pleasure may constitute falling into a trap. With few exceptions, a hotel or restaurant that wants to maximize its potential simply cannot afford to treat all people the same.

The Saturday night hotel guest does not behave the same as the Wednesday night one—even when it is the same person. Likewise, the Monday night restaurant customer is not the same as the Saturday night one. The anniversary dinner is not the same as the business dinner. One restaurant of one of the authors' acquaintances had a heavy weekday lunch patronage of businesspeople but wondered why they never appeared for dinner or on weekends. Subsequent research revealed that these customers found the restaurant convenient for lunch but did not find it satisfactory as a place to bring their spouse or significant other for dinner.

User segments have an advantage over geographic, demographic, and psychographic segments. Because of their nature and narrowness, they are more predictable. In other words, if we know what influences them (i.e., why they constitute a segment), the chances are good that they can be influenced. This is not necessarily the case simply because we know someone's age, income, sex, or geographic origin. Exhibit 12-15 illustrates segmenting customers on usage categories—in this case, those planning a wedding.

Benefit Segmentation

Benefit segments are based on the benefits that people seek when buying a product. Benefits are very akin to need satisfaction. Following are just a few of the possible benefits sought in a hospitality purchase:

- ■ Comfort
- ■ Prestige
- ■ Low price
- ■ Recognition
- ■ Attention
- ■ Romance

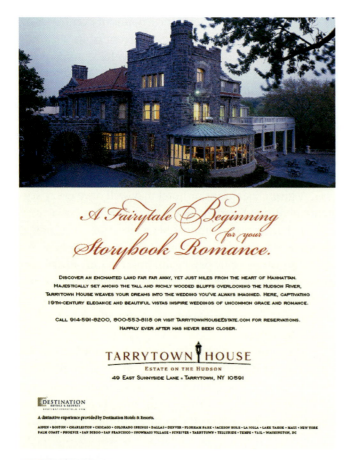

EXHIBIT 12-15 Tarrytown House segments by benefit categories, as shown in this advertisement.

Source: Destination Hotels & Resorts. Used by permission.

EXHIBIT 12-16 This advertisement shows all of the benefits of staying at a Fairmont Hotel in Bermuda.

Source: Fairmont Hotels and Resorts, Bermuda. Used with permission.

■ Quiet
■ Safety

Benefit segments may be the most basic reasons for true market segments and the most predictable of all segments. Knowing what benefits people seek provides a basis for predicting what people will do.

Benefit segmentation is a market-oriented approach consistent with the marketing concept. From these segments other characteristics can be derived, such as demographics, psychographics, usage patterns, and so forth; in other words, benefit segments can be used to identify relevant descriptive variables and consumer behavior. Benefit segmentation is also concerned with total satisfaction from a service rather than simply individual benefits. This phenomenon has been termed the **benefit bundle** and is a significant factor in segmenting markets by benefits. An example is shown in Exhibit 12-16. This advertisement shows all the benefits of staying at a Fairmont Hotel in Bermuda.

There are two important distinctions between benefit segmentation and other forms of segmentation. Benefits *are* the needs and wants of the customer. More than that,

benefits are what the product or service does for the customer. Other segmentation strategies only assume a relationship between the segment variables and customer needs and wants. We all know that McDonald's makes a special effort to appeal to children, a well-defined demographic segment. The next time you go to a McDonald's, look around at the people and see if you can place them into a segment category. Chances are it will be a benefit segment: quick and cheap.

Second, understanding benefits enables marketers to influence behaviors. Other segmentation variables are often merely descriptive. The marketer can only try to appeal to what exists and its assumed relationship. Consider the singles or mature category, both fairly large market segments. The marketer might think that each group is relatively homogeneous and as such can be treated as one major segment. Nothing could be further from the truth. In fact, within the large group are smaller homogeneous segments. This can be illustrated by the story told in Exhibit 12-17. This story explains how at one point those 55 and older were thought to be similar in terms of their wants and needs regarding vacation travel. Research proved otherwise.

| EXHIBIT 12-17 | Market Segments Occur at All Age Groups |

It is hard to believe now, but in 1984 the conventional wisdom was that those 54+ were similar in terms of their wants and needs when it came to vacation travel. This illusion was shattered when two elderly hotel patrons on a bus tour were overheard speaking to each other in very sharp tones. One person was complaining to the other that there were too many activities on the tour and he was too tired to enjoy himself. The other person, his cousin, was the tour organizer. She explained to him that, if he wanted to rest, he should have taken a vacation. This was not a vacation, but a trip; and with a trip, the goal was to see as much as possible in the time allotted. A research project based on this discussion revealed that, within the state of Pennsylvania in the USA, those 55+ could be divided into three market segments based on the benefits they desired from travel. The study was undertaken first in 1986 and then again in 1996. A third study was started in 2006. Results of the 1996 study are presented here.

The analysis revealed that those 55+ years of age and residing in the state of Pennsylvania could be divided into three different segments based on their reasons for pleasure travel. Each segment was given a name based upon the characteristics of that segment. One segment is referred to as the *Escape and Learn Group*, members of the second segment are referred to as *The Retirees* and members of the third segment are called the *Active Story Tellers*.

ESCAPE AND LEARN GROUP

This group is named the *Escape and Learn Group*. While ratings on the different variables are greater than many of the same ratings made by members of *The Retirees*, they are less than the ratings given by members of *Active Story Tellers*. Highest ratings for reason to travel were "visit new places," "get rest and relaxation," "escape the everyday routine," and "experience new things."

Slightly under 50% (48.8%) are retired or unemployed and 51.2% work full time or part time. The median age is 65, which is the middle age range of the three clusters. This group has the most members with incomes of $50,000 or more. Specifically, more than one-third (34.2%) have incomes of $50,000 or more, which is a directionally larger percentage than the same income for *The Retirees* and statically larger from the same income for *Active Story Tellers*. The fact that this group has more people in the highest income category may explain why they like to visit new places and experience new things. They may like to go new places since if they do not like their vacation destination, they can afford to go somewhere else.

Slightly fewer than 7 of 10 (68.6%) travel 2 or more times per year; this is the least traveling done by any of the groups. While at first this may be surprising given their income, it should be noted that more than one-half of the members of this group work full or part time. Members of this group are slightly more likely than members of *The Retirees* to use guidebooks to help determine overnight accommodations. This may be a result of visiting a new place. Members of *Escape and Learn Group* tend to travel with a friend or relative compared to a group (directionally different than scores of member of other clusters).

THE RETIREES

This group is named *The Retirees* because 57.2% of this group is retired or unemployed. This is directionally higher than the percentage of retirees in the other two groups. The median age of members of this group is 66, which is directionally higher than the median age of the other two groups. Almost 50% of the members of this segment earn less than $30,000 per year. This is directionally higher than a similar income for the other groups.

Members of this cluster "prefer to return to a destination rather than visiting a new one." Despite this one feature, this is the segment we know the least about in terms of their primary reasons for travel. This group represents 19.3% of the sample.

ACTIVE STORY TELLERS

This group represents 34.8% of the sample. The median age of this group is 62 and the mean is 63.5, which is the youngest of all three groups. Given this age grouping, it is not surprising that more members of this group have been retired less than one year compared to members of the other two groups. Specifically, 9.7% of the members of this group have been retired less than a year, compared to 3.7% for members of the *Escape and Learn Group* and 2.9% for members of *The Retirees*. Overall, 50% of the members of this group are retired.

Members of this group are more likely than members of other groups to travel because they want to:
1. Escape everyday routine
2. Be able to experience new things
3. Spend time with immediate family
4. Meet people and socialize
5. Visit festivals
6. Seek intellectual enrichment
7. Tell friends about the trip
8. Engage in physical activities
9. Seek spiritual enrichment
10. Be with members of the opposite sex
11. Visit museums and historic sights

Members of *Active Story Tellers* are also more likely than members of other groups to:
1. Believe anticipation of trip is as exciting as trip itself
2. Enjoy telling friends about trip
3. Have pleasure trips filled with activities
4. Usually more tired after they return than before they left
5. Use trips to build friendships
6. Believe they are still as active today on pleasure trips as they were 5 years ago
7. Use guidebooks to help determine overnight accommodations

The above should demonstrate that those 55+ are not just one segment, but many. Again, not surprising in 2006, but new in 1986.

Source: Shoemaker, S. (2000). Segmentation of the senior pleasure travel market: 10 years later. *Journal of Travel Research, 39,* 11–26.

In summary, benefit analysis can be a powerful segmentation tool. Its best use lies in good research—research that can pay off in terms of understanding customers and what motivates them.

Price Segmentation

Price segmentation is actually a form of benefit segmentation, only it is more visible and more tangible. There are two ways to look at price segments: one is between product classes; the other is within a **product class**. Price segments within a product class, at least in hospitality, are limited. A lower price may increase the value of the benefit bundle, other things being equal, but customers will generally not make major trade-offs for a small gain in price; that is, they won't accept a poor location or poor service just to save a few dollars within the same product class. Price segmentation is nearly nonexistent in these cases in hospitality.

Segmentation between product classes is different. Five-star hotels and budget motels both provide lodging, but they are each a different product class. Gourmet restaurants and fast-food restaurants are also separate product classes. The inference is that one product class does not truly compete with another on the same occasion, given the same circumstances. If we go to New York City, we do not choose between the Waldorf-Astoria and Days Inn. In these cases, price is clearly a segmenting factor. Although the initial determination by the customer may be based on price range, the other elements of the bundle will influence the final choice. No one rationally pays more for something without expecting to get more. In cases like these, markets are segmented within broad price ranges.

In the U.S. hotel industry today, Smith Travel Research defines five segments based on average room rates in specific metro markets. In nonmetro areas, the luxury and upscale segments are collapsed to form four price segments. These segments, and how they are defined, are shown in Exhibit 12-18.

Amazingly, with today's modern construction, the physical product is not all that different (within ranges), and in some cases, neither is the price. In many cases, lower prices have been obtained by lower construction and operating costs and through elimination of public space and food and beverage facilities. Of course, as one moves up the ladder, the furniture gets better, the walls and the carpet get thicker, the atrium gets higher, and the bathroom (sometimes) gets larger and has more amenities. No longer, necessarily, does one find a sagging bed in a budget motel or scratched, broken, and torn furniture or tiny (or nonexistent) soap in the bathroom. In other words, the basic needs are still fulfilled.

Why, then, are customers willing to pay more for relatively little? And is this really price segmentation? Well, in many cases they are not, and in many cases it really isn't. Those cases in which customers are willing to pay more are largely because of the intangibles and tangibles that they receive in return: service, prestige, professionalism, larger, higher quality, among others. These are benefits, and the net result is actually benefit, not price, segmentation.

Web Browsing Exercise

Visit the websites of the Marriott brands shown in Exhibit 11-19 (http://marriott.com/default.mi). How does each brand's website reflect its market segment? How are the sites similar? How are they different?

The other answer to why customers will pay more for relatively little is somewhat ambiguous because, for most, price is a major consideration in any purchase and varying price sensitivities will stratify any market. In the final analysis, however, within the same product class, it is rarely price alone that determines the segment. Price is only the risk that the willing and able buyer will take based on the intensity of the problem and the perceived value and expectation of the solution. This analysis applies to both the hotel and restaurant industries. In Exhibit 12-19, you can see how Marriott has touched on just about all of the **segmentation variables** we have discussed.

International Segmentation

Segmentation takes on a different perspective for hospitality companies in the international arena. The potential market is so diverse that special care must be taken with regard to customer mix. For the individual restaurant, segmentation strategies are developed based on whether the intended market is native, international, or both. The hotel restaurant will likewise segment both by its in-house market and by the local market it wishes to attract.

Hotel companies in countries other than the United States, at least those in major cities, have long had to deal with wide geographic and cultural segmentation. Groupe Accor's Formule 1, Etap, Ibis, Mercure, Novotel, and Sofitel divisions all segment both on the native market and on various international markets. In some small countries, such as Singapore, the upscale hotels are almost totally dependent on the international market. Even in large countries such as India and China this is also largely true in major cities. In the United States relatively few hotels segment on the international market at all. However, as international tourism and business travel into the United States continues to grow rapidly, many hotels in gateway cities such as New York, Los Angeles, and Miami actively seek out foreign visitors.

When a hotel company targets business from foreign lands, the picture changes. The company must first seek geographic and cultural definition of its markets. The Nikko (now Westin) hotel in New York City and the New Otani in Los Angeles (both Japanese-owned hotels) initially sought to capture the Japanese market. More specifically, they segmented on both the Japanese business and pleasure travel markets. Other companies, like those from France such as Meridien and Sofitel, do not necessarily seek the same nationality as their origin. Instead, this segment will be just one of a number of segments they hope to attract. When either these companies or U.S. companies locate in other parts of the world, they seek a diverse international clientele.

International hotel marketers must first make conscious decisions about the geographic segments they wish to attract. The Japanese market, the Taiwanese market, the Australian market, the German market, the European market, and the North American market all have special

EXHIBIT 12-18	Price Segments in the U.S. Lodging Industry

LUXURY
- COLONY
- CONRAD
- FAIRMONT HOTEL
- FOUR SEASONS
- HOTEL SOFITEL
- INTER-CONTINENTAL
- LOEWS
- LUXURY COLLECTION
- MANDARIN ORIENTAL
- PAN PACIFIC
- PREFERRED
- THE PENINSULA GROUP
- PRINCE HOTELS
- ST. REGIS
- REGENT HOTELS
- RITZ-CARLTON
- STARHOTELS
- W HOTELS
- THE WALDORF-ASTORIA
  COLLECTION

UPPER UPSCALE
- CAESARS
- CONCORDE HOTELS
- DORAL
- DOUBLETREE HOTELS
- EMBASSY SUITES
- EMBASSY VACATION RESORTS
- GAYLORD ENTERTAINMENT
- HELMSLEY HOTEL
- HILTON HOTELS
- HILTON GAMING
- HYATT
- JURYS HOTELS
- LANGHAM HOTELS
- LE MERIDIEN
- MARRIOTT
- MARRIOTT INTERNATIONAL
- MARRIOTT CONF. CENTER
- MILLENNIUM HOTELS
- NEW OTANI HOTELS, THE
- NIKKO
- OMNI
- PRIME HOTELS
- RENAISSANCE
- SHERATON HOTEL
- SONESTA HOTEL
- SWISSOTEL
- WESTIN

UPSCALE
- ADAM'S MARK
- AMERISUITES
- AYRES
- XANTERRA PARKS & RESORTS
- ASTON
- CHASE SUITES
- CLUB MED
- COAST HOTELS USA
- COURTYARD
- HILTON GARDEN INN
- CROWNE PLAZA
- FOUR POINTS
- HARRAH'S
- HAWTHORN SUITES
- HAWTHORN SUITES LTD
- HOMEWOOD SUITES
- HOTEL INDIGO
- HOTEL NOVOTEL
- OUTRIGGER
- RADISSON
- RESIDENCE INN
- RESORT QUEST HAWAII
- SIERRA SUITES
- SPRINGHILL SUITES
- STAYBRIDGE SUITES
- SUMMERFIELD BY WYNDHAM
- WOODFIELD SUITES
- WOODFIN SUITES
- WYNDHAM HOTELS

MIDSCALE W/F & B
- BEST WESTERN
- CLARION
- DOUBLETREE CLUB
- GOLDEN TULIP
- HARVEY HOTEL
- HAWTHORN INN & SUITES
- HOLIDAY INN
- HOLIDAY INN SELECT
- SUNROUTE CO LTD
- HOWARD JOHNSON
- JOLLY HOTELS
- LITTLE AMERICA
- MARC
- OHANA HOTELS
- PARK PLAZA
- QUALITY INN
- QUALITY INN SUITES
- RAMADA
- RAMADA PLAZA
- RED LION

- ROMANTIK HOTEL
- WESTMARK
- SUNSPREE RESORT
- WESTCOAST
- WYNDHAM GARDEN HOTEL

MIDSCALE W/O F&B
- AMERIHOST
- AMERICINN
- BAYMONT INNS & SUITES
- BRADFORD HOMESUITES
- CABOT LODGE
- CANDLEWOOD HOTEL
- CLUBHOUSE INNS OF AMERICA
- COMFORT INN
- COMFORT SUITES
- COUNTRY INN & SUITES
- DRURY INN
- DRURY LODGE
- DRURY PLAZA HOTEL
- EXTENDED STAY DELUXE
- FAIRFIELD INN
- HAMPTON INN
- HAMPTON INN & SUITES
- HEARTLAND INN
- HOLIDAY INN EXPRESS
- INNSUITES HOTELS
- LA QUINTA INNS
- LA QUINTA INNS & SUITES
- LEES INN OF AMERICA
- MAINSTAY SUITES
- PHOENIX INN
- RAMADA LIMITED
- SHILO INN
- SIGNATURE INNS
- SILVER CLOUD
- SLEEP INN
- TOWNPLACE SUITES
- WELLESLEY INN
- WELLESLEY SUITES
- WINGATE INN

ECONOMY
- 1st INTERSTATE INN
- ADMIRAL BENBOW
- AMERICA'S BEST INNS
- AMERICA'S BEST SUITES
- AMERICA'S BEST VALUE
- BAYVIEW INT'L HOTELS
- BUDGET HOST INN
- COUNTRY HEARTH INN
- CRESTWOOD SUITES

- CROSS COUNTRY INN
- CROSSLAND SUITES
- DAYS INN
- DOWNTOWNER MOTOR INN
- E-Z 8
- ECONO LODGE
- INNS OF AMERICA
- EXEL INN
- EXTENDED STAY AMERICA
- FAMILY INNS OF AMERICA
- GOOD NITE INN
- GREAT WESTERN
- GUESTHOUSE INNS
- HOMEGATE
- HOMESTEAD STUDIO SUITES
- HOWARD JOHNSON EXP. INN
- INNKEEPER
- INNCAL
- INTOWN SUITES
- JAMESON INN
- KEY WEST INN
- KNIGHTS INN
- LEXINGTON HOTEL SUITES
- MASTER HOSTS INN
- MASTERS INN
- MCINTOSH MOTOR INN
- MICROTEL INN
- MOTEL 6
- NATIONAL 9
- PARK INN
- PASSPORT INN
- PEARTREE INN
- RED CARPET INN
- RED ROOF INN
- ROADSTAR INN
- RODEWAY INN
- SAVANNAH SUITES
- SCOTTISH INN
- SELECT INN
- SELECT SUITES
- SHONEY'S INN
- STUDIO 6
- STUDIO PLUS
- SUBURBAN EXTENDED STAY
  HOTELS
- SUN SUITES HOTELS
- SUPER 8
- THIFT LODGE
- TRAVELODGE
- VAGABOND
- WANDLYN INN

Source: Retrieved September 16, 2005, from *www.smithtravelresearch.com/SmithTravelResearch/misc/GlossaryAds.aspx.* Copyright 2006, Smith Travel Research Publishing. Used by permission.

significance for hotels in ASEAN (Association of Southeast Asian Nations) countries (Philippines, Singapore, Malaysia, Thailand, Indonesia, and Brunei). This is true whether the hotels are operated by companies from the native country, the United States, Hong Kong, Japan, or any other country. This situation is even more apparent in Hong Kong, where, like Singapore, very few guests will be national residents.

It is also possible, of course, for some of these hotels to have guests from over 20 different countries at one time

EXHIBIT 12-19	Marriott Segmented Hotel Brands	
Brand Name	**Double Occupancy Price Range**	**Market Segment**
Fairfield Inn	$72–89	Upper-economy business and leisure travelers
TownePlace Suites	$79–109	Moderate-level travelers with weekly or multiweekly stays
SpringHill Suites	$79–115	Business and leisure travelers seeking more space and amenities
Courtyard	$75–179	"Designed for the road warrior"; quality and affordable accommodations
Residence Inn	$85–179	Travelers looking for a "residential-style" hotel
Marriott Hotels & Resorts	$119–400	"Achievers" who seek consistent quality—business and leisure
Renaissance Hotels & Resorts	$130–500	More discriminating travelers who want attention to detail—business and leisure
Ritz-Carlton	$175–900	Luxury, unique, personalized stay for senior executives
JW Marriott Hotels & Resorts	$199–219	Luxury, unique, architectural detail; for senior executives
Ramada International Hotels & Resorts	$79–90 or $200 in select cities	Locations reflecting the character and culture for the traveler wanting consistently excellent and affordable service
Marriott ExecuStay	$1,900–4,500/ month Housing	Temporary housing needs, customized, relocation; insurance adjusters, corporate and military travelers
Marriott Executive Apartments	$135–500	Home-style living with hotel amenities, for business executives
Marriott Vacation Club International	$89–500	International resorts, luxury, business and leisure travel
Marriott Conference Centers	$120–300	Meeting resort for conventions and executive resorts

or another, as we have previously shown. Resources would be spread too thin, however, if a hotel made concentrated efforts to appeal to all of them. Many hotels try to avoid the stigma of being a one-origin hotel—a Japanese hotel, an Arab hotel, or an American hotel.

A case in point is the Oberoi hotel in Mumbai (formerly known as Bombay), which tried to shed the image of catering primarily to the international traveler, while its rival, the Taj Hotel, skimmed off the cream of the Indian market. Another case is a former Holiday Inn in Antwerp, Belgium, that wanted to dispel the image of being an "American" hotel, especially when the American market weakened. Focusing too narrowly on a major share of just one market can be misleading and counterproductive when you consider that no one geographic market is large enough to maintain necessary occupancy, in spite of the potential of obtaining a major share of that market.

Fine-Tuning Segments

It can be a mistake to segment on very broad geographical or cultural areas. All Europeans are clearly not the same, nor are all Muslims, all French, or all Americans. Thus, some international hotel companies are beginning to fine-tune their segmentation strategies with a global perspective. This could mean, for example, a certain level of business executive regardless of geographic origin. This segment, composed of diverse cultures, is more difficult and expensive to reach, but increasingly, global communication media and distribution channels are easing the task.

Fine-tuning follows the pattern of good segmentation strategy—that is, complementary target markets. One way to fine-tune is to look at the business market as something other than one vast market and segment on benefits and usage. Moller and colleagues found that business segments included a larger share of top and middle management personnel who travel more than the average business customers and do more work during their stay at the hotel. Another segment had additional, fairly unique, features. Its members were keen on hotel advice, using the "right" hotels and included a high share of U.S. and UK visitors. This segment also displayed more loyal patronizing behavior than other segments, was more favorable toward international "luxury" chains, and exhibited a more active recreation pattern.[7]

Radisson/SAS Hotels of Brussels was particularly successful in using psychographic segmentation—concentrating on the "efficiency-minded" segment. In Stavanger, Norway, Radisson/SAS operates an "efficient" businesspersons' hotel without the usual flourish of varied restaurants and lounges usually associated with upscale hotels.

The pitfalls of concentrated segmentation are more acute with international markets. Some geographic markets collapse overnight, as occurred with the fall of the North American market in Europe as a result of terrorism activities, the Gulf War in 1990, and the Iraq War in 2003. The same thing happened in Florida in the 1990s with the

German market, as foreign tourists were the victims of violent crimes that received tremendous publicity. Of course, there is no way to foresee these types of events, but being forewarned means not depending on one segment too heavily.

Globalization of Markets

Theodore Levitt considered that the era of multinational marketing must move to one of "globalization of markets." Levitt argued,

> Though companies always customize for specific segments, success in a world whose wants become more homogenized requires of such companies strategic and operating modes that search for opportunities to sell to similar segments throughout the globe to achieve the scale economies that keep their costs competitive.
>
> Seldom are these days a segment in one country unique to that country alone. It is found everywhere, [and is] thus available to sellers from everywhere. Small local segments in this fashion become globally standardized, large and therefore subject to global competition, especially price competition . . . the successful global corporation does not abjure customization or differentiation for the requirements of markets that differ in product preferences, spending patterns, shopping preferences. . . . but the global corporation accepts and adjusts to these differences only reluctantly, only after relentlessly testing their immutability—after trying in various ways to circumvent and reshape them.[8]

Does Levitt argue against segmentation? If a country or even a segment within that country is not homogeneous, can the world be one homogeneous marketplace? Does this apply to the hospitality industry? Is a hotel room or a restaurant meal basically the same worldwide with minor modifications? Should the marketer adjust only after testing the waters? In the final analysis, other than catering to cultures and differences, if you agree with Levitt (and many don't), it is probably benefit segments that are the "similar segments throughout the globe," and whose "immutability" can be relied on.

Segmentation Strategies

No segments exist in isolation, and there is considerable overlap and sharing of the variables. Also, few hotels or restaurants today can survive on only one market segment. It is likely that there will be numerous segments and numerous segmentation strategies. The foundation of any segmentation strategy is behavioral differences. No segment is meaningful if it does not behave differently from another segment—the same factor that leads to conflict between segments. Whether you use geography, demographics, psychographics, benefits, or usage, the test of the segment is the differentiation of behavior. Thus, in the final analysis, the behavior of segments is the true test of their validity. Consider the following example:

> A suburban hotel suffering from slow weekend occupancy surveyed the market for new sources of business. Two distinct segments were discovered, but neither one was large enough to create the desired weekend occupancy. It was decided to market to both, and separate strategies based on the needs and wants of each segment were developed and implemented. The segments were romantic couples who wanted to get away for a peaceful and quiet weekend and families who wanted to take their children for a minivacation with lots of activities. It wasn't long before the two segments collided head on. The potential damage is obvious.

The two segments in the preceding example behave differently, so they are both valid segments. The problem arose only when the two came together. A similar example occurred in Las Vegas when the city tried to be family orientated. It did not take long to discover that tourist families with children did not gamble; in fact, the children "got in the way" of the gamblers. Las Vegas has since repositioned itself to be more adult and convention oriented.

Knowing how customer behaviors change, it is readily apparent that segments also change over time. We have argued already that one of the advantages of segmentation is the ability to stay closer to the customers and understand them better. This advantage should never be neglected, and a constant alert must always be maintained for changing, merging, or dividing segments. Too much segmentation can lead to too many markets and an inability to serve anyone well or profitably.

In the final analysis, market segmentation is a scientific procedure requiring scientific analysis. It cannot be a casual or haphazard exercise. What strategic thinking management does is seek the "ideal business mix." Exhibit 12-20 shows the tests to which each market segment should be subjected. Exhibit 12-21 shows the relationship between market analysis and segmentation, and marketing strategies.

The necessity of market segmentation in the hospitality industry has become increasingly critical because of the intense competition that has become even more evident over time. In many cases, market segmentation may be a prerequisite to growth. In some cases, large or major segments may have reached their level of fulfillment. Smaller segments, unimportant individually but critical in the aggregate, may be the next wave.

Product differentiation, as a *singular* market strategy, may have seen its day in the hospitality industry. As product classes become more crowded, however, it will remain as a key competitive strategy within the same product classes.

EXHIBIT 12-20 **Tests for Segmentation**

- **Is it homogeneous?**   Homogeneity on every aspect is not possible or even necessary, but certain key aspects should be identified in this respect. These aspects form the basis of the segment.
- **Can it be identified?**   Certainly we can identify segments based on gender or geographic origin, but other measures are not so easy. For example, suppose we wanted to segment on psychographic dimensions of conservative, moderate, and liberal. The segment would be of little value if we could not identify those who fit those dimensions.
- **Can it be measured?**   Suppose we could identify a conservative segment. We would then need to be able to measure the level of conservatism and the accompanying needs and wants.
- **Can it be reached economically?**   The segment will not be much use to us, beyond present customers, if we cannot build on

it. Through media, direct mail, or even internal marketing we need to be able to get to the segment.
- **Can a differential in competitive advantage be maximized and preserved?**   In the hospitality industry this is one of the toughest tests of segmentation, but one that should be constantly sought if not always reached.
- **Is it compatible with others segments we may have at the same time?**
- **Is the segment large enough and/or profitable enough?**   There is a large bus tour segment for hotels that many would find unprofitable. There is a very small segment of visiting royalty that a few hotels may find very profitable. The cost and effort of serving each segment must be weighed against the return.

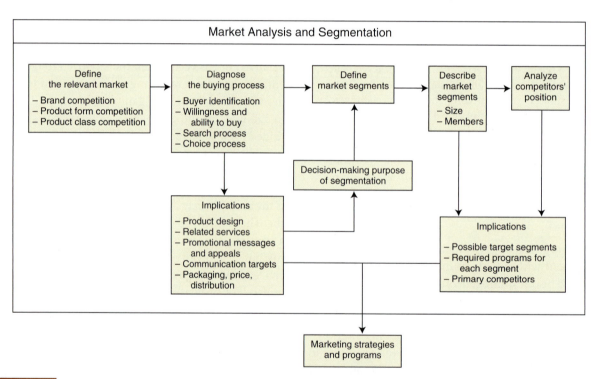

EXHIBIT 12-21   Relationship between market analysis and segmentation strategies.

Source: Guiltinan, J. P., & Paul, G. W. (1993). Marketing management: Strategies and programs (5th ed.). New York: copyright 1993 by The McGraw-Hill Companies, Inc.

Target Marketing

Target markets are drawn from segments. They might be called subsegments, but the word *target* has a more active connotation that is important. Once we have segmented the market and examined the market potential, we must select those specific markets that we can best serve by designing our products and services to appeal directly to them. Many of the same segmentation rules apply; we just refine them more. For example, earlier in the chapter we

segmented the restaurant market on gourmet and then targeted a smaller portion of that segment. There are three strategies for selecting target markets:

1. An *undifferentiated* targeting strategy assumes that customers within a segment have similar needs so only one type of product or service is offered to that segment. This is common practice in the hospitality industry; the business traveler is an example.
2. A *concentrated* targeting strategy is when a firm selects a target group within one market segment and

pursues it aggressively. For example, Ritz-Carlton targets executives who demand top hotel experiences, whereas Microtel goes after business travelers who merely need a place to sleep.

3. The third strategy is *differentiated multitarget* marketing. Marriott International is the perfect example, targeting specific business needs with Marriott Hotels, Courtyard by Marriott, Fairfield Inn, and Residence Inn, all serving distinct target markets within the business segment and doing so without the confusion that Choice International has created with its overlapping products. Within any one hotel, multitarget strategy is also in effect. Numerous hotels have "towers—a hotel within a hotel," concierge floors, or "business plan" rooms with special services that target differentiated business travelers with specific business needs.

Concentrated or differential **target marketing** means aiming specifically at one or more portions of a market. One travel researcher found, for example, that the vacation market segment could be broken down into 10 target markets. Each one represents an isolation of interests and behavior based on benefits, usage, demographics, and psychographics. Each one has different needs and wants and requires a different package, a different positioning, and different communication. These target markets and some of their specific characteristics are shown in Exhibit 12-22.

Tourism Marketing Application
A trend in tourism marketing is the promotion of gay and lesbian travel. We discuss this trend in detail in our interview with Terry Jicinsky of the Las Vegas Convention and Visitors Authority in Chapter 21. Puerto Vallarta, Mexico, is a destination that specifically promotes itself to gay and lesbian travelers. Two travel companies specifically target this market via the Web: www.gay.com and www.gaytravel.com. A magazine that targets this market segment is www.outtraveler.com (accessed March 25, 2006).

As with segmentation, there are criteria for choosing target markets. They overlap the segmentation criteria, but are a little more precise. These are shown in Exhibit 12-23.

Target marketing is practiced at the unit level also. A property may use concentrated targeting, select one market, and serve it well. The Delta Queen Steamboat Company, which operates three-day to one-week cruises on the Mississippi River, effectively targets the mature traveler market that likes to gamble. The risk of concentrated targeting is that of putting all your eggs into one basket. If environmental or other changes negatively affect the demand, you may not have any market left to serve. On the other hand, a hotel may select several markets to serve, but there are risks to this strategy too, as we noted earlier. These

---

EXHIBIT 12-22 Vacation Target Markets

- **The Carriage Trade:** Desire a change of scene but not of style, secure in wealth and position, play golf and tennis year around, and when traveling, tend to vacation as a family.
- **The Comfortables:** The largest group, insecure, seek social and psychological comfort, like recommended restaurants, guided tours, and organized activities.
- **The Venturers:** Want to see new things; have a thirst for fresh ideas, information, and education; seek the new and the different; don't travel in groups; and collect experiences.
- **The Adventurers:** The venturer advanced one step—seeks risk, danger, and the unknown.
- **The Inners:** Jet-setters, go somewhere because of who is there rather than what is there; they "make" destinations such as Acapulco, Majorca, Costa del Sol.
- **The Buffs:** Strongly subject oriented; travel because of particular interest or hobby.
- **The Activists:** Not content to sit by the pool and bask in the sun; want constant activities.
- **The Outdoorsers:** Campers, hikers, birdwatchers, bicyclists, and other outdoor recreationists.
- **The Restless:** Travel for something to do, tend to be senior citizens, retired, widowed; collect travel experiences and travel all the time including off-seasons.
- **The Bargain Hunters:** Can afford to travel, but compulsively seek the best deal.

EXHIBIT 12-23 Target Market Criteria

- What is the potential revenue and market share?
- What are the demand characteristics?
- Are they able and willing to buy?
- How are they currently being served by the competition?
- Are they compatible with the objectives of the firm?
- Are they compatible with each other?
- Do they fit the resources of the firm?
- Do they fit the tastes and values of the firm?
- What is the feasibility of exploiting them?

EXHIBIT 12-24	Unique Target Markets

- **Equinox Hotel, Manchester, Vermont:** Mastering falconry-handling birds of prey; Land Rover–handling four-wheel-drive vehicles on ice-slicked roads or steep terrain; fly fishing.
- **Hyatt, Scottsdale, Arizona:** Hopi Indian learning center; "hop on a Harley" motorcycle riding.
- **Forte Hotel, Guyana:** Timberland, a rainforest retreat.

- **Mauna Lani Bay Hotel, Hawaii:** Explore hidden pools, ravines, guava forest, and horse back.
- **Praia do Forte, Brazil:** Eco resort: Turtle mating and procreation.
- **Four Seasons, Chicago; Vista, Pittsburgh:** Cigar smoking salons and dinners.

markets must be compatible and seek similar benefits from the establishment.

Take the case of one very successful resort in the Virgin Islands. One target market was honeymoon couples and the other was high-income senior executives and their spouses, usually over 55 years old (employees referred to these markets, tongue-in-cheek, as newly-weds and nearly-deads, respectively). At first glance, these segments do not appear to have much in common, but in reality they complemented each other. Both segments wanted isolation, peace, and quiet. The resort was on a small remote island, and rooms did not have air conditioning, radios, television, or telephones. The resort pursued these two markets aggressively and ran an annual occupancy rate of over 85 percent. To increase low season occupancy rates, the resort decided to book group leisure travelers from Italy. These guests were on holiday and rightfully sang and danced until the wee hours of the morning, alienating the resort's traditional target markets. Needless to say, this experiment was quickly ended. Consider, however, the unique target markets in Exhibit 12-24. These are obviously quite small, but may also be high rated.

Mass Customization

While we have talked about criteria for market segments and target markets, such as homogeneity, size, and so forth, modern technology is bringing us closer to target markets of one, sometimes referred to by the oxymoron, **mass customization**. This is largely because of the computer databases that contain vast amounts of guest information. The goal of such databases is to look at the customer not as a segment of many, but as a segment of one.

Marketers are taking the database far beyond a simple electronic Rolodex of names and addresses. It is possible to talk to customers as individuals and then reconstruct the product/service to aim at target groups and to reward loyal customers. Databases can measure what the customer does, not just what she says she does. This information can drive the entire marketing strategy. Much of this, of course, is based on the heavy user segment that accounts for a large

proportion of sales. We discuss databases in more detail in Chapter 20.

Databases are rich sources when they combine demographics with buying habits. These will become even more potent marketing tools in the future. All of this, of course, is relationship marketing on which we spent all of Chapter 4, but the flip side of that is mass customization. The economic logic behind mass customization is, today, as inevitable and irresistible as the logic of the assembly line 100 years ago. It *will* happen, and marketers will have to think in terms of share of customer, rather than market share. Mass customization, if done correctly, will result in keeping a satisfied, loyal, long-term customer. It is the ultimate form of customer differentiation to capture the greatest possible share of every single individual's business. It is the key to success in tomorrow's hospitality business. Once target markets have been determined, the next step is to tailor the marketing effort to the needs and wants of each market.

Tourism Marketing Application

Footprint® Vietnam Travel is one company that offers personalized tours. Travelers can go to this firm's website (www.footprintsvietnam.com) and choose their destination, how much they would like to spend, the types of activities, and the type of accommodation. Footprint® Vietnam Travel will then design a personalized tour for them.

■ Summary

Differentiation, market segmentation, and target marketing are different but complementary marketing strategies. In a highly competitive marketplace, each one alone (and all of them together) is critical to the marketing effort.

Differentiation is used to create real or perceived differences between products and services offered by hospitality organizations. The objective is for the customer to perceive a positive difference between our offering and that of the competition and thus react more favorably toward ours.

The differences among customers are the basis for market segmentation. Segmentation is the strategy wherein the firm attempts to match its marketing effort to the unique behavior of specified customer groups in the marketplace through the use of key segmentation variables.

Several criteria guide the process of segmentation and differentiation. It is necessary first to identify the bases for segmenting the market. Profiles of the resulting segments are then determined and matched with the firm's capabilities, followed by the projection of potential markets and segment attractiveness. The market is then segmented, and target markets are selected from the identified segments. Positioning is developed for each target market, and the marketing mix is tailored accordingly.

Each segment or target market must be examined competitively. When others are targeting the same market, as will usually be the case, a final differentiation strategy is needed. Increasingly, customer differentiation is the goal of organizations. The trend is to move away from segments of many to segments of one. The segments of one are examples of mass customization though the use of database marketing.

■ Key Terms

demand analysis	cohorts
metropolitan statistical areas (MSAs)	PRIZM NE
	usage segmentation
family life cycle	market segmentation
DINKs	benefit bundle
DEWKs	product class
echo boomers	segmentation variables
activities, interests, and opinions (AIOs)	differentiation
	target marketing
values and lifestyles (VALS)	mass customization

■ Discussion Questions

1. Distinguish between product differentiation and product segmentation. Discuss how they relate. Which would you use, and how, if your product were a pure commodity? Why?
2. Consider a restaurant with which you are familiar. Apply strategies for differentiation and segmentation. Discuss.
3. Using the same restaurant as Question 3, discuss the various segmentation variables. How do they fit? How can they be better targeted?
4. The text argues that price segmentation is really benefit segmentation. Explain and discuss.

5. What is the difference between a target market and a market segment? Give some examples and explain them.
6. Considering your answers to Questions 2 and 3, how would you develop a marketing program for a restaurant?
7. Develop a list of unique target markets for a specific hotel or restaurant that would meet the target market criteria in Exhibit 11-23.
8. Using yourself as the guinea pig, develop a mass customization program for you as a customer.

■ Group Projects

1. Try segmenting your group on the different segmentation criteria discussed in the chapter. Then, given a specific time, place, and purpose, try to pick a hotel or restaurant product for each segment.
2. Develop a mass customization program for each member of your group. Are the programs feasible? How would you set up the programs?

■ References

1. Levitt, T. (1980, January-February). Marketing success through differentiation—Of anything. *Harvard Business Review*, 73. Copyright 1980 by the President and Fellows of Harvard College; all rights reserved.
2. Levitt, T. (1986). *The marketing imagination.* New York: Free Press, 128.
3. Retrieved September 16, 2005, from my.webmd.com/hw/health_guide_atoz/ty6172.asp.
4. Retrieved September 16, 2005, from www.choicehotels.com/ires/en-US/html/CorporateHistory?sid=Lgwc.DLG8ggFmq.8.
5. Plummer, J. T. (1974, January). The concept and application of life style segmentation. *Journal of Marketing*, 33–37. Published by the American Marketing Association.
6. Retrieved September 16, 2005, from www.cohorts.com/building_foundation_3.html.
7. Moller, K. E. K., Lehtinen, J. R., Rosenqvist, G., & Storbacks, K. (1985). Segmenting hotel business customers: A benefit clustering approach. In T. Bloch et al. (Eds.), *Services marketing in a changing environment.* Chicago: American Marketing Association, 72–77.
8. Levitt, T. A. (1983, May/June). The globalization of markets. *Harvard Business Review*, 92–102.

CHAPTER 13

Branding and Market Positioning

Overview

Think about the hotel chain Four Seasons. What words immediately come to mind? You may think of words such as *luxury, pampering, high-thread-count sheets*, and perhaps *expensive*. Now, think about the company Marriott. What words come to mind now? Words such as *consistency, good value, functional*, and *sameness from property to property* probably come to mind. Four Seasons and Marriott are both companies. But they also are brands. When people hear their names, words and associations immediately come to mind.

Brands have been defined as "the impressions received by consumers resulting in a distinctive position in their mind's eye based on perceived emotional and functional benefits." Essentially, these impressions form a promise to the customer regarding what they will receive when staying at one of these properties. *Market positioning* refers to the activities that a firm undertakes to place the brand in customers' minds so they understand what the brand is and who its competitors are. Without effective positioning, a property can get lost in the customer's mind and hence in the marketplace.

I. Introduction to Hospitality Marketing
1. The Concept of Marketing
2. Marketing Services and the Hospitality Experience
3. The Marketing Mix and the Product/Service Mix
4. Relationship/Loyalty Marketing

II. Marketing to Build a Competitive Advantage
5. Strategic Marketing
6. The Strategic Marketing System and Marketing Objectives

III. The Marketplace
7. Understanding Individual Customers
8. Understanding Organizational Customers
9. The Tourist Customer and the Tourism Destination

IV. Situational Analysis
10. Understanding Competition
11. Marketing Intelligence and Research

V. Functional Strategies
12. Differentiation, Segmentation, and Target Marketing
13. *Branding and Market Positioning*
14. The Hospitality Pricing Mix
15. The Communications Mix: Advertising
16. The Communications Mix: Sales Promotions, Merchandising, Public Relations, and Publicity
17. The Communications Mix: Personal Selling
18. Hospitality Distribution Systems
19. Channels of Distribution: Bringing the Customer to the Product
20. Interactive Marketing: Internet and Database Marketing

VII. Feedback

VI. Synthesis
21. The Marketing Plan

John Griffin joined Le Meridien in 2001 after moving from Sydney, Australia. Griffin previously held a range of roles with American Express in advertising and customer relationship management, including areas of new product development. In the years prior to joining Le Meridien, he worked with global agencies Leo Burnett and Wunderman, managing a range of Australian and global accounts in the financial services, technology, and pharmaceutical industries. Griffin leads a worldwide marketing team handling brand development, advertising and research, loyally marketing, new product development, customer intelligence, and partnerships.

Marketing in Action

John Griffin, Vice President, Worldwide Marketing, Le Meridien

What is your definition of a brand?

It's a series of tangible and intangible elements that can connect with emotion to create a perception in a consumer's mind about a product or service.

I would assume that the branding statement say what the brand is all about. Is that correct?

It says what the brand is all about and should relate to the position that we want to hold in a consumer's mind.

What are the issues Le Meridien considers as they develop a branding strategy?

First and foremost, we need to make sure that our strategy resonates with customers. Then, our range of hotels and the services that we provide in those hotels must have the ability to deliver on the brand proposition that we envision. As a service industry, the branding strategy has to work as much for staff as for customers, It has to touch all aspects of our business comprehensively and consistently—staff, customers, and sales interactions. Even our internal departments need, in some way, to be able to connect with what the branding statement is about. Put simply, it's as much cultural as it is an external marketing premise. And as we work through our product and develop our communication approaches, we're constantly looking at the fact that we are maintaining our differentiation against our competition and that the branding statement remains reflective of the evolving trends and needs in the marketplace at the time.

Do you do a lot of research to determine what the position of the brand is prior to developing the brand statement? What kind of research do you do to determine that?

We look to customers to help us refresh and evolve our brand direction through a variety of research methods—from qualitative and quantitative brand research to behavioral trends of existing and potential customers, We go into the marketplace on a regular basis to look at our target audience, how their needs are changing, and how the brand proposition that we put forward meets that need. Having been in existence since the early '70s, our challenge is to ensure that the equity built through our brand history is leveraged to its best advantage and evolved in such a way that it retains and builds on the inherent strengths of the brand whilst steering its position to future success.

What does your Le Merdien brand stand for in your customer's view?

For many global hotel brands, it's hard to determine exactly what they stand for. While consumers can recognize many hotel brand names, there are very few whose positioning is clearly understood by or connected to their target audience. What helps define our brand is our European heritage and origins. Our name, Le Meridien, is unmistakably French, and our origins were indeed French. We leverage our name and provenance by using the elements of style and sophistication that are associated with being European.

How would you compare the brand image to that of Marriott or Hilton?

Hilton and the Marriott enjoy a strong breadth of location and a well-established reputation for consistent standards. Wherever you are in the world, you feel at home at a Hilton. We aim to take a different stance by focusing more on what makes our properties different in each and every location and by embracing the local culture that we actually occupy. Using architecture, service, and food, we focus on combining the best of the environment in which we operate in a local country with the elements that come from our brand heritage of "Frenchness" and "Europeanness."

What should students understand about branding?

One of the most important things about branding is that it actually transcends the printed page. It's as much cultural as physical. A high degree of the experiences in our industry are intangible. Branding is also a living thing—it should always be at the forefront of the business, being worked with by the business and creating the personality for our communications and approach to the market.

Branding needs to provide the tangible foundation for the promise being made and do it in such a way that it sets your product apart from the competition. To succeed, a branding strategy must apply consistently across all aspects of corporate and individual hotel communications so as not to confuse the customer and waste valuable resources competing among ourselves. If there's a disconnect between the two, then we're potentially blurring the brand message.

How do you ensure that?

The first and most tangible element is to ensure that we have a strong set of brand guidelines that we know can apply across the board to a diversity of properties. Within those guidelines, we cover end-to-end communication, from what appears in physical materials in our hotels through to how our advertising looks, our in-house com-munications, and our Web development. The most important thing is to be flexible enough within the guidelines to allow the brand to be articulated in a way that best suits the many markets in which we do business. The aim is to keep the brand guidelines alive and make them relevant, which means we can talk as one brand.

Do you have branding managers within the region?

We have small branding teams in each region that are tasked with having dialogue on a regular basis with the hotels. Those individuals will often act as a sounding board for how the brand applies to new hotel development. They will attend ongoing seminars and conferences with the hotels and talk about branding. They're essentially consultants focused on helping the hotels find solutions for the branding challenges they face.

So they would work with the general manager, the marketing director for each property?

General managers, marketing and sales directors, yes.

In terms of the career path for someone who wants to do branding and would like to be eventually in your position, what kind of a career path would you recommend for students and what kind of courses should they be taking and what kind of careers should they look for to move into the right direction of branding?

Having sufficient experience with a breadth of different roles at the property level first enables you to understand the challenges in creating a guest experience. Time in a corporate office role then allows you to see the other side of the experience. It can even help to have exposure to the marketing discipline from outside of our industry as well—it enhances the ability to understand a brand in the consumer's mind, especially that we aren't the only ones competing for space. Look at taking a graduate diploma or equivalent in marketing, to expose you to the mix of disciplines and, most importantly, be willing to try different experiences to broaden your overall understanding of the business.

Are you suggesting then that students who earn a degree in hospitality should go into operations to fully learn the business, and then go back to graduate school to focus on corporate communications, advertising, and branding? After graduate school they might get a job in a different industry in a branding role and then eventually go back to hotel business.

For any business, but particularly hospitality, matching the operational delivery to the marketing promise is essential.

Therefore, what really makes an effective marketer is the ability to have worked and understood how the operation applies to the branding promise and vice versa. In my experience, there's always a healthy tension between marketing and operations on delivering the brand, and your ability to succeed as a marketer is to be able to understand and work with the bounds of the operation. Don't over-promise—but also find the right way in which you can influence the organization to grow and deliver better in the future. And, yes, the disciplines of branding can be developed in other categories than ours—particularly the ability to understand customer dynamics.

What other ideas should we be thinking about in terms of branding?

I can't emphasize enough that branding is as much cultural as it is physical and visible. Association with HR in communicating and delivering at all levels is a must-do. The interaction between marketing and the hotel teams is critical for a consumer to truly understand what the brand means to them and therefore how our employees have to be able to deliver. For too long in our industry there has been a perception that you can change the flag over the door and it doesn't make much of a difference. To truly change that, you have to create a passion about the brand going right through the business. It's a huge challenge, but one that's worth overcoming.

How do you build or create that culture down at the property level?

Start with the core of the brand proposition, then look at the different traits and behaviors that surround the brand and how we want to be perceived by our customers. Look at this from a communications standpoint, but in conjunction with human resources, focus on delivery via behavioral training, reward and recognition, and team interaction—all based around the core premise of what the brand stands for. If all these elements come together in the right way, we have the Holy Grail—an understanding of what it means to be part of the brand in a very different way than just an academic exercise related to marketing

The main point of many of your comments is that branding is a 360-degree way of looking at the business. It is something that has to be integrated into the whole culture of the organization. Is this a fair assessment?

Yes, and you can boil it down to leadership. It requires an active role in demonstrating the same behaviors as set by the brand that then should cascade to our employees for the benefit of our guests—that's the creation of a brand culture, Without the focus from the top and an integrated combination of strategy, product, visual and behavioral integration, we make it hard for ourselves and our customers to understand what we stand for—and then want to associate with the brand.

What companies do you think are doing a good job with their brand definition?

In our industry, brands such as Mandarin Oriental and Banyan Tree show their strength in creating a unified brand position from the promise to the delivery, which I think is clearly communicated and well understood by their target audience. Outside of our industry, companies like Apple and American Express are great examples in the way they define their brand—through their internal culture particularly.

Given the recent purchase of the Le Meridien brand by Starwood Hotels & Resorts, which took place subsequent to this interview, how do you equate your comments on Le Meridien's brand and culture with a potential future as part of a multibranded hotel company?

The success of your business ultimately rests with your customers and starts with your staff. How you train them, how you interact with them, and the belief that the culture that you set up with them then helps define the brand, even in a multibranded environment. As I said before, the stronger your brand and your culture, the better your position to succeed—and this success can come in a number of ways. The challenge for Le Meridien as part of a larger, multibranded company will be to help retain La Différence that makes it the brand it is. Being part of a multibrand company can only help crystallize those differences and how they help distinguish the brand.

Used by permission from John Griffin

Marketing positioning is the natural follow-through of market segmentation and target marketing. In fact, it is on those strategies that positioning is built because they define the market to which the positioning is directed. Therefore, we must select and understand our target markets before we can develop effective and efficient positioning strategies. The objective of positioning is to create a distinctive place in the minds of potential customers—a place where customers know who the firm is, how the firm is different from the competition, and how the firm can satisfy the customers' needs and wants. It is about *creating* the perception that the firm is best able to solve customers' problems.

The firm that does not create a distinctive place in customers' minds faces several pitfalls:

1. The firm is forced into a position of competing directly with stronger competition. For example, an independent midscale hotel may be pushed into a losing competition with a clearly positioned Courtyard.
2. The firm's position is unclear so that it lacks true identity and customers do not know what it offers and what needs are fulfilled. In other words, there is no clear perception. This often happens when a property or chain tries to be all things to all people.
3. The firm has no position in customers' minds so that it lacks top-of-the-mind awareness and is not part of the customer's **evoked set.** A name like Joe's Restaurant, for example, provides no perception or image. Contrast this with a name like Kentucky Fried Chicken. Even if you had never heard of the restaurant, you would have an idea of the type of items sold there.

There are actually two kinds of positioning in marketing: objective positioning and subjective positioning. Each has its appropriate place and usage. Each is concerned with its position vis-à-vis the competition. Before we explain these, however, we need to deal with three customer attributes that are important when positioning.

Salience, Determinance, and Importance

In evaluating and developing effective positioning strategies, we need to understand how customers perceive and differentiate among salient, determinant, and important product or service attributes or benefits. One might, for example, position on a salient benefit with poor results because those benefits are not necessarily important in the customer choice process. To develop branding and positioning strategies, we must be able to determine why the customer is buying our product or service. Once this reasoning has been determined, the positioning of the product or service becomes more natural.

Salience

Salient attributes are those that are "top of the mind." They are the ones that readily come to mind when you think of an object. Because of this, a list of strictly salient attributes obtained from customers may be totally misleading in describing how they make choices. If you were asked, "Why did you buy that shirt?" you might say because it was on sale. If we then assumed that the next shirt you buy will be one on sale, we could be making a completely erroneous assumption. What really determines your choice could be the style of the shirt; the sale price was just an inducement.

Salient factors may be determinant factors, but they are not determinant when they are not the true differentiating factor the customer is looking for or when they are common truoughout the product class. Consider, for example, the chocolates on the pillow. This could be very salient and be remembered by customers, but it is doubtful that they would base their choice of hotel on chocolates.

Now consider location. Take a survey of almost any set of hotel customers and ask what is important to them in choosing a hotel. At the top of the list will almost always be location, as descriptive, multiple-answer questionnaires will always reveal. Location is a very salient attribute, but if six restaurants are within four blocks of each other in Chicago or right next to each other as in "fast-food rows" everywhere, or eight resort hotels are within five miles of each other in Palm Springs, as is the case in so many areas today, location is not likely to be a determinant factor. In marketing, we most often use salient factors to get attention and create awareness.

Determinance

A study that looked at the influence of different value drivers for hotels found that although location and amenities were important for business travelers, price was overall the most important determinant of value. For leisure travelers, amenities are the most important determinant of value.[2]

Determinant attributes are those that actually determine choice, such as reputation, price/value, or level of service. These are the attributes most closely related to customer preferences or actual purchase decisions; in other words, these features predispose customers to action. These attributes are critical to the customer choice process. The problem is that customers do not always know exactly what forms the basis of their choice.

An example here is bathroom amenities. Bathroom amenities may not be very salient, but they could be quite important after we have become used to having them. If every hotel in the product class has them, however, they are hardly determinant any more. There is a caveat here, however. If we were now to remove the extended line of bathroom amenities, they might become negatively determinant; that is, people might say, "I won't go there because they don't have good bathroom amenities." The implication is that perhaps hotels in this product class should now have the amenities, but promoting them or positioning on them would be to little avail.

This is also true of location and cleanliness, supposedly the main reasons that people choose hotels. People don't choose hotels simply because of location and cleanliness; however, they do choose against specific hotels because of their lack of location and cleanliness. In marketing, we most often use determinant factors to persuade customers to make a choice.

Importance

Importance attributes are those that are important to the customer after having made a choice. The previous example of bathroom amenities demonstrated this. It is important that they be there, once the customer is accustomed to their being there, but they are still not determinant. Once the choice has been made, what was salient or determinant fades into the background unless, of course, they are found not to exist. Now it is important that the room be clean and the bed be comfortable. In marketing, we most often use importance factors to arouse interest and create a benefit bundle that will lead to determinance.

Salience, determinance, and importance are complementary concepts, and they are all significant in the positioning effort. It is critical to understand the place of each. Recall the discussion in the chapter on individual customers regarding selective perception, selective acceptance, and selective retention. All three may occur with salient factors. Determinant and important factors are more likely to cause selective retention, because we remember what features helped provide the memorable experience or offered a solution to our problem. Much positioning that is done only on salient factors—for instance, location or an atrium lobby—is less than successful when these factors are not determinant. In summary, good positioning requires that creating an image, differentiating the product or service, and making a promise are all based on determinant and/or importance factors.

We now discuss different types of positioning.

Objective Positioning

Objective positioning is concerned almost entirely with the *objective* attributes of the physical product. It means creating an image about the product that reflects its physical characteristics and functional features. It is usually concerned with what actually exists. For example, take the statement "The car is red." We can all see that it is red. If the company that makes this car makes only red cars, we might call it "the red car company." We would carry an image of these cars as opposed to those made by "the green car company." Or, we could say, "That building is tall." Again, we would all likely agree.

That's a little simplistic, so let's apply it to the hospitality industry. Econo Lodge is a low-cost motel; Hyatt Regency's Cerromar Beach Resort & Casino in Puerto Rico is on the beach; Ruth's Chris Steakhouse sells steaks. All of these businesses conjure up specific images based on the name itself—it derives from an objective, concrete, specific attribute. If we know anything about the product (for instance Marriott Marquis), we know at least that much.

Objective positioning need not always be concrete, however. It may be more abstract than these previous examples. Ferraris are not only red; they also go fast. A Ritz-Carlton is a luxury hotel; McDonald's offers quick service; Le Cirque 2000 offers gourmet meals and fine wines. Again, these images derive from the product itself.

Objective product positioning can be very important and is often used in the hospitality industry. Westin has the Heavenly Bed; Red Lobster positions on seafood; and Olive Garden, on Italian food. The Plaza Athenee, located in New York City, positions on its proximity to Central Park and the fact that it is a boutique hotel with 115 guest rooms located in the residential area of the East Side. If a product has a unique characteristic or unique functional feature, that feature may be used to objectively position the product, to create an image, and to differentiate it from the competition, as shown in the ad in Exhibit 13-1. The suggestion of Exhibit 13-1 is that, while there are lots of spas, very few offer the natural and private setting found at a Marriott Hotel & Resort.

Less successful objective positioning occurs when the feature is not unique, as shown in Exhibit 13-2, which shows a table in the restaurant. In other words, this ad creates no real position in our mind about this, although it may create awareness, which is probably its intent. Totally unsuccessful approaches include a picture of two people in a hotel room or, worse, a picture of an empty restaurant with waiters standing at attention.

Subjective Positioning

Subjective positioning is much more difficult in practice than objective positioning. It is concerned with *subjective* attributes of the product or brand. Subjective positioning is the image, not of the physical aspects of the product, but other attributes as perceived by the customer—they belong not necessarily to the product, but to the customer's mental perception of the product. These perceptions and the resulting image may or may not reflect the true state of the product's characteristics. They may simply exist in the customer's mind, and we might find many who would disagree with particular perceptions and images. What the marketer hopes is that the people in the target market will agree on a

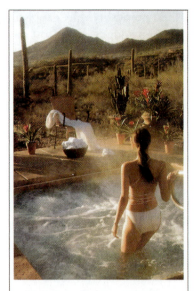

THESE FIVE RESORTS SET THE STANDARD FOR LUXURY.

We deliver luxury stripped of pretense and brimming with relevance. Sophisticated, unobtrusive and very personal. It is based on the recognition that it's all about you. You'll enjoy this luxury in surroundings of uncommon beauty in five of the most enviable locations in all of North America. We invite you to take a visual tour of each JW Marriott Resort & Spa by visiting the web site below. **Arrive.**℠

JW MARRIOTT.
HOTELS & RESORTS

JW Luxury Experience from $264 – $579.
Premium accommodations, with breakfast in bed and the Wall Street Journal included.

Visit www.jwresortluxury.com or call 888-770-0139.

JW Marriott Starr Pass Resort & Spa, Tucson, Arizona

JW Marriott Las Vegas Resort & Spa, Nevada

Camelback Inn, A JW Marriott Resort & Spa, Scottsdale, Arizona

JW Marriott Desert Ridge Resort & Spa, Phoenix, Arizona

Desert Springs, A JW Marriott Resort & Spa, Palm Desert, California

Resort featured in photo: JW Marriott Starr Pass Resort & Spa, Tucson, Arizona. Rates vary by resort. Please contact us for full amenities and limitations.

EXHIBIT 13-1 Marriott positions its spas on privacy and natural beauty.

Source: Marriott International. Used by permission.

favorable image or characteristic, whether or not it is factual. This is the test of effective subjective positioning.

Hilton Hotels' former ad campaign, "When American business hits the road, American business stops at Hilton," and its slogan "America's Business Address" are examples of attempts at subjective positioning. The desired image, obviously, was that businesspeople prefer Hilton Hotels. One reason that people might not accept this positioning is because it lacks uniqueness and does not differentiate from the competition. For example, one Hilton advertisement showed an empty conference room with a conference table surrounded by chairs. These are objective product characteristics that clearly are no different from characteristics at thousands of other hotels. Hilton's new campaign is "Take me to the Hilton." According to Robert Dirks, who was senior vice president of brand management and marketing at the time the campaign began in April 2004, the goal was to position Hilton as the number one solution to many of the concerns expressed by modern-day travelers, such as lack of personalized service, uncomfortable environment, and poor technology.[3]

Tangible Positioning

There are two very important differences in the types of positioning when they are used in the hospitality industry. The first occurs in **tangible positioning**, because the industry's product has almost reached **commodity status**. In other words, many of the rooms in hotels of the same product class are almost exactly alike. The same is true, to a lesser degree, in restaurants. Consider, for example, McDonald's versus Burger King or the upscale New York restaurant Le Cirque 2000 in the New York Palace versus the upscale Les Celebrites located in the Essex House Hotel Nikko New York. We need to understand what this almost commodity status means for positioning.

Consider the ultimate commodity, salt. How would you use positioning to create a unique image and differentiate your salt from someone else's salt? Morton tries it with the **positioning statement** "When it rains, it pours." This is intended to imply that Morton salt is free-flowing even when the weather is damp, whereas other salts are not. It is not necessarily true that others are not, but if you buy into it, you do so because you differentiate Morton's salt from other salts based on the physical characteristic of being free-flowing. Salt is a very tangible good; it would be difficult to argue that salt is exotic, tantalizing, or romantic.

Those arguments, however, could be made for cosmetics, and they certainly are, as we all know. Cosmetics are mostly tangible. However, their successful marketing is

EXHIBIT 13-2 This table in a restaurant tells us nothing about the restaurant.

Source: Magnus Rew © Dorling Kindersley, Courtesy of the Four Points Sheraton Hotel, Orlando.

based on mental perceptions of intangible results. As the founder of Revlon Cosmetics said, "In the factory we make cosmetics; in the drugstore we sell hope." If we are selling a near-commodity product such as a hotel room that is mostly tangible, then we need to develop intangible mental perceptions that may or may not actually belong to the product—hence the expression, "Sell the sizzle, not the steak." As Bob Osgoodby, publisher of the *Add Me Newsletter,* stated, "While the 'nuts and bolts' of your product or offer are important, that is not normally what gets someone's initial interest and makes the sale."[4]

Consider again a hotel ad showing a picture of a couple in a hotel room. A hotel room is very tangible. It looks like thousands of other hotel rooms. As with salt, it is very hard to develop a mental perception of a hotel room that creates an image and differentiates it from other hotel rooms. Two people in the room are also tangible. What's more, they are no different from two people in any other hotel room. Now you see the problem that advertisers have been struggling with for years: How do we position a tangible product that has very little means of differentiation?

It is difficult, but not impossible. For example, what is more dull, plain, ordinary, and undifferentiated than a prefrozen, overcooked hamburger? But notice the next McDonald's commercial that you see. Notice the emphasis on people, fun, good times, convenience, and so on. They have particularly capitalized on these intangible elements with their new "I'm Lovin' It" campaign. Exhibit 13-3 shows an attempt to create a subjective position from the tangibleness of a unique dish of green ice cream. The idea is that if the ice cream is unique, the

freshly made

green tea ice cream

delivered to your door

what can we do for you?

THE
ALEX
overnight or over time

203 impeccable guest rooms and deluxe suites

concierge services beyond expectation

flat-screen TVs in all bedrooms, bathrooms & living rooms

24-hour room service from Riingo® and award-winning chef, Marcus Samuelsson

The Alex Hotel. 205 East 45th Street at Third Avenue. New York, NY 10017
212.867.5100 www.thealexhotel.com

EXHIBIT 13-3 This advertisement is an example of subjective positioning.

Source: The Alex. Used by permission.

rooms in the hotel are probably also unique. Subjective positioning of tangible features requires developing intangible images.

Tourism Marketing Application
Objective and subjective positioning works very well for tourist destinations because the objective part focuses on the attributes of the area while the subjective focuses on what the attributes represent. Consider the Tahiti. The beaches are the attributes, while the subjective belief relates to images of love, relaxation, and beauty. More examples of position in tourism can be found at this website: www.hotel-online.com/Trends/AsiaPacificJournal/PositionDestination.html (accessed March 26, 2006).

Intangible Positioning

The second important difference in the positioning of hospitality products resides in the converse situation, which is **intangible positioning**. What we are largely marketing is not tangible; it is intangible. Some would say that is nonsense, because what's more important than the room or the meal? They would be right, but that's what we are selling and not what we are marketing. If we were selling rooms and beds or steaks and sushi bars, what difference would it make where the customer went, assuming a comparable level of quality? And that is an assumption we have to make within the same product class, so it doesn't get us very far.

So, again, what we are largely marketing are intangibles. The tangibles are essential and necessary, but as soon as they reach a certain level of acceptance, they become secondary. Because tangibles are so difficult to differentiate, to be competitive we have to market the intangible aspects of the product or service. Even when tangible (e.g., a steak), they have a measure of intangibility because they are consumed rather than taken home to be possessed. We have referred to this as *tangibilizing the intangible.* The intangible elements are abstract. To emphasize the tangible elements is to fail to differentiate from the competition. To emphasize the abstract (e.g., with phrases such as "escape to the ultimate") is to compound the intangibility. Thus, hospitality positioning needs to focus on enhancing and differentiating the intangible realities through the manipulation of tangible cues.

Some hotels do this with atrium lobbies. People don't buy atrium lobbies; they buy what the lobbies make tangible. We might not all agree, but some would say atrium lobbies are exotic, full of grandeur, majestic, or exciting. These are intangible images and nothing more than mental perceptions. Of course, check-in may be just as slow and the rooms may be no different from those in other hotels, but the image is there, not just the physical characteristics.

What we want to do is create a subjective "position" in the customer's mind. You can see now why positioning follows so closely on target marketing—we need to know what mental constructs are held by the customer in the target market and what tangible evidence sustains them.

Return for a moment to the steak-and-sizzle argument. If we want to sell the steak, as this argument goes, then we need to market the sizzle. But our steak is just like all the others, so what we have to do is sell the sizzle, the intangible. How do we tangibilize the sizzle? There is probably no better example, even 30 years later, than what Jim Nassikas did at the Stanford Court Hotel in the 1970s. (This hotel, located in San Francisco, is now a Marriott Renaissance Hotel.) In fact, he was so successful in positioning the Stanford Court that Nassikas virtually stopped advertising and still ran one of the highest occupancies and ADRs in San Francisco. He positioned his hotel "for people who understand the subtle difference." When he did use advertisements, he used headings such as: "You gloat over a great hotel the way you do over a rare antique find. We designed The Stanford Court for you." Another example was "You're as finicky about choosing a fine hotel as you are about the right patisserie. We designed The Stanford Court for you." A more modem example is the advertisement for Mandarin Oriental Hotel Group with the tagline "She's a fan." This is shown in Exhibit 13-4.

Positioning, then, is a relative term. It is not just how the brand is perceived alone, but how the perceived image stands in relation to competing images. It is the customer's mental perception, which may or may not differ from the actual physical characteristics. It is most important when the product is intangible and there is little difference from the competition on physical characteristics. For two examples of this kind of restaurant positioning, see the ads in Exhibit 13-5 and 13-6.

Effective Positioning

Our discussion thus far has dwelled largely on *image,* the mental picture the customer has of the product or service. We have also discussed the need for the image to *differentiate* the brand from the product class. These are two essential criteria for effective positioning, but there is one more.

This will take us back to the basic marketing concept, the notion of needs and wants, and problems and solutions—the promise we make to the customer. It also takes us back to our chapter on understanding individual customers, in which we discussed consumer behavior in terms of customer attitudes. Images and differentiation mean

EXHIBIT 13-4 This advertisement for Mandarin Oriental tangibilizes the intangible.

Source: Mandarin Oriental Hotel Group. Used by permission.

EXHIBIT 13-5 This advertisement for Whaler Inn tangibilizes the intangible.

Source: Fairmont Hotels. Used by permission.

creating beliefs. Next we have to develop the affective reaction, the attitude toward the belief, and the action that will create the intention to buy.

Thus, effective positioning also must *promise the benefit* the customer will receive, it must create the expectation, and it must offer a solution to the customer's problem. And that solution, if at all possible, should be different from and better than the competition's, especially if one of the competitors is already offering the same solution.

David Ogilvy, a longtime advertising guru and former head of the international firm Ogilvy and Mather, stated: "Advertising which promises no benefits to the customer does not sell, yet the majority of campaigns contain no promise whatever. (That is the most important sentence in this book. Read it again.)"[5] Notice how the ad in Exhibit 12-4 fills all three of the good positioning requirements: it creates an image, differentiates itself, and promises a benefit. If we're

lucky, we can capture all of this in a single positioning statement, as Mandarin Oriental did.

Here are some better-known positioning statements, some of which are current and some of which are not, with which many of us are familiar. As you read each one, consider the image, the differentiation, and the promised benefit, as well as the tangible and intangible aspect.

- U.S. Army—An Army of one.
- U.S. Army—Be all that you can be.
- Marines—The Few, The Proud, The Marines.
- Toyota Today—Moving forward.
- Toyota Old—Get the feeling.
- IBM—Solutions for a small planet.
- McDonald's Today—I'm loving' it.
- McDonald's Old—You deserve a break today.
- Burger King—Have it your way.
- Hilton—Take me to the Hilton.

EXHIBIT 13-6 This advertisement for County Seat Café tangibilizes the intangible.

Source: Folks Restaurant Management Group, Inc. Used by permission.

- General Electric Today—Imagination at work.
- General Electric Old—We bring good things to life.
- Microsoft Today—Your passion, our commitment.
- Microsoft Old —Where do you want to go today?
- Holiday Inn Express—Stay smart.
- Motel 6—We'll leave the light on for ya.
- Embassy Suites—Twice the hotel.
- Nike—Just do it.
- Hyatt—This is the Hyatt Touch.

Exhibit 13-7 discusses why Shangri-La Hotel Group developed its positioning statement "Between Heaven and Earth." Exhibit 13-8 shows the advertisement that conveys this position.

Tourism Marketing Application

Tourism destinations also have positioning statements. For Las Vegas, it is "What happens in Vegas Stays in Vegas." For Nepal, the positioning statement is "Naturally Nepal, Once Is Not Enough." For the state of Missouri, the positioning statement is "Rediscover Your Missouri." For the region of Andaman and Nicoba in India, it is "An all season Indian holiday amidst health, nature, and adventure." For India as a county, it is "Incredible India." The slogan for Uganda is "Gifted by Nature." Thailand's sloagn is "Thailand Grand Invitation 2006"—a change from the old slogan, which was "Thailand Happiness on Earth." Thailand was not the only country to change its positioning statement. South Korea moved from "Dynamic Korea" to "Korea: Something More." Singapore changed from "New Asia—Singapore" to "Uniquely Singapore." Bangladesh changed from "Exotic Bangladesh" to "Bangladesh—Beautiful Surprise." Finally, the Philippines changed from "Rediscovery: Philippines" to WOW (wealth of wonders) Philippines!" The campaign for Australia is "So Where the Bloody Hell Are You?" It used to be "See Australia in a Different Light."

EXHIBIT 13-7 **The Message behind Shangri-La's Position Statement "Between Heaven and Earth."**

"Where will you find your Shangri-La?" But where is Shangri-La? Where is the paradise that James Hilton's *Lost Horizon* described? Is it in the Yunan province, or is it a place at all? Shangri-La is a state of mind, of peace and tranquillity, a feeling, a moment in time, somewhere between Heaven and Earth.

The ad campaign places the Shangri-La moment, the experience that you have when you stay at the Shangri-La, between Heaven and Earth. It showcases the magical moments that our audience will enjoy and asks them the question, "Where will you find your Shangri-La?"

The ads have a very graphic look and feature the words *Heaven* and *Earth* in a heavy bold typeface. The words frame people experiencing and enjoying magical Shangri-La moments. The scenes in the ads are reflecting the real location of the different Shangri-La hotels and resorts within the group.

Source: Shangri-la Hotels and Resorts. Used by permission.

How do we determine the desired position for our product or service? Exhibit 13-9 provides a brief checklist for this purpose. This tells us that one may position in a number of different ways, all related to segmentation strategies. As discussed, positioning may be achieved on specific product features, product benefits, or a specific usage or user category. In sum, an effective position is one that clearly distinguishes from the competition on factors important to the relevant target market in everything an operation does. Exhibit 13-10 is a checklist of positioning approaches.

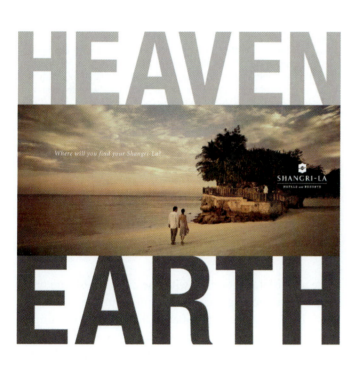

EXHIBIT 13-8 This advertisement differentiates Shangri-La from similar properties.

Source: Developed for Shangri-la Hotels and Resorts. Used by permission.

Positioning's Vital Role

We have dealt with positioning so far in the context of advertising, only because it is easier to illustrate that way. However, this is by no means the only context in which positioning should be used. Positioning should be a single-minded concept, an umbrella from which everything else in the organization flows. Bill Dowling, a hotel marketing consultant, wrote in 1980 that "Properly targeted, single-minded positioning affects everything a hotel [or restaurant] does or stands for—not only advertising but also all of its promotions, brochures and facilities—even its decor."[6] This is as true today as when it was first written.

Positioning also affects policies and procedures, employee attitudes, customer relations, complaint handling, and the myriad of other details that combine to make a hospitality experience. Positioning plays a vital role in the development of the entire marketing mix. Hospitality services compete on more than just image, differentiation, and benefits offered. There must be a consistency among the various offerings, and it is the positioning statement that guides this consistency. Likewise, although positioning can be applied for a given unit, a specific service, chain operations should develop a consistency if the company desires to use one unit to generate business for another.

Kyle Craig, former president and CEO of S&A Restaurant Corp., operators of the Steak & Ale, Bennigan's, JJ Muggs, and Bay Street chains and also past president of Kentucky Fried Chicken's domestic business, pioneered the repositioning of Kentucky Fried Chicken by changing its name to KFC and launching its first nonfried chicken products. He stated:

> When we talk about a marketing niche we are really talking about positioning. You must position your concept as offering a unique product or service. The key is to understand the customer decision and then use it to your advantage to successfully stimulate sales. Once you understand what the customer wants and match that against what your chain has to offer, you have a better chance of success.

EXHIBIT 13-9	**Checklist for Determining a Desired Position**

- Analyze product attributes that are salient and/or determinant and/or important to customers.
- Examine the distribution of these attributes among different market segments.
- Determine the optimal position for the product/service in regard to each attribute, taking into consideration the positions occupied by existing brands.

- Choose an overall position for the product, based on the overall match between product attributes and their distribution in the population and the positions of existing brands.

Source: From Marketing Planning, and Strategy, 5th edition, by Jain. © 1997. Reprinted with permission of South-Western, a division of Thomson Learning: www.thomsonrights.com. Fax 800-730-2215.

EXHIBIT 13-10	Checklist for Positioning Approaches

POSITIONING BY ATTRIBUTE, FEATURE, OR CUSTOMER BENEFIT

This approach emphasizes the benefits of particular features or attributes of the service or product. The Heavenly Bed pioneered by Westin, now part of Starwood, is an example of this approach. Another example is how the Tucson Convention Center promotes itself as having the largest convention space in the Southwest.

POSITIONING BY PRICE OR QUALITY

Price is a powerful positioning tool because it is perceived to say a great deal about the product. It also supports a level of quality. This is one reason that upscale hotel chains maintain high rack rates and then discount them severely. To lower the published price is perceived as lowering the image and positioning downward.

Price/quality does not have to be high price/high quality. It can also be used to represent low price/high quality. An example is Red Roof Inns and Motel 6. Although these companies offer low prices, they also provide quality; that is, the product performs as it was designed to do.

POSITIONING WITH RESPECT TO USE OR APPLICATION

Here a service is positioned on the reasons for using it. Often hotels will direct this positioning toward specific markets that have been segmented by purpose of use. Wingate Inns says, "We are built for business, every amenity, absolutely free, everywhere you are." Harrah's in Lake Tahoe goes after incentive travel business with, "Tell your best people to go jump in the lake." The Ventana Canyon Golf & Racquet Club in California sets itself apart as a place for meetings that require golf as an essential amenity. McDonald's formerly used "You deserve a break" as a contrast to cooking at home.

POSITIONING ACCORDING TO THE USERS OR CLASS OF USERS

This positioning features the people who use the product. Choice Hotels uses advertising showing famous, but active, senior citizens as users of their hotels. Fisher Island, a luxury residential development in Florida, positions itself as the place "Where people who run things can stop running." Westin once used the line: "If the *Wall Street Journal* were a hotel, it would be a Westin."

POSITIONING WITH RESPECT TO A PRODUCT CLASS

This technique is often used to position a product in a certain product class. Preferred Hotels, a referral group of independent hotels, shows their exclusivity with the statement, "We made it impossible to join. That's why every hotel wants to get in." The Beverly Wilshire hotel claimed: "If Hollywood is indeed ruled by czars, the Regent Beverly Wilshire is their palace." A famous example is 7UP cola, which positioned itself as the un-cola, to separate itself from Coke and Pepsi. It could do this because its syrup is clear, unlike most colas. Caress also positioned itself as a bath oil rather than a hand soap. Such strategies, at least initially, made them the only products in their newly defined category.

POSITIONING VIS-À-VIS THE COMPETITION

This approach is sometimes called "head-on" positioning and is used to bring out differences among services. Visa credit cards compete with American Express by showing examples of places all over the world where they do not accept American Express and only Visa cards are accepted. Another example is Avis' now famous campaign against Hertz: "We're #2 so we try harder."

... Finding a niche is tough but delivering the restaurant experience the niche demands is tougher.... Once the concept matches customer needs there are two litmus tests. First, your position must be believable in the customer's mind. Second, you must deliver on the promise on a consistent basis. Also, watch out for a niche that is restaurant-driven rather than customer-driven[7]

Subjective positioning is a strategy for creating a unique product image with the objective of creating and keeping customers. It exists solely in the mind of the customer. It can occur automatically, without any effort on the part of the marketer, and any kind of positioning may result. Two very dissimilar products may be perceived as the same; two similar products may be perceived as different. What the marketer hopes to do is to control the positioning, not just let it happen. Failure to select a position in the marketplace and to achieve and hold that position by delivering it, moreover, may lead to various undesirable consequences.

Repositioning

Repositioning, as the name implies, constitutes changing a position or image in the marketplace. The process is the same as initial positioning with the addition of one other element—removing the old positioning image.

There may be a number of reasons for wanting to reposition. One reason may be that you are occupying an unsuccessful position in the first place. Another is that you may have tried and failed to fully achieve a desired position. Also, you might find that competitors, too many and/or too powerful, have moved into the same position, making it overcrowded. Another reason could be in perceiving a new niche opportunity of which you wish to take advantage.

All of these situations are relatively common in the hospitality industry. Hamburger chains have tried repositioning as "gourmet" hamburger restaurants. Friendly's, originally an ice cream and sandwich chain, repositioned itself as a family restaurant. Many restaurants that often change hands are constantly repositioning with new names. A more complete example of restaurant repositioning is given in Exhibit 13-11.

Tourism Marketing Application.
The bombings in Bali had a major impact on tourism to that country. Figures released in 2005 revealed that the number of tourists visiting Bali in November 2005

EXHIBIT 13-11	The Repositioning of Dunkin' Donuts.*

Dunkin' Donuts, like many large companies, has gone through multiple ownerships and multiple changes in positioning. The company started in 1950 in Quincy, Massachusetts. By 1963 there were 100 franchised stores on the East Coast of the United States, with expansion growing into the Midwest and Southwest by 1982. In 1990 the firm was purchased by Allied Domecq PLC, which also owns ice-cream shop Baskin-Robbins and sandwich shop Togo's.

At the time of the purchase by Allied Domecq, Dunkin' Donuts was losing much of its breakfast sales to companies such as McDonald's and Burger King, while at the same time losing its "coffee crowd"—which consisted of approximately 2.7 million people per day—to specialty coffee shops such as Starbucks. In 1994 William Kussell was brought in from Reebok to spice up the menu and reputation. He changed the old slogan, "America's Number One Donut Chain," to "Dunkin' Donuts: Something fresh is always brewing here" and began a play to become the breakfast king. He switched the strategy of selling doughnuts by the dozen to selling a more frequently consumed item: coffee.

Dunkin' Donuts introduced four or more blends of fresh-brewed coffee and hot and cold specialty drinks, all at a fraction of the Starbucks price. A 10-ounce. Dunkin' Donuts coffee costs, on average, $1.19, while a 12-ounce cup of Starbuck's coffee costs between $1.40 and $1.65, depending on store location. Value and no-nonsense service has now positioned Dunkin' Donuts against Starbucks and McDonald's in a serious battle for the breakfast buck. John Gilbert, Dunkin' Donuts vice president of marketing, states that "counterintuitively, Dunkin' Donuts is primarily a coffee company. Unlike our coffee competitors, we also sell delicious fresh baked goods, such as breakfast sandwiches on fresh bagels. Our business model is to sell a cup of coffee plus a baked good to every customer. It is this focus on selling beverages and baked goods together that has helped us thrive when our competitors are suffering in this low-carb era."*

In addition, Allied Domecq housed its three brands (Dunkin' Donuts, Baskin-Robbins, and Togo's) under one roof with the idea that each brand would cater to an audience at different times of the day. It was a failure, as customers were confused and franchisees complained that it was too much to manage all three brands. In the fall of 2005, the practice of housing the brands in the same building was terminated. The focus on coffee was, however, a success. As a result of the switch, 2005 sales were up 14% from the previous year, with coffee making up 62% of sales.

In addition to moving away from only donuts toward specialty coffees, oven-baked bagels, and fat-free muffins, the firm also started to remodel their stores: To ensure that they would get the new layout and color scheme just right, Dunkin' Donuts paid faithful Dunkin' Donuts customers to fill their food and beverage needs at Starbucks for a week. They also paid Starbucks customers to switch to Dunkin' Donuts for the same period of time. The company concluded that Dunkin' Donuts customers felt the Starbucks environment was "pretentious" and "trendy," and the focus on the individual seemed a bit bewildering and even disingenuous at times. The people who frequented Starbucks felt Dunkin' Donuts was "unoriginal" and "austere" by comparison and wanted to have more control over things such as how much sugar and cream should go into their drinks.

The tacky old Dunkin' Donuts pink decor was replaced with a more upscale "ripe raisin" hue. The square laminate tables were replaced with round imitation-granite tabletops and sleek chairs. Customers loyal to Dunkin' Donuts had only one concern: that the changes not result in longer waiting lines, which now average about two minutes per customer from the time they order to the time they get through the register. Starbucks, by comparison, has a goal time of about three minutes per customer. Dunkin' Donuts also elected not to install wireless Internet access because it did not fit with customers' imagine of Dunkin' Donuts.

In December 2005 Dunkin' Donuts was sold by Pernod Richard SA, which had acquired Allied Domecq PLC to an investment group consisting of Thomas H. Lee partners, Bain Capital Partners, and the Carlyle Group. The new CEO is Jon Luther.

Dunkin' Donuts has more than 6,000 stores in the United States and 29 other countries

Source: *Dunkin' Donuts Press Room. Retrieved from www.dunkindonuts.com/aboutus/press/PressRelease.aspx?viewtype=current&id=100042* on May 5, 2005; *http://online.wsj.com/article/SB114446712300420923-search.html?KEYWORDS=dunkin+donuts&COLLECTION=wsjie/6month* accessed on April 23, 2006. Also adapted from Dunkin' Donuts is on a coffee rush. *Business Week*, (1998, March 16), 107–108. Ashley Trevitz, from the University of Houston, helped to adapt this material.

---

was down 42.5% from the number visiting in November 2004. To reverse this trend and plan for the future, a conference on positioning, repositioning, crisis management, and image recovery was held in Bali in December 2005. The United Nations World Tourism Organization (UMWTO) organized this conference. "The aim was to help Bali to rapidly regain markets, by not only recuperating and rebuilding confidence in the short term, but also to plan for the future, so as to enable the destination to confront the challenges facing the industry and to refocus efforts to regain market shares and acquire new ones." (www.bali-tourism-board.com/news.php?tit=198&month=12&year=2005, accessed March 25, 2006)

 Web Browsing Exercise

Visit the websites for Dunkin' Donuts (www.dunkindonuts.com) and Starbucks (www.starbucks.com). How is their positioning reflected by their websites? Compare and contrast.

Repositioning might also be used to appeal to a new segment, to add a new segment while at the same time trying to hold on to an old one, or to increase the size of a segment. Club Med, as we have noted, repositioned to the family market but still keeps its old market (and some of its old image) at some well-defined properties. Another reason for repositioning could be that new ownership desires a new position or wishes to merge the position of a newly acquired property into that of other properties already owned. Finally, repositioning would be called for in developing a partially or totally new concept, downgrading a property that has become distressed, or upgrading one that has been refurbished.

Examples of repositioning are when Holiday Inn, before being bought by InterContinental Hotels, separated its upscale Crowne Plaza line by removing the Holiday name and marketing it separately. In New York City, Schrager Hotels renovated a rundown hotel, Morgans, and repositioned it as a chic, trendy hotel. They did similar renovations with the Paramount, Barbizon, and St. Moritz. When Schrager ran into financial trouble, Schrager Hotels was renamed Morgans Hotel Group. Affinia Hospitality, formerly Manhattan East Suite Hotels, repositioned the old two-star Beverly hotel into a four-star product called the Benjamin. Starwood Hotels bought the Doral Hotels, also in New York, and has repositioned them as its new luxury brand, W.

In another case, Ramada tried to go upscale with hotels called Ramada Renaissance Hotels. The Ramada name, however, had a downscale stigma that stuck and was eventually dropped to better position Renaissance hotels as upscale. Renaissance is now owned by Marriott, who kept only the Renaissance name. An example of a single property repositioning is given in Exhibit 13-12.

Renovating and repositioning old hotels has become a common practice today. Stephen Taylor described the situation:

> The art of repositioning is coming into its own. Repositioning, the economic [marketing] revival of troubled properties and the renovation and revitalization of old/

outdated ones, can provide an alternative to the more traditional routes taken when hotels stop making good economic sense.

The task of repositioning is not as simple as creating a market slot for a brand-new hotel. A repositioner has to deal with two customer images—the existing one and a new one that must be projected.

Repositioning is a two-pronged effort. In most cases, a negative image and customer ill-will must be overcome before a new impression can be created. To achieve the goals which define the success of a repositioning effort . . . it needs to be finely tuned to fit the specific situation and it takes thought, perceptiveness and careful planning. . . . The successful repositioning of any hotel property begins with an intensive examination of the market the repositioner intends to enter.[8]

The Art of Repositioning

Repositioning rests on a change of image. The appropriate procedure for doing this is shown in Exhibit 13-13.

The application of the first four criteria in Exhibit 13-13 is evident in the effort of the Waldorf-Astoria Hotel to reposition. This famous hotel is shown in Exhibit 13-14. The Waldorf was perceived as the hotel of royalty and top business executives and as being very expensive even though it was in the same price range as its competition. Management wanted to position to customers at the middle-management level. Research revealed lifestyles of this level of the Waldorf's customers. The repositioning campaign emphasized these lifestyles as well as the attributes and the affordability of the Waldorf.

EXHIBIT 13-12	Repositioning the Hotel Nikko Atlanta

When the Hotel Nikko Atlanta opened in the exclusive Buckhead area of the city, there were four other major hotels close by: Ritz-Carlton, Westin, Embassy Suites, and Holiday Inn. The city and the area were suffering low occupancy rates that affected all. In fact, the Westin was in foreclosure by its owners and later became a Marriott. Ritz was the occupancy leader with 75 percent occupancy and an ADR of $120 from a single rack rate of $140–$185. Westin was running 55 percent occupancy and an ADR of $100 from a single rack rate of $130–$170. The others were further below. Nikko set its rack rates at $135–$185 and positioned directly against the Ritz, whom it saw as its only real competition. A year later, Nikko was running 35 percent occupancy and drastically discounting to pick up market share. The situation did not improve even when the market picked up. A year later new management was brought in.

According to the new GM, "The hotel wasn't marketed right; it was more concerned with competing with the Ritz. Nikko management looked at what was good for operations. We were providing customers what we wanted, not what the customers wanted. While the customer experience at the Nikko could be just as good as one at the Ritz, that wasn't the way the customer perceived the hotel."

The Nikko first reconceived and then repositioned itself. The goal became to be the area's value leader among luxury hotels. Nikko's rack rate was dropped $15 below that of the Ritz while also adding room upgrades. That positioned the hotel lower than the Ritz but slightly higher than the JW Marriott (former Westin) and a new Swissotel. "The intent was to encourage more trial visits and create more awareness. Although we lowered the rates, average rates actually went up." Weekend packages were instituted for $125 on an executive floor and $139 in an executive suite, including valet parking and a $20 credit in the signature restaurant. In the first month, Nikko sold 1,000 packages generating more than $100,000 in revenue. "By finding the right market niche and positioning ourselves appropriately, we became the growth leader among our primary competitors. We've grown 18 percent in occupancy and 24 percent in revenue this year over last. Our closest competitor grew 10 percent and 16 percent, respectively," said the GM.

Source: Abstracted from Wolff, C. (1994, November). When reconception means repositioning. *Lodging Hospitality*, 28, 30. Copyright © Penton Media, Inc.

EXHIBIT 13-13	**Procedures for Repositioning**

1. *Determine the present position.* It is essential to know where you are now before you determine how you are going to get to where you want to go. In repositioning, this is absolutely critical because the customer's image may not be at all what you think it is. Before trying to change a perception, you have to know what that perception is.
2. *Determine what position you wish to occupy.* This calls for thorough and objective research of the market and the competition, as well as the resources and ability to occupy that position. One has to be very realistic at this stage and not simply engage in wishful thinking.
3. *Make sure the product is truly different for the repositioning.* Telling a customer that the product has changed and is therefore now attractive had better be followed through operationally.
4. *Initiate the repositioning campaign based on the three criteria of effective positioning.* These include image, differentiation, and promised benefits and should be formulated from the research of the target market.
5. *Measure to see whether the position has significantly changed in the desired direction.* This too is critical. It is naive to assume that perceptions have changed simply because they are expected to. Do not simply measure this in terms of sales or profits— changes there may be due to other causes. What you want to know is whether perceptions have truly changed.

EXHIBIT 13-14	This advertisement shows the effort of the Waldorf-Astoria to reposition.

Source: Ambient Images. Creative Eye/MIRA.com

Hilton, which owns the Waldorf, had a different repositioning problem for the elite Towers section at the hotel. Billed as an upscale "hotel within a hotel," this product did not match the affordability positioning of the Waldorf. The Towers successfully aligned itself with a different reservations system, Leading Hotels of the World, and marketed itself separately from the main hotel.

There are pitfalls associated with repositioning. The short-run effect may be a loss of sales while the repositioning is being accomplished. A gain in sales, on the other hand, may occur only because people are "giving it another chance." There may be a sales drop because the new position was a poor choice and the market is too limited or already dominated by a competitor. It is important to find out why something has happened; it is never good business sense to assume that you know why.

Developing Positioning Strategies

Strategies are necessary whether initially positioning or repositioning. This means doing a thorough situational analysis. Lovelock suggested the model shown in Exhibit 13-15 as appropriate for developing market positioning strategies. This model is no different from one a marketer might use for selecting target markets. A major distinction, however, would occur in the thrust of the research. In this case, we would need to know a great deal more about perceptions, what they mean, and what they reflect. A benefit is not a benefit unless it is perceived to be one.

Once again, positioning is not in the product, in the brand, or even in the advertising; it is in the customer's

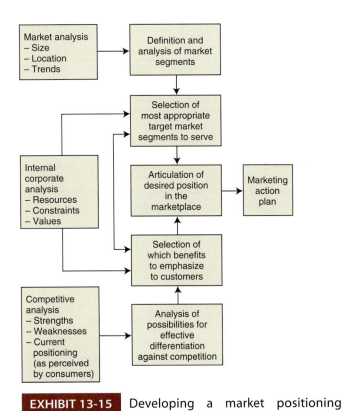

EXHIBIT 13-15 Developing a market positioning strategy.

Source: ©2004 Christopher H. Lovelock and Jochen Wirtz. Used by permission.

mind. It is definitely and positively not in management's mind. This is why it is so important for management to understand true positioning. It can be a perilous trap to assume that customers position in the same way as management does.

A checklist for developing positioning strategies is presented in Exhibit 13-16. This, of course, has to be based on the target markets.

 Web Browsing Exercise

Visit any website for a hotel, restaurant, and travel/tourism company. How, if at all, do these companies answer the questions asked in Exhibit 13-16? Compare and contrast. Choose a firm that does not address the issues in Exhibit 13-13 and rewrite the positioning statement based on the information you can find on the company.

Competitive Positioning

One way to visualize some of the elements in Exhibit 13-16 is through the use of positioning maps. We introduced this idea in Chapter 11. Because of its importance in marketing, we illustrate it again using a more detailed example in the appendix to this chapter.

EXHIBIT 13-16 **Checklist for Developing Positioning Strategies**

1. Company:
   - What are strengths and weaknesses, resources, management capabilities, present market position, values, objectives, and policies?
   - Where are we now?
   - Where do we want to go?
2. Product/Service:
   - What are facilities, location, attributes (salient, determinant, important), physical condition, level of service?
   - What is the product/service?
   - What does it do, in functional terms?
   - Why do/should people buy/come?
3. Brand Position:
   - What awareness, loyalty, and image do consumers have?
   - How does the brand compare to the competition?
   - What are the market segments?
   - What are the perceived attributes, and how are they distributed among the segments?
   - Where are we positioned?
4. Customers:
   - What are their segments and needs and wants?
   - What benefits do they seek?
   - What is the optimal position of attributes for each segment?

5. Competition:
   - Who are their customers, and why do they go there?
   - What does the competition do or not do better?
   - How are we differentiated?
   - What positions do the competition occupy?
6. The Marketplace:
   - What are the segments?
   - What is the generic demand?
   - What is our market share?
   - How are the segments reached?
   - Where does the market come from (e.g., geographic location)?
7. Opportunities:
   - What needs are unmet?
   - Can we meet them?
   - Can we improve on them?
   - What innovations are needed?
   - Are they worth going after?
   - Are there new uses, new users, or greater usage?
8. Decision:
   - What is the best overall position?

In developing positioning strategies, a critical element is positioning vis-à-vis the competition. It is necessary to first examine images and positions of all entities that may compete. One should then try to anticipate the effects of the proposed positioning and the reactions of competitors. Examining strengths and weaknesses of **competitive positioning** can identify positions to adopt and to stay away from and areas of dissatisfaction where a new positioning could generate new customers or lure others from the competition. If the segment is expanding, this process could also identify a growth opportunity.

Many hospitality entities today focus too closely on their immediate adjacent competition. As the economy becomes more global, newer markets and competitors must be understood to effectively market a hotel. There is a temptation to judge success by looking at the competition down the street.

Consider the example of a Marriott-franchised hotel in east Cleveland, Ohio, that was concerned about its rate structure for the upcoming year. After doing a quick review of the destination, marketers found that the hotel was competitive with the local hotel offerings. The determination of the pricing, however, should have come not from the local competition, but from the target markets. Research indicated that a majority of customers, business travelers, at this hotel could be segmented on similar characteristics and came from certain East Coast cities. Travel agencies from these "feeder cities" were booking thousands of room nights per quarter. These customers were used to paying $300 plus per night in New York and $250 in Boston and Chicago. Why, then, $159 in Cleveland? By positioning the hotel vis-à-vis its local competitors, money was being lost. When the hotel positioned itself against other destinations, the results improved dramatically.

The risks involved in positioning or repositioning are high. Thus, it is important to position on customers' perceptions, not management's, vis-à-vis the competition. The technique of perceptual mapping can be used to substantially reduce the risks. It helps the marketer do the following:

- Understand how competing products/services are perceived by the target markets in terms of strengths and weaknesses.
- Understand the similarities and dissimilarities between competing products/services.
- Position or reposition a product/service in the marketplace.
- Track the progress of a marketing campaign on the perceptions of the target markets.[9]

In analyzing the position of the competition, marketers also want to be able to protect the position they hope to establish. This means anticipating possible competitive reactions and taking measures to reduce their impact.

Positioning makes a statement of what the product is and how it should be evaluated. True positioning is accomplished by using all of the marketing mix variables. This includes the products and services offered, how they are presented to the customer, the price, and all the methods used to communicate to the customer. Not a single element of the marketing mix can be ignored because it is there for the consumer, whether or not the firm makes use of it.

Once the positioning goal has been established, every effort must be made to be certain that the product or brand actually achieves the position. Even with all of the necessary ingredients of good positioning, there is no assurance of success until "share of mind" is achieved. This is where promotional strategy comes into play. Whether it is implemented through advertising or in-house, desired positions do not wait to be discovered. Success here means the realization of all positioning efforts. Exhibit 13-17 provides a checklist for evaluating your positioning or desired positioning.

EXHIBIT 13-17　**Checklist for Evaluating Positioning Strategy**

1. Does it say who you are and what you stand for? Does it create a mental picture?
2. Does it set you apart and show how you are different?
3. Does it preempt a benefit niche and capitalize on an advantage?
4. Does it turn any liability into an asset?
5. Does it have benefits for the target market you are trying to reach?
6. Does it provide tangible evidence or clues?
7. Does it feature the one or two things that your target market wants most?
8. Is it consistent with strategy—for instance, does it expand or exchange usage patterns? Create new awareness? Project the right image?
9. Does it have credibility?
10. Does it make a promise you can keep?

Internal Positioning Analysis

Positioning maps help to determine positioning strategies vis-à-vis the competition. They are also very useful methods for analyzing one's own position on a number of attributes or benefits. In these cases, the usual procedure is to use expectations and salient, determinant, or importance factors as one scale and performance perception as the other. Customers then are asked their rating on each scale. Exhibit 13-18 shows how such questions might be asked. All attributes so measured can be shown on one two-dimensional plot such as the hypothetical example in Exhibit 13-19.

The hard questions that have to be asked are these:

- What is the expectation of the target market?
- How does it perceive us on these attributes?

Internal analysis indicates where the operation may be failing internally. Further, it aids in the best use of resources by indicating where they will count the most for the customer. Similar maps can be drawn for the competition to learn where they stand.

Exhibit 13-19 shows importance versus performance for a hypothetical casino. This figure reveals the following pieces of information:

- Quadrant I represents the area where the casino is doing a good job; it is performing well on features that are important to the customer. For instance, the feature *drinks served in timely manner* is an important feature for the customer. The casino appears to do well in providing this to its customers. A similar statement can be made for the feature *good F&B options*.
- Quadrant II represents the area where the casino is doing a poor job providing the features that are important to the customer. Both the feature *type of promotions offered* and *ease of parking* are very important to customers. However, the casino does very poorly on these features, indicating possible customer dissatisfaction.
- Quadrant III represents the area where features are not important to the customer and the casino does poorly in providing these features. The casino need not worry about features that fall into this quadrant.
- Quadrant IV is the area where the casino is overperforming. That is, it is doing a great job on features

---

EXHIBIT 13-18 **Typical Wording of Questionnaire for Importance versus Performance**

IMPORTANCE QUESTION WORDING

Please think for a moment about the reason for visiting a specific legalized gambling establishment in Las Vegas. Please tell me how important each reason is for you in your decision to visit one specific property over another. Please use a 1 to 10 scale where a 1 means the reason is not at all important and a 10 means the reason is very important in your decision to choose one legalized gambling establishment over another. You may use any number on this 1 to 10 scale. Do you understand how this 1 to 10 scale works? (IF NOT REPEAT SCALE.) How important is _____ in your decision to choose one place to visit over another?

PERFORMANCE QUESTION WORDING

Now I am going to read you a list of features that may or may not describe some of the casinos in the Las Vegas area. We'll use a 1 to 10 scale where 1 means it does not describe the casino at all and 10 means it describes the casino perfectly. If you have not been to the casino personally, please base your answers on what you have heard or what you believe to be true. The first feature is _____.

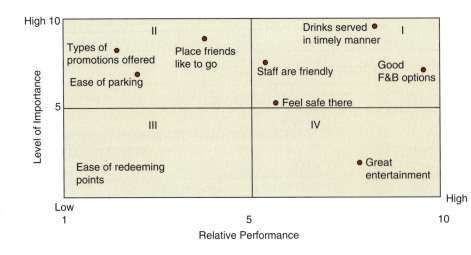

EXHIBIT 13-19 Importance versus performance for a hypothetical casino.

that are of little importance to customers. For instance, in this example customers believe that this casino offers *great entertainment;* however, this feature is not important to them.

Mangers need to focus on Quadrant II and IV. Basically, they need to provide less of the features in Quadrant IV and use the cost savings to improve the features in Quadrant II.

The reality is that if the target market doesn't perceive the image, it doesn't exist. If the target market doesn't believe that what you have to offer is a benefit, it isn't a benefit. If customers do not believe that you can deliver the benefit, your promises are meaningless. If the benefit isn't important to the target market, it isn't important, and if your benefit is not perceived as different from that of the competition, you haven't differentiated.

In short, images, benefit, and differentiation are solely the perception of the customer, not management. We keep repeating these statements intentionally—they are the most often forgotten or neglected truths of marketing. Let us also repeat, as a reminder, that these statements are especially pertinent to hospitality marketing because of the intangibility of the services offered and the simultaneous production and consumption of the offering, which permits evaluation only after the purchase, but also leaves plenty of room for wrong images before the purchase.

Hospitality research too often fails to identify the vital elements of benefits. Comment cards, for example, ask customers whether they liked certain features of the property or operation. What those features do for the customer or how important they are even when satisfactorily rated is not revealed.

The architecture of a property, the decor, and the furnishings are examples of attributes that may produce a benefit or may be tangible representations of intangible benefits, but are not themselves benefits. The benefit itself is what the attributes do for the customer—for instance, give a sense of security, a sensation of grandeur, an aura of prestige, or a feeling of comfort. The credibility of these benefits may diminish rapidly if an expectation is not fulfilled. Decor is soon forgotten if the service is slow and the wait staff is rude. The impression of security loses credibility if the guest notices that there are no cameras watching the exits, if doors that should be closed are open, or if lightbulbs are burned out. It is this fulfillment of expectations or lack of it that creates the perception of deliverability for the customer.

Finally, as previously mentioned, competing properties may be seen to offer the same senses of security, grandeur, prestige, and comfort. The tangible attributes have lost their ability to differentiate and, at the same time, are no longer determinants in the customer choice process. Benefits, then, like positioning, exist in the mind of the customer and are determinable only by asking the customer. This information is essential to proper positioning analysis.

In sum, positioning is the ultimate weapon in niche marketing. Stripped of all its trappings, positioning analysis answers the following questions:

1. What position do you own now (in the mind of the target market)?
2. What position do you want to own? (Look for positions or holes in the marketplace.)
3. Who must you outposition? (Manipulate what's already in the mind.)
4. How can you do it? (Consider the attributes or benefits that are salient, determinant, and important to the target market and that the firm can deliver.)

Branding and Positioning

Earlier in the chapter we briefly defined a brand. Now we define brand equity using the definition developed by David Aaker from the Haas School of Business at the University of California at Berkeley. Dr. Aaker defined brand equity as "a set of assets (and liabilities) linked to a brand's name and symbol that adds to (or subtracts from) the value provided by a product or service to a firm and/or that firm's customers. The major asset categories are: brand name awareness, brand loyalty, perceived quality and brand associations."[10]

Branded properties are becoming ever more important in the marketing realm. In the United States, approximately 70 percent of hotel properties are branded, but in Canada it is closer to only 30 percent. In other parts of the world, it can drop to 10 to 15 percent. Regardless, it is definitely on the increase because the brand name provides "instant recognition." Companies that control well-recognized and well-reputed brands will be successful over the long run, depending on how they handle their brand identity.

Branding is very important for hospitality companies because a strong brand allows a company to attract more franchisees, which translates into higher revenue; after all, an owner would rather become a franchisee of a strong brand than of a weak one. Branding enables firms to gain management contracts, access to capital, and higher-than-average revenue per available room. Branding also allows firms to spread costs for supplies and technical issues, such as web connectivity, across multiple properties.

Web Browsing Exercise

Search for a branded hospitality franchise. Compare a dozen or so different properties on attributes, price, and so forth. Are they consistent? Can you explain the differences as a customer? If so, how?

Technology has had a significant impact on brand marketing. Reservation systems are shifting from central reservation systems to Internet distribution. This had considerable implications for the benefits associated with branding. For one, it brings branded properties wider recognition because they can afford to pay the necessary fees to get better placement on the ending search engine page. The other advantage is that with multiple names appearing on the website, the customer will tend to examine only hotels they are familiar with and ignore the rest. The rationale for this is the risk associated with buying a hospitality product. As discussed in Chapter 2, this risk results from the intangibility of the hospitality product and the simultaneous consumption and production.

Product consistency and integrity of branded properties affect the positioning of the entire brand. Inconsistent brand portfolios that cannot meet this challenge will lose out in the competitive marketplace. In fact, protecting the brand's image and identity is one of the major goals of brand managers. Companies do this by implementing quality standards and frequent inspections of proprieties.

Exhibit 13-20 provides 10 guidelines for building strong brands. Understanding these components are essential to positioning a property to the market sector it serves and the clientele it will attract.

Hotel Restaurant Branding

An interesting part of the branding phenomenon has been the outsourcing of F&B outlets to recognized brand names. In the past, hotel F&B outlets have been notoriously unprofitable. For some, this is changing with new brand identities.

In 1998 Malayan United Industries, which owns the Regal and Corus brands (MUI Group is a diversified conglomerate, headquartered in Kuala Lumpur, Malaysia), acquired a controlling interest in the Restaurant Partnership, which owns and manages brands such as Simply Nico, Nico Central, Elena's L'Etoile, The Gay Hussar, and Thierry's. The Restaurant Partnership provides F&B solutions to the hotel industry through expertise and the installation of branded outlets. Hotel guests have traditionally "eaten out" on a majority of occasions, going instead to a recognized brand restaurant. The new trend is to put those brand names in-house to keep customers from going outside the hotel and as a point of differentiation among hotels.

Branded restaurants are very popular in both Las Vegas and Dubai. Exhibit 13-21 shows the commentary of Mike Feldott on the rise of branded restaurant concepts in hotels.

EXHIBIT 13-20   Ten Guidelines for Building Strong Brands

1. *Brand Identity:* Have an identity for each brand. Consider the perspectives for the brand-as-person, brand-as-organization and brand-as-symbol, as well as brand-as-product. Identify the core identity. Modify the identity as needed for different marketing segments and products. Remember that an image is how you are perceived, and an identity is how you aspire to be perceived.
2. *Value Proposition:* Know the value proposition for each brand that has a driver role. Consider emotional and self-expressive benefits as well as functional benefits. Know how endorser brands will provide credibility. Understand the brand–customer relationship.
3. *Brand Position:* For each brand, have a brand position that will provide clear guidance to those implementing a communication program. Recall that a position is the part of the identity and value proposition that is to be actively communicated.
4. *Execution:* Execute the communication program so that it not only is on target with the identity and position but achieves brilliance and durability. Generate alternatives and consider options beyond media advertising.
5. *Consistency over Time:* Have as a goal a consistent identity, position and execution over time. Maintain symbols, imagery and metaphors that work. Understand and resist organizational biases toward changing the identity, position and execution.
6. *Brand System:* Make sure the brands in the portfolio are consistent and synergistic. Know their roles. Have or develop silver bullets to help support brand identities and positions. Exploit branded features and services. Use sub-brands to clarify and modify the brand. Know the strategic brands.
7. *Brand Leverage:* Extend brands and develop co-branding programs only if the brand identity will be both used and reinforced. Identify range of brands and, for each, develop an identity and specify how that identity will be different in disparate product contexts. If a brand is moved up or down, take care to manage the integrity of the resulting brand identities.
8. *Tracking Brand Equity:* Track brand equity over time, including awareness, perceived quality, brand loyalty and especially brand associations. Have specific communication objectives. Especially note areas where the brand identity and position are not reflected in the brand image.
9. *Brand Responsibility:* Have someone in charge of the brand who will create the identity and position and coordinate the execution over organizational units, media and markets. Beware when a brand is being used in a business in which it is not the cornerstone.
10. *Invest in Brands:* Continue investing in brands even when the financial goals are not being met.

Source: Adapted with permission of The Free Press, a Division of Simon & Schuster Adult Publishing Group, from *Building Strong Brands* by David A. Acker. Copyright © 1996 by David A. Aaker. All rights reserved.

| EXHIBIT 13-21 | The Use of Branded Restaurants in Hotels |

WHAT HAS BEEN THE HISTORY OR BRANDED RESTAURANT CONCEPTS IN HOTELS?

There were three major trends in the past:

- A freestanding restaurant brand that was on the same property as the hotel, which had its own building and land for parking. An example of this would be the La Quinta hotel brand tied in with a coffee shop brand like Denny's or IHOP that served full breakfast.
- Then, as limited service hotel brands started giving away a complimentary breakfast in the lobby, the restaurant building was taken to the next level with either a Chili's, Applebee's, or TGI Friday's type of operation that promoted lunch and dinner and had a bar.
- The third trend was when a full service hotel wanted to promote a signature restaurant in the hotel as an alternate choice to the three meals a day restaurants. Steakhouses, such as Ruth's Chris, Morton's, the Palm, and McCormick & Schmick, fit that mix of great rooms matching with great brand restaurants.

WHAT ARE THE CURRENT TRENDS OF BRANDED RESTAURANTS IN HOTELS?

Over the last few years, many hotels want to take the brand environment to the next level so they have a competitive edge in the market.

Would you rather stay at the same type hotel with a Ruths' Chris or something that is less upscale? For example, a Hilton in Indianapolis recently opened with a McCormick & Schmick Seafood Restaurant as a hook to the competition. When the sales department sells, they are now selling an upscale dining experience as well. In addition to pairing with McCormick & Schmick, Ruth's Chris, and Morton's, Hilton has also paired with Benihana.

WHAT ARE YOUR FUTURE PREDICTIONS OF THE BRANDED RESTAURANTS IN HOTELS TREND?

The future designs of hotels will include freestanding looking spaces attached to the hotel that will drive hotel business opportunities and also function for the local resident market. In larger hotels, you may see the lifestyle section of the hotel take form with a mix of specialty retail and restaurants as part of the hotel. With the success of Las Vegas style restaurants at hotels, you will see this concept scope as part of mixed use that includes hotel development. Fast casual and fast food will probably not be part of the new hotel mix, as the sales-to-investment ratio does not work in a hotel environment.

Source: Milke Feldott. Used by permission.

The F&B branding trend works, generally speaking, in three ways. The first is for the hotel to lease the space for a flat fee and/or a percentage of sales. In this case, the hotel loses control to another operator. The second method is for the hotel to acquire a franchise and become a franchisee, paying fees and royalties to the franchisor. Marriott was one of the first to do this, with Pizza Hut in 1989.

The third method is to undertake a joint venture in which both the hotel and the restaurant operator share the costs and the profits. Radisson SAS Hotels use both the first and third methods to develop its strategy of having branded F&B outlets. For example, in Hamburg, Germany, their hotel has a Trader Vic's (U.S. brand); in Berlin, it has a TGI Friday's (U.S. brand); in Copenhagen, it has a Blue Elephant (Thai brand); and in Brussels, it has a Henry J. Bean's (UK brand).

Today, joint ventures are being undertaken by hospitality and nonhospitality companies. Recently, Nickelodeon (a family television network) joined forces with Holiday Inn to build a $110 million hotel in Orlando, Florida, the Nickelodeon Family Suites by Holiday Inn.[11] Giorgio Armani S.p.A. is awarding a long-term license to EMAAR Hotel & Resorts for the operation of a collection of luxury hotels and resorts. The agreement foresees the opening of at least seven luxury hotels and three vacation resorts within the next 10 years.[12]

Tourism Marketing Application

Before Walt Disney Parks and Resorts opened their theme park in Hong Kong, the company spent two years working with the China Youth League. This organization, supported by the state, runs after-school programs for children under 14 years of age. Disney taught students to draw Disney characters and explained how animation works. They also told Disney stories and "educated" children about Disney and its culture. As part of their planning, Disney also made sure that the park did nothing offensive to Chinese customs. For example, there are no floors numbered 4 (an unlucky number); a feng shui expert helped with overall design of the park, ensuring the proper placement of park accessories; and the main ballroom in the Hong Kong hotel measures 888 square meters because 8 is a lucky number. (www.bized.ac.uk/educators/16-19/tourism/destinations/activity/appeal.htm, accessed March 26, 2006)

Multiple Brands and Product Positioning

Hospitality companies develop multiple brands for growth purposes and for market niches. Sometimes this is through development of a new concept, sometimes through acquisition, and sometimes through both. Marriott, for example, developed the Courtyard (midprice) and Fairfield Inn (budget) lodging concepts to develop new segments, purchased Residence Inns for quick entry into extended stay properties, developed Marriott Marquis as convention hotels and Marriott Suites as luxury all-suites, and initiated JW Marriott's as upscale luxury hotels.

While development of multiple brands provides growth, it also provides protection from the competition against a single brand. Marriott saw other chains moving into lower-tier markets and threatening the middle-to-upper tier in which Marriott hotels were positioned. Marriott felt it might as well steal its own customers (also called **cannibalization**) as let someone else steal from them. It also realized that there were markets that the existing concept was neglecting.

Multiple brands, of course, are common practice in other industries—for instance, Procter & Gamble and General Motors. The restaurant industry has long had multiple brands, as in the case of Darden Restaurants, which owns Red Lobster, Olive Garden, Bahama Breeze, Smokey Bones, and an upscale restaurant concept, Seasons 52. Yum! Brands, formerly Tricon Global Restaurants, Inc., owns A&W Restaurants, Long John Silver's, Pizza Hut, Taco Bell, and KFC. Brinker International has seven distinct restaurant brand concepts.

In the cruise industry, Carnival Corporation & plc owns a variety of different cruise companies, each of which appeals to a specific market. The various companies it owns and a description of each company appear in Exhibit 13-22.

The issue here is one of multiple brands positioning for each brand. Yum! Brands has similar positioning strategies between its own brands as an outside competitor would toward its brands. Unfortunately, this may be self-defeating for the parent company if these chains cannibalized each other, which to some extent they now do by offering similar products. What they want to do, instead, is to position to different market segments, as Darden's five brands do.

The different market segments may include many of the same people. They belong, however, to a different segment when they use restaurants for different purposes, in different contexts, or at different times. Thus, the positioning of each chain should be managed so that they do not steal from each other and then the standard positioning rules can be applied. Ever since Quality Inns was successfully broken into Comfort Inns, Quality Inns, and Quality Royale (now Clarion), there have been a number of hotel chains with properties under the same or similar name, each trying to position to a different market segment. This is commonly referred to as brand extension.

Quality Inns subsequently created Sleep Inns and renamed itself Choice International Hotels with multiple brands. Management claims that there is no question about the difference between the brand names. Further, the purchase addition of Rodeway, Friendship, and Econo Lodge to the Choice fold may have created some very confused customers, particularly as the website for each brand lists the same 800 number. Choice now has seven brands with 13 different products, some being different versions of the same product, (e.g., Clarion hotels, suites, resorts, and inns). The overlap is obvious as shown in their own brand positioning portrayal.

A *Cornell Hotel and Restaurant Administration Quarterly* article by one of the authors of this text contained some comments on this situation:

> Yesawich said that the success of brands depends on creating a clear differentiation in the minds of customers. With only few exceptions, the advertising and promotion that has been initiated on behalf of new product concepts has failed to communicate clearly or convincingly the basis of the differentiation. Customers are quick to discern the availability of free drinks or free breakfasts, but it takes much more to constitute a new product in customers' minds. . . . If advertising doesn't communicate the perception of a new product, then maybe the product isn't really new at all. Some observers are concerned that customers may be confused by a chain that has one name on a variety of hotels. Yesawich noted that chains pursuing diversification by introducing new products under different names have so far met with greater success. "In general terms, a brand name is an asset, as long as it stands single mindedly for a specific package of value and benefits. Call it a personality," said Robert Bloch [then senior vice-president for marketing at Four Seasons]. The practice of "leaving a mid-price brand name on an upscale property, as some operators are doing, may confuse some customers."[13]

Sheraton and Hilton have wrestled with a similar image problem. The vast difference between the Sheraton Wayfarer Motor Inn in Bedford, New Hampshire, and the Sheraton St. Regis in Manhattan was about the same difference as the Berkshire Hilton Inn and the Waldorf-Astoria, two hotels sporting the Hilton name brand. Customers can be very confused with what position the brand name actually conveys. To deal with this problem, which has existed for many years, Hilton has recently developed Hilton Garden Inns, while Sheraton created Four Points and required all of the former "inns" to come up to standard to use this name or otherwise be disenfranchised.

Marriott debated long and hard when developing the Courtyard concept as to whether to call it a Marriott. The final decision was to call it Courtyard by Marriott with the Marriott in smaller letters. Today, the "by" has been dropped.

EXHIBIT 13-22	Companies Owned by Carnival Corporation & plc: Each Line Caters to a Different Segment

CORPORATE INFORMATION

Carnival Corporation & plc is a global cruise company and one of the largest vacation companies in the world. Our portfolio of 12 leading cruise brands includes Carnival Cruise Lines, Holland America Line, Princess Cruises, Seabourn Cruise Line, and Windstar Cruises in North America; P&O Cruises, Cunard Line, Ocean Village, and Swan Hellenic in the United Kingdom; AIDA in Germany; Costa Cruises in southern Europe; and P&O Cruises in Australia. These brands—the most recognized cruise brands in North America, the United Kingdom, Germany and Italy—offer a wide range of holiday and vacation products to a customer base broadly varied in terms of cultures, languages, and leisure-time preferences. The company also owns two tour companies that complement its cruise operations: Holland America Tours and Princess Tours in Alaska and the Canadian Yukon. Its combined vacation companies attract 6.8 million guests annually.

CARNIVAL CRUISE LINES

Carnival Cruise Lines is the best known cruise brand in North America and the most profitable in the world. The leader in the contemporary cruise sector, Carnival operates 21 ships that are expected to carry a record 3.3 million passengers this year—the most in the cruise industry. Guests aboard the "Fun Ships" enjoy a variety of dining, entertainment, and activity options, all in a festive and lively environment. Most recently, the line has launched several product enhancement initiatives that include an exclusive alliance with world-renowned French master chef Georges Blanc—who has maintained the coveted three-star Michelin rating for more than 25 years—and the new "Carnival Comfort Bed" sleep system featuring plush mattresses, luxurious duvets, and high quality linens and pillows.

PRINCESS CRUISES

One of the best known names in cruising, Princess is a global cruise and tour company operating a modern fleet of 15 ships carrying more than a million passengers each year. The company's ships are renowned for their innovative design and wide array of choices in dining, entertainment, and amenities, all provided in an environment of exceptional customer service. A recognized leader in worldwide cruising, Princess offers its passengers the opportunity to escape to more than 280 destinations around the globe, with sailings to all seven continents ranging in length from seven to 30 days.

HOLLAND AMERICA LINE

With 133 years of experience, Holland America Line is recognized as the undisputed leader in the cruise industry's premium segment. Its 13 ships sail to more than 300 ports of call on all seven continents. With more than 500 cruises a year, itineraries range from two to 108 days.

Completed in September 2006, Holland America Line's $225 million fleetwide Signature of Excellence enhancements feature programs and amenities that have established a new standard in premium cruising.

SEABOURN CRUISE LINE

The Yachts of Seabourn offer its 104 fortunate couples an intimate setting aboard its all-suite ships: Seabourn Pride Spirit and Legend. Rated among the highest ships in the world, they offer sumptuous ocean-view suites measuring 277 square feet or more, many with balconies. Seabourn is renowned for extraordinarily personalized service, with nearly one staff member per guest.

WINDSTAR CRUISES

Seattle-based Windstar Cruises operates three motor sailing yachts known for their pampering without pretense and their ability to visit the hidden harbors and secluded coves of the world's most treasured destinations. The unobtrusive service and attentive staff create a casually elegant atmosphere that effortlessly fosters camaraderie among guests and crew. Carrying just 148 to 308 guests, the luxurious ships of Windstar cruise to nearly 50 nations, calling at 100 ports throughout the Caribbean, Costa Rica, Panama Canal, Mediterranean, and Greek Isles.

P&O CRUISES

One of the most recognizable and respected names in travel, market-leading P&O Cruises has been operating cruise ships for more than 160 years and combines innovation, professionalism, and unrivalled experience on its fleet of five ships dedicated to the British market. Each ship is elegantly appointed, combining classic British tradition and hospitality with modern amenities. The result is a refined cruising experience with distinctive restaurants, comfortable accommodations, and enjoyable entertainment.

CUNARD LINE

Since the first paddle-wheeled steamer crossed the Atlantic in 1840, the name Cunard has been synonymous with the quest for new discoveries, legendary voyages, and majestic onboard pursuits. Royalty, celebrities and voyagers from every walk of life have enjoyed Cunard's White Star Service^{SM} across the globe. Guests enjoy a classic luxury experience based on the history and tradition of transatlantic liner service. Continuing the tradition of luxury ocean travel, *Queen Mary 2* and *Queen Elizabeth 2* are international icons evoking the nostalgia of the grand era of cruising and are the only traditional ocean liners in operation.

OCEAN VILLAGE

Ocean Village combines action and relaxation at sea and ashore into a fresh new take on holidays for thirty-to-fifty-somethings: younger, more upbeat passengers who want to get more out of their time away. With no formal dress codes, *Ocean Village's* casual on-board style includes high quality 24/7 buffet dining, plus waiter service options at the Bistro with a menu created by TV celebrity chef James Martin. Calling at six destinations every seven days, *Ocean Village* offers a choice of four itineraries—two in the Caribbean, two in the Mediterranean.

SWAN HELLENIC

Swan Hellenic focuses on discovery cruising for the discerning traveler on board *Minerva II*, whose interiors are designed to resemble a floating English country house with a capacity for 600 passengers. Expert speakers in wide-ranging areas such as botany, theology, geology, international diplomacy, gastronomy, and astrology accompany each cruise, bringing each destination vividly to life in highly informative lectures and seminars.

COSTA CRUISES

Based in Genoa, Italy, Costa Crociere is the leading cruise company in Europe and South America, operating a modern fleet of 11 ships with a basis-two capacity of 20,200 total lower berths. Costa, whose origins date back to mid-1800s with a fleet of freighters transporting fabrics and olive oil between Genoa and Sardinia, has grown to become one of the most famous and respected names in seagoing travel. A Costa cruise is distinguished by its "Cruising Italian Style" shipboard ambiance, which offers an on-board experience that combines the sophisticated elegance of a European vacation with the fun and spirit of the line's Italian heritage.

AIDA

AIDA Cruises is the number-one operator in the German-speaking cruise market, carrying more than 233,000 passengers in 2005. A total of four AIDA ships are currently in service: AIDAcara, AIDAvita, AIDAaura and AIDAblu, with a total lower berth capacity of 5,400 guests. These vessels currently operate in the Mediterranean, Northern Europe, the Caribbean, the Arabian Gulf, and around the Canary Islands. AIDA ships are dedicated to the German-speaking market and are renowned for their youthful style and casual service.

P&O CRUISES AUSTRALIA

The pioneer of Australian cruising, P&O Cruises celebrates its 75th anniversary in 2007—marking the 1932 departure of the 23,000-ton liner *Strathaird,* which sailed from Australia on a five-night round trip from Sydney to Brisbane and Norfolk Island.* Nearly 75 years later, P&O Cruises Australia continues to offer holidays tailored to Australian cruise passengers, and now carries a diverse clientele totaling more than 100,000 people each year. P&O Cruises Australia has expanded considerably over recent years and will soon boast three cruise ships.

Source: Carnival Corporation & plc. Used by permission.

Thus, Courtyard can trade on its famous brand name without creating expectations of the same product/service. The same was done with the Fairfield Inn brand line. Marriott, in fact, has probably been the only hotel company in the United States that has successfully differentiated its brands and kept them clearly in their product class. The problem for others is not necessarily in the name (only a possible compounding of the problem), but in the positioning.

Can hotel concepts under the same or similar names make the same claim? In other words, is each brand or product positioned to a different specific target market, each with specific needs that relate to the positioning? Second, if the first case is true, can these markets differentiate the positioning of each brand or product name so that they (the markets) know which one "belongs" to them? This is the case in point and is the concern of positioning any multiple brands, more so when the problem is compounded by similar names. If the answers to these questions are no, then there will be a clear case of cannibalization and customer confusion.

Multiple brand positioning can be done successfully, as Marriott has shown. Groupe Accor, a French firm, has developed lodging concepts called Formule 1, Ibis, Mercure, Novotel, and Sofitel and owns Motel 6 and Red Roof Inns in the United States. By French government rating, these are one-, two-, three-, and four-star properties, respectively. Each is based on the needs of a specific target market. Each is clearly differentiated from the other three; in fact, you might say that no customer would ever choose one when he or she wanted the other. However, in at least one place in Paris, a Novotel and Sofitel sit side by side with separate entrances and a common wall dividing them, a practice not uncommon among multibrand hotel companies in the United States. The traveler has a choice in the same location. Each was clearly positioned to its own market segment, but eventually Novotel started to cannibalize the Sofitel.

Starwood announced, in a press release in May 2006, the new positioning of all of its brands.[14] The Starwood brands are Sheraton, Four Points by Sheraton, Le Meridien, Luxury Collection, St. Regis, W, Aloft, and Westin. The core values of "chic, cultured, discovery are born of its European heritage. The brand seeks to engage its guests in a meaningful way—bringing alive its passion points of music, film, art, photography, food, design, architecture, and fashion. It will curate an experience for its guests, stimulating them and enriching their stay—revealing the curious in all of us."

Web Browsing Exercise

Using your favorite web browser, go to www.hotel-online.com/News/PR2006_2nd/May06_StarwoodStrategy.html. Read about the positioning statements for all their brands.

■ Summary

Market positioning is a valuable weapon for hospitality marketers. To position successfully requires recognizing the marketplace, the competition, and customers' perceptions. Positioning analysis on a target market basis provides the tools to identify opportunities for creating the desired image that differentiates from the competition and for serving the target market better than anyone else.

Positioning may be objective, where images of the physical characteristics of the product are used, or subjective, where customers' mental perceptions play a greater role. Positioning of a tangible good is often accomplished through association with intangible notions; alternatively, it is better to position intangible services with tangible clues.

Repositioning may be necessary when a hospitality firm is in an unacceptable position or when trying to appeal to a new market segment. Old hotels with poor images are often renovated, and repositioning them is crucial to their success. Six approaches to positioning were discussed. Marketers may select the ones that will be most effective after selecting the desired position.

The differences among salient, important, and determinant attributes must be considered especially if the firm is being positioned by benefit or attribute. All three are complementary, and it is crucial to understand their place.

As many hotel and restaurant chains grow by adding new brands and concepts, multiple brand positioning becomes important. Firms must prevent one brand from cannibalizing the other and also be able to create separate images and benefits for each one. Finally, internal positioning analysis can be used to examine one's own position and see how it is perceived by customers.

■ Key Terms

market positioning	commodity status
evoked set	positioning statement
salient attributes	intangible positioning
determinant attributes	repositioning
importance attributes	competitive positioning
objective positioning	cannibalization
subjective positioning	multiple brand positioning
tangible positioning	

■ Discussion Questions

1. What are the different kinds of hospitality positioning? Give examples of when you would use each one and why.
2. Discuss the problems a product can incur with a weak or undefined position.
3. Identify a hotel or restaurant you know that is in need of repositioning and outline the steps needed to achieve the repositioning.
4. Take two competing hotels you are familiar with and position them using the six approaches to positioning (Exhibit 12-10).
5. Discuss the salient, determinant, and important attributes of the same hotel or restaurant.
6. Develop a list of questions that you would pose to a focus group of customers of a cocktail lounge that seeks to establish a position in the marketplace.
7. How does competition affect the positioning of a product? Discuss.
8. Draw a positioning map (see Exhibit 13-19) for a group of restaurants or hotels with which you are familiar, based on your own perceptions.
9. Draw another positioning map showing your own expectations and perceptions of a particular property.
10. Discuss how a company may avoid problems of cannibalization among competing brands.
11. Conceptualize how a lagging brand may be repositioned for new uses.
12. What criteria may be employed to determine the viable position for a brand in the market?

■ Group Projects

1. Consider a hotel, restaurant, or chain not mentioned in the chapter and consider how it is positioned, both objectively and subjectively, and why. Does this positioning reflect reality?
2. Take a different hotel, restaurant, or chain that is poorly positioned and outline how you would reposition it.

■ References

1. Knapp, D. E. (2000). *The brand mindset.* New York: McGraw-Hill, xv.
2. Verma, R., Plaschka, G., Dev, C., & Verma, A. (2002, Fall). What today's travelers want they select a hotel. *HSMAI Marketing Review,* 20–23.
3. Hotelmarketing.com website. TIG Global launches group RFP tracking and reporting solution. Retrieved April 20, 2004, from www.hotelmarketing.com/index.php/content/article/hilton_hotel_resorts_launches_new_image_campaign/rketing.com.
4. Osgoodby, B. (2001, September 5). Sell the "sizzle." *Add Me Newsletter, 219.* Retrieved May 5, 2005, from www.addme.com/issue219.htm.
5. Ogilvy, D. (1985). *Ogilvy on advertising.* New York: Vintage Books, 160.
6. Dowling, W. Q. (1980, September). Creating the right identity for your hotel. *Lodging,* 58.
7. Quoted in Brennan, D. M. (1986, May 1). Niche marketing. *Restaurant Business,* 186, 189.
8. Taylor, S. P. (1986, Fall). Repositioning: Recovery for vintage and distressed hotels. *HSMAI Marketing Review,* 12–15.
9. Adapted form Jain, S. C. (1997). *Marketing planning and strategy,* p. 350. Cincinnati: South-Western Publishing.
10. Aaker, D. A. (1996). *Building strong brands.* New York: Free Press, 7–8.
11. Retrieved September 16, 2005, from www.hotel-online.com/News/PR2005_2nd/Jun05_Nickelodeon.html.
12. Retrieved September 16, 2005, from www.hotelmarketing.com/index.php/content/article/armani_hotel_and_resorts_launched/.
13. Witham, G. (1985, November). Hotel companies aim at multiple markets. *Cornell Hotel and Restaurant Administration Quarterly,* 39–51.
14. http://www.hotel-online.com/News/PR2006_2nd/May06_StarwoodStrategy.html accessed May 27, 2006.

CHAPTER 14

The Hospitality Pricing Mix

Overview

The pricing strategy is the part of the marketing strategy that defines the way to extract value from customers based on their willingness to pay for the value they get. Pricing strategy is critical to a firm because prices are the only part of the marketing mix that creates revenue for the firm. Because of the intangibility of services and simultaneous production and consumption, prices are also used by customers as a mechanism to help determine the quality they are being offered. Setting prices requires a thorough decision-making process that involves an understanding of costs, competition, demand, supply, channels of distribution, and, of course, the customer. This chapter discusses the nuances of arriving at the appropriate pricing mix.

I. Introduction to Hospitality Marketing
1. The Concept of Marketing
2. Marketing Services and the Hospitality Experience
3. The Marketing Mix and the Product/Service Mix
4. Relationship/Loyalty Marketing

II. Marketing to Build a Competitive Advantage
5. Strategic Marketing
6. The Strategic Marketing System and Marketing Objectives

III. The Marketplace
7. Understanding Individual Customers
8. Understanding Organizational Customers
9. The Tourist Customer and the Tourism Destination

IV. Situational Analysis
10. Understanding Competition
11. Marketing Intelligence and Research

V. Functional Strategies
12. Differentiation, Segmentation, and Target Marketing
13. Branding and Market Positioning
14. *The Hospitality Pricing Mix*
15. The Communications Mix: Advertising
16. The Communications Mix: Sales Promotions, Merchandising, Public Relations, and Publicity
17. The Communications Mix: Personal Selling
18. Hospitality Distribution Systems
19. Channels of Distribution: Bringing the Customer to the Product
20. Interactive Marketing: Internet and Database Marketing

VII. Feedback

VI. Synthesis
21. The Marketing Plan

John Shields
Corporate Director of Revenue Management, Hyatt Hotels Corporation

John Shields has held the position of corporate director of revenue management for Hyatt Hotels Corporation since September of 2003. In this capacity, he is responsible for the daily revenue management operation at all 122 domestic Hyatt properties. He is also responsible for developing and facilitating Hyatt's revenue manager training program. Reporting to Shields are five corporate revenue managers who work closely with each of their hotels to ensure compliance with Hyatt's revenue management initiatives. Previously, he worked in electronic distribution with Hyatt, specifically with the opaque distribution channels.

Shields began his hospitality career in 1980 as a housekeeping floor supervisor at the Grand Hyatt New York. From there, he held various positions in rooms operations at several Hyatt properties, working his way up to rooms executive at the Hyatt Oakland in 1988. He left Hyatt to pursue a general manager position at an independent hotel, but returned to Hyatt in 1992 as the director of revenue management at the Hyatt Regency Chicago. Shields held the position of corporate director of revenue management at Starwood Hotels and Resorts from 1997 until 2001, when he returned once again to Hyatt to work in electronic distribution.

Shields received his bachelor of science in management from Syracuse University.

Marketing in Action

John Shields, Corporate Director of Revenue Management, Hyatt Hotels

Briefly explain your career in revenue management.

I began my career in revenue management in 1992. Previous to that, I had about 12 years of experience in rooms operations and transitioned into revenue management at the Hyatt Regency Chicago, where I was the director of revenue management. I was the first revenue manager in the company and held that position until 1997, when I moved over to Starwood as an area director of revenue management. That grew into a regional role, which grew into a corporate role. I was eventually promoted to the corporate director of revenue management for Starwood, where we helped integrate the Sheraton-Westin brands into one revenue management operation. I built the regional revenue management team there and helped get revenue managers operational within the hotel. I was with them until 2001, then came back to the Hyatt in 2003 in the role of corporate director of revenue management. It was very similar to the role I had at Starwood; however, with Hyatt there was no corporate revenue management structure, nor did they have any revenue management structure on the property. My job was to put together the corporate team, which was responsible for overseeing the revenue management operation at the property. Altogether, I have about 13 years of experience in the area of revenue management.

How important is revenue management to Hyatt?

It's critical to the success of this company. For a long time, our competitors—Hilton, Marriott, and Starwood—all had very sound revenue management processes and a very developed revenue management culture within their organizations. Since 1995 Hyatt has had an automated revenue management system, but beyond that, had no revenue management function on the corporate level or on the property level. It was just a system. As a result, for many years we were at a competitive disadvantage for a number of reasons. Obviously, we're a private company and the others are public companies, which made a difference, but beyond that we were clearly at a competitive disadvantage because we did not engage in, nor did we practice, revenue management on a daily basis. In the last year and a half, we have developed a corporate revenue management structure that places revenue managers in every one of our hotels. This is because we've seen very good results as we go with that. It is critical to the success of this company competitively and has really been thrust to the forefront of what we do in Hyatt. There's been a huge growth in the last two years in revenue management culture within our organization. This is not just from the revenue management perspective, but also the sales organization and the operations side that have really embraced revenue management in the company. If we're going to move ahead and be competitive in this industry, revenue management is critical to our success.

How is revenue management tied in to pricing?

Pricing is part of revenue management; they are not separate entities within our company. Pricing is as integral a part of revenue management as the revenue management system is, as the distribution is, as the sales process is. As a matter of fact, it's a key component to revenue management. The hotels are responsible for developing their pricing. We price very competitively. We've really grown in that area, and in our book, pricing *is* revenue management.

Does each of your properties have a system for revenue management? Are the forecasting methods built right into the system?

There are two components to forecasting—the group component and the transient component. With our system, we have to input the group forecast, which is a manual input and is the revenue manager's job in conjunction with the director of sales. The transient piece is the automated piece, which looks at a combination of history and pace. As you get closer to the arrival date, it relies more on pace. However, there is the opportunity for human intervention—to go in and update your arrivals forecast if need be or things that may be happening that are going to adjust that forecast. Other than that, it is a systems-based forecast.

What is a typical day for a revenue manager?

I don't know that there is a typical day, but there is one part that is consistent on a day-to-day basis, which is the maintenance of the system. We call it the "nine at nine." There are nine basic steps that the revenue manger needs to do in terms of checks and balances of the system first thing in the morning. Beyond that, they're responsible for the development, implementation, and measurement of tactics and strategies that are designed to optimize revenue. They analyze transient pricing, distribution strategies, business trends, market economy, and competitive landscape. Every day, they're looking at our competitors and our pricing. Many of them now are moving into the function space area, managing function space as it applies to groups and catering. They lead the weekly strategy meeting, they lead the weekly group pickup meeting, and they attend the tentative sales meeting. That's really their focus—it's about developing strategy and analyzing the results of those strategies. A

lot of what they do on a daily basis, as our company grows, is interface with the managers and directors of sales for price analysis. Right now, they're in the process of the 2006–2007 strategy and will be for the next month.

Is there an area revenue manager?

Yes, there are five, and those five are deployed geographically throughout the country. Their job is interesting—it's part coach and part mentor to the revenue managers at the property. In some instances, their job is to really hold general managers, specifically, accountable for their support of the revenue management process at the hotel. We need to make sure that the general mangers support the tactics that we are using and understand our processes. Our job is to call them out when they make unwise decisions. We are there to coach and mentor, but we're also there to challenge. The five we deploy then report to me, and if they cannot get through to a general manager, I may pick up the phone.

Do revenue managers that you hire come from other companies?

The ones that we bring in do come from other companies. Since November of last year, we've probably recruited 20 from other companies. One has to remember in our company, they were dabbling in revenue management for years and did not really have a sophisticated revenue management process. The hardest part comes in especially in how they interact with people in sales and the sales process, as well as a successful transition from one company to the other.

How is revenue management at hotels different from revenue management at an airline?

My sense is that the airlines are very systems driven and very technology driven and that the decision-making process is very much bottled. There is some human component to what airlines do, but in hotels, I think you will find that it's a day-to-day battle with your competitor down the street. Pricing is not automated. In airlines, they see what everyone else is charging and can adjust quickly. At a hotel, there is an entire team involved. There's a huge human component in revenue management, as opposed to just using automated systems—although clearly revenue management systems are an integral part of what we do.

What are the most critical issues in revenue management today?

There are a number of them. The challenges are exciting in a lot of ways because a lot of it is about change. The biggest challenge is the human component of revenue management. There is not a lot of depth in the ranks of revenue management, and I think there was a misconception about what you could do with a specialization in revenue management. As a result, more people want to get involved in revenue management now than before. In addition, it is seen as a highly specialized discipline, and because of that it's not really on the career path, but it needs to be so we don't get those people who are coming up through the ranks. I think adding it to a curriculum helps them because it doesn't just become a discipline. Some of the other challenges that face revenue managers today are consolidation of companies and the growth of the Internet. We need to stay up on changes in technology.

The other thing that the Internet has done is that it has made consumers a lot more knowledgeable about the products that are out there and, in some cases, the growth of brands. The other critical issue is changing technology and keeping our systems and our technology up to date. We're looking at making some major changes to our revenue management system and are constantly trying to find ways to innovate and learn and put out the best products for our money as possible.

Used by permission from John Shields.

The Basis of Pricing

The marketing discipline grew out of the economic discipline. The basic theory of economics, simply stated, is that the economy responds to the customer. The basic theory of marketing is that the customer calls the shots. When it comes to setting prices, these basic theories need to be remembered. Prices need to be established with the long-term customer, not the short-term margin, in mind. Elliot Ross, of the well-known consulting firm McKinsey & Co., stated this concept well:

> [I]mproving pricing performance without the risk of damaging market repercussions [rests on understanding how the industry's pricing works and how customers perceive prices, based on] information about market and customer characteristics, competitor capabilities and actions and internal capabilities and costs. . . . Proactive pricers . . . time price changes to the anticipated reactions of customers and competitors rather than to . . . their own analysis of costs.[1]

Two other authors made the same point. James Abbey stated that pricing decisions should be based on solid "market research and thorough understanding of the economics of price changes," rather than "intuitive judgments of what the market will bear."[2] Management guru Peter Drucker also talked about the importance of pricing in his discussion of the five deadly business sins. The first three of his sins relate to pricing. As he stated:

> The past few years have seen the downfall of one once-dominant business after another. . . . But in every case the main cause has been at least one of the five deadly business sins—avoidable mistakes that will harm the mightiest business.
>
> ■ The first and easily the most common sin is *the worship of high profit margins and of "premium pricing."*
> ■ Closely related to this first sin is the second one: *mispricing a new product by charging "what the market will bear."*
> ■ The third deadly sin is **cost-driven pricing.** The only thing that works is price-driven costing. [Cost-driven pricers argue,] "We have to recover our costs and make a profit."

This is true but irrelevant: Customers do not see it as their job to ensure manufacturers a profit. The only sound way to price is to start out with what the market is willing to pay—and thus, it must be assumed, what the competition will charge—and designing to that price specification.[3]

This chapter addresses these warnings and comments. Following are the major categories to be considered in developing pricing strategies:

■ An understanding of what price is and how to change prices
■ An understanding of costs, cost-based pricing, value pricing, objectives of the firm, competitive pricing, market demand pricing, and customer pricing

We will discuss each in turn.

The role of pricing must be, first and foremost, customer based. Cost and profit considerations follow under the heading of "Can we afford to do it?" as indicated earlier. Recall from Chapter 1 that profit should be the test of the validity of management decisions, not the cause or rationale for them.

To motivate the discussion of price and to provide a frame of reference for the chapter, we first provide a brief overview of current pricing practices in the hotel and restaurant industry. At this time, we also discuss the future of pricing. Next, we discuss a definition of price. This is followed by a review of the drivers of profit and the different types of costs found in the hospitality industry. We then discuss two methods of pricing; cost-based pricing and value-based pricing. With an understanding of how pricing is accomplished, we turn our attention to the pricing objectives of the firm. Demand-based pricing and the use of revenue management are included in these objectives. We end the chapter with a discussion of international pricing and pricing across multiple channels of distribution.

Pricing Practices

Pricing practices continue to evolve. This evolution has been a result of more sophisticated computer models used to estimate demand; the teaching of revenue management in colleges and universities; and the realization that, because expenses and costs have been reduced as much as possible, it is necessary to look for other sources of revenue. Indeed, firms are beginning to have positions such as Chief Marketing Officer, which is at the same level as Chief Financial Officer. As discussed throughout the book, pricing is part of marketing. For a long time pricing and marketing were different functions. This is changing, as we discuss next.

Hotel Room Pricing

Hotel room pricing has changed remarkably over the years. This is illustrated in Exhibit 14-1. Notice that as one moves from left to right on this chart, profitability increases and pricing becomes less tactical and more strategic. Initially hotel pricing involved changing rates every season. There was some demand forecasting, but much of it pertained to examining occupancy the year before. This all changed with the advancement of sophisticated mathematical models that estimated demand by room type and rate. Marriott International was the first major hotel chain to implement such systems, and soon other chains followed. Currently very few hotels operate without some form of revenue management system. (We explain revenue management in detail in the appendix to this chapter.)

We argue that the majority of the hotel firms in 2005 were pricing somewhere between revenue per available customer and value-based pricing. Revenue per available customer includes room revenue as well as food and beverage, Internet charges, and the like. Harrah's Entertainment was the first to incorporate the lifetime of the customer (see Chapter 4) into its decision models. This means, for example, that if only one room is available in a hotel and two people want the room, Harrah's knows which guest will provide the most long-term economic value to Harrah's and will assign the room accordingly. The days of first come, first served are slowly going away. Internet firms such as Hotwire, Priceline, and Expedia.com are moving more and more into bundling, as it provides a great way to hide the cost of each individual component of the trip. Packaging is a form of bundling.

Restaurant Pricing

Restaurant pricing has traditionally used cost-based pricing and was seriously affected when inflation became rampant in the 1970s. The industry responded by continuously increasing prices. Whenever the cost of staples of the industry (e.g., butter, beef, sugar, coffee) went up, restaurant prices quickly followed suit. The result was that the customer eventually said, "Whoa!" and turned to other alternatives, including staying home.

Eventually, the industry caught on. It found new ways to do things, new items to put on menus, new ways to prepare menu items, and new ways to serve them (e.g., the salad bar) to cut labor costs. In the restaurant industry, cus-

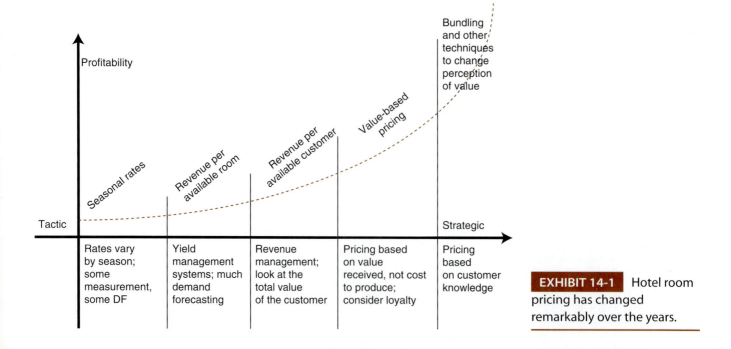

EXHIBIT 14-1 Hotel room pricing has changed remarkably over the years.

tomer reaction to price can be very swift, if only because it is relatively simple for someone else to enter the market with a new idea or a better price.

Taco Bell's introduction of the 59-cent taco in the late '80s is a prime example of finding new ways to do things. For example, they redesigned the actual taco to support the lower price. This was accomplished by slightly changing the amount of meat in the taco and its grade. Extensive customer research was undertaken to ensure that these changes did not impact the customer. In addition, they redesigned the process of preparation by moving the majority of preparation to central facilities. This allowed smaller kitchens and more seating area. Today most fast-food restaurants have 99-cent or dollar menus.

Restaurants today are experimenting with revenue management, which we discuss later in the chapter. They are also pricing much more with the customer in mind.

Tourism Marketing Application

Pricing in tourism is also changing, as described in Exhibit 14-1. Although initially the various parts of the travel component were priced separately, packaging is becoming more and more important, especially for online bookings. The reason for this is that tourist destinations realize that consumers consider not only the price of hotel rooms and meals in the choice of destination, but also the cost of getting to the destination. The arrival of the low-cost carrier (LLC) has been a boon to many destinations, making those destinations suddenly affordable to many visitors.

More and more computer programs have also made pricing much more transparent. New software in development at the time of this writing is called Flyspy. This software will enable consumers to determine very quickly the prices for the next 30 days of multiple flights to a destination. It is also possible to look up prices for another destination: the software will plot graphs comparing prices of multiple destinations so travelers can easily find the least expensive flight and the least expensive destination. More information on this form of pricing can be found at www.techcrunch.com/2006/02/20/flyspy-brings-the-new-web-to-airline-ticketing/ (accessed March 26, 2006).

What Is Price?

We begin the chapter by providing a definition of price. This definition will change depending on whose viewpoint one takes—the customers' or the manufacturers'. From the customers' viewpoint, price can be defined as "what the customer must give up to purchase the product or service."[4] The "what" may include actual money, time, a product or service (e.g., an exchange of rooms for free advertising), mental or cognitive effort, and transaction cost (steps necessary to take actual procession of the product or service). Notice that for the customer, these are costs of purchasing the product. Customers will often pay more for a reduction in both transaction costs and cognitive effort. Items sold in an in-room minibar are often more expensive that the same items in a grocery store for this very reason. It is easier to open the minibar than look for the nearest grocery store to purchase drinks and food items. From the manufacturers' perspective, price is defined as the products and services that they give to the customers versus what they receive in return.

With this definition of price, it should be easy to see that the firm has multiple ways to change price. These different ways are shown in Exhibit 14-2. Notice that one of the items listed is *change the quality of goods and services provided by the seller*. This method works extremely well in the hospitality industry because not all hotel rooms are alike; the number of beds in each room varies, as does the view offered. As discussed earlier, Taco Bell was able to lower its prices by changing the quality of the ingredients in a taco. This was done only after numerous consumer taste tests revealed that consumers could perceive no difference between a more expensive quality ingredient and a less expense alternative. They also slightly changed the quantity of ingredients offered. Another method of lowering prices is to *change the quantity of goods and services provided by the seller*.

 Web Browsing Exercise

Use your favorite browser and type www.pricingsociety.com/. What does the pricing society do? Why would a hotelier or restaurateur want to be a member of such an organization?

Another way to change prices, as shown in Exhibit 14-2, is to *change the acceptable form of payment*. For example, consider the Basin Harbor Club, which is located on Lake Champlain in Vergennes, Vermont. This resort, whose website is shown in Exhibit 14-3, encourages payment by check or cash, although they will accept credit cards as a last resort. This way, they keep prices lower. If they accepted credit cards, they would need to raise their rates to cover credit card fees. Similarly, one of the authors of this text conducted a study to determine the types of credit cards business travelers carried when traveling on business. The sponsor of the study was a major hotel chain that wanted a reduction in the surcharge fee charged by one of the major credit card issuers. When the results revealed that travelers

EXHIBIT 14-2	Ways to Change Prices

1. Change the quantity of money or goods and services to be paid by the buyer
2. Change the quantity of goods and services provided by the seller
3. Change the quality of goods and services provided by the seller
4. Change the premiums or discounts to be applied for quantity variations
5. Change the time and place of transfer of ownership
6. Change the time and place of payment
7. Change the acceptable form of payment

| EXHIBIT 14-3 | The Basin Harbor Club is located on Lake Champlain in Vergennes, Vermont. |

Source: Retrieved November 21, 2005, from www.basinharbor.com/ welcome_offseason.asp. Used by permission of The Basin Harbor Club.

were indifferent to which credit card they used, the hotel chain threatened to stop accepting the card unless the surcharge fee was lowered. The credit card firm lowered its fees. This saved the hotel chain from having to raise prices.

Prices can also be changed by *changing the time and place of transfer of ownership.* This is the basis for revenue management. The axiom is: "Tell me when you would like to arrive at the hotel and I will tell you the price." Or: "Tell me how much you would like to pay for your hotel room and I will tell you when you can arrive."

Other methods for changing prices can be seen in Exhibit 14-2.

Pricing as One of the Seven Ps

Pricing is one of the seven Ps because price is used by the firm to represent the value of the offering and the value of what is received. Price is of unique importance to marketers for a number of reasons:

1. It is the only revenue-producing part of the marketing mix.

2. It is used to match supply to demand so that financial objectives of the firm can be achieved.
3. It is a powerful force in attracting attention and increasing sales.
4. It establishes the market positioning of the product.
5. The pricing practice can have a major impact on customer loyalty.

For all of these reasons, price should be based on a thorough decision-making process by the seller that will communicate the worth of the total offering—a worth that is consistent with the market's perception of the offering's value. The importance of price in the marketing mix is explained as follows:

> Price is a dangerous and explosive marketing force. It must be used with caution. The damage done by improper pricing may completely destroy the effectiveness of the rest of a well-conceived marketing strategy. . . . As a marketing weapon, pricing is the "big gun." It should be triggered exclusively by those thoroughly familiar with its possibilities and dangers. But unlike most big weapons, pricing cannot be used only when the danger of its misuse is at a minimum. Every marketing plan involves a pricing decision. Therefore, all marketing planners should be equipped to make correct pricing decisions.[5]

In the final analysis, pricing, like the product and service, is customer driven. Using all of the models of pricing only gets the end price closer to what the customer will pay. If the price is too high, customers will not pay for the service. If the price is too low, many customers may also not pay for the service because it might be perceived as "too cheap" and they would worry about the quality. Ultimately, customers determine the price at which a product or service will be successfully offered. Because of this, the integration of product and price is critical. Notice how this is done in Exhibit 14-4.

Setting prices is a complex exercise, with any number of strategic and tactical implications. The hospitality industry has fixed physical plant products and locations. Sometimes we have to work with the product we have and set prices accordingly. In other words, rather than set the price to the target market, we may have to find the target market that will accept a given product at a given price. This is called **product-driven pricing**, but it is still the customer who will determine the acceptable price. Given this, it is worth noting Subhash C. Jain's comments:

> [W]hile everybody thinks businesses go about setting prices scientifically, very often the process is incredibly arbitrary. Although businesses of all types devote a great deal of time and study to determine the prices they put on their products, pricing is often more art than science. In some cases, setting price does involve the use of a straightforward equation . . . . But in many other cases, the equation includes psychological and other such subtle factors that the pricing decision may essentially rest on gut feeling.[6]

Before proceeding further, we first briefly review the drivers of profit, one of the goals of any pricing decision. The drivers of profit are shown in Exhibit 14-5. Notice that the two main components are sales revenue and costs. Sales revenue is determined by the multiplication of sales volume and price. It is the role of marketing to ensure that pricing strategies yield the optimum sales volume.

Obviously, costs play a major role in both profit and the determination of price; as such, it is important to understand the types of costs that impact the hospitality industry.

Types of Costs

The goal in this section is not to repeat the accounting class or finance class that you may have already taken. Rather, the goal is to review some of the basic concepts you will need to understand how to effectively set prices. One of the costs listed in Exhibit 14-5 is **variable cost**. Variable costs can be considered either direct or semivariable. Direct variable costs can be traced directly to the level of activity. The higher the activity, the higher the variable cost. These costs are also known as out-of-pocket costs. Kent Monroe, a leader in pricing, explained it this way:

> One test of a unit variable cost is whether it is readily discontinued or whether it would not exist if a product were not made. Direct variable costs include those costs that the product incurs unit by unit and include such costs as productive labor, energy required at production centers, raw material required, sales commissions, royalties and shipping costs. The major criterion of a direct variable cost is that it be traceably and tangibly generated by and identified with, the making and selling of a specific product.[7]

EXHIBIT 14-4   This advertisement shows the integration of product and price.

Source: Marriott International, Inc. Used by permission.

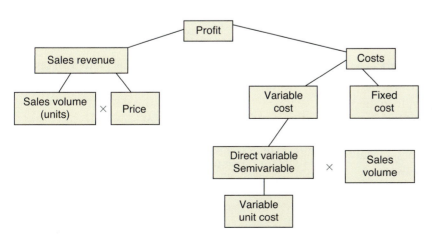

EXHIBIT 14-5   The drivers of profit.

Source: Adapted with the permission of The Free Press, a division of Simon & Schuster Adult Publishing Group from Power pricing: How managing price transforms the bottom line, by Robert J. Dolan and Hermann Simon. Copyright © 1996 by Robert J. Dolan and Hermann Simon. All rights reserved.

A second type of variable cost is semivariable. The best way to understand **semivariable costs** is to consider kitchen staples such as salt, pepper, baking soda, and the like. Other costs include the staff required to run the operation at a minimum. Semivariable costs are needed regardless of the level of activity, but unlike fixed costs, these costs rise markedly with an increase in activity.

Fixed costs are those costs that exist regardless of the level of activity. Following are some examples of fixed costs:

■ Rent/mortgage
■ Insurance
■ Taxes
■ Overhead
■ General administration

Cost-Based Pricing

Cost-based pricing comes in a number of versions in the hospitality industry. Most popular among these are the following:

■ Cost-plus pricing
■ Cost percentage or markup pricing
■ Break-even pricing
■ Contribution margin pricing
■ $1 per thousand pricing

We will cover each of these briefly.

Cost-Plus Pricing

Cost-plus pricing involves establishing the total cost of a product, including a share of the overhead, plus a predetermined profit margin. Its common use in pricing food and beverages is to relate the profit margin to the selling price. Thus, if desired profit is 20 percent of the selling price, an item that costs $4, plus $2 labor and $2 overhead, would be priced at $9.60. This results in $1.60 of profit for that item. Each product or product line is allocated an appropriate share of every type of expense as well as its own variable cost. The intent is that every product should be profit generating.

Cost-plus pricing ignores the notion that total income is a combined effort in which some products will not generate as much profit as others but will contribute to the whole. It is also subject to misallocation of costs such as depreciation, maintenance, and so on. Cost-plus pricing does not allow for flexibility in pricing decisions nor does it take into consideration customers' perceptions of a product's value. It is totally cost oriented and ignores demand. Attempts to apply different gross margin percentages to different menu items to account for different labor costs have done little to overcome the deficiencies of this method.

Cost Percentage or Markup Pricing

Cost percentage or **markup pricing** is also heavily favored by the restaurant industry. It features either a dollar markup on the variable ingredient cost of the item, a percentage markup based on the desired ingredient cost percentage, or a combination of both. A bottle of wine that costs $10 might be subject to a $5 markup, making the selling price $15. The markup percentage would give a 66.6 percent cost-percent-to-selling-price ratio ($10/$15). If, on the other hand, a 50 percent wine cost was desired, the bottle would be marked up by $10 to make the selling price $20 ($20 × 50%).* A common combination of both would be to mark the wine up 100 percent plus $2, making the selling price $22.** Room service liquor follows a similar, if somewhat illogical, pricing strategy. The fifth of Johnny Walker scotch that costs $20 across the street in a liquor store is offered through room service at $100 to protect the 20 percent target beverage cost of the hotel.

The food service industry appears to be enamored by this method of pricing. Food cost and liquor cost percentages become the standard by which results are measured. The three major fallacies of this method are as follows:

1. It is totally cost oriented.
2. It ignores customer perceptions of value, particularly in times of widely fluctuating costs.
3. It tends to price high-cost items up to a level that customers are unwilling to pay.

Break-Even Pricing

Break-even pricing is used to determine at what sales volume and price a product will break even or where costs are equal to sales. It distinguishes between fixed costs and variable costs. The break-even point is calculated as follows:

$$\text{Break even} = \frac{\text{Fixed costs}}{\text{Price} - \text{Variable cost}}$$

The break-even point is graphically plotted for several prices using the same fixed and variable costs. By plotting

---

*The formula for desired percentage cost (DPC) is DPC = cost/selling price. In this example, cost is $10 and DPC is 50%. Therefore, $50\% = \$10/x$ or $.50x = 10$, $x = \$20$.

**In this case, we are doubling our cost, so $10 becomes $20. When you add the $2, it becomes $22. If we want to know the DPC, we calculate DPC = 10 / 22 = 45%.

the revenue generated at various prices, a comprehensive picture of profit can be created if the demand is known at various levels. Exhibit 14-6A to 14-6C demonstrate the process. Exhibit 14-6A shows a hypothetical break-even analysis for **price-sensitive** restaurants. In this case, fixed costs are relatively low and unit variable costs are relatively high. Because of these factors, sales quickly pass the fixed cost line, but the profit margin remains relatively narrow regardless of the quantity sold. This leaves relatively little room for discounting for purposes of increasing volume. Exhibit 14-6B shows the break-even point for several prices. If demand at a certain price is equal to or greater than the break-even point, then that price would be profitable.

Exhibit 14-6C demonstrates a break-even analysis for **volume-sensitive** hotels. The fixed cost line in this case is higher, and it takes longer for the sales line to pass it. Once past it, the profit margin widens quickly as variable costs remain a relatively small percentage of unit sales. There is more

room for discounting to increase volume once the fixed and variable cost lines have been passed by the sales line.

Break-even analysis is a fairly efficient method of determining profit margins at various price levels if—and this is a big *if*—sales volume can be accurately predicted at the different price levels. Knowledge of customer perception and demand is still needed to predict this volume.

Contribution Margin Pricing

Contribution margin pricing occurs when pricing is used to help cover costs. For example, if the total variables cost of a meal is $3 and the meal is sold for $4, then $1 is available as a contribution to fixed costs. Contribution margin pricing is depicted in Exhibit 14-6D. In contrast to Exhibits 14-6A and 14-6B, the variable cost line is interjected into the plot at the same place as the sales line, starting at the zero intersection. This demonstrates the

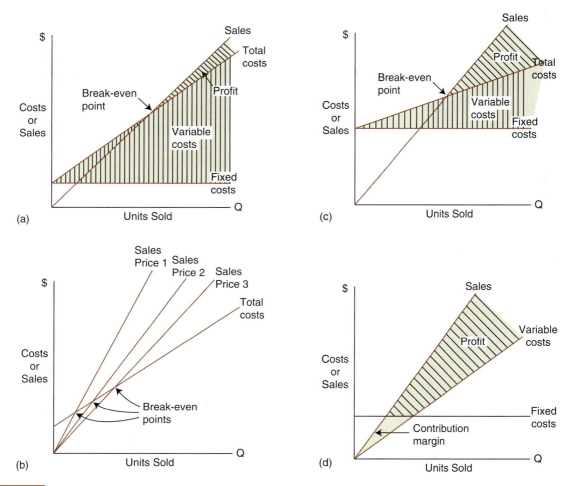

EXHIBIT 14-6 (a) Hypothetical break-even analysis for price-sensitive restaurants; (b) break-even point for several different prices; (c) break-even analysis for volume-sensitive hotels; (d) contribution margin pricing.

Source: Special thanks to Professor Catherine E. Ralston for help in developing these graphs.

concept of contribution, showing that if the product sells at a higher price than its variable cost, it makes a contribution to fixed cost even when sales are not high enough to produce a profit.

This technique is very useful for hotels in soft periods of demand. Room prices can be discounted substantially, if that is what it takes to have them occupied. Even though no profit results, a portion of the fixed cost that would occur if the room were not occupied would be covered. The success of this technique must be assessed by examining the total revenues from rooms sold. After all, selling more rooms at discounted prices may have the same effect as selling fewer rooms at higher prices. In addition, it is important to consider the cost of occupancy; that is, the cost of wear and tear on the fixed assets, the cost of staff burnout, and the cost of trying to raise prices once consumers have been trained to get the room for less.

Contribution margin pricing is another version of markup pricing that can be used to overcome the problem of overly high prices on high-cost items when pricing food and beverages. For example, a bottle of wine that cost $50 could be priced with a contribution margin of $25 for a selling price of $75. Wine cost percentage would then be 67 percent, a very high and forbidding percentage by industry standards. However, the contribution margin would be higher than on two $10 bottles sold at $20 each with a 50 percent wine cost.* There is a saying that goes "You bank dollars, not percentages."

$1 Per Thousand Pricing

The $1 per thousand pricing method for establishing the selling price of hotel rooms is no longer used, according to our knowledge. The rule is that the average room rate in a hotel should be $1 per every $1,000 of construction cost per room. Thus, if a hotel cost $80,000 per room to construct and furnish, the average selling price of the rooms should be $80. We include this archaic "rule of thumb" because it shows how far hotel pricing has developed.

Web Browsing Exercise

Use your favorite web browser to search for information on "cost-based pricing." What different types of information appear? Choose one of the pieces of information and be prepared to discuss the article in class.

---

*Again, the formula for DPC is DPC = Cost/selling price. In this example, DPC = $50/$75 = 67%. Two bottles of wine sold at $20 each yields a $20 contribution margin.

Value-Based Pricing

Value-based pricing can be considered the antithesis of cost-based pricing. It involves choosing a price after developing estimates of market demand based on how potential customers perceive the value of the product or service. It has nothing to do with the cost to produce the item. Perceived value is often defined as what one receives divided by the price one paid. An illustration of this method of pricing occurred when one of the authors of this text needed to have his big screen TV fixed. He called the first person he found in the phone book and without getting a bid (something one should never do), he had the repairperson come and fix the TV. The repairperson took off the back of the TV, jiggled a few wires, placed his soldering gun on another wire, and then closed the back of the TV. The whole process took less than 10 minutes. He then proceeded to write an invoice for $275. His response to the question, "How can you charge me so much when you were only here 10 minutes?" was, "How much did you pay for the TV?" When I responded $675, he said "I just saved you $400. I can't wait until everyone has a plasma TV." Because TVs cost so much to buy, he was able to charge more to fix them, because the cost of fixing the TV, although expensive, was still less expensive than buying a new plasma TV. The repairperson was, of course, correct. And, he was competitive in his pricing. Additional calls to other repair services found the same charge.

Value-based pricing has the advantage that it forces managers to do the following:

1. Review the objectives they have when marketing their product or service
2. Keep in touch with the needs and preferences of customers

Because we have discussed the customer in some detail already, we will not reiterate all of the elements that need to be considered in pricing the product. The reader knows by now that in using any marketing tool, such as pricing, the customer is the first consideration. We discuss the particulars of value-based pricing next.

In establishing prices, some elements are particularly pertinent in regard to the customer. The first of these is the perceived price–value relationship, as it is commonly called. The importance of this relationship is illustrated by a study of business travelers who both spend more than $120 per night for a hotel room and take six or more business trips per year. The study revealed that 28 percent of the 344 who spend more than 75 nights per year in hotels (38 percent of the total sample) claimed that the feature "is a good value for the price paid" is important in the decision to stay in the same hotel chain when traveling on business.[8]

 Web Browsing Exercise

Use your favorite search engine to search for articles using the words "value-based pricing." Read a couple of the articles and prepare a brief report on what you learned.

The Components of Value

The role of management is to increase the perceptions of price value so consumers will be willing to spend more money. One way to accomplish this goal is to focus on one or more of the six components of value. These value added features can be categorized into six types:

- *Financial* (e.g., saving money on future transactions, complete reimbursement if service failure, 10 percent discount at gift shop)
- *Temporal* (e.g., saving time by priority check-in)
- *Functional* (e.g., availability of check cashing)
- *Experiential* (e.g., active participation in the service)
- *Emotional* (e.g., more recognition)
- *Social* (e.g., interpersonal link with a service provider)
- *Trust* (e.g., the organization does what it says it will do)
- *Identification with the organization* (e.g., affinity with a sports team)

Each of these is disussed briefly in the following sections.

Financial Value. Exhibit 14-7 shows the different factors that impact financial value. The more **price sensitive** customers are, the more difficult it will be for the firm to get them to pay more for the product or service. Given that the reverse is also true, the role of the firm is to make customers less price sensitive. For example, Exhibit 14-7 reveals that if customers believe that there are many alternative solutions to their problems and needs, and that one firm's offerings are not unique and are easy to compare with other firms' offerings, they will be more price sensitive; that is, the firm will have more difficulty charging higher-than-average prices. The same is true if customers believe that it is easy to switch from one firm to another. One of the roles of loyalty programs, as discussed in Chapter 4, is to make it more difficult for customers to switch to other brands. If they do switch, they do not get the same level of service as they would if they stayed with the firm to which they were most loyal.

Exhibit 14-7 also shows that buyers are more price sensitive when the expenditure is large relative to their household income or travel budget. This is important to remember for hotels such as Four Seasons and Ritz-Carlton that charge premium prices. It is often difficult for a reservation agent who makes $15 per hour to sell a room that costs $600 per night, as $600 to such an agent is a lot of money. It would take a reservation agent 40 hours to earn $600. It is important to remember that the person who can afford a $600 hotel room makes much more than $15 per hour. As a percentage of her annual income or travel budget, $600 is very small. If the percentage were large, she would not be calling either Four Seasons or Ritz-Carlton. Although the price of the hotel room is a small percentage for guests, it is a large percentage for the reservation agent. For this reason, when quoting room rates, the agent is more likely to attempt to sell a less expensive room. In order to keep proper perspective, management needs to remind reservation agents that the price of the hotel room is fair from the guest's perspective.

One mistake hoteliers used to make was considering business travel to be inelastic. That is, business travelers would pay whatever rate was necessary to stay in a particular hotel. Part of the reason for this belief was that the money was not the traveler's money, but the firm's. This is the shared-cost effect shown in Exhibit 14-7.

The end-benefit effect suggests that reservation agents always ask customers why they are staying at the hotel. Customers who are staying at a hotel for a special occasion such as an anniversary are more likely to pay more (e.g., be less price sensitive) than customers who just need a room for the night before moving on to the next city.

The other two factors that impact financial value—the fairness effect and price quality—are self-explanatory and not discussed in detail.

Temporal Value. In the research mentioned earlier in this chapter, it was found that business travelers consider their time to be worth, on average, $150 per hour. This suggests that if a service process can be redesigned to save 15 minutes of the customer's time, the customer believes he has just saved $37.50. The advertisements by National Car Rental promoting the fact that customers do not have to spend time filling the rental car with gasoline because National charges only the prevailing rate for gasoline instead of the standard gasoline markup is an example of a value added strategy that from the customer's viewpoint saves time and money.

Customers continue to have less and less time. Anything the firm can do to save customers' time can be

EXHIBIT 14-7 **Factors That Impact Financial Value**

Perceived Substitute Effect: Buyers are more price sensitive the higher the product's price relative to prices of perceived substitutes

Unique Value Effect: Buyers are less sensitive to a product's price the more they value any unique attributes that differentiate the offering from competing products

Switching Cost Effect: The greater the product-specific investment that a buyer must make to switch suppliers, the less price sensitive that buyer is

Difficult Comparison Effect: Buyers are less price sensitive to the price of a known or reputable supplier when they have difficulty comparing alternatives

Price Quality Effect: Buyers are less sensitive to a product's price to the extent that a higher price signals better quality

Expenditure Effect: Buyers are more price sensitive when the expenditure is larger, either in dollar terms or as a percentage of household income

End-Benefit Effect: This is broken into two parts:
- Derived demand (the relationship between the desired end benefit and the buyer's price sensitivity for something that contributes to achieving that benefit)
- Share of total cost (the cost of the specific item to the total cost of the product)

Shared-Cost Effect: Impact of partial or complete reimbursement on price sensitivity

Fairness Effect: Based on the price previously paid, prices of similar products (includes location or situation), and if item is to avoid a loss versus achieve a gain

Source: Nagle, T. T., & Holden, R. K. (2002). *The strategy and tactics of pricing: A guide to profitable decision making* (3rd ed.). Upper Saddle River, NJ: Pearson Education, 82–101.

beneficial to the firm. Consider the success of the UPS Store, Kinko's, FedEx, and PostNet. All are designed to save customers' time.

Functional Value. Functional value pertains to the belief that the product or service does what it is designed to do. The main components of functional value are the RATER system, which was discussed at length in Chapter 3. Again, RATER stands for reliability, assurance, tangibility, empathy, and responsiveness. Management needs to ensure that every interaction with customers includes one or more of these components to convey to customers that they are receiving quality. Customers' perceived quality is a result of customer experiences; as such, they need to be managed by the organization. The objective quality of the atrium lobby (the tangible component of the RATER system) may be negated by the lack of perceived quality that is experienced by a rude and unresponsive desk clerk. This can instantaneously change a "fair" objective price to an "unfair" perceived price.

If the product or service does what it was designed to do, customers will pay more for it. For instance, consider something as simple as checking into a hotel. One must start this process not when the guest walks up to the front desk, but at the point the guest starts the reservation process. The steps one can immediately think of are making the reservation, arriving at the hotel, and walking up to the front desk. If the guest calls to make a reservation and is put on hold for too long or if the website is hard to navigate, the cost of the trip increases and perceived value decreases. If this happens, the customer may exit the relationship and stay with a competitor. Once the guest

gets to the hotel, if there are not enough convenient parking spaces near the hotel or if the valet attendant is not around, the guest may be inconvenienced, which decreases the perceived value. Finally, if it takes too long to check in and if the same information is requested at various points throughout the process (e.g., do we ask for guest's name and address both at reservation process and check-in?), perceived value might decrease.

Experiential Value. Experiential value occurs when guests are active participants in the service as compared to passive observers. Which is more fun, sitting at a concert watching quietly or singing along with the group and perhaps dancing in the aisle? A good example of experiential value is the chef's table in the kitchen. This is a table in the kitchen where customers dine on a preset menu selected by the chef. The purpose of such a table is to give customers the feeling of "being in the know" and "being in the heart of the action." Exhibit 14-8 shows the chef's table in Brennan's, a famous restaurant that has locations in New Orleans, Houston, and Las Vegas.

Emotional Value. Emotional value pertains to customers' need to be considered special. Las Vegas casinos spend much money to make their very heavy gamblers, known as whales, feel very special. Casinos cater to their every need, as well as to the needs of their friends and family members. Of course, one does not need to be in the casino business to treat customers as though they are high rollers. Ritz-Carlton, along with other companies, has made extensive use of database systems to keep track of customers' needs and wants. When the customer checks into the hotel or restaurant, his or her favorite room or table is available.

Social Value.   Most customers like to celebrate special occasions with friends and families. Research presented at the Milliken Food and Beverage Conference in 2005 stated that consumers dine out to celebrate the following:

- Birthdays (54 percent celebrate their own; 37 percent celebrate spouses'; and 28% celebrate their child's)
- Mother's Day (38 percent)
- Father's Day (22 percent)
- Valentine's Day (28 percent)
- New Year's Eve (13 percent)
- Easter (13 percent)

One of the authors of this text worked at the Tyler Place Family Resort in Vermont, where guests arrived on a Saturday afternoon, remained for a week, and departed the following Saturday morning. Activities were organized for all age groups. The resort offered programs for toddlers to teens, as well as family retreats and family reunions. Many guests came to this resort the same week each year so they could vacation with friends they had met on prior occasions. Customers who look forward to the opportunity to spend time with friends and family on vacation are willing to spend more money on such opportunities. The programs offered at the Tyler Place Family Resort are similar to those offered at Smuggler's Notch, which we discussed in Chapter 3.

Trust.   As discussed in Chapter 4, trust is a major antecedent of loyalty. And, customers who are loyal to an organization are willing to pay more to stay with that organization. Because services are intangible and one cannot evaluate the service prior to purchase, customers do pay more to purchase services from firms they trust and know to be reliable.

EXHIBIT 14-8   Brennan's of Houston advertises its chef's table on its website.

Source: Retrieved on November 21, 2005 from http://www.brennanshouston. com/kTable.htm. Used by permission from Brennan's of Houston.

Identification with the Organization.   The final component of value occurs when customers identify so strongly that price is removed from the equation. One example of such an affiliation is the relationship customers have with their favorite sports team. Another example is HOG, which is the Harley Owners Group. Firms can increase customers' feelings of affiliation by incorporating any of the following tactics into their marketing plans:

- Providing opportunities for public displays of association, such as logo apparel and sponsorship of community activities
- Actively aligning with and supporting social causes such as becoming an environmentally friendly hotel or restaurant and working with local area care organizations to "stamp out hunger"
- Providing opportunities for contact by creating a dialogue with customers through direct mail and e-mail
- Having distinctive human resources policies such as those offered by firms such as Starbucks

 Web Browsing Exercise

Use your favorite web browser to look up HOG. Be prepared to explain whether learning about HOG has changed your image of those who own motorcycles. What did you learn from this website that can be translated into the hospitality business? Do you think customers might pay more money for a Harley-Davidson because of this organization? Why or why not? Use your favorite web browser to also look at the human resources policy at Starbucks. What benefit does this policy have for customers? Does it enable Starbucks to charge more for its coffee? Why or why not?

Prospect Theory

Another way to increase the perceptions of price value is to frame the offer in the best possible light. For example, consider the following two options:

Option A: Luxury suite room at $159 and then for an additional $30 you get a guaranteed room on a high floor with a view of the Las Vegas Strip

Option B: Luxury suite room with a guaranteed room on a high floor for $189 or a room for $30 less anywhere in the hotel

Which option would you choose? When the $159 was quoted first, 13.6 percent of the participants elected to pay an additional $30 for a guaranteed Las Vegas Strip view. This means that 86.4 percent elected to keep the $159 rate. When the $189 rate was quoted first, 20.6 percent elected to take this rate; the remaining 79.4 percent elected to take the less expensive room. The additional revenue generated by quoting the $189 first was approximately $31,000 per month or $372,000 per year.

The preceding example can be explained in terms of prospect theory.[9] Prospect theory argues that when people make decisions, they do so by examining changes relative to a reference point. The area to the right of the reference point is called the gain domain, and the area to the left is called the loss domain. This is shown in Exhibit 14-9.

The key to whether one is in the gain domain or the loss domain depends on the reference point. This reference point is different from person to person. However, Kahneman and Tversky found that the reference point can be changed depending on how the decision is presented or framed.

In the previous example, Option A sets the reference point at $159 without a guaranteed room with a Las Vegas Strip view (a desirable trait) and then penalizes buyers an additional $30 if they want a guaranteed Las Vegas Strip view; that is, a loss relative to the reference point. This loss occurs in two places: the cash cost of $30 and the lack of the Las Vegas Strip view. In contrast, Option B first establishes a reference point of $189 with a guaranteed Las Vegas Strip view and then rewards buyers $30 who do not wish a Las Vegas Strip view—a gain relative to the reference point.

Prospect theory also works for restaurants. In a study on menu pricing, it was found that menu items with detailed descriptions and high prices were perceived to have the same price value as menu items with modest description and low prices. The differences in descriptions can be seen in Exhibit 14-10. Overall, it should be clear that there are multiple ways hospitality firms can increase perceptions of price value.

Reference Pricing

A second way to increase the perceptions of price value is known as reference pricing. As we know from Chapter 1, customers purchase problem solutions based on expectations. Let's turn that around and say that customers also have in mind a price they expect to pay for a given solution. This is called their **reference price**. Reactions to prices will vary around this reference or expected price, based on some kind of prior experience or knowledge. In understanding reference pricing, it is important to understand some critical pricing definitions. *Reference price* is the first pricing term firms need to understand. This is the price for which consumers believe the product should sell. The reference price is formed when consumers consider such things as the following:

■ Price last paid
■ Price of similar items
■ Price considering the brand name
■ Real or imagined cost to produce the item
■ Perceived cost of product failure

The last item is of considerable importance because it reflects consumers' imaginations of what could go wrong. As discussed in prospect theory, a loss (in this case a bad meal) is worse than the thought of a good meal. For example, the reference price for a meal at which one is celebrating a special occasion is higher than the reference price for a meal with some old college friends, even though the restaurant may be the same. The risk of failure is critical in the first case and less critical in the second.

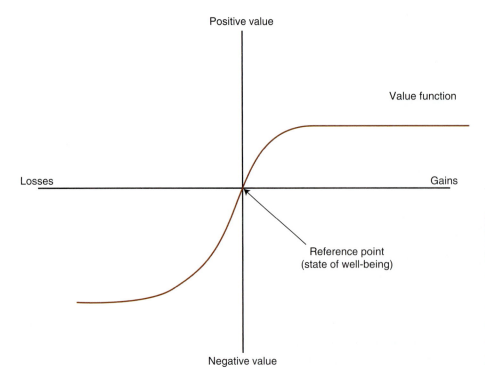

EXHIBIT 14-9 The area to the right of the reference point is called the *gain domain*, and the area to the left is called the *loss domain*.

Source: Value function in prospect theory by Stowe Shoemaker, Journal of Revenue and Pricing Management *2(3), October 2003, p. 277. Henry Stewart Publications. Reproduced with permission of Palgrave MacMillan.*

EXHIBIT 14-10	Differences in Menu Descriptions

MODEST DESCRIPTION

Spinach and Feta Dip
Spinach and Feta Cheese with Tomatoes and Pinenuts

Tilapia
Pan-Fried in Cornmeal. Served with Cabbage Slaw in a Lime Dressing

Boston Green Salad
Boston Bibb Lettuce with Roasted Peppers, Bacon, and Blue Cheese in a Red Wine Dressing

Apple Crisp
Apple Slices Baked with a Nut Topping
Served with Vanilla Ice Cream, Strawberries, and Whipped Cream

DETAILED DESCRIPTION

Spinach and Feta Dip
Organic Spinach Sautéed in Garlic and Combined with Authentic Athenian Feta Cheese, Sun-Ripened Yellow Tomatoes, and Toasted Pinenuts

Fresh Tilapia
Farm-Raised Tilapia Delicately Crisped in Stone-Ground Cornmeal and Topped with a Jicama and Napa Cabbage Slaw Tossed with Lime Ginger Dressing

Boston Green Salad
Crisp Boston Bibb Lettuce Tossed with Roasted Peppers, Crispy Pancetta Bacon, and Roquefort Blue Cheese in a Pinot Noir Dressing

Warm Apple Crisp
Washington State Jonagold Apples Are Sliced Thick and Baked with Our Delicious Crispy Nut Topping.
Served with House-Made Vanilla Bean Ice Cream, Juicy Strawberries, and Freshly Whipped Cream

The second definition firms need to understand is *reservation price*. This is defined as the maximum price the customer will pay for a product. For instance, if the customer's reservation price for a can of soda is 1 euro and the price is 1.01 euros, the customer will not buy the product. If the selling price is less than the reservation price, the customer will buy the product. Firms that price exactly to the reservation price are said to extract the entire *consumer surplus*. Firms that price less than the reservation price are said to be *leaving money on the table*. Obviously, firms do not want to leave money on the table.

In 1988 Taco Bell used a research methodology based on research originally conducted by Dutch economist Peter H. Van Westendorp to determine customers' reference or expected price. This methodology was further developed as price sensitivity measurement (PSM) by Kenneth Travers and others,[10] but until Taco Bell picked up on it, had been largely ignored in the hospitality industry. This process, explained briefly in Exhibit 14-11, puts a price value on a product as determined by the perception of the target market, which, in the final analysis, is the only way to set prices. Basically, this methodology helps determine the reference price and the reservation price.

Through the PSM pricing methodology, Taco Bell learned to bundle its products—for example, adding sour cream, including a soft drink, etc.—in a way and at a price where the customer perceived "value." For the fast-food industry giants, value pricing and bundling have reduced the former standard practices of discounts, coupons, and direct mail as key weapons in the fast-food wars.

Exhibit 14-11 explains how research can demonstrate the way customers, in some arbitrary fashion, establish an upper price level at which they deem the product to be too expensive and a lower price level below which the quality of the product would be suspect. This is based on expectations. Between these two is the "indifference" price—the price perceived as normal for that product in a given market, given one's expectations. There are certain hotels and restaurants at which we would expect to pay different prices. When we are surprised by an unexpected price, we may tend to become somewhat irate. Thus, it is the responsibility of the price setter to educate the customer about prices.

Expectations should be built into the pricing decision. Research can determine what the market thinks the product should cost. This can be especially useful in the pricing of services where a cost basis is lacking for developing an expectation. Findings may indicate that the service can be priced higher; contrarily, a lower-than-expected price may offer competitive advantage. Knowledge of price expectation can help firms avoid both overpricing and underpricing.

Psychological Pricing

Prices cause psychological reactions on the part of customers just as atmospherics do. As noted, high prices may imply quality and low prices may imply inferiority. This is especially true for services because of their intangibility. Thus, higher-priced services may sell better, whereas lower-priced services may sell poorly. This is contrary to the standard economic model. Psychological reactions, however, do not necessarily correspond to reality, and it is not unusual for customers to feel that they have made a mistake.

EXHIBIT 14-11 **PSM: Price Sensitivity Measurement**

PSM is based on psychological and sociological principles and aims to examine price perception by determining levels of customer resistance as they relate to quality perceptions and the market range of acceptable prices for a specific product or service. For each specific product or service, four questions are asked. The first two questions determine the Indifference Point (IDP, Graph I). This is the price at which an equal number of respondents feel the product or service is cheap, as feel it is expensive.

1. At what price on the scale do you consider the product or service to be cheap?
2. At what price on the scale do you consider the product or service to be expensive?

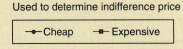

Used to determine indifference price

Indifference Price is point at which
the number who feel it is expensive but still buy is equal
to the number who feel it is cheap but still okay
to buy

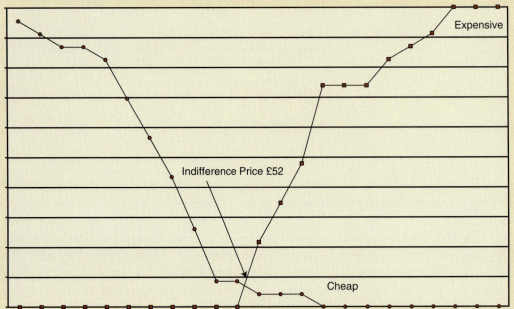

Graph I Cheap versus expensive.

The second two questions determine the Optimal Pricing Point (OPP, Graph II). This is the price at which customer resistance to purchase is at its lowest; that is, an equal number feel the product or service is too cheap as feel it is too expensive.

3. At what price on the scale do you consider the product or service to be too expensive, so expensive that you would not consider buying it?
4. At what price on the scale do you consider the product or service too cheap, so cheap that you would question the quality?

Optimal Pricing Point is point at which consumers' resistance to purchase is at its lowest; point where an
equal number feel the product is too cheap as feel it is too expensive.

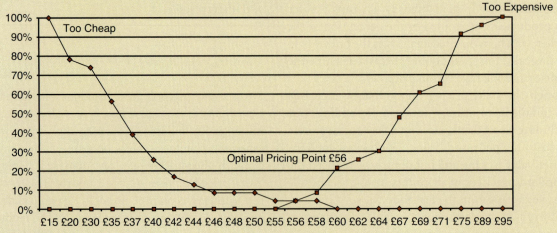

Graph II Too cheap versus too expensive.

When the four cumulative distributions are combined, it can be determined if there is "stress" in price consciousness (Graph III). The closer the OPP is to the IDP, the less price conscious are the respondents. As the gap widens, the greater is the number of customers who feel the "normal" price is too high—that is, they are more sensitive to price.

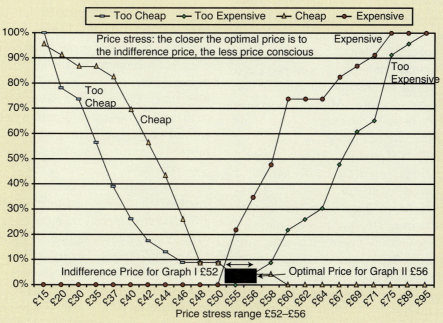

Graph III Price-stress analysis.

The final manipulation gives the Range of Acceptable Prices (RAP, Graph IV). The "too cheap" and "too expensive" curves are graphed with the reversed cumulative distributions of the "cheap" and "expensive," which are then labeled "not cheap" and "not expensive." The intersection of these two curves is the Point of Marginal Cheapness (PMC). This is the point where the number of respondents who feel the product or service is too cheap is equal to the number of respondents who feel it is not cheap.

The intersection of the "not expensive" and "too expensive" curves is the Point of Marginal Expensiveness (PME). This is the point where the number of respondents who feel the product or service is too expensive is equal to the number of respondents who feel it is not expensive.

The Range of Acceptable Prices (RAP) has the PMC as its lower price limit and the PME as its upper price limit. It would be unwise to price outside this range unless there is real change in the perceived value or positioning of the product or service. Thus, for example, Taco Bell found that it could move prices up (i.e., create great price value) by adding sour cream to tacos and changing the perceived value.

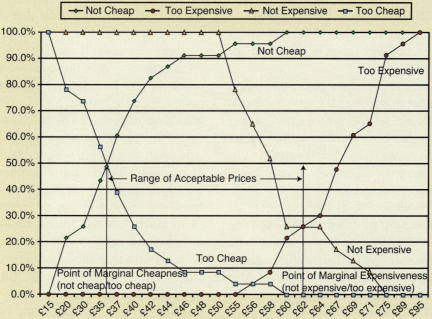

Graph IV Range of acceptable prices.

Source: Adapted from Lewis, R. C., & Shoemaker, S. (1997). Value pricing: Another view and a research example. *Cornell Hotel and Restaurant Administration Quarterly, 38* (2), 44–54.

This is also true in the hospitality industry because of the "visibility" factor. Being "seen" at an upscale restaurant or hotel is very important to some customers. For example, a businessman might buy inexpensive furniture for his apartment and drink ordinary wine at home. This same businessman, trying to make an impression on peers and customers, will rave about the antique furniture in the lounge and the expensive wine ordered with dinner—in other words, he wants to be seen with the product that offers the highest affordable visibility factor.

Buyers and nonbuyers of products also have different perceptions of price. This contrast can be demonstrated best with the case of upscale restaurants. Many such restaurants are perceived by those who have never been there to be far more expensive than is actually the case. Commander's Palace, one of New Orleans' finest restaurants, used large advertisements in the local paper detailing their attractively priced lunch specials to counteract this. In pricing, it is important to understand the price perceptions of nonusers as well as of users.

Another **psychological pricing** technique is called **price lining**. This technique clumps prices together so that a perception of substantially increased quality is created. For example, a wine list might have a group of wines in the $8 to $10 range and have the next grouping in the $14 to $16 range. The perception is a definitive increase in quality, which may or may not be the case.

Still another version of psychological pricing is called **odd-numbered pricing**. This is a familiar tactic to all of us. Items sell at $6.99 rather than $7.00 to create the perception of a lower price. Sometimes this is carried to extreme such as a computer that sells for $6,999.99 or a car advertised at $22,999. This tactic is often used in menu and hotel room pricing.

All these differences in customers' perception might seem to make pricing an impossible task. Perhaps that is why hotels and restaurants tend to ignore the customer and price according to other factors! Customer-based pricing is not impossible, however. Target marketing allows us to select relatively homogeneous markets for which the product and the price are designed.

The marketer should also be aware, very aware, of how the customer uses price to differentiate competing products and services. This is a key to positioning with price. Value perception is always relative to the competition, whether the value perceived is real or imagined. It is the marketer's job to understand this process.

As an example of what we have just said, consider the case of a major hotel chain that conducted price research in one of its major market areas. Exhibit 14-12 shows some of the findings and conclusions of the research.

Veblen Effects

There is a contrary phenomenon to almost everything we have said so far in this chapter. A century ago, Thorstein Veblen's *The Theory of the Leisure Class* coined the term *conspicuous consumption* to describe the human tendency to use purchasing as a way of raising social status. John Kenneth Galbraith's *The Affluent Society*, in the 1950s, argued that the modem corporation creates customer desires with advertising and needless brand proliferation. In 1998 Juliet Shor continued the theme with her book, *The Overspent American*.

For these authors, the result is a materialistic race no one can win; in contrast to most economists who view growth in customer spending as a sign of rising living standards. Viewing consumption as status seeking has considerable implications. Luxury items such as furs, jewelry, designer clothes, or a Mercedes may be purchased more to impress others than for any other reason. If this is the case, then there may be potential advantages to maintaining high hotel rates and restaurant prices. Flying first class to Paris, staying at the Ritz, and dining at a four-star Michelin restaurant may satisfy many needs, but most likely "conspicuous consumption" is one of them. To lower prices at these and similar places would, in effect, be counterproductive. Additionally, what looks conspicuous to one person may just be good value to another.

Value Added Service Pricing

Value added services are those that are added to the basic product or service that the customer buys to enhance the perception of value. These are worth evaluating because in some cases, they may not add true value, may simply increase the cost base, or may eventually be passed on to a customer (in the form of higher prices) who doesn't really want them or perceive a higher value.

Developing a product or service for customers' specific needs that augments the standard product is a part of loyalty marketing. Business services in a guest room, for which an additional charge is sometimes made, and turndown service at no charge are perfect examples. Many hotels, however, instead of tailoring added services to individual needs, sometimes provide customers with more services than they want or need at prices that don't reflect the value or their cost. Unfortunately, management sometimes does not even know which services customers with similar needs really want, which should be offered as part of the standard product, or which should be offered as value options that some would pay extra for. Furthermore, because of the intangibility of many ser-

EXHIBIT 14-12	Research Results on Pricing Effect in a Market

The research of a major hotel chain revealed a steady loss of regular-rated room nights and revenue—that is, there was enough increase in discounted transient room nights to make published rack rates virtually meaningless. Moreover, many of these rooms were being sold at rates below the corporate rate. This trend had led to declining average rates overall, with almost half the room nights being sold at deep discounts. Although published and corporate rates had been increased dramatically, discount rates had remained flat.

With respect to customers, this research also had some interesting findings. For one, the pricing strategy was building loyalty and repeat business with the "wrong" target markets. Customers were found to have a high degree of rate awareness that influenced their value perception and intention to return; corporate- and regular-rate customers felt the hotels were overpriced. The indifference price was found to be as much as $25 lower than the regular or corporate rates being charged. For discount customers, however, it was slightly higher than what they were paying. In addition, corporate- and regular-rate customers gave the hotels lower value ratings, and the higher the rate they paid, the less likely they were to return. Market share of high-rated customers was being lost to competitors. Furthermore, reservation incentive systems designed to obtain higher rates from customers were, in fact, damaging long-term profitability by alienating customers. One important conclusion of the findings was that by reducing high rates and raising discount rates, the customer mix could be changed so as to produce increased profits in the long run.

vices, they often don't know the cost of providing them; no matter how homogeneous a target market, one size does not fit all.

Because hotel managements rely almost solely on measures of customer satisfaction, they are often misled. Customers are always happy to get something for nothing, and when they do, they express satisfaction of the overall offering. The property, however, has to absorb the costs, of which they may be unaware, that may or may not have created real value in the first place.

The solution to this is called **flexible service offerings**—particular services valued by individual customers. A hotel should first "inventory" these services to find out what is being provided to whom and on what basis. They should then apply **activity-based costing** on a segment-by-segment or customer-by-customer basis. These acts apply especially to group bookings where services are often added just to get the booking. The same thing should be done for any new services that are being considered.[11]

Customers then need to be asked the value of the service to them. This leads to activity-based pricing. The following options are now available:

1. Do not offer the service.
2. Give the service away at no additional charge.
3. Raise the price equal to the cost of providing the service.
4. Raise the price less than the cost of providing the service.
5. Raise the price slightly higher than the cost of providing the service to camouflage a price increase on the standard product.

This approach allows hotels to fit the service to customer needs, as well as notify customers that they do not have to pay for something they don't want. Some hotels today have turn-down service on request only—but only after realizing how much it was costing them and how many customers didn't want it. British Airways has been very successful charging the customer for value added services. For those customers who just want the cheapest price available, British Airways has this price. This enables them to compete with the low-cost carriers (LCC). For those customers who want more services, ticket flexibility, and upgrade availability, British Airways offers customers such options. Exhibits 14-13A–D illustrate how customers can choose the price they want to pay and the value added service options.

Pricing Objectives

Objectives are what we want to accomplish. Without them, it is hard to determine where we are going or how we are going to get there. Pricing objectives fall into three major categories: financial, volume, and customer objectives.

Financial Objectives

Financial objectives are probably the most dominant, widespread, and enduring pricing objectives in the hospitality industry. Although absolutely essential to success or even survival, the heavy emphasis on financial objectives tends to overwhelm all other considerations. In some cases, this can actually lead to failure; in others, even in successful firms, it can lead to the inability to maximize potential.

Financial objectives take different forms, all of which are interrelated. Profit is the one that usually comes to mind first. We call this **pricing for profit maximization**, whether the emphasis is on gross profit or net profit. The first problem with the heavy emphasis on profit in pricing is that it tends to ignore many other considerations—in particular, the customer.

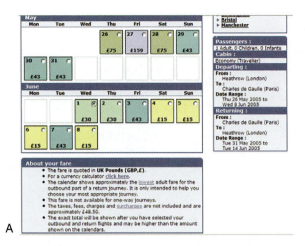

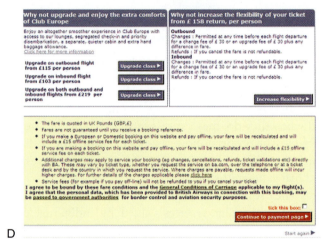

EXHIBIT 14-13 British Airways customers can choose the price they want to pay and the value added service options.

Source: British Airways. Retrieved from www.ba.com. May 12, 2005. Used by permission.

The second and related problem is that a built-in profit determination may be hard to achieve in the hospitality industry. In other industries, the relationship among cost, price, and profit is more direct and obvious. In the hospitality industry, it is indirect and vague. Product makers can calculate very closely their variable, indirect, and fixed costs. From that basis, they can add on a profit margin per unit. If they are good forecasters, they will do well because the products they don't sell today they will sell tomorrow, even if they have to discount them and reduce their profit margin.

In hotels and restaurants, the room or the seat not occupied tonight cannot be sold tomorrow, even at a discount. Yet a large part of the fixed and semivariable cost of selling that room or seat exists regardless. Even with these problems, there are tools for calculating desired profit margins that go beyond the scope of this section. Instead, we are more concerned with the setting of prices based on the thesis that the higher the price, the greater the profit. That

thesis will hold true if the price has no effect on patronage. For example, airline terminal bars and lounges are notorious for overpricing and operating with a cost of sales under 15 percent. It is doubtful that this practice has much effect on volume given the nature of the captive market. In most other instances, however, this will not hold true.

High prices alone will reduce volume in most cases. Thus, after setting high rack rates, hotels discount to get back the volume at a lower price. From a marketing point of view, something else occurs in the process—the hotel loses customers who are turned off by the high prices, don't know how to negotiate a discount, or simply don't like feeling that they are being taken advantage of. Even in times of high demand, too high prices force many travelers to seek alternatives. Websites like Hotels.com promote hotel discounts and provide a variety of alternatives to customers. These customers not only don't come or don't come back, but they also tell many others about the high prices. Essentially, pricing for profit maximization by maximizing prices ignores marketing forces.

Other financial objectives in pricing are **target return on investment (ROI)**, stabilization of prices and profit margins, and **cash flow pricing** (to maximize short-run sales in order to generate cash). All of these objectives have their place in pricing and, in fact, are necessary. Problems arise when one of them becomes the sole pricing objective.

Volume Objectives

Volume objectives are a second set of pricing objectives and take a number of forms. These objectives are particularly prevalent in the hotel industry because it is such a highly volume-sensitive business—that is, fixed costs are high but variable costs per room can run as low as 15 to 25 percent of departmental income. Once fixed costs have been surpassed, a small gain in volume supports a large increase in profit. This is the case with the airlines as well. In the restaurant business, a price-sensitive business (i.e., a small increase in price supports a large increase in profit), variable costs can run as high as 35 to 55 percent of sales. Both industries, of course, seek volume (with some noted exceptions, such as where high prices are designed to promote exclusivity). Lower variable costs, however, provide hotels with the ability to discount deeper to promote volume. Hotel restaurants also are in the unique position of "paying no rent," in contrast to their freestanding competitors.*

One major and commonly used measure of volume is market share, which we discussed in an earlier chapter. As a reminder, market share is the percentage of units sold (e.g., occupancy) or dollar volume share of the total business that an individual business is able to obtain within a competitive group. Market share has been shown in other industries to be a leading indicator of profit. It also measures how well one is doing vis-à-vis the competition and also how well in terms of one's own fair share.

To increase market share, a property has to do something better than the competition. This can be a better product, better service, better location, or better perceived value. One can also be "better" by lowering prices. This may or may not be self-defeating. For a restaurant, a quickly calculated break-even analysis can indicate at which point increased volume will overcome the lost revenue due to lower prices. For a hotel, it is more likely that competition will follow suit and market share will soon return to where it was before. It is probably foolish in most cases in the hospitality industry to lower prices for the sole purpose of increasing market share, as others will be bound to follow, hurting all.

Another volume objective is to build business by increasing the customer base. With this strategy, prices are usually lowered, either temporarily or in special promotions, to attract more customers with the hope that they will become permanent customers. This also can backfire, as it usually does with restaurants that run a two-for-one promotion. The reason it backfires is that many customers who take advantage of the promotion will never return to the property when they have to pay the regular price.

There can be much merit, however, to using price to build the customer base when doing so will build customer loyalty, especially during normally slow periods. For hotels, more customers in the rooms can also mean more customers in the food and beverage outlets.

Another volume objective is to increase occupancy or seat turnover. This is really no different from talking about increasing sales by lowering the price. Higher occupancy or seat turnover helps to cover relatively fixed labor costs and overhead. Again, for hotels it can mean more customers in the food and beverage outlets. Hotel management personnel in the past were often judged on their occupancy ratios and often rewarded accordingly, so there was a high incentive to price with the objective of increasing occupancy. More frequently today, however, hotel managers are awarded on their REVPAR, which helps to stop them from lowering rates just for the purpose of increasing occupancy.

A final volume objective is the contribution to fixed costs that is made by any incremental business, called a contribution margin. If the variable cost of a meal is $3 and the meal is sold for $4, then $1 is available as a contribution toward fixed costs. This is better than zero, which would result if the meal is normally sold for $8 but cannot be sold. The high fixed costs and volume sensitivity of hotels make this objective even more viable and are the reason for contracting with low-rated airline crews or other low-rated business in off-peak hours.

Volume and profit objectives in pricing often go hand in hand, but this is not always the case. Volume objectives tend to be more oriented toward the long term and, when done wisely, toward building the customer base.

---

*This creates an interesting paradox in many hotels. The following scenario is common: A sales manager books a large group at a favorable (to the hotel) room rate. To do so, she had to heavily discount the meals. The food and beverage manager and the chef scream—the prices will ruin their food cost percentage—disregarding the overall profit to be gained from the booking. In most cases, these F&B manager' bonuses are tied into producing a satisfactory food cost. This type of reward compensation forces managers to choose between customers and their own pockets. Some hotels counter this by assigning a portion of room revenues to F&B revenues.

Customer Objectives

The term *customer objectives,* as used here, means influence of the customer in a favorable way. This is truly the marketing objective of pricing. There are many ways that pricing can be used to do this, simply because it is the most visible part of the presentation mix. We will suggest a number of those ways.

One customer objective is to instill confidence in the customer by **price stability**. For a long time this was not common in the hotel industry, other than in some budget properties such as Microtel, Red Roof, and Econo Lodge and some middle-tier properties such as Courtyard and Hampton Inns. The rise of the Internet and other multiple channels of distribution made firms aware of the need for some price stability. We can also think of price stability in terms of rate parity, rate integrity, and rate transparency. Each of these is defined in Exhibit 14-14.

Hotel companies have negotiated rates with corporations that remain constant for some period of time. The rates are usually based on the guarantee of a certain number of room nights during the same period. This allows corporations to better budget their travel expenses when they are confident of a stable price.

Another customer objective is "inducement to try." Restaurant two-for-one programs are designed for this purpose, as are other special promotions. Restaurants run **loss leaders** (items on which they take a loss or lower margin with the hope of making up the profit on other items) just as retail stores do. Individual and new menu items may also be priced lower for this purpose. Some weekend and off-peak packages at hotels are another example of an inducement to try. "Opening specials" or **price penetration**, capturing as much of the market as possible as soon as possible, represent a specific case of inducement-to-try pricing. Hotels used to open at the highest price they thought the market would bear and avoided initial discounting on the assumption that natural demand would fill the new rooms. Exhibit 14-15 is an example of inducement-to-try pricing to obtain more customers.

The goal of penetration pricing is to generate sales volume even at the expense of high margins. Penetration pricing does not mean that prices are necessarily cheap, but they are low relative to what is normally charged. Penetration pricing works well if the following conditions are in effect:

- A large share of the market are willing to change suppliers in response to the price differential.
- Customers only really look at price and not the other features that would make them ignore the low price offer.
- Price is not a trivial expenditure to customers.

In most marketplaces, where there is greater supply, new demand is not created because a new hotel is opened. The meetings or business traveler market already exists, in another hotel. Or, the traveler stays someplace else because of the tight market. For example, many who would, prefer to stay in New York City, where they do business, stay in New Jersey instead because of more availability and lower room rates. Opening pricing is extremely important; the idea is to get existing customers in competitors' hotels to try the new product. Opening pricing can also be used to send a message to both customers and competitors. Consider the story of two hotels in New York

---

EXHIBIT 14-14	Key Terms in Customer Objective Pricing

RATE PARITY

The uniformity of retail rates across different channels of distribution that provide the same product. For example, a standard room for two nights, arrival on January 29 for two people, should be sold at the same price at a proprietary site, at a third-party wholesaler or through the GDS. If the same product was sold with different restrictions (e.g., nonrefundable, nontransferable, or fully prepaid), a different price could be applied to that product without affecting rate parity.

RATE INTEGRITY

The trust in the fair price of a hospitality product. It is usually achieved when customers believe they would not find lower prices for a given product through other channels. Many hotels and airlines are achieving this by guaranteeing having the lowest Internet booking fares.

RATE TRANSPARENCY

The perfect knowledge of the price for a specific hospitality product, due to the customer's ability to shop for rates across channels. The concept of rate transparency is similar to the concept of perfect information in economic theory.

RATE CANNIBALIZATION

A dilution in rates due to an increased rate transparency and a lack of rate parity. It occurs when customers shop the same product through different channels and book at the lowest rate encountered, even though they would have booked at higher rates. In other words, there is demand for higher price levels. Rate cannibalization causes a decrease in revenues without increasing demand.

Source: Green, Cindy Estis (2004). De-Mystifying Distribution. *TIG Global Special Report*. Hospitality Sales and Marketing Association International Foundation.

EXHIBIT 14-15 This advertisement for hotels.com is an example of inducement-to-try pricing to obtain more customers.

Source: hotels.com. Used by permission.

City that took exactly opposite opening pricing strategies, as shown in Exhibit 14-16.

The objective in the St. Regis situation, rather than inducement to try, is another customer objective called "enhancing the image," sometimes called prestige pricing. The attempt is to make the property appear so special, new, and different that it is worth the higher price. The practice of initial high pricing is called **price skimming**. The term derives from the notion of skimming the cream off the top, before the competition comes in and forces prices down.

Price skimming can be profitable when a company introduces a new product into the market.

The goal of price skimming is to capture high margins at the expense of high sales volume. It works well when the following conditions are in effect:

- Customers are price insensitive.
- Customers place a high value on a product's differentiating attributes.
- There is value attached to prestige and exclusivity.

EXHIBIT 14-16	Two Opening Pricing Strategies

Two hotels in New York City opened with the exact opposite introductory pricing strategies and ended up in the same position. The St. Regis and Four Seasons hotels both opened (the St. Regis after a massive renovation) in the New York marketplace when demand for guest rooms was soft. The St. Regis priced itself at the top of the market and declared it would rather run empty rooms than discount. In fact, it ran many vacant rooms until the economy picked up in the mid-1990s. Four Seasons opened its hotel with introductory rates of $179, astounding for a five-star hotel of that caliber. By the end of 2005, both hotels were flirting with an $850 average daily rate.

Another customer objective in pricing is to "desensitize" the customer to the price. One way to do this is to bundle items together and charge just one price. Outstanding examples of this practice are Club Med and the all-inclusive resorts of Jamaica. Club Med started the trend with its "one price covers all" policy, sometimes even including airfare. Alcoholic drinks and incidentals are extra, however, but you "pay" for them with colored beads that you buy (they go on your bill) at the front desk and wear as a necklace. You are desensitized until you check out, but it works. This is similar to what happens in the cruise industry.

The all-inclusive resorts have no extra charges; everything is "free" after you have paid one (substantial) price per week. An example of attempts to desensitize in restaurants is the use of fixed price menus with one inclusive price, common in France and other parts of Europe as *menu degustation* or *prix fixe*.

A good price–value relationship is reflected in another customer pricing objective that is a policy for many hospitality companies. This is another way to "desensitize" overall price and also a form of image enhancement, since the market is generally conceded to be very price value sensitive. Fast-food restaurants in the middle to lower price ranges use this technique all the time in their advertising. We discussed different ways to increase the perceived value earlier in this chapter.

Two other customer objectives are worth mentioning. One is to use pricing to differentiate the product, usually with higher prices. If the product appears essentially the same, then price can be used as a customer perception mechanism to differentiate one product from another: The 12-ounce prime New York sirloin for $24.95 certainly must be better than the same item for $19.95 somewhere else. Alternatively, Red Lobster frequently uses promotions such as 30 shrimp for under $10 ($9.99 to be exact). Another objective in the same vein is to introduce or promote added services or physical facilities. Concierge floors in hotels are priced in this manner, as are tableside flambé desserts in restaurants. While it is sometimes difficult to justify the price differences for these services in the formal product, other core elements, such as "prestige," may justify the cost to the buyer.

Determining Price

One of the most direct methods of determining price is to base it on what competitors charge, sometimes called the "going rate." One has little choice but to stay in line with other properties offering *the same product in the same product class.* Without valued differentiation, it is difficult to get higher prices, and lower prices will probably be met by competitors. Competitors' prices are readily available, at least the stated prices, making it easy to use them as a benchmark. For example, the Venetian, because of its size and location next to the convention center, is the **price leader** among convention hotels in Las Vegas. All other convention hotels are priced below the Venetian to remain competitive.

Competitive pricing is also known as **match pricing**. It is viable as long as there is no customer perception of significant differences among the entities, as long as one's cost structure allows pricing at that level, and assuming competitors' prices are set right at the beginning. These are all very big assumptions, which are usually not met. Match pricing also means that the market must be willing and able to buy at that level. It means that the customer is totally concerned about price.

For example, a new upscale hotel may price its rooms competitively with existing upscale hotels. That seems to work fine as long as the demand exists. If, however, present upscale hotels are running at low occupancy and the market has largely traded down, this may be sheer folly. It might be advantageous to position by pricing somewhere between the two tiers, with the advantage of a better product than one and a lower price than the other. If existing upscale hotels react by meeting this lower rate, the consequences will be the same. A positive effect, however, would be that at least the upscale properties together might take business back from the lower tier.

The other side of competitive pricing is that the *augmented* product is rarely ever the same, even in the same product class. This will make little difference—unless the customer perceives it to be so. One way to create that perception is with pricing as a tangible aspect of the presentation mix. When one prices above the direct competition, a statement is made that a better product is being offered. The reverse is true if one prices below the competition. In the final analysis, this is only a starting point; the market will make the final decision. Thus, it is inherently foolish to attempt to bait the customer with pricing if the product is not there to support it.

A good example is a hotel in New York City that at one point was running an average room rate of $139. New ownership and management took over and decided to go upscale after slightly refurbishing the hotel. Rack rates of $199 and $239 were posted. The market quickly perceived that the refurbishing was inadequate to justify this kind of price increase, and occupancy dropped. Not until rates were dropped to $159 did the hotel regain its market share. The same situation can also work in reverse: The same company opened a refurbished smaller hotel in a different location and priced rooms at $159. The market saw an incredible value as comparable hotels in the area were already at $199. Rates were successfully increased to $219. These two situations in the same company are examples of ignoring the market when setting prices.

In restaurants, there is far more variation in the product relative to the same product class. Atmospherics are probably important, along with the menu items, the chef's preparation, the quality of food and drinks, and other variables. Nevertheless, the need to maintain a strong pricing relationship with competitors is important. Restaurants have more opportunity to differentiate their product and should price accordingly, provided the market perceives that differentiation and is willing and able to pay for it.

Both restaurants and hotels will sometimes use penetration prices initially to create awareness and trial, steal customers, and build volume. Once the business is established, it is normal for prices to be increased. Sometimes this works and sometimes it backfires and business is lost, at which point it is far more difficult to lower prices and recapture the business. The image of being overpriced or having poor price value is an enduring one with the customer.

In setting prices, the marketer must always make conscious predictions about competitive reactions. Will they meet the prices? What will be the effect if they do or don't? What has become a classic textbook case is the case of Peoples Express Airlines. By drastically reducing airfares, Peoples captured enormous market share until the bigger carriers met them at the same price levels with a superior product. This and other reasons eventually led to the demise of Peoples. On the other hand, Southwest Airlines has remained one of the most profitable carriers with low costs that the large carriers have been largely unable to combat. It has done this by carefully focusing on the markets and segments it serves, which Peoples did not.

The final generic pricing strategy is **neutral pricing**. Here, management decides not to use price to gain market share; rather, they use other market variables. Those who practice neutral pricing believe the customer wants a coherent pricing strategy. They may or may not be concerned with competition and may or may not understand costs. Exhibit 14-17 summarizes fair pricing strategies.

The decisions of whether to practice penetration, skim, neutral, or match pricing are usually situation specific. We can only caution here that the marketer should conduct a thorough analysis of the complete situation—the product, the market, and the competition—before establishing pricing strategies. This is not a time for seat-of-the-

EXHIBIT 14-17	**Summary of Fair Pricing Strategies**			
	Skim	**Penetration**	**Match**	**Neutral**
Customers	Price insensitive; place high value on a product's differentiating attributes	A large share of the market must be willing to change suppliers in response to a price differential	Believe customer is concerned about price	Maintain coherent pricing strategy
Competition	Must have some source of competitive protection	Competitors lack the ability or incentive to match prices	Totally concerned with competition	May or may not be concerned with competition
Costs	Incremental unit costs represent a small share of product's price; even a small price premium will generate a large percentage increase in the contribution margin	More favorable when variable costs represent a small share of the price so that each additional sale provides a large contribution margin	No understanding of costs	May or may not understand costs
Strategy	Designed to capture high margins at the expense of high sales volume	Setting price far enough below economic value to attract and hold a large base of customers	Decision to directly match competitor's price	Strategic decision not to use price to gain market share

pants judgments. In fact, Exhibit 14-18 provides a good list of competitive information needed in developing a pricing strategy.

Market Demand Pricing

The term *market demand* covers a broad range of factors to be considered in any pricing decision. The appropriate term for the consideration of all these factors is **demand analysis**. Demand analysis should be a major portion of any feasibility study because it is the most critical element in establishing a market. Demand analysis means more than demand for a product; it means, instead, asking whether there is a market sufficient in size that is willing and able to buy this product.

Sufficient demand means that there is a large enough market that wants the product. Let's simplify the problem and say the product is a Rolls Royce automobile. *Able to buy* means those consumers who actually have the means to buy it. For a Rolls Royce, the market is now considerably smaller. *Willing to buy* means those who have the means and also have the desire to buy the car. Now we have a very small market.

With this information (and much else, of course) the makers of the Rolls Royce can make a pricing decision. The target market is very small so large quantities will not be sold; this eliminates economies of scale. To make a reasonable profit or return on investment, the car will have to be priced considerably higher than its variable cost. Will the target market pay this inflated price? Research can determine that willingness and ability exist. In fact, for this market, another $10,000, $20,000, or $30,000 is not going to make much difference in the decision to purchase the car. The car can thus be priced at the appropriate level.

The same process applies to steak dinners, lobster, flambé desserts, vacations, hotel rooms, suites, or any other product that is put on the market. If there is not sufficient market willingness and ability to buy, the product is doomed to fail. It does not matter what the costs are, how much advertising you do, what the guarantee is, or anything else. The critical question is simply: 'What is the market acceptance level of price?'

The answer is not the simplest to find. Many don't find it until after the product has been marketed, for better or worse. But, a careful analysis of the market beforehand can make the pricing decision a great deal easier.

Another concept of demand analysis is called demand or **price elasticity**. The concept is covered fully in economics texts so it will not be discussed in detail here.* Generally speaking, high elasticity means that the higher the price, the lower the demand and vice versa. In the case of the Rolls Royce, we could say that within the target market, the product is inelastic—a few more thousand dollars is not going to affect demand. We cannot ignore the elasticity concept, and this concept must be applied to the appropriate target market. This is especially true in the case of hotels and restaurants where there are numerous alternatives. Alternative options increase the elasticity of the product. This is exactly why hotel rooms are subject to major discounting in order to obtain sufficient business.

There are a number of other points in regard to market demand that affect pricing that we will not discuss in detail, but are listed in Exhibit 14-19. This list is not all inclusive but only suggests elements of the identified and appropriate target markets that must be considered.

In the appendix to this chapter (at the end of the book) we discuss revenue management. Revenue management attempts to maximize revenue on each room sold at each point in time. This cannot be done without understanding demand.

EXHIBIT 14-18	Competitive Information for Pricing Strategies

1. Published competitive price lists and advertising
2. Competitive reaction to price moves in the past
3. Timing of competitors' price changes and initiating factors
4. Information on competitors' special campaigns
5. Competitive product line comparisons
6. Assumptions about competitors' pricing/marketing objectives
7. Competitors' reported financial performance
8. Estimates of competitors' costs—fixed and variable

9. Expected price retaliation
10. Analysis of competitors' capacity to retaliate
11. Financial viability of engaging in a price war
12. Overall competitive aggressiveness

Source: Marketing planning & strategy (5th ed.) by Jain. © 1997. Reprinted with permission of South-Western, a division of Thomson Learning: www. Thomsonrights.com. Fax 800 730-2215.

---

*The simplest and most common equation for elasticity is percent change in price divided by percent change in quantity sold equals degree of elasticity; that is, the proportionate change in demand relative to the change in price represents the degree of elasticity. If lowering or raising price has little effect on demand, demand is considered inelastic and vice versa.

| **EXHIBIT 14-19** | **Demand Pricing Considerations** |

USAGE

How is the product used?
- Business purposes?
- Pleasure?
- Personal?

What are the users' lifestyles?
- Do they use it because it is convenient or do they make a special effort to come here?
- Do they buy on price?
- Do they shop for the best price?

Is it the main usage in this area or an alternative?
- Do they use it regularly or just for special occasions?
- Do they use the whole product or just part of it?
- Do they use it seasonally, cyclically, at certain times, on certain days, during certain periods?

Are there different target markets?
- How many are on expense accounts?
- How many use credit cards?
- How many come through agents who receive commissions?

ALTERNATIVES

What are the competitive options?
- Upscale?
- Downscale?
- Other locations?

What are nonprice alternatives such as staying with friends or staying home?

DEMAND GENERATORS

Where are **demand generators?**
- How much do they generate?
- At what level do they generate?

Ways to identify sources of demand:
- Local business forecasts/publications
- Convention bureau reports
- Airport information

- Office building occupancies
- Local government forecasts
- Special events
- Health/outlook of top clients

DEMAND SATISFACTION

Is there unfulfilled demand, or is the market saturated?
- What is the market acceptance level?
- Is the quality level satisfied?
- What is the generic demand as opposed to the brand demand?

Are the available product/service mixes appropriate?

How many customers are in the market?
- Is the number increasing? Decreasing?

Do demand differentials reflect differential costs?

ECONOMIC CONDITIONS

How are economic conditions?
- Good?
- Bad?
- Inflationary?

Is promotional and discount pricing in vogue?
- Will we have to compete?

OTHER QUESTIONS TO ASK FOR TRANSIENT DEMAND

Are there special events or groups occurring next year? What are the chances of winning that business?

What portions of the year seem to show lots of opportunity? What portions look soft?

Does rate and mix strategy make sense given how the year looks?

Does the information gathered suggest that room nights in each segment will be up, down, or flat?

Are there new sources of business entering the market?

Are there key sources of business leaving the market?

Price Customization and Revenue Management

Yield management, now called **revenue management,** started in the hotel industry in 1988. Under the revenue management system, prices are opened and closed based on fluctuating demand and advance bookings. Like airline passengers, hotel customers pay different prices for the same room depending on when and how their reservation is made. Through the sophistication of computer technology, different prices are set depending on demand, day by day or hour by hour. The basic concept is to make reservations available to various market segments based on the value of each segment. These market segments, in part, are determined by their willingness to pay a specific rate.

For example, when demand is soft, lower rates requiring advance bookings remain available or are reopened for sale shortly before the dates that are not fully booked. When demand builds, the lower rates are removed so that customers then booking will pay higher rates. In other words, all levels of pricing are controlled by opening and closing them almost at will, with any variation in demand. It is said that the competitive advantages of revenue management are enormous:

Revenue management can dramatically increase revenues; maximize profits; greatly improve the effectiveness of market segmentation; open new market segments; strengthen product portfolio strategy; instantly improve cash flow; spread demand throughout seasons and times of day; and allow management to price according to market segment demand.[12]

What Revenue Management Is

Revenue management is a systematic approach to matching demand for services with an appropriate supply in order to maximize revenues. Before revenue management, this was largely limited to balancing group with individual demand, based on complementary booking times. Today, through computer technology, the attempt is to juggle all bookings and rate quotations so that on any given night the maximum revenue potential is realized.

Revenue management plans the ideal business mix for each day of the upcoming year and prices the rooms accordingly. It then adjusts the mix and prices on an ongoing basis as reservations do or do not develop.

Several factors make the use of revenue management suitable to the hotel industry. First, a hotel room is a perishable product, so it is sometimes better to sell it at a lower price than not to sell it at all, because of low marginal production costs and high marginal capacity costs (i.e., contribution margin pricing). Second, capacity is fixed and cannot increase to meet more demand. Third, hotel demand is widely fluctuating and uncertain, depending on the days of the week and seasons of the year. Fourth, different market segments have different lead times for purchase. A convention group might reserve hotel rooms three years in advance; a pleasure traveler, two months; and a business person, a week. Fifth, hotels have great flexibility in varying their prices at any given time.

These factors are very similar to the airline industry and represent the requisite conditions for a successful revenue management program. Although an operational tool, revenue management requires hotels to be market oriented. Knowledge of market segments, their buying behavior, and the prices they are willing to pay is essential for maximum success.

Revenue Management Practices

The essential rules of revenue management for hotels have been said to be as follows:

- Set the most effective pricing structure.
- Limit the number of reservations accepted for any given night or room type, based on profit potential.
- Negotiate volume discounts with groups.
- Match market segments with room type and price needs.
- Enable reservations agents to be effective sales agents rather than merely order takers.[13]

We have added the following:

- Provide reasons for lower rates, such as advance purchase time, payment in advance, nonrefundability, length of stay, and so on, for a variety of market segments. Marriott has done this deliberately to put the trade-off decision in the hands of the customer. In industry jargon, this is called "fences."
- Be consistent across central reservation system (CRS), property reservationists, travel agents, and other intermediaries so that quoted rates are the same. This is rate parity discussed earlier in the chapter.

Some booking systems have incorporated a set of rules called inventory "nesting." Nesting assures that high value rates are never closed for sale when lower value rates are available. In other words, any rooms allocated to lower rates can also be sold at higher prices; if you know how to bargain, you win; if you don't, you get stuck. In another technique called "continuous nesting," instead of allocating a certain number of rooms to each rate program, a minimum rate for acceptance is established. Each reservation request is compared to the minimum rate, called the "hurdle" rate. Any request below the hurdle rate is rejected. A hurdle rate is set for each future date by room category. In continuous nesting, the total price for a multiday stay is compared to the sum of the hurdle rates across those days. If the total price does not exceed the sum of the hurdle rates, it is rejected. For example, if the hurdle rate is $100, $200, and $150 for Tuesday, Wednesday, and Thursday, respectively, someone wanting all three nights would have to pay $450 or $150 per night. All this leads to a variety of acceptances and rejections of room requests by various segments. The length of stay and the rates they are willing to pay are useful facts in accepting or rejecting a discounted group booking.

Although the practice of revenue management has its applications for the hotel industry, the authors feel strongly that a marketing approach needs to be employed in conjunction with revenue management. An operations approach to revenue management would be to offer the same room at different rates to the customer depending on what the market will bear, similar to the airlines. For all of the reasons a hotel stay is different from an airline flight, so too should be the marketers approach to revenue management.

The revenue management system of a hotel should be set up to offer different categories of rooms for different prices. A hotel has an opportunity to create many different types of guest rooms, some more desirable than others. An effective hotel revenue management system will open and close categories of rooms, giving the customer greater value for higher pricing.

Benefits of Revenue Management

We have only touched on the rudiments of revenue management, which are sufficient for an introduction to the process. Now we will look at the benefits.

Yield.   Yield is the ratio between actual and potential room revenue. Actual revenue is received from room sales. Potential revenue is what a hotel would have received if their rooms were sold at full price or rack rates. Keep in mind, of course, that for this to be realistic, the full price rates must be realistic. Rack rates that are rarely achieved have little meaning for true yield ratios. Also realize that a hotel will have any number of different rates, including suite rates. All these must be calculated to determine a true yield ratio. Unlike airlines, hotels cannot ignore the incremental revenue of food and beverages. Yield takes into account both occupancy and room rates and can be illustrated by the example in Exhibit 14-20.

Thus, a hotel can reach the same, a better, or a poorer yield through different combinations of average rates and occupancy. Effective revenue management requires hotels to have access to many kinds of information, but the most basic element is demand forecasting. Hotels must be able to forecast the demand for each rooms category from each of its market segments, for any date in the future (the near future, at least). Thus, customer purchase behavior must be well understood—especially the lead time for purchase and price elasticity.

Revenue management, if used effectively, allows a hotel to manage its limited inventory better to maximize revenues. Short-term gains, however, must not substitute for long-term profits. Loyal and repeat customers will not appreciate the lack of room availability or special rates to which they are accustomed. They are likely to be more interested in price stability, so it may be a mistake not to honor a long-term customer's request for his usual rate. Hotel employees who are affected by revenue management systems, especially in reservations, sales, and front office departments, must be involved in the process so that they understand that outside the promoted objectives of revenue management (i.e., to maximize revenues), it is still critically important to keep loyal customers.

Why Revenue Management Works

Robert Crandall, the former chief executive of American Airlines, once said, "If I have 2,000 customers on a given route and 400 different prices, I am obviously short 1,600 prices." This one sentence captures the essence of revenue management because it argues that rather than setting prices by segment (e.g., weekend traveler versus midweek traveler, business guest versus leisure guest, etc.), firms should set prices by individual customers. The goal of this section is to show why Robert Crandall is correct and to explain why many of the chain hotels offer so many different prices on a given night.

Dolan and Simon provided a great example as to why multiple pricing works using an airline.[14] This example, of course, is equally applicable to the hotel industry by substituting the word *room* for *airline seat*. Exhibit 14-21 shows that the airplane has 380 seats and the variable cost per seat is $100, which means that this is the minimum price the airline seat would sell for; anything less and the airline would lose money. The maximum reservation price is $3,900, which means that at $3,901, no one would buy the seat. The area of potential is represented by the triangle ABC. Recall from high school (yes, there was a reason you learned geometry) that the area of a triangle is ½ the base × the height; for this example, the area is $722,000 [½ × 380 × ($3,900–$100)]. The goal of pricing is to capture all or as much as possible of this $722,000.

Therefore, if one price were to be chosen, the optimum price would be somewhere between $100 and

---

<table>
<tr><td>**EXHIBIT 14-20**</td><td>**Calculating Yield**</td></tr>
</table>

Hotel A has 500 rooms and an average rack rate of $180. On August 1, it had occupancy of 70 percent or 350 rooms sold, at an average rate of $140. (REVPAR figures are shown only as a point of comparison.)
- Yield = *Revenue Realized*
- Revenue Potential
- Revenue Realized = $140 × 350 rooms sold = $49,000 REVPAR $98.00 (49,000/500)

- Revenue Potential = $180 × 500 = $90,000
- Yield = $49,000/$90,000 = 54.4%

Hotel A can realize the same yield or a higher yield if it sells fewer rooms at a higher rate or more rooms at a lower rate:

Average Rate	Rooms Sold	Revenue Realized	Yield	REVPAR
$160	306	$48,960	54.4%	$98
$120	408	$48,960	54.4%	$98
$170	300	$51,000	56.7%	$102
$130	400	$52,000	57.8%	$104

$3,900. It turns out that if there is a linear sales response curve similar to Exhibit 13-21, then the optimal price is the middle between the lowest and highest price [($100 + $3,900)/2], which is $2000.

Exhibit 14-22 shows that at a price of $2,000, 190 seats will be sold, because this is where the lines intercept the linear sales response curve. The area in the square formed is calculated by multiplying the base by the height (yes, geometry again). The base is equal to the sales price ($2,000) minus the variable cost ($100) or $1,900. The height is the number of seats sold. The revenue captured is then

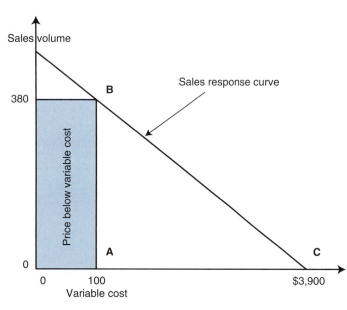

EXHIBIT 14-21 Airline sales response curve (1).

Source: Adapted from Dolan, Robert J., & Simon, Hermann. (1996). Power pricing: How managing price transforms the bottom line. New York: Free Press. Used by permission.

$361,000 or 50 percent of the total revenue. This means that 50 percent of the potential revenue was not earned. We can say the airline lost potential revenue of $361,000. Where did this revenue go? Exhibit 14-22 provides the answer.

The reader should note that in Exhibit 14-22 there is a group who did not buy the airline seat because their reservation price was under $2,000. This group is labeled X. There is another group who had a higher reservation price (labeled Y), but were able to buy the airline seat at a lower price. In this case, the airline left money on the table. The challenge is to transfer some of the revenue in X and Y to the firm. The firm does this by having more than one price.

To have more prices, however, the firm needs to create different products. In the airline industry, this is accomplished by different classes of services and restrictions on Saturday night stays, time of booking, and the like. For a hotel, a simple way to create different products is to treat rooms with a view as one type of room and rooms overlooking the parking lot as another type of room. Each room type can be priced differently. The price of a room for a guest staying four nights is also different from the price of a room for a one-night guest.

Exhibit 14-23 shows what happens when, instead of just one price, the airline adds two prices—a price for economy class and a price for business class. These prices are $1,367 and $2,633, which were determined at random for this example. The reader should immediately note that the areas of X and Y have decreased. This is because with a lower price, some of those who were priced out initially can now afford to fly. Similarly, some of those with a higher reservation price elected to fly business instead of economy. As shown in Exhibit 14-23, 127 people chose to fly business and 127 chose to fly economy. Again, these numbers are determined by the intersection of the prices with

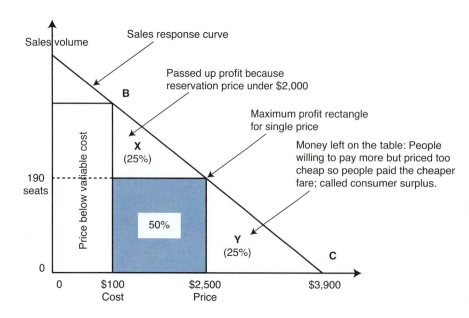

EXHIBIT 14-22 Airline sales response curve (2).

Source: Adapted from Dolan, Robert J., & Simon, Hermann. (1996). Power pricing: How managing price transforms the bottom line. New York: Free Press. Used by permission.

the linear response curve. The revenue for business class is $321,691 [($2,633 − ($100) × 127]. The revenue for economy is $160,909 [($1,361 − ($100) × 127]. The revenue for both classes combined is $482,600, which is an increase of $121,600 from just one price.

Please note again that the firm did not maximize revenue because some fliers were able to pay less than their reservation price and others still found the lower price too expensive. This suggests that perhaps another price, and hence another category of service, could be added. This is shown in Exhibit 14-24. Specifically, the categories of service are now first class ($2,950), business class ($2,000), and economy class ($1,050).

Exhibit 14-24 shows that each level of service (price point) has attracted 95 fliers. The revenue for economy class is $90,250 [(95 × ($1,050– $100)], for business class it is $180,500, and for first class it is $270,750. The combined total is $541,500, which means that by having three price points, the firm has captured 75 percent of the total possible revenue ($541,500/$722,000). Exhibit 14-25 summarizes the financial impact of multiple prices. It should be clear that if additional prices were added, more revenue would be captured.

The discussion of airline ticket prices should convince the reader that Robert Crandall is correct ("If I have 2,000 customers on a given route and 400 different prices, I am obviously short 1,600 prices". The key to multiple prices is that each price must represent a different product and that those who have a high reservation price will not be able to buy a lower-priced product. We now examine how to keep those with high reservation prices from buying less expensive products. This occurs through what is known as fences. Exhibit 14-26 shows some typical fences in the hospitality industry.

Fences must make sense to consumers. That is, customers must believe that the rate they are paying is based on their choices, not on greed by the firm. For instance, the consumer needs to think, "I need to pay more because having flexibility is more important than price." Or, "I am paying more because I cannot decide exactly what I want to do."

One fence that is not listed in Exhibit 14-26 is the "loyalty fence." This is a fence for frequent and loyal customers. The firm that offers multiple prices must be careful that the pricing decision does not destroy loyal customers' trust in the organization and, hence, their loyalty. In research undertaken in part by one of the authors, loyal hotel customers were presented with a hypothetical situation in which the hotel they were loyal toward increased its rate because of anticipated demand. Consumers were then asked how this would change their attitudes and behaviors toward the hotel that they claimed they were loyal toward. Findings indicated that 60 percent of the customers would ask the rate the next time they called for a reservation (normally, loyal customers do not ask about rates). In addition, 35.7 percent would call other hotels in the area to get their prices. Clearly, the loyal guest needs to be treated differently than the guest who comes for a one-night stay.

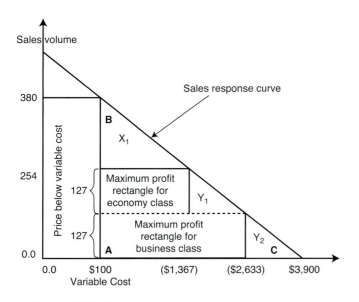

EXHIBIT 14-23 Airline sales response curve (3).

Source: Adapted from Dolan, Robert J., & Simon, Hermann. (1996). Power pricing: How managing price transforms the bottom line. New York: Free Press. Used by permission.

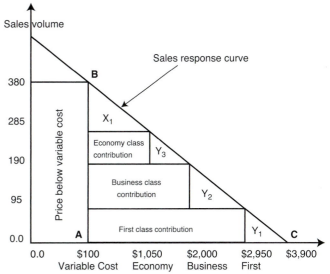

EXHIBIT 14-24 Airline sales response curve (4).

Source: Adapted from Dolan, Robert J., & Simon, Hermann. (1996). Power pricing: How managing price transforms the bottom line. New York: Free Press. Used by permission.

EXHIBIT 14-25	Summary of the Financial Impact of Multiple Prices					
	Single Ticket	First Class	Economy Class	First Class	Business Class	Economy Class
Price	$2,000	$2,633	$1,367	$2,950	$2,000	$1,050
Sales volume	190	127	127	95	95	95
Total passengers	190	254		285		
% increase passenger count from one price	N/A	33.6% (254 – 190)/190		50% (285 – 190)/190		
Contribution	$361,000	$482,600		$541,500		
Money left on table/passed up	$361,000	$239,400		$180,500		

EXHIBIT 14-26	Potential Fences			
Rule Type	Advanced Requirement	Refundability	Changeability	Must Stay
Advance purchase	3-day	Nonrefundable	No changes	Weekend
Advance reservation	7-day	Partially refundable (% refund of fixed $)	Change to dates of stay, but not number of rooms	Weekday
	14-day		Changes, but pay fee; must still meet rules	
	21-day	Fully refundable	Full changes; nonrefundable	
	30-day		Full changes allowed	

International Pricing

Pricing is an even more complex variable of the marketing mix in the international marketplace. There are two main reasons for this beyond the usual complexities of pricing. First, the monetary exchange rates fluctuate on a daily basis. These rates fluctuate radically during either national or international economic cycles and affect every international visitor as well as local guests. Second, pricing tactics by locally owned competitors can send rate structures into a tailspin.

The president of an international hotel company with worldwide properties once said to one of the authors, "We're not in the hotel business; we're in the monetary exchange business." Although this statement is not to be taken literally, it demonstrates the concerns of a company operating internationally. Probably one of the greatest problems in this segment is pricing both for the native of a host country and for the international traveler, each of whom may have totally different perspectives of the price–value relationship.

Various practices also occur in different countries. French hotels, for example, quote "straight" rates; in other words, for the ordinary traveler, the rack rate (or rate posted with the government by law) is usually the rate you

pay. * Thus, the bargaining process discussed earlier in the chapter does not occur in France, regardless of occupancy. At least you know what you are going to pay without all the hassle. Thus, France, or any other country, may become either a bargain or costly, depending on the exchange rate between that country and the one you are coming from at the time that you travel.

Traveling with exchange rates in mind is tricky business. Consider the following scenario: Once, an American could book a room in an American company–operated hotel in Acapulco through an American travel agency for

---

*This is also true in much of Europe. Many European countries also use an official or unofficial rating system based on the "number of stars system." There is minimum overlap in the rates between hotels with different star ratings. The ratings also indicate the physical facilities available. Thus, customers know pretty well what the property offers and at what rate range, when they choose a one-, two-, three-, four-, or five-star hotel, which have different meanings than in the United States. An Example in Paris of a five-star hotel is the Ritz; four-star, Le Meridien; three-star, Novotel; and two star, Ibis. One-star properties are close to hostels. There are efforts, however, to adopt a uniform rating system such as that used to rate hotels by Supranational (www.snrhotels.com/). Just about all hotels and restaurants in much of Europe add a 10 to 15 percent service charge for every service purchase.

$120 per night or could go to Mexico, exchange dollars for pesos, go to the hotel, and obtain the same room for $60. What may seem frustrating (or even devious) to the American customer is a major headache for the operator who is trying to make a profit while serving markets with totally different monetary values.

The same scenario is repeated worldwide, one way or another, in various international markets. It is no wonder that the tourist is bewildered, but it is no less wonder that the hotel company has a difficult problem on its hands. Now consider the same scenario when the market mix of the hotel is from many different countries, each with its own rate of exchange against the currency of the host country. The rate of exchange is also affected by the prevailing inflation rate in that country.

Furthermore, pricing tactics by locally owned competitors in developing countries can send rate structures into a tailspin. Consider the pricing tactics of "unscrupulous" competitors. These owners are primarily profit driven, not to mention high rate oriented. When business is good, everyone gets top price. When business is bad, many local owners operating in their own countries, as well as some foreign chains, will do anything to get business—which here means to cut room rates. With "deep pockets" for survival, these hotels discount to a level at which their international counterparts, who need to show a profit, cannot compete.

Pricing a hotel room in the international market can be extremely risky, yet this is a marketing tool that cannot be ignored. Heavy discounting when there simply isn't enough demand for the supply ends up being self-defeating for all. As an alternative destination for pleasure travel, for example, Singapore competes with Hong Kong. If the currency exchange rate in one of these countries is unfavorable, the international pleasure traveler may decide to go to the other instead. Thus, foreign country destination hotels compete on currency exchange rates over which they have no control.

Pricing across Multiple Channels of Distribution

The critical point that needs to be made here about pricing and the different channels of distribution is that there must be rate parity. As shown in Exhibit 14-14, rate parity means a uniformity of retail rates across different channels of distribution that provide the same product. The only way to stop brand price erosion is for parity to occur. As more and more reservations come through alternative channels, rate parity becomes more and more important.

The Last Word on Pricing

We close this chapter with some final conclusions. First, Exhibit 14-27 provides some guidelines from a customer pricing perspective on information that should be obtained for developing pricing strategies. Second, Exhibit 14-28 summarizes the pitfalls of pricing that have been found to

---

EXHIBIT 14-27   Information Needed for Pricing Strategies

1. The customer's value analysis of the product or service
2. The price level of acceptance in each major market
3. The price the market expects and the differences in different markets
4. The product's position on the life cycle curve
5. Seasonal and cyclical characteristics of the industry
6. Economic conditions now and in the foreseeable future
7. Customer relationship
8. Channel cost to figure in calculations and the mark up at each level
9. Advertising and promotion requirements and costs
10. The product differentiation that is needed

EXHIBIT 14-28   Common Mistakes in Pricing

1. Prices are too cost oriented. They are increased to cover increased costs and don't allow for demand intensity and customer psychology.
2. Price policies are not adapted to changing market conditions. Once established, they become "cast in cement."
3. Prices are set independent of the product mix rather than as an element of positioning strategy. Integration of all elements of the marketing mix is essential.
4. Prices ignore the customer psychology of experience, perception of value, and the total product. These are the true elements of price perception that will influence the choice process.
5. Prices are a decision of management, rather than of marketing.

occur most frequently. Because pricing is the most flexible part of the presentation mix, it requires constant evaluation. Those who evaluate their pricing should check their pricing strategies against this list.

■ Summary

Pricing is a complex marketing tool. However, it is first and foremost a marketing tool. Thus, by definition, pricing should be customer based and customer driven. Pricing is also a tangible aspect of the product or service offered. As such, it can be used to change and manipulate customer perception. The effective marketer must understand this process.

When establishing prices, it is critical to identify the target market objectives in terms of financial objectives, volume objectives, and customer objectives. The marketing mix strategy should be based on these objectives and the customers' needs and wants. Cost and competitive pressures establish constraints, but cost-oriented methods of pricing such as cost plus, cost percentage, break-even, and contribution margin pricing ignore the need for price-driven costing. Prices must also take into account overall market demand for the industry's products and services. Finally, marketers must understand customers' expectations and how they perceive the price–value relationship.

■ Key Terms

cost-driven pricing
product-driven pricing
variable cost
semivariable costs
fixed costs
cost-plus pricing
markup pricing
break-even pricing
price sensitive
volume sensitive
contribution margin pricing
value-based pricing
reference price
psychological pricing
price lining
odd-numbered pricing
value added services
Veblen effects
flexible service offerings

activity-based costing
pricing for profit
    maximization
target return on investment
    (ROI)
cash flow pricing
price stability
loss leaders
price penetration
price skimming
menu degustation
prix fixe
price leader
match pricing
neutral pricing
demand analysis
price elasticity
demand generators
revenue management

■ Discussion Questions

1. What pricing lessons can the hospitality industry learn from the boom times of the early 1980s, the tough times of the early 1990s, the boom times of the mid-to late 1990s, and the tough times of the early 2000s?
2. Discuss the three types of pricing objectives (financial, volume, and customer), how they are different, and how they overlap.
3. Why is using only cost percentage pricing methods not recommended as a marketing-driven option, especially in the hospitality industry?
4. Discuss why it is possible for the hotel industry to have room rates that can change on a daily basis. How would you deal with a guest who complains about her room rate because she has found that her friend is paying $20 less per night for the same type of room?
5. Is the maintenance of a stable price a viable objective? Why or why not?
6. Discuss your personal pricing elasticity in terms of restaurants; that is, at what point in the price value mode will you trade down?
7. Discuss how psychological pricing can make a product seem to have a higher price–value relationship.
8. Choose two common mistakes in pricing and apply them to a real-life hospitality establishment.

■ Group Projects

1. Obtain a copy of the *Wall Street Journal* or another major newspaper and locate the foreign exchange rates. Calculate the impact on different markets traveling to different countries, based on the currency of your own country (e.g., what does it cost an Italian to go to France, Thailand, or Japan and stay in the same price hotel in U.S. dollars?).
2. Define a certain type of room for a certain date in a certain hotel. See how many different rates you can get for this room.
3. Interview the managers of two or three hotels or restaurants. Determine how that property establishes various prices at various times (e.g., rooms, food, wine, liquor, and other services). Written or orally, evaluate these practices in the context of this chapter.

■ References

1. Ross, E. B. (1984, November-December). Making money with proactive pricing. *Harvard Business Review*, 145–155.

2. Abbey, J. (1983). Is discounting the answer to declining occupancies? *International Journal of Hospitality Management, 2* (2), 77–82.

3. Drucker, P. F. (1993, October 21). The five deadly business sins. *The Wall Street Journal*, p. A20.

4. Peter, J. P., & Olson, J. C. (2002). *Customer behavior and marketing strategy* (6th ed.) New York: McGraw-Hill Irwin, 459.

5. Bell, M. L. (1971). *Marketing: Concepts and strategy.* Boston: Houghton Mifflin, 857.

6. Jain, S. C. (1997). *Marketing planning & strategy* (5th ed.). Cincinnati: South-Western College Publishing, 400.

7. Monroe, K. B. (2003). *Pricing: Making profitable decisions* (3rd ed.). Boston: McGraw-Hill Irwin, 261–262.

8. Bowen, J., & Shoemaker, S. (1998). The antecedents and consequences of customer loyalty. *Cornell Hotel and Restaurant Administration Quarterly, 39* (1) 12–25.

9. Kahneman, D., & Tversky, A. (1979). Prospect theory: An analysis of decision under risk. *Econometrica, 47* (2), 263–291.

10. Travers, K. (n.d.). *PSM: A new technique for determining customer sensitivity to pricing.* Los Angeles: Plog Research.

11. Adapted from Anderson, J. C., & Narus, J. A. (1995, January-February). Capturing the value of supplementary services. *Harvard Business Review*, 75–83.

12. Makens, James, C. (1988, April). Yield management: A major pricing breakthrough. *Piedmont Airlines* (inflight magazine), p. 32.

13. Lieberman, W. (1993, February). Debunking the myths of yield management. *Cornell Hotel and Restaurant Administration Quarterly*, 34–41.

14. Dolan, Robert J., Simon, Hermann. (1996). Power pricing: How managing price transforms the bottom line. New York: Free Press.

CHAPTER 15

The Communications Mix

Advertising

Overview

This chapter begins with a repeat of the definition of the communications mix and the purposes it serves. This brief review addresses all the elements of the mix. Certain strategies should guide the communications effort. These are based on objectives and influenced by the stage of the consumer's knowledge and the type of influence that should be used. Proper research can improve the effectiveness of marketing communications by identifying the needs and objectives of the communications mix, as well as the success rate of any campaign.

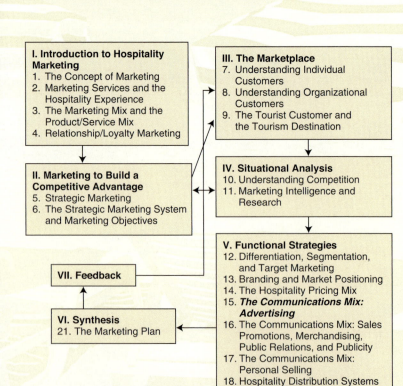

I. Introduction to Hospitality Marketing
1. The Concept of Marketing
2. Marketing Services and the Hospitality Experience
3. The Marketing Mix and the Product/Service Mix
4. Relationship/Loyalty Marketing

II. Marketing to Build a Competitive Advantage
5. Strategic Marketing
6. The Strategic Marketing System and Marketing Objectives

III. The Marketplace
7. Understanding Individual Customers
8. Understanding Organizational Customers
9. The Tourist Customer and the Tourism Destination

IV. Situational Analysis
10. Understanding Competition
11. Marketing Intelligence and Research

V. Functional Strategies
12. Differentiation, Segmentation, and Target Marketing
13. Branding and Market Positioning
14. The Hospitality Pricing Mix
15. *The Communications Mix: Advertising*
16. The Communications Mix: Sales Promotions, Merchandising, Public Relations, and Publicity
17. The Communications Mix: Personal Selling
18. Hospitality Distribution Systems
19. Channels of Distribution: Bringing the Customer to the Product
20. Interactive Marketing: Internet and Database Marketing

VII. Feedback

VI. Synthesis
21. The Marketing Plan

Larry Tolpin
President and Chief Creative Officer, Yesawich, Pepperdine, Brown & Russell

Larry Tolpin joined Yesawich, Pepperdine, Brown & Russell following 14 years with J. Walter Thompson and BBDO Worldwide. At JWT, he served as the company's worldwide creative director as well as being CEO and chief creative officer for JWT West and Canada.

At BBDO, Tolpin was the North American regional creative chairman, CEO and chief creative officer of BBDO South, and national creative director of BBDO Canada.

Tolpin has won over 500 major creative awards, including being named Creative Director of the Year three times by major trade publications. Prior to JWT and BBDO, Larry held senior posts at the Walt Disney Company and FCB West and was a managing partner of his own firm.

Marketing in Action

Larry Tolpin, President and Chief Creative Officer, Yesawich, Pepperdine, Brown and Russell

Please briefly explain how advertising campaigns are developed. Is this process different for print, radio, and TV campaigns?

When we start the creative process, I don't like to think about ads, I think about ideas. Our job is to provide fresh creative solutions to marketing problems. I always tell the creative team that they need to generate ideas that best crack the solution, whether it's through traditional or non-traditional advertising, public relations, a promotion, an event, or even a movie or book.

Regarding creating advertising for the various mediums, each medium has a different purpose. With TV as an example, which is a very visual medium in which you normally have 30 seconds or, if you're lucky, 60 seconds to do a TV commercial, obviously you have to be very single-minded and deliver a really simple message. Plus it must be surprising so that it will evoke some emotion with the viewer and get them to remember the commercial. Finally, it must sell.

Print is another story. You're competing against dozens of advertisements, and you have to be able to stop somebody before they flip a page. So you have to grab their attention right away and bring them into the body copy.

With the Internet or when you create "buzz" or "guerrilla" advertising, it's a whole different world. Guerrilla advertising could be—if you're selling adult beverages, as an example—something at the bottom of your glass or beer bottle with a message on it. It could be on a napkin, it could be in the bathroom, sometimes you see ads in the parking lot—literally, on the gate that goes up to let you in or out. I've seen ads on sidewalks in New York that say: "Look's like you need some new underwear." There are so many different ways of doing guerrilla advertising, especially if you're trying to reach young people who don't watch as much TV or folks that are on the go so much who you can't reach through traditional mediums.

How much consumer testing goes into a campaign?

It really varies. A lot of different agencies have different philosophies. I believe that the bulk of your testing should really go into your strategic thinking. Creativity does not happen in a vacuum. Breakthroughs in creativity are usually the result of breakthroughs in strategic thinking. Strategic leaps produce creative leaps.

If the strategy is a mirror image of everyone else in the category, the creativity will suffer a similar fate. If the strategy breaks new ground in the category, the creativity will too. It's more important to know exactly what you need to say—what's the one driving message to get across, what's the part that's going to invoke an emotional response to make the consumer say, "Wow, they're talking to me. I get it," versus necessarily testing the execution.

Sometimes we test "adcepts," which are concepts, but not as much as testing literally the body copy, or anything. It's very difficult to test emotions, especially in broadcast, when you try to test an emotional commercial on TV. Unfortunately, you are testing "animatics," which are still drawings or photographs, which totally lack emotion. Emotion is in the performance, the filming, the music. You can't ask a consumer to use their imagination because everyone thinks differently.

When we do direct response advertising, we will test different executions when the commercial is finished and we will know right away if someone clicks on your website or calls your number. The best advertising research is the journey around the consumer's head. What we really want to know is what dreams the consumer is dreaming and how we can position our brand in such a way that they will help these dreams come true. It's a technique borrowed from therapeutic counseling—tell me about your life and, in that story, I'll find a point of connection.

Pretesting of rough executions and ads is the refuge of the insecure. You are making the consumer the judge and jury of creative when it isn't even finished. Testing ends up putting a little fence around what you can talk about with consumers and usually kills great emotional ideas. The real challenge is to establish what concepts exist in the consumer's mind. If you can do that, you don't need to test.

How valuable is it to have celebrity spokespersons or celebrity voice-over?

Needless to say, it depends on the idea and the execution. I used to be the chief creative officer at BBDO, and we were known for using celebrities in many commercials. From Madonna to Britney Spears to Shaq for Pepsi to Tommy Lee Jones for Miller Brewing and to Donald Trump and Miss Piggy for Pizza Hut and Frito-Lay. Today, you hear Robert Redford for the voice of United Airlines, Angela Lansbury for Walt Disney World, Quentin Tarantino for Universal Studios, and William Shatner for Priceline.com.

We are currently talking to a few celebrities for a television project we are doing for Marriott. In short, when you use a celebrity, even just their voice, it lends instant familiarity and instant credibility and usually breaks through

a sea of commercials. Saying that, a great voice or celebrity can't save a bad idea.

What is the ideal length of time for an advertising campaign to run?

It really varies. If you're doing a commercial such as the 1984 Macintosh commercial, it only ran once during the Super Bowl. They had newspaper ads that ran before with a headline, "Don't go to the bathroom during this time or you're going to miss the best part of the Super Bowl." The commercial only ran once and it was almost like a big event around that commercial, with the premise "Why 1984 won't be the 1984 from Orwell's book." That was the introduction of Apple's Macintosh computer.

Sometimes you can run a good commercial, such as M&M's, for years. Or "A diamond is forever" from De Beers. In the travel industry, unfortunately, campaign themes seem to flip all of the time. When I worked on Delta, we used "Delta is ready when you are" because they used to have so many flights a day. But then a new ad manager changed it to "Delta Gets You There." I always thought that's the least an airline can do. Later on, they changed it to "Delta loves to fly and it shows." But after they started to lay off people, they needed to change it quickly. Just like United changed their theme line, "The friendly skies of United" after all of their cutbacks.

So I don't know if there is a definite answer to the question, How long should a campaign run? It's like the question, How much copy should you write? [It should stop] when the reader stops reading your ad. Or in the case of an ad campaign, it should stop running when it's not working anymore.

With the advent of products like TiVo, how do you stop consumers from speeding through a TV advertisement?

Truth be known, many of the commercials running these days are much better than the programming they run on. Even in the Super Bowl, a good portion of folks who watch the Super Bowl watch it mainly for the commercials.

Commercials must be intelligent with our choices of words if we hope to communicate clearly, but we must also entertain if we hope to engage and enchant the viewer. Remember, television is a visual medium. And the television execution is the vehicle to transport the idea and break through the clutter.

What are some key elements that get consumers to recall the advertisement?

As I said before, you must start with a great idea. An execution can't be an idea. It's only the vehicle to transport the idea. The fact is, you tend to remember execution for a short while. You tend to remember ideas for a long time.

When I was at BBDO, we used to create what we called "famous advertising." What I mean by that is to create advertising that people talk about, at home, around the water cooler, at Starbucks. Those were all based on great ideas with first class executions. I am a firm believer that it's more important to have a sharper nail than a heavier hammer. What I mean by this is that a great commercial or ad doesn't need as much in media support as a bad one.

We all remember our favorite TV spots, the ones we say, "Wow, I really loved that Anheuser Busch, Pepsi, or iPod commercial." And we also remember the ones we hate. But, unfortunately, we don't even notice most commercials. They're like wallpaper. The same goes for most print ads. That's because they lack a big idea and a great presentation.

In an earlier chapter of this book, we discussed VALS and other lifestyle segmentation strategies. How much are these lifestyle categories used in your advertising?

Before we start working on an ad, we definitely want a clearly defined group of not only demographics, but psychographics, because we want to know as much as we can about the consumer.

Where do you see hospitality advertising in five years, given the growing amount of competition for the consumer "eyeball"?

Hospitality advertising is so different from any other kind of advertising—you're competing against everybody, every day. Obviously the Internet is going to play a huge role because of how life has changed. We used to call up the airline or the travel agent; now, the bulk of people book online.

However, we still will have to do brand advertising. Whether that will be traditional or nontraditional, I don't know. I don't see television advertising going away soon. Perhaps network advertising will give way to more targeted spot buys on cable. Magazine, especially trade advertising, is here to stay. However, newspaper readership and advertising is declining every year, while the Internet is growing stronger and stronger.

Remember, the secret is to outsmart the competition, not to outspend them. Staying on the offense is key. You must embrace forward thinking because at the end of the day, the company with the best ideas wins.

For students who wish to enter the advertising field, how do you suggest they begin?

Well, there are different ways to begin, and it depends on where you want to go—the agency side or client side? For ad agencies, you can work in creative, strategic planning; account management; media planning and buying; public relations; and specialized areas such as branding, direct response, promotions, etc. On the client side, there are numerous opportunities as well, including marketing, advertising, public relations, interactive, and even in-house creative agencies for clients like Walt Disney World, Universal Studios, and most Las Vegas resorts.

There's an old expression that says account people come from MBA programs while creative people come from their mamas, because in most cases, either you're born creative or you aren't born creative. Schools can teach you the disciplines, but they can't teach you to be creative. If you're going to go on the client side or account management for an agency, it's good to have an MBA. If you're going into creative, I would recommend a degree in art, journalism, or English.

Unfortunately, very few universities have great advertising schools. Of course, there is the exception, but many students will get their undergraduate degree in the school of arts, communications, or business and then go to a two-year advertising specialty school, such as the Creative Circus in Atlanta or VCU in Virginia taught by advertising executives. The best things to do for students who want to go the agency route is to try and intern for an advertising agency or in-house agency. This way you can see if you like it and what you will need to succeed.

To wrap things up, let me quote Picasso, "A day without laughing is a wasted day." Whatever you do, find something you love to do. Work shouldn't be work. It should be fun. Or you will be miserable at it in more ways than one.

Any other comments or questions you think we should be asking?

To produce great advertising, you need three things in an ad agency:

- The management that wants it
- The creative people who can produce it
- Most important of all, the clients who will buy it

Rather than view creativity as dangerous, you should deem it mandatory. Apple, Nike, and Pepsi are household names because of the result of breakthrough advertising ideas. The client who protects the idea is just as important as the person who comes up with the idea.

Used by permission from Larry Tolpin.

The communications mix is what we have come to know as traditional marketing. Again, it is useful to repeat the definition: All communications between the firm and the target market that increase the tangibility of the product/service mix, that establish or monitor consumer expectation, or that persuade customers to purchase. Some elements of this definition need further explanation. Note the phrase *between the firm and the target market.* This tells us that communications are a two-way street. It is not simply what the firm does to communicate, but it is also the feedback from the target market that tells the firm how well it is communicating and how well it is providing the services promised. This, of course, is part of relationship marketing.

Second, the definition says that communications *increase the tangibility of the product/service mix.* As we have seen, the presentation mix does the same thing. The difference is that the presentation mix does this with tangible physical evidence of the product. Communications do it with words and pictures, not the product itself.

Third, communications *establish or monitor consumer expectations.* Not only do communications create expectations, but they also signal when expectations change or are not being met.

Finally, marketing communications *persuade customers to purchase*—we hope. Although communications, particularly in advertising and public relations, may be crafted to achieve such nonbehavioral outcomes as the creation of awareness or the modification of a brand image, the ultimate goal of most marketing communications is to induce purchase.

The Communications Mix

The communications mix contains five elements:

1. Advertising
2. Sales promotion
3. Merchandising
4. Public relations and publicity
5. Personal selling

We will discuss each of these in turn in this and subsequent chapters. First, in Exhibit 15-1 we relate an example to demonstrate the elements of the mix.

Communications Strategy

Communications strategies are concerned with the planning, implementing, and control of persuasive communication with customers. The strategy is the plan, and tactics represent the actions. This is an important distinction be-

cause it is very easy, in implementing marketing communications, to get bogged down in the tactics. When this happens, communications are often not consistent with strategic objectives.

For example, in personal selling we might call on a client hoping to convince him to book his next group meeting at our hotel. Knowing when his next meeting will be held, we might try to persuade him to book that period. That is a tactic. But if he has already reserved at another hotel for that meeting, the result is no sale, and we will have to go through the same process for his subsequent meeting.

Instead, we might use strategic persuasion. Our strategic objective is to persuade the client that our hotel, of all hotels, can best serve his meeting needs. We don't mention dates, we don't "sell" our product; we address his needs. Instead of a "no sale," we receive this response: "I've already booked our next meeting, but I'll get in touch with you for the one after that." If our persuasion has been successful, he will.

In advertising, the same concept applies. The first step in the development of a communications strategy is to decide what our objectives are and what we hope to accomplish. These are broad objectives that will serve as an umbrella for all communications efforts; that is, they will permeate the advertising, selling, promotion, merchandising, and public relations. Some, or all, of these elements may also have subobjectives, but they will all be subsumed under the main objectives. Similarly, we may have more than one objective at a time. In any case, we want the objectives to be congruent and not in conflict with each other.

There are many possible main objectives. Here, we list just a few:

- Create or change an image
- Position (both objectively and subjectively)
- Provide benefits
- Offer solutions to problems
- Create awareness
- Create belief
- Stir emotions
- Change attitudes
- Create expectations
- Stimulate action

These are all strategic objectives, and one or more may guide the communications process.

The communications process has six broad stages, which are shown in Exhibit 15-2. The first of these stages is "to whom to say it." This stage sets the guidelines in terms of featured attributes, positioning, benefits offered, promises made, and so forth. Consider the ads for two hotels (Exhibit 15-3, 15-4) and two restaurants (Exhibit 15-5, 15-6) for the purpose of relating the communications

EXHIBIT 15-1	Communications Mix in Practice

Jim and Paula Johnson saw a news item in the paper that a new restaurant was going to be created in a long-abandoned, historic stone mill down by the river. "It's about time," they thought, "that this town had a new restaurant. This one sounds intriguing. Any restaurant in an old stone mill has to be an exciting concept, and it would have to have good food."

Jim and Paula forgot about the restaurant, except when someone mentioned it during a bridge game or in casual conversation, until about six months later. Then they saw a half-page ad in the newspaper. The ad announced the grand opening of the Old Stone Mill restaurant on the next Friday night, featuring fine cuisine and excellent service. There was an enticing picture of the old stone mill by the river. They couldn't go Friday, but immediately made reservations for the next night, Saturday, when the grand opening special drink prices and hors d'oeuvres would still be featured.

On Saturday night they drove with some friends to the restaurant. They had difficulty finding it because the roads down by the river were confusing and not clearly marked. They finally found the restaurant but couldn't find any nearby parking spaces. It was a clear night with almost a full moon, however, and they found the walk to the restaurant invigorating. They looked forward to a great meal and a great experience. When Jim and Paula got to the restaurant, they found a long line waiting to get in. Because they had reservations, they passed by the line and went into the cocktail lounge. They had come early to take advantage of the special offer. They found the lounge packed, with no seating space available. The special hors d'oeuvres had all been devoured. They tried to find someone to take their drink order, to no avail, so they went looking for the hostess. They were 30 minutes early for their reservation, but the hostess told them there would be a two-hour wait for their table. "What the heck," they said, "it's always this way on Saturday night anywhere," and decided to wait. They were seated an hour and 45 minutes later.

They waited a long time for a waiter. The waiter suggested a menu item that he said was a special and a unique creation of the restaurant owners. Jim and Paula both decided to order it. They then waited a similar length of time until they were served. The waiter explained that the special dish required extra care and time to prepare. On the table, however, was a table tent featuring a carafe of house wine and some shrimp canapés at a special price. They ordered this to have while waiting for their dinner, and it came quickly. By the time the meal came, they were filled up on the canapés, salad, bread, and cheese and were not very hungry. The meal was delicious, but they had lost their appetites. They wanted to have another wine with dinner, but were never brought a wine list so didn't order it. Later, when they learned of the wine prices, they were just as happy that they hadn't. They didn't complain, but as they left, they vowed never to go there again and to tell their friends what kind of experience they had.

A month later, the ad rep from the local paper visited the same restaurant to solicit some advertising. The owners were glad to see him because they were having real problems. The restaurant had opened to rave review, although one restaurant critic mentioned the slow and inefficient service. At first, it was so busy that they couldn't keep up. Lately, however, business had dropped off dramatically. There had been very few complaints; in fact, almost everyone praised the food, the décor, and the concept. The owners figured that what they needed now was a good advertising campaign.

This story dramatizes the kinds of problems that arise in marketing communication. The Johnsons felt frustrated because they were not satisfied with the restaurant. They wished they had complained to the management. In that wish, they were typical of consumers who feel reluctant and frustrated in not communicating their true feelings to business organizations.

The restaurant owners also felt frustrated. Apparently people were not returning to the restaurant, and there had to be a reason. On the other hand, the owners knew their food was superior and their atmospherics were unique. They wished that they had spent more time talking to their customers to see what they liked and disliked about the restaurant. In that wish, they were typical of business owners who feel they could do a better job of communicating with their customers.

The example illustrates a lack of effective marketing communication. The restaurant has frustrated its customers by not being responsive to their needs. Customers complain to each other by word of mouth, but don't communicate their feelings to the restaurant management. Both parties would like to have a favorable relationship with the other but don't know how to go about it. What the restaurant needs now is a communications strategy that will address the requirements of both parties in an efficient and effective manner. The anecdote demonstrates all the elements of the communications mix: publicity, advertising, promotion, personal selling, direct mail and merchandising, as well as word of mouth. By the time we get through Chapter 17, we will see how all of these elements apply in this anecdote and how the restaurant owners should develop a communications campaign. This chapter will start the process.

process to an actual strategy. Each ad has a different strategic objective.

To Whom to Say It

The first stage of the communications strategy is to define the target market. The appropriate research should be done and the needs and wants of the target market clearly identified. The target markets for both Exhibits 15-3 and 15-4 are vacationers, but that's too simplistic. Do the target markets for the properties in the advertisements have the same needs and wants? Not really. The advertisement for the Fairmont Hotels in Bermuda (Exhibit 15-3) focuses on the sophisticated traveler, as evidenced by the use of the terms that refer to expensive gems such as sapphire, emerald, and diamond. In addition, the use of the phrases "pink sands of private beach" and "executive 18-hole golf course also suggests that properties must be very nice and expensive. Notice that nowhere is price mentioned.

 Web Browsing Exercise

As this book is getting ready to go to print, the latest marketing trend is podcasting. Use your favorite search engine and type in the word *podcasting*. Be prepared to discuss the definition of podcasting, its origins, its growth over the last couple of years, and its future. Also be sure to address how a hospitality organization (restaurant, hotel, or tourist destination) might use podcasting as part of its advertising strategy.

The advertisement for Ohana Hotels and Resorts (Exhibit 15-4), on the other hand, also focuses on the vacationer. However, the emphasis is not at all on the sophisticated traveler, but instead on the more casual family/

EXHIBIT 15-2	Six Stages of a Communications Strategy

Stage	Possible Strategic Element
1. To whom to say it	The target markets(s)—those who either use our product or who we want to persuade to use it.
2. Why to say it	Prior users—persuade to use again or more often: <ul><li>Offering new benefits</li><li>Offering specials at slow periods</li><li>Show improvements</li><li>Develop relationships</li><li>Recapture, reposition</li><li>Adopt as first choice</li></ul> Nonusers: <ul><li>Get interested, get attention</li><li>Make part of evoked set</li><li>Position</li><li>Arouse desire</li><li>Provide more information to evaluate, explain features</li><li>Persuade to use</li></ul>
3. What to say	<ul><li>Awareness, to desire, to buy</li><li>Awareness, interest, evaluation, trial</li><li>Logos, pathos, ethos</li><li>Cognitive, affective, conative.</li></ul>
4. How to say it	Humor, sex, cost/value, bargain, slice of life, lifestyle, mood, atmospherics, testimonial, service, quality, action, etc.
5. How often to say it	Depends a lot on budget, reach, effectiveness
6. Where to say it	Selecting the media or personal selling that would most likely reach the target market most effectively and efficiently

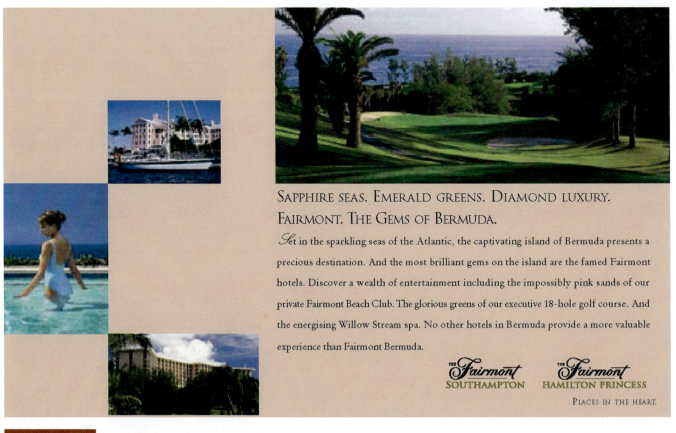

SAPPHIRE SEAS. EMERALD GREENS. DIAMOND LUXURY.
FAIRMONT. THE GEMS OF BERMUDA.

Set in the sparkling seas of the Atlantic, the captivating island of Bermuda presents a precious destination. And the most brilliant gems on the island are the famed Fairmont hotels. Discover a wealth of entertainment including the impossibly pink sands of our private Fairmont Beach Club. The glorious greens of our executive 18-hole golf course. And the energising Willow Stream spa. No other hotels in Bermuda provide a more valuable experience than Fairmont Bermuda.

THE *Fairmont*
SOUTHAMPTON

THE *Fairmont*
HAMILTON PRINCESS

PLACES IN THE HEART.

EXHIBIT 15-3	This advertisement for the Fairmont Hotels in Bermuda focuses on the use of exclusive gems to make tangible the high quality of the resort.

Source: Fairmont Hotels, Bermuda. Used by permission.

EXHIBIT 15-4   This advertisement for Ohana Hotels and Resorts focuses on words such as *family and friends* and is crafted to suggest it is a property where you can bring kids.
Source: Outrigger Hotels & Resorts. Used by permission.

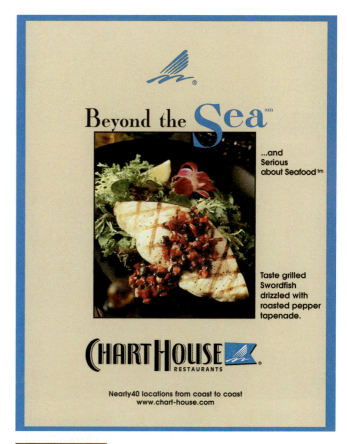

EXHIBIT 15-5   This advertisement for Chart House Enterprises, Inc., positions the restaurant as a place for fish.
Source: Chart House Enterprises, Inc. Used by permission.

friends traveler. This is evidenced by the pictures of the women in the very casual clothes, the focus on "you're among friends," and the highlighting of the buffet. The ad also shows the price per night. This is in contrast to the previous advertisement where price is not mentioned. The feeling for the Fairmont ad is, "If you have to ask the price, you cannot afford it."

The advertisement for the Chart House (Exhibit 15-5) is for the consumer who likes fresh seafood and casual, relaxed dining. This is suggested by the fact that they show a picture of the seafood. They are promoting the product, not the experience. In contrast, the advertisement for the Newport Room (Exhibit 15-6) is promoting a more formal experience. This is evidenced by the emphasis on the fact that the restaurant is "so elegant, it even comes with diamonds." Rather than showing an example of a food item, the reader is left to ponder what the restaurant might be like and the experience one would have eating there. Here one would imagine that users are definitely couples who dress for dinner, like really fine food and service, drink wine, and want romance, peace, and quiet.

Tourism Marketing Application

An example of a destination promoting to a specific target market is Queensland, Australia. Specifically: "Target markets for the Fraser Coast destination were identified as families, and couples aged over 45 without dependent children, from the primary source regions of Brisbane, South East Queensland (SEQ), Regional Queensland, and Northern New South Wales, and secondary source regions of Sydney and Melbourne. As indicated by research, intrastate consumer awareness of the Fraser Coast destination is sound (although limited), and based mainly around knowledge of Hervey Bay, Fraser Island, and Rainbow Beach. Therefore, the focus has been to continue building awareness of the key attractions within the region and to convert this awareness into a genuine desire to travel to the destination." (www. tq.com. au/industry/knowledge-banks/fraser-coast/ fraser-coast-destination-management-plan/ section-2—destination-analysis/2.5-destination-marketing.cfm, accessed on April 2, 2006)

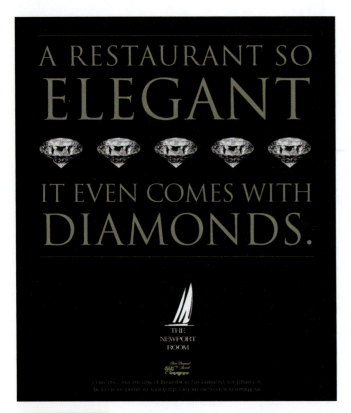

EXHIBIT 15-6 This advertisement for the Newport Room positions the restaurant as a fine dining establishment.

Source: Fairmont Hotels & Resorts, Bermuda. Used by permission.

Why to Say It

At this stage is where the marketing strategy comes in. We are concerned with what effect we expect the communication to have; that is, what we want to accomplish. Some of these purposes are shown in Exhibit 15-2.

The strategy for the Fairmont is to position the resort as a quiet, sophisticated alternative to other destination resorts in Bermuda and to tell the target market, "We are one of the gems of Bermuda." The ads are designed to communicate how the Fairmont hotel differs from the numerous other resorts on the island of Bermuda.

The strategy for Ohana is to position it as a family resort with an array of facilities and recreational amenities for the whole family or group of friends. Notice the advertisement for the buffet suggesting that you can cook your own food—certainly a good thing for those whose children are "picky" eaters. Also, suggesting that you "go early, it can get crowded" implies that it is not the place for those who want intimacy.

In Exhibit 15-5, the strategy is to position the Chart House as the place for fish. Again, it is positioned by attribute (seafood). Because the dish looks appetizing but not pretentious, it says that it probably offers a relaxed atmosphere.

In Exhibit 15-6, the strategy is to position the Newport Room as a preeminent fine dining restaurant, as evidenced by the use of five diamonds and the jacket and tie requirement. It hopefully makes the restaurant part of the "evoked set" the next time they want that perfect, romantic dining experience.

> **Tourism Marketing Application**
> India and Singapore provide an example of what to say. In August 2005, the tourism boards of India and Singapore announced that they planned to advertise that Kolkata (Calcutta), India, and Singapore could be visited as a single seamless attractive tourist package. The target market was business tourists from western countries. The distance between these two areas is 2870 KM. As a point of perspective, the distance between New York and London is 5585 KM. (www.bridgesingapore.com/4bsnews_7oct.htm, accessed April 2, 2006)

What to Say

This stage evolves from Stage 2 (why to say it). It deals with the method chosen to achieve the strategic objective and is based on knowing some things about the target market. It deals with four models of communications strategy. The first two deal with the consumer stage, and the second two deal with the communications effort.

Model 1. One thing we need to know about the target market is what stage it is in. Traditional models of persuasion assume that consumers move through essentially six steps that ultimately lead to purchase behavior (although this may not be true; think about all of the advertising you can remember for products or services that you *didn't* purchase and the phenomenon we call "impulse purchase"). The steps are not equal: Some may be achieved quite rapidly or even simultaneously, but when there is more psychological or economic commitment or risk involved in the purchase (high involvement), consumers will take longer to climb the steps and each step will be more important. The steps through which the consumer progresses describe the consumer's state of mind:

1. Is unaware of the existence of the product or service
2. Is aware of the existence of the product or service
3. Is knowledgeable about specific feature or benefits of the product or service
4. Has favorable attitudes toward the product or service
5. Prefers the product or service over other alternatives
6. Intends to purchase the product or service the next time the need arises

7. Actually purchases the product or service
8. Has purchased the product or service before

Model 2.   This model of consumer behavior, called the "adoption process model," contends that adoption, or the purchase of a product, is a process. The process starts with awareness because obviously consumers are unlikely to buy something about which they are not aware. Awareness can develop simply from walking down a street and seeing a restaurant entrance. It can also develop from seeing a billboard on the highway, seeing an advertisement in the newspaper, and, of course, from word of mouth. Apart from word of mouth, most awareness in the hospitality industry is usually created by advertising and public relations.

Once the consumer is aware, the next step in the hierarchy is interest. If consumers are interested, they seek further information and details about the product, such as its features, the cost, how to buy it, and so forth. This information may be, and often is, obtained from exposure to advertising. In many situations, however, it may come through the consumer's own initiative—that is, consumers will call or e-mail to obtain more information on their own. Personal selling also plays an important part in providing information when marketing to groups and meeting planners.

The third stage in this model is evaluation. At this stage consumers ask themselves a number of questions: Of what relevance is the product to me? Does it fulfill my needs? Does it solve my problems? Does it do it better than someone else's product? Is it worth the risk? Advertising, personal selling, and public relations can all play important roles at this stage. If the evaluation is favorable, the consumer then evolves to the next stage, trial.

Trial of the hospitality product usually means the same as purchase; there is really no other way to try it. The promotion and merchandising parts of the communications mix are often used to induce trial; beyond that, use is induced by the other mix elements. This is the fourth stage.

If the trial is favorable, consumers may "adopt" the product and become repeat customers. The final stage is

that they may then tell others, thus becoming sources of awareness, information, and evaluation for others who are at various stages of the evaluation process. Marketers can influence adoption through performance and relationship marketing, which is why the quality of these two factors is so critical to successful marketing.

Marketers should know the stage of their target market before developing marketing communications. This knowledge will strongly influence the communications strategy and objectives, which should be developed with reference to the two models of "influence," which are models 2 and 3.

Model 3.   Aristotle promulgated three basic rules of persuasion centuries ago:

- *Logos:* logic and reasoning (e.g., "It is a safe place to visit"). These are rational appeals.
- *Pathos:* emotions (e.g., "the destination provides the opportunity to 'refresh'"). These are emotional, mood appeals.
- *Ethos:* source credibility (e.g., "a respected restaurant critic gives it four stars"). These are belief appeals, evidence.

For the marketer, these rules represent commonsense treatment in communicating with the target market. Logos, pathos, and ethos are a refinement in Stage 3 of communications, shown in Exhibit 15-2.

Model 4.   We next use the stages of the customer's attitudes to judge the effect we want the communications to have and the strategy to obtain that effect. These stages are shown in Exhibit 15-7.

Using these models, we can evaluate the four ads shown earlier. The ads for the Fairmont Hotel and the Newport Room both use pathos (emotions) to pull readers into the advertisement and eventually encourage them to purchase. The Newport Room also uses ethos (source credibility via the five diamond award) to create a desire to buy and the trial stage.

Ohana's ad is based more on logos (logic and reasoning). It addresses the affective stage to develop favorable

EXHIBIT 15-7 **Attitudinal Components and Their Impact on Communications Strategy**

Consumer Stage	Effect Stage	Strategy
Cognitive: the stage of thoughts/beliefs	Create awareness, beliefs	Provide information, get attention, inform, remind
Affective: the stage of emotion	Change attitudes and feelings, get involved, evaluate	Position, create benefits and image, stir emotions, arouse
Conative: the stage of motivation and intention	Stimulate and direct desires, adopt	Move to action, reinforce expectation, persuade (see Exhibit 14-8)

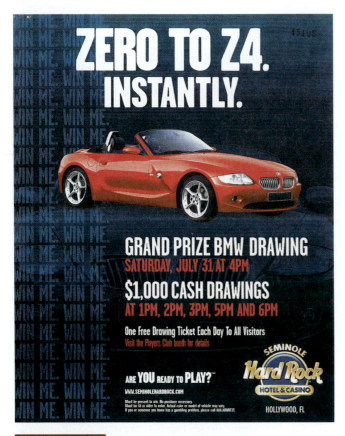

EXHIBIT 15-8   This advertisement for Hard Rock Café is meant to appeal to the conative consumer stage.

Source: Seminole Gaming. Used by permission.

attitudes toward the product and, finally, the evaluation and trial stages. The Chart House advertisement is also clearly aimed at the logos level. The fish looks good, so it must be. It attends to the affective stage to develop preference for the product over other possibilities and, finally, the trial stage.

How to Say It

Once the first three stages of communication strategy have been considered, the creative juices of everyone tend to focus on the advertising copy and its appeal to the customer, the execution stage. Of the many, many creative options, the search is for the one that will work best, the one that most precisely accomplishes the objectives consistent with the identified target market. Following are some of the elements used to generate appeal:

- Humor
- Sex
- Cronyism
- Surprise
- Complexity
- Price/value

- Slice of life
- Lifestyle
- Self-improvement
- Mood
- Testimonial
- Quality

Tourism Marketing Application

Tourist destinations certainly promote images of their destination, as discussed in Chapter 9. However, destinations may also use slogans or positioning statements (discussed in Chapter 13) to capture attention. Australia's tag line, "Where the bloody hell are you?" appears after the opener "I've bought you a beer" has created quite the buzz because of its shock value. Governments of Canada and England complain of the language and may ban the advertisements. The advertisement did accomplish its goal, which is to get people talking about Australia. (www.smh.com.au/news/world/bloody-hell-now-its-our-beer/2006/03/22/1142703389739.html, accessed April 2, 2006)

The creative strategy for the Fairmont is to emphasize the product's beautiful seas, physical ambience, high quality, and uniqueness. For Ohana, it is fun, family, friends, dancing, and food. The creative strategy at the Chart House is to "conch out," relax, and enjoy (lifestyle). And for the Newport Room, it is elegance, quality, romance, and atmospherics.

Compare these ads to the GAP model discussed in Chapter 2.

- How do the ads fit this model?
- What expectations do they create?
- What problems do they solve?
- What is the price–value relationship and the risk?

Also, consider all four ads in terms of the definition of the aims of the communications mix:

- Establish communications between the firm and the target market
- Increase the tangibility of the product/service mix
- Establish or monitor consumer expectations
- Persuade consumers to purchase

These are the things to be accomplished. Consider the ads also in terms of the following:

- Selective perception
- Selective attention
- Selective comprehension
- Selective acceptance
- Selective retention
- Salience, determinance, and importance

How Often to Say It

The next decision is both a consumer-driven and a budget-driven one. Repetition has been shown to help build awareness and enhance product recall over time. Perhaps ironically, continued repetition of the same message also produces an undesirable outcome called "wear out," or the gradual decline in the ability of the advertising execution to capture and retain the attention of the intended audience (this phenomenon is referred to as "habituation to a stimulus" in the psychology of learning). Therefore, careful thought and planning are required to determine the number of executions that will be used in the campaign, as well as their frequency of exposure.

 Web Browsing Exercise

Use your favorite search engine and type in the words "advertising recall." Read some of the sites listed and be prepared to discuss the factors that impact recall. How can hotels, restaurants, and tourism destinations create more recall?

Where to Say It

Where, as used here, applies to the various components of the communications mix. The examples used earlier were advertisements, but only for ease of illustration. If we use advertising, then we must select the appropriate media, offline or online, electronic or print, and out of home. Electronic media include television, radio, and now a multitude of online services. Print media include newspapers, magazines, and direct mail. Out-of-home media include billboards, bulletins, transit displays, and the like. The demography, lifestyle, and social values of the target audience are all evaluated when composing a media plan to ensure that the final media selection "reaches" the target both effectively and efficiently.

Research for the Communications Mix

If we have to know the target market in order to develop the optimal communications mix and strategy, it follows that the best results will be obtained through media research. This will entail a comprehensive review of the readership or viewership data gathered and measured by the media under consideration. In the long run, good research will ensure that communications dollars deliver the best return in terms of audience delivery and, hopefully, response.

We recognize that many properties, particularly individually owned restaurants, will not have such involved communications mixes as those described here. Even these properties, however, will most likely engage in merchandising, sales promotion, and some advertising, if not personal selling. Good public relations, however, can be used by any business. As such, research should be conducted both internally and externally. The following guidelines apply to even the smallest business, if in somewhat modified form. There are five major questions to be answered.

Where Are We Now?

In other words, How are we perceived? Examples might be "expensive," "luxurious," "good service," "good food," "full facilities," "atmospheric," "cheap," "unfriendly," "run down," "old and tired," or any number of other things. Here are other questions to be asked:

- How do we compare with the competition?
- What do their customers think of us?
- Are they aware of what we have to offer?
- Have they tried us? If not, why not?
- If they have tried us, do they return? Why or why not?
- What are their attitudes and feelings?

In short, the research question at this stage is, How are we viewed by prospective customers now? Management may believe that it has the finest food in town, but if the market doesn't believe this, it really doesn't matter whether management believes it or not. It is hard to go anywhere if you don't know the position from which you are starting.

Why Are We There?

This research step calls for an evaluation of the product and previous communications efforts. To embellish on the previous example, suppose analysis shows that our food is really not that good. If the objective is to be perceived as having the finest food in town, the product will have to be altered and a new communications effort initiated. If, in fact, we do have the finest food in town, then the communications objective will be to change the existing erroneous perceptions. Besides product evaluation, here are other aspects to be researched:

- Are prices perceived to be too high?
- What is the real quality level of our service?
- Is the competition doing the same thing, only better?
- Are our attributes and benefits what we think they are?
- Do we really solve consumers' problems? Are they the right ones?
- What puts us in this position?
- What are our strengths and weaknesses?
- What are the users' dissatisfactions?

- What is the profile of users?
- What is the usage pattern of users?
- Have we communicated what we want to communicate?

The research question at this stage is, How is our product used? If where we are now is not where we want to be, then we have to find out how we got there. Even if it is where we want to be, we still need to know how we got there. There is nothing like knowing what you are doing right and why.

Where Could We Be?

If where we are now is not where we want to be, then where could we realistically be? Let's say we are not perceived as having the best food in town, but that is where we would like to be. Is that realistic? Do we have the right staff in the kitchen? Can we afford to buy the finest ingredients without raising prices? Would we have to raise prices to achieve the "finest food" objective? Is there a market for it?

That's the product point of view. Perhaps we do have the finest food in town, just where we want to be, but the market doesn't see it that way. Then we would have to ask whether it is realistic to believe that we can change perceptions that, in this case, would be vis-á-vis the competition. Here are some other issues in this stage:

- What market position could we achieve?
- Are there new buyers and users out there?
- Can we increase awareness?
- Can we change beliefs or create new ones?
- Can we increase benefits and solve other problems?
- Do we have the right target markets? Are there others?
- Can we create new target markets?
- Can we steal from the competition?

The major research question at this stage is, What unmet needs, wants, and problems are there that we have the capability of fulfilling? The answers to these questions will establish our communication objectives.

How Can We Get There?

Now comes the creative thinking. When this is based on good, solid research, it comes easier and is more likely to work. The first and most obvious question is, What do we have to change? This could be any part of the product/service mix or of the presentation mix that is tangibilizing the product/service to the marketplace. Thus, we might have to change the product, the service, the price, the atmospherics, the facilities, the employees, or perhaps even the location. We might also have to change the distribution network or the target markets.

Once we have the product right (and not until then), we can commence the effort to change what we have to change via the communications mix. Howard Johnson's ad campaign, "If it's not your mother, it must be Howard Johnson's," stretched consumer credibility to a limit that very few restaurants could hope to achieve, and which Howard Johnson's never did. Such actions are often fatal; the customer doesn't like to be fooled, and certainly not twice. This is an example of trying to persuade with communications before the product is corrected.

Are We Getting There?

This is probably the most neglected stage of communications research. It really means starting over at the beginning, except that now the field is narrower because we know what we are looking for. This is research to measure the impact of communication. It asks, What have we or haven't we changed?

If the objective was to be perceived as having the best food in town, are we now so perceived? The campaign may have brought people, which can be temporary and misleading, but what we want to know is whether we have changed perceptions.

Some years after the Howard Johnson's campaign discussed earlier, after Marriott had bought the chain and resold the lodging properties to Prime Motor Inns (which went into bankruptcy and sold it to Hospitality Franchise Systems, who in turn sold it to Cendant), another communications campaign was undertaken.

Push/Pull Strategies

Push/pull strategies are important elements in developing the communications mix. This is especially true in an industry that deals so heavily with other customer providers or intermediaries, such as travel agents, tour operators, and external reservation systems.

Using a **push strategy** means "pushing" the communications mix down through the distribution channels. For example, a hotel company calls on travel agents, advertises in travel agent publications, uses media available on the computer screens of travel agents, provides travel agent bonuses, and so forth. This is intended to get their cooperation in sending customers.

Using a **pull strategy** means going directly to the market that will then go through the distribution channels to book their reservations with an idea in mind of what they want. Ads that say "Call your travel agent" are using this

EXHIBIT 15-9	The Impact of Word of Mouth

Janet Johnson, the Vice President of Marketing Communications at Marqui (www.marqui.com) has written extensively on the various types of word-of-mouth advertising and how to create WOM. Her firm works with a variety of tourism companies, including Motorcoach tour operators, destination marketing organizations, and cruise lines, as well as other businesses across multiple industries. The various types of WOM available to organizations include:

- **Buzz marketing:** Using high-profile entertainment or news to get people to talk about your brand.
- **Viral marketing:** Creating entertaining or informative messages designed to be passed along in an exponential fashion, often electronically or by e-mail.
- **Community marketing:** Forming or supporting niche communities that are likely to share interests about the brand (such as user groups, fan clubs, and discussion forums); providing tools, content, and information to support those communities.
- **Grassroots marketing:** Organizing and motivating volunteers to engage in personal or local outreach.
- **Evangelist marketing:** Cultivating evangelists, advocates, or volunteers who are encouraged to take a leadership role in actively spreading the word on your behalf.
- **Product seeding:** Placing the right product into the right hands at the right time, providing information or samples to influential individuals.
- **Influencer marketing:** Identifying key communities and opinion leaders who are likely to talk about products and have the ability to influence the opinions of others.
- **Cause marketing:** Supporting social causes to earn respect and support from people who feel strongly about the cause.
- **Conversation creation:** Using interesting or fun advertising, e-mails, catch phrases, entertainment, or promotions to start word of mouth activity.
- **Brand blogging:** Creating blogs and participating in the blogosphere in the spirit of open, transparent communications.
- **Referral programs:** Creating tools that enable satisfied customers to refer their friends.

In order to create WOM and encourage communications, Johnson recommends that the firm give people something interesting to talk about. For example, in their work with a cruise line they have included tips on the website about wine education, environmental tourism, and safety and security.

A second recommendation for creating WOM is creating communities and networks to connect people. Ms. Johnson's company has enabled guests taking a motorcoach tour to send electronic postcards to friends and relatives. They have also enabled newfound friends to stay connected on a secure website.

A third suggestion is to work with influential communities. In Chapter 16, we discuss Mrs. Serna, from the Conrad Punta del Este Resort and Casino, who has created a program wherein local children come to the resort for after-school meals and entertainment. In addition to positive results for the community, this program has also generated positive WOM for the resort.

A fourth idea is to create evangelist or advocate programs, enlisting people to be evangelists while they're taking advantage of your services. Starwood Resorts benefited from an employee evangelist called the Starwood Lurker, who was well known for solving problems with Starwood frequent traveler programs. The Lurker's full-time job is to monitor Internet discussion boards such as FlyerTalk (www.flyertalk.com).

A final method for generating WOM is the use of blogs. A *weblog* is a journal (or newsletter) that is frequently updated and is intended for general public consumption. Blogs often have hyperlinks, which enable the user to search other similar information or connect with others reading the same blog. Johnson states that 27 percent of adults who go online in the United States read blogs and that more than 28 percent of journalists now rely on blogs for reporting and research, according to a survey by EURO RSCG Magnet and Columbia University.

MEASURING WORD OF MOUTH

Roger Hallowell and Abby Hansen of Harvard Business School have stated that, in order to calculate the value of word of mouth, one needs to have the following information:* (1) Likelihood that customer will refer the property (2) Number of people to whom the recommendation will be made (3) Percentage of referrals that are empathetic (i.e., may act on what they hear) (4) Probability that those who are empathetic will buy the service (5) Lifetime value of the customer

Given this information, the formula for WOM is: WOM = *(a*b*c*d*e)*.

The lifetime value of the customer is calculated as:

a. Gross profit on an average purchase
b. Average number of purchases a customer makes each year
c. Average number of years customer will continue to purchase
d. Probability that customer will continue to purchase

LVIC = *(a*b)* + *(a*b*c*d)*, where *(a + b)* is the profit for the first year.

EXAMPLE

The information needed in the above formulas can easily be gathered from a survey questionnaire. To gather WOM information, one might ask the following questions:

a. How likely are you to recommend this property to a friend? Choose 1 for "not at all likely" to 10 for "very likely." (This 1-to-10 scale can then be changed into percentages. For example, a 9 would represent 90 percent.)
b. How many people will you tell about your experiences?
c. Of the people you tell, how many do you think will actually make a similar visit? (This is a combination of information in c and d above.)

If *a* = 9, *b* = 13 and *c* = 2, the results can be computed as follows:

a. Likelihood that customer will refer 90 percent
b. Number of people to whom the recommendation will be made = 13
c. 1/13 = .0769
d. LVIC = 725

WOM = (.9*13*.0769*725)= $652.30

Source: www.hotelmarketing.com/indexphp/content/article/060413_starwood_launches_blog_thelobbycom. Accessed August 16, 2006.

*Roger Hallowell and Abby Hansen (1999), *A Taste of Frankenmuth: A Town in Michigan Thinks About Word-of-Mouth Referral,* Harvard Business School Publishing, Product Number 9-800-029

method; that is, the company is "pulling" the customer up through the distribution channel. Both methods are common in the hospitality industry and often used simultaneously. The communication question is, Who are you targeting—the customer or the intermediary? This will guide the communications message.

Word-of-Mouth Communication

The most powerful form of communications, especially in the hospitality industry, is word of mouth (WOM). The reason is that hospitality products are considered **credence goods**. These are products or services that typically cannot be tested before purchase, so consumers are forced to seek outside advice on whether or not to purchase the service.

Elements of the communications mix can, of course, influence word-of-mouth behavior. In fact, creating WOM is a critical outcome of the communications mix. We may see an ad, read or hear publicity, or talk to a salesperson and from any one of those experiences develop a perception and expectation. We may then communicate that perception to someone else via word of mouth even though we really have no actual experience with the product. In this sense, the communications mix affects word of mouth and, indirectly, may persuade someone to purchase or not to purchase.

Word-of-mouth behavior originates from an actual experience with the product or the word of mouth of others who have had an actual experience. Thus, we control behavior more by what we do (relationship marketing) than by what we say. A strong foundation for good word-of-mouth communication is built by fulfilling the needs and expectations of our customers. When this is not done,

an important factor in recapturing a reputation is the way customer requests and complaints are handled.

Various types of word of mouth are currently entering the marketing lexicon. We highlight these in Exhibit 15-9. Exhibit 15-9 also shows ways to measure the impact of word-of-mouth advertising. Exhibit 15-10 discusses a new way to expose customers to products and get them talking. The method is called *undercover marketing*.

 Web Browsing Exercise

Use your favorite search engine and type in the phrase "undercover marketing" or "stealth marketing." Read some of the sites listed and be prepared to discuss undercover marketing or stealth marketing in more detail. What are the pros? What are the cons? Do you think this is a good idea for hotels and restaurants? How would you implement such a plan for hotels and restaurants?

Budgeting the Communications Mix

The amount that a company or an individual property may spend on its total communications effort is not easy to determine. There are no universally accepted standards as to how much should be spent in a given product or market situation. This is because the situation is compounded by a complex set of circumstances that is never constant within or among properties or companies. Our concern here will be with individual properties, not entire firms such as Mc-

---

EXHIBIT 15-10 Undercover Marketing

Forget television commercials and big billboards trying to get consumers to buy their products. The newest form of marketing being done completely "under the radar" is undercover marketing. Undercover marketing, or stealth marketing, is marketing to consumers when they do not even realize they are being marketed to. In today's marketplace, many customers have become bitter toward basic advertisement campaigns. People are going out of their way to avoid being marketed to, such as buying TiVø so they can fast forward commercials and showing up late at the movie theaters to avoid preshow advertisements.

Some marketing companies are starting to compensate for this through the use of undercover marketing. A marketing company will hire actors, who appear to be very approachable people, to use the product they are trying to promote in a visible location where potential consumers of the product are likely to congregate. The actors then begin conversations with the people at the location and promote the use of that product. Undercover marketing can be used everywhere, from a bar where people are trying to promote new types of alcohol to a PTA meeting where a hired mother endorses the benefits of the new laundry detergent she is using. The whole idea behind undercover marketing is that it is not invasive—it is marketing without the pressure of feeling like a pitch.

Sony Ericsson launched an undercover marketing campaign called the "fake tourist campaign" to promote its new camera phones. The company hired actors to walk the streets of New York, acting like tourists and stopping people on the street to ask them to take their picture. While the person was taking their picture, the fake tourist couple would talk about the benefits of their new camera phone.

The goal behind undercover marketing is to create buzz. Buzz is spontaneous; it is word of mouth from peer to peer. Consumers tend to trust word of mouth because they feel the recommendation was sincere and unsolicited. This is also known as viral marketing because it is like a virus. People tell more people until the virus has taken hold. Buzz has many other benefits as well—it is relatively cheap to generate and it can reach people who are isolated from other media sources.

Undercover marketing can also have some negative effects. There can be a backlash when the customer finds out. When a customer finds out that the chance encounter was not by chance, he or she can tend to get angry with the company. The angry customer then has the potential to generate negative buzz about this product. This is why it is vital that undercover marketing be conducted discreetly.

Whatever the risk, undercover marketing is becoming very popular in the advertising world. It has little cost associated with it and has the potential for a large return. Most important, it reaches consumers who have become negative toward the traditional forms of advertisement.

Sources: CBS Videos. (2004, July 25). 60 Minutes; Harmon, L. Secret agents of capitalism. Retrieved December 1, 2005, from www.metroactive.com/papers/metro/05.12.04/marketing-0420.html; and Wikipedia. Undercover marketing. Retrieved December 1, 2005, from http://en.wikipedia.org/wiki/Undercover_markettìng.

Donald's and Burger King that spend huge amounts and use television, or Marriott and Hilton that use the national print media.

What does the budget consist of? Let's start with some common practices. Independent restaurants typically do not have marketing departments. They may or may not fund advertising campaigns. If they do, the amount spent on them is most likely based on "gut feel." How good is business, how well are they known, and how far is their reach? Chances are, those who advertise will spend 2 to 3 percent of sales. In a city where advertising costs are higher, they may spend more. Restaurants that are part of a chain or a franchise will pay up to 4 percent of revenue to the parent company that does national or regional advertising for all units in the chain. Any local advertising they may do on their own comes under the 2 to 3 percent category.

 Web Browsing Exercise

Visit the franchisor information websites for Cendant (http://hotelfranchise. cendant.com/) and Yum! (www.yum.com/franchising/default.asp). What are the marketing percentages required? Compare and contrast.

In the hotel industry similar rules apply, only now reservation costs are added to the equation. A franchised Days Inn may also have no marketing department and do zero local advertising, but will pay the franchisor a set fee per room or a percentage of revenue for both advertising support and the reservation system. These amounts are contractually negotiated; for example, some recent figures are shown in Exhibit 15-11.

The recent shift in the allocation of media funds has been the most prevalent in the United States. Exhibit 15-12 shows the change in overall marketing spent by medium. Clearly, more marketing funds are moving toward the Internet at the expense of some traditional communication vehicles, such as television. This trend is slower in the hospitality industry because many hotels do not have budgets to accommodate broadcast media, but the change is happening nonetheless.

EXHIBIT 15-12	Five-Year Change in Advertising Spending

Communication Vehicle	% change in past five years
Direct mail	+2.4
Newspapers	−18.8
Broadcast TV	−15.2
Cable TV	+79.1
Radio	−5.6
Magazines	−9.9
Internet	+203.9

EXHIBIT 15-11	Marketing Costs

The local advertising done by franchise restaurants is similar to that of independent restaurants. In addition, if they have meeting space, they may have salespeople who also represent part of the operation's total marketing cost.

Most major hotels have marketing departments, so this is the more complex case. We'll deal with common practice which, of course, varies among properties. A major hotel usually bases its marketing budget on forecasts of total sales (rooms, food, and beverages). The budget includes the salaries of the marketing and sales staff as well as fees paid to the brand affiliation (or flag) for national or regional advertising and for the reservation system. These fees may be a percentage based on number of rooms or, in the case of advertising, on total revenue. Hotels also pay a fee to the brand to participate in its frequent traveler program. (These costs are usually forecast as a separate item outside the marketing budget.).The cost of local advertising is typically borne by the property.

What does all this amount to? In 2004, marketing expenses ranged from a low of 2.6% of total revenue for a limited service hotel to a high of 5.2% for a resort hotel. This equates to $416 per available room at limited-service hotels to $4,464 per available room at resort properties. The average U.S. hotel spent $1,882 per available room on marketing.*

Allocation of the money across the communications mix is another issue. Other than contractual fees, which are fixed, a property has considerable latitude regarding whether to spend on such items as advertising, promotions, collateral, research, or on the sales force. A hotel with a large proportion of meetings business will have a larger sales staff to support. The director of marketing will negotiate with management for the department's budget and its allocation, with one choice clearly affecting the other. Salaries and wages make up 43.6 percent of the average hotel's marketing budget, while employee benefits make up another 11.5 percent, according to a PKF study.** Of specific interest is the fact that more money is going into sales and less into advertising: selling makes up 28.3 percent of the marketing budget, while advertising contributes only 14.0 percent.

The greatest change in marketing expenses from 2003 to 2004 occurred in the category of salaries and wages, which grew by 9.7 percent. Total labor costs grew by 7.0 percent, and employee benefits increased by 4.7 percent. Although selling costs grew by 6.6 percent, advertising costs were down by 5.1 percent.

For all types of hotels except full-service, total revenue increased by a larger percentage than did marketing expenses, with limited-service hotels posting the largest relative gain: marketing expenses actually decreased by 0.5 percent, but total revenue showed a 5.8 percent gain. Full-service hotels spent 7.5 percent more on marketing but their total revenue grew by only 6.8 percent.

The Internet has presented a new challenge to hospitality marketers. Websites, banner advertisements, pay per click advertising, and other online communications vehicles all cost money, forcing the director of marketing to reduce expenses in other areas in order to fund Internet marketing. In this regard, it is interesting to note that the year 2005 represented the first year that Google and Yahoo's United States advertising revenues exceeded the combined advertising revenues of the biggest three broadcast television networks: stations, ABC, CBS and NBC.

*www.commercialpropertynews.com/cpn/article_display.jsp?vnu_content_id=1000969244 accessed July 31, 2006.

**www.commercialpropertynews.com/cpn/article_display.jsp?vnu_content_id=1000969244, accessed July 31, 2006.

BEFORE HURRICANE DENNIS. **AFTER HURRICANE DENNIS.**

Same Beach. Same Vacation. Only Now You Get Your 4th Night Free.*

Thankfully, some things never change. Even after a hurricane. You get the same beautiful beaches. Golf courses. Restaurants. And accommodations. But now you can get your 4th night free at the select accommodations below when you check in any Sunday or Monday and stay 3 nights before September 30. Plus, save even more with our special *Hit the Beach Value Card*, good for discounts at restaurants, attractions and shopping. Visit thebeachloversbeach.com for information. Or call 1.800.PCBEACH.

PANAMA CITY BEACH
CONVENTION & VISITORS BUREAU
The Beach Lover's Beach
thebeachloversbeach.com

BASIC CONDOMINIUM RENTALS 800-874-8600 www.basicmgt.com	BAY POINT MARRIOTT RESORT 800-874-7105 www.marriottbaypoint.com
BOARDWALK BEACH RESORT 800-224-GULF www.boardwalkbeachresort.com	BY THE SEA RESORTS 888-627-0625 www.bythesearesorts.com
COLDWELL BANKER RESORT MANAGEMENT 800-621-2462 www.panamabeachrentals.com	EDGEWATER BEACH RESORT 800-874-8686 www.edgewaterbeachresort.com
GET AWAY TO THE GULF 800-224-GULF www.getawaytothegulf.com	HOLIDAY INN SUNSPREE RESORT 800-633-0266 www.hipcbeach.com
MAJESTIC BEACH TOWERS 866-494-3364 www.majesticbeachtowers.com	PANAMA CITY BEACH 800-PCBEACH www.thebeachloversbeach.com
PINNACLE PORT VACATION RENTALS 800-874-8823 www.pinnacleportrentals.com	SANDPIPER BEACON BEACH RESORT 800-488-8828 www.sandpiperbeacon.com
SEA SIDE VILLAS CONDOMINIUM 800-784-5527 www.pcbseasidevillas.com	STERLING RESORTS 866-5RESORT www.sterlingresorts.com

*Some restrictions may apply.

EXHIBIT 15-14 This Panama City Beach advertisement has accomplished the five goals necessary for a successful hospitality ad.

Source: Panama City Beach Convention & Visitors Bureau, Inc. Used by permission.

The fourth component of an ideal advertisement—it will have positive effects on employees who must exceed the promise—is not included in this advertisement. However, the fifth component—it will capitalize on word of mouth—is used. Specifically, the two pictures and the headings, "Before Hurricane Dennis" and "After Hurricane Dennis" are counter to the beliefs one who listens or watches the media would have. This counterbelief will get people talking.

It is seldom easy to get all these elements into one advertisement; usually we have to settle for less. Even then, however, we should strive to differentiate with something other than grandiose claims that characterize some hotel and restaurant ads. Unless there is something truly unique about the property, that kind of ad doesn't fill the requirements and will not help the property gain more customers.

For example, consider a hotel advertisement scene that shows a couple in a room, usually with the woman sitting on the bed and the man standing in a sliding doorway, or they may be in a swimming pool or at a golf course or in a lobby. Fortunately, we do not see these types of advertisements very often. While the room, the pool, and the golf course are all part of the product, they do not differentiate it from other hotels in the same product class. They don't position the property, they promise no special benefit or problem solution, they don't tangibilize the service, they

don't provide reinforcement, they don't have positive effects on employees, they don't generate positive word of mouth, they are not very informative, and they hardly persuade the consumer to choose this hotel.

So much for graphics. How about copy? The same rules apply. Ads that simply list the physical facilities of the property (e.g., number of rooms, pools, restaurants, bars, etc.) also do not fulfill the criteria we have given. True, it may sometimes be necessary to provide this information, depending on the target market. However, the key is to make sure the copy provides this differentiation. For example, consider the advertisement in Exhibit 15-15. Notice that the copy includes differentiating terms such as "flexible function space," "Arnold Palmer signature golf courses," "team building site" and "30 miles north of Tampa International Airport."

Use of Advertising Today

If you cannot make an impact on the market through advertising, other than to create awareness and provide information, it might be better to save your dollars and put them to better use (for instance, in the product or in lower prices, which will generate positive word of mouth, a far more powerful force than most advertising). This is not to say that ad agencies are not creative. It is just that they don't

EXHIBIT 15-15 Notice how this advertisement's copy includes differentiating terms.

Source: Saddlebrook Resort Tampa. Used by permission.

EXHIBIT 15-16 South Seas Island Resort follows the rules and is quite effective in this advertisement.

Source: South Seas Island Resort. Used by permission.

always develop advertising in accord with the guidelines we have discussed. Note the creative ad in Exhibit 15-16 that does follow the rules and is quite effective.

Tourism Marketing Application

Outdoors is one place where consumers see advertising messages. The Ministry of Tourism in Greece uses outdoor advertising in multiple countries. These advertisements appear on buses, bus stop shelters, in subways, and on free-standing signs. An example of current advertising can be found on (www.gnto.gr/pages.php?pageID=876&langID=2, accessed April 2, 2006)

The consumer today is constantly bombarded with advertising messages from all directions (over 400 different messages each day by some estimates). The human mind is not capable of paying attention to all these messages. Instead, the mind will selectively perceive, attend to, comprehend, accept, and retain those to which it is most responsive. What the mind is most responsive to is those features, experiences, needs, and wants that solve a problem or fulfill a need or desire.

Hospitality properties and services are very similar in the same product class; some would say that they have even reached commodity status. The competition is selling the same thing, unique niches are harder and harder to find, services are easy to copy, and aggressive competitors are using innovative positioning strategies. These things mean that it is difficult to gain a competitive advertising advantage solely through the use advertising. In many cases, it may be too expensive to achieve effective awareness and persuasion levels by this means.

These factors demonstrate that advertising must be managed with extreme care. Successful advertising is not just copy and graphics, not even just clever copy and graphics, but derives from a well-thought-out and planned strategy. However, there is a strong tendency to look just at the execution (the copy) and ignore the strategy. Many copy decisions in advertising, in fact, are based on what someone likes rather than how it necessarily affects the customer. It is no wonder the famed retailer John Wanamaker once said, "I know that only half of my advertising is working; I just don't know which half."

Evaluating Advertising

Advertising effectiveness is measured in several ways:

1. A tracking measure can be inserted into the ad, such as a special toll-free telephone number or a request to "Ask for Mary, to get the special deal."
2. Image advertising can be measured by evaluating changes in pre- and postexposure perceptions of the property or brand. This technique entails conducting primary research with targeted prospects to assess their image of the property before exposure to the campaign, then replicating the research postexposure to see if perceptions have changed. A similar technique may be used to assess other surrogate measures of advertising effectiveness including changes in both unaided and aided awareness of the property or brand and similar shifts in stated purchase intention.
3. Advertising efficiency can also be measured by the theoretical cost per thousand prospects who are exposed to the message, as shown in Exhibit 15-17. In this case, assuming that the customer base is similar, *Departures* and *Architectural Digest* appear to be the best value for advertising, with *Travel and Leisure* and *Gourmet* being the most expensive "buys."

After all of the previously described phases of the advertising process are employed, the ultimate question is, Did it work? To answer this question, we must first estimate the cost of the program, including all of the components. Ad design, creative work, copy, production, and other costs are combined under the term *ad preparation*. These are added to the media and agency costs, and the total cost is compared to expected results. Exhibit 15-18 shows a calculation for weekend package advertising for a 400-room hotel.

To evaluate the potential return on investment for advertising a weekend package for this hotel, the total communications expense is calculated. Step 1 combines the cost of all of the ad preparation with the actual media and agency expenses.

Step 2 determines the net room rate generated by the sale of each weekend package room. Although the price is $100 per room, there is the cost to service the room, pay the travel agent, run the air conditioning, and so on. For this example, a typical cost of 30 percent of the sale price of the room was established.

The final step matches the advertising cost with the results expected. In this case, the hotel has to generate an additional 12 rooms sold per weekend night to return the investment. Each additional room sold generates an incremental gross margin of $70 for the property. In this case, the hotel decided that there was a good chance that 12 more rooms per weekend night could be sold. With this type of tracking in place, both the advertising agency and the hotel management have clear expectations of the campaign and the net result after it's over.

Look at a similar model for the hotel's restaurant. Sunday brunch covers have been declining for some time. The advertising agency designs a similar campaign to advertise the Sunday brunch. Exhibit 15-19 shows the results of the potential return on investment.

In this case, the hotel wisely declined. The restaurant had only 200 seats, and the return on the advertising investment could never be recovered. Because there is no single preferred method for the measurement of advertising

EXHIBIT 15-18	Expectations of an Ad Campaign for Weekend Packages
Step 1	
Ad preparation	$2,000
Media placement	15,000
Total communications expense	$17,000
Step 2	
Weekend package room rate	$100
Departmental profit	70%
Net margin on room rate	$70
Step 3	
Total communications expense	$17,000
Net margin on room rate	$70
Room nights needed	243
10-Week media Placement	10
Room nights needed per weekend to break even	24
Two nights per weekend (Fri/Sat)	2
Additional room night sales per weekend night to break even	12

EXHIBIT 15-17	Evaluating Advertising by Cost per Thousand			
Publication	**Circulation**	**Size of Ad**	**Cost**	**Price per Thousand**
Condé Nast Traveler	785,262	Full page, color	$38,220	$20.02
Travel and Leisure	1,008,844	Full page, color	$47,583	$21.20
Architectural Digest	815,282	Full page, color	$46,288	$17.61
Departures	362,878	Full page, color	$30,238	$12.00
Town & Country	440,464	Full page, color	$21,000	$20.97
Gourmet	880,661	Full page, color	$35,393	$24.88

EXHIBIT 15-19	Expectations of an Ad Campaign for Sunday Brunch

Step 1

Ad preparation	$2,000
Media placement	15,000
Total communications expense	$17,000

Step 2

Sunday brunch price	$20
Departmental profit	15%
Net margin per cover	$3

Step 3

Total communications expense	$17,000
Net margin per cover	$3
Covers needed	5,666
10-Week media placement	10
Covers needed per Sunday brunch	567

EXHIBIT 15-20	Do the collateral rules apply to this website for the Victoria Jungfrau Hotel?

Source: Victoria-Jungfrau. Used by permission.

results, the most prudent approach to measurement is one that incorporates some combination of the methods outlined in this chapter.

> **Tourism Marketing Application**
> The Tourism Center at the University of Minnesota provides a methodology for measuring the effectiveness of advertising for a tourism destination using survey data from a random sample of travelers who visited a specific destination. Information on their approach and appropriate forms can be found at www.tourism.umn.edu/research/surveyhowto.html (accessed April 2, 2006).

Collateral

The same rules for advertising explained in this chapter also apply to brochures, direct mail, and other forms of advertising that are commonly referred to as **collateral** in the industry. Much hotel print advertising has progressed beyond the stereotypical ads we have described during the past few years. Hotel collateral, on the other hand, has progressed only in rare instances and generally consists of relatively uninspiring visuals and copy. In at least 75 percent of all hotel brochures, you couldn't tell one hotel from another, even if you changed the name, address, and picture of the hotel. Websites have provided a new outlet for creativity, however, and become mandatory "brochures" on the Internet.

Because collateral is a frequently used form of advertising for hotels, we recommend you evaluate the website shown in Exhibit 15-20. Do the rules apply? Now examine Exhibit 15-21. How would you rate this advertisement based on our discussion throughout the chapter?

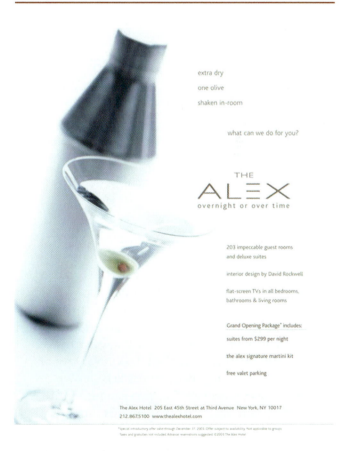

EXHIBIT 15-21	Evaluate this advertisement based on our discussion throughout the chapter.

Source: The Alex. Used by permission.

EXHIBIT 15-22	Campaign Management: What Is It, and Why Should I Care?

There is nothing to hide—no technical jargon to befuddle you. Campaign management is exactly what it sounds like—and it sounds like something we've all been doing for years. So what's the fuss? We have all been managing our own marketing campaigns [here in the Canadian Tourism Commission (CTC), or as tourism businesses] with varying degrees of success over the years. So, as the saying goes, if it ain't broke, why fix it?

Well, what if I told you that it can work better? Is that reason enough? The fact is that campaign management—and, more specifically, automated campaign management (CM)—provides so much more than just a basic tracking tool. It is an extension of customer relationship management. When properly implemented, automated CM can be used to launch, change, and redeliver campaign materials, calculate the return on investment, streamline your marketing activities, profile customers, and generally allow more flexibility in your campaigns.

From the CTC's perspective, this is a set of tools with which to refine communications with travel consumers while building our knowledge and understanding of them. The "currency" at the CTC is data. Just as one would strive, in the stock market, to be better informed and therefore better able to invest our currency to generate more in return, we can use the "currency" of data that we gather to enable us to be more flexible in our campaigns.

Prior to the automation of CM, there was no central place in an organization where management could see every aspect of a campaign: creative, timing, results, current status. And each aspect had to be "actioned" manually. For example, on a launch day, a reminder would be sent to management; then a call would be placed to the advertising company, which would contact the web company, which would send the distribution list to the fulfillment house, which then actually launched the content. With an automated system, all the details are handled in one location with a simple, coordinated production and delivery system.

The cost savings are substantial and the final product is far better than it once was. The design and delivery to reach 50,000 customers with a campaign e-mail blast could easily run into the tens of thousands of dollars. In the past the CTC would launch a marketing effort and then be forced to wait for months to see the results, and if an ad was underperforming there was little that could be done. With an effective CM system, this problem can be remedied in one-third the time and at one-third the cost. By monitoring the status of the campaign in near-real-time it is easy to see how consumers are interacting with the creative and determine what content is working and what should perhaps be changed. Making the

necessary adjustments can be handled at low cost and quickly, making an entire campaign flexible to the demands of the target market.

Further to the actual campaign itself, CM will turn marketing communications into a two-way street. No longer will information be flowing only from you to the consumer; with CM you will receive a great deal in return. The automation of e-mail, the Web, and (to some degree) print campaigns not only allow you to track how a customer interacts with your creative; it also allows you to create customer profiles.

Consider the e-mail blast for a recent high-end fishing campaign as an example. In addition to tracking "e-mail bouncebacks," who opened, and so on, it would be possible with a CM platform to determine which link a recipient clicked on—whether for salmon fishing in BC, walleye fishing in Northern Saskatchewan, or trout fishing in Quebec. Maybe a link about family fishing trips grabbed their attention. All of this information is added to their profile, giving the CTC feedback on our consumer base and making possible a more targeted message on follow-up.

Add a simple online poll—When were you last on a fishing trip in Canada?—and the information keeps flowing. The profile will be filed under past visitors, Canada traveler, fishing/soft adventure, and so on. Should the CTC wish to send a campaign inviting past visitors to "Explore Canada again!" this contact will receive the correspondence. Subscribers to printed material (such as the *Pure Canada* publication) can be segmented in a similar fashion and added to the database.

Now imagine, if you will, all of the CTC's consumer profiles, customer knowledge, marketing know-how, and website content being managed from a single platform. The advantages are many: for the first time the CTC will be able to create and launch a personalized product-specific campaign to a selected audience while tracking customer reactions and adjusting aspects that may be underperforming, all the while receiving consumer feedback and building the strength of the customer database. And this is just the tip of the iceberg!

Automated campaign management is a powerful tool, and as such it requires careful planning in order to maximize the benefits. This is a challenging situation for small businesses to tackle, but there are options available.

Source: Adapted from Campaign Management. www.canadatourism.com/ctx/app/en/ca/magazine/article.do?path=templatedata\ctz\magArticle\data\en\2006\issue03\marketing\online_revealed. Used by permission.

Tourism Marketing Application

The Canadian Tourism Commission (CTC) argues that firms should use automated campaign management systems for tracking the effectiveness of a campaign. Such a system is explained in detail in Exhibit 15-22. The article, which was shortened, was written by Jens Thraenhart, Executive Director of Marketing Strategy & Customer Relationship Management, Canadian Tourism Commission. An interview with Mr. Thraenhart appears at the beginning of Chapter 17.

■ Summary

In this chapter we discussed the foundations of the communications mix and its major component, advertising. We discuss other foundations, database marketing, and interactive markets in Chapter 20. The foundations apply to all aspects of communications, and successful implementation depends on a comprehensive knowledge of the market gleaned through appropriate marketing research, which was discussed in Chapter 11.

In small firms, the various parts of the communications mix will often become the responsibility of just one person or one department, thereby easing their coordination. In larger firms, there may be both an advertising and public relations firm on retainer, with only personal selling handled by in-house staff. In these cases, a special effort is needed to be certain that all of the elements of the communications mix are synchronized. In either case, the mix should emanate from the marketing needs of the firm and be consistent with its overall marketing strategy.

Word-of-mouth communications are a potent force in the hospitality industry, and recommendations from persons who have personally experienced a product or service play an important role in the selection process. Complaints and praise are ways that customers choose to communicate. These can be more effective than any advertising campaign, yet equally destructive if negative.

It should be clear that effective advertising is not simple to orchestrate. Although it is easy to employ advertising techniques, it is not so easy to do so successfully. The common theme in the development of advertising is that its success depends on its ability to address the needs of the customer. Advertising should have clear goals and should be developed only after asking the right research questions.

This chapter offers a foundation and a methodology for the successful development and execution of an advertising campaign. The most common reason for failure in delivering these subsets of the communications mix is a lack of research and planning. With an effective planning process in place and a good research evaluation mechanism, both revenues and customer satisfaction can be maximized. In the next chapter we continue with the communications mix and four of its other elements—sales promotions, merchandising, public relations, and publicity. The last element of the communications mix is personal selling, and we will devote all of Chapter 16 to the examination of this discipline because of its importance to the overall property or brand marketing communications plan.

■ Key Terms

push strategy	collateral
pull strategy	complementary-sell
affective stage	conative stage
cognitive stage	cross-sell

ethos	advertising
evoked set	pathos
logos	slice of life
maintance	tracking

■ Discussion Questions

1. Discuss word-of-mouth communications and how they are affected by the communications mix. Give specific examples. How does this affect the need or lack of a need to advertise?
2. Spot the five elements of the communications mix in the anecdote given in the beginning of the chapter of the couple trying out a new restaurant. How could the restaurant have communicated better? How could the couple? Is the answer to the restaurant's problem now to advertise? Discuss.
3. Evaluate the ads in the chapter other than Exhibits 14-3 to 14-6. Discuss the strategy and tactics of these ads and how they are or are not implemented.
4. Select a local restaurant and ask the five major questions that must be answered by market research to develop the communications mix.
5. Why is it so critical to understand the target market before developing the communications mix? Discuss this in detail, with specific examples.
6. Pick out some ads from a recent newspaper or magazine. Which are effective? Which are not? Explain.
7. Record a hospitality company commercial. Bring it to class and analyze it.

■ Group Projects

1. Consider a local hotel or restaurant and put together an advertising campaign that follows the guidelines laid out throughout this chapter. Be prepared to present this to the class.
2. Conduct a research project for a local establishment that follows the first four guidelines in the chapter under the heading Research for the Communications Mix.

The Communications Mix

Sales Promotions, Merchandising, and Public Relations and Publicity

Overview

This chapter will discuss three more elements of the communications mix: sales promotions, merchandising, and public relations and publicity. The chapter begins with a review of the definition of the communications mix that was presented in Chapter 14. We do this to remind the reader what the communications mix is and to emphasize its importance in marketing. The communications mix is what is often thought of, incorrectly, as marketing. Again, the definition is as follows: All communications between the firm and the target market that increase the tangibility of the product/service mix, that establish or monitor consumer expectations, or that persuade customers to purchase.

Some elements of this definition need further explanation. Note the phrase *between the firm and the target market*. This tells us that communications is a two-way street. Communications is not simply what the firm does to communicate, but it is also the feedback from the target market that tells the firm how well it is communicating and how well it is providing the services promised.

Continued on page 434

432

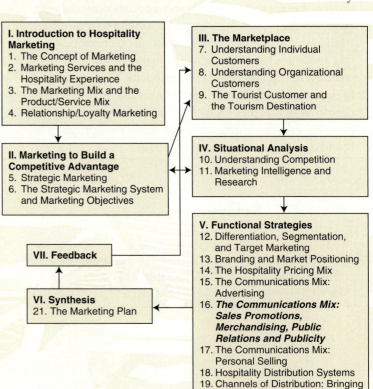

I. Introduction to Hospitality Marketing
1. The Concept of Marketing
2. Marketing Services and the Hospitality Experience
3. The Marketing Mix and the Product/Service Mix
4. Relationship/Loyalty Marketing

II. Marketing to Build a Competitive Advantage
5. Strategic Marketing
6. The Strategic Marketing System and Marketing Objectives

III. The Marketplace
7. Understanding Individual Customers
8. Understanding Organizational Customers
9. The Tourist Customer and the Tourism Destination

IV. Situational Analysis
10. Understanding Competition
11. Marketing Intelligence and Research

V. Functional Strategies
12. Differentiation, Segmentation, and Target Marketing
13. Branding and Market Positioning
14. The Hospitality Pricing Mix
15. The Communications Mix: Advertising
16. ***The Communications Mix: Sales Promotions, Merchandising, Public Relations and Publicity***
17. The Communications Mix: Personal Selling
18. Hospitality Distribution Systems
19. Channels of Distribution: Bringing the Customer to the Product
20. Interactive Marketing: Internet and Database Marketing

VII. Feedback

VI. Synthesis
21. The Marketing Plan

Jennifer Ploszaj
Global Director of Brand Communications & Public Relations
InterContinental Hotels & Resorts

Jennifer Ploszaj currently serves as director of global brand communications and PR for InterContinental Hotels & Resorts, the luxury brand of InterContinental Hotels Group. In this role she has overall responsibility for communications and public relations for the 140 InterContinental hotels around the world.

Ploszaj's career spans more than 15 years, with a focus in communications and marketing in the luxury hotel segment. Prior to 2005, Jennifer was vice president of communications for Noble House Hotels & Resorts, a privately held boutique luxury resort company based in Seattle. In that role, she managed all communications including advertising and marketing and led the company to win more than 20 HSMAI awards for advertising and marketing excellence. Jennifer also spent time working in San Francisco during the dotcom boom and led the communications efforts for a NASDAQ-listed online marketing company.

Marketing in Action

Jennifer Ploszaj, Global Director of Brand Communications & Public Relations, InterContinental Hotels & Resorts

What is the role of a public relations specialist at the property level and at the corporate level?

We'll start with the property level because I think that's probably the most tactical area in which you can make the biggest impact from a hotel standpoint. The role of the public relations specialist or director is to drive local and regional awareness. The role of PR directors in each individual location, whether it be Beirut, San Francisco, or Hong Kong, is to drive awareness within their local community, as well as within their key source markets. For example, the PR director in Paris focuses largely on French media; U.S. media, which is also a big source market for the hotel; and German media, which is another big source market for the hotel. [The local property approach] is the same approach as marketing, so it's very tactical; it's getting people in the door, getting people to try, getting people to write about the hotel within the regions in which they can drive business. The local approach is about driving awareness of the hotel in the local and regional markets, but also driving trial of the property.

The corporate or global role is to drive awareness for the brand across the board and across the globe This is where a PR director is focused on brand positioning and key messages. The global role is more of an awareness approach as opposed to a tactical approach, which is what the local PR directors embark upon. We approach PR as the fifth *P* in the marketing mix, so our role is to support and supplement the overall brand marketing plan. The other piece of corporate PR is to ensure that individual staff in the local and regional markets are on message—that what they're doing and what they're communicating supports the overall brand positioning.

What are some challenges that face PR executives today?

I think the biggest challenge today for PR is that it must be more strategic than it was in the past. PR in the past was often viewed as very superficial. Today, many hotel structures have a PR job description that is not well defined. Sometimes they don't really know where it fits within the mix or where it fits within the structure of the organization. In today's competitive environment, it's critical that PR be closely aligned with marketing. Particularly as most hotel companies are now moving toward a

Continued on page 434

Principles and Practices of Sales Promotions

Sales promotions are marketing communications that serve specifically as incentives to stimulate sales on a short-term basis. In addition, sales promotions can also be effectively used to stimulate trial purchases. In hospitality, they are frequently used to bring in business during periods of slow demand and corresponding low occupancy. In most of these cases, the lure is tied to some form of discounting or the bundling of products and service at one price that gives the perception of a price discount. Marriott's Two-For-Breakfast weekend package is an example of such bundling, as is the combination of travel, rooms, meals, sightseeing, and so forth, in one all-inclusive price. Exhibit 16-1 shows a package for Bali that includes airfare, transfers to and from the hotel to the airport, and lodging.

Casinos use their player tracking system, which is essentially a loyalty card, to reward customers. The types of promotions casinos offer include cash back, double points, free food and merchandise, or discounts on food and merchandise. Exhibit 16-2 shows a promotional mailing for Harrah's Entertainment.

An example of a sales promotion in the restaurant business was when McDonald's offered reduced prices on "Teenie Beanie Babies" with the purchase of a Happy Meal. It is also a sales promotion when restaurants offer discount coupons or two entrees for the price of one. Sales promotion involves the development of creative ideas aimed at producing new customers or driving more frequent purchases in support of the total marketing effort. Sales promotions must be in tune with overall objectives and must complement other elements of both the communications mix and the marketing mix. Sales promotions, by definition, although they should provide customer satisfaction, are not likely to build long-term customer loyalty. The only exception is when they are used to reward loyal guests, as suggested in part by Exhibit 16-2.

Sales promotions are typically oriented toward the short term. If they are perceived to run all the time (for e.g., cash back promotions run by the automobile companies), they rarely succeed in the long term. The reason for this is that the promotion becomes part of the product; that is, it no longer performs as originally intended. The promotion becomes, instead, something you are forced to give customers as part of the customary transaction because the customers have come to expect the offer. In fact, they may not buy unless the offer is in place.

EXHIBIT 16-1   An advertisement that offers an all-inclusive package.

Source: Singapore Airlines. Used by permission.

EXHIBIT 16-2   A promotional mailing for Harrah's Entertainment.

Source: Harrah's Las Vegas. Used by permission.

Sales Promotions and Marketing Needs

Sales promotions are designed to fulfill a specific marketing need. It follows, then, that the first thing to be done when developing a sales promotion is to define that need. There are myriad reasons for the development of promotions. To create new business, to create awareness, and to create trial purchase are typical. Some others are to increase demand in slow periods, to take business from the competition, or to meet the competition in its own promotional efforts. Whatever the reason, there is one major warning with regard to promotions: They should be tied to something positive such as a new or better facility, a new product, or a special time or offering.

Promotions tied to negative features—for instance, lack of business when it is expected to be good—tend to backfire. An example of this is restaurant two-for-one promotions offered by companies that print guidebooks or mail circulars. These promotions are designed to generate business by bringing in new customers. In the best situations, they succeed in doing this, but the customers they bring in may not be from the designated target market, and few of them may ever return. Although there may be a temporary increase in business, it is obtained at a cost: If food cost percentage is 35 percent, it is now 70 percent. At the same time, regular customers who would normally pay the full price are also dining at half price. The net gain is minimal, if not negative. Feltenstein stated:

> The trick is to discount in such a way that you do not sabotage the integrity of your menu. Disguise the lure so that it's perceived as something other than an attempt to discount mainline items. . . . In the consumer's mind, there is always a correlation between product and price. . . . But over time, discounting is bound to raise questions in the consumer's mind about the integrity of your pricing structure. . . . If you must discount . . . [and] there are times when discounting is a sound promotional technique— then put together a separate package to your regular offering, that will engender no recognizable negative effect on your customer's perception of the value and price of your menu. . . . [Once] you get the customer in the store, remember it is going to take more than a cents-off coupon to bring him or her back.[1]

   Web Browsing Exercise

Use your favorite web browser and search the words "restaurant promotions." What do you find? What did you learn about such promotions?

Guidelines for Sales Promotions

The following sections contain some general guidelines for promotions that should apply to most cases.

Tourism Marketing Application

The primary goal of the Malaysia Tourism Promotion Board, or Tourism Malaysia, is to promote tourism to Malaysia. To this end, between September 2005 and December 2005, a contest was

Designing the Successful Sales Promotion

What, then, are the steps that need to be taken to ensure a successful promotion? The following sections detail these steps.

Identify the Gap

One purpose of a sales promotion from the management perspective is to increase revenues. It makes sense to plan promotions when the facility is not at capacity; the idea is to create new demand. Many promotions are designed to build revenues during slack times or sell products that are traditionally in low demand.

The New York Palace completed an extensive renovation in 1997 and repositioned itself at the top of the New York City luxury market. Specifically, the Towers section of the hotel competed head on with the established St. Regis and Four Seasons hotels. Although the physical product was five-star quality, the customers' perception of the hotel remained confused. Customer research indicated that the St. Regis and Four Seasons were well liked by travelers, and changing their behavior would prove difficult. The problem was that the competition was doing a good job, and there were no real reasons for their customers to look elsewhere. Palace management was convinced, however, that once customers tried the Towers, they would return. Getting trial usage became the marketing problem to be solved. A sales promotion was created to give the customer a reason to try the Towers. The promotion offered a round trip airline ticket on Delta Airlines to anyone staying in the Towers for one night.

The tickets were purchased through a special program offered by Delta for $249. Rates in the Towers began at $525 and, with an average stay of two nights, each booking paid for the sales promotion. Future stays created incremental revenue and guest loyalty.

Web Browsing Exercise

Use your favorite web browser to search the web for specific "hotel web promotions" or "restaurant web promotions." What options appear? Pick one or two of the firms that interest you and be prepared to discuss what you found in class.

Design the Sales Promotion

There are two areas to address when designing the promotion: the customer and time. Normally, the customer should be considered before putting any type of promotion together. However, management might design a promotion because of excess inventory. Perhaps some wine was bought in too large a quantity and needs to be sold. A wine promotion is created, regardless of the needs of a customer, but the promotion itself is designed to satisfy needs. The promotion must be consistent with the positioning of the restaurant or hotel. A disco promotion at the Ritz is not in keeping with the positioning of the hotel. Similarly, a caviar promotion at a family restaurant is equally inappropriate.

The second important aspect in the design of the promotion is the timing and planning. It takes time to plan a promotion. The promotional material needs to be prepared and supplies need to be ordered to guarantee that when guests arrive at the facility, not only is the promotional item available, but employees are aware of the promotion.

The proper delivery of a promotion includes the integration of a variety of items in the communications mix. Advertising, merchandising, and public relations all need time to be coordinated. Promotions that do not have the proper timing and planning are usually a failure

Throughout the design of the promotion, a clear and concise message must be put forth to the customer. This may not be as necessary for promotions centered on established events, but promotions that are attempting to present a novel concept have to be clear. A St. Patrick's Day promotion can be easily understood by most customers because the event carries with it a certain level of expectation; however, a novel promotion may have to be explained to customers and also to all employees.

Analyze the Competition

Competition should be analyzed before a sales promotion is developed. If all of the restaurants in town are offering a turkey dinner for Thanksgiving, what will make this promotion different? A close watch on competitive activity can give the promotion designer a head start on potential problems.

Allocate the Resources

No sales promotion will be successful if customers are unaware of the activity. A major reason for the failure of a promotion is underestimating the resources needed to bring in customers. Just putting the corned beef sandwich on the blackboard of the restaurant will not be enough exposure to have a successful St. Patrick's Day promotion.

All parts of the communications mix should be evaluated for their ability to bring customers to a promotion. Public relations, advertising, and even direct sales can be used to get the message to potential participants. E-mail can be a cost-effective way to deliver the promotion. In hotels, traditional merchandising methods such as table tents, signage in the elevators, and employee buttons can carry the theme of the promotion.

Establish Goals

How should success be judged? If a sales promotion is to satisfy both the customer and management, how many extra rooms, covers, or cases of wine can be reasonably expected to sell? What level of sales must be achieved simply to cover the cost of the promotion? Goals should be set in advance for evaluating the promotion at the conclusion of the event. Goals also need to be realistic, and a measurement form should exist before the promotion takes place.

Research the Promotion

Many times a promotion is planned without any communication with the potential customers to see whether the promotion is something in which they would actually like to participate. Only after lots of money has been spent is it judged a failure, while up-front consumer research might have avoided the failure. Research can also be undertaken to understand the likely response of a firm's customers to promotions of its competitors. For instance, one of the authors tested 10 possible promotions for a major hotel firm. Half of the promotions were ones the firm was thinking of offering; the other half were promotions competitors had offered in the past. The goal was to determine what would happen should the promotions be offered. Exhibit 16-8 shows the wording used in the questionnaire to test the promotions.

Firms can also test promotions by taking a small sample of likely customers and dividing them into two separate groups—one group for each of two possible promotions. Each group is then sent one of the promotions. The promotion that yields the highest return is then used for the whole population scheduled to receive the promotion.

Understand the Break-Even Point

It is imperative to understand the economic consequences of the sales promotion before its execution. For example, there may be too many resources allocated to the promotion to ever make meeting the goals financially feasible.

A restaurant promotion might use a $500 advertisement in the local paper to reach the maximum number of potential customers. If the promotion is slated for a Thursday evening in a restaurant that normally sells 75 covers, a realistic goal for a successful promotion might well be 125 customers on the night of the event. However, if the average check for the event is planned at $15, with a gross profit margin of $4.50, the additional profit would be $225, obtained at a cost of $500, Clearly, this would not represent an effective use of marketing funds.

Break-even analysis should be conducted early in the sales promotion planning. We saw one supposedly great promotion developed by a hotel team that at its most successful point—and success was widely anticipated—would have lost $100,000. The greatest "success" of this promotion, had it been carried out, would have been its failure. Both overallocation and underallocation of resources must be carefully analyzed in relation to the success of the promotion.

Pricing is an important factor in sales promotions and not just because of profits. Is the promotion so expensive to the customer that there will be little demand for the product, or is it so inexpensive that the market will be apprehensive of the quality? Sometimes simplicity may be the way to go, as shown in Exhibit 16-9.

Execute the Sales Promotion

The execution stage of the promotion is as important as all the others. Execution includes delivery of the product to the customer in the framework of the created expectation. Promotion delivery is more critical than normal delivery because the customer is excited and anticipatory. The promotion has created a demand. Demand has created a special reason to use the product, and customer expectations are unusually high.

Proper execution includes employee participation. The entire staff needs to understand the promotion and its specific involvement. When a bartender shows up for work in the middle of an Oktoberfest without knowing

---

| EXHIBIT 16-8 | **Example of Wording to Test Possible Sales Promotions** |

FOR 50 PERCENT OF THE SURVEYS

I am going to read you a list of possible promotions a hotel chain could offer. For each promotion, please indicate how likely you would be to stay at that chain instead of the chain you normally stay at most often to take advantage of the promotion. 1 means *not at all likely* and 9 means *very likely*. Assume the chains are similar in terms of quality, consistency, and price, but the chain offering a promotion is slightly less convenient.

FOR 50 PERCENT OF THE SURVEYS

I am going to read you a list of possible promotions a hotel chain could offer. For each promotion, please indicate how <u>many more dollars</u> you would be willing to pay to take advantage of this promotion. Assume the chains are similar in terms of quality, consistency, and convenience, but the chain offering a promotion has a rate premium.

THE LUXURY OF HOMELIKE ACCOMMODATIONS IN THE CITY

AN ATMOSPHERE OF TRANQUILITY AND PEACE

A PHILOSOPHY OF WELLNESS

EXCLUSIVENESS, WARMTH, COMFORT

From Milan..........

ENJOY REAL HOSPITALITY

ENJOY **REAL** HOSPITALITY

ENJOY REAL **HOSPITALITY**

Unique resorts in unique locations to provide you with the ultimate holiday, fun and relaxation.

For further information please contact us at: info@planhotel.com www.planhotel.com

..........To Maldives

EXHIBIT 16-9 This advertisement for Town House Hotels shows them providing a range of hotels in different locations.

Source: Plan Hotels. Used by permission.

the service steps involved, trouble can be anticipated. Employee involvement, perhaps even in the design stages of the promotion, will increase the chances for optimal delivery of the correct product.

Execution also means maintaining the proper inventory of goods to be sold. If the restaurant runs out of bratwurst during the Oktoberfest and has to substitute hamburgers, the customers' expectations will not be met. Part of the planning process of the promotion is the development of goals. Purchasing should be based on the attainment of these goals, at a minimum. It is more desirable to have some waste than to not fulfill expectations.

Tourism Marketing Application

An organization that promotes *cultural tourism* (defined as "traveling to experience the places and activities that authentically represent the stories and people of the past and present. It includes historic, cultural and natural attractions") recommends that, in order to track the success of a promotion, one must look at some of the following indicators: economic impact (e.g., increase in tax revenues, new tourism jobs created, and increase in retail sales to out-of-town customers), increase in number of visitors and their length of stay, increase in inquiries, overall visitor satisfaction, media coverage, and expanded capacity of heritage and cultural organizations. (www.culturalheritagetourism, accessed April 3, 2006)

Evaluate the Sales Promotion

All sales promotions should have an evaluation mechanism installed that includes asking the following questions:

- Were the goals met?
- Would the customers have come anyway?
- Were resources optimally allocated?
- Did it generate revenues sufficient to cover the costs?

Although these questions are certainly relevant and necessary, they constitute only half the equation designated for success. The second half consists of the following questions:

- Were the customers satisfied?
- Were there any unusual complaints?
- Do comments reflect any information that might be useful for future promotions?

All of these questions should be addressed in the evaluation process to allow a total assessment of the event.

Evaluation of a promotion is one of the more difficult analyses to undertake. In a personal correspondence with one of the authors, Judd Goldfeder of the Customer Connection, a firm specializing in restaurant loyalty programs, stated:

> While we try to do all we can to objectively and accurately measure the sales generated by a frequent diner program, no analysis can provide absolute evidence that any program produces a definitive amount of incremental sales. Therefore, the best we can do is make some subjective assumptions, temper them with common sense and good business judgment and reach a "comfort zone" regarding what portion of sales were generated as a direct result of the program versus guest patronage that would have occurred anyway.

Despite the preceding comments, there are two tests management can undertake to help understand whether "customers would have come anyway." Exhibit 16-10 shows one such test, and Exhibit 16-11 shows a second.

The first test shown is a traditional pretest/posttest with a control group. In this test, the target population is divided into two similar groups based on such characteristics as buying behavior, loyalty toward the firm, and the like. Notice that in Exhibit 16-10, groups are determined by their RFM (recency, frequency, monetary value). These are the rows in the table. Each group is then split into a test group and a control group (represented by the columns). The test group receives the sales promotion offer, while the second group receives nothing. Purchase behavior of the two groups is tracked after the promotion. To be successful, the purchase behavior of the test group should be much higher than the purchase behavior of the control group. If this is the case, then the promotion impacted behavior. If the purchase behavior is the same for the two groups, then the promotion had no impact. Obviously, the difference between the two groups should exceed the cost of the promotion. The calculation appears in Exhibit 16-10.

A second way to judge the success of a promotion is to use what is called "they would have come anyway analysis." In this analysis, management makes basic assumptions about the percentage of customers who came because of the promotion and those who would have come anyway. By examining the different percentages of each group and the cost of the promotion, management can gain an estimate of whether the promotion was a success. Obviously, this analysis can be undertaken before the promotion begins.

When all feedback has been analyzed, the final stage is formulating the next promotion. What other promotions can be developed to fill in gap periods or to sell slower-moving products or time periods? The process of promotional development begins all over again.

Exhibit 16-12 provides ideas for restaurant promotions from the Quantified Marketing Group, a restaurant consulting company.

Principles and Practices of Merchandising

Merchandising is primarily an in-house marketing technique designed to stimulate immediate purchase behavior through means other than personal selling or the purchase of time or space in the media. In a sense, merchandising is marketing to the captive customer once the customer comes into the hotel or restaurant to purchase a room or a meal. Many customers will buy nothing other than the basic product. The goal of merchandising is to provide opportunities for customers to purchase related or auxiliary products and services.

The goal of merchandising, however, should not be just to stimulate sales; it also has a more long-term goal of increasing customer satisfaction. When the dessert tray is presented at the end of the meal, the goal is to have customers order dessert and thereby increase the check average. It is also to have customers feel even more satisfied because they have finished their meal in a very pleasing manner. If hotel guests order room service, they add to their overall bill. Also, we hope, their stay has been made just a little bit better and we have a few more satisfied customers. In a casino, the merchandising may include an on-the-floor promotion of a specific game.

Like everything else, we approach merchandising from a marketing perspective—fulfilling customers' needs and wants and solving their problems. It may also be to provide a unique or exciting experience, as in the case of the casino. If we are able to do this, the higher check averages and the larger bills will follow. If, instead, we put all the emphasis on the increased revenue, we are likely to fall into the same old trap of forgetting about the customer.

Basic Rules of Merchandising

The opportunities for merchandising in a hotel or restaurant are almost endless and, like sales promotions, are limited only by the imagination. There are a few rules that affect all merchandising, which, again, are not unlike those for sales promotions.

EXHIBIT 16-10	Tests to Determine the Success of Promotions

BASIC FORM OF PREPROMOTION/POSTPROMOTION WITH CONTROL GROUP

Code	Group	Number of Visits
01	Prepromotion test group (e.g., receives promotion)	5.3
02	Postpromotion test group (e.g., receives promotion)	7.8
03	Prepromotion control group (e.g., does not receive promotion)	5.4
04	Postpromotion control group (e.g., does not receive promotion)	5.6

Effect of the promotion = (02−01)−(04−03)
(7.8−5.3)−(5.6−5.4)
(2.5−0.2)
2.3 increase in number of visits because of promotion

POPULATION DIVIDED BY RFM (ROWS) AND TEST CONTROL GROUP (COLUMNS)

Count of Account	R (Recency)	F (Frequency)	M (Monetary Value)	Test Group	Control Group
90	5	5	3	45	45
99	5	5	4	50	49
106	5	5	2	53	53
123	5	5	5	62	61
281	5	5	1	140	141
Subtotal: 699				350	349
105	5	4	1	53	51
135	5	4	2	66	68
139	5	4	3	70	69
154	5	4	4	77	77
167	5	4	5	84	85
Subtotal: 700				350	350
152	5	3	5	76	76
156	5	3	4	78	78
146	5	3	3	73	73
159	5	3	2	80	79
86	5	3	1	43	43
Subtotal: 699				350	349
125	5	2	5	63	62
145	5	2	4	73	72
160	5	2	3	80	80
148	5	2	2	74	74
122	5	2	1	61	61
Subtotal: 700				351	349
132	5	1	5	66	66
146	5	1	4	73	73
164	5	1	3	82	82
152	5	1	2	76	76
106	5	1	1	53	53
Subtotal: 700				350	350
Total: 3,498				1,749	1,749

Purpose

All merchandising should have a purpose. The commonly expressed purpose—to increase sales—is true, but not sufficient. Instead, let's say that the overall purpose is to increase customer satisfaction and loyalty. Of course, we could also say the purpose is to fulfill needs and wants and solve problems. Much of merchandising does that, but in this case we go a little bit beyond the basic marketing concept.

Sometimes just knowing that something is available and can be had if wanted will establish the need or want or increase satisfaction—even when that thing is not consciously needed or wanted. A good example is the year-round swimming pool in an urban hotel. Proportionally,

EXHIBIT 16-11	They Would Have Come Anyway Analysis*	

% Who Would Have Come Anyway	Total Sales of Those Who Would Have Come Anyway	Incremental Revenue Less Cost of Program
5%	$69,720 (.05 × 1,394,408)	$1,263,688 (.95 × 1,394,408– $61,000
10%	$139,441	$1,193,967
15%	$209,161	$1,124,247
20%	$278,882	$1,054,526
25%	$348,602	$984,806
:**		
50%	$697,204	$636,204
:		
75%	$1,045,806	$287,602
:		
90%	$1,254,967	$78,441
95%	$1,324,688	$8,720
100%	$1,394,408	-61,000

*Cost of the promotion is $61,000, and total revenue of time period is $1,394,408.
**The ":" indicates that numbers no longer go in 5% increments. Obviously, a spreadsheet could be created for each percentage from 0 to 100.

EXHIBIT 16-12	Restaurant Promotions from the Quantified Marketing Group

10 TACTICS FOR DRIVING F&B SALES
Restaurant Promotions Tactic 1: Publicity Stunts

Stunt is a word with negative connotations for restaurant owners, but I wanted to use a word that conjured up images that are different than traditional press relations efforts. Sending a standard press release about a new menu may result in a small write-up. To cut through the clutter and generate extensive exposure, you need a newsworthy angle. Something like a celebrity chef cook-off, really unique contest or other major event. Think beyond typical events like golf tournaments and simple fundraisers. Challenge your staff or marketing firm to think what you'd have to do to make it into the Guinness Book of World Records. Challenge them to think much bigger and come up with ideas that tie in to what your club stands for but also have potential for national exposure. If you create events that have only local appeal, you'll be limited with your media exposure potential and may not even make the local paper. If you think much larger, you won't have to worry about getting coverage. A well-constructed publicity stunt can be worth its weight in gold in terms of positive exposure for your restaurant. And everybody wants to be associated with a winner.

Restaurant Promotions Tactic 2: Public Relations

Public relations has been called advertising that you don't have to pay for. If you have a successful public and media relations program, you'll get increased exposure and prestige without spending a fortune. For this to work, though, you'll need to create and publicize newsworthy stories. Hiring a new chef isn't always enough to garner the kind of attention you deserve. Create other angles that are unique and make your restaurant stand out. Also, review your restaurant's marketing and advertising expenses over the last three years. Then determine the percentage that was spent on traditional advertising compared to public relations. It's worthwhile to spend 15–30 percent of your budget on a solid public relations program. Find a firm that has creativity and excitement about your restaurant. If that firm doesn't seem genuinely curious and interested in your restaurant and what it has to offer, it'll have a hard time creating interest with the media.

Some higher-end restaurants are understandably concerned about publicity stunts and other marketing activities that seem to fly in the face of the exclusivity of their establishment. My answer to that is simple—these tactics won't be appropriate for everyone. That being said, if you are one of the restaurant owners that cringes at the thought of creating buzz in the community at large, I urge you to think about your position.

Everyone wants to be associated with a winner. For some of your regulars the whole reason they belong in the first place is because it's exclusive and their being a part of that is an extension of their self-brand and identity. Creating buzz won't distract from that; it will reinforce it in many cases. They key is how the publicity comes across. If done correctly, it supports your position in the market, exclusivity and prestige.

Restaurant Promotions Tactic 3: Bouncebacks

This is an underutilized tool that bounces guests from peak times to off-peak times and can also work to encourage frequency in your food and beverage operations. While simple in theory and execution, this tactic can produce far more in revenues per dollar invested than traditional advertising. An you do is offer incentives at the point of purchase on popular services to encourage the guest to try your restaurant another time. For instance, if you're busy for lunch and need to drive sales for dinner, offer bounceback certificates that can only be redeemed during dinner hours. Test different offers and delivery vehicles and track response rates for each to hone in on what works best with your clientele.

Restaurant Promotions Tactic 4: Stop Discounting

Discounting tells your customers and prospective customers. "We don't deserve full price, so we'll be happy to lower our rates to make up for the difference." This point was driven home to me during my tenure with The Breakers of Palm Beach, a lavish resort whose guests spend a small fortune to walk the halls. Discounting the price would be to discount the 105 years spent building a brand. Instead of discounting, consider no strings offers that do not rely on percentages. Examples include value-added perks

(continued)

such as free valet parking, complimentary services, merchandise, etc. And, in a related topic, never offer coupons, only offer certificates. There is a big difference in perception.

Restaurant Promotions Tactic 5: Business Socials

A no brainer, right? Well, you'd be surprised how unreceptive or apathetic some restaurant owners are to hosting business socials with outside organizations at their establishment. However, if you select the right group to partner with, you can leverage their resources to promote your restaurant, and you can also target your core audience. Host socials where the food is center stage. Arrange photo opportunities that include your displays in the background and submit to local media. Partnering with a business or charitable organization works on many levels and can help you stretch your marketing budget while still delivering higher returns on investment than can be achieved with traditional advertising.

Restaurant Promotions Tactic 6: Sampling

Tasting is believing and if you would grade your food a B minus or above, you need to get it in potential customers' mouths. That's the best way to build recognition and it is more effective and less expensive than advertising. Every public event that draws your core audience is an opportunity to offer samples of your product. Pick the best 2–3 items on your menu that can be easily transported and get some solid representatives of your restaurant out to meet and greet at these off-property functions

Restaurant Promotions Tactic 7: Host Food Events

Hosting food events such as the "Taste of (insert your town)" is a great way to position your restaurant as a center of the food scene in your market. It allows you to leverage the reputation, profile and credibility of all of the other participants, and it can also help you share the expense of holding the event. Hosting an event also provides your restaurant with the opportunity to recruit additional manpower and resources for promoting the event and gives that added edge with garnering local publicity.

Restaurant Promotions Tactic 8: Toss Up Tuesdays

Promote this program through your next newsletter and other internal marketing vehicles to your existing customer base. Pick Tuesdays (or your slowest food day) and flip for the food tab. Guests will have a 50 percent chance of getting their food bill paid by the restaurant. This attracts your guests' attention much more than a "buy one get one free" restaurant promotion. Guests are also more likely to have higher check averages than normal because there is a chance they won't have to pay. It creates a tremendous attention among your core guest base.

Restaurant Promotions Tactic 9: Menu Bingo

This is a great tactic for encouraging frequency and getting members to try different items on the menu. You simply create bingo cards that have

different menu items in boxes. Have the cards designed with five columns and five rows. You can also promote other non-food items such as merchandise, cookbooks, and gift certificates. Guests have an allotted period of time—60 days for example—to complete a connection just as they would with a bingo card. Once they try five items in any direction, they receive a free gift basket or other incentive that is roughly equal to one of the items purchased.

Restaurant Promotions Tactic 10: Birthday Program

Research shows that 50 percent of all Americans eat out on their birthday. This presents an opportunity for establishments with solid birthday programs. So why don't restaurateurs do more to take advantage of this? You've got me, but it does offer a chance for you to swoop in and capture your increased share of the market. A birthday program can be executed through new automated tools like those that are available through e-mail marketing service providers. You simply plug in the birthday and e-mail address of your members, and a secure and nicely designed e-mail is sent to them at a time you determine in advance. The system knows who and when to send the e-mail to and also tracks view rates for reporting that allows you to know how well your program is working. You can also have the e-mail include a redemption code that will allow you to track what percentage of the e-mails are bringing in guests and calculate a return on investment. Recent research has shown that retention based e-mail marketing is 300 to 400 percent higher than traditional vehicles such as direct mail and faxes. It's a great way to communicate and manage your club's birthday program.

The restaurant industry has been conditioned to believe that only traditional marketing efforts can be applied to grow sales because it's what everyone else is doing. Fact is, the restaurant industry is getting more competitive and will continue to do so. In the face of increased competition, the most effective strategy is to differentiate your restaurant from the others and create excitement in a way that reinforces your positioning strategy. Again, restaurant promotions are only gimmicky if they are created that way; it is entirely possible to execute these restaurant promotions in a way that is completely in alignment with the image of your restaurant no matter how exclusive.

Remember, differentiation and exciting tactics like the ones described here are particularly potent for your food and beverage operations.

Smart marketing is best achieved through non-traditional techniques that are executed inside your restaurant and among your existing customer base. Opportunities abound if you look at your situation through the right lens. Use the preceding ideas to spark your own thinking of similar underutilized programs in your own operation and reap the rewards as other successful restaurants are around the country.

Source: Adapted from the work of Aaron D. Allen, founder/CEO of Quantified Marketing Group (www.quantifiedmarketing.com).

very few guests use these pools, but research has shown that they like the idea that the pools are there to use if they wish. A positive, however, is turned into a negative when the pool is not open at reasonable times that people want to use it because of operational convenience. The same is very true of fitness areas. It is human nature to want to feel that we can have something if we want it; merchandising creates that feeling and increases satisfaction and loyalty.

The other reason we go beyond the basic marketing concept is that merchandising is involved in the *creation* of

wants. Marketing can stimulate basic needs, but it can also create wants. Restaurant diners might feel a need for chocolate after dinner (might even want it, in fact), but repress that need because of the concern about the number of calories in the dessert. However, along comes the pastry cart with all those goodies, and now, instead of not ordering any dessert, customers at the table may order a couple of desserts to share. Restaurants have tremendous merchandising opportunities. The most powerful one, sometimes neglected, is the menu itself, which can range from mundane and blasé to exciting and provocative. In our chapter on pricing, we provided an example of a study that tested the impact of very descriptive menu items. Not only did participants in the study feel that the menus were of great price value, but they viewed the menu items as more appealing.

By the same token, hotel guests do need to eat; merchandising can make them want to eat in one of the hotel's restaurants. Cards are put up in the elevators, and signs may be displayed in the lobby and in promotional flyers that are placed on the desk in the guest room. In many hotels, guests also see and hear about the in-house restaurants on the television in their room. In many European hotels, merchandising is practiced upon check-in, when the desk clerk asks if the guests would like a dinner reservation made for them. The in-room dining menu is a great opportunity for selling in-room dining, but only if the menu is clean, looks appealing, and does not show the previous guest's order in the menu. Unfortunately, all too often such menus do not fit these criteria, causing hotels to miss a great merchandising opportunity.

All merchandising ploys need to have their purpose understood. One purpose, as we mentioned, is to create the feeling, "If you want it, we have it." Another might be to create excitement, as with an exotic drink, a flambé dessert, or a "spinning salad bowl," which made Don Roth's Blackhawk Restaurant in Chicago famous. Another purpose might be entertainment, such as that provided by slot tournaments held by casinos. Other possible purposes are convenience (room service), relaxation (aperitifs), contentment (after-dinner cognac), or information (in-room directories).

A merchandising technique used by Marriott in some of its hotels, which can also be used in restaurants, occurs when you are first seated at your dining room table. A waiter or waitress immediately approaches with a basket of house wines, offered by the glass. The customer has immediate service, and a need identified by the customer has been met. Even if there is a delay in ordering the meal, instant satisfaction has been created. Some hotels also use the same approach at breakfast: You are immediately greeted by a server with a pot of coffee in one hand and a pitcher of fresh orange juice in the other.

Compatibility and Consistency

Merchandising efforts should be compatible and consistent with the rest of the marketing effort in terms of quality, style, tone, class, and price. They should reinforce the basic product/service mix, since these efforts themselves are part of the augmented product. Hotels that have an eye on the growing family vacation travel market should consider opening a child care center where parents can leave their children with trained, licensed professional staff. Some resorts offer 24-hour child care service. However, this market and this service may not be compatible in a hotel with a strong transient business traveler base.

Practicality

The rule here is if you can't do it right, don't do it. Failure to follow this rule results in lost customers, not satisfied ones. The child care center is an example in which serious problems can result if the service is not offered in a professional way.

Visibility

Let the customer know about what you are trying to sell and how to get it. Elevator cards merchandising restaurants often fail to say where the restaurants are or what hours they are open. In today's modern hotels, where restaurants might be anywhere, it can literally be a mind-boggling experience to find one. One mistake management often makes is that they forget that for many customers this may be the first time in the hotel. In-room directories sometimes are so confusing that the guest either turns to the telephone or gives up. We have even seen directories with full pages on the swimming pool and health club facilities but no indication of how to get there or what to wear on your way. Many people don't use pools simply because they are too embarrassed to go there in a bathing suit and do not want to change in dressing rooms. The Royal Garden Hotel in Trondheim, Norway, solved this customer problem by identifying a swimming pool/health club elevator specifically for that purpose.

On the other hand, visibility doesn't mean total clutter. Some restaurant tables or hotel desktops have so many table tents, flyers, and brochures on them that there isn't room for anything else and it is too confusing to find what you want. They also can get in the way of the necessary work space that many business travelers need. Some people just remove them without looking so they can put down their own things.

Clutter can also occur on the casino floor or, more important, hanging from the casino ceiling. Some casinos have so much merchandising hanging from the ceiling that the consumer does not see anything through the clutter. It is always good to put yourself in the shoes of the customer.

Simplicity

Make your merchandising efforts easy to understand and your merchandise easy to obtain. Be clear about how much it will cost, how long it will take and when it is available and provide any other information that will make it unnecessary for the customer to have to make additional inquiries. Customers tend to just give up when they have to go through too much effort to purchase a service. Placing a star next to an "extra hot" menu item provides quick information to customers and increases sales of those items for those who are looking for something very spicy. It also makes sure that those who do not like spicy foods do not order such items.

Knowledgeable Employees

Make sure all of your employees know about the product or service you are promoting, what it is, how it works, how you get it, what you do with it, and so forth. The key to the success of any in-house promotion is the knowledgeable employees who publicize it to the customers. Many hotels advertise their customer loyalty program at the front desk, yet when customers ask why they should join, employees cannot articulate all the benefits because they have never been trained about the program.

Merchandising is just one more marketing tool for creating and keeping customers. It is also a communications tool because it says to the customer, "Here is what else we can do for you." Wisely used, merchandising is a powerful tool; it is a revenue producer and, more important, a customer satisfier. Too often, however, it becomes a customer annoyer.

Examples of Good Merchandising

Examples of good merchandising techniques abound. One case in point is the business centers that are frequently found in hotels that cater to business travelers. These business centers offers a variety of administrative support services such as typing and dictation, together with copying, fax machines, Internet access, and computer terminals. Business centers are usually located somewhat off the lobby, with a separate room in which to work. These services cost money for the guests, and hotels can make a profit on them. More important, they fill a need of the traveling businessperson and create a better guest experience, especially if they are priced fairly. Even though many guests travel with laptops, business centers still get much business as they have moved beyond renting computer time to many other services (copying, shipping, etc.)

Another example of good merchandising in a business-related restaurant is the offering of a 45-minute guaranteed lunch to cater to the limited time many people have for lunch. While no additional charge is made for this service, the restaurant has differentiated itself from its competitors by satisfying a need through merchandising.

The emergence of pizza on finer hotels' room service menus is a merchandising opportunity that fills a need of many customers. Many people do not want a full, heavy meal in their room. Some just want to watch television and have something "fun," as if they were at home. The pizza (merchandised often with beer) fills the need of the customer while putting money into the hotels' cash registers. Courtyard hotels has recently redesigned their lobbies to include 24-hour "mini-markets" that sell food products and other items that travelers may require. This type of merchandising can only increase revenues. Price does not become the deciding factor; instead, the product (and its ease of accessibility) becomes the reason for the purchase. Those customers who really wanted pizza in the first place might have called for a delivery from outside or gone out of the hotel; either way, the money would have been spent outside the hotel or not at all. More important, once again, you have satisfied a customer by fulfilling a need. Exhibit 16-13 shows a young entrepreneur in Istanbul, Turkey, selling his services.

The inclusion of minibars in guest rooms is satisfying to customers and increases hotel profits. Minibars are self-contained units that have beer, wine, liquor, juices, and soft drinks together with snacks. An inventory is taken of the unit's contents before the guest checks in, and all items consumed are posted to the bill on checkout. The probability is low that a guest would call room service for only one beer. With a minibar in the room, customers can lean over while watching television or reading and open a beer at their convenience. Minibars are now featuring many nonfood items such as playing cards and disposable cameras. Again, however, improper merchandising can lose customers. Too many minibar contents are overpriced, and customers are not particularly pleased when they have to pay the high prices. Because of the lack of items that guests want and the overpricing of these items, many buy outside and use the minibar as a refrigerator. This is an opportunity lost.* Smart hoteliers are talking with their guests before their arrival and asking what items they would like to see in the minibar. This way, the food items are things the guest will like and will be more likely to order. Some are

---

*We have asked some management why they charge so much for items in the minibar. The answer is unanimous—too many customers abuse the system, raising the costs. For example, they will take out a bottle of beer, drink it, fill it with water, put the cap back on, and return it to the minibar. Some of the newer versions of minibars at least partially prevent this. However, we have not seen the prices going down in these situations.

EXHIBIT 16-13   A young man selling his services in Istanbul, Turkey.

Source: Jeff Greenberg, Omni-Photo Communications, Inc. Used by permission.

also including the minibar items in the price of the room or pricing the items fairly.

Merchandising is marketing to the "captured" customer. Do not translate *captured* into *captivity*. Instead, translate *capture* into *opportunity*: Here's an opportunity to make the customer even more satisfied.

 Web Browsing Exercise

Go to the website for the National Association for Retail Marketing Services (www.narms.com). What did you learn about this organization? Do you think you might want to belong? Why or why not? What sort of companies belong to this organization?

Tourism Marketing Application

The International Association of Amusement Parks and Attractions (IAAPA) is an organization that helps attractions and amusement parks with their merchandising efforts. Not only do they publish magazines for their members, but they offer educational seminars on a variety of topics. Information about this organization can be found at www.iaapa.org/attractionstourist.htm (accessed April 3, 2006)

Public Relations and Publicity

Public relations is used to present the product or service to the media and the community in the best possible light. Positive publicity is the desired outcome. Public relations

and publicity are grouped together because of their commonality, which is the "free" use of the media to present management's view to the community at large. Instead of buying space in a newspaper or time on a radio station to get the firm's information out, the organization obtains it for free—provided the media think the organization is newsworthy or of interest. Usually, though, the organization does not control the actual placement and appearance of the information.

Every organization exists in a community that influences its success. It wants to have a positive image in the community and to be seen as a contributor to the overall well-being of society. Although publicity can derive from public relations, the difference is that publicity constitutes only the information the media freely and without influence choose to use. Thus publicity may be positive or negative. Public relations, on the other hand, constitutes attempts to manage publicity and to "plant" information in the press or to create a favorable image for reasons other than its formal product. In politics this is called **spin control,** a phrase that is used quite frequently.

Public relations, as well as publicity, also occurs through word of mouth. Although much of this may be started by the media, other aspects may be spontaneous. For example, a restaurant makes a special effort to employ people with special challenges. This fact may never strike the media, but the word gets around and the restaurant is looked at as a "do-gooder." This reflects positively on other aspects of the restaurant.

To the public, public relations and publicity may be the most believable forms of the communications mix, although recent research conducted by one of the authors suggests that consumers are increasingly suspicious about the contents of information they see, read, and hear in the media. A salesperson pitching a product or a slick advertising campaign may be subject to skepticism from consumers. When an independent source, such as a newspaper, writes about the product in a seemingly unbiased setting, credence is lent to the message unmatched by any other media format. A potential customer for a restaurant is more likely to try the veal special recommended by a restaurant reviewer than to try the same dish touted by a full-page ad proclaiming its excellence. A negative review can also totally counteract the positive impact of a full-page ad.

Tourism Marketing Application

The World Tourism Organization (www.world-tourism.org) sponsored two conferences in 2006 focusing on the best practices of tourism communications. Called TOURCOM, the meetings were held in Bamako, Mali, for Africa and in Rosario, Argentina, for the Americas. WTO believes that public relations play a key role in the international tourism process. As one person stated at a TOURCOM meeting in Amman, Jordan, in 2005: "The media are an equally important partner of destinations to tour operators and airlines." Information about TOURCOM can be found at www.world-tourism.org/newsroom/Releases/2006/february/tourcom.htm (accessed April 3, 2006).

Public Relations (PR)

Public relations is the planned management of the media's and community's perception of the hospitality enterprise. Although the press certainly cannot be told what to publish, a public relations effort can steer the story toward the best features of the product and away from negative images. Public relations efforts are designed to create stories that capture writers' attention with the hope that the writers will, in turn, communicate "the good news" to the desired readers or target market. Exhibit 16-14 is an example of a **PR news release**.

We can demonstrate these points with some examples. After Hurricane Katrina hit the Gulf Coast region, hoteliers in the region were faced with running their businesses while showing compassion. Area hotels provided food and shelter for evacuees and relief workers, helped coordinate medical care, organized fundraisers, and relaxed policies for pets and the number of people per room. At the corporate level, response was widespread and swift, aimed at helping both evacuees and employees of affected properties. Immediately after the hurricane struck, staff members of the Millennium Hotels and Resorts across the United States held a Basic Essentials Drive that collected over 12,000 donations of toiletries, food, clothes, medicine, paper products, and baby items for distribution to those in need. In addition, Millennium helped provide long-term assistance to displaced hospitality industry members by posting nationwide employment opportunities to the Travel Industry Association of America's (TIA) job bank.[2] Starwood ran a weeklong, worldwide online auction on Yahoo! to raise money for the Starwood Relief Fund benefiting Starwood associates affected by Katrina, offering honeymoon, spa, and gold packages at Starwood properties around the world, celebrity packages, and various other auction items, representing a combined retail value of over $1 million.[3] Marriott developed a program for Marriott Rewards members to convert their rewards points into monetary donations to the Red Cross.[4]

Another example is that of McDonald's, a company widely acclaimed for its public relations efforts. For McDonald's, public relations is a fundamental part of the brand marketing strategy. Ronald McDonald homes for families of ill children at nearby hospitals are nationally famous. When disaster strikes anywhere near a McDonald's, some of the first people on the scene are McDonald's employees with coffee and hamburgers for the victims and workers on the scene. When a man went into a McDonald's in California and shot and killed customers, McDonald's immediately closed the store and provided financial aid to the victims' families. When the company wanted to reopen the store a few months later, the townspeople strongly opposed it. McDonald's quickly complied by closing the store permanently. A great deal of positive publicity came from its public relations efforts to manage this tragedy.

In such cases and more often in less serious situations, public relations is used to formulate an image in the consumer's mind of what the company or product represents. Public relations–engendered publicity enabled McDonald's to capitalize on a possible negative image. Hosting Ronald McDonald homes has nothing to do with the production of hamburgers. The story is "created": The company cares for children (and perhaps, one thinks subliminally, has the same care while preparing the food). McDonald's comes across as a "good guy" in a bad situation.

Exhibit 16-15 provides a brief interview with Ms. Serna, whose husband is vice president and general manager of the Conrad Punta del Este Resort & Casino in Uruguay. In this interview she explains how the resort is very active in helping the children of Uruguay. Exhibit 16-16 shows employees from the Conrad Punta del Este Resort & Casino giving back to the community.

Undertaking Public Relations. Public relations efforts are not just initiated to deal with negative happenings or simply to create positive happenings; instead, they rep-

EXHIBIT 16-14 **Publicity Helps with Promotions**

FOR IMMEDIATE RELEASE

Contact: Jennifer Ploszaj
            InterContinental Hotels & Resorts

DO YOU LIVE AN INTERCONTINENTAL LIFE?
InterContinental Hotels & Resorts Launches Global Advertising Campaign

LONDON (September 22, 2005)—InterContinental Hotels & Resorts announced today it will launch a new global brand advertising campaign on September 26.

InterContinental's new advertising campaign is the result of positioning work that has been ongoing since late 2004. The brand's new tagline challenges its audience to answer the question, "Do you live an InterContinental Life?"

"At a time when other hotel brands are working to keep people in a 'bubble', InterContinental wants to provide our guests with memorable and unique experiences that will enrich their lives and broaden their outlook," said Jenifer Zeigler, senior vice president, global brand management, InterContinental Hotels & Results. "We believe the new social currency is about being 'in the know.' And we deliver that to our guests through great travel experiences."

The campaign launch consists of a television commercial filmed in Sydney, Australia, featuring Australia's Challenge Yacht, named Spirit, built for the 1992 Americas Cup in San Diego. The campaign's first print executions feature photography shot on the beaches and in the local markets of Bali, Indonesia.

"At InterContinental, we believe travel is a great thing," said Zeigler. "Launched in 1946, InterContinental Hotels became the symbol of glamour, sophistication and success that years later, continue to define international travel."

The television spot will air on CNN International as well as in-flight programming on British Airways, United, American, Emirates and Singapore airlines. The print media schedule includes insertions in *The Wall Street Journal, The New York Times, Newsweek, Time Magazine, Forbes, The Financial Times, Economist, The Times* and *Business Week* as well as major in-flight publications.

The campaign launches on Monday, September 26 and continues through the 2005 business travel season.

###

<u>Note to Editors:</u>

InterContinental Hotels Group PLC of the United Kingdom [LON:IHG, NYSE:IHG (ASRs)] is the world's largest hotel group by number of rooms. InterContinental Hotels Group owns, manages, leases or franchises, through various subsidiaries, more than 3,500 hotels and over 537,000 guest rooms in nearly 100 countries and territories around the world. The Group owns a portfolio of well recognized and respected hotel brands including InterContinental® Hotels & Resorts, Crowne Plaza® Hotels & Resorts, Holiday Inn® Hotels and Resorts, Holiday Inn Express®, Stay-bridge Suites®, Candlewood Suites® and Hotel Indigo™, and also manages the world's largest hotel loyalty program, Priority Club® Rewards, with over 26 million members worldwide. In addition to this, InterContinental Hotels Group has a 47.5% interest in Britvic, one of the two leading manufacturers of soft drinks, by value and volume, in Great Britain.

InterContinental Hotels Group offers information and online reservations for all its hotel brands at <u>www.ichotelsgroup.com</u> and information for the Priority Club Rewards program at <u>www.priorityclub.com.</u>

For the latest news from InterContinental Hotels Group, visit our online Press Office at <u>www.ihgplc.com/media.</u>

Source: InterContinental Hotels Group. Used by permission.

resent an ongoing task and are an important part of marketing planning. In this capacity, public relations plays the following roles:

[I]mproving awareness, projecting credibility, combating competition, evaluating new markets, creating direct sales leads, reinforcing the effectiveness of sales promotion and advertising, motivating the sales force, introducing new products, building brand loyalty, dealing with consumer issues and in many other ways.[5]

Public relations efforts also create images for the local, public, and financial communities as well as for the firm's employees. They create favorable attitudes toward a firm, its

EXHIBIT 16-15   **Interview with Ms. Serna**

I WOULD LIKE TO TALK TO YOU A LITTLE BIT ABOUT THE CONRAD PUNTA DEL ESTE RESORT AND CASINO, BECAUSE YOU ARE THE PUBLIC FACE FOR THE COMMUNITY. PLEASE TELL ME ABOUT SOME OF THE ACTIVITIES YOU ARE INVOLVED WITH HERE IN PUNTA DEL ESTE.

I am very happy with the support provided by the Conrad Punta del Este Resort and Casino. They have enabled me to work very closely with many of the poor children and families here in the community. We help over 500 families by giving them meals Monday through Friday. The children of the families we help come to the hotel for their snack at 4:30 in the afternoon after school. After they eat their snack, the children pick up their meal packet, which the casino makes, and then bring the packet home to their family. We want the children to have a snack first because we want to make sure that they share the food they bring home with their family. The resort hotel and casino pays for everything.

WHAT OTHER EVENTS ARE YOU INVOLVED IN PERSONALLY OR THROUGH THE RESORT?

The children need lots of help and something different to do every day, so we plan many activities on a daily basis. The children really like to play football [soccer]. We put together different activities—playing with computers, dancing, etc. I organize a prize for the best in each competition—things like that.

DO YOU ORGANIZE ANY PARTIES SPECIFICALLY FOR THE CHILDREN?

Yes. I try to make the parties as beautiful as possible. Here, it is not like America, where there are beautiful things everywhere. Here, people are not used to very pretty things, so I give them what I can at these parties. Again, the resort pays for everything.

HOW HAS YOUR WORK IN THE COMMUNITY HELPED THE RESORT?

It is wonderful. It is something all employees like to do. The company gives employees enough time to put everything together; they are very understanding with everything. It is a great morale builder for the resort.

Source: J. Serna. Used by permission.

EXHIBIT 16-16   The Conrad Punta del Este Resort & Casino organizes activities geared specifically toward poor children in the community.

Source: Conrad Punta del Este Resort & Casino. Used by permission.

products, and its efforts. Public relations can also create pre-opening publicity for hotels and restaurants through news releases that the media will carry. The result is the press may attend a grand opening or ribbon cutting. It invites dignitaries who make news and in whom the press and the public are interested. On an ongoing basis, public relations efforts keep the press and hence the public informed as to what is happening at the property or with the firm. Preopening public relations efforts are extremely important in getting a hotel or a restaurant off to a good start. At this point, we are marketing not only an intangible product but also one that does not yet exist. Several marketing objectives must be met during this time, including creating name recognition, establishing an image, building excitement, and cementing positive ties to the local community. Preopening public relations typically begins many months in advance of opening and gathers momentum as opening day approaches. Exhibit 16-17 shows a sample timetable for preopening public relations.

EXHIBIT 16-17	**Sample Timetable for Preopening Public Relations for a Hotel**

This schedule begins six months before the hotel opening, at which time the announcement of construction plans and the groundbreaking ceremony will have been completed.

150–180 days before opening	1. Hold meeting to define objectives and to coordinate public relations effort with advertising; establish timetable in accordance with scheduled completion date.
	2. Prepare press kit (printed and electronic form).
	3. Order photographs and renderings.
	4. Begin preparation of mailings and develop media lists.
	5. Contact all prospective beneficiaries of opening events.
	6. Reserve dates for press conferences at off-site facilities.
	7. Create a special "press room" on the website.
120–150 days before opening	1. Send announcement with photograph or rendering to all media.
	2. Send first progress bulletin to agents and media (as well as corporate clients, if desired).
	3. Begin production of permanent brochure.
	4. Make final plans for opening events including commitment to beneficiaries.
90–120 days before opening	1. Launch publicity campaign to national media.
	2. Send mailings to media.
	3. Send second progress bulletin.
	4. Arrange exclusive trade interviews and features in conjunction with ongoing trade campaign.
	5. Begin trade announcement.
	6. Post all press releases in the online press room.
60–90 days before opening	1. Launch campaign to local media and other media with a short lead time; emphasize hotels' contribution to the community, announcement of donations and beneficiaries, etc.
	2. Send third and final progress bulletin with finished brochure.
	3. Commence "behind-the-scenes" public tours.
	4. Hold "hard hat" luncheons for travel writers.
	5. Set up model unit for tours.
30–60 days before opening	1. Send preopening newsletter (to be continued on a quarterly basis).
	2. Hold soft opening and ribbon-cutting ceremony.
	3. Hold press event to announce opening.
	4. Establish final plans for opening gala.
The month of opening	1. Begin broadside mailing to agents.
	2. Hold openings festivities.
	3. Conduct orientation press trips.

Source: Adapted from the work of Aaron D. Allen, Founder/CEO of Quantified Marketing Group (www.quantifiedmarketing.com).

Large companies or properties usually have their own public relations firms, which are hired on a monthly retainer to develop and maintain favorable publicity for the organization. But even smaller companies that cannot afford PR agencies, as they are called, must practice public relations in-house on an ongoing basis. Doing this involves managing employee relations. It also involves relationships with taxi drivers and local police, the press, the competition, member of the distribution channels (such as airlines, travel agencies, tour operators), purveyors (who can be excellent carriers of good tidings), shareholders, bankers, and all manner of other publics with which the firm interacts.

Hotel and restaurant managers should belong to the appropriate community and public service organizations such as the Rotary, Chamber of Commerce, community task forces, and other groups. One could almost say that everything management does contributes in some manner to the public relations program. Even the employees of the firm may be excellent public relations ambassadors; in fact, for some firms they may be the most important of all. What your employees say about you and the way you operate reflects heavily on the image that will be created in the public's mind. Public relations efforts may also serve well in times of need as a defensive weapon; but more important, as a continuous and ongoing offensive weapon.

Planning Public Relations. The rules that govern the proper planning of the communications mix also apply to public relations. These include the following:

- Purpose
- Target market (in this case it may not be the customer at all, but might be the press, the financial community, the industry, employees, and intermediaries)
- Setting of tactics
- Integration with the product or service
- Integration with the firm's overall marketing efforts

Purpose. The purpose of a specific public relations program effort should be established before any further planning occurs. The purpose must be definitive and quantifiable. For example, a restaurant might be under a new management that has to overcome a perception in the marketplace of slow service. In this case, it is unlikely that an advertising campaign would really convince anyone that the service was better. Improving the customers' perception of the restaurant's service would be the purpose of the public relations campaign. The quantifiable measurement, as in advertising, would be positive shifts in local opinions about the restaurant's service standards and, ultimately, an increased number of covers.

A hotel might have an image in the marketplace of being too expensive for the local customers and might thus be avoided by them. The purpose of the public relations effort would be to dispel this perception by improving the price–value relationship image in the local marketplace. The success of this program may be measured by increased usage of guest rooms by local customers or in increased restaurant or lounge business outside of usual occupancy trends. In both of these situations, market research should be used to correctly evaluate customer perceptions, both before and after the public relations effort. Only then can the effort be correctly focused.

Target Markets.   When planning public relations, one must consider the benefit to the customer in the target market. Choosing a target market for a public relations effort is as important as choosing the correct market for any marketing communications effort. You must ask, How will the target market be influenced by the communications? This involves not only short-term benefits, but long-term ones as well, because hotels and restaurants are a major part of the community in which they exist. They are the most public of all commercial enterprises, so much so that they often become "public places" where people meet. It is these same people, as well, who answer such questions from out-of-towners as, Where should I stay? or Where's a good place to eat? Public relations will influence local responses to these questions even when the people themselves have never stayed or eaten at the property. Public relations efforts create an image in the mind of the consumer and reinforce that image in many ways.

Along with identifying a target audience comes the task of reaching these prospects. Although the geographic location of the customers needs to be understood, the correct media to reach that geographic area must be analyzed as well. Although a computer trade journal may appear to be a good place to advertise for a corporate meeting, this is probably not where a potential vacationer would be reading an article on the benefits of staying in a hotel.

While "selling stories" may sound unusual, good public relations experts will have a network of editors to whom they can do just that by calling on them personally. This relationship with editors and writers can be critical to breaking a story. For this reason, the discipline of public relations is becoming more of a science and less of an art form.

The public relations expert will push a story as much as a salesperson sells a product. Calls are made to the editors, they are wined and dined, and thank-you notes and flowers are sent in appreciation of the placement of a story or press release. A press release is a document that contains the message or story the hospitality enterprise wishes to communicate that is prepared in a manner that is consistent with the expectations of the media. A press release always contains the contact name and number of the public relations professional who wrote the story, background information on the facility, and the body copy of the story. It is then "pitched" or "sold" to the media.

Personal contacts with the media are what differentiate a good public relations firm from a poor one. Anyone can write stories and send them to papers and broadcast media, but only a true professional has the contacts to follow up until the article is published or the story makes the nightly news.

Positioning   A cohesive message must be developed before a public relations campaign is launched. Ideally, the public relations message will complement the message appearing in the other forms of the communications mix. If the advertising message is telling customers that service is the main advantage of the product, the public relations stories should also reinforce that theme. If food quality is the focus of the marketing effort, stories on the chefs and their background will augment this effort.

The positioning must also be kept within the framework of the overall purpose of the public relations effort. If a public relations effort is undertaken to change the customer's perception of slow service, then the positioning should also follow this generic format. It is very easy to get distracted during a public relations campaign and begin many activities unrelated to the original purpose or positioning of the product. Positioning is where the "spin" is put on the story.

Developing Tactics.   Before the public relations program is employed, it is important to begin to develop stories on the product itself. Good starting points in a public relations campaign include looking at personnel, customers, and history. Exhibit 16-18 suggests 10 "surefire" ways to obtain publicity.

Personnel   Numerous personnel stories can be developed and submitted based on the employees who work every day in a hotel or restaurant. The Clarion Hotel in New Orleans received much media attention when an off-duty

EXHIBIT 16-18	Opening a New Hotel? Announcing a Renovation? Here Are 10 Surefire Ways to Get the Publicity You Need to Get Heads in Beds

If you are in the planning stages for the opening of a new hotel or a significant renovation, and you expect to get noticed by the media upon project completion, you would be wise to keep the following 10 tips in mind.

1. When possible, be unique and different with your hotel's design and amenities. This may be stating the obvious, but the media—whether local or trade—ultimately is not going to be as interested in a hotel that is cookie cutter, has no interesting story to tell, and is no different than its market competitors. Because the Courtyard by Marriott—Los Angeles/San Fernando Valley went beyond brand standards with extra amenities and a unique boutique-style design, it was of greater interest to the media and was featured in numerous publications including *Hotels* magazine and *L.A. Direct*.

2. Just as you should start early designing your marketing strategy and hiring the most qualified sales staff, start just as early establishing your public relations strategy and selecting a qualified public relations professional. Most hotels do not have the money or the need to employ a full-time public relations professional, but there are highly qualified consultants available who can guide you through the planning process. Be sure to select a professional who has lodging industry experience. An experienced representative knows the best way to make an impact. Once you have selected your consultant, clarify your expectations before reaching an agreement.

3. Once you and the consultant have established an agreement that details both parties' expectations, work with that person to establish a media target list. The list should include names, titles, e-mail addresses, phone numbers and a brief description of the media outlet each person represents. Ask to review the spreadsheet. It should include names from the following: local newspapers, area business magazines, radio and TV stations, chambers of commerce, industry association newsletters and convention and visitors bureau publications. The spreadsheet also should include contact information for industry trade publications as well as industry electronic newsletters—Hotel Online, for example.

4. Decide what type of press release strategy will work best for your hotel: just one press release, a series of releases, or a complete press kit that includes press releases, hotel background and highlights, as well as other material such as owner/management company information. The consultant should know what is best for your property. The person you hire should communicate with you consistently during every step of the publicity process, get your approval on each piece of written material, inform you of successes and provide proof of them.

5. Select a professional photographer to shoot high-quality digital photos of the interior and exterior areas of your hotel. An amateur is less likely to understand what angles and lighting are necessary for good composition. The photographer should provide images to you and your public relations professional in both high- and low-resolution formats (high-res for print publications and low-res for online reproduction). With the assistance of your consultant, select several photos that can be used on an ongoing basis to help brand your hotel. These images also can be used on any of the many travel websites where your hotel will be listed.

6. As mentioned above, determine what is most unique about your hotel. Highlight it in the headline of each press release. When the Noble Investment Group recently opened the Courtyard by Marriott at UAB (University of Alabama-Birmingham), what was highlighted in the release's headline was the fact that the hotel was downtown Birmingham's first new hotel In 15 years. Editors often will give more attention to stories that are unique and different.

7. Meet the media. One way to do that is to work with your public relations consultant to organize a media reception and hotel tour. A well-organized and creative consultant should be able to manage the distribution of invitations, follow-up and RSVPs. A good time to hold a reception is very soon after the hotel's opening. A pre-opening exclusive also may be given to a prominent media outlet if the opening or renovation merits that—typically done at a larger, historic, or landmark hotel.

8. Hold an open house and invite the business community and/or public. Give away a few free weekends, pay to have a local celebrity appear, or invite a radio or TV station, if possible, to do a remote broadcast from the hotel lobby. Once again, use your public relations professional to help coordinate invitations, write a press release and follow-up with the media to drum up interest in this type of event.

9. One way to gather the media, the business community and public officials at the same time is to hold a ribbon cutting ceremony. Hire a professional photographer to record the event. Work with your public relations professional to coordinate the invitations, press release and follow-up. Invite the mayor, area government representatives, business leaders and other dignitaries.

10. In public relations, repetition is everything. It takes multiple impressions to help brand your hotel. If you are happy with the quality of the work performed by your public relations representative, establish an ongoing relationship. Openings and renovations are not the only reasons to issue a press release. Other possible reasons: personnel appointments, special events, celebrity appearances, sales promotions, to announce an award, respond to a crisis event or publicize a volunteer program.

If you select a public relations professional with a proven track record and industry experience, you will have a lot less to worry about before, during and after the hotel opening/renovation process.

Source: Hasek, G. (2005, December). *Opening a new hotel? Announcing a renovation? Here are 10 surefire ways to get the publicity you need to get heads in beds*. Retrieved December 13, 2005, from www.hotel-online.com/News/PR2005_4th/Dec05_Hasekcommunications.html. Glenn Hasek is president of Hasek Communications, Middleburg Heights, Ohio.

bellman chased and apprehended the attacker of a foreign tourist who had ventured into an unsafe area of the city.

For restaurants, the background of the chef can provide an interesting story. If the chef has won any awards or trained outside of the country, the local media are often willing to convey the story to their readers.

Customers　Sometimes customers become a story in themselves. A honeymoon couple from 30 years back checking into the same room can generate tremendous interest in the press. A customer who dines regularly in a restaurant conveys an image of contentment that might cause readers to try the product. And when celebrities or politicians dine in a restaurant or stay in a hotel, the public has a natural curiosity.

Positioning also becomes an important element in using customers as a lead story for a hotel or restaurant. Be sure, however, that the customer being featured is the right representative for the desired target market.

History A story line developed about the building, neighborhood, or owner's or manager's background can also provide a format of interest to the public. Examples include any of the hotels developed by Donald Trump, Steve Wynn, or Ian Schwager.

Measuring Success. As with all communications vehicles, measuring success is important in public relations; unfortunately, the impact of public relations is particularly difficult to track. Without special 800 numbers for advertisements, traffic to specific websites, or the redemption of coupons from direct mail pieces, the results attributable to a public relations program may be elusive at best. One method used frequently by practitioners is based on the value of the exposure created in the medium relative to its equivalent value in terms of paid advertising. Put simply, for each column inch of editorial or "unpaid" story line (or broadcast time on television), the equivalent advertising rate is calculated to determine the corresponding "value" of the public relations effort. Exhibit 16-19 shows how a promotion for a prominent New York City hotel tracked this in terms of advertising equivalents. The PR release ran in the last quarter of the year. Many prestigious magazines have "closing dates" 90 days prior to the cover date of publication. A tracking service provided clippings of the stories that appeared in the publications shown in the exhibit. The column inches were determined by the actual copy, and the cost per column inch was determined by each publication's rate card. In this case, the promotion yielded $144,905 of "unpaid" media coverage that reached 1,729,550 people. This worked out to a little over eight cents per person reached. Exhibit 15-9 discusses word of mouth and explains how to calculate its impact. This should be part of measurement of any promotional campaign.

Guidelines. Additional guidelines for public relations have been suggested by Rod Caborn, executive vice president public relations for the firm Yesawich, Pepperdine, Brown & Russell.[6]

1. The most common mistake hotels make are that they do not budget for PR expenses. In order to get results, you need to spend some money.
2. Be careful who you hire, as PR titles are often bestowed on people who have no training or experience in public relations. It is best to use reputable PR firms.
3. Like a good marketing plan, it is imperative to have a written PR plan. Without such a plan, PR will not happen.
4. PR people must understand your marketing plan. You can't expect results unless you let them in on your plans and objectives. Make sure they understand that PR is part of the marketing mix.
5. A consistent, ongoing PR program should provide consistent, ongoing results.
6. It takes innovative ideas to get deserved PR coverage.
7. Remember: Great public relations depends upon creative management.

 Web Browsing Exercise

Use your favorite web browser and type in "hospitality public relations." Be prepared to discuss what you find. Be sure to investigate the types of services offered.

Publicity

When "natural" stories like those discussed earlier have been fully developed, other methods need to be employed to keep the press interested in the hospitality enterprise. Publicity now needs to be "created" so that editors will continue to have something to write about.

The creation of publicity events is not as simple as it may sound. The purpose of the event needs to be established together with a target medium, and an evaluation of the event needs to follow. Publicity, in this sense, is like pro-

EXHIBIT 16-19	Measuring Public Relations Success			
Publication Article Appeared	Circulation	Column Inches	Cost per Column Inch	Advertising Equivalency of Placed Article
Avenue magazine	80,000	11	$399	$4,389
Cornell Quarterly	6,000	4	$45	$180
Gourmet	880,774	124	$1,104	$136,896
Lodging magazine	46,000	1	$169	$169
Travel America	416,776	8	$370	$2,960
Barron's	300,000	1	$311	$311
	1,729,550			$144,905

motion, except that publicity is aimed specifically at the media to generate more public relations. Promotions can be held without publicity; publicity helps with promotions.

Publicity begins with inviting the appropriate editors and radio or TV station managers to the property for a specific event. Again, the personal relationship developed by the public relations manager is critical for successful attendance by the right people.

The event must be organized so that everything goes perfectly. If an event is not executed well, the hotel or restaurant may be the object of negative publicity. In addition, any other potential customers who hear of it by word of mouth may be turned off. While this might be catastrophic, it is nothing compared to the potential lost business that one editor could produce by writing a critical review in a newspaper with a circulation of 300,000 readers.

At the event, press releases with background information are made available to the press. A prepared press release will answer questions such as the number of seats available in the restaurant, the name of the manager, and so on. The public relations professional will "work the event" by attending and "pitching" the points personally to the attendees from the media. The end of the actual promotion signals the beginning of the placement work for the public relations effort. Thank-you notes, special commemorative gift, and/or flowers are typically sent to remind the attendees of the importance of the event. Follow-up calls are made to cajole the writers to place the story in the best light and to request favorable placement from the editors. Having a story placed in a newspaper or on radio or television is not the only measure of success. The physical placement of the story in the medium (relative to other stories) is as important as getting the story into the media.

After all of this work is finished, the last stage of the public relations/publicity effort is program evaluation. Have more customers been generated? Was the perception in the marketplace altered to the satisfaction of the management team? The evaluation process is as important as any other phase of the effort. Restaurant covers and rooms sold can be tracked at the property, but changes in customer perceptions are more difficult to measure. These measures are typically taken through consumer research that measures both "pre" and "post" campaign images.

Effective public relations programs always include a provision for the unexpected—the negative publicity that can follow a natural disaster or otherwise unfortunate event. When hurricane Wilma devastated the resort community of Cancun, local hoteliers had an immediate need to communicate quickly and accurately with the worldwide media covering the story. Marriott managed the tragedy in a masterful manner, chartering buses to take guests to a regional airport several hundred miles away, then picking up the tab to fly them home. Other properties that were less well prepared were the object of repeated negative stories that featured disgruntled guests who had no food, water, or clean shelter for days. Accordingly, every public relations plan must include a provision for "crisis communications" setting forth policies on such critical issues as who will serve as the official spokesperson to the press, what arrangements will be made to get timely and accurate information to the press, how often the press will be briefed, and so on.

Handling negative publicity is an art unto itself. Exhibit 16-20 is abstracted from an article on franchisees' and franchisers' cooperation in handling negative publicity.

How should franchise companies best handle media questions regarding events that take place at individual

---

EXHIBIT 16-20   Handling Negative Publicity

It is not unusual for hotels, resorts, restaurants, and related hospitality businesses to find themselves the object of negative attention in the press, frequently a result of circumstances beyond their control. And, although management is generally not able to control the actual content of the resulting press coverage, it can ensure balanced reporting of the circumstances and the event through observance of the following guidelines:

- *Be prepared.* Every hospitality enterprise should anticipate the ultimate occurrence of some type of crisis or catastrophic event through the preparation and maintenance of a crisis communications plan. The latter should specify the policies and procedures that would apply in the event of an emergency or other event that could result in negative coverage of the business in the press.
- *Stick to the facts.* Report and comment on only what you know to be true, not on what you think may be true or on speculation that has yet to be confirmed;
- *Tell your story through a single spokesperson.* This individual should be identified in the crisis communications plan, and he or

she should be the sole source of contact with the media. This precaution will minimize the potential for miscommunication about the facts and/or the business's actions in the aftermath of the event.
- *Tell your story in a timely manner.* There's nothing more suspicious than silence in the aftermath of some type of unfortunate event, so be sure to provide the press with periodic updates as you sort out the facts and determine the most appropriate course of action.
- *Tell the truth.* This seems to be an obvious guideline, yet intense scrutiny from the press often tempts those in the hot seat to soften the news, particularly if it is bad.
- *Do the right thing.* This is the Golden Rule of media: If a customer, stakeholder, or employee has legitimately been wronged as a result of an action taken by the business, then management should acknowledge the failure and do the right thing to make proper amends, even if the corresponding action has adverse financial implications for the business.

properties? "There needs to be an open dialogue with the press, so that no one thinks a property is trying to hide something," says Scott Brush. an independent consultant. Regardless, the public will look to the brand to make a corporate statement, as provided by the following example.

An 18-year-old woman was killed in a freak accident at a Ramada Inn. The woman, who was wet from a downpour, was electrocuted as she slid her card key into the metal door of her room. Both the hotel's GM and Ramada's PR manager released immediate statements saying the case was under investigation and no new information could be provided at the time. Later, negative publicity arose from preliminary findings, when it was shown that some failure in the guest room's air conditioning or its supply cord caused the unusually high voltage that triggered the electrocution. Ramada's parent company had no formal crisis management program but consulted with the general manager and issued statements as needed. It only got involved as much as the franchisee wanted it to. In this case, that wasn't enough to stop the adverse publicity.

Radisson has a crisis communications plan in place for each hotel and, in such situations, maintains a channel of communication with the press. If a reporter wants to make a national story out of something, there is no way to stop him. But you can't run away from the issue and say "no comment," says Radisson. Often, Radisson will set up a spokesperson at the property. However, Radisson believes that a hotel should establish its own relationship with the media. Very often, when an accident occurs, the hotel is just as much a victim as the actual victim. Radisson tries to keep a local story from becoming a national story. But if it is unable to prevent this, corporate gets very involved and stands side by side with the franchisee to protect the brand and the investment.

Choice Hotels International has a 24-hour crisis hotline for its franchisees. Choice's corporate PR office will also write statements for a property and guide property management on how best to answer questions from the press. Hilton and Sheraton follow a very similar practice. Their corporate offices can be contacted 24 hours a day through special hotlines.

Tourism Marketing Application

An article published in *Kathamandu Post Basanta Raj Misras* states: "Tourism in Nepal has been hit not only by the insurgency but also by the wrong perception created by the inflated news and other types of misinformation campaign. The misconception has kept significant number of tourists off Nepal, despite an improved security situation in the country." To counteract the negative publicity, the government of Nepal has set up a crisis management center comprising high-level officials throughout various branches of government. The goal of this center is "to disseminate correct and authentic news and fight against negative publicity by establishing strong relationships with foreign media, adopting appropriate marketing strategy, suggesting policy measures, and handling seen and unforeseen incidents." (www.strategypage.com/messageboards/messages/76-270.asp, accessed April 3, 2006)

■ Summary

This chapter offers a foundation and methodology for the successful execution of sales promotions, merchandising, and public relations programs. The most common reason for failure in delivering these subsets of the communications mix is lack of planning. Sales promotions usually have short-term objectives. They must be developed with reference to the interests of a specific target market, and both employees and customers must be aware of the product or service being promoted. Different products have to be promoted in different ways, but eventually, results must be measured. Merchandising is primarily in-house marketing, and the planning process includes assessing the needs of the customer then providing the product to the customer in a cost-effective manner. With a strong planning process in place and a proper evaluation mechanism, both revenues and customer satisfaction can be maximized.

The public relations component of a hospitality marketing plan is a very important element of the communications mix. In fact, it may be the most important element in that it is generally the most believable for the consumer. A potential customer is more likely to be influenced by reading or hearing a third party's praise for a product than by an advertising campaign.

The public relations campaign should be focused and quantifiable within targeted positioning objectives. Publicity remains a subset of the public relations umbrella, to be used after all "natural" stories have been highlighted by press coverage. Negative publicity requires special handling. In the next chapter we continue with the last element of the communications mix, personal selling. We devote an entire chapter to that subject because of the predominance of its use in driving revenues to hospitality enterprises.

■ Key Terms

sales promotions
merchandising
spin control

public relations
PR news release

■ Discussion Questions

1. Develop a hypothetical promotion to sell more California wine in a restaurant using all of the steps outlined for a successful sales promotion.
2. Discuss the basic rules of merchandising using a real-life example.
3. Develop an example of good merchandising for a hotel or restaurant using at least two of the other elements of the communications mix.
4. What are the components of a good public relations plan? Discuss how you might apply them to a local restaurant.
5. Discuss the similarities and differences between sales promotions and merchandising.
6. Contrast public relations and publicity and discuss the implications of each.
7. A major role of public relations may be to deal with unexpected crises that result in bad publicity. Discuss how hospitality organizations can create positive public relations when faced with disasters such as accidental death or serious injury caused by a drunken customer.
8. Develop a preopening public relations plan for a restaurant using Exhibit 16-17 as a guide.

■ Group Projects

1. Suppose you have developed a totally new service for a hotel that you believe is unique and not done by others. Define the service. Then develop a promotion and merchandising campaign for it internally and a PR program for it externally.
2. Do the same as project 1 for a local restaurant menu item.

■ References

1. Feltenstein, T. (1987, November 9). How to discount your product without sabotaging your image. *Nation's Restaurant News,* F20.
2. Retrieved November 2, 2005, from www2.millennium hotels.com/MCIL.nsf/unidlookup/E742B59BD6400B 1548257098000C43A6?opendocument.
3. Retrieved November 2, 2005, from www.starwoodhotels. com/luxury/about/news_release_detail.html?obj_id= 0900c7b9804db82b.
4. Retrieved November 2, 2005, from http://marriott.com/ news/detail.mi?marrArticle=102037.
5. Haywood, R. (1984). *All about PR.* London: McGraw-Hill. Excerpted from Buttle, F. A. (1986). *Hotel and food service marketing.* London: Holt, Rinehart and Winston, 400.
6. Conversation with Rod Caborn, Executive Vice President/Public Relations of Yesawich, Pepperdine, Brown & Russell, November 2005. Updated from Adams, J. (1987, June 8). Good P.R. plan can be potent marketing tool for hotels. *Hotel & Motel Management,* 60.

CHAPTER 17

The Communications Mix

Personal Selling

Overview

Personal selling is the only part of the communications mix that involves direct interaction between the seller and the buyer. It is especially suitable when both the product and the buyer's needs are complex. In the hospitality industry, it is used primarily by large hotels and chains that actively solicit corporate accounts and meetings and conventions. Personal selling involves face-to-face contact in which the salesperson has a high degree of control over the information exchange with the customer and can receive immediate feedback in the negotiation process. The salesperson can then tailor the offer to meet customers' needs and solve their problems.

This chapter also discusses the sales process. Starting from scratch, the sales process has a definite sequence. **Prospecting** is the process of finding qualified customers. **Qualifying** a prospect means making sure they are willing and able to buy. The sales approach is tailored to the customer by learn-

Continued on page 464

462

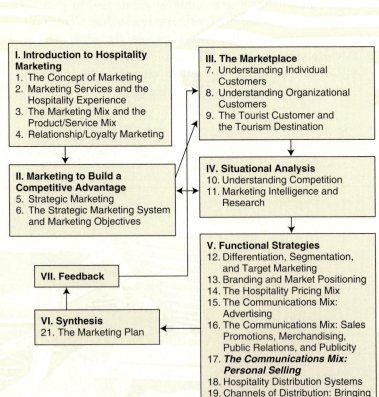

I. Introduction to Hospitality Marketing
1. The Concept of Marketing
2. Marketing Services and the Hospitality Experience
3. The Marketing Mix and the Product/Service Mix
4. Relationship/Loyalty Marketing

II. Marketing to Build a Competitive Advantage
5. Strategic Marketing
6. The Strategic Marketing System and Marketing Objectives

III. The Marketplace
7. Understanding Individual Customers
8. Understanding Organizational Customers
9. The Tourist Customer and the Tourism Destination

IV. Situational Analysis
10. Understanding Competition
11. Marketing Intelligence and Research

V. Functional Strategies
12. Differentiation, Segmentation, and Target Marketing
13. Branding and Market Positioning
14. The Hospitality Pricing Mix
15. The Communications Mix: Advertising
16. The Communications Mix: Sales Promotions, Merchandising, Public Relations, and Publicity
17. *The Communications Mix: Personal Selling*
18. Hospitality Distribution Systems
19. Channels of Distribution: Bringing the Customer to the Product
20. Interactive Marketing: Internet and Database Marketing

VII. Feedback

VI. Synthesis
21. The Marketing Plan

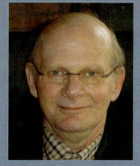

David Green
Chairman of the Board, David Green Organization

Mr. Green was a pioneer in integrating database marketing, telemarketing, and direct sales representation into a unified marketing model. In 1969, after successfully completing the first-ever sales and marketing management-training program of Sheraton Hotels Corporation, Mr. Green became one of Sheraton's top producers in New York and Boston. Two years later he leveraged his relationships with meeting planners and hotel peers to launch the David Green Organization.

David is a frequent guest presenter at trade events on various topics, including "How to Build Customer Databases," "Selecting the Right Database," and "Telemarketing as an Effective Tool." An all-New York City basketball star, David played for City College of New York, where he earned a B.A. degree.

Marketing in Action
David Green, Chairman of the Board, David Green Organization

There are various ways hotels communicate to customers—advertising, the Internet, public relations. How do you see personal selling being integrated into the overall marketing and communication strategy of the hotel?

At a property level, I think the focus is salespeople. A sales individual is what is referred to as a "high-touch channel," meaning that the design of salespeople is to go and spend time with the more profitable accounts of the property. It is really a function of employing people against the right accounts. The relationship has a lot to do with the activity, the frequency, and the opportunity for the hotel. It is relation selling that is solution-driven selling. It's the opportunity to send back to people a level of service that is ultimately a tipping point in these kinds of opportunities. When you are looking at salespeople in general, the ones who are rewarded handsomely or are well paid are the ones who avoid the small programs—to the extent that you are really focusing on the relationship to continue the journey of delivering that kind of business to the actual property.

Can you tell me a little about some of the characteristics you see in successful salespeople?

Certainly passion has to be part of the equation. Also curiosity, the ability to listen well and then respond in the right kind of communication are important characteristics—to be prepared to say no when you can't do the right thing for your client. A lot of integrity is involved. The ability to understand the organization and understand the customer is also important. An interesting piece to that equation is that in today's environment, the decision makers are individuals and not necessarily companies; therefore, the more knowledge you have about that individual, the closer you can get to them and communicate what is important to them compared to what is not important. Also, every time you have an opportunity to work with your customer is an opportunity to let that relationship develop.

Conversely, I think what is going to happen to that world is that it is going to shift, so it is not so much an individual's wrong decision as it is the company's. In today's environment, it is not the meeting planner and the corporate travel department who are making these decisions, but

Continued on page 464

Overview *(continued)*

ing what the customer's real requirements or problems are. This often requires a lot of probing. Benefits and features are presented after learning the customer's needs. Being able to deal with customers' attitudes is a skillful process. The salesperson has to learn to overcome skepticism, indifference, and objections. Closing the sale means asking for and getting a commitment. Once the sale is closed, regular follow-up is important, and at the time of the event all promises made must be kept.

Marketing in Action *(continued)*
David Green Chairman of the Board, David Green Organization

rather the CFOs and distribution managers. In some cases, the bonding really goes from company to company and not from person to person. Not to say that the relationship is being eliminated, but it is the company itself that is really driving decisions.

Who in your view has a successful hotel sales organization?

I think Hyatt is very engaged, Marriott certainly, and Starwood. I think all of the significant chains, but that's not to exclude the independent and small brands, which are very focused on training and understand the characteristics of a salesperson. They are basically hunters and farmers.

Could you describe the hunting and farming concept further for us?

The hunting process is more prospective. It's reaching out trying to find new customers. And that kind of skill set takes the ability of a person who has stamina and is excited by the opportunity of finding new customers. They are more receptive on the front end—meeting, uncovering new opportunities—compared to perhaps booking a piece of business. The skill sets there are quite different compared to a farmer, who is more engaged in actually working with a customer in order to really penetrate increased activities and opportunities. The hunter is really starting from a base of zero, having to reach out and identify the opportunity to make the call, to build the dialogue to get that first opportunity.

Do you think it is important for a sales organization to have both?

Absolutely! With the competitive environment going on, you have to also extend it to loyalty—or the lack of it at times—in light of what could happen with your better clients. Meetings could be eliminated later or downgraded, companies could be sold, contacts could be changed, or competition shows up. There are more parts that you need to look at. With that in mind, I think you have to have a plan going on in order to replace customers that may go away. Therefore, you have to integrate sales departments with hunters and farmers.

Can you tell me a little bit about how your team prospects for new business?

Our team benefits to a great extent from the call center we have. I believe that prospecting is important to the sales process. Ideally, what you want is channels at the call center or Internet to deliver opportunities for these kinds of people. More selling time is made available and the hunting is sourced to a department or an infrastructure that has the skill sets and is charged with just reaching out and finding new customers, depending upon the size of the operation. Some hotels don't have the luxury, and some larger companies have the luxury and appreciate that a sale is a sale.

You touched on something there. How do you think the Internet is affecting the sales process?

It is a vehicle or a channel where the buyer can reach out to do research any time of day. Traditionally, they would do it during the day, whereas now they are doing it later on or on a laptop 24/7. They are reaching out to a website to gather information about a property and its capabilities or just looking at different locations to see what makes it unique. It's at their convenience, at their time. What it also suggests is that they may go online to learn more about hotels—at least those that can handle their requirements—and ultimately refer back to the actual hotel, to their sales department, or to a representative.

Do you see the Internet becoming a bigger and bigger part of the equation as life goes on?

Absolutely, because I think what will eventually happen will be the sites and their content will continue to improve. I think the technology will also continue to improve in terms of what you might be able to do online in the future. A small meeting of under 50 people could be literally executed online, with the ability to deliver individual information and your requirements to the actual property electronically online and they can respond within a few seconds with information about the rate, meeting facilities, etc.—eliminating human intervention but being able to fully execute online. I think that is the next generation of what will occur. What is interesting is that about 75 percent of all meetings are for under 50 people.

The dynamics there are interesting, if it were to be fully automated. If you look at hotels with your company, maybe 60 percent of the people at a property level are handling small meetings. Just imagine if this could be eliminated and fully automated; you would be able to redeploy those people into another capacity.

Can you describe a successful campaign that your organization has executed for a customer?

We have done different programs in light of really using the call center. For example, we did a program for the Los Angeles Convention and Visitors Bureau, trying to find new customers, which mirrored the potential growth of a certain segment of the city of Los Angeles. They wanted to reach out to different technology companies based in the East Coast as opposed to the West Coast, because technology companies in the West Coast usually meet in the East Coast. So the idea was to find technology companies that really resembled the comforts that they were experiencing in Los Angeles. They were multinational companies that had revenue bases of $1 million or upwards, and we began to reach out to different communities on the East Coast to simply mirror the profile of these kinds of companies that were meeting out in the West Coast. It was a very successful campaign. So we took insights, we took revenue stats, SIC, etc.

What is SIC?

SIC is an industry segment specific to technology. They were not hardware companies; they were software companies. So we really broke down the SIC—not just technology, but the kind of technology. And the idea here was even

though the core campaign did not necessarily deliver, it was delivered back to them in future opportunity by saying, yes, they do have meetings similar to what you like to pursue; yes, they are based in the East Coast. You begin to see dialogue with people within these organizations, and over time you begin to encourage them to look at your city for their next venue. And the fact you did that, the likelihood is that you would be included when they begin this kind of conversation about sites in the future, particularly in the West Coast. So it was about identifying what it's like beginning to build a campaign, beginning to build a relationship, and it's the fact that you begin to look at location because of what you accomplished, which was the project focus in the long run.

How do you think personal selling will change in the next five years?

I think a variety of things will happen. I think perhaps compensation will change. I think the hotel will get different types of compensation schedules that will get employed inside the hotel community and outside, meaning it will feel the compensation should be charted into results. If that is the case, bonuses are introduced, lower salaries are instated, and commissions are established. Really it is designed to find people who operate willingly in terms of what they book and what they make. And the skill sets certainly continue to evolve in that regard, once again, commission driven. Not just how to help you with your meeting, but really how else we can support these venues, whether you have the services or you find the services to welcome these organizations. So it's almost like saying your hotel or hotel company becomes the full-stop engagement. They can work with the organization many different ways, and that is based on a knowledge and a trust that they create and establish with the organization. I think it's huge when you talk about that. It's a kind of training. It is a skill set, it is solution driven, and that kind of training has to be introduced because the plan results are changing. They are being asked to do more with less. So, if they can find a resource that can work with them and can accommodate their requirements, I think they are more responsive to that kind of a relationship. You are seeing hotel companies and airlines doing this, so it is really a full service and demonstrates a level of experience that truly exceeds their reputation. At the end of the day that is what it is all about.

Used by permission from David Green.

Personal selling is the direct interaction between a seller and a prospective buyer for the purpose of making a sale. Personal selling may be one of the more challenging aspects of the communications mix. While public relations communicates through stories and the media, advertising communicates through copy and artwork, and merchandising communicates through in-house promotions, the salesperson communicates through direct oral presentations to the customer.

Obviously, every employee should be a "salesperson" for his or her organization. In this chapter, however, we will discuss selling from the perspective of hospitality organizations that specifically designate people to carry out the direct sales function.

Organized personal selling is not universally used in the hospitality industry. Rarely will you meet a salesperson from the local Pizza Hut, McDonald's, or even Motel 6. On the other hand, full-service hotels and restaurants with extensive catering facilities for groups employ salespeople as an essential part of their communications mix.

Whether personal selling is used by an organization depends on several factors, including the following:

- Targeted source of revenue
- Complexity of the products and services offered
- Quantities in which products and services are purchased
- Price that is paid

In the fast-food or budget hotel case, the products and services are relatively simple, the customer knows what they are, individuals or small groups in relatively small quantities usually purchase them, and the price is low. For the buyer, it is a low-risk, low-involvement purchase. Hiring a salesperson would not be cost effective or even productive. The interaction between the buyer and seller is easy and straightforward.

Contrast this with the 1,600-room Hilton Americas in Houston. One salesperson may book a group of 500 rooms for three nights at $150 per room night. This is $225,000 worth of room revenue alone, negotiated between the salesperson and a meeting planner. In addition, there are food and beverage functions, hospitality suites, general session and breakout rooms, representing possibly another $100,000, and dozens of other details to be worked out. The same is true of a resort such as the Broadmoor in Colorado Springs. These are high-risk purchases with high involvement on the part of the buyer who wants every detail to go perfectly. The products and services are complex and need much explanation, negotiation, and confirmation before a contract is signed. A good salesperson will decrease the risk factor by offering assurance and providing examples.

Besides **sales managers** at the unit level, chains such as Marriott, Hyatt, and Hilton employ national and international sales managers to represent the entire chain to accounts that have ongoing needs for many hotels in many locations. Personal selling has been found to be most appropriate in the following situations:

- The product requires that the customer receive assistance, perhaps a personal demonstration and trial, and the purchase decision requires a major commitment on the buyer's part.
- The final price is negotiated, not fixed, and the final price and quantity purchased allow an adequate margin to support selling expenses.
- Distribution channels are short and direct, and channel members require training and assistance.
- Advertising media do not reach all of the intended markets, and the information sought by potential customers cannot be provided thoroughly through advertising.
- The market sees personal selling as an essential part of the product.

The hospitality product and organizational markets clearly lend themselves to the personal selling component of the communications mix. Buying the product requires a major commitment on the purchaser's part. Even a small meeting of only 30 people for three days in a suburban hotel can easily exceed $10,000. Assistance is necessary in application—that is, understanding customers' goals and helping them achieve them. Personal demonstrations and trial are common such as site inspections, trial stays, and booking a small meeting before a large one. Pricing for meetings, group bookings, and corporate accounts is normally negotiated. Distribution channels are short and direct, and intermediaries require training and assistance. Advertising is inadequate and too expensive to reach and fulfill the needs of the buyer and explain the benefits. Finally, the marketplace sees the salesperson as an integral part of the product. As hotels in the same product class have essentially become a basic commodity, salespeople can develop relationships that provide a competitive edge.

All the rules of the communications mix apply to sales. However, there are differences between personal selling and the other components of the communications mix, as seen in Exhibit 17-1.

Following are several advantages to using personal selling:

1. Selling is really about solving a customers' problem. Customer problems become needs. Personally selling enables the salesperson to determine what those problems are and then show how the salesperson's product solves the problem.

EXHIBIT 17-1	**Characteristics of the Communications Mix**				
Communications Mode	**Personal Selling: Direct and Face-to-Face**	**Advertising: Indirect and Nonpersonal**	**Publicity: Usually Indirect and Nonpersonal**	**Sales Promotion: Usually Indirect and Nonpersonal**	**e-mail**
Communicator's control over the situation	High	Low	Moderate to low	Moderate to low	Moderate to high
Amount of feedback	Much	Little	Little	Little to moderate	Moderate
Speed of feedback	Immediate	Delayed	Delayed	Varies	Varies
Message flow	Two-way	One-way	One-way	Mostly one-way	Can be two-way or one-way
Control over message content	Yes	Yes	No	Yes	Yes
Sponsor identified	Yes	Yes	No	Yes	Yes
Speed in reaching large audiences	Slow	Fast	Usually fast	Fast	Fast
Message flexibility	Tailored to prospect	Uniform and unvaried	No direct control over message	Uniform and varied	Tailored

Source: Adapted from McDaniel, C., Jr., & Darden, W. M. (1987). *Marketing.* Newton, MA: Allyn & Bacon, 526. Used by permission.

2. Personal selling can be used to make services tangible and describe products and services in greater detail.

3. The sales presentation can be tailored to customers' needs. Solutions to specific customer's problems can be offered.

4. Prospective buyers can be identified and qualified before engaging personal selling so that overall communications mix dollars may be more effectively spent.

5. Personal selling can reduce risk and is more effective in getting customers to close the deal and sign the contract.

6. Personal selling is the only part of the communications mix that permits direct feedback from the customer.

7. Personal selling provides an excellent opportunity for relationship marketing.

The Sales Process

The steps in the personal sales process are as follows:

1. Prospecting
2. Qualifying prospects
3. The sales approach
4. Handling objections
5. Closing the sale
6. Following up

The sales process also has two other very important aspects that must be kept in mind during the sales interaction: knowing how to sell the product given unique client needs and knowing what to sell. The successful sales team knows not only how to sell, but what to sell most efficiently.

Prospecting

Prospecting is the term used for finding new customers. The goal of prospecting is to convert unqualified names of potential customers into sales leads. Sales leads turn into making sales calls, in person or by phone, to qualified customers who are not currently using the product. Prospecting is more difficult than calling on existing customers because new customers do not necessarily know the product, although they may certainly have some perception of it. New customers need to be convinced that the product they are currently using does not satisfy their needs as well as your product would. One axiom goes like this: If you want to sell your product to our company, be sure your product is accompanied by a plan that will so help our business that we will be more anxious to buy than you are to sell.

It is highly unlikely that a meeting planner will "create" a meeting just because of your facility. The meeting either will already exist, having occurred before at a competitor's hotel or in another area, or will have been partially developed and waiting to be placed in a property. In direct sales, the most common way to get new customers is to take them away from competitors. Prospecting has evolved over the past decade as the real challenge for selling in a competitive marketplace.

Cold calling (calling on a prospect without notice) used to be the main method to drum up new business. One technique was for a sales team to "**blitz**" an area or office building by making calls, unannounced, on companies within the buildings. This method is still in place in some organizations, but is not generally recommended because of its limited effectiveness. Few like to have a salesperson walk in "cold" and ask to speak to the person that books meetings or banquets. Many salespeople also do not like cold calling and the risk of rejection that comes with it. On the other hand, some individual salespeople use cold calling, not necessarily "blitz," to successfully set up appointments and obtain pertinent information.[1]

More sophisticated methods of generating leads or prospects have emerged. Many sales directors are recognizing the cost of sales calls and realize that sending salespeople out on calls without appointments is an expensive way to do business. Depending on the experience of the salesperson, the location, the account, and other variables, a sales call can cost $55 to $500 or more, after salary, benefits, office space, secretarial support, collateral, and travel are factored in as part of the cost of doing business. At even $50 per call, the salesperson becomes an expensive resource, not to be used without a well-devised plan. Direct mail and **telemarketing** (which also may be called cold calling or prospecting) or sometimes a combination of both are used effectively to set up sales calls in advance and make for concentrated sales efforts with advance notice. Once a face-to-face rapport is established, salespeople often use the telephone and the Internet as much as possible because of the time and cost associated with many face-to-face calls.

Tourism Marketing Application

One of the major methods of prospecting used by tourist destinations is regional travel marts, such as the one sponsored by the Pacific Area Travel Association. Travel Mart 2007 will be held in Bali. "The Director General for Indonesian Culture and Tourism Marketing, Mr. Thamrin Bachri, said that Indonesia would promote special-interest tours including golf, community-based tourism, eco-tourism, village tours, and marine tourism at the Mart. The PATA Bali and Nusa Tenggara Chapter sees the successful bid as "a real breakthrough in boosting the declining visitor arrivals at Bali." Former Chapter Chairman and Bali Discovery Tours President and Director John M. Daniels said, "PATA's decision to select Bali as the venue for PATA travel Mart 2007 represents excellent timing. The event will bring top-travel industry members from around the world to see firsthand the enduring charms of our tropical island and the significant new investments over the past few years." (www.tourismindiaonline.com/highlightpages/highlights2.html#Bali%20To%20Host%20PATA%20Travael%20Mart%202007, accessed April 6, 2006).

Qualifying Prospects

In this step of the sales process, the salesperson determines whether prospects are qualified to make the purchase by asking the following questions:

- Can they afford it?
- Do they have business in this destination?
- Do they have the authority to make the decision?
- How serious are they about using our facilities, or are they using us for leverage against another property?

Qualifying is done during prospecting, during telemarketing, or as a follow-up to direct mail or advertising responses. The qualifying process turns hundreds of names into a few sales leads. One way to generate sales leads are through a direct mail, whether it is through the post office or through the Internet. A mailing list or e-mail list is purchased, and a mailing piece is developed and mailed with a response request or card and, often, some kind of incentive. For example, a facility may want to increase its share of a certain market, such as medical meetings. Certain parameters that fit the property, such as the size of the meeting and geographic preference, are established. A creative direct mail piece is created to generate a response for more information. A sales manager or telemarketer would then follow up the lead to determine the customer's needs. This method is effective in qualifying prospects because only those who are genuinely interested in the service will bother to respond to the solicitation.

Exhibit 17-2 illustrates a promotional piece used by Unisys to promote its customer loyalty system; Exhibit 17-3 shows a piece designed by ICLP to show its client list.

 Web Browsing Exercise

Go to www.unisys.com/transportation and work your way through the website. Determine what Unisys does as a company. What different solutions does the company offer for customer loyalty? What is the AirCore solution?

Telemarketing is another, more direct method to generate and qualify leads. This time the prospect is phoned. The telemarketer may just find out whether there is a need for the facility and then turn the lead over to the

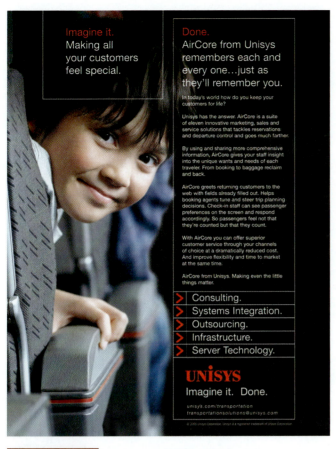

EXHIBIT 17-2 A promotional piece by Unisys.

Source: Unisys. Used by permission.

sales manager for professional follow-up. Many travel managers are besieged by sales managers and telemarketers on a daily basis, however, and keep their voice mail on to screen unwanted calls. Yet, on the other hand, sales mangers play an important part in fulfilling a travel manager's responsibilities because frequent contact keeps them apprised of the best deals with the best product.

Advertising to meeting planners is also common practice for large hotels, resorts, and hotel chains. Media that reach professional meeting planners include such trade publications as *Meetings & Conventions, Successful Meetings, Corporate Meetings & Incentives, The Meeting Professional, Convene,* and a host of other titles. It is also possible to advertise on the Meetings Industry Megasite (www.mimegasite.com), as shown in Exhibit 17-4. The business press, including newspapers and magazines, are frequently used as well. Advertising appearing in these sections may provide special incentives or direct solicitations of meeting planners. Responses are followed up with more information; for example, sending brochures, meeting room specifications, facilities, and so on. Some properties also send out videos or DVDs to provide more graphic and direct presentations. Eventually, a personal sales call or a telephone call followed by an invitation to make a "site inspection" will be in order. It can take many prospects to get a few customers, as shown in Exhibit 17-5.

dallas   london   singapore   zurich
dubai   mumbai   sydney
hong kong   san francisco   taipei
kuala lumpur   shanghai   tokyo

ICLP the global loyalty agency

managing profitable relationships
world-class | consulting • creative • client services

EXHIBIT 17-3 A promotional piece by ICLP, "the global loyalty agency global client experience."

Source: ICLP. Used by permission.

EXHIBIT 17-4 Advertising on websites is another way to reach a target market.

Source: Retrieved from www.mimegasite.com—VNU Business Media – USA. Used by permission.

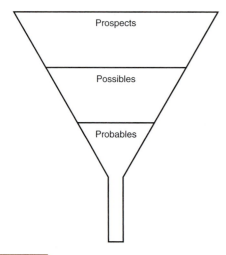

EXHIBIT 17-5 Many prospects but few customers.

 Web Browsing Exercise

Use your favorite search engine and look up the term "sales process." Examine two or three of the sites. What did you learn? If possible, find a site that offers an article explaining the sales process in more detail.

The Sales Approach. The sales approach, which entails communicating personally with customers, is not an easy skill to master. In past years, when the demand for guest rooms exceeded supply, the selling process was simple—order taking. A salesperson would simply answer the phone or call back customers who had telephoned earlier and take their orders. The sales process is now very different. In most markets, supply exceeds demand, and the telephones no longer ring by themselves. An effective sales process is what makes the telephone ring.

There is a right way to sell and a wrong way to sell, yet it is still a very personal skill. Many salespeople in the hos-pitality industry think they are selling by knocking on office doors without appointments (cold calling) and leaving behind brochures. Today, good salespeople get "inside the buyers's head." The sales process has evolved to where good salespeople are good problem solvers.

Theodore Levitt chronicled the evolution of the sales process. In past practice and perhaps still too often today, the seller tried to unload onto a buyer what the seller decided to offer. "This was the basis for the notion that a salesperson needs charisma, because it was charisma that made the sale rather than the product selling itself." Over time, selling progressed to where the seller "penetrates the buyer's domain to learn about his needs, desires, fears and the like and then designs and supplies the product in all its forms. Instead of trying to get the buyer to want what the seller has, the seller tries to have what the buyer will want. The 'product' is no longer merely an item but a whole bundle of value satisfactions." The progression process for the buyer is from need to benefit to feature.[2]

Today, once a buyer has been prospected, **successful selling** is more about long-term relationships between sellers and qualified buyers. The point is not just keeping customers. It is more a matter of what the buyer wants. The buyer wants a seller who will keep in contact and deliver on the promises made. Thus, an interdependence develops between the seller and the buyer.

The Ritz-Carlton Hotel Company learned the lesson of the buyer–seller relationship when it hired a research firm to study its relationships with meeting planners. The research revealed that Ritz-Carlton was perceived as deficient during the period after the sale and before the event, a period of sometimes a year or more. Buyers felt, "Now, that they've got my business, they don't care about me," when there was no contact from the hotel until just before the event. Buyers wanted an ongoing relationship during the interim that assured them that their business was appreciated.

Similarly, some companies, such as Marriott and Hyatt, have specific account managers who work with only a few major accounts such as IBM and GE. These people "live" with these companies so as to get inside their culture and fully understand their needs when planning a meeting or event. This is a good example of relationship selling.

The art of selling begins, like all marketing, by understanding the needs of the customers. This is critical for a successful sale. Once again, the idea is to solve a customer's problems. First, one must determine what they are. Sometimes this calls for an interpretation. For example, a customer might say, "I need a good hotel close to the airport for my meeting." This means that one of the customer's requirements is convenience. The salesperson's property might not be near the airport, and the sale might be lost.

Possibly, however, offering pickup and transportation—overcoming the distance by offering convenience—might save the sale. In any event, the salesperson must determine the real problem in order to address it.

Sometimes a customer will express an opportunity, not a need. The salesperson has to understand the subtle difference. A need is a customer want or desire that can be satisfied by the hospitality entity, whereas an opportunity is a statement of a problem without the expressed desire to solve the problem. Let's look at the difference:

- ■ "I need a hotel with a location near the airport." (need)
- ■ "The hotel we use now is too far from the airport." (opportunity)

In the first statement, the problem is explicit. The first statement expresses the desire to solve the problem. The second sentence is an opportunity that calls for further interpretation. Suppose the salesperson responds by telling the customer how close his hotel is to the airport. The customer then might reply: "That's nice, but it doesn't matter. My boss lives on the other side of town and doesn't want to travel all the way to the airport. I personally think the hotel we use now is out of the way, but what can you do?" What the salesperson interpreted as an opportunity was actually not a conscious need. By addressing a perceived opportunity with a benefit not important to the customer, the salesperson alienated the customer. The location of the hotel was a problem for the meeting planner, but not one that he had a desire to solve. It is not uncommon for a salesperson to sell to an opportunity, rather than to a real need; however, he must first know the difference.

Probing

How do you ensure that you are not selling to an opportunity? By asking the right questions. Asking the customer questions is defined as **probing.**

Probing comes in two forms, **open probes** and **closed probes.** Open probes encourage customers to speak freely and to elaborate on their problems. Closed probes limit customer response to a yes or no answer or a limited range provided by the salesperson. An example of open probes might be "Tell me about what is important to you when you select a restaurant?" or "What is the nature of your conference?" In both cases, the customer is encouraged to freely discuss her feelings (and hopefully reveal some needs). The other probe is called a closed probe. The closed probe may sound like this: "Is location important to you?" or "Do you prefer chain or independently run restaurants?"

The customer can answer yes or no to the first question and has a limited option for the second question.

Tourism Marketing Application

Helen C. Broadus of the Africa Travel Association recommends, in order to sell Africa more effectively as a destination, that salespeople ask the following probing questions of their prospects:

- Have they taken a trip to Africa before?
- How physically active are they?
- What kinds of tourism activities do they like?
- Are they interested in wildlife viewing, exploring local cultures, or educational/historical venues?
- Would clients be comfortable on trips where they are up close and personal with the people and/or the wildlife, or do they prefer more luxurious accommodations in a relaxed atmosphere?"

(www.africa-ata.org/ata_tips.htm, accessed April 6, 2006)

Let's go back to differentiating between needs and opportunities. To confirm that an opportunity is a need, a closed probe is appropriate. Let's review the selling example already presented:

Salesperson: "Tell me a little bit about your meetings." (open probe)

Customer: "Oh, we have had many lately, but the hotel we use now is too far from the airport." (opportunity)

Salesperson: "Is an airport location important to you in choosing a hotel?" (closed probe)

Customer: "Not really, my boss lives on the other side of town and doesn't want to change now."

The salesperson has avoided talking about something the customer did not need. The salesperson would then open probe further until a customer need or a new opportunity is identified. In some cases, however, the salesperson might address the objective by further probes (why the boss won't change) and suggest a probable solution before going on to new opportunities.

Once the need has surfaced, the salesperson has to support the need. Supporting is done in two stages:

1. Acknowledging the need
2. Introducing the appropriate benefits and features to the customer

Acknowledging the need tells the customer that the salesperson understands the problem to be solved. The salesperson then introduces the solution (benefit and feature). A salesperson's acknowledging statement might be: "I understand your need for a large ballroom, as a screen projection can take up quite a bit of room. However, there will be plenty of room for all, so no one will feel cramped or crowded."

Benefits and Features

Once the needs of the customer have been established through a series of probes, the customer is introduced to the product benefits and features. A feature is a tangible or intangible subset of the product the customer will buy or a characteristic of the service being offered. It is also important to recognize those features that differentiate the product from those of the rest of the competition. These distinctive features should be especially emphasized if they are important to the customer.

The most important thing to remember is that customers do not buy features; they buy benefits. A benefit is the value of the feature to the customer and should be mentioned first to get attention. Unless the benefit is clearly explained, the customer may not understand why the feature is important. A feature might be a ballroom with high ceilings; the benefit to the customer might be that they can produce a high-tech show because the room's high ceilings can accommodate complicated audiovisual requirements. A feature might be a good location; the benefit to the customer might be that the attendees of the meeting do not have far to drive from the office.

To encourage the potential customer to buy the product, the good salesperson will attempt to match the benefits and features to the customer's objectives and needs. Features that may not provide any benefit to the customer should be excluded from the presentation. A primary mistake made in direct sales is to misunderstand the needs of the customer and present features and benefits of the product that are unimportant.

One of the authors was training a salesperson on the selling process and encountered the following scenario:

Salesperson: "Tell me what is important to you when you choose a hotel for your meetings." (open probe)

Customer: "I want a hotel that can handle a large checkout all at once. The last hotel we went to took one and a half hours for our guests to pay their bills!" (need)

Salesperson: "Was the problem the billing or the time to get through the line?" (closed probe)

Customer: "The time to get through the line."

Salesperson: "I can see why it is important for the group to check out effortlessly. Like most hotels now, we are able to check out the guest without the guest coming to the front desk. Unlike most hotels, however, we are able to provide a zero balance due on the bill we slip under their door on the last night of their stay."

In this case, the salesperson was doing fine (satisfying the needs of the customer), until she introduced a feature (video checkout) without clearly articulating how the benefit worked. The customer thought that the hotel had a video camera in the lobby to record checkouts. The customer was perplexed as to how this would ease the checkout process. The correct presentation would have been as follows:

Salesperson: "I can see why it is important for the group to check out effortlessly. At our hotel, there is no waiting in line at all (benefit). Attendees can call up their bill on their in-room television and check out right there! (advantage). We have video checkout to make leaving the hotel easier" (feature).

Once the feature was translated into the value for the customer, the customer accepted the benefit.

Salespeople must sometimes translate the features of the facility into the benefits because, although the customer may have some idea of the feature being sold, he may be skeptical, have a misunderstanding, or have the wrong impression from previous experience. For example, a health club may not seem to be in need of translation into benefits, but the quality of health clubs in hotels differs greatly. Some "health clubs" are rooms with two or three treadmills, whereas other hotels offer space with spas, Jacuzzis, state-of-the-art training equipment, personal instructors, and so on. If a health club is relevant to the customer, then the benefits should be explained.

The same holds true for other generic hotel features. A concierge in a Le Meridien Hotel may be sophisticated, multilingual, and resourceful. A concierge in a Ramada Inn may be the manager's secretary. Both are marketed as concierge services, with very different benefits to customers. Convention services in one hotel may consist of a staff of 10; in another, the bell person may also set the room. Translating what the features do for the customer is important in the sales process once you have determined what is important to the customer. Exhibit 17-6 shows a sample benefits/features form to be used in the selling process.

Once the need has surfaced and been supported, other needs are sought to which the salesperson can respond by further probing. When all the needs have been uncovered and responded to, it may be time to begin thinking about closing the sale. However, before this is accomplished, it is necessary to understand customer attitudes, to see if they may need to be changed.

Customer Attitudes

The salesperson can have an easy customer, as shown in the scenarios outlined earlier, or more likely, difficult customers. Recognizing customer attitudes is important for the successful selling effort and closing the sale.

The most common attitudes encountered on a sales call are **skepticism,** misunderstanding, **indifference,** and ob-

Objective-Benefit-Feature (OBF) Chart

Market segment: _____

Customer industry/organization:_____

Customer title/job function: _____

General customer needs (by priority):

1. _____	4. _____	
2. _____	5. _____	
3. _____	6. _____	

Customer Objectives	Benefits	Features

EXHIBIT 17-6   A sample benefits/features form for selling.

jection. Skepticism is when a customer doubts the benefit introduced to satisfy the need. A customer may say, "I do not think that your food is as good as you say it is." The salesperson would overcome skepticism or misunderstanding in a customer by introducing a "proof source." A proof source is a vehicle that proves to the customer that the benefit introduced is as presented by the salesperson. A testimonial letter from another satisfied customer may be the proof needed to convince the skeptical customer that the food is actually as good as the salesperson says it is. A restaurant review from a local food critic may also be a good proof source. An independent source, in writing, may be all that is needed to convince the skeptical customer. A misunderstanding is something that needs to be clarified.

A more difficult customer attitude is indifference. When a customer is satisfied with another facility or has internal options, the customer is considered indifferent. The customer may say, "I am already using the banquet facilities at the Fontainbleau Hotel" (i.e., "Why should I change?"). This customer is indifferent and not open to considering alternatives. The salesperson must provide her with a reason to consider options. The other type of indifference may stem from internal options. Internal options can be meeting rooms at the office; therefore, the customer would see no need to have meetings at a hotel. In this case, the benefits of not having distractions during a meeting might be emphasized. By meeting off-site, attendees stay focused because they are not in close proximity to their offices.

Tourism Marketing Application

Governments spend much money attempting to understand consumers' attitudes towards their country, as discussed in detail in Chapter 9. As an example of this type of research, the Government of Scotland commissioned a study of visitors from European countries in March of 2006. The Minister for Tourism, Sport and Culture, Patricia Ferguson, said: "The survey also tells us what visitors want to experience when in Scotland, which helps us target different markets as we drive to increase tourism revenues by 50 percent by 2015."

Chief Executive of VisitScotland, Philip Riddle, said: "The results coming back from the Tourism Attitudes Survey are a wonderful endorsement from visitors to Scotland, but they're also a very useful tool for us to really understand what they are looking for, no only when choosing a holiday in Scotland but when they are actually here. From this survey we now have an understanding of everything visitors from these countries like to see and do, from what they like to eat to where they like to sleep, how long they tend to stay, and even down to what gifts they like to buy before heading home." (www.scotexchange.net/news_item.htm?newsID=37779, accessed April 6, 2006)

The solution for handling an indifferent customer is to probe for unrealized needs. These unrealized needs are often the weakness of the competitor. Let's stay with the Fontainbleau example. The well-prepared salesperson would know the weakness of the competition—in this case, the small size of the parking facility. The salesperson knows that there are never enough parking spaces at this hotel and would probe to determine whether there was a need to satisfy this problem.

The sales conversation might go like this (but probably not this easily!):

Customer: "I appreciate your coming by to see me, but I do not see the reason for the call. I am using the Fontainbleau for my banquets, and I am satisfied at this time." (expressing indifference)

Salesperson: "I see. Do you mind if I ask you some questions anyway?"

Customer: "Go ahead."

Salesperson: "I know that you hold some very large functions. Is it important for you to have enough parking for all of your guests?" (closed probe for unrealized needs)

Customer: "As a matter of fact, it is. At the last meeting the speaker was late to the podium because she couldn't find a place to park." (expressing an opportunity)

Salesperson: "Then having enough parking for you and your guests is critical for a successful banquet?" (closed probe to determine need)

Customer: "Certainly."

The salesperson has now uncovered a need and addressed the need by supporting it.

It is easy for salespeople to place a competitor in a bad light. This practice is not recommended, however, because many customers are turned off by this selling strategy. In the previous sales conversation, the professional salesperson referred vaguely to a problem that he knew was a disadvantage of the Fontainbleau, but never directly mentioned the hotel.

The final customer attitude is one of objection. **Objection** occurs when there is a real problem with your product offering that cannot be changed. If the customer wants a hotel near the airport and yours is not, then you have an objection. If the customer wants a restaurant with a private dining area for a group and yours does not have one, then you have an objection. Or, the objection that cannot be changed may be on the customer's side. For example, corporate mandates and prescribed hotel lists may dictate that travelers will not be reimbursed if they use your hotel.

Objections are very hard to overcome. It is important to view objections as positive customer feedback rather than as personal reverses during the sales process. Anticipating specific objections is the best way to prepare for them. The strategy for solving the objection is to present benefits already accepted that outweigh the objection presented or verify why the objection is important and figure out an alternative. Although the customer may want an airport location, the fact that your hotel is newly renovated and has a better pool and more flexible meeting space may outweigh the location objection, as might the fact that it is nearer the office and most attendees are driving.

A restaurant customer desiring a private room for a meal may be presented with more parking facilities, better food, and billing privileges. After all, customers make trade-offs between the different attributes of a product or service to choose the one that offers the best bundle of benefits. After reviewing the entire buy decision, the restaurant customer may be convinced to choose the restaurant without the private dining room. The focus, once again, should be on the objective and needs of the customer. You can overcome the objection by either providing a solution acceptable to the customer or agreeing that it cannot be overcome and therefore hoping that the benefits of using your facility will outweigh the disadvantages.

Tourism Marketing Application
Tourist destinations can also be perceived poorly because media tend to report only tragic events, thus giving the impression that a whole country suffers the same calamity. Africa is one such country where this occurs. Rick Taylor, Johannesburg-based head of South Africa Tourism's National Convention Bureau and an at-large member of MPI (Meeting Planners International), stated: "Our growth strategy is to eliminate seasonality and get geographical spread, promoting the entire country—building on our asset base like a corporation or sports team. The image problem does exist. People come here with preconceived notions of starving children and wild animals walking the streets, but when they arrive they're gob-smacked by the sophisticated nature of the destination. We have to convey the message that not all of Africa fits the CNN image—that we're open for business, and the time is now. South Africa's one of the world's top value destinations. I estimate about a three-to-one value compared to the United States." (www.mpiweb.org/CMS/mpiweb/mpicontent.aspx?id=2940, accessed April 6, 2006)

Closing

The close, or signed contract, should come naturally without having to ask for it. If you have done a good job selling and if you have handled all objections and solved all the problems, the client may tell you he is ready to sign. Asking for a close prematurely puts too much pressure on the buyer and may lose the sale. **Closing** a sales call entails asking the customer for a commitment. Hence, a sales call close might be getting to meet the decision maker's boss on the next visit, having the customer visit the hotel, or making a presentation to the board that will make the decision.

The ultimate closing is when the salesperson "asks for the business." (This entire process, of course, does not necessarily all take place in one meeting.) At this point, the salesperson summarizes all of the benefits accepted by the customer and then asks for the customer's commitment.

It should be apparent that the sales approach is a difficult one at best. With many new facilities in each market, the selling process is more competitive than ever. The salesperson that has the correct selling skills and uses them on the sales call will close on a larger portion of business.

Follow-Up

Follow-up means regularly contacting the customer until the event takes place. One of the most common complaints of meeting planners in the hospitality industry is that the person who made the sale is not around when the services are actually being performed. A convention or meeting may be booked in a hotel 2 to 10 years in advance. The promises made by someone who may no longer be at the property or who may be out trying to sell to another account should still be kept when the event takes place. Too often, operations says, belatedly, "We can't do that." Also, human error in incorrectly tracing a file can cause untold havoc. To create good word-of-mouth communications and to get customers to come back, follow-up is extremely important. Often, it is the internal service manager who does this, but it can also be the senior management, as shown in Exhibit 17-7 from ETAP hotels in Essen. Working closely with management may be as important to the salesperson as working with the customer.

EXHIBIT 17-7 AT ETAP Hotels in Essen, senior management follows up with the customer.

Source: Yavuz Arslan/DAS FOTOARCHIV. Peter Arnold, Inc. Used by permission.

Thus, the role of the professional salesperson is evolving. The "order taker" of the mid-1990s became the "order getter" in the early 2000s. Clearly the effects of September 11 changed the selling scenario drastically. Suddenly there were very few buyers. Security became a need that was not discussed prior to the terrorist attacks. Price became a serious issue as all companies cut back spending on travel until events became more stabilized. Today, successful salespeople will have to be relationship managers. This is especially important in service businesses where trust, credibility, and confidence that promises will be kept form essential parts of the relationship between the buyer and the sales representative. Of course, the working relationship of the salesperson with operations is also critical, as noted previously. Customers sometimes ask the impossible. However, sometimes the impossible can be done with the right knowledge and working relationship.

Web Browsing

Go to the website of Hospitality Sales & Marketing Association International (www.hsmai.org). Explore the website and be prepared to discuss the following:

- ■ The goals of the organization
- ■ Why it would be good to be a member
- ■ The different programs they offer
- ■ Membership dues for students and others

Sales Management

A variety of skills is needed to manage an effective sales force. Proper **account management**, organization of the sales team, development of personnel, and motivation of the workforce all combine to make a sales team efficient. The skills necessary to manage the selling process are very different from the skills needed to sell. The best salesperson in an organization may be promoted to sales director and fail. The gap between good selling skills and good management skills is a wide one.

Account Management

The method of managing customers and the sales process is called the **account management system**. The account management system balances the resources of the sales team with the profile of the customer base. The account management system allows the sales team to manage its customer accounts like a portfolio of stocks, spending time on the customers that will produce the most business, while balancing many smaller accounts in case one large account is lost.

The foundation of the account management system is the following sales equation:

$$\text{Past customers} + \text{New customers} = \text{Goals}$$

Past customers (or repeat guests) provide some of the business, and new customers provide the rest. If the products and services delivered are what the customer expects, new customers will become past customers, making everyone's job easier. First, past customers need to be analyzed and prioritized in terms of the business they provide. An example of this prioritization process is offered here:

Category	Potential Rooms Usage per Account
A	500 +
B	100 to 499
C	less than 100

The past customer base is then placed into each category, and each customer account should be called according to its potential business. Customers who provide the most business are called on more than are customers who provide less business. The account management system ensures that the smaller potential customers also get called on a regular basis.

Calculations are then made as to the total number of calls that the sales team needs to make to past customers, as follows:

Category	Number of Customer Accounts	Number of Calls per Year	Total Calls per Year
A	150	12	1,800
B	300	6	1,800
C	500	2	1,000
Total	950	20	4,600

This calculation shows that 4,600 sales calls per year will properly cover the past customer base. Next, the call schedule is calculated, including new customers:

Position	Average Number of Calls per Week	Annualized
Director of sales	20	960
Sales manager #1	40	1,920
Sales manager #2	40	1,920
Sales manager #3	40	1,920
Total		6,720

With the past customers prioritized and the resources allocated, the sales equation is again used to determine whether the sales department has the proper perspective on past and new customers.

Past customers	+	New customers	=	Goals
4,600	+	2,120	=	6,720
68.5 %	+	31.5 %	=	100 %

The goals are derived from the resources available. Past customers are calculated from the account management system. New customers, or the prospecting effort, are calculated by subtracting the past customers from the goals. If the goals are less than or equal to the past customers, then new customers (prospecting) are being neglected.

For a **mature property**, one that has been in the marketplace for at least three years within the same product class and positioning, the preceding model is ideal for the allocation of resources. The sales team should focus about 70 percent of its time on past customers, and the remaining 30 percent should be dedicated to finding new customers. In new hotels, restaurants, and catering facilities, the sales equation may be the reverse; with a small existing customer base, the need for prospecting is intensified. Also, in some organizations, an account manager helps to maintain accounts so that the salesperson can be out creating new ones. The sales equation can be used to focus a sales team on its priorities.

The next step of the account management system is to assign revenue potential to each of the accounts. The following example continues the hotel scenario, with the understanding that room nights could easily translate to restaurant covers, airline seats, or other hospitality sales units. Room night revenue potential for each account is determined so the sales team can begin to develop the appropriate action steps needed to fill the gaps in revenues:

Category	Number of Accounts	Room Nights
A	150	75,000
B	300	90,000
C	500	30,000
Total	950	195,000

From this calculation, the director of sales can determine that if all of the past customers on the account management system are called regularly, the hotel can potentially book 195,000 rooms from past customers. In most cases the goal or budget is higher than that. Let's look again at the sales equation in terms of room nights:

Past customers	+	New customers	=	Goals
195,000	+	15,000	=	210,000

Now the selling task is clearer. Set the parameters and call goals, make sales calls on all of the past customers, and the hotel should sell 195,000 rooms. The goal, however, is 210,000 rooms. Therefore, the sales team has to prospect, or find, 15,000 new room nights.

Selling 210,000 rooms in one year may seem like an awesome task, and, without making the task smaller, it is. Therefore, the next step of the account management system is the breaking down of large tasks into smaller ones, or the **lowest common denominator (LCD)**. The following example illustrates how LCD works:

Need to sell 210,000 rooms sold	History says we will get 195,000 past customers
so need 15,000 new rooms	if each person stays 2 nights
need 7,500 new customers	if average account is 50 rooms per year
then need 150 new accounts	since there are 48 weeks per year
we need 3 new accounts per week	and if there are 3 sales managers
then 1 new account per week opened per sales manager (LCD)	

The sales team can now go out and sell 210,000 rooms for the year. Without applying LCD to the problem, however, the results are usually unfocused. The sales team becomes very busy trying to sell 210,000 rooms, but many times not productively. However, the sales team, after working through the LCD system, can define its strategy—manage the account management system and open one new account per sales manager per week.

Sales Action Plan

The marketing plan is the overall vision for business development during the upcoming year. It encompasses all of the marketing activities, as follows:

- Advertising
- Online marketing
- Public relations
- Direct mail
- Sales promotion
- Other communication vehicles

The **sales action plan** narrows the broader vision of the marketing plan and assigns detailed tasks to the sales managers. The sales action plan allows the sales team to take the marketing plan and step it down to the execution phase of the process. It enables the sales team to execute the portion of the marketing plan for which they are responsible. A typical sales action plan is shown in Exhibit 17-8.

The sales action plan follows the phases of the account management system—calling on past customers and new customers. Goals are established through LCD for bookings and new accounts. The salesperson can clearly see what needs to be done on a monthly, weekly, and daily basis.

EXHIBIT 17-8	Sales Action Plan

Name: Mary Jones

Quarter: 3rd

- Referrals from current customers
- Newspaper leads, etc.

SALES EQUATION/SALES CALLS

Past customers	+	Prospecting	=	Goals
100	+	60	=	160 per month
25	+	15	=	40 per week
5	+	3	=	8 per day

BOOKING GOALS

480 per month   120 per week   30 per day

NEW ACCOUNTS OPENED

20 per month   5 per week   1 per day

PROSPECTING RESOURCES

- Meeting planner directories
- Convention and visitors bureau leads

ACTION PLAN BY WEEK

Week 1	Sales calls to Hartford
Week 2	Make appointments for trade show
Week 3	Attend trade show
Week 4	Develop direct mail for groups
Week 5	Sales calls to Boston
Week 6	Send direct mail to planners
Week 7	Local sales calls
Week 8	Local sales calls
Week 9	Follow up leads from direct mail
Week 10	Follow up leads from direct mail
Week 11	Follow up leads from direct mail
Week 12	Develop next quarter sales action plan

The sales action plan is formatted to accommodate 12 weeks of work. Each quarter, a new sales action plan is written to reflect the next 12-week period of work. This planning process allows the sales team to be flexible and to change activities to reflect market conditions. The umbrella marketing plan is written to give the direction and overall focus for the sales team. Within the next 12 months, many assumptions made during the formation of the marketing plan may change. The quarterly sales action plan allows the team to adjust its course quickly.

The quarterly plan may also be broken down further into a weekly plan. Exhibit 17-9 shows a sample format by the week and by the day and the weekly productivity report.

Organization of the Sales Team

The number of sales calls that should be made on a yearly basis determines the size of the sales force. Staffing the sales office should result from a mathematical calculation of sales calls needed to satisfy current customers and those needed to find a reasonable amount of new customers. This is different from the industry practice of determining the number of salespeople by the number of available rooms in the hotel or the customary practice of adding a salesperson when sales are down (and eliminating them when sales are up). In those situations, resources may be overallocated or underallocated. On a mathematical basis, a salesperson will usually handle between 250 and 350 accounts a year, depending on the market mix of the property.

Once staffing guidelines are established, salespeople are usually organized by geographic territory, market (e.g., business, leisure), event type (e.g., weddings), national accounts (e.g., IBM), and/or product line. For example, in terms of potential customers for a hotel, the city of Cleveland can be divided in half. To keep the sales process orderly, one sales representative may be assigned to the east side while another is assigned to the west side.

Tourism Marketing Application

The city of London, England's Tourist Board and Convention Bureau, as it was called—it is now called Visit London—changed its business model in 2005 after attending a meeting where members were exposed to different ways of running a sales organization. Initially the team consisted of people with tourism backgrounds who were reactive rather than proactive, and focused primarily on the leisure market. After receiving major funding, they now sell, market, promote, and act as the voice of the tourism industry for London. They promote London not only to Londoners and the rest of the United Kingdom, but to overseas markets as well. Instead of being only a reactive team, they split into two groups: a sales team and an account management or client services team. The sales team feeds leads to the account management team, which follows up with the actual bid. They also changed the focus of our public relations team to look after both leisure and business travel. In terms of measuring their success, they focus on the economic benefit to the city of their efforts versus focusing on room nights driven. (www.mpiweb.org/CMS/mpiweb/mpicontent.aspx?id=2940, accessed April 6, 2006)

Sales Team Activity Report

Name _____	Week ending _____

Sales Activity and Results

Action Steps	Day / Date	Monday	Tues.	Wed.	Thur.	Friday	Totals Week	MTD
Personal sales calls	Objective							
	Result							
Telephone sales calls	Objective							
	Result							
New account development	Objective							
	Result							
Interhotel referrals	Objective							
	Result							
Wholesale/volume accounts signed	Objective							
	Result							
Sales contact totals	Objective							
	Result							

SEE BACK PAGE FOR PRODUCTIVITY QUOTAS AND RESULTS

Key Account Activity and Results

ORGANIZATION	OBJECTIVE	RESULT	ACTION STEP

EXHIBIT 17-9 Sales action plan format.

The type of service within the hotel that the salesperson represents determines product lines. Three types of product offerings are sold through direct sales: group, transient, and catering. The group product line is for customers who purchase a number of sleeping rooms at the same time. The group salesperson may or may not sell the function space simultaneously. A bus tour would be considered a group but would have no need for function space. A corporation might have the same number of guest room requirements as the bus tour but have extensive meeting space needs. Depending on the size of the hotel, there may be more than one group salesperson; for example, there may be a need for a separate convention salesperson if this is a major market for the hotel.

Transient salespeople sell to customers who have a need to book guest rooms on an individual basis. Corporate sales managers call on corporate travel planners. The catering salesperson normally handles meetings and social events such as weddings, which do not require a large number of sleeping rooms. This person sells the ballroom space for functions with food and beverage, if possible.

Different organizations, of course, have different organizational structures and duty assignments. One company may have its outside sales force out of the office and

WEEKLY PLAN

PRIORITIES FOR THIS WEEK:	RESULTS
1.	
2.	
3.	
4.	
5.	

DAY: **DATE:**

	SCHEDULED ACTIVITY	OBJECTIVE	RESULTS	ACTION STEP
8 AM				
9 AM				
10 AM				
11 AM				
12 NOON				
1 PM				
2 PM				
3 PM				
4 PM				
5 PM				
EXPENSES:				

DAY: **DATE:**

	SCHEDULED ACTIVITY	OBJECTIVE	RESULTS	ACTION STEP
8 AM				
9 AM				
10 AM				
11 AM				
12 NOON				
1 PM				
2 PM				
3 PM				
4 PM				
5 PM				
EXPENSES:				

DAY: **DATE:**

	SCHEDULED ACTIVITY	OBJECTIVE	RESULTS	ACTION STEP
8 AM				
9 AM				
10 AM				
11 AM				
12 NOON				
1 PM				
2 PM				
3 PM				
4 PM				
5 PM				
EXPENSES:				

EXHIBIT 17-9   Sales action plan format *(Continued).*

cold calling four days a week, with one day in the office writing call reports. Sales leads get passed to inside salespeople who close sales and maintain accounts. Another company may have sales managers who spend half their time inside and half outside. Leads are generated, pursued, and finalized. An inside support person, an account manager, is available inside to maintain accounts. Other companies may have variations of these approaches.

Keeping an effective sales organization on a focused track requires a very disciplined effort. The director of sales needs to cue salespeople as to when business is needed most. For example, weddings may book a ballroom a year in advance. Large groups, such as an Elks Club convention, may also want the ballroom for the same weekend, but will also reserve a large number of sleeping rooms. If a wedding with a few overnight rooms were already booked for the ballroom, the Elks Club business might be lost. Conversely, if the wedding were turned away and the Elks Club did not choose the hotel, the ballroom might be empty on that date. Such decisions are made on a daily basis.

 Web Browsing Exercise

Go to www.dgoinc.com, which is the website for the David Green Organization. David Green was interviewed for this chapter, as shown in the Marketing in Action feature at the beginning of the chapter. What does the website tell you about the organization? What advantages does it offer hotels? Who are its primary competitors?

WEEKLY PRODUCTIVITY REPORT

Name _____ Week Ending _____

DEFINITE BOOKINGS

ORGANIZATION	NEW	EXISTING	DATES	RATES	COVERS/ SUITE NIGHTS	CATERING/SUITE REVENUE

CANCELLED DEFINITES

TENTATIVE BOOKINGS

ORGANIZATION	NEW	EXISTING	DATES	RATES	COVERS/ SUITE NIGHTS	CATERING/SUITE REVENUE

CANCELLED TENTATIVES

PRODUCTIVITY SUMMARY

DEFINITES — WEEKLY TOTALS, MONTHLY TOTALS, QUOTAS | COVERS/SUITE NIGHTS | AVERAGE RATE | CATERING/SUITE REVENUE | CATERING/SUITE REV. QUOTA

TENTATIVES — WEEKLY TOTALS, MONTHLY TOTALS, QUOTAS | COVERS/SUITE NIGHTS | AVERAGE RATE | CATERING/SUITE REVENUE | CATERING/SUITE REV. QUOTA

EXHIBIT 17-9 Sales action plan format, *(Continued)*.

Product Line Management

Most hotel sales offices are structured to sell the three distinct products already discussed: the transient product for the individual traveler, such as Marriott Rewards and Starwood Preferred Guest; the group product that offers the customer the opportunity to purchase both sleeping rooms and function facilities for a meeting; and the catering product for the customer who needs function or meeting space without guest rooms (the term for this last type of business is *freestanding*).

Many customer accounts have a need for more than one product and in some cases all three. For example, a planner at IBM might have occasion to need transient guest rooms, group space, and freestanding function space in the same hotel. Many present methods, however, divide the sales effort and provide for three different salespeople to represent the three products in the same hotel.

Most other industries do not operate in this manner. For instance, you can buy an entire range of automobiles or insurance coverage from the same person. Why, then, does the hotel industry make the same IBM customer talk to three different representatives to buy very similar products in the same location? It seems that old habits die hard. Trying to purchase various hotel products from the same hotel can easily mean negotiating with six to seven salespeople in one year.

The **product line management** approach to sales, in which one sales representative services all three products for the same customer (sometimes called one-stop shopping), is a method to gain a competitive edge over sales offices organized in the traditional format. A variation of this is "**meetings express**" sales positions. This "book 'em and cook' em" approach to selling is gradually becoming more commonplace. Specifically, for smaller meetings, the meetings express person sends the contract, blocks the rooms and function space, selects the menu, handles the rooming list, and sends the thank-you letter after the meeting occurs.

Either of the preceding methods means that customers who have a need for more than one hotel product are handled by the same salesperson in order to offer continuity during the sales process. Those customers who have a need for only one product (e.g., a wedding) should be handled in the regular manner (in this case, by the catering salesperson). The difficulty with the product line approach, and one that has slowed its acceptance, is that each salesperson must be familiar with all of the hotel's products and how to sell them.

Development of Personnel

The development of personnel is critical to the success of a sales organization. If the wrong people are hired, business will be lost. If good salespeople leave to go to a competitor for better opportunities, which frequently happens, there is an additional opportunity to lose business. If a position remains open for any length of time, necessary sales calls to existing and new customers will not be made. Companies need to be conscious of this problem and address the reasons for it. Through better selection and training, Ritz-Carlton reduced its sales force turnover from 40 percent to 10 percent once they had identified the problem that salespeople well trained by other hotel chains did not necessarily fit into the Ritz-Carlton mode.

Another reason for high turnover is the "**move up and out**" **philosophy**. Promotions often involve relocation. If a salesperson is unwilling to relocate, the only other way to further a career is to move to another hotel. Also, salespeople are highly visible, not only to their clients but also in networking functions. This high exposure provides increased opportunities for other positions.

Development of an effective sales staff begins with recruitment. There should be an ongoing effort to locate and know the best salespeople in the marketplace. Although new talent can be solicited at the college graduate level, there is still a void at the experienced salesperson level. Organizations such as Hotel Sales & Marketing Association International (HSMAI) are good forums for getting to know the better salespeople in an area.

Training is critical to the development of salespeople. Although there are many existing sales training programs, the challenge is to use them. At least one month of training is necessary for new salespeople to minimally learn the product and understand the needs of customers. Even seasoned salespeople need to be constantly trained through role-playing and sales meetings to keep their skills sharp. Training also indicates the level of commitment that the company has toward the individual development of a salesperson's career. Exhibit 17-10 shows a simplified diagram of a salesperson's relationship qualities.

Tourism Marketing Application

There are organizations that provide extensive training for salespeople, whether in the hotel or in the destination area. One such organization is the Convention Industry Council, which was formed in 1949 by four organizations: American Society of Association Executives (ASAE), American Hotel and Motel Association (AH&MA), Hospitality Sales & Marketing Association International (HSMAI), and International Association of Convention and Visitor Bureaus (IACVB). (www.conventionindustry. org) This organization offers a program called the Certified Meeting Planner or CMP. According to the website, "The CMP designation recognizes those who have achieved the industry's highest standard of professionalism. Established in 1985, the CMP credential was developed to increase the proficiency of meeting professionals in any component or sector of the industry by:

- Identifying a body of knowledge
- Establishing a level of knowledge and performance necessary for certification
- Stimulating the advancement of the art and science of meeting management
- Increasing the value of practitioners to their employers
- Recognizing and raising industry standards, practices, and ethics
- Maximizing the value received from the products and services provided by Certified Meeting Professionals."

(www.conventionindustry.org/cmp/index.htm, accessed April 7, 2006)

Ethics

All salespeople should also develop a code of **ethics**, both personally and through the company. Because they will encounter ethical dilemmas, salespeople should have certain guiding principles to allow them to conduct their business

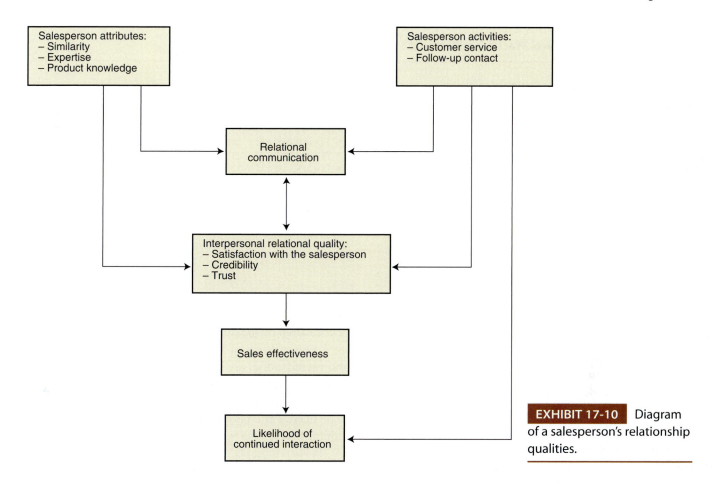

EXHIBIT 17-10 Diagram of a salesperson's relationship qualities.

with honesty and integrity. Examples of unethical practices are shown in Exhibit 17-11.

Thomas McCarthy, a hotel marketer who provides hotel sales seminars, provided another perspective on ethics. McCarthy also writes the marketing column for *Lodging Hospitality* and is a member of the HSMAI Hall of Fame. Although McCarthy asked these questions a while ago, the information is still insightful. He asked a group of hotel sales and marketing people whether they thought the following situations were ethical.

1. You offer one company, which has an average of 10 reservations a month, a $100 rate. The company accepts. On the same day you offer another company the same rate for the same number of reservations. The prospect says it's too high so you offer a $90 rate.
2. A hotel has a weekend policy that if walk-ins ask for the weekend rate they get it for $69; if they don't ask, they are charged $85.
3. A report indicates that an association has signed a contract with another hotel for next year's meeting. Your boss tells you to call the association and offer 50% off the other hotel's rate if it will break the contract and come to your hotel.

Results to #1: 37 percent of respondents said the action was unethical. Results to #2: 60 percent said the practice was unethical. Results to #3: 67 percent said the request was unethical. All three practices are common. McCarthy offered the following two questions to answer when quoting rates:

1. If the public knew about this policy, what would be the reaction? If the reaction would be negative, there's something wrong with the policy.
2. If someone asked why one customer got a lower rate, could it be explained in a way that a logical person would accept and understand? If not, the practice is probably unethical.

Apply these two questions to the three scenarios above and see what you think.[3]

The Internet has provided another wrinkle to the ethics dilemma facing today's salespeople. Let's say a group was booked three years prior for $100 per night. On Hotels.com today (check-in), there is a $79 rate available to the Internet customer. Does the salesperson notify the meeting planner that lower rates are available and drop the group rate by $21 or let the front desk handle it upon check-in?

EXHIBIT 17-11	Unethical Practices in Personal Selling

THE SALESPERSON'S COMPANY
- Misrepresentation of call reports
- Misrepresentation of expense accounts
- Use of company assets for personal benefit
- Conflict-of-interest situations
- Disclosure of proprietary company information
- Disparagement of the company

THE SALESPERSON'S CUSTOMERS AND PROSPECTS
- Misrepresentation of yourself
- Misrepresentation of your company
- Misrepresentation of your products or services
- Use of high-pressure selling tactics

- Inappropriate gift-giving
- Disclosure of proprietary customer information

THE SALESPERSON'S COMPETITORS
- Disparagement of a competitor's company
- Disparagement of a competitor's product or service
- Disparagement of a competitor's sales representative

Source: Professional selling: A relationship management process. 1st edition by Coppett, Staples. © 1990. Reprinted with permission of South-Western, a division of Thomson Learning: www.thomsonrights.com. Fax 800 730-2215.

 Web Browsing Exercise

Go to the website for *Lodging Hospitality* (www.lhonline.com) and access some of the past articles by Thomas McCarthy. What are the big issues in marketing, as evidenced by his columns? Read a column and be prepared to discuss it.

Motivation

Salespeople need to be consistently motivated to be effective. Although this may be true of all job categories, it is especially true of salespeople, who represent the product on a daily basis. Unlike their counterparts in the operations aspect of the hotel business, salespeople are usually paid a salary plus commission or performance bonus. Normally, the operations people are paid a bonus based on the financial progress of the property and, one hopes, on customer feedback. Salespeople are paid on their productivity, which is based on quotas. Quotas are developed based on the territory, the market, and the product sold. This quota is normally derived from the budget that the hotel has set for the sales team that year. Once quotas are established, the salespeople are paid for achievement over and above the quota. Some incentives are paid monthly; others are paid quarterly or yearly. It is likely that the more immediate the gratification, the more motivated the salesperson will be.

Productivity, of course, is not the easiest thing to measure because it is not simply a matter of room nights sold or revenue gained. To put this in perspective, Exhibit 17-12 cites from an article by Eric Orkin, who is an expert in yield management.

Orkin's point is that "if you use averages to measure performance, people will make decisions to improve the averages whether or not the numbers are good for the hotel. The value of a room night is a reflection of the probability that it can be sold and the rate it can command." If

salespeople are motivated by goals, then those goals must be measured by measures other than averages.

Other forms of motivation, such as incentive trips and merchandise, are becoming part of the motivational toolbox of sales organizations. These are also based on quotas and may be used when a short-term sales gap needs to be filled. For an example of a short motivation tool, see Exhibit 17-13.

Sales and Operations

"Sales sells and operations provides" is an expression that describes what is often seen as the relationship between sales and operations. As previously mentioned, that relationship is a critical one and needs further explanation here, because a conflict between sales and operations can be incredibly damaging to a hotel's relationship marketing effort. In fact, this situation represents a real need for internal relationship marketing.

Knowledge of the product and the capabilities of the organization is essential to successful selling. Constant and continuous communication between sales and operations is imperative to effective marketing for a hospitality organization. If what the salesperson sells cannot be delivered, the hotel will in most cases eventually lose the customer (and the salesperson!). It is natural for a salesperson to want to make promises to make the sale.

Salespeople have two difficulties in this regard, which they need to overcome. One is perception. Operations people see salespeople largely when they are in-house entertaining clients (e.g., having lunch, giving tours) and see their job as a "cushy" one. The second one is that salespeople have no direct authority over operations people, yet they need to make certain that their promises are executed prop-

---

EXHIBIT 17-12 **Using Averages to Measure Sales Performance**

In the hotel industry, we use averages to understand how we are doing and to help make decisions. But the premise is unsound: there is no average room night. Consider the following sales chart for one month:

Sales Manager	Room Nights Sold	Average Rate	Total Revenue
Alan	600	$100	$60,000
Barry	583	$103	$60,000
Cathy	700	$85.71	$60,000
Debra	680	$ 99	$67,320

Who did the best job? Debra is the revenue leader with a good ADR. Barry has the highest ADR but the lowest room night volume. Alan is in the middle. Cathy has the highest room night volume but may be "giving away" the rooms.

Now consider the following expanded sales chart:

Sales Manager	High Demand Days		Medium Demand Days		Low Demand Days	
	Room Nights	ADR	Room Nights	ADR	Room Nights	ADR
Alan			600	$100		
Barry	583	$103				
Cathy	250	$103	250	$97	200	$50
Debra	680	$ 99				

The picture of efficiency and productivity now changes. Debra is selling high demand room nights at discount. Barry may be missing opportunities on off-peak days. Alan is okay. Cathy is the star. She is selling low demand, as well as high demand days; her ADR is justified because many of her room nights would otherwise have remained unfilled.

Source: Orkin, E. (1994, February). Breaking the law of averages. *Lodging Hospitality,* 24–25. Copyright © Penton Media, Inc.

$$

HOW TO MAKE MORE MONEY AND SCORE BIG BROWNIE POINTS WITH THE D.O.S.

1ST WAY! For every actual group roomnight in February booked after 1/11/99, you will receive $2.00

Minimum rate Monday-Thursday $79
Minimum rate Friday-Sunday $69

Example: Computerland Group 10 roomnights for 3 nights at a rate of $89 = $60 for Sales Manager

2ND WAY! Whoever exceeds 300 actual group room nights in the month of February will receive $100 BONUS on top of the "1st Way" promotion!

Cathy/Tracy: If you <u>exceed</u> the budgeted Club goal of 300 roomnights in February, you will both receive $100

Get on your mark, set . . . Book 'em DANNO!!!!!

(*Please note the rate restriction of $99 over Super Show)

Amy <u>will</u> be accepting bribes for any inquiry calls!
Simply put your name and offer in a sealed envelope and return ASAP.

$$

EXHIBIT 17-13 An internal memo to motivate a sales force.

---

erly. This can cause friction in the lines of authority needed to get the job done and keep promises to customers.

A thorough knowledge of the product and the capabilities of the organization will go a long way toward keeping these promises from creating unreasonable ex-

pectations for the customer. If the salesperson is not sure that the hotel can deliver, then she should confirm with operations before making the promise. This not only provides a confirmation, but it also gets operations into the act so that there is more likelihood that someone will follow through. The services manager position in large hotels helps avoid these problems. This person works closely with the salesperson and also personally attends to the function when it takes place.

If both parties are truly tuned in to solving the customer's problems and each party fully understands the problems of the other, a satisfactory resolution is almost always possible. This is both internal and relationship marketing at their best. The marketing and management leadership of the property or the company sets the tone and should make sure that it happens. The salesperson must go back to dissatisfied customers and ask for their business once more.

■ Summary

The sales process is becoming more complex in the competitive marketplaces of today. The selling process is not unlike the marketing process; understanding the needs of the customer is the primary focus of the sales organization and is the foundation of effective selling. The selling process involves the skilled use of probing, supporting, and closing to manage the sale. Different customer attitudes are encountered on each sales call—skepticism, indifference, and objection. All three are handled with professional selling skills.

Having the ability to sell is only half of the selling process. Planning the sales function is also important. Tools such as an account management system, LCD, and a sales action plan all assist the sales manager to focus on what is important. Maintaining a balance of resources to call on past and new customers is critical to the success of the entire organization.

Finding new customers has become a difficult task, because each hospitality entity is vying for a smaller base of customers to fill expanding numbers of hotel rooms and meeting space. New methods to find customers, through direct mail, online marketing, and telemarketing, have replaced "cold calling" as methodologies for generating leads.

A sales organization needs to have a clear definition of the markets that it wants to attract and a recognition that it needs to penetrate competitors' business in order to increase its own. Additionally, the organization has to be knowledgeable and consistent about its goals through the sales organization and be prepared to sell the customer with appropriate features and benefits. The sales office that carefully organizes the sales team and develops and motivates its people effectively will be the most productive. As the marketplace absorbs more new hotels and demand remains stagnant, the competitive fight for the same business will intensify. Properties that establish a strong plan based on the components discussed in this chapter will have the competitive edge necessary to win fair market share.[4]

■ Key Terms

prospecting	follow-up
qualifying	account management
sales managers	account management
cold calling	system
blitz	mature property
telemarketing	lowest common
successful selling	denominator (LCD)
probing	sales action plan
open probes	product line management
closed probes	meetings express
skepticism	"move up and out"
indifference	philosophy
objection	ethics
closing	

■ Discussion Questions

1. Describe the correct selling scenario for a customer who responds to your questions like this: "I am currently using a facility with which I am very satisfied."
2. Develop three proof sources for a banquet facility.
3. For an account management system, create a call schedule and a sales equation given the following information:

Account Base:	Category	Number of Files
	A	100
	B	250
	C	300
Positions:	Director of sales, sales manager #1	

4. Break down the task in Question 3 to its lowest common denominator.
5. Compose a benefits and features chart for a hotel and discuss how you would use it to address a specific target market.
6. Discuss the needs and difficulties in organizing a sales force by territory and by product line.
7. Explain the difference between an opportunity and a need; then give an example of each.
8. Find a prospect list of groups from the Internet.

■ Group Projects

1. Assume you are the sales team for the hotel in Question 5. Select three competitive hotels and assess their weaknesses. Prepare four weaknesses per competitor to be used to overcome the customer attitude of indifference.
2. Make a list of five open questions and five closed questions to ask a potential customer to uncover his needs. In class, with a separate group, set up a role-playing scenario in which you ask the questions and respond to the answers.

■ References

1. For a positive view on cold calling and how to do it successfully, see Gitomer, J. H. (1994). *The sales bible.* New York: William Morrow, 94–108. Gitomer's recommended opening line is, "Can you help me?"
2. Levitt, T. (1986). Relationship management. In Levitt, T. (1986). *The marketing imagination.* New York: Free Press, 111–126.
3. McCarthy, T. T. (1994, January). Fair rates improve profits and image. *Hotel & Resort Industry,* 12–13.
4. The nature of this book limits our discussion on personal selling. For further, more complete information, an excellent source is Shaw, M., & Morris, S. V. (2000). *Hospitality sales and marketing.* New York: John Wiley & Sons.

CHAPTER 18

Hospitality Distribution Systems

Bringing the Product to the Customer

Overview

Distribution systems are conduits for getting the product to the customer or the customer to the product. They have become an increasingly critical marketing tool for the hospitality industry, although they come in a number of different forms. This chapter should be read with Chapter 19: together, these two chapters represent both the current and future distribution strategies that occur in the hospitality industry. Chapter 18 provides a brief discussion of what distribution channels are and how distribution systems work. It also explains how hospitality firms use various forms of distribution to increase their size or reach—for example, making sure that there is a restaurant or hotel where the customer needs one. Size is important, for it is one of the building blocks of competitive advantage.

Chapter 19 examines how the distribution channel is used to bring the customer to the product.

I. Introduction to Hospitality Marketing
1. The Concept of Marketing
2. Marketing Services and the Hospitality Experience
3. The Marketing Mix and the Product/Service Mix
4. Relationship/Loyalty Marketing

II. Marketing to Build a Competitive Advantage
5. Strategic Marketing
6. The Strategic Marketing System and Marketing Objectives

VII. Feedback

VI. Synthesis
21. The Marketing Plan

III. The Marketplace
7. Understanding Individual Customers
8. Understanding Organizational Customers
9. The Tourist Customer and the Tourism Destination

IV. Situational Analysis
10. Understanding Competition
11. Marketing Intelligence and Research

V. Functional Strategies
12. Differentiation, Segmentation, and Target Marketing
13. Branding and Market Positioning
14. The Hospitality Pricing Mix
15. The Communications Mix: Advertising
16. The Communications Mix: Sales Promotions, Merchandising, Public Relations, and Publicity
17. The Communications Mix: Personal Selling
18. *Hospitality Distribution Systems*
19. Channels of Distribution: Bringing the Customer to the Product
20. Interactive Marketing: Internet and Database Marketing

Jens Thraenhart
Executive Director, Marketing Strategy & Customer Relationship Management, Canadian Tourism Commission

As executive director for the Canadian Tourism Commission, Jens Thraenhart oversees the development and implementation of approaches, programs, and initiatives to ensure the effective management and expansion of integrated solutions to e-marketing, e-business, CRM, and technology development initiatives aimed at increasing the penetration of Canadian tourism in targeted markets.

Thraenhart's 15-plus years of international hospitality experience include hotel and restaurant operations, revenue management, sales and marketing, e-business, strategic planning, and hospitality consulting. He has worked with such companies as Fairmont, Four Seasons, Ian Schrager Hotels, Kempinski, and Marriott, including founding and operating a successful food catering company and managing an independent luxury golf resort in Germany.

Thraenhart holds an MBA-accredited masters of management in hospitality from the School of Hotel Administration at Cornell University, and a joint bachelor of science in international hospitality management from the University of Massachusetts, Amherst, and the University Center "Cesar Ritz" at Brig, Switzerland. He chairs the HSMAI International Travel Internet Marketing Organization. Most recently he was director of Internet strategy for Fairmont Hotels and Resorts.

Marketing in Action

Jens Thraenhart, Executive Director, Marketing Strategy & Customer Relationship Management, Canadian Tourism Commission

What is your background?

I'm originally from Germany and started my own catering business when I was 18 years old, then went to hotel school in Switzerland. I began working in hotel operations from food and beverage, rooms divisions, reservations, and housekeeping. I was the general manager at an independent hotel when I was 25 and worked for chains like Four Seasons, Kampinski, and Fairmont. I ran my own Internet company out of New York and a company focused on upscale leisure funded by Lehman Brothers. It was during an exciting time with the Internet before the bubble burst and there were a lot of opportunities and we were able to launch the company, raise capital, and do all of that. It was really a company that had the concept of dynamic packaging before it became a buzzword and coupled it with personalization. What we should have done instead of building a consumer model is to have built a B2B (business-to-business) model.

I also did some consulting with hotel companies, helping them to figure out the Internet back in 1998, before many hotel companies were looking at e-commerce.

I worked on and off with Fairmont in Boston—I was front office manager, I was revenue manager, and then also I was at the corporate office in San Francisco as a strategic planning analyst. I rejoined them after the Internet company and after the stock crash, to head up their Internet e-commerce operations, and then was promoted to head up marketing and owner services, owner relation strategy for the new private residence club division of the Fairmont. I also started the Hotel Internet Marketing Committee at the Travel Internet Marketing Organization for HSMAI, the Hospitality Sales & Marketing Association International, and that has been very successful. We're doing around two Internet marketing strategy conferences a year, and we now have over 800 HSMAI members that opted to get information. Basically all the major hotel companies are part of the Hotel Internet Marketing Committee. We are in the process of adding other verticals such as cruise and destinations to Travel International Marketing Organization and expanding the concept to other regions of the world.

Not only do search engines deliver relevant consumers with increased purchase motivation, giving consumers access to the exact product or service being sought—kind of like a reverse direct marketing tool—but also, search engine visibility on the Internet increases brand equity by building recognition, recall, and affinity. Most importantly, though, the Internet in its most analytical form can be used to learn more about our target audience.

Consider this: What if we knew the last 100 words a consumer target-searched for on the Internet and which websites are being visited after leaving our own site? The knowledge of both pre- and post-click consumer behavior on our website is invaluable. This sort of intelligence allows us to tailor offline and online messaging, products, and services to meet the wants and desires of our audience. Consistently meeting these needs over time is what builds increased lifetime value of a customer. That is why the Internet is becoming a more and more integrated and vital component to the sales and marketing mix and will dictate how offline marketing strategies are planned and executed. The travel and hospitality providers who are able to leverage the power of the Internet and technology in order to create value to consumers will be the ones who will benefit from this evolution.

What do you see as the top five trends?

Convergence. There's going to be more and more consolidation as it relates to online and offline marketing, and it's not about the Internet. It's about touching the consumer and developing models where you look at what goal drives which marketing media and which distribution channel.

Metrics. There is a lot of potential in learning about the consumer and turning the website into a virtual focus group, then taking the data and converting it into intelligence and overlaying with the existing customer data.

Trademark protection. Trademark protection will get more and more attention from marketers and there is a lot going on relating to **phishing.*** Just a few weeks ago, one of the big hotel companies was attacked by a few guys out of the Philippines who got hold of some e-mail addresses out of their loyalty program and basically sent out an e-mail requesting updates. It looked like an e-mail and the website of that hotel company. People then updated their information, including credit cards and so on, which went right to the guys in the Philippines, which is troubling enough, but then the other thing is there are no laws right now to allow someone to press charges.

Emerging applications. I hear a lot about whether hotel companies should start their own blogs, but I think it's a lot bigger than that. I think it's understanding what blogs are, that consumers write about the hotels, which could be damaging to the brand and have a trademark effect. You've got to look at both sides as it relates to emerging applications. Wireless is another one. There are other new technologies coming forth, so there's a lot more that's going to happen and you need to stay on top of developments.

Search engine marketing. Search engine marketing is going to be more and more important because that's how the Internet is being used, but I think it's going to evolve in terms of applications and personalization and so on. I think marketers need to stay on top on how search engine marketing will evolve.

Metasearch Kayak (partnership with AOL), Fairchase (owned by Yahoo), and Mobissimo, Bezurk, just to name a few major metasearch companies, make it easy for people to scan various travel websites for hotel rates and airline fares. It all comes back to the consumer, and there will be more and more sites coming up with very consumer-centric applications. In the end, it's really about driving convenience.

Where do you see the dot travel initiative fitting in, if at all?

I see the value of the dot travel domain extension as making it easy for consumers to find relevant travel and tourism websites. Dot travel is more than just a domain extension endorsed by travel and tourism trade associations worldwide, such as WTO (World Tourism Organization), WTTC (World Travel Tourism Council), PATA (Pacific Asia Tourism Association), ITAC (Travel Industry Association of Canada), and so forth, but also including a web directory and a sophisticated authentication process. This authentication process ensures that only relevant companies register their respective domain name, providing value to consumers.

The CTC has been an early supporter of the dot travel concept. Because Canada.travel is simple, short, and relevant (it consists of two very critical keywords), the search engine will quickly find content from within the entire CTC family of websites. When Canada.travel content is among the first few items to display after a quick online search, the result will be more unique visitors to the site and, by default, to any partner's content, adding value to the online campaigns.

In short, the dot travel initiative is another enabler to leverage the value of the Internet to travel and tourism

---

*Phishing is defined by Wikipedia as a form of criminal activity characterized by attempts to fraudulently acquire sensitive information, such as passwords or credit cards, by pretending to be a legitimate person (www.en.wikipedia.org/wki/phishing, accessed April 8, 2006)

providers worldwide by providing convenience to consumers and increasing economic value, especially to smaller operators with limited resources.

What type of skill sets would you envision a student needing to be successful in this environment in the future?

When people look at a career in e-commerce or Internet marketing, the first thing they need is marketing skills: sales skills, distribution management skills, revenue management skills, as well as technology skills. These skills are very important to build a base to be successful. Even more important are financial skills, because you're always dealing with business models, so if you don't have the financial skills, it will be hard to be successful. Because you're managing change in an organization, it's very important to have organizational behavioral skills: being able to communicate new marketing mediums and introduce new technologies into the organization. For many people, the Internet is still a very confusing big black hole, so it's important to be able to translate it so it's aligned to the corporate strategy and the marketing strategy and with what a consumer is actually looking for. If someone has all those different skill sets, it's a very exciting career.

Used by permission from Jens Thraenhart

How Distribution Channels Work

The distribution system consists of all channels available between the firm and the end user (i.e., the customer) that increase the probability of getting the end user to purchase the product. There are two ways to look at distribution channels. The first is to answer the question, How do I get my product to where the customer is located? And the second question is, How do I get the customer to where my product is? We discuss the first question in this chapter. The second question is discussed in Chapter 19.

Distribution channels are important; one leading analyst group estimates that 85% of the Fortune 500 companies sell their products through distribution channels.[1] A formal definition of distribution systems is: a set of different organizations, independent or not, that are involved in the process of making a product or service available for use or consumption. An important point to remember about distribution is that the goal is to get the product to where the customer is now or is going to be in the future.

Branded Hospitality Companies

Marriott International, Four Seasons, Intercontinental Hotel Group, Accor Hotels, SAS Radisson, Rezidor, and Shangri La are a few examples of branded hotel companies. These companies may own all of a particular asset, part of it, or none of it. The defining element of these types of companies is that they use the brand on the top of the asset, regardless of the actual owner. The hotels are marketed by the brand and all properties that carry the brand name adhere to strict service standards. As discussed in Chapter 13, branded companies are becoming more important because a strong brand allows a company to attract more franchisees, which translates into higher revenue. Branding also enables firms to gain management contracts, access to capital, and higher-than-average revenue per available room. This increase in size allows firms to spread the costs of supplies and technical issues, such as web connectivity, across multiple properties. Successful brands work because, to the consumer, a brand is a promise—a promise that she will be treated with respect, will receive excellent care, will get good value for her money, and will reap the rewards of whatever other promises the brand makes.

Franchises

Cendant Hotels is the largest hotel franchisee, with nine brands and over 6,000 hotels. Cendant manages Days Inn, Ramada Hotels, Howard Johnson, Knights Inn, and Wingate Inns, as well as Avis Rent-a-Car and many other nonhospitality franchises. As a franchisor, Cendant is an attractive alternative to more restrictive forms of marketing alliances. In addition to having an internationally recognized brand name, members benefit from worldwide reservation and marketing services, the mass buying and bargaining power of thousands of hoteliers, and the experience and services of a professional headquarters staff. Costs of all major services and programs are included in the annual fees and dues.

Franchise fees are usually based on annual revenue of a hotel, with up to 5 percent of the rooms' revenue paid to the franchisor. The idea is that there is a partnership between the franchisor and franchisee, so the better the hotel does financially, the better Cendant does.

 Web Browsing Exercise

Look up Cendant on your favorite search engine. Be prepared to discuss the company's history and the brands it owns. Is it different from other hotel companies? If so, how? What seems to be its competitive advantage(s)?

Reservation Services

Some hotels choose to market themselves independently and choose a reservation service only for connectivity to channels of distribution. By using SynXis or Pegasus, the hotel can link directly to the GDS or Internet without having a brand affiliation. Reservation services do not offer ancillary marketing programs. Each hotel is on its own to bring business to the channels.

Originally founded as the Hotel Industry Switch Company (THISCO) in 1988, Pegasus Systems, Inc., provided electronic commerce and transaction processing solutions to the hotel industry and operated its own customer travel reservation site, TravelWeb.com. Pegasus also offered the premier electronic switching service for reservation processing, which allows central reservation systems to connect seamlessly to global distribution systems (GDS) and/or to the Internet with a single electronic interface. Pegasus services also included Pegasus Commission Processing, the largest provider of travel agent commission payment processing services.

An established, well-known company within the hospitality industry, REZsolutions was formed in 1997 with the merger of Utell International and Anasazi, Inc. Utell, the world's largest hotel reservation and marketing company, which was founded in 1930 and has maintained a long-standing presence in Europe and Asia, merged with Anasazi, a leading supplier of hotel reservation technology solutions. The result was a fully integrated portfolio of hotel industry information technology products and services, which included the following:

■ Central reservation systems
■ A property management system
■ Hotel and brand representation services
■ Global reservations distribution through:
  Call centers
  Global distribution systems (GDS), such as Sabre and Galileo
  Connectivity with the Internet

The union of these two companies signified the birth of a powerful new entity that is uniquely positioned as a total solution provider for reservations distribution, offering a second-to-none comprehensive portfolio of products and services to the global hospitality industry.

Representation Firms

A representation (rep) firm is a channel of distribution that, figuratively speaking, brings a hotel to a marketplace. These companies market a hotel to customers for a fee and are hired to act as sales organizations for independent properties that don't have sales or reservation networks of their own. Major chains may also use representation firms to enhance their regional sales efforts. Representation firms have their own sales forces and represent a number of hotels through regional offices in different geographical areas.

These are called *soft brands* because they are essentially two brands: the brand of the representation firm and their own independent brand. Hotels get the best of both worlds: they can choose them as a way to maintain their independence while still accessing numerous marketing programs. The Leading Hotels of the World, WORLDHOTELS, Preferred Hotels & Resorts, Small Luxury Hotels of the World, and Relais & Châteaux all are considered soft brands. These brands all have the following:

■ Standards for membership
■ Connectivity to electronic channels of distribution
■ Sales initiatives
■ Marketing programs
■ Participation in trade shows

Exhibit 18-1 shows an advertisement for Preferred Hotels & Resorts.

Representation firms go much further than reservation companies in promoting their member hotels. Apart from the worldwide reservation network and a link to all global distribution systems, they often have a sales force actively selling their member hotels and publish an annual directory featuring these hotels, with detailed information on their services and facilities. They may print other marketing collateral, such as special programs, newsletters, and flyers. They also undertake advertising and public relations campaigns on behalf of their member hotels.

Once a representation firm has been engaged, it uses all of the normal communications mix, such as personal selling, direct mail, advertising, sales promotion, and public relations, to get customers to buy certain hotels. Sales calls are the most used form of the communications mix, followed by direct mail. David Green Organization of Chicago is an example of a representation firm that has been in the business for a long time. Newer, more segmented representation firms, such as Associated Luxury Hotels, have begun to carve niches in the representation marketplace.

Supranational, a European-based firm, is another example of a rep firm. Supranational's purpose is to unify the reservation network without sacrificing the identity of the individual property or chain. It is a very active sales and marketing company. Supranational represents entire hotel companies, as well as a number of independent properties around the world, which are rigorously selected.

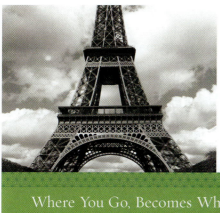

EXHIBIT 18-1 Preferred Hotels Group is an example of a hotel representation company.

Source: Preferred Hotel Group. Used by permission.

 Web Browsing Exercise

Use your favorite search engine to look up information on WORLDHOTELS, Supranational, David Green Organization, Preferred Hotel Group, and Leading Hotels of the World. Compare and contrast the companies. What are the strengths and weaknesses of each firm? If you were the director of marketing for a hotel, would you use any of these services? Why or why not?

In total, Supranational represents over 1,100 hotels, including more than 40 hotel chains in 75 countries and has 23 reservation offices worldwide. IcelandAir Hotels in Iceland; Fiesta Americana; and Fiesta Inns in Argentina, Brazil, and Mexico are members of this system. The selling point for customers, usually travel agents, is that by calling the reservation office of the local hotel company of any of the member chains, they can book reservations directly anywhere in the world in any of the member chains' properties. Additionally, Supranational has an active sales force in all key markets, and each member hotel group is responsible for selling and marketing Supranational hotels in its local market. That is, each member of the system attempts to market its counterparts, in hopes that the counterparts are doing the same for them. A 4 percent commission on revenue is paid to the partner when this occurs. Supranational is a nonprofit organization operated by hoteliers for hoteliers.

Supranational also publishes a wide range of marketing programs, including directories with the following:

■ International hotel classifications
■ Newsletters
■ City savers
■ Spotlight flyers
■ Guaranteed U.S. dollar programs
■ Incentive programs

Its global distribution system, Columbus, is considered to be among the most cost effective and advanced in the industry. It links into all the major airlines' systems.

A good rep firm also offers other services to customers, such as meeting planners, in prescreening hotels to be sure they will meet customers' needs. This includes doing the following:

■ Checking for space availability
■ Negotiating the most attractive rates
■ Providing other information about hotels

Representation firms operate on a retainer basis or are paid a fee when the group checks out of the hotel, or some combination of the two. Once a hotel has retained the services of the representation firm, the firm prints a brochure on the facility and markets it in clusters with other hotels in its network. Sales representatives of these companies operate in much the same way as a hotel's sales department. They maintain a client base and files and make sales calls to convince customers to use a facility in their portfolio rather than an alternative. Having a franchise does not preclude the use of representation firms. Some operators like the opportunity to have as many people selling their hotels as possible.

A representation firm can be more cost effective for a hotel company than establishing individual sales offices in feeder cities. A **feeder city** is a geographic area from which business is derived, but where a company may or may not have a property of its own. For example, Chicago is a major feeder city for New York City, as are Los Angeles, Paris, and London. If Chicago were a major feeder city for a hotel in Phoenix, it might not be cost effective for the Phoenix hotel to have a sales representative make frequent sales trips. Also, setting up a regional office to call on customers can be very expensive. Instead, a representation firm may be retained in the feeder city to make local calls as the most cost-effective method to build the channel of distribution.

On the surface, representation firms, which are usually located in major metropolitan centers, usually offer an effective support system to the marketing distribution effort. Sometimes, however, there are disputes as to where the booking originated. For example, a hotel might have an IBM account in its file system when the representation firm uncovers a piece of business from the same company but from a different contact. The question arises as to whether the firm should be paid for the booking. Such details need to be worked out before the representation agreement is consummated. If handled properly, this channel of distribution can supplement property-specific distribution efforts very effectively. Exhibit 18-2 provides a summary of the various methods that companies use to get their product or service to the customer.

There is a growing need in the hospitality industry to use distribution systems as never before. Distribution systems make it easier for customers to find the product. When demand for hotel rooms and restaurants exceeded supply, customers managed to find their way to the product offered. This is not the case today, with the proliferation of new hospitality products all vying for the same customer. It therefore becomes necessary to get the product to the customer. Next, we review how distribution systems work for manufactured goods and hospitality services.

Channels for Manufactured Goods

In the bricks-and-mortar world of manufactured goods, the producer of the goods uses either a wholesaler or a broker to assist with the distribution of the product or ships the product directly to a retailer. A wholesaler is an intermediary who buys or takes merchandise from the producer on consignment and sells it to the retailer. A broker serves a similar function but may or may not actually acquire the merchandise. The retailer, defined as whoever actually sells the product to the end user, represents the point of sale where the customer can purchase the product. Wholesaler, broker, and retailer are all part of the distribution system. They are all considered to add value to the product as it passes through their hands. This value can benefit the manufacturer (i.e., the wholesaler warehouses the product for the manufacturer or the broker handles all shipping and transportation of goods to the final destination) or the customer (i.e., the retailer handles all service issues related to the product.). Hence, the term VAR, which stands for value added reseller, is often used to describe the wholesaler, broker, and retailer.

As an example, Procter & Gamble works through brokers and wholesalers to get its product to retailers, of which there are tens of thousands worldwide. Coca-Cola distributes through franchisees that buy syrup in bulk, make and bottle the final product, and deliver it to innumerable retailers. Ford Motor Company distributes through its retailers, the local car dealerships, which sell Ford cars to the public. Variations of such distribution systems are endless.

In the past, companies found it necessary to use separate distribution systems, not only because of the prohibitive costs of developing their own, but also because distributors, particularly retailers, can get closer to the customer. All of this changed, however, with the development of the Internet.

In today's world, companies can sell their products directly to customers without having to go through another party. The process of going directly to the customer and not through established channels is known as **disintermediation.**[2] The most successful example of this strategy is Dell Computer. Most manufacturers of consumer products (e.g., Sony, Hewlett-Packard, and Levi Strauss) now sell their products directly to customers, although they also continue to sell their products through the traditional bricks-and-mortar channels mentioned earlier, as well as to other retailers who also market on the web. For instance, Sony will sell its products on www.sony.com, as well as through www.bestbuy.com and traditional bricks-and-mortar Best Buy stores. Southwest Airlines sells over 50 percent of its seats on the Internet.[3] Southwest does not participate in the traditional GDS links to travel agents, savings millions in commissions on a yearly basis. Today, many airlines charge a small booking fee for booking over the phone or give bonus miles for booking online.

Despite the rise of disintermediation, intermediaries are not going away. Rather, new intermediaries are being created to help connect the buyer and seller in cyberspace. These intermediaries are being created to make it easier for customers to search and buy products online by providing customers with the ability to compare products and prices in one location, rather than having to search multiple places. One such example is Bizrate.com, which compares prices for over 30,000 stores on products ranging from electronics to travel and leisure products (www.bizrate.com), as shown in Exhibit 18-3. Chaffey and colleagues (2003) referred to this process as reintermediation.[4]

Channels for Hospitality Firms

Although the principles are the same in the brick and mortar world, the distribution system for the hospitality industry becomes more complex. Unlike traditional

EXHIBIT 18-2   **Summary of Channel Types**

Channel	Examples
Methods to Get the Product to the Customer	
Ownership of Facilities	JC Resorts CNL Financial Group; also branded hotel companies
Management and Ownership of One Facility of Multiple Facilities. AKA Branded Hotel Companies with their own brands (or flags). May have ownership of some or all facilities.	Marriott International, Rezidor, Intercontinental Hotel Group, Accor
Management without Ownership	Marriott International, Redidor, Intercontinental Hotel Group, Accor
Franchises/ Franchising	Cendant, Marriott International Rezidor, IHG; Accor
Strategic Alliances	
Methods to Get the Customer to the Product	
Representation Firms	Leading Hotels of the World
Reservation Services	Pegasus, REZsolutions
Offline Travel Agents	Amex
Incentive Travel Organizations	Martiz
Consortia	GIANTS, Virtuoso
Corporate Travel Departments	Any large firm
Tour Wholesalers	Liberty Travel, Tui
GDS Based	Galileo: Travel Port; Sabre: Travelocity: Amadeus: E-Travel
Centralized Reservation System	
Travel Management Companies	American Express, Carlson Wagonlit, Rosenblueth
Convention Meeting Planner Organizations	CVB
Discount Brokers/Consolidators/Wholesalers	TUI
Destination Management Organizations	http://www.pra.com
Online Intermediaries for Business or Groups	Expedia Corporate, Travelocity Business, Orbitz for Business, Groople
Online Intermediaries for Transient, Business, and Packages	Expedia Corporate, Travelocity Business, Orbitz for Business, Groople

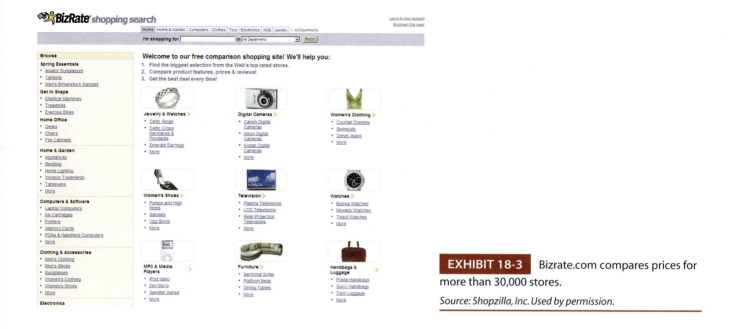

EXHIBIT 18-3 Bizrate.com compares prices for more than 30,000 stores.

Source: Shopzilla, Inc. Used by permission.

goods that are manufactured somewhere else and then shipped through the distribution chain to the consumer, the hotel or restaurant is also the retailer. This means that, unlike a manufacturer, the hotel or restaurant must be where the customer is. Firms such as Legal Seafoods, the local deli, and Dominos– or other local pizzerias—are exceptions to these rules because it is possible to have their food items delivered. Such companies are not the norm. In contrast to traditional bricks and mortar manufacturing, because of the unusually high perishability rate of the hospitality product, a separate wholesaler or retailer (such as a travel agent) rarely takes physical possession of the product to be marketed and delivered to the end customer at a later date. (They may, however, take nominal possession, such as a wholesaler who purchases a block of rooms or airline seats to be packaged and sold to the ultimate customer at a markup.) Recall from discussions throughout the book that one of the generic building blocks of competitive advantage is size, which is also known as *distribution reach*.

A 2005 report by PhoCusWright (PhoCusWright 2005 Consumer Survey, used by permission) revealed that, in 2004, one in four consumers in the United States booked leisure or unmanaged business travel online, and this figure is estimated to grow to 38 percent by 2007. For European consumers, the 2004 figure was 9 percent, and the estimated figure for 2007 is 27 percent. Asia Pacific lags behind these numbers, but given that 29 percent of the worldwide internet population is in this region, the potential for growth is enormous. For 2004, the percentage

of those who booked leisure or unmanaged business travel was 3 percent, and this figure is expected to grow to 25% in 2007.

It is clear from these figures that both online agencies and hotel websites will increase in importance. It is estimated by Credit Suisse/First Boston that traditional bricks and mortar travel agencies will suffer a decline in bookings as a result (by 15%), while calls to the CRS will decrease by roughly 23%. The relatively small decrease in estimated travel agency bookings will be primarily for simple, low risk transactions (e.g., the purchase of a round-trip airline ticket or a hotel reservation for three nights), which supports our earlier discussion that the traditional bricks and mortar travel agency still plays an important role in the distribution channel.

Each of the distribution channels represents a cost to the hotel. The estimated costs of customers using the various distribution channels are shown in Exhibit 19-6. The drive to reduce the cost of getting the guest into the hotel is behind most lodging brands' desire to move more reservations to the hotel's own website.

Structure of Distribution

Firms are considered to be either fully or partially vertically integrated. They are considered fully vertically integrated if they own the supplier of the raw materials used in the creation of their goods and if they own the retailers who sell their goods and services. That is, they provide both forward (e.g., supply the raw goods needed to make the product) and backward (e.g., the manufacturer owns the retailers) integration. Today, full **vertical integration** is rarely practiced in the manufacturing sector because the cost of doing so is too high. In the past, IBM was a fully integrated company making all the components for its computers and then selling them to customers. However, with the shift to open standards of hardware and software, it was no longer profitable to practice full integration. There were too many companies who could make the components more cheaply than IBM itself could make them.[8]

An example of a fully integrated hospitality firm is the tour company Nouvelles Frontières (NF) of France. NF either owns its own travel agencies or franchises them, which in turn sell only NF tours and packages. NF operates its own airplanes (but also uses common carriers); NF also owns a number of hotels (but also uses others). Another company similar to NF is TUI. Exhibit 18-4 shows an advertisement for one of their companies. In the restaurant industry, Starbucks practices full integration, as it owns its

own coffee bean fields in Colombia as well as the stores that sell the coffee. In the same vein, McDonald's also owns cattle ranges and potato farms. However, both Starbucks and McDonald's also buy their supplies from other sources in addition to the suppliers they own. Friendly Ice Cream Corporation is another example. Not only does it manufacture its own ice cream, but it distributes the ice cream in 530 company and franchised restaurants throughout the Northeast and through more than 4,500 supermarkets and other retail locations.[9]

Partially integrated firms own only part of the system—either on the manufacturing side or the retailer side. An example of partial integration would be Tandy Corporation, which owns the retailer Radio Shack and distributes to Radio Shack stores, the only stores that sell its products. Because Tandy Corporation buys raw materials from others, it only practices backward integration. Dell Computer and Apple Computer are other firms that practice partial integration. Both buy the components of their computers from someone but distribute all or some of their computers directly to the customer. Dell does this directly, whereas Apple sells through its retail stores and other retail stores, as well, of course, as on the Internet. In the hospitality industry, an example of a firm that is partially vertically integrated is TUI Austria Holding AG, which owns both a tour company and the travel agents that sell its tours. Again, it is partially integrated because, unlike our earlier example of Nouvelles Frontières (NF) of France, TUI only integrates forward.

It should be noted that when generic marketing texts refer to integration, they often address it as vertical marketing systems (VMS). In this usage, a VMS is any unified combination of suppliers, producers, wholesalers, or retailers working together to deliver a product or service to the end customer. A *corporate* VMS is one like Nouvelles Frontières, Carlson Companies, or Starbucks, in which one company owns all parts of the system. An *administered* VMS is one in which one of the members dominates the system by virtue of its power in the system. At one point, Häagen-Dazs, which is owned by Pillsbury, had so much power that it prohibited retail stores that carried its product from carrying Ben and Jerry's ice cream. To both create public awareness of this power and to get its product into stores that also carried Häagen-Dazs, Ben and Jerry's created its infamous advertising campaign with the slogan "What's the doughboy afraid of?"[10] A *contractual* VMS is one controlled by a contract. Examples of a contractual VMS include, but are not limited to, franchising arrangements, hotel representative companies, and membership organizations.

All three types of VMS are actually vertical distribution systems (VDS); regardless, these designations really do not fit the service sector. In service industries, where there

EXHIBIT 18-4   An ad for Jetair, one of the TUI companies.

Source: Jetair-TUI Belgium. Used by permission.

is simultaneous production and consumption, the producer and the retailer are one and the same. Production takes place at the end of the chain, at the outlet, and on site. Thus, we don't use the term *VMS*. Instead, we just use the term *integration*.

Distribution and the Building Blocks of Competitive Advantage

Size, or distribution reach, is critical for the hospitality firm because the firm needs to be where the customer is or where he plans to go in the future. A customer is more likely to join a specific hotel's frequent guest program if there are hotels located where guests can both earn and spend their points. In order for a chain to be successful in the frequent guest program game, and therefore be able to gain franchise agreements and management contracts, distribution is critical. It was this philosophy, in part, that prompted Hilton Hotels Corporation to buy the Promus chain. With the purchase of Promus, Hilton added a large number of hotels to its portfolio. Because the costs associated with "being where the customer is" are normally quite high, hospitality firms must eventually decide how to distribute their product. Manufactures do this by moving the product through middlemen, brokers, etc. until it reaches

the retail store where the customer buys the product. Firms must eventually decide whether to:

1. make slower progress by owning (at least partially) and managing each unit,
2. manage without owning,
3. franchise its name to be managed by others, or
4. form strategic alliances.

These choices essentially reflect the four types of business models that comprise the hospitality industry, as listed here:

- Franchisor (they sell the use of their name)
- Franchisee (they buy the use of another's name)
- Both franchisor and franchisee
- Both owning and being part of a strategic alliance

Some companies do all four independently, whereas others may do a combination of the four. Exhibit 18-5 illustrates some of the complexity associated with the four types of business models and hotel development.

For restaurant companies, growth occurs largely through franchising. However, because of a recent trend wherein hotels are outsourcing some, if not all, of their food and beverage facilities to restaurant companies, restaurants are gaining access to additional customers by leasing space in hotels. For example, the restaurant Panevino, which is owned and operated by Restaurant Associates, is located in

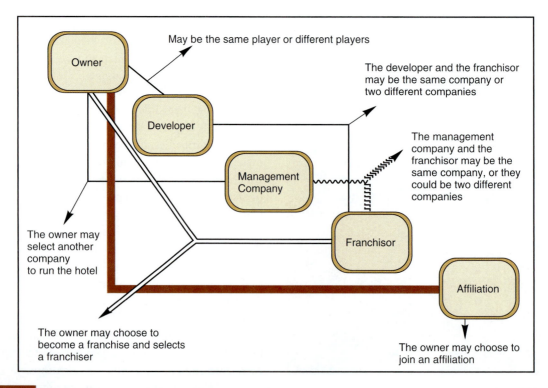

EXHIBIT 18-5 The players in hotel development.

Source: Lane, H. E. (1997). Hospitality world. New York: John Wiley & Sons, 350. Used by permission.

the Embassy Suite Hotel on 22nd Street in Washington, DC. Restaurant Associates is part of the Compass Group.

Major hotel companies such as InterContinental, Hilton, Sheraton, and Marriott are primarily hotel managers who operate hotels for owners, who could be themselves, be an individual, a partnership, a trust, a bank, or an insurance company, or some combination of these. They also franchise their names to others. In 1993, in fact, Marriott Corporation divided into two companies: Marriott International, Inc., which manages hotels and resorts and franchises its name to those owned by others; and Host Marriott, which is a real estate investment trust (REIT) company that gets favorable tax treatment because it is a REIT and buys and owns properties, sometimes managed by Marriott International, but also by Hyatt, Delta, Four Seasons, and others.

The Compass Group, shown in Exhibit 18-6, is an example of a similar structure in the restaurant and food service industry. The Compass Group is the world's largest food service organization. Not only does it own its own brands, but it also runs franchised brands. Exhibit 18-6 summarizes the different operating companies under the Compass Group brand.

The different types of business models found in the hospitality industry are discussed in detail next.

> **Tourism Marketing Application**
> The Walt Disney Company is an example of an integrated firm. Not only do they own theme parks, but they have a travel firm to get you to a Disney park and they also own hotels and cruise ships.

Ownership of Facilities

One ownership model is to own the property (or asset) and have others manage it. Host Marriott is an example of an ownership structure that owns but does not manage. Another example is CNL Hospitality Properties, Inc., which is an affiliate of CNL Financial Group, Inc. This is a privately held real estate and finance company. According to company information, CNL owns interests in a portfolio of 124 hotels with more than 25,000 rooms in 37 states with 19 nationally recognized hotel brands.[11] One of the more famous brands is the Hotel del Coronado, located in San Diego, California, which the company purchased in 2003 and then sold in 2005.[12]

The owners of these facilities typically hire former hoteliers to oversee the management company that runs the hotel. These employees are called asset managers. The Hotel Asset Managers Association (HAMA) is an organization that allows such managers to share information and learn new things. Following is its mission statement:

> HAMA is an association of professional individuals who are dedicated to the enhancement of hotel and hospitality asset values. The purpose of the organization is to:
>
> - improve asset management through education of members
> - communicate to the hotel industry the concerns of ownership
> - serve as a network
>
> Our business is to provide intense semi-annual forums and industry communications to fulfill the purpose of the organization. HAMA promotes ethical standards of conduct and mutual respect among members and the hospitality industry.[13]

> **Tourism Marketing Application**
> Governments can also own hotels. For example, the government of Spain plans to own 100 hotels by the year 2010. These hotels are called *paradores,* and they are usually situated in prime locations. They may be in historic buildings such as castles, convents, and palaces, and they are relatively pricey four-star hotels. (www.bbc.co.uk/languages/spanish/lj/cultural_notes/hotel.shtml, accessed April 8, 2006, and www.concierge.com/cntraveler/articles/detail?articleId=6022, accessed April 8, 2006)

 Web Browsing Exercise

Visit the website for HAMA (www.hamainfo.com/HAMA_com.htm). How does one become a member of this organization? What current information is listed about this organization? For example, where is the next meeting? Who speaks at these types of meetings? What are the advantages of joining?

Management and Ownership of One Facility or Multiple Facilities

A combination of management and ownership provides the brand name with the best integrity from a product delivery point of view. If a company both manages and owns a facility, there is a greater chance that customers will find consistency, both in terms of the physical product and the intangible service elements, throughout the network of properties. This consistency in the physical product comes about because the parent company controls the allocation of funds and can ensure that properties are maintained to

| EXHIBIT 18-10 | Changing Direction: Reflagging Can Help Increase Rate, and Occupancy |

Among the various tools at the disposal of a third-party management company, few can impact a hotel as much as a brand change. Typically, a reflagging is used to take a hotel property's profile up in search of better room rate, occupancy or both. And the local market conditions will dictate what kind of reflagging is necessary to keep a hotel viable.

"Virtually every reflagging we have done is to move the hotel up a notch," said Judy Hoffman, senior v.p. of marketing for San Diego-based Trigild International. Trigild manages 68 hotels generating annual sales revenue in excess of $50 million. Trigild has had past experience, for example, in taking over two budget hotels in freeway locations.

"We did major renovations and flagged one a Days Inn and the other a Ramada Ltd., and it made a huge difference," Hoffman said. "We don't see the point of reflagging if you are going to make a lateral change; we haven't done it to be equal with competing hotels." A sound reflagging strategy is to convert a hotel into the primary flag in its segment, such as Holiday Inn Express, she said. But Hoffman also acknowledged that Internet marketing has had a profound impact on the option of reflagging. In some cases, the money spent acquiring a franchise license might be put to better use on an increased marketing budget with an emphasis on Internet advertising.

"We have one [independent] property that sits on the beach in San Diego for which we exceed the market in occupancy but don't get quite the same rate or [revenue per available room], but when you factor everything in, our bottom line is significantly better keeping it unbranded," she said. In other cases, a flag switch is part of a major renovation. Daniel Vosotas, president of Trans Inns Management, which is based in Farmington Hills, Mich., said his company took the 204-room Best Western in Farmington Hills and converted it to a Courtyard by Marriott two years ago. The step up into a Marriott flag involved improvements to virtually every aspect of the hotel, he said. The hotel had been in the Trans Inns portfolio for some time, but the opportunity to convert it to another leading hotel brand had not been available, Vosotas said.

When the Courtyard flag did become available, Vosotas took advantage of Best Western's one-year membership agreement and started the conversion process. "From an economic standpoint, Best Western wasn't providing the reservation volume or the rate, and we couldn't justify spending the money on a renovation and keeping it in the Best Western system," he said. Vosotas cautioned, however, that the reflagging in and of itself will not create success at a higher room rate, but that the process is meant to complement what should already be a soundly operating property.

Although Portsmouth, N.H.-based Ocean Hospitalities has done its share of up-market reflaggings, President Doug Greene said the downward lodging cycle has created scenarios that might not even include keeping the hotel in your portfolio, let alone rebranding with the flag of your choice. "We do a lot of bank-owned properties and sometimes the lender will either buy the hotel, or fix it up and put another brand on it," he said. David Akridge, Ocean's v.p., said sometimes it is appropriate to move down the food chain; and with large franchisors like Cendant Hotel Group and Choice Hotels International, there is the opportunity to move up and down in a franchise organization. "Say there are capital issues for a Brand X hotel, the owner can make the decision to downgrade the flag, reasoning that any brand would be better than no brand," he said.

Both executives stressed that Ocean's recent business has been a mixture of switches. "We have been doing foreclosures with banks, so the flag is already off the property, but we have also been doing new construction with premium brands and high-end conversions," Greene said. Akridge is optimistic that even as hotel real-estate churns and older properties are reflagged, legitimate demand is being created. "An old Holiday Inn will move down the food chain, giving the new owner a new opportunity to capture new business," he said. "The hotels that are 35-[years old] to 40-years old move down the food chain and are replaced by new hotels."

Source: Reprinted with permission from Hotel and Motel Management. Copyright © 1998. All rights reserved.

---

products. Contrarily, Holiday Inn has franchised over 95 percent of its product line at all levels. Some companies, such as Four Seasons, Fairmont, Omni Hotels, Hyatt Hotels and Resorts, Mandarin Oriental, Peninsula Hotels, Oberoi of India, and Shangri La of Hong Kong, do not franchise at all. The philosophy of these companies is that the level of service they are attempting to deliver can be maintained only by direct control. So, instead of letting others own and run a property with their flag, they run the properties themselves.

The examples we have given are intended to be illustrative only of the complexity of the owning, managing, and franchising maze. The **reflagging** phenomenon (i.e., brand switching) that is occurring makes what is true today false tomorrow (see Exhibit 18-10). We describe the advantages and disadvantages of owning a franchise in Exhibit 18-11.

Strategic Alliances

Strategic alliances represent another form of geographic distribution channels. As mentioned in earlier chapters, this is where hotel, restaurant, and tourism companies form alliances with telephone, credit card, or other companies that have complementary customers and mutually beneficial objectives. These alliances are unique, however, because the firms are not in the same business. Strategic alliances between companies that are in the same business (e.g., lodging and food service) are becoming increasingly popular. Again, this is a way to gain greater distribution but still maintain independence and avoid some of the liabilities. An excellent case in point is that of SAS Hotels and Radisson, which is told in Exhibit 18-12.

EXHIBIT 18-11   Advantages and Disadvantages of Franchising

FRANCHISEE ADVANTAGES

First consider the advantages that you, as the owner of a hotel and franchisee, would enjoy. These advantages speak to the benefits you would receive by being part of a larger organization, such as brand-name recognition, an established customer base, purchasing economies, technical assistance, quality control, reduced financial risk, and a central reservation system.

The franchisee enjoys the benefit of an established product or service having customer acceptance and is therefore free of worries about traditional startup costs, such as developing a market presence. In the case of such companies as Sheraton Hotels, Hilton Hotels, and Holiday Inns, franchisors spend a sizable portion of their advertising budgets on national campaigns to keep the public aware of their hotel and restaurant services. The franchisee is customarily charged an advertising fee based on the gross revenues of a franchised unit for this service. Brand-name recognition—the fact that customers have heard of the chain and associate a specific image with it—is a key advantage to the franchisee. Moreover, a franchisee saves all the time, effort, and expense of building a reputation that is required for an individual entrepreneur, thus enabling the franchise unit to maintain its competitive edge.

A second advantage to the franchisee is the availability of managerial and technical assistance provided by the franchisor. Depending on the policy of the specific franchisor, the range of assistance available may or may not include managerial training; site selection; layout and design; furniture, fixtures, and equipment purchasing; inventory control; and promotional plans for the grand opening.

Another advantage to the franchisee is the franchisor's oversight of quality control standards. This is important not only to assure a consistent customer image but also to maintain employee pride in the workplace.

In many instances, franchisees benefit financially from the franchisor's advice and guidance on how much inventory to carry, thus avoiding waste and spoilage of perishables and unprofitable storage of low-demand items. Franchisees also benefit from purchasing economies, as the chain as a whole can negotiate better rates for things like soap and towels, as well as credit card fees and long-distance telephone services.

The carefully designed procedures of a franchised system minimize the financial risks for the franchisee and therefore tend to increase—but not to guarantee—the likelihood of generous franchise earnings.

Finally, substantial business is often referred to individual hotels via a central reservation system and chain directories, the cost of which is shared by all units in the chain. This makes the marketing dollars of individual units go much further.

FRANCHISEE DISADVANTAGES

Next, consider the disadvantages that you as the owner or franchisee would face. You would give up the advantages and be constrained by the rules of the franchise organization.

Failure of the franchisee to read carefully the fine print in the franchise agreement or failure to secure legal advice before signing such an agreement may cause a prospective franchisee to succumb to false or misleading sales practices of franchise promoters. Like any other contract, the franchise contract spells out in detail precisely what the franchisor will provide. Consulting with an attorney who understands the practical as well as the legal implications of a franchising agreement will enable a prospective franchisee to focus on those factors most likely to make the franchising relationship a successful one.

Because franchisors typically realize substantial revenues from franchise fees, as well as continuing royalties from franchisees, it may come as a shock to prospective franchisees that the financial obligation up front, when the franchise agreement is signed, can be steep. The ongoing fees also cut into the profit one could make as an independent property.

Franchisees may be required to provide certain amenities and facilities to be part of the chain, such as swimming pools or 24-hour front desk service. These and other service costs are borne by the franchisee and may turn out to be higher than expected and thus severely diminish the franchisee's expectations of a satisfactory return on the investment.

Territorial rights of the franchisor may overlap those of a franchisee and thus limit the revenue that the franchisee might otherwise expect to realize. For example, many of the larger hotel chains, early on, granted franchises that prohibited the franchisor from making any other franchise agreements within a specified geographical area. This was designed to protect a franchisee from having the franchisor grant another franchisee the right to operate another unit in the immediate neighborhood (e.g., two Sheratons on the same street). In recent years, however, segmentation of hotel markets has resulted in the creation of different hotel brands with separate corporate identities. When these new brands are granted franchises, they have often disregarded the territorial restrictions agreed to by the parent company and its franchisees. Thus, the original franchisees are hurt by competition from another franchisee—essentially from the same company—being permitted to locate within territory originally designated exclusively for the parent company franchisee.

For example, suppose a franchisee was granted a Holiday Inn franchise from Holiday Inn several years ago and was given the exclusive rights to the city of Denver. Subsequently, Holiday Inn launched two brands, Holiday Inn Suites and Holiday Inn Select. It may be that the rights to those franchises are given to someone else in the same market area, potentially hurting the original franchisee's sales.

With respect to a franchisee's desire to terminate the franchise, such occasions are generally covered by the language of the agreement. An uncooperative franchisor, however, may withhold approval of such a transaction if, for any reason, the franchisor believes the franchisee to have violated any provision of the franchise agreement.

FRANCHISOR ADVANTAGES

Next, consider the advantages of franchising from the point of view of the franchisor. Franchising is the ticket to growth for a franchise organization, and its members have a vested ownership interest.

Franchisors regard business expansion through a franchising network as the most attractive means of achieving rapid growth without the necessity of having to inject large sums of their own money or incurring substantial debt through borrowing from banks or insurance companies. Thus, the franchisee's investment in a particular franchise enables the franchisor to share the heavy burden of a rapidly growing hotel or restaurant empire, while at the same time allowing the franchisor valuable time for evaluating market opportunities in a wide variety of competitive environments.

Moreover, some franchisors suspect that a manager may be less enthusiastic about the operation of a company-owned unit than one who is a resident of the local community. The personal investment of the franchisee-manager motivates that person to work hard in pursuit of financial success. Franchising creates motivated owner-managers.

FRANCHISOR DISADVANTAGES

Finally, consider the disadvantages of franchising as seen by the franchisor. Multiple owners can mean a lack of consistency and control, and finding qualified franchisees can be difficult.

The idea of using the franchisee's money to keep a franchisor's business expansion plan afloat is not without its drawbacks. In the first place, overseeing a quickly expanding chain of hotel franchisees is always a formidable challenge. If less desirable franchisees are allowed to enter the system, it reflects badly on the whole organization.

In addition, there can be no guarantee that a franchisee will not discover, sooner or later, that they would be able to do just as well—if not better—by operating the business without the franchisor. After the franchise agreement expires, the franchisee may not renew.

Furthermore, although the supply of prospective franchisee applicants may appear to be inexhaustible, some franchisors report a lack of applicants whose experience, financial backing, and motivational drive are sufficiently persuasive to warrant taking a chance on their ability to become successful franchise operators.

Source: Retrieved November 29, 2005, from www.findarticles.com/p/articles/ mi-m3072/is_4_220/ai_n15725252. Wendy Valle 866-344-1315, wvalle@ reprintbuyer.com. Reprinted with permission from *Hotel & Motel Management.* Copyright © 1998. All rights reserved.

| EXHIBIT 18-12 | A Powerful Strategic Alliance |

SAS International Hotels (SIH), a division of the Scandinavian Airline System (SAS), started in 1960 with its first hotel in Copenhagen, their most important gateway city. During the next 28 years, SIH owned or leased and operated 21 more hotels in Scandinavia, as well as one each in Kuwait, Vienna, and Hamburg. In order to expedite its growth process, in 1989, SIH invested US$500 million for a 40 percent equity position in InterContinental Hotels (ICH), then owned by a Japanese company. ICH had more than 40,000 hotel rooms in more than 80 cities worldwide. The advantage to SIH was a worldwide reservation and distribution system in most of its important destinations. The intent was an eventual merger.

Unfortunately, because of the Gulf War and a general downturn in the international economy, SIH (SAS International hotels) was forced to absorb 40 percent of ICH's losses and taxes plus pay high interest on its borrowings. In addition, management cultures and approaches were incompatible. In 1992, SIH divested its equity position in ICH, taking a huge write-off on its balance sheet and facing bankruptcy.

SAS planned a merger with Swissair, so SIH entered into a marketing alliance with Swissotels, a subsidiary of Swissair. Swissotels, however, lacked the critical mass that SIH needed to grow internationally. Meanwhile, Radisson Hotels of Minneapolis was trying to penetrate the European market and had a marketing alliance with Mövenpick Hotels of Switzerland, also lacking a critical mass. In 1994, SIH and Radisson broke off their separate agreements and formed a strategic alliance called RadissonSAS.

SIH obtained all rights to the name and development of RadissonSAS hotels in Europe, the Middle East and North Africa. Neither company invested in the other. Radisson got immediate properties, brand identity and distribution in SIH territory. SIH got immediate brand identity, a global reservation system and distribution in the western hemisphere. The two companies shared many other economies of scope. This is a real strategic alliance that mutually benefits both parties and SIH. In November 2005, RadissonSAS operates over 133 hotels in Europe, the Middle East and Africa with another 39 projects under development.

Source: Retrieved November 7, 2005, from www.radissonsas.com/servlet/ContentServer?pagename=RadissonSAS/Page/rsasSimpleArticle&cid=1054883823930&c=Page&language=en.

Tourism Marketing Application

The United States government works with Xanterra Parks and Resorts to provide concession operations at the North and South Rims of Grand Canyon, Yellowstone, Mount Rushmore, Everglades, Bryce, Zion, Death Valley, and Petrified Forest. Xanterra purchased the Fred Harvey Company in 1968, which had provided this service since the mid-1800s. A history of The Fred Harvey Company and Xanterra Parks & Resorts® can be found at www.grandcanyonlodges.com/Our-History-722.html (accessed April 8, 2006).

It is interesting that SIH and Radisson have continued this pattern of mergers and joint agreements. For example, as of 2005, Carlson Hospitality, owner of the Radisson brand, had acquired 25 percent of Rezidor SAS.

In another version, Choice Hotels International, essentially a franchisor, entered into a strategic alliance in 1998 with Flag International, Australia's largest lodging chain, now called Flag Choice Hotels Ltd. Thus, Choice gets distribution through 481 Flag properties across Australia; New Zealand; Fiji; and Papua, New Guinea. Flag gets master franchise rights and a worldwide reservation and directory distribution system. Marriott International has a marketing alliance with New Otani of Japan, giving both companies distribution in each other's primary markets.

Alliances among airlines are well known. The Star Alliance includes such airlines as United, Air Canada, Thai, ANA, Lufthansa, Air New Zealand, Singapore Airlines, and SAS. In 2004, US Airways became the 16th member of the Star Alliance.[20] The oneworld alliance includes British Airways, American Airlines, Qantas, Iberia, Cathay Pacific, LAN, Finnair, and Aer Lingus. Set to join oneworld at the turn of 2006/2007 is Royal Jordanian, the first carrier from an Arab region to join. The biggest carrier in the Asia-Pacific region, Japan Airlines, is also seeking membership and would become the largest member of oneworld in terms of group revenue.[21] Although these airlines compete with each other on some routes, each sells the others' products and **code sharing** allows them to book each other's routes, share frequent travel points, and offer "seamless" travel worldwide.

Another example of a strategic alliance is between universities or sporting goods manufacturers and soda companies. For instance, Duke University is a Nike School, meaning that all the athletic teams wear Nike gear. Nike pays Duke University for this privilege, as well as providing all athletic teams with equipment. In turn, Nike receives product exposure. Frequently, the brand of soda sold on campuses is related to the contracted food service management company. For example, Chartwells has an exclusivity agreement with Coke, so campuses with Chartwells are "Coke Schools." The University of Nevada, Las Vegas is a "Pepsi School," meaning that only Pepsi is sold on campus. Strategic alliances are increasingly popular as companies seek faster growth, geographical distribution, and **economies of scope**.

EXHIBIT 18-13 Legal Sea Foods delivers its food to customers.

Source: Legal Sea Foods, Inc. Used by permission.

Restaurant Distribution

Unlike all the geographic distribution systems we have discussed, restaurants have one other system that hotels cannot duplicate. Unique in hospitality, they send the product to the customer. Although there have long been lots of take-home food products and home delivery of pizza, the latest pattern includes hotel delivery. Pizza Hut, Domino's, and the like, work with hotels to deliver pizzas to hotel guests. More than that, we now have better restaurants doing the same thing through an outside distribution system. Takeout Taxi is one company that delivers meals on behalf of restaurants it serves in the United States. Takeout Taxi bills itself as "the nation's largest

multi-restaurant delivery service." The restaurants range from local restaurants to big chains like Chi Chi's and TGI Friday's. It has developed a database of restaurant customers and uses it to develop highly targeted promotional programs for the restaurants.

Another example of sending the product to the customer is Waiter.com. According to the company website, this company pioneered the concept of online restaurant ordering in 1995, in Silicon Valley. They started with 60 local restaurants for delivery or take-out and today there are over 1,300 restaurants nationwide. Featured restaurants include TOGO'S Eatery, Chili's Grill & Bar, Boston Market, Round Table Pizza, Domino's, the Olive Garden, and California Pizza Kitchen. Not only do they offer convenient delivery, but they also offer a frequent dining program.

 Web Browsing Exercise

Visit the websites for Takeout Taxi (www.takeouttaxi.com/) and Waiter.com (www.waiter.com/cgi-bin/SCMMOS/RegSys/AutoRegHome.cgi). Prepare a short report about these firms. What do they actually do? Where are they located? How does a restaurant join this organization? To which market will they appeal?

Lettuce Entertain You of Chicago, which owns about 30 restaurants, uses a firm called Room Service Deliveries to deliver meals to hotel rooms. Many hotels in city areas, primarily those that do not have a restaurant of their own, have a selection flyer in every room listing 5 to 15 restaurants, with menus, that can be called to order delivery. This service is especially popular in all-suite hotels because the food can be refrigerated and reheated.

A final example of a firm that delivers its product to the customer is Legal Sea Foods, which is based in Boston (www.legalseafoods.com). This firm ships its famous seafood around the United States. Exhibit 18-13 shows an advertisement for Legal Sea Foods.

■ Summary

Distribution systems are methods of marketing a hospitality entity that are gaining greater importance in an increasingly competitive environment. In a business in which the product is perishable and production and consumption are simultaneous, we need to find many ways to allow customers to purchase our products and services easily.

Geographic distribution strategies such as management contracts, franchising, and strategic alliances allow a firm to reach new markets without incurring large capital investment and financial risk. However, firms can lose operational control by lending their names to franchisees all over the world. Regardless, geographical distribution means being in the right places.

■ Key Terms

phishing	reflagging
feeder city	code sharing
disintermediation	economies of scope
territorial rights	

■ Discussion Questions

1. Discuss the advantages and disadvantages of franchising as a method of increasing the channels of distribution.
2. Discuss the similarities and dissimilarities among brands, franchises, reservation companies, and representation firms.
3. Why do some hotel companies franchise aggressively while others do not?
4. Why are channels of distribution inherently different for the hospitality industry than for the goods industry?
5. Discuss the different forms of integration. What are the advantages and disadvantages of the different forms? Why would you use one form over another?

■ Group Projects

1. Assume your group has a small, but growing, chain of 15 upscale 300-room hotels in three countries. Using the web, compare reservation systems, their cost and effectiveness, to determine which system or systems you would use. Explain.
2. You have been asked by a wealthy client to find a restaurant franchise for her children to operate. Investigate two restaurant companies that franchise. Using the web, investigate the requirements to become a franchisee. Prepare a detailed report of the costs and benefits of one company over another.

■ References

1. Greenberg, P. (2002). *CRM at the speed of light: Capturing and keeping customers in real time* (2nd ed.). Berkeley: McGraw-Hill/Osborne Media.
2. Chaffey, D., Mayer, R., Johnson, K., & Ellis-Chadwick, F. (2003). *Internet marketing: Strategy, implementation and practice* (2nd ed.). Harlow: FT Prentice Hall, 52.
3. Retrieved November 7, 2005, from phx.corporate-ir. net/phoenix.zhtml?c=92562&p=irol-news Article&ID=751757.
4. Chaffey et al., 52.
5. Yesawich, Pepperdine, Brown & Russell/Yankelovich Partners. (2005). *National Travel MONITOR*.
6. KPMG LLP. (2005, March). *KPMG's Global hotel distribution survey 2005: Managing pricing across distribution channels.* Retrieved November 29, 2005, from www.kpmg.co.uk/industries/tlt/pubs.cfm.
7. Chaffey et al., 54.
8. Hill, C., & Jones, G. (2003). *Strategic management: An integrated approach* (6th ed.). Boston: Houghton Mifflin, 308.
9. Friendly Ice Cream Corporation website. Retrieved September 5, 2005, from http://phx.corporate-ir.net/ phoenix.zhtml?c=102153&p=irol-irhome.
10. Inc. Magazine. (1999, May). *It was 20 years ago today: A look back at the people and trends that shaped our world, 1979–1999* [Electronic version]. Retrieved November 29, 2005, from www.inc.com/magazine/19990515/ 4696.html.
11. Retrieved November 7, 2005, from www.cnlhotels. com/documents/090203.pdf.
12. Retrieved November 7, 2005, from www.cnlhotels.com/ documents/Del%20Agreement%2010-31-05%20FI-NAL.pdf.
13. Hospitality Asset Managers Association website. Retrieved November 29, 2005, from www.hamainfo.com/ HAMA_mst.htm.
14. National Real Estate Investor. (2003, July 1). Retrieved September 5, 2005, from http://nreionline.com/property/ hotel/real_estate_top_hotel_owners/index.html.
15. Eyster, J. (1997). Hotel management contracts in the U.S.: The revolution continues. *Cornell Hotel and Restaurant Administration Quarterly, 38* (3), 14–20.

16. Ibid.

17. Retrieved September 5, 2005, from www.hotelbusiness. com/links/archive/archive_view.asp?ID=19688&search_ variable=meridien%20hotels.

18. Retrieved November 29, 2005, from www.ehotelier. com/news/01/Jan7.htm#OUTRIGGER.

19. Koppel, A. (Anchor). (2003, October 25). Dollar signs: Opening a franchise. *CNN Live Saturday* [Television broadcast]. Transcript #102503CN.V27.

20. Retrieved November 7, 2005, from www.staralliance. com.

21. Retrieved November 7, 2005, from www.oneworld.com/.

Overview

Distribution systems are conduits for getting the product to the customer or the customer to the product. They have become an increasingly critical marketing tool for the hospitality industry, although they come in a number of different forms. This chapter should be read with Chapter 18: the two chapters together represent both the current and future distribution strategies that occur in the hospitality industry. Chapter 18 provides a brief discussion of what distribution channels are and how distribution systems work. It also shows how hospitality firms use different forms of distribution to increase their size or reach—for example, making sure that there is a restaurant or hotel where the customer needs one.

Chapter 19 examines how the distribution channel is used to bring the customer to the product, either directly or through an *intermediary*—an entity between the hospitality product and the customer. Intermediaries include travel agents, distribution service providers, and the like. The various distribution channels overlap, and the industry is not absolutely uniform in its use of nomenclatures. This can become quite confusing, but we have done our best to sort it out, as evidenced in Exhibit 18-2. Making the most of distribution channels means selecting the right channels and managing them to optimize their benefits.

Channels of Distribution

Bringing the Customer to the Product

I. Introduction to Hospitality Marketing
1. The Concept of Marketing
2. Marketing Services and the Hospitality Experience
3. The Marketing Mix and the Product/Service Mix
4. Relationship/Loyalty Marketing

II. Marketing to Build a Competitive Advantage
5. Strategic Marketing
6. The Strategic Marketing System and Marketing Objectives

III. The Marketplace
7. Understanding Individual Customers
8. Understanding Organizational Customers
9. The Tourist Customer and the Tourism Destination

IV. Situational Analysis
10. Understanding Competition
11. Marketing Intelligence and Research

V. Functional Strategies
12. Differentiation, Segmentation, and Target Marketing
13. Branding and Market Positioning
14. The Hospitality Pricing Mix
15. The Communications Mix: Advertising
16. The Communications Mix: Sales Promotions, Merchandising, Public Relations, and Publicity
17. The Communications Mix: Personal Selling
18. Hospitality Distribution Systems
19. *Channels of Distribution: Bringing the Customer to the Product*
20. Interactive Marketing: Internet and Database Marketing

VII. Feedback

VI. Synthesis
21. The Marketing Plan

Spencer Rascoff is CFO and vice president of marketing at Zillow.com, an Internet startup focused on the real estate industry. Prior to joining Zillow.com, Rascoff was vice president of lodging for Expedia and Hotels.com, where he was responsible for overseeing their partnerships with over 20,000 individual hotels and hundreds of hotel chains. In 1999 he cofounded Hotwire.com, a leading Internet travel company, and ran several prod-uct lines there. In 2003 Hotwire was sold to InterActiveCorp, the parent company of Expedia at the time.

Prior to Hotwire, Rascoff served as an investment professional at the Texas Pacific Group, a leading private equity firm. Previously, Rascoff worked as an investment banker in the mergers and acquisitions group at Goldman Sachs in New York. He also held other investment positions at Bear Stearns and Allen & Company.

Rascoff graduated cum laude from Harvard University.

Marketing in Action
Spencer Rascoff Cofounder of Hotwire.com

How, why and when was Hotwire started?

The Texas Pacific Group (TPG) Started Hotwire. Texas Pacific Group is a very large buyout firm that does leverage buyouts and other investing in companies and they got their start in the early '90s when they brought Continental Airlines out of bankruptcy and turned it around before selling much of their Continental stake to Northwest. So, they're actually on Northwest Airlines' board of directors and own a lot of Northwest. TPG then brought America West, which they still control, out of bankruptcy. In Europe, TPG is involved with Orion Air. So, through their background in the airline industry, they decided to try and get together a group of airlines here in the U.S. to create Hotwire. Back in 1999, they sat down with American, United, Continental, Northwest, US Airways, and America West and said, "How can we build a better mousetrap and create an alternative distribution model for our supply partners that works for both suppliers and customers?" Hotwire was launched in 2000, and in 2003 it earned about $1 billion in gross bookings. This made it the third or fourth largest online travel site. If it was an offline travel agency, it would be the sixth largest offline travel agency in the country.

Can you give us your impression of the Internet channel?

In the days before the Internet, suppliers sold distressed inventory through offline consolidators, which achieved some element of segmentation due to their inconvenience and lack of customer service. Frequently, they're operating in a different language than the native language of the country. Here in the United States, for example, when we started Hotwire, we asked Continental and American Airlines how an American in the U.S. could get the cheapest flights to Europe. They told us that the cheapest flights to Europe were sold through Italian-language and Spanish-language consolidators here in the U.S. Therefore, in the days before the Internet, they managed to segment customers sort of crudely, if you will. Then along came the Internet, and a lot of these consolidators started putting these fares online. Cheap Tickets started putting them online. Hotel Reservations Network started putting them online, and the segmentation lines were blurred because now, all of a sudden, higher-value, higher-paying customers were able to find these fares or these hotel rates. Then along came Priceline, which invented a new product—a really revolutionary product—that segmented customers not by geography or by language, but by product type. They said, "Let's create a product that is fundamentally so unappealing to an affluent customer, to a brand-loyal customer, that although they will be aware that it exists on Priceline, they just won't purchase on it. So, let's make it nonrefundable. Let's make it so you don't know the flight times, you don't know the carrier, you don't know the routing, you don't get frequent flier points. In the case of the hotel, you don't know the name of the hotel, you don't know the precise location of the hotel, you don't know the brand, etc. And, by the way, let's have them name their own price."

Well, about two years after Priceline launched, when we (the founders of Hotwire) were talking to the airlines, we asked, "What is important to you about this model and what is unimportant?" What the airlines told us at the time was that what was important was the ability to segment customers by whether they're brand loyal or brand neutral. What was not important to them was the "name your own price" aspect of the model. In that case, since it is quite cumbersome for customers to name their own price, we suggested dropping that aspect of the model, but keeping the segmentation, which is what is important to suppliers. This is what we did.

Who is the Hotwire customer?

Our customers primarily travel on the weekend. About 75 percent of our customers stay on a Thursday, Friday, or Saturday night with an average length of stay of about two and a half nights. In terms of college education, about 50 percent have four or more years in college with a median income of $75,000. Hotwire tends to attract the same type of customer as an Expedia customer, but because the customer is traveling on leisure rather than on business, they want to save money because it's on their own dime.

How much does the Hotwire customer spend on ancillary items at a hotel?

Data from 2003 showed that the average customer spent $28 per room night on incidental spend. Specifically, about half of Hotwire's customers dined in the restaurant, about 40 percent paid for parking, and about 10 percent paid for some sort of in-room entertainment. This compares with about $29 per day on average for that same group of customers when they purchase through the hotel websites directly and about $28 (essentially the same price) when they book through Expedia directly. So, it's a misperception that opaque customers spend less money once they're in the hotel.

Why is packaging becoming so important to the web?

The Hotwire package product takes our existing hotel inventory and bundles it with an air product, but it shows the name of the hotel. In that sense, it is price opaque but not

brand opaque. The customer will know it's a Wyndham or Hilton or Sheraton, but they won't know the price point associated with the hotel component. Instead, it will be a single price combined with air and hotel or air, hotel, and car. Packages have been wildly successful. In 2003 Hotwire was the second biggest package seller on the web, after Expedia.

Packaging has enormous customer appeal for one reason. Packages give the customer the ability to get a great deal while sacrificing less. What does the customer give up by buying a package? He gives up the ability to know what portion of the transaction is allocated to which travel product. He does not care about that anyway—he only considers where he is staying. For instance, consider a package to the Caribbean. Hotwire cannot give away a room behind a brand shield in the Caribbean, which makes sense. It's what Hotwire calls the "spouse factor." It's one thing if you're going to stay at the Milwaukee airport, if it ends up being a bad hotel because Hotwire rated it incorrectly. But if you're going all the way to the Caribbean for seven nights with your wife and kids, you want to see the name of the hotel. You want to see photos. You want to see how big the pool is. You want to see what color the walls are. You want to learn about the restaurants. You want to know if there's a golf course. You want to see pictures of the golf course, etc. That's really important. Hotwire is doing about 10 times as many room nights in the Caribbean, Mexico, and Hawaii through packages as they are through our brand-shielded, room-only product.

How do you see Hotwire as different from Priceline?

In terms of suppliers, we really serve very similar needs. We allow them to sell distressed inventory. In the hotel case, however, the "posted price" model had some very fundamental advantages over the "name your own price" model. That is the ability to stimulate incremental demand. In other words, we are able to advertise prices in our online marketing, our newsletters, our offline marketing, and our radio ads. We're able to say, "We've got great hotels in New York from $99! Come check us out!" The "name your own price" model requires your marketing to say, "We've got great hotels in New York! Come guess how much they are!" It makes it very difficult for Priceline to generate incremental travelers who might not have gone into New York for the weekend because they don't know what they're going to pay. In other words, the "name your own price" model suffers from what I call the babysitter problem. It is a nonrefundable purchase on both Priceline and Hotwire, but on Priceline you already have to have your babysitter lined up before you bid for the room. So you've got to sit down at your computer and say, okay, I want to go to New York for the weekend. I'm going to check with my wife. I'm going to get a babysitter. I'm going to tell the kids we're going to New York for the weekend, and I'm going to bid. Okay, I bid $100. Oops, the bid got rejected. Now I've got to go cancel the babysitter, etc. Whereas on Hotwire, you do a search, you see the prices. You say, "Oh, it's $100! That's great!" Now, I'm going to go call the babysitter, check with my wife and see if she wants to travel, etc. So, the "posted price" model is really able to generate incremental travel, which is very difficult to do with the "name your own price" model.

There's one other element that appeals to a lot of our upscale hotels about the "posted price" model, as opposed to a "name your price" model, which is the ability to up-sell customers to a higher star category. Frequently, we have customers who think they are, say, three-star customers. But they see, "Wow, for an extra $5 or $10, I can stay in a four-star or a four and a half or five-star hotel." This encourages a natural trade-up in the "posted price" model, which you really don't get in the "name your price" model because you have to actually name what star category you're bidding for.

Who owns the data on the customer?

Until the customer appears at the hotel, it's a Hotwire customer. The Hotwire privacy policy with our customers says that our hotels can't market to our customers without asking permission from the customer directly. Once a customer shows up at the hotel's front door, however, that person is the hotel's customer, and at that point the hotel should get as much of their information as possible in order to market directly to them. Many of Hotwire's partners, most specifically our Las Vegas partners, are very sophisticated about marketing to our customers. A Hotwire guest will show up at the Venetian and the hotel will see it's through Hotwire and at that point they'll sign up the customer for their rewards program and will ask for their e-mail address and then will market directly to that customer. It's a great way for a brand to take a brand-indifferent customer and turn them into a brand-loyal customer.

Used by permission of Spencer Rascoff.

Hospitality Channels of Distribution

Once a hospitality organization has chosen a method to ensure that there is a product where the customer is, it must determine the appropriate channel to bring the customer to the hospitality product. Exhibit 18-2 (page 497) showed the different channels available to hospitality firms to accomplish this task. In this chapter we discuss those various channels in depth—except for representation firms and reservation services (which were discussed in Chapter 18) and convention management organizations (which were discussed in Chapter 8)—enumerate the strengths and weaknesses of each, and highlight strategies to manage the channels. The channels include: (1) representation firms, (2) reservation services, (3) consortia, (4) incentive travel organizations, (5) offline travel agents, (6) centralized reservation systems, (7) GDS-based systems, (8) tour operators/discount brokers/consolidators/wholesalers, (9) corporate travel departments, (10) travel management companies, (11) convention meeting planner organizations, (12) destination management organizations, (13) online intermediaries for businesses or groups, and (14) online intermediaries for transient, business, and packages.

Consortium

The Merriam-Webster dictionary defines **consortium** as "an agreement, combination or group formed to undertake an enterprise beyond the resources of any one member."[1] Consortia occur for both travel agencies and hotels. In our discussion with hoteliers, most think of consortia as only referring to travel agencies, for example, GIANTS (Greater Independent Association of National Travel Service—now known as the Ensemble Travel Group), eTravCo, MAST (Midwest Agents Selling Travel), the Leisure Travel Group, and Virtuoso. However, using the Merriam-Webster dictionary as our guide, we define consortium in the hospitality industry as a loosely knit group of independently owned and managed properties (e.g., hotels or travel agencies) with different names, a joint marketing distribution purpose, and a common consortium designation.

The purpose of the consortium is to open a channel of distribution by maximizing combined marketing resources while amortizing the associated marketing expenses. Consortia are more common in the United States. Consortia distribute hotel inventory at preferred rates to affiliated travel agencies. Many of the affiliated agencies are "in-plants," or travel agencies dedicated to one company. Bear Stearns, the global investment banking firm in New York City, had American Express as its in-plant. American Express travel agents were dedicated to Bear Stearns business, working at the offices at 245 Park Avenue. The American Express consortia provided reduced rates for Bear Stearns travelers.

 Web Browsing Exercise

Use your favorite web browser to look up eTravCo (www.e-travco.com), Ensemble Travel (www.ensembledirect.com), and Virtuoso (www.virtuoso.com). Be prepared to discuss each in more detail. What did you learn from each of the sites? What is the win for the travel agent? What is the win for the customer? How do these sites relate to what was discussed in Chapter 17?

Incentive Travel Organizations

An **incentive travel organization** is another example of a channel of distribution. These are companies that specialize in handling strictly incentive reward travel. Many organizations and firms have incentive contests to reward top-performing employees, salespeople, dealers, or retailers. Travel rewards are a popular form of incentive. An advertisement appears in Exhibit 19-1. We also discussed this market in Chapter 8.

Major corporations often have their own in-house travel departments or individuals to handle incentive arrangements. Many companies have used travel agents. More and more, however, both large and small companies are relying on incentive houses to organize their trips. Carlson Marketing Group is one of the leading incentive travel providers with offices in 30 major cities in the United States and in 20 countries worldwide. Maritz travel, based in the Midwest, is also an established incentive house.

The reason for the use of such companies as Carlson and Maritz is that incentive travel is a special type of corporate travel. For companies that use this kind of reward frequently, there is a constant need for destinations that are new, different, and exciting—in other words, that offer a real incentive for performance. Second, there is a real need for the trip to be letter-perfect. A poor trip destroys the morale of the very employee that one is trying to reward. Keeping up with all of this, on a worldwide basis, is expensive and time-consuming.

Incentive houses, because of their collective accounts, can partial out the costs of their expertise. Almost always, someone will have visited and thoroughly inspected the destination, the hotels, the restaurants, and the ground services before putting together the incentive package. The incentive house then "sells" it to the company and helps the company to "sell" it to those who seek the reward.

For upscale hotels, particularly in resort areas or foreign destinations, it can be a real boost to the distribution channel to be on the approved list of a major incentive house. In these cases, a property does not simply buy an incentive house's services. In effect, it earns them by doing things right. By contrast with consortia, reservation networks, rep firms, and travel agents, the customer, not the hotel, pays for the incentive house's service. It is important to note that incentive planners deal directly with individual properties as opposed to representatives of specific hotel chains in order to be personally certain of the product.

Each channel member involved with incentive travel is integrally dependent on the other members in the channel for performance. If customers are dissatisfied with the trip, they may choose another incentive house for the next program. Each channel member has to make sure that everything goes as promised. For example, if the ground transportation is an hour late in picking up a group at the airport, the entire trip can be spoiled. Future business may be lost not only to another incentive house, but to another destination.

Remember How Rewarding Choice Can Be?

American Express® Gift Cheques and Reward Cards give your sales representatives the ability to *choose* rewards that are meaningful to them while giving you a *simple* solution to all your incentive applications – from sales contests to reseller promotions. Motivate your team with the right reward and the revenue they deliver will be your reward.

Give the reward of choice.
Call **877/353-4438**
or visit **www.aeis.com**

MAKE LIFE REWARDING® | Incentive Services

GIFT CHEQUES ■ REWARD CARDS ■ ONLINE REWARD MANAGEMENT

EXHIBIT 19-1 An American Express Incentives Services advertisement offering rewards to top-performing salespersons.

Source: American Express Incentives Services. Used by permission.

Traditional Offline Travel Agents

Travel agents represent an important intermediary in the distribution of hospitality products and services. Travel agents are compensated through a sales commission, usually based on the rate of the service sold. As a rule of thumb in most cases, a 10 percent commission is paid to travel agents who book cruises and hotel rooms, whereas rental car firms pay a lesser rate. Most airlines, once a major source of commission revenue for travel agencies, no longer pay commissions, and this has forced many agents to add a transaction fee for making airline and other travel reservations. In fact, travel agents do not so much sell airline seats, hotel rooms, or rental cars as they sell their time and knowledge of travel service suppliers. A 10 percent commission on a $100 room is $10. A travel agent can access this hotel room through a GDS in three to seven seconds.

If that same travel agent had to look up the property in a directory, dial the 800 number, get put on hold, speak to an agent, and then confirm the booking, they would make the same $10 for 10 minutes' worth of work. In today's highly competitive environment, agencies that take 10 minutes for a $10 commission will not be in business very long.

Travel agencies also form consortia, using the strength of many individual agencies to combine marketing and negotiating clout as a channel member. In North America, travel agencies are larger than their counterparts in other parts of the world. This is because size is needed to handle the large accounts and negotiate the best arrangements, a necessary ability for being the agent of choice. Further, by banding together in consortia, groups of agencies have been able to bargain collectively with travel suppliers to gain access to preferred rates or other customer benefits. These are subsequently used as enticements to lure and retain business clientele, who could not otherwise obtain the same benefits. Through the control of information, agents exert great influence in all segments of the travel market. Virtuoso, formerly Allied Percival International (API), is an example of a consortium of upscale travel agencies. Virtuoso negotiates airline, hotel, and car rental rates on the basis of its combined travel expenditures among all of its participating members. Each member retains its autonomy while benefiting from volume-negotiated rates. Their positioning statement is as follows:

> Virtuoso is a consortium of the top-selling leisure travel agencies in the United States. Together member agencies have over 1 billion dollars of buying power. What does this mean to you, our customers? It means **we have clout!** As a Virtuoso member agency, we can get you the best **value** for your money on some of the best hotels, tours, resorts, and cruise lines. Our customers also enjoy a number of attractive, free enhancements and amenities. Note the word "value," not "cheap." Whether you buy a house, a car or a vacation, you want the best value—not the cheapest. As a member, we work to give you the best possible value.[2]

Tourism Marketing Application

Destinations market to travel agents by attending trade fairs, such as the ITB Berlin, which is the largest travel trade show in the world. Visitors come from all sectors of the industry: tour operators, travel agencies and their employees, hotel managers, and the like. (www.itb-berlin.de) For example, the Maldives Tourism Association held a Maldivian Evening at ITB in 2006 that was attended by more than 500 tour operators, travel trade, and media. Guests were entertained by Maldivian traditional dancers and heard live music performed by the Sultans. (www.visitmaldives.com/mu/latest/update.

php?subaction=showfull=id&=;1142406896&archive=&start_from=&ucat=&, accessed April 9, 2006.

As the Internet continues to grow in importance as a mechanism for booking travel, many believe that the travel agent's role in the distribution of travel services will become smaller and smaller. A report by YPB&R/Yankelovich Partners stated that such thinking is premature.[3] In fact, they stated that although there were approximately 20 percent fewer ARC (Airlines Reporting Corporation) appointed agency locations in 2003 than in 1999, the remaining agencies were booking 140 percent more per year than they did in 1999. This is not surprising when one considers the changing role of the travel agency.

The Travel Agent Role.   The customer is faced with a blizzard of changing conditions in the marketplace. Rates change at a pace that is unparalleled in the history of travel. Airlines, collectively, are reported to change fares as many as 80,000 times a day. The proliferation of hotels offering thousands of packages, incentives, and varying rate structures to varying people at varying times makes booking a difficult task at best. The rental car industry has followed suit with the airlines and hotels, offering special promotions and incentives every day. Many of these promotions have conditions attached to them, such as booking an airline seat 30 days in advance with cancellation penalty clauses. Add to all of this the overlapping frequent traveler awards and you have a very complex problem for the ordinary traveler.

Exhibits 19-2A and 19-2B, adapted from a report by the investment bank Credit Suisse/First Boston, shows two types of transactions with which the customer is faced. In the first part of Exhibit 19-2A, labeled Routine, the customer knows what he wants. Here, the agent is basically selling her time; specifically, the time it takes to book the transaction. For this type of transaction, the customer is most likely to book online and avoid the travel agent service charge. The second type of transaction in Exhibit 19-2A, labeled Complex, reflects the scenario described in the previous paragraph. In this scenario, the travel agent sells Knowledge, which is exactly what the customer is looking for in a travel agent. Exhibit 19-2B further illustrates complex leisure transactions.

One of the *complex* transactions that travel agencies are now booking, in addition to the leisure activities of tours, cruises, honeymoons, and all-inclusive packages, are meetings and conventions. An executive vice president of American Express noted at a 2003 industry conference that meeting space is the fastest growing portion of the business for them.[4]

EXHIBIT 19-2A	Types of Transactions

Routine	Complex
Customer knows exactly what she wants, e.g., flight from New York to London	Customer has idea of what she wants, e.g., vacation to Europe
Agent determines everything and sells client details of how to make vacation happen, e.g., flight time, cost, airline	Agent determines everything and sells "knowledge, expertise, and experience"
Fees-usually nominal—to agent for booking and, perhaps, agreement with airline	Fees—usually much higher than for routine transaction—to agent for: booking, perhaps airline agreement, perhaps fees for hotels & other bookings
Agent selling time to book	Agent selling their time to investigate

Source: Adapted from Credit Suisse/First Boston Lodging Intermediation. (2003, May 12). A white paper on shifting online lodging distribution dynamics; and Minor, J., Angel, S. M., & Hart R. (2003, May 14). The internet dilemma: Third-party sites complicate a promising distribution. New York: Lehman Brothers Inc., Global Equity Research.

Complexity

		Low	Medium	High
Content	Low	Car rental	Airline flight	Multi-destination travel
	Medium		Weekend getaway	International travel arranged by firm pre-agreement
	High	High-price purchase (justify price)	High-price purchase	tours, cruises honeymoon

EXHIBIT 19-2B	Relationship Between Complexity and Content

Source: Adapted from Credit Suisse/First Boston Lodging Intermediation. (2003, May 12). A white paper on shifting online lodging distribution dynamics; and Minor, J., Angel, S. M., & Hart R. (2003, May 14). The internet dilemma: Third-party sites complicate a promising distribution. New York: Lehman Brothers Inc., Global Equity Research.

How Agencies Book Travel. Agencies that were on manual systems only a short time ago now have sophisticated database equipment to manage their bookings. Other automated systems are largely reservation terminals provided by the major GDS systems (discussed later) creating direct links between travel agents, hotels, and airlines.

Working with Travel Agents. Travel agents need clear, concise information on the product and cooperation with the delivery of the product. The hotel company that can provide the least complicated products to travel agents and deliver them to the customer will likely get the most bookings. The more agents have to decipher very difficult booking procedures, the less likely they are to recommend the brand or property in the future.

All rates and information furnished to travel agents on a property need to be as current as possible. Travel agencies have their own customer bases and will be blamed by their customers for poor service at a facility they recommend if their expectations go unfulfilled. For example, the fact that lengthy renovations are planned should be communicated to travel agents before they hear it from their customers. The short-term loss of revenue from agents' not booking the facility during the renovation period will appear small compared with the possible customer dissatisfaction and loss of future bookings.

Cooperation with agents also requires the payment of commissions on a timely basis. The agency has performed the desired service of bringing the product through the channel of distribution. For that service, it needs to be paid in a timely manner. Because most agencies are small, cash flow is very important to their survival. A company or hotel can very quickly get the reputation of being slow or of not paying on commissions. Agencies will go out of their way to avoid recommending the property if they are not receiving their commissions. Contrarily, agents are quick to recommend those brands or properties that pay commissions promptly.

Further, cooperation with travel agents includes upgrading their important clients at no extra charge, offering complimentary stays to allow them to experience the product firsthand, doing special promotions to gain their loyalty, and, in general, working with them in every way possible. Failure to do this is to bite the hand that feeds you. Given the importance of travel agents in the overall distribution system, particularly for resorts and offshore destinations, hospitality companies today often market directly to them. The testimonial letters shown in Exhibit 19-3 illustrate that, despite the advent of the web, the travel agent is still important.

A familiarization trip (commonly referred to as a "fam" trip) is a popular method used to expose the hotel product to intermediaries in the channel of distribution. A familiarization trip is just that; the hotel has a group of travel agents visit the facility to familiarize them with the features and benefits. Word-of-mouth advertising is the most believable form of communication. If travel agents are impressed with a facility during a familiarization trip, they will convey their enthusiasm to customers, and bookings will increase.

Travel agents are also reached through other distribution channels. Advertising in travel agent publications, such as *Travel Weekly* and *Travel Agent,* is one such channel. Other effective methods include online marketing promoting visitation of "agent-only" websites, direct marketing, and, yes, even the low-tech fax!

> ### Tourism Marketing Application
> Destinations also use familiarization trips as a way to create awareness of their offerings. For example, the state of Vermont runs such trips to qualified meeting planners considering holding meetings in the state. As they state on their website, the convention bureau, working together with its members, identifies, qualifies, and selects appropriate meeting planners to suit a specific region and then plans a FAMtrip that will entertain, educate, and ultimately draw business to the state. (www.vermont.org/groups/fams.html, accessed April 9, 2006). Another example is Myanmar, which is located between India and China and next to Thailand. The Myanmar Tourism Promotion Board offers FAM trips for 8 days and 7 nights covering Yangon, Bagan, Mandalay, and Inle Lake. These trips are not free, but they are offered at a reduced price. For example, traveling from Bangkok prices range from $875, and from Europe they start at $1200. (www.myanmar-tourism.com/mystical_fam_trips.htm, accessed April 9, 2006)

Hotels can also get information to travel agents through the GDS system either through advertising or text messaging. Research by NFO Plog Research, one of the large research firms studying the hotel industry, found that 90 percent of travel agents they surveyed in October 2003 used the GDS and GDS shopping displays for hotel information either as much or more in 2003 than in 2001. In addition, 53 percent of all travel agents who recalled GDS advertising reported that they made a booking at least once as a result of a GDS advertisement.[5] The advantage of GDS advertising/text messaging is cost. For example, a $20,000 investment can reach 200,000 targeted GDS potential buyers (through their agents), whereas the same investment in a local newspaper may reach only a handful of buyers.

Travel agents are as important worldwide as they are in the United States. In major destination areas such as Singapore, Hong Kong, and Manila, many agents operate as "inbound" agencies—that is, they deal primarily with people coming into the country as opposed to those going out. This means setting up ground arrangements, hotel bookings, local tours, and so forth.

EXHIBIT 19-3   Testimonial letters show that travel agents are still important.

Source: Adapted from Richcreek Vacations. Used by permission.

Central Reservation Systems

The central reservation system (CRS) function, which allows booking from an 800 number, is integrated with both

EXHIBIT 19-4 Footprint Vietnam Travel advertisement.

Source: www.footprintsvietnam.com/plan_trip_or_customized_travel_tours. htm. Used by permission.

include "unspoiled," "eco-friendly," and "real destinations, not tourist traps." The website also uses testimonials to help reassure the customer of the reliability of this organization.

An example of a wholesaler is GOGO Tours, which does millions of dollars of business in the Caribbean, as well as elsewhere. It takes an allotment of rooms from a specific hotel at, for example, 20 percent off the gross rate, in different rate categories, with cutoff time periods to sell them. Other wholesalers work on a "sell and report" basis; that is, they report sales only after they are made, free of a cutoff time. The hotel advises sellout periods. GOGO's inventory appears in the computers of its nationwide neighborhood stores, airline GDS, and agents-only website at **www.gogowwv.com.** The rooms are sold by travel agents at their regular rates, as though they called the hotel directly. The hotel, of course, has paid GOGO a commission. GOGO pays a commission to the travel agent.

The wholesaler market includes people using a variety of transportation options. The wholesaler negotiates with the airlines, cruise lines, railroads, hotels, car rentals, and bus companies to develop travel options to be resold as a total package. Groups come from every realm of the spectrum, from a high school hockey team to an upscale corporate trip to the Super Bowl to individual travelers. Wholesalers negotiate the best deals from the suppliers and then re-sell the product at a price that includes their profit margins. Many of the tour operators belong to the United States Tour Operators Association (www.ustoa.com).

Web Browsing Exercise

Visit www.ustoa.com/. Explore the site and be prepared to discuss the following:

- Why should a customer travel with USTOA members?
- How can the customer save by booking a package instead of booking separate reservations?
- What are the mission and goals of the organization?
- What activities does the organization undertake?

International wholesalers exist both domestically and abroad. Domestic wholesalers under the umbrella of, for instance, Visit USA, are called inbound operators; they handle tours and groups organized overseas and manage their travel needs while in the United States. Their outbound counterparts handle the reverse travel internationally. This is true of all countries serving international markets.

Ad hoc groups are organizations that are already formed and want to book a tour to a previously visited or new destination. An example of an ad hoc group is a Lions Club tour to the Ozarks in Arkansas or an archeology club tour to Mexico. The tour operator again takes possession of the inventory of hotel rooms and restaurant seats, but the risk is much lower because a solid booking is in place. A series group, on the other hand, might be a solicited group of couples or retirees that want to tour the French vineyards with specific, predetermined departure dates.

The tour operator needs the full cooperation of channel members to be successful. Ad hoc groups are the least complicated to administer. Wholesale tours, on the other hand, are very risky; some hotels and restaurants have strict cancellation guidelines and, if the tour doesn't sell, the wholesaler can end up holding a large, perishable inventory.

Good channel management can work two ways. If a wholesale tour broker is attempting to coordinate a tour series to a destination, the hotels and restaurants should remain flexible to help in the development of the distribution network. The fall foliage season in New England may not be the time to help a channel member create a new series, because demand for the hotel product at that time exceeds the supply. If the wholesaler is attempting to bring in business at a less busy time, such as spring, every attempt should be made to encourage the effort. Short-term decisions regarding cancellation clauses could prejudice an active channel member in the future.

The other side of the coin is that, when business is slow, the operators will wield clout to obtain the lowest possible rates. In heavy destination areas such as the Algarve coast in Portugal, where extensive overbuilding has occurred, British tour operators have bargained for tens of thousands of room nights to bring room rates down to ridiculously low levels.

Web Browsing Exercise

Go to www.gogowwv.com. Explore the site and answer the following questions:

- Why should a consumer use a travel agent?
- What is the history of GOGO?
- Why would a hotel want to work with GOGO?
- Does the Internet have the potential to make a company such as GOGO become extinct? Why or why not?

Internet Channel Intermediaries

As discussed already, customers can book rooms in a hotel in a variety of ways, including the following:

- Calling the hotel directly
- Calling the hotel's central reservation center
- Going through a designated hotel representative
- Visiting a traditional bricks-and-mortar travel agency
- Walking directly into the hotel

Now, however, customers can also book hotels by using an online travel agency (e.g., Travelocity or Expedia) or directly through the hotel or resort's own website. Exhibit 19-5 presents an interview with Max Starkov and Jason Price from e-business strategies and provides insight into the future.

Each of the distribution channels represents a cost to the hotel. The estimated total costs of customers using the different distribution channels are shown in Exhibit 19-6. The drive to reduce the cost of getting the guest into the hotel is behind most lodging brands' desire to move more reservations to the hotel's own website.

One example of an online agency shown in Exhibit 19-6 is a hotel consolidator. The most well-known player is Hotels.com. The hotel consolidator typically follows one of two strategies: a merchant model strategy or an agency model strategy. In the merchant model strategy the consolidator contracts for inventory from the hotels at a fixed rate, often referred to as the net rate. For example, one hotel in Las Vegas sets its consolidator rates for its suite reservations once a day for the next 14 days and twice a week for the next 90 days. Regardless of how often rates are set, these net rates are usually sold to the consolidator at a deep discount. The goal, of course, is to sell the rooms that cannot be sold using normal channels to ensure as high an occupancy as possible. Usually, a specific amount of inventory is taken on a consignment basis under a one-year contract. There are times, however, when the hotel consolidator cannot sell the room through traditional channels. The online hotel consolidators then either sell their allocated rooms to their affiliated websites (e.g., Hotels.com may sell its allocated rooms to Travelocity) at a marked-up price or sell them on their own website at a certain markup (usually anywhere from 20 to 30 percent). Rooms that are booked in this way go directly to the hotel's central reservation system via a switch.

The hotel consolidator may also follow an agency model strategy. This model is very similar to the bricks-and-mortar travel agency model. The hotel gives the consolidator commissionable rates and then pays a commission on any rooms that are booked. Online travel agencies include Lastminute.com, Travelocity.com, Expedia.com, and Orbitz.com. In this model, the consolidator typically books through the GDS system.

It should be noted that a hotel consolidator might follow both strategies simultaneously. As stated by the investment bank Lehman Brothers in a research report, "Most of the merchant model sites also offer reservations under the traditional travel agent model (in which the site receives an industry-standard 10 percent commission for booking a reservation for a guest), but these offerings are usually buried after several pages of more merchant model listings.[7]

The hotel consolidator following the merchant model approach may use an opaque approach to selling rooms.[8] The two firms that practice this approach are Hotwire.com and Priceline.com. The opaque model works in one of two ways, depending on whether the customer is buying a single part of the travel package (e.g., only a hotel room) or the whole package (e.g., hotel room, airline

The explosion of the "merchant model" after 9/11 caught the hospitality industry by surprise. Over the last four years many hoteliers have been struggling to decrease their dependence on the online merchants and to develop direct online distribution strategies of their own. Hoteliers are also trying to find answers to several critical questions: does the cost of doing business with online merchants outweigh the cost of not doing business with them? What will be those crucial developments in the online hospitality marketplace over the next five years and what can hoteliers do to prepare for and take advantage of them now? This paper provokes thoughts that may help shape executive decisions under the current circumstances.

BACKGROUND

The *merchant model* is a simple wholesale arrangement that involves net rates and room allotments with cutoff dates. The concept is nothing new and existed long before Hotels.com and Expedia, in the form of the FIT wholesale model fashioned with tour operators. Companies like Gulliver's have operated in this space for decades. The only difference is that in the past hoteliers did not allow wholesalers and tour operators to publish discounted/wholesale hotel rates (net + markup) if not bundled with other travel services.

Due to a lack of understanding of how online distribution worked, exacerbated by the industry-wide desperation after 9/11, hoteliers did not impose the same restriction on the online merchants. As a result hoteliers saw their discounted rates posted all over the Internet—on merchant sites and thousands of affiliates—and suffered severe consequence to rate and brand integrity.

While hoteliers gave up rooms at steep discount, online merchants became darlings on Wall Street. Hotels.com had a market capitalization of over $3 billion at one point. This unhealthy industry practice was best illustrated by one industry executive who described the state of confusion as "Selling Waldorf-Astoria on Hotels.com is like buying Armani in Wal-Mart." Since those days, hoteliers have sobered up, but the hangover still lingers and too many hoteliers are still having difficulty weaning themselves away and adopting better online distribution strategies.

THE INTERNET IS ALL ABOUT EFFICIENCY

The Internet is all about transparency, efficient distribution of information, and inexpensive e-commerce transactions. It is the most efficient marketing and distribution medium ever invented. It is simply the best direct-to-consumer distribution channel ever created and it definitely favors supplier–buyer relationships. Nowhere is this better illustrated than between hotel and customer. Hoteliers that embraced their own direct online distribution efforts first and merchants second now enjoy as much as 40% to 60% of total revenues from their own websites.

In this sense the abnormally high margins of the merchant model (18%-30%) constitute a temporary anomaly, not the rule. This is because the merchant model contradicts the very nature of the Internet as an efficient and direct-to-consumer channel. The marketplace cannot tolerate deficiencies and abnormally high profit margins except on a temporary basis in periods of major industry transitions or during the emergence of entirely new distribution and marketing media (i.e., the Internet).

Travel is all about selling a dream, an anticipated experience. Selling a hotel stay over the Web does not require warehouses, complicated wholesale and retail arrangements, fulfillment centers, etc. Hoteliers know their product, destination, and customers better than anybody else. Just think about what a smart hotelier can do by employing rich media on the Web (virtual tours, photo galleries, floor plans, interactive applications, etc). In this sense to market well online hoteliers do not need third party intermediaries, and can do the job themselves.

The proverbial "pendulum" has shifted back in favor of hoteliers. Major brands and savvy hoteliers are regaining control of the online distribution channel and have already proven that they can "dictate the terms of the online game" via tight control over properties, rate parity, best rate guarantees and successful loyalty programs (e.g. 75% of all Internet sales for Marriott come from the brand website)

THE MERCHANT MODEL IS ALREADY EVOLVING

The merchant model, used as the main business model by leading online intermediaries, is becoming more flexible due to the changing market conditions and increased pressure by travel suppliers: corporate contracts, lower mark-ups (e.g. 18%-22%), direct interfaces to the major brand CRSs, and last room availability on the hotel site. All of these concessions would have been unthinkable just two years ago.

This trend will inevitably accelerate over the next years as travel suppliers and major hotel brands continue to apply pressure on the online intermediaries in an environment of improved economic conditions and positive changes in consumer purchasing behavior.

The online merchants are embracing the dynamic packaging model as the next high profit margin generator. Dynamic packaging is a reincarnation, on a higher technology level, of the traditional FIT packaging that has existed since the advent of the GDS. This business model enjoys an increasing popularity among the online intermediaries. Why? It allows intermediaries to charge much higher markups (e.g. 25%-35%) compared to the merchant model (e.g. 18%-25%). At the same time travel suppliers prefer dynamic packaging to the merchant model because it makes their distressed inventory and pricing opaque.

Forrester predicts that dynamic packaging sales will quadruple between 2004 and 2009. Sixty-eight percent of online travelers would consider purchasing a dynamic package (PhoCus Wright Survey). All major online intermediaries have embraced the dynamic packaging model. Expedia, Travelocity and Orbitz report their dynamic packaging modules are the fastest growing segment of their overall bookings.

COMEBACK OF THE AGENCY MODEL?

The agency model (i.e., the old travel agency model that relies on supplier commissions, usually 10%) is beginning to regain at least some of its past luster as a result of the rate parity introduced by all major brands, and the lower merchant markups negotiated by some of the major hotel brands (e.g. 18%). One of the typical merchants, Lodging.com, has negotiated straight commission override deals with some of the major brands.

DEVELOPMENTS IN HOSPITALITY OVER THE NEXT FIVE YEARS

Hospitality eBusiness Strategies firmly believes that the following crucial developments in the hospitality industry over the next five years will benefit hoteliers and other travel suppliers and help lessen their dependence on the online intermediaries and transform the merchant model as we know it:

ONLINE DISTRIBUTION HAS BECOME THE #1 CHANNEL IN HOSPITALITY

- In 2005 over 25% of all hotel room revenue will be booked online. Another 25% of hotel bookings will be directly influenced by the Internet but done offline. In 2006 this percentage will exceed 27%-29%. Overall travel booked online will exceed 31%-35% of total bookings over the next 2 years (PhoCus Wright, HeBS). We expect that by 2009 over 50% of all hotel bookings will be performed online.
- The Direct vs. Indirect ratio in the online channel will follow closely with the offline channel (75:25) and will become as favorable as 80:20 in favor of the direct channel due to the diminishing role of call centers, travel agents, and traditional tour operators; rate parity; and better channel control on behalf of the major brands).

DISAPPEARANCE OF THE TRAVEL AGENCY COMMISSION

- In our view the standard travel agency commission, which is currently 10%, will disappear over the next 5 years in the same manner as it vanished in the airline and car rental sectors.
- The main reasons we believe standard agency commissions will disappear are: the diminishing importance of this channel and the GDS in general; the shift toward Internet distribution and rapidly changing consumer purchasing habits that favor suppliers; increased online expertise by the major brands, franchisees, and independents alike; the improved economic situation. Once again: the Internet is all about efficiency and distribution and provides a powerful alternative to the travel agency channel, which is a highly inefficient channel of distribution.
- Travel agency locations in the US have decreased by 10% every year over the past 5-6 years. From nearly 35,000 travel agencies in the US back in 1995, there were only 21,787 travel agencies in 2004, according to ARC, and as per current trends there will be less than 19,500 travel agencies by end of 2005. A growing number of travel agency bookings for hotels are already noncommissionable (preferred corporate rates, group rates, etc.).
- For the first time in 2004 the Internet hotel bookings surpassed GDS hotel bookings and this trend will continue in the future. In 2006-2007 the Internet will generate twice as many hotel bookings as the GDS. Even now an increasing number of travel agency GDS bookings are noncommissionable transactions - as a rule preferred corporate rates are net, noncommissionable rates.
- In our view over the next several years the agency commission will shrink from the current 10% level to 8%, 5% and then will become a simple flat "Booking Reward" payment per reservation, most probably $5-$10 per booking by 2009. After that even this flat fee may disappear for good.

DIRECT CORRELATION BETWEEN AGENCY COMMISSION AND MERCHANT DISCOUNT

The lower the standard travel agency commission becomes, the lower the merchant model discount granted by hoteliers will be. Volume producers will be rewarded with commission/flat booking reward payment overrides in the range of 50%-100% above the standard travel agency commission or flat booking rewards that exist at the time. If the standard agency commission is at the 5% level, wholesalers will get discounts at the 7%-10% level. No hotelier will be willing to grant a merchant discount to the tune of 25%-30%.

In this environment the marketplace will not tolerate the merchant model with its abnormally high margins and it will become a thing of the past.

THE END OF THE MERCHANT MODEL

We believe that the merchant model as we know it will not exist five years from now in the U.S. 2005 will deepen and finalize the process of hoteliers getting the upper hand over online intermediaries.

From the major brands to savvy hotel management companies (HMC) to the individual hotel owner operator, each is firmly gaining control of their relationships with the third parties, and has instituted "preferred" or "approved" partner programs (similar to IHG). Franchisee direct contracts with the online intermediaries will disappear and will be folded into the corporate agreements with "preferred" or "approved" third parties. HMCs with multiple properties in the same destination can offer consumers a choice of hotels with their own destination sites, and independents are becoming increasingly choosy and very careful with their third-party relationships. The overall trend is to work with fewer "hotel friendlier" and carefully chosen online intermediaries.

Major hotel brands and many savvy hoteliers already operate in a rate parity and best rate guarantee environment and will continue to do so in the foreseeable future.

In the near future major brands and smart hoteliers will start introducing restrictions on how net wholesale rates can be marketed on the Internet by the third parties, which will gradually lead to a requirement that net rates should be bundled with other services and cannot be exposed "naked" on the Web (i.e. like it is today with the merchant model). As noted, such a requirement existed in the past.

HeBS firmly believes that the merchant model and the agency model will evolve over the next few years and converge into a "commission override" model where higher booking volume production will earn the intermediaries better commissions or overrides above existing travel agency commission levels, but at a fraction of today's abnormally high discounts of 18%-30%. As discussed above we expect the current 10% commission to shrink to 8% then 5%, in the end becoming a flat fee of $5-$10.

This convergence model will still require the online intermediaries to build direct interfaces to the major hotel brand CRSs to reduce distribution costs. Some of the savings realized by the hotel brands may be shared with the intermediaries.

Online intermediaries will further embrace and perfect the dynamic packaging model, thus turning themselves into typical online wholesale packagers/tour operators. Dynamic packaging and addition of local sightseeing and entertainment will be the only chance of the online intermediaries to generate higher profit margins.

In addition to the dynamic packaging model that will become the norm, the online intermediaries will embrace the advertising model and start offering enhanced listings and positioning, pay-per-click (PPC), and display advertising programs to supplement their decreased margins. A recent survey by Expedia actually probed hoteliers' attitude toward PPC and other advertising models.

CONCLUSIONS

Over the next 5 years the merchant model as we know it will disappear. It will be transformed into a commission override convergence model. Travel agency commissions will shrink from the current 10% level to 8% then 5%, in the end becoming a flat fee of $5-$10. Online merchant operators will start earning volume discounts above current agency commission levels but at a fraction of today's levels.

Online intermediaries will further embrace the dynamic packaging model, thus turning themselves into typical online wholesale packagers/tour operators, and start offering new advertising programs, such as enhanced listings and positioning, PPC and display advertising.

WHAT CAN HOTELIERS DO?

Hoteliers should establish a "Preferred Partner" program and introduce stringent requirements the online intermediaries have to meet in order to qualify. Hoteliers have to create "Preferred Partner Guidelines" outlining these requirements. Hoteliers have to limit the number of third-party intermediaries they are doing business with and focus on their direct online distribution and marketing strategies. Hoteliers have to start negotiating commission overrides to preferred partners as opposed to net rates.

Hoteliers should focus all of their efforts and resources on building and expanding their existing direct online distribution and marketing strategies. Consider seeking advice from an experienced Internet distribution and marketing hospitality consultancy to help navigate the Internet and utilize the direct online channel to its fullest potential. Learn from experts who can teach hoteliers and their staffs best practices and provide crucial professional development, as well as guide a hotel company's direct Internet distribution and marketing strategies, online brand building strategies, e-CRM, website optimization and search engine marketing strategies.

Used by permission from Max Starkov.

EXHIBIT 19-6	Estimated Costs to Hotel to Book a Room Costing $220 Using Different Methods

Customer Books via:	Total Cost to Hotel
Toll-free call to CRS	$3–$5
Through traditional travel agent	$22–$27
Toll-free call directly to hotel	$3–$5
Branded website	$5
Online travel agency— merchant model	$18–$24
Online Travel agency—agency model	$66
Direct through hotel website	$5–$15

EXHIBIT 19-7	Hotwrite web page.

Source: Expedia.com. Used by permission.

ticket, and car.) If the customer is buying only a single part of the package, the customer does not know the specific brand she will be buying until after she has actually made the booking. However, she does know the quality rating and the general location of the hotel. If the customer is buying a package, the hotel brand is shown to the customer, whereas other parts of the package (e.g., the airline portion) may or may not be opaque. The customer also does not know how much she is paying for each component of the total package. Hence, this is often referred to as price opaque but not brand opaque. In either case, prices are nonrefundable and nonchangeable. Exhibit 19-7 shows the Hotwire webpage.

The opaque model allows a hotel to discount without letting its brand-loyal customers trade down to those lower price points. The example frequently used by Spencer Rascoff is that of the outlet mall:

> When you think about how apparel retailers sell their excess inventory; for example, how Polo/Ralph Lauren or Brooks Brothers gets rid of their excess inventory, they traditionally do not discount heavily in their own flagship stores. The reason is that their brand loyal customers go into those stores prepared to pay full price. If customers see the discounted price, they will naturally trade down to those discounts. To move excess inventory, the apparel industry has created a network of outlet malls throughout the country that have either inferior or no customer service. In addition, they have tainted products in some cases, they have limited selection and they have inconvenient locations. These are the revenue management fences that the apparel industry has created to move their excess inventory through a different network or channel than their retail structure. The opaque channels are essentially the outlet malls of the travel industry, allowing suppliers to discount without brand dilution.

In the hospitality industry, what the opaque model does is allow a hotel to sell excess rooms without diluting the brand. For instance, if a Hilton has extra rooms to sell and can't sell them at $150, but they could sell at $75, they do not want to say "Hilton" next to the $75 because people are going to think about Hilton differently if they see Hilton for $75. So, instead, Hilton will want an opaque channel, like Hotwire, to sell a four-star hotel for $75 and let the customer be pleasantly surprised when they find out that it is a Hilton.

From a revenue management standpoint, the opaque model allows suppliers to segment customers into brand-loyal, high-value, paying-full-price customers on the one hand and discount incremental, brand-disloyal customers on the other. It's allowing suppliers to create these two types of customers each buying a different product in the prepurchase stage. One buys a branded product and pays for the security of knowing where they will be staying and the type of room, while the other has no idea until after the purchase is made.[9]

As mentioned, the two firms that practice this approach are Hotwire.com and Priceline.com. Priceline and Hotwire are very different from a customer perspective. Priceline is known as a "name your price" model, whereas Hotwire is known as a "posted price" model. With Priceline the hotel customer first determines both the general geographic location in which he wishes to stay and the star category of hotel he wishes to purchase. He then bids what he is willing to pay for this hotel room. The bid is either accepted or not. Once the bid is accepted, the customer then finds out in which hotel he will be staying. The accepted bid cannot be changed or canceled. Priceline.com has evolved over time and now also offers the consumer the capability of shopping and comparing more than 60,000 hotels around the world.

Similar to Priceline, on Hotwire.com the customer first selects the general location where she would like to stay. Hotwire then shows the customer multiple prices for different categories of hotels. For instance, she might see a four-star hotel for $75, a three-star for $60, and a five-star for $180. The customer then selects the hotel based on the price she is willing to pay. Once she has selected this price, the customer then finds out in which hotel she will be staying. The accepted bid cannot be changed or canceled.

From a hotel perspective, the two businesses are actually quite similar. They are similar because they don't show the name of the hotel until after the purchase is completed. This allows the hotelier to protect his brand. The reservation is entirely electronic. In Priceline's case, it goes through the Worldspan GDS. In Hotwire's case, it goes through the Pegasus switch. But either way, they are both electronic, as opposed to being fulfilled by fax or phone call to the hotel.

In the Marketing in Action feature at the beginning of the chapter, Spencer Rascoff, one of the founders of Hotwire, discusses the creation of Hotwire, the profile of the Hotwire customer in 2003, and the future of Hotwire. In the late fall of 2003, Hotwire was purchased by Hotels.com and is now part of InterActive Corporation. Time will tell how this purchase will impact this channel.

The interview with Rascoff also shows that customers can book hotel rooms directly by going to the hotel's landing page. Travelzoo is an example of a firm that sends customers to the landing page of a specific hotel. Essentially, Travelzoo works like the travel section of the local newspaper, with the exception that it reaches more than 9 million users who have requested to receive its newsletter with special travel offers. The hotel controls the rates that appear on the landing page. Once the customer gets to the landing page, he can book the hotel directly by calling the hotel's reservation department. The landing page can also direct the customer to a specific page on the hotel's own website.

Web Browsing Exercise

Visit www.travelzoo.com/ and spend time exploring the site. How does this site differ from the sites examined in the Web Browsing Exercises earlier in this chapter? What is the consumer proposition? What is the firm's proposition?

To get to the hotel's reservation page on the hotel's website, customers can either go directly to the website and be forwarded to the reservation page or they can be directed to the reservation page by one of the secondary websites via links. An example of a secondary website that links customers to a hotel is Travelaxe.com.

Future Challenges of Online Distribution

Bill Carroll, a professor at Cornell University and a consultant to PhoCusWright and major hotel firms, states that the Internet has fundamentally changed travel and hospitality distribution. We concur. In discussions with Dr. Carroll, we identified some of the key challenges facing marketing managers in the hospitality industry as a result of the Internet. Although an entire chapter could be dedicated to these challenges, we are able to present only a sampling of these challenges.

The first challenge is that the consideration set for travel options has expanded exponentially as search engines provide multiple travel options within seconds. This means that the competitive set may be not only other properties in your destination, but other destinations around the world. As discussed throughout this text, the focus must be on what the customer is actually buying and what problems are being solved. The solutions to these problems can be found instantaneously and may be outside the normal geographic area that a marketing manager typically thinks about.

An example of an Internet firm that aids consumers in their search for solutions is Kayak.com (www.kayak.com). As stated on their website:

> Kayak is considered a meta-search engine and that means our website searches hundreds of other websites in real time for the best travel deals available. Kayak.com lets you look at a full range of airlines, hotels, and car rental agencies quickly and efficiently based on the exact criteria you select." They go on to say that they "are not a travel agency. With a travel agency, you pay a fee to get an airline reservation, a hotel room, or a rental car. There are no fees with Kayak.com. We do not sell airline tickets or hotel rooms or rental car reservations. Instead, we direct you to other travel sites where you can make these purchases directly. Our way of helping you plan your travel gives you a more comprehensive list of your travel options. Really fast. And with no biases or hidden agenda. In short, you are in control of your travel choices. Since we search hundreds of travel websites (including travel agency sites), you now have to search only one: Kayak.com. Kayak.com makes money when people click onto advertising on our website. Plus, we make money when people click on the results

from our travel partners like airlines, hotels, and rental car companies. This is a revenue model (for all of you MBAs) similar to that of Google.[10]

A second challenge is the challenge of price transparency and consistency. Two issues addressed in earlier chapters were brand integrity and customer loyalty. A component of both is trust. That is, the consumer must trust that the brand will look after the customer's best interest and not practice opportunistic behavior. When prices vary for no particular reason, trust erodes. Firms such as Travelaxe.com (www.travelaxe.com) enable the consumer to compare the prices of a particular hotel across a variety of websites. If the hotel is not careful in managing its prices across the various distribution channels, it will be immediately apparent to the customer. It is because of this that many firms have gone to "best available rate" on their own website. Yet, pricing issues still can occur. Hence the pricing of the different distribution channels must be watched constantly.

A third challenge facing hospitality industry executives is the need to manage transaction costs. As shown in Exhibit 19-6, the various channels have different costs. Marketing managers will need to better understand their customers and determine ways to drive them through the most efficient channel. A critical component of this goal is understanding the types of information customers want to see about a specific destination or property. Consumers will go to the sites that provide such information, and it may not be the home page of the hospitality firm.

A fourth challenge brought about by the Internet is the reallocation of marketing dollars. A survey of 25 travel marketing executives by PhoCusWright and New York University in 2005 found that "42 percent of the respondents were spending 20 percent or more of their marketing budget on online channels in 2005, compared to 25 percent spending 20 percent or more in 2004. More than three-quarters of the hospitality respondents (78 percent) planned to increase spending on search engine optimization, while 74 percent planned to increase spending on web site design and functionality."[11]

A fifth challenge is the advent of what is known as *Web 2.0. Wikipedia* (http://en.wikipedia.org/wiki/Web_2.0) defines Web 2.0 as a "phrase coined by O'Reilly Media to refer to a supposed second generation of Internet-based services that let people collaborate and share information online in a new way—such as social networking sites, wikis (a type of website that enables users to easily add, remove, or otherwise edit and change some available content, sometimes without the need for registration) and folksonomies. (The process of *folksonomic tagging* is intended to make a body of information increasingly easier to search, discover, and navigate over time. A well-developed folksonomy is

ideally accessible as a shared vocabulary that is both originated by and familiar to its primary users.) Examples of Web 2.0 are myspace.com and tripadvisor.com. Because of such websites, marketers need to keep well informed about what people are saying about the organization.

Part of Web 2.0 is what is known as *RSS–real simple syndication*. RSS enables consumers to customize the information that they wish to receive so they don't need to look the information up daily. For example, Expedia.com allows consumers to sign up for RSS, which allows Expedia to deliver the latest prices on trips that consumers are interested in. Marriott is also using RSS and claims that "great deals now come your way, not the other way." Truly, this is the foundation of revenue management discussed in Chapter 14: tell me when you want to come and I'll tell you the price. Tell me what you want to pay and I'll tell you the price."

A sixth challenge, suggested by Carolina Colasanti of Starwood Hotels, is what she calls **onward distribution.** This is the process whereby negotiated rates to wholesalers are passed on to other websites either intentionally or unintentionally. Ms. Colasanti states that, whereas most websites have good intentions, some can easily dilute your brand by catering to a different market and boasting deeply discounted room rates and making negotiated rates available to the public, undercutting your own "best available rates" and breaking the promise of a "best rate guarantee." This scenario can, however, be avoided by ensuring you have an "onward distribution" clause on all of your contracts with those suppliers.

A seventh challenge is the rise of third parties that are going after the group market. Passkey Research reveals that one in four rooms are associated with a group and that 15 percent of this 25 percent are a result of citywide events. Of the remaining 85 percent, 33 percent are less than 25 people.[12] An example of a firm entering this market is Groople.com (www.groople.com), as shown in Exhibit 19.8. Groople.com and other similar firms provide the consumer with multiple options. Although such choice is good for the consumer, it is harder on the hotel.

A final challenge for hospitality firms is the increase in packaging. This is a good challenge because it allows the hospitality organization to mask the price of the individual components. The challenge arises in the software needed to create dynamic packaging, which is what the consumer demands.

> **Tourism Marketing Application**
> The Czech Tourist Authority has implemented a pull and push strategy. Specifically, the pull strategy involves associating the Czech Republic with the

EXHIBIT 19-8 Groople web page.

Source: Groople. Used by permission.

favorable images that help drive travel motivations, such as friendly, wonderful history and architecture, and interesting castles and chateaus. The push strategy is to begin to develop long-term relationships with tour operators and travel agents. (www.czechtourism.com/upload/1082967278 promotionstrategy.pdf)

 Web Browsing Exercise

Use your favorite search engine to look up "online travel distribution." Pick one or two sites and be prepared to discuss the information presented. Has the world of online travel distribution changed much since the publication of this book (2007)? If so, how?

Promotional Tie-Ins

The category of strategies called promotional tie-ins is the catchall for the burgeoning attempts of the industry to expand its market base through intermediaries. Under this umbrella lies the couponing used by restaurants and hotels alike. The numerous dining clubs sprouting up throughout the country present a good example of the promotional tie-in channel of distribution. In this method, a number of restaurants participate in a dining club, whereby the intermediary organization prints, markets, and distributes the

coupons representing everything from a free dessert to a two-for-one dinner offering. This is similar to the entertainment book we discussed earlier in this book.

Hotel companies have been represented by various couponing organizations, primarily selling a 50 percent discount off rack or corporate rates to their members, often, but not necessarily, on weekends and during slow periods. With today's rampant discounting this, like some car rental discounts, is often not a good deal. One can often negotiate for less, but the coupon-using customer usually does not know this.

Another area of tie-ins for hotels is with the airlines. A majority of airline customers eventually become hotel customers. Hotels work with airlines to arrange specific marketing packages to mutual destinations. Now, the channel of distribution grows longer. After the hotel enters an agreement for distribution with an airline, a second channel member, the travel agent or tour operator, moves in. Each intermediary, while offering new customers, takes a commission.

Tourism Marketing Application

The state of Hawaii understands the value of promotions, as exemplified by their working relationship with Hollywood Studios. One example is their tie-in with the movie *50 First Dates*, which starred Drew Barrymore and Adam Sandler. The promotional campaign included a sweepstakes for a trip to the island. For those who did not win, the promotion also included information on products and hot spots featured in the movie, as well as a promotion entitled "50 Dates in the 50th State," which included a list of romantic ideas for couples vacationing on Oahu. "For the right projects, where there's a win–win, we try to partner so that we help to promote the project and help get viewership while doing destination marketing within that," says Walea Constantinau, film commissioner for the Honolulu Film Office and the island of Oahu. (www.hollywoodreporter.com/thr/film/feature_display.jsp?vnu_content_id=1000921405, accessed April 9, 2006)

Hotel and rental car companies are, out of necessity, integrating their offers with the airline reservation systems. By combining technology, these channel members present a unique opportunity to the customers (in this case, travel agents) to take advantage of "one-stop shopping." Through direct access to global distribution systems, agents can make flight arrangements, get a rental car, and book a sleeping room without ever using the telephone.

None of this channel participation is without cost. Without constant supervision and evaluation, channels of distribution can sometimes become cost prohibitive. For example, "super-saver" room rates could indeed bring in less than the cost of the channel of distribution. At $49, the commissions paid to the airline network, the travel agent, the contribution to the advertising, the contribution to the frequent traveler plan, and the franchise fee could actually bring the net revenue to below the cost of providing the service!

Selecting the Channel of Distribution

The selection of distribution channels is important. The length of the channel needs to be analyzed. In no uncertain terms, shorter is better; the longer the channel of distribution, the higher the cost and the more potential problems arise for the management of that channel.

By *short* or *long,* we refer to the number of intermediaries in the channel. Each intermediary has to make a profit, and each one involves some measure of coordination. Therefore, the fewer middlemen involved, the more profit and the less chance for errors. At some point, there may seem to be a need to add on channels. If the new intermediary can be reasonably expected to bring in more customers at a profit for the originator, the channel should probably be expanded. If the channel member cannot deliver the needed number of customers and the profit, the decision should be negative.

International Markets

As discussed in Chapter 18, Internet bookings are increasing in both Europe and Asia Pacific. An analysis of the Chinese market by Michael David Blanding, a student in the hotel school at Cornell University, reveals examples of challenges faced in the international arena. He writes that there are three primary challenges to online distribution in China.[13] The first and perhaps most prominent barrier to e-commerce in China is the cash-based nature of Chinese society and the fact that very few Chinese carry international credit cards. Instead, most carry a debit card from one of the many domestic Chinese banks. This situation presents a challenge because most hotel companies use a single payment platform for all of their many language websites. This payment platform normally requires that the customer enter an international credit card number to make the booking. Since very few Chinese have the necessary credit card, many bookings are abandoned before being finalized, and the customer calls the property to book directly.

To overcome this obstacle, the more forward-thinking hotel companies have created alternative payment options for their Chinese-language websites. In China, it seems that the more payment options a website has in place, the better the website performs. Some websites have the flexibility to accommodate up to eleven different payment styles. Some common payment solutions among successful Chinese e-businesses include:

- Payment by mobile phone (phone number is tied to bank account and money is transferred via text message)
- Cash pick-up (employees are dispatched to come to consumer's door within four hours of online purchase and make cash transaction)
- Domestic bank card
- Post office payment

The second obstacle is that, given the fact that e-commerce is still relatively young in China, very few Chinese have a track record of successful online transactions. As a result, little trust has been built up for the Internet as a distribution channel and many Chinese harbor concerns regarding the safety and security of personal information given out over the Internet. To ease this common concern, the more culturally sensitive hotel companies translate their website security statement into Chinese and emphasize their web security in Chinese advertising.

A final challenge for Chinese Internet users is the tendency to question the reliability of information provided online. Chinese are skeptical of room descriptions and hotel amenity lists found on hotel websites. To address this concern, many major players in the Chinese hospitality industry are enriching the content of their websites by including more virtual tours, floor plans, and photographs of the properties.

Although the hospitality industry is based heavily on standardization, success in the Chinese Internet market is contingent upon a hotel company's willingness to break the traditional mold of its cookie-cutter e-commerce platform and cater to the unique needs and concerns of the Chinese consumer.

Channel Management

In a typical conventional distribution system, the retailer carries many brands, including those of competing companies. Control and management of the channel therefore lies in the strength of the product being sold. If an item is in very high demand, the producer of this product may be able to set the terms of the system and may manipulate the retailer into carrying and merchandising other, weaker products as well. When the product is weak, the retailers will dictate the terms of the system to reach the customer.

The same principles of control and channel management apply to the hospitality industry, except that the producer of the product is also the retailer. Thus, if the product is strong, the retailer (the property) has control over the wholesaler (for example, a tour operator). If the product is weak, the wholesaler assumes the control. An example is when one of the authors of this text started selling his hotel to motorcoach tour operators. At the beginning, he had very little power over such operators, and they usually set the terms and conditions (e.g., the price and the dates when the tour would arrive.) Once the end customer became aware of this author's property and began to contact the hotel directly for tours, the power shifted. Suddenly, motorcoach operators were asking when they could come and were paying the price suggested by the hotel.[14]

The study of channel management is an academic discipline in itself, and multiple books have been written on the topic. In this section we present some rules of thumb.

Relationships among Channels

Good channel management stems from the formulation of a good working relationship among channels from the start. All agreements pertaining to the workings of the channel should be in writing and should be updated as market conditions change. There is rarely an all-win situation. If a channel member is not deriving some reasonable value from the network, that member will not participate actively and distribution will eventually become more difficult and more costly.

For example, a hotel could develop a good working relationship with a representative firm for marketing the property. The representative firm then markets the hotel through sales calls, brochures, direct mail, and so on. A booking results and a commission becomes due. If the hotel begins to dispute the validity of the origin of the bookings or delays the payment, the relationship with the channel of distribution becomes ineffective. The representative firm will not be anxious to market the facility in the future and will spend its time selling more cooperative hotels. This becomes a no-win situation. The hotel is dissatisfied with the productivity of the channel member, and the representative firm will move on to more lucrative endeavors.

Each channel member seeks to create customers for a profit, but without some give and take on a regular basis by all channel members, the system becomes tedious and disruptive. The hospitality firms that have carefully selected their partners and are managing them well will be consis-

tently increasing their customer base while others are looking for new channel members.

> ### Tourism Marketing Application
>
> A four-year project undertaken in New Zealand attempts to better understand tourism destination distribution by investigating (1) the factors that influence the behavior and motivation of different channel members, (2) how the success of the channel is influenced by the type of relationships within the channel, and (3) how channels differ by type of market segment. This project is called "Innovation in New Zealand Tourism through Improved Distribution Channels." (*Source:* Douglas G. Pearce and Christian Schott (2005). Tourism distribution channels: The visitors' perspective, *Journal of Travel Research*, Vol. 44, August 2005, pp 50-63)

Evaluation of the Channel

Evaluation is critical for the continued success of any program. If a hospitality entity is unable to tell how many bookings a representation firm produced or how many coupons were turned in from the dining guide, then intelligent channel management is impossible. Often, channel members can report the statistics. If unit management is unable at least to spot-check these numbers, the channel member will be in control when it comes time to negotiate the next agreement.

For example, the hotel that engages in a channel agreement with an airline sets an objective. The objective needs to be set in a quantitative format to be useful in the evaluation process. The success of the channel of distribution might be defined as raising the productivity of the airline reservation service from 100 rooms per month to 120 per month.

It is also beneficial to understand the break-even point of the channel. In the preceding example, it might take an additional 10 rooms per month to cover the additional commissions and some combined advertising costs. After a predetermined amount of time, the channel is evaluated. If it is producing less than 110 rooms per month, careful consideration might be given to either increasing the marketing support for the program or dropping the channel member completely.

Evaluation is more than just a tally of dinner covers or room nights. A channel may be driving the volume, but if the customer is unhappy, the effort is not only short-sighted but also dangerous.

A dining guide can market a two-for-one dinner promotion in a number of ways. If customers expect two lobsters for the price of one when making reservations and find out the promotion applies only to chicken, they will be sincerely disappointed. If the hotel guest was expecting deluxe accommodations and the agreement with the channel member was to offer a run-of-the-house room, the guests who get the inferior rooms will not be happy with their purchase. They may not be unhappy enough to complain but, even worse, they may be unhappy enough not to come back.

The marketing-driven company with good channel management skills will ensure customer satisfaction throughout the process. If a channel member is producing customers that are consistently unhappy, it would be better never to have used that distribution method in the first place.

During channel management, two ongoing factors are needed to ensure continued success: motivation and recruitment. For motivation, it must be recognized that most channel members are carrying many similar products into the marketplace. Travel agents have a variety of hotels and airfares from which to choose. The representative firms have several hotels in their portfolio that match the needs of their customers. The number of promotional tie-ins available to both the customers and the channel members are mind-boggling. Franchising options for the developers and independent managers are plentiful.

Web Browsing Exercise

Use your favorite search engine and type in the words "channel management." Investigate two or three of the suggested sites. What do you find? If a site offers a white paper, which is a paper that presents a particular point of view or opinion and is different from an academic paper in that it is not peer reviewed, download and read. What new things did you learn?

Motivation

Some type of motivation must be continuously offered by the channel leader in order to promote continued success. Unless the product offered is so desirable that several channel members are bidding on the rights to carry it, motivational techniques are necessary.

The push strategies mentioned earlier are the primary source of motivational support for channel members. Incentive trips for outstanding travel agents or the best franchisee in the system will go a long way toward smoothing operating channels of distribution. Many companies in the customer goods and industrial products industries have full-time staff members who do nothing but organize and implement channel incentives to keep members interested in their products.

Incentives need not be in the form of travel. Customer goods such as appliances and televisions can make the bonus system easier to attain and provide short-term gratification for participants. The drawback of the magnificent incentive trip to Europe may be that it takes a year to

win and only a very few employees will ever have a chance to collect the prize.

Although the motivational options available are almost unlimited, an area that also needs attention is that of top management. All of the sales representatives can win trips and toasters, but the president of the company is often ignored. Travel agency owners do not need toasters and trips; what they need is the personal attention that allows their views to surface to someone important. An invitation to dinner by a senior executive of the hospitality company may buy more loyalty than 1,000 toasters. Too often, in the rush to motivate a channel member, the owner of the business is left out of the process.

Recruitment

The second ongoing task for the channel manager is to recruit new channel members. If this task is not organized and planned, the channel is in perpetual danger. Unfortunately, the danger is subtle because a company may not realize that it is exposed until a member drops out. For example, a travel agency may be one of your best producers in the Florida market. It sends an unusually high number of guests to your hotel because it has done a good job marketing your facility and has built up a good clientele.

One day, the travel agent calls and says it is dropping your facility in favor of your competition down the street. Immediately, the reservations slip and business starts falling. This scenario is very realistic for a number of managers. First, the competitor had a good recruitment program in place and replaced its channel member with yours, thereby improving its distribution network overnight. Second, without having had a good recruitment program, your hotel now has to begin the process of finding a strong replacement channel member. As you are now in dire need, the negotiations will swing in favor of the new channel member.

There will always be times that a channel member leaves or needs to be replaced. This is part of doing business. However, a good channel manager will have alternatives ready and prescreened according to the criteria mentioned earlier in the chapter.

Recruitment is also necessary to provide alternatives to channel members who are not performing satisfactorily. It is far easier to deal with an unsatisfactory situation once you have other options than to have to recruit channel members when you are at a disadvantage.

 Summary

Consortia, affiliations, reservation networks, and representation firms bring the customer to the product, especially in faraway places. Incentive houses, travel agents, and tour operators are intermediaries who distribute hospitality services to customers and also bring them to the product. And the Internet is rapidly changing the way all bring hospitality products and services to market.

The backbone of any channel of distribution is channel management. Any marketing-driven organization will take the time to evaluate its current distribution system and organize a cohesive plan for improvement. A competent channel manager should then be assigned to monitor and consistently reevaluate the network to obtain the maximum benefits for the company. This channel manager may take the form of the director of sales, the general manager, or the resident manager at the unit level of the hotel. The corporate marketing office should assume responsibility for the chainwide agreements. Finally, the satisfaction of the customer is the true test of a channel's success. Without this, none of the steps outlined are productive or needed.

For hotels, at least, channel management is a far more productive and critical part of the marketing mix today than it was prior to the Internet.

■ Key Terms

consortium	intermediary
global distribution system (GDS)	distribution service provider (DSP)
incentive house	corporate or managed business traveler
ad hoc groups	
series groups	onward distribution

■ Discussion Questions

1. Explain in your own words each of the following: consortia, incentive houses, GDS, tour operators, CRS, wholesalers, and discount brokers.
2. Given what you have learned about pricing (Chapter 13), loyalty (Chapter 4), and sales (Chapter 15), how would you go about setting up a training program for CRS employees to maximize hotel revenue?
3. What is the difference between a "name your price" model and a "posted price" model? Why would a hotel company want to use one versus another? Why would a consumer?
4. Describe the difference between a push and pull strategy. When might it be best to use one instead of the other?
5. What are the key issues in channel management?

■ Group Projects

1. Pick a specific hotel and a specific date. Use all the various channels available to book a room at that hotel on that night. Does the price change by channel? What other information did you find out?
2. Prepare a report that provides an overview of the different channels available to a hotel. Discuss the strengths and weaknesses of each channel and when you might use one channel over another.

■ References

1. *Merriam-Webster's collegiate dictionary* (11th ed.). (2003). Springfield, MA: Merriam-Webster, Inc.
2. Retrieved November 30, 2005, from www.rennekamp.com/provident.html.
3. Yesawich, Pepperdine, Brown & Russell/Yankelovich Partners (2003). *National Leisure Travel MONITOR*.
4. Keung, P., & Moffett, E. (2003, November 19). Recap of PhoCusWright travel industry conference. CIBC World Markets: Equity Research.
5. Cohen, R. (2003, October). Travel agents still rely on GDS for hotel selection. *Hotel Online.* Retrieved September 5, 2005, from www.hotel-online.com/News/PR2003_4th/Oct03_GDSTerminals.html on.
6. Morrison, A.M., Bruen S.M., and Anderson, D.J. (1998). Convention and visitor bureaus in the USA: A profile of bureaus, bureau executives, and budgets. *Journal of Travel and Tourism Marketing,* Vol 7, No. 1, 1-19.
7. Minor, J., Angel, S. M., & Hart, R. (2003, May 14). *The internet dilemma: Third-party sites complicate a promising distribution.* New York: Lehman Brothers Inc., Global Equity Research, United States, 6.
8. Rascoff, S. (2003, July). Personal communication.
9. Ibid.
10. http://corp.kayak.com/about.html
11. PhoCusWrite's Online Travel Overview, Fifth Edition. Used by permission.
12. Passkey research 2006
13. Correspondence with Stowe Shoemaker August 2006. Used by permission.
14. Shoemaker, S. (1984). Marketing to older travelers. *Cornell Hotel and Restaurant Administration Quarterly, 25* (2), 84–91.

Interactive Marketing

Internet and Database Marketing

Overview

In the early years of hospitality marketing, to make a hotel reservation the customer contacted the hotel, airline, or car rental company directly by either telephone or telex.* Other travelers simply walked into a hotel and asked for a room for the night—hence the term *walk-in reservation*. The customer relationship was directly with the hospitality entity. Similarly, when hospitality marketing representatives needed to talk with a customer, it was usually through the telephone, a fax machine, or direct

---

* A teleprinter (teletypewriter, teletype, or TTY) is a largely obsolete electromechanical typewriter that can be used to communicate typed messages from point to point through a simple electrical communications channel, often just a pair of wires. Teletypewriters are still in use by the deaf for typed communications over the telephone, usually called a *TDD* or *TTY*.

Continued on page 538

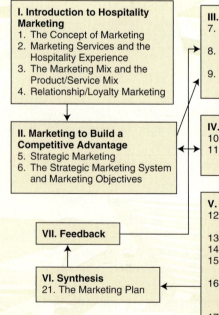

I. Introduction to Hospitality Marketing
1. The Concept of Marketing
2. Marketing Services and the Hospitality Experience
3. The Marketing Mix and the Product/Service Mix
4. Relationship/Loyalty Marketing

II. Marketing to Build a Competitive Advantage
5. Strategic Marketing
6. The Strategic Marketing System and Marketing Objectives

VII. Feedback

VI. Synthesis
21. The Marketing Plan

III. The Marketplace
7. Understanding Individual Customers
8. Understanding Organizational Customers
9. The Tourist Customer and the Tourism Destination

IV. Situational Analysis
10. Understanding Competition
11. Marketing Intelligence and Research

V. Functional Strategies
12. Differentiation, Segmentation, and Target Marketing
13. Branding and Market Positioning
14. The Hospitality Pricing Mix
15. The Communications Mix: Advertising
16. The Communications Mix: Sales Promotions, Merchandising, Public Relations, and Publicity
17. The Communications Mix: Personal Selling
18. Hospitality Distribution Systems
19. Channels of Distribution: Bringing the Customer to the Product
20. *Interactive Marketing: Internet and Database Marketing*

John Springer-Miller launched Springer-Miller Systems out of a 150-year–old farmhouse in Stowe, Vermont. He was awarded various projects in the first few years, including a student management system that became the standard for public schools in Vermont, a complaint management solution for Ben & Jerry's Ice Cream, and a guest history system for the Golden Eagle Resort right in Stowe. The guest history system, [SMS]Host, soon evolved into a complete system for hotels and resorts, and the market quickly embraced the world's only "guest-centric" hospitality management solution. It has been the exclusive focus of SMS since 1989, and frequent enhancements have made it the most powerful system available to the industry.

Marketing in Action

John Springer-Miller, President and CEO, PAR Springer-Miller Systems

Please explain a little bit about yourself and give some background on your company.

I started this company in 1983 and did quite a bit of custom database work in the early days. One of my favorite projects was something we did for Ben & Jerry's Ice Cream, which in the early '80s was in their great growth phase and built their factory about eight miles away from our offices. We did a complaint management system for them that helped keep track of production information, customer complaint information, shipping information, employee information and production, and things like that. It was pretty neat to be able to match things up and, when a customer complained about a carton of ice cream, be able to figure out through the database who actually had anything to do with that carton of ice cream along the way—which trucking company, which store, which fruit feeder operator was putting the cherries into the Cherry Garcia at the time, and so on. It was interesting, and that was one of the bigger projects that we worked on in the early days.

In 1985 and 1986, we had a couple of customers and a couple of neighbors here in Stowe, Vermont, which is a resort community. It's a big ski resort town, and a couple of hotels in this area were looking for systems to help them remember their guests. Nobody on the market was doing anything about that. In those days, all of the hotel systems that existed threw out the information—pretty much the day after checkout. They knew how to make a reservation, check somebody in, and post a folio, but then the day after the guest checked out, all of the information got deleted and nobody had any way to remember their customers. So, we built a guest history system that was designed around the idea of, at first, sucking information out of other property management systems and providing a customer profile. That goes back to 1985.

Then we quickly realized that the best way to build a profile would be to book the reservation. We just started adding more and more transaction types to the system in the first year or so that we were doing this as a means of thinking this is how we're going to build a better history system. The whole idea just kind of snowballed. We now have something like 30 modules that pretty much tackle every aspect of managing a complex hospitality environment, from fine dining point of sale to spa and golf management, transportation, and luggage.

Everything that involves customer contact is what we've been focused on. We took the product national in

Overview *(continued)*

mail pieces. Although these methods of making a reservation and communicating with the customer still exist today, the way both of these activities occur is changing rapidly. We discussed many of the ways the hospitality firms get their product to customers in Chapters 17 and 18.

Those chapters focused mainly on the architecture and channels needed to reach the consumer—for example, the Internet, GDS system, and the like. In contrast, this chapter focuses on how hospitality entities can best use these channels to communicate effectively with customers.

Marketing in Action *(continued)*
John Springer-Miller, President and CEO, PAR Springer-Miller Systems

1989 and have just continued along with the same concepts ever since. We've just always been focused, almost with single-minded blinders, on the idea that if we can put customer information at every point of guest contact, then the guest service levels will improve and the customer information will grow as a result of that contact. And that continuous cycle has been our model forever. We did it for individual properties and we built out every aspect of a property that we could get to, in terms of dealing with the different points of customer contact. Then we started on a multiproperty model in 1990 and built that up and have done a lot with that.

We developed the Central Reservations Enterprise model back in the mid-nineties to do large and diverse and widely geographically distributed properties. I think the first Enterprise system we installed was in 1995 for a customer that has ski resorts and beach resorts that are spread out all over Hawaii and the western United States. We developed the system by which they could have all their customer information in one place and still, regardless of where they were on a property, access that information.

But for us, it's always been a matter of how we can leverage customer information into the guest experience and therefore, both at the system level and at the human level, have ways to get the right information to the right place at the right time so that some form of service can improve. And, we keep doing it! We're now doing a chain of hotels that we're doing some pretty neat new in-room technology for, with the same concept of in-room services being another place where you have guest contact with customers. For instance, on the telephone, you can push a button and up pops a list on your LCD telephone screen of all the members of your group and you can touch one and speed-dial their room. It's just a matter of all of the

things that interact with a guest from a technology perspective, understanding the guest, and intuitively using guest information as part of the natural work flow for those processes.

Some of the things you've just mentioned, such as with all your groups being able to speed-dial the group members without having to call down to the front desk and ask to be connected, are very interesting. Can you give us some more examples of companies that you have worked with that have done some really neat things with your software and have added some value to the guest's stay?

There are a lot of examples. When you say value, I think from our perspective, we first interpret that as value from a service perspective, from a recognition and benefit perspective. In 1992 we were contracted by Hilton Hotels to do all of their properties in North America, and we developed the first significant two-way central reservations interface so that, in real time, information was flowing back and forth between the mainframe in Dallas and all of the properties. We have done about 240 Hiltons that eventually had the software installed. Part of that development process for Hilton was to develop all of the Hilton HHonors functionality within our application. That kind of point-based loyalty program is one type of customer benefit that big hotel chains continue to rely on. We do a lot of work with that. However, for example, we've done work with smaller hotel chains where they don't have the kind of central fulfillment issues that a company like Hilton or, say, Hyatt has. So we have set up systems by which a group of hotels can provide points to their users, to the customers, but have the fulfillment be a real-time process regardless of where they go on the property.

There's one scenario: Our rate management system, for instance, does points-based rates as well as currency rates. By the way, there's another little side trip to all of this, which is that anything that we do that is designed to provide better customer service and guest recognition is also a revenue tool in our perspective. Every aspect of that becomes a revenue driver. So, in this points system, which at first glance seems like a loyalty program—you know, you come and stay and you get some points—but it is also designed as a service-level driver. A customer has enough points to get a standard room for a couple of nights and they call to book a reservation. During that reservation process, the system prompts the reservation agent to the fact that that customer has a certain value on hand and that they can do certain things with it. It may be that they can get a standard room for a couple of nights, or maybe they want a different kind of room—maybe we're going to try to get them to play golf with their points or something like that. But then we also will prompt the operator that says they can get a standard room, but if they want, they can upgrade to a deluxe room or a suite and use their points plus $50 a night. So, we in effect use the points as a revenue driver instead of just as a loyalty program. In many cases, the system might pull up the suites and say that we know you're going to book a suite because we know who you are and we know what you want. It just leverages the customer information all along the way.

Another kind of interesting example of that is the use of gift certificates, which is very widespread within our customer base. This is one of my favorite little approaches to using a revenue driver based on customer service. Most properties—spas, resorts, golf resorts, beach resorts, ski resorts, and many different types of hotels—have gift certificates of various kinds, either for promotional purposes or because it's a good kind of business. You get people to lend you money interest free for long periods of time. I think the national statistics within our customer base is that something like 82 percent of the gift certificates actually get redeemed. So in those cases, they're actually just giving you money, which is in many ways also interesting. But one of the reasons our customers have such a high rate of return on gift certificates is because they use those as drivers instead of just having it be a passive instrument. They will tell our system, for instance, to generate a personal piece of correspondence or a personalized e-mail to all of the guests that have a gift certificate that is $100 or less or such-and-such a value that is going to expire within the next 90 days.

They'll issue out a piece of correspondence reminding the customer that they have value that will be lost if they don't do something with it. From a customer perspective, that's a really interesting service. Because now you have a hotel calling you and saying, "Hey, you've got $100 and if you don't use it, you're going to lose it! You don't want that to happen, do you?" And that feels like really good service, but at the same time, the customer is booking a $500 or $1,000 stay as a result of that. It's just a really good lever and a really good driver. That kind of thing happens a lot with our products.

Are your products available around the world or mostly in North America now?

Around the world. We have offices in Europe and Asia, as well as four locations in the United States and in Canada. At this point, we do quite a bit of business in Southeast Asia, an increasing amount of business in Europe, and a fairly significant business in the Middle East. We have a couple of significant accounts that we're doing in Saudi Arabia right now. We are pretty much all over. The kinds of customers that we are seeing more of are international chains. We have not been a company that has gone after chain business. We've always been a company that has focused on a certain type of customer, and the driver for us is we want to find customers that are really focused on customer service and guest recognition because that's what we're all about. But that can be a resort or it can be the New York Palace. It can be the Mandarin Oriental in Miami or it can be the Bellagio in Las Vegas. They are all different kinds of customers, but they all have something in common. They are trying to focus on better guest service.

One of the things that is interesting in the industry right now is that we're finding that having larger chains like Hilton as customers was an aberration for us back in the 1990s. It wasn't a customer that we were trying to go after. They showed up on our doorstep and said, "We want to use your system," and so we worked for them. Now, however, we're finding that chains—whether it's Hilton or Hyatt or a lot of the larger hospitality companies—are trying to find ways to leverage the technology to deliver better service. Most of them at least come to us and explore what it is that we're doing and how we're doing it and how they might be able to use it. We're seeing a lot more of that kind of activity. We're doing a lot more international chains.

Used by permission from John Springer-Miller

The First Generation of Electronic Marketing (E-Marketing)

"What comes around goes around" is a popular saying and one that applies to the hospitality industry. The original idea of hospitality was a one-on-one relationship with the customer, from the beginning of the reservations process to the end of the stay. In the very old days, this was handled by the general manager, who prided himself—and yes, it usually was he—in knowing all the guests and their preferences. Guests usually called the general manager directly. This process was circumvented with the rise of the travel agent and the advent of the GDS, as guests started booking with their travel agent who communicated electronically with the hotel, usually only sending the guest's name and his or her preferences. The relationship was with the travel agent, not the guest. Now, the individual relationship with the guest is starting to return with the advent of loyalty programs, as discussed in Chapter 4. Another reason for this return of the individual relationship is the popularity of the Internet. The Internet has given hospitality entities an opportunity to communicate directly with the customer again. However, many hotels are still reliant on travel agency bookings for filling rooms. The influence of travel agents has waned considerably, however, as more consumers discover and use the Internet to book reservations directly with travel suppliers.

In fact, according to U.S. government statistics, the employment of travel agents is expected to decline through 2012. One of the rationales given for this is that, because airlines no longer pay commissions to travel agencies in the United States, this has reduced revenues and caused some agencies to go out of business.[1] This does not mean that travel agents will disappear or that they are sitting by doing nothing. The American Society of Travel Agents (ASTA) is working hard to get out a strong "We're not dead yet" message. It's motto "Without a Travel Agent, You're On Your Own" appeals to travelers who want to know that someone will act as their advocate if something goes wrong.[2]

We provide a brief history of the GDS in Exhibit 20-1.

The Role of the Internet in Transforming Marketing

The year 1996 is widely considered the year in which the Internet became a consumer medium in America. Only 11 percent of U.S. households had access to the Internet then, and today the penetration rate is approaching 80 percent (almost half of which now have high-speed access). And several countries are more "wired" than the United States, including South Korea, the Scandinavian countries, and Canada. The second channel of distribution in the e-commerce arena is the Internet. (Recall that the first one was the GDS.) This medium is designed to reach the consumer directly, without the need for intermediaries. Although this is still an evolving medium, the influence of the Internet on the hospitality industry is growing in significance.

The Internet began simply as a way to distribute information. The second generation of Internet marketing ushered in the new applications for marketing and direct selling. Simple transactions, such as buying a book or CD, were the foundation of Internet commerce. As technology improved, the size and complexity of transactions increased. Cars, cruises, and expensive jewelry all began to trade regularly on the Internet. And auctions became the rage (witness the rapid growth of eBay.) Every major brand, regardless of its goods or services offering, has an Internet strategy in the emerging environment of electronic distribution.

According to *The Economist,* citing Nielsen//NetRatings—a firm that analyzes Internet usage—54 percent of American consumers start with an online travel agent, such as Expedia.com, Travelocity.com, or Orbitz.com.[3]

Early in the developing stages of the Internet, opportunistic companies such as Expedia, Travelocity, Hotels.com (these are called third party sites or online travel agencies) and many others stepped into the distribution process to become Internet travel agents and wholesalers. Technology at the time made the booking process somewhat cumbersome. Many hotels had e-mail requests for reservations on their websites. The e-mail went to the reservation office, and the agent checked availability, responded with a rate, and awaited the customer's reaction again via e-mail for the booking. The confirmation was then sent to the consumer. Given this time-consuming process, combined with the fact that consumers were hesitant to send their credit card information over the **unsecured Internet,** many consumers continued to use the old-fashioned method of booking, especially because there was no real price difference. With the economy strong, hotels had no incentive to discount rooms.

The tragedy of September 11, 2001, in the United States accelerated the impact of the Internet on the distribution of travel services. Hotels suddenly had hundreds of vacant rooms to fill because travelers were wary of traveling. To sell these rooms, hoteliers turned to the third party websites on the Internet who advertised discounted hotel rooms. Consumers, fearful of the economy, cut back on expenses and became even more focused on finding the best deal. Those deals were now available on the Internet.

EXHIBIT 20-1	A Brief History of the GDS

In the 1970s the airline industry created a computer platform to distribute all inventory and manage reservations, later called the Global Distribution System (GDS), which was comprised of similar computer programs making reservations for airline seats. This was the first generation of electronic marketing (e-marketing) in the travel industry. American Airlines owned a GDS by the name of Sabre Systems to make reservations on its flights, as well as on other airlines. All of the other carriers had similar systems that were also developed during this time. Travel agents were then recruited to use these systems to make reservations on airlines for their customers. The GDS platform was eventually reconfigured to accommodate hotel rooms and rental cars as well.

The distribution strategy by the airlines was brilliant. Travel agents worked on commission—10 percent of the value of the booking at the time. The airlines thus created thousands of sales agents without the overhead costs of payroll, rent, equipment, and so on. The travel agent made good money as well, as 10 percent of a $3,000 airline ticket was a generous reward for a few minutes' work on the telephone.

The GDS fundamentally changed the relationship most hospitality entities had with their customers. Travel agents used the GDS to make reservations for hotels and car rentals as well as airline seats. Hotels began to make sales calls and develop marketing programs to attract the intermediaries (e.g., the travel agents) instead of the end customer. The idea was to make travel agents loyal to the hotel, thereby ensuring bookings from the customer. All of the major hotel companies encouraged customers to "consult with your local travel professional" to reaffirm their support for travel agents and continue to support this relatively inexpensive distribution system.

Today, the GDS consists of five companies all working from a similar technology platform: Sabre, Galileo, Worldspan, Amadeus, and Abbacus. Sabre and Galileo are used primarily in the Americas distribution, Amadeus and Abbacas in Europe, and Worldspan for the balance of the globe. Figure 1 shows how the GDS appears to the travel agent looking for rooms in Lima, Peru. Notice that, in this example, three hotels appear, each offering a different rate. Rates here are presented lowest to highest.

Each travel agent has a computer at her desk connected to one or more of the four GDS platforms, offering inventory of airline seats, rooms, or cars. Agents choose a hospitality entity, and the reservation is electronically submitted to the hotel, airline, or car rental company. Airlines and car rental companies have their own proprietary software to interface with the GDS. Hotels have a variety of options. Brands such as Marriott and Accor provide their proprietary software to the hotels they manage and franchise. Independent hotels until recently had to choose a representation firm to provide connectivity to the GDS. Leading Hotels of the World, Utell, and others mentioned earlier in this text served this function. Technology breakthroughs in 2002 enabled hotels to connect directly to the GDS, and representation firms began to assume the same status as travel agents. Basically, rep firms are intermediaries who, to some extent, have been circumvented by technology.

The GDS platform began to peak in early 2002 and continues to decline as the new e-marketing platform, the Internet, is coming into its maturity.

FIGURE 1 What the travel agent sees on the GDS when looking for a hotel in Lima, Peru.

Many reservations were made by these third party sites, which had improved the booking process to make the reservation process less cumbersome and more consumer friendly.

The business model underlying the initial third party sites was modeled after the traditional travel agent commission structure—each company garnered a 10 percent commission for delivering a booking to a hotel. After

the September 11, 2001, incident, hotels rushed to these sites to find customers for their empty hotels. A new financial model, called the merchant model, then evolved whereby the third party site negotiated net rates from the hotels, then marked up the price to what the market would bear. For example, a hotel may have offered a $60 net rate to Hotels.com, who then in turn sold the same room online for $100—a 40 percent markup. There was no risk for the online sellers from the merchant model sites; they had the flexibility of selling the room for any rate above $60 and could still make money. If the market for the room fell below $60, the online seller would simply go back to the hotel and ask for a lower rate. To compete with these third party sites and begin to gain control of their inventory, hotel brands such as Marriott, Hilton, and Starwood began to build their own sites to attract customers and became direct competitors of the third party marketers on the Internet. InterContinental Hotels became the first brand to remove its inventory from the third party sites in an effort to standardize rates across all channels of distribution and regain control of its customers.

With the arrival of 2004, we began to observe a fundamental shift back to the original customer relationship with hotels, one on one. Clearly the days of customers calling hotels to make reservations had past, but consumers began to recognize that they could get more information, competitive room rates, and good service by going directly to the hotel/airline/car rental websites. Although there was an emerging theory that consumers who booked online were more likely to be the recipients of inferior service upon arrival, fully 84 percent of travelers agreed with the following statement: "People who book reservations through a third-party intermediary are treated the same as those who book reservations either directly with the hotel or resort through the hotel or resort's dedicated Web site."[4] E-mail addresses were then captured and hospitality entities were again communicating directly with the consumer, albeit by electronic sources.

The Internet has enabled the individual hotels to begin to regain control of their customer relationships as well. Many nonchain hotels began to construct their own websites and thereby compete with the major chains.

Tourism Marketing Application

A 2005 study by the Travel Industry Association of America entitled *Travelers' Use of the Internet* found that 79 million Americans turned to the Internet for travel or destination information in 2005, a significant increase from 2004. Almost half of online travel planners use destination websites—such as those maintained by convention and visitor bureaus—to plan trips.

"Survey findings from the TIA report also indicate that 82 percent of travelers who plan their trips online now also book reservations online, with more than 64 million Americans purchasing or reserving an airline ticket, hotel room, rental car, or package tour online this past year—up from 70 percent in 2004.

According to Dr. Suzanne Cook, Senior Vice President of Research for the Travel Industry Association of America, "The USDM.net Destination Web Site Survey Report findings are in line with other research that shows Americans are turning to the Internet to plan and book their trips in greater numbers than ever before. Consumers appreciate the ease and convenience the Internet provides for online travel research, planning, and booking." (www.hospitality-1st.com/PressNews/USDMnet-033006.html, accessed April 9, 2006)

An Overview of Hospitality Website Design

Internet marketing begins with a website. The website for a hotel should be thought of as the new millennium version of an old standard in the hospitality business: the rack brochure. As such, it should be a reflection of the personality of the hotel. Proper visuals, text, and related information are critical to convey the hotel's image online.

Given that many hospitality companies are currently trying to drive business to their own brand websites to bypass expensive intermediaries, issues such as what should be included on a hospitality website and how these features should be presented have become increasingly important. However, designing and creating effective websites is not an easy task. Good design means integrating technical skills, such as a knowledge of HTML, CGI scripting, and Flash programming, with good artistic taste and graphic design skills. And this is, of course, before the issue of content is considered, where knowledge of online consumer behavior and an in-depth familiarity with the company in question are useful in knowing what to include to help sell the product. This section gives an overview of some of the most important issues that should be considered when designing a website for a hospitality company and highlights how many aspects of the design process need to be integrated to maximize the benefits that can be gained from a web presence.

When assessing what features to include on a hospitality website, it is clear that the needs of the customer must be foremost in the designer's mind. A potential customer's motivation for visiting a hospitality website is usually quite clear—to find out information about the product as part of his decision-making process and, assuming the website designer does a good job of convincing him that the product is a good match for his needs, to make a reservation. This means that meaningful but sales-orientated descriptions need to be combined with appropriate graphics to give the website visitor a true feeling for the atmosphere and experience at the unit in question, be it a hotel, restaurant, or other form of hospitality operation. Of course, what exactly is required will vary significantly depending on the market segment. For companies operating in the economy segment, quite basic graphical elements and limited, more factually focused text tend to be effective (see Exhibit 20-2). After all, who wants to look at 360-degree photos of a typical motel room? However as the product becomes more up-market or more complex (for example, luxury hotel, resorts, cruise ships, etc.), developers usually need to combine both increasingly detailed textual information with higher-quality graphical elements—perhaps even multimedia—to effectively have an effect on the consumer decision-making process.

EXHIBIT 20-2   The website for Motel 6 is a good example of an economy hotel.

Source: Retrieved November 30, 2005 from www.motel6.com. Used by permission of accorhotels.com.

An overused but valuable phrase when it comes to website design is that "content is king." However, most industry observers agree that many hospitality website designers fail to provide visitors with the information they need to make a purchase decision. Consider, for example, the number of hotels that neglect location information on their sites. Although most (but not all!) list the address, this is only a small part of their location, as proximity to attractions, activities, major businesses, and other points of interest, as well as access to information from airports or train stations, are an essential part of a property's location and play an important part in converting a potential customer.

Unfortunately, while some developers do not include enough content, others go to the opposite extreme. With the low marginal cost of adding data to a website, it's easy to overwhelm potential customers with a haze of irrelevant (to them) detail. For a website to be effective, it must provide visitors with quick and easy access to the information they require. For that reason, it is a good idea to stream your website toward the needs of different target consumer groups. Although this could be something as simple as having different parts of your website for leisure customers and corporate customers, some companies are going further and providing different sections—and sometimes even completely separate sites—for customer segments such as meeting planners, travel agents, tour operators, and wedding organizers, to name just a few (see Exhibit 20-3). Although at a basic level each type of customer needs similar information, each also has specific needs that are of no interest to the others, and frequently the format in which they need information presented is very different. Effectively servicing each segment means developing separate targeted solutions for each one, derived from the same source but all focused clearly on matching the information needs of the particular segment.

EXHIBIT 20-3   Temecula Creek Inn is an example of a company providing different website sections—and sometimes even completely separate sites—for various customer segments.

Source: JC Resorts. Used by permission.

Once the website visitor has been converted and wants to proceed to the next stage and make a booking, a good website must provide appropriate booking facilities. Online reservations offering last room availability and instant confirmation are now an essential component of effective hotel websites, while more and more restaurants are finding it beneficial to provide some sort of reservation facility on their sites, be it online or through a call-back system. In today's fast-paced world, convenience is key, and the reservation facility provided needs to be as intuitive and easy to use as possible. The benefits of providing the right facilities are clear—capturing the sale while the consumer is still on the site and reducing the risk of her defecting to competitors. Getting it wrong undoubtedly results in lost business.

While matching the information content and the facilities provided to the customer is essential, the aesthetics, or "look and feel," of the site are also important. In many cases, this will flow naturally from the corporate image and offline promotional material of the company in question. However, it is important to realize that the web is a different medium from paper, and elements such as animation and sound can be used quite effectively to reinforce the promotional message. As discussed earlier, more up-market companies typically need a richer look and feel, incorporating richer graphical and multimedia elements than their economy or midmarket competitors. However, care must be taken that multimedia are not just added gratuitously. The (now thankfully passé) trend of having Flash animations (known as splash screens) when you first entered a website is a typical example of hyperactive designers showing off their animation skills while at the same time often alienating the customer. The decision criteria as to what to include should be based on whether it either helps build the image of the company or aids in the selling process.

Closely related to aesthetics is the issue of website navigation. Through conditioning, web surfers have come to expect that sites conform to certain conventions with respect to navigation. Deviations from these conventions just tend to confuse the website visitor. For example, we have come to expect that navigation menus will be either down the left-hand side or across the top of the screen. Although other solutions may look nice and be more innovative, they also tend to frustrate visitors and drive them to alternative sites. Website navigation must follow industry norms to help users find the information or feature that they are seeking as quickly and easily as possible. Site maps and search facilities can also help with this and should be included where appropriate.

And lastly, all sites should be designed for two different audiences. One is the potential client of the company; the other is much more discerning—the search engine. Even if your company has, from a consumer perspective, a superbly designed and amazingly functional site, this is pointless unless people can find your site on the web. While your domain name (or, more probably, names) is undoubtedly important, in practice, a good site must also be listed prominently under appropriate search phrases on the major search engines. The most effective way to achieve this is known as organic search engine manipulation, which in effect means designing your pages to maximize their position in the search engine indexes. Some of the techniques include ensuring that each page concentrates on a single subject (yet another reason for streaming different sections of your site toward different customer segments as discussed previously), reinforcing this theme by including appropriate words and phrases throughout the page's headings and text, prompting the search engine using the page's hidden meta tags, and linking each page to other similarly themed pages. However, trying to manipulate search engines is a complex and ever-changing black art, so you should consider the use of a specialist company to help design (and subsequently redesign) your pages to be more search engine friendly.

It's often said that companies moving online go through different phases, or generations, of sites. Their initial first- or second-generation sites tend to take existing offline promotional material and move it online without taking advantage of the power of the new medium. For today's sophisticated web consumers, such "brochureware" sites do little to either enhance the image of the company or generate incremental sales. Providing customers with in-depth targeted information and appropriate facilities to make it as convenient as possible for them to do business with you is the key to success. Both Exhibits 20-4 and 20-5 provide excellent examples of this. Exhibit 20-4 is for the Country Club Lima Hotel, and Exhibit 20-5 is for Gayot.com, which is one of the leading hospitality information websites in the world.

Finally, the website has to be functional. A website may be visually pleasing, but if the customer finds it is hard to navigate, its effectiveness is greatly diminished. Following are four **best practices** for website design in the hospitality industry:

1. The reservation **mask** should be at the front of the page to enable customers to make their online reservations.
2. The e-mail acquisition section should be on the home page.
3. The site should have text conveying **best value** to the customer, to ensure that the customer stays on the

local site and does not shop for a better rate elsewhere on the Internet.

4. Security for the transaction needs to be conveyed to the customer. Consumers are still concerned about online commerce, particularly outside of the United States. Many consumers are wary of credit card theft on the Internet.

The websites in Exhibits 20-4 and 20-6 illustrate each of these best practices.

Tourism Marketing Application

A study by USDM.net (www.usdm.net/), an interactive marketing agency that focuses on the travel industry, found that, in 2005, 55 percent of consumers surveyed who visited 11 U.S. official tourism office destination websites subsequently visited the destinations and during their stay spent an estimated $9 billion collectively on lodging, dining, shopping, entertainment, and transportation. These findings demonstrate that websites are important for destinations as well as for hotels and restaurants. They also suggest the need

for hoteliers to make sure that their website is linked to the destination where they are located. (www.modernagent.com/x/modernagent/visitor/resources/editorial.cds?n=11006, accessed April 9, 2006).

EXHIBIT 20-5 Gayot.com's website, one of the leading hospitality information websites in the world.

Source: www.gayot.com. Used by permission of Goutmillav Inc., DBA Gayot.com.

EXHIBIT 20-4 Country Club Lima Hotel website illustrates 4 best practices for website design.

Source: Country Club Lima Hotel. Used by permission.

EXHIBIT 20-6 This Rancho San Bernardo Inn ad conveys best value to the customer.

Source: JC Resorts. Used by permission.

Web Browsing Exercise

Go to a hospitality website and judge the website based on the criteria listed. Find an example of a good website and a poor website. Be prepared to discuss what changes you might make to the websites and why.

Once the website is developed, the site needs to be marketed. The primary marketing vehicles for websites are the search engines. Google, Yahoo, and MSN are the most popular search engines as of this writing and collectively account for over 9 out of every 10 **keyword** searches initiated by Internet users. Hotels may be listed in the search engines two ways: organically or through paid placement.

Organic search refers to the **free listing** of a hotel or resort property on the Internet. Rankings in the various search engines (where they appear in order once the search results have been displayed) are the direct result of the information contained in the website. The concept is similar to the traditional Yellow Pages provided by the telephone companies for use by customers searching for a business by category of service.

Certain keywords—phrases that consumers use to search for sites online—are programmed onto the websites to allow the search engines to find them. For example, a customer looking for a luxury hotel in London may look on Google and find the results in Exhibit 20-7.

The first free listing in Exhibit 20-7 is www.land marklondon.co.uk/, a listing for an upscale hotel in London. A customer may choose to look at this site or any of the others appearing on the various pages of listings resulting from this search. Research has revealed that most customers using search engines rarely go past the third page, however; therefore, positioning on the first page is the desired outcome of any search.

Search engines charge for the listings on their sites. This pay per click model of listing hotels according to their appearance in the search results allowed hotel marketers to increase traffic to their sites. Each keyword or keyword grouping is auctioned, with the highest bidder getting the highest placement, the second highest bidder getting second placement, and so on. A customer looking for a luxury hotel in St. Louis would see the organic listings on the left side of the page and paid listings on both the right side of the page and at the top under "Sponsored Listings." Exhibit 20-8 shows how pay per click listings from Google work, and Exhibit 20-9 shows an actual pay per click listing.

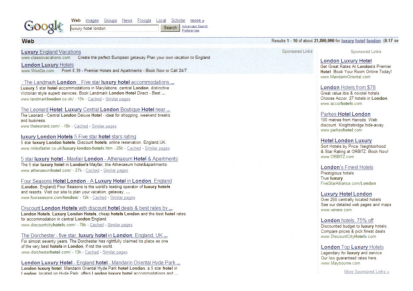

EXHIBIT 20-7 Organic search listings.

Retrieved November 30, 2005, from www.google.com/search?hl=en&q=luxury+hotel+london. Source: Google Inc. Used by permission.

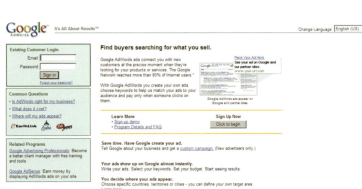

EXHIBIT 20-8 How pay per click listings work.

Retrieved November 30, 2005, from http://adwords.google.com/select/. Source: Google Inc. Used by permission.

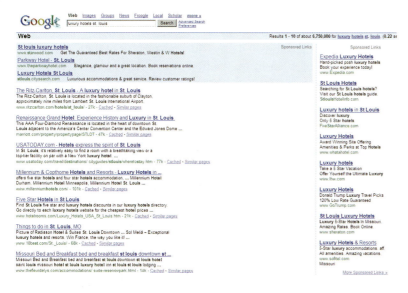

EXHIBIT 20-9 A pay per click listing.

Retrieved November 30, 2005, from www.google.com/ search?hl=en&q=luxury+hotels+st.+louis, Source: Google Inc. Used by permission.

The first listing for "Luxury Hotel St. Louis" is for the Ritz-Carlton. There are other opportunities to market the hotel online, with links to local attractions and destination-related sites. Consumers looking for sights to see in certain areas may click onto the accommodations pages of these types of sites.

> **Tourism Marketing Application**
> A website called Destination Webrings, run by travelnotes.org (www.travelnotes.org/Webrings/ destinations.htm), provides the consumer with a list of "some of the exceptional travel websites tucked away in a webring and not ranked highly on search engines." The website shows destination websites by country and things to do while there. For a destination that cannot afford a sponsored link on one of the major search engines, this may be a way to be noticed.
>
> WebRing is a firm that businesses can use to create webrings (dir.webring.com/rw). A webring is defined this way: "similar sites are grouped together in rings and each site is linked to another by a simple navigation bar. Rings form a concentration of sites, allowing visitors to quickly find what they are looking for. Each Ring is created and maintained by an individual website owner called the RingMaster. RingMasters determine the look and feel of the Ring, approve and manage member sites, and encourage other sites to join." (dir.webring. com/h/what.html, accessed April 9, 2006)

The Internet has also increased marketers' ability to track their efforts online. Each customer visit can be traced with a "cookie," or electronic impression of the visit. This

peter o'connor@adtech[1]	1 Ko	Document texte
peter o'connor@2o7[2]	3 Ko	Document texte
peter o'connor@serving-sys[2]	1 Ko	Document texte
peter o'connor@www.pcmag[2]	1 Ko	Document texte
peter o'connor@rd[1]	1 Ko	Document texte
peter o'connor@dilbert[1]	1 Ko	Document texte
peter o'connor@PW060808[1]	2 Ko	Document texte
peter o'connor@www.unison[1]	1 Ko	Document texte
peter o'connor@anad.tacoda[1]	1 Ko	Document texte
peter o'connor@my.yahoo[1]	1 Ko	Document texte
peter o'connor@247realmedia...	1 Ko	Document texte
peter o'connor@adforum[2]	1 Ko	Document texte
peter o'connor@orbitz[1]	1 Ko	Document texte
peter o'connor@ctix8.cheapti...	1 Ko	Document texte

EXHIBIT 20-10 Example of a cookie.

cookie can be followed throughout the site, showing the marketer the origin of the visitor to the site (Google, Yahoo, banner advertisement on the Theme Park Site, etc.) and what they did when they went into the site. Technology now exists to track the actual bookings from online marketing efforts; thus, a return on investment can be calculated for every online marketing campaign. A diagram of a cookie for one site is shown in Exhibit 20-10.

Managing Customer Information

The GDS offers limited information on individual guests aside from what the customer needs to make a reservation. All of this information is transferred into the hotels' property management system (PMS). Extraction of this data can be cumbersome, however. In contrast, the Internet allows the consolidation of many fields of customer data, but careful consideration must be given to the techniques used to acquire customer data on the Internet. Many countries, particularly in Europe, have stringent laws governing the acquisition and use of e-mail data. There are two sources of e-mail data: **spam** and consensual data. Spam consists of unwanted e-mail that is sent to lists of e-mail names acquired from a variety of third party sources. Many companies can provide thousands of e-mail names for marketing

purposes, yet consumers are becoming increasingly wary of unsolicited e-mails.

Exhibit 20-11 provides an analysis of the CAN-SPAM Act of 2003 in the United States. As one can see, the requirements stated in this law are clear; however, as discussed in Exhibit 20-11, there is debate as to its success.

Consensual data are gathered only with the customer's permission. This is also called **permission-based marketing**. Customers are given the option to provide their e-mail address in order to receive additional information or

---

| EXHIBIT 20-11 | **CAN-SPAM Act 2003** |

According to Grimes, the purpose of the CAN-SPAM Act is not to prohibit commercial e-mails, but to regulate the way companies can use e-mail as a legitimate marketing tool.[a] To do this, the act contains very specific provisions that govern how e-mail should be used to communicate with customers (or potential customers). It is worth noting that the legal requirements of several other regions, particularly South Korea, Japan, and the proposed legislation in Singapore are broadly similar to the U.S. requirements.[b] These requirements focus on the subject line, the "from" line, physical contact details, and opt-out facilities:

1. Subject lines must not be misleading and must include a clear indication that the e-mail is an advertisement (unless "prior affirmative consent" has been given by the recipient). In this way, recipients can know at a glance whether a particular e-mail is a marketing message and can delete the message without reading its content, thus saving time and minimizing inconvenience.
2. Messages must have a functioning and nonmisleading e-mail address in the "from" line of the header. This must serve as the reply-to address and must remain active for at least 30 days following the transmission of the message.
3. The body of the message must contain a valid physical postal address.
4. The message must include easy-to-locate, clear, and explicit instructions detailing how to opt out of future mailings. Such opt-out requests must be honored within 10 working days.

Although the act provides for both substantial criminal and civil penalties (damages of $250 per message sent in violation, up to an aggregated maximum of $2 million, as well as jail time for specific infractions), and a variety of companies have already been prosecuted, the overall effects of the act seem to have been minimal. A January 2004 survey carried out by TMCnet found that 99 percent of a sample of commercial e-mail failed to comply with the guidelines.[c] However, this is not surprising given that the act only came into effect on January 1 and thus companies would not have had adequate time to react. However, another study one year later examined the practices of 100 U.S.-based heavily trafficked websites. Once again the researchers found some degree of violation. For example, 30 percent of companies failed to include a valid postal address in their e-mail content, and a significant number of companies did not comply with the opt-out requirement. Even after unsubscribing, the researchers continued to receive e-mails from the surveyed sites or their partners in nearly 15 percent of cases.[d]

It is clear from the preceding discussion that companies' use (or misuse) of e-mail as a communications medium has become an important issue. Consumers have become concerned about how their personal data are being used for commercial purposes, and unless these concerns are addressed, users may refuse to provide the transactional data necessary for operations to online sites.[e] According to Hoffman, "almost 95% of web users have declined to provide personal information to web sites at one

time or another," and a recent survey by the Trans-Altantic Consumer Dialogue—an international consumer advocacy group—found that over half of respondents were shopping less online or not at all because of concerns that any personal data they submitted would result in more spam.[f]

Travel companies, particularly hotels, collect extensive personal data about their customers.[g] Even when the reservation function (in which all users have to provide personal identifying data to successfully complete a booking) was ignored, O'Connor found that over 90 percent of hotel chains collected personal identification information, including e-mail addresses, as part of their normal website operations. Furthermore, when a guest stays in a hotel property, such companies have the potential to collect further in-depth data about both expressed preferences and actual behavior, which if used for marketing purposes could potentially be a valuable resource. Although at present, organizational and technical issues generally prevent this from occurring, such barriers are gradually being overcome and such scenarios are likely in the future.[h] Given such access to extensive personal data, the question must be asked as to whether hotel companies behave ethically with their resources.

Source: O'Connor, P. (2006). An analysis of e-mail marketing practices of international hotel chains: Compliance with legislative requirements. *Proceedings of the ENTER Information and Communications Technology in Tourism Conference,* Lausanne, Switzerland. New York: Springer.

a. Grimes, G. (2004). Issues with SPAM. *Computer Fraud & Security, 5,* 12–16.

b. IDA Singapore. (2004, March). Proposed legislative framework for the control of e-mail spam (Joint IDA-AGC Consultation Paper), Infocomm Development Authority, Singapore.

c. TMCnet. (2004). MX Logic finds nearly 100 percent of SPAM not compliant with new CAN-SPAM law. Retrieved February 9, 2005, from www.tmcnet.com/usubmit/2004/Jan/1022594.htm.

d. Spring, T. (2005). Spam law test. *PC World,* January, pp. 20–22.

e. Cheng, T. (2004). Recent international attempts to an spam. *Computer Law & Security Report, 20* (6), 472–479.

f. Hoffman, D. Noval, T., & Peralta, M. (1999). Building consumer trust online. *Communications of the ACM, 42* (4), 80–85

g. O'Connor, P. (2003). Privacy and the online hotel customer: An analysis of the use of fair information practices by international hotel companies. *Proceedings of the ENTER Information and Communications Technology in Tourism Conference,* Helsinki, Finland; Frew, A., Hitz, M., O'Connor, P. (eds.), Springer Computer Science, New York, 382–392.

h. Piccoli, G., O'Connor, P., Capaccioli, C., & Alvarez, R. (2003, August). Customer relationship management—A driver for change in the structure of the U.S. lodging industry. *Cornell Hotel & Restaurant Administration Quarterly,* 61–73.

become eligible for a prize. The best method to acquire e-mail addresses of prospects is to tell them exactly what they will be receiving in return for their e-mail address. "Fill in the e-mail form and we will send you quarterly newsletters of interesting news about our hotel" would be a good way to assure customers they will not be blitzed with unwanted marketing messages every day from the hotel.

The hotel would then develop a newsletter to communicate directly with the customer. Exhibit 20-12 shows an e-mail solicitation from Basin Harbor Club. In terms of how often one should communicate with guests, the answer is: as often as the guest wants to hear from you. The success of permission-based marketing is based on the data collected in the database. We discuss databases in the next section. Exhibit 20-13 details how Greti Mennig communicates with her guests at the Restaurant Zum See. She shows that you can create a relationship the old-fashioned way.

Tourism Marketing Application

One website destination prints the following information on their website. This is an example of the presentation that all destinations should use to keep their customers informed about privacy issues.

Automatic Information

When you visit our Site, we may collect some information automatically, such as your Internet address, the identity of your Internet Service Provider, the Website from which you linked (if any), and the time and date of your visit. This information is not linked to personally identifiable information. This information is used to compile aggregate statistics about the total number of daily visitors to our Site, the pages most frequently visited and how long you stay at each page. By collecting this information we get a better understanding of your needs and what products and services we can develop to meet those needs. All the information we gather helps us understand your preferences so we can continually improve your online experience with us.

Internet Protocol Address

We may use your Internet Protocol address to help diagnose problems with our server and to administer the Site. Your Internet Protocol address is used to help identify you for the duration of a session and to gather broad demographic information. This information will not be sold to any third party.

Click Stream Data

As you browse the Internet, a trail of electronic information is left at each Web site you visit. This information, which is sometimes called "click stream" data, can be collected and stored by a Web site's server. Click stream data can tell us the type of computer and browsing software you use, the address of the Web site from which you linked to the Web Site, and in some instances, your e-mail address. We may use click stream data to determine how much time visitors spend on each page of the Site and how they navigate through the Site. We will only use this information to improve the Site. Any collection or use of click stream data will be anonymous and aggregate, and will not contain any personally identifiable information. (www.outdoorexpeditions.com/privacy.asp, accessed April 9, 2006)

Web Browsing Exercise

Go to www.landsend.com and investigate how this U.S.-based clothing retailer allows the guest to determine the frequency of communication. Now go to different hotel websites and see what type of communication options are presented.

The e-marketing solicitation in Exhibit 20-12 clearly states where the e-mail came from, in this case, Basin Harbor. Although it is not sham, the e-mail also offers the consumer the ability to **opt out** of the e-mail campaign. By simply clicking on the appropriate area on the e-mail, the receiver can remove himself from the list for the next marketing campaign.

Some e-databases require more customer information, such as a request for proposal (RFP) at a hotel. A simple e-mail address is not sufficient for the salesperson to respond to the needs of the customer. The company name, arrival/departure dates, meeting space requirements, and so on, all need to be filled out by the customer in order to receive a relevant quote from the hotel. All of these fields of data can then be stored and sorted for future campaigns. For example, a hotel may find that March is a slow month for group bookings. The electronic database of RFPs can be sorted by requested meeting dates (in this case, March), and an e-mail can be designed to offer special packages that entice meeting planners to host their functions during these dates.

Other sources of e-mail addresses come from the on-line reservation systems, also known as **booking engines**. Unlike the GDSs, the booking engines require the e-mail address of the consumer in order to deliver the confirmation. The hotel has access to this information on past customers and can sort the data by arrival dates for timely marketing messages. This ease of customer communication often tempts hotel marketers to mail lots of information

e-BREEZE

Blows Most Anytime!

BASIN HARBOR CLUB
On Lake Champlain Vermont

Issue 9 December 2005

Message from the Beach Family

Recipe Files:
Endive and Smoked Salmon Mousse

Gift Certificates: The Perfect Gift

Breezeway Specials

From the Wine Cellar

Our Friends at Dakin Farm

Season's Greetings from Basin Harbor

Like much of the East, we have gone from unusual early winter warmth to seasonal temperatures and even a bit of snow. Lake Champlain is at a record high for December, and the water is only eight inches from the bottom of the diving board. Even the North dock is barely above water. It will be very interesting to see what the water level will be come spring!

As we write this, Heidi Rumble-Bassett, Lodging Services Manager, is expecting the birth of her son at any minute, so she and her husband, Justin, will have a memorable Christmas for sure!

Bob and Pennie and their families celebrated Thanksgiving this year with Bob, Sr., in Naples, Florida, at the Naples Beach Hotel. If you're looking for a family-friendly spot to get away this winter, the Watkins Family would love to see you (www.naplesbeachhotel.com). It was wonderful to get away and get some sun but we were all glad to come home for the holidays.

As 2005 goes out, we give thanks for family, friends, and our many blessings. Best wishes for happy holidays and a joyous, healthy New Year to one and all.

Recipe File: Endive and Smoked Salmon Mousse

Winter "Registration"

The Royal Lees: Turreted Harbor Road

A classic for easy entertaining this holiday season. Makes about 2 1/2 dozen appetizers.

6 oz. Smoked Salmon
2 T Olive Oil
1 T Lemon Juice
2 T Chives, snipped
1/4 tsp. White Pepper
4 Belgian Endives
Horseradish
Cream Cheese, softened
Lemon Wedges, extra small

1. Mix coarse, chopped salmon with olive oil, lemon juice, snipped chives and pepper. Cover and refrigerate until flavors blend, about 1 hour.
2. Remove 6-8 outer leaves from each of the endives. Refrigerate.
3. When ready to serve, spoon a portion of the filling onto each endive leaf. Add a small dollop of cream cheese followed by a small amount of horseradish and garnish with a tiny lemon wedge.

Enjoy.

The Breezeway Shop

The doors are closed and the inventory is put away for the winter but we are always here to provide you with the perfect BHC gift. If it's not on the site, www.basinharbor.com/store.asp, then call us and we will tell you if we have it! We have some great Christmas specials for you. And don't forget, we will wrap it for you!

-Micro Chenille blankets at $49. Baby blankets at $36
-Tapestry Bags at $20

The Gift Everyone Loves to Get!

$10 dollars. $50 dollars. $200 dollars. Whatever the amount, your friends and family are sure to enjoy a gift certificate to Basin Harbor Club. They may be used in the Pro Shop, the dining rooms, the Breezeway Gift Shop, massages or for lodging. Or you can personalize them for specific activities or services like a Spa Pedicure or a 30 minute golf lesson. Call Brooke or Mary Lou in Reservations and have them send a little bit of BHC to someone. We will even include a lovely green gift box with ribbon and sticker. 800-622-4000 or email them at info@basinharbor.com

-Ribbon Tote Bags at $18

Back for a holiday showing, we have our 14kt Adirondack Chair Charm. $225

And as you can see our Kit and Bitty Baby love the new Adirondack Chair, perfect size! $50

Happy Shopping.

Tips from the Wine Cellar

Don't forget some bubbly for the holidays!

Marquis de la Tour, France - $10 approx
Graham Beck, South Africa -$15 approx
Gruet Winery Blanc de Noir, New Mexico - $18 approx

If you can find these wines, they are a great value and quality for your festive gatherings.

And if you are looking for that perfect company gift or that hard to find person who lives across the states, remember our friends at Dakin Farm.
We serve their great cob smoked bacon and their hams, ribs, cheeses, preserves, ummmm...lots of wonderful delicacies. They ship anywhere and their gift boxes are eagerly anticipated by all.
www.dakinfarm.com

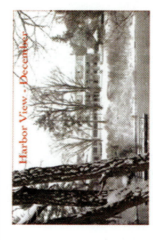

Harbor View - December

Forward this email to a friend.
Click here to be removed from our mailing list.

www.basinharbor.com 800.622.4000
4800 Basin Harbor Road, Vergennes, Vermont 05491

EXHIBIT 20-12 E-mail solicitation from Basin Harbor Club.

Source: Basin Harbor Club. Used by permission.

EXHIBIT 20-13	How Greti Mennig Maintains Her Customer Database

HOW DO YOU MAINTAIN A LONG-DISTANCE RELATIONSHIP WITH YOUR GUESTS?

In writing or via e-mail. But it is more that I am contacted by my clients and we do not send out newsletters.

HOW DO YOU KEEP TRACK OF YOUR GUESTS?

I remember them over the years. It is so nice having customers coming back every year. Many guests feel very close to me too; they tell me all kind of stories about the past year.

WHAT SORT OF COMMUNICATION DO YOU USE WITH YOUR GUESTS (E.G., E-MAILS, PRINTED BROCHURES, HANDWRITTEN NOTE)?

As we are a family-style restaurant, most of the time I do handwritten notes; then I even started to learn how to use e-mails and I write to my Japanese clients who send me pictures. It is nice to have the possibility to get in touch with them. Luckily, we do not have to spend money to have a database and send out large mailing lists. We do have the advantage that once the guests are in Zermatt, they would come back to Zum See year after year, as we are part of their holiday and we do complement their ski holiday with our hospitality.

HOW OFTEN DO YOU COMMUNICATE WITH YOUR GUESTS?

Usually once a year. I write many cards for Christmas because I have the time to write just before the winter season starts. These are our most loyal guests who come to Zum See for about 10 years. But our guests become friends of ours, and we really start having a relationship with them over the years.

HOW DO YOU DETERMINE WHICH GUESTS TO COMMUNICATE WITH?

Many of our guests do write to me for Christmas, telling me how their year was, that they are looking forward to coming to Zermatt again. I reply to these cards; then I send cards only to our long-term repeat customers. The good thing with Zum See is that all the guests are repeat customers.

ON AVERAGE, HOW LONG DO YOU KEEP COMMUNICATING WITH GUESTS? WHAT IS THE LONGEST RELATIONSHIP YOU HAVE HAD WITH ONE OR MORE OF YOUR GUESTS?

The longest is 22 years, with a lady that came on the first day we opened. They now come with their children and grandchildren. It is lovely that we do have such loyal guests; for most of them Zum See is part of their holiday in Zermatt.

Source: Used by permission of Greti Mennig.

---

under the theory that a 4 percent response rate of 1,000 customers is clearly not as good as a 4 percent response rate of 10,000 customers. This mentality can, however, destroy the relationship with the guest. Exhibit 20-14 summarizes the top 10 successful secrets of e-mail marketing by Larry Chase, an expert in the area of Internet marketing and co-founder of *Web Digest for Marketers* (www.wdfm.com).

Web Browsing Exercise

Use your favorite search engine and look up the website www.wdfm.com. Find an article of interest to you on this site and be prepared to talk about it in class.

Web Browsing Exercise

Go to a hospitality firm's website and request to be put on its mailing list. Evaluate the e-mails you receive in terms of the 10 secrets presented in Exhibit 20-14.

Database Marketing

Database marketing used to be known as direct marketing, but it is much more than that. Direct marketing implies a one-way communication: from the firm to the customer. Database marketing, however, involves two-way communications. It is both part of the communications mix and also part of interactive marketing. Its most important usage is that of managing relevant data on customers to identify them for the purpose of developing a long-standing relationship of repeat business; to send desired messages at the right time, in the right form, to the right people; and to develop the right product that satisfies their needs and wants. Essentially, databases are decision-support systems.

The information in the systems typically includes internal data on customers and purchased data (list sources) on both customers and prospects. The information can be used to generate mailing lists and prospect lists for salespeople and to identify market segments. A direct communications channel with customers and prospects is provided through a computerized customer database. Database marketing augments more traditional communications vehicles, such as advertising and personal selling. Before the late 1990s, database marketing was generally limited to the use of brochures and letters with offers sent by mail. Today's marketing environment includes e-mail marketing in the database marketing offerings. E-mail marketing has become an integral component of a comprehensive database marketing strategy.

BUILDING YOUR LIST—BE SELECTIVE ABOUT WHO IS ADDED TO YOUR LIST OR YOU'LL CREATE MORE WORK FOR YOURSELF.

If you want to build an email list of existing customers, be sure to obtain their permission first instead of adding their names without telling them. Give your customers a value proposition that makes them want to be on your email list. This approach gives you the opportunity to strengthen the bond between you and your customers. If you add an email address without permission, recipients might complain and possibly abandon the relationship with you altogether.

HTML VS. TEXT? NO CONTEST . . . IT'S HTML FOR HIGHER RESPONSE RATES.

HTML helps direct the reader's eye where to go next and where to put one's attention. What's more, a good graphical layout communicates a better brand impression. HTML also lets you track open rates, click-throughs, and pass-alongs (recipients who pass your email communication along to friends/colleagues). All-text email does not allow for tracking.

RELEVANCY—MAKE CERTAIN YOUR EMAILS ARE EXTREMELY RELEVANT AND VALUABLE TO THE RECIPIENTS.

In the recipient's mind, you have to be known for sending high-quality messages; otherwise, you will be ignored or recipients could unsubscribe or complain. Your name in the "From" field represents your brand and reputation for sending messages that directly appeal to the recipient. The "Subject" field represents the timely and relevant proposition.

HOW OFTEN TO SEND EMAIL?

Start off slowly. Get the kinks out by sending monthly or quarterly before going weekly depending on your business. Whether you're building a house list in order to send offers, or starting an email newsletter, you are essentially getting into the publishing business. The challenges of publishing deadlines and production may not be familiar to you. So take it slow at first. You can always increase the frequency of your email communications later. How often should you send? The answer is as often as your subscribers want to hear from you.

EMAIL LENGTH—KEEP IT SHORT AND PACKED WITH VALUE.

People are overwhelmed with the number of email messages they receive daily. In addition, they are inundated with direct mail, telemarketing, print magazines, and TV ads and will only pay close attention to what is immediately important. Your enemy is the delete key; make every word and graphic work hard to deliver value to the reader. Small chunks of information are more digestible than a 2,000-word article. When it comes to straightforward offers, shorter is usually better. When it comes to informational and educational content, readers typically have a greater attention span.

CONTENT—GIVE THEM SOMETHING THEY CAN'T LIVE WITHOUT.

The "look-and-feel" should say "Come on; I'm easy to read." Whether you're preparing editorial or commercial content, make sure it is distinctive and can't be found anywhere else. Industry news and analysis, useful insights from your experience, or product tips are examples of content that can jump off the screen and into the minds of your readers. Make your content so good that your readers pass it along.

DON'T TURN YOUR EMAIL INTO A VISUAL CIRCUS; REMEMBER . . . LESS IS MORE.

It's uncomfortable staring into a screen for long periods of time to read documents. You want to offer your readers an inviting "look-and-feel" that's attractive and easy-to-understand at a glance. Make your emails look like an oasis when compared to the sea of chaos found in the rest of the recipient's Inbox.

TEST EVERYTHING.

Test your subject header, your content, your offer, your pricing, your call to action, delivery days and times. Reinforce navigational cues by stating the wanted action, such as "Click Here," "Go" or "Buy Now," etc. Don't assume the reader knows to click on an embedded link or graphic. Get the most mileage out of your email marketing efforts by tracking everything you can, and then improving on those results. Use "split copy testing." Send one offer worded in a certain way to part of your list and the same offer worded differently to another part of your list and see which does better. Try to do it at the same point in time so results reflect similar market conditions.

MULTIMEDIA EMAILS.

There are many compelling reasons for marketers to consider using multimedia in their email campaigns. Recent statistics show multimedia ads on websites draw above average click-through rates. This is probably because they're more dynamic and possibly more involving. Just because multimedia emails are technically feasible to produce and distribute, does this mean you should jump in now? Not necessarily. Your particular audience may or may not want to see multimedia playing in their Inbox. If you give your recipients something they're not ready for or want, you could seriously damage your relationship with them. Certain market niches may be more apt to accept and want multimedia emails, such as gamers and people in high-tech industries.

WHAT TO EXPECT AFTER YOU HIT "SEND."

It's always exciting monitoring the launch of an email campaign using your on-screen console because it's happening in real time. It's like watching election returns. In both cases, you're watching people vote. In your case, people are voting with their mouse for your offer, your content, your product upgrades, etc. Some feedback you'll like, some you won't, and still other feedback will be unexpected. Open rates tell you the success of your subject header and "From" fields. Click-throughs tell you how interesting your offer or content is to the reader. Expect to see at least six kinds of responses as soon as you hit the "Send" button.

1. Valid responses: These most important, non-automated replies are from real people requesting specific information or action on your part.
2. Hard bounces: These are abandoned email addresses. Delete them from your email list.
3. Soft bounces: These are typically mailboxes that are full and can't accept any new inbound emails. Leave these email addresses on your list for the time being. If the same soft bounces occur regularly, then delete those addresses as well.
4. Spam filter rejections: These messages tell you your email has not been delivered. You will probably receive more and more of these notifications as recipients institute controls to cut down on spam, which is growing rapidly. According to Jupiter Research, the number of unwanted email messages per email user will increase from 2,551 messages in 2003 to 3,639 unwanted messages in 2007. In some cases, you can manually interact with these emails so your message is delivered to the recipient.
5. Spam filter messages: Pay attention to these messages because they tell you why your email has been filtered out. Some spam notifications will actually give you their rating system and show you the words that sent you over the allowable threshold. You may want to avoid some of these words in the future in order to stay under that threshold.
6. "Out of office" replies: Be prepared to receive many of these replies, especially around holidays and the last two weeks of August.

Source: Chase, L. Top ten success secrets of e-mail marketing. *Web Digest for Marketers*. Retrieved December 12, 2005, from www.wdfm.com. Used by permission of Web Digest for Marketers.

Database marketing works well with certain market segments of the hospitality industry. Restaurant customers respond well to database marketing, as do weekend package customers for hotels. Individuals tend to respond to database marketing better than organizational customers. There appears to be a correlation between the size of the purchase and the response to database marketing. For example, a promotion offering a dinner for two that may cost $100 brings a better response rate than a promotion to a meeting planner who may spend $100,000 in a hotel.

Database information enables companies to target individuals or small segments of like customers. This is very useful for sales and sales management support and for direct marketing programs. Database marketing has three main benefits:

1. It provides a strategic advantage through the more effective use of marketing information internally.
2. It improves the use of customer and market information.
3. It forms a basis for developing long-term customer relationships, especially with those customers who account for a large portion of a firm's business.

E-mail allows a degree of tracking consumer behavior that was not available in the past. Ten years ago, one of the authors would send a direct mail solicitation to customers to come to his hotel. A redemption offer would be enclosed to encourage the customer to buy a hotel room. Elaborate mechanisms and standard operating procedures were established to collect the coupons at the front desk to track the results. E-mail can now be tracked by "click through" rates (how many customers opened the e-mail), by the number of **unique visitors** to the landing page on a website (how many customers actually viewed the offer), or by actual bookings (how many customers made a reservation). A return on investment for each campaign can be viewed by the marketer. Exhibit 20-15 is an interview with Judd Goldfeder, president of the Customer Connection.

A form of database marketing is telemarketing or using the telephone to reach customers or prospective customers. This technique, however, has its limits. In some industries, its usage is so frequent that it becomes annoying to those who are contacted and hence counterproductive. The U.S. government recently responded to the numerous complaints by citizens tired of receiving unsolicited sales calls at home. A website was established to allow consumers to register their telephone numbers as part of a government mandated "do not call" list (www.donotcall.gov). The response was overwhelming, with over 50 million Americans voting with their mouse to remove their names from telemarketers' lists.

However, once the customer gives you permission, your name can go into the database. In this way, databases

complement advertising and personal selling. From either of those sources information may be obtained to set up the database, which is then used for further contact.

Proprietary marketing databases are those developed by an individual company for its own use. They provide a competitive advantage in enabling a company to focus on a particular market segment. Examples in the hotel industry include databases that contain guest history information or information on the participants in frequent guest programs. Preferred room type, pillows, amenities, and other preferences may be loaded into these databases to enable a hotel to be more responsive to each customer's personal requests upon arrival and without hassle. This is a powerful aspect of relationship marketing. Some systems, such as Ritz-Carlton's, enable any Ritz-Carlton in the world to tap into these preferences after a customer has stayed at any other Ritz-Carlton at another location. A similar program, introduced by Wyndham International, invites guests to populate a database with their personal preferences (Wyndham ByRequest) so these may be arranged prior to the guest's stay at any property in their system.

E-mail confirmations now allow hotels to thank the customer for making the booking, ask if the customer would like a spa treatment or tee time during their stay, and then send a thank-you note upon departure.

Customized marketing databases are used to profile prospective customers. Data obtained from outside sources are customized to fit the property's customer profile. Customer information is obtained before the customer is actually contacted so that product information can be filtered appropriately in advance. Also, contacts can be made with potential customers who have similar profiles to present customers. These prospects have a greater probability of becoming future customers. Exhibit 20-16 is an interview with Mike Marker and Al Martinez Fonts of Saddlebrook Resort.

 Web Browsing Exercise

Use your favorite search engine to find current laws requiring the collection, storage, and use of customer information. Given that many hospitality firms are international, be sure to investigate the laws of multiple countries. Be prepared to discuss in class what you have found.

Database Marketing Components

Database marketing has four fundamental components—strategy, data, information, and knowledge.

Strategy.   Strategy begins with the development of objectives for the marketing program. Who is the target customer, where do they live, what do they buy, where else do

EXHIBIT 20-15	Interview with Judd Goldfeder, President of the Customer Connection

HOW CRITICAL IS IT TO MEASURE THE EFFECTIVENESS OF CONSUMER RESPONSE?

If I am the one spending the dollar, then I like to know what kind of return I'm getting on my dollar. So I think it's very important for two reasons. One, am I doing the right thing and making money at what I am doing? Two, I think it is important to measure response to know whether you should do it again. The ways that we measure are two fairly simple ways. One of them is, if you're sending a redeemable promotion—let's call it a coupon—you might send that coupon on a receipt they got when they dined the last time via e-mail or you might mail it to them, but nevertheless it is a coupon that they have to bring back in to use. When the coupon is redeemed, we have the restaurant return those to us, marking on them how much money the people spent, how many people were in the party, and we can then put that back into their database and the database for that particular promotion and measure the response to it.

One of the things that I have heard frequently is, "Why do I want to market for my guests—They would have come anyway." We send a communication of any kind to a group of members. We can identify that group in a database—let's say we sent something to 1,000 people and there are 700,000 members—because we're a frequency program. We know every time those people buy, so we can look at the date on which they got the communication, look back 30 days, and use that as a benchmark for their frequency per day. We then look after they received whatever they got and see how that affected their frequency of dining. We can see whether they would have come in anyway, whether we're getting people to come more often, or whether we're getting people who have not been coming at all.

So, we think it is imperative in terms of measuring the response, because you want to know what you're getting for your money. You want to know what strategies you would want to repeat, and which ones were not such a good idea. We first started a frequency for one of our clients in 15 restaurants in a local market to see if the frequency program was going to increase sales. They found at the end of the test that a control group whose sales were up in one market did the same advertising or marketing as the group who were in the frequency program. In the control group, where there was no frequency program, sales for the restaurant went up about 2 percent compared to the prior period, and in the test group, where they had a frequency program, sales were up about 14 percent overall.

HOW DO YOU DETERMINE CONTROL AND TEST GROUPS? WHAT TYPES OF METHODS DO YOU USE?

In the one situation where we were investing a whole frequency program, we had a control group of restaurants in northern California and a test group of restaurants in southern California, so they were isolated geographically and there was little crossover. In our environment, we were going to send a promotion. We can send it to half of a group and hold out on another group that are, for the most part, the same as the group that is getting the promotion. We then see how often each group has visits and see what effect the promotion had. We're right now testing e-mailing birthday cards as opposed to mailing them, because people think that e-mail is the next thing to heaven because it doesn't cost much, but the redemption rate appears to be half or less than it is with mail. By testing things like that, they can make an economic decision—whether it is worthwhile investing more money in order to get a higher return.

DO YOU KNOW WHY E-MAIL IS NOT WORKING AS WELL?

In my opinion, it's because it's impersonal, people who don't know about it won't open the e-mail, and it's more businesslike. A postcard comes in the mail, the whole family sees it, and it may hang on the refrigerator, getting more visibility. Steak & Ale had a 500,000-member mail database, and they were spending large amounts of money. It was poorly structured, but they decided that mail cost them too much money and told everyone that they were converting to e-mail. They made two or three efforts to get everyone's e-mail, and I was at a conference where one of the people from the company said, "The mangers and the customers were all ticked off, but it's too bad—it saved us money."

SOME COMPANIES ARGUE THAT YOU DON'T WANT TO DO TEST AND CONTROL GROUPS BECAUSE, IF YOU DON'T GIVE ALL OF YOUR CUSTOMERS THE SAME THING, THEY'RE GOING TO HEAR ABOUT IT AND GET ANGRY, SO IT'S BETTER TO JUST GIVE ALL OF THE CUSTOMERS THE SAME THING AND NOT WORRY ABOUT IT. WHAT IS YOUR OPINION ON THIS IDEA?

We have for the past 15 years—since we've been doing frequency—been able to segment people into those who come often, moderately often, or never. We have sent different offers or no offers to different members all the time and do the 800-member phone service system, and will very rarely get that type of a call. We get very few comments—in terms of the percentage of what's mailed out, it's nil.

Source: Used with permission from Judd Goldfeder.

they go, and so on? Once the strategy is conceived and integrated with the other marketing vehicles such as advertising and public relations, the data are assembled.

Data. Data start with the actual names, addresses, telephone numbers, dates of arrival and departure, room preferences, purchase habits, credit card usage, and so forth. The initial database should contain data on past customers. New customer prospects, obtained from list sources, can then be added. As discussed earlier, for the data to be meaningful, they have to be accurate (easier said than done). The advantage of loyalty programs is that they help ensure the accuracy of the data. One way to ensure the accuracy of the database and avoid breaking any database marketing rules is to gain customers' permission to communicate with them.

Permission means giving customers the ability to easily change their information online, opt in (sign up for the mailing), provide preferences (e.g., the type of information they would like to receive and the frequency with which these e-mails arrive), and opt out (cancel membership or mailings.)

Information. The information portion of database marketing consists of the analysis of the data. The demography and psychographics of customers need to be

EXHIBIT 20-16	Interview with Mike Marker and Al Martinez Fonts, Saddlebrook Resort

PLEASE PROVIDE A LITTLE BACKGROUND ON YOUR RESORT.

Our resort was built primarily to hold corporate meetings. We are a self-contained, independently owned resort away from the city of Tampa. We're in a suburban setting and have everything you need for a meeting. Just like any other product, we appeal to some groups more than others. For companies that wish to introduce more hush-hush ideas—such as when Heineken introduced Heineken Light or medical companies that have developed new medical equipment—we are the ideal place because we're secluded, secure, and out of the way. You are not going to get people walking in off the street and see something they're not supposed to see. We have the ability to have off-duty county police officers here for security at night in certain areas. We can lock all the doors.

We currently have 82,000 square feet of function space so we have a lot of flexibility. Currently about 80 percent of our business comes from such meetings. Prior to 9-11, we handled approximately 500+ meetings per year; now, however, we're at about 450 meetings per year. Since 9-11, we have seen a trend toward smaller meetings rather than larger meetings, regional meetings instead of national, and smaller East Coast or West Coast meetings instead of one big one. This helps the companies save on expenses. In terms of the size of groups we cater to, I would say an average number would be anywhere from 100 to 150 people. We have catered to as few as 20 people and as many as 900 people.

HOW MANY ROOMS ARE THERE AT THE RESORT?

We have 550 suites. The majority of these suites have two private bedrooms with private bathrooms, which means we have 800 actual rooms. It is kind of strange because, even though we have 800 rooms, if somebody asks how many keys you have, it's 550.

DO A LOT OF PEOPLE BUNK TOGETHER?

Yes, because they have their own private bed and bath. The only things they share are the dining room, living room, and kitchen. "Bunking together" really isn't the right word because it's a two-bedroom suite. The key to these corporations is that they want to make sure the attendees get their own bedroom and bath, which the two-bedroom suite allows you to do. It is not an easy sell—bunking together—doesn't sound very appealing. They need to see it, and then it becomes easier to sell because they see that they have their bedroom, their own bathroom, their own TV, their own door to close off so they have their privacy. As I said, the only things they have in common are the living, dining, and kitchen areas.

HOW DO YOU REACH THESE GROUPS?

We use a lot of direct mail. We are blessed with a lot of repeat business, which means that our database is very good, accurate, and up-to-date. That's why our direct mail program works. We keep changing and improving and adding new things to the resort, which is where the direct mail program comes in. The direct mail pieces are unique because they are subject-related to the different changes we constantly make. We send a letter from our CEO, and they go to about 9,000 meeting planners in our database.

Besides the direct mail program we have an advertising schedule. We are very versatile in our advertising, but we mainly advertise in *Successful*

Meetings and *Conventions Magazine*. We have always believed in large photography and good color photography to sell our amenities. We've gone beyond *Successful Meetings* and *Conventions Magazine* in the last couple of years into magazines geared toward pharmaceutical and other executives. We do not advertise our meetings market in the consumer market, such as in *Forbes, Fortune,* or the *Wall Street Journal*. A lot of people will call me and say, "Yeah, but these are read by executives; and, yes, they are. However, for the type of meetings that we attract, meeting planners do not get their information from such magazines.

Since our meetings are sold as a package, which includes food and beverage, recreation, etc., we are not interested in just the room nights. We need to approach those meeting planners who are charged with the responsibility for all phases of the meeting. These people are reading the trade books and trade magazines.

The other thing that we've done over the last couple of years is to start gathering e-mail addresses. We communicate through a personal e-mail to that particular client. We have been very successful at sending "not sales" sales messages. We get the most response from e-mail messages that include a recipe from our chef—either a spring recipe or a fall recipe. We get a lot of comments back thanking us, because we aren't trying to sell them anything. It's more like, "Hey, we wanted to share this with you."

In addition to direct mail and advertising, we have a staff of nine salespeople—only one of these is charged with the leisure side of the business. All of the other folks are geographically assigned to specific sales areas. For example, we have one person who is assigned to all corporate group business in the state of Florida. We have other people assigned to the Northeast, Midwest, etc., and those people stay in touch with the meeting planners. We do a lot of business with third parties nowadays because that's getting more and more dominant, so we form a partnership with them whenever and wherever we can.

That's the sort of thing that we do in terms of marketing, and, of course, the salespeople attend selective trade shows—not the really big ones, because they become diluted. We have more of a target audience, rather than a shotgun approach. It's different when you're talking to us because we're one property in one place.

WHAT IS AN EXAMPLE OF A THIRD PARTY?

Examples of third party firms are Conferon, Conference Direct, Helms-Brscoe, Prestige Resorts, etc. These organizations have independent salespeople—approximately 90 percent of which probably come from the hotel industry. The salespeople are independent contractors with their own contacts. They earn a commission for each property that they match with the meeting, which is how they get paid. We also retain other third party sales groups, such as the Krisam Group, Hintont & Grusich, and the David Green Organization because they have offices in New York; Chicago; Washington, D.C.; and Dallas, where we cannot afford to have our own offices because we're an independent property. They have their own portfolio of clients, and they act as an extension of our offices. A chain would have their offices across the country.

Source: Used with permission from Mike Marker and Al Martinez Fonts.

analyzed. Other factors, such as why they use a particular hotel or restaurant, can be added.

Knowledge.   The knowledge stage of a database program includes segmentation, clustering, and modeling.

Segmentation, as discussed earlier in the text, includes gathering "like" customers together. For example, a hotel might have a list of customers who buy weekend packages segmented under a **leisure** code. A restaurant might have a list of customers who attend Sunday brunch. These segments are then clustered. It is important to realize that the leisure traveler may also eat brunch at the same property. Or, the leisure customer might come to New York City on weekends in April and live in Northern New Jersey, another cluster.

Once customers are clustered, the search for new lists (and potentially new customers) begins through modeling. The assumption is that nonusers will cluster in a manner similar to that of current customers, and list sources screened in this manner will have a higher yield than those with no known similarity to current customers.

Using the Database

Database marketing should first be employed to contact past customers. Many property management systems (PMS) in hotels capture extensive data on customers that have used the hotel in the past and are familiar with the property. The first step in a database marketing campaign is to assemble the list of past customers. This list may come from the PMS, registration cards, old invoices, credit card companies, business cards, or e-mail addresses from the website.

Consensual marketing may also be used to build databases, and the concept is just as the term implies. Customers offer their e-mail addresses in exchange for newsletters, information on special packages, and the like. The customer is giving the supplier permission to send information.

The list of past customers is then put on some type of computer program. Simple lists can be assembled on traditional software, such as Word or Excel. More complex lists need to be built on database programs such as Paradox. Once the list of past customers is organized, certain fields are established to allow the organization to segment the customers. A field is an indication on the database that one characteristic is different from another. Fields can be established for the residence of the guest (by media market, as defined by the guest's postal code), date of reservation, date of checkout, market segment type, amount spent per visit, and so on.

For example, in a hotel, corporate and leisure customers typically plan and book their accommodations differently. To make the example simple, a hotel determines that most customers checking out Monday through Friday are corporate guests, whereas customers checking out Saturday and Sunday are more likely to be leisure. These are two different types of customers with two different sets of needs. Accordingly, fields are set up within the database to allow the marketer to choose corporate and leisure customers to contact.

The hotel then decides to "talk to" both its corporate and leisure customers. Two different collateral pieces or e-mail campaigns are developed, one aimed at the corporate customer, the other at the leisure customer. The advertising agency creates two mailers designed to thank the past customers for their business and encourage future usage. A newsletter is created to inform corporate customers about the different programs within the hotel. The leisure customer is mailed a promotion encouraging return during certain slow weekends.

Once the collateral is developed, the piece is "dropped," or mailed to the customers. To track the database marketing effort, a "trigger" or response mechanism is placed in the collateral to measure success. A trigger might be a special telephone number for the promotion or a certificate to be redeemed in the restaurant. Advertising campaigns work similarly, yet database marketing is unique in its ability to be tracked and documented.

Database marketing can be tracked through a variety of methods, particularly on the Internet. Advertising can be image oriented (to communicate a positioning statement to a customer) or retail oriented (offering specific prices to be tracked for response). Contrarily, database marketing has been tracking driven, typically requiring returns of between 2 and 5 percent of the total prospects contacted to be deemed successful. Like advertising, database marketing now has an image component that remains untrackable. For example, many restaurants and hotels routinely send customers newsletters on upcoming programs. These newsletters are untrackable in terms of covers or room nights, but nonetheless keep the hospitality entity in touch with its customers. E-mail marketing allows similar communications with customers.

Once a facility covers its past customers, it can obtain new customers through database marketing. New customers can be found by profiling past customers. The theory behind profiling is that similar customers tend to buy similar facilities. By analyzing the fields of the past customers, a very good picture of new customers begins to emerge. Past customer fields can yield information regarding age, location, income, type of car driven, purchase habits, media usage, local business contacts, number of visits to restaurants in a month, and so forth. Given this information, the savvy database marketer seeks lists of "like" customers. Exhibit 20-17 provides an example of how a major chain used database software to help it in its marketing.

Electronic commerce cannot be successful without an up-to-date and accurate database. The hospitality industry is lucky because consumers make very few other purchases that require them to provide their name, address, and method of payment before they actually consume the product. This is one reason frequent buyer programs have become so important in the grocery business; these programs provide the information the business

EXHIBIT 20-17	A Major Chain Uses a Hosted, Internet-Based CRM Service to Help Manage Its Customers

A major chain operates luxury and first-class hotels in 56 countries worldwide. At the end of 2001, the global travel and hotel industry was experiencing the fallout from the 9/11 tragedy. At the same time, the downturn in the global economy meant that corporations were intent on reducing all costs, including travel, conferences, and accommodation.

The key to profitability for this chain is to maximize the occupancy rate of its 34,000 bedrooms and hundreds of banqueting and meeting rooms. "We required a system to manage more efficiently our corporate customer relationships across more than 50 countries," comments the senior VP for marketing and sales.

The chain had a customer management system. However, it was overcomplicated and not user friendly, resulting in low usage. This meant there was limited sharing of information on corporate accounts across the chain's 100-person international sales team. "Ease of use is key, because if you have low compliance, the system falls down," says the senior VP for marketing and sales.

£300,000 IMMEDIATE SAVINGS IN IMPLEMENTATION COSTS

The firm hired a major consultancy group to review the CRM options—including hotel-specific applications—and make recommendations. The report came back with a recommendation of traditional CRM, which would take 18 months to implement and cost at least £300,000 during the implementation phase, even before adding software licensing fees.

"The firm was undergoing a major restructuring and we could not afford to wait around for 18 months to implement CRM. We needed to move much more quickly than that," says the senior VP for marketing and sales. "We asked the consultants to go back to the drawing board and look at Internet-hosted solutions."

The firm's regional sales office in Italy had been using salesforce.com, and reports were positive from the local management and sales staff. The consultants considered this and other hosted applications and recommended salesforce.com. Salesforce.com delivers CRM on demand via the Internet. As a result, there is no need to buy, install, or maintain hardware, software, networks, or hosting. Neither did the firm have to invest in upfront licensing charges. The service is provided on demand for a monthly fee per user. "We selected salesforce.com because of its flexibility, low cost, ease of use, and speed of implementation," says the senior VP for marketing and sales. "By going this route rather than the originally suggested traditional CRM approach, we immediately saved £300,000 in implementation costs."

GROWING CORPORATE ACCOUNT REVENUE DURING DOWNTURN

Salesforce.com was implemented globally within three months. Today, the chain uses salesforce.com Professional Edition across 140 users. There is now much greater transparency of corporate accounts on a global basis. Prior to the implementation of salesforce.com, the company was trying to track 6,000 to 7,000 accounts. This included significant duplication and wasted effort. "We have now focused this down to approximately 2,500 corporate accounts."

Salesforce.com helps the chain to manage its business more productively. For example, it can dip into the system and implement short-term incentive schemes for sales staff. "During a quiet period we might implement an extra bonus for business generated over the next 60 or 90 days. This has proven to be a very effective facility," says the senior VP for marketing and sales.

Another benefit is that it helps to project the firm as a single brand across the world rather than a loose confederation of operations. "I am a salesperson, not a computer expert," explains the vice president of sales—Europe & Africa. "The fact that salesforce.com is easy to use ensures compliance across my salespeople. Before this we had important customer information scattered across individual laptops. Now we can access real-time information on a corporate account anywhere in the world. The fact that we know we handle that account in another market helps us in the sales process."

"The Internet has made the hotel industry more of a commodity," adds the senior VP for marketing and sales. "There is less loyalty with the facility to source hotels and prices at the click of a mouse. This emphasizes the need to maximize customer service and know the customer better. Salesforce.com helps us to achieve this." Between 2001 and 2004, corporate business for hotel chains was under considerable pressure. At the same time, the chain went through its own restructuring, which resulted in the shedding of some properties. "Despite this, we have managed to grow global corporate account revenue at a time when companies were cutting back," says the senior VP for marketing and sales. "Salesforce.com has played a significant role in this achievement."

Source: Retrieved July 7, 2005, from www.salesforce.com/customers/casestudy.jsp?customer=lemeridien. Copyright © 2000–2006 salesforce.com, inc. Customer Relationship Management (CRM). All rights reserved.

needs to better understand the purchasing patterns of their customers. As discussed in Chapter 4, practically all the chain hotels have frequent guest programs. Just like grocery store programs, these programs exist so that the chains can record the purchase behaviors of their customers. However, for the grocery store, it is usually one or two locations, while for the major chains, the purchases can take place anywhere in the world.

The database contains much more than names and addresses, however. A good database will contain the recency of purchase, the frequency of purchase, the monetary value of the purchases, and the specific items purchased. As the cost of data storage has declined, hospitality firms can also collect customers' preferences; for example, whether they like feather pillows or specific types of drinks in the minibar or before going to bed. All of this information is then used to develop a long-term relationship with the guest. Both Ritz-Carlton and Four Seasons are well known for keeping track of such information. These are two chains that do not use frequency programs to collect this information, however. They are able to do this because, unlike many other hotel chains that have different ownership structures (e.g., franchisees), Ritz-Carlton and Four Seasons are corporately managed, providing them with more control over collecting customer information. Their relatively small size also enables the use of centralized databases. Independent properties can obviously create customer databases quite easily because they have control over the collection of such information.

> **Tourism Marketing Application**
> Destination websites should provide the website visitor with a means to request more information about the website. This link provides the destination with the opportunity to create a dialogue with the site visitor. The website for Pitcairn Island provides the site visitor with many opportunities to receive additional information. (www.lareau.org/pitc.html, accessed April 9, 2006)

Ways to Use the Database

One way to use the database is customer segmentation. As discussed in Chapter 4, not all customers are equal. Some are more valuable to the firm than others. A way to determine the value of individual customers is to look at their recency, frequency, and monetary value. This is known as RFM analysis. The basic idea is that customers have a three-digit code attached to their records; one code for recency, one for frequency, and one for monetary value. Although code numbers can be assigned in different ways, traditionally each code ranges in value from 5 to 1, with 5 being the most recent or frequent or the highest monetary value and 1 being the least recent or frequent or the lowest monetary value. The actual value is determined by sorting the database one code at a time. The sorted database is then divided into quintiles. This is done for each of the three codes. So, a customer with a code of 555 would be in the most recent customer grouping, the most frequent customer grouping, and the highest monetary value grouping. This customer would clearly be one of the best customers.

A customer with a value of 111, however, would be one of the worst. Different communication strategies can then easily be developed based on this coding scheme. For instance, a customer with a 335 would clearly be targeted for a "come see us again" type promotion, whereas a customer with a 551 might not receive anything. Although this customer has been with the firm recently and comes frequently, he spends little money with the firm. It would be recommended that research be undertaken to find out why this customer spends so little money on the property.

A second way to use the database is to communicate with the customer, as was detailed previously in the discussion of e-mail marketing. The most important tactic for this strategy is to deliver a consistent message with product usage. For instance, once a week, airlines usually send special web fares to their most valuable customers. However, if one customer lives in Dallas, she should not be getting special web fares flying from Boston. If the message is not targeted based on buying behavior, the message becomes spam and after a while is automatically deleted without ever being opened. Thus, when a Dallas fare does become available, it will most likely be missed.

A third way to use the database is for customer management. That is, give the customers what they want before they have to ask for it. This is the hallmark of Four Seasons and Ritz-Carlton. It is also the hallmark of the systems designed by Springer-Miller Systems, as described in the Marketing in Action feature at the beginning of this chapter. Customer management also involves providing the customer with choices.

A fourth way to use the database is to improve the delivery of sales promotions. This improvement comes in two ways. One, because it is sent directly to specific customers, the competition may never know about it and hence be unable to offer a similar promotion. This is called stealth communication. Two, promotions can be sent at a time when the customer is most likely to buy but needs some sort of reminder or inducement. Harrah's Entertainment is a world leader in knowing this type of information. An example of this would be that, when the customer is close to moving to his next tier of reward benefits, he will be more likely to respond to a targeted promotion than would someone far away.

Databases are also a great way to conduct customer and product marketing research. A problem with comment cards is that they are not representative of everyone using the hospitality product. Usually, only those extremely happy or those extremely unhappy respond, leaving the majority in the middle unaccounted for. If customers provide the firm with their e-mail addresses and permission to contact them, this will help the firm contact a representative sample of customers. Following is an example of how a firm might get permission for this type of research:

> We occasionally contact a random sample of customers to gain their feedback on how well we are doing. Would you be willing to be contacted for such a survey? If so, please provide us with your e-mail address. If you are contacted, you will be eligible to win a $500 gift certificate.

The final way databases can be used is to increase the channels of distribution. As discussed in Chapters 17 and 18, the least expensive way to book reservations is for guests to book them themselves through the firm's own website. The database can aid in this by reminding the customer to always book directly. Exhibit 20-18 discusses the top 10 trends for the next 10 years for Internet marketing.

Larry Chase of the *Web Digest for Marketers* has been publishing his e-mail newsletter for 10 years. His newsletter analyzes and reports on the meaningful trends in Internet marketing. His prediction for the 10 trends for the next 10 years in Internet marketing are shown here verbatim from his newsletter.

1. *Pay Per Call Rings In:*   Any salesperson worth his or her salt knows that a call is worth many times more than a click. Having 1-to-1 contact with a prospect live on the phone is so much more likely to result in a sale. Some say the likelihood is ten-fold. So it's no wonder this nascent industry has many people watching closely. There will be issues with "fake" phone calls that will be reminiscent of click fraud problems today. But look for the pay-per-call industry to catch on fire within the next 1 1/2 years, despite these concerns. I am devoting an entire issue of *Web Digest for Marketers* to the subject of Pay Per Call later this year.

2. *Feed Marketing Flourishes:*   You've got RSS (Real Simple Syndication). You've got podcasting (where you can download and time-shift audio content to your iPod or MP3 player). Now you've even got Video Podcasting where you can download MP4 videos into Sony's PlayStation Portable unit for viewing when you're mobile. As the use of RSS grows quickly, and more consumers buy iPods or MP3 players, these formats will grow in usage. And where there are ears and especially eyeballs, marketers are never too far behind. The podcasts may employ the sponsorship model, or subscription (further off), or simply be done for the coolness factor, customer retention, or PR pop that you'll get if you do it early enough. RSS ad units will settle into some format that offers a decent ROI for the advertiser. There are already coupons being fed via RSS. Expect to see more point-to-point syndication feed models as we move forward in time.

3. *Email Marketing Will Survive:*   Spam issues will recede dramatically, because they have to. Too much is at stake. We may resort to the payment of email postage for guaranteed delivery, or maybe not. But the email platform is now like a fax machine. While there are fancier applications, email is easy, cheap, effective and everywhere.

4. *Personal Agents Propagate:*   Watch for the growth of "agent software" to help you sift through the morass of online information. There's too much relevant stuff for mere humans to sift through now. Agent software learns your habits by following your moves online and on your computer as well as by asking about your preferences. Some early forms of this exist now, but it will become much more sophisticated. Your agent will bring you both B2B and B2C offerings, whether the latest on-target ad deal or the best tennis racket at the best price.

5. *Reverb Marketing, In Stereo:*   eMarketer points out that many Internet users already use multiple forms of media at once. Even as I write this I'm listening to CNBC in the background. Smart marketers will synchronize their messaging so the end user hears and sees complementary messages at or near the same time. This will be the new definition of what media planners call "Road Blocking." Since the end user's attention is split between different media, it will be essential that messages reinforce each other. HINT: Visual gags on TV spots or simply showing the 800 number on screen won't be as effective, because a significant segment of people won't be watching the screen. Even today we're starting to use TV like radio.

6. *Audio Blogs/Video Blogs (V-Blogs):*   Blogs are obviously here to stay. Some of the cutting-edge blogs are starting to offer content in audio and even in video. This will not only affect journalism, but it will impact the retail business as well. Imagine a personality-driven QVC blog on your computer screen.

7. *IPTV Adds Interactivity:*   Microsoft and others are currently exploring TV over Internet protocol. But don't expect TV on the Net to look and act like the TV you see on your television screen. After all, we already have television, so who needs the redundancy? IPTV (or as some say TVIP) will take a different twist. While Madison Avenue types will say, "At last, we can now feed TV commercials over the Net!", consumers will not want to see those ads on their computer screens. They already TIVO over on them on their TV screens, right? IPTV will be much more interactive. In addition to an 800 number, with IPTV you'll be able to click and buy right then and there. One form might be a video catalog wherein you click on the product or infomercial of interest. To really make this happen, compression schemes will need to get better in order to prevent buffering at the consumer end.

8. *Commercial Content On Demand:*   Messages from marketers need to be so appealing that the audience actually requests the message. This evolutionary process is already underway as "push marketing" is giving way to "pull marketing." The costs of paper, postage, TV and print production are getting too expensive and are not performing as well as they used to. Commercial content that the end user wants isn't far-fetched. Look at *Lucky* magazine or niche catalogs such as *Outdoor Adventure Sports*. B2B marketers have been using high-value ads for years. The advertisers in *Web Digest for Marketers* generate sales leads by offering high-value PDF downloads on subjects of particular interest to the target audience they're trying to reach. The how-to workshops at Home Depot are a prime example on the B2C side. It doesn't take a seer to see that the days of "hot air advertising" are so over.

9. *Publishing Faces Tectonic Shifts:*   Research is already showing that many people in their 20s are not picking up the newspaper habit the way their parents did. Add to this demographic shift the cost of newsprint, postage (for magazines) and handling, and it's likely to cause tectonic shifts in the publishing industry. Many people already read newspapers and magazines online. My bet is that special issues will appear in print, and that many publishers will ultimately have to figure out how to make a go of it with free content online (i.e., advertiser-supported), perhaps by asking their readers for demographic information that enables the publisher to sell targeted advertisements at a premium, as you'll frequently find with trade publications. At the same time, in select industries people will pay for online subscriptions that deliver real value. This is already apparent (the *Wall Street Journal* has 700,000 paid subscribers), but it's not for every content provider out there. For a look at the next level, check out www.cnbcdowjones.com, where you can get just the editorial clips of CNBC, sans commercials, for $99(US) a year. You get 250 plays per month. I subscribe, and find it to be a great time saver.

10. *Direct Marketers Will Take Over the Internet:*   Oops, this has already happened, but not the way I predicted 10 years ago. There are two types of direct marketers on the Net. Those who started out as online marketers have come across the language and practices of DM without realizing it. They talk of response rates by way of clickthroughs, cost per lead, cost per sale, and so on. This group would do well to study the DM masters who have written extensively on the subject over the past 80 years. Then there are the traditional direct marketers, some of whom get it, and some of whom are still riveted on the shriveling response rates of print mailings and catalogs and on ever-increasing postage costs. The irony here is that traditional direct marketing folks are the ones who understand human nature best. Because of their extensive experience, they can smell what will work and what won't. It's baked into their genes now. This group would do well to look at

the Net as the incredible opportunity it is, rather than focusing on what was. What was is not coming back. The good news for traditional DM'ers is that the Internet has not repealed the laws of human nature. So while the tools of DM are changing, the underlying principles that have driven DM since the time of Ben Franklin are still exactly the same.

BONUS TIP

11. *Internet-Free Zones Become the Hot New Trend:* The Internet will become as ubiquitous as cell phones are today. Some enter-

prising travel package company will then begin offering "Internet-free zones"—no cell phones, no Internet, no fax machines, and you won't have to climb the Himalayas to escape the media onslaught. This won't be an option for many people. It seems already that people desperately need to stay connected to others, lest they connect with themselves.

Source: Reprinted with permission from wdfm.com/toptenmarketingtips. htm. Accessed December 10, 2005. Used by permission of *Web Digest for Marketers.*

■ Summary

Interactive active marketing is the future. The advances in data storage and computer technology have enabled astute marketing executives to reconnect with the customer. The information gathered from loyalty programs (Chapter 4), comment cards, guest surveys, and registration forms can all be used to customize the customer's interaction with the hospitality entity. This customization includes not only the physical product, but also the way the firm communicates with the guest.

Interactive marketing is multifaceted. It includes website development, database creation, and the development of creative ways to communicate with the customer. As stated throughout the chapter, this communication has to be two-way. Customers have to be given the ability to opt in and opt out. In addition, they need to be able to tell the hospitality organization the frequency with which they would like to be contacted. Recall from Chapter 1 that the definition of marketing is "solving customers' problems, giving them what they want or need at the time and place of their choosing and at the price they are willing to pay (or a sacrifice they are willing to make)." If done correctly, interactive marketing provides customers with the necessary information to make decisions that benefit the firm. If done incorrectly, it drives the customers to other firms. And, as discussed, it may break government laws.

As Larry Chase pointed out, the next 10 years will bring forth many changes to interactive marketing. It is worthwhile to pay attention to these changes, because the competition surely is.

■ Key Terms

unsecured Internet	spam
best practices	permission-based marketing
mask	opt out
best value	booking engines
keyword	unique visitors
free listing	

■ Dicsussion Questions

1. Find two examples of hotel websites: a good example and a poor example. Use the criteria listed in this chapter to judge the websites selected.

2. The chapter lists the top 10 trends for Internet marketing. Using the web, information you learned in other classes, and other sources that you can find, how many of these trends have already come true? Are any incorrect?

3. Explain the history of the GDS. Who are the major players described in the book? Given the rapid change occurring in the industry, are these the same players as today? Who are current owners of these players? Has ownership changed since this book was published?

4. What are the latest statistics in terms of how people make travel arrangements? Have current statistics changed from what is presented in this chapter?

5. E-ticketing is becoming very important to the airline industry. Based on what you have read in this chapter and other chapters in this text, why is this the case?

What value does it bring to the organization? What percentage of the airlines offer e-ticketing at the time you are reading this (hint: check the website www.iata.org)?

6. Contact someone in a local hospitality organization in your area and discuss with them their e-mail strategy. Be prepared to bring an example of one of their e-mails back to class. Compare the e-mail with the e-mail recommendations listed in this text.

■ Group Projects

1. Visit a local hospitality firm and ask to speak to the marketing director. Ask whether they have a database of customers and how they use this database. Compare their use of databases to the ones suggested in this chapter. Which ones do they use? Which ones do they not use? Does the hospitality firm use its database in a way not mentioned?

2. Develop a website for a fictional hospitality firm. If you do not know how to use web development software, then map out the website so that someone who is an expert in web design would be able design the website for you. Be detailed about exactly what you want and why.

3. You have been asked to give the keynote address to the national travel agency association in your country. This is their annual meeting that will be attended by the majority their members. The topic of your talk is "Surviving the Future." What do you tell them? Be sure to use all information in this text as well as other outside sources of information.

■ References

1. U.S. Department of Labor Bureau of Labor Statistics. (2005). *Occupational outlook handbook, 2004–05 edition*. U.S. Government, Washington DC (www.bls.gov/oco/home.htm)
2. Retrieved December 12, 2005, from www.hotelmarketing. com/index.php/content/article/travel_agents_find_routes_to_survival/.
3. Flying from the computer. Retrieved September 29, 2005, from *The Economist* print edition at www.economist.com/displaystory.cfm?story_id=4455692.
4. Yesawich, Pepperdine, Brown & Russell. (2005). *National Travel MONITOR*.

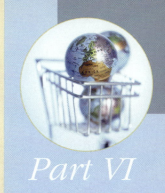

Part VI

Synthesis

The Marketing Plan

Overview

The marketing plan is the management tool that turns the strategic planning process into specific action steps for the forthcoming year. The marketing plan is a working document, used throughout the year to guide the organization in its strategic direction toward the achievement of detailed goals and objectives. In addition to the marketing plan, we discuss data collection in this chapter. Workable, effective, and realistic marketing plans may be developed only through the gathering of complete and adequate information followed by its thorough and objective analysis. Following are some key points:

- External environment data includes international and domestic trends both in the environment and in the marketplace.

- Competitive environment data collection helps marketers review the status of direct competitors, including their physical condition, market segments, behavior, and other pertinent matters.

Continued on page 566

564

I. Introduction to Hospitality Marketing
1. The Concept of Marketing
2. Marketing Services and the Hospitality Experience
3. The Marketing Mix and the Product/Service Mix
4. Relationship/Loyalty Marketing

II. Marketing to Build a Competitive Advantage
5. Strategic Marketing
6. The Strategic Marketing System and Marketing Objectives

VII. Feedback

VI. Synthesis
21. *The Marketing Plan*

III. The Marketplace
7. Understanding Individual Customers
8. Understanding Organizational Customers
9. The Tourist Customer and the Tourism Destination

IV. Situational Analysis
10. Understanding Competition
11. Marketing Intelligence and Research

V. Functional Strategies
12. Differentiation, Segmentation, and Target Marketing
13. Branding and Market Positioning
14. The Hospitality Pricing Mix
15. The Communications Mix: Advertising
16. The Communications Mix: Sales Promotions, Merchandising, Public Relations, and Publicity
17. The Communications Mix: Personal Selling
18. Hospitality Distribution Systems
19. Channels of Distribution: Bringing the Customer to the Product
20. Interactive Marketing: Internet and Database Marketing

Terry Jicinsky is senior vice president of marketing for the Las Vegas Convention and Visitors Authority (LVCVA). The LVCVA, with a current annual budget of just over $190 million, is notably the largest convention and visitors bureau in the world. The organization is responsible for marketing the brand of Las Vegas and Southern Nevada as one of the nation's premier vacation, gaming, and convention destinations.

A 17-year resident of Las Vegas, Jicinsky's responsibilities with the LVCVA encompass the oversight of all advertising, marketing, sales, and public relations efforts. With close to 22 years of experience in the travel and tourism industry, Jicinsky's career path has covered aspects ranging from consumer travel research to Internet marketing, database marketing, and hotel management. Before joining the LVCVA in 1992, his work experience included consulting positions with the national accounting firms of Laventhol & Horwath and Coopers & Lybrand, as well as management positions with Marriott hotels.

Jicinsky is a graduate of the Las Vegas Chamber of Commerce Leadership Program, class of 2002; is an alumnus of the University of Wisconsin, Stout; and attended the University of Nevada, Las Vegas.

Marketing in Action

Terry Jicinsky, Senior Vice President of Marketing, Las Vegas Convention and Visitors Authority

How is your marketing plan for the Las Vegas Convention and Visitors Bureau developed? What is the process you go through?

In the example of Las Vegas, it's clearly a collaborative effort in that all of our stakeholders and partners play a role in developing that marketing plan. For example, our sales force is integral to helping us understand the market segments we're trying to reach with the marketing plan. Our advertising agency plays a key role in helping us understand the branding message we're sending out. Our board of directors, representing the community as a whole, plays a role in helping us understand how we tie in with the hotel product and the attractions in Las Vegas.

How many market segments are there that you go after in Las Vegas?

We go after almost every market segment there is, but at the broadest level, we focus on two very broad-based market segments, those being the leisure/pleasure traveler and the convention/trade show traveler. As Las Vegas evolves from a gaming destination to a full-service resort destination, the gaming message over the years has become a smaller and smaller component of the overall branding campaign. So now, it's part of the mix, but in each of those market segments, it's becoming less and less of the primary component. As a proportion of total expenditure, the gaming budget continues to decrease, but nongaming becomes a larger portion of the total travel wallet.

When you develop the marketing plan, what are the critical issues you consider?

First and foremost, we consider what the hotel community and the attractions are offering our consumer. As a destination marketing organization, we are in that position where we actually market something that we don't control; rather, the hotels and attractions control the actual experience. The first element of building our branding campaign and our marketing campaign is understanding how the product is evolving, and making sure our message is in tune with what the actual product offering is. It's a branding campaign about the destination as a whole that is reflective of every stakeholder we have.

Continued on page 566

Overview *(continued)*

■ Internal environment data collection brings together all the relevant information about the property and its customers to reveal its strengths and weaknesses.

Once the data have been collected, they have to be analyzed:

■ Environmental analysis dissects the trends and forces prevailing in the business environment and examines their potential impact.

■ Competitive analysis reveals the trends of the competition—their strengths and weaknesses, successes and failures—in order to seek opportunities for competitive advantage.

■ Demand analysis reveals overall customer needs in the marketplace and how they are being fulfilled.

■ Property needs analysis addresses internal opportunities to improve the customer base where business is now weak.

■ Internal analysis dissects the current business and customer base and examines the property's overall market situation.

■ Market analysis brings all other phases of the data analysis together to focus on the customer in the search for business development opportunities.

Finally, we discuss the mission statement. After all of the data collection and analysis has been completed, the mission statement, including broad objectives and positioning strategy for the next year, is created for the business unit. This mission statement follows the conclusions of the research, not the other way around. Customer opportunities and objectives follow from the marketing plan.

Marketing in Action *(continued)*
Las Vegas Convention and Visitors Bureau

How often is your marketing plan developed, and what does that entail?

We produce a five-year marketing plan that is updated every 18 months. It is actually a full rewrite of the campaign. We will add another 18 months to the back of the campaign so that we always have a working five-year document, or a five-year road map. In reality, it's really in the current 18 months that we have tangible action plans in place, and that's why we update them every 18 months. The integral part of the marketing plan itself is a very robust research program that focuses on tracking our successes on a month-to-month basis. For example, we do a U.S. population-based advertising awareness survey, where we measure the awareness of the campaign itself across the United States with the traveling public, and we create an index of how we compare from month to month in the awareness factor. A sister program to that is what we call a perception study, done every six months, which is a much more in-depth consumer research program, where we measure the people's perception of Las Vegas as a vacation destination, and then we tie that back to goals and objectives of the advertising campaign.

Do you report those findings back to your various stakeholders?

No, those are perceived to be internal tracking mechanisms because of the competitive nature, and we do not necessarily release those to the general public. From the general public standpoint, we track visitor counts into our destination on a monthly basis, we track citywide hotel occupancy on a monthly basis, we track average daily room rate, and those are the numbers we report back to our stakeholders. These are much more the tangible performance measures, where the awareness survey and the perception study are more internal documents to help us fine-tune the actual brand and campaign itself.

How much do you consider what other convention bureaus are doing when you do this research?

We're very cognizant of what our competition is doing, especially on the leisure side, and not only the primary leisure destinations such as Orlando or beach communities such as Miami or Los Angeles. But also as the proliferation of gaming has taken place over the last decade, we're very cognizant of what's happening in the destinations that have riverboat casinos or those that have Indian gaming, and our primary goal is to distinguish our destination from those other destinations, whether they would be direct competitors in the gaming world or whether they're just direct competitors for the leisure dollar, such as Orlando or a beach community. We're very cognizant of what their marketing pitches are, and our focus is on motivating more people to come to Las Vegas, versus where they could spend their leisure dollar.

Getting the All Star game for the NBA must be a huge feather in your cap.

Attracting the 2007 NBA All Star game was really a milestone for our destination. First and foremost, it is the first time the NBA has agreed to play an All Star game in a city that doesn't have an NBA franchise. We were very excited to be the first community to do that. Second, it really raises the profile of Las Vegas in the sporting world. Throughout our history, we've always found a high correlation between sporting enthusiasts and people who like to gamble. There's that degree of risk-taking, that degree of involvement in your leisure activity whether you're actually playing a sport or sitting in an arena as a fan. There's that same connection to the casino experience, whether you're actually participating in the activity. Anytime we can tie our brand to a sporting event proves to be very successful for us.

So these major sporting events really fit in the whole brand awareness mentality?

The National Finals Rodeo is another example of that, where 10 days out of the month of December every year, Las Vegas turns into a Country and Western community, and we have the premier rodeo event of the world headquartered in Las Vegas. The NASCAR race we have every spring is another example of tapping into that NASCAR world and cobranding Las Vegas and NASCAR racing.

How much involvement does the individual hotel have?

The individual hotels are very involved, and the individuals they assign to fulfill that role are really at the level of the individual market segments. For example, when we're developing a campaign for citywide trade shows and conventions, we'll work with the hotel directors that specialize in the meetings world for their hotels. When we're working at campaigns that target the leisure traveler, we'll work with the sales directors at the hotels that work with wholesale tour operators or international marketing elements. We'll tie their marketing segment approach into our market segment approach for those specific markets. When we work on diversity or minority marketing programs, we will work with those hotel executives that specialize in their diversity marketing programs.

What would be an example of a diversity marketing program?

Right now we have programs specific to four diversity submarkets: the Hispanic market, the African American market, the Asian market, and the gay and lesbian market.

Is the Hispanic market more gambling, or more just leisure/entertainment?

We have had most of our success with the Hispanic market to be centered around the Spanish holidays, as well as generational family travel, where the grandparents, parents, and adult children travel together. So, many of our programs in this market segment are specific to these criteria.

What about the African American market?

For the African American segment, most of the programs are focused on special events, or special entertainers, so we have jazz concerts that might have specific entertainers that are heavily followed by the African American community. This fall, we have a syndicated radio personality, Tom Joyner, who will be doing live broadcasts from Las Vegas for a week, and then we have specific minority marketing programs targeting the African American market in partnership with his airing of the show in Las Vegas.

What about the gay and lesbian market?

The gay and lesbian market is our newest market, and we're still in the process of developing programs. We are looking for opportunities that will capitalize on special events that may be of interest to this market, as well as some customer service issues that are letting them know that this marketing segment is welcome in the community and will be treated appropriately.

When you develop these five-year and 18-month marketing plans, how long does it typically take to put them together, and how many people are actually involved?

We've been doing it for 20 years now, so our system is pretty well in place. Our marketing plans are drafted in a three-month window prior to the release of the physical document. We'll start the strategy meetings first with our stakeholders internally, and then working with the hotel community and our board of directors. Then, as a final element, the full report is presented to our board of directors for final adoption.

Does your advertising agency help with that plan, or do you do it all yourself?

We are in a partnership with our advertising agency, and the advertising agency is actually the author, so they do the interview process, they work with the research companies to complete the research and to integrate the research, and they are the day-to-day liaison with the groups that have been involved. The advertising agency is also the final author.

So consumer research plays a key role in developing the marketing plan?

Consumer research plays a key role in developing the Las Vegas marketing plan. The Las Vegas CVB was one of the first CVBs that had a dedicated internal research department which we can trace back to 1972, the first year that we started incorporating and dedicating resources to research, and that has been a key element of all of our marketing plans.

How long did you hold the position as head of research for the Convention Bureau?

Seven years.

And from there you moved into your current position?

No, actually from there I went to director of Internet marketing for three years, developing Internet marketing programs. From the Internet director position, I went to vice president of marketing.

What other insights could you give to undergraduate and graduate students that might help them with marketing plans?

Specific to marketing and destination, I think the biggest thing that Las Vegas has learned over the years is that, while understanding the product and understanding the individual stakeholders' needs, the biggest thing to take into account when developing a marketing plan is understanding individual consumer experience. So, in addition to just focusing on your product offering and the tangible things, the most successful marketing plans really understand the experience of visiting the destination. There is a difference between simply marketing your destination based on the "what" and the "who." Really, marketing is based on the "why," and how it transcends the visitor experience.

Used by permission from Terry Jicinsky.

The marketing plan is the working document that the hospitality enterprise develops to guide specific action steps during the forthcoming year. Although sometimes marketing plans are written for future years, they are usually written for just one year at a time. Plans to capture business that may materialize several years down the road, for example, from major groups and conventions may also be used.

The marketing plan of a business unit is derived from its strategy and mission statement, which, in turn, derives from the corporate strategy and corporate mission statement.* In many hospitality firms, the corporate level and the business unit level are one and the same, so the strategic plan and the marketing plan will be at one level only. On the other hand, many hospitality firms do not do strategic planning, develop annual marketing plans, or even have mission statements. This can be a mistake. Marketing plans are quite common in hotel chains and large restaurant companies, but not so common in smaller businesses, especially restaurants. Our focus here is on the individual property, the most common application in hospitality.

Requirements for a Marketing Plan

There are three key elements to a successful marketing plan:

1. It is workable.
2. It is realistic and flexible.
3. It has measurable, achievable goals.

Too many plans fail in one or more of these respects which, by their nature, overlap each other.

The marketing plan has to remain simple and easy to execute. Two-hundred-page marketing plans with a list of 100 action steps may be impressive, but are not workable. Too many businesses confuse activity with productivity. The result is poor performance and frustration. The marketing plan that is the simplest, listing just the key items to be completed, will be the most focused and successful.

The marketing plan must also be realistic and flexible. Although an analogy to a road map is somewhat old, it is still valid today. A road map is useful if one is lost in a highway system, but not in a swamp whose topography is constantly changing. A simple compass that indicates the general direction and allows you to use your own ingenuity in overcoming difficulties is far more valuable.[1]

The topography of the hospitality industry changes rapidly these days. Marketing plans, even more than strategic plans, should always be adaptable to changes in the business topography. Thus, marketing plans must constantly be reviewed and reevaluated. This is not to say that they should be changed at the sign of the slightest aberration; a good marketing plan has some stability to it. It simply means that you must not be locked into a position when the situation changes and there is evidence that this position no longer is the most effective one. The impact of the rapidly changing distribution channel of the Internet provides a good example. Strategies set in January for marketing on the Internet will most likely change by June of the same year, if not sooner!

The marketing plan must be appropriate for the business in terms of capacity, image, scope, and risk, as well as feasible in terms of time and resources available for exe-

---

*It may be helpful to refer back to Exhibit 5-4 to review the differences between strategic marketing and marketing management.

cution. This would seem to be a fairly obvious statement, but it is often violated. Owners' demands, corporate demands, management's demands, and others lead to many marketing plans that simply have little or no chance of success. Although a marketing plan will have objectives, they should be based solely and entirely on the characteristics of the market and the resources available to implement the plan. Wild-eyed dreams and wishful thinking will not overcome the realities of the marketplace just because someone higher up says, "**Raise the numbers**" (a hotel industry expression meaning increase occupancy and average rate).

The marketing plan should assign specific responsibilities, with times and dates for accomplishment of measurable and achievable goals, both individually and as a total effort. As an example: "Raise occupancy four percentage points," or "Raise REVPAR four dollars." Continuous follow-up ensures that these responsibilities will be met or changed, as need be. This provision requires that the plan be thoroughly understood by everyone in the organization. A good plan indicates how marketing activities are integrated with all of the other activities of the operation. What this means is that responsibility for implementing the marketing plan does not stop at the door of the marketing office. Although the details of the entire plan will not go to every person in the workforce, the essence of the plan should do exactly that.

A Bangkok hotel, for example, planned to attract a market segment of German families with children on vacation at a package rate. The promotion was a success and the families came, but no one had made adequate plans, as promised in the promotion, for children's activities, babysitters, or even extra beds to be placed in the rooms.

A Valentine's Day promotion at a large New York City hotel was part of a well-written marketing plan. The hotel "sold out" on the promotion, making it a financial success. Unfortunately, the front office manager forgot to tell the garage that the promotion included free parking. The result was a one and a half hour wait to park and another hour to retrieve a car the next day. A full hotel with angry customers is not an example of a well-executed marketing plan.

Any plan that succeeds in attracting the market but fails to fulfill its promises, explicit or implicit, to that market will be self-defeating in the long term. Personnel cannot deliver what marketing promises if they don't know what those promises are or don't have the tools to deliver them.

A good marketing plan provides direction for an operation. It states where you are going and what you are going to have to do to get there. It builds employee and management confidence through shared effort and teamwork toward common goals. It recognizes weaknesses, emphasizes strengths, and deals with reality. It seeks and exploits opportunities. And last but certainly not least, a good marketing plan gets everyone into the act.

Some marketing plans are no more than a description of the facility, a list of possible competitors and their facilities, an advertising and sales plan, and a forecast and budget. These are necessary but not sufficient elements for a marketing plan to succeed. Like everything else we have said in this book, the test of the marketing plan is embodied in the question, How will the customer be served?

 Web Browsing Exercise

Use your favorite search engine and type in the words "marketing plan." Examine in detail one or two of the sites you find. Be prepared to discuss in detail in class what you found and what you learned.

Development of the Marketing Plan

As in strategic planning, the marketing plan begins with a situation analysis. Here, however, we are dealing with greater specifics. Our goal is to decide how our marketing resources will be used to best attract and serve designated markets.

Therefore, it is best to begin with a short, simple version of the mission statement of the individual property, which sets forth its broad mission, keeping in mind the corporate philosophy and the master strategy. For example, consider the hotel that picks up on the corporate mission and adds a short mission for each of its functional departments, as shown in Exhibit 21-1.

 Web Browsing Exercise

Find a corporate mission statement for a hotel, restaurant, or travel/tourism company. Using the example from Exhibit 21-1, add a short mission statement for each department or position. Be prepared to discuss in class.

Following is the property mission statement from a five-star (four-star deluxe by French nomenclature) hotel in Paris, part of a small luxury chain, that we will be using as an example throughout this chapter.

- Grand expectations . . .
- Pleasant surprises . . .
- We will consistently serve our guests, employees, and owners by exceeding expectations and continually enhancing our standards of service excellence.
- Listening, not hearing . . .
- Doing, not just acting . . .
- Anticipating, not just serving . . .
- Caring, genuinely.

EXHIBIT 21-1	Mission Statement

CORPORATE

The corporation is a socially sensitive organization committed to its team members and customers, and to the communities in which we do business. We are committed to the recognition and satisfaction of human needs through integrity, quality, and communications. As an industry leader, we create a quality product and a quality work environment, which will result in superior financial performance and long-term asset appreciation.

FUNCTIONAL AREAS

- *Human Resources:* We are the human tools that ensure the success of our team members by providing a healthy environment through competitive recruitment, development recognition, and compensation.
- *Housekeeping:* We will do our best to provide you with clean and comfortable accommodations each and every day.
- *Engineering:* We are committed to doing it right the first time.
- *Food & Beverage:* We provide each and every guest with an exceptional dining experience, using the freshest ingredients available and presenting our products in an interesting, efficient, friendly, and professional manner.
- *Front Office:* We are empowered and committed to providing quality service and a friendly atmosphere—at your home away from home.
- *Reservations:* There are no hesitations when you make reservations—no matter which channel you use.
- *Sales:* We will demonstrate and encourage a level of service that inspires our fellow team members. We will respect each team member as we work together to achieve excellence and have fun in the process.

This will establish the context within which the marketing plan will be developed, which will be restated later as mission objectives.

A further statement at this point should include what has worked well in the past and broad objectives for the coming year, such as to increase actual market share from 8 to 10 percent* or, qualitatively, to reach or expand new markets or to project a better image.

The next step is to complete the first major portion of the plan, data collection.

Data Collection

Data collection can be divided into three parts: external, competitive, and internal.

External Environment

External data are about the environment, including international and domestic trends. There are also numerous industry trends to be considered, such as the growth or decline of various market segments, building trends affecting future supply, room occupancy, eating-out trends and new concept trends. We discussed much of this in Chapters 5 through 9. Let it suffice here to say that the marketing plan should include data on any competitor in the forthcoming year from which we can reasonably expect to take customers or to which we could conceivably lose customers.

Then there are external impacts such as state, regional, or national tourism promotions; major new tourist attractions; new industries in the area; new office buildings being built; airline routes added or removed; plant closings; companies merged and moved; new origin markets of visitors; and new convention centers being built. Every factor does not affect every operation; the key is to recognize those that may affect yours. The marketing plan has to deal with these factors, prepare for them, and, whenever possible, capitalize on them or counteract them.

For example, we know of one restaurateur who operated a very successful restaurant for a number of years until business began declining quite drastically. Because this operation was in the country and some distance off a main highway, the operator concluded that people were simply not traveling as often or as far because of the cost of gasoline. Closer analysis revealed, however, that his competition was doing better than ever. In fact, the tastes of the market had changed and new markets had emerged. Instead of adapting to the market by changing his menu, which had remained pretty much the same for 30 years, he watched his business gradually disappear.

Competitive Environment

The second area of data collection deals with competitive data. It is important that the local marketing team collect data on all feasible competitors within logical boundaries. Understand that "logical boundaries" may mean the hotel or restaurant across the street or one that is 3,000 miles away. The competition for the convention market for the Hotel del Coronado in San Diego includes the Homestead Resort in Virginia; the Greenbrier Resort in West Virginia; the Cloister in Sea Island, Georgia; the Breakers Resort in Florida; and the Hyatt Regency in Maui, not to mention many others.

---

*An interesting side note: Jack Welch, CEO of General Electric for many years and considered by many to have been one of the top CEOs in industry, is noted for saying, "I don't want my fair share; I want my UNfair share."

A motel in North Overshoe, Maine, competes with a motel in South Skislope, Maine, even though they are 30 miles apart. The Club Med in Eleuthera, Bahamas, competes with the all-inclusive resorts in Jamaica. A restaurant in the city competes with the one in the suburbs. And McDonald's competes with the convenience store, but, by the same token, neither one competes with the French restaurant located between them. **Competition**, as defined by the marketing plan, is any business competing for the same customer with the same or a similar product or a reasonable alternative that the customer has an opportunity to purchase at the same time and in the same context. As we discussed in earlier chapters, the best way to understand who is the competition is to ask your current customers where they would have stayed had they not stayed with you. Another way is to call a hotel you know is full on a given night and ask where they recommend you stay instead.

As in everything, of course, there may be exceptions. We may want to expand this perspective in a period of slow economic growth. At these times, it may be necessary to reach down-market from the current level of customers in order to maintain acceptable profit margins. This happened after the terrorist attacks on the United States on September 11, 2001. With very little travel, hotel rates dropped significantly, and what may have been out of a customer's budget range suddenly became affordable.

The marketing team must take an objective stance when it comes to evaluating the competition. While we all like to believe we have the best product to sell in our product class, this may lull us into a false sense of security and the competition can move by us very quickly. The marketing plan must be truly objective and realistic about the products evaluated for the best results. After making a list of all of the competitors for your product, the minimum information shown in Exhibit 21-2 will be needed.

Once again, keep in mind that competition is all relative. Traditional boundaries of location may no longer apply. For a restaurant in New York City, the competition may encompass a three-block radius that is less than one-quarter square mile. For a five-star resort, the competition might be located thousands of miles away. When determining who your competition is, the question must be asked, Where else do/might my customers or potential customers usually go?

If you do not know who your competition is or care to validate your assumptions, just ask the customer. They will tell you what other hotels they prefer to patronize in the destination. They will tell you the other restaurants in which they dine when they are not in your establishment.

In the development of the marketing plan, it is also critical to keep in mind the fact that you want new customers and that you are looking for opportunities to attract them. This means that sometimes you have to break the "rules" of competition. For example, a Hilton property might normally be positioned against Sheraton, Hyatt, and Westin. In good times, this might be correct. However,

---

EXHIBIT 21-2 **Competitive Information Needed in the Marketing Plan**

DESCRIPTION

A brief description is needed of the physical attributes of the competing hotel or restaurant or lounge (or, for marketing tourism destinations, countries, states, or cities). Examine strengths as well as weaknesses. Determine such things as when the product was last renovated, plans for upgrading in the near future, physical facilities, and all features that compete with yours—that is, the product/service mix. The description should include both tangible and intangible features, relative quality, personnel, procedures, management, reservation systems, distribution networks, marketing efforts and successes and failures, promotions, market share, image, positioning, chain advantages and disadvantages, and so forth. All of these items will be important in the final analysis. A physical inventory and description—number of rooms, meeting space, F&B outlets, and so on—is simply not enough. All strengths and weaknesses need to be defined.

CUSTOMER BASE

Who are your competitors' customers? Why do these customers go there? Are they potentially your customers? Part of the marketing plan will focus on creating demand for your product. Much of the plan will focus on attracting customers away from your competitors. It will be difficult to take customers from your competition if you do not know who their customers are. In a restaurant situation, for example, do your competitors have a high volume of senior citizens eating at traditionally quiet times,

a group that you desire? Does their lounge have a successful happy hour that you could augment for your lounge, and, if so, what type of people go there? Does a competitive hotel have a higher percentage of transient guests than your own? What particular market segments does the competition attract?

PRICE STRUCTURE

Where is your competition in relation to price? Although food and beverage prices are relatively easy to obtain, the product delivered for the price is also important. Is their $6.95 chef's salad as good as yours for $8.95? When analyzing prices, you must compare apples with apples. Published guest room prices are relatively easy to discover. Negotiated prices with volume producers take a little more effort but usually can be obtained from purchasers or directories made available to the public.

FUTURE SUPPLY

It is important to determine whether any new projects will affect your competitive environment in the future. This information can normally be obtained from the chamber of commerce or other local sources. The fact that a new 300-room hotel is scheduled to break ground soon will be very important when developing your marketing plan. Likewise, if the building that houses a major food and beverage competitor is scheduled for demolition to make way for a new office park, this could also influence your decision-making process for the following year.

when occupancies are low—as mentioned earlier after the terrorist attacks of 2001 in the United States—the Hilton hotel might consider customers that it could capture at a profit from other competitors. If rooms are going vacant, a "normal" Holiday Inn customer might be a target of the marketing plan for the same Hilton. A Holiday Inn customer paying $95 for a room that is offered at $125 but costs only $25 to clean may be a good customer to have when the room might otherwise be vacant. In addition, there might be a longer-term benefit—retaining this person as a regular customer. On the other hand, the Red Roof Inn customer who only wants a room at $59 would not be considered an alternative target.

Internal Environment

The third area of collection is that of internal data. One hopes that accurate and adequate records have been kept and much of this information will be readily at hand. Once you have prepared your first marketing plan, you will have said, at least a dozen times, "I wish I knew that." Thus, you will have set up procedures so that next year you will know "that."

The first category of internal data that hotels and restaurants should have at all times is current data on occupied rooms by market segment: occupancy ratio, fair market share, actual market share, revenues, average rate (total and by market segment), REVPAR, market segments served, restaurant covers, seat turnovers, check average, food-to-beverage ratios (total and for each outlet), and ratios as a percentage of gross revenue. These figures should be broken down, seasonally, by month, week, and day of the week. This is also the place to identify market segments and target markets—past, present, and future. These are "hard" data and the easiest to obtain, but this is not the place to stop. Now list what you know about the markets:

- Who they are?
- What do they like?
- What are their needs and wants?
- Why do they come here?
- Where would they go if they didn't come here?
- What are their complaints?
- What are their characteristics, attitudes, opinions, and preferences?
- What is the market's perception and awareness?

If you are unable to answer these questions, it is time to start doing some research. At a minimum, start talking to your customers. Have personnel in every single department keep logs on all customer comments—good, bad, and otherwise.

Formal research is even better. A basic tenet of all effective marketing is that you must know your market. Yet it is surprising how few hospitality establishments do. This is why so many marketing plans, rather than addressing what they will do for the customer, deal with bricks and mortar, physical facilities, inaccurate definitions of the competition, too broad market segments (e.g., the business traveler), vague budgets and forecasts, and unfocused advertising. Marketing intelligence is discussed in length in Chapter 11.

The second category of internal data collection is the objective listing of resource strengths and weaknesses, including the bricks and mortar. What is the condition of the property? Where is it weak and where is it strong? How can or should it be improved? What does it offer in terms of facilities? How attractive is the location?

Then, the hardest part—how strong is management? The marketing team? Personnel training, experience, and attitude? How are guests being treated? What do complaints look like? How successful have marketing efforts been in the past? What is customers' image of the property? What is the property's position in the marketplace? This is the time for realistic objectivity, not glossing over or wishful thinking. Finally, make a list of what you do not know—that is, what additional research you may need.

To give an idea of how all of this comes together, some extracts from the data collection portion of the actual marketing plan of a five-star hotel in Paris are shown in Exhibit 21-3.*

Data Analysis

Thus far, we have been discussing only the collection of data. It is wise to complete this stage first without attempting any **data analysis**, because you want to obtain the complete picture. Analyzing different factors in isolation can be misleading.

Analysis follows the same flow as the data collection process. Essentially, we want to draw some conclusions about market position, market segments, customer behavior, environmental impacts, growth potential, strengths and weaknesses, threats and opportunities, performance trends, customer satisfaction, resource needs and limitations, and other factors that will be pertinent to the marketing plan.

Environmental and Market Trend Analysis

The first data to look at are environmental and market trends. Are they positive or negative? How will or can they affect us? How can we take advantage of or compensate for

---

* The entire marketing plan is 78 pages, so we can show only excerpts.

EXHIBIT 21-3	**Data Collection Abstracts from a Paris Hotel Marketing Plan**

ECONOMY

The economy in France is wrestling with the creation of the postwar socialist state, the European Union (EU), and the euro. The latter, especially, is having multiple effects on pricing and operating costs. High unemployment has put pressure on the government to reduce benefits to workers to increase jobs. Neighboring European states, as well as China and India, are producing quality goods with one-third of the fixed labor costs. In addition, there is unrest within a segment of the population who do not feel as if they have been treated fairly. Riots captured world attention, and potential tourists and potential new businesses considered other locations within Europe.

EXTERNAL IMPACTS

Although Paris remains a strong destination in the worldwide marketplace, pricing has become an issue. Five-star hotel rooms are more expensive in Paris than in Los Angeles, New York, and London. The result is occupancy that is way down, making most hotels unprofitable. Customers are coming to Paris from other European destinations for only one- and two-day trips, leaving rooms empty almost half the time.

Internal impacts—while service levels remain high, workers share a growing anxiety about the French economy. At this writing, the country has a high unemployment rate and Euro Disney continues to lose money. Will jobs be combined or eliminated to meet owners' needs? Will the customers return after the renovations or be absorbed by another hotel in the area?

FUTURE OF OUR MARKETS

The European Union made travel among citizens of member countries much easier. The single currency has been a success for the participating countries. Overall, the economy of Europe itself is growing, led by the United Kingdom, Paris' largest feeder market. Tourists, however, are more prone to short holidays and weekends and packages, especially in summer, our busiest season. Company individual bookings have also declined.

---

them? What are our alternatives? How long will they last? What courses of action are possible and feasible? How do these fit together?

Exhibit 21-4 provides insight into dining trends by Robin Uler, senior vice president of food & beverage, spas and retail services, and Brad Nelson, vice president of culinary and corporate chef for Marriott International, Inc. Exhibit 21-5 provides insight into the do's and don'ts of hotel technology presented by Terence Ronson of Pertlink Limited (www.pertlink.net). Both exhibits provide examples of information that is very necessary for the development of marketing plans.

 Web Browsing Exercise

Use your favorite search engine and look up dining trends. How, if at all, have dining trends changed since the publication of this book? How would you recommend that a restaurant incorporate these trends into its marketing plan? Be prepared to discuss in class.

Competitive and Demand Analysis

What are the potentials and opportunities in the marketplace? This requires a close analysis of all the demand factors, various market segments, and target markets—for instance:

- What are the strongest market segments?
- What is their potential for further growth?
  - Steady?
  - Growing?
  - In decline?
- What is their contribution in room nights?
- What is their contribution in covers?
- What is their contribution in revenue?
- What can be done to accelerate a growing trend?
- What can be done to begin growth in a steady trend?
- What can be done to reverse the direction of a declining trend?
- What other segments are there, perhaps untouched, that could be developed?
- How do these segments affect our market mix?
- Are they compatible?
- Can they be expanded to fill gaps such as seasonal or day-of-week fluctuations?
- What types of business would complement these segments?
- What types of action could be taken to attract more business during low-occupancy periods?
- How does the competitive situation affect all these factors?

Property Needs Analysis

Here, we have added a new category. A property needs analysis is an analysis of major profit areas to see what gaps have to be filled. These gaps could be in occupancy, market share, average room rate, market segment mix, food sales, beverage sales, seasonal needs, and many other areas. In other words, instead of looking at where we can cut costs, we want to look at where we can increase revenues. When we have done that, we can match property needs with market needs to determine target markets and how to reach and serve them.

Needs analysis also means identifying other marketing problems. For example, there might be marketing strategies that are not working, image changes that are

EXHIBIT 21-4   Robin Uler and Brad Nelson's Top Food Trends for 2006

Robin Uler, senior vice president of food & beverage, spas, and retail services, and Brad Nelson, vice president of culinary and corporate chef for Marriott International, Inc. (NYSE: MAR), give their forecast for what's up and coming on the dining front in the coming year. Uler and Nelson are responsible for identifying and implementing culinary trends for 2,700 hotels in many of the world's greatest cities.

BACK TO BASICS AND SIZED TO ORDER

Gone are the days of starched collars, jackets and ties, and three-hour dining experiences. Guests are looking for great food served with friendly, professional care in a "buzzing" contemporary environment that offers a "sense of place." Menus will reflect this as well. Chef-crafted plates of varying sizes create a variety of tastes and flavors, and allow for a more social, casual dining experience than traditional "courses." Also, this allows diners to "graze" and determine portion control.

BREAKFAST IS BACK

The "most important meal of the day" is becoming even more important. Approachable comfort food, eggs cooked to order, and healthy options with "good carbs," low in fat and high in protein and nutrition, are starting diners' days. French toast and waffles are a growing trend. Big, fluffy buttermilk, blueberry, and apple streusel pancakes, sweet and savory waffles, and flavorful French toast are being seen more and more in restaurants and catering. New takes on breakfast basics, such as the Lemon Souffle Pancakes that are found at the restaurants of Renaissance hotels, are becoming more and more popular.

IN GOOD COMPANY

Communal tables have become a staple in many contemporary restaurants. But that will be taken a step further with the advent of "gathering areas." Many food and beverage arenas will be the new living room/dining room. Enclaves for small groups and quick quality snacks and beverages will be making their way into the hospitality industry. These will be community gathering places as well as havens for harried travelers.

TAKEAWAY

Takeout service at full-service restaurants and related venues is growing, as the combination of stress and lack of time, but with a sense of wanting the best, is leading the market's drive for more upscale foods that can be quickly delivered or purchased and consumed on the run. Many upscale markets offer this already, but this will expand into the restaurant realm. Note that restaurants will be sure to have items available to go that adapt well to traveling.

FROM THE KITCHEN TO THE BAR

With the advent of more and more premium spirits on the market and the push for evermore creative cocktails, the pairing of food and spirit in one will be on the menu. It is now as important for the bartender to be a trained "mixologist" as it is for culinary professionals in the kitchen to be trained chefs. From the appetizer paired with a special cocktail to tea- and truffle-flavored vodkas, food and drink will be a bar and restaurant menu highlight. Look for premium liquors to be paired with freshly squeezed juices and herbs, as in the thyme Cosmo or basil Mojito.

HEALTHY FOOD ... NOT DIET FOOD

As Americans become more aware of nutrition combined with waistline watching, diners are seeking healthy options on menus. Individual preferences and needs vary and trendy diet fads come and go, so menus are reflecting a variety of healthy dining offerings, from low-carb to low-fat to lower calorie, depending on preference. At full-service Marriott hotels, for example, a "Fit for You" program allows diners to select a healthy meal based on their preference, whether it be low-carb, low-cholesterol or low-fat.

SOFT, COMFORTABLE, HIP

The pendulum will start swinging away from the very angular, overly retro or stark look of many restaurants in favor of the softer and more opulent ambience. Clean, not Victorian, but comfortable and contemporary, utilizing funky domes, cut crystal, etc. for service. Gone will be the sparse white plates, replaced by a more elegant but comfortable feel.

THERE'S ALWAYS ROOM FOR ...

Highly flavored gel squares and desserts made with gelatin sheets and fresh purees are popping up on tables. From Chef Gordon Ramsey's Rhubarb Parfait to gel bites that taste like fresh mango, key lime, and other exotic fruits to the return of aspic, it's okay to admit we all love this childhood favorite and can now enjoy the slightly more sophisticated version. Puddings too are making the transition. Flavors like Amaretto Bourbon spiced rice pudding are taking diners back to childhood favorites—but with a more creative twist.

HERITAGE—BOOMERS ARE BEGINNING TO REMEMBER ...

Foods from Scandinavia and Eastern Europe—cured salmon, goulash, stuffed cabbage and the like—will make an appearance but with a contemporary twist, perhaps with a "new" kind of cabbage or Spaetzle. Look for a representation of this type of cuisine with a more modern element.

NON-"ENGINEERED" PRODUCT

More and more diners are looking for purity of product. The "microgreen" . . . well, not so much. Diners will be looking for a more "natural" product, like buttery Boston lettuce and sweet bib varieties. Menu items will be "ingredients-based." Fresh, wholesome, and locally grown. Foods that are true to the actual product and true to its roots. Many chefs are utilizing their local farmers, purchasing product grown practically in their own back yards. Some, like Melissa Kelly of Primo in Tucson, Arizona; Rockland, Maine; and Orlando, Florida, cultivate their own gardens on the restaurant grounds and are attuned to utilizing the "whole" product—no waste.

SO LONG AMUSE-BOUCHES!

We taste while shopping in the market, so why not when dining? When visiting an upscale grocery or even bulk food stores, tasting is almost essential, whether it's the fresh fruit, the cheese, or an item on sale. Look for chefs to send out samples of signature appetizers and side dishes in small tasting portions, showcasing the chef's style and creativity through a real menu item.

Source: Uler, R., & Nelson, B. (2005, December 8). Dining trends for 2006: Marriott food and beverage execs, Robin Uler and Brad Nelson, give their forecast for what's up on the dining front. Retrieved December 16, 2005, from www.hotel-online.com/News/PR2005_4th/Dec05_FoodTrends.html. Used by permission from Marriott International.

| **EXHIBIT 21-5** | **64 Do's and Don'ts of Hotel Technology** |

1. Do understand that when buying technology for your hotel you start a journey that has no destination.
2. Don't go to the expense of placing a plasma TV in the room, if it cannot be seen when working at the desk.
3. Do put at least three guest use power sockets at the desk inside the guestroom.
4. Do put a power socket by the bedside specifically for the guest to use.
5. Don't deploy a VoD system just so your guests can watch porn—make it more of an information center.
6. Don't overprice HSIA (high speed internet access—wired and wireless).
7. Do teach your staff how to offer first line tech support to guests who may have connectivity issues—don't just rely on the IT dept.
8. Do put an A/V connection panel in your room so the guest does not have to fumble around trying to connect their notebook, camera or MP3 player to the back of the TV.
9. Do create always-on power sockets so guests can leave their notebooks on (and connected to the internet) while they are out of the room.
10. Do try to work for a few hours at the desk in your own hotel rooms and see if you like it. Come to think of it, you should also sleep in the bed, use the toilet and take a shower . . .
11. Do try and make a booking via your own hotel website, and see how easy it is.
12. Do remember that business travelers are not only men.
13. Do not put "last updated" on your website, especially if you don't do it frequently.
14. Do not give away (outsource) your services (like broadband) to 3rd party companies unless you really have no option.
15. Do think carefully about selecting an "interfaced solution" versus an "integrated solution."
16. Do focus on your cabling infrastructure ensuring it's robust and flexible enough to evolve with the business.
17. Do place a chair at the desk that is easy to slide in and out, and not just a dining table type. Make sure it can move up and down also—not all people are the same height.
18. Don't just place 3-in-1 coffee in your tea/coffee making facilities—place good and simple plain coffee also.
19. Do not clutter the desk with loads of collaterals—make it free and clear, ready for the guest to use.
20. Do check the TV channels reception in your rooms, and not just the channels you like to watch.
21. Do remember that guests are carrying more items of technology these days, with varying (international) power plugs.
22. Do understand that your guests perceive the phone on the desk, or the one beside the bed, to be too expensive to use—and by default will prefer to use their mobile phone.
23. Don't place a clock at the bedside if it cannot be read when the lights are off and the room is dark.
24. Do bear in mind that the experience of staying in your hotel will most likely start at your website. If that's unattractive, so will be your hotel.
25. Do note that if you replace CRT type displays on your reception counter with flat panels, consider viewing angles, the working position of staff and how to maintain eye contact with guests.
26. Do replace paper based banquet event signage or the type that uses white plastic or brass letters with multimedia display panels.
27. Do think about disabling all the USB ports on your hotel's PCs. They are open to abuse and pilferage of (valuable) data.
28. Do make it easy for people to work anywhere in your hotel—give them access to power sockets.
29. Do have an electronic currency exchange rate indicator at your Front Desk.
30. Do bear in mind that if your lights are programmed to turn off when the room key is removed from its holder, you should give guests at least one minute to exit the room before turning off the power.
31. Do select in-room safes that have internal power sockets so items can be charged while safely stowed away.
32. Do not have staff use Walkie-talkies, unless they have discreet ear pieces.
33. Do cut cables instead of leaving long trailing or curled up wires in rooms.
34. Do place a rechargeable flashlight by the bed that automatically illuminates during an emergency or power failure.
35. Do not place a PC in each of your guestrooms. It's a waste of money.
36. Do think about placing a full size keyboard inside the desk drawer for guest use. But at the same time, consider how to keep it clean.
37. Do remember that if you plan to place a glass surface desk in a guestroom, it's almost impossible to use a mouse, unless you place a mouse mat.
38. Do understand that technology will fail and most likely at the worst possible time—like the Friday afternoon of a long weekend. Be prepared!
39. Do not overcharge for services in the Business Center—like printing a singe A4 page—especially if your room rates are already high.
40. Do not believe that just by deploying technology in your hotel service levels will increase. This is a people business.
41. Do make the lighting levels in your guestrooms dimmable—from very bright to a nice warm and cozy mood.
42. Do place a shaving mirror close to the shaver socket.
43. Do try and place the in-room safe at a reasonable height and not one where you have to get down on all fours to try and enter the PIN.
44. Do be conscious that, if you put labels on switches that are next to the bed, the guest may be reading them upside down—and without spectacles.
45. Do have a switch which has a small glowing light that the guest can easily find when waking up in a darkened room, often disoriented by jet lag and unfamiliar surroundings.
46. Do understand that the guest may only stay in your hotel for one day, and cannot spend time working their way through complex remote control devices, often labeled in a language that is unfamiliar to them.
47. Don't place a speaker volume control in the bathroom, unless it works.
48. Do remember that guests trust their mobile phones as alarms more than they do your call center to wake them up.
49. Do have excellent bathroom lighting—consult with a woman to tell you if it's the right level.
50. Do have the Room Attendant pay attention to the noise level of the room fan coil, and report it to engineering (for immediate remedial action) if it's noisy.
51. Do stock the most popular type mobile phone battery chargers in your Business Center.
52. Do have DVD players available for guest use.
53. Don't just have PCs in your Internet corners, have a MAC as well.
54. Do print your Instant Messenger address on your Business card.

(continued)

EXHIBIT 21-5	64 Do's and Don'ts of Hotel Technology *(Continued)*

55. Do insist that your staff use a spell checker on all documents before sending them out.
56. Do make sure that all software used in your business is legal.
57. Do use the freely available technologies like RSS, Google Earth and Podcasting to help promote your business.
58. Do put an internet browsing station in your staff canteen or recreation area. Encourage your staff to check email during breaks and get familiar with the technology.
59. Do get your technology vendors to update you twice a year on what is happening with their products.
60. Don't just look at the hospitality industry when thinking about technology—look everywhere.
61. Do consider making information about your property downloadable into a PDA for easy reference by your guests.

62. Do not change any configuration or settings on a guest's computer unless you have their written approval on a liability waiver form.
63. Do perform regular system backups, and keep your data backup off-site.
64. Do make sure that the staff who escort a guest to a room informs them that your hotel has in-room HSIA installed, and offers to help make the connection.

Source: 64 do's and don'ts of hotel technology. Retrieved December 15, 2005, from www.hotel-online.com/News/PR2005_4th/Dec05_PertlinkChecklist. html. Used by permission from Terence Ronson of Pertlink Limited (www. pertlink.net).

EXHIBIT 21-6	Hypothetical Competitive Universe of ABC Hotel

Hotel	# Rooms	Available/year	% Rooms FMS*	Rooms Occupied	Sold	AMS**	Variance	Rank
ABC	200	73,000	20%	67	48,910	20%	0	3
Westin	350	127,750	35%	73	93,258	38.2%	3.2	1
Hyatt	250	91,250	25%	72	65,700	26.9%	1.9	2
Hilton	200	73,000	20%	50	36,500	14.9%	(5.1)	4
Total	1,000	365,000	100%	67	244,368	100%		

*FMS (fair market share) is the number of available rooms per hotel divided by the total number of available rooms.
**AMS (actual market share) is the number of rooms sold per hotel divided by the total number of rooms sold.

needed, ineffective advertising or promotion, pricing problems, a loss of business to a particular competitor (perhaps because of a new facility, new product or service, or even better marketing), or changing needs of a market segment that we cannot meet.

In short, property needs analysis is the identification of problems to be overcome. It makes the case clearer if we can apply some quantitative measurements to our analysis, which are no more than best estimates based on all of the data assembled. To demonstrate this, we will use a simplified case to determine what the overall increase or decrease for the product will be for the forthcoming year. Ideally, this would be done by market segment.

In this example, we will say that we are anticipating an increase of 2 percent in the demand for both group and transient hotel rooms in the product class category. From the data collected, a competitive universe can be compiled as shown in Exhibit 21-6.

Assume, also, for the purpose of this discussion, that a Crowne Plaza of 200 rooms is opening next year with a projected occupancy of 55 percent. Its forecasted market mix is 50 percent group and 50 percent transient.

Now, for the purpose of developing the marketing plan, we have some quantitative data with which to work. One thing is immediately obvious: ABC Hotel has a relatively low occupancy and is barely achieving its fair market share. After all the data collected in the situation analysis have been analyzed, two main areas of concentration must be addressed: creating new business and capturing competitors' business.

Creating New Business. Given the current situation, what plans can be developed to create new demand for the product? McDonald's created new demand for its product by opening for breakfast. Package weekends have created new demand for hotel products in the past. Spas are the latest amenity driving demand for many hotels and resorts. Creating new demand in the hospitality industry, however, may be the toughest part of marketing. The important point to remember is that we are creating demand that until now did not exist for a product. This usually means creating a new use.

The advertisement by the Fairmont Hotel in Exhibit 21-7 is an example of a promotion to create new business. In this case, the target market is people who want to spoil themselves. The objective of the hotel, of course, is to build weekend business. This is different from, for example, selling a corporate meeting package where meeting planners have already decided what they need and are only concerned with where to find it. That constitutes direct marketing against the competition, rather than creating a new use for the product. Other parts of the marketing plan will carry out and specify the implementation of this promotion in terms of the specific target market.

Capturing Competitors' Business.   Most marketing plan program executions are concentrated in the area of capturing business from the competition. Specifically, let's return to the competitive universe depicted in Exhibit 21-6. ABC Hotel's main competitors are Westin, Hyatt, and Hilton, plus the new Crowne Plaza being built. A demand analysis for these five hotels, two of which are capturing more than fair market share while ABC and Hilton are not, might appear as shown in Exhibit 21-8.

A red flag should be raised with this scenario. Although the forecast reveals an increase in demand for the hotel product, the increase in supply will be greater than the increase in demand. Each hotel will now be fighting for a smaller piece of the pie. If ABC Hotel does everything the same as the year before, it will be drawing on a smaller pool of rooms and occupancy will drop even further. In fact, ABC and its four competitors are now competing for 209,105 rooms versus 244,368 in the previous year, after the new Crowne Plaza takes its share.

ABC's marketing team can now see the task that lies before it. Just to maintain the occupancy of the year before, it will have to create new demand for the product, aggressively attack competitors for new business, and maintain its own customer base, which the competition will be trying to lure away with their marketing plans. It will also have to exceed its new FMS by 2.95 percentage points, something it hasn't been able to do in the past. ABC's strength may be as a transient hotel, whereas this may be a weakness of the other properties. In this case, ABC might choose to direct its major marketing effort toward that market.

Another possibility is that ABC has neglected the group market and needs to concentrate greater effort in that direction. Of course, it may have to make major efforts in both directions. Let us assume, for the sake of argument and because it is easier to demonstrate, that there is a high degree of price sensitivity in the market within either one or both of these segments. In either case, specific marketing plans must be made to attack the competitive hotels in order to capture rooms from them. The plans might call for

lowering prices specific days of the week or times of the year when ABC's occupancy suffers the most.

The ABC example is clearly an oversimplified one. There are innumerable other factors affecting any similar situation and numerous alternative approaches. In fact, we haven't even mentioned the customer in this discussion, and that database would be the first one to consider! The point we want to make is that there is an absolute need for complete and adequate data and information followed by a thorough analysis of all possible considerations. It is only through such methods that workable, realistic, and effective marketing plans are developed.

Internal Analysis

We now turn to the internal analysis. Using the realistic and objective data we have gathered, we start by asking questions such as those shown in Exhibit 21-9. We would do this by segment and target market. Strategies by segment for a hotel might include efforts directed against group sales, consortia, national sales, local corporate, weekends, or international markets. Catering might include segments such as freestanding, local corporate, evenings, and social markets. Descriptions on how each market should be addressed should be outlined in this section.

The list of internal analysis questions could go on indefinitely. Once again, we have to state that workable, effective, and realistic marketing plans can be developed only through the gathering of complete and adequate information and its thorough and objective analysis.

Market Analysis

Our final step in analysis focuses on the market itself, the customer. Because this entire book is about the hospitality customer, it would be redundant to repeat here all that we have said about this ever-changing individual who is the reason for the existence of any hospitality enterprise. For purposes of developing the marketing plan, this step means determining where the gaps are, where needs are unfulfilled, where problems are not being solved, and where there are niches the competition is not filling.

This analysis must be matched with the environmental trends, the competitive and demand analysis, the property needs analysis, and the internal analysis. We would, of course, combine all of these analyses by segment and target market. We are then ready to develop a mission statement for the property, determine opportunities, establish objectives, and begin preparation of the actual marketing plan, which will include a plan and course of action for each segment or target market.

EXHIBIT 21-7 This advertisement by the Fairmont Hotel is an example of a promotion to create new business.

Source: Fairmont Hotels and Resorts, Bermuda. Used by permission.

EXHIBIT 21-8 **Hypothetical Demand Analysis**

	Total	Group Segment	Transient Segment	New ABC FMS	@20% AMS
Rooms sold previous year	244,368	146,231	98,137		
Next year projection with 2% increase in demand	249,255	149,156	100,099		
New supply from Crowne Plaza	40,150	20,075	20,075	16.7%	49,851

EXHIBIT 21-9 **Internal Analysis Questions**

- What is the gap between what your customers want and need, what you promise them, and the product/service you provide?
- How well do you meet or exceed customer expectations?
- How does the market's estimation of your product/service agree with yours? What makes you think so?
- What items, product improvements, or services are needed to improve customer satisfaction?
- Are you actually delivering what you think you are?
- What patterns are appearing in guest comments? What types of problems seem to recur? What areas seem to need improvement?

- Do you have the proper organization to accomplish what you are trying to? For instance, although the manager is a strong operations person, does she understand the customer?
- Do you reward your staff strictly on bottom-line results? If so, does it show up in matters affecting the customers?
- Do you know, identify, and deal with your real strengths and weaknesses?

The Mission and Marketing Position Statement

The mission statement at the beginning of the marketing plan flows from the strategic mission statement and from the corporate mission statement. It differs from the former, however, in that it is a broad statement of objectives at the unit level. The general guideline of the corporate mission statement is a good starting point. In multi-unit organizations, however, there can be great variety. Many chains have diversified products selling in diversified markets for di-

versified uses. Corporate strategies established in corporate headquarters in Atlanta, Chicago, New York, London, Paris, or Tokyo do not necessarily fit the situation in India, Germany, Kuwait, Minneapolis, or Los Angeles.

The situational analysis of the marketing plan provides the test of the strategy and necessitates rewriting the local mission statement. Therefore, only after the situational analysis has been completed do we recommend writing the marketing plan mission statement and, if necessary, adjusting the strategic mission statement. Recall, moreover, that the latter is the long-term mission; the marketing plan mission is set forth one year at a time. This mis-

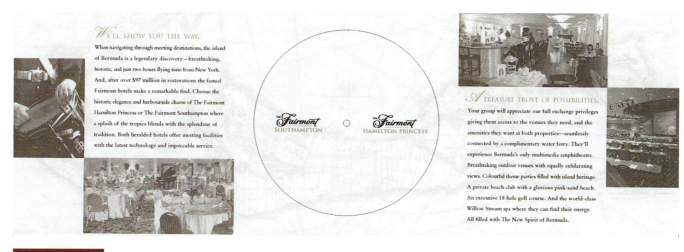

EXHIBIT 21-7 *(Continued).*

EXHIBIT 21-10 **Marketing Plan Opportunity Analysis of Paris Hotel**

A. Market segments relating to existing customer mix
  1. Corporate groups
  2. Corporate individual bookings
  3. Leisure travelers from abroad
  4. Weekend packages with special features
  5. Special off-season incentives
B. New markets
  1. Packages for individual travelers
  2. U.S. upscale travel agencies

  3. Incentive market—London, New York
  4. High-ranking government officials
C. Image
  1. More professional and colorful F&B promotions
  2. Improved reputation of service and cuisine
  3. Provide better background information about city, emphasize price/value
  4. Professional advertising to improve hotel image

sion statement will have specific objectives such as "to be the business traveler's hotel of choice in the city." More specific objectives will be contained in the statement of objectives, such as "increasing our ratio of business customers to pleasure travelers from 55 to 65 percent."

Further, the intended "position" in the eyes of customers will be identified. This statement flows from the strengths and weaknesses of the competition as well as the property for which the plan is written. For example, our Paris hotel example would be positioned, at minimum, as one of the top five luxury hotels in Paris. Other attributes, such as a "corporate luxury hotel," might also be part of the positioning to that market segment.

Opportunity Analysis

If we have done a thorough job of data collection and analysis, we should now be able to determine the opportunities available. The section heading is self-explanatory and can best be discussed by example. Therefore, we abstract again from the marketing plan of the Paris hotel previously mentioned, as shown in Exhibit 21-10.

The opportunities in Exhibit 21-10, although perhaps too general, have been developed after analysis of the market, market segments, the competition, trends, the needs of the property, and so forth. Its brief form belies the groundwork that goes into identifying the opportunities. Sometimes this groundwork is not done—that is, someone says something like, "How about the incentive market? We don't have any of that business. That's an opportunity! Let's put it down." Of course, a thorough study of the incentive market, its needs and wants, and the organization's ability to serve them is necessary first. Opportunities, in the true sense, are not just something that are "out there"; they are, instead, a match among customer needs, an organization's competencies, and, one hopes, a lapse in the competition.

Objectives and Methods

The next step in the marketing plan is to establish the objectives and how they will be accomplished. Again, this is better explained through an actual illustration, so we continue to use the marketing plan of the French five-star hotel, as shown in Exhibit 21-11.

EXHIBIT 21-11   Objectives and Methods from Paris Hotel Marketing Plan

A. To increase yearly occupancy from 58 to 64 percent
  1. Review annual forecast on a monthly and weekly basis to ensure an overall and continuous view of occupancies and early actions where problem periods or days exist.
  2. Develop and advertise more attractive, unique weekend packages to increase weekend occupancy by 15 percentage points.
  3. Orient the room rate structure to the market and similar destinations worldwide.
  4. Conduct permanent hard and aggressive sales actions to increase the following:
    a. Corporate rate business—increase 10 percent from present 38 percent of occupancy
    b. Seminars and small conferences, especially in winter
    c. Winter weekend business with high-end travelers
    d. Incentive travel year-round—now 1 percent of occupancy, increase to 5 percent
B. To keep up with the competition and increase our actual market share among direct competitors in Paris from 14.7 to 16.5 percent (FMS is 15.2 percent)
  1. Provide better technological amenities for business travelers.
  2. Make better use of database on regular customers and their needs.
  3. Spruce up hospitality service and well-trained staff.
  4. Continuous sales follow-up on existing corporate clients.
  5. Continuous sales calls to potential new customers.
  6. Offer clients "just a little more" in rooms and restaurant, which will make their stay with us different from the others.
  7. Develop more creativity in sales and F&B.
C. To level out occupancy throughout the year
  1. Develop attractive (but not bargain) offers during weak periods for seminars and conferences; emphasize price/value.
  2. Develop winter all-inclusive packages for individuals.
  3. Develop new initiatives, such as room here and lunch on Champs-Elysées.
  4. Develop incentive tie-ins with exclusive Parisian boutiques.
D. To level out occupancy over the week
  1. Lower rates for winter seminars during the week.
  2. Develop packages for individuals to be distributed to London travel agents with special commission rates.
  3. Create special activities for upscale consortia to sell in the United Kingdom, Japan, and the United States.
E. To increase average rate from €520 to €580
  1. Increase corporate rates and add value with business amenities.
  2. Increase rates in the commercial business market by 10 percent.
  3. Build higher rate in suites through luxury room amenities, upgrades, and services
  4. Try to reduce low-rate contracts during the high season.
  5. Develop exclusive weekend packages at higher prices where the market is not price sensitive.
F. To increase F&B sales by 10 percent overall and average check in signature dining room from €220 to €260
  1. Improve signature restaurant image with better selling of individual items (vs. degustation menu) and wines.
  2. Appeal more to in-house guests through the following:
    a. Tasteful promotional material in rooms, lobby, reception, and other guest service areas
    b. Food promotion frames inside and in front of elevators
    c. Sales-trained people in bar, restaurant
    d. Training guest service agents to ask at check-in if guests want to reserve table in restaurant
  3. Develop the local market through promotions.
    a. Special chef presentation dinner promotions
    b. Wedding promotions for exclusivity and security
    c. Charity dinners at the high end
    d. Attract traders in the financial sector with an after-work promotion

EXHIBIT 21-12   Possible Marketing Plan Objectives

- Changes in marketing direction (defined by competitive set or business mix or both)
- Defensive or offensive marketing moves
- New opportunities (new market segments)
- Other specific product line objectives (e.g., increase food, beverage, spa, or other revenues)
- Market share objectives—overall and by market segment, such as geographic, demographic, psychographic, group, FIT, package, etc.
- Pricing objectives (defined as an indexed value against other properties in the competitive set)
- Sales and promotion objectives
- Advertising objectives (in terms of awareness or intention)
- Channel, distribution, and intermediary objectives, such as the percentage of business from travel agents
- Research objectives
- Image and positioning objectives
- Double occupancy objectives
- Customer loyalty and repeat business objectives
- Customer satisfaction objectives
- Revenue per occupied room objectives

The objectives listed in Exhibit 21-11 are specific and fairly typical of hotel marketing plans. Many are directly measurable. **Action plans** are designed to carry out each one. There could be many other kinds of objectives, including strategic ones, particularly those that derive from the identification of market needs, such as those in Exhibit 21-12.

We caution once again not to try to accomplish too many things at once. Make objectives reasonable so you can attain them well.

Marketing efforts must be directed to existing customers as well. Relationship marketing can always be improved. These customers may, in fact, represent your best opportunity and the target of the most important objectives. This part of the plan addresses current patrons and should be designed to make them "competition proof." Because the main emphasis of the marketing plan will be on capturing competitors' business, so too will be the emphasis of competitors' marketing plans. If the focus is entirely on bringing in new customers and present customers are forgotten, then the marketing plan is simply going to be one of robbing Peter to pay Paul. Replacing current customers with new customers is never cost efficient.

A documented plan to keep guests coming back and reduce exposure to competitors' attempts to steal customers should be an integral part of any marketing plan. Once again, however, this does not necessarily mean giveaway programs. The basic task of marketing is to fulfill the brand's promises, not give away the product.

Action Plans

Action plans dictate how the marketing plan will be carried out. They assign specific responsibility to individuals and dates for accomplishment. An action plan is a detailed list of the action steps necessary for carrying out the strategies and tactics for reaching each objective. One format for an action plan is shown in Exhibit 21-13, but there are numerous variations on the theme.

Action plans deal with the various parts of the marketing mix, which, of course, result in the implementation of the marketing plan. For example, the action plan for the communications mix might incorporate advertising (both offline and online), direct mail, personal sales efforts, promotions, merchandising, and public relations campaigns. Each of these is coordinated for maximum impact of the strategies that derive from the conclusions drawn from the creation of business and competitive strategies section of the plan.

The action plan should be developed for a full year and updated quarterly for all products and actions, consistent with the stated performance goals by market segment and time of year.

In the previous example of the promotion for the New York Palace shown in Exhibit 21-7, advertising support may be necessary in designated months to create awareness and accommodate requests for more information. An ad in a travel agency directory might be intended to offer an alternative to competition when targeting travel agencies.

Yearly schedules for other support elements of the communications mix are needed to coordinate the entire

---

EXHIBIT 21-13 **Marketing Plan Action Plan**

XYZ HOTEL MARKETING ACTION PLAN

NAME: Quarter:

BOOKING GOALS

1000 MONTH   250 WEEK   50 DAY

NEW ACCOUNTS OPENED

20 MONTH   5 WEEK   1 DAY

Action Plan by Week: **Person Responsible:**

Week 1 _____ Begin advertising campaign, corporate group   _____

Week 2 _____ Trade show schedule, third quarter   _____

Week 3 _____ Direct mail, corporate transient   _____

Week 4 _____ Good accounts function, associations   _____

Week 5 _____ Public relations for catering   _____

Week 6 _____ Public relations for catering   _____

Week 7 _____ Focus groups, meeting planners   _____

Week 8 _____ Focus groups, travel agents   _____

Week 9 _____ Image advertising campaign begins   _____

Week 10 _____ Strategy session, tour and travel   _____

Week 11 _____ Direct mail, past users   _____

Week 12 _____ Develop comarketing partners   _____ plan. A direct mail campaign might be used in conjunction with the advertising for the promotion to generate the best response. Without action plans, too many things are forgotten too often or are done too late to be effective.

There are other concerns as well. The communications mix is expensive to execute. The savvy marketing executive will constantly be looking for ways to maximize the impact of communications dollars. Cooperatively funded advertising is possible with related travel partners such as American Express. Airlines are increasingly willing to work with hotels to generate business through collective advertising and direct mail. Credit card companies are doing dual promotions with restaurants and lounges on a consistent basis to differentiate their products and combine resources. The Internet now requires resources for individual hotels to allocate money and personnel to this growing channel of business. All of these efforts require considerable advance planning and specific actions executed on time.

Except for the final forecast and component budgets, the marketing plan is now complete. Remember, this should be a "fluid" document, ready to be changed with shifts of the marketplace. This is not to suggest that the entire marketing plan be rewritten every time there is a major change in the business climate or competitive environment; if the situational analysis was done properly, the conclusions drawn should not change readily or dramatically.

Some opportunities, however, that arise during the year should be incorporated into an effective marketing plan. For example, if an opportunity arose to do a combined direct mail piece to selected customers of a reputable credit card company, it should not be passed up just because it is not in the marketing plan. Resources may be reallocated if appropriate and necessary.

The Marketing Forecast

Making accurate performance forecasts is one of the most difficult marketing responsibilities. Regardless, the best attempt possible is essential. Forecasts represent a venture into the unknown that are subject to any number of vagaries in the marketplace. Accuracy is ensured only by access to the best information available, thorough analysis, and the learned judgment of the forecaster.

Many hotel marketing plan formats require the projection of room nights for every day of the forthcoming year to forecast, by segment and day of the week, the upcoming year's business. It is not uncommon for forecasters to use some figure, say 5 percent, as the projected increase in sales over the previous year. Such a method is purely arbitrary

and may have no basis in market fact. It is better to start with a zero base each year and build the forecast according to the strategies set forth in the marketing plan. In this way, room nights, covers, and other sources of revenue are based on the performance objectives that have been realistically established. Monetary amounts, such as average room rate per segment, or average breakfast, lunch, and dinner check are used as the multipliers to forecast revenue.

Exhibit 21-14 illustrates a forecast form used by one hotel company. Again, there are many variations on the theme according to the particular situation or needs of the operation.

The Marketing Budget

The industry-wide average for marketing expenditures for average U.S. hotels falls between 4.5 and 5.5 percent of gross revenue (rooms, food, beverage, and miscellaneous). There are no reported averages for restaurants except a general figure of 2 to 3 percent of revenue spent on advertising for an individual sit-down, mid-to-upper-scale operation. As a rule of thumb, the marketing payroll expenses are normally one half of the total marketing budget, although this will vary depending on the importance of group business to the property and corresponding size of the sales force. Traditionally, resorts have slightly higher **marketing budgets** as a percentage of gross revenue because of the seasonal nature of their business, as do properties that are relatively new or find themselves battling a number of new or aggressive competitors. The overall trend in the industry has been toward increasing the marketing budget as a total percentage of revenue as the cost of implementing various aspects of the marketing program has continued to rise. For instance, marketing expenses increased 6.1 percent in 2004.

Exhibit 21-15 displays a report issued by PKF Hospitality Research that explains in detail marketing budgets in the hospitality industry.

Web Browsing Exercise

Use your favorite search engine to search for updated marketing budget statistics. Be prepared to discuss how, if at all, these statistics compare to what is presented in the book. What trends, if any, do you notice? How might an individual property respond?

The marketing budget should be a natural extension of the marketing plan—no more and no less. Once a strategy has been developed to create, steal, or keep customers, adequate funds need to be allocated to ensure success.

EXHIBIT 21-14	Hotel Occupancy Forecasting Form, by Month							

	Last Year Actual Rooms Occupied	Last Year Actual Average Rate	Last Year Actual Revenues	Budget Revenues	Budget Average Rate	Budget Rooms Rented	Month	
							January	February
Pure/transient								
Meeting conversion								
Travel & tour								
Individual								
Wholesaler								
Group								
Total travel & tour								
Contract								
Charter								
Other								
Total contract								
Commercial								
Preferred company								
Preferred guest								
Other								
Total commercial								
Special programs								
Weekend package								
Other								
Other								
Other								
Totals								
Rooms available								
% of Occupancy								

The budget will normally include the following components, regardless of the size or type of the operation. This even includes a case in which, for example, the manager of a restaurant (chain, individual, or within a hotel) performs all the marketing and sales duties. Parts of that person's salary and expenses should be allocated to the marketing budget.

■ Payroll will include all sales and administrative staff, plus any secretarial or related work.
■ Communication includes all advertising, promotion, direct mail, public relations, collateral, and related items.
■ Travel includes all related travel.
■ Office expenses include telephone and related office supplies.

■ Research includes all research expenses.
■ Entertainment includes entertainment of clients or prospective clients both in-house and out.
■ Agency fees and expenses include all professional services purchased from outside marketing service suppliers.

The preceding are broad and fairly obvious categories of expenditure. A further breakdown depends on the needs of the operation. It is important that marketing expenses be clearly and appropriately assigned. Exhibit 21-16 shows one hotel's monthly spreadsheet for allocating particular expenses to a given month.

The budget should be carefully prepared, not done haphazardly or by guesswork. If you are not your own boss, you will probably have to have it approved by someone. In

EXHIBIT 21-15	PKF Study Finds Hotels Increase Marketing Budgets by 6.1 Percent in 2004—Hotels Continue to Shift Marketing Dollars from Advertising to Person-to-Person Selling

Marketing expenses at U.S. hotels increased 6.1 percent in 2004 as hotels attempted to lure guests back and take advantage of a strongly rebounding lodging climate, according to a recent study published by a leading hospitality consultant. The study further indicates that a growing number of hotel marketing departments are shifting more of their sales budgets to activities that involve person-to-person contact, such as trade shows, meals, and entertainment, rather than advertising, brochures, and billboards. In fact, this marks the fifth consecutive year that hotels have cut their local advertising budgets. These observations come from an analysis of the data collected for the recently released 2005 edition of *Trends in the Hotel Industry* published by PKF Hospitality Research (PKF-HR), an affiliate of PKF Consulting.

On the income side of the ledger, hotels earned an additional 7.6 percent in revenue for the year. The question is how much of that revenue increase was driven by the increase in marketing expenditures. "With the lodging industry in its first full year of recovery after three long years of recession, it is tough to differentiate how much impact local sales efforts had on revenue gains, versus the influence of improving local economies," said R. Mark Woodworth, executive managing director of Atlanta-based PKF-HR.

Woodworth pointed out that hotels spend most of their marketing dollars on labor-related expenses. "Salaries and wages comprise 43.6 percent of the average hotel's marketing budget, while employee benefits make up another 11.5 percent. Advertising made up 14.0% of expenditures; selling made up 28.3%; the remaining 2.6% of expenses was divided among the other categories. When digging down into where the additional dollars were spent, we found that labor costs within the marketing department grew 7.0 percent, while all other expenses in the department grew just 3.5 percent. For reference purposes, total hotel labor costs grew 6.3 percent from 2003 to 2004. Given the current spending trends, these ratios will most likely grow in the future," Woodworth observed.

According to Stephen Fertig, president of the International Society of Hotel Consultants, the increase in labor costs can be attributed to the re-hiring of personnel laid off during the recession, as well as changes in the profile of the typical hotel marketing department employee. "The additional payroll dollars are being spent on sales personnel skilled at managing distribution channels, guest loyalty programs, and yield management systems. In other words, the role of marketing in the industry has taken on a more sophisticated hue."

For this special analysis it is important to note that franchise fees and assessments were not included in the marketing department expenses. These fees and assessments typically cover national advertising campaigns, as well as frequent guest programs. Therefore, this examination can be viewed as a study of unit-level marketing expenditures.

Labor costs, advertising, and selling expenses are just some of the 200 discrete hotel revenue and expense items captured by PKF-HR for its 2005

Trends in the Hotel Industry report. The 2005 report marks the 69th annual review of U.S. hotel operations conducted by PKF. The 2005 sample draws upon year-end 2004 financial statements received from more than 5,000 hotels across the country.

SELLING, NOT ADVERTISING

With regard to non-labor-related expenses within the marketing department, the study finds a continued shift away from advertising to selling. From 2003 to 2004, the dollars spent on selling increased 6.6 percent, while the money allotted to advertising declined 5.1 percent.

"At the unit level, hotel managers are clearly showing a preference for person-to-person contact as opposed to mass communication," Woodworth said. "This could be an indication that the chain-affiliated hotels are relying more on the national advertising campaigns conducted by the franchise companies. In addition, use of the Internet to advertise has tended to cost less than the historical forms of visual media."

DIFFERENCES BY PROPERTY TYPE

Except for limited-service hotels, marketing expenses typically run between 4.5 and 5.5 percent of total revenue. In 2004 the average U.S. hotel spent $1,882 per available room (PAR) on their local sales efforts. This expense ranged from $416 PAR at limited-service hotels to $4,464 PAR at resort properties. All-suite hotels spent $1,228 PAR, and convention hotels spent $2,648 PAR.

"Obviously there is a big difference in the size of the marketing budgets for resorts and limited-service hotels. However, it is interesting to note that these two property types were the only ones to show an increase in their advertising dollars during 2004. The leisure orientation of these two property types most likely influenced this spending tactic relative to the choices made by sales and marketing managers at more commercial oriented hotels," Woodworth concluded.

RETURN ON INVESTMENT

As a direct, or indirect, result of spending 6.1 percent more to market their properties in 2004, U.S. hotels earned an additional 7.6 percent in revenue for the year. Resort, all-suite, and convention hotels all shared similar experiences of revenue gains exceeding growth in marketing expenditures. Full-service hotels, unfortunately, were only able to convert their 7.5 percent increase in marketing dollars into a 6.8 percent gain in revenue. At the other end of the spectrum, limited-service hotels actually spent 0.5 percent fewer marketing dollars in 2004, yet enjoyed a 5.8 percent boost in revenue.

Source: Used by permission. PKF Hospitality Research.

---

that case, you may have to justify each cost item as one that will produce tangible results.

The marketing budget should also be a fluid tool, responding to changes in the marketing plan. It is critical to protect the integrity of the budget and plan throughout the planning year. The plan and budget should be changed if results are falling short of forecasts. For instance, the "Sex in the City Weekend" might be considered cost effective if it produced 50 rooms for a given Friday and Saturday night. If, after three or four week-

ends, the demand never exceeds 35 room nights, the responsive marketing team will reevaluate the feasibility of the package.

The decision might be to revise the components of the package, try the promotion again at a later date, or scrap it altogether and allocate the funds elsewhere. Problems occur when managers think only in terms of short-term response (i.e., improving short-term financial performance by cutting costs) rather than executing longer-term strategies to increase and retain customers.

EXHIBIT 21-16	Monthly Spreadsheet for Allocating Expenses to a Given Month

	Date	Market Segment
Sales Trips/Trade Shows		
Washington (WSAE)	5/00	Group
Atlanta/Delta & agents	5/00	Tour and Travel Agent/ Wholesalers
Incentive house trip	5/00	Tour and Travel agent
Advertising		
Hotel Travel Index 1 pg 4c	Quarterly	Tour and Transient
Florida Resident Ad 2 col 5″	1 week	Special
Southern Living 4″ ad	Monthly	Transient
Airport Display	Monthly	Transient
Travel Agent Marketplace	Bimonthly	Tour and Travel agent
Travel Weekly 20″ 4c	6X	Tour and Travel agent
F&B Advertising		
Florida Tour News	6X	Food and Beverage
Orlando Magazine 1/2 pg BW	Monthly	Food and Beverage
Dining Out 1 ph BW	Monthly	Food and Beverage
Orlando Sentinel	5X	Food and Beverage
Local news	1X	Food and Beverage
Special Promotions		
Mother's Day Coll. & Menu	Annual	Food and Beverage
Samantha's Calendar	Monthly	Food and Beverage
Direct Mail		
Business reply	Ongoing	Group
Samantha's mailing	Monthly	Food and Beverage
Mother's Day mailing	Annual	Food and Beverage
Collateral Proration		
5,000 rack brochures	Ongoing	Group
5,000 IT brochures	Ongoing	Tour and Travel agent
7,000 F&B brochures	Ongoing	Food and Beverage

The lows on the short term occur frequently in the careers of sales and marketing professionals as they are rewarded for business now, not later. Although there is no clear-cut answer to the dilemma, the need to create and keep customers should be the paramount consideration for any successful organization. Short-term rewards are sought too many times at the expense of future business.

Marketing Controls

It is critical to monitor the performance of the marketing plan throughout the year and at the end of the year.

The first step, of course, is to continuously match performance against the desired results and to detect when and where deviations occur. The extent of each deviation should be measured, and the worst ones should be addressed. The cause of the deviation should be determined and dealt with either by bringing it into line or adjusting the plan.

Benchmark measurements are established in advance. These could include any of the following, as well as others:

- Market share versus expected fair share
- Occupancy (both achieved and indexed against the competitive set)
- Covers served
- Seat turnovers
- Check averages
- F&B ratios
- Revenue per available guest room
- Average room rate by segment
- Product mix
- Business mix by segment
- Advance bookings
- Advertising inquiries
- Website traffic
- Return per marketing dollar
- Customer satisfaction
- Complaints and compliments
- Repeat business
- Revenue
- Profit

A feedback system should be established to synchronize with the benchmarks. You should be able to answer questions such as the following:

- Is the product/service meeting the needs of the segment(s)?
- Is the segment growing, static, or declining?
- Is the segment profitable?
- Is customer perception as intended?
- Is your positioning correct?
- How are you doing vis-à-vis the competition?
- Are you solving customers' problems?
- Are weaknesses showing?
- Are strengths being exploited?
- Is there price resistance?
- Are you having selling problems?
- What are the reasons for the variances?

If your answers to the preceding questions indicate that you are not where you want to be, you may have to

EXHIBIT 21-17   A new trend for many travelers is the practice of taking their pets with them while they travel. Here is Belle, resting during one such trip.

make changes where necessary or shift to contingency plans. You may have to reanalyze your strategy or plan or perform a new situational analysis. Marketing plans are not static, but dynamic; they are executed under dynamic conditions and must be monitored in the same way.

A final word: The marketing-driven organization must not permit the demands of short-term performance to dictate decisions and actions that may result in the loss of customers. The marketing budget and plan should be adjusted to reflect the needs of the customers, not those of the accountants. To do otherwise is not unlike deferring maintenance to improve short-term bottom-line figures, then having to buy new equipment at some inopportune time in the future. Nevertheless, accountants must have their say. Thus, plans and budgets must ultimately stand the test of cost-effective results and proven revenues.

Exhibit 21-17 shows that it is critical that one keep track of current trends when developing a marketing plan. One of the latest trends is traveling with pets. In fact, there is a website dedicated solely to this phenomenon. The firm BringYourPet (www.bringyourpet.com) is "a leading resource of free information to the hundreds of thousands of traveling pet owners in the United States and abroad looking for quality pet-friendly accommodations. BringYourPet.com caters to pet owners who enjoy bringing their pets with them" (www.bringyourpet.com, accessed April 23, 2006). Websites such as this one will continue to be developed to capture customers' unmet needs or solve their problems. The marketer who practices marketing leadership will and should always be on the lookout for new ways to take better care of the customer.

■ Summary

The marketing plan and the marketing budget are fluid tools designed to create, capture, and retain customers. Their development is based on a sound and realistic situational analysis that requires good data collection, primary research where necessary, and thorough analysis. Instead of relying on traditional methods to deal with unique situations, the marketing team needs to develop innovative strategies based on insightful information. The funding made available to implement these strategies must then be sufficient to get the job done.

Exhibit 21-18 has been designed as a template to use to develop a marketing plan. The chapter fills in many of the empty spaces with explanations, but the actual data must come from those who work the plan.

■ Key Terms

marketing plan	data analysis
raise the numbers	action plans
competition	marketing budgets
data collection	benchmarks

■ Discussion Questions

1. Discuss the key differences between strategic marketing and marketing management in the development of the marketing plan.
2. Formulate a situational analysis for a restaurant or hotel where you have worked or with which you are familiar. Analyze the internal and external factors.
3. Construct a detailed property needs analysis for the same restaurant or hotel that will form the basis of a marketing plan.
4. Develop an internal marketing plan for a real or hypothetical hotel or restaurant.
5. Why is the realistic and objective analysis of the data collection critical to a successful marketing plan? Discuss. What happens when this is lacking?
6. Write a mission statement for the restaurant or hotel analyzed in Question 2.

■ Group Projects

1. Develop a marketing plan for a hotel or restaurant with which you are all familiar. If that is not possible, develop a plan for one of the cases that can be found on the CD that is bundled with this book.

| **EXHIBIT 21-18** | **Marketing Plan Template** |

1. Overall mission statement (Chapters 5 and 6)
   Broad-based as guideline, subject to revision later
2. Situational analysis (Chapters 5 and 6)
   The situational analysis describes the business climate of the hospitality entity. This portion of the plan gives an overview of the business, recapping what worked well in the current year and what needs to be accomplished for the upcoming year. It also indicates environmental and industry trends.
   a. Recap of past year, what worked well, what didn't, and broad needs for next year
   b. Environmental trends
      Possible major shifts that affect customers or operations: political, economic, social, technological, ecological, regulatory
   c. Market trends
      Provide the foundation for the marketing plan, including possible major or minor shifts that affect customers: international, national, regional, local. Statistics are gathered for analysis. Market potential is an important part of this. Macro statistics can be obtained from sources such as the local visitors and convention bureau or the National Restaurant Association. Micro statistics such as local trends can be obtained from Smith Travel Research for rooms or Fasttrack for food and beverage.
   d. Competitive trends and forces—current and forecasted
      Needed to anticipate competitive moves and strengths and weaknesses, both current and forecasted. A competitive review needs to be completed at least yearly. Current supply of hotel rooms or restaurants should be documented with not only the obvious statistics, such as number of guest rooms, seats, or square footage of function space, but also a determination of the direction of each competitor in terms of the overall marketplace. Strengths and weaknesses of each should be documented. Any new or lost supply of rooms or restaurants should be identified.
3. Internal data (Chapter 11)
   Provides all pertinent data and statistics on the operation, both financial and customer information, including segments and target markets.
4. Data analysis (Chapter 11)
   Involves analyzing the data collected in steps 2 and 3. We add, however, one new category called property needs analysis. In this category we analyze the internal gaps to be filled so that we can match them with the opportunities revealed by analyses of the other stages.
5. Mission and market position statement (Chapter 12 and 13)
   The mission and objectives for the forthcoming year are detailed. Although this is not done until all the previous work is done, it will be inserted at the beginning of the marketing plan right after the broad mission statement.
   The market positioning strategy follows. With the statistics gathered and the competitors reviewed, the hospitality entity has to define clearly where it belongs in the constellation of competitive brands. For example, Mary's Restaurant will be positioned just below Cathy's Restaurant, directly in competition with Jenny's Restaurant, and above Meagan's Restaurant. The market position statement gives direction for the marketer as well as the employees as to what the hospitality entity expects of itself.
6. Opportunity analysis (Chapters 5, 6, 7, 8, 10, 11)
   Involves identifying all the opportunities in the marketplace revealed by all the previous analyses that are consistent with the mission and market position adopted. Once the positioning has been established, a strategy for each market segment needs to be developed. This can be as simple as breakfast and lunch for Mary's Restaurant or 22 segments of customers at the Grand Hyatt in New York City. Each segment has to be defined and addressed in the marketing program.
7. Objectives and methods—objectives are measurable where appropriate (Chapter 11)
   Define precisely where we want to go and how we plan to get there.
8. Action plans
   Establish specific responsibilities for every member of the team and some who are not directly part of the marketing team. For example, a chef may be brought in here, if not before, to get involved in the action.
9. Marketing communications (Chapters 15 through 17).
   Each segment responds to different communications. For example, the corporate group market has to be called on by salespeople. The "two-fers" for a restaurant read newspaper ads or listen to the radio. The marketing communications portion of the marketing plan establishes how we are going to reach our customers and tell them what we have to offer.
   Clearly, multiple communication vehicles are available to reach each market segment. The corporate customer not only responds to a salesperson, but also reads the business press, corporate directories, and other periodicals.
10. Market forecast and revenue projections (Chapters 11 and 14)
    The revenue forecast takes all of the assumptions of the marketing program and establishes a financial goal for the upcoming year. In many cases revenue goals by market segment are determined to track the progress of the marketing programs.
11. Marketing budget
    With the data collection in place and strategies outlined by segment, the allocation of marketing resources such as advertising, public relations, direct sales, and database marketing may begin to support the strategies.
12. Marketing controls
    The old expression "What gets measured gets done" applies here. This is the follow-up to stay on track, see what is working and what is not, and decide whether any changes or new directions are needed.

2. If you can, obtain an actual hotel marketing plan. One of you may be able to obtain one where you work, or your instructor may have some copies. Do a thorough analysis of this plan, good and bad, as outlined in this chapter.

■ Reference

1. Hayes, R. H. (1986, April 20). Why strategic planning goes awry. *New York Times*, Section 3, Page 2, Column 3.

Segmenting the U.S. Travel Market According to Benefits Realized

Stowe Shoemaker

Reprinted with permission from Travel and Tourism Research, *Volume XXXII, Number 3, Winter 1994. Copyright © 1994 by the Travel and Tourism Research Association and the Business Research Division, University of Colorado at Boulder. All rights reserved. 0047–2875 USPS 677–920*

Abstract

This research studied the differences between what consumers say they want and what they actually buy. A segmentation study was conducted based on the benefits derived from travel using the sampling methodology that was non-destination specific. The sampling methodology employed also allows for the findings to be generalizable to the U.S. traveling public. Four market segments are identified—three that are big enough to warrant different marketing strategies—and discussed in detail. Where appropriate, they are compared to the segments identified by previous researchers.

The travel and leisure literature is replete with articles explaining why people travel (Bonn 1982; Bryant and Morrison 1980; Crandall 1980; Mazanec 1984; Rubenstein 1980). The implicit assumption in all these studies is that the consumer will choose the destination or type of holiday or vacation that will best satisfy his/her desires or needs. It is this logic that has led researchers to study the motivations for travel.

Travel researchers have also studied consumer's preferences for and perceptions of vacation destinations (Matejka 1973; Schewe and Calantone 1978; Goodrich 1977; Woodside and Lysonski 1989; Um and Crompton 1990; Chon, Weaver, and Kim 1991). The impetus for these studies is to understand the determinance of destination choice. It is hoped that such information will then enable marketers to define their destination in terms of desired benefits. However, many travel researchers, on both a national scale and in non-proprietary published studies, have yet to understand and divide groups of consumers into smaller segments based on benefits they receive. This is not to say that past researchers have failed to use benefits realized as a way to infer travel motivations. Both Dann (1981) and Pearce and Caltabiano (1983), for example, understood that past experience is a good way to infer travel motivations (or desired benefits).

Dann (1981) argued that researchers face problems measuring travel motivation because tourists may not wish or may be unable to reflect on real travel motives. In addition, they may either be unable or unwilling to express their real travel motives to themselves or professional interviewers. To overcome these limitations, Pearce and Caltabiano (1983) examined travel motivations by having respondents describe one positive and one negative experience from their last holiday. Maslow's hierarchy of needs (Maslow 1943) was then used as a descriptive tool to code these responses. The study's findings indicate that positive experiences were associated with the fulfillment of psychological, love, self-actualizing needs. In contrast, negative experiences were associated with threatening psychological and safety needs. The authors use these results to argue that rather than promoting a combination of attributes, travel marketers should instead demonstrate how attributes satisfy given needs.

Woodside and Jacobs (1985) argued that "learning actual benefits realized from experiencing specific travel destinations may be useful for deciding on making physical improvements in destination facilities and revising advertising messages" (Woodside and Jacobs 1985, p. 7). They examined the different consequences and benefits realized from travel to Hawaii by three nationalities of visitors—

588

Canadians, Americans, and Japanese. Each nationality responded differently to the questions posed. For example, unlike Canadian and Japanese visitors, mainland Americans were more likely to describe their Hawaii visit as a learning experience and as being exciting without being dangerous. On the other hand, Canadian visitors claim their trip was very restful (unlike the Japanese and mainland Americans), while only Japanese visitors claim they spent more time with their immediate family while on vacation than when at home. These findings suggest that advertising strategies to each group should be different if they are to be effective. What will entice one nationality to visit Hawaii will not entice another.

The study presented here adds to the previous work of Pearce and Caltabiano (1983) and Woodside and Jacobs (1985) by not only looking at past travel experience as a way to infer desired benefits, but also by using these inferred benefits to create smaller homogenous market segments. It also adds to these previous works by being more generalizable. Unlike Woodside and Jacobs' (1985) research, this study is not destination specific. Generalizability is also enhanced by the use of random probability sampling methodology.

For this study, ratings of the last destination visited while on vacation were used to infer the desired benefits. The last vacation destination was chosen rather than the "typical" vacation destination because there may be no such thing as a "typical" vacation destination. For example, some travelers may take a Caribbean cruise one time, a Las Vegas trip the next, and a family visit all within a short period of time. We did not want respondents to average all the vacation destinations they have visited together in response to our questions. Before examining the specifics of this study, a brief review of past studies pertaining to why people travel and influences of destination choice is useful.

Literature Review

One of the earliest published studies addressing the issue of why people travel was written by Lundberg (1971). From a review of various studies, Lundberg developed a list of 18 motivations which were believed to influence travel. These motivations range from the desire to engage in educational and cultural activities to the desire to have a change of weather (for instance, to get away from the cold) and participate in sports (e.g., to swim, ski, or fish). These 18 motivations, subdivided into four groups, appear in Exhibit 9A-1.

Crompton (1979) looked at the motivations for pleasure travel by conducting 39 unstructured, in-depth interviews with a convenience sample of respondents from Texas and Massachusetts. Although sample size was quite small and the sample far from representative, Crompton's findings have been substantiated by other studies (Crandall 1980; Rubenstein 1980).

Crompton identified nine motives, seven of which he classified as "social psychological" and two of which he classified as "cultural." The social psychological motives identified were escape from a perceived mundane environment, exploration and evaluation of self, relaxation, prestige, nostalgia/regression, enhancement of kinship relations, and facilitation of social interaction. The two cultural motives identified were novelty and education.

Other authors (Etzel and Woodside 1982; Goodrich 1978; Calantone, Schewe, and Allen 1980) used many of these same motivations to classify respondents into different market segments. For example, Young, Ott, and Feigin (1978) using a national probability sample collected by the Canadian government, divided the U.S. travel market into six market segments using benefits/motivations as a discriminating variables. These six market segments

---

EXHIBIT 9A-1	**What Makes People Travel?**

EDUCATIONAL AND CULTURAL MOTIVES
1. To see how people in other cultures live, work, and play
2. To see particular sights
3. To gain a better understanding of what goes on in the news
4. To attend special events
5. To participate in history (visit temples or ruins) or participate in current events

RELAXATION AND PLEASURE
6. To get away from the everyday routine
7. To have a good time
8. To achieve some sort of sexual or romantic experience

ETHNIC
9. To visit places your family came from
10. To visit places your family or friends have gone to

OTHER
11. Weather (for instance, to avoid winter)
12. Health (sun, dry climate, and so on)
13. Sports (to swim, ski, fish or sail)
14. Economy (inexpensive living)
15. Adventure (new areas, people, experiences)
16. One-upmanship
17. Conformity (keeping up with the Joneses)
18. Sociological motives

Adapted from Lundberg (1971).

EXHIBIT 9A-2	Six Market Segments Identified by Benefits Sought

Segment 1: Friends and Relatives—Nonactive Visitor (29%)
These vacationers seek familiar surroundings where they can visit friends and relatives. They are not very inclined to participate in any activity.

Segment 2: Friends and Relatives—Active City Visitor (12%)
These vacationers also seek familiar surroundings where they can visit friends and relatives, but they are more inclined to participate in activities—especially sightseeing, shopping, cultural activities, and other entertainment.

Segment 3: Family Sightseers (6%)
These vacationers are looking for a new vacation place which would be a treat for the children and an enriching experience.

Segment 4: Outdoor Vacationers (19%)
These vacationers seek clean air, rest and quiet, and beautiful scenery. Many are campers and availability of recreation facilities is important. Children are also an important factor.

Segment 5: Resort Vacationers (19%)
These vacationer are mostly interested in water sports (e.g., swimming) and good weather. They prefer a popular place with a big city atmosphere.

Segment 6: Foreign Vacationers (26%)
These vacationers look for vacations in a place they have never been before; a place with a foreign atmosphere and beautiful scenery. Money is not of major concern but good accommodations and service are. They want an exciting and enriching experience.

From Young, Ott, and Feigin (1978)

ranged from the desire to visit family and relatives and do little else to the desire to visit a place they have never been before. A detailed description of these segments appears in Exhibit 9A-2.

With so many complete studies on the reasons for travel, the reader may wonder why one more study is necessary. It is important to remember that past studies have looked at consumers in terms of what they would like to do. This one builds on the studies by Pearce and Caltabiano (1983) and Woodside and Jacobs (1985) by understanding consumers in terms of what they did.

This perspective is necessary because, as Ajzen and Fishbein (1980) and Mazis, Ahtola, and Klippel (1975) have shown, attitudes towards brands and products (or destinations) do not predict behavior. For example, in one study by Ajzen and Fishbein (1980), consumers stated that their two most preferred brands of automobiles were Mercedes and Jaguar. But, when asked which brands they will most likely purchase, respondents chose Chevrolet (Ajzen and Fishbein 1980). A similar anthology can be made for travel destination. For example, consumers' response to a question probing attitude towards a Caribbean vacation might be "Terrific! A great place to vacation! Sand, sun and fun!" but response to questions regarding the likelihood of vacationing there might be "No. Why not? Because of cost, family pressure, and other such reasons."

The study presented here is also unique in that the results are representative of the U.S. traveling public and the derived benefits are not destination-specific. This is in contrast to many studies where the sample is either confined to a geographic region or is based on a convenience sampling methodology.

Research Design

The broad purpose of this research was to determine the behavior patterns and attitudes consumers have towards vacationing in several destinations around the United States. Of specific interest was travelers' perception of a specified west coast destination. Owing to the proprietary nature of the research, the destination cannot be identified; however, its identity does not affect the results of this study. The questionnaire topics included:

- Previous travel experience and future vacation plans,
- Favorite vacation spots,
- Factors important when choosing a vacation destination,
- Descriptive attributes of the last vacation destination visited,
- Images of selected cities, and
- General demographic characteristics

Only the topics pertaining to travel behavior, vacation destinations, and demographics are addressed in this article.

The sample was a qualified random sample of U.S. households with telephones. Respondents were selected to meet the following qualification criteria:

- Be actively involved in the decision-making process for household vacations or pleasure trips, and
- Have taken at least one overnight pleasure or combined business and pleasure trip a specified minimum distance from their home in the past 12 months, or be planning a pleasure, or combined business and pleasure trip of the same specified minimum distance in the next 12 months.

The required minimum distance traveled was 500 miles from home in all regions with the exception of the Pacific states. Because of the Pacific states' proximity to one of the cities under study, the minimum distance of travel required to qualify in this section of the country was just 300 miles. The client believed that a major potential market lived between 300 and 500 miles from the destination under study; therefore a minimum distance of 300 miles was selected for this region. It was important that consumers living in this area have a chance to express their opinions. As this relates to the study, all questions regarding past or planned travel referred to this minimum mileage level. Although screening criteria included combined business and pleasure trips, the wording of the questions pertained to vacation pleasure travel only.

To ensure a representative cross-section of the U.S. population, the sample for this study was divided by state into six separate pre-specified geographic regions. The six regions and appropriate sample sizes were Eastern (196), Southern (199), Midwest (202), Southwest (196), Pacific (199) and Northwest/Mountain (204). A breakdown of these six regions by state is available from the author. The number of respondents from each state was selected proportionately based upon its total population within its assigned region. Quotas are set to guarantee that the ending sample reflected the population of these pre-specified regions. The final sample size was 1,196.

Respondents were chosen via computer-generated random-digit-dial telephone (RDD), the numbers provided by Scientific Telephone Samples, a national supplier of RDD samples. Phone samples were supplied in replicates and each number in one replicate was attempted three times before moving on to another replicate. When using telephone samples, it's customary to have the entire phone sample printed in replicates, with each replicate representative of all the phone numbers in the specified area. Replicates are used to ensure that an entire range of numbers in the selected area is called before the study is completed. Exact incidence figures are unavailable but the qualification rate was quite high. Because of the funding considerations, no attempt was made to study the opinions of the smaller percentage of nonrespondents.

Interviewing was conducted via telephone in August and September 1990 from a central location telephone bank in Las Vegas, Nevada. To enhance the quality of data collected, on-line computer terminal interviewing (Sawtooth's Ci2 software) was employed. Sample characteristics, along with the U.S. population characteristics, appear in Exhibit 9A-3. Discrepancies, particularly with respect to education and income under $25,000, are hypothesized to be a result of the screening criteria.

Analysis of Respondents

Travel Behavior

Exhibit 9A-3 also reveals that for a majority of the respondents, the decision regarding where to travel is made jointly with other family members or friends. More than 80% of the respondents claimed their last vacation occurred during 1990 or 1989 (63.8% and 21%, respectively). On the average, respondents from the Pacific region took 2.25 trips while those from the other five regions averaged 1.62 trips in the prior year. The higher number of trips by respondents in the Pacific region may be related to the minimum distance required—300 miles for the Pacific group versus 500 for the other regions. Respondents indicated that they will continue to travel in the future, as only 12.8% stated they would travel less. Popular destinations include the state of Hawaii, countries in Europe, and the U.S. cities Los Angeles, New York City, and San Francisco.

Exhibit 9A-4 shows the most frequently mentioned last vacation destinations. The "last destination" rated was the location named in response to the question, "Where was the last place you went for a vacation-pleasure trip where you traveled at least 500 miles from home?" In addition to their last vacation destination, respondents also rated two other places as possible vacation destinations. As

EXHIBIT 9A-3	Sample Characteristics (U.S. Population Figures)	

Demographic Characteristics

Sex	Sample	(US Population)
Male	54.6%	(48.8%)
Female	45.4	(51.3)

Marital Status

Married	64.0%	(61.1%)
Not married	35.3	(27.3)
No answer	0.7	
Widowed/divorced	—	(11.6)

Age of Respondents (U.S. population percentage based on those 18 or older)

18–24 years	12.1%	(13.6%)
25–29	12.9	(11.3)
30–34	14.5	(12.1)
35–39	12.9	(11.1)
40–44	12.5	(10.0)
45–54	15.2	(14.0)
55–64	11.3	(11.6)
64–74	8.6	(9.9)

Education (U.S. population figures based on those 25 or older)

Some high school or less	2.9%	(24.8%)
High school graduate	19.8	(30.0)
Some college/technical	39.3	(24.9)
College graduate	19.8	(13.1)
Some post-graduate/post-graduate degree	18.2	(7.2)

(continued)

EXHIBIT 9A-3	Sample Characteristics (U.S. Population Figures) (Continued)

Income	Sample Characteristics
Less than $25,000	21.8%
$25,001–$30,000	15.9
$30,001–$40,000	15.6
$40,001–$50,000	11.7
$50,001–$60,000	12.2
$60,001–$70,000	8.8
$70,001–$80,000	5.8
$80,001–$100,000	4.0
Greater than $100,000	4.2
Income (U.S. household income 1989)*	
Less than $25,000	(41.8%)
$25,000–$34,999	(15.8)
$35,000–$49,999	(17.9)
$50,000–$74,999	(15.0)
$75,000–$99,999	(5.1)
Greater than $100,000	(4.4)

Behavioral Characteristics
Pleasure Trip Decision Maker

Individual makes most decisions by self	36.7%
Decision-making shared equally with others	63.3

Year of Last Pleasure Trip at a Minimum Specified Distance

1990	63.8%
1989	21.0
1988	6.1
1987	2.2
Prior 1987	6.9

Average Number of Trips Taken During Past 12 Months

Among total sample	1.72%
Pacific region (300 or more miles from home)	2.25
Non-Pacific region (500 or more miles)	1.62

Plans for Future Trips

More trips	40.0%
Same number of trips	47.2
Fewer trips	12.8

Three Places Respondents Would Really Like to Visit in Next Few Years**

Hawaii	17.6%
Europe/Russia	17.1
Los Angeles	16.2
New York City	15.8
San Francisco	15.3
Seattle/Tacoma/Portland	13.2
Orlando	12.2
Washington, D.C.	9.9
Southern urban areas	9.7
Colorado	9.4

*Questionnaire not designed to match U.S. government defined categories.
**Figures add up to more than 100% due to multiple responses.

EXHIBIT 9A-4	Most Frequently Named Vacation Destinations (by Region)

Midwest

Last Destination (sample size)	(202)
Other Florida areas*	9.9%
Orlando area	7.4
Los Angeles area	5.4
Southern urban areas	5.0
Canada	4.5
Las Vegas area	4.5

Southwest

Last Destination (sample size)	(196)
Colorado	6.1%
Southern urban areas	6.1
Los Angeles area	5.6
Other Texas**	5.6
Southwestern urban areas	4.6

Northwest/Mountain

Last Destination (sample size)	(204)
Los Angeles area	10.3%
Seattle/Tacoma/Portland	7.8
Southwestern urban areas	5.4
Idaho/Wyoming/Montana	4.9
Europe/Russia	4.0

East

Last Destination (sample size)	(196)
Orlando area	9.7%
Other Florida areas*	8.7
Southern urban areas	7.1
Caribbean Islands	6.1
Miami/Palm Beach/Fort Lauderdale	5.6

South

Last Destination (sample size)	(199)
Southern urban areas	13.69%
Other Florida areas*	11.6
Europe/Russia	5.0
Orlando area	4.0
Urban Ohio	3.5

Pacific

Last Destination (sample size)	(199)
Los Angeles area	12.6%
Seattle/Tacoma/Portland	6.0
Southwestern urban areas	5.5
Las Vegas area	4.5
San Diego	4.5
San Francisco	4.5

*Does not include Orlando, Miami, Fort Lauderdale, or Palm Beach.
**Does not include Dallas, Fort Worth, or Houston.

would be expected, the location of the most recent pleasure trip varied when analyzed by region. This is probably due to geographical proximity to the respondent's home.

Destination Planning Concerns and Image of Last Vacation Destination

Respondents were asked to rate a variety of potentially influential attributes of vacation destination selection on a scale of concern ranging from 1 to 10. The question was worded as follows:

> I'd like you to think about the factors which you may, or may not, be concerned with when deciding which places you would like to go for a vacation or pleasure trip. To do this we'll use a 1 to 10 scale where "1" means you are "not at all concerned" with that aspect when planning where to vacation, and "10" means you are "very concerned" with that factor when deciding on a vacation destination. You can use any number 1 to 10. The higher the number, the more concerned you are with that feature when thinking about where to go for vacation or pleasure.

Exhibit 9A-5 shows the responses to these attributes.

The attributes of value for the money, low crime rate and high personal safety, rest and relaxation, and natural sights and scenery received the highest ratings with means scores above 8.00. On the other end of the scale (under means score of 5), guided tours, major sporting events, golf/tennis, and gambling seemed to be of lesser concern.

Although it is not shown, t-tests (alpha<.05) revealed that those who have taken or are planning to take two or fewer trips per year are more concerned with:

■ Price/value,
■ Crime rate and safety of an area,
■ The location's suitability for children, and
■ The availability of amusement parks and guided tours.

In contrast, heavier travelers (three or more trips taken or planned in a one-year period) are more interested in night life and cultural activities such as theaters or museums.

While "concern" ratings represent "ideal" conditions that a traveler is seeking in a destination, ratings of the last vacation destination that respondents visited provide a picture of what they will tolerate. To this end, respondents rated their last vacation destination on the same set of attributes using a 1 to 10 scale. This time, "1" meant the attribute did not describe the last vacation destination at all, while "10" meant it described the last vacation destination visited exactly. Exhibit 9A-5 also shows the responses to these attributes and how they differ from the ideal.

Exhibit 9A-5 reveals some interesting differences between what respondents say is a concern and what they actually do. For example, while travelers claim to be concerned with going "somewhere new" (mean response of 7.43), this attribute did not characterize the last vacation destination for most (mean response of 2.61). Similarly, low crime is said to be a major concern (8.07), but the last vacation destination visited was not perceived to be especially safe (6.31).

In contrast, the attribute "know someone who's been there" (5.22) was of relatively minor concern in choosing a vacation destination, but was said to describe the last vacation destination more than any other attribute (mean rating 8.96). This suggests that consumers may be using risk avoidance strategies when choosing a vacation destination. Support for this argument is found by examining "critical" attributes. These are attributes where the concern ratings are approximately equal to the actual behavior. These attributes are hotels available in all price ranges, how much it costs to get there, cleanliness of the air, experiencing different cultures, and the availability of amusement or theme parks.

In terms of travel frequency (not shown in Exhibit 9A-2 or 9A-3), heavy travelers' (three or more trips) last vacation destination was more likely to be a place they were very familiar with and a place they would like to re-visit. Moreover, these travelers also favor mountain regions, areas with low crime rates, and places with little traffic congestion. In contrast, light travelers (one trip) were more apt to drive to their last vacation destination and visit areas with major amusement parks.

Multivariate Analysis of Last Vacation Destination Descriptive Rating Data

Full use of the information contained in the last vacation destination rating data was gained by applying various multivariate techniques to the data. The ending sample size after the multivariate procedures were completed was 942; cases with incomplete information were removed prior to the multivariate procedures (listwise deletion). In addition, because outlying cases can adversely affect results, they were removed prior to determining the final solution. First, principal component analysis (PCA) (Dillon and Goldstein 1984) was used to group the descriptive ratings for the last vacation destination (excluding the variables "I am very familiar with this city," "I really want to go there," and "realistically, it's a place I plan to visit in the next couple of years") into a smaller number of components. These variables were not included because of the desire to use them as dependent variables in another part of the analysis, which is not discussed in this article. This analysis reduced the original 39 variables to 19 variables (12 principal components plus

EXHIBIT 9A-5	Image of Last Destination Visited in Comparison with Destination Planning Concerns*		
Attribute Sample Size	**Last Destination (1,196) (A)**	**Concern (1,196) (B)**	**Planning Difference**
Know someone else who has been there	8.96	5.22	+3.74**
Rest and relaxation	8.42	8.04	+0.38**
All members of party will like it equally	7.99	7.80	+0.19
Number of places and points of interest to see	7.98	7.58	+0.40*
Number of activities and things to do	7.97	7.43	+0.54**
Hotels available in all price ranges	7.87	7.87	0.00
Natural sights and scenery	7.77	8.01	−0.25**
Opportunity for recreation or sports	7.70	6.53	+1.17**
Friendliness of local residents	7.59	7.18	+0.41**
How much it costs to get there	7.50	7.58	−0.08
Climate/weather	7.48	7.87	−0.39**
Fine dining/elegant, sophisticated restaurants	7.48	5.63	+1.84**
Value for the money	7.44	8.20	−0.76**
Popular place to go	7.39	5.50	+1.89**
Cleanliness of air	7.39	7.32	+0.07
Near the water (ocean, river, lake)	7.34	7.10	+0.24
Ability to drive to the destination	7.31	6.38	+0.93**
Famous city/place	7.27	5.66	+1.61**
Learn new things/personal enrichment	7.08	7.26	−0.18
Night life and entertainment	6.96	6.02	+0.94**
Golf/tennis	6.94	3.61	+3.33**
Vacation packages include everything	6.91	6.13	+0.78**
Good city services	6.78	6.02	+0.76**
It's a place for children	6.72	5.10	+1.62**
Cultural activities (museums, galleries, opera, theater, dance)	6.70	6.29	+0.41**
Guided tours	6.63	4.68	+1.95**
Experiencing different cultures	6.62	6.64	−0.02
Sunbathing	6.58	5.01	+1.57**
Ability to walk to sights and activities	6.37	6.74	−0.37**
Low crime rate	6.31	8.07	−1.76**
A place where friends or relatives live	5.93	6.15	−0.22
Traffic/congestion	5.53	6.30	−0.77**
Amusement or theme parks	5.44	5.39	+0.05
Major professional sporting events	5.44	4.25	+1.19**
Beaches	5.18	6.40	−1.22**
Mountains	5.15	6.58	−1.43**
A place not many people go to	4.22	5.72	−1.50**
Gambling	3.09	3.56	−0.47**
Somewhere I've never been before	2.61	7.43	−4.82**

*Among the total sample.
**Indicates that the mean rating for last destination and concern is significantly different at 95% confidence level.

seven original variables, which did not load highly on any one of the derived components and were used in later analysis). These new combination variables, along with their PCA loadings and mean scores, are shown in Exhibit 9A-6.

Next, K-means clustering was used to cluster respondents into a smaller set of relatively homogenous groups. The input variables in this cluster analysis were the PCA scores on the 12 derived components and the normalized scores of the additional seven attributes, shown in Exhibit 9A-6. Again, the last vacation destination ratings were used rather then the concern ratings because of the desire to understand consumers' vacation destination choice in terms of the destination they actually visited rather than their "ideal" vacation destination.

Factor and Variables*	Factor Loading	Mean
Educational possibilities		
Can experience different cultures	.792	6.62
Can learn new things/get personal enrichment	.747	7.08
There are cultural activities (museums, galleries, opera, theater, dance)	.726	6.70
No. of places and points of interest to see	.643	7.98
Can get guided tours	.628	6.63
Famous city/place	.583	7.27
There are a number of activities	.509	7.97
There are major sporting events	.424	5.44
Environmental aspects of destination		
Clean air	.824	7.39
Low crime rate/a safe place	.775	6.31
Friendly local residents	.747	7.59
There is little traffic/congestion	.710	5.53
Resort set		
Can play golf/tennis	.702	6.94
Hotels or accommodations all price ranges	.657	7.87
Fine dining/elegant, sophisticated restaurants	.600	7.48
Good night life, entertainment	.485	6.96
Sun sports		
Good beaches	.863	5.18
Near water (ocean, river, lake)	.773	7.34
Good place for sunbathing	.701	6.58
Destination popularity		
It's a place not many people go to	−.827	4.22
It's a popular place to go	.594	7.39
Value		
Reasonable cost to get there	.764	7.50
Can drive to the destination	.757	7.31
Good value for the money	.527	7.44
Scenery		
Good mountain areas	.869	5.15
Natural sights and scenery	.611	7.77
Friends/relatives		
A place where friends or relatives live	.858	5.93
Place to gamble		
Can gamble there	.882	3.09
Convenience		
Can walk to sights and activities	.721	6.37
Good city services, transportation, etc.	.554	6.87
Something new		
Somewhere I've never been before	.937	2.61
Recommendation		
Know someone else who has been there	.925	8.96

*Variables not included: Can get vacation packages (6.91); can rest and relax, don't have to do anything (8.42); good climate/weather (7.48); there is opportunity for recreation/sports (7.70); place for children (6.72); all members will like it equally (7.99); there are amusement or theme parks (5.44).

Derived Market Segments

Various cluster solutions were examined, ranging from 3 to 10 clusters; they produce either considerable overlap among clusters or very unequal sample sizes between clusters. (The "correct" number of clusters is typically determined by heuristic procedures [Aldenderfer and Blashfield 1984]. For this study, the heuristics included minimum overlap between clusters and derived clusters with enough cases to warrant different marketing strategies.) The solution with the best fit yielded four market segments. While four was the proper number of market segments derived, one of the groups was considered too small to analyze (32 people, or 3.4%). As such, only the three largest groups will be discussed here.

To determine which variables were important to each market segment, a perceptual map was created using discriminant analysis. (See Shoemaker 1989 for more discussion about the use of cluster and discriminant analysis and travel research.) The resultant map appears in Exhibit 9A-7. In addition, various cross tabulations were performed using demographic and other variables to provide a clearer picture of the derived segments.

Information pertaining to consumer sources of information about specific destinations (e.g., from travel agents, AAA, friends or relatives, or tour operators) was not available. This question was asked, but only as it pertained to obtaining information about the destination under study. In retrospect, this information may have provided valuable insight. Respondents were, however, asked which, if any, travel publication they subscribed to. Only 15.1% claimed to subscribe to such a publication. These responses were too varied to be meaningful and are not presented in this article. No questions were asked about television viewership or newspaper and non-travel magazine readership.

Exhibit 9A-7 shows the three largest groups plotted relative to the combined last vacation destination attributes (represented by vectors). The degree to which these variables separate the groups is indicated by the length of this vector, while the proximity to each market segment and direction shows how influential the attributes inclusive in that factor are to the respondents in each segment.

When reading the map, it is important to remember that each group's individuality depends not only on which attributes are most important to the respondents, but also on which are less important. Therefore, it is also necessary to consider the continuation of the lines in the negative direction.

As can be seen from the map, the largest segment to emerge from the analysis consists of 37.8% of the traveling public. This one segment was followed by two additional segments representing 30.7% and 28.1% of the sample (the fourth segments relative size excludes it from being noteworthy). Each market segment has been given a name based on those factors/variables which define the group and separate them from the others: Get Away/Family Travelers, Adventurous/Educational Travelers, and Gamblers/Fun Oriented. Additional information pertaining to each cluster segment appears in Exhibit 9A-8, which shows the "top-three box scores" (rating of 8, 9, or 10) for each attribute by derived market segment.

The largest market segment is the Get Away/Family Travelers, so named because among other things, the place they last visited tended to be geared towards families. This market segment is also most similar to segments I (Friends and Relatives—Nonactive Visitor), III (Family Sightseers), and IV (Outdoor Vacationers) identified by Young, Ott, and Feigin (1978). For example, rating their last vacation destination as a good place for children, 64.3% of the members of this group gave it a rating of either an 8, 9, or 10—compared to just 42.4% and 40% for the Adventurous/Educational Travelers and Gamblers/Fun Oriented clusters, respectively. Similarly, the number of people that claimed their last vacation trip was to a place where friends or relatives lived was equally high (70.5% compared to 45.8% and 34.7%). The length and direction of these attribute vectors visually display these relationships.

Members of this cluster, like members of segment IV (Young, Ott, and Feigin 1978), are also more likely to visit destinations with "scenery" than are members of the other two clusters. Specifically, just under three-quarters said their last destination had "natural sights and scenery," compared to 54.9% and 63.0% for the Adventurous/Educational and Gamblers/Fun Oriented clusters.

Other variables which can be considered more important to the members of this group include:

- Visiting places where they can rest and relax and not do anything if they don't want to (90.4%),
- Friendly local residents (79.8%),
- The ability to drive to the destination (73.6%),
- Can learn things/get personal enrichment (57.3%),
- Low crime rate/a safe place (55.1%),
- Good mountain areas (44.7%), and
- There is little traffic/congestion (43.8%).

Interestingly, the popularity of the vacation destination is relatively unimportant to this group while it is important to members of the other two clusters (46.3%, compared to 62.8% and 75.1% for Adventurous/Educational Travelers and Gamblers/Fun Oriented segments, respectively). This probably is most likely related to Family Travelers' tendencies

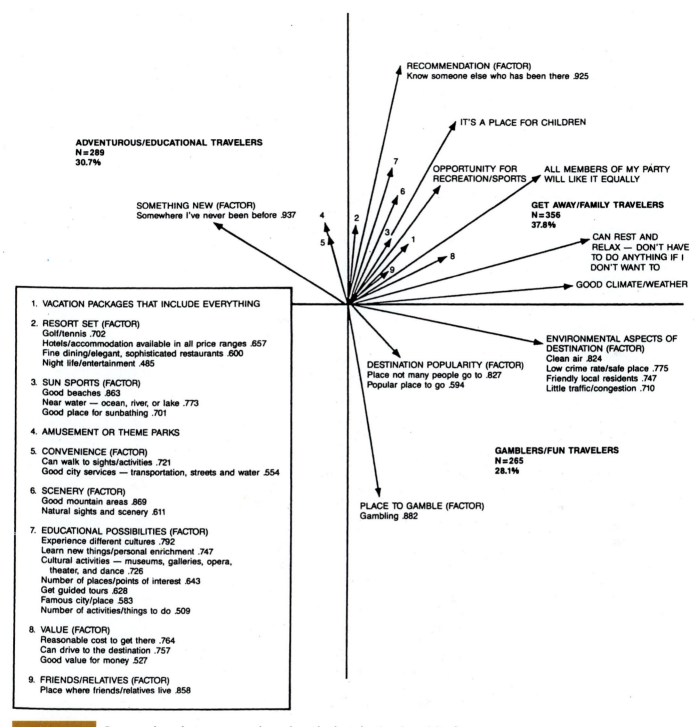

ADVENTUROUS/EDUCATIONAL TRAVELERS
N = 289
30.7%

RECOMMENDATION (FACTOR)
Know someone else who has been there .925

IT'S A PLACE FOR CHILDREN

OPPORTUNITY FOR
RECREATION/SPORTS

ALL MEMBERS OF MY PARTY
WILL LIKE IT EQUALLY

SOMETHING NEW (FACTOR)
Somewhere I've never been before .937

GET AWAY/FAMILY TRAVELERS
N = 356
37.8%

CAN REST AND
RELAX — DON'T HAVE
TO DO ANYTHING IF I
DON'T WANT TO

GOOD CLIMATE/WEATHER

ENVIRONMENTAL ASPECTS OF
DESTINATION (FACTOR)
Clean air .824
Low crime rate/safe place .775
Friendly local residents .747
Little traffic/congestion .710

DESTINATION POPULARITY (FACTOR)
Place not many people go to .827
Popular place to go .594

GAMBLERS/FUN TRAVELERS
N = 265
28.1%

PLACE TO GAMBLE (FACTOR)
Gambling .882

1. VACATION PACKAGES THAT INCLUDE EVERYTHING

2. RESORT SET (FACTOR)
   Golf/tennis .702
   Hotels/accommodation available in all price ranges .657
   Fine dining/elegant, sophisticated restaurants .600
   Night life/entertainment .485

3. SUN SPORTS (FACTOR)
   Good beaches .863
   Near water — ocean, river, or lake .773
   Good place for sunbathing .701

4. AMUSEMENT OR THEME PARKS

5. CONVENIENCE (FACTOR)
   Can walk to sights/activities .721
   Good city services — transportation, streets and water .554

6. SCENERY (FACTOR)
   Good mountain areas .869
   Natural sights and scenery .611

7. EDUCATIONAL POSSIBILITIES (FACTOR)
   Experience different cultures .792
   Learn new things/personal enrichment .747
   Cultural activities — museums, galleries, opera,
      theater, and dance .726
   Number of places/points of interest .643
   Get guided tours .628
   Famous city/place .583
   Number of activities/things to do .509

8. VALUE (FACTOR)
   Reasonable cost to get there .764
   Can drive to the destination .757
   Good value for money .527

9. FRIENDS/RELATIVES (FACTOR)
   Place where friends/relatives live .858

EXHIBIT 9A-7 Proposed market segments based on the last destination visited.

to visit places where their family or friends live as opposed to places that are exciting or popular destinations.

Similarly, the availability of vacation packages that include everything is also relatively unimportant to members of this group. For example, only about one-third claim their last vacation destination offered vacation packages compared to 54.9% for the Adventurous/Educational group and 76.2% for the Gamblers/Fun Oriented cluster. The number of different priced hotels or accommodations is also relatively unimportant. Again, since this group may be staying with family or friends, accommodation costs would be relatively less important.

| EXHIBIT 9A-8 | "Top Three Box Scores" for "Last Destination" Ratings by Market Segment |

Variable	Total Sample (*n* = 1,196)	(A) Get Away/ Family Travelers (*n* = 356)	(B) Adventurous/ Educational (*n* = 289)	(C) Gamblers/ Fun Oriented (*n* = 265)
Know someone else who has been there	85.1%	93.5%C*	93.1%C	78.1%
Can rest and relax	75.3	90.4B	53.8	88.7B
Number of activities/things to do	67.5	61.0	71.9a	80.4AB
All members of party will like it equally	67.1	74.2B	56.6	79.2B
Realistically, it's a place I plan to visit in the next couple of years	66.8	76.1B	58.3	71.7B
No. of places and points of interest to see	66.7	68.5	71.5	67.5
Hotels/accommodations in all price ranges	65.5	58.1	66.3A	80.4AB
I really want to go there	63.2	71.9B	47.6	77.0B
Can drive to destination	63.0	73.6BC	63.5	58.1
There are natural sights and scenery	62.2	72.5BC	55.9	63.0b
There is opportunity for recreation or sports	61.8	53.7	66.7A	78.9AB
Near the water (ocean, river, lake)	61.1	69.7C	63.9	58.9
Friendly local residents	60.3	79.8BC	40.3	67.5B
Clean air	60.0	72.5B	41.0	70.9B
It's a popular place to go	59.0	46.3	62.8A	5.1AB
Famous city/place	58.7	45.5	71.2A	65.3A
Elegant, sophisticated restaurants	58.0	45.5	69.8A	67.2A
Good climate/weather	57.8	67.7B	36.5	81.1AB
Reasonable cost to get there	57.5	66.6B	49.3	69.8B
Very familiar with this city	54.8	64.3B	50.0	61.9B
Good value for the money	54.1	63.5B	33.0	74.0AB
Can play golf/tennis	51.5	48.0	51.4	64.9AB
Can get vacation packages which include everything	50.9	35.1	54.9A	76.2AB
Good night life and entertainment	50.8	36.0	61.1A	64.5A
A place where friends or relatives live	50.5	70.5BC	45.8C	34.7
Can learn new things/get personal enrichment	49.6	57.3Bc	44.4	49.4
Good place for sunbathing	47.9	40.4	44.4	66.8AB
It's a place for children	47.5	64.3AB	42.4	40.0
Cultural activities (museums, galleries, opera, theater, dance)	46.9	45.2c	58.7AC	37.7
Can get guided tours	46.6	41.0	57.0A	56.2A
Good city services	45.2	46.1	45.5	49.1
Can experience different cultures	44.0	45.5	44.8	41.5
Can walk to sights and activities	43.5	49.2b	41.7	42.6
Low crime rate/a safe place	39.8	55.1BC	25.0	44.5B
Good beaches	36.5	36.8	35.1	44.2aB
There are amusement or theme parks	35.7	36.2c	42.7aC	29.8
There are major professional sporting events	34.9	28.9	48.6AC	33.6
Good mountain areas	34.0	44.7BC	27.1	30.9
There is little traffic/congestion	31.9	43.8BC	21.9	32.1B
It's a place not many people go to	20.0	29.2BC	19.1C	10.2
Can gamble there	14.6	7.6	9.7	29.8AB
Somewhere I've never been before	13.5	7.0	25.0AC	8.7

*Capital letters mean significantly different at 95% than the number under the column with the same letter. Lowercase is significant at 90%–94%.

In terms of their last vacation destination, only about one-fourth of the Get Away/Family Travelers visited any beach/ocean/coastal destination. In contrast, more than one-third of the members of the other two segments chose this type of area to vacation. With regard to specific destination areas, 9.8% traveled out of the country, 9.3% visited a non-metro southern city, 7% went to Florida (not including Orlando), 3.7% visited San Francisco, another

3.7% explored Seattle/Tacoma/Portland, and the remaining visited less frequently named destinations. (The table pertaining to this information is not shown.)

No statistical difference was found between the various cluster segments on the demographic variables age and ethnicity. However, with an average age of 40, Get Away/Family Travelers are slightly older (significant at p = .08) than the Gamblers/Fun Oriented segment (average age 38). Compared to the other two groups, this segment has more members earning less than $25,000 per year—another possible explanation for their staying with family/friends when on vacation.

The second largest market segment consists of 289 travelers, or 30.7% of the traveling population. This group is similar in behaviors to concerns expressed by segment 6 (Foreign Vacationers) in Young, Ott and Feigin (1978). They are named Adventurous/Educational Travelers because one-fourth of their members' last vacation was to a place they had never been before. In contrast, only 7.0% of Get Away/Family Travelers and 8.7% of the Gamblers/Fun Oriented segment did the same. Additionally, more than one-half visited a place that had cultural activities such as museums, galleries, opera, theater, and dance. Finally, only 58% claimed they would visit their last vacation destination again within the next couple of years—suggesting the desire to visit new places.

More than two-thirds of this group also visited a place that:

■ Someone else they knew had been to (93.1%),
■ Offers a number of places/points of interest to see and a number of activities (71.5% and 71.9%, respectively),
■ Is a famous city/place (71.2%),
■ Has fine dining/elegant sophisticated restaurants (69.8%),
■ Provides the opportunity for recreation or sports (66.7%) and
■ Offers hotels or accommodations in all price ranges (66.3%).

One of the key aspects separating this group from the other two groups is that Adventurous/Educational Travelers are not concerned that the vacation destination be a place to rest and relax. Support for this is found by looking at Exhibit 9A-7: The vector representing this variable moves away from this market segment. Other areas of less concern include:

■ Whether all members of party will like it equally,
■ Environmental aspects of the destination (friendly local residents, traffic/congestion, low crime rate, and clean air), and
■ Cost to get there and the value for the money.

Behaviorally, members of this cluster take pleasure/vacation trips on the average of 1.6 times per year, significantly less than the Gamblers/Fun Oriented segment (2.0 trips), but statistically equal to members of the Get Away/ Family Travelers (1.7 trips). Adventurous/Educational Travelers make on the average 1.1 business trips and 0.72 combined business/pleasure trips per year. In terms of future trips, 43.6% claim they will travel more often next year. This figure is slightly higher than the percentage of Get Away/Family Travelers who claimed the same (36.2%) and more than the figure recorded by the Gamblers/Fun Oriented segment (34.3%).

One in eight respondents in this segment claimed Los Angeles was the last destination they visited. In fact, Los Angeles received more mentions than any other destination. Other areas included any foreign country (9.0%), Orlando (5.2%), Seattle/Tacoma/Portland (4.5%), southern urban areas (4.5%), and Hawaii (3.1%).

As discussed, there are no differences among the three groups in terms of sex, ethnicity, and marital status. The average age of this group is 39, which is also statistically equal to the age of the members of the other two groups. Approximately 13% of the respondents in this group live in California—compared to 11.2% for the Family Travelers and 7.9% for the Gamblers.

The third largest market segment accounts for 28% of the market. Members of this group are most similar to members in segment 5 (Resort Vacationers) identified by Young, Ott, and Feigin (1978). This group is named the Gamblers/Fun-Oriented cluster. As their name suggests this group places a high importance—as evidenced by the place they chose to visit last—on those variables associated with "gambling" and "fun." Specifically, members of this group last visited a place where:

■ One can gamble (29.8% versus 7.6% and 9.7% for the Family Travelers and Adventurous segments);
■ Opportunity for recreation or sports exists (78.9%), including golf/tennis (64.9%);
■ Popularity of the destination is high (75.1%);
■ Good night life and entertainment are available (64.5%); and
■ Fine dining/elegant sophisticated restaurants (67.2%) are available.

In addition, this group is also concerned about price/value. Specifically,

■ More than 80% vacationed at a place where hotels or accommodations are available in all price ranges,
■ Almost three-quarters rate their last destination a good value for the money, and
■ An equal percentage claim they could get vacation packages that included everything.

Finally, members of this group are more concerned that the destination have good beaches (44.2%), be a good place for sunbathing (66.8%), and have good climate/weather (81.1%). Attributes not as much a concern to this group include, but are not limited to:

- Cultural activities—museums, galleries, opera, theater, and dance (37.7%),
- Friends or relatives in residence there (34.7%),
- Amusement or theme parks (29.8%), and
- Lower popularity, i.e., a place not many people go to (10.2%).

Las Vegas was the most frequently mentioned last destination visited (9.1%) by members of this group. This is followed by Orlando (7.9%), other Florida destinations (7.9%), the Caribbean Islands (6.4%), Hawaii (5.7%), and Mexico (4.9%).

In terms of place of residence, 16.6% live in Texas—significantly different from Adventurous Travelers (9.0%) and directionally higher than Get Away/Family Travelers (13.3%).

More information about the three groups and their last vacation destination can be found in Exhibit 9A-8.

Implications

The findings in this study add support to the arguments made by Pearce and Caltabiano (1983) and Woodside and Jacobs (1985); namely, a good way to understand travel motivations (or desired benefits) is to infer them from consumers' past travel experience. Additionally, learning the benefits realized from a travel experience can offer useful insights for developing marketing strategies.

For example, the Gamblers/Fun Oriented group may be enticed to a destination by the variety of beaches, the great weather, and the "fun" that can be had. Adventurous/Educational Travelers may like to hear about the cultural and personal enrichment opportunities available in the area. Family Travelers, on the other hand, may be attracted to marketing tactics that stress that there is something for everyone, that one can rest and relax, and that the destination offers a good value. Cruise ships immediately come to mind as something this group might like.

The segments identified via benefits realized are similar to those identified by Young, Ott, and Feigin (1978), suggesting validity to the new derived segments. Although the Young, Ott, and Feigin (1978) study was undertaken more than 10 years ago, similar market segments were identified, even though that study looked at benefits sought while this one looked at benefits realized. Specifically, the behaviors of Get Away/Family Travelers were similar to the desires of segments 1, 3, and 4 shown in Exhibit 9A-2. Similarly, Adventurous/Educational Travelers' benefits were similar to the wants of the Foreign Vacationers (segment 6) while Gamblers/Fun Oriented are closely identified with Resort Vacationers (segment 5) shown in Exhibit 9A-2. These similarities do not suggest that it does not matter whether one looks at benefits sought or benefits desired; they only imply that there is support for the derived segments.

As mentioned, although consumers say that a particular attribute is a major concern when choosing a vacation destination, the lack of that attribute will not rule out that destination as a place to visit on vacation. For example, while travelers claim to be concerned with going "somewhere new" (mean response 7.43), this attribute did not characterize the last vacation destination for most (mean response 2.61). For destinations that may not be considered completely safe, or may have some other perceived disadvantages, this is good news.

For five of the attributes (hotels available in all price ranges, how much it costs to get there, cleanliness of the air, experiencing different cultures, and the availability of amusement or theme parks) the difference between concern rating and last destination rating was quite small ($\leq = .08$). these attributes may be considered critical because for these attributes "ideal" matches "behavior." The nature of the attributes suggests that some consumers may be employing a "risk avoidance" strategy when choosing a vacation destination. This belief is reinforced by the finding that the mean rating for the attribute "know someone else who has been there" was 8.96 for the last destination. From a managerial perspective, this suggests that tourism marketers must develop strategies that reduce perceived risk of choosing a vacation destination. It also suggests that tourism marketers need to know more about how consumers use different benefits to remove or reduce perceived risk. As I have argued, the way to do this is to look not at benefits sought, but at benefits realized.

The ability to derive meaningful benefit segments based on past experience suggests that past experience may be useful in other types of segmentation strategies. For example, many travel researchers have used life-style/psychographic variables as a means of segmentation (Schewe and Calatone 1978; Hawes 1977; Woodside and Pitts 1976; Solomon and William 1977; Abbey 1979). Yet many of the life-style/psychographic attributes are written in the present tense. It would be interesting to examine whether and how responses would change if the characteristics were written to measure actual behavior. For example, how would responses have changed if instead of writing "I take pride in traveling places where my friends have never been," Abbey (1979) had written, "On my past vacation I traveled to a place where my friends have never been." Similarly, instead of writing "I would welcome an evening of ballet while on vacation," Abbey could have written "On past vacations, I have gone to the ballet." The results from the study presented in this article suggest that the answers to the revised questions may have been different. Similar comments can be made for other segmentation strategies such as person/situation segmentation (Dickson 1972), which "occurs when markets are divided on the basis of the usage situation in conjunction with individual differences of consumers" (Peter and Olson 1990, p. 583). Future research should address these issues.

Future research should also investigate whether and how the inferred destination benefits vary by type of vacation. After all, as shown in Exhibit 9A-1, the motivation for travel ranges from the desire to engage in educational and cultural activities to the desire to have a change of weather. This study looked at just the last vacation without further dividing it into other such subgroups. Clearly, such information would add insight into the inferred benefits and derived market segments. Similarly, life-style characteristics would have also made the derived clusters "come alive." Schewe and Calatone (1978) provide a good example of how the two go hand-in-hand. Future research needs to include questions to measure these aspects.

Limitations

Like most research projects, this one suffers from the "if only I had asked that question" syndrome. Clearly, respondents should have been asked how and where they obtained information about their last vacation destination. Additionally, the question "which travel publication do you subscribe to" should have been "which travel publication do you read, and how often." Similarly, information regarding television viewership and general magazine and newspaper readership would have been useful.

Respondents would have also been asked how frequently they visited their last vacation destination and how typical this last vacation destination was of the places they go to when on vacation. Although respondents were asked whether they would visit the destination again in the next couple of years, they were not asked directly how much they enjoyed the vacation destination. This would have been useful.

Similarly, it would have been useful to know whether any situational constraints affected their last vacation destination choice. As mentioned above, questions pertaining to life-style/psychographics would also have been useful.

These limitations do not invalidate the findings presented. Their absence only makes the data less rich than they might have been. Hopefully, future travel researchers will incorporate these suggestions into their studies.

Summary

The study presented is based on the thesis suggested in the works by Dann (1981), Pearce and Caltabiano (1983), and Woodside and Jacobs (1985), who believed that the best way to truly understand consumers' motivations for vacation travel or benefits sought from a vacation destination is to study consumers' past travel behavior. Because consumers may be unable or unwilling to express their real travel motives, it is best not to look at the benefits they seek, but rather to look at the benefits they realized. As Ajzen and Fishbein (1980) and this study have demonstrated, what consumers say they want and what they will actually buy can be quite different.

The research went beyond the earlier works cited by (1) performing a segmentation study based on the derived benefits and, (2) using a sampling methodology that was not destination-specific. The sampling methodology employed also allows for the findings to be generalizeable to those U.S. citizens who fit the qualification criteria.

Four market segments were identified, one quite small; therefore, only three were discussed in detail. Some have benefits desired similar to those presented by Young, Ott and Feigin (1978). The three segments identified in this study were named Get Away/Family Travelers (37.8%), Adventurous/Educational Travelers (30.7%), and Gamblers/Fun Oriented Travelers (28.1%). While our clusters were deemed the most appropriate for reasons presented earlier, additional cluster solutions were also investigated.

References

Abbey, James R. (1979). "Does Life-Style Profiling Work?" *Journal of Travel Research, 18* (Summer): 8–14.

Ajzen, Icek, and Martin Fishbein (1980). *Understanding Attitudes and Predicting Social Behavior.* Englewood Cliffs, NJ: Prentice Hall.

Aldenderfer, Mark S., and Roger K. Blashfield (1984). *Cluster Analysis: Series: Quantitative Application in the Social Sciences.* London: Sage Publications.

Bonn, Mark A. (1982). "The Relative Utility of Sociodemographics, Psychographic Scales and Benefits for Segmenting Pleasure Vacation Markets." Doctoral dissertation, Texas A&M University.

Bryant, Barbara E., and Andrew J. Morrison (1980). "Travel Market Segmentation and the Implementation of Market Strategies." *Journal of Travel Research, 18* (Winter): 2–8.

Calantone, Roger J., Charles Schewe, and C. T. Allen (1980). "Targeting Specific Advertising Messages at Tourist Segments." In *Tourism Marketing and Management,* edited by D. E. Hawkins, E. L. Shafer, and J. M.

Rovelstad. Washington DC: George Washington University, pp. 133–147.

Chon, Kye-Sung, Pamela A. Weaver, and Choi Yong Kim (1991). "Marketing Your Community: Image Analysis in Norfolk." *Cornell HRA Quarterly, 31* (February): 31–37.

Crandall, Rick (1980). "Motivations for Lesiure." *Journal of Leisure Research, 12* (1): 45–53.

Crompton, John (1979). "Motivations for Pleasure Travel." *Annals of Tourism Research, 4:* 408–424.

Dann, Graham M. S. (1981). "Tourist Motivation: An Appraisal." *Annals of Tourism Research, 8:* 187–219.

Dickson, Peter R. (1972). "Person-Situation: Segmentation's Missing Link." *Journal of Marketing, 46:* 56–64.

Dillon, William R., and Matthew Goldstein (1984). *Multivariate Analysis: Methods and Applications.* New York: Wiley.

Etzel, M. J., and A. G. Woodside (1982). "Segmenting Vacation Markets: The Case of the Distant and Near-Home Travelers." *Journal of Travel Research, 16* (Spring): 10–14.

Goodrich, Jonathan N. (1977). "Benefit Bundle Analysis: An Empirical Study of International Travelers." *Journal of Travel Research, 16* (Fall): 6–9.

———— (1978). "The Relationship Between Preferences for and Perceptions of Vacation Destinations: Applications of a Choice Model." *Journal of Travel Research, 17* (Fall): 8–13.

Hawes, Douglass K. (1977). "Psychographics are Meaningful . . . Not Merely Interesting." *Journal of Travel Research, 15* (Spring): 1–7.

Lundberg, Donald E. (1971). "Why Tourists Travel" *Cornell HRA Quarterly* (February): 75–81.

Maslow, Abraham H. (1943). "A Theory of Human Motivations." *Psychological Review, 40:* 370–396.

Matejka, J. K. (1973). "Critical Factors in Vacation Area Selection." *Arkansas Business and Economic Review, 6:* 17–19.

Mazanec, Josef A. (1984). "How to Detect Travel Market Segments: A Clustering Approach." *Journal of Travel Research, 23* (Summer): 17–21.

Mazis, M. B., O. T. Ahtola, and R. E. Klippel (1975). "A Comparison of Four Multi-Attribute Models in the Prediction of Consumer Attitudes." *Journal of Consumer Research, 2:* 38–52.

Pearce, Phillip L., and Marie Caltabiano (1983). "Inferring Travel Motivation from Travelers' Experiences." *Journal of Travel Research, 22* (Fall): 25–30.

Peter, J. Paul, and Jerry C. Olson (1990). *Consumer Behavior and Marketing Strategy* (2nd ed.). Boston: Irwin.

Rubenstein, Carin (1980). "Report on How Americans View Vacations." *Psychology Today,* May: 62–76.

Schewe, Charles D., and Roger J. Calantone (1978). "Psychographic Segmentation of Tourists." *Journal of Travel Research, 16* (Winter): 14–20.

Shoemaker, Stowe (1989). "Segmentation of the Senior Pleasure Travel Market." *Journal of Travel Research, 27* (Winter): 14–21.

Solomon, Paul J., and George R. William (1977). "The Bicentennial Traveler: A Life-Style Analysis of the Historian Segment." *Journal of Travel Research, 15* (Winter): 14–17.

Um, Seoho, and John L. Crompton (1990). "Attitude Determinants in Tourism Destination Choice." *Annals of Tourism Research, 17:* 432–448.

Woodside, Arch G., and Lawrence W. Jacobs (1985). "Step Two in Benefit Segmentation: Learning the Benefits Realized by Major Travel Markets." *Journal of Travel Research, 24* (Summer): 7–13.

Woodside, Arch G., and Steven Lysonski (1989). "A General Model of Travel Destination Choice." *Journal of Travel Research, 27* (Spring): 8–14.

Woodside, Arch G., and Robert E. Pitts (1976). "Effects of Consumer Life Styles, Demographics, and Travel Activities on Foreign and Domestic Travel Behavior." *Journal of Travel Research, 14* (Winter): 13–15.

Young, Shirley, Leeland Ott, and Barbara Feigin (1978). "Some Practical Considerations in Market Segmentation." *Journal of Marketing Research, 15:* 405–412.

Understanding the Marketing Research Process: A Guide to Using an Outside Research Supplier

Stowe Shoemaker

Reprinted with permission from International Journal of Hospitality Management, *Vol. 13 No. 1, pp 36–56, 1994. Copyright © 1994 Elsevier Science Ltd. Printed in Great Britain. All rights reserved. 0278-4319(94)E0004-4*

Abstract

The competitive environment facing the hospitality industry has forced executives at all levels to learn more about the needs and wants of their customers and how their own business can meet these needs. Marketing research is one of the ways executives learn about their customers. In his article in the *Cornell Quarterly*, Peter Yesawich explained how an individual property can conduct its own studies using in-house resources. This article adds to the work of Yesawich by explaining how to use an outside marketing research contractor to undertake specific studies. Specifically, this article provides an overview of the different types of marketing research contractors, their strengths and weaknesses, and ways to choose and evaluate them. The information is directed at those who realize the need for marketing research but are unfamiliar with either the process of marketing research or how to buy it. The reasons for using an outside contractor and the steps involved in a marketing research study are also explored.

Introduction

It is no secret that the hospitality industry has become quite competitive. This competitive environment has forced executives at all levels to learn more about the needs and wants of their customers and how their own business can meet these needs. Marketing research is one of the ways executives learn about their customers.

What is marketing research? Churchill (1991) defines marketing research as "the function linking the consumer to the marketer through information used to identify and define marketing opportunities and problems; generate, refine, and evaluate marketing actions; monitor marketing performance; and improve understanding of marketing as a process." Specific kinds of questions marketing research can help answer include, but are not limited to:

- What is the position of the firm relative to its competition?
- What is a firm's market share?
- Who are the customers and why do they buy the product?
- Which types of new products or promotions are likely to be the most successful and why?
- Which advertising messages are most likely to succeed?

The idea of using marketing research to understand one's customers is certainly not new to the larger, multi-unit firms involved in the hospitality industry. Marriott, for example, used research to develop its Courtyard property (Goldberg, Green, & Wind, 1984), and Hilton Hotels used research to create its BounceBack Weekend promotion (Quirk's Marketing Research Review, 1989a). Similarly, Marie Callender's Restaurants use research to stay in touch with the needs of their customers in the Los Angeles area (Quirk's Marketing Research Review, 1989b).

Marketing research need not, however, be limited to multi-unit chains with their own marketing research departments. Individual properties can also use marketing research either by using limited in-house internal resources, or by using outside marketing research contractors. Yesawich (1987) has already shown how an individual property can conduct its own studies using in-house resources. This article adds to the work of Yesawich by explaining how to use an outside marketing research contractor to undertake specific studies. Specifically, it provides an overview of the different types of marketing research contractors, their strengths and weaknesses, and ways to evaluate and choose them. The information is directed at those who realize the need for marketing research but are not familiar with either the process of marketing research or how to buy it.

Before examining the different types of marketing research contractors, it is first necessary to review both the reasons for using an outside contractor and the steps involved in a research study. Only with such an understanding will one be able to properly use an outside contractor.

Reasons for Using an Outside Contractor

One reason for using outside contractors is that they can supply expertise that is not readily available in-house. Those with expertise in a given area can usually perform the tasks more efficiently and more accurately. They are also more likely to foresee potential problems before they surface.

A second reason is cost. It may be less expensive to out-source all or part of the study than incur the expense of one or more full-time employees. An article in the *New York Times* drove home this point: "Companies are looking closely at virtually everything they do and applying the market test: can it be done at least as well and cheaper by an outside supplier?" (Lohr 1992).

A third reason is flexibility. Use of outside contractors allows one to conduct more than one study at a time and keep in-house people focused on what they do best. Finally, contractors may be more objective and less subject to internal politics (Dillon, Madden, & Firtle, 1987). This helps ensure that an unbiased approach will be taken to the study. The type of contractor one needs depends, of course, on the phase of the study being contracted out. These phases are discussed next.

Steps in a Research Project

Exhibit 11A-1 shows the major steps involved in a research project. The major steps are purposely divided into many smaller steps. The first five steps: defining the management problem (the problem confronting the decision maker), identifying the research purpose (what you intend to do with the findings), the research problem (questions to be answered to fulfill the research purpose), research objectives (things that need to be known to answer the research problem), and determining what we expect to know (all the pieces of information necessary to fulfill the objectives), are the most critical as every step that follows flows from these first five (Lewis & Chambers, 1989). Lewis and Chambers provide an excellent detailed explanation, using a mini-case, of each of these five steps.

The sixth step involves the search for secondary data— data gathered for some other purpose. Examples of secondary data include articles published in trade or academic journals, census data, store audit, and diary panel data. For hotels, a prime source of secondary data is guest registration forms (Dev & Ellis, 1991). The next step involves exploratory data collection, such as focus group or in-depth interviews. Exploratory data collection is undertaken both to help the marketer gain ideas and insights from the target audience and to learn the "language" of the customer. For example, the terms "rack rate" and "yield management" are part of the hotel industry's jargon, not of its customers. Therefore, if one is interested in the customers' opinions on these issues, they need to be phrased in such a way that the respondents would understand the question.

The eighth step is the data tabulation plan. The data tabulation plan is included early because it forces the researcher to think about possible relationships among variables and how to analyze these relationships (i.e., what statistical tests to apply). This, in turn, determines the level of measurement needed for each variable on the questionnaire.

The ninth step is the study design. Questions addressed here include the methodology (i.e., mail survey vs. telephone survey vs. in-store survey, or any combination of these three), the questionnaire design and layout, and instructions for the supervisors. The study design is followed by the sample selection and implementation. Included in this area are the purchase of a sample (either random digit or listed) and procedures to ensure that the final sample is representative of the target population.

Steps 10 through 15 deal with the actual data collection or, in the vernacular of research professionals, the "fielding" of the study. Notice that each of these steps is undertaken to guarantee that the data collection follows the study design.

Once the data has been collected, it is necessary to edit the questionnaires (check for incomplete surveys, quotas, etc.) and begin building the numeric codes for the open-ended (free response) questions. For example, the author recently completed a proprietary study where respondents were asked to name what they particularly liked and disliked about their stay at a specific hotel. All these likes and dislikes had to be categorized into logical groups (e.g., mentions pertaining to facilities, service staff, and atmosphere and/or decor) and assigned numbers so that a count could be made of each type of mention. Similar to the data collection phase, the coding phase needs to be controlled to ensure consistency and accuracy. Coding also has to be verified. All these activities are shown in steps 16–20.

Steps 21 and 22 include inputting the responses into the computer for later analysis. Again, it is important that the keypunching (the process of typing the numeric responses into the computer) be verified. This ensures that the data in the computer accurately reflects the information found in the questionnaires. The final two stages before the analysis

1. Identify the Management Problem
   - The problem confronting the decision maker
2. Define the Research Purpose
   - The research purpose derives from the management problem. The purpose of the research is what you intend to do with the findings—that is, what kinds of business decisions you plan after you have the results.
3. Define the Research Problem
   - The research problem defines the questions to be answered to fulfill the research purpose. For example, if the management problem is declining business, the research problem is to answer the question: "What is causing business to decline?"
4. Define the Research Objectives
   - The research objectives are those things that need to be known to answer the research problem.
5. Define What We Expect to Know
   - What we expect to know is all the pieces of information that are necessary to fulfill the objectives.
6. Search Secondary Data
   - Includes published articles, past studies, government documents, etc.
7. Exploratory Data Collection
   - Includes focus group interviews and in-depth personal interviews
8. Determine the Tabulation Plan
   - Determine the number of banner points
   - Determine the cost of additional tables once the study is processed
   - Determine the type of statistical tests to be used
   - Determine if advanced multivariate techniques should be applied to the data
9. Study Design
   - Prepare the questionnaire (write, pretest, print, collate, mark rotation patterns, column number questionnaire)
   - Schedule interviewing dates with field services/phone banks
   - Prepare interviewer and supervisor instructions
   - Determine study methodology (e.g., pre-recruit personal interview, in-store intercept, mall intercept, telephone, mail, or any combination of above)
   - Prepare study budget
10. Sample Selection
    - For telephone studies, purchase RDD [random digit dial] samples for area probability samples or reserve directories for listed area samples
    - For mail surveys, purchase or gather lists, check lists for duplicates, check for proper zip codes
    - For mall intercepts, select malls whose shopper demographics match the target population
    - For in-store sampling, select stores that are representative of the system, have enough customers to ensure a large number of completed surveys, and can handle the interruptions caused by interviewing
    - Prepare sampling instructions and quota sheets to ensure that the final sample is representative of the target population
11. Field Control
    - Brief supervisors and interviewers on job specifics
    - Ensure that all job supplies (e.g., questionnaires, etc.) are in the proper locations prior to the start of the study
    - Make sure there are sufficient controls to detect problems before they become too costly
    - Arrange a mechanism for alerting the home office to any problems that may arise
    - Coordinate shipment of extra supplies to the field and completed work to home office
12. Field Supervision
    - Prepare a list of items that the supervisor should be especially concerned with when overseeing the study
    - Prepare a mechanism to ensure that the supervisor spends time on your job and not on other studies that are being conducted simultaneously
    - Prepare interviewer evaluation sheets for the supervisors so that the interviewers can be judged uniformly
13. Field Interviewers
    - Develop a mechanism to ensure that the interviewers are selected, trained, evaluated and retrained or terminated
    - Develop a procedure to ensure that interviewers new to a study receive a proper briefing
    - Prepare guidelines for codes of dress and behavior while "on duty"
14. Field Quality Checks
    - Design a system to monitor the quality of the interviewing
    - Check skip patterns and answers by interviewer for possible cheating
    - Examine respondent names and phone numbers for possible "professional respondents"
15. Validation
    - Determine the percentage of interviews that need to be validated
    - Determine method of validation (e.g., phone call, postcard, etc.)
    - Decide who is responsible for the validation: the home office or the field service
16. Editing
    - Prepare editing instructions and go over them with the editors
    - Decide who is responsible for the editing: the home office or the field service
17. Code Building
    - Determine how large a sample should be used to develop the codes and how the sample should be selected
    - Determine if codes should be recorded verbatim or collapsed and, if collapsed, where and how
    - Determine how to code missing or nonsensical answers
18. Coding
    - Determine how coding should be done (i.e., one question at a time or one survey at a time)
    - Determine what happens to the "all other" category (i.e., how large can it get)
    - Determine the physical layout of the coding area so that coders can see the codes easily
    - Determine if questions should be asked as they occur or should there be a "question" pile
19. Coding Control
    - Determine the controls for coding accountability (e.g., each coder is assigned a specific question or a specific set of pre-numbered questionnaires)
20. Coding Verifications
    - Determine what percentage of the coding should be verified
    - Determine when verification should be done (e.g., at the beginning or continuous)
21. Keypunching
    - Examine the keypunchers' qualifications
    - Determine the extent of control and supervision over the keypunchers
22. Keypunch Verification
    - Determine the percentage of work to be verified
    - Determine who is responsible for verification
23. Cleaning Procedures
    - Determine how errors are to be corrected (e.g., will each error be checked against the actual questionnaire or will the computer delete incorrect responses)
    - Ensure that the person cleaning the data is familiar with the questionnaire
    - Create a system to record how much cleaning was necessary
24. Print Final Data Results
25. Analysis and Interpretation
    - Analyze the data and write the report

This Table is adapted from both Charles S. Mayer (1967), "Evaluating the Quality of Marketing Research Contractors," *Journal of Marketing Research*, Vol IV(May), pp. 134–141; Robert C. Lewis and Richard Chambers (1989), *Marketing Leadership in Hospitality*, New York: Van Nostrand; and the author's own experience as a marketing research contractor.

involve cleaning up the data (e.g., looking for improper key punches) and printing the responses in a readable format. The final phase of the research project is the analysis, interpretation, and writing up of the findings. Normally included in the final report are the strategic and tactical recommendations to address the issues explored in the research.

Sources of Research

The company sponsoring the research can subcontract either all or part of the research steps shown in Exhibit 11A-2. There are basically six types of contractors to which to outsource a firm's research needs. These six types of contractors are shown in Exhibit 11A-2 and discussed next.

Full Service Suppliers

The first type of outside contractor is the full service supplier. As its name suggests, the capabilities of this group include all phases of the study from defining the research purpose to writing the final report. Practically all parts of the project are handled by full service suppliers, although they may subcontract out some or all of the data collection. Examples of well known full service suppliers include Audits and Surveys, Market Facts, Walker Research, and Yankelovich Clancy Shulman. Two firms specializing in hotels and restaurants include IHR Research (Irvine, CA) and DK Shifflet and Associates (Washington, DC).

The typical organizational chart of a full service supplier is shown in Exhibit 11A-3. Reporting directly to the President or Senior Partner (the first level) are the Junior Partners or Vice Presidents. The role of those at this second level depends to a great extent on the size of the company. In large organizations, there are separate VPs for servicing clients and supervising the in-house staff functions. In smaller companies these roles may be served by the same person.

| EXHIBIT 11A-2 | Steps Typically Involved in a Research Project and Those Usually Responsible for Their Completion |

Steps	Research Buyer	Full Svc Suppliers	Data Tabulation Houses	Advertising Agencies	Data Collection Companies	Consultants	Focus Group Moderators
1. Identify Management Problem	x	x		x		x	
2. Define the Research Purpose (decisions to be made)	x	x		x		x	
3. Define the Research Problem (questions to be answered to fulfill the purpose)	x	x		x		x	
4. Define the Research Objectives (what needs to be known to answer research problem)	x	x		x		x	
5. Define What We Expect to Know	x	x		x		x	
6. Search Secondary Data	x	x		x		x	
7. Exploratory Data Collection		x		x	x	x	x
8. Determine the Tabulation Plan	x	x		x		x	
9. Study Design	x	x		x		x	
10. Sample Selection	x	x		x	x	x	
11. Field Control		x			x	x	
12. Field Supervision		x			x		
13. Field Interviewers		x			x		
14. Field Quality Checks		x			x		
15. Validation		x			x		
16. Editing		x			x		
17. Code Building	x	x		x		x	
18. Coding		x				x	
19. Coding Control		x				x	
20. Coding Verifications		x				x	
21. Keypunching			x				
22. Keypunch Verification		x	x			x	
23. Cleaning Procedure		x	x			x	
24. Print Final Data Results		x	x				
25. Analysis and Interpretation	x	x		x		x	x

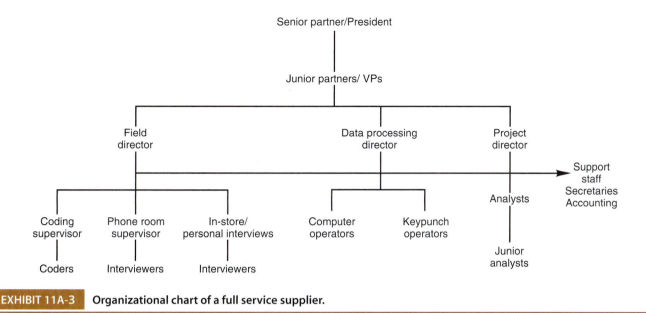

EXHIBIT 11A-3 **Organizational chart of a full service supplier.**

Under the VPs/Junior Partners are the specific staff functions: the field director, the data processing director, and the project directors. Those employees at the director level have overall responsibility for all activities within their area. For example, the field director is responsible for the coders and telephone and in-store interviewers. Similarly, the data processing director is responsible for all employees involved in the data processing. Under the project directors (those who have overall responsibility for design, implementation, and management of research projects) are the analysts (who handle the details involved in executing the project—such as designing and pretesting the questionnaire) and junior analysts (who handle routine assignments such as secondary data analysis and simple statistical analysis). In larger companies, project directors will work directly for a specific VP. In contrast, project directors at smaller firms will report to many VPs/Junior Partners. While the larger firms will conduct research for a variety of industries, the smaller full service firms tend to specialize in specific industries.

Full service marketing research firms typically advertise in the yellow pages under Marketing. They can also be found in *The Researcher SourceBook* (Published by Quirk Enterprises: Minneapolis, MN). Other sources of information include the *Dun's Directory of Service Companies* (published by Dun's Marketing Services in Parsippary, NJ), *The AMA Directory* (published by the American Marketing Association in Chicago, IL), the MRA directory (published by the Marketing Research Association in Rocky Hill, CT), and the *Green Book* (published by the New York Chapter of the American Marketing Association located in New York City.)

Well-established and recommended full service marketing research firms are best used by those who have never

undertaken a marketing research study. Because these firms will help define the research purpose, the research problem, and the research objectives, the novice research buyer can be confident that the research will produce actionable results. This confidence does come at a cost, however. It is usually more expensive to subcontract all facets of a study.

Data Tabulation Houses

The second type of outside contractor is the data tabulation house. As their name suggests, data tabulation houses are responsible for tabulating the survey results and supplying their clients with a set of data tables that present the findings in readable and usable format.

Data tables usually provide all the necessary statistical tests to test for differences between various subgroups (e.g., are men different from women in terms of their attitudes toward the hotel), as data tabulation houses normally have a variety of statistical programs at their disposal. Some so-called "tab" houses will also provide more sophisticated multivariate statistical analyses.

In addition to supplying readable and statistically tested tables, tab houses are also responsible for data entry. This is the process of turning the completed questionnaires and written responses into numbers that the computer can read and tabulate. The proliferation of personal computers and canned PC statistical programs such as SPSS, SYSTAT, and SAS have made it possible to use tab houses simply as reliable and quick data entry professionals.

Data tabulation houses can have any number of employees. Most, however, have one owner, a few full-time employees, and many part-time keypunch operators and computer operators. Data tabulation houses typically advertise in the yellow pages under Marketing Research or Computer Services. Another good source is a full service marketing research supplier in the area who can make recommendations.

Data tabulation houses are an excellent place to tabulate guest comment cards or other internally generated data (e.g., guest registration cards, internally generated questionnaires, etc.). Because they normally have access to many computers and employees to work on the computers, job turnaround is usually quite fast. For those who do not need a fast turnaround, it may be possible to negotiate a lower rate by taking advantage of non-peak pricing. Most tab houses will also help you design the layout of your comment card or registration card for easy input, again helping save money. (It would not be advisable to have them help you design your questionnaires as their expertise is in data tabulation and keypunching, not in questionnaire designing.)

Advertising Agencies

Advertising agencies are a third source of outside research support. The type and extent of the service provided by them varies by company. For example, some firms have their own internal data collection capabilities while others use full service suppliers or field services (to be discussed next) to do much of the work (Dillon, Madden, & Firtle, 1987). The types of marketing research conducted by advertising agencies include conducting focus group interviews, pre-testing advertising copy, measuring advertising effectiveness (by examining awareness and recall either in a controlled or "real world" setting), and conducting or overseeing market segmentation or positioning studies.

The number and types of employees in the research department will depend upon the number of clients and the types of studies. Larger agencies will normally have a senior research director who will supervise any number of junior research directors. The junior research directors supervise any number of project directors. Research directors and their project directors tend to work for a group of clients. In contrast, a smaller agency may have one research director and a small group of project directors working for all the clients of the agency. Advertising agencies, like the other contractors mentioned so far, can be found in the yellow pages under Marketing or Advertising.

While advertising agencies normally offer competent research services, it may be advisable to have an independent source conduct one's research, especially if the research involves advertising effectiveness. This is because rarely will an advertising firm present results which show that the advertising is ineffective. In addition, the internal politics of an agency may favor a certain type of advertising campaign and, intentionally or unintentionally, the research may be biased to favor that campaign. For these reasons, this author advises that such research be conducted independently.

Data Collection Companies

Data collection companies are responsible for recruiting and interviewing respondents. One type of data collection company is the field service company or firm. Anyone who has been approached in a shopping mall and asked to complete a survey has encountered this type of data collection company first hand.

Field services have evolved over the last 15 years from a cottage industry to professionally run businesses. Early field services were independent and run from a supervisor's home with friends as interviewers. Now, most have a national affiliation, operate from a professional office building or a shopping mall, and have trained and MRA (Marketing Research Association) certified interviewers (Jacobs, 1990). Four of the larger nationally affiliated field services are Equifax/Quick Test Opinion Centers, Consumer Pulse, Heakin Research, and Quality Controlled Services.

Field services vary in terms of their offerings. At one end are the firms that only supply interviewing and field control (e.g., insuring interviewers are sampling the right people, etc.). At the other end are firms that not only supply interviewing and field control but also have their own focus group facilities, test kitchens, phone banks for pre-recruiting respondents, and coding and tabulating services. Field services are located in all the major cities and towns throughout the United States. This enables companies to sample respondents from any region of the country.

The second type of data collection company is the national central location telephone facility (CLT) or WATS house. As their name implies, these companies are used primarily to conduct interviews over the telephone. CLTs range in size and scope. Some offer instantaneous data collection by having all interviews conducted on the computer, while others still collect data using paper and pencil. Most have the technology which enables a supervisor to monitor interviews and some have the technology which enables the client to call from his/her home or office to monitor interviews in progress.

Just as the field services have evolved into much more professional organizations, so have the CLTs. Initially, there were very few CLTs doing national calling. Instead, most telephone interviewing was done in decentralized local facilities within each market, or from the interviewer's home (Gershowitz, 1990). Lists provided by the client or phone books were the normal source of phone numbers. But, according to Howard Gershowitz, an executive of a major CLT, much of this has changed with the increased competition brought about by the divestiture of AT&T (Gershowitz, 1990). Suddenly, affordable long distance calling was made available to everyone.

The affordability of long distance calling meant that instead of having calling done from many areas to save long distance phone charges, a study could be completed from one area. This led to bigger staff within a CLT (rather than 10 people under five different roofs, now there could be 50 under one) and more control over training and supervision. The advances in computer generated random digit phone samples by such companies as Survey Sampling and Scientific Telephone Samples also reduced the need for local phone books while at the same time providing better quality samples (for more information on random digit phone samples, see Churchill, 1991).

The best source of data collection companies is the MRA directory. Similarly, data collection companies are listed in *The Researcher SourceBook* published by Quirk Enterprises.

Whenever a personal interview is involved, it is always advisable to have professionally trained interviewers collect the data. Interviewers need to be independent and cannot let their own feelings or their position influence the respondent. While guests may feel uncomfortable telling an employee the truth about their experience, they probably will have no problem telling an independent outsider about their true feelings. A second reason for using professionally trained interviewers is that they have also learned the "tricks" on how to entice consumers to participate, thus increasing the response rate and lowering the cost per completed interview. Finally, the use of professional interviewers will help guarantee that all responses, both good and bad, are given to those financing the survey.

Consultants

The fifth type of outside contractor is the consultant or, as defined by the *New York Times,* the "hired gun" (Lohr, 1992). Lohr predicts that there will be an increase in the use of consultants due to the current corporate downsizing movement. He believes that many who cannot find jobs, or take early retirement, will turn to consulting as a way to earn income.

Consultants are different from full service suppliers in that they tend to out-source most of their work except the analysis and interpretation. An example is Wendy Liebmann, a former marketing executive, who founded a New York–based marketing research consulting firm in 1986. Her client list has grown, but the firm still operates with a core of three professionals. Tasks like field research are farmed out to others. "We believe in hiring outside specialists just as our clients hire us as specialists" (Lohr, 1992).

Consultants usually advertise in the yellow pages under Marketing. Another good source is the AMA membership directory. A third source is the *Directory of Consultants* (published by the International Society of Hospitality Consultants located in Memphis, TN). A fourth source is *The Researcher SourceBook*. Many university faculty also offer their services on a contractual basis.

Consultants are best used to help separate the management problem from the symptoms. They also can help define the research purpose, the research problem and the research objectives, and can help with the study design. Their other strength is that they can help develop marketing strategies based on the research. Because many of the consultants out-source much of the work, it is important to ask which parts of the job will be out-sourced and to whom. It is also important to know the types of companies the consultant has worked for and the types of studies they have undertaken. Consultants have different strengths and research buyers contracting their services need to be sure that the strengths they are buying are the ones needed.

Focus Group Moderators

This final group of contractors is concerned mainly with conducting and preparing the results of focus group interviews. Greenbaum (1988) lists ten criteria of evaluation for good focus group moderators. These criteria are listed in Exhibit 11A-4. As shown in this table, they include such characteristics as a "friendly" leader, knowledgeable but not all knowing, excellent memory, empathetic, and a good writer.

Many full service suppliers have a moderator among their staff, but advertising agencies and field services often hire these independent contractors on a per-project basis. Because of this, advertising agencies and field services are a good source for names of moderators. Again, another good source is *The Researcher SourceBook*. (For more detailed information on focus groups, see Templeton, 1987.)

Choosing Research Contractors

When choosing a specific marketing research contractor, it is important to remember that when one chooses an outside contractor, one enters into a relationship. Like all relationships, this too needs to be built on a series of trusts. There is trust that the contractor will live up to all the presale promises, will keep the study confidential, and that every phase of the study will be undertaken with the utmost care so as not to bias the results. Additionally, one needs to trust that the staff assigned to the job will have expertise in the areas the hiring firm needs, and trust that only the truth will be reported—even if it is unpopular or unexpected.

EXHIBIT 11A-4	Ten Criteria of Good Focus Group Moderators

1. Quick Learner
   - Must be able to quickly understand what the client (research buyer) is seeking from the focus group and must be able to absorb and understand the inputs from the group respondents.
2. A "Friendly" Leader
   - Must be able to develop rapport with group respondents quickly. Should be viewed as an authority figure (to maintain control) and at the same time as the type of person one would like to have a conversation with.
3. Knowledgeable But Not All Knowing
   - Moderator needs to communicate to the group that he/she has some knowledge of the subject matter but is not an expert. If members of the group feel that the moderator is the expert, they will ask questions rather than provide the answers.
4. Excellent Memory
   - Must be able to recall comments made early in an interview so that statements made later can be cross-checked for consistency of the participant's viewpoints.
5. Good Listener
   - Must be able to hear all the information people convey, in terms of both content and implication.

6. A Facilitator, Not a Performer
   - The moderator's goal is to obtain information from the group, not to entertain them or the clients who are watching. Too much moderator-generated humor will result in less-than-satisfactory inputs from the participants.
7. Flexible
   - Must be able to deviate from the prearranged discussion points to capitalize on inputs of valuable discussion.
8. Empathetic
   - Must be able to relate to the nervousness of some respondents. If the respondent senses this empathy, he/she is more likely to participate actively in the discussion.
9. A "Big Picture" Thinker
   - Must be able to separate the important observations from the less significant ones and follow up on these themes, if appropriate. Must be able to draw together all the inputs and present the overall message generated by the discussion.
10. Good Writer
    - Must be skilled in writing clear, concise summaries of the sessions that provide the client with meaningful and action-oriented conclusions and recommendations.

This table is adapted from Gilbert A. Churchill (1991), *Marketing Research: Methodological Foundations*, 5th ed. Chicago: The Dryden Press, p. 141. The original source of this table is from Thomas L. Greenbaum (1988), *The Practical Handbook and Guide to Focus Group Research,* Lexington, Mass.: Lexington Books, pp. 50–54.

Trust, of course, is developed over time. This is of little help to those who are buying research for the first time or trying a new contractor. There are companies, however, that are experienced research buyers. It is good to use these companies as references before buying. Any respectable contractor will be more than happy to supply a list of references.

It is also important to remember that it takes years of training and experience to be able to properly design and write questionnaires, coordinate the various aspects of a study, and interpret the results. The contractor one chooses should have experience in the type of work being contracted out. One would not, for example, want to contract out the analysis phase to a contractor whose specialty is data processing.

Given the need for trust and experience, it is the research buyer's responsibility to ask the following questions:

- How long has the firm been in business and what sort of experience does the firm have in the type of studies being contracted out?
- What other companies has the contractor worked with in the past?
- Who will be involved in the day-to-day supervision of the study?
- What is the experience and educational background of those who will be working on the project?
- What quality control steps are taken in the areas of data input, field work, coding, and data processing?

- What, if any, parts of the study will be sub-contracted and to whom?
- How often can the buyer expect progress reports?
- What is the estimated cost and how far can the final price vary from this estimate (most studies are bid +/−10%)?
- How flexible is the contractor in accepting last minute changes (e.g., will last minute changes cost the bid price to sky rocket)?

Because relationships work both ways, it is necessary to be honest and forthright in terms of needs and expectations when seeking bids from contractors. Larry Stanek, Vice President and Director of Marketing Information at Kraft, Inc., argues that the research buyer is responsible for letting the contractor know the following:

- An explanation of the problem,
- Background on the marketing situation,
- A statement of the decisions involved,
- A list of critical information that is to be obtained/that will impact decision making,
- A review of what criteria will be applied in arriving at a decision, and
- A statement of (realistic) timing or cost constraints (Stanek, 1985).

To this list, this author would add the following: the number of other contractors bidding for the job, the number and types of data analysis tables needed, a realistic estimate of the effective study incidence (ESI), and the type of methodology that is unacceptable.*

First, a contractor must have a reasonable chance to win the bid because of both the time and money needed to prepare a thorough proposal. If too many bids are sought, a contractor may choose not to submit a bid. This will only hurt the research buyer in the long run if contractors decide it is not worth submitting a bid. Stanek (1985) recommends seeking no more than three proposals.

Second, the number of tables needed and the ESI need to be provided to the contractor because they will directly affect the cost of the study. If both are understated, the contractor will ask for more money or take shortcuts to ensure the desired profit margin. Neither solution benefits the research buyer.

Finally, if the research buyer wants a specific methodology (e.g., a telephone survey) he/she owes it to the contractor to tell them this information before the bid is submitted. This way, the contractor can prepare the best possible bid based on the desired methodology.

Evaluating Marketing Research Contractors

A detailed evaluation scheme is provided by Charles Mayer (1967) in an article which appeared in the *Journal of Marketing Research.* Mayer believed that the proper way to evaluate a marketing research contractor is to examine how well he/she performs each of the research steps shown in Exhibit 11A-1 and the qualifications of the support staff performing these tasks. He devised a system of points for each phase of the study based on its contribution to total quality. Out of a total of 200 points, 30 are awarded to the general assessment of physical and technical capabilities, 85 are awarded to sampling and fielding, and the final 85 are awarded to coding and tabulating. Mayer stated that each section is then further subdivided and points are awarded to each subsection for various quality producing components.

Evaluating contractors then becomes a matter of examining the number of points allocated to each potential contractor. Mayer states, however, that:

The highest quality research is not always necessary. Since high quality and high costs usually go hand in hand, a research buyer may at times settle for less than the highest quality work. He should recognize

the trade-off that he is making. Having decided on a specific level of quality, he should invite tenders only from those contractors who can supply that level [of quality]. With specific reference to the rating system, only contractors with comparable ratings (within a 20 point range) should be asked to bid on the same job. (Mayer, 1967)

Julie Rathbone (1992), a former research manager at Foodmaker (parent company to Jack-In-The-Box Restaurants), used the following criteria to judge an outside contractor:

- Reputation (what do their past and present customers say about them?),
- Confidentiality (the supplier cannot also work for Foodmaker's major competitors),
- Ability to operate with little direction,
- Ability to derive creative designs once the objective of the study is known,
- Cost, and
- Ability to keep time deadlines.

Rob Radomski (1992), at Holiday Inn Worldwide, stated the following criteria (in no particular order):

- *"Accessibility*—If I call, I want to be able to talk directly to someone. If the project manager is not by his/her phone, I want to be able to ask when he/she will return, and get an answer (NO VOICE MAIL!—that sends a "don't care" message. An office paging system would really impress me). If there is an emergency, and the project manager is not available, I would like to have the ability to talk to someone else who is knowledgeable about the project and can act on the request.
- *Honesty*—If it's (the project/report) going to be late, tell me as soon as you know . . . don't wait until the day it was due (we're setting due dates on the other end). If there's a problem in the field, let us know immediately. Don't cover it up (we'll find out eventually). Honesty, regardless of the disaster, means we call you again. Dishonesty means we call someone else.
- It's preferable to work with a single project manager from the initial phone call to the end of the job. The approach where an account/sales manager turns an awarded job over to a project manager is often ineffective. The continuity of ideas is broken and the account manager is usually not a researcher.
- Other criteria include general competence, fair pricing and personal liking.

Churchill (1991) argues that "when evaluating suppliers that seem equally competent, a manager must rely on

---

*Effective study incidence (ESI) is defined as the total number of respondents screened and found eligible divided by the total number screened. For more information on incidence, see "Incidence Guidelines," Council of American Survey Research Organizations and Marketing Research Association, 1988.

his or her intuitive assessment regarding the soundness of the research design proposed, the supplier's responsiveness to the manager's (buyer's) specific questions, and the supplier's understanding of the subtler aspects of the marketing problem."

Enough cannot be said about the value of the experience a contractor can bring to a study. Although a contractor is good in one type of study, it does not mean he/she is good in all types of research. Therefore, it is important to choose a contractor who understands the idiosyncrasies of the buyer's business and customers.

In addition to relevant experience, it is critical that the buyer trust and respect the contractor. This trust comes about only after working together. Trust, however, can be developed by checking references and asking lots of questions prior to committing to a study. Finally, the buyer needs to be able to communicate with the contractor. If trust, respect, and communication are not there, then one should choose another contractor—no matter how qualified the current contractor is.

Summary

Because one cannot be an expert in everything, at some time it will be necessary to seek the advice and help of others. Naturally, one needs to feel secure in buying this help. This article has attempted to help the research buyer feel more secure by explaining the steps involved in a research study and how to buy and evaluate marketing research contractors.

Another way to feel more secure in buying and using marketing research is to contact a local university or community college about marketing research courses. Such courses are universally available and the knowledge gained will enable the research buyer to help design the study and interpret the results.

The competitive environment of the '90s suggests that those who truly understand their customers' needs and wants, and their competitors, will prosper. Those who don't will suffer. Good marketing research is the best way to reach that understanding.

References

Churchill, G. A. (1991). *Marketing research: Methodological foundations* (5th ed.). The Dryden Press: Chicago.

Dev, C. S. & Ellis, B. D. (1991). Guest histories: An untapped service resource. *The Hotel and Restaurant Administration Quarterly, 32*, No. 2 (August), 28–37.

Dillon, W. R., Madden, T. J. & Firtle, N.H. (1987). *Marketing research in a marketing environment.* Mirror/Mosby College: St Louis Times.

Gershowitz, H. (1990). Entering the 1990s—the state of data collection—telephone data collection. *Applied Marketing Research,* Vol. 30, No. 2 (Second Quarter), 24–26.

Goldberg, S. M., Green, P. E. & Wind, Y. (1984). Conjoint analysis of price premiums for hotel amenities. *Journal of Business, 57*, No. 1, pt. 2, s110–s147.

Greenbaum, T. L. (1988). *The practical handbook and guide to focus group research* (pp. 50–54). Lexington Books: Lexington, MA.

Hilton uses research in creation of vacation promotion (1989). *Quirk's Marketing Research Review,* (June/July), 18, 34–35.

Jacobs, H. (1990). Entering the 1990s—the state of data collection—from a mall perspective. *Applied Marketing Research,* Vol. 30, No. 2 (Second Quarter), 24–26.

Lewis, R. C., & Chambers, R. (1989). *Marketing leadership in hospitality.* Van Nostrand: New York.

Lohr, S. (1992). More workers in the U.S. are becoming hired guns. *The New York Times,* 14 August, A1, D2.

Mayer, C. S. (1967). Evaluating the quality of marketing research contractors. *Journal of Marketing Research,* Vol. IV, (May), 134–141.

Radomski, R. (1992). Fax transmission to the author.

Rathbone, J. (1992). Personal conversation with the author.

Stanek, L. P. (1985). The three bid system: A client's point of view. *Journal of Data Collection,* Vol. 25, No. 2 (Fall), 17–19.

Syndicated study keeps restaurant chain in touch with its customers (1989). *Quirk's Marketing Research Review,* (August/September), 14.

Templeton, J. F. (1987). *Focus groups: A guide for marketing & advertising professionals.* Probus Publishing Company: Chicago.

Yesawich, P. C. (1987). Hospitality marketing for the '90s: Effective marketing research. *The Hotel and Restaurant Administration Quarterly, 28*, No. 1 (May), 48–57.

Brand Positioning: An Example

Firms that operate in an extremely competitive market must understand how their brand is "positioned" relative to the other brands in their market. To illustrate how positioning takes place, we use an example from a study undertaken in Las Vegas, Nevada. The data in the study have been changed, but the relationships are reflective of Las Vegas at the time of the study. For illustrative purposes, assume that the study was performed for the Rio. The study was also completed before Bellagio and other of the newer casinos were built; hence, the following is used to illustrate how positioning is accomplished and not to illustrate consumers' perceptions of the different hotel casinos in Las Vegas. If the study were undertaken again today, the data would be completely different.

Focus groups, in-depth interviews with gamblers, and a review of the academic literature revealed that the decision to visit a specific casino was based on 27 possible attributes—each attribute having different levels of importance for different customers. These attributes were used to measure the different casinos in the Las Vegas market.

To understand the competitive position of the Rio, it is necessary to compare the Rio to the other 31 casinos that were in the market at the time of the study. Again, the Rio was chosen arbitrarily to be the point of reference; any casino on the map could fulfill this role. Because it was impractical to ask each respondent to rate each of the 31 other Las Vegas properties on 27 measured attributes, the rating sequence was set up on a balanced "incomplete block" design. An incomplete block design was used so that information could be gained on all casinos without asking each respondent to rate all 31 competitive brands. Instead, each respondent rated four casinos—the Rio plus three other casinos. The use of the incomplete block design ensured that each casino was rated an equal number of times. More importantly, an incomplete block design ensures that the casinos are balanced with respect to each other so that no biases are introduced. This is especially important given that customers will judge each casino, in part, relative to the other casinos they rate. (Note: Only those casinos opened at the time of interviewing were included in the study, which is why firms such as Bellagio and Wynn do not appear on the accompanying maps.)

Multidimensional scaling (MDS) was the statistical technique used to examine the relationship among all the rated casinos. Specifically, the MDS algorithm KYST (an acronym for Kruskal, Young, Shepard, and Togerson, the developers of the model) was used to create the information needed to visually represent customers' current perceptions of the casinos in Las Vegas.

The KYST algorithm "works" by first taking the "distance" between casinos—created from the differences in mean scores between the casinos on the 27 attributes[*]—and constructing a set of coordinates that accurately represent these distances. The coordinates that were output from the KYST program appear in Exhibit 13A-1. These coordinates are then used to plot the casinos in perceptual space. Exhibit 13A-2 visually shows the coordinates listed in Exhibit 13A-1. Exhibit 13A-2 was constructed using a set of axes whose origin represents a theoretical average or neutral zone.

Exhibit 13A-2 reveals that the Rio is positioned to the right of the middle of the right half of the graph. At the far right are the brands MGM Grand, Flamingo Hilton, and Caesars Palace. At the opposite side of the perceptual map are Santa Fe, Main Street Station, Sunset Station, Boulder Station, Texas Station, and Fiesta.

Generally speaking, there are two methods of interpretation of an MDS perceptual map. The first is subjective in nature. Here, one looks at the distance between casinos. The closer the casinos are to each other, the more they are perceived to be similar. Conversely, the farther apart they are, the more dissimilar they are perceived to be. Based on this method, the Rio is considered most similar to the Las Vegas Hilton. The Rio is also more similar to Caesars Palace

---

[*]The calculation for the distance between casinos A and B is given by the Σ (mean attribute 1 for casino A – mean attribute 1 for casino B)^2 + . . . + (mean attribute 26 for casino A – mean attribute 26 for casino B)^2]$^{1/2}$. This is the Euclidean distance formula.

EXHIBIT 13A-1	Coordinates from KYST Program

The final configuration of 32 points in two dimensions has a stress of 0.036.

	x	y	Brand
1	0.242	−0.113	Bally's
2	−0.978	0.343	Binion's Horseshoe
3	−1.557	−0.138	Boulder Station
4	1.635	−0.031	Caesars Palace
5	0.058	−0.038	Circus Circus
6	0.411	−0.026	Excalibur
7	−1.469	0.051	Fiesta
8	1.407	0.014	Flamingo Hilton
9	−1.139	0.026	Gold Coast
10	0.733	0.367	Golden Nugget
11	0.453	−0.121	Hard Road
12	0.692	0.188	Harrah's
13	−0.440	0.189	Imperial Palace
14	−1.127	0.423	Lady Luck
15	0.788	0.048	Las Vegas Hilton
16	0.717	−0.111	Luxor
17	−1.538	−0.037	Main Street Station
18	1.350	0.190	Mirage
19	1.578	0.109	MGM Grand
20	0.122	0.089	Monte Carlo
21	0.802	−0.198	New York New York
22	−0.211	0.037	Orleans
23	−0.549	−0.093	Palace Station
24	0.982	0.004	Rio
25	0.044	−0.323	Sahara
26	−0.063	−0.392	Sam's Town
27	−1.660	−0.091	Santa Fe
28	−0.230	−0.064	Stratosphere
29	−1.323	0.013	Sunset Station
30	−1.067	−0.182	Texas Station
31	0.959	−0.234	Treasure Island
32	0.377	0.101	Tropicana

and the MGM Grand than it is to Sunset Station and the other casinos on the left side of the map.

What one needs to do is to think about the properties of the casinos occupying extreme positions in the derived space and then attempt to identify possible attributes that can explain the relative positions. It appears that the casinos at the far left along the *x* axis represent properties more geared to locals, whereas the brands on the far right along the *x* axis represent more "Strip" properties. Another interpretation is that casinos on the left are more "downscale," whereas casinos on the right are more "upscale."

It could be argued that casinos at the very top of the *y* axis represent casinos that are "downtown" properties. As one moves south on the *y* axis, one moves away from the downtown properties and closer to the Strip or off-Strip properties. Putting all this information together leads to the following interpretation:

- *Upper Right Quadrant:* At the very top, downtown upscale properties catering to out-of-town guests. As one moves toward the lower right quadrant, one moves to "Strip" properties catering to out-of-town guests.
- *Lower Right Quadrant:* "Strip" properties catering to out-of-town guests.
- *Upper Left Quadrant:* At the very top, downscale properties catering to out-of-town guests.
- *Lower Left Quadrant:* Downscale "off-Strip" properties catering to locals.

The difficulty in subjective interpretation should be obvious. This leads to Method 2, which is not at all subjective. Rather, it is very quantitative.

The second method is termed *property fitting.* Property fitting places the 27 attributes that the respondents used to rate the different casinos in the same perceptual

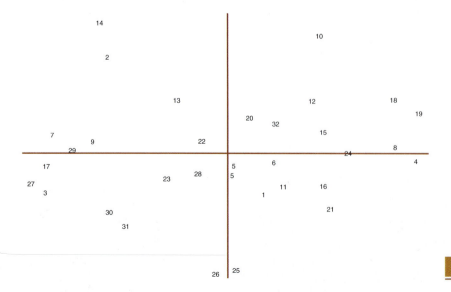

EXHIBIT 13A-2

space as the casinos, thus aiding in interpretation of the casinos' positioning. These attributes are placed in the same perceptual space using multiple regression. Essentially, the mean rating of each of the 27 measured attributes is taken individually and regressed on the derived space coordinates (from the KYST algorithm). In multiple regression terms, the dependent variable is the mean rating, and the independent variables are the derived space coordinates—the x and y point for each brand. One important by-product of the regressions, besides the R^2, which shows how important each variable is in defining the perceptual space, is the beta weights—one for each stimulus point. These beta weights are used to calculate the coordinates for the attribute vector. The coordinates for the property fitting appear in Exhibit 13A-3. Exhibit 13A-4 presents the positioning of the rated casinos along with the vectors derived via property fitting.

A perpendicular line drawn from the hotel to each vector reveals the influence of these attribute vectors on the placement of the hotels. Although the vectors are shown pointing only in the positive direction, it is useful to remember that they continue in the negative direction as well. Casinos on the negative side of the line are thought to have less of that particular attribute. Notice that the vectors (lines) are of similar length. This is by design because, unlike in discriminant analysis, the vectors do not indicate the relative importance.

An examination of both Exhibits 13A-2 and 13A-4, along with Exhibit 13A-5, which provides the key to the perceptual maps, reveals that the Rio is positioned closely between the Las Vegas Hilton to the left and the Flamingo Hilton on the right. Based on the location of the Rio, the features that describe the Rio better than other features—as indicated by where the perpendicular line from the center of the hotel crosses the vector—are as follows:

- Drink orders are taken and delivered in a timely manner (#12)
- Overall, it is a place I am very satisfied with (#5)
- A hotel where I would stay if visiting Las Vegas (#10)
- My favorite machine or table game is always available (#18)
- It is a place my friends like to go (#6)

Note that many of the same features refer to MGM Grand, Caesars Palace, and the Flamingo Hilton. However, since these brands are to the right of the Rio, participants perceive these brands to offer more of these features than the Rio currently offers. That is, the feature *Overall, it is a place I am very satisfied with* is more likely to describe the MGM Grand than the Rio. If one examines Exhibit 13A-6, the "top-two" (rating of a 9 or 10) score for the MGM Grand was 40.8, whereas for the Rio, the same score was 37.6.

The Mirage is positioned relative to the following features:

- Table limits within comfort range (#13)
- Overall, it is a place I will return to (#4)
- Cashier's cage is properly staffed (#15)
- I get complimentaries (#21)
- Positive past experience (#17)

The following features differentiate New York New York and Treasure Island from the other brands:

- I feel safe there (#1)
- Restaurants I eat at on the property offer great price value (#9)
- Always have good entertainment in the bars or lounge areas (#8)
- A good place to take out-of-town guests (#3)
- Employees are friendly and courteous (#2)

The property fitting also suggests that Sam's Town is positioned in the lower center of the exhibit because of the belief that "convenient parking is always available." If one were to extend the line labeled 14 in the opposite direction, it would pass through Lady Luck and Binion's Horseshoe. This suggests that these casinos are positioned there because of the belief that they do not offer convenient parking. Given their downtown location, this makes perfect sense.

Harrah's and the Golden Nugget's positions are a result of the following beliefs:

- They seem to have better odds than other places (#24)
- They send mailings ("I receive mailings from the casino," #27).
- Their machines pay off better (#23)
- "It is a place I play at regularly" (#25)
- Respondent has had positive past experiences (#17)
- "I get complimentaries" (#21)

Potential Repositioning Strategies

Exhibits 13A-2 and 13A-4 suggest that if the Rio wants to compete with MGM Grand, the Mirage, and Caesars Palace, it needs to improve operationally so that consumers will say, "Overall, it is a place I am very satisfied with" (#5) and that it is "a hotel where I would stay if visiting Las Vegas" (#10). Following are other variables pointing in the direction of these three brands:

- My favorite machine or table game is always available (#18)
- Drink orders are taken and delivered in a timely manner (#12)
- Slot machines are filled in a timely manner (#20)
- Makes me feel more special than other places (#19)

Directional Cosines of Fitted Vectors in Normalized Space

	x	y	
1	0.8703	−0.4925	I feel safe there
2	0.9177	−0.3973	Employees are friendly and courteous
3	0.8117	−0.5841	A good place to take out-of-town guests
4	0.9012	0.4334	Overall, it is a place I will return to
5	0.9760	0.2177	Overall, it is a place I am very satisfied with
6	0.9840	−0.1783	It is a place my friends like to go
7	0.9569	−0.2903	I want to eat at one of the restaurants on the property
8	0.8139	−0.5811	Always have good entertainment in the bars or lounge area
9	0.7510	−0.6603	Restaurants I eat at on the property offer great price value
10	0.9988	−0.0494	A hotel where I would stay if visiting Las Vegas
11	0.9349	−0.3550	Can get change in a timely manner
12	0.9978	0.0662	Drink orders are taken and delivered in a timely manner
13	0.8768	0.4808	Table limits within comfort range
14	0.4167	−0.9090	Convenient parking always available
15	0.9175	0.3977	Cashier's cage is properly staffed
16	0.9484	−0.3170	Type of people who play there are like me
17	0.7495	0.6620	Positive past experience
18	0.9964	−0.0843	My favorite machine or table game is always available
19	0.9291	0.3700	Makes me feel more special than other places
20	0.8673	0.4979	Slot machines are filled in a timely manner
21	0.7507	0.6606	I get complimentaries
22	0.8277	−0.5612	Type of promotions offered
23	0.5350	0.8449	Machines pay off better
24	0.3417	0.9398	Seems to have better odds than other places
25	0.5931	0.8051	Is a place I play at regularly
26	0.9037	−0.4282	Benefits provided by slot club
27	0.5035	0.8640	I receive a mailing from the casino

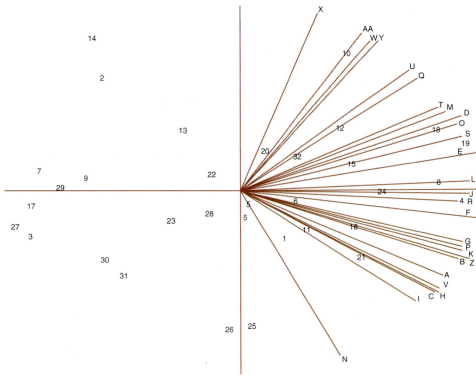

EXHIBIT 13A-5	Keys to Vectors			
I feel safe there	1	Cashier's cage is properly staffed	15
Employees are friendly and courteous	2	Type of people who play there are like me	16
A good place to take out-of-town guests	3	Positive past experience	17
Overall, it is a place I will return to	4	My favorite machine or table game is always available	18
Overall, it is a place I am very satisfied with	5	Makes me feel more special than other places	19
It is a place my friends like to go	6	Slot machines are filled in a timely manner	20
I want to eat at one of the restaurants on the property	7	I get complimentaries	21
Always have good entertainment in the bars or lounge area	8	Type of promotion offered	22
Restaurants I eat at on the property offer great price value	9	Machines pay off better	23
A hotel where I would stay if visiting Las Vegas	10	Seems to have better odds than other places	24
Can get change in a timely manner	11	Is a place I play at regularly	25
Drink orders are taken and delivered in a timely manner	12	Benefits provided by slot club	26
Table limits within comfort range	13	I receive a mailing from the casino	27
Convenient parking always available	14		

- Table limits within comfort range (#13)
- Cashier's cage is properly staffed (#15)

One way the Rio may wish to reposition itself is to move into the perceptual space to the far right of the Flamingo Hilton between the MGM Grand and Caesars Palace. This move makes logical sense because respondents already believe that the Rio possesses the necessary features (e.g., *Drink orders are taken and delivered in a timely manner, My favorite machine or table game is always available,* and *A hotel where I would stay if visiting Las Vegas*). The problem is, respondents believe that the MGM Grand and Caesars Palace already own these attributes. That is, respondents believe the MGM Grand and Caesars Palace are better at delivering on these features—hence, the higher ratings.

A second way to reposition—and perhaps a move that makes more strategic sense—is for the Rio to reposition itself in the area between Caesars Palace and Treasure Island. This area is currently free of any casinos. The Rio would need to develop the following features further to move into that position:

- It is a place my friends like to go (#6)
- I want to eat at one of the restaurants on the property (#7)
- Restaurants I eat at on the property offer great price value (#9)
- Can get change in a timely manner (#11)
- Employees are friendly and courteous (#2)
- Benefits provided by slot club (#26)

The figures present interesting options for the management of the Rio. A first question is, Should the Rio reposition itself? If so, how? Exhibit 13A-4 displays their overall position in the market along with potential areas to move to. An immediate question is, Should the Rio be the worst property in the tier of top properties, or should it position itself as the top property in the second tier of properties? These are not trivial questions. The answer involves much discussion and an honest analysis of the Rio's internal strengths, weaknesses, and commitment.

EXHIBIT 13A-6 Descriptive Ratings of Selected Brands (% Rating Feature a 9 or 10)

	Importance	Rio	Caesars Palace	MGM Grand	Flamingo Hilton	LV Hilton	Mirage	Treasure Island	Harrah's
		A	B	C	D	E	F	G	H
(Sample size)	(571–597)	(380–504)	(53–77)	(60–76)	(57–66)	(52–69)	(49–72)	(39–66)	(51–68)
Overall, it is a place I am very satisfied with	65.9	37.6	39	40.8	37.5	36.2	28.6	31.8	29.4
I feel safe there	62.2	45.2	56.2	57.3A	48.3	55.6	43.7	43.1	44.8
Overall, it is a place I will return to	59.4	40.4	37.7	42.7	37.5	38.6	38.9	30.3	36.2
Employees are friendly and courteous	57.8	36.7	35.1	36.5	28.6	26.6	30.4	38.8	31.3
Positive past experience	49.1	29.5	31.1	34.7	33.9	29.2	31	23.3	29.4
Machines pay off better	49.1	11.1	12.5	20.3F	15.3	15.8	7.9	12.2	16.1
I can get complimentaries	46.1	19.7	26.2	22.2	22.8	34.6AG	18.3	17	21
A hotel where I would stay if visiting Las Vegas	45.5	32.9GH	33.8	40.5DGH	24.6	37.7GH	30.4	21.3	20.9
Convenient parking always available	45.4	27.1	32.4	27.8	30	34.9	22.1	21.8	23.8
Restaurants I eat at on the property offer great price value	42.6	32.1EFGH	24	25	24.6	19.7	16.2	13.3	17.5
Seems to have better odds than other places	42.4	10.5	13.7	15.3	18.3	17.5	10.4	8.8	13.6
My favorite machine or table game is always available	39.2	23.5	29.7	33.8H	27.9	27.4	27.9	22	17.2
Is a place I play at regularly	38.6	17.4G	14.3	28.4ABG	17.7	16.7	21.4G	9.1	22.9G
Table limits within comfort range	38.1	28.1	31.9	27.1	35.7	31.6	21.5	33.9	33.8
A good place to take out-of-town guests	37.5	36.7H	49.3ADH	43.8H	30.6	37.3	35.7	50.8ADH	22.6
Drink orders are taken and delivered in a timely manner	36.3	24.4	24.6	30.6	34.9GH	24.6	25.4	16.9	18.8
Makes me feel more special than other places	36	22.4	25.6	29.7	25.4	28.8	21.7	19	20.6
Cashier's cage is properly staffed	35.5	23.1	34.8	27.8	35.6	33.3	20.3	20	23.9
Can get change in a timely manner	34.8	27.5	30	30.6	38.7H	27.1	25	30.5	18.2
I want to eat at one of the restaurants on the property	32.6	38.8GH	33.3	31	29.7	29.9	36.8H	24.2	21.2
It is a place my friends like to go	32.5	36.2G	35.1	44.6GH	28.8	34.9	34.8	27	20.9
Slot machines are filled in a timely manner	30.7	22.7	28.4	27.3	25.4	29.3	20.6	17.4	24.6
Type of promotions offered	30.5	14.2	17.7	22.1	16.1	16.7	14.8	15.2	21
Always have good entertainment in the bars or lounge area	25.9	32.5H	30	34.3H	25.8	27	26.9	38.5H	19
I receive a mailing from the casino	25.7	13.7	9.1	16.4	12.1	17.2	12.5	14.3	22.6B
Type of people who play there are like me	25	26.6	21.5	22.5	27	28.8	23.9	20.3	20.6
Benefits provided by slot club	22.2	13.9	20.8	15	10.9	21.2	18.4	17.9	17.6

Capital letter = Significantly different from the number listed under the identified column at the 95% confidence interval

Revenue Management

Thomas Gorin, Ph.D.

Manager, Revenue Management, Continental Airlines.

The purpose of revenue management is to maximize the firm's revenues, given the assumption that costs are essentially fixed costs, or that variable costs are very low. Revenue management typically applies to the travel industry, where airline seats, hotel rooms, or rental cars have high fixed costs and relatively lower variable costs. For example, given that a plane will fly a given route, the incremental cost of carrying an additional passenger is very low (additional meal, small amount of fuel) relative to the cost of flying the aircraft. Given these assumptions, revenue maximization is equivalent to profit maximization.

Revenue management (also know as yield management) is best suited to environments in which the firm's product is perishable and is either sold to the customer within a specific time frame or remains unused and disappears from the firm's inventory without generating revenue. Revenue management was developed by the airlines in the early 1960s and quickly spread to other industries, such as hotels, rental car companies, and cruise lines, because airplane seats (hotel rooms, rental cars, and cruise ship cabins) are perishable products that must be sold for the flight (night, day, or cruise) of interest, lest they go unused.

The basic premise behind revenue management—whether it be applied to airlines, hotels, cruise lines, or rental car companies—is to make inventory (seats, rooms, cabins, cars, etc.) available at lower prices to customers who would otherwise not have purchased them, while at the same time ensuring that the lower prices are not purchased by customers who are willing to pay the higher prices. Revenue management is often described as consisting of two distinct components: differential pricing and inventory control.[1]

Differential pricing is the practice of differentiating products by offering different amenities or restrictions, and hence setting different prices for each combination of product, amenities, and restrictions. The different purchasing patterns of business and leisure customers and the offer of differentiated products add to the complexity of the revenue management problem and have created the need for inventory control and the development of computerized revenue management systems.

Inventory control determines how many products of each type to make available throughout the selling period. In particular, it sets the amount of low-price products to make available to ensure that later-purchasing, higher-price customers are able to purchase the remaining products at a higher price without turning away needed low-price demand.

Because of the low pricing power of firms in a highly competitive environment such as the airline industry, revenue management is often thought of only as inventory control (since pricing is assumed to be somewhat out of the firm's control). For the purpose of this discussion, and since pricing has already been discussed in Chapter 14, we focus on inventory control and illustrate the discussion with examples from the travel industry.

Inventory control consists of three distinct components: overbooking, forecasting, and optimization. Overbooking recognizes that travelers may fail to show for their reserved hotel room (airline seat or other product) and artificially inflates the available inventory in an attempt to minimize the number of empty rooms on any given night. Forecasting can be viewed as the critical component of inventory control, because it generates the forecasts of demand for each type of room, which will be used by the optimizer to determine the availability of each product type. Forecasting and optimization involve various levels of refinement from basic day-to-day methods to more advanced length-of-stay systems (in the case of hotel rooms).

History of Inventory Control

Revenue management is based on the premise that one is selling fixed inventory, which may be time (e.g., spa services), hotel rooms or airline seats. Because this inventory is the product, it is important that inventory be under the control of the owner of the inventory and not a third party (e.g., online travel agent). We discuss methods of inventory control next.

Overbooking

Most of the history of revenue management and inventory control relates to the airline industry where revenue management was born. Airlines have been overbooking their aircraft (accepting more bookings than capacity) for close to three decades in an attempt to reduce the revenue loss associated with passenger no-shows. The objective of overbooking algorithms is to determine the total number of seats to sell on a flight, while balancing the loss of revenue associated with an empty seat and the cost of "bumping" a passenger. As stated by the Department of Transportation (DOT):

> Overbooking is not illegal, and most airlines overbook their scheduled flights to a certain extent in order to compensate for no-shows. Passengers are sometimes left behind or bumped as a result. When an oversale occurs, the Department of Transportation (DOT) requires airlines to ask people who aren't in a hurry to give up their seats voluntarily, in exchange for compensation. Those passengers bumped against their will are, with a few exceptions, entitled to compensation.[2]

Airline overbooking research dates back to the 1950s with Beckman's static optimization model.[3] Later statistical models include the work of Taylor, Simon, Rothstein, and Vickrey.[4] Although the practice of overbooking is slightly less evident in the hospitality industry, it is nevertheless used to also maximize the occupancy rate: The nature of a hotel room makes overbooking a more delicate matter relative to an airline seat where a delay caused by overbooking may be acceptable to the passenger.

Overbooking models can be as simple as applying historical averages of show-up rates to the company's inventory to determine the number of units of product to make available beyond capacity in order to maximize utilization. More advanced overbooking methods use statistical models and allow analysts to choose the amount of acceptable risk involved in overbooking, account for revenues and costs associated with overbooking, or use customer information to identify unique attributes that might affect the likelihood of each individual customer to no-show.

Basic Optimization Systems: Booking Monitoring

The first and most basic inventory control systems consisted of simple databases recording booking behavior of airline passengers or hotel guests, which allowed the revenue management analysts to perform "post-departure" analyses of the booking behavior of travelers. The major shortcoming of these systems lay in their inability to automatically identify critical patterns in the booking cycle.

These systems were thus later improved to identify unusual booking behavior and focus the attention of analysts on departures from the norm. These computerized systems consisted of large databases that allowed analysts to define "usual" booking patterns and set thresholds beyond which unusual activity was flagged for analyst review. These monitoring systems were not advanced enough to provide automated responses to changes in booking patterns or demand. However, some systems could provide recommendations to the analysts as to the appropriate course of action. The final decision remained in the analyst's hands.

Advanced Optimization Systems

The latest step in revenue management systems involved the addition of mathematical models to forecast demand and optimize inventory allocation based on historical data collected in booking databases as well as recent behavior as monitored by these same databases. These mathematical models involve deterministic or statistical optimizers that communicate directly with the firm's reservation system and automatically set the availability of each individual product without user intervention.

These third generation systems marked a crossroad in revenue management by moving from user-dependent systems to user-independent systems (see Exhibit 14A-1). In these third generation optimizers, the analyst monitors the performance of the system and makes corrections for unusual events and departures from "standard" behavior that could not be forecasted by the system. The role is therefore reversed from first and second generation systems, where the analyst decided on the course of action based on booking behavior.

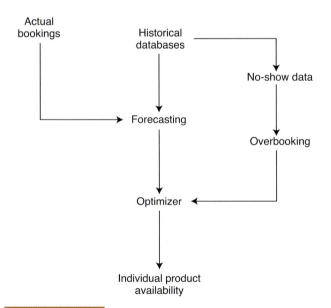

EXHIBIT 14A-1 Third generation revenue management system architecture.

Overview of Inventory Control Techniques

In this section we focus on the individual components of third generation inventory management systems: overbooking, forecasting, and optimization.

Overbooking

As previously mentioned, overbooking is the practice of accounting for traveler no-show when determining the optimal number of inventory units to make available for sale, with the goal of filling all units. Numerous methods can be used to overbook—from simple deterministic overbooking to more advanced stochastic methods. Deterministic overbooking uses a fixed estimate of the no-show value to set the overbooking level, whereas stochastic methods estimate the probability distribution of the no-show rate and use this information to make predictions of future no-shows. The stochastic approaches to overbooking have the advantage of capturing changes in traveler behavior that may not be captured in deterministic methods, and further account for the stochastic nature of demand and customer behavior.

The simplest deterministic method uses a predetermined fixed value of overbooking, based on analyst knowledge of demand. For example, an airline might choose to overbook all of its flights by five seats. More advanced methods might use forecasts of demand—costs of empty seats and revenue gain of additional seats—as deterministic inputs to a linear program that would solve for the optimal overbooking level based on these assumptions.

Traditionally, however, overbooking relies on stochastic models in which no-show rates are estimated based on historical data, and the optimal overbooking level is then derived from this historical data based on a predetermined stochastic model.[5] An example of such models is a calculation of simple straight averages of historical no-show rates subsequently applied to future periods.

More advanced stochastic models apply confidence intervals techniques to historical data and thus incorporate the history's variability in the calculation of no-shows. These systems thus adjust the forecasted no-show rates (from the simple average) based on an input confidence interval. For example, if the analyst chooses to set the no-show to ensure that the probability of a denied boarding (in the case of airlines) be less than 5 percent, the recommended no-show rate will be significantly lower than the average, based on the variability of historical no-show rates. Exhibit 14A-2 illustrates how this method would change the forecasted no-show rate from the average based on the distribution of historical no-show rates.

Finally, state-of-the-art overbooking techniques include estimates of revenues gained from overbooking, costs incurred from overbooking, and traveler-specific attributes in the calculation of overbooking levels. The following equation gives the example, in the airline case, of the calculation of the total cost of denied boardings and spoiled inventory (unsold product, such as empty seats or hotel rooms) as a function of the distribution of no-shows,

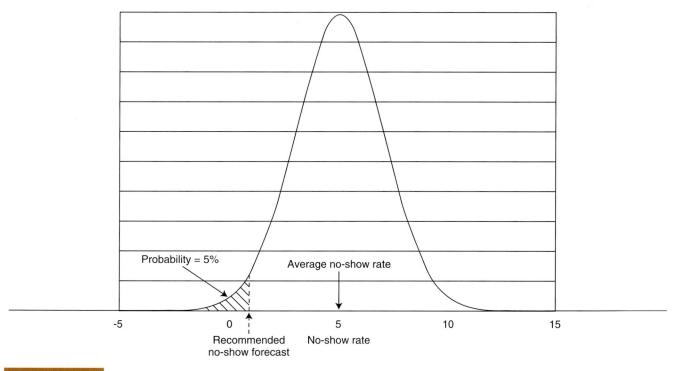

EXHIBIT 14A-2   Example of confidence-based no-show rate.

the cost of a denied boarding and a spoiled unit of inventory, and the assumed no-show rate. The no-show rate that minimizes this cost is chosen as the optimal no-show rate.

$$TotCost\ (Assumed\ NS \mid NS\ dist) =$$

$$DBCost \times \sum_{n \geq 1} Pr(DB > n \mid NS\ dist)$$

$$+\ SpoilageCost \times \sum_{n \geq 1} P(Spoilage > n \mid NS\ dist)$$

where *DB* represents denied boardings,
Spoilage represents spoiled inventory, and
DBCost and *SpoilageCost* represent the cost of DBs and spoilage.

In other applications of advanced overbooking calculations, Neuling, Riedel, and Kalka[6] discussed the use of data mining techniques in the calculation of airline overbooking, whereas Garrow and Koppelman[7] used choice models to identify the attributes most likely to explain no-show behavior, and Gorin and colleagues combine cost-based and attribute-based no-show forecasting techniques.[8]

Forecasting

More often art than science, forecasting is the process of predicting future demand based on historical data. Littelwood[9] and Smith[10] provided the basis for initial research in forecasting of airline demand, which led to numerous models of demand forecasting.[11]

Typical demand forecasts are based on historical booking periods, which are further divided into rolling historical periods and holiday or special events periods. Rolling history uses the most recent historical data to forecast demand for future booking periods. Holiday and special events history recognizes that special events or holidays differ from nonholiday periods and use year-over-year data as a historical period. Once the appropriate historical data have been identified, forecasting is typically done using stochastic approaches. For example, future demand can be estimated as the average demand for the historical data, or as the sum of historical "pickup"* between today and departure (in the case of airlines). In the example shown in Exhibit 14A-3, the historical data include flights up to June 6 (referred to as today). Future flights have bookings recorded in history and require forecasts of demand or pickup for the remaining time periods before departure. The remaining demand for

the flight departing on June 13 can be calculated as the average historical pickup for all flights in the historical data. In this example, the pickup for the last week before departure is

$$\frac{10 + 15 + 20 + 5}{4} = 12.5, \text{ and the forecasted demand}$$

for the flight departing on June 13 is *CurrentBooked + PickUp* = 95 + 12.5 = 107.5. Similar calculations and forecasts can be done for the flights on June 20, June 27, and so forth. For all flights departing after June 20, the forecasted pickup in the last week would be the same as previously calculated. The pickup forecast for periods further out would include the most recent data and could be calculated as

$$\frac{20 + 15 + 20 + 5 + 10}{5} = 14$$

between 7 and 13 days before departure, for example.

As more history becomes available, the forecasts of demand for this last time period can be updated. For the flights beyond June 13, and booking periods between 7 days and 13 days before departure and so on, data can be extracted from the departed flights as well as the undeparted flight on June 13. The forecasted pickup thus incorporates the most recent historical data available. L'Heureux[12] described the details of this forecasting mechanism.

Other methods also rely on historical data, but determine the forecasted demand as a weighted average of the history or use exponential smoothing techniques to put more emphasis on recent data.

Although actual calculations of a forecast for demand are relatively simple, three major challenges remain. The first challenge pertains to the capacity constraints imposed on demand. Typically, the availability of hotel rooms, airline seats, rental cars, or even boat cabins is limited and can be less than demand. As a consequence, historical observations are constrained observations of demand and therefore do not reflect the actual demand, but underestimate it. As a result, it becomes necessary to unconstrain (or detruncate) demand to estimate what historical demand would have been without capacity restrictions. Unconstraining (detruncation) techniques also involve stochastic approaches and can be based on booking behaviors for low-demand periods (when demand did not exceed capacity) relative to high-demand periods.

The second challenge in forecasting, once unconstrained demand has been estimated, involves estimating the impact of seasonal traffic on demand. As observed by many travel industry specialists, demand is cyclical and depends on the season. Airlines typically expect lower demand in the fall and winter, while they forecast much higher demand in the spring and summer. It therefore becomes imperative to account for these seasonal patterns when forecasting future

---

*Pickup refers to the number of travelers who book between the current period and departure. For example, pickup between 90 days before departure and departure is different from demand at departure, and allows for adjusting demand as departure gets closer.

EXHIBIT 14A-3	Example of Historical Data Used in Forecasting Future Demand							

	Week of							
Bookings between days	Past data			Today	Future data			
	16 May	23 May	30 May	6 Jun	13 Jun	20 Jun	27 Jun	4 Jul
0–6	10	15	20	5	?	?	?	?
7–13	20	15	20	5	10	?	?	?
14–20	15	10	10	15	10	15	?	?
21–27	10	10	10	15	20	20	15	?
28–34	10	20	10	10	5	10	10	10
35–41	15	15	10	20	5	5	10	5
42–48	15	15	5	15	10	5	10	5
49–55	10	15	5	10	15	10	15	15
56–62	10	5	5	10	20	15	15	5
Total bookings	**115**	**120**	**95**	**105**	**95**	**80**	**75**	**40**

demand so as to avoid forecasting fall demand using unadjusted summer history. Such an approach (in the case of airlines) would invariably overestimate demand for fall travel and underestimate spring demand, ultimately causing the airlines to forego substantial revenues by rejecting low-fare demand in the low-demand months and accepting too much low-fare demand in high-demand months.

Finally, the level of detail involved in a forecast also poses a significant challenge to forecasters. Indeed, the level of aggregation of historical data and future demand is critical in creating a reliable and accurate forecast. Too much aggregation yields too little information on future demand, whereas too much detail leads to highly variable estimates of demand that are useless. Demand can be broken into finer and finer portions, which better reflect the attributes of individual passengers and thus become more coherent groupings of demand. However, as groupings increase, so too does variability of this demand. For example, when considering the hotel inventory control problem, should the forecaster focus on individual night stays and forecast demand for future nights individually? Or, should the forecaster attempt to account for length-of-stay data? Individual night forecasts yield less variable forecasts but lose the information of length of stay, which would allow the optimizer to decide between a single-night customer and a multinight customer. Similarly, the length of the booking periods studied to calculate pickup information affects the reliability of a demand estimate.

All of these challenges have been addressed in some form by revenue management tools, but no optimal solution has yet been devised. Exhibit 14A-4 summarizes forecasting methodology and identifies some of the most critical challenges in forecasting.

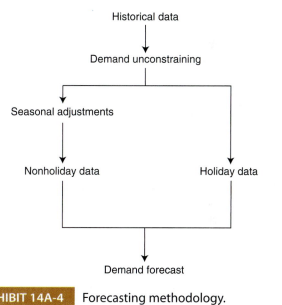

EXHIBIT 14A-4 Forecasting methodology.

Inventory Control and Optimization

Given overbooking levels and forecasts of demand for future flights, hotel night stays, rental cars, or cruise line cabins, the inventory optimizer sets the availability within each product category to maximize revenues. Three major approaches exist in this final step in inventory control:

1. Deterministic control
2. Stochastic optimization
3. Advanced dynamic programming methods

Deterministic linear programs use forecasted demand as a deterministic input to a linear program, which then sets the amount of seats (hotel rooms, etc.) available at any given price. These linear programs allocate inventory and meet the capacity constraints imposed by hotel or aircraft size and can be reoptimized once a preset threshold of bookings/cancellations is reached. Following is general formulation of the inventory control linear program:

$$\max(\text{Revenue}) = \max\left(\sum_{i,j} X_{i,j} \times R_j\right)$$

subject to:

$$\sum_{i,j} X_{i,j} \leq cap$$

$$\sum_{j} X_{i,j} \leq D_i$$

where

D_i represents demand of type i,
$X_{i,j}$ represents the allocation of demand type i to product type j, and
R_j represents the price of product j.

Stochastic approaches take into consideration the variable nature of demand for travel services or other products and compute the expected marginal revenue to be achieved from selling one additional unit of a specific product category. Based on the expected additional revenue from each product compared to the other products available, booking (availability) limits are set within each category. The expected revenue from each incremental unit of product type depends on the distribution of demand for each product.

These stochastic methods are the most commonly used in the travel industry because they have the advantage over deterministic methods of accounting for variability in demand. However, some limitations of these methods are that they often assume independence of product type demand: If a particular product type is unavailable, the customer may not be willing to buy any other product type. In addition, these stochastic methods also make assumptions on the distribution of demand. For simplicity purposes, it is often assumed that demand follows a normal distribution.

Exhibits 14A-5 and 14A-6 illustrate an example of a stochastic approach to inventory control. Exhibit 14A-5 shows the average demand and standard deviation for each product type, as well as the associated price of each product.

Assuming that the demand for each product type is independent and normally distributed, it then becomes possible to calculate the expected revenue from selling at least one seat at the highest price. This value is equal to the probability of selling at least one unit of Product 1, multiplied by the price of Product 1. This process is repeated for each additional unit of each product. In other words,

Expected Revenue$_j$ (unit i) = P(selling at least i units of product j) × Price (product j)

The expected revenues for each product type and unit sold are then ordered in decreasing order, and inventory is allocated based on this ranking. Exhibit 14-A6 shows the final ranking of each unit of each product and the associated inventory allocations. These allocations are then fed into the reservation systems.

The previous example describes a generic stochastic approach to optimization, but there are numerous variations on this theme, all attempting to achieve the same goal—optimal inventory allocation with the goal of maximizing revenue. Belobaba[13] published the first leg-based airline seat inventory management algorithm for nested fare classes, known as the expected marginal seat revenue algorithm (EMSR), upon which this example is based. Building on this research, Belobaba,[14] Curry,[15] Brumelle and McGill,[16] and others developed heuristic extensions as well as theoretically optimal formulations of the multiple nested class seat protection model.

Advanced dynamic programming methods involve the relatively new field of dynamic programming, and involve far greater computing power than do deterministic or stochastic approaches. Without going into the details of dynamic programming, these methods divide the remaining booking periods into sufficiently small time increments so as to ensure that, at most, one booking will occur within each time frame. From any point in the booking period, every possible alternative will be considered and the alternative leading to the highest revenue will be chosen. This process is repeated at each time increment to ensure that the best option is always chosen from that point onward, and, ultimately, that revenues are maximized. These methods show promising results in simulation settings, but have been difficult to implement because of the required computing power. In addition, optimization times are generally too long to allow for the frequent reoptimization needed by these methods.

EXHIBIT 14A-5	Forecasted Average Demand and Standard Deviation by Fare Product Type		
		Demand	
Product Type	**Price**	**Average**	**Standard Deviation**
1	$400	10	5
2	$200	15	5
3	$150	20	5
4	$100	20	5

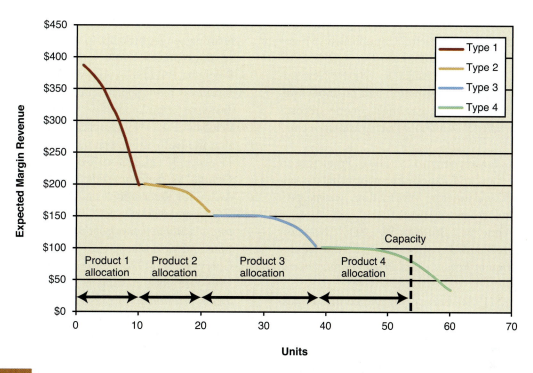

EXHIBIT 14A-6   Expected marginal revenue curve and associated inventory allocation for each product type.

Conclusion

Revenue management techniques have been used for close to three decades, and have produced significant revenue gains for the companies using them effectively. In 1993, American Airlines estimated annual gains attributable to revenue management at $500 million or more.[17] More recent studies show that these revenue gains depend on the competitive environment, but that revenue management generally benefits the company using it. For more details on the evolution of the science of revenue management, refer to McGill and Van Ryzin, who provide a thorough description of the history and evolution of airline revenue management.[18]

In the process of improving the efficiency of revenue management, numerous avenues are currently being explored. Forecasting remains a very difficult discipline in constant need of improvement. Current forecasting methods, while suited to differentiated pricing environments, are rather inadequate at forecasting demand in undifferentiated environments, as currently faced by airlines. Optimization relies on very restrictive assumptions, such as the independence of fare product demand and the normal distribution of that demand. Last, alternative approaches to revenue management currently investigate the possibility of moving away from traditional methods and forecasting altogether to use choice model approaches. Choice models

determine the probability that a passenger will choose any of the alternatives that are available to him or her and thus differ from traditional forecasting methods. However, the calibration of such choice models remains a challenge in the transportation industry.

References

1. Belobaba, P. P. (1987). *Air travel demand and airline seat inventory management* (Report R87-7). MIT Flight Transportation Laboratory, Cambridge, MA.
2. Retrieved November 21, 2005, from http://airconsumer. ost.dot.gov/publications/flyrights.htm#overbooking.
3. Beckman, J. M. (1958). Decision and team problems in airline reservations. *Econometrica, 26,* 134–145.
4. Taylor, C. J. (1962). The determination of passenger booking levels. In *AGIFORS Symposium Proceedings 2.* Fregene, Italy; Simon, J. (1968). An almost practical solution to airline overbooking. *Journal of Transport Economics and Policy, 2,* 201–202; Rothstein, M. (1968). *Stochastic models for airline booking policies.* Unpublished doctoral dissertation, Graduate School of Engineering and Science, New York University; Rothstein, M. (1985). O.R. and the airline overbooking problem. *Operations Research, 33,* 237–248; and Vickrey, W. (1972). Airline overbooking: Some further solutions. *Journal of Transport Economics and Policy, 6,* 257–270.

5. Belobaba, P. P. (1999). Flight overbooking models and practice. Airline Management. Unpublished, Massachusetts Institute of Technology, Boston.

6. Neuling R., Riedel S., & Kalka K. (2004). New approaches to origin and destination and no-show forecasting: Excavating the passenger name records treasure. *Journal of Revenue and Pricing Management, 3* (1), 62–73.

7. Garrow, L. A., & Koppelman, F. S. (2004). Predicting air travelers' no-show and standby behavior using passenger and directional itinerary information. *Journal of Air Transport Management, 10* (6), 401–411.

8. Gorin, T., White, M., Brunger, W. (2006). No-show forecasting: A blended cost-based, PNR-adjusted approach. *Journal of Revenue and Pricing Management, 5* (1).

9. Littlewood, K. (1972). Forecasting and control of passenger bookings. In *AGIFORS 12th Annual Symposium Proceedings* (pp. 95–117). Nathanya, Israel.

10. Smith, B. C. (1984, March). Overbooking in a deregulated airline market. *ORSA/TIMS Conference Proceedings.*

11. Zickus, J. S. (1998). *Forecasting for airline network revenue management: Revenue and competitive impacts.* Master's thesis, Massachusetts Institute of Technology, Cambridge, MA; and Gorin, T. O. (2000). *Airline revenue management: Sell-up and forecasting algorithms.* Massachusetts Institute of Technology, Cambridge, MA.

12. L'Heureux, E. (1986). A new twist in forecasting short-term passenger pick-up. In *AGIFORS Symposium Proceedings* (pp. 248–261).

13. Belobaba, P. P. (1987). *Air travel demand and airline seat inventory management* (Report R87-7). MIT Flight Transportation Laboratory, Cambridge, MA.

14. Belobaba, P. P. (1989). Application of a probabilistic decision model to airline seat inventory control. *Operations Research, 37* (2), 183–197; Belobaba, P. P. (1992, May). *Optimal vs. heuristic methods for nested seat allocation.* AGIFORS Reservations and Yield Management Study Group; and Belobaba, P. P. (1994). *Network seat inventory control without network optimization.* AGIFORS Reservations and Yield Management Study Group, Hong Kong.

15. Curry, R. E. (1990). Optimal airline seat allocation with fare class nesting by origins and destination. *Transportation Science, 24* (2), 193–204.

16. Brumelle, S. L., & McGill, J. I. (1993). Airline seat allocation with multiple nested fare classes. *Operations Research, 41*, 127–137.

17. Smith, B. C., Leimkuhler, J. F., & Darrow, R. M. (1992). Yield management at American Airlines. *Interfaces, 22* (1), 8–31.

18. McGill, J. I., & van Ryzin, G. J. (1999). Revenue management: Research overview and prospects. *Transportation Science, 33* (2), 233–256.

Glossary

account management management of customers' accounts.

account management system management of the sales process.

accounts payable any outstanding bills of a firm; money owed to suppliers for goods and services purchased for the normal operations of the venture.

action plans plans that detail putting the marketing plan into action by specific assignment. While the marketing plan and mission statement are both developed and reviewed annually, the action plans are updated at least quarterly to keep the planning process current.

activity-based costing determining the cost of providing a value added service.

activity-based pricing the pricing or nonpricing of providing a value added service.

actual market share (AMS) the share of business generated in a competitive area that a property actually obtains, relative to other properties in the same product class.

ad hoc groups organizations already formed that book tours.

advocate a customer who encourages others to buy from a firm.

affective stage the stage at which the buyer has emotions and feelings toward the product.

affiliation a group of hotels that carry the same common name, not necessarily in the same product class, or that affiliate with another group, also with the same common name.

airline market an organizational customer that purchases rooms for airline personnel in an extended time frame up to one year, subject to renewal.

alternative evaluation process by which firms provide different components of the product (e.g., room with a view or one without) so consumer can evaluate the various offerings prior to making specific choice.

ambient conditions conditions present in the immediate surrounding area.

association meetings organizational customers that use hospitality services for organizations such as the Elks Club and Alzheimer's Association, which may also be conventions.

attitudes the affective component of the belief, attitude, intention trilogy of the buying process.

attitudes, interests, and opinions (AIO) used in lifestyle segmentation to measure people's activities in terms of (1) how they spend their time; (2) their interests and what degree of importance they place on their immediate surroundings; (3) their opinions in terms of their view of themselves and the world around them; and (4) some basic characteristics such as stage in life cycle, income, education, and where they live [i.e., demographics and geographic location].

augmented product the totality of all benefits received or experienced by the customer.

baby boomers those born from 1946 through 1964.

bases for differentiation the product/service cannot be easily duplicated, appeals to a particular need or want, and creates an image or impression that goes beyond the difference itself.

behavior primacy theory the theory that behavior is not always based on needs but may, in fact, be a reaction to the environment.

benchmark a point of reference served by a particular measurement or standard by which performance is measured.

benefit bundle the group of benefits that consumers get from a purchase.

blitz multiple calls more or less at random: the preferred term today is *concentrated sales effort*.

blog short for weblog. A journal (or newsletter) that is frequently updated and is intended for general public consumption. Blogs generally represent the personality of the author or the website. Blogs often have hyperlinks, which allow the reader to easily search other similar information or connect with others reading the same blog.

bottom-line orientation a style of management that strictly focuses on the bottom-line profitability of the business, without regard to the impact on customers or their changing needs or wants.

brand blogging creating blogs and participating in the blogosphere in the spirit of open, transparent communications; sharing information of value that the blog community may talk about.

break-even pricing pricing above the point at which costs are equal to sales.

business strategies the "how" of the strategic marketing system.

>**competitive strategy** defining the competition for products and services; also defining when, where, and against whom the hospitality entity will compete.

>**market strategy** strategy for reaching the market with the product.

>**positioning strategy** creating the image of the product or service in the mind of the customer.

>**product strategy** focusing on the offering of different products and services to satisfy the needs of the customer.

>**target market strategy** defining the right target market within a broader market segment.

buy time the time span between an actual event and when the product is bought; also, the calendar time that a group books.

buying decision process the customer has a problem (need/want) that can be solved or satisfied by the hospitality offering. To resolve this, a decision process is followed.

>**beliefs** derived from perceptions and, in the consumer's mind, reflecting the position of the hospitality offering.

>**high involvement** when a purchase has high relevance; for example, a customer actively researching a honeymoon destination.

>**low involvement** when a purchase has low relevance; for example, a customer chooses one fast-food restaurant over seven others.

>**perceptions** perceptions of the product or service are critical in the buying decision process.

>**search process** initially the customer searches past experiences to solve the problem, but may graduate to seeking outside information.

>**stimuli** these provide impetus for the buy/not buy decision.

buzz marketing using high-profile entertainment or news to get people to talk about your brand.

cannibalization   taking customers away from one of your own products.

cash flow pricing   maximizing sales at a low price to generate cash.

cause marketing   supporting social causes to earn respect and support from people who feel strongly about the cause.

choice intentions   customers choose what they intend to do. Whether the customer actually does what he or she intends to do cannot be determined until after the fact.

client   someone who regularly buys services.

closed probes   probes that limit the customer's response to a yes or no answer, or an answer within a limited range provided by the salesperson.

closing   Asking the customer to weigh the pros and cons of the decision and ultimately accept the product.

code sharing   when different airlines in an alliance can access each other's flight schedules to plan seamless trips for passengers.

cognitive dissonance   a state of mind after behavior is performed that is not consistent with a new attitude; for example, "Why did I buy that? I could have found one cheaper."

cognitive stage   the stage at which the buyer has beliefs about a product.

cohorts   a firm that supplies psychographic segmentation of consumers. Their typology defines 31 different market segments. See also *VALS, PRIZM NE.*

cold calling   calling on a prospective customer without notice.

collateral   promotional material such as brochures, flyers, directions, and so on, used for customer information and to create interest.

commitment   a willingness to work at maintaining a relationship.

commodity status   when there is little or no differentiation in the product among producers.

communications mix   all communications between the firm and the target market that increase the tangibility of the product/service mix, that establish or monitor consumer expectations, or that persuade consumers to purchase.

community marketing   forming or supporting niche communities that are likely to share interests about the brand (such as user groups, fan clubs, and discussion forums); providing tools, content, and information to support those communities.

competition   anyone competing for the same customer with the same or a similar product, or a reasonable alternative, that the customer has a reasonable opportunity to purchase at the same time and in the same context.

competitive advantage   the edge by which all organizations hope to beat the competition.

competitive intelligence   information obtained on the competition that can be used to understand what it is doing and, perhaps, to develop better strategies and tactics to obtain competitive advantage.

   defensive keeping track of competitors' moves to avoid being caught off-guard.

   offensive identifying new opportunities.

   passive obtaining information in order to make a specific decision.

competitive intensity   the fierceness in the marketplace with which competitors compete; for example, matching prices and offerings, or even skullduggery.

competitive positioning   positioning the hospitality offering vis-à-vis the competition. This positioning can be done by any number, or combination, of attributes.

competitive strategy   being different in a way that gains competitive advantage.

conative stage   the stage at which the buyer has the intention or readiness to buy.

concept of marketing   creating customer value and helping customers to be better off by fulfilling their expectations and solving their problems.

conference centers   facilities specifically built and designed to accommodate corporate and other meetings and are within or connected to a hotel.

conference coordinator   a hotel employee who handles the details of a meeting before and during the meeting.

consortium   a group of individual properties with different names that carry a common designation that groups them into the same product class.

contrary needs   things that customers do not want that lead to need dissatisfaction (e.g., a missed wake-up call).

contribution margin   the contribution that price makes to fixed costs, over and above variable costs.

convention and visitors bureau (CVB)   a local, business-supported, nonprofit organization that facilitates the selling of a city or destination to groups.

convention centers   freestanding independent facilities specifically built and designed to accommodate large conventions and trade shows; they provide catering service but not lodging.

convention planners   organizational customers who arrange conventions and may purchase or organize hospitality services for large organizations or associations.

conversation creation   using fun advertising, e-mails, catch phrases, entertainment, or promotions to start word-of-mouth activity.

core product   what the customer is really buying (see *formal product*).

core services   services that are based on central rather than peripheral market needs, such as checking into a hotel or being seated in a restaurant.

corporate or managed business traveler   a business traveler who must follow the rules and regulations of the corporate travel department. Corporate travel departments range from a corporate travel director who develops corporate travel policies and writes contracts with travel suppliers (e.g., hotels and airlines) to full in-house travel agencies.

cost-driven pricing (also cost-based pricing)   prices that are based on the costs involved, rather than on the market.

cost leadership strategy   outperforming competitors by producing at a lower cost.

cost-plus pricing   pricing based on cost plus a profit margin.

crafted strategies   strategies that evolve, as time passes, from either planned or emergent strategies.

creating a customer   building a relationship that creates loyalty.

credence goods   products or services that typically cannot be tested before purchase, so consumers are forced to seek outside advice on whether or not to purchase the service.

CREST   Consumer Reports in Eating Share Trends, a marketing and research firm that monitors expenditures and behavior in food service industries.

customer analysis   analyzing customers in terms of how to focus on them.

customer loyalty ladder   an effort to move the customer from the state of awareness to being a brand advocate.

customized databases   databases developed from outside information and customized to fit a company's prospective customer profile.

customized products   products designed to fit the specific needs of a particular target market.

customized service   service designed to meet specific needs and wants.

data analysis   the analysis of all the information collected so it can be synthesized to provide the course and structure of the marketing plan.

   competitive analysis a dissection of the competition and everything it does or does not do in the search for competitive advantage.

   demand analysis searching the overall customer needs and demand factors for rooms or restaurant or other services.

   environmental and **market trend analysis** an analysis of the trends in the business environment in order to look at their potential impact for opportunities and threats.

   internal analysis an analysis of the trends of the current customer base and the successes and failures of the property in order to look for strengths and weaknesses.

market analysis the consideration of all other phases of the data analysis together to focus on the customer, in the search for opportunities.

property needs analysis identifies the areas in which the property needs improvement in developing the market.

databases computerized information on customers that contains personal information so that they can be reached and served better.

data collection the gathering of complete and adequate information for the marketing plan.

competitive environment data collection includes the status of direct competitors and any information that can be obtained about them, including such things as their renovation status, markets, and related business development plans.

external environment data (technological, economic, social, regulatory, political, and ecological) includes international and domestic trends. Industry trends such as the increase or decrease in demand from certain market segments, new room or restaurant supply, and new concept trends are also included.

internal environment data encompasses how well the property is operating, the current customer base, and the strengths and weaknesses of the property.

death spiral the spiral of cutting back on costs, leading to less business, leading to more cost cutting.

decline stage if the product is not maintained in the mature stage, the end of the product is near; however, there could be rebirth in the future.

default sample a type of nonprobability sample in which the sample of participants is biased based solely on the fact that they chose to participate.

demand analysis measuring the market to calculate existing or future potential demand.

demand generators sources of demand such as businesses, office buildings, highways, events, and so on.

descriptive quantitative research research that tells us how many, how often, whether respondents like or dislike something, and the demography of the respondents.

designated market areas (DMA) a geographic division of customers within which the majority of households consume media that emanate from a central source, as developed by ACNielsen. This geographic division is determined by television viewers.

determinant attributes attributes of a product or service that actually determine the purchase choice.

DEWK "dual employed with kids" families.

differentiation the concept of making the product or service distinctively different from those of other firms, or appear to be so.

differentiation strategy achieving competitive advantage by producing in a manner that is perceived to be unique.

DINK "double income, no kids" families.

distinctive competence things a firm does particularly well that give it a competitive advantage.

distribution service provider (DSP) a firm that provides the switch that links the central reservation system with the GDS. Examples of a DSP are Wizcom, Thisco, Pegasus, and Trust.

distribution mix all channels available between the firm and the target market that increase the probability of getting the customer to the product.

diversification entering into a new business activity that is related or unrelated to the current business.

echo boomers the largest generation of young people since the 1960s, so called because they are the genetic offspring and demographic echo of their parents, the baby boomers.

economies of scope savings that occur when two or more business units share resources such as distribution systems (especially reservations) and advertising.

effective positioning positioning that creates an image and differentiates the product from that of the competition. Effective positioning promises and delivers the benefits the customer will receive when purchasing the product or service and creates expectations and offers solutions to the customers' problem.

emergent strategy a strategy that is developed and shaped by the business, rather than planned.

employee empowerment allowing the employee to make decisions that will solve customers' needs. Employee empowerment is part of internal marketing in that it brings the decision-making process to the closest point of contact with the customer.

employee relationship marketing applying marketing principles to those who serve the customers and building a mutual bond of trust with them.

environment items, both tangible and intangible, that create the atmosphere experienced by the customer. The following environmental forces impact the hospitality industry:

economic recession, inflation, discretionary income, and currency exchange rates are just some of the more visible economic impacts that affect the hospitality industry.

natural natural environmental concerns such as product usage and waste disposal that concern customers and governments.

political government and antigovernment movements and positions that affect consumers and businesses, such as feminism, discrimination, funding, tourism support, uprisings, border crossings, truth in menu, monetary policy, and freedom of choice.

sociocultural cultural values, customs, habits, trends, taste, demographic changes, and so forth, that affect consumer behavior.

technological advances in technology from electronic door locks to computerization to information systems that drive change and create marketing opportunities.

environmental scanning analyzing the forces that cause change; literally scanning the environment in search of future impacts. The OT part of SWOT analysis (opportunities and threats) that are created because of environmental change.

ethics a code of moral decisions that people choose to apply to their everyday lives.

evangelist marketing cultivating evangelists, advocates, or volunteers who are encouraged to take a leadership role in actively spreading the word on your behalf.

evoked set the products that immediately come to mind when a person is considering a purchase.

experience the total outcome to the customer from the combination of environment, goods, and services purchased.

experience-based marketing a form of marketing that involves spending time with customers, constantly monitoring competitors, and developing a feedback system that turns this information into new product/service intelligence.

external customers consumers who buy goods and services from a firm. Organizations need to focus on both internal customers (e.g., employees, suppliers, etc.) and external customers.

fair market share (FMS) a property's "fair" share of business based on its capacity relative to the competition in the same product class.

family life cycle the age cycle that runs from young single to widow/widower.

feasibility study a business study is based on present and future competitive data and consumer demand that is used to determine whether a project is feasible; it is followed by financial analysis.

features aspects of a facility that may or may not be important to the potential customer.

feedback loops mechanisms to measure the success of the strategic marketing process. Loops question the risk if the master strategy is pursued and provide feedback on whether the strategy is working once it is in place.

feeder city/country a geographic location that regularly feeds customers into another city or cities, country or countries.

fit how activities match and complement each other to gain the strongest possible force.

FIT (free independent traveler) a nonorganized visitor who does not belong to a group.

fixed assets assets used to produce revenue and not intended for sale; also known as long-term assets (factory equipment, vehicles, property, office furniture, etc.).

fixed costs costs that don't change regardless of sales (e.g., insurance and real estate taxes).

flexible service offerings value added services offered only to customers who value them.

focus group 8 to 10 people who represent the type of people expected to use the product.

focus strategy serving the needs of a limited customer group based on a distinctive competency.

follow-up regularly contacting the customer until the event takes place.

formal product what customers think they are buying (see *core product*).

franchise authorization granted to someone to sell or distribute a company's goods or services in a certain area, or a business established or operated under such authorization.

franchisee an organization or person that purchases a brand name to distribute the product or service.

franchisor the parent company of a franchising distribution network.

functional strategies the "what" of the strategic marketing strategy:

communications this strategy outlines the use of the communications mix: advertising, promotion, merchandising, public relations, direct sales, and websites.

distribution this strategy outlines how a hospitality entity brings the customer to the product or service.

presentation this strategy employs elements of the presentation mix: physical plant and atmosphere, employees, customers, location, and pricing.

pricing one of the first visible signs to the market, this strategy must be consistent with the other four functional strategies.

product/service this strategy focuses on what level of product/service to offer and how.

generic building blocks efficiency, quality, innovation, and customer responsiveness.

genXers generation Xers; adults born since 1964.

global distribution system (GDS) a computerized reservation system that includes airline, hotels, ground services, and so on; most often used by travel agents.

goods the physical factors over which management has direct, or almost direct, control.

government market organizational customers who purchase hospitality services for government employees.

grassroots marketing organizing and motivating volunteers to engage in personal or local outreach.

growth stage after the introductory stage, the stage where the product is growing or dropping in sales.

heterogeneity of services the inconsistent delivery of service levels provided by many different employees, affected by many different customers.

hospitality customers a variety of hospitality customer types display different buying behaviors:

business customers the largest segment for the hospitality industry, these customers have needs such as convenience, location, business services, and, at some point, price.

international customers a growing segment as a result of lower airfares and increasingly easier access to most countries.

mature travelers a strong segment of the hospitality industry. Seniors are traveling to hotels and eating in restaurants at an ever-increasing rate.

package customers travelers that are buying hotel rooms wrapped with value added items such as continental breakfast, free drinks, or parking.

pleasure travelers these travelers tend to be more price sensitive, stay over in hotels or eat in restaurants over the weekends, and visit relatives and attractions during their stays. Resorts represent the upper end of the pleasure travel segment.

hospitality product the combination of goods, services, environment, and experience that the hospitality customer buys.

importance attributes attributes of a product or service that are important to a consumer in making a choice, or after making a choice.

impulse buying an unplanned or shifted purchase.

incentive houses companies that provide high-quality incentive planning for organizations.

incentive planners a subsegment of the corporate market; provide trips as rewards for top performers within the end user organization.

indifference when a prospect is happy with current usage and doesn't really care what benefits and features a property has.

indirect costs costs that are part of selling the product but not in the product itself, such as advertising.

inferential quantitative research research that allows us to generalize to a larger population based on the findings from a probability sample, in which each person in the population being studied (e.g., business travelers) has an equal chance of being selected.

influencer marketing identifying key communities and opinion leaders who are likely to talk about products and who have the ability to influence the opinions of others.

infrastructure the underlying foundation or basic framework of a system or organization.

in-plant a division of a travel agency located on corporate premises to handle travel management.

intangibility the attribute of services that the customer cannot grasp with any of the five senses; that is, customers cannot taste, feel, see, smell, or hear a service until they've consumed it, and one cannot easily grasp it conceptually.

intangible positioning creating a tangible, objective image based on intangible attributes such as service and guest experience.

intermediaries go-betweens that bring the customer and the property together, for example, travel agents, tour operators.

intermediary an agent that sits between the hospitality product and the customer. Intermediaries include travel agents, distribution service providers, and the like.

internal customers employees, staff, and so on.

internal marketing see *employee relationship marketing.*

introductory stage a product's entry into the marketplace.

knowledge-based marketing mastering the technology in which a company competes, with knowledge of competitors and customers, the competitive environment, and one's own organization's capabilities and way of doing business.

latent demand a need with no suitable product to fill it.

lead time see *buy time.*

liabilities the debts of a company and other financial obligations; the opposite of assets.

lifetime value of a customer the total value of a customer based on repeat purchase and word of mouth to others, minus costs.

loss leaders low-priced items to attract customers who hopefully will buy other higher-priced items.

lowest common denominator (LCD) the breakdown of new room nights needed to achieve goals so that each sales manager has a smaller specific goal to achieve.

loyalty circle a loyalty-building framework consisting of three components: the process in which customers buy your service, value creation, and communication. For loyalty to exist, each component of the circle must occur, as the customer can exit the relationship anytime. The goal of hoteliers is to keep the customer in the circle by executing equally well the three functions of the circle.

loyalty marketing see *relationship marketing*.

macro industry competition any other organization that competes for the same customer dollar.

maintenance advertising advertising to keep the name in front of the market for quick recognition and as part of the evoked set.

maintenance stage the stage at which a firm maintains the business it is currently receiving and develops new users, new uses, and new variations on the theme.

management effectiveness a characteristic of companies that operate smoothly and produce well.

market segmentation a process of separating and selecting customers that have similar needs and wants on one or more dimensions. The customer comes first, before the product.

market share a property's or company's share of the business regardless of whether it is fair. For example Marriott might have an X percent share of all lodging business in the United States.

market strategy a business strategy based on matching the right product with the right market.

marketing budgets the financial planning required to fund the implementation of the marketing plan.

marketing concept the theory that the customer has a choice and does not have to buy a product, or your product—thereby creating the need to market or attract the customer to the product.

marketing definition the process of identifying evolving consumer preferences, then capitalizing on them through the creation, promotion, and delivery of products and services that satisfy the corresponding demand. This is done by solving customers problems and giving them what they want or need at the time and place of their choosing, and at the price they are willing to pay.

marketing forecast this portion of the marketing plan requires forecasting the statistics for the forthcoming year of rooms sold, covers sold, financial results, and so on, to accurately forecast future results.

marketing leadership a characteristic of hospitality enterprises that integrate marketing into every phase of their operation through opportunity, planning, and control. Marketing leadership combines a vision for the future with systematic planning for solving customers' problems.

marketing orientation an emphasis on the importance of the customer and on creating value for and from customers by recognizing their changing needs and wants.

marketing plan the management tool that brings the strategic planning process to the unit managers. The marketing plan provides the road map to operate during the year. The marketing plan needs to be a working document, used throughout the year to guide the organization in the pursuit of its mission.

markup pricing marking up prices over the cost or adding a price based on some rule of thumb.

Maslow's hierarchy a hierarchy of needs that begins with physiological needs, such as thirst and hunger, moves to safety needs, social needs, esteem needs, and finally the need for self-actualization, but not always necessarily in that order.

mass customization rather than making the same product for everyone, the trend is to allow customers to personalize the product or service to their specifications; e.g., requesting a certain type of pillow in the room or specific items in the minibar.

master marketing strategy a strategy that reviews the strengths, weaknesses, opportunities, and threats of the hospitality entity and shapes its long-range marketing objectives.

match pricing a strategy in which a firm sets its prices to match those of the competition. Firms that use this strategy believe that customers base their buying decisions strictly on price.

mature property a property that has been in the marketplace for at least three years within the same product class and positioning.

mature stage the stage at which the product is at a standstill and can be supported only by loyal customers.

mature travelers age 55 and over, these travelers usually spend over 50 percent of their time away from home, usually traveling to visit new places.

meeting planner a professional who plans the group travel and meeting arrangements of end users. In some cases this person also plans incentive travel.

meetings express a salesperson who handles all details of small groups.

menu degustation literally, a "tasting" on a menu of a small amount of many different things at one price.

merchandising the promoting of additional items for purchase by the customer who is already purchasing something from us.

metropolitan statistical areas (MSAs) federally defined large metropolitan areas based on supposed economic boundaries.

MICE acronym most often used for meeting, incentive, conference, and exhibition market.

microcompetition any business that competes for the same customers in the same product class at the same time.

mission statement a statement that defines the purpose of a business and may include many ways to achieve that in terms of all stakeholders. It should drive all subsets of the business.

motorcoach tour this organizational customer represents the market of people traveling by bus to various attractions and destinations.

"move up and out" philosophy a philosophy that results from the fact that promotions often involve relocation; if a salesperson is unwilling to relocate, the only other way to further his or her career is to move to another hotel.

multiple brand positioning offering different levels of product and service for different target markets.

multivariate analysis measuring various effects of different factors on a specific market segment.

National Tourism Organization (NTO) a government agency that promotes the nation's tourism in the international market. The goal is to advocate for the county as a destination by increasing public awareness and marketing positive images.

neutral pricing a strategy in which a firm uses other marketing tools (e.g., differentiation, positioning) to gain a competitive advantage and increase market share. The goal is to maintain a coherent marketing strategy and not confuse the customer with constantly changing prices. Firms that use this strategy are less concerned with what competitors are charging.

niche an area of the market that specializes in a certain type of product.

nonprobability sample a sampling method in research in which each member of the population does not have an equal chance of being selected. Also known as a convenience sample.

nontraditional marketing the concept of designing and delivering a product or service based on the needs of the customer.

objection a product failing that cannot be changed.

objective positioning creating an image about a product based on the objective attributes of the physical product. Resorts, for example, often position themselves objectively by offering branded golf courses (e.g., an Arnold Palmer course) or branded spas (e.g., Clarion Spa). Objective positioning is based on features that we would all more or less agree upon.

odd-numbered pricing   prices such as 99 cents in the last digits, rather than being rounded up to the next whole number, to give a lower cost perception.

one dollar per thousand pricing   an archaic concept that average daily rate (ADR) should be $1.00 for every $1,000 of construction cost.

one-stop shopping   see *product line management*.

onward distribution   the process whereby negotiated rates to wholesalers are passed onto other websites, either intentionally or unintentionally. This process can easily dilute a brand, as these websites boast deeply discounted room rates and make negotiated rates available to the public, undercutting hotels' own "best available rates" and breaking the promise of a "best rate guarantee."

opaque   not transparent; difficult to view

open probes   questions that encourage the customer to speak freely and elaborate on their problems.

operations orientation   a style of hospitality management that focuses on the execution of the operation to provide a smooth-running organization.

opportunities   marketing opportunities begin with finding unmet customer needs and serving customers in new and better ways in a changing environment.

opt out   an opportunity for the consumers to remove themselves from a list used in a marketing campaign.

organizational customer   this customer is both the meeting planner and travel manager, buying hospitality services for the end user, an organization, and the people in the organization who will actually use the product.

organizational planner   a generic term, regardless of title, for the purchaser of hospitality services for a group or an organization that has a common purpose.

package market   a way to attract customers during a low-demand period. The offering of a combination of room and amenities to consumers for an inclusive price.

pathos   using emotions to persuade.

perception is reality   if the customer doesn't perceive it, it doesn't exist for that customer.

perceptual mapping   a method of visually comparing competitors' products against one's own, based on consumer perception.

per diem   a fixed daily allowance for employees to spend on travel, for which they are reimbursed by the company.

perishability   the life cycle of the hospitality service. For example, a room is only available for a 24-hour period, making it very perishable.

permission-based marketing   when customers are given an option to provide consent to allow a firm to use their personal contact information for future mailings or giveaways.

pleasure traveler   a person traveling for a nonbusiness purpose, a weekend or other package user, or one who travels for shopping, visiting friends, going to the theatre, and so on.

population   all of the people in whom one is interested for a particular study.

positioning statement   a singular expression by a property or brand that captures its intended position in the marketplace.

postconference meeting   a meeting to recap the event to determine whether there were shortfalls in expectations.

preconference meeting   a meeting to arrange details and resolve conflicts during the conference planning/execution process. The planner and the hospitality enterprise meet prior to the event to ensure there are no misunderstandings as to the expectations of either party.

presentation mix   all of the elements used by the firm to increase the tangibility of the product/service mix in the perception of the target market at the right place and time.

price   what the customer sacrifices to purchase the product or service.

price-driven costing   the price is based on the market, after which the product is developed at the appropriate cost.

price elasticity   a measure of demand based on price movement.

price leader   the dominant player in the marketplace that establishes prices that others have to follow.

price lining   a psychological technique that clumps prices together to affect perception.

price penetration   obtaining as much market share as soon as possible at a specific price point that is low compared to what is normally charged.

price point   the amount a customer is willing to pay

price sensitive   the characteristic of a business with high variable costs where an increase in price is the primary way to increase profits on the same volume.

price sensitivity measurement (PSM)   based in psychology and sociology, a measurement system that examines price perception by determining levels of customer resistance as they relate to quality perceptions and the market range of acceptable prices for a specific product or service.

price skimming   charging high prices to "skim off" the top of the market before having to lower prices.

price stability   instilling customer confidence by keeping prices constant.

price value pricing   a method of pricing based on the value the customer derives from the purchase and not the actual cost to produce the item. For example, one can charge more for a soufflé than the cost of ingredients and the labor involved in preparing it because it is an item people do not usually make at home.

pricing mix   the combination of prices that consumers pay for a product or service.

pricing for profit maximization   when the basis of the pricing mix is how much profit can be made.

prix fixe **menu**   a full menu from start to finish at one fixed price.

PRIZM   a typology for psychographic segmentation of consumers. This typology defines 66 different market segments based on ZIP codes. PRIZM stands for *potential rating index ZIPcode markets*. See also *cohorts*, VALS.

PR news release   a favorable news item that is released to the media in the hope that it will be published.

probability sample   a sample in which every member of the population has an equal chance of being selected.

probing   asking prospective customers questions to research their real problems and needs.

product   an offering or a bundle of benefits designed to satisfy the needs and wants, and solve the problems of, specified target markets; composed of both tangible and intangible elements—may be as concrete as a chair or a dinner place, or as abstract as a feeling.

product class   a group of similar products basically serving the same needs (e.g., fast food vs. gourmet, upscale vs. budget).

product-driven pricing   the product drives the price because that is all the customer will pay for it.

product life cycle   a product goes through several stages during its lifetime. These stages are introduction, growth, maturity, and decline.

product line management   one salesperson sells all products to large user customers.

product (property) research   an aspect of marketing research that identifies and quantifies a property's most marketable features.

product seeding   placing the right product into the right hands at the right time, providing information or samples to influential individuals.

product segmentation   a form of segmentation wherein different products are designed for different segments; e.g, luxury hotels are designed for wealthy travelers and budget hotels are designed for the less affluent.

product/service mix the combination of products and services, whether free or for sale, that are aimed at satisfying the needs of the target market.

product/service orientation a style of hospitality management with a primary emphasis on creating great products or services in order to attract customers.

proof source a credible source used to overcome a prospect's objections.

property management systems (PMS) computerized systems in a property that make it more efficient to handle operations, reservations, and customer needs.

proprietary databases databases developed by individual companies for their own use.

proprietary research research conducted on behalf of a particular organization for the particular use of that organization—as opposed to general use.

prospect theory the theory that consumers make decisions by examining changes relative to personal reference points.

prospecting the process of finding qualified customers who are likely to buy the product.

psychological pricing pricing that takes into consideration what may be in customers' minds or how they react.

publicity news that is told by the media, or word of mouth, as a result of some event. It may be positive or negative.

public relations favorable information that is spread by the media and is often "planted."

pull strategy "pulling" the customer up through the distribution channel to the product.

push strategy "pushing" the product down through the distribution channel to the customer.

qualifying *(a prospect)* making sure customers are willing and able to buy.

qualitative research typically exploratory research conducted on small groups of people that seeks to understand consumer attitudes and behaviors. This research cannot be generalized to a larger population.

quota sample a type of nonprobability sample in which respondents are selected based on certain characteristics. Also known as a judgment sample.

QSC quality, service, cleanliness.

raise the numbers a hotel industry expression meaning increase the average rate and occupancy.

rate buckets rate brackets for customers gaining discounts based on volume.

rate cannibalization a dilution in rates due to an increased rate transparency and lack of rate parity.

rate integrity trust the consumer places in the fair price of a product.

rate parity the uniformity of retail rates across different channels of distribution that provide the same product.

RATER a way to remind customers that the experience they are receiving meets their expectations focusing on the dimensions of service quality: reliability, assurance, tangibility, empathy, and responsiveness.

rate transparency the perfect knowledge of a price for a specific product, due to the consumer's ability to compare rates.

reactive acting as a result of changing preferences, needs, or unanticipated problems.

real simple syndication (RSS) enables consumers to customize the information that they wish to receive without having to look the information up daily. For example, Expedia.com allows consumers to sign up for RSS, enabling Expedia to deliver the latest prices on trips consumers are interested in.

reference group people who influence a person's attitudes, opinions, and values.

reference price an expected price based on a prior experience or knowledge.

referral program tools that enable satisfied customers to refer their friends.

reflagging a colloquial industry term for changing management or franchise names.

relationship marketing marketing to protect an existing customer base through an ongoing process by creating new value for customers and sharing this over a lifetime association. Relationship marketing ensures a loyal base of customers.

reliability in research, findings can be projected to a larger population if it is the intent of the researcher to do so; also, if the study is repeated, similar findings will emerge.

repositioning changing the image of a product or service. There are a number of reasons for repositioning but they all arise from lack of performance or market recognition in the present position.

representation (rep) networks these companies have sales offices and market to represent different properties under different names.

research design a road map for research from beginning to end that includes specifying the research purpose, defining the research problem, establishing the research objectives, and determining what one expects to result.

reservation price the maximum price a consumer will pay for a product.

return on investment (ROI) the ratio of profits to investment that is generated by a business.

revenue management a systematic approach to matching demand with supply in order to maximize revenue.

REVPAC (revenue per available customer) the lifetime, or lifetime span, revenue generated from a single person or company.

REVPAR (revenue per available room) average revenue obtained per room on a given night or period of time; calculated as total room revenue divided by the number of available rooms.

REVPAS (revenue per available seat in a restaurant) total revenue divided by the number of seats available per month.

REVPOR (revenue per occupied room) average or specific revenue derived from room night including all hotel expenditures by the occupant.

ROI See *return on investment (ROI)*.

RSQFT (revenue per square foot in a restaurant) total revenue divided by the number of square feet available.

sales action plan a plan for the forthcoming quarter for reaching goals.

sales equation past customers plus new customers equal a sales goal.

sales managers those who represent the company property in the sales process.

sales promotions special promotions of a short-term nature to sell a product by offering special benefits such as special prices or features.

salient attributes attributes of a product or service that are "top of mind" reasons for considering a product.

sample a group derived from the population at large; from it we hope to learn the characteristics of many based on a few.

secondary research examining or reading about someone else's research (either primary or secondary) such as in a library.

segmentation variables there are a variety of methods to segment a given market, including the following:

> **benefit segmentation** grouping customers based on the advantage of gain that they seek when buying a product.

> **demographic segmentation** grouping customers based on income, race, age, culture, nationality, religion, gender, education, and other similar categories.

> **geographic segmentation** grouping customers by where they come from, either residence or place of business.

international segmentation grouping customers according to the heterogeneity of consumer preferences across national markets.

price segmentation grouping customers that choose products in a similar price range.

psychographic segmentation grouping customers by personality traits, self-concepts, and lifestyle behaviors.

usage segmentation see below.

selectivity customers choose what holds their attention. The four stages include attention, comprehension, acceptance, and retention.

selling orientation a style of hospitality management with a primary emphasis on salespeople and promotions that communicates a message to customers in order to sell products.

semivariable costs costs that are somewhat fixed regardless of sales units, but can be varied in some circumstances, such as servers and staff payroll.

series groups various people brought together to form a travel group.

service augmentation building extras into a service, especially those that are difficult for the competition to copy.

service product the core performance or service purchased by the patron.

service quality management improving service quality by management's focus on process improvement; can be viewed as a type of competitive advantage.

services the nonphysical and intangible items that management does, or should, control.

servicescape the physical environment in which service is provided.

SERVQUAL a marketing research model and tool designed to measure service quality.

seven Ps a term applied to a common marketing mix for goods: product, price, place, promotion, process, physical attributes, and people.

simultaneous production and consumption when production and consumption of the product(s) occur in the same place.

single-minded promotion a promotion with a single focus that can be easily understood by the public.

situational analysis the first step in developing strategies: finding out where we are now including external factors (opportunities and threats) and internal factors (strengths and weaknesses).

skepticism when a customer doubts that the benefit will satisfy his or her need.

slice of life people using the product in a normal lifestyle setting.

SMERF market organizational customers who purchase hospitality services in the social, military, education, religious, or fraternal categories.

spam unwanted e-mail that is usually the result of unsolicited electronic mass mailings; the electronic equivalent of "junk mail."

spin control converting negative publicity to a less negative or positive form by those affected.

stabilization pricing when a company keeps the price of a product stable at one level where it has a known profit margin.

standard products products that appear similar and standard to the customer, albeit in different locations.

standard product with modifications a product that has been embellished with new elements but the basic product remains essentially the same.

strategic alliance an effort made by firms to cooperate in areas such as advertising, marketing, customer base, and financing activities in order to maximize business.

strategic business unit (SBU) a unit of a business that serves a clearly defined product-market segment with its own strategy.

strategic effectiveness performing different activities from competitors or performing similar activities in different ways.

strategic leadership leadership that thinks strategically, rather than tactically, by viewing the big picture beyond the everyday management aspects.

strategic marketing system the open system of strategies that flows from the corporate mission or vision through each level with two feedback control loops.

strategic planning a systematic planning process that reviews business objectives, matches service with customers, identifies competition, allocates resources, and implements measurement tools.

strategic thinking long-range thinking about the big picture and the impact of environmental forces.

strategic visioning envisioning the future by exploring potential change, understanding the forces driving change, analyzing the impacts, and formulating strategic competitive methods.

subjective positioning positioning that presents an image, not a physical product, to the customer. Attributes such as service and prestige are less tangible than the physical characteristics of the product. Positioning tangible features requires developing intangible mental perceptions. Intangible positioning requires tangible evidence to create the image.

substitutability a subjective assessment of whether something is viewed as an acceptable alternative.

successful selling the result of long-term interdependent relationships between sellers and qualified buyers.

sustainable competitive advantage an advantage over the competition that can be sustained for at least some period of time; that is, it is not quickly replicated.

SWOT analysis an analysis that looks at an organization's internal strengths and weaknesses as well as external opportunities and threats in order to establish a master marketing strategy.

synthesis the process of putting back together the parts from an analysis to form a new and succinct whole.

tactics the specific action steps employed to execute the strategy.

tangibility the attribute of products or components that the customer can grasp with any of the five senses.

tangible positioning creating an intangible, subjective image based on a tangible attribute.

target marketing the process of choosing subsegments of customers and allocating marketing resources toward developing an individual product or service for each target market.

target return on investment the return expected in profit from the cost of the investment.

telemarketing a method of marketing using phones to call prospective buyers and guests.

temporal value value that relates to time increments, that is, saving time.

tenets of consumer behavior consumer behavior is purposeful and goal oriented; consumers have free choice; consumer behavior is a process; consumer behavior can be influenced; and there is a need for consumer education.

territorial rights the area in a franchise agreement in which the franchisee has the exclusive right to operate properties.

thirteen Cs a comprehensive categorization of all aspects of marketing: customer, categories or offerings, capabilities of the firm, cost, control of process, collaboration, customization, communications, customer measurement, customer care, chain of relationships, capacity control, and competition.

threats competition and environmental situations that can affect businesses negatively.

tip of the iceberg phenomenon the concept that top management is largely unaware of what customers need.

total assets the combined value of all items of monetary value held by the individual or firm; include the tangible (inventory and equipment), as well as the intangible (feeling of goodwill and reputation within the market).

total quality management (TQM) the concept that quality is a process that can be managed. TQM usually sets a high focus on process measurement as a means to improvement.

tracking keeping tabs on advertising effectiveness by response or other cues.

trade-off model the idea that if a solution to a customer's problems, needs, or wants meets his or her level of expectation and the value of that product or service justifies the sacrifice or risk, that sacrifice or risk becomes more justifiable, and a higher level of satisfaction becomes more likely.

trade shows organizational customers that purchase hospitality services for industry groups displaying products, such as the Toy Fair and the Printing/Stationery Show.

traditional marketing the use of advertising and salespeople to communicate to customers what a company wants to sell.

travel agent valuation a type of competitive advantage that seeks to improve relationships with the travel agent industry to secure a greater volume of business.

travel manager a person who oversees, negotiates arrangements, and sometimes plans the individual travel and entertainment of the end users. In some cases this person also plans meetings.

trust the belief that an individual or entity can be relied on to keep their word and promise, explicit or implicit.

turn-down service the practice of some upscale hotels of nightly turning down the bed, checking the towels, emptying wastebaskets, and so on.

"twofers" two for the price of one.

twofold purpose of marketing to create and retain customers.

undercover marketing marketing to potential consumers without their knowledge or awareness of the marketing effort.

unique visitors Internet users who land on a website and actually view the offer.

unmanaged business travel the individual business traveler who makes arrangements for himself or herself, as opposed to corporate travel, which is managed by an individual at the firm.

unsecured Internet transactions made over the Internet that may be prone to electronic eavesdropping.

usage segmentation an umbrella concept of segmenting a market based on how a consumer uses a product or service, including the following:

  frequency segmentation customers are segmented by the frequency with which they visit an establishment.

  heavy, medium, and light users customers are segmented by the degree of their usage of a product.

  monetary value segmentation customers are segmented by how much they are worth to the organization.

  nature of purchase segmentation customers are segmented by how they made the decision to purchase the product or service.

  purchase occasion segmentation customers are segmented by special purchase occasions such as anniversaries or birthdays.

  purpose segmentation customers are segmented by the reason for the purchase, such as business or pleasure.

  recency segmentation customers are segmented by how recently they visited the organization.

RFM a database analysis score used to identify customers on the basis of recency, frequency, and monetary segmentation values. Companies use the RFM score to direct targeted mailings.

  timing segmentation customers are segmented by the time of day or time of year that they purchase, and also by how far in advance.

  where they go segmentation customers are segmented by any routine of where they make their purchase. For instance, segmentation based on the fact that they always go to Starbuck's because it is on the way to work.

validity a characteristic achieved when data represent true and accurate measures of the variables under study.

VALS a typology for psychographic segmentation of consumers. This typology defines 8 different market segments. See also *cohorts, PRIZM NE.*

value the perception of a fair return in goods, services, or money for something exchanged. Marketing creates value for customers by understanding and delivering on their needs and wants. Value is a judgment assigned by consumers to the expected or completed consumption of specific goods and services.

value added services services added to the standard product, sometimes charged for, sometimes not, to increase the perceived value.

value chain the four major components or generic building blocks that add value to a company's offering: efficiency, quality, innovation, and customer responsiveness.

value pricing pricing based on customer sensitivity of the price–value relationship in a product.

values and lifestyles (VALS) a consumer psychographic segmentation tool for categorizing the way people think, live, and do. This typology defines eight different market segments. See also *cohorts, PRIZM NE.*

variable costs costs that vary directly with each unit sold, such as food cost.

Veblen effects the theory of conspicuous consumption in which people buy expensive things to raise their social status.

vertical integration when a company makes and sells its own products, it is called backward or upstream vertical integration. When it controls use of the product, it is called forward or downstream vertical integration. When it does both, the company is considered fully vertically integrated.

viral marketing entertaining or informative messages designed to be passed along in an exponential fashion, often electronically or by e-mail.

volume sensitive a business with high fixed costs but low variable costs so that larger volume creates a larger profit percentage, such as hotels and airlines.

whatever the market will bear charging the price that people will pay because they have little other choice.

what it does for the customer the absolute critical test of whether a product fulfilled customer needs and wants and solved problems.

word-of-mouth an informal form of oral communication; considered to be a very powerful form of communication and advertising in the hospitality industry.

yield the ratio between actual revenue and potential revenue.

yield management sometimes called revenue management, the practice of pricing according to demand cycle patterns, such as hourly, daily, weekly, monthly.

yuppies young, urban professionals on the fast track—a class of the baby boomers.

zero-based budget a budget set to a specific performance goal.

zone of tolerance the area between desired service and adequate service that the customer will tolerate, even if not totally satisfied.

Name Index

Aaker, David, 365–366, 371
Abbey, James, 375, 407
Adams, J., 461
Adelson, Sheldon, 17
Ahlstrand, B., 147
Alonzo, V., 223
Anderson, J. C., 407
Angel, S. M., 520, 523
Applegate, L. M., 115
Araskog, Rand, 30
Arndt, M., 35

Bachri, Thamrin, 468
Ballotti, Geoff, 31
Barlow, J., 107, 116
Barsky, J., 195
Beckman, J. M., 620, 625
Bell, R.A., 222, 407
Belobaba, P. P., 624, 625, 626
Bitner, M. J., 53, 55, 57
Bollenbach, Steve, 30, 31
Borden, Neil, 62–63, 81, 82
Bowen, J. T., 91–92, 101, 104, 111, 113, 115, 116, 407
Brennan, D. M., 371
Broadus, Helen C., 471
Brumelle, S. L., 624, 626
Brush, Scott, 460
Burke, Adam, 85–89

Caborn, Rod, 458
Caktiong, Tony Tan, 70
Camacho, Frank, 30
Cannie, J. K., 115
Cantalupo, James R., 18, 19, 20, 124
Carlzon, Jan, 32, 45, 57
Chaffey, D., 498, 512
Chase, Larry, 552
Chase, R. B., 57
Choi, S., 57
Cohen, R., 535
Cook, Suzanne, 542
Craig, Kyle, 357
Crandall, Robert, 401
Cross, S., 116
Curry, R. E., 624, 626

Daniels, John M., 468
Darlington, Sean, 63
Darrow, R.M., 626

Day, S., 35
Dirks, Robert, 352
Dolan, Robert J., 401–403, 407
Dow, Roger, 60
Dowling, Bill, 357, 371
Drucker, Peter, 19–20, 57, 166, 277, 279, 375, 407

Elliott, S., 35
Ellis-Chadwick, F., 512
Eyster, J., 512

Feldott, Mike, 366–367
Feltenstein, T., 83, 437, 461
Ferguson, Patricia, 475
Fonts, Al Martinez, 554, 556
Friedman, Thomas, 136

Galbraith, Kenneth, 390
Gardyn, Rebecca, 186, 195
Garrow, L. A., 622, 626
Gates, Bill, 123
Geller, A., 287, 308
Gershowitz, Howard, 608
Gilly, M. C., 116
Gilmore, J. H., 57
Gogi, P., 35
Goldfeder, Judd, 445, 554
Goodman, J., 106, 107, 116
Gordon, I., 82, 96, 112, 115, 116
Grainger, D., 20
Green, David, 463–465
Greenberg, Jack M., 18
Greenberg, P., 512
Griffin, John, 347–349
Gursoy, D., 225, 229, 247–248, 250

Hart, R., 520, 523
Hayes, R. H., 587
Haywood, R., 461
Hazard, Robert, 277, 319
Heskett, J. L., 107–109, 115, 116
Hill, C., 512
Hilton, Barron, 30
Himelstein, Bruce J., 149–151
Hirohide Abe, 253–255
Hughes, K. A., 83

Jain, S. C., 70, 82, 162, 166, 255, 260–261, 279, 287, 308, 358, 371, 379, 398, 407

Jaworski, B. J., 31
Jicinsky, Terry, 343, 565–568
Johnson, Howard B., 32
Johnson, K., 512
Jones, G., 512
Jones, T. O., 24, 115, 116
Jurowski, C., 229, 250

Kahneman, D., 386, 407
Kalka, K., 622, 626
Kelley, R. E., 113, 116
Keung, P., 535
Kimes, S. E., 57
Knapp, D. E., 371
Knutson, B., 308
Kohli, A. K., 31
Koppel, A., 513
Koppelman, F. S., 622, 626
Kranes, David, 50, 57
Kroc, Ray, 18, 33
Kurth, Brian, 319

Lampel, J., 147
Landro, L., 83
Lee, P. Y., 57
Lehtinen, J. R., 345
Leimkuhler, J. F., 626
Leopold, Gary, 37
Leven, Michael A., 15–17, 48, 261, 504, 505
Levitt, Theodore, 46, 50, 57, 69–70, 90, 115, 318, 341, 345, 470, 487
Lewis, R. C., 35, 57, 92, 115, 116, 308
L'Heureux, E., 622, 626
Lieberman, W., 407
Liebmann, Wendy, 609
Limsky, Drew, 69, 82
Litt, M. R., 147
Littlewood, K., 626
Lovelock, C. H., 57
Loveman, G. W., 115, 116

Makens, James, C., 407
Mandelbaum, R., 222
Marker, Mike, 554, 556
Marriott, Bill, 33
Marzella, Dennis, 281–284
Maslow, Abraham, 172–174, 193, 194, 195
Mayer, Charles, 611
Mayer, R., 512
McCarthy, E. J., 62, 81, 82

McCarthy, Thomas, 483–484, 487
McCleary, K. W., 247–248, 250
McGill, J. I., 624–625, 626
McKenna, R., 34
Mennig, Max and Greti, 3–5, 65, 71, 129, 151, 284, 552
Miller, D., 163, 166
Minor, J., 520, 523, 535
Mintzberg, Henry, 134, 146, 147
Moffett, E., 535
Møller, C., 116
Moller, K. E. K., 340, 345
Monroe, Kent, 379, 407
Morris, B., 116
Morris, S. V., 116, 487
Moss, Nan K., 181
Muller, C., 166

Narus, J. A., 407
Nash, L., 195
Nassikas, Jim, 317, 354
Nebel, Eddystone C., III., 111–112, 116
Nelson, Brad, 573
Neuling, R., 622, 626
Ngonzi, E. N., 57
Nightingale, M., 35, 57
Norton, David, 311–314

Ogilvy, David, 355, 371
Olsen, Michael, 263
Olson, J. C., 407
Orkin, Eric, 484
Osgoodby, Bob, 353, 371

Partlow, C. G., 116
Peppers, D., 101, 115
Peter, J. P., 407
Peters, T. J., 35
Piccoli, G., 115
Pine, J. B., II, 57
Pizam, A., 308
Plaschka, G., 371

Pletcher, Leanne, 232
Plog, S. C., 218, 223
Ploszaj, Jennifer, 432–435
Plummer, Joseph, 324, 345
Pollack, Mary Lou, 61
Porter, Michael, 6, 123–124, 132, 147, 254, 257–258, 260, 275, 276, 279
Portman, John, 28, 277
Price, Jason, 525–526
Pride, W. M., 35

Rascoff, Spencer, 515–517, 528–529, 535
Rathbone, Julie, 611
Ray, Kathy, 113
Reed, Robert, 145
Reichheld, K., 115
Renaghan, L. M., 63, 81, 82, 166
Revlon, Charles, 21
Riedel, S., 622, 626
Rodomski, Rob, 611
Rogers, M., 101, 115
Ronson, Terence, 573
Rosen, Harris, 16
Rosenqvist, G., 345
Ross, Elliot, 375, 407
Roth, Don, 449
Rothstein, M., 620, 625
Rutherford, D., 214, 222, 223, 229, 250

Salma, Umme, 250
Sasser, W. Earl, 24, 107–109, 115, 116
Schlesinger, L. A., 108–109, 115, 116
Schrager, Ian, 60, 458
Schultz, Howard, 16
Seal, K., 222
Shaw, M., 223, 487
Shields, John, 373–375
Shoemaker, S., 56, 57, 90–92, 101, 104, 111, 113, 115, 116, 223, 407, 535
Shor, Juliet, 390
Silvestro, R., 116
Simon, Hermann, 401–403, 407

Simon, J., 620, 625
Siskos, Catherine, 504
Skinner, Jim, 124
Smith, B. C., 622, 626
Springer-Miller, John, 537–539
Stanek, Larry, 610
Starkov, Max, 525–526
Sternlicht, Barry, 30–31, 59–61, 140
Storbacks, K., 345

Taylor, C. J., 620, 625
Taylor, Stephen, 360, 371
Thraenhart, Jens, 430, 489–493
Tiplady, R., 250
Tolpin, Larry, 409–411
Travers, Kenneth, 387, 407
Trump, Donald, 30, 458
Turkel, Stanley, 67
Tversky, A., 386, 407

Uler, Robin, 573, 574
Umbriet, W. T., 214, 222, 223
Uysal, M., 229, 250

Vanderpool-Wallace, Vincent, 225–227
van Ryzin, G. J., 625, 626
Veblen, Thorstein, 390
Verma, A., 371
Verma, R., 371

Warcholak, E. S., 206, 222
Warren, Peter, 59–61
Waterman, R. H., Jr., 35
Wener, R., 57
Wilson, Kemmon, 9, 33
Withiam, G., 371
Wynn, Steve, 318, 458

Zeithaml, V., 53, 55, 57
Zemke, D., 55, 57
Zickus, J. S., 626

Subject Index

Accor Hotels, 6, 67–68, 132, 140, 158, 493, 503
Account management systems, 476–478, 627
AC Neilsen, 322
Acquisition strategy, 129, 130
Action plans, 580, 581–582, 627
Activities, interests, and opinions (AIO), 323
Activity-based costing, 391, 627
Actual market share, 264, 627
Add Me Newsletter, 353
Ad hoc groups, 522, 627
Adoption process model, 417
ADR (average daily rate), 265
Advertising
   collateral, 429
   communications mix, 162, 424–430
   differentiation, 318
   evaluating, 428–429
   expectations, 54
   impulse buying, 21
   intangibility, 42–43
   Larry Tolpin on, 409–411
   as part of marketing, 19
Advertising agencies, 608
Advocates (customers), 98, 627
Affective stage of communications strategy, 417, 627
Affinia Hospitality, 360
Affluent Society (Galbraith), 390
Africa Travel Association, 471
Age, 191, 241–242, 323
AH&MA (American Hotel and Motel Association), 482
AIO (attitudes, interests, and opinions), 324, 627
Airbus A380, 9
Airline crew market, 216–218, 259, 627
Airlines, generally, 510, 522 (*see also specific airlines*)
Aladdin Casino, 73
Alex Hotel, 60–61
Allied Percival International (API), 519
Allie's, 131, 153
All-suites hotel concept, 66, 70, 277, 314, 320 (*see also specific hotels*)
Alternative evaluation, 177–178, 295, 627
Amadeus (GDS), 522
Ambient conditions, 50, 161, 627
Amenities, 181, 261, 316, 350
American Bus Association, 219

American Express, 18, 207, 208, 286, 517
American Hotel and Motel Association (AH&MA), 482
American Resort Development Association, 296
American Society of Association Executives (ASAE), 199, 482
American Society of Travel Agents (ASTA), 540
Amerisuites, 87, 320
API (Allied Percival International), 519
Apple iPod, 21
Aramark Harrison Lodging, 211
Arbitron, 322
Area-wide demand, 293–294
ASAE (American Society of Association Executives), 199, 482
ASEAN (Association of Southeast Asian Nations), 339
Asian American Hotel Owners Association (AAHOA), 15
Assets and liabilities, customer, 89
Association meetings, 213–214, 627
Association of Southeast Asian Nations (ASEAN), 339
Assurance, as a dimension of quality, 6, 55, 56
ASTA (American Society of Travel Agents), 540
Atmosphere, 50, 161
Atria Hotels, 214
Atriums, 277, 315, 354
Attitudes, customer, 176, 178. *See also* AIO
Augmentation, 65–66, 101, 627
Automated campaign management (CM) systems, 430
Avendra, 134
Average daily rate (ADR), 265
Avian flu epidemic, 230
A&W Restaurants, 368

Babson Executive Center, 210–211
Bahama Breeze, 368
Bali bombings, 358–359
Barbizon, 360
Basin Harbor Club, 377–378, 549
Bass Breweries, 129, 130
Beer Stock Exchange, 45, 50
Behavior primacy theory, 173, 627
Beliefs, 177, 627

Bellagio, 129, 275, 315
Benchmark measurements, 585, 627
Benefit bundle, 336, 627
Benefit segmentation, 335–337
Benjamin Hotel, 360
Berkshire Hilton Inn, 368
Best Inns, 48, 131
Best practices, for website design, 544–545
Bizrate.com, 496
Blackhawk Restaurant, 449
Blitzing, 468, 627
Booking engines, 549
Boston Market, 18, 29, 73, 511
Boston Marriott Copley, 204
Bottom-line management, 29, 132, 627
Branding
   competitive advantage, 5
   distribution, 493, 494
   intangibility, 43
   John Griffin on, 347–349
   multiple, 367–370
   positioning, 365–370, 613–618
   reflagging, 508
Breakers Resort, 570
Break-even pricing, 380–381, 627
Brennan's, 384
BringYourPet.com, 586
Bristol Hotel (Paris), 71
British Airways, 63, 493
Budgeting, 422–424, 582–585
Bundling purchase concept, 65, 376
Burger King
   advertising, 333, 423, 425
   alternative evaluation, 177
   bottom-line management, 132
   competition, 256
   differentiation, 318
   international franchises, 193, 532
   positioning, 352
   product life cycles, 72
   standardization, 68
Burj Al Arab, 319
Business centers, 42
Business planning strategies, 131–134, 157–160, 627
Business travelers, 69, 169–170, 180–184, 205–208
Buying decision process, 174–180, 627
Buy times, 201–203, 627

California Pizza Kitchen, 511
Campaign management (CM) systems, 430
Canadian Tourism Commission (CTC), 430, 490
Candlewood Suites, 504
Caneel Bay Resort (St. John), 100
Cannabilization, 368, 370, 394, 627, 633
CAN-SPAM Act (2003), 548
Capacity control, 62
Capital, competitive advantage and, 5
Caribbean Tourism Organization, 225–227
Carlson Companies, 499, 508–510
Carlson Hospitality, 131
Carlson Marketing Group, 518
Carlyle, 188
Cash-flow pricing, 393, 627
Catskills, 78
Ceasar's Entertainment, 122
Celebrity advertising, 410
Cendant, Inc., 32, 420, 493, 522
Central location telephone facility (CLT), 608
Central reservation system (CRS), 521–522
Certified Meeting Planner (CMP), 482
Champions, 318
Change, 32, 568
Channel management, 532–534
Chart House, 413–418
Chi Chi's, 511
Chili's Grill and Bar, 511
China Coast restaurants, 29
China National Tourism Administration (CNTA), 231
Choice Hotels
    branding, 368
    competition, 158, 256
    crisis management, 460
    differentiation, 318, 319, 343
    franchises, 504, 507
    industry change, 277
    segmentation, 73, 191
    strategic alliances, 510
CIC, 199
Claridge, 134
Clarion Hotels, 158, 318, 319, 456–457
Claritas, 312, 330
Click stream data, 549
Clients, 98, 627
The Cloister, 570
Closing (sales calls), 475, 628
CLT (central location telephone facility), 608
Club-Corp USA, 134
Club Med, 8, 163, 190, 359–360, 395, 571
CMP (Certified Meeting Planner), 482
CMP (complete meeting package), 211
CNL Hospitality Properties, Inc., 501
CNTA (China National Tourism Administration), 231
Coca-Cola, 16, 178
Code sharing, airlines, 510, 628
Cognitive dissonance, 178, 179, 628

Cognitive stage of communications strategy, 417, 628
Cohorts, 312, 325, 332
Cold calling, 468, 480, 628
Collateral advertising, 429, 628
Colony Square Hotel (Atlanta), 28
Columbus (global distribution system), 495
Comfort Inns, 158, 318, 319
Comfort Suites, 314
Commitment, 103, 628
Commodity status, 352, 628
Communications mix
    advertising, 54, 162, 424–430
    budgeting, 422–424
    definition, 628
    destination marketing, 244–249
    hospitality marketing mix, 64
    merchandising, 445–451
    publicity, 458–460
    public relations, 451–458
    push/pull strategies, 420
    research, 419–420
    sales promotions (see Sales promotions)
    strategy, 412–419
    word of mouth, 422
Compass Group, 501, 506
Competitive advantage, 5, 6, 158–159, 276–278, 362–363, 628
Competitive analysis (see also Research)
    choosing the right competition, 259–260
    competitive intensity, 260–263, 628
    in destination marketing, 242
    Hirohide Abe on, 253–255
    macrocompetition, 256–257
    microcompetition, 257–258
    overview, 255–256, 259–263, 573
    using, 275–276
Competitive intelligence
    customer satisfaction index (CSI), 267–268
    definition, 628
    feasibility studies, 278
    Hiroshide Abe on, 254
    Internet, 266
    market share, 264–265
    perceptual maps, 268–269, 270–271
    purchased data, 267
    REVPAC (revenue per available customer), 263–264
    REVPAR (revenue per available room), 265
    REVPOR (revenue per occupied room), 263–264
    types and objectives of, 271, 272–273
    yield index, 254, 265
A Complaint Is a Gift, 107
Complaints. See Service recovery
Complete meeting package (CMP), 211
Computer technology. See Technology
Conative stage of communications strategy, 178, 417, 628

Conceptitis, 259
Conference centers, 41–42, 210–211, 215–216, 628
Conferences, 188
Connaught (London), 134
Connecticut Commission on Culture and Tourism (CCT), 440
Conrad, 87
Conrad Punta del Este Resort & Casino, 452
Consortia, 517
Conspicuous consumption, 390
Construct validity, 305
Consultants, research, 609
Consumer Financial Decision's Macro Monitor, 325
Consumer Pulse, 608
Consumer Reports in Eating Share Trends (CREST), 285
Contrary needs, 173–174, 628
Contribution margin pricing, 381–382, 628
Control, 33, 585–586
Convene, 469
Convention and visitors bureaus (CVBs), 215–216, 229, 628
Convention centers, 215–216, 628
Conventions, 8, 200–201, 213–214
Conversion research studies, 294
Co-op advertising, 424
Copley Connection, 204
Copley Place Shopping Galleries, 204
Core product, 65–66, 628
Corporate Meetings & Incentives, 469
Corporate meetings market. See Business travelers
Corporate travel market. See Business travelers
Costs, 375, 379–382, 628 (see also Bottom-line management)
Countermediation, 498
Country Club Lima Hotel, 544–545
Courtyard Marriotts
    branding, 368, 370
    customers, 7–8, 74
    customized product, 69
    differential multitarget marketing, 343
    franchises, 507
    growth strategies, 123
    merchandising, 450
    mission and objectives, 152
    multiple brand positioning, 368
    new venture strategy, 131
    price stability, 394
    product life cycle, 73
    segmentation, 319
Crafted strategies, 134, 136, 628
Creativity, 5
CREST (Consumer Reports in Eating Share Trends), 285, 628
Cross Sphere, 219
Crowne Plaza, 145, 360, 504, 507
CRS (central reservation system), 521–522

Cruise lines, 143, 145, 368
CSI (customer satisfaction index), 267–268
Cultural tourism, 444
Culture, 5, 56
Currency exchange issues, 142, 404–405
Customer Connection, 445, 554
Customer expectations. *See* Expectations
Customers (*see also* Business travelers;
    Destination marketing;
    Organizational customers;
    Relationship/loyalty marketing)
    airline crews, 216–218
    analysis of, 95–97, 628
    association, conventions, and trade
        shows, 213–216
    buying decision process, 174–180
    characteristics, 172–174
    corporate travel managers, 205–211
    creating and keeping, 20–21
    early adopters, 75
    expertise of, 246–247
    group tour and travel market, 218–221
    heterogeneity, 45–46
    incentive meeting planners, 211–213
    information acquisition by, 246–249
    innovators, 74
    laggards, 78
    leisure travelers, 170–171, 184, 186–193
    meeting planners, 201–205
    Michael Levine on, 16–17
    middle majority, 74
    presentation mix, 161
    pricing, 378–379
    public relations, 458
    research, 53, 290–293, 296–300
    responsiveness, 7–8
    sales calls, 472–474
    simultaneous production and
        consumption of services, 47
    SMERF market, 218
    solving problems, 21–26
    tenets of consumer behavior, 172
    Thomas Storey on, 169–172
    trade-off model, 21–26
Customer satisfaction index (CSI),
    267–268
Customization, 68–69, 100–101, 344, 628
CVBs (convention and visitors bureaus),
    215–216, 229

The Daily Bench Limited, 264, 267, 285,
    286, 288
Dairy Queen, 532
Daniel (restaurant), 23
Darden Restaurants, 74, 123, 131, 276, 368
Data analysis, 304, 572–578, 628
Database marketing, 552–559, 628
Data collection, 303, 344, 570–572, 608, 628
Data tabulation houses, 607–608
David Green Organization, 463–465, 494
Davidson-Peterson, 288

Days Inns
    advertising, 423
    differentiation, 316, 318
    distribution channels, 493
    franchises, 493, 504, 507
    segmentation, 338
    value, 19
Death spiral, 78, 629
Decision Analyst, 285
Decline stage, product life cycle, 78–79, 629
Default samples, 302, 629
Delta Hotels, 111, 501
Delta Queen Steamboat Company, 343
Demand analysis, 320, 398–399, 629
Demographics, 243–244, 323
Denny's, 532
Descriptive quantitative research,
    298–299, 629
Designated market areas (DMAs), 292,
    322, 629
Destination marketing
    communications, 244–249, 260
    competition, 242–244
    distribution mix, 163
    economic importance of travel and
        tourism, 227–228
    local residents' attitudes, 228–229
    national tourism organizations' role,
        229–231
    pricing, 377
    segmentation, 242–243
    strategies, 232, 234–242
    Vincent Vanderpool-Wallace on, 225–227
Destination Webrings, 547
Determinant attributes, 350, 629
DEWK (dual employed, with kids), 323, 629
Differential pricing, 619
Differentiation, 132–133, 158, 276,
    311–318, 627, 629
DINK (dual income, no kids), 323, 629
Direct mail, 162
Disintermediation, 496
Disney, 27, 70–71, 193, 367
Distinctive competence, 155, 629
Distribution
    brands, 493
    definition, 629
    franchises, 493, 504–508, 509, 532
    hospitality/marketing mix, 64, 162–163
    international markets, 531–532
    manufacturing *versus* hospitality, 496, 498
    ownership models, 500–504
    representation firms, 494–496
    reservation services, 494
    restaurants, 511
    strategic alliances, 508, 510
    strategies, 530–531
    structure, 498–500
Distribution service provider (DSP), 522
Diversification, 129, 629
Diversity marketing, 567

D.K. Shifflet, 288
DMAs (designated market areas), 292, 322
Domino's Pizza, 277, 511
"Do not call" list, 554
Doral, 41–42, 360
Doubletree, 316
DSP (distribution service provider), 522
Dunkin' Donuts, 507

Early adopters (customers), 75
EBIDTA (earnings before interest, depreci-
    ation, taxes, and amortization), 20
Echo boomers, 323, 629
Ecological environments, 143, 145, 239
Econo Lodges, 351, 368, 394
Economic environments, 142, 182,
    234–235
Economic impacts, 228, 229
Economies of scope, 510, 629
Ecotourism, 143
Efficiency, 6, 7
EMAAR Hotels & Resorts, 367
E-marketing. *See* Internet
Embassy Suites, 8, 206, 314, 316, 500–501
Emergent strategies, 134, 136, 629
Empathy, 6, 55, 56
Employees
    competitive advantage, 5
    empowerment, 111, 122, 629
    internal marketing, 108–114, 629
    mission and objectives, 152
    presentation mix, 161
    public relations, 456–457
    rewards systems *versus* guests needs, 54
    sales promotions, 439, 450
    training, 54
Ensemble Travel Group, 517
Environmental change, 256–257, 277
Environmental scanning, 128, 136, 234,
    284, 296, 629
Environments
    demographic, 239, 240–242
    ecological, 239, 629
    economic, 234–235, 629
    macro, 234
    political/legal, 235, 238–239, 629
    sociocultural, 239, 629
    technological, 137, 139, 235, 629
Equifax/Quick Test Opinion Centers, 608
Ernst & Young (E&Y), 288, 296
Essex House, 159, 256, 352
Etap, 68, 338
Ethics, 482–483, 629
Ethos, 417
eTravCo, 517
EuroDisney, 193
Evaluation/fit, 163
Events marketing, 566–567
Evoked set, of customer awareness, 350, 629
Exchange rates, 404–405
Expectations, 23–25, 25–26, 41–42, 54, 176

Expedia.com, 139, 376, 498, 525, 540
Expedition travel, 49
Experience-based marketing, 34, 52, 629
E&Y (Ernst & Young), 288

Face validity, 305
Fads, 256–257
Fairfield Inns, 123, 343, 368, 507
Fair market share, 264, 629
Fairmont Hotels & Resorts, 134,
    413–418, 508
Family life cycle, 323, 629
Family travelers, 186
FAMtrips, 521
FDI (foreign direct investment), 140
Feasibility studies, 278, 629
Feedback loops, 150, 585–586, 629
Feeder cities, 495, 629
Fences, 403
Fiesta Americana, 495
Fiesta Inns, 495
Fit, as a corporate strategy, 129, 163, 629
FIT (free independent [or international]
    traveler), 193, 629
Fitness centers, 42
Fixed costs, 380, 629
Fixed demand, 43–44
Flag International, 510
Flexible service offerings, 391, 629
Flyspy, 377
Focus groups, 102, 297, 303, 609, 629
Focus strategy, 133–134, 158
Follow-up, after a sales call, 475, 629
Foodservice Europe and Middle East, 285
Food service trends, 145
Footprint® Vietnam Travel, 344, 523–524
Forecasting, 582, 619, 622–623
Foreign direct investment (FDI), 140
Formal product, 65, 629
Formule1 lodging chain, 6, 7, 68, 132,
    338, 370
Four Course Compost, 145
Fournou's Ovens, 317
Four Ps marketing mix, 62, 630
Four Seasons hotels
    branding, 493
    brand message, 38
    customer expectations, 41
    differentiation strategy, 132
    focus strategy, 134
    franchises, 508
    management and ownership, 503, 504
    price-sensitivity, 383
    service, 37, 276
    strategic alliance, 131
    value, 19
Four Seasons Hotel Company, 69
Franchisees, 68, 506–507, 630
Franchises
    advantages and disadvantages, 509
    definition, 630

distribution networks, 493, 504–506, 532
    future of, 507–508
    within hotels, 367
    marketing, 423, 493
    restaurants, 500–501
Free independent traveler (FIT), 193
Free listings, Internet, 546
Freestanding meeting space, 481
Frequency programs, 86, 93, 98, 103–104,
    162, 290
Friendly's, 358–359, 499
Friendship Lodge, 368
Functional-level strategies, 134, 160–163, 630

Galileo, 522
Garden Inns, 319
Gay and lesbian market, 343
Gayot.com, 544–545
GDS (global distribution system), 493, 494,
    521, 522, 540, 541
Geographic segmentation. *See* Location
George V Hotel, 6
GeoVALS, 325
GIANTS (Greater Independent Association
    of National Travel Service), 517
Gillette, 74
Giorgio Armani S.p.A., 367
GIT (group inclusive tour), 219
Global distribution systems (GDSs), 493,
    494, 521, 522, 540, 541, 630
GOGO Tours, 524
Golfplan, 32
Goods, 40–41, 51, 630
Goodwill equity, 93
Google, 546
Government regulations. *See* Regulations
Government travel market, 218, 630
Granada Royale Hometels, 320
Greater Independent Association of National
    Travel Services (GIANTS), 517
Greenbrier Resort, 570
Groupe Accor, 158–159, 256, 338, 370
Group inclusive tour (GIT), 219
Group tour and travel market, 218–221
Growth stage, product life cycle, 75–76, 630

HAMA (Hotel Asset Managers
    Association), 501
Hamburger University, 506
Hampton Inns, 87, 394
Harrah's Entertainment, 5, 122, 311–314,
    376, 436
Hawthorne Suites, 48, 73, 131, 504
Heakin Research, 608
Henry Bean (restaurants), 318
Heterogeneity of services, 44–47, 630
Hierarchy of needs model, 172–174, 631
Hilton hotels
    advertising, 423
    branding, 348
    business models, 500, 503

competitive advantage, 8
    distribution channels, 493
    franchises, 507
    Internet, 542
    multiple branding, 368
    positioning, 352
    repositioning, 360
    sales, 466
    sales promotions, 439–440
    segmentation, 319, 460
Hilton Americas (Houston), 466
Hilton Garden Inns, 319, 368
Hilton Guest Profile Manager, 101
Hilton Hawaiian Village® Beach Resort &
    Spa, 140
Hilton HHonors Worldwide, 85
Hilton Hotel's Corporation's OnQ, 101
Hilton International, 70, 160, 507
Hilton's HHonors program, 262
Hilton Waikoloa, 232
Holiday Inn Express, 504
Holiday Inns
    branding, 493
    franchises, 504, 508
    international market, 70
    joint venture with Nickelodeon, 367
    marketing leadership, 18
    repositioning, 360
    standardization, 67, 68
Homestead Resort, 570
Hospitality Franchise Systems, 420
Hospitality marketing mix, 63–64
Hospitality product, 47–52, 64–66, 630
Hospitality suites, 214
Host Marriott, 501, 503
The Hotel, 9
Hotel Asset Managers Association
    (HAMA), 501
Hotel del Coronado, 501, 570
Hotel Indigo, 504
Hotel Industry Switch Company
    (THISCO), 494
Hotel Nikko Atlanta, 360
Hotel Nikko New York, 352
Hotel Pennsylvania, 188, 256
Hotel restaurants, 317–318, 366–367
Hotel Roosevelt, 256
Hotel Sales & Marketing Association
    International (HSMAI), 15, 482
Hotels.com, 44, 498, 525
Hot Shoppes, 123–124
Hotwire.com, 44, 134, 139, 258, 376,
    515–516, 525, 528, 529
Howard Johnson hotels, 18, 29, 32, 156,
    177, 420, 421, 493
HSMAI (Hotel Sales & Marketing
    Association International), 15, 482
Human resources, 6, 54
Hyatt
    acquisitions, 87, 320
    competitive analysis, 253–255

franchises, 508
functional-level strategy, 134
marketing opportunities, 277
market strategy, 160
revenue management, 373–375
sales, 466, 470
strategic planning, 131
Hyatt Regency (Atlanta), 28
Hyatt Regency Cerromar Beach Resort & Casino, 351
Hyatt Regency (Maui), 570

IAAPA (International Association of Amusement Parks and Attractions), 451
IACC (International Association of Conference Centers), 211
IACVB (International Association of Convention and Visitor Bureaus), 482
Ian Schrager Hotels, 60
Ibis, 338, 370
IBM, 18
Iceland Air Hotels, 495
IHR Research Group, 303
Image, 244–245
Importance attributes, 350, 630
Impulse buying, 21, 630
Incentive houses, 212, 518, 630
Incentive meeting market, 211–213
Indian Ocean tsunami, 229
Indifference, customer attitude of, 472–473, 630
Industrialization of services, 46, 50
Industry life cycle, 72
Inferential quantitative research, 299, 630
Information acquisition (travelers), 246–249
Innovation, 6, 8
Innovators (customers), 74
In-plants, 208, 517, 630
Intangibility, 40–43, 630
Integration, 498–500
InterActive Corporation, 529
InterContinental, 119, 129, 130, 134, 160, 360, 432–435, 493, 542
InterContinental (Atlanta), 28
InterContinental Hotels Group (IHG), 504
Internal information gathering, 290–293
Internal marketing, 108–114, 630
Internal validity, 305
International Association of Amusement Parks and Attractions (IAAPA), 451
International Association of Conference Centers (IACC), 211
International Association of Convention and Visitor Bureaus (IACVB), 482
International franchising, 532
International hotel, strategic plan for, 156–157, 162
International pricing, 404–405
International product/service mix, 69–71, 73

International segmentation, 338–340, 341
International tourism, 186, 192–193 (see also Destination marketing)
Internet
    advertising, 424, 429, 442
    branding and selling, 38, 366
    communications mix, 162
    corporate meeting planners, 198
    database marketing, 552–560
    data management, 547–552
    distribution, 122, 139, 515–516, 525–530
    ethics, 483
    innovation, 8
    marketing, 42, 263, 540–542
    marketing research, 304
    marketing trends, 560–561
    product/service mix, 61
    REVPAR (revenue per available room), 265
    security, 540
    website design, 542–547
Internet Protocol address, 549
Interstate Hotels, 159
Interviews, 297
Introductory stage, product life cycle, 73–75, 630
Inventory control. See Revenue management
Inventory nesting, 400
ISM Marketing, 37
It's a Grind, 103
ITT Sheraton. See Sheraton
Ivory Soap, 72

Jacob Javits Convention Center, 215
J.D. Power & Associates, 306
Joint ventures, 367
Jollibee, 70
Judgmental samples, 302
Jurni Network, 103–104
JW Marriott, 130, 368

Keyword searches, 546
KFC (Kentucky Fried Chicken), 70, 131, 140, 357–358, 368
K-Minus program, 7
Knights Inns, 493
Knowledge-based marketing, 34, 630
Knowledge relationships, 101
KYST algorithm, 613

Laggards (customers), 78
Laguna Beach Resort, 145
Landry's Restaurants, 73
Langham Hotel, 315
La Quinta, 318
Lastminute.com, 525
Las Vegas, 8, 73
Las Vegas Convention and Visitors Authority (LVCVA), 565–568
LCD (lowest common denominator), 477

Leadership, 17, 32–33, 123–124, 131, 631
Leading Hotels of the World, 494, 522
Lead times, 201–203, 630
Le Cirque, 317, 351, 352
Legal Sea Foods, 511
Leisure travelers, 170–171, 184, 186–193
Leisure Travel Group, 517
Leisure Travel MONITOR, 282
Le Meridien, 160, 347–349, 472, 504
Le Parker Meridien, 256
Les Celebrites, 352
Lettuce Entertain You Enterprises, 317, 511
Lifetime value of a customer, 93–97, 114–115, 171, 630
Lindblad Expeditions, 49
Location, 5, 159–160, 161, 295, 350
Lodging Hospitality, 483
Logos, 417
London tourism (Visit London), 478
Long John Silver's, 368
Loss leaders, 394, 630
Low-cost carriers (LCCs), 377, 391
Lowest common denominator (LCD), 477, 630
Loyalty circle, 101–102, 630
Loyalty. See Relationship/loyalty marketing
Luxury Collection, 159
LVCVA (Las Vegas Convention and Visitors Authority), 565–568

Macrocompetition, 256–257, 630
Maintenance stage, product life cycle, 77, 630
Mall intercepts, 302
Management (see also Channel management; Revenue management)
    bottom-line orientation, 29, 122
    competitive advantage, 5–6
    crisis situations, 460
    employee empowerment, 111–114, 122
    marketing orientation, 29, 30–32
    operations orientation, 26–27
    product/service orientation, 28
    selling orientation, 28–29, 122
Mandalay Resorts, 129
Mandarin Oriental Hotel Group, 316, 354–355, 508
Manhattan East Suite Hotels, 360
Mansion on Turtle Creek, 276
Maritz Travel, 518
Market behaviors, 244, 284
Market demographics, 243–244, 323
Marketing
    concept of, 15–17, 19, 29, 31–32
    creating and keeping customers by, 20–21
    definition, 631
    experience-based, 34
    knowledge-based, 34
    Michael Leven on, 15–17
    as part of the value chain, 6
    permission-based, 548–549

Marketing, *(continued)*
  product, 37
  sales *versus*, 15
  service, 37
  traditional, 25–26, 42
Marketing leadership. *See* Leadership
Marketing management. *See* Management
Marketing mix
  complexity of hospitality
    product/service mix, 66–69
  developing new products and services,
    79–81
  Four Ps, 62
  hospitality marketing mix, 63–64
  hospitality product, formal and
    augmented, 65–66
  hospitality product/service mix, 64–65
  international product/service, 69–71
  overview, 62
  Peter Warren on, 59–62
  the product decision, 71
  the product life cycle, 71–79
  Seven Ps, 62–63
  13 Cs, 62–63
Marketing plan *(see also* Planning)
  budgeting, 582–585, 631
  data analysis, 572–573, 576–577
  data collection, 570–572
  development, 569–570
  forecasting, 582, 631
  mission and marketing statements,
    578–582
  requirements, 568–569
  template, 587
  Terry Jicinsky on, 565–568
Marketing Research Association (MRA), 608
Market Metrix, 173
Market psychographics, 244
Market research. *See* Research
Market share, 264–265, 631
Market strategy, 159–160, 631
Markup pricing, 380, 631
Marriotts *(see also* Courtyard Marriotts)
  advertising, 275–276, 423
  branding, 348, 493
  competition, 256, 261
  customer responsiveness, 7–8
  differential multitarget marketing, 343
  differentiation, 158, 316
  distribution channels, 493
  franchises, 367, 507
  frequency programs, 98–99
  Internet, 542
  management and ownership, 504
  marketing leadership, 18
  market strategy, 160
  merchandising, 449
  mission and objectives, 152
  motivating employees, 111
  positioning and repositioning, 351,
    360, 368

  pricing, 376
  publicity and public relations, 452, 459
  sales and promotions, 436, 466, 470
  segmentation, 319, 338
  sports bars, 317–318
  strategic alliances, 510
  strategic planning, 129, 134, 343, 501,
    503, 573
  SWOT analysis, 155
  timeline, 125
Marriott Copley Place, 152
Marriott Distribution Services, 124, 129
Marriott Long Wharf, 152
Marriott Marquis, 351
Marriott Renaissance Hotel (San
  Francisco), 354
Marriott Restaurant Division, 153
Marriott Rewards System, 131
Marriott's Automated Reservation System
  for Hotel Accommodations
  (MARSHA), 131
Maslow's hierarchy of needs model,
  172–174, 631
Mass customization, 344, 631
Master marketing strategy, 153–154, 631
MAST (Midwest Agents Selling Travel), 517
Match pricing, 396, 397, 631
Materials management, 6
Mature property, 477, 631
Mature stage, product life cycle, 76–78,
  256, 631
Mature traveler markets, 191, 631
McDonald's
  advertising, 333, 423, 425
  augmented products, 66
  bottom-line management, 132
  competition, 256, 571
  customers, 18, 20
  demand, 576
  differentiation, 318
  distribution channels, 493
  ecological environment, 145
  franchises, 504–505, 507
  Hamburger University, 506
  international, 70, 74, 193, 532
  location, 159–160
  marketing concept, 18
  nontraditional marketing, 19
  opportunity, 276
  positioning, 351, 352, 353
  product life cycles, 72, 77
  public relations, 452
  sales promotions, 436
  segmentation, 336
  standardization, 68
  strategic leadership, 126
  trade-off model, 23–24
  value chain activities, 6
  vertical integration, 499
MDS (multidimensional scaling), 613
Measurement, 306, 439–440, 585–586

Media Mark Research Inc. (MRI), 325
Media research, 288
Meeting planners, 188, 200–205, 469, 631
The Meeting Professional, 469
Meeting Professionals International (MPI),
  197, 199
Meetings & Conventions, 469
Meetings express sales positions, 482, 631
Meetings Industry Megasite, 469
Menlo Consulting Group, 288
Menu degustation, 395, 631
Merchandising, 162, 445–451, 631
Merchant model, 525–527, 541–542
Mercure, 338, 370
Meridien, 338
Merrill Lynch, 324–325
Metropolitan statistical areas (MSAs),
  322, 631
MGM Grand, 8
MGM Mirage Resorts, 123, 129
Microcompetition, 257–258, 631
Microsoft, 123
Microtels, 48, 67–68, 158, 261, 394, 504
Middlebury Inn, 20, 218–219
Middle majority (customers), 74
Midwest Agents Selling Travel (MAST), 517
Milford Plaza, 188, 256
Mission statements, 149, 151, 569,
  578–582, 631
"Moments of truth," 45, 47, 51
Monthly Eating-Out Monitor, 288
Morgans Hotel Group, 360
Motel 6, 140, 370
Motorcoach tours, 219–221, 631
Mövenpick, 317
"Move up and out" philosophy, 482, 631
MPI (Meeting Professionals
  International), 199
MRA (Marketing Research Association), 608
MRI (Media Mark Research Inc.), 325
MSAs (metropolitan statistical areas), 322
MSN, 546
MUI Group, 366
Multidimensional scaling (MDS), 613
Multiple brand positioning, 367–370, 631
Multivariate analysis, 299, 631

National Conference Center, 210–211
National Restaurant Association, 296
National Tour Association (Cross
  Sphere), 219
National tourism organizations (NTOs),
  228, 229–231
National Travel MONITOR, 282, 285, 498
Natural environment, 143, 145
Needs hierarchy, 172–174
Neutral pricing, 397, 631
New Otani, 338
Newport Room, 413–418
New ventures, 129
New York Hilton Towers, 256

New York Palace, 134, 317, 442
New York Sheraton, 256
NF (Nouvelles Frontières), 129, 499
Niche, 631
Nickelodeon Family Suites by Holiday Inn, 367
Nielson Media Research, 292
Nikko (Westin), 338, 352, 360
Noncontact employees, 11
Nonprobability samples, 302, 631
Nontraditional marketing, 19, 631
Norcal Waste Systems, 145
Nouvelles Frontières (NF), 129, 499
Novotel, 140, 338, 370
NPD, Inc., 285
NTOs (national tourism organizations), 228, 229–231, 631
Numi Tea, 152

Oberoi Hotels, 160, 340, 508
Objective positioning, 351, 631
Objectives, 149–153, 391–396, 393
Odd-numbered pricing, 390, 631
Ohana Hotels and Resorts, 413–418
Olive Garden, 123, 276, 351, 368, 511
Omni Hotels, 159, 256, 508
On Achieving Excellence (Peters), 105
One dollar ($1) per thousand pricing, 382, 631
One-stop shopping, 482, 631
Online distribution systems, 525–530
Online marketing. *See* Internet
Operations orientation, 26–27, 44, 631
Opportunities, 18, 33, 155, 257, 471, 632
Opryland Hotel, 111
Optimization, 619, 620, 623–624
Opting out, 549, 632
Orbitz.com, 525, 540
Organic Internet search, 546
Organizational customers
    airline crew market, 216–218
    association, convention and trade shows, 213–214
    Charlotte St. Martin on, 197–200
    conference centers, 210–211
    convention and visitors bureaus, 197–198
    corporate meetings market, 208–211
    corporate travel market, 205–208
    definition, 632
    government market, 218
    group tour and travel market, 218–221
    incentive meeting planners, 211–213
    meeting planners, 197, 200–205
    SMERF market, 218
Organizational design, 163
Outdoor advertising, 427
Overbooking, 619, 620, 621–622
Overspent American (Shor), 390

Pacific Area Travel Association, 468
Packages, 171, 188–191, 376, 436, 632

Palms (casino), 133
Panama City Beach, 425–426
Pan American Airlines, 160
Pannell Kerr Forster (PKF), 288
Paradores, 501
Paramount, 360
Parc Central Hotel, 159
Parker Meridien, 159
PAR Springer-Miller Systems, 537–539
Partnerships, 88
Passports, 141
Patents, 5
Pathos, 417, 632
PCMA (Professional Conference Managers Association), 199, 218
Peabody Hotel, 111, 314, 316
Pegasus, 493, 494, 522, 529
Peninsula Hotels, 508
Peoples Express Airlines, 397
Pepsico, 131
Perceptions, 175–176, 484–485, 627, 632
Perceptual maps, 268, 270–271, 632
Per diem, 217, 632
Perishability, 43–44, 632
Permission-based marketing, 548–549, 632
Personal interviews, 297, 303, 609
Personal selling, 162, 412 (*see also* Sales)
Personnel, sales, 482–484
Pertlink Limited, 573
P.F. Chang's, 123
PFK Hospitality Research, 582
Phishing, 492
Physical plant, presentation mix and, 161
Pierre, 131, 134
Pizza Hut, 70, 131, 367, 368, 511
PKF (Pannell Kerr Forster), 288
Planet Hollywood, 29, 73, 132, 316
PlanHotel Resorts, 190
Planning
    business level, 131–134, 157–160
    corporate level, 129–131
    definition, 128
    emergent strategies (crafted), 134, 136
    events, 201–205
    feedback loops, 163–164
    functional level, 134, 160–163
    role, 128
Plaza Athenee, 351
Plaza Hotel, 315
Pleasure travelers, 632 (*See also* Leisure travelers)
PMS (property management systems), 522, 547–548, 557–558
Political/legal environment, 139–141, 238–239
Populations, in research, 301, 632
Porter's five forces, 254, 257–258
Positioning
    branding, 365–370
    competitive, 362–363
    customer attributes, 350–351

definition, 628
defensive, 276
effective, 354–357, 629
intangible, 354
internal analysis, 364–365
John Griffin on, 347–349
objective, 351
overview, 160, 349–350
public relations, 456
repositioning, 358–361
role, 357–358
strategies, 361–362
subjective, 351–352
tangible, 352–354
Positioning statements, 352, 356, 418, 632
Postconference meeting, 205, 632
Posttesting, 283
Potential Rating Index Zip Code Markets (PRIZM), 312, 330, 332
Preconference meeting, 205, 632
Preferred Hotels & Resorts, 494, 522
Presentation mix, 64, 161, 632
Prestige pricing, 395
Pretesting, 283
Price elasticity, 398–399, 632
Price leaders, 396, 632
Priceline.com, 44, 134, 258, 376, 515–516, 525, 528, 529
Price lining, 390, 632
Price penetration, 394, 632
Price point, 6, 632
Price resistance, 142
Price segmentation, 337–338
Price sensitivity, 381, 383, 632
Price sensitivity measurement (PSM), 387, 632
Price skimming, 394, 632
Price stability, 394, 632
PricewaterhouseCoopers, 296
Pricing
    basis, 375
    cash-flow, 393
    changing, 377–378
    cost-based, 379–382
    definition, 377
    determining, 396–398
    differential, 619
    hotel rooms, 376
    intangibility, 43
    international, 404–405
    market demand (demand analysis), 398–399
    market research, 295
    mix, 64, 162, 632
    multiple channels of distribution, 405
    objectives, 391–396
    optimization, 44
    presentation mix, 161
    profit maximization, 391, 632
    psychological, 387, 390
    restaurants, 376–377

Pricing, *(continued)*
    revenue management, 399–403
    seven Ps, 378–379
    value-based, 382–387, 632
Prime Motor Inns, 29, 420
Prix fixe, 395, 632
PRIZM (Potential Rating Index Zip Code
    Markets), 312, 330, 332
Probability samples, 302, 303, 632
Probes, open and closed, 471, 632
Product, 337, 632
Product differentiation. *See* Differentiation
Product-driven pricing, 378–379
Production, as part of the value chain, 6
Product life cycle, 71–79, 632
Product line management, 481–482, 632
Products
    augmented, 65–66
    benefits and features, 472
    core (salient), 65–66
    customized, 68–69
    designing, 65
    formal, 65
    physical, 49
    service, 49
    standard, 67–68
    strategy, 158
Product/service mix
    augmented product, 65–66
    concept, 63–64
    core product, 65–66
    definition, 632
    designing the product, 65
    formal product, 65
    hospitality product/service mix, 64–65,
      66–69
    international, 69–71
    management orientation, 28
Professional Conference Managers
    Association (PCMA), 199, 218
Profit, 19, 93–97, 151 (*see also* Bottom-line
    management)
Promotion, 162, 244–245, 531
Promus Hotels, 8, 500
Property management systems (PMS), 522,
    547–548, 557–558, 632
Property research, 294–296, 573, 576
Proprietary research, 296, 632
Prospects (customers), 97–98
Prospect theory (pricing), 385–386, 632
PR (public relations) news release, 452, 632
Psychographic segmentation, 324–326,
    330, 332–333
Psychological pricing, 387, 390, 633
"Public domain" research, 289
Publicity, 458–460, 633
Public relations, 162, 262–263, 432–435,
    451–458, 633
Purchase cycles, 201–203
Push/pull strategies, 420, 530,
    533–534, 633

Qualifying prospects, 468, 633
Qualitative research, 296, 297–298, 633
Quality, 6, 55 (*see also* RATER [reliability,
    assurance, tangibility, empathy,
    responsiveness])
Quality Controlled Services, 608
Quality Inns, 158, 277, 318, 319, 368
Quality Royale (Clarion), 319, 368
Quantified Marketing Group, 445
Quantitative research, 296, 298–300
Questionnaires, 299, 303
Quiet Zone, Crowne Plaza, 69
Quota samples, 302, 633

Radisson Hotels, 131, 277, 460, 507,
    508–510
Radisson/SAS Hotels, 340
Raising the numbers, 568, 633
Ramada, 360, 460, 472, 493
Random samples, 302
Rate buckets, 207, 633
Rate cannabilization, 633
Rate integrity, 394, 633
Rate parity, 198, 394, 405, 633
RATER (reliability, assurance, tangibility,
    empathy, responsiveness), 6, 55, 56,
    67, 98, 384, 633
Rate transparency, 394, 633
Real estate investment trusts (REITs), 31,
    140, 501, 633
Red Lobster, 123, 276, 351, 368
Red Roof Inns, 140, 370, 394
Reference groups, 176, 633
Reference price, 386–387
Reflagging, 508
Regent, 131
Regulations, trade, 139–141
Reintermediation, 496
REITs (real estate investment trusts), 31,
    140, 501
Relais & Châteaux, 494
Relationship/loyalty marketing
    Adam Burke on, 85–89
    building customer loyalty, 98–101
    complaints and service recovery,
      104–108
    customer life cycles, 97–98
    customers as assets, 89
    definition, 91
    description, 90–92
    frequent guest and loyalty programs, 92,
      103–104, 540
    goals, 90
    internal marketing, 108–111
    lifetime value of a customer, 93–97
    the loyalty circle, 101–102, 630
    management practices, 111–114
    marketing, 34
    need for, 92–93
    RATER and, 55
Reliability, 6, 55, 56, 304–305

Renaissance hotels, 123, 130
Repeat customers. *See* Customers
Repetition, 419
Repositioning, 358–361
Request for proposal (RFP), 549
Research
    communications, 419–420
    conducting customer satisfaction
      ratings, 306
    designing the marketing information
      system, 286
    developing customer profiles, 296–300
    developing the research design,
      300–304, 633
    establishing reliability and validity,
      304–306
    gathering internal information, 290–293
    using marketing intelligence, 293–296
    using outside contractors for, 603–612
    using to yield measurement metrics, 306
The Researcher SourceBook (Quirk
    Enterprises), 609
Reservations, 8, 387, 494, 633
Residence Inns, 73, 152, 343, 368
Resort leisure market, 188, 295, 396
Responsiveness, 6, 55, 56
Restaurant Associates, 500–501
Restaurant Partnership, 366
Restaurants
    business travelers, 182
    CREST (Consumer Reports in Eating
      Share Trends), 285
    demand, 44
    distribution systems, 511
    failure rates, 74
    franchises, 500–501
    in hotels, 317–318, 366–367
    innovation, 8
    market opportunities, 277–278
    multiple brand positioning, 368
    pricing, 376–377, 394
    prospect theory, 386
    research, 284
    revenue per available seat (REVPAS), 267
    revenue per square foot (RSQFT), 267
    sales promotions, 447–448
    sociocultural changes, 143
Restaurant Zum See, 3–6, 9, 20
Restructuring, 129, 131
Return on investment (ROI), 20, 393,
    424, 633
Revenue management
    definition, 633
    history of inventory control, 619–620
    inventory control techniques, 621–625
    John Shields on, 373–375
    as a managerial discipline, 44
    overview, 400–403, 619
Revenue per square foot (RSQFT), 267, 633
REVPAC (revenue per available customer),
    263–264, 266, 633

REVPAR (revenue per available room), 254, 265, 633
REVPAS (revenue per available seat), 267, 633
REVPOR (revenue per occupied room), 263–264, 266, 633
Reward programs, 122
REZsolutions, 494
RFM (recency, frequency, and monetary value), 334, 445
RFP (request for proposal), 549
Riedel Glassware, 6
RingMaster, 547
Risk/fit loop, 163
The Rittenhouse Hotel, 9
Ritz-Carlton
   customer expectations, 41
   customer responsiveness, 7–8, 384–385
   differentiation, 315, 318–319
   differentiation strategy, 158
   focus strategy, 134
   functional-level strategy, 134
   mission and objectives, 152
   motivating employees, 111
   ownership, 123, 130
   packages, 188
   positioning, 351
   price-sensitivity, 383
   product/service mix, 160
   proprietary database, 554
   sales, 470
   service marketing, 37
   target marketing, 343
Ritz-Carlton (Atlanta), 28
Ritz-Carlton (Chicago), 69
Ritz-Carlton (Egypt), 503
Rodeway Inns, 73, 368
Roger Smith Hotel, 315
ROI (return on investment), 20, 393, 424, 633
Ronald McDonald homes, 452
Room rates, 376
Room service, 51–52
Room Service Deliveries, 511
Rosenbluth Travel, 207
Rosewood Hotels, 132–133
Round Table Pizza, 511
Royal Caribbean Cruise Line, 9
Royal Garden Hotel, 449
Roy Rogers, 153
RSQFT (revenue per square foot), 267
Ruth's Chris Steak House, 316, 351

Sabre Holdings, 103–104, 522
Saks, 38
Sales
   action plan, 477–478, 633
   communications mix, 162, 466–467
   David Green on, 463–465
   management, 28–29, 466, 476–482, 633
   marketing, 15, 19

versus operations, 484–486
   personnel development, 482–484
   process, 467–476
   prospecting, 464–465
   successful, 470
Sales promotions, 436, 437–441, 442–445, 633
Salient attributes, 350, 633
Samples, 301–302, 633
Sandals, 190
S&A Restaurant Corp., 357
SARS virus outbreak, 230
SAS Hotels, 45, 277, 508–510
SAS Radisson, 493
SAS (Scandinavian Airlines System), 32–33
Satisfaction, 24, 179–180, 306
Savoy, 134
Scarborough Research, 325
Schrager Hotels, 360
Search engines, 546
Sears Roebuck and Company, 18
Seasons 52, 368
Secondary research, 288, 633
Security (Internet), 540, 545
Segmentation
   benefit, 335–337, 633
   customer research, 291
   David Norton on, 311–314
   definition, 631, 632, 635
   demographic, 323, 633
   destination marketing, 242–243
   differentiation, 318–320
   fine-tuning, 340–341
   geographic, 322–323, 633
   international, 338–340, 341, 633
   price, 337–338, 633
   process, 320–321
   psychographic, 324–326, 330, 332–333, 633
   Stowe Shoemaker on, 588–602
   strategies, 341
   usage, 333–335, 633
Selectivity, 175, 633
Self-service, 40, 46
Semivariable costs, 380, 633
Senior Living Service Communities, 124
Seniors HHonors, 191
September 11, 2001, 228, 476, 540–541, 571
Series group tour operators, 522–523, 633
Services
   complaints (see Service recovery)
   definition, 634
   delivery, 51, 54
   environment, 50, 51
   gaps, 43, 52–57 (see also Zone of tolerance)
   Gary Leopold on, 37–39
   versus goods, 40
   heterogeneity, 44–47
   hospitality product, 48–52
   intangibility, 40–43

management orientation, 28
   perishability, 43–44
   product, 50, 51
   quality, 52–55, 633 (see also RATER)
   simultaneous production and consumption, 47
Service America (Albrecht and Zemke), 30
Service recovery, 53–54, 87, 104–108
Servicescape, 50, 634
SERVQUAL model, 52, 634
Seven Ps marketing mix, 62–63
Shangri-La Hotel Group, 356, 508
Sheraton, 29–31, 37, 110, 159, 368, 460, 504, 507
Sheraton Boston Hotel, 204
Sheraton Center Towers, 256
Sheraton Grand (Washington, DC), 113
Sheraton St. Regis, 368
Sheraton Wayfarer Motor Inn, 368
S&H Green Stamps, 98
SHR (Swedish Hotel and Restaurant Association), 141
Signs and symbols, 50
SIH (Rezidor SAS Hospitality), 131
Simmons Market Research Bureau, 325
Simultaneous production and consumption of services, 47, 634
SITE (Society of Incentive Travel Executives), 212
Situational analysis, 154–156, 634 (see also Competitive analysis; Competitive intelligence; Research)
Size, competitive advantage and, 6, 8
Sizzler, 70
Skepticism, sales calls and, 472–473, 634
Sleep Inns, 158, 318, 368
Small Luxury Hotels of the World, 494
Smartertravel.com (offseason travel), 54
SMERF (social, military, education, religious, and fraternal) market, 218, 634
Smith Travel Research (STR), 264, 267, 285, 286, 288, 338
Smokey Bones, 368
Smuggler's Notch, 67, 385
Society of Incentive Travel Executives (SITE), 212
Sociocultural environment, 142–143
Sofitel, 140, 338, 370
South Seas Resort, 20
Southwest Airlines, 7, 122, 132, 133, 397
Spam, 548, 634
Spatial layout, 50
Spin control, 451, 634
SRI Consulting Business Intelligence (SRI-BI), 312, 324–325
St. Moritz, 360
St. Regis, 159, 316–317, 395, 442
Standardization, 46, 50, 634
Stanford Court Hotel, 317, 354
Starbucks, 16, 68, 69, 499, 503

STAR reports, 267, 285
Starwood Hotels and Resorts
    acquisitions, 29–30
    Barry Sternlicht, 30–31, 59–61, 140
    differentiation, 315, 349
    Internet, 542
    management and ownership, 504
    public relations, 452
    repositioning, 360
Staybridge Suites, 504
Stealth marketing, 422
Steigenberger Hotels, 145
Strategic alliances, 508–510, 634
Strategic business units (SBUs), 151, 160, 634
Strategic marketing (*see also* Objectives)
    business strategies, 157–160
    Christian Hempell on, 119–121
    communications, 412–413
    competitive marketing, 122–123
    definitions of strategy, 124, 127
    environmental scanning, 136
    feedback loops, 163–164
    functional strategies, 160–163
    versus management effectiveness,
        121–122
    master marketing strategy, 153–156
    planning, 127–134, 136 (*see also*
        Planning)
    selection and failure, 164–165
    strategic leadership, 123–124, 634 (*see
        also* Leadership)
    tactical initiatives, 87
    types of environment, 137, 139–144,
        145 (*see also* Environments)
STR (Smith Travel Research), 264, 267,
    285, 286, 288, 338
Studio 6, 140
Subjective positioning, 351–352, 634
Substitutability, 295, 634
Successful Meetings, 469
Suite hotels, 66, 70, 277, 314, 320 (*see also
    specific hotels*)
Summit Hotel Management Company, 504
Supranational, 494–495
Survey Sampling and Scientific Telephone
    Samples, 609
Suspects (prospective customers), 97–98
Sustainable competitive advantage, 276, 634
Swedish Hotel and Restaurant Association
    (SHR), 141
Sweet Tomatoes, 297–298
SWOT (strengths, weaknesses,
    opportunities, and threats) analyses,
    149–150, 154, 155–156, 634
Synthesis, of feedback analyses, 163, 634
SynXis, 493, 494

Taco Bell, 7, 110, 131, 277, 368, 377, 387
Tactical initiatives, 87
Tactics, 87, 124, 127, 634
Taj Hotels, 158, 340

Takeout Taxi, 511
Tangibility, 6, 40, 49, 55, 56, 634
Target marketing, 157–158, 321–322,
    342–344, 413, 415, 456, 634
Target return on investment (ROI), 393, 634
TARP Worldwide, 105–106
Tarrytown House, 201
Tauck Tours, 219
Technology
    brand marketing, 366
    choice, 33
    data collection, 303, 344
    do's and don't's, 575–576
    enabler *versus* crutch, 86
    environment, 137, 139, 235
    meetings, 198
    pricing, 377
Technology Portals, Inc., 46
Telemarketing, 468, 469, 634
Tenets of consumer behavior, 172, 634
Territorial rights, 504, 634
Texas Pacific Group (TPG), 515
TGI Friday's, 70, 318, 505, 511
Thai Wah Group, 145
Theory of the Leisure Class (Veblen), 390
Thirteen Cs marketing mix, 63, 74–79
THISCO (Hotel Industry Switch
    Company), 494, 522
Threats, as opportunities, 155, 257, 634
TIA (Travel Industry Association of
    America), 60, 192, 229, 230, 288,
    296, 542
Time, value of, 383–384
TiVo, 410
Todd English Restaurants, 318
TOGO's Eatery, 511
TOURCOM, 452
Tourism. *See* Destination marketing
Tour operators, ad hoc and brokers,
    522–525
TPG (Texas Pacific Group), 515
TQM (total quality management), 77,
    122, 634
Tracking, 428, 634
Trade issues, 139–141
Trade-offs, 21–26, 178, 634
Trade shows, 8, 211, 213–214, 634
Traditional marketing, 25–26, 634
Travel agencies, 518, 519
Travel Agent, 521
Travel agents, 518–521, 540
Travelaxe.com, 529
Travel Business Roundtable, 229
TravelCLICK, 264, 267, 286
Travel Industry Association of America
    (TIA), 60, 192, 229, 230, 288, 296, 542
Travelnotes.org, 547
Travelocity, 139, 498, 522, 525, 540
TravelStyles, 288
TravelWeb.com, 494, 498
Travel Weekly, 521

Travelzoo, 529
Tricon Global Restaurants, Inc., 368
Trust (distribution service provider), 522
Tsunami disaster of 2004, 175, 229
TUI Austria Holding AG, 499
Turtle Island Resort, 240–241
Tyler Place Family Resort, 385

UNWTO (United Nations World Tourism
    Organization), 227, 359
Undercover marketing, 422, 635
Unions, 214
Unique visitors, 554, 635
Unisys, 468
United Bus Owners of America, 219
United States Tour Operators
    Association, 524
Unsecured Internet, 540, 635
U.S. Travel Data Center, 289
Usage segmentation, 333–335, 635
USFS (US Franchise Systems, Inc.), 3–5,
    48, 504, 505
USTTA (United States Travel and Tourism
    Administration), 229
Utell, 493

Vail Resort Company, 103
Validity, research, 304–306, 635
VALS (values and lifestyles) system, 312,
    324–325, 332, 411, 635
Value, 19, 383–387, 544, 635
Value added services, 390–391, 635
Value-based pricing, 382–383, 635
Value chain, 6, 120, 134, 160, 635
Variable costs, 379, 635
VAR (value added reseller), 496
VAT (value-added tax), 141
VDS (vertical distribution systems),
    499–500
Venetian Hotel, 17, 333
Vertical integration, 129, 499, 635
Victoria-Jungfrau Hotel, 51
Victoria Station, 29
Virtuoso, 517, 519
VMS (vertical marketing systems), 499
Vocation Vacations, 319
Volume pricing objectives, 393
Volume-sensitivity, 381, 635
VWP (visa waiver program), 139

Waiter.com, 511
Waldorf-Astoria, 188, 315, 338, 360, 368
Waldorf Hotel, 504
Warren Kremer Paino Advertising, LLC, 59
Waterlot Inn, 315
Wayne Manor, 128
W concept (Starwood), 315
Web Digest for Marketers, 552
WebRing, 547
Wendy's, 158, 256, 276, 318
Westin, 28, 260, 262, 351

Westin Hotel Copley Place, 204
Westin's Guest Office®, 69
White Castle, 73
Wingate Inns, 8, 493
Wizcom, 522
Woodside Travel, 207
Word of mouth communications, 422, 635
WORLDHOTELS, 493, 494
Worldspan, 522, 529
World Tourism Organization, 452
World Wide Web (WWW). *See* Internet

W (Sheraton brand name), 159
WTO (World Trade Organization), 139–140
Wyndham ByRequest, 101, 139, 554
Wyndham International, 554
Wynn Resorts, 201

Xanterra Parks and Resorts, 510

Yahoo, 546
Yesawich, Pepperdine, Brown & Russell,
    281–284, 285, 288, 296, 409–411, 458

Yield, 401, 635
Yield index, 254, 265
Yield management, 635 (*See also* Revenue
    management)
Yum! Brands, 131, 368

Zero-based budgets, 424, 635
Zillow.com, 515
Zone of tolerance, 52, 55–56, 635
Zum See Restaurant, 3–6, 9, 129

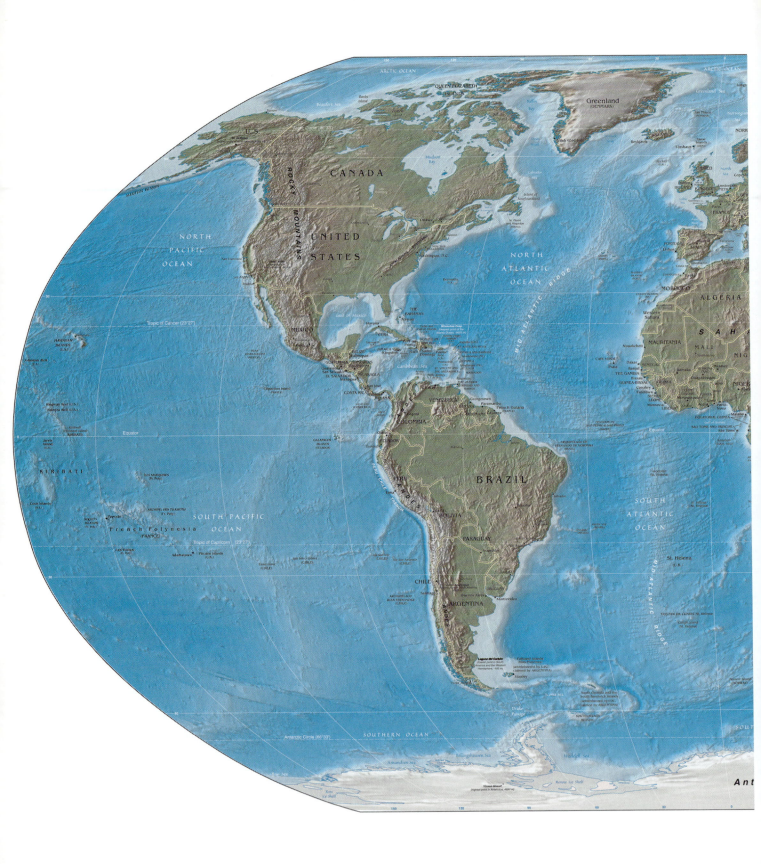

651

Arctic Ocean

Russia
ASIA

Greenland
(Denmark)

Beaufort Sea

ARCTIC CIRCLE

75° N

Gulf of
Alaska

60° N

Labrador
Sea

45° W

Bering
Sea

Hudson
Bay

Canada

150° W

Great
Lakes

45° N

Pacific
Ocean

United States
of
America

Atlantic
Ocean

600 mi

600 km

Bermuda
(U.K.)

30° N

Mexico

Gulf of
Mexico

75° W

60° W

TROPIC OF CANCER

Bahamas

NORTH
AMERICA

Cuba

CARIBBEAN

Jamaica

Dominican Rep.

Belize

Caribbean Sea

Puerto
Rico

15° N

Guatemala

Honduras

Trinidad

El Salvador

Nicaragua

Venezuela

Pacific
Ocean

N

CENTRAL AMERICA

Costa Rica

Panama

Colombia

SOUTH
AMERICA

135° W

120° W

105° W

90° W

©GraphicMaps.com

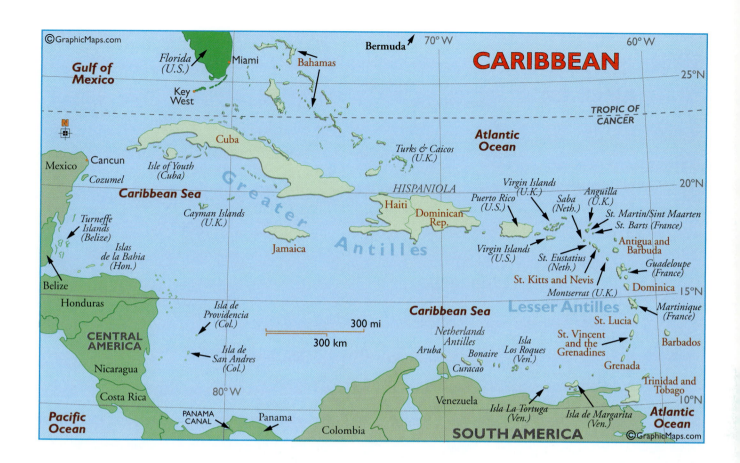

©GraphicMaps.com

CARIBBEAN

Bermuda

70° W   60° W

Florida (U.S.)   Miami

Bahamas

25°N

Gulf of Mexico

Key West

TROPIC OF CANCER

Greater Antilles

N

Cuba

Turks & Caicos (U.K.)

Atlantic Ocean

Mexico   Cancun

Isle of Youth (Cuba)

HISPANIOLA

Virgin Islands (U.K.)

Anguilla (U.K.)

20°N

Cozumel

Caribbean Sea

Puerto Rico (U.S.)

Saba (Neth.)

St. Martin/Sint Maarten

Cayman Islands (U.K.)

Haiti

Dominican Rep.

St. Barts (France)

Turneffe Islands (Belize)

Virgin Islands (U.S.)

St. Eustatius (Neth.)

Antigua and Barbuda

Islas de la Bahia (Hon.)

Jamaica

St. Kitts and Nevis

Guadeloupe (France)

Belize

Montserrat (U.K.)

Dominica

15°N

Honduras

Isla de Providencia (Col.)

Caribbean Sea

Lesser Antilles

Martinique (France)

CENTRAL AMERICA

300 mi

St. Lucia

Nicaragua

Isla de San Andres (Col.)

300 km

Netherlands Antilles

Aruba

Bonaire

Isla Los Roques (Ven.)

St. Vincent and the Grenadines

Barbados

Costa Rica

80° W

Curacao

Grenada

Trinidad and Tobago

Pacific Ocean

PANAMA CANAL

Panama

Venezuela

Isla La Tortuga (Ven.)

Isla de Margarita (Ven.)

10°N

Atlantic Ocean

Colombia

SOUTH AMERICA

©GraphicMaps.com

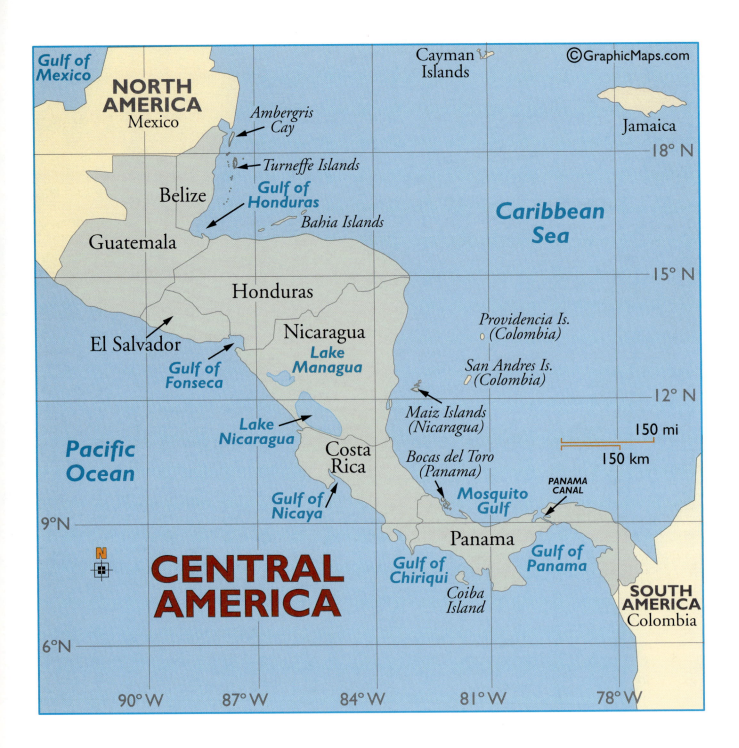

Gulf of Mexico

NORTH AMERICA
Mexico

Cayman Islands

©GraphicMaps.com

Jamaica

Ambergris Cay

18° N

Belize

Turneffe Islands

Gulf of Honduras

Bahia Islands

Caribbean Sea

Guatemala

15° N

Honduras

El Salvador

Nicaragua

Providencia Is. (Colombia)

Lake Managua

San Andres Is. (Colombia)

Gulf of Fonseca

Lake Nicaragua

Maiz Islands (Nicaragua)

12° N

Pacific Ocean

Costa Rica

Bocas del Toro (Panama)

150 mi

150 km

Mosquito Gulf

PANAMA CANAL

Gulf of Nicaya

9°N

Panama

CENTRAL AMERICA

Gulf of Chiriqui

Gulf of Panama

SOUTH AMERICA
Colombia

Coiba Island

6°N

90° W   87° W   84° W   81° W   78° W

654

SOUTH AMERICA

Pacific Ocean

Atlantic Ocean

NORTH AMERICA
Caribbean Sea
Mexico
Central America
Venezuela
Colombia
Guyana
Suriname
French Guiana (France)
EQUATOR 0°
Galapagos Islands (Ecuador)
Ecuador
Brazil
Peru
Bolivia
Easter Island (Chile)
TROPIC OF CAPRICORN
Paraguay
Chile
Argentina
Uruguay
Pacific Ocean
Falkland Islands (U.K.)
Scotia Sea
Atlantic Ocean
South Georgia Is. (U.K.)
Southern Ocean
ANTARCTICA
ANTARCTIC CIRCLE 0°

15° N
45° W
0°
15° S
75° W
30° S
45° S
60° W
45° W
30° W
15° W
105° W
90° W
60° S

©GraphicMaps.com

600 mi
600 km

N

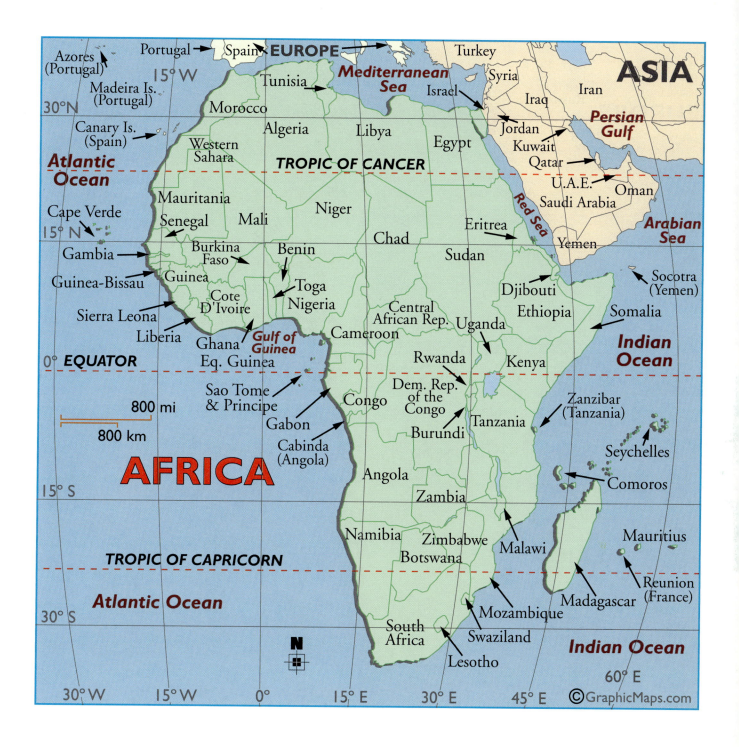

AFRICA

657

©GraphicMaps.com

659

©GraphicMaps.com

Russian Federation

Kazakhstan

Altay

Karamay

Kyrgyzstan

Bishkek

Urumqi

Turpan Pendi

Tian Shan Mts.

Kashi

Takla Makan Desert

Afgn.

K2

Kunlun Shan Mts.

Islamabad

Pakistan

Plateau of Tibet

New Delhi

Nepal

Kathmandu

HIMALAYAS

Lhasa

Mount Everest

Thimphu

Bhutan

Mekong River

500 mi

500 km

Dhaka

Bangladesh

India

Burma (Myanmar)

Indian Ocean

Sri Lanka

Ulan Bator

Mongolia

Gobi Desert

Yumen

Altun Shan Mts.

The Great Wall

Yinchuan

Lanzhou

Baotou

Datong

Tianjin

Huang He (Yellow River)

Xi'an

CHINA

Chengdu

Chongqing

Chang Jiang (Yangtze River)

Nanning

Pearl River

Nanjing

Wuhan

Nanchang

Guangzhou

Macau

Hong Kong

Hainan Island

Laos

Hanoi

Vientiane

Thailand

Rangoon

Bangkok

Phnom Penh

Cambodia

Vietnam

Heihe

Amur River

Harbin

Jilin

Jixi

Changchun

Da Hinggan Ling Mts.

Xiao Hinggan Ling Mts.

Shenyang

Fushun

Anshan

Beijing

Dalian

Jinan

Qingdao

No. Korea

Pyongyang

So. Korea

Seoul

Yellow Sea

Japan

Shanghai

Ningbo

Fuzhou

Taipei

Taiwan

Shantou

South China Sea

Manila

Philippines

Pacific Ocean

N

©GraphicMaps.com

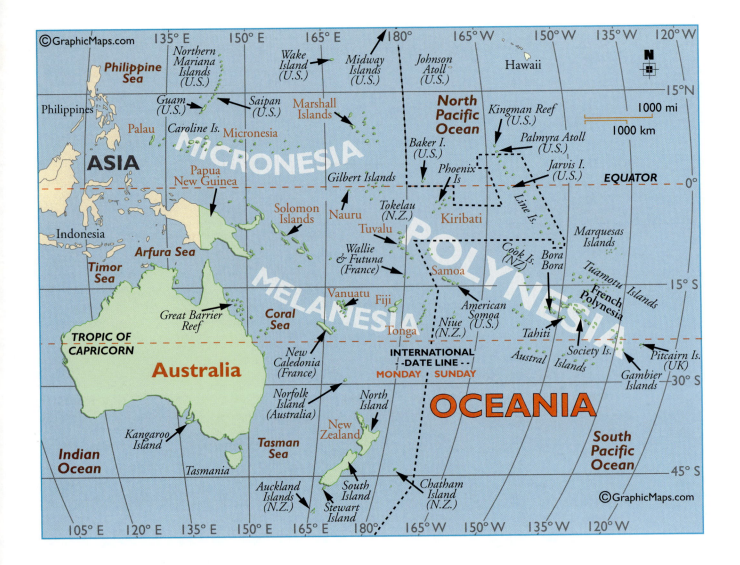

Part Opener and Chapter Opener Photo Credits

Pages i, iii: Jupiter Images/Corbis

Page 13: Corbis RF

Pages 14, 36, 58, 84: Steven Puetzer, Getty Images–Iconica

Page 117: Mitchell Funk, Getty Images Inc.–Image Bank

Pages 118, 148: Grant V. Faint, Getty Images Inc.–Image Bank

Page 167: Richard Wahlstrom, Getty Images Inc.–Image Bank

Pages 168, 196, 224: Gary S. and Vivian Chapman, Getty Images Inc.–Image Bank

Page 251: Douglas Peebles, eStock Photography LLC

Pages 252, 280: GMBH/Look, eStock Photography LLC

Page 309: Jean Louis Batt, Getty Images, Inc.–Taxi

Pages 310, 346, 372, 408, 432, 462, 488, 514, and 536: Pierre-Yves Goavec, Getty Images Inc.–Image Bank

Pages vii, ix, xvii, xxiii, xxv, 563: Corbis Royalty Free

Page 564: BananaStock, Jupiter Images Picturequest–Royalty Free

Pages 650–662: © GraphicMaps.com

Background (chairs and umbrella) pages 3, 14, 36, 58, 84, 118, 148, 168, 196, 224, 252, 280, 310, 346, 372, 408, 432, 462, 488, 514, 536, and 564: Philip Coblentz, Getty Images/Digital Vision